Crisis Intervention Strategies

SEVENTH EDITION

RICHARD K. JAMES

University of Memphis

BURL E. GILLILAND

D0068940

BROOKS/COLE
CENGAGE Learning

Australia • Brazil • Japan • Korea • Mexico • Singapore • Spain • United Kingdom • United States

Crisis Intervention Strategies,
Seventh Edition
Richard K. James, Burl E. Gilliland

Acquisitions Editor: Seth Dobrin

Assistant Editor: Naomi Dreyer

Assistant Editor: Suzanna Kincaid

Media Editor: Elizabeth Momb

Marketing Program Manager: Tami Strang

Content Project Manager: Rita Jaramillo

Art Director: Caryl Gorska

Manufacturing Planner: Judy Inouye

Rights Acquisitions Specialist: Dean Dauphinais

Production Service: Scratchgravel Publishing Services

Text Researcher: Ashley Liening

Copy Editor: Margaret C. Tropp

Cover Designer: Design Is Play

Compositor: MPS Limited

Library of Congress Control Number: 2012933593

ISBN-13: 978-1-111-18677-7

ISBN-10: 1-111-18677-4

Advantage Loose-leaf Edition:

ISBN-13: 978-1-111-77061-7

ISBN-10: 1-111-77061-1

Brooks/Cole
20 Davis Drive
Belmont, CA 94002-3098
USA

Cengage Learning is a leading provider of customized learning solutions with office locations around the globe, including Singapore, the United Kingdom, Australia, Mexico, Brazil, and Japan. Locate your local office at **www.cengage.com/global.**

Cengage Learning products are represented in Canada by Nelson Education, Ltd.

To learn more about Brooks/Cole, visit **www.cengage.com/BrooksCole**

Purchase any of our products at your local college store or at our preferred online store **www.CengageBrain.com.**

Printed in the United States of America
1 2 3 4 5 6 7 16 15 14 13 12

The seventh edition of this book is dedicated to the men and women of the international forces that have served and are serving in the Middle East to protect the United States and other freedom-loving countries from terrorism. In particular, this seventh edition is dedicated to the frontline medical and mental health staff that strive to keep soldiers medically and psychologically fit and the homeland follow-up staff of the armed services and the Veteran's Administration that strive to stop PTSD and other physical and psychological maladies of those who have served. Hopefully, what they do and what the Army's new Comprehensive Fitness Program proposes to do will stave off some of the traumatic psychological wake of combat.

This book is also dedicated to the past and present students in the counseling department at the University of Memphis whom we have known, taught, and become extremely proud of over 35 years here. If you watch the videos that accompany this book, you'll see them in action. Those students are the new kids on the block, taking their first run at crisis intervention. They make mistakes but they are good one-trial learners, and they represent hundreds of other students who have gone through our program and gone on to become excellent crisis interventionists who, because of their skills, save lives where others probably couldn't. Although Burl Gilliland died nearly 10 years ago, I think I speak for him as well in saying that we learned as much from you as you learned from us. Thank you for allowing us to teach and learn from you.

Brief Contents

PART I   Basic Training: Crisis Intervention Theory
              and Application   1

1   Approaching Crisis Intervention   3

2   Culturally Effective Helping   28

3   The Intervention and Assessment Models   50

4   The Tools of the Trade   75

5   Crisis Case Handling   95

6   Telephone and Online Crisis Counseling   119

PART II   Handling Specific Crises: Going Into the Trenches   147

7   Posttraumatic Stress Disorder   149

8   Crisis of Lethality   209

9   Sexual Assault   248

10   Partner Violence   297

11   Chemical Dependency: The Crisis of Addiction   349

12   Personal Loss: Bereavement and Grief   414

13   Crises in Schools   474

PART III   On the Home Front: Crisis in the Human
Services Workplace   539

14 Violent Behavior in Institutions   541

15 Crisis/Hostage Negotiation   579

16 Human Services Workers in Crisis: Burnout, Vicarious
Traumatization, and Compassion Fatigue   612

PART IV   No Man's Land: Facing Disaster   647

17 Disaster Response   649

Index   712

Contents

PART I Basic Training: Crisis Intervention Theory and Application 1

CHAPTER 1
Approaching Crisis Intervention 3

A Brief History of Crisis Intervention 3
Grassroots Movements 4
The Importance of Volunteerism 5
The Need for Institutionalism 5
The Media and the Societal Impetus
   for Crisis Intervention 6
The Case Against Too Much "Helping" 7

Definitions of Crisis 7
Individual Crisis Definitions 7
Behavioral Emergencies 8
Systemic Crisis Definitions 8
Metastasizing Crisis 9

Characteristics of Crisis 10

Transcrisis States 11
Transcrisis Differentiated From Posttraumatic
   Stress Disorder 11
Transcrisis Points 12

**Theories of Crisis
and Crisis Intervention 13**
Basic Crisis Intervention Theory 13
Expanded Crisis Theory 14
Applied Crisis Theory 16

Crisis Intervention Models 17
The Equilibrium Model 17
The Cognitive Model 17
The Psychosocial Transition Model 18
The Developmental-Ecological Model 18

The Contextual-Ecological Model 18
Psychological First Aid 19
The ACT Model 20

Eclectic Crisis Intervention Theory 20

Characteristics of Effective Crisis Workers 21
Life Experiences 21
Personal Characteristics 22

Rewards 23

Summary 23

References 24

CHAPTER 2
Culturally Effective Helping 28

Multicultural Perspectives in Crisis Intervention 28
Culturally Biased Assumptions 29
Universal Versus Focused Views 30
Working on the Individualist/Collectivist–
   High/Low Context Continuum 30
Emic Versus Etic Models of Multiculturalism 32
Awareness of Both Ecology and Multicultural
   Competencies 35

**Shortcomings of a Multiculturalist Approach
to Crisis Intervention 36**

Culturally Effective Helping 38
Positive Aspects of an Effective Multicultural
   Counselor 39
When in Rome, Italy . . . or Georgia 40
Language Barriers 40
Religion and Spirituality 40
Support Systems 42
Occupation as a Cultural Barrier 42
Geographic Locale as a Cultural Barrier 43
The Dilemma of Local Consultation 44

The Necessity of Acting   45
Training   45
Where It Stands Now . . . Sorta   45

Summary   46

References   46

CHAPTER 3
The Intervention and Assessment Models 50

Introduction   50

A Hybrid Model of Crisis Intervention   51
Task 1. Predispositioning/Engaging/Initiating
Contact   52
Task 2. Problem Exploration: Defining the Crisis   53
Task 3. Providing Support   54
Default Task: Safety   55
Task 4. Examining Alternatives   56
Task 5. Planning in Order to Reestablish Control   56
Task 6. Obtaining Commitment   58
Task 7. Follow-up   58

Assessment in Crisis Intervention   59
Assessing the Severity of Crisis   60
The ABCs of Assessing in Crisis Intervention   60
The Triage Assessment System   61
The Triage Assessment Form   61
Alternate Forms of the TAF   67
Psychobiological Assessment   69
Assessing the Client's Current Emotional
Functioning   70
Assessing Alternatives, Coping Mechanisms,
and Support Systems   71
Assessing for Suicide/Homicide Potential   71

Summary   72

References   73

CHAPTER 4
The Tools of the Trade 75

Introduction   75

Listening in Crisis Intervention   75
Open-Ended Questions   75
Closed-Ended Questions   76
Restatement and Summary Clarification   76
Owning Feelings   77
Facilitative Listening   79

Basic Strategies of Crisis Intervention   81

Climate of Human Growth   83
Communicating Empathy   83
Communicating Genuineness   86
Communicating Acceptance   87

Acting in Crisis Intervention   87
Directive Counseling   88
Collaborative Counseling   89
Nondirective Counseling   89
Action Strategies for Crisis Workers   89

Summary   93

References   94

CHAPTER 5
Crisis Case Handling 95

Handling Crisis Cases Versus Long-Term Cases   95

Case Handling at Walk-In Crisis Facilities   96
Types of Presenting Crises   96
Case Handling at a Community Mental Health
Clinic   99

Police and Crisis Intervention   101
Changing Role of the Police   101
Police and the Mentally Ill/Mentally Disturbed   101
The Crisis Intervention Team (CIT) Program   102

Transcrisis Handling in Long-Term Therapy   105
Anxiety Reactions   106
Regression   106
Problems of Termination   107
Crisis in the Therapy Session   107
Psychotic Breaks   108
People With Borderline Personality Disorder   108

Counseling Difficult Clients   111
Ground Rules for Counseling Difficult Clients   111
Confronting Difficult Clients   112

Confidentiality in Case Handling   112
Principles Bearing on Confidentiality   112
The Intent to Harm and the Duty to Warn   113

Summary   115

References   116

CHAPTER 6
Telephone and Online Crisis Counseling 119

Case Handling on Telephone Crisis Lines   119

Telephone Counseling Strategies   121
Making Psychological Contact   122
Defining the Problem   122
Ensuring Safety and Providing Support   123
Looking at Alternatives and Making Plans   124
Obtaining Commitment   124
Errors and Fallacies   125

**Regular, Severely Disturbed,
and Abusive Callers   126**
Understanding the Regular Caller's Agenda   126

Handling the Severely Disturbed Caller   128
Other Problem Callers   131
Handling the Problem Callers   133

Hotlines   134

The Internet's Growing Role in Crisis Intervention   135

Behavioral Telehealth   135
The Appeal of Online Counseling   136
Problems of Online Counseling   136
Netiquette   137
Predispositioning   138
Need for Training   140
Virtual Reality   140

**Legal, Ethical, and Moral Issues of Telephone
and Internet Counseling   141**

Does It Work?   141

Summary   142

References   142

PART II   Handling Specific Crises: Going Into the Trenches   147

CHAPTER 7
Posttraumatic Stress Disorder 149

Background   149

Dynamics of PTSD   152
Diagnostic Categorization   152
Complex PTSD   153
Conflicting Diagnoses   153
The Question of Preexisting Psychopathology   153
Physiological Responses   154
Affective-State-Dependent Retention   155
Children and Neuropathology   155

Incidence, Impact, and Trauma Type   156
Incidence   156
Residual Impact   156
Importance of Trauma Type   156
Vietnam: The Archetype   157
Intrusive-Repetitive Ideation   159
Denial/Numbing   159
Increased Nervous Symptom Arousal   160
Dissociation   160
Family Responses   160

Maladaptive Patterns Characteristic of PTSD   161

The Traumatic Wake of Iraq and Afghanistan   163
The Comprehensive Solider Fitness Program   163

Treatment of Adults   164
Assessment   164

Phases of Recovery   169
Importance of Acceptance   170
Risks of Treatment   171
Multiphasic/Multimodal Treatment   171
Psychotropic Medication   172

Individual Intervention   172
Emergency/Outcry   172
Extinguishing Intrusive Images   173
Numbing/Denial   173
Reflection and Transition   175
Integration   177

Group Treatment   178
Support Groups   178
The Life Adjustment Group   183
Family Treatment   184

**Eye Movement Desensitization and Reprocessing
(EMDR)   184**
The Controversy Over EMDR   184
EMDR Therapy   185

Children and PTSD   188
Support Systems   188
Types of Trauma   189
Etched Memories   189
Developmental Issues   190
Other Responses to Type I Trauma   190
Type II Traumas   191
Intervention Strategies   192
Therapy   193

Moving Beyond the Trauma   195

Summary   196

References   196

CHAPTER 8
Crisis of Lethality 209

Background   209
The Scope of the Suicide Crisis   209
Suicide and the Moral Dilemma   210

The Dynamics of Suicide   211
Psychological Theories   211
Sociological Theory   212
Interpersonal Theory   212
Existential-Constructivist Framework   212
Other Explanations   213
Characteristics of People Who Commit Suicide   214
Similarities Between Suicide and Homicide   215
Analyzing Suicide/Homicide Notes/Videos   215

Myths About Suicide   216

Assessment   217
Suicide Clues   217

Assessment Instruments   219
Clinical Interview   219
Using the Triage Assessment Form in Addressing
    Lethality   220

Intervention Strategies   222
The Three I's   222
Older Adults   231
Guidelines for Family, Friends, and Associates   236
The Psychological Autopsy   237
Postvention   237

Losing a Client to Suicide   241

Summary   241

References   242

CHAPTER 9
Sexual Assault 248

The Scope of the Problem   248
Underreporting   249
The Unique Situation of Sexual Abuse/
    Rape Survivors   249
Defining Rape   249

The Dynamics of Rape   249
Social/Cultural Factors   250
Personal and Psychological Factors   250
Myths About Rape   251

Date and Acquaintance Rape   253
Date Rape Risk   254
Preventing Date, Acquaintance, and Other Forms
    of Rape   254

Intervention Strategies for Rape and Battery:
    The Case of Melody   255
Immediate Aftermath   255
The Following Three Months   259

Adult Survivors of Childhood Sexual Abuse   261
Psychological Trauma and Sequelae   261
False Memories   262

Intervention Strategies for Adult Survivors:
    The Case of Heather   263
Assessment   264
Treatment of Adults   265
Discovery and Admission   265
Grounding   266
Validation   267
Extinguishing Trauma   267
Prolonged Exposure/Cognitive Restructuring   268
Grief Resolution   269
Support Groups for Adult Survivors   270

Sexual Abuse in Childhood   271
Dynamics of Sexual Abuse in Childhood   272
Dynamics of Sexual Abuse in Families   273
Phases of Child Sexual Abuse   274

Intervention Strategies With Children   275
Assessment   275
Therapeutic Options   276
Need for Affirmation and Safety   277
Regaining a Sense of Control   277
Education   278
Assertiveness Training   278

Intervention Strategies for Child Sexual Abuse:
    The Case of Elizabeth   278
Disclosure   279
Immediate Aftermath   279

Prosecuting the Perpetrator   281
Interviewing the Child   281
Preparing the Child for Testimony   282
Aftermath   282

Counseling   283
Group Counseling   283
Boundary Issues   284
Group Support Work With Nonoffending Parents   284
Preventing Revictimization   284
Individual Counseling   284

Summary   288

References   289

CHAPTER 10
Partner Violence 297

The Incidence of Partner Violence   298

Emerging Approaches to Partner Violence   299

Dynamics of Partner Violence   300
Psychosocial and Cultural Dynamics   300
Psychological Factors   304
Stressors   305
Myths About Battering   306
Profiling the Batterer   307
The Cycle of Violence   307
Realities for Abused Women   308

Intervention Strategies   309
Assessment   309
Components of Intervention   312

Shelters   318
Counseling Women at Shelters   319
Follow-Up   322

Intervention With Children   322

Courtship Violence   325
Stalking   325

Gay and Lesbian Violence   326
Prevalence of Violence   326
Complicating Factors   327
Crisis Intervention Involving Gay and Lesbian
    Violence   327

Treating Batterers   329
   Intervention Models   329
   Treatment Models   330
   Hybrid Models   330
   Treatment Goals   330
   Assessment   331
   The Intake Interview   331
   Motivation   332
   A Typical 24-Session Anger Management Group   332
   Program Success   337

Summary   338

References   339

CHAPTER 11

Chemical Dependency: The Crisis
   of Addiction 349

Sociocultural Determinants of Substance Abuse   350

Alcohol: Number One Abused Substance   351

Models of Addiction   352

Definitions of Commonly Used Terms   354

The Dynamics of Addiction   356
   Defense Mechanisms   356
   Enabling and Codependency   358

Children in Alcoholic Families   360
   Family Rules in Alcoholic Families   361
   Adult Children of Alcoholics   363

Treatment Approaches   365
   Alcoholics Anonymous (AA)   365
   Cognitive-Behavioral Therapy (CBT)   366
   Inpatient Treatment: The Minnesota Model   367
   Outpatient Programs   367
   Contingency Management (CM)   368
   Community Reinforcement Approach (CRA)   368
   Reinforcement-Based Treatment (RBT)   369
   Inpatient or Outpatient?   370
   Contemporary Model   370

Multivariate Diagnosis   371
   Matching Treatment to Client   371
   Dual Diagnosis   371

Intervention Strategies   372
   Motivation and Stages of Change   372
   To Drink or Not to Drink   374
   Assessment   375
   Crisis Points in Chemical Dependency Treatment   381
   Detoxification   385

Principles of Treatment   385
   Treatment Techniques   385
   Treatment Goals   385
   Treatment Protocol   386
   Individual Therapy   387

The Treatment Group   388
   Learning Relationship Skills   389
   Accepting Responsibility   389
   Getting Past Denial   390
   Confrontation   391
   Limit Testing   393
   Treatment Secrets   393
   Disrupting Irrational Mental Sets   394
   Overcoming Environmental Cues That Lead
      to Drinking   395
   Treating the Family   396
   Aftercare and Relapse Prevention   399

Summary   402

References   403

CHAPTER 12

Personal Loss: Bereavement and Grief 414

Terms Critical to Understanding Loss   416

Dynamics of Bereavement   417
   Cultural Dynamics   417
   Sociocultural Mores   418
   Spirituality and Religion   419

Conceptual Approaches to Bereavement   420
   Stage/Phase Models   420
   A Counterpoint to Traditional Models   421
   Assessment Tools   423

Types of Loss   423
   Death of a Spouse   423
   Loss Due to Caregiving   424
   Death of a Child   425
   Bereavement in Childhood   425
   Bereavement in Adolescence   428
   Bereavement in Elderly People   429
   HIV/AIDS   430
   Job Loss   431
   Separation and Divorce   432
   Death of a Pet   433
   Complicated/Prolonged Grief, Bereavement,
      and Mourning Reaction   433

Intervention Strategies   435
   Being There for Grievers: A Worker Imperative   436
   Fitting Technique to Style of Grief   437
   Cognitive-Behavioral Approaches   438
   Narrative Therapy   438
   Attachment Theory and Therapy   439

Dealing With Loss   439
   Sudden Death of a Spouse   439
   Traumatic Death of a Child   442
   Bereavement in Childhood   447
   Separation and Divorce   449
   Death of a Pet   453

Bereavement in Elderly People   454
Bereavement in an HIV-Infected Client   456
Complicated Grief: Death of a Mother   457
The Crisis Worker's Own Grief   461

Is There Any Lemonade in All These Sour Lemons?   462

Summary   463

References   464

CHAPTER 13

Crises in Schools..............................474

**The New-Millennium, Violence-Proof School
Building   474**
Conflicting Statistics   476
Violence and Youth   478

Gangs   479
Types of Gangs   479
Emergence of Suburban and Rural Gangs   480
Gang Intervention/Prevention Programs   480

Bullying   485
Cyberbullying   486
Individual Intervention   487

The Estranged Violent Juvenile Offender   488
A Comparison of Traits, Characteristics, and
Behaviors of SVJOs and EVJOs   489
Case Study: Seung-hui Cho   493
Screening the EVJO   493
Interviewing the Potential EVJO   495
Acting   498

School-Based Suicide Prevention and Intervention   499
Risk Factors/Predictors/Cues   500
Preadolescent Suicide   500
Child and Adolescent Cases of Suicidal Ideation   501
Postvention   505

**Legal and Ethical Issues of Potentially Violent
Behavior   509**
Confidentiality and Duty to Warn   509
Consistency of Intervention   511
The Problem of "Doing Something" in a University
Setting   511

Planning for a Crisis   515
The Crisis Response Planning Committee   516
The School Crisis Response Team (SCRT)   517

Implementing the Crisis Plan   519
Physical Requirements   519
Logistics   519
Responding to the Crisis   520

Bereavement in Schools   523
Group Work   524
Defining the Boundaries   525

Transcrisis Intervention   525
The Case of Josh   525

Epilogue   527

Summary   528

References   529

**PART III   On the Home Front:
Crisis in the Human
Services Workplace   539**

CHAPTER 14

Violent Behavior in Institutions................541

Precipitating Factors   542

Institutional Culpability   543
Universities and Their Counseling Centers   543
Denial   544

Staff Culpability   545

Legal Liability   545

Dynamics of Violence in Human Services Settings   546
Violence Potential Assessment Instruments   546
Bases for Violence   546

Intervention Strategies   549
Security Planning   549
Commitment and Involvement   549
Worksite Analysis   549
Hazard Prevention and Control   550
Training   552
Record Keeping and Program Evaluation   555
Stages of Intervention   555

The Violent Geriatric Client   564
Mild Disorientation: The Case of Cliff   564
Distinguishing Between Illusions and
Hallucinations   567
Severe Disorientation: The Case of Grace   568

Follow-up With Staff Victims   569

Summary   571

References   571

CHAPTER 15

Crisis/Hostage Negotiation....................579

Dynamics of Hostage Taking   580
Types of Hostage Takers   581
The Mentally Disturbed   581
Other Hostage Takers   586
Stages and Dynamics of a Hostage Situation   588

Intervention Strategies   591
Communication Techniques   592
Containing the Scene   593
Gathering Information   594
Stabilizing the Situation   594

Persuading the Hostage Taker to Give Up   596
Negotiating in a Hostage Situation: The Case
     of James   598
The Crisis Worker as Consultant   603
If You Are Put in the Role of Negotiator   603
If You Are Held Hostage   604

Intervention After Release   605
Crisis Intervention With Hostage Survivors   606
Crisis Intervention With the Hostage Negotiator   608

Summary   609

References   609

**CHAPTER 16
Human Services Workers in Crisis:
     Burnout, Vicarious Traumatization,
     and Compassion Fatigue** 612

Helping Professionals: Prime Candidates   612

Defining Burnout   613

Dynamics of Burnout   614
Cornerstones of Burnout   614
Research on Burnout Dynamics   615
Myths That Engender Burnout   616
Symptoms of Burnout   617
Levels of Burnout   617
Stages of Burnout   617

Worker–Client Relationships   619
Countertransference   619
Secondary Traumatic Stress/Vicarious
     Traumatization/Compassion Fatigue   620
Compassion Satisfaction   621

The Culpability of Organizations   621

Self-Recognition of Burnout   622

Intervention Strategies   622
Assessment   623
Intervention Through Training   624
Intervention With the Organization   624
Self-Care   629

Private Practitioners and Burnout   629

Intervention With the Individual: A Case Study   630

Epilogue: Cross-Cultural Comparisons   639

Summary   640

References   640

**PART IV   No Man's Land:
     Facing Disaster   647**

**CHAPTER 17
Disaster Response** 649

A Brief History of Disaster Mental Health Provision   649

Where the World Is   652

**International Terrorism and Human-Made
     Disasters   652**

New Directions and New Visions   654

System Overview   655
Microsystem   656
Mesosystem   656
Exosystem   659
Macrosystem   659
Chronosystem   660

**Defining Principles of a Crisis Intervention
     Ecosystem   664**
National Crisis Response Teams   665
Vertically and Horizontally Integrated Local
     Emergency Management Systems   668
Mental Health Components of Local EMAs   673
What Happened With Katrina?   674
Psychological First Aid and Psychosocial Support
     as Applied to Disaster Survivors   676
When More Than PFA Is Needed   676
The Current State of Affairs   677

The People of Disasters: Responders and Survivors   678
Crisis Workers at the Disaster   678
Thoughts of a Mental Health Worker on Katrina
     One Year Later   679
Lessons I Learned From Katrina   681

Case Study of the Benefield Family   683

Focus on the Worker   696
Debriefing   696
Debriefing Emergency Workers   697
Debriefing Crisis Workers   699

Final Thoughts   702

Summary   702

References   703

Index 712

Preface

Purpose of the Book

The primary purpose of this book is to present applied therapeutic counseling in general, and crisis intervention in particular, in a way that effectively describes actual strategies to alleviate the crisis. In our experience, most clients who enter counseling or psychotherapy do so because of some sort of crisis in their lives. Although "preventive" counseling is the ideal, personal crisis generally provides the impetus that impels real clients into contact with a helping person. This book provides a perspective that puts you into the crisis situation as it is occurring, enabling you to experience what crisis workers are experiencing as they operate.

Rationale

The Primacy of Crisis Intervention

The two Chinese characters embedded on the front cover of the book and at the beginning of each chapter symbolize both "danger" and "opportunity." Those two elements are the essence of *crisis*—the human dilemma that is common to all cultures. We believe that practically all counseling is initiated as crisis intervention. As much as the helping professions would prefer otherwise, people tend either to avoid presenting their problems to a helper until those problems have grown to crisis proportions, or to become ensconced in situational dilemmas that wind up in unforeseen crises. Our ideal objective, as human service workers, is to establish primary prevention programs so effective that crisis intervention will seldom be needed. However, it appears that people will not be as quick to adopt preventive measures for their psychological health as they are for their physical health.

The Case for an Applied Viewpoint

The materials and techniques we promote in this book come from two sources: first, the authors' own experiences in teaching and counseling in crisis situations, and second, interviews with people who are currently in the trenches, successfully performing counseling and crisis intervention. We have obtained input from many different individuals in the helping professions, whose daily and nightly work is dealing directly with human dilemmas, and have related their views to the best of current theory and practice from the professional literature. Through many hours of dialogue, these experts have provided the most contemporary strategies and techniques in use in their particular fields. They have also reviewed the content of each crisis category and have provided much helpful commentary and critique of the ecology and etiology, tactics and procedures, terminology, and developmental stages of the specific crises with which they work. Therefore, what you read in the case-handling strategies comes directly from the horse's mouth.

Where controversies exist in regard to treatment modalities, this text attempts to present as many perspectives as possible. Dr. Gilliland has been dead for 10 years, so if you encounter problems with the tactics and techniques presented in the current edition, the fault is undoubtedly in Dr. James's rendition of the current research and therapeutic modalities.

The authors have endeavored to incorporate, synthesize, and integrate the case-handling strategies of the resource people in a comprehensive, fluid, and dynamic way that will provide crisis workers with a basic set of tenets about effective crisis intervention. This book is not about long-term therapy or theory. Nor is it a volume dealing with crisis from only one theoretical perspective, such as a psychoanalytic approach or a behavioral system. The book incorporates a wide diversity of therapeutic modalities and reflects our eclectic approach to crisis intervention.

Specific crises demand specific interventions that span the whole continuum of therapeutic strategies. The strategies presented in this book shouldn't be construed as the only ones available for a particular crisis. They are offered as "best bets" based on what current research and practice indicate is appropriate and applicable. Yet these strategies may not be appropriate for all practitioners with all clients in all situations.

Good crisis intervention, as well as good therapy of any other kind, is a serious professional activity that calls for creativity and the ability to adapt to changing conditions of the therapeutic moment. To that extent, crisis intervention at times is more art than science and is not always prescriptive. Therefore, we caution you that there are no clear-cut prescriptions or simple cause-and-effect answers in this book.

The Case for an Experiential Viewpoint

The fact that no single theory or strategy applies to every crisis situation is particularly problematic to those who are looking for simple, concrete answers to resolve the client problems they will face. If you are just beginning your career in the human services, we hope that while reading and trying out activities in this book you will suspend your judgment for a while and be open to the experience as you read about crisis workers attempting to implement theory into practice.

Moral Dilemmas. An issue that permeates many of the topics covered in this book concerns the emotions they generate and the beliefs about what is morally "right" and what is morally "wrong" that pervade those topics. People have been willing to go to prison or die because of the strong beliefs they hold about many of these topics. Where such moral issues and beliefs abound, we have attempted to deal with them in as even-handed a manner as possible. This book is not about the morality of the issues covered, but rather about what seems to work best for the people who are experiencing the dilemma. We ask you to read the book with that view in mind and, at least for a while, suspend your moral

view of the situation or problem as you read about crisis workers attempting to grapple with heart- and gut-wrenching problems.

Finally, because of a virtually unlimited supply of different crisis situations, we have had to make tough decisions about what kinds of problems to illustrate in the most generic and comprehensive way so as to reach the broadest possible audience. We understand and empathize very deeply with readers who may have suffered terrible crises that are not mentioned in this book and who are puzzled, chagrined, and angry that we have not given space and time to the particular crisis that they have suffered through. For that we apologize. The space available means that we simply cannot include all situations. However, what we would like you to do, rather than rail at our callous treatment in ignoring your particular dilemma, is to imagine how the strategies and techniques you are reading about might apply to the particular crisis you have experienced. We hope that what we say about those crises will help you come to understand the dynamics of your own crisis a bit better.

Basic Relationship Skills. The listening and responding skills described in Chapter 4 are critical to everything else the worker does in crisis intervention. Yet on cursory inspection these techniques and concepts may seem at best simplistic and at worst inane. They do not appear to fix anything because they are not "fixing" skills. What they do is give the crisis worker a firm basis of operation from which to explore clearly the dilemma the client is facing. Basic listening and responding skills are the prerequisites for all other therapeutic modalities.

Our experience has shown us over and over that students and trainees who scoff at and dismiss these basic relationship skills are the ones who invariably have the most trouble meeting the experiential requirements of our courses and workshop training sessions. We feel very strongly about this particular point and thus ask you to read Chapter 4, The Tools of the Trade, with an open mind. Students and veterans who operate in a client-centered mode may find some of what we propose to be pretty close to heresy, because a lot of these tools are directive and judgmental regarding the action to be taken—particularly when client safety is concerned. Again we ask you to suspend judgment and give these tools a good tryout in this new venture.

Role Play. If this volume is used as a structured learning experience, the case studies in each chapter are a valuable resource for experiential learning. So are the exercises your instructor will give you, as are the videos. It is essential that you observe effective crisis intervention models at work and then follow up by actually practicing and enacting the procedures you have observed. Intensive and extensive role play is an excellent skill builder. A critical component of training is not just talking about problems but practicing the skills of handling them as well. Talking about a problem is fine, but attempting to handle a live situation enables the trainee to get involved in the business of calming, defusing, managing, controlling, and motivating clients. Role play is one of the best ways of practicing what is preached, and it prepares human services workers for developing creative ways to deal with the variety of contingencies they may face. Role play gives human services workers the chance to find out what works and doesn't work for them in the safety of a training situation and affords their fellow students and trainees an opportunity to give them valuable feedback.

A major problem in role play is the perception of standing up in a class or workshop and risking making a complete fool of oneself. We want to assure you that in our classes and training sessions we don't expect perfection. If our students and trainees were perfect at crisis intervention, they wouldn't be taking instruction from us in the first place! Therefore, put your inhibitions on the shelf for a while and become engaged in the role plays as if the situations were real, live, and happening right now. Further, be willing and able to accept critical comments from your peers, supervisors, or instructors. Your ego may be bruised a bit in the process, but that's far better than waiting until you are confronted with an out-of-control client before you think about what you are going to do. Over and over, our students report that this component of instruction was the most profitable to them and was also the most fun!

Give the exercises that go with each chapter your best effort, process them with fellow students or trainees, and see what fits best with your own feelings, thoughts, and behaviors. Many times our students and trainees attempt to imitate us. Although it is gratifying to see students or trainees attempting to be "Dr. J.," it is generally an exercise in futility for them. What they need to do is view us critically as we model the procedures and then incorporate their own style and personhood into the procedures. We urge you to do the same.

More "Stuff." Some of these chapters are *really* long. We didn't put all that "stuff" in there to beat you to death with verbiage. We did it because the field of crisis intervention keeps expanding rapidly, as does the knowledge base. Therefore, you need to know the "stuff" to do your job effectively. If you just watch the PowerPoint presentations or the video clips, you might get enough knowledge to pass your instructor's tests. However, you won't know enough to help your client or yourself when you get in a tight spot. So read, read, read.

Finally, if you are never, ever going to be a crisis interventionist, but you are a "consumer," this book can still be very useful. Sad to say, but just through living, you are going to encounter a lot of the crises in this book that are going to afflict you, your loved ones, your friends, your workplace, and the ecosystem in which you live. This book can give you the basic knowledge to deal with the crisis or know when it's time to get help.

Organization of the Book
Part I, Basic Training
Part I of the book introduces the basic concepts of crisis intervention. It comprises Chapters 1, 2, 3, 4, 5, and 6.

Chapter 1, Approaching Crisis Intervention. Chapter 1 contains the basic rationale and the theoretical and conceptual information needed for understanding applied crisis intervention.

Chapter 2, Culturally Effective Helping. Chapter 2 is concerned with how crisis and culture interact. Dealing effectively with people from diverse backgrounds who are undergoing a crisis or have survived a disaster mandates an understanding of and sensitivity to multicultural issues. "Social locations" for both worker and client play a major role in crisis intervention work.

Chapter 3, The Intervention and Assessment Models. Chapter 3 introduces the new task model for crisis intervention as well as the triage assessment system for rapidly assessing the severity of the crisis in a multidimensional way.

Chapter 4, The Tools of the Trade. Chapter 4 provides a conceptual as well as a skill-building model of crisis intervention that applies to all crisis categories. It describes listening and relationship skills, strategies, and practical guidelines for initial intervention in all types of crises.

Chapter 5, Crisis Case Handling. Chapter 5 presents an overview of how crises are handled. Long-term therapy is compared with crisis intervention. Different venues where crisis intervention operates are explored to give an overview of the general tactics and strategies that are used.

Chapter 6, Telephone and Online Crisis Counseling. The majority of crisis intervention is now done on the telephone. The wave of the future for crisis counseling will most likely be the Internet. This chapter explores the issues and techniques that are involved in these two mediums of communication.

Part II, Handling Specific Crises: Going Into the Trenches

Part II (Chapters 7 through 13) addresses a variety of important types of crises. Each chapter in Part II describes the background and dynamics of the particular crisis type to provide a basic grasp of the driving forces behind the dilemma. Although some theory is presented to highlight the therapeutic modalities used, comprehensive theoretical systems are beyond the scope of this book. For sources of that information, turn to the reference section at the end of each chapter.

In Part II we provide scripts from real interventions, highlighted by explanations as to why the crisis workers did what they did. Techniques and cases are used to support live tryout, experiencing, and processing of the cases and issues in each chapter.

Chapter 7, Posttraumatic Stress Disorder. Posttraumatic stress disorder (PTSD) is the linchpin chapter of this section. Many of the chapters that follow deal with problems that may be precursors of PTSD or, alternately, may represent its manifestations.

Chapter 8, Crisis of Lethality. Chapter 8 focuses on strategies that crisis workers need in working with people who are manifesting lethal behavior. Suicidal and homicidal ideation flows through many other problems that assail people the human service worker is likely to confront, and is a consideration for all providers of crisis intervention services in regard to the safety of both those clients and the interventionists.

Chapter 9, Sexual Assault. Chapter 9 address a societal crisis that practically every human services worker will eventually encounter—clients who have either experienced or been affected by sexual assault. Sexually assaulted clientele are a special population because of the negative moral and social connotations associated with the dehumanizing acts perpetrated on them.

In addition to examining the immediate aftermath of sexual assault on both children and adults, this chapter also examines adult survivors of sexual/physical abuse experienced in childhood.

Chapter 10, Partner Violence. Chapter 10 deals with a crisis that many people in domestic relationships face: being treated violently by their partners. This chapter provides strategies to help people who are suffering abuse in any kind of domestic relationship. The chapter also deals with emerging treatment techniques for the batterers.

Chapter 11, Chemical Dependency: The Crisis of Addiction. Chapter 11 deals with one of the most pressing issues of our day, addiction to substances. Because chemical addiction is such a pervasive scourge on our society, no human services worker in the public arena can escape dealing with its effects. Crises of codependency and the long-term effects of substance abuse that create crises in the lives of adult children of addicts are also examined in this chapter.

Chapter 12, Personal Loss: Bereavement and Grief. Chapter 12 presents a type of crisis that every person will sooner or later face: personal loss. Even though the phenomenon of loss has been with us as long as the human species has existed, many people in our contemporary culture are poorly prepared and ill-equipped to deal with it. This chapter provides models and strategies for coping with unresolved grief. It uses ultimate loss—death—to examine a variety of problems associated with termination of relationships, both for the client and for the crisis worker.

Chapter 13, Crises in Schools. Schools have become a focal point for the violence perpetrated by gangs and disenfranchised and socially isolated children and adolescents. This chapter examines crises as they impact schools from preschool through higher education. It considers what crisis workers need to do in assessing, screening, and working with the potentially violent individual student who is estranged from the social mainstream of the school. It also deals with what the crisis worker needs to know in dealing with a problem that has become endemic in youth—suicide. The chapter describes what goes into making up a crisis response team for a school building and a school system, and how such teams respond when a crisis occurs. Finally, some of the legal and ethical ramifications of dealing with minors who are contemplating or have engaged in acts of violence are considered.

Part III, On the Home Front: Crisis in the Human Services Workplace

Part III (Chapters 14 through 16) concentrates on the problems of crisis workers themselves and their employing institutions.

Chapter 14, Violent Behavior in Institutions. Chapter 14 tackles the little publicized, and badly neglected, type of crisis that workers in many institutions face daily: violent behavior within the walls of the institution. Regardless of the organizational setting in which they are employed, workers will find in this chapter useful concepts and practical strategies that they and the institution can put to immediate use with agitated and potentially assaultive clients.

Chapter 15, Crisis/Hostage Negotiation. Chapter 15 presents another issue that human services workers pay little attention to, until it happens to them. The taking of hostages has become well-publicized through terrorism and other acts of violence. However, many hostage takings occur within the confines of human services work settings. This chapter provides basic crisis negotiation strategies and survival techniques that may enable a human services worker to contain and survive a hostage situation.

Chapter 16, Human Services Workers in Crisis: Burnout, Vicarious Traumatization, and Compassion Fatigue. Chapter 16 is about you and all human services workers who are in the helping professions. No worker is immune to stress, burnout, and the crises that go with human services work. This fact is particularly true in crisis work. This chapter should prove valuable for any worker anywhere whose work environment is frenetic and filled with crisis intervention or whose personality tends to generate compulsive behavior, perfectionism, or other stressors that may lead to burnout.

Part IV, No Man's Land

Part IV focuses on an ecosystem view of crisis and crisis intervention. It also provides an up-close-and-personal picture of the crisis workers who operate at the scene of a disaster.

Chapter 17, Disaster Response. Chapter 17 explores the theoretical basis and operating paradigm for large-scale disasters. It also describes a variety of crisis workers as they respond to a natural disaster, both how they take care of survivors and how they take care of themselves.

In summary, we have been less concerned with intellectualizing, philosophizing, or providing theoretical interpretations than with focusing on practical matters of how to respond in crisis situations, in order to give you an understanding of some of the general types of crises you will face and the basic skills you will need to do something about them.

New to the Seventh Edition

- New videos, available on DVD and through CourseMate (both available for packaging with the text), correlate with the text and demonstrate crisis intervention techniques, enabling students not only to understand the theoretical underpinnings of crisis intervention but also to apply them in crisis situations, thus learning how the theories play out in crisis scenarios.
- This updated edition includes references to seminal historical works as well as new research.
- Chapter 1, Approaching Crisis Intervention, now includes an expanded history of crisis intervention.
- Chapter 2, Culturally Effective Helping, contains extensive new material, in particular the use of Brown's social location theory as it applies to crisis. Videos developed for the text include a live scenario using the new theory.
- The discussion of basic intervention skills is now divided into two chapters in order to make the content easier for students to manage. Chapter 3, The Intervention and Assessment Models, presents the new hybrid task/step crisis intervention model and an expanded version of the Triage Assessment Form. Chapter 4, The Tools of the Trade, covers the basic techniques used in crisis intervention.
- The discussion of case handling in Chapter 5, Crisis Case Handling, has been updated, with more coverage of borderline personality disorders and legal changes that affect how crisis intervention clients may be handled.
- Chapter 6, Telephone and Online Crisis Counseling, now offers much more discussion of Internet and telehealth applications.
- The coverage of PTSD in Chapter 7, Posttraumatic Stress Disorder, has been substantively updated and enhanced, with new content on the new military wellness programs as well as the use of traumagrams.
- Chapter 8, Crisis of Lethality, has updated and expanded coverage of both assessment and intervention strategies for lethal clients.
- Case material in Chapter 9, Sexual Assault, has been refined to better illuminate issues in all three

segments discussed in the chapter: adult sexual assault, adult survivor of childhood sexual assault, and child assault.

- Chapter 10, Partner Violence, has expanded commentary on shelters and community models of intervention.
- Chapter 11, Chemical Dependency, has expanded coverage of behavioral treatment models and how they are used in inpatient and outpatient programs.
- Chapter 12, Personal Loss, has undergone major changes. The former stage models have largely been supplanted by process-oriented models such as the dual process and adaptive models of grieving.
- Chapter 13, Crises in Schools, now includes more on bullying and cyberbullying, as well as contagion suicide.
- Chapter 14, Violent Behavior in Institutions, has expanded coverage on treatment of workers who have been the victims of assault.
- Chapter 15, Crisis/Hostage Negotiation, introduces the SAFE and REACT models that are currently being used in hostage negotiation.
- Chapter 16, Human Services Workers in Crisis, which addresses burnout among human services workers, now includes expanded coverage of compassion fatigue and compassion satisfaction.
- Chapter 17, Disaster Response, provides more historical background on disaster response systems and how they have grown. New communications and planning techniques are discussed, along with the role of psychological first aid in disaster workers' responses to survivors.

Student Ancillaries
DVD for Crisis Intervention Strategies
Video clips demonstrate various crisis intervention scenarios through the use of role play by Dr. James and his students. Included scenarios address job loss, cultural adaptation, borderline personality disorder, domestic violence, psychological autopsy, alcohol addiction, critical incident stress debriefing, PTSD, rape, adult survivor of childhood sexual assault, violent students, burnout, survivors of disaster, and suicide. Instructors can package the DVD with the student textbooks at the bookstore when placing their textbook order. If the DVD did not come packaged with this text, it can be purchased separately at www.cengagebrain.com.

CourseMate Website for Crisis Intervention Strategies, *Seventh Edition*
The CourseMate website includes a suite of student resources such as quizzes, activities, an eBook, and exemplar videos developed to accompany this text. These video clips demonstrate various crisis intervention scenarios through the use of role play by Dr. James and his students. Included scenarios address job loss, child neglect, cultural adaptation, borderline personality disorder, domestic violence, psychological autopsy, alcohol addiction, critical incident stress debriefing, PTSD, rape, adult survivor of childhood sexual assault, violent students, burnout, survivors of disaster, and suicide. Instructors can package a printed access code with the student textbooks at the bookstore when placing their textbook order. If the printed access code did not come packaged with this text, instant access can be purchased separately at www.cengagebrain.com.

Instructor's Ancillaries
Online Instructor's Manual
The instructor's manual includes classroom exercises, role plays, and case studies, as well as practice test questions.

Online Test Bank
The Online Test Bank contains true/false, multiple-choice, and short essay questions with page number text references.

Acknowledgments

In writing a book that covers so many diverse areas of the human condition, it would be extremely presumptuous of us to rely solely on our own expertise and theories of truth, beauty, and goodness to propose crisis intervention techniques as the one true path of enlightenment to dealing with crises. We decided that the only realistic way to present the most current, reliable, and practical techniques of crisis intervention would be to go straight to the people who do this work day in and day out. They are not "big names," but rather people who go methodically about the business of crisis intervention daily in their respective venues. They work in such diverse occupational roles as ministers, police officers, psychologists, social workers, psychiatrists, nurses, marriage and family counselors, correction counselors, and school counselors. They work in every kind of agency and institution that deals with people and their dilemmas. They range geographically from across the United States to across the world. They are an encyclopedia of practical knowledge, and we are deeply in their debt for the help, advice, time, interviews, and critiques they have provided. This book would not be possible without their assistance, and we thank them one and all.

We would also like to thank the students in our crisis intervention classes at the University of Memphis. If you watch the videos that accompany this text, you are going to meet some of them up close and personal—both as crisis interventionists and as wild and crazy clients! You will see that as rookies they are not perfect, but they are pretty darn good. They had fun making the videos, and we hope you will have as much fun practicing these skills as they did. We want them to know we appreciate them deeply and have stood in awe and admiration in regard to how many of them have gone on to excel in this field.

A special thanks to Emily Meadows, doctoral student and counselor at Memphis Catholic High/Middle School, for her excellent work in creating the online practice quizzes and PowerPoint presentations. You might want to thank Emily yourself because you are going to find those are really helpful in learning the material and maybe even in getting an A.

We extend our grateful appreciation to the following professionals who have served as our editors and other gophers: Seth Dobrin, Senior Acquisitions Editor; Naomi Dreyer, Assistant Editor; Suzanna Kincaid, Editorial Assistant; Elizabeth Momb, Media Editor; Tami Strang, Marketing Program Manager; Rita Jaramillo, Content Project Manager; Caryl Gorska, Art Director; Judy Inouye, Manufacturing Planner; Dean Dauphinais, Rights Acquisitions Specialist; Anne Draus, production manager at Scratchgravel Publishing Services; Greg Draus, illustrator and art wizard; Ashley Liening, text researcher; and Peggy Tropp, copyeditor. They have practiced their own crisis intervention skills when we have become oppositionally defiant to written comments and suggestions.

Finally, we would certainly like to acknowledge the following reviewers for their cogent comments and insightful critiques.

Seventh Edition:
Lorraine Barber, Community College of Philadelphia
Renee Henry, Central Texas College

Stephany Hewitt, Trident Technical College
Debra Johnson, Lindenwood University
Nicole Williams, Anne Arundel Community College

Sixth Edition:
Annette Albrecht, Tarleton State University
Sarah Altman, Southwestern Community College
Irene Mass Ametrano, Eastern Michigan University
Larry Ashley, University of Nevada, Las Vegas
Faye Austin, Springfield College
Ed Barker, Liberty University
Ken Bateman, Amberton University
Evelyn Biles, Regent University
John Boal, University of Akron
Patricia Bromley, University of Wisconsin–Platteville
Robert M. Burns, Hesser College
Tommy Caisango, Webster University
Nancy G. Calley, University of Detroit Mercy
William F. Cavitt, Troy University, Florida Region
Barbara Chandler, University of Alabama
Joseph C. Ciechalski, East Carolina University
Cynthia A. Cook, Saint Louis University
Carolyn Dallinger, Simpson College
Ronald Dickerson, Trident Technical College
Eustace Duffus, Prairie View A&M University
James Duffy, Springfield College
Kelly Duncan, Northern State University
Louis F. Garzarelli, Mount Aloysius College
Patricia Harris, Sandhills Community College
Daphne Henderson, East Tennessee State University
Pilar Hernandez, San Diego State University
James Herndon, Columbia College

Jan Hockensmith, Olivet Nazarene University
Debbie L. Hogan, Ferrum College
Pearl Jacobs, Sacred Heart University
Jean Keim, University of Arizona South
Bonnie Kendall, Columbia Basin College
Larry Kontosh, Florida Atlantic University
Alan M. Lavallee, Delaware Technical & Community College
Eric Ling, Mount Olive College
J. Barry Mascari, Kean University
Virginia McDermott, University of New Mexico
Richard Mizer, Columbia College/Ft. Leonard Wood
Christine Mouton, University of Central Florida
Jean Nuernberger, Central Missouri State University
Suzette Overby, Riverland Community College
Derrick Paladino, University of North Texas
Sue Passalacqua, California State University, Fullerton
Debra Pender, Southern Illinois University/Northern Illinois University
Beth Potter, Anne Arundel Community College
Michael Poulakis, University of Indianapolis
Mary Rogers, Black Hills State University
Lori Rudolph, University of New Mexico
Christopher Schanno, Drexel University
Shanta Sharma, Henderson State University
Debbie Simpler, Belmont University
Jakob Steinberg, Fairleigh Dickinson University
Darlene Townsend, Northwest Nazarene University
Joy S. Whitman, DePaul University
Shannon Wolf, Southwestern Baptist Theological Seminary

Basic Training

Crisis Intervention Theory and Application

Part I introduces you to the fundamental concepts, theories, strategies, and skills needed to understand and conduct effective crisis intervention. Chapter 1 presents a brief historical overview of the field and introduces the conceptual dimensions of crisis work. Chapter 2 deals with the ecosystemic and multicultural considerations involved in providing crisis intervention. Chapter 3 serves as a key to the application of assessment and intervention strategies in crisis intervention. Chapter 4 describes the basic skills and techniques crisis interventionists use. Chapter 5 explains the major components of effective case management in crisis intervention. Chapter 6 discusses two of the main ways that crisis intervention is delivered—by telephone and Internet.

CHAPTER 1

Approaching Crisis Intervention

A Brief History of Crisis Intervention

We open the seventh edition of this book with a brief history of crisis intervention. While crisis itself has probably been in existence ever since Eve ate the apple in the Garden of Eden, formal crisis theory, research, and intervention comprise one of the newest fields in psychotherapy. Probably most laypersons would think of formal crisis intervention as historically having to do with large-scale disasters, such as hurricanes or 9/11, and most typically performed by government agencies like the Federal Emergency Management Agency (FEMA) or by charitable organizations like the Red Cross. While the Red Cross and the Salvation Army have been involved in disaster relief for approximately the past century, FEMA has been in existence only for about 30 years, and until quite recently none of these organizations has had much to say or do about crisis intervention from a mental health perspective. Like Topsy in Harriet Beecher Stowe's classic, *Uncle Tom's Cabin,* "it just sorta growed." Understanding just how much it has "growed" in such a short time will help you understand why there's still a lot we don't know. But what we do know in 2012 is light-years ahead of what we knew when the first edition of this book appeared in 1987. If you could find a first edition in your library, it would look very little like this book does now.

Suicide prevention is probably the longest running intervention program in which individual crisis is addressed from a mental health standpoint. The first identifiable crisis phone line was established in 1906 by the National Save-a-Life League (Bloom, 1984). Dr. Edwin

Shneidman's (2001) landmark research into the causes of suicide, which started in the 1950s, has spanned six decades. Suicide has achieved such importance that it has become an "ology" and has a national association devoted to its study.

However, most people who study the field would probably say the benchmark for crisis intervention was the Cocoanut Grove nightclub fire in 1942, in which more than 400 people perished. Dr. Erich Lindemann (1944), who treated many of the survivors, found that they seemed to have common emotional responses and a need for psychological assistance and support. Out of Lindemann's work came the first notions of what may be called "normal" grief reactions to a disaster. Gerald Caplan (1961) was also involved in working with the Cocoanut Grove survivors. His experience led to some of the first attempts to explain what a crisis is and to build a theory of crisis. However, not until the 1960s did the first attempts occur to provide a structure for what would become crisis intervention.

The Community Mental Health Centers Act of 1963 completely changed the way mental health services were delivered in the United States. As the large state insane asylums were closed down and replaced by community mental health centers, one of the primary mandates of those centers was to provide emergency services and crisis intervention 24/7. While the community mental health concept was laudable, the idealistic notion that patients would be docile, medication compliant, and fully functional proved to be problematic. Depending on what statistics are used, fully a quarter to a half of residents of local jails have identifiable mental disorders. Those prisoners got there because they were deemed out of control enough to warrant a psychiatric detention order, and since there is no place else to put them, they go directly to jail! It is little wonder, then, that mobile mental health crisis teams, police officers, and emergency room staff now get training in crisis intervention with the mentally ill.

To really understand the evolution of crisis intervention, though, is to understand that several social movements have been critical to its development, and these did not start fully formed as "crisis intervention" groups by any means. Three of the major movements that helped shape crisis intervention into an emerging specialty were Alcoholics Anonymous (AA), Vietnam veterans, and the women's movement of the 1970s. Although their commissioned intentions and objectives had little to do with the advancement of crisis intervention as a clinical specialty, they had a lot to do with people who were desperate for help and weren't getting any. These groups all started as grassroots movements.

Grassroots Movements

The need for crisis intervention services remains unrecognized by the public and by existing institutions until a critical mass of victims comes together to exert enough legal, political, or economic pressure to cause the particular crisis category, malady, or social problem to become formalized. Until that time, it remains informal, nonprofessional, and unsubsidized. The problem is responded to or handled mainly through ad hoc, informal means by former victims, current victims, friends, or significant others who are affected by the problem. The free storefront clinics for Vietnam veterans that grew out of a refusal of the Veterans Administration to handle their problems and the attempt by Mothers Against Drunk Driving (MADD) to deal with the crisis of drunk driving in the face of resistant state legislatures are excellent examples of grassroots responses to unmet needs.

Initiators of crisis intervention services are generally concerned with one particular crisis category that personally affects them in some way. Typically, the crisis gets far enough out of hand to cause noticeable problems before remedial responses are initiated. At first, the initiators are mavericks who are starting a victims' revolt. The revolt is against an entrenched status quo or power structure that shows little awareness of or responsiveness to the problem. The victims' revolt somehow manages to get a fledgling crisis agency started despite the benign neglect and reluctance of mainstream society. In the 1970s, Vietnam veterans'

efforts to get posttraumatic stress disorder (PTSD) categorized as a mental disease and get financial support for research and treatment are a classic example of this revolt. So are the efforts of the National Organization for Women and other women's groups in the 1970s to raise the curtain on domestic violence and child abuse in the United States and to get state legislatures to deal with them as criminal acts.

The fledgling crisis agency is initially funded by private donations, as with the many telephone call-in lines for victims of domestic violence that were started at local YWCAs in the 1970s. The services are often provided by ad hoc workers who are quite informally organized. The crisis agency gains access to public funding only after the agency has attained validation and some recognition by a substantial portion of the power structure. If, after a time, the crisis agency does not attain credibility sufficient to garner substantial private support or a modicum of public support, the agency begins to falter and eventually folds and ceases to operate.

It is this grassroots influence that often captures the attention of the media, impels people to join as volunteers, and causes a greater number of clients and victims to seek the services of the agency. Initially, community leaders may deny that the crisis exists, minimize its seriousness, or express doubt that it represents a recurring problem. But when the crisis persists, they finally come to realize that someone must become proactive—someone must exert the leadership, energy, time, resources, and resolve to confront the crisis. Thus the formation of an agency is sanctioned or even encouraged. If the fledgling agency born from the need to contain the crisis succeeds and is publicly recognized as fulfilling a need, the quest to expand and mature begins. As mainstream institutions, such as governmental structures, become aware of the problem and as volunteer centers reach the saturation point at which needs are obviously going unmet, some governmental or institutional funding is provided.

Pressure politics, public relations, and public image building affect the course and growth of an organization and the problem it seeks to solve. For example, the plight of the Vietnam veterans suffering from PTSD was largely ignored until the problem spilled over from the streets into the seats of power and authority—from personal crisis to politics. When the PTSD problem began to affect members of Congress, the power of the federal government and the resources of the Veterans Administration were brought to bear not only to create a network of veterans centers throughout the country, but also to slash bureaucratic red tape to ensure that services for Vietnam veterans were taken to the streets where PTSD sufferers were living rather than requiring veterans to report to regular VA hospitals. The activism of those veterans in the 1970s can be seen today in the comprehensive frontline treatment and exit programs of the armed services and the extensive use of veterans outreach centers across the United States. In fact, the United States Department of Veterans Affairs now sponsors the National Center for PTSD: Advancing Science and Promoting Understanding of Traumatic Stress. The Center aims to help U.S. veterans and others through research, education, and training on trauma and PTSD.

An excellent example of this political process is currently occurring in the United States with the controversy surrounding and the continuing reorganization of the Federal Emergency Management Agency. A great deal more will be said about this organization and its short, checkered history in Chapter 17.

The Importance of Volunteerism

Contrary to the popular misconception that paid veteran crisis workers descend on a large-scale disaster like smoke jumpers into a forest fire, most crisis intervention in the United States is done by volunteers. Volunteer workers perform all kinds of services in most crisis agencies—from menial chores to answering the phone to frontline crisis intervention with clients. Volunteerism is often the key to getting the fledgling crisis agency rolling. The use of trained volunteers as crisis workers has been a recognized component of many crisis centers and agencies for years (Clark & McKiernan, 1981; Roberts, 1991, p. 29; Slaikeu & Leff-Simon, 1990, p. 321). Probably the greatest number of frontline volunteers are used in staffing 24-hour suicide hotlines in major cities. Such hotlines require an enormous number of crisis workers because the crisis service never ceases—it must be provided 7 days a week, 52 weeks a year. Roberts (1991, p. 29) reported that more than three-quarters of all crisis centers in the United States indicate that they rely on volunteer crisis workers and that such volunteers outnumber professional staff by more than 6 to 1. Although volunteers cannot replace professionals, highly selective screening procedures and effective preservice and inservice training programs usually make the volunteer cadre in crisis centers the mainstay of hotline services in this country. Typically, as the numbers and needs of the clientele increase, the agency reaches the point where compassion

and volunteerism alone cannot handle all of the complex personal, social, economic, public relations, psychological, and political problems that assail it.

The Need for Institutionalism

As crisis agencies become well known and as their clientele are drawn from a wider segment of the community (to the point that the work cannot be handled by the communication system of grapevine, word of mouth, notepad, e-mail, and Twitter), the agency sees that if it is to continue to grow and serve its clients, it must institutionalize. The seeds of bureaucracy are thus born.

To manage all of its vital functions, the agency must centralize and formalize most aspects of its operation. It takes on a formal board of directors, establishes rigorous auditing and record-keeping functions, and requires more money, paid staff, and staff support. As crisis agencies become crisis organizations, they gain more power, prestige, and notoriety. They tend to attract the attention of the human services professions because they offer fertile fields for funded research, placement of practicum and internship students, and employment of graduates. Crisis agencies sometimes attain eminent success, to the point that it becomes a vested interest of the human services professions to formalize the competencies of the personnel of such successful agencies through certification, licensure, and accreditation. The progression from the humble origins of Alcoholics Anonymous as a support group formed by fellow alcoholics in the 1930s to the current classification of alcoholism as a disease, the proliferation of thousands of treatment centers around the world, huge government funding for research and prevention, university courses on the subject, and the state licensure or certification of substance abuse counselors provides an outstanding example of the evolution from self-help by a group of recovering alcoholics in crisis to the full institutionalization of the crisis of drug abuse.

As a specialty evolves, it develops its own empirical base, professional research, and writings. For example, for crisis intervention we have publications such as *Crisis Intervention, Journal of Interpersonal Violence, Victimology, Violence and Victims, Journal of Family Violence, Death Studies, Journal of Traumatic Stress, Suicide and Life Threatening Behavior, Child Abuse and Neglect, Journal of Child Sexual Abuse, Aggression and Violent Behavior,* and *Violence Against Women.* The amount of data and information in the field has expanded so much that the *Encyclopedia of Psychological Trauma* (Reyes, Elhai, & Ford, 2008) includes 720 large pages covering everything from A (Abuse, child physical) to W (Workplace violence).

Specialty areas may also attain a distinct level of recognition by building a base of national or regional affiliates, as with various topic- or malady-centered hotlines, chat rooms, and websites; AA chapters; spouse abuse centers; and victim assistance programs. Local, state, regional, and national conferences are organized to provide for exchange of ideas and problem-solving strategies. These conferences range from specialty areas that bring together some of the greatest research minds in the field—such as the First Annual Conference on Trauma, Loss, and Dissociation in 1995—to "in the trenches" conferences such as the Annual Convening of Crisis Intervention Personnel, which provides practical, hands-on programs for crisis interventionists, and the Crisis Intervention Team (CIT) convention for police officers who deal with the mentally ill. The emergence of hundreds of crisis-oriented organizations in the 1970s, 1980s, and 1990s (Maurer & Sheets, 1999) and the realization of the role that immediate intervention plays in alleviating traumatic stress (Mitchell & Everly, 1995) attest to the dramatic transformation and professional acceptance of crisis intervention from a psychological backwater field to a pervasive specialty. Probably the best testament to the center stage on which crisis intervention is now playing is the birth in 2006 of the American Psychological Association's newest division, Division 56, Trauma Psychology, along with the provision of counseling (Council for Accreditation of Counseling & Educationally Related Programs, 2009) and school psychology (National Association of School Psychologists, 2010) professional accreditation standards for training graduates in crisis intervention. One of the major players in the field of trauma, Christine Courtois (Courtois & Gold, 2009), has eloquently stated the critical need for inclusion of psychological trauma training in all helping service curricula.

The Media and the Societal Impetus for Crisis Intervention

Why, from the 1970s to the present, has the crisis intervention movement experienced such extraordinary growth? Probably no single factor alone can explain why. In the United States, the bombing of the Murrah Federal Building in Oklahoma City, 9/11, Hurricane Katrina, Virginia Tech, Northern Illinois University, and a variety of public school shootings have all given rise to the demand for crisis intervention. Yet such natural and manmade disasters have been with us since

the city of Pompeii was buried by Mt. Vesuvius and Rome was sacked and burned. What has changed public perception to the extent that the acronym PTSD—which in the first edition of this book was a brand new term that lots of psychologists were unfamiliar with or didn't believe was a valid diagnostic—is now common parlance?

The media's role in creating awareness of crises and crisis intervention has probably generated the most profound change in public consciousness of what it means to be in crisis after a large-scale disaster. When Matthew Brady's pictures of the windrows of dead from the American Civil War battle of Antietam were put on display in New York in 1863, this first use of photographic media changed forever how people would perceive wars and the psychological trauma that invariably comes with them. Public perception of war as glorious changed forever as its horror and carnage were brought to the American dooryard by Brady's harrowing pictures. Since that time, the ability of the media has advanced from the still-life daguerreotypes of Brady to real-time sound and video of New Orleans citizens sitting on top of flooded buildings, of Baghdad residents running from a car bombing, of the jumpers from the Twin Towers. It is unclear exactly what impact such real-time media has on the public, but clearly it does have an impact and changes our perception of the world as ever smaller, more interconnected, and certainly more dangerous, unsafe, and crisis prone (Marshall et al., 2007).

There are valid reasons for the widespread acceptance of crisis intervention as a therapeutic specialty. People in general have become more positive in their acceptance of outreach strategies following a crisis and are more knowledgeable about its psychological ramifications such as PTSD. There is less "blaming the victim" as somehow inadequate. Probably most important from a pragmatic point of view, it is cost effective (Roberts, 1991). People in human services and political leadership positions have discovered that when they either ignore crisis situations or leave solutions entirely to the experts who have little political clout, lasting solutions elude them, and the leaders themselves are blamed and held publicly responsible. Reactive responding has not worked very well. Leaders have discovered that endemic crises will not easily go away, that reaction or no action may result in the problems' becoming pandemic or out of control. In a sense, then, political expediency has dictated not only the widespread acceptance of effective crisis intervention strategies but also that crisis intervention become proactive, preventive, and integrated on the local, national, and international levels. One need go no further than the aftermath of Hurricane Katrina to understand the full impact of what this paragraph is about.

The Case Against Too Much "Helping"

With the rise of postintervention psychological assistance in the last 20 years, an interesting phenomenon has started to emerge. "Do-gooder" individuals and paternalistic bureaucracies appear on the scene and want to "straighten" things out and "help" people. Van den Eynde and Veno (1999) report the case of an Australian community that literally had to kick government "help" out of town after the discovery of a case of long-term mass pedophilia in their midst. Even though the community clearly had the situation under control, the government authorities kept insisting they did not. What they had to do to get the government out of their town is interesting reading indeed.

In a worst-case scenario, crass commercialization, pseudoscience, vicarious thrills, and outright fraud mark the traumatic wake of a crisis (Echterling & Wylie, 1999; Gist, Lubin, & Redburn, 1999; Gist, Woodall, & Magenheimer, 1999; Lohr et al., 1999). Gist, Lubin, and Redburn (1999) have coined the term "trauma tourism" to describe the burgeoning industry in postintervention psychological trauma replete with trade shows, trade publications, talk shows, and charitable giving.

The assumption is that disaster invariably leads to psychopathology, and psychopathology sells. If people are seen as incapable of caring for themselves and are traumatized and in a panic state after a disaster, it follows that they must be somehow infirm and unequal to the task and need assistance. A paternalistic government is then tasked with taking care of them. This view may be even more true with "noble savages," transients, indigenous people, or other marginalized and disenfranchised groups who are seen as socially or technically unsophisticated and in need of benevolent and well-intentioned guidance and protection (Gist, Lubin, & Redburn, 1999; Kaniasty & Norris, 1999; Ober et al., 2000). On the other hand, such groups of disenfranchised and dislocated persons, particularly if they are migrants or undocumented aliens, may be given short shrift from the authorities and may be persecuted if they come to the attention of bureaucracies that are dealing with a crisis (Brown, 2009, pp. 215–226).

The fact is that in most instances victims of disaster do not panic. They organize themselves in a collective manner and go about the business of helping one another and restoring equilibrium (Kaniasty & Norris, 1999). Called the "altruistic or therapeutic community," the typical immediate collective response to a disaster is characterized by the disappearance of community conflicts, heightened internal solidarity, charity, sharing, communal public works, and a positive "can-do" attitude (Barton, 1969; Giel, 1990). So, as of 2012, crisis intervention has emerged from a psychological backwater 25 years ago when we started writing the first edition of this book to a veritable tidal wave of interest, albeit it at times controversial and full of heated debate.

Definitions of Crisis

This book is mainly about doing crisis intervention with individuals. To a lesser extent, it is also about systems in crisis and how the crisis interventionist functions within those systems, whether in institutions such as hospitals, schools, and mental health centers or as service providers after large-scale disasters. To that end we start this book in a pretty boring way by giving you not only a history lesson but also a long list of definitions of crisis as it applies to both individuals and systems. We apologize for that, but we do this because we want you to understand that this business is still so new that a definition of an individual or a system in crisis is by no means fixed or absolute. As a matter of fact, as you are going to find throughout this book, there is a whole lot about crisis and crisis intervention that is not fixed or absolute! Consider, then, the following definitions of individuals in crisis.

Individual Crisis Definitions

1. People are in a state of crisis when they face an obstacle to important life goals—an obstacle that is, for a time, insurmountable by the use of customary methods of problem solving. A period of disorganization ensues, a period of upset, during which many abortive attempts at solution are made. (Caplan, 1961, p. 18)
2. A crisis arises from a traumatic event that is unpredictable and uncontrollable. There is an inability to influence it by one's actions. The nature of the event changes values and priorities, and indeed changes everything. (Sarri, 2005, pp. 19–24)
3. Crisis is a crisis because the individual knows no response to deal with a situation. (Carkhuff & Berenson, 1977, p. 165)

4. Crisis is a personal difficulty or situation that immobilizes people and prevents them from consciously controlling their lives. (Belkin, 1984, p. 424)

5. Crisis is a state of disorganization in which people face frustration of important life goals or profound disruption of their life cycles and methods of coping with stressors. The term *crisis* usually refers to a person's feelings of fear, shock, and distress *about* the disruption, not to the disruption itself. (Brammer, 1985, p. 94)

6. Crisis is a temporary breakdown of coping. Expectations are violated and waves of emotion such as anger, anxiety, guilt, and grief surface. Old problems and earlier losses may surface. The event's intensity, duration, and suddenness may affect the severity of response to the crisis. (Poland & McCormick, 1999, p. 6)

7. Crisis is a loss of psychological equilibrium or a state of emotional instability that includes elements of depression and anxiety which is caused by an external event with which individuals are unable to cope with at their usual level of ability. (Kleespies, 2009, p. 15)

8. Crisis in a clinical context refers to an acute emotional upset arising from situational, developmental, or sociocultural sources, and results in a temporary inability to cope by means of one's usual problem-solving devices. (Hoff, Hallisey, & Hoff, 2009, p. 4)

9. A crisis may be a catastrophic event or a series of life stresses which build rapidly and accumulate such that the person's homeostatic balance is disturbed and creates a vulnerable state, which, if not resolved, avoided, or redefined will cause self-righting devices to no longer be effective and plunge the person into psychological disequilibrium. (Golan, 1978, p. 8)

It should immediately become clear that the term *crisis* has different meanings to different people and is used to describe a variety of incidents, settings, situations, and the adaptations, albeit less than adequate, that people attempt to make in response to them. To summarize these definitions, for an individual, crisis is the perception or experiencing of an event or situation as an intolerable difficulty that exceeds the person's current resources and coping mechanisms. Unless the person obtains relief, the crisis has the potential to cause severe affective, behavioral, and cognitive malfunctioning up to the point of instigating injurious or lethal behavior to oneself or others.

Behavioral Emergencies

A *behavioral emergency* occurs when a crisis escalates to the point that the situation requires immediate intervention to avoid injury or death. Direct or intentional behavioral emergencies fall into the general categories of engaging in self-injurious behavior, perpetrating violent interpersonal behavior, and being a victim of violence (Kleespies, 2009, p. 13). Suicide/homicides resulting from broken romances provide a classic example of these categories.

We believe that *indirect and noncommissioned* behavioral emergencies can also occur. Indirect behavioral emergencies occur when people make bad decisions and wind up placing themselves in potentially lethal situations. Indirect behavioral emergencies are crises that happen with no directed purpose or intentionality to do something harmful to oneself or others. Drunk driving, boating, snow skiing, swimming, and project construction may all turn into behavioral emergencies that have the potential for injurious or lethal behavior and call for intervention. A parent who, after receiving a phone call informing her that her child has been seriously injured in a school bus accident, becomes hysterical, leaves her newborn at home with a pot of cooking oil boiling on the stove, and drives 90 miles an hour to the hospital is creating a behavioral emergency to put it mildly. Persons with borderline personality disorder are the archetype of people whose unstable lifestyles continuously set them up to fly into crisis after crisis and oftentimes move quickly into behavioral emergencies by impulsively deciding to commit suicide or committing *parasuicide* (accidentally doing something or going into a situation a reasonable person wouldn't and getting themselves killed).

More often than we would like to imagine, crisis interventionists will deal with people whose behavior has escalated to the point that they can be considered to be behavioral emergencies. For that reason, when you first make the acquaintance of the Triage Assessment Form in Chapter 3 you will note that scores of 10 (maximum) on the form's scales all have lethal feeling, behaving, and thinking as part of their assessment anchors.

Systemic Crisis Definitions

"Individual crisis" is really something of an oxymoron, because as most crises unfold, they rarely remain confined to one person. They ripple out and affect numerous other people who interact with the person in crisis. To think that the crisis created by a date rape or an alcoholic mother affects only the young woman who was assaulted or the housewife who drinks is to have a very wrong notion indeed about what a crisis is and what you may have to do and with whom you may work. Therefore, when we consider a definition of crisis, we are bound to look at how that crisis affects the system.

Systemic crises may come in many forms. They may be economically based, perhaps affecting only the families of a small produce chain that goes bankrupt when the refrigeration in their warehouse fails or as large as a worldwide recession that throws millions of people out of work. They may be natural disasters, as small as a tornado tearing up a small Kansas farming community or as large as a pandemic flu epidemic that kills millions. They may be manmade, ranging from a structural failure that causes a building to collapse to wars that kill and displace millions of people. They may be psychologically based, ranging from fear of a school bully to an entire nation rendered paranoid by the terrorist attacks of 9/11. As you will see in the last chapter of this book, large-scale disasters that become systemic crises most generally fit the public perception of what crisis intervention is about. Indeed, the role of crisis interventionists as mental health service providers in that setting is becoming larger and larger. Consider, then, the following definitions of a system in crisis, in which the term "system" ranges across families, churches, businesses, neighborhoods, communities, large cities, geographical flood plains, and nations:

1. A crisis that threatens the organization is unexpected, demands a rapid response in a short time frame, and threatens its basic values. (Hermann, 1963, p. 63)
2. Communities in crisis have several characteristics in common with individuals. Within the group there is an atmosphere of tension and fear. Rumors run rampant. Normal functioning is at a standstill and schools and businesses are closed and health and emergency resources may be in short supply. (Hoff, Hallisey, & Hoff, 2009, p. 209)
3. Communities in crisis go through chronological stages following a disaster that are known as the impact, heroic/rescue, honeymoon, disillusionment, and reconstruction/recovery phase. Each phase has identifiable characteristics and sequential timelines, and depending on how the various systems in the community react, may move forward positively or not. (Roberts, 2005, p. 205)
4. A systemic crisis is a negative event or outcome, which includes the element of surprise, disruption of operations, and is a threat to the property, financial and physical resources, well-being of individuals within the system, and the reputation of the system to provide for the well-being of its constituency. (Zdziarski, Dunkel, & Rollo, 2007, p. 6)

To sum up what we believe generally defines a systemic crisis: When a traumatic event occurs such that people, institutions, communities, and ecologies are overwhelmed and response systems are unable to effectively contain and control the event in regard to both physical and psychological reactions to it, the crisis has become systemic. The size of the system may range from a family, to a mental health clinic, to a nation, but the main identifying factor is that the system is in disequilibrium and previous response systems and coping mechanisms no longer work. If adequate intervention doesn't occur, the potential exists for irreparable damage or termination of the system. Sandwiched between individual and systemic crises is another type of crisis with which the interventionist is likely to be faced, which we have called a "*metastasizing* crisis."

Metastasizing Crisis

A *metastasizing* crisis occurs when a small, isolated incident is not contained and begins to spread. The analogy to the spread of cancer is apt because what may start out as a focal and localized problem that could have been easily cured with early, preemptive intervention is not diagnosed or remedied, but is allowed to grow through benign neglect and suddenly becomes endemic within the system. At that point it is anything but easy to excise or remedy. A school system's neglect in dealing with isolated cases of bullying can soon lead to a culture of bullying that moves out of the classroom and into cyberspace to pervade and wreak havoc on students' lives 24 hours a day. *Predispositioning* both personnel and resources can go a long way toward what is called *primary* intervention, which seeks to proactively handle problems before they metastasize and get out of control. From that standpoint many crisis interventionists are also engaged in *primary prevention*, stopping a problem before it starts, as well as *secondary intervention*, minimizing the harmful effects that have already occurred (Caplan, 1964).

Characteristics of Crisis

The following discussion of characteristics of crisis represents an expanded definition of what *crisis* means.

Presence of Both Danger and Opportunity.   Crisis is a *danger* because it can overwhelm the individual to the extent that serious pathology, including homicide and suicide, may result. Crisis is also an *opportunity* because the pain it induces impels the person to seek help (Aguilera & Messick, 1982, p. 1). If the individual takes advantage of the opportunity, the intervention can help plant the seeds of self-growth and self-realization (Brammer, 1985, p. 95). People can react in any one of three ways to crisis. Under ideal circumstances, many individuals can cope effectively with crisis by themselves and develop strength from the experience. They change and grow in a positive manner and come out of the crisis both stronger and more compassionate (Danish, 1977).

Others appear to survive the crisis but effectively block the hurtful affect from awareness, only to have it haunt them in innumerable ways throughout the rest of their lives. Yet others break down psychologically at the onset of the crisis and clearly demonstrate that they are incapable of going any further with their lives unless given immediate and intensive assistance (Rapoport, 1967).

Seeds of Growth and Change.   In the disequilibrium that accompanies crisis, anxiety is always present, and its discomfort provides an impetus for change (Janosik, 1984, p. 39). Often anxiety must reach the boiling point before the person is ready to admit the problem is out of control. One need look no further than the substance abuser for affirmation of this assertion. By waiting too long, for example, the substance abuser may become so entrenched that he or she may need a therapeutic jackhammer to break the addiction down into manageable pieces. Even here, however, a threshold point for change may be reached, albeit in last-ditch desperation, when the abuser finally surrenders to the fact that something must be done.

No Panaceas or Quick Fixes.   People in crisis are generally amenable to help through a variety of forms of intervention, some of which are described as *brief therapy* (Cormier & Hackney, 1987, p. 240). For problems of long duration, however, quick fixes are rarely available. Many problems of clients in severe crisis stem from the fact that the clients sought quick fixes in the first place, usually through a pill. Such a "fix" may dampen the dreadful responses but does not change the instigating stimulus, so the crisis deepens.

The Necessity of Choice.   Life is a process of interrelated crises and challenges that we confront or not, deciding to live or not (Carkhuff & Berenson, 1977, p. 173). In the realm of crisis, *not to choose is a choice,* and this choice usually turns out to be negative and destructive. *Choosing to do something* at least contains the seeds of growth and allows a person the chance to set goals and formulate a plan to begin to overcome the dilemma.

Universality and Idiosyncrasy.   Disequilibrium or disorganization accompanies every crisis, whether universal or idiosyncratic (Janosik, 1984, p. 13). Crisis is universal because no one is immune to breakdown, given the right constellation of circumstances. It is idiosyncratic because what one person may successfully overcome, another may not, even though the circumstances are virtually the same. It is foolhardy to maintain a belief that one is immune to psychic assaults, that one can handle any crisis in a stable, poised, and masterful fashion. Thousands of "tough" veterans of the Vietnam, Afghanistan, and two Gulf Wars suffering from posttraumatic stress disorder (PTSD), who have turnstiled through VA hospitals, veterans' centers, and other medical facilities, are convincing proof that when a crisis boils over, disorganization, disequilibrium, disorientation, and fragmentation of an individual's coping mechanisms can occur no matter how conditioned against psychological trauma the person may be.

Resiliency.   Yet the National Comorbidity Survey found that while their nationally representative sample had better than a 50% prevalence of traumatic events for both men and women, only about 5% of men and 10% of women contracted PTSD (Kessler et al., 1995). One of the key jobs of the crisis interventionist is finding the right combination of support systems and coping mechanisms, and forming them into action plans that will tap the reservoir of resiliency that most people have to move them through and beyond the crisis.

Perception.   As paradoxical as it may seem, the precipitating event is not the major cause of the crisis. It is the *perception* of the event that plays a huge role in a crisis. How individuals interpret events has a great deal to do with how amenable the crisis will be to resolution

(Callahan, 2009, p. 21). As the old adage states, "One man's fruit may be another man's poison." It is no accident that the Cognitive scale in the Triage Assessment Form that you will encounter in Chapter 3 is the most complex of the three scales. How people appraise precipitating events and what the interventionist can do to reframe and temper catastrophic interpretations of the event will have a great deal to do with how well and how quickly the crisis is alleviated.

Complicated Symptomology. Crisis is *not* simple; it is complex and difficult to understand, and it defies cause-and-effect description (Brammer, 1985, p. 91; Kliman, 1978, p. xxi). The symptoms that overlie precipitating crisis events become tangled webs that crisscross all environments of an individual. When an event reaches a flash point, there may be so many compounding problems that crisis workers must intervene directly in a variety of areas. Furthermore, the environment of people in crisis strongly affects the ease or difficulty with which the crisis can be handled. Families, individuals, partners, institutions, and employees may all directly affect problem resolution and a return to stability. When large numbers of people are affected at the same time by a crisis, the entire ecological system of a neighborhood, community, geographical region, or country may need intervention. A stark but global example of such a nationwide ecological crisis occurred in the United States in the immediate aftermath of the September 11, 2001, terrorist attacks (Bass & Yep, 2002; Pyszczynski, Solomon, & Greenberg, 2003).

Transcrisis States

Crises have typically been seen as time limited, usually persisting a maximum of 6 to 8 weeks, at the end of which the subjective discomfort diminishes (Janosik, 1984, p. 9). That view is now changing, and the effects of the original crisis may extend a good bit beyond that time frame (Callahan, 1998; Salzer & Bickman, 1999). Indeed, the impact of a crisis may last a lifetime (van der Kolk & McFarlane, 1996). What occurs during the immediate aftermath of the crisis event determines whether or not the crisis will become a disease reservoir that will be transformed into a chronic and long-term state. Although the original crisis event may be submerged below awareness, and the individual may believe the problem has been resolved, the appearance of new stressors may bring the individual to the crisis state again. This emotional roller coaster may occur

frequently and for extended periods of time, ranging from months to years. An adult who has unresolved anger toward a dead parent and transfers that anger to other authority figures, such as supervisors or employers, is in a *transcrisis state.*

The adult may have apparently attained functional and normal mental health. However, this appearance is gained at the cost of warding off and repressing the "unfinished business" of making peace with the lost parent. Later, during the stress related to getting along with another authority figure, the person blames that authority figure and has no conscious awareness that the unfinished repressed material (submerged as a transcrisis state) is at the root of the problem. Although the person with the transcrisis state may come to identify the problem as poor relationship skills and enter counseling to improve those skills, this action is also a symptom of the psychological roller-coaster ride that started with the unfinished business. The relationship skills may be temporarily improved, but the source of the transcrisis state may not have been recognized or expunged. It has merely subsided, and a temporary state of equilibrium has been achieved, but the original trauma will usually reemerge and instigate a new crisis the moment new stressors are introduced. Dynamically, this pattern is defensive repression. Therapeutically, this transcrisis state calls for crisis intervention techniques.

Transcrisis Differentiated From Posttraumatic Stress Disorder

People familiar with posttraumatic stress disorder (PTSD) may ask, "So how is a transcrisis state different from PTSD?" First, PTSD is an identifiable anxiety disorder (American Psychiatric Association, 2000) caused by an extremely traumatic event, and very specific criteria must be present for a diagnosis of PTSD to be made. Although a person who is suffering from PTSD may be in a transcrisis state, not all people who are in a transcrisis state suffer from PTSD. Indeed, it would probably be more appropriate to look at all the different kinds of anxiety and personality disorders found in the fourth edition of the *Diagnostic and Statistical Manual–Technical Revision* (DSM-IV-TR; American Psychiatric Association, 2000) as representative of transcrisis states because of the chronic kinds of thinking, feeling, and acting that keep these individuals constantly in psychological hot, if not boiling, water.

But it is not just persons with anxiety and personality disorders who may be in a transcrisis state. A broad range of people, from so-called normal individuals who are constantly fired from jobs because of their uncontrollable tempers to those with psychoses who quit taking their medicine because it has unpleasant side effects, are also representative of individuals in transcrisis states. Armsworth and Holaday (1993), in their review of affective, behavioral, cognitive, and physiological-somatic effects of trauma, identified a number of factors that, although not found in PTSD descriptors, would probably be inherent in many transcrisis states. The key differentiating element of a transcrisis state is that, whether it is due to trauma, personality traits, substance abuse, psychosis, or chronic environmental stressors, the state is residual and recurrent and always present to some degree. Although people in a transcrisis state are generally capable of functioning at some minimal level, they are always at risk, and any single small added stressor may tip the balance and send them into crisis. Therefore, when we assess individuals in crisis, our focus is not only on the current clinical/diagnostic state of the individual, but also, and as importantly, on the repetitious cycle of problems and the historical precursors that may have caused the crisis to arise. A medical analogy would be the person suffering from a chronic sinus condition who continually takes nasal decongestant and so can function, albeit at a less than optimum level. However, if the person is exposed to a virus, the sinus condition may progress to an infection and eventually pneumonia.

Being aware that someone is operating in a transcrisis state also gives us important information regarding the kind and degree of therapeutic intervention to provide, in both the short and the long term. We probably would deal far differently with the salesperson who just turned 45, lost her job with a company she had been with for 20 years, has been unemployed for 6 months, and is now clinically depressed and suicidal, than we would with the salesperson who just turned 45, lost her job for the 20th time, has been unemployed for 6 months, and is now clinically depressed and suicidal. Although immediate intervention in regard to the suicidal ideation of both women might be very similar, our view as to what caused the depression, how we would treat it, and what transcrisis issues we might expect would be very different.

Transcrisis Points

Transcrisis points occur frequently in transcrisis states within the therapeutic intervention. These points are generally marked by the client's coming to grips with new developmental stages or other dimensions of the problem. Transcrisis points do not occur in regular, predictable, linear progression. For example, an abused spouse may go through transcrisis point after transcrisis point talking to a crisis worker over the telephone before making a decision to leave the battering relationship, often calling crisis workers a dozen times in the course of a few days. The abused spouse may then make a decision to leave the battering relationship and go to a spouse abuse shelter, only to find that the necessity of making a geographic move or finding a job instigates a crisis almost as potent as the battering.

Human services workers who practice long-term therapy are often shocked, confused, and overwhelmed by the sudden disequilibrium their clients experience. Handling these transcrisis points can be the equivalent of standing in the middle of a Los Angeles freeway and attempting to stop traffic. Behaviorally, such clients may vacillate from a placid to an agitated state so fast that the worker puts out one brush fire only to be confronted by yet another. It is at these transcrisis points that standard therapeutic strategies and techniques are suspended and the therapist must operate in a crisis intervention mode.

Transcrisis points can be seen as benchmarks that are crucial to progressive stages of positive therapeutic growth. These points are characterized by approach-avoidance behavior in seeking help, taking risks, and initiating action steps toward forward movement. Encountering these transcrisis points, a person will experience the same kind of disorganization, disequilibrium, and fragmentation that surrounded the original crisis event. Leaping one hurdle does not necessarily mean that the entire crisis is successfully overcome. Survivors of a catastrophe may expunge the event from memory and then be faced with repairing gaping wounds in personal relationships that have been torn apart by their long-term pathological behavior. People who have spinal cord injuries may be successfully rehabilitated physically, but may retreat into substance addiction or become depressed and/or suicidal as they attempt to begin a new lifestyle from a wheelchair.

Therefore, it is not only the initial crisis with which the worker must contend but also each transcrisis point, as it occurs, if clients are not to slip back into the pathology that assailed them in the first place. Transcrisis points should not be confused with the jumps and starts that go with working through typical adjustment problems. Although these points may be forecast with some degree of reliability by workers who are expert in the particular field, their onset is sudden, dramatic, and extremely potent. In that regard, these psychological aftershocks can be just as damaging as the initial tremor and may require extraordinary effort on the part of the human services worker to help the client regain control. This book is also concerned with these transcrisis states and points; the cases portrayed represent both components.

Theories of Crisis and Crisis Intervention

No single theory or school of thought encompasses every view of human crisis or all the models or systems of crisis intervention. We present here a brief overview of theories relevant both to crisis (as a phenomenon) and to crisis intervention (as an intentional helping response). Janosik (1984) conceptualizes crisis theory on three different levels: basic crisis theory, expanded crisis theory, and applied crisis theory. The newly emerging ecosystem theory has been expanded into a comprehensive chapter (Chapter 17) in this text.

Basic Crisis Intervention Theory

The research, writings, and teachings of Erich Lindemann (1944, 1956) gave professionals and paraprofessionals a new understanding of crisis. Lindemann helped caregivers promote crisis intervention for many sufferers of loss who had no specific pathological diagnosis but who were exhibiting symptoms that appeared pathological. Lindemann's basic crisis theory and work made a substantive contribution to the understanding of behavior in clients whose grief crises were precipitated by loss. He helped professionals and paraprofessionals recognize that behavioral responses to crises associated with grief are normal, temporary, and amenable to alleviation through short-term intervention techniques. These "normal" grief behaviors include (1) preoccupation with the lost one, (2) identification with the lost one, (3) expressions of guilt and hostility, (4) some disorganization in daily routine, and (5) some evidence of somatic complaints (Janosik, 1984, p. 11). Lindemann negated the prevailing perception that clients manifesting crisis responses should necessarily be treated as abnormal or pathological.

Whereas Lindemann focused mainly on immediate resolution of grief after loss, Caplan (1964) expanded Lindemann's constructs to the total field of traumatic events. Caplan viewed crisis as a state resulting from impediments to life goals that cannot be overcome through customary behaviors. These impediments can arise from both developmental and situational events. Both Lindemann and Caplan dealt with crisis intervention following psychological trauma using an equilibrium/disequilibrium paradigm. The stages in Lindemann's paradigm are (1) disturbed equilibrium, (2) brief therapy or grief work, (3) client's working through the problem or grief, and (4) restoration of equilibrium (Janosik, 1984, pp. 10–12). Caplan linked Lindemann's concepts and stages to all developmental and situational events and extended crisis intervention to eliminating the affective, behavioral, and cognitive distortions that precipitated the psychological trauma in the first place.

Differentiating Basic Crisis Theory From Brief Therapy. The work of both Lindemann and Caplan gave impetus to the use of crisis intervention strategies in counseling and brief therapy with people manifesting universal human reactions to traumatic events. Whereas *brief therapy theory* typically attempts to remediate more or less ongoing emotional problems, *basic crisis theory,* following the lead of Lindemann and Caplan, focuses on helping people in crisis recognize and correct temporary affective, behavioral, and cognitive distortions brought on by traumatic events. Although brief or solution-focused therapy may be the equivalent of crisis intervention (in that it seeks to restore the person to a state of homeostasis or equilibrium), not all brief or solution-focused therapy is related to crisis intervention.

Perhaps the following example will clarify the difference between the two. A student fails one algebra test and concludes that he or she can never pass algebra, therefore cannot become an engineer (as the parents are perceived to expect/demand). The student progresses to a feeling of helplessness, then to hopelessness, and then contemplates suicide. Here, crisis intervention that focuses on suicide prevention is clearly indicated. Another student fails one algebra test and, feeling uncomfortable, disappointed, and confused, makes an appointment to see the school counselor. Here, the modality becomes a typical brief or solution-focused therapy situation wherein the emphasis is on how to improve study habits and test-taking skills.

Differentiating between brief or solution-focused therapy and crisis intervention depends on how intensely the client views the problem as intolerable or on how much emotional disequilibrium the client experiences. Severe emotional disequilibrium over the event may escalate the person into crisis and the therapist into a crisis intervention modality.

Expanded Crisis Theory

Expanded crisis theory was developed because basic theory, which depended on a psychoanalytic approach alone, did not adequately address the social, environmental, and situational factors that make an event a crisis. As crisis theory and intervention have expanded, it has become clear that an approach that identifies predisposing factors as the main or only causal agent falls short of the mark. A prime example of this restrictive view was the erroneous diagnosis, by practitioners who first encountered PTSD victims, that pathology preceding the crisis event was the real cause of the trauma. While preceding factors can certainly create a fertile field for PTSD and other psychopathology, it has become apparent that given the right combination of developmental, sociological, psychological, environmental, and situational determinants, anyone can fall victim to transient pathological symptoms. Therefore, expanded crisis theory draws not only from psychoanalytic theory but also from general systems, ecosystems, adaptational, interpersonal, chaos, and developmental theory. The following are synopses of these major theoretical components of an expanded view.

Psychoanalytic Theory. Psychoanalytic theory (Fine, 1973), applied to expanded crisis theory, is based on the view that the disequilibrium that accompanies a person's crisis can be understood through gaining access to the individual's unconscious thoughts and past emotional experiences. Psychoanalytic theory presupposes that some early childhood fixation is the primary explanation of why an event becomes a crisis. This theory may be used to help clients develop insight into the dynamics and causes of their behavior as the crisis situation acts on them.

We have come almost completely full circle in our view of this approach. First thought to be the only valid way to view pathology resulting from trauma, then dismissed as patently false and an excuse for the government not to meet the medical needs of veterans suffering from PTSD, currently treatment approaches see predisposing factors as one of the many factors that can contribute to PTSD and other psychopathologies.

Systems Theory. Systems theory (Haley, 1973, 1976; Hardy, 1997) is based not so much on what happens within an individual in crisis as on the interrelationships and interdependence among people and between people and events. Belkin (1984) adds that this theory "refers to an emotional system, a system of communications, and a system of need fulfillment and request" in which all members within an intergenerational relationship bring something to bear on the others, and each derives something from the others (pp. 350–351). Indeed, Slaikeu (1990, p. 6) defines crisis as "a helping process aimed at assisting a person or a *family* so that the probability of debilitating effects is minimized and the probability of growth is maximized."

Systems theory represents a turning away from traditional approaches, which focus only on what is going on within the client. A standard systems approach to crisis may be thought of in interpersonal terms. System theory is contextual in that it suggests that we look at the environment within which the person lives and the dynamic interactions the person has within that environment, which can provide information into the predisposing factors, onset, length, intensity, and resolution (Slaikeu, 1990, p. 34). Normally the "environment" in basic systems theory can be thought of as the extended family unit, the neighborhood, school, job, social clubs, fraternal or civic organizations, beauty parlors, bars, church, and so on. Chapter 11, Chemical Dependency: The Crisis of Addiction, makes a compelling argument for this theory's approach.

Ecosystems Theory. Ecosystems theory (Bronfenbrenner, 1995) broadens out the base of the system and looks at crisis in relation to the environmental context within which it occurs (James, Cogdal, & Gilliland, 2003; Myer & Moore, 2006). Systemic interactions may occur from the microsystem (family and community) out to the macrosystem (nation) or vice versa. There is great value in looking at crises in their total social and environmental settings—not simply as one individual being affected in a linear progression of cause-and-effect events (Hardy, 1997; James & Gilliland, 2003, pp. 336–368).

The fundamental concept of ecosystems theory is analogous to "ecological systems in which all elements are interrelated, and in which change at any level of those interrelated parts will lead to alteration of the total system" (Cormier & Hackney, 1987, p. 217). Passage of time, proximity to the epicenter of the crisis, and what develops over time and the environment all contribute to the ultimate resolution of the crisis. Ecosystems theory comes into play most typically when large-scale disasters occur and affect very large macrosystems. The expanding role of communication systems and their ability or inability to link systems is a critical ingredient that will be explored in Chapter 17, Disaster Response.

Adaptational Theory. Adaptational theory, as we use the term, depicts a person's crisis as being sustained through maladaptive behaviors, negative thoughts, and destructive defense mechanisms. Adaptational crisis theory is based on the premise that the person's crisis will recede when these maladaptive coping behaviors are changed to adaptive behaviors.

Breaking the chain of maladjusted functioning means changing to adaptive behavior, promoting positive thoughts, and constructing defense mechanisms that will help the person overcome the immobility created by the crisis and move to a positive mode of functioning. As maladaptive behaviors are learned, so may adaptive behaviors be learned. Aided by the interventionist, the client may learn to replace old, debilitating behaviors with new, self-enhancing ones. Such new behaviors may be applied directly to the context of the crisis and ultimately result in either success or reinforcement for the client in overcoming the crisis (Cormier & Cormier, 1985, p. 148). People who have learned ineffective coping skills and continue to use them even though they continually wind up in psychological hot water best manifest this approach. Changing ingrained and entrenched behaviors and thoughts that create transcrisis invariably means changing adaptive mechanisms and coping skills—not an easy job!

Interpersonal Theory. Interpersonal theory (Rogers, 1977) is built on many of the dimensions Cormier and Hackney (1987) describe as enhancing personal self-esteem: openness, trust, sharing, safety, unconditional positive regard, accurate empathy, and genuineness (pp. 35–64). The essence of interpersonal theory is that people cannot sustain a personal state of crisis for very long if they believe in themselves and in others and have confidence that they can become self-actualized and overcome the crisis. When people confer their locus of self-evaluation on others, they become dependent on others for validation of their being (Raskin & Rogers, 1995). Therefore, as long as a person maintains an external locus of control, the crisis will persist.

The outcome goal in interpersonal theory is returning the power of self-evaluation to the person. Doing so enables the person once again to control his or her own destiny and regain the ability to take whatever action is needed to cope with the crisis situation. In terms of crisis intervention, interpersonal theory is reflected in the initial tasks of Predispositioning, Problem Exploration, and Providing Support in our overall crisis intervention model to be introduced in Chapter 3.

Chaos Theory. Why is a meteorologist (Lorenz, 1993) who thinks a butterfly cruising along in a jungle path in the Amazon capable of starting a hurricane in the Atlantic getting a reference in a crisis intervention book? Furthermore, what in the world do words like *fractals, bifurcations, intermittences, folded towel diffeomorphisms,* and *smooth noodle maps* have to do with crisis? These are all concepts that seek to capture the structural complexity underlying chaos theory, and Edward Lorenz in his attempts to better predict weather patterns is seen as its founder. The primary reason we include chaos theory is, as you may well imagine, that in most crises there is a lot of chaos! But lo and behold, it turns out that chaos isn't random and that it has all kinds of ramifications for a range of other occupations, including crisis interventionists. Early conceptualizations of chaos theory by scientists in the fields of meteorology, mathematics, and physics viewed the theory as applying to systems or events that appeared random but, on closer inspection, revealed an underlying order (Gleick, 2008). Paradoxically, what happens in chaotic systems appears to be random and unpredictable so that there is no possibility of determining what future outcomes will be, but in fact there is (Lorenz, 1993, p. 9).

Chaos theory is really sort of a theory of evolution when applied to human functioning such as crisis intervention. It is evolutionary in that it is essentially an open-ended, ever-changing, "self-organizing" system whereby a new system may emerge out of the crisis (Butz, 1995, 1997; Chamberlain, 1993, 1994). A chaotic (crisis) situation—which Postrel (1998, p. xv) calls "emergent complex messiness"—evolves into a "self-organizing" mode whenever a critical mass of people come to perceive that they have no way to identify patterns or preplan options to solve the dilemma at hand. Because the chaotic situation falls outside of known alternative solutions, physicists and human services workers necessarily resort to spontaneous, trial-and-error experimentation to try to cope with the crisis. The "messiness" of the crisis lies not in disorder but in an order that is unknown, unpredictable, and spontaneous, an ever-shifting pattern driven by millions of uncoordinated, independent factors that necessitate experimentation, yet may finally result in a global clarification of the crisis. Such experimentation may lead to false starts, temporary failure, dead ends, spontaneous innovation, creativity, improvisation, brainstorming, cooperative enterprise, and other "evolutionary" attempts to make sense of and cope with the crisis (Gleick, 2008, pp. 33–42). Indeed, chaos theory has many parallels with another emerging field called evolutionary psychology which, as you can also well imagine, is not without its controversial aspects (Confer et al., 2010).

The crisis intervention attempts in the wake of British Petroleum's Deep Horizon well blowout provide a vivid example of chaos theory at work—in both a positive and a negative sense. So it is not just the "messiness" of an utterly new phenomenon like the blowout of the deep well in the Gulf of Mexico and attempts to look at and fix the disaster at one fixed point such as the wellhead. While that point is critical, it is also reductionistic in terms of chaos theory and doesn't look at the total gestalt, or "big picture," of the economic, ecological, and psychological costs of the crisis. All the tangled threads and points on the fabric of the crisis don't portray the underlying and interlocking patterns that provide information about the big picture and the potential ramifications of these dynamic systems on one another and on the total system after the crisis erupts.

Okay, so you didn't sign up for a course in higher mathematics or physics, which is where chaos's roots are, and the foregoing paragraphs are making your hair hurt! But a basic understanding of this exotic and esoteric theory should give you two important pieces of information. First, big crises call for a lot of different people working from a lot of different perspectives in a well-coordinated manner who can connect the myriad dots in a chaotic situation, see the underlying patterns, make sense of them, and change to meet changing conditions as new eddies and vortexes swirl out of the crisis. Myer and his associates have attempted to demonstrate what this theory looks and acts like when combined with ecosystemic theory after a disaster on a college campus (Myer, James, & Moulton, 2011).

Second, transcrises come close to manifesting chaos theory at work. Lots of times transcrises don't make sense and don't appear to have any discernable pattern, but much like the theoretical mathematician, just because you don't have an equation to solve the problem doesn't mean that one doesn't exist. There is an underlying pattern, and that's why all professional crisis interventionists use the right side of their brain a lot because dealing with crisis calls for a lot of creative thinking.

No other writers at present are discussing chaos theory as it applies to crisis intervention, but our guess is that they will as we attempt to unravel and understand the genetics that make up this field.

Developmental Theory. Because many crises have their bases in developmental stages that humans pass through, developmental theory must play a part in crisis intervention. Developmental stage theorists such as Erikson (1963), Levinson (1986), Levinson and Levinson (1996), and Blocher (2000) clearly believe that movement through various developmental life stages is critical. Developmental tasks that are not met and accomplished during particular life stages tend to pile up and cause problems. As individual needs and wants butt heads with the demands and expectations of society, and the individual fails to move on to the next life stage, the potential for crisis arises. Neglected, abused, and bullied children; alienated and isolated adolescent drug abusers; people who lack education or lack vocational satisfaction or success; or those exposed to domestic violence, divorce, suicide, homicide, and a host of other problems may be unable to meet life stages effectively. When an external, environmental, or situational crisis feeds into preexisting developmental crises, intrapersonal and interpersonal problems may reach the breaking point.

Applied Crisis Theory

Brammer (1985, pp. 94–95) characterizes applied crisis theory as encompassing three domains: (1) normal *developmental crises*, (2) *situational crises*, and (3) *existential crises*. Given the ecosystem theory perspective, we have added a fourth domain, (4) *ecosystemic crises*.

Developmental Crises. Developmental crises are events in the normal flow of human growth and evolution whereby a dramatic change or shift occurs that produces abnormal responses. For example, developmental crises may occur in response to the birth of a child, graduation from college, midlife career change, retirement, or even the aging process. Developmental crises are considered normal; however, all persons and all developmental crises are unique and must be assessed and handled in unique ways.

Situational Crises. A situational crisis emerges with the occurrence of uncommon and extraordinary events that an individual has no way of forecasting or controlling. Situational crises may follow such events as terrorist attacks, automobile accidents, kidnappings, rapes, job loss, or sudden illness and death. The key to differentiating a situational crisis from other crises is that a situational crisis is random, sudden, shocking, intense, and often catastrophic.

Existential Crises.   An existential crisis includes the inner conflicts and anxieties that accompany important human issues of purpose, responsibility, independence, freedom, and commitment. An existential crisis might accompany the realization, at age 40, that one will never make a significant and distinct impact on a particular profession or organization; remorse, at age 50, that one chose never to marry or leave one's parents' home, never made a separate life, and now has lost forever the possibility of being a fully happy and worthwhile person; or a pervasive and persistent feeling, at age 60, that one's life is meaningless—that there is a void that can never be filled in a meaningful way.

Ecosystemic Crises.   Ecosystemic crises typically occur when some *natural* or *human-caused* disaster overtakes a person or a (large or small) group of people who find themselves, through no fault or action of their own, inundated in the aftermath of an event that may adversely affect virtually every member of the environment in which they live. Such crises may be the result of natural phenomena such as hurricanes, floods, tsunamis, earthquakes, volcanic eruptions, tornadoes, blizzards, mudslides, drought, famine, and forest or grassland/brush fires. Other instances of ecosystemic crises may be *biologically derived,* such as a disease epidemic or the effects of a huge oil spill; *politically based,* as in war, a refugee crisis associated with war, or ethnic cleansing; or *severe economic depression,* such as the Great Depression of the early 20th century.

Crisis Intervention Models

Three basic crisis intervention models discussed by both Leitner (1974) and Belkin (1984) are the *equilibrium model,* the *cognitive model,* and the *psychosocial transition model.* These three generic models provide the groundwork for many different crisis intervention strategies and methodologies. Two new models that target ecological factors that contribute to crisis are the *developmental-ecological model* (Collins & Collins, 2005) and the *contextual-ecological* model (Myer & Moore, 2006). Two field-based practice models are *psychological*

first aid (Raphael, 1977; U.S. Department of Veterans Affairs, 2011), which is used in the immediate aftermath of disasters and terrorist attacks, and Roberts' (2005) ACT model, which is more generic but primarily trauma based.

The Equilibrium Model

The equilibrium model is really an equilibrium/disequilibrium model. People in crisis are in a state of psychological or emotional disequilibrium in which their usual coping mechanisms and problem-solving methods fail to meet their needs. The goal of the equilibrium model is to help people recover a state of precrisis equilibrium (Caplan, 1961). The equilibrium model seems most appropriate for early intervention, when the person is out of control, disoriented, and unable to make appropriate choices. Until the person has regained some coping abilities, the main focus is on stabilizing the individual. Up to the time the person has reacquired some definite measure of stability, little else can or should be done. For example, it does little good to dig into the underlying factors that cause suicidal ideation until the person can be stabilized to the point of agreeing that life is worth living for at least another week. This is probably the purest model of crisis intervention and is most likely to be used at the onset of the crisis (Caplan, 1961; Leitner, 1974; Lindemann, 1944).

The Cognitive Model

The cognitive model of crisis intervention is based on the premise that crises are rooted in faulty thinking about the events or situations that surround the crisis—not in the events themselves or the facts about the events or situations (Ellis, 1962). The goal of this model is to help people become aware of and change their views and beliefs about the crisis events or situations. The basic tenet of the cognitive model is that people can gain control of crises in their lives by changing their thinking, especially by recognizing and disputing the irrational and self-defeating parts of their cognitions, and by retaining and focusing on the rational and self-enhancing elements of their thinking.

The messages that people in crisis send themselves become very negative and twisted, in contrast to the reality of the situation. Dilemmas that are constant and grinding wear people out, pushing their internal state of perception more and more toward negative self-talk until their cognitive sets are so negative that no amount of preaching can convince them that anything positive will ever come from the situation. Their behavior soon follows this negative self-talk and begets a self-fulfilling prophecy that the situation is hopeless. At this juncture, crisis intervention becomes a job of rewiring the individual's thoughts to more positive feedback loops by practicing and rehearsing new self-statements about the situation until the old, negative, debilitating ones are expunged. The cognitive model seems most appropriate after the client has been stabilized and returned to an approximate state of precrisis equilibrium. Basic components of this approach are found in the rational-emotive work of Ellis (1982), the cognitive-behavioral approach of Meichenbaum (1977), and the cognitive system of Beck (1976).

The Psychosocial Transition Model

The psychosocial transition model assumes that people are products of their genes plus the learning they have absorbed from their particular social environments. Because people are continuously changing, developing, and growing, and their social environments and social influences (Dorn, 1986) are continuously evolving, crises may be related to internal or external (psychological, social, or environmental) difficulties. The goal of crisis intervention is to collaborate with clients in assessing the internal and external difficulties contributing to the crisis and then help them choose workable alternatives to their current behaviors, attitudes, and use of environmental resources. Clients may need to incorporate adequate internal coping mechanisms, social supports, and environmental resources in order to gain autonomous (noncrisis) control over their lives.

The psychosocial model does not perceive crisis as simply an internal state of affairs that resides totally within the individual. It reaches outside the individual and asks what systems need to be changed. Peers, family, occupation, religion, and the community are but a few of the external dimensions that promote or hinder psychological adaptiveness. With certain kinds of crisis problems, few lasting gains will be made unless the social systems that affect the individual are also changed, or the individual comes to terms with and understands the dynamics of those systems and how they affect adaptation to the crisis. Like the cognitive model, the psychosocial transition model seems to be most appropriate after the client has been stabilized. Theorists who have contributed to the psychosocial transition model include Adler (Ansbacher & Ansbacher, 1956), Erikson (1963), and Minuchin (1974).

The Developmental-Ecological Model

Collins and Collins (2005) have developed a developmental-ecological model of crisis intervention that integrates developmental stages and issues with the environment within which the individual operates. In this model, the crisis worker needs to assess both the individual and the environment as well as the interrelationship between the two and then factor in the developmental stage within which the person is operating. Any situational crisis must always be considered in relationship to the stage of development the person is in, and the potency of the crisis may depend on how well there has been stage mastery of the tasks affected by the crisis.

The Contextual-Ecological Model

Myer and Moore (2006) have developed an ecological model that focuses on contextual elements of the crisis. Their first premise is that contextual elements may be seen as layered. These layers are dependent on two elements: proximity to the crisis by physical distance, and reactions that are moderated by perception and the meaning attributed to the event.

The second premise of this model is that reciprocal impact occurs between the individual and systems affected by the event. Understanding the reciprocal effect of the crisis involves recognition of two elements: the interaction among the primary and secondary relationships, and the degree of change triggered by the event. Primary relationships are those in which no intervening component (other individuals or systems) interacts with or mediates the connection. An example of a primary relationship would be between an employee and a company. If an accident occurred and the company immediately took a number of steps to support employees and assure them that safety measures had been increased so that such an accident would be unlikely to happen again, the employees might feel secure, safe, and satisfied with the company's efforts. A secondary relationship is mediated by at least one other individual or system. For example, if the employee's family members were so terrified for the safety of their loved one that no amount of assurances would satisfy them, then the primary relationship between the employee and the company would be affected.

The third premise is that time directly influences the impact of a crisis. The two major time elements are the amount of time that has passed and special occasions such as anniversaries and holidays following the event.

Myer and Moore (2006) propose a formula for gauging the impact of the crisis on the individual or system. The formula can be summarized as a function of proximity to the event, reaction to the event, relationship to the event, and amount of change caused by the event, which is then divided by the amount of time that has passed. What is critical in this formula is understanding that no single component can be considered separately. Close proximity alone may not have as much bearing on the impact of the crisis as the degree of change resulting from it. While this highly theoretical model as of yet has no empirical basis, nor does it yet have a great deal of utility for intervention, it poses questions and generates premises that can help us understand the impact of the crisis as it interacts between and within a variety of systems and individuals.

Psychological First Aid

Slaikeu (1990, p. 6) breaks crisis intervention into two parts: First-order intervention, or *psychological first aid*, seeks to address the immediate crisis situation and provide immediate relief, possibly to a wide range of individuals. Second-order intervention, or *crisis therapy*, seeks to resolve the crisis and is generally provided by trained, licensed human services professionals. In this book, most of what would be seen as psychological first aid and initial crisis therapy is what we define as crisis intervention.

The National Institute of Mental Health (2002) defines psychological first aid as establishing the safety of the client, reducing stress-related symptoms, providing rest and physical recuperation, and linking clients to critical resources and social support systems. Raphael (1977) first coined the term *psychological first aid* in her discussion of crisis work with an Australian railway disaster. She described a variety of activities that provided caring support, empathic responding, concrete information and assistance, and reuniting of survivors with social support systems. Paramount in psychological first aid is attending to Maslow's needs hierarchy and taking care of survival needs first. Many counselors, social workers, and psychologists helped meet basic support needs of food, shelter, clothing, and other survival needs during the aftermath of Hurricane Katrina before they ever did any "counseling."

Controversy has arisen over who should get care, what kind of care should be provided, how it should be delivered, by whom, and under what circumstances immediately after a traumatic event—especially after a mass disaster. Much of this controversy has arisen in regard to critical incident stress debriefing (Mitchell & Everly, 1995) and the notion that everybody exposed to a traumatic event needs to talk about it as quickly after the event as possible to stave off PTSD. A huge controversy has erupted over this treatment approach (to be discussed in Chapter 17), to the point that the prevailing approach for immediate disaster intervention is now psychological first aid that is nonintrusive and does not promote discussion of the traumatic event (Young, 2006). The notion is that not all people will need psychological help and the initial paratraumatic symptoms that most people manifest will self-eradicate in a short period of time (National Institute of Mental Health, 2002).

The National Center for PTSD (U.S. Department of Veterans Affairs, 2011) has published a field manual, *Psychological First Aid: Field Operations Guide*, that offers an evidence-informed modular approach for assisting people in the immediate aftermath of disaster and terrorism, to reduce initial distress and to foster short and long-term adaptive functioning. The manual states that it is for use by first responders, incident command systems, primary and emergency health care providers, school crisis response teams, faith-based organizations, disaster relief organizations, Community Emergency Response Teams, Medical Reserve Corps, and the Citizens Corps in diverse settings. This approach to psychological first aid includes eight core actions (U.S. Department of Veterans Affairs, 2011, p. 18):

1. **Contact and Engagement**
   Goal: To respond to contacts initiated by survivors, or to initiate contacts in a nonintrusive, compassionate, and helpful manner.
2. **Safety and Comfort**
   Goal: To enhance immediate and ongoing safety, and provide physical and emotional comfort.
3. **Stabilization** (if needed)
   Goal: To calm and orient emotionally overwhelmed or disoriented survivors.
4. **Information Gathering: Current Needs and Concerns**
   Goal: To identify immediate needs and concerns, gather additional information, and tailor psychological first aid interventions.
5. **Practical Assistance**
   Goal: To offer practical help to survivors in addressing immediate needs and concerns.
6. **Connection with Social Supports**
   Goal: To help establish brief or ongoing contacts with primary support persons and other sources

of support, including family members, friends, and community helping resources.

7. **Information on Coping**

Goal: To provide information about stress reactions and coping to reduce distress and promote adaptive functioning.

8. **Linkage with Collaborative Services**

Goal: To link survivors with available services needed at the time or in the future.

Psychological first aid provides the bare-bones basics of crisis intervention. It is designed to be palliative. It is not designed to cure or fix anything, but rather to provide nonintrusive physical and psychological support. Social workers would be very comfortable with this model because a great deal of it resembles social work services. If we consider the first four tasks (Predispositioning, Problem Definition, Providing Support, Safety) of the model of crisis intervention you will meet in Chapter 3 as being close to what is meant by psychological first aid, then psychological first aid is clearly necessary. Whether it is also *sufficient* in providing immediate crisis intervention services is another matter. Certainly not all people need immediate psychological assistance, nor should they have it forced on them, but the high adrenal moments of a lot of crisis intervention make us believe that something more than psychological first aid is needed to defuse emotional volatility, deescalate life-threatening behavior, and reframe and cool the insane, irrational, hot cognitions that typify many crisis situations.

The ACT Model

The ACT model proposed by Roberts (2005) is an acronym:

*A*ssessment of the presenting problem, including emergency psychiatric and other medical needs and trauma assessment

*C*onnecting clients to support systems

*T*raumatic reactions and posttraumatic stress disorders

The model has seven generally linear stages: crisis assessment, establishing rapport, identifying major problems, dealing with feelings, generating and exploring alternatives, developing plans, and providing follow-up (pp. 104–106). This model has been designed to deal with the onset of a traumatic event and, probably even more appropriately, with what Kleespies (2009) calls behavioral emergencies.

Eclectic Crisis Intervention Theory

Eclectic crisis intervention involves intentionally and systematically selecting and integrating valid concepts and strategies from all available approaches to helping clients. Eclecticism is thus a hybrid of all available approaches. It operates from a task orientation, as opposed to concepts. Its major tasks (James & Gilliland, 2003, p. 374; Lazarus, 1989; Thorne, 1973, p. 451) are (1) to identify valid elements in all systems and integrate them into an internally consistent whole that does justice to the behavioral data to be explained; (2) to consider all pertinent theories, methods, and standards for evaluating and manipulating clinical data according to the most advanced knowledge of time and place; and (3) to identify with no specific theory, keep an open mind, and continuously experiment with those formulations and strategies that produce successful results.

Throughout this book, the reader will find an eclectic approach integrated into the interventions presented. Much of what happens will depend on the situation with which we find ourselves. "Situation" may be defined as including the type of crisis, the physical and ecological setting in which it occurs, individual characteristics, cultural background, and significant others who may be directly or indirectly involved. Probably more important than all the factors that affect clients are the knowledge, strength, and skills that interventionists bring to the crisis.

The eclectic approach fuses two pervasive themes: (1) all people and all crises are unique and distinctive, and (2) all people and all crises are similar. We do not see these themes as mutually exclusive. All people and all crises are similar in that there are global elements to specific crisis types. The dynamics of bereavement are generic and provide us with general guidelines for intervention. However, treating individual cases of bereavement is anything but generic. How a family perceives the impact of the death of a member depends on a number of factors: the deceased member's place in the family, what each member of the family does in response to the death, and how the changed family system now operates. Treatment of surviving family members who have lost a child after rearing five others, as opposed to those who have lost their only child, born late in the parents' life, who had become the focus of existence for the couple, may call for far different intervention strategies even if bereavement is the generic issue.

An eclectic approach does not mean taking a therapeutic shotgun and aimlessly blasting away at the crisis. Using an eclectic approach means not being bound by and locked into any one theoretical approach in a dogmatic fashion. Rather, it means being well versed in a number of approaches and theories and being able to assess the client's needs so that appropriate techniques can be planned and fitted to them. Many human services workers avow an eclectic approach but actually use the word to rationalize not being able to do anything very well. Being a true eclectic means doing lots of hard work, reading, studying, experiencing, and being supervised and critiqued by other professionals. It also means taking risks and being willing to abandon an approach that on first inspection might seem reasonable and proper but, once entered, proves fruitless for the particular situation.

Eclecticism performed well is equal parts skill and intuition. Paying attention to your feelings as much as to your cognition about the situation is crucial. Changing to a more effective intervention is often based on nothing more scientific than a feeling that something is amiss. Although having a feeling is little justification, in the scientific sense, for doing something, it can nevertheless be a sound basis for action. There is no known formula for deciding when to move from a nondirective to a highly directive stance with a client in crisis, nor is there an equation that tells a therapist that mental imagery may be more effective than confrontation as an intervention technique. An eclectic approach done well is the zenith of the performing art of crisis intervention.

Characteristics of Effective Crisis Workers

Almost everyone can be taught the techniques in this book and with practice can employ them with some degree of skill. However, the crisis worker who can take intervention to the performing art level is more than the sum of techniques read about and skills mastered. A master of this art is going to have not only technical skill and theoretical knowledge but also a good deal of the following characteristics.

Life Experiences

The worker handles a crisis or not to the extent that he or she is a whole person or not (Carkhuff & Berenson, 1977, pp. 162–163). A whole person has a rich and varied background of life experiences. These life experiences

serve as a resource for emotional maturity that, combined with training, enables workers to be stable, consistent, and well integrated not only within the crisis situation but also in their daily lives. However, life experiences alone are not sufficient to qualify one to be a crisis worker and can be debilitating if they continue to influence the worker in negative ways. This issue is central to crisis intervention because many people who work as volunteers, support personnel, and professionals are products of their own crisis environments. They have chosen to work with people experiencing the same kind of crisis they themselves have suffered, and they use their experiential background as a resource in working with others. For example, recovering addicts may work in alcohol and drug units, battered women work in spouse abuse centers, and PTSD victims counsel in veterans' centers. These professionals have had firsthand experience with the trauma their clients have experienced. Does this background give them an edge over other workers who have not suffered the same pain?

The answer is a qualified yes—qualified in that the person who carries emotional baggage into the helping relationship may be even less effective than the person who has had few if any life experiences. One sees examples of emotional carryover into the intervention process in the proselytizing recovering alcoholic who vilifies others to assuage his own insecurities and fears about "falling off the wagon" and in the child abuse worker, herself a former victim of sexual abuse, who castigates mothers for their failure to confront abusing fathers.

Such human services workers may have tremendous difficulties because they mingle many of their own problems with those of their clients. The workers alternate among feeling states characterized by sympathy, anger, disappointment, and cynicism, which are detrimental both to themselves and to their clients. We do not believe crisis workers must have "lived in the crisis" to be able to understand and deal with it effectively. We do believe that interventionists who have successfully overcome some of life's problems and have put those problems into perspective will have assets of maturity, optimism, tenacity, and tough-mindedness that will help them marshal their psychological resources to assist their clients.

You should also be cautioned that on-the-job training in this business is a very arduous way to win one's spurs, particularly for a worker who has led a sheltered, constricted life and decides through misguided idealism to become a Florence Nightingale and fix the problems of the world. This rose-colored view does little for clients in general and may do considerable harm to workers as their good intentions pave the road to burnout. We hasten to add that chronological age has very little to do with having or not having self-enhancing life experiences and a broader, more resilient viewpoint. We know people ranging in age from 21 to 65 who are emotional adolescents. When threatened by face-to-face encounters with the real world, they may be characterized by rigidity, insularity, and insecurity. The ideal crisis worker is one who has experienced life, has learned and grown from those experiences, and supports those experiences in his or her work by thorough training, knowledge, and supervision. This individual constantly seeks to integrate all these aspects into his or her therapeutic intervention in particular and into living in general.

Personal Characteristics

Poise.   The nature of crisis intervention is that the worker is often confronted with shocking and threatening material from clients who are completely out of control. Probably the most significant help the interventionist can provide at this juncture is to remain calm, poised, and in control (Belkin, 1984, p. 427). Creating a stable and rational atmosphere provides a model for the client that is conducive to restoring equilibrium to the situation. Effective crisis workers are as steady and well-anchored psychologically as the Rock of Gibraltar. This does mean that effective crisis workers are made of stone and are not frightened, tense, anxious, and at times unsure of themselves. However, in the very act of making self-disclosing owning statements of his or her own frailties and shortcomings, the worker models the assuredness, transparency, and congruency that are prized professional assets in any professional human service worker (Carkhuff, 1987; Rogers, 1961)

Creativity and Flexibility.   Creativity and flexibility are major assets to those confronted with perplexing and seemingly unsolvable problems (Aguilera & Messick, 1982, p. 24). In our courses and training workshops, students and trainees often have difficulty conducting role plays with peers because they have no formula for getting the "right" answer. Although practice in tough role-play situations builds confidence, how creative individuals are in difficult situations depends in large measure on how well they have nurtured their own creativity over the course of their lives by taking risks and practicing divergent thinking.

Energy and Resiliency.   Functioning in the unknown areas that are characteristic of crisis intervention requires energy, organization, direction, and systematic action (Carkhuff & Berenson, 1977, p. 194). Professional training can provide organizational guidelines and principles for systematic acting. What it cannot do is provide the energy requisite to perform this work. A crisis worker must also be resilient. By its very nature crisis work has many "downs" when, no matter how capable, no matter how committed, no matter what was tried or done, "success" was not achieved. Crisis workers must have "bounce back" potential. They take care of themselves physically and psychologically and make wise use of their available energy.

Quick Mental Reflexes.   Crisis work differs from typical therapeutic intervention in that time is a critical factor. Crisis intervention requires more activity and directiveness than ordinary therapeutic endeavors usually do. Time to reflect and mull over problems is a rare commodity in crisis intervention. The worker must have fast mental reflexes to deal with the constantly emerging and changing issues that occur in the crisis. The worker who cannot think fast and accurately is going to find this business very frustrating indeed.

Assertiveness.   One of the major problems that interventionists who have been trained in formal professional programs experience in attempting to apply the skills in this book is their reticence at times to be proactive, assertive, and directive. These therapeutic stances run counter to what has been hammered into them with regard to not being judgmental, not breeding client dependence, not imposing their values on the client, being accepting, and unconditionally positively regarding their clients as human beings of worth. While we believe wholeheartedly in those dictums, and employ them whenever possible, crisis intervention has different rules.

Many clients who are in crisis do not talk or act nicely. For that reason you need to be able to assertively set limits to behavior, both in regard to maintaining your own integrity and keeping the client stabilized so that intervention can occur. Clients are likely to have exhausted their repertory of coping skills and drained their psychological resources to the point that their ability to take action, think constructively, or control feelings is gone. At such times crisis interventionists cannot be passive. You are the expert on the scene, you have the fund of knowledge needed, and you need to employ your skills, knowledge, and abilities in as clear and directive manner as you possibly can. The nine intentional helping strategies described in Chapter 4 are predominately interventionist driven and have little passivity or reactivity. Much like competitive athletics, if you are going to do this well, you need to get your game face on and get actively involved.

Other Attributes.   Crisis workers have found the following attributes to be of utmost importance to themselves and their clients: tenacity, the ability to delay gratification, courage, optimism, a reality orientation, calmness under duress, objectivity, a strong and positive self-concept, and abiding faith that human beings are strong, resilient, and capable of overcoming seemingly insurmountable odds. Poll yourself: Do you have these attributes? We also want you to understand that admission into the inner circle of the profession is not reserved solely for a few supermen and superwomen. Most interventionists we know, certainly including ourselves, are at times perplexed, frustrated, angry, afraid, threatened, incompetent, foolish, vain, troubled, and otherwise unequal to the task. We allow ourselves and our students and trainees at least one mistake per day and go on from there. We would very much like you to remember that cognitive billboard,

"You get one free," and place it squarely in the forefront of your mind.

Rewards

Standing up to the intense heat of the crisis situation to help people through seemingly unsolvable problems is some of the most gratifying and positively reinforcing work you can do in the psychotherapy business. The intense personal rewards that accrue to crisis workers lead me to believe that this work would be high on Glasser's (1976) list of positive addicting behaviors.

Now consider for a moment yourself as a client. Everyone is at times subject to the whims of a randomly cruel universe, and the kinds of crises that are dealt with in this book are apt to be visited on us all. Understanding how to navigate through these constellations of problems is a valuable resource. How well we live depends on our ability to handle the problems that confront us when we least expect them. As you read through the material, you may find yourself "living into" some of these problems and asking yourself, "I wonder how I'd fare if I were a client?" We believe that this too is a worthwhile perspective if you can look beyond the dilemmas to the coping techniques and bank them for future reference and use.

SUMMARY

Historically, crisis intervention has developed and evolved in about the last 60 years. Its origins have typically been in grassroots organizations, groups of people who came together to solve a specific crisis that was assailing them. Through both natural and human-made crises and the influence of the media, crisis intervention has moved from a backwater psychological specialty into the mainstream of helping skills.

Our composite definition of *individual crisis*, derived from the sources given at the beginning of this chapter, is *a perception or experiencing of an event or situation as an intolerable difficulty that exceeds the person's current resources and coping mechanisms. Unless the person obtains relief, the crisis has the potential to cause severe affective, behavioral, and cognitive malfunctioning up to the point of instigating injurious or lethal behavior to oneself or others.* Because systems play an equally important part in the business of

crisis intervention, we define systemic crisis as follows: *When a traumatic event occurs such that people, institutions, communities, and ecologies are overwhelmed and response systems are unable to effectively contain and control the event in regard to both physical and psychological reactions to it, the crisis has become systemic.* These general definitions are enhanced by considering several important principles and characteristics of crisis:

1. Crisis embodies both danger and opportunity for the person experiencing the crisis.
2. Crisis is usually time limited but may develop into a series of recurring transcrisis points.
3. Crisis is often complex and difficult to resolve.
4. The life experiences of crisis and other human services workers may greatly enhance their effectiveness in crisis intervention.
5. Crisis contains the seeds of growth and impetus for change.

6. Panaceas or quick fixes may not be applicable to many crisis situations.
7. Crisis confronts people with choices.
8. Emotional disequilibrium and disorganization accompany crisis.
9. The resolution of crisis and the personhood of crisis workers interrelate.

Understanding transcrisis states and transcrisis points helps in understanding many crises. Clients experiencing crises rooted in their transcrisis states or transcrisis points show recurring traumalike symptoms derived from earlier traumatic events. Transcrisis states and points have parallels with and differences from PTSD.

Basic crisis theory views crisis as situational or developmental rather than pathological in nature. *Expanded crisis theory* adds to and enhances basic theory by incorporating and adapting components from psychoanalytic, general systems, ecosystems, adaptational, interpersonal, chaos, and developmental theory.

Five fundamental crisis intervention models are equilibrium, cognitive, psychosocial transition, developmental-ecological, and contextual-ecological. The *equilibrium model*, probably the most widely known model of the five, defines equilibrium as an emotional state in which the person is stable, in control, or psychologically mobile. It defines disequilibrium as an emotional state that accompanies instability, loss of control, and psychological immobility. The *cognitive model* views the crisis state as resulting from faulty thinking and belief about life's dilemmas and traumas. The *psychosocial transition model* assumes that people are products of both hereditary endowment and environmental learning and that crisis may be caused by psychological, social, or environmental factors. The *developmental-ecological model* considers developmental stages in relation to the ecological system within which the individual develops. A *contextual-ecological model* looks at layers, relationships, and time when it examines a crisis. The *psychological first aid* and *ACT* models are both practice-based field models that deal with disasters and trauma-related crises. An eclectic theoretical position incorporates and integrates all valid concepts of crisis intervention.

Effective crisis workers share a number of positive personal characteristics. They maintain poise, quick wittedness, creativity, tenacity, assertiveness, and resiliency, among a host of other attributes, while confronting the difficult issues of clients in crisis.

REFERENCES

Aguilera, D. C., & Messick, J. M. (1982). *Crisis intervention: Theory and methodology* (4th ed.). St. Louis, MO: C. V. Mosby.

American Psychiatric Association. (2000). *Diagnostic and statistical manual of mental disorders–technical revision* (4th ed.). Washington, DC: Author.

Ansbacher, H. L., & Ansbacher, R. R. (1956). *The individual psychology of Alfred Adler.* New York: Greenberg.

Armsworth, M. W., & Holaday, M. (1993). The effects of psychological trauma on children and adolescents. *Journal of Counseling and Development, 72*(1), 49–56.

Barton, A. M. (1969). *Communities in disaster.* Garden City, NY: Doubleday.

Bass, D. D., & Yep, R. (Eds.). (2002). *Terrorism, trauma, and tragedies: A counselor's guide to preparing and responding.* Alexandria, VA: American Counseling Association.

Beck, A. T. (1976). *Cognitive therapy and the emotional disorders.* New York: International Universities Press.

Belkin, G. S. (1984). *Introduction to counseling* (2nd ed.). Dubuque, IA: William C. Brown.

Blocher, D. H. (2000). *Counseling: A developmental approach* (4th ed.). New York: John Wiley & Sons.

Bloom, B. L. (1984). *Community mental health: A general introduction* (2nd ed.). Pacific Grove, CA: Brooks/ Cole.

Brammer, L. M. (1985). *The helping relationship: Process and skills* (3rd ed.). Upper Saddle River, NJ: Prentice Hall.

Bronfenbrenner, U. (1995). Developmental ecology through space and time: A future perspective. In P. Moen, G. H. Elder, Jr., & K. Luscher (Eds.), *Examining lives in context: Perspectives on the ecology of human development* (pp. 619–647). Washington, DC: American Psychological Association.

Brown, L. (2009). *Cultural competence in trauma therapy: Beyond the flashback.* Washington, DC: American Psychological Association.

Butz, M. R. (1995). Chaos theory, philosophically old, scientifically new. *Counseling and Values, 39,* 84–98.

Butz, M. R. (1997). *Chaos and complexity: Implications for psychological theory and practice.* Washington, DC: Taylor & Francis.

Callahan, J. (1998). Crisis theory and crisis intervention in emergencies. In P. M. Kleespies (Ed.), *Emergencies in mental health: Evaluation and management* (pp. 22–40). New York: Guilford Press.

Callahan, J. (2009). Emergency intervention and crisis intervention. In P. M. Kleespies (Ed.), *Behavioral emergencies: An evidence-based resource for evaluating and managing risk of suicide, violence, and victimization* (pp. 13–32). Washington, DC: American Psychological Association.

Caplan, G. (1961). *An approach to community mental health.* New York: Grune & Stratton.

Caplan, G. (1964). *Principles of preventive psychiatry.* New York: Basic Books.

Carkhuff, R. R. (1987). *The art of helping* (6th ed.). Amherst, MA: Human Resource Development Press.

Carkhuff, R. R., & Berenson, B. G. (1977). *Beyond counseling and therapy* (2nd ed.). New York: Holt, Rinehart & Winston.

Chamberlain, L. (1993, August). *Strange attractors in patterns of family interactions.* Paper presented at the Annual Convention of the American Psychological Association, Toronto.

Chamberlain, L. (1994, August). *Is there a chaotician in the house? Chaos and family therapy.* Paper presented at the Annual Convention of the American Psychological Association, Los Angeles.

Clark, S. C., & McKiernan, W. (1981). Contacts with a Canadian "street level" drug and crisis centre, 1975–1978. *Bulletin on Narcotics, 33,* 23–31.

Collins, B. G., & Collins, T. M. (2005). *Crisis and trauma: Developmental-ecological intervention.* Lahaska, PA: Lahaska Press.

Confer, J. C., Easton, J. A., Fleischman, D. S., Goetz, C. D., Lewis, D., Perriloux, C., & Buss, D. M. (2010). Evolutionary psychology: Controversies, questions, prospects, and limitations. *American Psychologist, 65*(2), 110–126.

Cormier, L. S., & Hackney, H. (1987). *The professional counselor: A process guide to helping.* Upper Saddle River, NJ: Prentice Hall.

Cormier, W. H., & Cormier, L. S. (1985). *Interviewing strategies for helpers: Fundamental skills and cognitive behavioral interventions* (2nd ed.). Pacific Grove, CA: Brooks/Cole.

Council for Accreditation of Counseling & Related Educational Programs. (2009). *CACREP 2009 standards and procedures manual.* Retrieved from http://www.cacrep.org/template/page

Courtois, C. A., & Gold, S. N. (2009). The need for inclusion of psychological trauma in the professional curriculum: A call to action. *Psychological Trauma: Theory, Research, Practice, and Policy, 1,* 3–25.

Danish, S. J. (1977). Human development and human services: A marriage proposal. In I. Iscoe, B. L. Bloom, & C. C. Speilberger (Eds.). *Community psychology in transition* (pp. 44–77). New York: Halstead.

Dorn, F. J. (Ed.). (1986). *The social influence process in counseling and psychotherapy.* Springfield, IL: Charles C Thomas.

Echterling, L. G., & Wylie, M. L. (1999). In the public arena: Disaster as a socially constructed problem. In R. Gist & B. Lubin (Eds.), *Response to disaster: Psychosocial, community, and ecological approaches* (pp. 327–352). Philadelphia: Brunner/Mazel.

Ellis, A. E. (1962). *Reason and emotion in psychotherapy.* New York: Lyle Stuart.

Ellis, A. E. (1982). Major systems. *Personnel and Guidance Journal, 61,* 6–7.

Erikson, E. (1963). *Childhood and society* (2nd ed.). New York: Norton.

Fine, R. (1973). Psychoanalysis. In R. J. Corsini (Ed.), *Current psychotherapies* (pp. 1–33). Itasca, IL: F. E. Peacock.

Giel, R. (1990). Psychosocial process in disaster. *International Journal of Mental Health, 19,* 7–20.

Gist, R., Lubin, B., & Redburn, B. G. (1999). Psychosocial, ecological, and community perspectives on disaster response. In R. Gist & B. Lubin (Eds.), *Response to disaster: Psychosocial, community and ecological responses* (pp. 1–16). Philadelphia: Brunner/Mazel.

Gist, R., Woodall, S. J., & Magenheimer, L. K. (1999). And then you do the Hokey Pokey and you turn yourself around.... In R. Gist & B. Lubin (Eds.), *Response to disaster: Psychosocial, community and ecological responses* (pp. 269–290). Philadelphia: Brunner/Mazel.

Glasser, W. (1976). *Positive addiction.* New York: Harper & Row.

Gleick, J. (2008). *Chaos: Making a new science.* New York: Penguin Books.

Golan, N. (1978). *Treatment in crisis situations.* New York: Free Press.

Haley, J. (1973). *Uncommon therapy.* New York: Norton.

Haley, J. (1976). *Problem-solving therapy.* New York: McGraw-Hill.

Hardy, K. V. (Therapist). (1997). *Family systems therapy* (Videotape No. 0-205-32931-4, T. Labriola, Producer). In J. Carlson & D. Kjos, *Family systems with Hardy: Psychotherapy with the experts.* Boston: Allyn & Bacon.

Hermann, C. F. (1963). Some consequences of crisis which limit the viability of organizations. *Administrative Science Quarterly, 8,* 61–81.

Hoff, I. A., Hallisey, B. J., & Hoff, M. (2009). *People in crisis: Clinical and diversity perspectives.* New York: Routledge, Taylor, & Francis Group.

James, R. K., Cogdal, P., & Gilliland, B. E. (2003, April*).* An *ecological theory of crisis intervention.* Paper presented at the American Counseling Association convention, Kansas City, MO.

James, R. K., & Gilliland, B. E. (2003). *Theories and strategies in counseling and psychotherapy* (5th ed.). Boston: Allyn & Bacon.

Janosik, E. H. (1984). *Crisis counseling: A contemporary approach.* Monterey, CA: Wadsworth Health Sciences Division.

Kaniasty, K., & Norris, F. (1999). The experience of disaster: Individuals and communities sharing trauma. In R. Gist & B. Lubin (Eds.), *Response to disaster: Psychosocial, community and ecological approaches* (pp. 25–62). Philadelphia: Brunner/Mazel.

Kessler, R. C., Sonnega, A., Bromer, E., Hughes M., & Nelson, C. B. (1995). Posttraumatic stress disorder in the National Comorbidity Survey. *Archives of General Psychiatry, 52*-1048–1060.

Kleespies, P. M. (2009). *Behavioral emergencies: An evidence-based resource for evaluating and managing risk of suicide, violence, and victimization*. Washington, DC: American Psychological Association.

Kliman, A. S. (1978). *Crisis: Psychological first aid for recovery and growth*. New York: Holt, Rinehart & Winston.

Lazarus, A. (1989*). The practice of multimodal therapy*. Baltimore: Johns Hopkins University Press.

Leitner, L. A. (1974). Crisis counseling may save a life. *Journal of Rehabilitation, 40*, 19–20.

Levinson, D. J. (1986). A concept of adult development. *American Psychologist, 41*(1), 3–133.

Levinson, D. J., & Levinson, J. D. (1996). *The seasons of a woman's life*. New York: Knopf.

Lindemann, E. (1944). Symptomatology and management of acute grief. *American Journal of Psychiatry, 101*, 141–148.

Lindemann, E. (1956). The meaning of crisis in individual and family. *Teachers College Record, 57*, 310.

Lohr, J. M., Montgomery, R. W., Lilienfeld, S. O., & Tolin, D. F. (1999). Pseudoscience and the commercial promotion of trauma treatments. In R. Gist & B. Lubin (Eds.), *Response to disaster: Psychosocial, community and ecological approaches* (pp. 291–321). Philadelphia: Brunner/Mazel.

Lorenz, E. N. (1993). *The essence of chaos*. Seattle: University of Washington Press.

Marshall, R. D., Bryant, R. A., Amsel, L., Suh, E. J. Cook, J. M., & Neria, Y. (2007). The psychology of ongoing threat: Relative risk appraisal, the September 11 attacks and terrorism related fears. *American Psychologist, 62*(4), 304–316.

Maurer, C. M., & Sheets, T. E. (Eds.). (1999). *Encyclopedia of associations* (34th ed.) (Vol. I, Parts 1–3). Farmington Hills, MI: Gale Research.

Meichenbaum, D. H. (1977). Cognitive-behavior modification: An integrative approach. New York: Plenum.

Minuchin, S. (1974*). Families and family therapy*. Cambridge, MA: Harvard University Press.

Mitchell, J. T., & Everly, G. S., Jr. (1995). Critical incidents stress debriefing (CISD) and the prevention of work-related traumatic stress among high risk occupational groups. In G. S. Everly, Jr., & J. T. Lating (Eds.), *Psychotraumatology* (pp. 267–280). New York: Plenum Press.

Myer, R. A., James, R. K., & Moulton, P. (2011). *This is not a fire drill: Crisis intervention and prevention on college campuses*. Hoboken, NJ: John Wiley & Sons.

Myer, R. A., & Moore, H. (2006). Crisis in context theory: An ecological model. *Journal of Counseling & Development, 84*(2), 139–147.

National Association of School Psychologists. (2010). *NASP Professional Standards (2010)*. Retrieved from http://www.nasponline.org/standards/2010standards.aspx

National Institute of Mental Health. (2002). *Mental health and mass violence: Evidence-based early psychological intervention for victims/survivors of mass violence* (NIH Publication No. 02-5138). Washington, DC: U.S. Government Printing Office.

Ober, C., Peeters, L., Archer, R., & Kelly, K. (2000). Debriefing in different cultural frameworks: Responding to acute trauma in Australian Aboriginal contexts. In B. Raphael & J. P. Wilson (Eds.), *Psychological debriefing: Theory, practice, and evidence* (pp. 241–253). New York: Cambridge University Press.

Poland, S., & McCormick, J. S. (1999). *Coping with crisis: Lessons learned*. Longmont, CO: Sophris West.

Postrel, V. (1998). *The future and its enemies: The growing conflict over creativity, enterprise, and progress*. New York: Free Press.

Pyszczynski, T., Solomon, S., & Greenberg, J. (2003). *In the wake of 9/11: The psychology of terror*. Washington, DC: American Psychological Association.

Raphael, B. (1977). Preventive intervention with the recently bereaved. *Archives of General Psychiatry, 34*, 1450–1454.

Raphael, B. (1986). *When disaster strikes: How individuals and communities cope with catastrophe*. New York: Basic Books.

Rapoport, L. (1967). Crisis-oriented short-term case work. *Social Services Review, 41*, 31–44.

Raskin, N. J., & Rogers, C. R. (1995). Person-centered therapy. In R. J. Corsini & D. Wedding (Eds.), *Current psychotherapies* (5th ed.). Itasca, IL: F. E. Peacock.

Reyes, G., Elhai, J. D., & Ford, J. D. (Eds). (2008). *The encyclopedia of psychological trauma*. Hoboken, NJ: John Wiley & Sons.

Roberts, A. R. (Ed.). (1991). *Contemporary perspectives on crisis intervention and prevention*. Upper Saddle River, NJ: Prentice Hall.

Roberts, A. R. (Ed.). 2005). *Crisis intervention handbook* (3rd ed.). New York: Oxford University Press.

Rogers, C. R. (1961). *On becoming a person*. Boston: Houghton Mifflin.

Rogers, C. R. (1977). *Carl Rogers on personal power: Inner strength and its revolutionary impact*. New York: Delacorte.

Salzer, M. S., & Bickman, L. (1999). The short and long term psychological impact of disasters: Implications for mental health intervention. In R. Gist & B. Lubin (Eds.), *Response to disaster: Psychological, community, and ecological approaches* (pp. 63–82). Philadelphia: Brunner/Mazel.

Sarri, S. (2005). *A bolt from the blue: Coping with disaster and acute trauma*. London: Jessica Kingsley.

Shneidman, E. (2001*). Comprehending suicide: Landmarks in 20th century suicidology*. Washington, DC: American Psychological Association.

Slaikeu, K. A. (Ed.). (1990). *Crisis intervention: A handbook for practice and research* (2nd ed.). Boston: Allyn & Bacon.

Slaikeu, K. A., & Leff-Simon, S. I. (1990). Crisis intervention by telephone. In K. A. Slaikeu (Ed.), *Crisis intervention: A handbook for practice and research* (2nd ed., pp. 319–328). Boston: Allyn & Bacon.

Thorne, F. C. (1973). Eclectic psychotherapy. In R. Corsini (Ed.), *Current psychotherapies* (pp. 445–486). Itasca, IL: F. E. Peacock.

U.S. Department of Veterans Affairs. (2011). *Psychological first aid: Field operations guide.* Retrieved January 11, 2011, from http://ptsd.va.gov/prfessional/manuals/psych-first-aid.asp

van den Eynde, J., & Veno, A. (1999). Coping with disastrous events: An empowerment model for community healing. In R. Gist & B. Lubin (Eds.), *Response to disaster: Psychosocial, community and ecological approaches* (pp. 167–192). Philadelphia: Brunner/Mazel.

van der Kolk, B. A., & McFarlane, A. C. (1996). The black hole of trauma. In B. A. van der Kolk, A. C. McFarlane, & L. Weisaeth (Eds.), *Trauma stress: The effects of overwhelming experience on the mind, body, and society* (pp. 3–23). New York: Guilford Press.

Young, B. H. (2006). The immediate response to disaster: Guideline for adult psychological first aid. In E. C. Ritchie, P. J. Watson, & M. J. Friedman (Eds.), *Intervention following mass violence and disaster: Strategies for mental health practice* (pp. 134–155). New York: Guilford Press.

Zdziarski, E. L., Dunkel, N. W., & Rollo, J. M. (2007). *Campus crisis management: A comprehensive guide to planning, prevention, response and recovery.* San Francisco: John Wiley & Sons.

CHAPTER 2
Culturally Effective Helping

Multicultural Perspectives in Crisis Intervention

Laura Brown is the past president of Division 56, Trauma Psychology; she is a diplomate (recognized as knowing a lot and contributing a lot) in clinical psychology, has received numerous awards, and has authored what we believe is the best book on cultural competence when it comes to doing trauma therapy, *Cultural Competence in Trauma Therapy: Beyond the Flashback* (2008). So we can pretty much assume she knows what she's talking about when she says, "After three decades of working intentionally with trauma I can say with utter certainty that I know that I have no idea of how any particular person will have experienced and made sense, or not, of her or his traumatic experiences" (p. 16). Therefore, as you read this chapter, understand that one of the best minds in this field is confessing to her ignorance when it comes to ferreting out all the ways that culture affects her clients. The message is that we're a long way from knowing all we need to know to effectively weave multiculturalism into crisis intervention. However, we do know more than we did in the last edition of this book, and the way research is moving (Brown, 2008, 2009; D'Andrea & Heckman, 2008; Ponterotto & Mallinckrodt, 2007; Ridley & Shaw-Ridley, 2011; Worthington & Dillon, 2011; Worthington, Sott-McNett, & Moreno, 2007), we're going to know more and more. So please understand that this chapter isn't a GPS for multicultural competency in crisis intervention that will precisely target your destination, but more like a compass that will point you in the right general direction.

In the United States, whether we realize it or not, we live in a pluralistic culture (Sue & Sue, 2002), and the same could be said for practically every country in the world. So just what is this abstract and amorphous thing called "culture"? And how does it become "multi"? Furthermore, what makes it important in the crisis business?

Adler (1997) defines culture as "that complex whole which includes knowledge, beliefs, arts, laws, morals, customs and capabilities acquired by a person as a member of society. It is a way of life of a group of people, the configuration of all the more or less stereotyped patterns of learned behavior which are handed down from one generation to the next through the means of language and imitation" (p. 14). Members of a given culture hold all of the foregoing to be pretty much self-evident truths to live by, as a way of making order and sense out of their lives. Thus, they are generally able to live with one another in an overall peaceful, profitable way with some sense of control over their lives and the community within which they reside. The "multi" part comes into play when we start to mix up people from different cultural communities with different assumptions about all those variables Adler is talking about.

The role that culture plays in crisis intervention has to do with what Savicki (2002) has termed *uncertainty avoidance*—and, as you will see in this book, attempting to avoid uncertainty and get back in control of a situation gets a lot of playing time. Uncertainty avoidance has to do with the degree to which cultures feel threatened by uncertainty and ambiguous situations, so rules, procedures, rituals, and laws may be formulated to buffer uncertainties of individual judgment (Savicki, 2002, p. 27). What this means in crisis intervention is that a crisis worker who ventures into a different culture had better be aware that the residents of that culture are basing their ability to get though the crisis on their own set of cultural survival standards, and those don't necessarily square up with the worker's.

Kiselica (1998, p. 6) identifies four attributes that are widely accepted as necessary for crisis workers and other mental health workers who intervene with clients in the multicultural world in which we work: (1) self-knowledge, particularly an awareness of one's own cultural biases; (2) knowledge about the status and cultures of different groups; (3) skills to effect culturally appropriate interventions—including a readiness to use alternative strategies that better match the cultures of crisis clients than do traditional strategies; and (4) actual experience in counseling and crisis intervention with culturally different clients. Sue (1992, p. 12; 1999a, 1999b) reminds us that failure to understand clients' worldviews may lead human services workers to make erroneous interpretations, judgments, and conclusions that result in doing serious harm to clients, especially those who are culturally different. A vast majority of the world's population lives by non-Western perspectives, and a lot of those perspectives are making their way to the United States through immigration. Despite the fact that the world is culturally pluralistic, many of our books, professional teachings, research findings, and implicit theories and assumptions in the field of counseling and crisis intervention are specific to North American and European cultures. Such theories and assumptions are usually so ingrained in our thinking that they are taken for granted and seldom challenged even by our most broad-minded leaders and professionals (Pedersen, 1998; Ponterotto & Pedersen, 1993; Ridley, 1995).

As an example, critics of "culture-blind" crisis interventionists propose that their reductionistic and outmoded logical positivism (based solely on observable scientific facts and their relationship to each other and natural laws of nature) has no place in dealing with widespread violence and social upheaval in large, ethnically different populations caught in long-term wars, rebellions, or other social disasters. They further believe that Western traumatologists adopt a naive view that trauma leads in linear fashion to PTSD in all people in all cultures. Social constructivists in particular rail at this normative view of trauma. They believe it may be much more appropriate to look at trauma, and the crisis intervention that follows it, in much broader social terms, such as safety, grief, injustice, and faith, as opposed to distinct clinical categories of PTSD and depression (Silove, 2000).

There is also a great deal of debate on the validity of any measures that are used to assess the various aspects of crisis that are dealt with in this book, because cultural bias and cultural artifacts can skew results to make clients look very different from what they actually are and lead to erroneous treatment decisions (Brown, 2008; Cokley, 2007). Further, the biggest assessment measure of all, the *Diagnostic and Statistical Manual, Fourth Edition Revised* (DSM IV-R), of the American Psychiatric Association (2000), has come under fire (Brown, 2008; Zalaquett et al., 2008) for its limited inclusion of social and cultural factors in the diagnoses of mental disorders. These critics believe that the normative, disease-based, medical model of the DSM IV-R, which emphasizes client deficits, top-down expert-professional-to-client relationships, medication as a major form of treatment, and universal interpretation for persons from various cultures, flies in the face of a counseling view of idiosyncratic behavior and often leads to ethnocentric and grossly inaccurate diagnoses (Zalaquett et al., 2008).

Ivey (1987) and Arredondo (1999) emphasize that counseling and therapy should begin with counselors' awareness of their own assumptions, values, and biases regarding racial, cultural, and group differences before considering individual variations on those themes. Ivey (1987) states that "only by placing multicultural counseling at the core of counseling curricula can we as counselors truly serve and be with those whom we would help" (p. 169). That statement is probably exponentially true for crisis workers. Specifically in regard to crisis, Brown (2009, p. 167) believes that more than any other form of distress, persons who have suffered complex trauma do so in relation to their psychosocial cultural context, and to deny the social identities they bring out of that culture is a pretty effective way to stop intervention before it starts.

Culturally Biased Assumptions

Unintentional and unexamined cultural and racial assumptions can impair functioning of counselors (Arredondo, 1999; Ober et al., 2000; Ridley, 1995; Thompson & Neville, 1999). That statement holds doubly true for crisis workers given the cross-cultural circumstances within which they often operate—particularly in large-scale disaster relief. Pedersen (1987) discusses the following 10 culturally biased assumptions that crisis workers would do well to remember:

1. People all share a common measure of "normal" behavior (p. 17) (the presumption that problems,

emotional responses, behaviors, and perceptions of crises are more or less universal across social, cultural, economic, or political backgrounds).

2. Individuals are the basic building blocks of all societies (p. 18) (the presumption that crisis intervention and counseling are directed primarily toward the individual rather than units of individuals or groups such as the family, organizations, political groups, or society).

3. The definition of problems can be limited by academic discipline boundaries (p. 19) (the presumption that the identity of the crisis worker or counselor is separate from the identity of the theologian, medical doctor, sociologist, anthropologist, attorney, or representative from some other discipline).

4. Western culture depends on abstract words (pp. 19–20) (the presumption of crisis workers and counselors in the United States that others will understand these abstractions in the same way as workers intend them).

5. Independence is valuable and dependencies are undesirable (p. 20) (the presumption of Western individualism that people should not be dependent on others or allow others to be dependent on them).

6. Formal counseling is more important than natural support systems surrounding a client (pp. 20–21) (the presumption that clients prefer the support offered by counselors over the support of family, peers, and other support groups).

7. Everyone depends on linear thinking (pp. 21–22) (the presumption by counselors and crisis workers that each cause has an effect, and each effect is tied to a cause—to explain how the world works—and that everything can be measured and described in terms of good or bad, appropriate or inappropriate, and/or other common dichotomies).

8. Counselors need to change individuals to fit the system (p. 22) (the presumption that the system does not need to change to fit the individual).

9. The client's past (history) has little relevance to contemporary events (pp. 22–23) (the presumption that crises are mostly related to here-and-now situations, and that crisis workers and counselors should pay little attention to the client's background).

10. Counselors and crisis workers already know all their assumptions (p. 23) (the presumption that if counselors and crisis workers were prone toward reacting in closed, biased, and culturally encapsulated ways that promote domination by an elitist group, they would be aware of it).

All 10 assumptions are flawed and untenable in a pluralistic world. Cormier and Hackney (1987) warn that human services workers who do not understand their own cultural biases and the cultural differences and values of others may misinterpret the behaviors and attitudes of clients from other cultures. Such workers may incorrectly label some client behavior as resistant and uncooperative. They may expect to see certain client behaviors (such as self-disclosure) that are contrary to the basic values of some cultural groups. The culturally insensitive counselor or crisis worker may also stereotype, label, or use unimodal, inappropriate, or ineffective counseling approaches and concepts in an attempt to help clients from other cultures (pp. 256–258). Specifically in the field of crisis intervention, there has been criticism of the Western-based trauma model and particularly the elevation of PTSD as a pathological entity that has been coined in self-serving ways by victims' groups, politicians, and profiteering lawyers and therapists when there is little empirical evidence to support such an assumption (Silove, 2000; Summerfield, 1999).

Universal Versus Focused Views

There are both universal and focused views on multicultural counseling. A universal view considers not only racial and ethnic minorities, but other minority or special populations as well. A focused view looks at multicultural counseling in relation to "visible and racial ethnic minorities" (Sue, Arredondo, & McDavis, 1992). More encompassing parallel terms you may run into in a multicultural text for these views are the *etic* and *emic* models. An etic model views people one dimensionally—focusing, for example, on their race, sex, age, hair color, or preference for junk food. We agree with Brown (2008, p. 12) that using racial designation, ethnic label, or any one characteristic, trait, preference, or other category to identify people may have little or nothing to do with the crises they are encountering and is probably a pretty poor unimodal cultural lens through which to view a person who has been traumatized. To view culture from such a narrow perspective is, we believe, asking for a lot of trouble in crisis intervention.

Working on the Individualist/Collectivist– High/Low Context Continuum

From a multicultural perspective, we may generally look at communication along an individualist/collectivist continuum. *Individualism* is a worldview that centralizes the personal—personal goals, personal uniqueness, and personal control—and peripheralizes the social group or social context within which the individual operates. *Collectivism* is based on the assumption that groups bind and mutually obligate individuals, that the personal is simply a component of the larger social group or context and subordinate to it (Oyserman, Coon, & Kemmelmeier, 2002). These concepts are important because they tend to dictate how the client sees him- or herself in relation to self-concept, sense of well-being, emotional control, and relational and attributional styles (Williams, 2003), which are all critical components in how crisis intervention strategies are formulated and applied to traumatized individuals. For instance, a person who lives in a collectivist culture—and they certainly do exist in the United States—who suffers a traumatic event that may be construed as shameful may have that extrapolate out to all members of the family, with family often defined as extending a good deal beyond a biological basis (Brown, 2009, p. 161).

In a meta-analysis of 170 studies on the individualist/collectivist worldview, Oyserman, Coon, and Kemmelmeier (2002) found that individualism centers on one's self-concept rather than one's family life, as opposed to collectivism, in which the opposite is true. In regard to "sense of well-being," individualists see well-being as related to a sense of personal control; collectivists do not. Even more important in terms of crisis intervention, individualism proponents tend to see the event in terms of their own personal preferences, whereas collectivist proponents interpret the event in relation to what they believe the expectations of others might be. A rather startling discovery contradicts the accepted belief that people who are collectivist consider the group, and particularly the family, as taking precedence and obligation over individual well-being. They found essentially no difference between individualists and collectivists regarding "sense of family obligation." When a dilemma was presented, collectivists responded by identifying themselves as part of a cooperative group, whereas individualists considered themselves to be individuals participating as part of a team effort. Finally, communication and conflict resolution styles were found to vary in relation to individualism and collectivism. Individualism consistently predicted goal-oriented, low-context, direct communication; collectivism opted for indirect, high-context communication. In confrontational situations, individualists adhered to a confrontational and arbitrational approach; collectivists preferred an accommodation and negotiation approach.

But how do people in a collective society operate under stress and traumatic conditions? The Heppners and their associates (2006) conducted research in establishing a collectivist coping styles inventory that attempts to discern how stressful and traumatic events are handled from an Asian perspective. Indeed, the 3,000 Taiwanese college students in the study endorsed coping strategies very different from those of their Western counterparts. Their acceptance, fatalism, efficacy, and interpersonal harmony strategies when faced with stressful events are unlike any other factors endorsed on traditional coping strategy inventories in the Western world. Family support and religious and spiritual resources are also different from their Western counterparts. Filial piety and elder support are important, and advice is generally sought within the sanctity of the family.

The Chinese kanji characters of crisis and opportunity that appear on the cover of this book are evident in the Taiwanese students' approach to coping with crisis. The Confucian and Buddhist philosophies that one endures suffering, looks for positive meaning, and exercises control and restraint predominate in their responses. Finally, their avoidance and emotional detachment from the stressful event and private emotional outlets are also different. Whereas in the United States we might expect an outpouring of emotion and immediate public support and grief following a traumatic event (Halpern & Tramontin, 2007, p. 98), the results from this study suggest that these students seek outside help as a last resort, and when they do it is most often in a confidential and anonymous manner. Their coping strategies revolved around avoiding shame and seeking help in safe, anonymous ways. The Heppners and their associates (2006) suggest that these students might go to a mental health professional who was unknown to them or their families or go into a chat room on the Internet to discuss their problems. The point is that, at least for these Taiwanese students, when under stress or traumatized, they might seek mental health help very differently than would their American counterparts.

High/Low Context Approaches.   To put the foregoing analysis in operational terms useful to the crisis worker, the individualist/collectivist continuum uses what Hall (1976) calls a high/low context approach. In low-context cultures, one's self-image and worth are defined in personal, individual terms. In high-context cultures, one's self-worth and esteem are tied to the group. In low-context cultures, information is generally transmitted explicitly and concretely through language;

in high-context cultures, information is transmitted in the physical context of the interaction or internalized in the person. In high-context cultures, facial expressions, gestures, and tone of voice are as important as the meaning of words that are said. Thus, in high-context cultures, the individual will expect the other person to know what the problem is so that he or she does not have to be specific and become embarrassed and lose face by talking directly about the issue. This communication style can be very problematic to a crisis worker who operates from a low-context style in which specific and concrete information is sought to determine what is needed to take care of the problem.

From the high-context client's standpoint, the low-context worker's attempt to gather specific information about the client's personal and social status in relationship to the crisis may be seen as intrusive, rude, and offensive. A high-context culture uses stories, proverbs, fables, metaphors, similes, and analogies to make a point (Augsburger, 1992). Thus, a high-context crisis worker might be very delicate, ambiguous, sensitive, and somewhat circumlocutory in discussing personal and social issues related to the crisis. In trying to help a low-context client, a crisis worker using such a communication style might be viewed as not being remotely aware of what the frustrated client's needs are.

As a result, one of the major problems in crisis intervention with culturally different people lies in both sending and receiving communications that are understandable, clearly communicating what we are attempting to do while not exacerbating an already potentially volatile situation. While it is impossible to know the nuances of every culture and the subtleties of the client's native language, one of our rules of the road in crisis intervention in which cultural differences are an issue is that there are these two broad camps, and we need to find out which one the individual is operating in and act accordingly.

Crisis worker: (*speaking to an East African male, a recent immigrant, who has been injured in a train wreck and doesn't know what has happened to his family*) I understand you are from Somalia. I don't know a lot about your country or customs, so please let me know if what I am saying doesn't agree with what you think is right and I'll do my best to explain why that is so here in the U.S. and how we might be able to still fit your cultural background as we try to find out about your family and get you the medical help you need.

We also need to clearly own that we may be culturally ignorant and thus appear to be insensitive to the crisis client's needs. Such admissions early on go a long way in letting the client clarify what his or her needs are. Those owning statements are true whether we are dealing with survivors of an east Kentucky coal mine explosion, war refugees in Liberia, or survivors and their families from the 9/11 attacks.

High/Low Uncertainty Avoidance Approaches. High and low context cultures get a lot of space in professional human service publications. What doesn't, and is particularly appropriate to crisis intervention, is understanding whether the culture one is entering is operating on high or low uncertainty avoidance principles (Savicki, 2002, p. 27). High uncertainty avoidance cultures develop a broad range of rules and regulations and procedures to cover a multitude of contingencies. In other words, if you are entering that high uncertainty avoidance culture, you had better understand they have a playbook of what is right and proper that will rival that of a playbook from the National Football League (if you are not a football fan, those books are huge and enormously complicated). If you don't understand and operate within it, you'll wind up butting your head against a very large cultural wall. On the other hand, if you are entering a low uncertainty avoidance culture you may well be frustrated by a "Relax! Be happy ! We're all alive! We have food and water! Hurricanes come and go! We'll rebuild tomorrow!" view. That sort of a "chill out" worldview can sabotage the herculean efforts of highly motivated disaster workers who are operating on short time frames and deadlines, leaving them embittered and burned out from the experience.

Emic Versus Etic Models of Multiculturalism

An emic model encompasses the smorgasbord of components that make up individuals, not just what their individual parts are, but more the total gestalt of how they come together. So please meet the emic model of Dr. Dick James, 60-something, father soon to be grandfather who is mostly happy about it, husband who thinks he's been married longer than he's been alive sometimes, hard of hearing from too many years in construction working his way through school and gets yelled at for not wearing his hearing aid enough, fisherman and hunter who pals around with one of his daughters doing those activities, white guy who grew up in a university town but had blue-collar parents, now has digestive trouble eating pizza and drinking beer, trains police officers to deal with the emotionally disturbed and severely agitated mentally ill, played baseball and ran track in an integrated high school in the '60s that he loved so has had some lifelong friends who are both white and black, has been a school counselor in a blue-collar Midwestern town, a Presbyterian who goes pretty regularly to church but has been a Baptist and a Methodist and has a lot of friends who are Catholic and Jewish, writes books like this one instead of the great American novel he thought he would when he was an English major at Eastern Illinois University, has a sense of humor that leaks out and sometimes gets him in trouble and likes to send jokes over the Internet and make people laugh, and had his first real crisis when he got shot in the chest at age 21 while with a girl who he would have probably married . . . if he hadn't gotten shot, and so on.

These are what Laura Brown (2008, p. 24) calls *social locations*, and both she and we believe they are important from a multicultural standpoint when you are doing this work. So if you compare all that to just Dr. James old dude, or Dr. James professor, or Dr. James white guy, or any other unitary, focused view of Dr. James, you surely aren't getting the view you got a couple of sentences ago and our guess would be you might not respond in quite the same way if you were doing crisis intervention with him. Thus, we take a universal/emic rather than a focused/etic view in crisis intervention. Therefore, when we speak of cultural diversity, we are speaking in the broadest possible terms in regard to all factors that somehow make clients "different" from the interventionist. Hopefully, the following analogies illuminate what is meant by a universal/emic view.

Your worldview, if you are a New York City social worker and you have spent your entire life in the city and are now trying to help a Midwestern farmer who has just lost everything in a flood, is going to be as different from his worldview as ours would be from Pakistani survivors of an earthquake we were attempting to help. Or how about your first encounter (assuming you are heterosexual) with a gay man who has just discovered he is HIV positive from his longtime, supposedly faithful partner? Or consider a staunchly devout Baptist woman who believes divorce is a sin but who is being severely beaten by her preacher husband. Does that mean you will be ineffective and should not go to Keokuk, Iowa, or we should not go to Karachi, Pakistan? Never work with gay men or Baptist women? Certainly not! What it does mean is that "multiculturalism" does not necessarily stand out in large neon lights saying "I am from Ethiopia or Nepal, and I am different from you" or "I have red, black, yellow, or green (there may

be some of those aliens from Area 51 in Roswell, New Mexico, reading this, and we don't want to leave them out) skin." In a statement that absolutely captures the essence of what is meant by a universal view, Halpern and Tramontin (2007) quote New York regional mental health officials: "In the large and diverse state of New York, when you know one county in the state you know one county" (p. 316). So how in the world do you do this business if there is that much diversity, not just in the world, but in one state?

Laura Brown (2008, p. 12) has used Hays's ADDRESSING model (2001, 2008) as one of the bases for her book on multiculturalism and trauma. The ADDRESSING acronym encompasses Age, acquired and Developmental Disabilities, Religion, Ethnicity, Social class, Sexual orientation, Indigenous heritage, National origin, and Gender. D'Andrea & Daniels (2005) have developed a comparable model called RESPECTFUL (Religious/spiritual, Economic class, Sexual identity, Psychological development, Ethnic/racial identity, Chronological age, Trauma and threats to well-being, Family, Unique physical issues, and Language and location of residence). From our own experience we would add geographic locale, living area (urban, suburban, rural), occupation, education, and marital or partner status. We believe these variables are the major components that capture the essence of how the crisis interventionist needs to think about clients and work with the multiple identities that intersect with the crisis.

Compounding the issue even more is the fact that you, the interventionist, are bringing all these social locations into the equation too. Consider Figure 2.1 and how the social locations of Dr. James fit (or not) with Leron, an individual you will meet in Chapter 3, who is having a really bad day. Dr. James will do a quick assessment of Leron's affective, behavioral, and cognitive functioning and immediately start identifying his social locations, which he believes may affect his intervention with Leron. By owning who he is, he is attempting to engage the client, the first task of the crisis intervention model you will meet in Chapter 3. Besides dealing with the very obvious social locations that differ between crisis workers and their clients, you need to be aware of *all* the baggage you carry into this particular environment that may hinder your efforts. Thus, Dr. James's social location of hearing impairment may not be visible, but on a noisy street it can be problematic to say the least if he misinterprets what he hears and is too proud not to mention this fact early on to a client who may see him as a whole lot of other things that are not helpful if he can't

Dr. James's ADDRESSING social locations

Born and raised in Illinois

Mentally alert

Lives in Memphis

Caucasian

Health generally good, hard of hearing

Past middle age

Upper middle class

Police consultant

Counseling psychologist

Family raised, lives with wife

Ph.D.

Crisis interventionist

Employed as a professor

Angry with housing authority

Depressed over loss of family
and inability to find work

Drunk **CRISIS SETTING**

Police on the scene,
traffic stopped

Middle of a major thoroughfare in rush hour traffic

Threatening, armed with two broken bottles

Lives in Memphis

Born in Mississippi

Poor history with police

Middle-aged

Homeless

Male

Lower middle class, moving to lower class

Out-of-work forklift operator

Family left

African American

Health deteriorating

Three years of high school

Drinking heavily

Leron's ADDRESSING social locations

FIGURE 2.1 ADDRESSING Social Locations: Dr. James and Leron

respond clearly and correctly. Likewise, he needs to be sensitive to the fact that one of Leron's present social locations is intoxication and it may be more the whiskey than the man doing the talking. So while our crisis interventionist may or may not have trouble because of his skin color, perceived social class difference based on his clothes and the way he talks, and the fact that he is a police consultant, he needs to be cognizant that those

factors may indeed be operating. For the master practitioners of crisis intervention, it is critical to their success that they are sophisticated enough to know when social locations they inhabit may become the major dynamic they are dealing with (Brown, 2009, p. 40) and what they need to do about it.

To that end crisis workers need to practice what Day-Vines and her associates (2007) called *broaching*.

Broaching refers to the crisis worker's consistent display of openness to invite the client to explore issues of diversity and a recognition that race, ethnicity, or some social location other than the crisis worker's may be contributing to the crisis.

Leron: What the hell you doin' out here you honkie, cracker? 'Lessen you from Channel Five I ain't got nuthin' fo' you. I wants the whole world to know about them Nazis down at the housin' 'thority what done kicked me out fo' no good reason.

Dr. James: I realize that I'm a white guy who isn't homeless and furthermore that I have a police T-shirt on that says I work for the man. I understand that may affect your ability to trust me that I can help you out, but the T-shirt also says CIT which means I am a person who trains police officers to deal with folks who have problems that frustrate them and cause them to take actions they normally wouldn't do unless they felt they had no other options, and that seems to be about where you are right now. So if you have questions about who I am, I'll be glad to answer them. By the way, one of the "Who I ams" is that I'm a little hard of hearing and it's noisy out here so I'd appreciate it if you could speak up a bit so I am sure I get everything you are saying. So I wonder if you might not trust me enough to tell me what got you out here in the middle of one of the busiest streets in Memphis to get the attention you seem to need.

To make things even more problematic, it isn't just "culture" that factors into this increasingly complex picture but the "ecology" you are working in as well. By "ecology" we mean the living environment in which the intervention occurs. It is 98 degrees Fahrenheit out on that street where Leron is. Do you suppose that adds to the problem? As we will see in Chapter 17, long-term residence in a displaced persons facility wears very thin when it is hot, there are no bathing facilities, and head lice are rampant. Your intervention will change and be influenced by a number of ecological variables. Are you working in a nice air-conditioned office with one person, or in an evacuation center with the power going on and off that is full of people 24/7 who haven't had a bath in a while and you haven't either? Are you working in the panhandle of Oklahoma in 100-degree weather in July with a blast furnace wind blowing all the time and you are from Minnesota? Or perhaps you are from an Iowa farming community where the tallest building is a grain elevator and you find yourself on Michigan Avenue in Chicago buried in the canyon of skyscrapers. So it isn't just culture by itself, it is also the ecological landscape you are operating in that is going to affect how and what you do.

Awareness of Both Ecology and Multicultural Competencies

Figure 2.2 is a diagram of the effects of ecology/culture on client–worker interactions. Notice that the "crisis" triangle has a component at each corner: the crisis worker, the client, and their ecological/cultural determinants. The two-way arrows connecting the three corners indicate the mutual and dynamic interaction that constantly occurs among all the possible ecological/cultural factors that affect both crisis worker and client: family, race, religion, locale, physical ability, sex, economic class, vocation, physical needs, social affiliations, and so on. The triangle itself represents the environment in which you are working and the ecological background and cultural attitudes, beliefs, and heritages you and the client bring into that setting.

Two examples illustrate this interaction well. The relationship of age to PTSD is an outstanding example of the effect of cultural context. Norris and Alegria (2006) report that among three samples of disaster survivors, manifesting PTSD occurred at higher rates in younger Mexicans, middle-age Americans, and older Poles. Clearly, there was no one consistent effect of disaster by age. Rather, the cultural context of the country and the variation in historical social roles that are dictated in those countries would seem to have a great deal of influence on how the crisis will unfold when age is a factor.

Ghafoori and Hierholzer (2010) studied personality disorders (PDs) among black, white, and Hispanic combat veterans who were diagnosed with PTSD. They sought to examine whether there were differences among the three groups on Cluster A PD (odd or eccentric behavior, including paranoid, schizoid, and schizotypal disorders), Cluster B PD (dramatic or erratic behavior, including histrionic, narcissistic, antisocial, and borderline disorders), and Cluster C (anxious

FIGURE 2.2 The Dynamic Effect of Ecology/Culture on Client–Crisis Worker Interactions

or inhibited behaviors, including avoidant, dependent, and obsessive-compulsive disorders). Based on previous literature reviews, the researchers hypothesized that blacks would have more Cluster A symptoms, blacks and Hispanics would have an increased likelihood of manifesting Cluster B symptoms, and the association between race, ethnicity, and PD symptoms would not be fully explained by combat exposure, PTSD, or the potential confounding variables of age, education, and income. What they found was in sharp contrast to what they had hypothesized. Their outcomes indicated that Hispanic veterans were significantly more likely to have personality disorders that fit under Category A compared to the other two groups. They also found that those veterans who had Cluster A symptoms were one and a half times more likely to have PTSD. Finally, they found that greater level of combat exposure was likely to manifest in Cluster C symptoms for all groups.

So if you are in the PTSD treatment business with combat veterans, it ought to become apparent that the interaction between environment and ethnicity will have some profound effects on what these clients bring into the therapeutic setting, and is certainly going to dictate that your treatment plan is most likely going to be different given the different clusters of PDs with which you are faced.

When the crisis worker is factored into the equation, then intervention becomes even more complex. Internal versus external locus of control is a particularly aggravating problem that may bedevil crisis workers. Most crisis workers have a high internal locus of control and believe that through personal effort, one can start to regain psychological homeostasis and equilibrium (Atkinson, Morten, & Sue, 1998). Understand, then, that no therapy is done in a sterile vacuum, free from the multiple effects of the ecological/cultural background. That statement is even truer in the highly charged emotional context of crisis intervention.

The wise crisis interventionist understands this complexity and, when faced with an out-of-control client whose ecological context and background may be extremely different from his or her own, goes slowly and carefully. The wise worker is highly sensitive to and asks questions about the person's preferred mode of receiving assistance. As an example, Weisaeth (2000) reports on deciding *not* to do critical incident stress debriefing (CISD) with a U.N. peacekeeping battalion of Fiji Islanders who were doing duty in South Lebanon. After an artillery attack that left many dead and wounded civilians they had been sheltering in their compound, the Fijis worked through their stress by using a very intense and emotional group ceremonial ritual that involved a mildly intoxicating drink called *kawa.* Weisaeth wisely decided to drop any attempt at a standard CISD because it was apparent the Fijis had their own quite adequate way of dealing with the trauma. Any attempt to shoehorn CISD into the Fiji cultural tradition might have caused a great deal of resistance and done more harm than good.

A recurrent comment we are confronted with in our classes comes from an apparent belief that "to counsel one, you gotta be one!" We believe that this stance is neither true nor workable. Particularly in crisis intervention, we seldom have the freedom to choose which clients we will get or take, and we generally do not have the luxury of making referrals simply because the client's ecological/cultural background does not fit nicely into our own. What we can do and must do is be acutely sensitive to the emerging needs of the individual, and in Carl Rogers's terms (Raskin & Rogers, 1995), prize that person in regard to his or her distinctive individuality in the context of the crisis situation. Above all else, research on the outcomes of therapy tells us that establishing a relationship built on trust and credibility is far and away the most important condition for a successful outcome of any kind of therapeutic endeavor (Capuzzi & Gross, 1995, pp. 12–25).

Shortcomings of a Multiculturalist Approach to Crisis Intervention

First and foremost, there is a lot of controversy over what the terms *ethnicity, race, ethnic and racial identity,* and *culture,* as definable and measurable constructs, actually mean (Cokley, 2007). That's problematic for multiculturalism in general and multicultural counseling in particular in trying to serve an increasingly culturally diverse society (Trimble, 2007), because if we can't define those words, then explaining what multicultural counseling is and how we go about doing it is really going to be difficult (Ponterotto & Mallinckrodt, 2007).

The multicultural approaches to crisis intervention described here do not have universal support among helping professionals. Those professionals are definitely not opposed to the concepts or the consideration of the various forms of diversity that are encountered in the helping and mental health services, nor are we. However, several serious questions must be posed about the current multiculturalist view of counseling. Those questions particularly apply to crisis intervention.

Perhaps the most prevalent alleged shortcoming is the flawed assumption on the part of many "multiculturalists" that the current theories of counseling, psychotherapy, and crisis intervention are inherently biased and oppressive (Weinrach & Thomas, 1998; Wubbolding, 2003). Another critique asserts that many of the current "cultural competency" practices are themselves too exclusive (Weinrach, 2003). Still another alleged shortcoming of the current multiculturalist approach is that much of the pertinent literature on multicultural competencies has not been subjected to peer review or empirical research (Brandsma, 2003; Sullivan & Cottone, 2010). A pretty sophisticated study by Owen and his associates (2011) that had clients rate therapist multicultural competencies along with the outcome of therapy found that multicultural competency didn't account for very much of therapy success, although their study has certainly been taken to task by other multicultural researchers (Ridley & Shaw-Ridley, 2011; Worthington & Dillon, 2011). As such, critics of the current multicultural movement believe that they are merely the unfounded views of those disaffected with the current theories and practices of mental health, and their complaints are expected to be accepted on faith with no evidence to back up their claims. Trimble (2007) puts the issue straight forward when he states that if we can't define these concepts clearly and concretely we have no business trying to measure them.

As a very vivid example, there has been a major assumption that certain Asian and Latino cultures have a much more collectivist view than Americans or Western Europeans in regard to how issues and problems are handled. The belief has long been held that Americans and Western Europeans are much more individualistic in their worldview. In a very large meta-analysis of this worldview hypothesis, Oyserman, Coon, and Kemmelmeier (2002) found that Indonesians were not significantly different from European Americans, Australians, and Germans in regard to individualism, and that European Americans were lower in individualism than people from more than half the countries in Latin America. A truly startling finding was that Americans were significantly higher in collectivism than the Japanese and no different in collectivism than Koreans. Oyserman and his associates' meta-analysis of 170 multicultural studies raised critical questions about the blind acceptance and division of cultures into collectivist and individualist camps.

Kim, Liang, and Li (2003) found that Asian American counselees responded more positively to European American counselors than to Asian American counselors. In attempting to unravel this puzzling outcome, the researchers found that European Americans displayed more positive animation (smiling, postural shifts), which seemed to lead to more positive attribution to the counseling by the Asian American clients, as opposed to less positive ratings for the Asian American counselors, who were more passive and unemotional. This finding brings into question whether being passive, noncommittal, and seemingly uninvolved is indeed the best approach to take with a client who is Asian—or at least one who is Asian American.

Shectman, Hiradin, and Zina (2003) examined the notion of group self-disclosure in Israeli Jewish, Muslim, and Druze adolescents. They hypothesized that because of the standard view that Muslims come from a collectivist culture and the Druze come from a very tightly knit rural collectivist culture far removed from the cultural mainstream, both groups would be far less likely than Jewish adolescents to self-disclose in group counseling. What they unexpectedly found was that while, true to form, the Druze adolescents self-disclosed little, the Muslim adolescents self-disclosed a great deal more than the Jewish adolescents. They hypothesized that these results may be due to the biculturation of Muslim youth, who may have a much greater need for an avenue to self-disclose than their Jewish counterparts. The behavior of the adolescents in this study does not operate along a linear pattern of the stereotypical notion of how ethnic groups self-disclose. It appears that if there is a moderately strong bicultural identity, participants may take advantage of the communication possibilities they are offered.

What these studies indicate is that to arbitrarily organize worldview differences—and therefore counseling approaches—along racial, ethnic, and nationality lines is indeed questionable and is likely to cause the very stereotyping of individuals that multiculturalism rails against (Cohen, 2009). Parallel to this criticism, questions arise as to how and to what extent validated cross-cultural studies are conducted to provide a solid research base for such competencies (Wubbolding, 2003), particularly when small samples of undergraduate foreign students are used as the basis to extrapolate questionable interpretations to entire ethnic populations (Oyserman, Coon, & Kemmelmier, 2002). Oyserman and his associates' (2002) meta-analysis confronted multicultural counseling with a number of uncomfortable facts. One in particular was debunking the notion that the individualist–collectivist construct is a valid means of understanding how cultures operate. That notion was a sacred cow to many multiculturalists and assumed to be self-evident. While there are certainly general differences *between* ethnic, racial, and national groups, and we see the individualist–collectivist concept as a nice theoretical model, we would argue that the differences *within* groups are just as critical.

Because this book is used in a number of countries (for example, there is a Chinese translation), it is worth mentioning that multiculturalists in the United States seem to be unaware or unwilling to state how the multicultural competencies apply to those working in contexts outside the United States (Johannes, 2003) and very few studies are looking at cross comparisons. We bring these issues up because we are a long way from knowing what we need to know about multiculturalism and how it operates in crisis intervention. Thus, you should be a very discerning consumer of what proponents of a multicultural counseling view extol as ultimate truth and beauty when they are arbitrarily generalized to all therapeutic situations and settings. To that point, if you are reading this book in Korean or any other translation, we would be very interested in hearing from you on how you believe your particular culture views helping people in crisis and whether what this book has to say about crisis agrees with your society's views on the matter.

Culturally Effective Helping

The plain and simple truth is that we don't know a lot about how culture, crises, and crisis intervention interact (Brown, 2008, pp. 256–257). Very little research has been done in the area. Certain cultures don't even have words for trauma (Silove, 1998)! However, we do know that deeply held cultural beliefs and previously learned ways of dealing with the world rapidly surface when individuals are placed in a crisis situation (Dass-Brailsford, 2008). When a traumatic event occurs, there is a high probability that people will revert to their long-held cultural beliefs no matter where they live and work at the moment (Brown, 2009, p. 154).

There is a good deal of evidence that minorities in the United States use mental health services a great deal less than European Americans do (Breux & Ryujin, 1999; Chen & Mak, 2008; Sue, 1977). That underutilization becomes very problematic when a disaster strikes, because research indicates that ethnic minorities tend to suffer more in a disaster than the majority group (Norris & Alegria, 2006).

Certainly much human-made crisis revolves around lack of cultural understanding and conflicts between cultures. Eidelson and Eidelson (2003) have documented how distorted beliefs may produce excessive death, suffering, and displacement as a result of conflicts among and between groups regarding ethnicity, nationality, religion, or other social identities and issues. These researchers focused on five core belief domains that propel both individuals and groups to make dangerous assumptions about people who are different from themselves. The domains are identified as revolving around assumptions regarding superiority, injustice, vulnerability, distrust, and helplessness. Deeply entrenched patterns for understanding, perceiving, and interpreting events appear to govern and produce emotions and behaviors that may ultimately lead to conflicts and problematic and destructive crises. Distorted and dysfunctional beliefs appear to be at the core of many of the problems that crisis interventionists and other helping professionals face.

A current example of such a distortion is the widespread belief among New Orleans African Americans that levees were blown up to save white residential districts from Hurricane Katrina's floodwaters. There is, in fact, a historical precedence for blowing up New Orleans levees to save parts of the city. The fact that it did not happen in Katrina's case makes little difference to those people who lost everything but the shirts on their backs. How do you think you would be received if you attempted to do crisis intervention with these individuals—particularly if you were white, and more particularly if you told them you didn't believe that the levees were intentionally blown up? Do you give up before you start? Not hardly!

Past history and experience may play a pivotal role in how recipients of service perceive crisis intervention. Mexican American families whose homes had been damaged in the 1989 Northern California Loma Prieta earthquake refused to go to mass shelters in schools and auditoriums. They continued to live in tents and also refused to go back to their damaged homes. The same was true after the 1995 Northridge earthquake near Los Angeles, even after authorities assured the Mexican Americans that it would be safe. The reason for their refusal was that aftershocks from the 1985 earthquake in Mexico City had killed and injured many people who had gone to such shelters or had returned to damaged homes. It finally took bicultural, bilingual "assurance teams" of crisis workers to convince the recent immigrants in California to go to shelters or return to their homes (Myers & Wee, 2005, pp. 59–60).

Positive Aspects of an Effective Multicultural Counselor

Sue (1992) states that multicultural helping is enhanced when the human services worker "uses methods and strategies and defines goals consistent with the life experiences and culture values of the client" (p. 13). Belkin (1984) points out that cross-cultural counseling need not be a negative experience; that it may effectively resolve client problems as well as provide a unique learning experience for both client and helper; and that the main "barrier to effective cross-cultural counseling is the traditional counseling role itself, which is not applicable to many cross-cultural interactions" (p. 527). Belkin further states that the principal cross-cultural impediments are (1) language differences, (2) class-bound values, and (3) culture-bound values (p. 534). Belkin concludes that perhaps the most positive discovery and/or belief of the effective cross-cultural counselor is that humans everywhere are more alike than they are different (p. 543).

Cormier and Hackney (1987) cite several strategies that culturally effective helpers use. For instance, such helpers (1) examine and understand the world from the client's viewpoint, (2) search for alternative roles that may be more appealing and adaptive to clients from different backgrounds, and (3) help clients from other cultures make contact with and elicit help from indigenous support systems (p. 259). Cormier and Hackney also specify that to be culturally effective, helpers should not (1) impose their values and expectations on clients from different backgrounds, (2) stereotype or label clients, client behaviors, or cultures, and (3) try to force unimodal counseling approaches upon clients (pp. 258–259).

As an example of such unimodal expectations, Sue (1992) notes that traditional helpers may tend to emphasize the need for clients to verbalize their emotions. He points out that some clients (such as traditional Japanese) may have been taught as children not to speak until addressed; that many cultures highly value restraint in expressing strong feelings; and that patterns of communication, contrary to ours in the United States, may "tend to be vertical, flowing from those of higher prestige and status to those of lower prestige and status" (p. 12). The unenlightened worker

seeking to help such a client may perceive the client to be inarticulate, unintelligent, lacking in spontaneity, or repressed (p. 13).

School crisis worker: (*speaking softly to a recently immigrated Japanese family whose son has just been severely injured in a high school football game and is going to be out of school for an extended period*) I would like to be helpful to your family in this difficult time for you, not knowing how well your son will recover from his injuries and what that means as far as his academic work and chances of going on to college are. I have had experience in dealing with these kinds of issues with a number of students and their parents and could certainly act as your advocate if you would like someone from the school to do that. It is what I do, and it would be my pleasure and honor to do it for you if you so desire. I'll leave my business card and you may call me at any time.

At the other end of the continuum, Dass-Brailsford (2008) notes that African American culture, particularly in the South, uses physical contact to establish connections, so hugging, ritual handshakes, demonstrative grieving, and joyful exclamations all have healing and bonding power.

School crisis worker: (*speaking animatedly and emphatically to an African American family whose son has just been severely injured in a high school football game and is going to be out of school for an extended period*) (Gives mother a heartfelt embrace and then shakes father's hand and grasps his forearm.) I hate this for you and Rashad. It is a terrible blow, not knowing how this will affect his football career and chances for college. You must be really scared and anxious to know how this will all play out. If you would let me be the point man on this with the school, I'd appreciate the opportunity to help you. I've done this with a lot of kids. I know Rashad and can get things coordinated with his teachers and see that the college applications go out like they're supposed to. I'll get on that tomorrow, or if you want to think on it I'll wait for your call, but understand you and Rashad are important to this school and we'll be with you. You are part of the Arlington High School family and that's how it is.

If the parents of our football player happen to be Hispanic, and the parents don't speak English and you took French in high school, you are going to need a translator you can trust who has the cultural background to know exactly how to put your words in tone, decibel level, gestures, body language, and directed to mom, dad, or both so that you convey your intent as closely as possible (Zalaquett, Carrion, & Exum, 2010). That means you are going to have to do a little planning ahead if you are counseling individuals who don't speak the language that most people in your country do.

So now you are thinking, "This is impossible. I can't begin to know the words and the culture of everyone I meet, so I'm bound to screw up." Not so! If you pay attention to Cormier and Hackney's points a few paragraphs back, you are going to be pretty much on course. The major themes in both of the foregoing examples are that the worker demonstrates empathy, caring, and positive regard while searching for a role that is compatible with the client's worldview, and offers to act as advocate without injecting his or her own values or conditions into the situation. While at times we do make mistakes in entering into clients' cultural worlds, there are very few clients who do not respond positively when these general facilitative conditions are in operation.

When in Rome, Italy . . . or Georgia

Understanding the cultural milieu in which he or she operates is of critical importance to the crisis worker who performs fieldwork or outreach services. The crisis interventionist's notion of what kind of help is needed and what is or is not appropriate help is a manifestation of his or her own cultural and societal upbringing, education, and views (Kaniasty & Norris, 1999). Cultural differences are particularly problematic when the worker is transported to and works on the "turf" of the client and has little time to become attuned to the cultural and ecological framework within which the client operates. We are not simply talking about "foreigners," either. Within the United States, residents of Jackson, Tennessee, made homeless by an F4 tornado; survivors of those killed in the Oklahoma City federal building bombing; American Indian families whose children were killed in the school shooting at Red Lake, Minnesota; or transient street people in dire need of social, medical, and mental health services may have views about what constitutes helpful intervention that are very different from the crisis worker's. Such individuals may take umbrage at the crisis worker's attempts to intrude into their world (Hopper, Johnston, & Brinkhoff, 1988). It is absolutely incumbent upon workers to be aware of these cultural subtleties, because victims and survivors will be (Golec, 1983).

Language Barriers

Although it may be difficult enough to work with people in crisis from the same generic cultural background and who speak the native language as a first language, the manifestation and communication of first-generation Americans' or immigrants' personal problems may be very different from what the crisis worker is used to handling. As a result, assessment and intervention become more complex and difficult. Confidentiality issues are also problematic because translators or children of parents who do not speak English have to act as interpreters. People in the United States with "green cards" or student visas run the risk of having information about their mental health status given to government agencies, which may then make negative evaluations about their immigration status. This issue is further compounded by language problems that make communicating clients' needs and crisis workers' offers of services subject to misinterpretation. Particularly for foreign students, having to leave school because of "mental problems" may cause tremendous loss of face in their families and in their home countries. If not handled sensitively, the worker's attempts to provide help may exacerbate rather than mollify the crisis (Oropeza et al., 1991).

If the crisis worker is not fluent in the native language, how can information be conveyed? While not the ideal, a good translator is critical to this endeavor, as opposed to using a family member as translator—particularly since the children, who because of their schooling know more English than their parents do, would probably serve as family translators. The need to discuss intimate details and preserve family roles makes it paramount that third-party translators be available (DeWolfe, 2000).

Crisis worker: (*speaking through a translator to a Pakistani family who lost all their belongings in a house fire and whose only members who are fluent in English are their children*) Please tell Mr. and Mrs. Maqsood that I apologize for not speaking Urdu. I can either speak through you or through their children, and I would like to know which they might prefer.

Religion and Spirituality

Religion and spirituality are so loaded with emotionality that many human service workers regard it as an exposed electrical wire, not to be touched on pain of death for fear they will be seen as either proselytizing for their religion or insensitive to other spiritual beliefs. However, to deny or act as if religion, faith, and spirituality are not part of any crisis is to neglect a large part of a crisis response for most people. Exclusive of pastoral counseling, it is interesting that little space is given to the effects that religion has in the counseling business

(Schlosser et al., 2010). Yet for most people trauma is the ultimate challenge to meaning making, and for most people, that meaning making is attached to some kind of faith (Brown, 2009, p. 228).

Perilla, Norris, and Lavizzo (2002) found that after Hurricane Andrew, besides being exposed to more of Andrew's wrath because of their poor economic state, Latinos and non-Hispanic blacks showed *differential vulnerability* to traumatic effects compared to whites. That is, they were more traumatized than whites, and at least part of this difference related to their fatalistic view that they had little control over the situation. They believed that whatever God willed would happen. Crisis workers who face such fatalism do themselves and their clients no service when they attempt to persuade clients to change their worldview from an external to an internal locus. In fact, the crisis workers would do far better to use the religious and spiritual beliefs that minorities have to guide their intervention (Myers & Wee, 2005, pp. 60–61).

There is a reason that the triage assessment system you will encounter in Chapter 3 has a spiritual/moral component. Religious and spiritual beliefs play a huge role in the outcome of a crisis as people attempt to make sense of events that seemingly make no sense at all. Faith plays a large part in how people try to come to terms with a randomly cruel universe that crashes down on the notion of a supreme being that runs a just and moral world. As Bingham (2010) states for African Americans, "What is difficult to understand is that the church is far more than family" (p. 22), and if you are not attuned to the importance of their church and faith for many African Americans (Grills, 2004), numerous other ethnic minorities (Taylor, Chatters, & Levin, 2004) and for that matter many Southern whites, you are probably going to have trouble helping them through the crisis.

It should not be surprising that recent immigrants who have seemingly adapted to the culture of their new country rapidly revert to old and customary ways of behaving in a crisis (Augsburger, 1992), just as the Caribbean and Latin American clients of Shelby and Tredinnick (1995) did after Hurricane Andrew struck south Florida. Shelby and Tredinnick spent considerable space reporting on the cultural differences they encountered doing disaster relief work in the aftermath of Hurricane Andrew. The large Caribbean and Latin American populations they dealt with had punitive religious interpretations of the disaster and punitive child-rearing practices, particularly under stress, that

differed greatly from what the crisis workers believed to be ethically and morally right. The workers had to be very sensitive in not challenging these deeply held beliefs. In short, while it may appear to you to be voodoo, if it is bringing solace and respite, crisis workers need to put their own beliefs on the shelf and encourage spiritual coping behaviors that help people heal (Dass-Brailsford, 2008).

So just what do you do when you are confronted with spiritual issues? What the workers did with Andrew survivors was allow them to process feelings of guilt and responsibility in line with their religious interpretation of the event, without passing any judgments on the merit of those beliefs. Furthermore, educating parents with ethnically different views of child rearing about the ways children generically respond after a trauma, along with the normal developmental issues they face, may indeed be a tall order given the brevity of crisis intervention. Such interventions, although needed, may be something the crisis worker wishes to consider very carefully.

To offload this tricky issue by merely suggesting that persons consult with their minister, priest, rabbi, or imam is to abdicate your responsibility as the crisis worker. Further, while you may certainly seek advice and counsel from a religious leader of a particular person's faith, that by no means guarantees that you will be congruent with that particular individual's sense of meaning making. There is also no way in the world you can become an expert in all the religions and practices of people in crisis that you will encounter. What we believe is that you can do what Schlosser and his associates (2010) propose and what has worked for us by making an owning statement that directly addresses the issue.

Crisis worker: (*working with a client whose family members have just been killed and injured in a landslide*) You have not mentioned your faith or religious affiliation. When I have been involved in similar situations with people who have lost loved ones, for many people faith is an important part of how they deal with such terrible tragedies. Even though one's faith is a deeply personal matter, and I may know very little about your religious faith, I am wondering if you would like to talk about that with me, or perhaps I can find a leader of your faith with whom you can talk if you would prefer that. One way or the other, I want you to know that I am going to be here with you to help you work your way through this difficult time.

After that, you generally need to practice the listening and responding skills you will encounter in Chapter 4.

For people who are in a transcrisis state due to a loss of faith and have unresolved grief, we will have more to say about spirituality and faith in Chapter 12, Personal Loss: Bereavement and Grief.

Support Systems

As you will soon see, providing support is so critical that we designate it as a separate task in our crisis intervention model (Chapter 3). Social supports—family, friends, peers, and professionals when no other supports are there or those former social support systems have been abandoned—are critical because they work (Taylor, 2007)! However, how people in crisis utilize social support systems is not always linear or direct. Shelby and Tredinnick (1995) found that African American and Hispanic populations tended to rely on extended support systems much more heavily than did European Americans. Dais-Railsford (2008) had a number of conversations with social service authorities, convincing them that children whose biological parents were missing post-Katrina were not abandoned but in the care of other competent adults who would care for them and keep them safe. For some cultures, "family" means a lot more than the residents in the house at 708 S. Grove Street. Therefore, the workers' efforts needed to focus more on systemic approaches that dealt with extended family networks rather than individuals.

As helpful as social support may be, for some people the cultural prohibitions against opening oneself up to receive social support may be like going from the frying pan into the fire. In their research on Asians and Asian Americans, Kim, Sherman, and Taylor (2008) found that the college students they studied were far more hesitant than their European American counterparts to seek any support systems because their inability to handle the crisis would bring shame not only on themselves but on their families as well. One reason for this reluctance, they suggest, may be that the very act of seeking support would require the students to self-disclose personal issues, which would put even more stress on them. Reframing such support in more culturally acceptable terms may be one way of allowing individuals to receive help. Organista and Munoz (1996) suggest using manuals and homework assignments, much like a teacher and a classroom assignment, to avoid the stigma of being seen by a mental health worker and receiving psychotherapy.

Crisis worker: (*dealing with a female Asian college student who is thousands of miles from home and who has been sexually assaulted and is largely noncommittal or oblique in her response to the assault*) Li Mai, suffering and enduring what you have is hard for any woman. It is very difficult to speak of such personal violations for almost every woman I have encountered who has undergone what you have. It is very common to not want to talk about a sexual assault because of all the negative emotions that go with it—particularly the guilt for thinking you were not cautious enough or the shame if it becomes known. However, I also know there are some things that you need to know about and could use some help with. You might wish to think of me more as a teacher who can give you important information which you can then use as you see fit. Or perhaps a coach who can help you make adjustments, just like a soccer player or a figure skater so that they are able to perform better. I hope you will think about what I have said and perhaps frame this incident in that manner and see me as that teacher or coach.

The shame of self-disclosure about a perceived moral or personal failing is not to be taken lightly. One of the hallmarks of domestic violence is the embarrassment and shame if word gets out that the person is being physically abused. Certainly no Jewish women are ever beaten by their spouses because that does not happen in the Jewish religion/culture. Whoa! Unless the city of Memphis has a different Jewish population than most other places in the world, the domestic violence reports that flow into our Family Trouble Center would indicate otherwise. However, such myths have a powerful social influence and pressure people not to seek support (Zimberhoff & Brown, 2006). Myth busting is part and parcel of a lot of the crises in this book, and providing education is a primary task of the worker.

Crisis worker: I want you to be aware that there's a notion that Jewish women do not get beaten by their husbands. Or at the very least good Jewish wives and mothers don't get beaten. Yet the fact is that we have many, many reports that in Memphis, Tennessee, Jewish women do get beaten, and I don't think there are that many bad Jewish wives and mothers around, so I want you to understand that is a myth and you are not the only Jewish wife who has been beaten. In fact, I would like you to come to a group of women in a support group who are coming out of the kind of battering relationship you have been in. It may interest you to know that there are three women in the group I am thinking of that are in fact Jewish.

Occupation as a Cultural Barrier

The ecological model in Chapter 1 may also be applied to the "culture" of particular occupations. It is interesting that most multiculturalists, with the exception of Laura Brown (2008, p. 25), give little or no acknowledgment to occupation as a major social location. An occupation is inextricably tied to most of our lives and is how we identify ourselves. Go to a party, meet a stranger, and after some initial pleasantries, we'll bet that somewhere in there will be a "So what do you do?" or "Where do you work?" question.

The occupational agriculture of Chandler Mountain, Alabama, is far different from the financial culture of Wall Street, New York. We believe that to not take occupation into consideration as a defining part of one's culture and ecosystem is to be absolutely oblivious to a major contributing factor in how one lives. Police work is an excellent example. Police officers might be thought of as psychologically at risk due solely to the high stress and potentially lethal situations they face. However, that is far from true.

Any crisis worker who proceeded to deal with a police officer based on the erroneous notion that high stress caused by exposure to lethal situations was the sole factor contributing to a crisis would be very mistaken. Police officers constitute a distinct occupational culture and closed ecosystem because of their authority roles, their segregation from the rest of society, their irregular work schedules, the reactive nature of their job, the constant exposure to the negative side of life, the constant emotional control they must maintain, and the definitive manner in which they must judge right and wrong (Winter & Battle, 2007).

A major issue that bedevils law enforcement officers is their married life. They have one of the highest divorce rates of any occupation. They do not usually talk about their jobs or their feelings because they sense their spouses are uncomfortable hearing about such matters. Their job stress occurs because of "burst stress." That is, they may go from a long period of tedium and boredom to an immediate high-adrenaline moment. Over the long run, that psychological roller-coaster ride is extremely stressful. Furthermore, because law enforcement officers see the failure of the mental health system every day in the United States, they are likely to have a very jaundiced view of the mental health profession as a whole (Hayes, 1999).

It is not to seek thrills that trainers of the Memphis Police Department Crisis Intervention Team (CIT) ride patrol shifts with CIT officers. Although those rides provide us with valuable on-the-scene experience, they also help us appreciate the ecosystem within which the officer operates. The alliance with CIT officers that emerges from riding the Saturday night shifts with them helps break down occupational barriers

and establish our own "bona fides" as being "culturally aware" of what the officers are going through. No amount of reading or expertise that we know of compensates for lack of knowledge and sensitization to this cultural milieu.

Indeed, this cultural bonding practice is now being field-tested by Winter and Battle (2007) on police officers who have had disciplinary referrals or bad conduct complaints. In this practice, called "embedded therapy" by Dr. Betty Winter of the Memphis Police Department, crisis workers ride in patrol cars with these troubled officers. As one might imagine, the officers initially exhibit a great deal of suspicion and hostility toward the workers. However, an eight-hour shift in the same patrol car breaks down barriers as the crisis worker empathically listens and responds to the officer's concerns. Fairly quickly, gripes about the officer's uncaring commanders turn to more personal and interpersonal issues as the crisis worker bonds with the officer and gains his or her trust. Early reports of improved conduct and lack of further disciplinary action for these targeted officers are encouraging (Winter & Battle, 2007).

Geographic Locale as a Cultural Barrier

Lenihan and Kirk (1999) have developed a rural, community-level crisis intervention plan for very small towns and rural areas that lack the typical crisis infrastructure and support systems available to even medium-sized communities. Many small communities and isolated rural areas are assailed by crises, yet these crises are not large enough to call for federal responses. However, the state emergency management agency may send crisis workers from neighboring counties and state agencies to assist the target community. Or the community itself may request volunteer help from universities, charities, civic groups, and local governments in close proximity. People in these areas may be very suspicious of outsiders, even those from neighboring communities, attempting to "tell them what to do." Yet collective fear, rumor, parochialism, and inaccessibility to services can keep the community traumatized and immobile without such help. Lenihan and Kirk propose that intervention strategies must absolutely address the cultural issues that will exist between outside service providers and recipients of service before any meaningful work can be done. They advocate an immediate assessment of the traumatic event's effect not only on individuals, but on the culture as well. In a sense, they are "triaging" the whole community. They propose that no outside crisis response team can do an adequate job if it does not first seek out, identify, and consult with a broad cross section of community leaders about how and with whom crisis intervention should proceed.

Particularly important is ascertaining what the community's belief systems are and if there are subcultures within the system that may have different responses from those of the community at large (Chemtob, 2000). Any crisis response must be integrated into the community leadership and organizations such as social clubs, churches, civic groups, and fraternal organizations. Providing sensitive consultation for community leaders without "ramming it down their throats" is imperative. The same is true of using basic listening skills in hearing what the community has to say, instead of a bull-in-a-china-shop, officious, expert, "we know what's best for you" approach (van den Eynde & Veno, 1999).

Evaluating and finding the natural leaders of the community and teaming up with them are important in forming workable alliances and providing the citizens an anchor of familiarity, security, and control at the scene. Any action plans should be developed cooperatively and should be concrete, doable, and manageable, considering the available community financial and human resources (Lenihan & Kirk, 1999). In short, outside interventionists in such communities do best when they function as guides and helpers who operate along a continuum of directive to nondirective intervention. That is, the interventionist should be only as directive as the degree to which the client (the community) is immobilized.

An ecological model posits that the efficacy of trauma-focused interventions depends on the degree to which those interventions enhance the person–community relationship and achieve a fit both within and between individual and cultural contexts (Harvey, 1996). If you view the ecology of such rural communities as having a great deal of resiliency, self-reliance, and belief in the community as the primary source of support, then you should also get a vivid picture of how delicately you intrude on such a community. The road to hell is paved with good intentions, so you need to know what road you are traveling on as you go into crisis intervention!

The Dilemma of Local Consultation

A real dilemma occurs in consulting and working with the local authorities. On the one hand, they know best the infrastructure and needs of the community.

Involving community representatives and leaders as intermediaries and consultants can give workers much easier access to the population and can provide helpful tips in regard to local taboos or cultural artifacts that can interfere with service delivery (Chemtob, 2000).

On the other hand, because outside workers are not invested in the local infrastructure and are not enculturated, they may blithely go about their business and in the process attempt to redress a variety of long-held social injustices and practices (Golec, 1983). The wise crisis worker who goes into a different geographical area needs to understand that this dilemma *always* exists, whether the location is Kabul, Afghanistan, or Collettsville, North Carolina. We are *absolutely not* proposing that crisis workers go about the business of changing and redressing all the perceived evils and shortcomings they may run into. However, as with Shelby and Tredinnick's (1995) report on the cultural reactions of their clients to a disaster, we are not so sure that one should stand passively by while victims project their frustrations by beating their children. What we do urge is that crisis workers *absolutely* need to be aware of this dilemma.

So should crisis workers leave well enough alone? Certainly the ability of a community to take care of itself is paramount. Members of the community understand the political, religious, and cultural roots and infrastructure far better than outsiders. Yet when a disaster strikes, and the community's resources are exceeded, there is a good deal of research that indicates such altruism does not extend to the poor, the elderly, the less educated, and ethnic minorities. Such groups may be disenfranchised and denied a part in the "democracy of a common disaster" (Kaniasty & Norris, 1995). Although the elderly, in particular, may be seen as needing assistance with physical complaints or illness, such attention does not necessarily extend to dealing with property damage or keeping a roof over their heads, food on the table, and medicine in their cabinets (Kaniasty & Norris, 1997; Kaniasty, Norris, & Murrell, 1990).

Kilijanek and Drabek (1979) coined the term "pattern of neglect" in regard to the lack of aid received by the elderly in their study of a Kansas tornado's devastation of Topeka. The "squeaking wheel gets the grease" is probably even more true in the wake of a disaster. "YAVIS" clients—those young, attractive, verbal, intelligent, and socially well-connected clients from higher socioeconomic backgrounds—get better service because they have the power, influence, and verbal articulation to get help. People whose social locations differ from those of

YAVIS clients tend to do less well and are not knowledgeable enough, not verbal enough, not able enough, not young enough, and not assertive enough to get the help they need (Brown, 2009). Crisis interventionists need to be acutely aware of this pattern and take pains to ensure that all individuals who seek and desire assistance in the traumatic wake of a disaster obtain it.

The Necessity of Acting

When we are in the heat of the moment in a crisis, observing the "niceties" of another culture that tends to deal obliquely and subtly with problems may not be in the best safety interests of those clients. The foregoing statement is made very conditionally. That is, whenever possible we want to take as much time as we can to understand the client's issues and perceptions, and that holds true of the collective populace as well. Certainly, being sensitive to the clients' cultural and ecological background is part of a patient and thorough problem exploration.

We further believe that one of the worst therapeutic errors a worker can make is to attempt to "hurry" the process. Crisis intervention should never be hurried. Although it may seem paradoxical, the fastest way to resolve a crisis is to take your time to understand what is going on. Still and all, if we have a client who is "running amok" (a Filipino cultural term for going absolutely, violently crazy), his cognitive processes are going to be seriously impaired, his behavior is going to be threatening, and his emotions will be out of control. What that means in the reality of the situation is acting rapidly and in a very concrete manner to assure his and others' safety. Finally, helping anybody, no matter how culturally different, is complex in a crisis. Something that is a crisis for one family may not be for another.

Many culturally diverse families have years of coping with crisis and are extremely resilient. If a person from a different cultural background is a recent immigrant, these successes may be minimized in the immigrant's new country or territory and seen as irrelevant or inconsequential. They are not! The astute crisis worker will attempt to recognize and marshal these past successes to the current dilemma. Normalizing the crisis experience is particularly important for the culturally diverse who may already be isolated socially and believe no one else is having similar responses. Empowerment, particularly for the culturally diverse, is the watchword in crisis intervention (Congress, 2000).

There is a delicate balance between helping and interfering. This is a constant bipolar dilemma for both recipients and providers of service after a disaster. On the one hand, the recipient appreciates the help, good intentions, and sincere concern. On the other hand, those same providers may be met with confusion, skepticism, and perceived psychological threat by the same recipients (Wortman & Lehman, 1985). Our experience has been that this bipolar dilemma can occur not only on the same day but in the same hour!

Training

The American Red Cross training for mental health disaster relief certification has course work in diversity training and cross-cultural differences. The National Institute of Mental Health (2002) report and recommendations for dealing with the traumatic wake of mass violence cautioned practitioners that disaster mental health training needs to incorporate cross-cultural training, because variations in understanding the meaning of thoughts, behaviors, and feelings by ethnically different persons can influence the validity of assessments, treatment protocols, and general interaction with survivor populations. Whether the crisis worker is going to Kobe, Japan, or Long Beach, Mississippi, understanding that it is culturally alien turf is critical to crisis work. The U.S. Department of Health and Human Services' *Developing Cultural Competence in Disaster Mental Health Programs: Guiding Principles and Recommendations* (2003) contains a variety of helpful suggestions for working with people in a large-scale disaster.

Where It Stands Now . . . Sorta

Multiculturalism has evolved though stages of raising consciousness levels. At present, the criticisms leveled in the past about treatment modalities that are biased toward ethnocentric European American populations seem unfounded or questionable at best. What does seem reasonable and shows some success is *cultural adaptation* that modifies evidence-based treatments to accommodate the cultural beliefs, attitudes, and behaviors of the cultural group to whom one is providing services (Whaley & Davis, 2007). To that end—and this is certainly easier said than done in the field of crisis where chaos theory tends to run rampant when service delivery is most critical—carefully controlled studies need to occur that measure both traditional therapeutic approaches against well-described cultural adaptations of those therapies and cultural specific practices that look nothing like our current intervention models. Moreover, there need to be more ethnic minorities involved in those studies (Atkinson, Bui, & Mori, 2001)—in itself a tall order since, as previously stated, minorities are not overly keen on using mental health services. It would also be very interesting to see what effect client–interventionist congruency, in terms of Brown's (2008) social locations hypotheses, has on treatment. To this point we have been unable to find any research that asks the most essential question arising from this chapter: "How sensitive was the interventionist in regard to your social locations, and was it helpful when she was?"

SUMMARY

While not a great deal is yet known about exactly how ecological/cultural determinants interact with crisis, it is clear that they do. This interaction has significant implications for crisis interventionists as they work with people from different cultural backgrounds. One of the major differences interventionists need to recognize is the different methods of communication and allegiances between individualist/collectivist–high/low context systems. Social locations, the many facets that make up each person's life, are as important "within" culture/ethnicity variables as the "between" variables that differentiate one group from another. This chapter espouses a universal/emic as opposed to a focused view in defining multiculturalism and cautions the reader to be a discerning consumer in regard to what prevailing multicultural views may hold for the practice of crisis intervention.

Particularly important to crisis interventionists is disabusing themselves of tunnel vision perspectives, assumptions, and unconscious biases they may have about people from different cultures. If you want to get a really good multicultural cross section of how people around the world deal with trauma, then read Ani Kalayjian and Eugene Dominique's (2010) two volumes on *Mass Trauma and Emotional Healing Around the World: Rituals and Practices for Resilience and Meaning Making.*

To see some of the concepts discussed in this chapter in action, refer to your *Crisis Intervention in Action* DVD, or see the clips online on the Counseling Course-Mate website. To access this site, go to www .cengagebrain.com, where you'll also find an eBook, additional study tools, quizzes, and more. As you watch the scenario, think of your own social locations. How do you think they might be an asset or a hindrance? When you get to the PTSD chapter, you are going to run into something called a traumagram. It might well be called your trauma social locations. How do you think those might affect what you would do with this young Kenyan, or for that matter anybody else in crisis? Even though the counselor is an African American, what advantage or disadvantage does that give her in working with an African?

REFERENCES

Adler, N. L. (1997). *International dimensions of organizational behavior.* Cincinnati, OH: South-Western.

American Psychiatric Association. (2000). *Diagnostic and statistical manual of mental disorders–technical revision* (4th ed.). Washington, DC: Author.

Arredondo, P. (1999). Multicultural counseling competencies as tools to address oppression and racism. *Journal of Counseling and Development, 77*(1), 102–108.

Atkinson, D., Bui, U., & Mori, S. (2001). Multiculturally sensitive empirically supported treatments: An oxymoron? In J. G. Ponterotto, J. M. Casas, L. A. Suzuki, & C. M. Alexander (Eds.), *Handbook of multicultural counseling* (2nd ed., pp. 542–574). Thousand Oaks, CA: Sage.

Atkinson, D., Morten, G., & Sue, D. W. (1998). *Counseling American minorities.* Boston: McGraw-Hill.

Augsburger, D. W. (1992). *Conflict mediation across cultures.* Louisville, KY: Westminster/John Knox Press.

Belkin, G. S. (1984). *Introduction to counseling* (2nd ed.). Dubuque, IA: William C. Brown.

Bingham, R. (2010). My life is a balance between . . . In J. G. Ponterotto, J. M. Casas, L. A. Suzuki, & C. M. Alexander (Eds.), *Handbook of multicultural counseling* (3rd ed.; pp. 19–25). Thousand Oaks, CA: Sage.

Brandsma, L. L. (2003, January). Letters: Much ado about multiculturalism, part 4. *Counseling Today, 45*, 31.

Breux, C., & Ryujin, D. H. (1999). Use of mental health services by ethnically diverse groups within the United States. *Clinical Psychologist, 52*, 4–15.

Brown, L. (2008). *Cultural competence in trauma therapy: Beyond the flashback.* Washington, DC: American Psychological Association.

Brown, L. (2009). Cultural competence. In C. A. Courtois & J. Ford (Eds.), *Treating complex traumatic stress disorders: An evidenced-based guide* (pp. 166–182). New York: Guilford Press.

Capuzzi, D., & Gross, D. R. (Eds.). (1995). *Counseling and psychotherapy: Theories and interventions.* Upper Saddle River, NJ: Prentice Hall.

Chemtob, C. M. (2000). Delayed debriefing after a disaster. In B. Raphael & J. P. Wilson (Eds.), *Psychological debriefing: Theory, practice, and evidence* (pp. 227–240). New York: Cambridge University Press.

Chen, S. O., & Mak, W. S. (2008). Seeking professional help: Etiology beliefs about mental health illness across cultures. *Journal of Counseling Psychology, 55*(4), 442–450.

Cohen, A. B (2009) Many forms of culture. *American Psychologist, 64*, 194–204.

Cokley, K. (2007). Critical issues in the measurement of ethnic and racial identity: A referendum on the state of the field. *Journal of Counseling Psychology, 54*(3), 224–234.

Congress, E. P. (2000). Crisis intervention with culturally diverse families. In A. E. Roberts (Ed.), *Crisis intervention handbook: Assessment, treatment and research.* New York: Oxford University Press.

Cormier, L. S., & Hackney, H. (1987). *The professional counselor: A process guide to helping.* Upper Saddle River, NJ: Prentice Hall.

D'Andrea, M., & Daniels, D. (2005, Spring). Sport psychology: A multidimensional-multicultural competency model. *ESPNews, 19*(1), 9.

D'Andrea, M., & Heckman, E. F. (2008). A 40-year review of multicultural counseling outcome research: Outlining a future research agenda for the multicultural counseling movement. *Journal of Counseling & Development, 86*, 356–363.

Dass-Brailsford, P. (2008). After the storm: Recognition, recovery and reconstruction. *Professional Psychology Research and Practice, 39*(1), 24–30.

Day-Vines, N. L., Wood, S. M., Grothaus, T., Craigen, L., Holman, A., Dotson-Blake, K., & Douglass, M. J. (2007). Broaching the subject of race, ethnicity, and culture during the counseling process. *Journal of Counseling & Development, 85*, 401–409.

DeWolfe, D. J. (2000). *Training manual for mental health and human service workers in major disasters* (2nd ed.). DHHS Publication No. ADM 90-538. Retrieved January 15, 2002, from http://www.mentalhealth.org/publications/allpubs;ADM90-538/index.htm

Eidelson, R. J., & Eidelson, J. I. (2003). Dangerous ideas: Five beliefs that propel groups toward conflict. *American Psychologist, 58*, 182–192.

Ghafoori, B., & Hierholzer, R. W. (2010). Personality patterns among black, white, and Hispanic combat veterans. *Psychological Trauma Research, Theory, Practice, and Policy, 2*(1), 12–18.

Golec, J. A. (1983). A contextual approach to the social psychological study of disaster recovery. *International Journal of Mass Emergencies and Disasters, 1*, 255–276.

Grills, C. (2004). African-centered psychology: Basic principles. In T. Parham (Ed.), *Counseling persons of African descent: Raising the bar of practitioner competence* (pp. 32–56). Thousand Oaks, CA: Sage.

Hall, E. (1976). *Beyond culture.* Garden City, NY: Anchor Press/Doubleday.

Halpern, J., & Tramontin, M. (2007). *Disaster mental health: Theory and practice.* Belmont, CA: Brooks/Cole.

Harvey, M. R. (1996). An ecological view of psychological trauma and trauma recovery. *Journal of Traumatic Stress, 9*(1), 3–23.

Hayes, L. L. (1999, May). Breaking the blue wall of silence: Counseling police officers. *Counseling Today, 41*(11), 1, 6.

Hays, P. A. (2001). *Addressing cultural complexities in practice: A framework for clinicians and counselors.* Washington, DC: American Psychological Association.

Hays, P. A. (2008). *Addressing cultural complexities in practice: Assessment, diagnosis, and therapy* (2nd ed.). Washington, DC: American Psychological Association.

Heppner, P., Heppner, M. J., Lee, D., Wang, Y., Park, H., & Wang, L. (2006). Development and validation of a collectivist coping styles inventory. *Journal of Counseling Psychology, 53*(1), 107–125.

Hopper, M. J., Johnston, J., & Brinkhoff, J. (1988). Creating a career hotline for rural residents. *Journal of Counseling and Development, 66*, 340–343.

Ivey, A. E. (1987). Cultural intentionality: The core of effective helping. *Counselor Education and Supervision, 26*, 168–172.

Johannes, C. K. (2003, January). Letters: Much ado about multiculturalism, part 4. *Counseling Today, 45*, 31.

Kalayjian, A., & Dominque, E. (Eds.). (2010). *Mass trauma and emotional healing around the world: Rituals and practice for resilience and meaning-making: Vol. 1. Natural disasters.* Santa Barbara, CA: Praeger/ABC-CLIO.

Kalayjian, A., & Dominque, E. (Eds.). (2010). *Mass trauma and emotional healing around the world: Rituals and practice for resilience and meaning-making: Vol. 2. Human-made disasters.* Santa Barbara, CA: Praeger/ABC-CLIO.

Kaniasty, K., & Norris, F. (1995). In search of altruistic community: Patterns of social support mobilization following Hurricane Hugo. *American Journal of Community Psychology, 20*, 211–241.

Kaniasty, K., & Norris, F. (1997). Social support dynamics in adjustment to disaster. In S. Duck (Ed.), *Handbook of personal relationships* (2nd ed., pp. 596–619). London: Wiley.

Kaniasty, K., & Norris, F. (1999). The experience of disaster: Individuals and communities sharing trauma. In R. Gist & B. Lubin (Eds.), *Response to disaster: Psychosocial, community and ecological approaches* (pp. 25–62). Philadelphia: Brunner/ Mazel.

Kaniasty, K., Norris, F., & Murrell, S. A. (1990). Received and perceived social support following natural disaster. *Journal of Applied Social Psychology, 20,* 85–114.

Kilijanek, T., & Drabek, T. E. (1979). Assessing long-term impacts of a natural disaster: A focus on the elderly. *Gerontologist, 19,* 555–566.

Kim, B. S. K., Liang, C. T. H., & Li, L. C. (2003). Counselor ethnicity, counselor nonverbal behavior, and session outcome with Asian American clients: Initial findings. *Journal of Counseling & Development, 81*(2), 202–207.

Kim, H. S., Sherman, D. K., & Taylor, S. E. (2008). Culture and social support. *American Psychologist, 63*(6), 518–526.

Kiselica, M. S. (1998). Preparing Anglos for the challenges and joys of multiculturalism. *Counseling Psychologist, 26,* 5–21.

Lenihan, G. O., & Kirk, W. (1999, April). *Rural community level crisis intervention.* Paper presented at the Twenty-Third Annual Convening of Crisis Intervention Personnel, Chicago.

Myers, D., & Wee, D. F. (2005*). Disaster mental health services.* New York: Brunner-Routledge.

National Institute of Mental Health. (2002). *Mental health and mass violence: Evidence-based early psychological intervention for victims/survivors of mass violence: A workshop to reach consensus on best practices.* NIH Publication No. 02-5138. Washington, DC: Government Printing Office.

Norris, F. H., & Alegria, M. (2006). Promoting disaster recovery in ethnic-minority individuals and communities. In E. C. Ritchie, P. J. Watson, & M. J. Friedman (Eds.), *Interventions following mass violence and disasters* (pp. 319–342). New York: Guilford Press.

Ober, C., Peeters, L., Archer, R., & Kelly, K. (2000). Debriefing in different cultural frameworks: Responding to acute trauma in Australian Aboriginal contexts. In B. Raphael & J. P. Wilson (Eds.), *Psychological debriefing: Theory, practice, and evidence* (pp. 241–253). New York: Cambridge University Press.

Organista, K. C., & Munoz, R. F. (1996). Cognitive behavior therapy with Latinos. *Cognitive Behavioral Practice, 3*(2), 255–270.

Oropeza, B. A., Clark, F., Fitzgibbon, M., & Baron, A. (1991). Managing mental health crises of foreign college students. *Journal of Counseling and Development, 69,* 280–283.

Owen, J., Leach, M. M., Wampold, B., & Rodolfa, E. (2011). Client and therapist variability in clients' perceptions of their therapists' multicultural competencies. *Journal of Counseling Psychology, 58*(1), 1–9.

Oyserman, D., Coon, H. M., & Kemmelmeier, M. (2002). Rethinking individualism and collectivism: Evaluation of theoretical assumptions and meta-analyses. *Psychological Bulletin, 128,* 3–72.

Pedersen, P. (1987). Ten frequent assumptions of cultural bias in counseling. *Journal of Multicultural Counseling and Development, 15,* 16–24.

Pedersen, P. (1998). *Multiculturalism as a fourth force.* New York: Brunner/Mazel.

Perilla, J., Norris, F., & Lavizzo, E. (2002). Ethnicity, culture, and disaster response: Identifying and explaining ethnic differences in PTSD six months after Hurricane Andrew. *Journal of Social and Clinical Psychology, 21,* 28–45.

Ponterotto, J. G., & Mallinckrodt, B. (2007). Introduction to the special section on racial and ethnic identity in counseling psychology: Conceptual and methodological challenges and proposed solutions. *Journal of Counseling Psychology, 54*(3), 219–233.

Ponterotto, J. G., & Pedersen, P. (1993). *Preventing prejudice: A guide for counselors and educators.* Newbury Park, CA: Sage.

Raskin, N. J., & Rogers, C. R. (1995). Person-centered therapy. In R. J. Corsini & D. Wedding (Eds.), *Current psychotherapies* (5th ed.). Itasca, IL: F. E. Peacock.

Ridley, C. R. (1995). *Overcoming unintentional racism in counseling and therapy: A practitioner's guide to intentional intervention.* Newbury Park, CA: Sage.

Ridley, C. R., & Shaw-Ridley, M. (2011). Multicultural counseling competencies: An analysis of research on clients' perceptions: Comments on Owens, Leach, Wampold, and Rodolfa. *Journal of Counseling Psychology, 58*(1), 16–21.

Savicki, V. (2002). *Burnout across thirteen cultures: Stress and coping in child and youth care workers.* Westport, CT: Prager.

Schlosser, L. Z., Foley, P. F., Stein, E. P., & Holmwood, J. R. (2010). Why does counseling psychology exclude religion? A content analysis and methodological critique. In J. G. Ponterotto, J. M. Casas, L. A. Suzuki, & C. M. Alexander (Eds.), *Handbook of multicultural counseling* (3rd ed., pp. 453–466). Thousand Oaks, CA: Sage.

Shectman, Z., Hiradin, A., & Zina, S. (2003). The impact of culture on group behavior: A comparison of three ethnic groups. *Journal of Counseling and Development, 81*(2), 208–216.

Shelby, J. S., & Tredinnick, M. G. (1995). Crisis intervention with survivors of natural disaster: Lessons from Hurricane Andrew. *Journal of Counseling and Development, 73,* 491–497.

Silove, D. (1998). Is PTSD an overlearnt survival response? An evolutionary learning hypothesis. *Psychiatry, 61,* 181–190.

Silove, D. (2000). A conceptual framework for mass trauma: Implications for adaption, intervention and debriefing. In B. Raphael & J. P. Wilson (Eds.), *Psychological debriefing: Theory, practice, and evidence* (pp. 337–350). New York: Cambridge University Press.

Sue. D. W. (1977). Community mental health services to minority groups: Some optimism, some pessimism. *American Psychologist, 32*(6), 616–624.

Sue, D. W. (1992, Winter). The challenge of multiculturalism: The road less traveled. *American Counselor, 1*, 5–14.

Sue, D. W. (1999a, August*). Multicultural competencies in the profession of psychology.* Symposium address delivered at the 107th Annual Convention of the American Psychological Association, Boston.

Sue, D. W. (1999b, August). *Surviving monoculturalism and racism: A personal journey.* Division 45 Presidential Address delivered at the 107th Annual Convention of the American Psychological Association, Boston.

Sue, D. W., Arredondo, P., & McDavis, R. J. (1992). Multicultural counseling competencies and standards: A call to the profession. *Journal of Counseling and Development, 70*, 477–486.

Sue, D. W., & Sue, D. (2002). *Counseling the culturally diverse: Theory and practice* (4th ed.). Hoboken, NJ: Wiley.

Sullivan, C., & Cottone, R. R. (2010). Emergent characteristics of effective cross-cultural research: A review of the literature. *Journal of Counseling & Development, 88*(3), 357–362.

Summerfield, D. (1999). A critique of seven assumptions behind psychological trauma programmes in war-affected areas. *Social Science and Medicine, 48*, 1449–1462.

Taylor, R. J., Chatters, L. M., & Levin, J. S. (2004). *Religion in the lives of African Americans: Social, psychological, and health perspectives.* Thousand Oaks, CA: Sage.

Taylor, S. E. (2007). Social support. In H. S. Friedman & R. C. Silver (Eds.), *Foundations of health psychology* (pp. 145–171). New York: Oxford University Press.

Thompson, C. E., & Neville, H. A. (1999). Racism, mental health, and mental health practice. *Counseling Psychologist, 27*, 155–223.

Trimble, J. E. (2007). Prolegomena for the connotation of construct use in the measurement of ethnic and racial identity. *Journal of Counseling Psychology, 54*, 247–258.

U.S. Department of Health and Human Services. (2003). *Developing cultural competence in disaster mental health programs: Guiding principles and recommendations.* DHHS Pub. No. SMA 3828. Rockville, MD: Center for Mental Health Services, Substance Abuse and Mental Health Services Administration.

van den Eynde, J., & Veno, A. (1999). Coping with disastrous events: An empowerment model for community healing. In R. Gist & B. Lubin (Eds.), *Response to disaster: Psychosocial, community and ecological approaches* (pp. 167–192). Philadelphia: Brunner/Mazel.

Weinrach, S. G. (2003, January). Letters: Much ado about multiculturalism, part 4. *Counseling Today, 45*, 31.

Weinrach, S. G., & Thomas, K. R. (1998). Diversity-sensitive counseling today: A postmodern clash of values. *Journal of Counseling and Development, 76*,115–122.

Weisaeth, L. (2000). Briefing and debriefing: Group psychological interventions in acute stressor situations. In B. Raphael & J. P. Wilson (Eds.), *Psychological debriefing: Theory, practice, and evidence* (pp. 43–57). New York: Cambridge University Press.

Whaley, A. L., & Davis, K. E. (2007). Cultural competence and evidence-based practice in mental health services. *American Psychologist, 62*(6), 563–574.

Williams, B. (2003). The worldview dimensions of individualism and collectivism: Implications for counseling. *Journal of Counseling and Development, 81*(3), 370–372.

Winter, B., & Battle, L. (2007, March). *Rolling sessions: Squad car therapy.* Paper presented at Thirty-first Annual Convening of Crisis Intervention Personnel and CONTACT USA Conference, Chicago.

Worthington, R. L., & Dillion, F. R. (2011). Deconstructing multicultural counseling competencies research: Comment on Owen, Leach, Wampold, and Rodolfa. *Journal of Counseling Psychology, 58*(1), 10–15.

Worthington, R. L., Sott-McNett, A. M., & Moreno, M. V. (2007). Multicultural counseling competencies research: A 20-year content analysis. *Journal of Counseling Psychology, 54*, 35–361.

Wortman, C. B., & Lehman, D. R. (1985). Reactions to victims of life crises: Support attempts that fail. In I. G. Sarason & B. R. Sarason (Eds.), *Social support: Theory research and application* (pp. 463–489). Dordrecht, The Netherlands: Martinus Nijhodff.

Wubbolding, R. E. (2003, January). Letters: Much ado about multiculturalism, part 3. *Counseling Today, 45*, 30–31.

Zalaquett, C., Carrion, I., & Exum, H. (2010). Providing disaster services to culturally diverse survivors. In J. Webber & J. B. Mascari (Eds.), *Terrorism, trauma and tragedies: A counselor's guide to preparing and responding* (3rd ed., pp. 19–24). Alexandria, VA: American Counseling Association Foundation.

Zalaquett, C. P., Fuerth, K. M., Stein, C., Ivey, A. E., & Ivey, M. B. (2008). Reframing the DSM-IV-R from a multicultural/social justice perspective. *Journal of Counseling & Development, 86*(3), 364–371.

Zimberhoff, A. K., & Brown, L. S. (2006). "Only the goyim beat their wives, right?" *Psychology of Women Quarterly, 30*, 422–424.

CHAPTER 3

The Intervention and Assessment Models

Introduction

The purpose of this chapter is to present an applied crisis intervention model that describes in detail the major tasks involved in dealing with a crisis. The Triage Assessment System is introduced as a rapid but systematic technique for the crisis worker to use to adjudicate the severity of a client's presenting crisis situation and gain some sense of direction in helping the client cope with the dilemma. Finally, this chapter shares some ideas on using referrals and gives some suggestions regarding counseling difficult clients. This chapter and Chapter 4, The Tools of the Trade, are a prerequisite for succeeding chapters, and we urge you to consider this foundation material carefully.

The model of crisis intervention you are about to encounter emphasizes an immediacy mode of actively, assertively, intentionally, and continuously assessing, listening, and acting to systematically help the client regain as much precrisis equilibrium, mobility, and autonomy as possible. Two of those terms, *equilibrium* and *mobility*, and their antonyms, *disequilibrium* and *immobility*, are commonly used by crisis workers to identify client states of being and coping. Because we will be using these terms often, we would like to first provide their dictionary definitions and then give a common analogy, so their meaning becomes thoroughly understood.

Equilibrium. A state of mental or emotional stability, balance, or poise in the organism.

Disequilibrium. Lack or destruction of emotional stability, balance, or poise in the organism.

Mobility. A state of physical being in which the person can autonomously change or cope in response to different moods, feelings, emotions, needs, conditions, influences; being flexible or adaptable to the physical and social world.

Immobility. A state of physical being in which the person is not immediately capable of autonomously changing or coping in response to different moods, feelings, emotions, needs, conditions, influences; inability to adapt to the immediate physical and social world.

A healthy person is in a state of approximate psychological and behavioral equilibrium, like a motorist driving, with some starts and stops, down the road of life—for both the short and the long haul. The person may hit some potholes but does not break any axles. Aside from needing to give the car an occasional tune-up, the person remains more or less equal to the task of making the drive. In contrast, the person in crisis, whether it be acute or chronic, is experiencing serious difficulty in steering and successfully navigating life's highway. The individual is at least temporarily out of control, unable to command personal resources or those of others in order to stay on safe psychological pavement.

A healthy person is capable of negotiating hills, curves, ice, fog, stray animals, wrecks, and most other obstacles that impede progress. No matter what roadblocks may appear, such a person adapts to changing conditions, applying brakes, putting on fog lights, and estimating passing time. This person may have fender benders from time to time but avoids head-on collisions. The person in a dysfunctional state of equilibrium and mobility has failed to pass inspection. Careening down hills and around dangerous curves, knowing the brakes have failed, the person is frozen with panic and despair and has little hope of handling the perilous situation.

The result is that the person has become a victim of the situation, has forgotten all about emergency brakes, downshifting, or even easing the car into guardrails. He or she flies headlong into catastrophe and watches transfixed as it happens. The analogy of equilibrium and mobility applies to most crisis situations. Thus, it becomes every crisis worker's job to figuratively get the client back into the driver's seat of the psychological vehicle. As we shall see, sometimes this means the client must temporarily leave the driving to us, sometimes it means sitting alongside the client and pointing out the rules of the road, and sometimes it means just pretty much going along for the ride!

All of that being said, the crisis worker will meet a number of individuals who were not poster children for psychological equilibrium before the crisis. Many people who were displaced by Hurricane Katrina, for example, were physically and psychologically fragile before the hurricane. We will have more to say about such people, who are more typically in a state of transcrisis, in Chapter 5, Crisis Case Handling.

A Hybrid Model of Crisis Intervention

Perhaps the biggest change in the seventh edition of this book is our notion of how a model for crisis intervention operates. There are numerous models for crisis intervention (Aguilera, 1998; Kanel, 1999; Kleespies, 2009; Lester, 2002; Roberts, 2005; Slaikeu, 1990). All of these models depict crisis intervention in some linear, stepwise fashion. Indeed, through 20-plus years of publishing this book we did much the same, with the admonition that changing conditions might well mean that the interventionist would have to recycle and move back to earlier steps. In our earlier model we depicted crisis intervention as starting with problem exploration, examining safety concerns, looking for support, examining alternatives to present behaving, planning how to restore equilibrium, and finally gaining a commitment to take action. We no longer believe that a stage or purely step model captures the way crisis intervention works, and here's why.

The problem that we have struggled with as we try to teach students like you about crisis intervention is that at times crisis is anything but linear. A lot of the times crisis intervention absolutely epitomizes chaos theory—with starts, stops, do-overs, and U-turns. At times doing crisis work is a lot like being a smoke jumper,

controlling a psychological brush fire on this side of the mountain only to be faced with a new one on the other side of the valley. Fighting those psychological fires according to a neat, progressive, linear plan is easily said but not so easily done. Therefore, we have combined our former linear model with a systems model we helped develop (Myer, James, & Moulton, 2011), resulting in what could more appropriately be called a hybrid model for individual crisis intervention that is generally linear in its progression but can also be seen in terms of tasks that need to be accomplished. While certainly some of these tasks would usually be done in the beginning, middle, or end of a crisis, changing conditions may mean you have to accomplish some task you would normally do later, first. Or indeed, a task you thought was already accomplished comes apart and has to be done over not once, but multiple times.

A further problem with a strict linear model is that each step should be discrete, following from step one to step two and so on, with particular techniques to employ in each of those steps. In crisis intervention, issues suddenly erupt that defy discrete, stepwise techniques. Focus on getting a commitment from a person to do something, which would normally come at the end of a crisis session, may need to happen immediately if that person is standing out in the middle of a busy intersection at rush hour! Likewise, gaining that commitment to get out of the street may call for assertion techniques that are anything but what we might normally do when making initial contact with a client. Consider the following analogy.

Picture yourself as a linesperson on the cross arm of a power pole, hard hat on, heavy insulated clothing, leather over insulated gloves, dug in with your climbing spikes, attempting to repair a high-voltage (crisis) transmission line in North Dakota in January with the wind blowing sleet in your face at 20 miles an hour. On your utility belt are a variety of tools. You know the steps required to get the transformer hooked back up and the sequential manner in which you will employ the tools on your belt to get the job done. The problem is, Mother Nature is not happy and the wind picks up and a coupling breaks loose or a new fuse you just put in blows and you have to start all over again! If you can picture this analogy in your mind's eye, you are well on the way to understanding how crisis intervention works. As we describe the model, we will give you some examples of when you have to change tools to meet the changing conditions up on that pole.

The model you are about to examine is the hub around which the crisis intervention strategies in this book revolve, and the tasks/steps are designed to operate as an integrated problem-solving process. It is not complex, but rather is designed to be simple to implement, easy to use, and adaptable to just about any crisis we can think of you would likely encounter.

Task 1. Predispositioning/Engaging/Initiating Contact

Predispostioning may be seen as first and foremost getting ready to do something. It is usually the first step in a crisis model: placing oneself, or something, in a position to be of use in some future occurrence. Typically, systems such as the armed forces and government agencies such as FEMA use predispositioning to get supplies, equipment, and personnel ready to meet some future emergency. Indeed, in Chapter 17, Disaster Response, you will see predispositioning in operation on a very large scale. In the counseling literature, predisposition was originally studied by Prochaska, DiClemente, and Norcross (1992) in regard to what motivated people who were suffering from addiction to decide to change. Since their seminal work, the concept of predisposing clients to get them ready for counseling has become widespread.

In crisis intervention, predisposition is somewhat different. It means predisposing individuals to be receptive to our intervention when, in many instances, they may not be at all enthused about our presence or be so out-of-control that they are only vaguely aware of us. Therefore, predisposition has a lot to do with the attitudinal set and predisposition of how the crisis worker enters the situation. A number of clients the crisis worker will meet do not act, talk, look, or even smell nice! The ability to convey empathy and be authentic as to who and what you are doing without pretense is critical (Kleespies & Richmond, 2009).

Particularly with a first contact, predispositioning the client as to what to expect is critical. Along with letting the client know what is going to occur, it is important to make contact in such a way that the client can see the interventionist as an immediate ally and support, and not another in a long line of people, representative of bureaucracies and institutional authorities, who have been anything but helpful in resolving their problems. One of the most critical initiating components of crisis intervention is how the worker introduces him- or herself to a client who has never met the crisis interventionist—which is a fairly common occurrence in this business. It is not just to fill time that our practicum training with aspiring crisis intervention

team police officers now devotes an initial session specifically to how the officer introduces him- or herself to a recipient of services (Memphis Police Department, 2010). Our primary objectives in predisposing an individual to accept crisis intervention are twofold: (1) to establish a psychological connection and create a line of communication and (2) to clarify intentions with regard as to what is going to happen.

Establishing Psychological Connection. First and foremost, you need to introduce yourself in a way that is nonthreatening, helpful, and assumes a problem-solving as opposed to an adversarial approach.

Leron: (*standing in the middle of a main city street in five o'clock rush hour traffic waving two broken whiskey bottles*) The God damned house authority. NO place to live. Kicked me out, the rotten bastards. Everybody needs to know them for the crooks they are.

CIT officer: (*slowly approaching the subject from a distance with hands visible, empty, and open*) Man! You really are angry with them to make this kind of statement out in the middle of Union Avenue during rush hour. My name's Scott Lewis, a CIT officer with the Memphis Police Department. I didn't catch your name. Mind telling me?

One of the most important elements in making first contact is getting the client's name and introducing yourself in a nonthreatening manner. Note that Scott approaches the subject slowly, not only because he is armed with two whiskey bottles (which has to do with another task that is pretty important here, providing for the client's safety and your own), and responds to his current affective and behavioral state of being. Before he ever asks a question about why this has happened, he immediately states his name and asks for the client's. Also note that his full name, not his rank or the police department, comes first.

Another advantage with the approach used by Scott is that he allows Leron to maintain some control over the situation. The housing authority has already taken his home and barred him from his belongings. Imagine if Scott rolled onto the scene and immediately began demanding Leron get out of the street and put down the whiskey bottles. Scott would likely get the response "screw you, cop." Scott would be seen as just another authority figure who doesn't listen. By establishing a problem-solving, helpful connection, Scott allows Leron to maintain momentary control of the situation. By reflecting Leron's anger, the crisis worker immediately attempts to convey empathic understanding of the extreme measures the client has taken in attempting to problem-solve.

Clarifying Intentions.   Clarifying intentions means informing the client about what the crisis intervention process is and what the client can expect to happen. For many clients who are in crisis, this will be their first contact with a crisis interventionist, and they will have little if any idea of what is going to happen or how it is going to happen. Leron most likely has had experiences with the police that will lead him to believe that nothing positive is going to happen with Officer Lewis. Thus, the CIT officer needs to quickly apprise him of what will happen.

CIT officer: Okay I can see right off you clearly have some issues with the housing authority. Right now I am going to listen very closely to what got you out here. I may ask you some questions so I get a clearer notion of the problem. We've got some time and I am going to take the time to hear you out. I'll also probably kinda sum up what you're saying so I'm sure I heard you right. So I wonder if we could move this over underneath that shade tree cause it's hot and not very safe out here.

Leron: (*weaving unsteadily and sweating profusely*) No! As soon as I do that, those other cops will bum rush me. Long as I'm out here they got to pay attention and that News 5 chopper stays up there. Lost my job through no fault of my own and now kicked out.

CIT officer: Okay. I hear what you're saying about keeping the evil stuff the housing authority has done to you in the public's eye. However, sooner or later we're going to need to get out of the street. I'd like that to be sooner since it is 98 degrees out here and my guess is you're getting thirsty and would like to get it settled and get out of the sun. Nobody's going to bum rush you. It's between you and me right now. That's the way I'd like to keep it.

Officer Lewis uses basic listening and responding statements that own what is going to happen in the next few minutes. He also states the immediate end goal of the crisis resolution for him as "getting out of the middle of the street." He clearly states his intention to listen, get the client's perspective, and do no harm to him while this is going on. While the client's end goal may be completely different—bringing the housing authority to justice in some manner—the interventionist states from the outset in pretty clear terms what he is going to do. In clear, concise statements, the interventionist creates a line of communication by using open-ended questions, reflection of feelings, and owning statements (all of which you will learn about in the next chapter) that reinforce and encourage the client to tell his story.

The major intentional strategy here is allowing the client to cathart but also keeping the client in real time and not allowing the interaction to degenerate into all the perceiving injustices ever perpetrated on him.

This introduction "stuff" may sound pretty simplistic, but in the heat of the moment it is surprising how that can go by the wayside. It may also seem like a "once and done" deal, but even for a client who has known the interventionist for a long time and is currently out of touch with reality, anchoring the client by stating who the interventionist is, clarifying intentions, and stating what needs to happen is a critical ingredient for a successful intervention.

Task 2. Problem Exploration: Defining the Crisis

A major initial task in crisis intervention is to define and understand the problem from the client's point of view. This is particularly difficult in the middle of a chaotic situation where there are complex biopsychosocial contributors interacting with one another (Kleespies & Richmond, 2009). Unless the worker perceives the crisis situation as the client perceives it, all the intervention strategies and procedures the helper might use may miss the mark and be of no value to the client. Intervention sessions begin with crisis workers practicing what are called the *core listening skills*: empathy, genuineness, and acceptance or positive regard (Cormier & Cormier, 1991, pp. 21–39).

Problem definition of a crisis does not mean going on a psychological archaeological dig to dredge up and sift every artifact of the client's past. Defining the crisis does mean attempting to identify the precipitating event across the affective, behavioral, and cognitive components of the crisis. This task serves two purposes. First, the interventionist sees the crisis from the client's perspective. Second, defining the crisis gives the interventionist information on the immediate conditions, parties, and issues that led to eruption of the problem into a crisis.

CIT officer: I understand that the housing authority screwed you over somehow. So tell me what got you so mad and frustrated you needed to get everybody's attention.

As Leron angrily expounds on the housing authority's injustices toward people and himself, Officer Lewis uses an expansion strategy to broaden the client's view of the problem without letting the problem escalate. He restates the client's complaint and follows with an open lead.

Inevitably other issues will surface as the interventionist attempts to define the crisis. In the case of Leron, Officer Lewis may suspect that Leron is dependent on alcohol, given the fact that he has two empty whiskey bottles in his hands and is having trouble keeping his balance. He also is now aware that Leron has recently been laid off from his job. While these issues need attention, at the moment the interventionist needs to remain focused on the crisis—getting Leron out of the street and assisting him to access the resources needed to address the eviction from his apartment. The other issues should be placed on the back burner and may well be discussed after the crisis has been resolved.

CIT officer: So they lost your application for delayed payment while you wait for unemployment to kick in, then said you hadn't filed and kicked you out. I understand how that could make you so mad. So how about putting those bottles down and stepping over to that shade tree. I see you're sweating pretty hard out here in the hot sun and bet you could use some water. I just happen to have some bottles in my lunch cooler. I've got a couple of ideas about how to get you out of this predicament.

Task 3. Providing Support

The third task in crisis intervention emphasizes communicating to the client that the worker is a person who cares about the client. Workers cannot assume that a client experiences feeling valued, prized, or cared for. In many crisis situations the exact opposite will be true. The support step provides an opportunity for the worker to assure the client that "here is one person who really cares about you." We believe that providing support occurs in three ways.

Psychological Support.   First and most immediate is providing psychological and physical support. Deep, empathic responding using reflection of feelings and owning statements about the client's present condition serves as a bonding agent that says emphatically, "I am with you right here." In Task 3, the person providing the support is the crisis worker. This means that workers must be able to accept, in an unconditional and positive way, all their clients, whether the clients can reciprocate or not. The worker who can truly provide support for clients in crisis is able to accept and value the person no one else is willing to accept. While Officer Lewis is attempting to get Leron out of the street, he also offers genuine support and help in getting the client out of his predicament with the housing authority.

Logistical Support.   In a more general sense, support may be not only emotional but instrumental and informational (Cohen, 2004). At times the client may not have money, food, clothing, or shelter. Little psychological support will be desired or progress made until the basic necessities of living and surviving are met. Physical support means giving clients concrete assistance to help weather the crisis. This support comes in many forms, ranging from providing pamphlets to arranging transportation of clients to organizations that have the resources needed to help them to simply giving them a drink of water.

CIT officer: I can't imagine what it's like not to have a job or a roof over your head. Where's your family in all this?

Leron: Tormeda and the kids done went to her momma's in Arkansas. Nothin' to eat and no place to live ceptin' the street. Momma took her back cause I ain't no account and cain't feed 'em or put a roof over dere heads.

CIT officer: The words "terrifying" and "hopeless" come to mind. I can see why this might come down to the only solution you can think of. I really do want to help you out with this and get you back on your feet, and I do maybe have an idea or two about how to do that. But I don't want to see you arrested and if we don't move this out of the middle of the street so I can share some of my ideas with you, nothing will happen except you going to jail. So you have a choice. What's your wish? Help getting this resolved or jail?

Leron: Jail don't sound good . . . been there, done that.

CIT officer: I hear that. I don't want to see you in jail either, so come on over here and let's look at some options.

Leron: (*walks slowly over to the curb and sets the bottles down*) Okay, I be done. I be givin' you a shot at dis. I guess I be needin' some hep.

In this exchange, Officer Lewis forms a bond with Leron. Officer Lewis does not judge Leron, instead he encourages him to stay out of jail. This encouragement helps Leron regain a belief that the situation is not as dire as it seems and maybe with help a solution can be found. Encouragement is a critical component in crisis intervention because, for most clients, what they are going through is anything but encouraging. Catching clients' even feeble attempts to problem-solve gives them a chance to regain some hope, validates that they still have capabilities, and starts reframing thinking toward a proactive, problem-solving mode (Courtois & Ford, 2009, pp. 86–87).

Social Support.   Third, providing support means activating clients' primary support system: family, friends, coworkers, church members, and so forth. For many people in crisis, this primary support system may be absent (a car accident 600 miles from home), fed up with their behavior (lying and stealing from them to subsidize an addiction), or unequal to the task of providing support as a result of the crisis (symptoms of posttraumatic stress disorder). Conversely, clients may feel too embarrassed or guilty to ask for help from their immediate support system such as Sunday school members (loss of job and inability to contribute to their church financially). At such times, the interventionist is not only the initial point of contact and immediate psychological and physical anchor, but also the "expert" who provides information, guidance, and primary support in the first minutes and hours after the initiating event (Aguilera, 1998; Cohen, 2004).

Informational Support.   At other times, clients do not have adequate information to make good decisions. The need for informational support is particularly critical in the next step, examining alternatives. One of the best techniques a crisis interventionist can be in command of is the ability to provide information on where, how, who, and what resources clients can access to get out of the predicament they are in. That is particularly true of people who after a disaster are trying to access the basic necessities of living (Ruzek, 2006).

Default Task: Safety

Safety is a default task that is *always* operational. Safety is a primary consideration throughout crisis intervention for a variety of reasons that are both physically and psychologically based. The task of assessing and ensuring the client's and others' safety is always part of the process, whether it is overtly stated or not. When we speak of safety, we are concerned about the physical safety not only of the client but also of those who may interact with him or her and, just as important, about keeping ourselves safe. Whether by commission or omission, clients often put themselves in hazardous situations as a result of their affective, behavioral, and cognitive reactions to the crisis. Leron's attempt to publicize his plight clearly puts him, the general public, and the officer at risk. While Leron's crisis is with the housing authority, the immediate crisis of Leron in the middle of a main street with two broken whiskey bottles in his hands is a safety issue. Nothing is more paramount in a crisis than ensuring safety.

We have personally known three human service workers who have been killed at the hands of clients in crisis. One of your authors could very easily have been added to that list early in his career when he talked a violent juvenile into handing over a gun pointed a foot from his face. He didn't think the weapon would work. After the youth was taken into custody, blanks were loaded in the gun and it fired very well, to the shock of a shaken 24-year-old junior high school counselor who thought he was immortal! There are no dead heroes in this business, only dead interventionists. We will have a great deal more to say on the subject of the interventionist's safety in Chapter 14, Violent Behavior in Institutions.

Generally, when we think about safety in a crisis, we assume that someone is engaging in lethal behavior toward self or others. But limiting the task of ensuring safety to issues of life and death overlooks many clients whose safety is in jeopardy. The fact is that in much crisis intervention people do not intend to cause harm to themselves or others but engage in activities that have a high potential for that to happen. You can extend the task of ensuring safety to include meeting the daily needs of clients such as finding shelter and food.

CIT officer: Leron, I want to keep you safe, man, and the middle of Union Avenue at rush hour is anything but that. I can get you some help not only as far as the housing authority is concerned but also in regard to getting some food in your belly and a roof over your head, but that has to start happening over in my squad car. Otherwise the TAC team will come and take you in to custody and none of that will happen. When did you eat last?

Leron: Don't remember . . . yesterday maybe . . . no, a couple of days ago I think. Got some stuff out of the back of one of them restaurants on Beale Street.

Officer Lewis is working to protect Leron from inadvertently being injured. Food and the offer of shelter are used to entice Leron off the street. This offer makes a clear point that all crisis interventionists' need to heed: If a person's basic physical needs are not being met, it is unlikely that the crisis will diminish until those needs are met.

Safety also includes assuring clients that they are psychologically safe. As we shall see in Chapter 9, Sexual Assault, many clients who have been subject to vicious assaults by sexual perpetrators have suffered secondary victimization, being revictimized by authority figures, government bureaucracies, religious entities, social service agencies, and, yes, incompetent therapists (Ochberg, 1988). Making it safe for a client in crisis to trust the interventionist comes before everything else and is a critical part of creating the trust and bond necessary to move forward (Courtois & Ford, 2009). Safety is a default task that is merged and subsumed in all the other tasks in the model, from predispositioning to follow-up.

Tasks 1, 2, 3, and the Safety task involve a lot of listening activities, although they are not necessarily passive or devoid of action, particularly when safety issues are involved. Taken together, these four steps most nearly represent what has become known in the field as *psychological first aid* (see Chapter 1).

Task 4. Examining Alternatives

Examining alternatives addresses an area that both clients and workers in crisis intervention often neglect—exploring a wide array of appropriate choices available to the client. In their immobile state, clients often do not adequately examine their best options. Some clients in crisis actually believe there are no options. Clients may develop tunnel vision and become stuck in an endless merry-go-round of attempting to engage in the same futile behavior.

Alternatives can be viewed from three perspectives: (1) *Situational supports* are people known to the client in the present or past who might care about what happens to the client. (2) *Coping mechanisms* are actions, behaviors, or environmental resources the client might use to help get through the present crisis. (3) *Positive and constructive thinking patterns* on the part of the client are ways of reframing that might substantially alter the client's view of the problem and lessen the client's level of stress and anxiety. The effective crisis worker may think about an infinite number of alternatives pertaining to the client's crisis but discuss only a few of them with the client. Clients experiencing crisis do not need a lot of choices; they need appropriate choices that are realistic for their situation. Some of these coping skills may be already present in the client but under the stress of the crisis may be forgotten or dismissed as ineffective because they were used "back when" or "back there" and are no longer workable in the here and now.

Leron: Used to have money in ma pocket. Had me a car 'n' a house 'n' food on de table. Fok lift op . . . e . . . ray . . . tore and damn good. Could figger stuff out. Fo'man on ma crew. Lotsa ideas 'bout movin' on up, din da compnee go bust. No mo'! Ain't got no job, no skills, no family, no nuthin' ceptin' damn housin' a-tho-it-tee.

CIT officer: Leron, it sounds like right now you're out there all alone against this big monster called MHA. I've got an idea. Okay, so your application for rent reduction got lost in the bureaucracy when you got laid off and they made it sound like it was your fault and blamed you for not submitting it when in fact you did. Your gripes to them haven't gotten you anywhere, and now you want everybody to know that they are trying to weasel out of their mistake. I've got one idea that might help, and that's the pro bono law advocacy student association of the Memphis University Law School. They take on stuff like this. I can take you down there and introduce you to somebody I know there, but I've got another concern. I wonder when was the last time you had something to eat and a place to lay your head down where you felt safe, could get some sleep and get some energy back?

By offering to physically transport Leron to the law school, Officer Lewis indicates that he is involved with Leron beyond his being a nuisance to get off the street. He also makes a hunch about Leron's physical condition, and that hunch segues into one of the most important tasks of crisis intervention, which is safety.

Examining alternatives is literally a "right here, right now" activity. Rapidly changing conditions may mean discarding old options that worked a half hour ago for completely new ones. One of the hallmarks of a world-class crisis worker is the ability to be resilient and rapidly brainstorm new ideas and implement them in a hurry.

CIT officer: (*noticing Leron's unsteady gate*) Leron, how much have you had to drink today?

Leron: 'Bout most of them two bottles.

CIT officer: I can understand why you'd need all that liquid courage to do this. Okay! Maybe we need to think about getting you sober before you talk to anybody down there. What about me taking you out to the Bartlett Salvation Army halfway house, getting some food in your stomach, cleaned up, some sleep so you got it all together and can talk real straight to the folks at the advocacy center.

Task 5. Planning in Order to Reestablish Control

A hallmark of people in crisis is the feeling of the loss of control. Chaos reigns and every effort to manage the situation has failed. Reestablishing control means helping clients create a plan to guide them in the resolution of the crisis. Such a plan needs to consider what options are available to the client and what choices need to be made in regard to those options. One of the primary strategies in planning to reestablish control is mobilizing the client.

The fifth step in crisis intervention, making plans, flows logically and directly from Task 4 alternatives. Much of the material throughout this book focuses either directly or indirectly on the crisis worker's involvement with clients in planning action steps that have a good chance of restoring the client's emotional, behavioral, and cognitive equilibrium. A plan should

(1) identify additional persons, groups, and other referral resources that can be contacted for immediate support, and (2) provide coping mechanisms—something concrete and positive for the client to do now, definite action steps that the client can own and comprehend. The plan should focus on systematic problem solving for the client and be realistic in terms of the client's coping ability.

While it may be that crisis workers have to be very directive at times, as much as possible it is important that planning be done in collaboration with clients so that clients feel a sense of ownership of the plan. At the very least, explaining thoroughly what is about to occur and gaining client acquiescence is extremely important. The critical element in developing a plan is that clients do not feel robbed of their power, independence, and self-respect. The central issues in planning are clients' *control* and *autonomy*. The reasons for clients to carry out plans are to restore their sense of control and to ensure that they do not become dependent on support persons such as the worker. It should be emphasized that planning is not what clients are going to do for the rest of their lives. Planning is about getting through the short term and getting some semblance of equilibrium and stability restored. Most plans in crisis intervention are measured in minutes, hours, and days, not weeks, months, or years.

CIT officer: I can't give you much more time. I gave you a choice. Those alternatives are to do something about the issue rather than going to jail. What do you want to do? I need for you to put those bottles down and walk over here and get in the car. Are you willing to do that and get some help for your problem and some food in your stomach?

Leron: (*hesitates and shrugs; puts bottles down and walks over to the car*) Okay . . . maybe you can get me some help.

(*Next afternoon at the legal aid office.*)

Legal aid worker: Mr. Brown, I believe we can exert some leverage on the housing authority and can make a case for you. This will take at least a couple of weeks, though, and I understand you have nowhere to stay.

(*Officer Lewis before dropping Leron off at the Salvation Army has made a promise to pick him up and take him to the legal aid office.*)

Officer Lewis: Leron, have you thought perhaps you might go over to Arkansas?

Leron: Man, I don't want to be beholden to my mother-in-law. She don't care much for me no how.

Officer Lewis: Well, you don't have a job, so you could go back out to the Salvation Army new halfway house. You'd qualify to get in it based on being out of work and the fact that your use of alcohol helped get you into that predicament.

Leron: Man, I ain't no charity case.

Officer Lewis: I hear that and understand you got your pride, but what about using their job counseling program out there to help you get back to work? I mean it's not like you're going there forever, and you'd be right there if anything comes in. They'd also do some job counseling.

Leron: Well, when you put it that way, could be okay.

Many times in crisis the alternatives are not what the client wants but what is necessary. When Officer Lewis reframes the stay at the Salvation Army as not charity but a way of getting Leron back to work, it becomes much more palatable and makes the alternative a much more positive and desirable one. Being able to reframe the alternative is empowering and one of the key ingredients in getting clients involved and energizing them to move forward.

Psychoeducation. At the time of the first edition of this book in 1987 there was not a great deal of information about many of the maladies in this book. Thus, interventionists didn't have a lot of information to give clients about the psychological course of the aftermath of a crisis. However, in the intervening quarter of a century, a tremendous amount of reliable and valid information has been discovered about the course of the crises discussed in this book. Giving clients this information, called *psychoeducation,* can be of tremendous benefit in helping them understand what is going on with them psychologically.

Psychoeducation means providing information to victims and survivors about what is happening and probably going to happen to them psychologically in the aftermath of a traumatic event. Psychoeducation has become an extremely important treatment component in helping people in crisis get control back in their lives, not only in preemptive work such as educating people about suicide, domestic violence, and sexual assault, but also in understanding what happens in the traumatic wake of a crisis such as the terrifying flashbacks and nightmares of PTSD (Briere & Scott, 2006; Courtois, Ford, & Cloitre, 2009; Kleespies, 2009). We considered making psychoeducation a task in and of itself. However, for the present we have put it under planning because of the critical part it plays in helping to mobilize the client. Psychoeducation means providing clients with information about their condition, what they can expect in the way of affective, behavioral, and cognitive dimensions of it, and how they can develop coping skills to alleviate it.

We would not expect a first grader to have much knowledge or many psychological resources to deal with bullying, so we would be pretty directive in providing the child with information and strategies to deal with it. Likewise, for a person who knew nothing about how to deal with housing bureaucracies, options to get out of an unemployment line, and the common depressive symptoms that might exacerbate those problems into a full-blown crisis, the crisis worker's best treatment option is to start providing information and instructing the client about what needs to be done and how to take care of oneself psychologically while doing it.

Rehabilitation counselor: (*at Salvation Army Treatment Center a week later*) Leron, we have a lot of information that I believe will help you as far as getting employable is concerned. We also found out that you are most likely clinically depressed. That's important information because it goes a lot toward answering why you have been in such a rut, unable to do much about your problems, and why you wound up in the middle of the street a frustrated and angry man. We're going to set you up with an appointment to get some medication for that and also to get some counseling. I am going to give you a lot of information on why we think this is a good plan, so if you have any questions, stop me and I'll try and answer them.

Task 6. Obtaining Commitment

The sixth task, obtaining commitment, flows directly from Task 5, and the issues of control and autonomy apply equally to the process of obtaining an appropriate commitment. It may seem overkill to devote a specific task/step to commitment as opposed to just making it a part of planning. However, getting a specific commitment from a client in crisis to do something differently than what has not been working is a big deal. The commitment step is clear, concise, and behaviorally specific. As a result, it is clear to the client what he or she is going to do and what the worker will do.

CIT officer: So tell me what we're going to do.

Leron: We gonna get out to the Salvation Armee and get me sobered up, din two' morro you gonna come git me 'n' tak me dow to legal aid 'bout 4:30, if'n I git in de polelesse car now and don't be givin' you no mo' trouble.

If the planning step is done effectively, the commitment step is apt to be easy. Many times the commitment step is brief and simple, consisting of asking the client to verbally summarize the plan. Sometimes a handshake may be used to seal the commitment. In some incidents where lethality is involved, the commitment may be written down and signed by both parties. The objective is to enable the client to commit to taking one or more definite, positive, intentional action steps designed to move that person toward restoring precrisis equilibrium. The worker is careful to obtain an honest, direct, and appropriate commitment from the client before terminating the crisis intervention session. No commitment should be imposed by the worker. Commitments should be free, voluntary, and believed to be doable. The core listening skills are as important to the commitment step as they are to the problem definition or any other step. Any hesitation on the part of the client to commit to the plan of action should be reflected and queried by the worker. A worker-imposed plan or commitment will not work.

Task 7. Follow-up

When we speak of follow-up in crisis we are not talking about days, weeks, or months. Long-term follow-up after a disaster is a special condition we will deal with in Chapter 17, Disaster Response. We are generally speaking of following up in a time frame of minutes, hours, and days. Follow-up in crisis intervention has to do with keeping track of clients' success in maintaining precrisis equilibrium, not whether they are maintaining long-term goals or changing deep-seated personality traits.

CIT officer: (*stopping by Salvation Army halfway house the next day*) Leron, glad to see you. You look lots better today. Clean and sober. I checked with the coordinator and they have you set up for some vocational evaluation. While I'm not your social worker, I did stop by the U of M law students' pro bono advocacy service and they are willing to look into your problem with MHA. I think you can get a voucher here to get a bus down there. You've got my card, let me know if I can do anything for you.

Short-term follow-up is also important as a reinforcing event that tells clients you are still in this with them. Engaging in follow-up is extremely important when clients have little other social support system.

The model we have been describing in some detail is summarized briefly in Figure 3.1.

ASSESSMENT

Overarching and continuous throughout the crisis:
Evaluating the client's present situational crisis in terms of the client's coping ability,
mobility, support systems needed, physical resources required, and degree of threat to self and others.
Making judgments as to type and kind of action needed, based on the crisis worker's action continuum.

TASKS

Overarching default task: Ensuring safety. Continuous assessment of how safe the client, others in the environment, and the worker are throughout the crisis. Putting in place and implementing procedures that will ensure the safety of *all* those involved in the crisis, including the crisis worker.

1. **Predispositioning/engaging/initiating contact.** Making initial positive contact with the client. Setting the stage for what the worker is going to do, what the client can expect from the worker, and how the worker will operate throughout the crisis.

2. **Exploring the problem.** Defining the problem as it currently manifests itself across the affective, behavioral, and cognitive domains of the individual. Exploring the intrapersonal, interpersonal, and systemic effects of the crisis as it operates in the current environment within which the person operates.

3. **Providing support.** Determining what kinds of support systems have worked in the past, what support systems are currently available, and what support systems will be needed. More

specifically, determining how much the worker will need to function as the main support system during the crisis and indicating to clients how that will happen.

4. **Examining alternatives.** Considering immediate short-term options to deescalate the crisis and defuse the situation. Examining the choices the client currently has available in a realistic and time-efficient manner; includes finding situational supports, installing coping mechanisms, and reframing thinking to be more positive and solution focused to generate achievable short-term goals.

5. **Making plans.** Generating a short-term plan from the alternatives that are positive and doable, and translating into immediate action steps the client can comprehend, own, and implement.

6. **Obtaining commitment.** Obtaining a verbal or written commitment to a plan that can be comprehended, owned, and put in operation by the client.

7. **Follow-up.** Immediate, short-term follow-up by the worker to ensure that the plan is working and that the client and others are safe.

Crisis Worker's Action Continuum

Crisis worker is nondirective	Crisis worker is collaborative	Crisis worker is directive

(Threshold varies from client to client)		(Threshold varies from client to client)
Client is mobile	Client is partially mobile	Client is immobile

The crisis worker's level of action/involvement may be anywhere on the continuum according to a valid and realistic assessment of the client's level of mobility/immobility.

FIGURE 3.1 Model of Crisis Intervention

Assessment in Crisis Intervention

Assessment is a pervasive strategy throughout crisis intervention. This action-oriented, situation-based assessment is the basis for systematically applying our task model. Thus, the entire task process is carried out under an umbrella of assessment by the crisis worker. Because many of the assessments in crisis situations occur spontaneously, subjectively, and interactively in the heat of the moment, we are not dealing here with formal techniques such as *DSM-IV-TR* diagnostic criteria or assessment instruments that are typically used in ongoing clinical evaluations. Kleespies and Richmond (2009) have a laundry list of mental status exam questions that cover everything from orientation/memory to visual/spatial organization. While these may be extremely useful in a set-piece intake assessment session at a hospital, lots of times there is neither the time nor the setting to engage in even a verbal comprehensive mental status examination.

Assessment is critically important because it enables the worker to determine (1) the severity of the crisis; (2) the client's current emotional, behavioral, and cognitive status—the client's level of mobility or immobility in these three areas; (3) the alternatives, coping mechanisms, support systems, and other resources available to the client; (4) the client's level of lethality (danger to self and others); (5) and how well the worker is doing in de-escalating and defusing the situation and returning the client to a state of equilibrium and mobility.

Assessing the Severity of Crisis

It is important for the crisis worker to evaluate the crisis severity as quickly as possible during the initial contact with the client. Crisis workers generally do not have time to perform complete diagnostic workups or obtain in-depth client histories. Therefore, a rapid assessment procedure, such as the Triage Assessment System (Myer, 2001; Myer et al., 1991, 1992) and its assessment siblings the Triage Assessment Checklist for Law Enforcement (TACKLE; James, Myer, & Moore, 2006) and the Triage Assessment System for Students in Learning Environments (TASSLE; Myer et al., 2007), are recommended as a quick and efficient way of obtaining information relevant to the specific crisis situation. These triage systems enable the worker to gauge the severity of the client's current functioning across affective, behavioral, and cognitive domains. The degree of severity of the crisis may affect the client's mobility, which in turn gives the worker a basis for judging how directive to be. The length of time the client has been in the present crisis will determine how much time the worker has in which to safely defuse the crisis.

The ABCs of Assessing in Crisis Intervention

Crisis is time limited; that is, most acute crises persist only a matter of days or weeks (the exception being large-scale disaster events such as the recent Japanese earthquake) before some change—for better or worse—occurs. The severity of the crisis is assessed from the client's subjective viewpoint and from the worker's objective viewpoint. Objective assessment is based on an appraisal of the client's functioning in three areas that may be referred to as the ABCs of assessment: *affective* (feeling or emotional tone), *behavioral* (action or psychomotor activity), and *cognitive* (thinking patterns).

Affective State. Abnormal or impaired affect is often the first sign that the client is in a state of disequilibrium. The client may be overemotional and out of control or

severely withdrawn and detached. Often the worker can assist the client to regain control and mobility by helping the client express feelings in appropriate and realistic ways. Some questions the worker may address are: Do the client's affective responses indicate that the client is denying the situation or attempting to avoid involvement in it? Is the emotional response normal or congruent with the situational crisis? To what extent, if any, is the client's emotional state driven, exacerbated, or otherwise influenced by other people? Do people typically show this kind of affect in situations such as this?

Behavioral Functioning. The crisis worker focuses much attention on *doing, acting out, taking active steps, behaving,* or any number of other psychomotor activities. In crisis intervention, the quickest (and often the best) way to get the client to become mobile is to facilitate positive actions that the client can take at once. People who cope with crisis successfully and later evaluate their experiences favorably report that the most helpful alternative during a crisis is to engage in some concrete and immediate activity. However, it is important for the worker to remember that it may be very difficult for immobilized people to take independent and autonomous action even though that is what they need to do most.

These are appropriate questions that the worker might ask to get the client to take constructive action: "In cases like this in the past, what actions did you take that helped you get back in control? What would you have to do now to get back on top of the situation? Is there anyone who, if you contacted them right now, would be supportive to you in this crisis?" The fundamental problem in immobility is loss of control. Once the client becomes involved in doing something concrete, which is a step in a positive direction, an element of control is restored, a degree of mobility is provided, and the climate for forward movement is established.

Cognitive State. The worker's assessment of the client's thinking patterns may provide answers to several important questions: How realistic and consistent is the client's thinking about the crisis? To what extent, if any, does the client appear to be rationalizing, exaggerating, or believing part-truths or rumors to exacerbate the crisis? How long has the client been engaged in crisis thinking? How open does the client seem to be toward changing beliefs about the crisis situation and reframing it in more positive terms of cooler, more rational thoughts, or is the client engaged in a downward spiral of catastrophic thinking with no hope of ameliorating the crisis?

The Triage Assessment System

Because rapid and adequate assessment of a client in crisis is one of the most critical components of intervention (Hersh, 1985), assessment has a preeminent place in the crisis intervention model, as an overarching and ongoing process. Constant and rapid assessment of the client's state of equilibrium dictates what the interventionist will do in the next seconds and minutes as the crisis unfolds (Aguilera, 1998). Unhappily, many assessment devices that can give the human services worker an adequate perspective on the client's problem are unwieldy and time consuming, and require that the client be enough in control to complete the assessment process or be physically present while undergoing evaluation. Although we might gain a great deal of helpful information with an extensive intake form, a background interview, or an in-depth personality test, events often occur so quickly that these are unaffordable and unrealistic luxuries.

What the interventionist needs in a crisis situation is a fast, efficient way of obtaining a real-time estimate of what is occurring with a client. Such a tool should also be simple enough that a worker who may have only rudimentary assessment skills can use the device in a reliable and valid manner. It should enable the assessment to be performed rapidly by a broad cross-section of crisis workers who have had little if any training in standardized testing or assessment procedures. What you are about to encounter (see Figure 3.2) is a composite of several forms of the Triage Assessment Form (TAF), which we believe admirably fits the foregoing criteria.

The Triage Assessment Form

Variations of the general TAF have been tested with police officer trainees, veteran crisis intervention team police officers who deal with the mentally ill, school counselors, community agency workers, secretaries, undergraduates, agency and crisis line supervisors, volunteer crisis line counselors, university professors, residence hall staff, and counselors-in-training (Blancett, 2008; Conte, 2005; Logan, Myer, & James, 2006; Myer, 2001; Myer et al., 1991, 1992; Pazar, 2005; Slagel, 2009; Watters, 1997). Before training, none of the groups had any familiarity with the TAF.

Ratings of these groups were compared with expert triage ratings on a variety of different crisis scenarios (Minimal Impairment, Moderate Impairment, and Severe Impairment). These researchers found that police officer trainees tended to overrate and label the Moderate Impairment scenario as Severe Impairment (probably because they were very sensitive to not underrating the severity for fear of criticism or making a mistake that could cause a fatality). Veteran crisis intervention team police officers' ratings almost replicated the expert ratings (Logan, Myer, & James, 2006; Pazar, 2005). The most problematic area of the scale appears to be the Moderate Impairment range (Watters, 1997). Veteran mental health workers either underrated or overrated Moderate Impairment scenarios. When queried, those veteran mental health workers who gave lower ratings than the experts indicated that they had seen, heard, and handled far more problematic behavior and felt Moderate was too high a rating. Conversely, other veteran mental health workers interpreted subtle responses in the Moderate scenarios to imply greater threat than what was being portrayed, and thus gave higher ratings than the experts. Overall, the ratings of all the other groups, such as the school counselors and volunteers, were deemed reliable and comparable with the ratings of the experts. All groups were congruent with the Minimal Impairment and Severe Impairment range (Blancett, 2008; Logan, Myer, & James, 2006; Pazar, 2005; Watters, 1997). What the research seems to imply is that the scales should be taken at face value, and the less interpretation made of what the affect, behavior, and cognition implies, the more congruent ratings will be. In other words, trying to read too much or too little into what is being observed appears to invalidate the instrument when clients are operating in the moderately impaired range.

Although simple to use, the TAF is also elegant in that it cuts across affective, behavioral, and cognitive domains, or dimensions, of the client; compartmentalizes each dimension as to its typical response mode; and assigns numeric values to these modes that allow the worker to determine the client's current level of functioning. These three severity scales represent mechanisms for operationally assigning numeric values to the crisis worker's action continuum in Figure 3.2. The numeric ratings provide an efficient and tangible guide to both the degree and the kind of intervention the worker needs to make in most crisis situations. Perhaps more important, they not only tell the worker how the client is doing, but also tell the worker how he or she is doing in attempting to deescalate, defuse, and help the client regain control. The rationale and examples for each of the scales are discussed on pages 65–67.

SEVERITY SCALES

	1 No Impairment	2/3 Low Impairment	4/5 Minimal Impairment	6/7 Moderate Impairment	8/9 Marked Impairment	10 Severe Impairment
F E E L I N G S	Stable mood, control of feelings. Normal variation of affect appropriate to daily functioning.	Feelings are generally appropriate. Emotions are under control with minimal effort. Responses to questions are not overly emotional. Brief periods during which negative mood is experienced slightly more intensely than situation warrants. Brief outbursts or periods of melancholy.	Feelings are somewhat appropriate but noticeable negativity and lability. Emotions are generally controlled but primarily focused on crisis event. Responses to questions/requests may vary from rapid and agitated to slow and subdued. Increasingly longer periods during which negative mood is experienced slightly more intensely than situation warrants. Client perceives emotions as being substantially under control.	Feelings are primarily negative and are exaggerated or significantly subdued. Considerable efforts to control labile emotions are not always successful. Responses to questions/requests are highly emotional yet somewhat appropriate and controlled with effort. Affect incongruent with situation. Extended periods of intense negative moods. Mood is experienced noticeably more intensely than situation warrants.	Feelings are particularly pronounced or may be severely constricted. Extremely limited control of emotions that negatively influence all areas of life. Responses to questions/requests are emotional and mostly not appropriate even with maximum effort. Negative affect experienced at markedly higher level than situation warrants. Affect obviously incongruent with situation. Mood swings, if occurring, are pronounced.	Feelings are extremely pronounced, from hysterical to nonexistent. No ability to control feelings, regardless of potential danger to self or others. Cannot respond to questions/requests because of interference of emotions. Decompensates. Feels unreal as if viewed from a TV. Depersonalizes: That's not really me.
B E H A V I O R S	Behaviors are socially appropriate. Daily functioning unimpeded. Behavior is stable and nonoffensive. Threat or danger nonexistent.	Behaviors mostly effective, outbursts short and minimal. Tasks needed for daily living are minimally compromised. Behaviors minimally unstable, mildly offensive. Behaviors, while problematic, are no threat to self or others. Client performs those tasks necessary for daily functioning, but does so with noticeable effort.	Behaviors are ineffective, yet not dangerous. Behaviors can be controlled by self or upon request by worker with some difficulty. Behaviors minimal threat to self or others. Client neglects some tasks necessary for daily living; functioning is somewhat compromised.	Behaviors are maladaptive but not immediately destructive. Behaviors are very difficult to control even with repeated requests. Behavior is becoming a threat to self or others and increasingly difficult to control. Ability to perform tasks necessary for daily functioning is being compromised.	Behaviors worsen crisis situation. Behavior is inconsistent and very hard to control even after repeated requests to do so. Behavior is threat to self or others. Ability to perform tasks necessary for daily functioning is markedly absent.	Behaviors are totally ineffective. Behavior is erratic and not predictable even after repeated requests to change it. Behaviors are highly destructive, possibly to cause harm to self or others. Cannot perform even simple tasks necessary for daily living.

FIGURE 3.2 Triage Assessment Form for Crisis Intervention.
Source: Compiled from Triage Assessment Form (TAF), Triage Assessment System for Students in Learning Environments (TASSLE), Triage Assessment Checklist for Law Enforcement (TACKLE). Crisis Intervention & Preventions Solutions Inc. Pittsburgh, PA. Reprinted with permission.

SEVERITY SCALES (continued)

	1 No Impairment	2/3 Low Impairment	4/5 Minimal Impairment	6/7 Moderate Impairment	8/9 Marked Impairment	10 Severe Impairment
T H O U G H T S	Decisions are logical and reasonable. Concentration intact. Client displays normal problem-solving and decision-making abilities. Client's perception and interpretation of crisis event match with reality of situation.	Decisions are a bit erratic but safe and generally considerate of others' feelings, thoughts, and well-being. Thinking influenced by crisis, but under control. Able to carry on reasonable dialogue, understand and acknowledge views of others with minor difficulty. Problem solving generally intact. Client's thoughts may drift to crisis event but focus of thoughts is under volitional control. Problem-solving and decision-making abilities minimally affected. Client's perception and interpretation of crisis event substantially match with reality of situation with only minor distortions.	Decisions are increasingly irrational but have no potential for harm to self or others. Somewhat inconsiderate of others' feelings, thoughts, and well-being. Thinking focused on crisis but not all consuming. Ability to carry on reasonable dialogue restricted due to failure to recognize different perspectives. Problem solving somewhat limited. Occasional disturbance of concentration. Client perceives diminished control over thoughts of crisis event. Client experiences recurrent difficulties with problem-solving and decision-making abilities. Client's perception and interpretation of crisis event may differ in some respects from reality of situation.	Decisions are mainly irrational and may potentially pose a threat to self or others. Increasing disregard for others' thoughts, feelings, and well-being. Thoughts are limited to crisis situation and are becoming all consuming. Ability to understand and respond to questions inconsistent. Problem solving blocked by lack of concentration. Frequent disturbance of concentration. Intrusive thoughts of crisis event with limited control. Problem-solving and decision-making abilities adversely affected by obsessiveness, self-doubt, and confusion. Client's perception and interpretation of crisis event may differ noticeably from reality of situation.	Decisions are impulsive and highly irrational with clear potential to harm self or others. Thoughts about crisis have become obsessive with expressions of confusion and self-doubt. Ability to understand and respond to questions is highly erratic. Problem solving ability absent due to inability to concentrate. Client plagued by intrusiveness of thoughts regarding crisis event. The appropriateness of client's problem-solving and decision-making abilities likely adversely affected by obsessiveness, self-doubt, and confusion. Client's perception and interpretation of crisis event may differ substantially from reality of situation.	Decision-making ability completely shut down. Thoughts present a clear and present danger to self and others. Thoughts are chaotic and completely controlled by crisis. Ability to understand and respond to questions nonexistent. Gross inability to concentrate on anything except crisis event. Client so afflicted by obsessiveness, self-doubt, and confusion that problem-solving and decision-making abilities have shut down. Client's perception and interpretation of crisis event may differ so substantially from reality of situation as to constitute a severe distortion of reality, including paranoia, hallucinations, and other psychotic symptoms.

CRISIS EVENT

Identify and describe briefly the crisis situation: _____

_____

_____

AFFECTIVE DOMAIN

Identify and describe briefly the affect that is present.

(If more than one affect is experienced, rate with #1 being primary, #2 secondary, #3 tertiary.)

ANGER/HOSTILITY: _____

_____

_____

FIGURE 3.2 (continued)

CRISIS EVENT *(continued)*

ANXIETY/FEAR: _____

_____

_____

_____

SADNESS/MELANCHOLY: _____

_____

_____

_____

FRUSTRATION: _____

_____

_____

_____

BEHAVIORAL DOMAIN
Identify and describe briefly which behavior is currently being used.
(If more than one behavior is utilized, rate with #1 being primary, #2 secondary, #3 tertiary.)

APPROACH: _____

_____

_____

AVOIDANCE: _____

_____

IMMOBILITY: _____

_____

COGNITIVE DOMAIN
Identify if a transgression, threat, or loss has occurred in the following areas and describe briefly.
(If more than one cognitive response occurs, rate with #1 being primary, #2 secondary, #3 tertiary.)

PHYSICAL (food, water, safety, shelter, etc.): _____

_____

Transgression_____ Threat_____ Loss_____

PSYCHOLOGICAL (self-concept, sense of emotional well-being, ego integrity, self-identity, etc.): _____

_____

Transgression_____ Threat_____ Loss_____

SOCIAL RELATIONSHIPS (positive interaction and support, family, friends, coworkers, church, clubs, etc.): _____

_____

Transgression_____ Threat_____ Loss_____

FIGURE 3.2 *(continued)*

CRISIS EVENT *(continued)*

MORAL/SPIRITUAL (personal integrity, values, belief system, spiritual reconciliation): _____

_____

_____

Transgression_____ Threat_____ Loss_____

TRIAGE ASSESSMENT (X = Initial Assessment / O = Terminal Assessment)

Feelings: **Behaviors:**

Anger_____ Fear_____ Sadness_____   Approach_____ Avoidance_____ Immobile_____

● ————————————————————— ●   ● ————————————————————— ●

 1   2   3   4   5   6   7   8   9   10.   1   2   3   4   5   6   7   8   9   10

Thinking:

Transgression_____ Threat_____ Loss_____

● ————————————————————— ●

 1   2   3   4   5   6   7   8   9   10

Initial Total Score: (X)_____   Terminal Total Score (O)_____

Describe the observations that led you to check the characteristics above: _____

_____

_____

FIGURE 3.2 *(continued)*

The Affective Severity Scale. No crisis situation that we know of has positive emotions attached to it. Crow (1977) metaphorically names the usual emotional qualities found in a crisis as yellow (anxiety), red (anger), and black (depression). To those we would add orange (our students chose this color) for frustration, which invariably occurs as clients attempt to meet needs. These needs range all across Maslow's needs hierarchy, from inability to get food, water, and shelter (Hurricane Katrina) to interpersonal issues (attempts to regain boyfriend/girlfriend) to intrapersonal issues (get rid of the schizophrenic voices) to spiritual concerns (God can't let this happen). Frustration of needs is often the precursor of other negative emotions, thoughts, and behaviors that plunge the client further into crisis. Even more problematic, some very famous psychologists have investigated the relationship between frustration and aggression and found that aggression is always a consequence of

frustration (Dollard et al., 1939, p. 1). That outcome particularly does not bode well when the client is in crisis.

Undergirding these typical emotions may lie a constellation of other negative emotions such as shame, betrayal, humiliation, inadequacy, and horror (Collins & Collins, 2005, pp. 25–26). Clients may manifest these emotions both verbally and nonverbally, and the astute crisis worker needs to be highly aware of incongruencies between what the client is saying, how the client is saying it (voice tone, inflection, and decibel level), and what the client's body language says.

Invariably, these negative emotions appear singularly or in combination with each other when a crisis is present. In their model, Myer and associates (1992) have replaced the term *depression*, because of its diagnostic implications, with *sadness/melancholy*. When any of these core negative emotions becomes all-pervasive such that the client is consumed by them, the potential for these emotions to motivate destructive behavior becomes extremely high.

The Behavioral Severity Scale.   While a client in crisis is more or less behaviorally immobile, immobility can take three different forms. Crow (1977) proposes that behavior in a crisis approaches, avoids, or is paralyzed in the client's attempts to act. Although Crow's proposal may seem contradictory, it is not. A client may seem highly motivated but be acting maladaptively toward a specific target or acting in a random, non-goal-directed manner with no specific target discernible. Alternatively, the client may attempt to flee the noxious event by the fastest means possible, even though the immediate threat to the client's well-being is gone. Whereas in many instances taking stock of the situation before acting is an excellent plan, clients transfixed in the face of immediate danger need to flee or fight. Although a great deal of energy may be expended and the client may look focused, once the crisis goes beyond the client's capacity to cope in a meaningful and purposeful manner, we would say that the client is immobilized, stuck in the particular approach, avoidance, or static behavior in a continuous loop no matter how proactive he or she may seem to be. At the severe impairment end of the continuum, maladaptive behavior often takes on a lethal aspect in regard to either the client or others.

The Cognitive Severity Scale.   Ellis has written at length about the part that thinking plays in emotions and behavior (Ellis, 1971; Ellis & Abrahms, 1978; Ellis & Grieger, 1977; Ellis & Harper, 1975). In a crisis situation, the client's cognitive processes typically perceive the event in terms of transgression, threat, loss, or any combination of the three. These "hot" cognitions, as Dryden (1984) calls them, can take on catastrophic dimensions at the extreme end of the continuum.

Such highly focused irrational thinking can cause the client to obsess on the crisis to the extent that little, if any, logical thinking can occur within or beyond the boundaries of the crisis event. The event itself consumes all of the client's psychic energy as the client attempts to integrate it into his or her belief system. The client may generate maladaptive cognitions about intrapersonal, interpersonal, or environmental stimuli. Transgression, threat, or loss may be perceived in relation to physical needs such as food, shelter, and safety; psychological needs such as self-concept, emotional stability, and identity; relationship needs such as family, friends, coworkers, and community support; and moral and spiritual needs such as integrity and values. To differentiate between transgression, threat, and loss, think of these dimensions in terms of time. *Transgression* is the cognition that something bad is happening in the present moment, *threat* is the cognition that something bad will occur, and *loss* is the cognition that something bad has occurred. When cognitions of the crisis move to the severe impairment end of the continuum, the perception of the event may be so extreme as to put the client or others at physical risk. Sometimes the client's thinking moves from "It's a pain in the neck that this is happening, but I'll get over it" to "It's absolutely intolerable, I will not stand for this, and I'll never get over it." This kind of shift, from cool to hot cognitions (Dryden, 1984), is setting the client up to make some bad decisions. Such decisions most probably will result in even worse behavioral consequences for the client and others.

Certainly the innate intellectual capacity of clients has much to do with how they respond cognitively to a crisis and how the crisis worker should respond to them. Given the same crisis, a client with borderline intelligence may perseverate on the need to obtain basic nurturance while an intellectually gifted person might brood on the existential issue of whether God had a hand in the crisis.

There are four basic areas of cognitive functioning that are likely to become involved in a crisis: physical, psychological, social relationships, and moral/spiritual beliefs. These look a lot like Maslow's needs hierarchy, and in some ways they are and some ways they aren't. In a disaster, as you will see in Chapter 17, people are pretty much concerned with getting food in their bellies and a roof over their heads first and worrying about other things second. On the other hand, it is not uncommon for all of these dimensions to come into play at once. Physical: "I am hungry, cold, and don't know how much longer I can stand it on top of this roof." Psychological: "I screwed up by not listening and preparing for the hurricane." Social: "Where is my family? Have they survived?" Moral/Spiritual: "How could God have done this to us?"

Some of you who are reading this book may take issue with the moral/spiritual component if you are agnostic, atheist, or just think the supreme being is currently on vacation in an alternate universe. But whatever your spiritual persuasion and whether you believe deities are named the Great Spirit, Allah, God, Vishnu, a large Douglas fir tree, your personal fitness trainer, guru, or preacher, or Charlie Brown's Great Pumpkin, we believe as others do that spirituality is a key component in the crisis business. We like Pargament and Sweeney's definition (2011) of spirit in their work developing the spiritual fitness component of the new U.S. Army's Comprehensive Soldier Fitness Program (see Chapter 7, Posttraumatic Stress Disorder). They define *spirit* as "the essential core of the individual, the deepest part of the self, and one's involving human essence" and *spirituality* as "the continuous journey people take to discover and realize their essential selves." Pargament (2007) adds that it is looking for the *sacred* in one's life. If you think that people who are in crisis don't get down to the core of their being and at times try like crazy to figure out what is sacred, morally right, and how their spirit and spirituality tie into this business, and that this is not really worthy of your consideration, you would be dead wrong.

Comparison With Precrisis Functioning. Although it may not always be possible, the worker should seek to assess the client's precrisis functioning with the TAF as a guide to determine how effectively the client functioned prior to the event. Comparing precrisis ratings with current ratings lets the worker gauge the degree of deviation from the client's typical affective, behavioral, and cognitive operating levels. The worker can then tell how atypical the client's functioning is, whether there has been a radical shift in that functioning, and whether that functioning is transitory or chronic. For example, a very different approach would be used to counsel someone with chronic schizophrenia suffering auditory hallucinations compared to an individual experiencing similar hallucinations from a prescription drug. Such an assessment can be made in one or two questions without having to ferret out a great deal of background information.

Rating Clients. In rating clients on the TAF, we move from high to low. This backward rating process may seem confusing at first glance, but the idea is that we rule out more severe impairment first. So if we were rating affect, we would first look at whether the client fits any of the descriptors under Severe Impairment. If not, we would then consider the descriptors under Marked Impairment. If we were able to check off at least half of those descriptors, the client would receive a rating of 9. If we could identify fewer than half of the descriptors, the client would receive an 8. We would repeat this rating process across all three dimensions to obtain a total rating. Based on the total rating, which will range from 3 to 30, we generally group clients into three categories. A 3–10 rating means minimal impairment; these clients are generally self-directing and able

to function effectively on their own. A rating of 11–19 means that clients are more impaired; they may have difficulty functioning on their own and need help and direction. Clients with a total score of 20 or above are moving deeper into harm's way; they are likely to need a great deal of direction and a secure and safe environment. Scores in the high 20s almost always mean that some degree of lethality is involved, whether it is premeditated or clients are simply so out of control that they cannot stay out of harm's way.

Rating clients on the triage scale also means rating the crisis worker! How is this so? If the worker is effective in stabilizing a client, the triage scale score should go down. If it does not, then the worker probably needs to shift gears and try another approach. While the TAF is not absolutely precise and is not intended to be, it does give a good numerical anchor that the crisis worker can use in making judgments about client disposition and the effectiveness of the intervention. Our students very quickly become skillful at making these ratings on sample cases, and so will you.

One rating issue that constantly arises is the question, "What do you mean by severe? Shouldn't a mother who just got news that her son was badly injured in a school bus accident be pretty hysterical and out of control?" That is certainly true. However, what puts the mother into a crisis category and allows us to rate her as "severely impaired" on the TAF is twofold. First, even though the feelings, thoughts, and behaviors may seem reasonable responses given the horrific situation, what kind of potential trouble does that get the mother into? Are her feelings, thoughts, and actions liable to exacerbate the situation further? Second, it is not just the intensity but also the duration of the feelings, thoughts, and actions. We might reasonably expect an initial response that is highly volatile, but if after 4 hours that same degree of emotional energy were still present, it would be obvious that the client is out of control, in crisis, and in need of assistance.

Alternate Forms of the TAF

The TAF has been modified for use with police departments (Logan, Myer, & James, 2006), higher education/student affairs personnel (Armitage et al., 2007), and disaster relief workers (James, Blancett, & Addy, 2007), based on the increased interaction with and need to provide services or actions for mentally ill and emotionally disturbed individuals. All these alternate forms of the TAF have been developed because of the expanding needs of a variety of workers who do not have a mental health background yet who come in contact with emotionally disturbed individuals for whom they are expected to render service of some kind. All of the following variations of the TAF have been modified for ease and simplicity of use and are now undergoing field testing.

The Triage Assessment Checklist for Law Enforcement (TACKLE; James, Myer, & Moore, 2006) was developed in cooperation with a focus group of police officers and mental health workers from the Montgomery County, Maryland, police department. It is used by police officers to make on-the-scene assessments of how they are doing in defusing and deescalating emotionally out-of-control recipients of service, to provide the officers with concrete behavioral assessments for placing recipients of service under legal confinement for psychiatric evaluation and/or commitment, and to provide behavioral assessments in legal proceedings to back up actions taken against recipients of service (see Chapter 14, Violent Behavior in Institutions).

The Triage Assessment System for Students in Learning Environments (TASSLE; Myer et al., 2007) is used by campus residence-life personnel to make on-the-scene decisions about out-of-control students. Its primary use is by residence hall assistants and dorm directors in providing behavioral assessments to campus police and counseling centers in decisions on whether students represent a threat to themselves or others and whether the students constitute a disruption to the community learning environment (see Chapter 13, Crises in Schools). Other specific forms have been developed for civilians after a disaster—the Triage Assessment Severity Checklist–Civilian (TASC-C); James,

Blancett, & Addy, 2007)—families (Slagel, 2009), and organizations (Conte, 2005).

The second section of the TASSLE form is titled "Observations" (see Figure 3.3). This section is divided into three columns listing some of the behaviors that may be seen with an individual in crisis. Several of the items have been identified as critical for either getting students support or removing them from the residence hall. A general guideline is the more items you check, the more likely a person will either need support or should be removed. Most often checking numerous items means the individual's rating on the severity scales will also be high. High scores on the severity scales generally mean an increased need for support services and an increased potential for hospitalization.

The first column addresses psychological problems. Check appropriate descriptors in this section based on your observations and questioning of individuals. You may not be able to gather all this information because clients may be uncooperative or simply unable to respond to questions. A good source for some of this information is other people who may know the client. Asking them about the individual may give you the information needed to check the appropriate descriptors in this column. The second column focuses on clients that are dangerous to themselves or others. They may be only threatening harm or actually making suicidal or homicidal gestures. If they are simply threatening harm, you will need to make a judgment as to whether the person is an immediate danger to self or others. Simply making

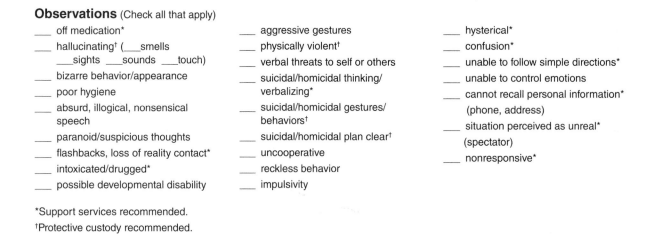

Observations (Check all that apply)

___ off medication*

___ hallucinating[†] (___smells
___sights ___sounds ___touch)

___ bizarre behavior/appearance

___ poor hygiene

___ absurd, illogical, nonsensical speech

___ paranoid/suspicious thoughts

___ flashbacks, loss of reality contact*

___ intoxicated/drugged*

___ possible developmental disability

___ aggressive gestures

___ physically violent[†]

___ verbal threats to self or others

___ suicidal/homicidal thinking/ verbalizing*

___ suicidal/homicidal gestures/ behaviors[†]

___ suicidal/homicidal plan clear[†]

___ uncooperative

___ reckless behavior

___ impulsivity

___ hysterical*

___ confusion*

___ unable to follow simple directions*

___ unable to control emotions

___ cannot recall personal information* (phone, address)

___ situation perceived as unreal* (spectator)

___ nonresponsive*

*Support services recommended.

[†]Protective custody recommended.

FIGURE 3.3   Triage Assessment System for Students in Learning Environments (TASSLE): Observational Checklist.
SOURCE: Myer et al., 2007.

threats to harm oneself or others does not automatically mean the student needs support services or removal. A standard guideline is if a person has a plan formulated and if the means to carry out the plan are available, that person is a threat and needs to be monitored in a safe place by qualified mental health workers until the threat has abated.

The third column relates to the severity scales most directly. Listed in this column are feelings, behaviors, and thoughts persons may experience when in a crisis. These correspond to characteristics on the severity scales. Generally, you can complete this section based on your observations and experience with students. Four of the descriptors have been identified as being critical: (1) hysterical, (2) confusion, (3) unable to follow simple directions, and (4) nonresponsive. Individuals who fit these descriptors are vulnerable, mentally fragile, and unable to care for themselves.

In summary, the TAF and its derivative alternate forms provide multiple three-dimensional combinations of the domains of assessment regarding the degree of impairment the crisis is causing, target specific areas of functioning, and let the crisis worker evaluate the client quickly and then construct specific interventions aimed directly at areas of greatest immediate concern.

Psychobiological Assessment

Although psychobiological assessment for psychopathology is beyond the scope of this book and most crisis situations, in terms of both immediacy of assessment and the assessment skills required of most human services workers, there is clear evidence that neurotransmitters play an exceedingly important role in the affective, behavioral, and cognitive functioning of individuals both during a crisis and, for some, long after a crisis (Briere & Scott, 2006; Solms &Turnbull, 2002; Strawn & Geracioti, 2008; van der Kolk, 1996a; Vermetten & Bremmer, 2002; Yehuda, 2006; Yehuda & LeDoux, 2007). It is becoming pretty clear that the limbic system in the brain plays a part in "catching" and "carrying" PTSD. It also appears possible that the gene pool you jumped out of may have something to do with how susceptible you are to PTSD, because there is substantive evidence that a lesser volume of certain limbic system components makes people more susceptible to PTSD. The good news is that certain drug therapies and psychotherapies can potentially increase the volume and change neurotransmitter conductivity that goes with symptomatic improvement in PTSD (Felmingham et al., 2007; Gilbertson et al., 2002; Shin, Rauch, & Pittman, 2006; Vermetten et al., 2003).

For at least three reasons, human psychobiology can be an important consideration in crisis intervention. First, evidence exists that when people are involved in traumatic events, dramatic changes occur in the discharge of neurotransmitters, such as endorphins, and in the central and peripheral sympathetic nervous systems and the hypothalamic-pituitary-adrenocortical axis. These two systems regulate one another. When PTSD enters the picture, the balance of these two systems is not maintained and the responses of both systems are affected (Raison & Miller, 2003). These neurological changes may become residual and long-term and have subtle and degrading effects on emotions, acting, and thinking (Burgess-Watson, Hoffman, & Wilson, 1988; Solms & Turnbull, 2002; van der Kolk, 1996b). Client education about the psychobiological effects of trauma is important in letting clients know they are not going "nuts" and that the urges of their bodies to spring into physical action even though the original stressor is long past have a neurological basis (Halpern & Tramontin, 2007, p. 83).

Second, research indicates that abnormal changes in neurotransmitters such as dopamine, norepinephrine, and serotonin are involved in mental disorders that range from schizophrenia (Crow & Johnstone, 1987) to depression (Healy, 1987). Decreased levels of cortisol and neuropeptide Y have been demonstrated in individuals living in chronic stressful conditions and have also been found in persons with PTSD and appears to be a predictor of it (Morgan et al., 2001; Southwick et al., 1999). Psychotropic drugs are routinely used for a host of mental disorders to counteract such neurological changes. A common problem faced by human services workers and police officers is the deranged or violent client who has gone off medication because of its unpleasant side effects or an inability to remember when to take it (Ammar & Burdin, 1991; Miller, 2006). Individuals with psychosis who have gone off their medication and taken their reactivated psychosis out onto the streets are legion and are the bane of crisis intervention team police officers.

Third, both legal and illegal drugs have a major effect on mental health. Although the way illegal drugs change brain chemistry and behavior has gained wide attention, legal drugs may promote adverse psychological side effects in just as dramatic a manner. In particular, combinations of nonpsychotropic drugs are routinely given to combat several degenerative diseases in the elderly. At times, these drugs may have interactive effects that generate unanticipated psychological disturbances. One has to read no further than the consumer trade books on prescribed drugs to obtain a rather frightening understanding of the psychological side effects prescription drugs can cause.

Therefore, the human services worker should attempt to assess prior trauma, psychopathology, and use, misuse, or abuse of legal and illegal drugs in an effort to determine whether they correlate with the current problem. "Talking" therapies do little good when neurobiological substrates are involved. If the human services worker has reason to suspect any of the foregoing problems, an immediate referral should be made for a neurological/drug evaluation. Officer Lewis's question about how much Leron had been drinking is almost a default question in regard to use or misuse of both prescription and nonprescription medications.

The following questions are practically mandatory during initial exploration activities with a person in crisis and should be asked in a nonaccusatory way.

Crisis worker: Lots of times people have a reaction to medication or changes in medication. Are you on any medication right now? Is it for emotional problems? Have you stopped taking it? Are you on any medications for other physical problems? Have you stopped taking or changed medications? Did you have any alcoholic beverages with your medication? Has there been any way you feel like you have changed or felt different since you went on or changed or went off a medication?

Assessing the Client's Current Emotional Functioning

Four major factors in assessing the client's emotional stability are (1) the *duration* of the crisis, (2) the *degree* of emotional stamina or coping at the client's disposal at the moment, (3) the *ecosystem* within which the client resides, and (4) the *developmental stage* of the client.

The duration factor concerns the time frame of the crisis. Is it a onetime crisis? Is it recurring? Has it been plaguing the client for a long time? A onetime crisis of relatively short duration is called *acute* or *situational*. A long-term pattern of recurring crisis is labeled *chronic, long-term,* or *transcrisis.*

The degree factor concerns the client's current reservoir of emotional coping stamina. During normal periods of the client's life the coping reservoir is relatively full, but during crisis the client's reservoir is relatively empty. Assessing the degree factor, then, involves the

crisis worker's determining how much emotional coping strength is left in the client's reservoir. Has the client run out of gas, or can the client make it over a small hill?

The ecosystem is a very large extraneous variable that can dramatically influence client coping (Collins & Collins, 2005; Halpern & Tramontin, 2007; James, Cogdal, & Gilliland, 2003; Myer & Moore, 2006). Geographic region and accessibility, communication systems, language, cultural mores, religious beliefs, economic status, and social micro- and macrosystem interactions are only some of the ecosystemic variables that may have subtle or profound effects on a client's emotional coping ability. No individual's crisis can be taken out of the ecosystemic context in which it occurs, and to believe it can be somehow treated separately without considering that context is to make a grave intervention error.

Developmental stages (Collins & Collins, 2005) certainly play a part in the client's emotional functioning during a crisis. Merely transitioning from life stage to life stage has its own potential for crises (Blocher, 2000; Erikson, 1963). Understanding the developmental tasks of different life stages, which may frame a client's view of a crisis and how the client responds to it, is critical for crisis workers. Further compounding the issue, developmental tasks are sometimes not accomplished at a particular life stage, and developmental crises occur (Levinson, 1986). It does not take much imagination to foresee that adding a situational crisis may have a tremendous impact on a "stuck-in-stage" individual's emotional coping skills.

The Client's Current Acute or Chronic State. In assessing the crisis client's emotional functioning, it is important that the crisis worker determine whether the client is a normal person who is in a *onetime* situational crisis or a person with a *chronic,* crisis-oriented life history. The onetime crisis is assessed and treated quite differently from the chronic crisis. The onetime crisis client usually requires direct intervention to facilitate getting over the specific event or situation that precipitated the crisis. Having reached a state of precrisis equilibrium, the client can usually draw on normal coping mechanisms and support people and manage independently.

The chronic crisis client usually requires a greater length of time in counseling. That individual typically needs the help of a crisis worker in examining available coping mechanisms, finding support people, rediscovering strategies that worked during previous crises, generating new coping strategies, and gaining affirmation and encouragement from the worker and others as sources of strength by which to move beyond the present crisis. The chronic case frequently requires referral for long-term professional help.

The Client's Reservoir of Emotional Strength. The client who lacks emotional strength needs more direct responses from the crisis worker than the client who retains a good deal of emotional strength. A feeling of hopelessness or helplessness is a clue to a low reservoir of emotional strength. In some cases, the assessment can be enhanced by asking open-ended questions for the specific purpose of measuring that reservoir. Typically, if the reservoir is low, the client will have a distorted view of the past and present and will not be able to envision a future. Such questions can reveal the degree of emotional stamina remaining: "Picture yourself after the current crisis has been solved. Tell me what you're seeing and how you're feeling. How do you wish you were feeling? How were you feeling about this before the crisis got so bad? Where do you see yourself headed with this problem?" In general, the lower the reservoir of emotional strength, the less the client can get hold of the future. The client with an empty reservoir might respond with a blank stare or by saying something like "There are no choices" or "No, I can't see anything. The future is blank. I can see no future." The worker's assessment of the client's current degree of emotional strength will have definite implications for the strategies and level of action the worker will employ during the remainder of the counseling.

Strategies for Assessing Emotional Status.   The crisis worker who assesses the client's total emotional status may look at a wide array of factors that affect both the duration (chronic versus acute) and the degree (reservoir of strength) of emotional stability. Some factors to be considered are the client's age, educational level, family situation, marital status, vocational maturity and job stability, financial stability and obligations, drug and/or alcohol use, legal history (arrests, convictions, probations), social background, level of intelligence, lifestyle, religious orientation, ability to sustain close personal relationships, tolerance for ambiguity, physical health, medical history, and past history of dealing with crises. A candid look at such factors helps the crisis worker decide whether the client will require quick referral (for medical treatment or examination),

brief counseling, long-term therapy, or referral to a specific agency.

Ordinarily, no one factor alone can be used to conclude that the client's reservoir of emotional coping ability is empty. However, some patterns can often be pieced together to form a general picture. A person in middle age who has experienced many disappointments related to undereducation would be viewed differently from a young person who has experienced a first career disappointment. A person who has experienced many serious medical problems and hospital stays would feel different from a person who is having a first encounter with a medical problem. The foregoing example is a *facilitative* affective assessment of the individual. By "facilitative assessment," we mean that data gleaned about the client are used as a part of the ongoing helping process, not simply filed away or kept in the worker's head.

Assessing Alternatives, Coping Mechanisms, and Support Systems

Throughout the helping process the crisis worker keeps in mind and builds a repertory of options, evaluating their appropriateness for the client. In assessing alternatives available to the client, the worker must first consider the client's viewpoint, mobility, and capability of taking advantage of the alternatives. The worker's own objective view of available alternatives is an additional dimension.

Alternatives include a repository of appropriate referral resources available to the client. Even though the client may be looking for only one or two concrete action steps or options, the worker brainstorms, in collaboration with the client, to develop a list of possibilities that can be evaluated. Most will be discarded before the client can own and commit to a definite course of action. The worker ponders questions such as, What actions or choices does the client have now that would restore the person to a precrisis state of autonomy? What realistic actions (coping mechanisms) can the client take? What institutional, social, vocational, or personal (people) strengths or support systems are available? (Note that "support systems" refers to people!) Who would care about and be open to assisting the client? What are the financial, social, vocational, and personal impediments to client progress?

Assessing for Suicide/Homicide Potential

Not every crisis involves the client's contemplating suicide or homicide. However, in dealing with crisis clients, workers must always explore the possibility of harm to self or others, because destructive behavior takes many forms and wears many masks. Crisis workers need to be both wary of and competent in their appraisal of potential suicidal and homicidal clients. What may appear to the crisis worker as the main problem may camouflage the real issue: the intent of the client to take his or her life, or someone else's life. Contrary to popular belief, most suicidal and homicidal clients emit definite clues and believe they are calling out for help or signaling warnings. However, even the client's closest friends may ignore those clues and do nothing about them. For that reason, every crisis problem should be assessed as to its potential for suicide and homicide. The most important aspect of suicidal/homicidal evaluation is the crisis evaluator's realization that suicide and homicide are always possible in all types of clients.

SUMMARY

The hybrid model in this chapter has to do with tasks to be accomplished during a crisis that do not always move in a stepwise linear progression. Overarching all tasks is safety—not only for the client, but for others and the worker as well. Making initial contact in a crisis is not always easy. That's why we have designated predispositioning, engaging, and initiating contact as a new primary task that is critical in laying the groundwork for the intervention to follow. Problem exploration includes affective, behavioral, and cognitive dimensions of the current crisis; it involves finding out what got the immediate crisis going and generally does not delve into all the past issues of the client. Providing support means finding what human resources are available to help the client and what role the crisis worker will play in either finding or being part of the support system. Examining alternatives and options, making plans, obtaining commitments, and following up are neither extensive nor long-term. They are target-specific attempts to find short-term solutions to restore precrisis equilibrium.

A major difference between crisis intervention and other human services endeavors, such as counseling, social work, and psychotherapy, is that the crisis worker generally does not have time to gather or analyze all the background and other assessment data that might normally be available under less stressful conditions. A key component of a highly functioning crisis worker is the ability to take the data available and make some meaningful sense out of it. This may be somewhat unsettling to those human services workers who are accustomed to having complete social and psychological workups available to them before they proceed with intervention. However, the ability to quickly evaluate the degree of client disequilibrium and immobility—and to be flexible enough to change your evaluation as changing conditions warrant—is a priority skill that students

should seek to cultivate. That's why you have been introduced to the hybrid task model and the Triage Assessment Form.

From onset to resolution of the crisis, assessment is a central, continuous process. The crisis worker must not assume that because the crisis appears on the surface to have been resolved, assessment is no longer needed. The balance sheet of assessing the client's crisis in terms of severity, current emotional status, alternatives, situational supports, coping mechanisms, resources, and level of lethality is never complete until the client has achieved his or her precrisis level of mobility, equilibrium, and autonomy. Only then are the psychological debts of the client reconciled. The resumption of precrisis equilibrium does not imply that the client needs no developmental or long-term therapy or medical treatment. It does mean that the crisis worker's job is done, and the acute phase of the crisis is over.

 To see some of the concepts discussed in this chapter in action, refer to your *Crisis Intervention in Action* DVD, or see the clips online on the Counseling CourseMate website. To access this site, go to www.cengagebrain.com, where you'll also find an eBook, additional study tools, quizzes, and more. Suppose you are part of the team working with Amy, who is in a terrible personal and economic mess. Using the assessment techniques in this chapter, what rating do you give her in the beginning as opposed to the end of the session? What's your basis for doing so? Now become Dr. James for a moment. What do you have to say to the team as far as their ability to get through the tasks in the model is concerned?

REFERENCES

Aguilera, D. C. (1998). *Crisis intervention: Theory and methodology* (8th ed.). St. Louis, MO: Mosby.

Ammar, A., & Burdin, S. (1991, April). *Psychoactive medication: An introduction and overview.* Paper presented at the Fifteenth Annual Convening of Crisis Intervention Personnel, Chicago.

Armitage, D., Rice, D., James, R., & Groenendyk, P. (2007, July). *Triage for psychological disorders.* Paper presented at the Association of College and University Housing Officers Convention, Seattle, WA.

Blancett, J. (2008). *A reliability and validity study of the Triage Assessment System for Students in Learning Environments.* University of Memphis, Memphis, TN.

Blocher, D. H. (2000). *Counseling: A developmental approach* (4th ed.). New York: John Wiley & Sons.

Briere, J., & Scott, C. (2006). *Principles of trauma therapy: A guide to symptoms, evaluation, and treatment.* Thousand Oaks, CA: Sage.

Burgess-Watson, I. P., Hoffman, L., & Wilson, G. V. (1988). The neuropsychiatry of posttraumatic stress disorder. *British Journal of Psychiatry, 152,* 164–173.

Cohen, S. (2004). Social relationships and health. *American Psychologist, 59,* 676–684.

Collins, B. G., & Collins, T. M. (2005). *Crisis and trauma: Developmental-ecological intervention.* Lahaska, PA: Lahaska Press.

Conte, C. (2005). *Examination of the reliability and validity of the Triage Assessment Survey: Organizations.* Duquesne University, Pittsburgh, PA.

Cormier, W. H., & Cormier, L. S. (1991). *Interviewing strategies for helpers: Fundamental skills and cognitive behavioral interventions* (3rd ed.). Pacific Grove, CA: Brooks/Cole.

Courtois, C. A., & Ford, J. D. (Eds.). (2009). *Treating complex traumatic stress disorders: An evidence-based guide.* New York: Guilford Press.

Courtois, C. A., Ford, J. D., & Cloitre, M. (2009). Best practices in psychotherapy for adults. In C. A. Courtois & J. D. Ford (Eds.), *Treating complex traumatic stress disorders: An evidence-based guide* (pp. 82–103). New York: Guilford Press.

Crow, G. A. (1977). *Crisis intervention: A social interaction approach.* New York: Association Press.

Crow, T. J., & Johnstone, E. C. (1987). Schizophrenia: Nature of the disease process and its biological correlates. *Handbook of physiology* (Vol. 5). Bethesda, MD: American Physiological Society.

Dollard, J., Doob, L. W., Miller, N. E., Mower, O. H., & Sears, R. R. (1939). *Frustration and aggression.* New Haven, CT: Yale University Press.

Dryden, W. (1984). *Rational emotive therapy: Fundamentals and innovations.* London: Croom Helm.

Ellis, A. (1971). *Growth through reason.* Palo Alto, CA: Science and Behavior Books. Hollywood, CA: Wilshire Books.

Ellis, A., & Abrahms, E. (1978). *Brief psychotherapy in medical and health practice.* New York: Springer.

Ellis, A., & Grieger, R. (1977). *Handbook of rational-emotive therapy.* New York: Springer.

Ellis, A., & Harper, R. A. (1975). *A new guide to rational living* (Rev. ed.). Hollywood, CA: Wilshire Books.

Erikson, E. H. (1963). *Childhood and society* (2nd ed.). New York: Norton.

Felmingham, K., Kemp, A., Williams, L., Das, P., Hughes, G. Peduto, A., et al. (2007). Changes in anterior cingulate and amygdala after cognitive behavior therapy of posttraumatic stress disorder. *Psychological Science, 18,* 127–129.

Gilbertson, M. W., Shenton, M. E., Ciszewski, A., Kasai, K., Lasko, N. B., Orr, S. P., et al. (2002). Smaller hippocampal volume predicts pathologic vulnerability to psychological trauma. *Neuroscience, 5,* 1242–1247.

Halpern, J., & Tramontin, M. (2007). *Disaster mental health: Theory and practice.* Belmont, CA: Thomson Brooks/Cole.

Healy, D. (1987). Rhythm and blues: Neurochemical, neuropharmacological, and neuropsychological implications of a hypothesis of circadian rhythm dysfunction in the affective disorders. *Psychopharmacology, 93,* 271–285.

Hersh, J. B. (1985). Interviewing college students in crisis. *Journal of Counseling and Development, 63,* 286–289.

James, R. K., Blancett, J., & Addy, C. (2007, March). *Adapting the TACKLE form to civilian use: The Triage Assessment Severity Checklist for Civilians.* Paper presented at the Thirty-First Convening of Crisis Intervention Personnel and Contact USA, Chicago.

James, R. K., Cogdal, P., & Gilliland, B. E. (2003, April). *Crisis intervention in the ecosystem.* Paper presented at the American Counseling Association Convention, Kansas City, MO.

James, R. K., Myer, R., & Moore, H. (2006). *Triage Assessment Checklist for Law Enforcement (TACKLE) manual and CD.* Pittsburgh, PA: Crisis Intervention and Prevention Solutions.

Kanel, K. (1999). *A guide to crisis intervention.* Pacific Grove, CA: Brooks-Cole.

Kleespies, P. M. (2009). *Behavioral emergencies: An evidence-based resource for evaluating and managing risk of suicide, violence, and victimization.* Washington, DC: American Psychological Association.

Kleespies, P. M., & Richmond, J. S. (2009). Evaluating behavioral emergencies. In P. M. Kleespies (Ed.), *Behavioral emergencies: An evidence-based resource for evaluating and managing risk of suicide, violence, and victimization* (pp. 33–58). Washington, DC: American Psychological Association.

Lester, D. (2002). *Crisis intervention and counseling by telephone.* Springfield, IL: Charles C. Thomas.

Levinson, J. D. (1986). A conception of adult development. *American Psychologist, 41*(1), 3–13.

Logan, J., Myer, R., & James, R. (2006). *How to TACKLE an excessive force complaint.* Paper presented at the Second Annual Crisis Intervention Team Conference, Orlando, FL.

Memphis Police Department. (2010). *Crisis intervention training manual.* Memphis, TN: Author.

Miller, L. (2006). *Practical police psychology.* Springfield, IL: Charles C. Thomas.

Morgan, C. A., Wang, S., Rasmusson, A., Hazlett, G., Anderson, G., & Charney, D. S. (2001). Relationship among plasma cortisol, catecholamines, neuropeptide Y, and human performance during exposure to uncontrollable stress. *Psychosomatic Medicine, 63,* 412–422.

Myer, R. A. (2001). *Assessment for crisis intervention: A triage assessment model.* Belmont, CA: Thomson Brooks/Cole.

Myer, R. A., James, R. K., & Moulton, P. (2011). *This is not a fire drill: Crisis intervention and prevention on college campuses.* Hoboken, NJ: John Wiley & Sons.

Myer, R. A., & Moore, H. (2006). Crisis in context theory: An ecological model. *Journal of Counseling & Development, 84,* 139–147.

Myer, R. A., Rice, D., Moulton, P., Cogdal, P., Allen, S., & James, R. (2007). *Triage Assessment System for Students in Learning Environments (TASSLE) manual and CD.* Pittsburgh, PA: Crisis Intervention and Prevention Solutions.

Myer, R. A., Williams, R. C., Ottens, A. J., & Schmidt, A. E. (1991). *Three-dimensional crisis assessment model.* Unpublished manuscript, Department of Educational Psychology, Counseling, and Special Education, Northern Illinois University, DeKalb.

Myer, R. A., Williams, R. C., Ottens, A. J., & Schmidt, A. E. (1992). A three-dimensional model for triage. *Journal of Mental Health Counseling, 14,* 137–148.

Ochberg, F. M. (1988). *Post-traumatic therapy and victims of violence.* New York: Brunner/Mazel.

Pargament, K. I. (2007). *Spiritually integrated psychotherapy: Understanding and addressing the sacred.* New York: Guilford Press.

Pargament, K. I., & Sweeney, P. J. (2011). Building spiritual fitness in the Army. *American Psychologist, 66*(1), 58–64.

Pazar, J. (2005). *A reliability study of the triage assessment scale.* Unpublished doctoral dissertation, University of Memphis.

Prochaska, J. O., DiClemente, C. C., & Norcross, J. C. (1992). In search of how people change: Applications to addictive behaviors. *American Psychologist, 47,* 1102–1114.

Raison, C. L., & Miller, A. H. (2003). When not enough is too much: The role of insufficient glucocorticoid signaling in the pathophysiology of stress-related disorders. *American Journal of Psychiatry, 169,* 1554–1565.

Roberts, A. R. (2005). *Crisis intervention handbook: Assessment, treatment, and research* (3rd ed.). New York: Oxford University Press.

Ruzek, J. L. (2006). Models of early intervention. In E. C. Ritchie, P. J. Watson, & M. J. Friedman (Eds.), *Interventions following mass violence and disasters: Strategies for mental health practice* (pp. 16–34). New York: Guilford Press.

Shin, L. M., Rauch, S. L., & Pittman, R. K. (2006). Amygdala, medial prefrontal cortex and hippocampal function in PTSD. *Annals of the New York Academy of Sciences, 1071,* 67–79.

Slagel, L. (2009). *Examination of the reliability and validity of the Triage Assessment Survey: Families.* Duquesne University, Pittsburgh, PA.

Slaikeu, K. A. (1990). *Crisis intervention: A handbook for practice and research* (2nd ed.). Boston: Allyn & Bacon.

Solms, M., & Turnbull, O. (2002). *The brain and the inner world: An introduction to the neuroscience of subjective experience.* New York: Other Press.

Southwick, S. M., Bremer, J. D., Rasmusson, A., Morgan, C. A., Arnsten, A., & Charney, D. S. (1999). Role of norepinephrine in the pathophysiology and treatment of posttraumatic stress disorder. *Biological Psychiatry, 46,* 1192–1204.

Strawn, J. R., & Geracioti, T. D., Jr. (2008). Noradrenergic dysfunction and the psychopharmacology of posttraumatic stress disorder. *Depression and Anxiety, 25,* 260–271.

van der Kolk, B. A. (1996a). The body keeps the score: Approaches to the psychobiology of posttraumatic stress disorder. In B. A. van der Kolk, A. C. McFarlane, & L. Weisaeth (Eds.), *Traumatic stress* (pp. 214–241). New York: Guilford Press.

van der Kolk, B. A. (1996b). Trauma and memory. In B. A. van der Kolk, A. C. McFarlane, & L. Weisaeth (Eds.), *Traumatic stress* (pp. 279–297). New York: Guilford Press.

Vermetten, E., & Bremmer, J. D. (2002). Circuits and systems in stress: Part 2. Applications to neurobiology and treatment in posttraumatic stress disorder. *Depression and Anxiety, 16,* 14–38.

Vermetten, E., Vythilingam, M., Southwick, S. M., Charney, D. S., & Bremmer, J. D. (2003). Long-term treatment with paroxetin increases verbal declarative memory and hippocampal volume in posttraumatic stress disorder. *Biological Psychiatry, 54,* 693–702.

Watters, D. (1997). A study of the reliability of the Triage Severity Scale. (Doctoral dissertation, University of Memphis.) *Dissertation Abstracts International, 58-08A,* 3028.

Yehuda, R. (2006). Advances in the understanding neuroendocrine alterations in PTSD and their therapeutic implications. *Annals of the New York Academy of Sciences, 1071,* 137–166.

Yehuda, R., & LeDoux, J. (2007). Response variation following trauma: A translational neuroscience approach to understanding PTSD. *Neuron, 56,* 19–32.

CHAPTER 4

The Tools of the Trade

Introduction

Accurate and well-honed listening skills are necessary and indeed sometimes sufficient skills that all therapists, but particularly crisis interventionists, must have. For that reason, listening skills are a major component of the crisis intervention model. Our preferred conceptual model for effective listening comes from person-centered counseling (Egan, 1982, 1990; Rogers, 1977). In this chapter, we present brief descriptions of generic techniques that are applicable to many types of crisis. Excerpts from real-life clients, called Rita, Jake, and Jean, are scattered throughout the rest of this chapter to illustrate helpful (as well as unhelpful) strategies.

Listening in Crisis Intervention
Open-Ended Questions

Often workers are frustrated by a client's lack of response and enthusiasm. Workers may make statements such as "All my clients ever do is grunt or shake their heads indicating yes or no." We can do something about getting fuller, more meaningful responses if we ask questions that are not dead ends. Open-ended questions usually start with *what* or *how* or ask for more clarification or details. Open-ended questions encourage clients to respond with full statements and at deeper levels of meaning. Remember that open-ended questions are used to elicit from clients something about their feelings, thoughts, and behaviors and are particularly helpful in the Problem Exploration task. Here are some guidelines for forming open-ended questions.

1. *Request description:* "Please tell me . . . ," "Tell me about . . . ," "Show me . . . ," "In what ways does . . . ?"
2. *Focus on plans:* "What will you do . . . ?" "How will you make it happen?" "How will that help you to . . . ?"
3. *Expansion:* "Tell me more," "Could you give me some more details?" "How about expanding on that a bit," "So then what happened?"
4. *Assessment:* "How is that different from before?" "What are you doing about that? "When that happened, how did you handle it?" "Who might you get to help you?"
5. *Stay away from "why" questions:* Beginners in the crisis intervention business invariably are intrigued and puzzled by the odd and bizarre things people in crisis think, feel, and do. As a result, beginners feel compelled to find out why a person thinks, feels, or does those "really crazy" things. It is our contention that "why" questions are generally poor choices for obtaining more information. Even though they may provide the client with an opening to talk more, they also make the client defend his or her actions. Notice the response of Jake, the husband of Rita, whom you will meet later in this chapter, as the crisis worker queries him about the reasons for his behavior.

CW: Why do you continue to beat your wife?

Jake: Hey! If she'd be a little more affectionate, I wouldn't have to beat her up! It's her fault!

As this example demonstrates, what generally happens is that clients become defensive and attempt to intellectualize about the problem or externalize it to somebody or something else without taking responsibility for or ownership of the problem.

Closed-Ended Questions

Closed-ended questions seek specific, concrete information from the client. They are designed to elicit specific behavioral data and yes or no responses. Closed questions usually begin with verbs such as *do, did, does, can, have, had, will, are, is,* and *was.* Contrary to what typically occurs in long-term therapy, closed-ended questions are often used early on in crisis intervention to obtain specific information that will help the crisis worker make a fast assessment of what is occurring. In most counseling programs closed-end questions are a "no-no!" because they indeed tend to close off interaction rather than facilitate dialogue. Thus, using closed questions is problematic for many graduate students whose instructors have harped at them, "Keep it open!" Whereas in long-term therapy the formulation of a plan of attack on the problem might be weeks or months in the making, crisis intervention often calls for instigating plans of action immediately. Closed-ended questions are particularly suited to obtaining commitments to take action. They are also highly appropriate in regard to safety issues. We don't mince words about safety issues, and we are not interested in circuitous responses. "Are you going to kill yourself?" may seem insensitive, coarse, and callous. It is not! We'll have a great deal more to say about this issue in Chapter 8, Crises of Lethality.

Here are some guidelines for forming closed-ended questions.

1. *Request specific information:* "When was the first time this happened?" "Where are you going to go?" "Are you thinking of hurting her?" "Have you gone back there?" "Does this mean you are going to kill yourself?"
2. *Obtain a commitment:* "Are you willing to make an appointment to . . . ?" "Will you confront him about this?" "Do you agree to . . . ?" "When will you do this?"
3. *Increasing focus:* "Do you understand what I am saying?" "Can you do this for me now?" "Are you on track with me?"
4. *Avoid negative interrogatives:* A negative interrogative is a closed question often used as a subtle way to coerce the listener into agreeing with the speaker. *Don't, doesn't, isn't, aren't,* and *wouldn't* all tend to seek or imply agreement. The negative interrogative statement "Don't you believe that's true?" really is a camouflaged exclamatory statement saying, "I believe that's true, and if you have an ounce of sense you'll agree with me!"

CW: Don't you think it'd be a good idea if you stay away from Rita?

Such statements generally have little place in a crisis interventionist's repertoire of verbal skills. A far better way of asking for compliance is with an assertive owning statement.

CW: Jake, I understand how difficult it is for you, but for the sake of both you and Rita, I'd really like you to continue to build on last week's success by agreeing to the "stay away from her" contract again this week.

Restatement and Summary Clarification

Restatement and summary clarification are critical ingredients in crisis intervention. Clients in crisis may have difficulty expressing themselves because of their disjointed thought processes or the chaos that is going on around them in the environment. By restating what the client is saying in the crisis worker's own words, the crisis worker can gain agreement from the client on what the client is attempting to say, feel, think, and do. Further, good restatement is particularly important in crisis because it tells the client that "Somebody is listening to me!" Restatement generally has to do with the content of the crisis event rather than the underlying feelings and thoughts about it. A sort of a default way of looking at this technique is using a famous line coined by Sgt. Joe Friday in the TV series *Dragnet*, "All we want are the facts," and then giving those facts back in your own words. Restatement can also serve as an effective break point for a client who is freewheeling in an ideational flight of emotions or thoughts.

CW: Time out a second, Jake. You've put a lot out here and my memory banks are getting pretty full. Let me summarize what you've said, and let's see if we are on the same track.

Restatement sounds simple. It is simple if the crisis worker focuses totally on the client's world. Restatement is not simple if the crisis worker is distracted by environmental stimuli or becomes preoccupied with his or her own thoughts, questions, evaluations, agenda, biases, or stereotypes about what the client is saying. So be wary! There are usually lots of environmental stimuli in a crisis, and it is easy to become distracted. Finally, summary clarification ribbon-wraps the dialogue. That is, it packages the preceding dialogue and lets both client and crisis worker know they are on the same wavelength. Particularly at the commitment stage, the crisis worker or, better yet, clients may be asked to summarize what the plan is and how they are going to go about doing it.

CW: I want you to summarize what the game plan is, then, when the urge starts to overtake you to go see Rita.

Jake: Okay, so I do this thought-stopping thing when the urge to give her a call or cruise by her house starts going off in my head. I don't go to my favorite bar because that just adds to it. Instead I go to the driving range and start hitting golf balls or go get on my game machine and kill aliens. When I get settled down, I write down all my thoughts and feelings and bring them into you next session. As a last resort, I call the crisis line.

Owning Feelings

Owning means communicating possession: "That's mine." Often in conversation we avoid specific issues by "disowning" statements with phrases such as "They say . . . ," "I heard the other day that you . . . ," "It's not right for you to . . . ," and "Don't you think you ought to . . . ?" Whether intentional or not, such verbal manipulation functions to avoid ownership of responsibility for what's being said or to avoid awareness of one's own thoughts and feelings concerning an issue.

Using owning or "I" statements is probably more important in crisis intervention than in other kinds of therapy because of the directive stance the crisis worker often has to take with clients who are immobile and in disequilibrium. It is further important in creating a direct bond between client and worker, particularly when a behavioral emergency is occurring and the worker wants the undivided attention of a wildly out-of-control client. Therefore, we illustrate a number of different types of owning statements the crisis worker may find useful for particular problems that occur during intervention. Although used more often in crisis intervention than in normal therapeutic settings, owning statements should nonetheless be employed sparingly, because the crisis worker's main job is to focus on the client and not on him- or herself. Given that admonition, when working with clients in crisis, it is very important to own your feelings, thoughts, and behaviors because many clients are using you as a model. So if you imply "We think this way" (meaning I and the director of the clinic, the school principal, the chief of police, the population of North America, the world, or God), then the client does not have much of a chance against that awesome cast and is liable to become dependently compliant or defensively hostile.

CW: (*authoritatively*) You know that the Family Trouble Center is a branch of the police department, and we can have you arrested, don't you?

Jake: (*defiantly*) Yeah, well, so what? I might as well be in jail anyway.

Collaborative Owning Statements. Early on in crisis intervention the use of "we" is generally not advised because it implies not only the interventionist's thoughts but a host of others' as well. The only parties we are concerned about is the person in crisis and the interventionist. Everybody else can get put on the bench and stay out of the game, at least for the time being. That being said, at some point "we" are going to strike a deal and make movement toward a short-term goal if at all possible. A critical component in eliciting cooperation and compliance from people who are sometimes less than cooperative is to build here-and-now relationships that emphasize a collaborative approach that says "you" are not alone, but "we "are in this together, using what Weiner and Mehrabian (1968) term *relational markers*. Relational markers shorten the psychological distance between the client and the worker through the use of such words as "this," "these," "we," "our," "here," and "now" as opposed to "that," "those," "mine," "there," and "then." Notice the difference between the two words "this" and "that" in the crisis worker's response to Jake's statement that it is really hard to change.

CW: Jake, I know it is tough, but *this* (*right now, right here*) is something we can work out. While I can't do much about *that* (*past time, out there*) stalking behavior, we can start on *this* (*right now, right here*) self-monitoring anger management model.

Using this language sets the stage for examining alternatives, making plans, undertaking commitments, and engaging in safer behavior. It distances the stalking and jealous behavior and brings the new concept up close and personal. It also acknowledges Jake's attempts and desire to change and how tough it is to do that all alone, but indicates that now help has arrived. The crisis worker's response hooks "we" together with "this" thing right here in front of us, as opposed to "you" and "that" thing way out there which is much harder to get a handle on.

Disowned Statements. Many of us chronically disown many human qualities that indicate we are less than perfect! Beginning crisis workers are particularly vulnerable to this fallacy because they do not want to be seen as inadequate, insecure, or otherwise unequal to the task. Small wonder that clients learn to distrust or become dependent on such all-knowing, well-integrated individuals. Let us take, for example, my feeling of confusion.

If I pretend I understand when in fact I am confused, the client who is listening to me is going to be doubly confused. Being willing to own my confusion or frustration and attempt to eliminate it is a trust-reinforcing event for two reasons: (1) both client and worker can reduce the need to pretend or fake understanding of one another and begin to see more clearly where communications are getting crossed, and (2) the client can begin to become actively involved with the worker in an attempt to work together.

CW: Right now I don't know what to think. You say you love her, yet your actions do everything to drive her away.

Jake: I know 'cause it confused me too! Well, it's like I want her to love me, and then I get jealous and paranoid, and like a switch gets flipped, and then I lose it. It frustrates me. I'm my own worst enemy, and I hate myself for it.

Conveying Understanding. Clients in crisis often feel that no one understands what they are going through. The "I understand" statement is an owning statement that clearly conveys to the client that you do understand that what is happening right now is causing the client distress. This does not mean that you understand what the client is going through, because you don't. I cannot understand what it is like to have prostate or breast cancer. I can understand the fear and anxiety that the client is presently demonstrating and acknowledge that. The "I understand" statement may have to be combined with what is commonly called a "broken CD" (repeated) response because the individual may be so agitated or out of touch with reality that he or she does not hear what is being said the first time.

CW: OK, Jake, I do understand it's frustrating when she gives you the cold shoulder, and all the ways you try to win her affection don't work.

Jake: (*pounding his fist on the table and yelling*) Every damn thing I do anymore is wrong!

CW: I understand right now that it's so frustrating the only thing that seems to work is lashing out at her physically.

Value Judgments. At times the crisis worker has to make judgment calls about the client's behavior, particularly when the client is in danger of doing something hurtful to him- or herself or to others. Owning statements speak specifically to the worker's judgment about the situation and what he or she will do about it.

Jake: (*making threatening gestures and with a trembling voice*) I . . . I . . . just caaann't taaake much more . . . of this. I'll huuurt her . . . huuurt her real bad.

CW: (*making a judgment*) The way you say that really concerns me. I believe that would not be in your best interests and wouldn't get you what you want, which is back with Rita. I'd have to call the police to see that you are both kept safe.

However, using owning statements does *not* generally mean making value judgments about the client's character, because such judgments are putdowns and do nothing to change behavior.

CW: (*sarcastically*) Yeah, you're a really big man to have to punch your wife out because you aren't as smart as she is. That really shows me a lot. I think maybe a stint out on the county work farm might take some of that energy out of you.

Positive Reinforcement. To be genuine in crisis work is to say what we feel at times. When a client has done well and we're happy and feel good about it, we say so. However, such positively reinforcing statements should always be used in regard to a behavior, as opposed to some personal characteristic.

CW: Jake, I know this is about the last place you'd like to be, and I think it took a lot of guts to come in here and admit to me you've got some problems.

Positive reinforcement is used a great deal in crisis intervention to gain compliance. Many times taking mini-steps to get a client to calm down or stop engaging in a dangerous behavior is tied to positive reinforcement.

CW: (*Jake is standing up and pounding his fist on the table, swearing.*) I need for you to take a deep breath and let it out gently. (*With difficulty, Jake complies.*) Great! That shows me you can get control of your emotions.

We often use positive reinforcement to successively approximate a client toward a larger goal we are seeking to achieve.

CW: Good! You were able to take a deep breath. Now could you cue yourself that every time you start pounding your fist, you will take at least three deep breaths, lower your arms, and allow yourself to relax and picture that tranquil lake scene? Just do that now. Excellent, I see you starting to relax. Can you feel the tension draining out? Terrific! Just continue to do that and feel the difference. See how great that feels and how you have gained mastery over your emotions? It shows me you have the guts to handle your emotions.

However, the use of positive reinforcement is also a double-edged sword. Many times in crisis intervention, reinforcing a client for a behavior may breed dependency or be seen as anything but reinforcing by the client. So be careful about what behavior gets reinforced.

Jake: (*sneeringly*) Guts my ass! If it weren't for the cops, I sure as hell wouldn't be in this stink hole with a jerk like you doing this crap.

CW: (*owning feelings*) I'm sorry you feel that way, but I meant what I said.

Personal Integrity and Limit Setting   When a client starts to browbeat, control, or otherwise put us on the hot seat, it does little good to try to hide our anger, disappointment, or hurt feelings. Furthermore, it is important to set clear limits with clients who are starting to get out of control or are trying to manipulate the crisis worker.

Jake: (*sneeringly*) What do you know? You're nothing but a snot-nosed girl! I don't have to take this crap!

CW: (*calmly, owning feelings and setting limits*) I don't appreciate the demeaning comments, the language, or your attitude toward me. I'd like an apology, and I'd also like you to be civil. If you can't, I'll assume you'd rather explain your problems to your probation officer, and we'll terminate the session.

Assertion Statements.   Finally, because crisis intervention often calls for the crisis worker to take control of the situation, requests for compliance in the form of owning statements are often very directive, short, and point specific. These owning statements, also known as *assertion statements*, clearly and specifically ask for a specific action from the client.

CW: I want you to commit to me and yourself that you'll stay away from her for the next week. I want you to sign this contract that you'll do that for your own safety and hers as well.

Jake: (*wistfully wringing his hands*) I dunno, that's a long time. I really miss her right now.

CW: I understand it's hard, particularly when you'd like to do something, but I need for you to sign this paper, so I can be sure you're committed to doing this.

Facilitative Listening

In summary, listening is the first imperative in crisis intervention. When the word *listening* is used, the term is being applied broadly to several important behavioral and communications skills discussed in this chapter.

To function in a facilitative way, workers must give full attention to the client by

1. Focusing their total mental power on the client's world.
2. Attending to the client's verbal and nonverbal messages (what the client does not say is sometimes more important than what is actually spoken).
3. Picking up on the client's current readiness to enter into emotional and/or physical contact with others, especially with the worker.
4. Emitting attending behavior by both verbal and nonverbal actions, thereby strengthening the relationship and predisposing the client to trust the crisis intervention process.

One important aspect of listening is for the worker to make initial owning statements that express exactly what he or she is going to do.

CW: Rita, I can see you're really hurting. To fully understand what's going on and what needs to be done, I'm going to focus as hard as I can on what you're saying and how you're saying it. As well as listening to what you say, I'm going to be listening for those things that aren't said, because they may have some bearing on your problems too. So if I seem to be really concentrating on you, it's because I want to fully comprehend in as helpful and objective a way as possible what the situation is and your readiness to do something about it.

The second important aspect of listening is to respond in ways that let the client know that the crisis worker is accurately hearing both the facts and the emotional state from which the client's message comes. Here we are searching for both the affective and content dimensions of the problem. The crisis worker combines the dilemma and feelings by using restatement and reflection.

CW: As you lay the problem out—the abuse by your husband, the job pressures, the wonderful yet guilt-ridden times with Sam—I get the feeling of an emotional switchboard with all the lines plugged in and even crossed over, and you're a beginning operator who might be able to handle one or two incoming calls, but now you're just sitting paralyzed wishing you'd never taken the job, wondering how you can get out, wanting answers, but having so many problems that you don't even know the right questions to ask.

The third facet of facilitative listening is facilitative responding. It provides positive impetus for clients to gain a clearer understanding of their feelings, inner motives, and choices. Facilitative responses enable clients to feel hopeful and to sense an inclination to begin to move forward, toward resolution and away from the central core of the crisis. Clients begin to be able to view the crisis from a standpoint of more reality or rationality, which immediately gives them a sense of control. Here the crisis worker targets an action.

CW: So, given all the wires running into the switchboard, which ones do you want to pull, and which ones do you want to keep plugged in? You've given me all kinds of information about how well you've handled the business up to this crisis point. Look back on how you handled that particular phone line. What worked then that might work now? Using that as an example, can we sort each one of these out and get the circuits plugged in or just say that particular call isn't important right now and unplug the line?

The fourth dimension of facilitative listening involves helping clients to understand the full impact of the crisis situation. Such an understanding allows clients to become more like objective, external observers of the crisis and to refocus on it in rational ways rather than remaining stuck in their own internal frame of reference and emotional bias.

Rita: I feel like the whole world is caving in on me. I wonder if I'll ever be able to get out from under all the mess I'm in now.

CW: You're sounding emotionally frozen by what is happening. I'm wondering what would happen if we could step back for a moment and look at it as if we were third-party observers to your situation—as if you were someone else in a soap opera. What would you say to that person?

Rita: Well . . . (*moment of thought*) . . . I'd say she's not the first or only one to experience lots of trouble—that things may look horrible now, but that eventually things get worked out—especially if she's lucky and can bear up long enough.

CW: Then looking at it from outside yourself does give you an additional view.

Helping clients refocus is not a solution in itself. It is an extension of the art of listening that may facilitate forward movement when clients are emotionally stuck.

These four aspects of listening don't operate in a fragmented or mechanical way. Such listening requires skill, practice, an emotionally secure listener, and both physical and emotional stamina on the part of the listener. The following dialogue gives a brief but comprehensive demonstration of how facilitative listening is combined in its many dimensions. The client now is

Jean, Rita's daughter. Don't be perplexed at the shift in clients. One person in crisis may well put a significant other into a crisis situation also. In this instance, Rita's problems have boiled over into her 13-year-old daughter's life.

Jean: I feel put down and ignored by my mother. Every time anything is mentioned about Sam—that's her secret boyfriend—she gets mad and leaves the room. Everything has changed. It's like I'm no longer important to her. I don't know what's happening or what to do.

CW: You're feeling hurt and disappointed, and you're also bewildered by her responses to you.

Jean: (*crying and very upset*) I . . . I feel like I no longer count. I'm feeling like I'm in the way. Like I'm suddenly no good. . . . I feel like now I'm the problem.

CW: You're blaming yourself even though you're trying to understand what has happened and what you should do.

Jean: (*crying is slowing down*) By Sunday night I felt like killing myself. I planned to do it that night. I was feeling abandoned, alone, and hopeless. I just wanted to find some way to end the hurting. I didn't think I could go on another day. I felt like I was no longer her daughter—like she had either disowned me or had been living a lie. I don't know if I can go on.

CW: Even though you were feeling you were at the brink of death, you somehow managed to pull out of it. What did you do, and what are you doing now to keep from killing yourself?

Jean: (*not crying—pondering the crisis worker's last response*) Well, Marlene and her parents came by. I spent the night with them. That really helped. It was lucky for me that they came by and invited me. They were so kind and understanding. I had a bad night. Worrying about all that stuff. But they, especially Marlene, helped me so much.

CW: Let's see if you can tell me what you have learned from that experience that can help you the next time you feel like killing yourself.

Jean: (*pause, as if studying the crisis worker's response*) To get away . . . with someone who cares and understands.

CW: Tell me someone you can contact whenever you feel hopeless and lonely and suicidal so that next time you won't have to depend on luck.

Jean: Well, I'd call Marlene again . . . or my uncle and aunt. They'd be quick to invite me over . . . and there are several friends at school I could call. (*Dialogue continues.*)

This segment of dialogue contains several of the elements of listening that have been described. It contains accurate reflective listening, open-ended questions, and attention to the client's safety (without asking closed questions, giving advice, or encroaching on the client's prerogatives and autonomy). Also, the crisis worker keeps the focus right on the central core of the client's current concerns, paving the way for the client's forward movement from the immediate crisis toward safer and more adjustive actions. The worker's selective responses are geared toward enabling the client to become aware of and pursue immediate short-term goals. The worker does not digress into external events, past events, the mother, the secret boyfriend, gathering background information, or conducting long-term therapy.

Basic Strategies of Crisis Intervention

Myer and James (2005) have formulated nine strategies used in crisis intervention. The basic core listening and responding skills already discussed are the foundation of these strategies. There is no formula for using these strategies. They may be used singly or in combination. Their use depends a great deal on the crisis context, the triage level of the client, and on what task of the crisis intervention model the interventionist is working. Here are the nine strategies.

Creating Awareness. The crisis worker attempts to bring to conscious awareness warded off, denied, shunted, and repressed feelings, thoughts, and behaviors that freeze clients' ability to act in response to the crisis. Creating awareness is particularly important for Task 2, Problem Exploration.

CW: It would be easier to just put it out of your mind, but I wonder what shoving it back will get you? You came here, so I'm pretty sure you want to get this out in the open and get some resolution. What would all this mess look like if it were sitting out there on the table?

Allowing Catharsis. Simply letting clients talk, cry, swear, berate, rant, rave, mourn, or do anything else that allows them to ventilate feelings and thoughts may be one of the most therapeutic strategies the crisis worker can employ. To do this, the crisis worker needs to provide a safe and accepting environment that says, "It's OK to say and feel these things." By so doing the crisis worker clearly says he or she can accept those feelings and thoughts no matter how bad they may seem to be. A word of caution here! Allowing angry feelings to continue to build and escalate may not be the wisest course of action. This strategy is most often used with people who *can't* get in touch with their feelings and thoughts, as opposed to those whose feelings are already volcanic. This strategy is most likely to be used for Task 2, Problem Exploration, and Task 3, Providing Support.

CW: It's tough to talk about it. After all, it is an affair you are having. Perhaps you think I'll pass moral judgment on you for that. I won't! What I would most like you to do is to open up those push-pull feelings. Tell me more about being scared and angry at the same time.

Providing Support. Often the crisis worker is the *sole* support available to the client. As such, the crisis worker attempts to validate that the clients' responses are as reasonable as can be expected given the situation. Many times clients believe they must be going crazy, but they need to understand that they are not "crazy" and that most people would act in about the same way given the kind, type, and duration of the crisis. Oftentimes in crisis, in an attempt to calm clients, workers state that it is "normal" to have such and such reactions. Nothing could be further from the truth. There is nothing "normal" at all about stress reactions associated with a sexual assault. Such attempts are at best placating and at worst discounting of the client. A far better description, we believe, is the word "common." Clients need to understand that while there is nothing "normal" about their feeling, acting, and thinking in a crisis situation, it is certainly "common" to most people. This kind of affirmation is particularly critical to clients who feel they have no support system available to them. That being said, the crisis worker *never* supports clients' injurious or lethal feelings, thoughts, or actions toward themselves or others.

Providing support is particularly useful when the client is attempting to move into action. In standard therapy, supervisors often express a great deal of concern about breeding dependence on the therapist. It should be clearly understood that when we are dealing with clients in crisis they may well need to be dependent on us for a short while. That doesn't mean we are going to adopt clients and take them home with us! It does mean that when the client is drained of emotional, cognitive, or behavioral resources, we are supportive, and we provide a shoulder to lean on.

Rita: I don't know which way to turn, what to do. This is not me! I am so confused and so alone. My God! How did I ever get in this awful mess?

CW: Right now you may feel that way, but I am in this with you, and I am going to stay in it until we get some control and direction back for you.

Rita: I don't know how there can ever be any control. (*Starts sobbing.*)

CW: We are going to get some control, and I am going to stay with you until that happens.

Promoting Expansion.   The crisis worker engages in activities to open up clients' tunnel vision of the crisis. Oftentimes clients are so wrapped up in the crisis and are continuously engaging in self-defeating thoughts and behaviors that they are unable to see other perceptions and possibilities. Increasing expansion helps clients step back, reframe the problem, and gain new perspectives. This strategy is primarily used to help clients resolve stuck cognitive reactions. By confronting clients' narrow and restrictive views, crisis workers help clients consider other perspectives. This strategy is particularly effective with clients who are not able to recognize environmental cues that may help them to perceive alternate meanings of events and possible solutions to them.

CW: This may be distasteful, but I want you to think about this. You know one possibility would be to get a restraining order. That is pretty common in most domestic violence situations, but it is used in other instances too.

Emphasizing Focus.   Conversely, at times the problem is that clients are too expansive and need to narrow their freewheeling, out-of-control flights of ideation about the crisis that have little basis in reality. The crisis worker attempts to partition, compartmentalize, and downsize clients' all-encompassing, catastrophic interpretations and perceptions of the crisis event to more specific, realistic, manageable components and options. This strategy has utility across all tasks of the crisis intervention model.

CW: Given this huge mess, what is the one thing you need to do right now to get some relief? What could you focus on that would tell you immediately that some pressure was off rather than trying to take care of everything and everybody?

Providing Guidance.   The term "guidance" has come to have somewhat of a negative connotation in the field of counseling because it implies that clients are incapable of helping themselves. However, many times clients in crisis do need guidance and direction. They don't have the knowledge or resources available to

make good decisions. Thus, the crisis worker provides information, referral, and direction in regard to clients' obtaining assistance from specific external resources and support systems. For example, one of the handiest tools that crisis workers have is a directory of all the social services available in their catchment area. This strategy is used almost exclusively to respond to clients' behavioral reactions.

Rita: I have no idea how to go about getting a restraining order.

CW: Up until now you would have had no reason to. However, the staff at the Family Trouble Center can do that for you and would be glad to help you do it. I can give you that number if you want.

Promoting Mobilization.   The crisis worker attempts both to activate and marshal clients' internal resources and to find and use external support systems to help generate coping skills and problem-solving abilities.

CW: There is a support group of women I know of that meets regularly at St. Michael's Catholic church. They all struggle with some of the same relationship issues that you are having. Hearing and interacting with them might give you some new ideas on how to go about solving this knotty problem. You have some good ideas and are pretty geared up to act on them, but it might not hurt to get their perspectives.

Implementing Order.   The crisis worker methodically helps clients classify and categorize problems so as to prioritize and sequentially attack the crisis in a logical and linear manner.

CW: It seems overwhelming, but let's put it into pieces you can manage. Break it down. If this were your business instead of your love life, how would you parcel the problem out, and what order of priorities would you give to each part? What's the first thing you would do? While it might not make it perfect, what would it take to make this situation more tolerable?

Providing Protection.   Providing protection is paramount in crisis intervention, so important that it is its own overarching task in our model. The crisis worker safeguards clients from engaging in harmful, destructive, detrimental, and unsafe feelings, behaviors, and thoughts that may be psychologically or physically injurious or lethal to themselves or others.

CW: I want to make the clearest personal statement I can to you Rita. I really fear for your safety. I would not confront

Jake alone after work at the garage. I understand you don't want a big scene in front of other people, but to do that alone with nobody around seems to me a really dangerous thing to do.

When these nine strategies are used with the basic verbal crisis intervention skills in this chapter, they form the backbone of crisis intervention techniques. By using them with the Triage Assessment Form, crisis interventionists should have a comprehensive real-time assessment of how they are doing as they move the client through the model.

Climate of Human Growth

According to Rogers (1977), the most effective helper is one who can provide three necessary and sufficient conditions for client growth. These conditions he named *empathy, genuineness,* and *acceptance* (pp. 9–12). These therapeutic conditions are particularly critical to doing effective crisis intervention. To create a climate of empathy means that the crisis worker accurately senses the inner feelings and meanings the client is experiencing and directly communicates to the client that the worker understands how it feels to be the client. The condition of genuineness (also called *realness, transparency,* or *congruency*) means that the worker is being completely open in the relationship: nothing is hidden, there are no facades, and there are no professional fronts. If the worker is clearly open and willing to be fully him- or herself in the relationship, the client is encouraged to reciprocate. The term *acceptance* (also referred to as *caring* or *prizing*) means that the crisis worker feels an unconditional positive regard for the client. It is an attitude of accepting and caring for the client without the client's necessarily reciprocating. The condition of acceptance is provided for no other reason than that the client is a human being in need. If these conditions of empathy, genuineness, and acceptance can be provided for the client, then the probability that the client will experience positive emotional movement is increased.

Communicating Empathy

In describing the use of empathy to help clients, we will focus on five important techniques: (1) attending, (2) verbally communicating empathic understanding, (3) reflecting feelings, (4) nonverbally communicating empathic understanding, and (5) silence as a way of communicating empathic understanding (Cormier & Cormier, 1991; Gilliland & James, 1998, pp. 116–118).

First, however, it is necessary to differentiate empathy from sympathy and distancing.

Sympathy. Beginners in the field confuse empathy with sympathy. Sympathy is fine at the right time and conveys support, but it means essentially taking on the person's problems and feelings rather than attempting to experience and convey what the person is feeling. Mostly we think of sympathy as a sad feeling with tears attached to it. It can just as well be righteous indignation and anger. Particularly when we are attempting to do exploration with a client in crisis, we will do better to put sympathy on the shelf for a while.

CW: You poor thing. That's terrible! Nobody should be allowed to get away with that kind of behavior. How about I call the police right now!

The behavior, indeed, may be terrible, but the crisis worker will do better to make a deep, reflective response that captures the client's feeling.

CW: You seem really torn—kicking yourself for being a fool, but still wanting and hoping the relationship to be something and go somewhere. It sounds like you know it is over, but you don't quite know what to do yet.

Distancing. At times, crisis workers may be so overwhelmed and frightened by what they are confronted with that they seek to distance themselves from the overwhelming affect by engaging in what we call "funeral home counseling." Here are a few examples of what people say when they have no idea what to say but feel they need to say something. These attempts to be palliative are generally not helpful and can, in fact, hinder intervention. Lots of times these statements are centered on a religious/spiritual theme: "It's God's will." "God works in mysterious ways." "Heaven wouldn't be heaven if it were only filled with old people." "He/she's in a better place." Another way of distancing is by rationalizing, discounting, and minimizing: "Well, you still have your health." "It could have been worse." "Don't feel guilty about it." "Try to get your mind off it." "Just try and relax a little." These statements probably say more about the *worker's* crisis state than they do about the client's. A far better way, when aspiring crisis workers don't know what to say, is to say nothing or to own the feeling of what they are experiencing. At times, owning our own inability to find words to convey the depth of feeling is probably one of the best ways to indicate that you do feel for the client.

CW: (*reaches out and touches Rita's arm and says nothing for a few moments*) I wish I had something to say that would take this pain and confusion away and make this all right, but right now I just don't.

Attending. The first step in communicating empathy has little to do with words and a lot to do with looking, acting, and being attentive. The foregoing crisis worker response is much more about attending than saying or doing. In most initial counseling and therapy sessions, the client enters with some anxiety related to the therapy itself in addition to the stress brought on by the crisis. In crisis situations, such anxiety is increased exponentially. Shame, guilt, rage, and sorrow are but a few of the feelings that may be manifested. Such feelings may be blatant and rampant or subtle and disguised. Whatever shape or form such feelings take, the inattentive crisis worker can miss the message the client is attempting to convey. Worse, an inattentive attitude implies lack of interest on the part of the worker and does little to establish a trusting relationship.

The effective crisis worker focuses fully on the client, both in facial expression and in body posture. By nodding, keeping eye contact, smiling, showing appropriate seriousness of expression, leaning forward, keeping an open stance, and sitting or standing close to the client without invading the client's space, the crisis worker conveys a sense of involvement, concern, commitment, and trust. Vocal tone, diction, pitch, modulation, and smoothness of delivery also tell clients a great deal about the attentiveness of the crisis worker. By attending closely to the client's verbal and nonverbal responses, the crisis worker can quickly tell whether he or she is establishing an empathic relationship or exacerbating the client's feelings of distrust, fear, and uncertainty about becoming involved in the relationship.

Attentiveness, then, is both an attitude and a skill. It is an attitude in that the worker focuses fully on the client right here and now. In such moments the crisis worker's own concerns are put on hold. It is a skill in that conveying attending takes practice. It is just as inappropriate for the crisis worker to look too concerned and be in too close proximity as it is to lean back with arms folded and legs crossed, giving a cold stare. Here is an example of an appropriate blend of both verbal and nonverbal skill in attending to a client empathically.

Rita: (*Enters room, sits down in far corner, warily looks about the room, crosses her legs and fidgets with her purse, and avoids direct eye contact, manifesting the appearance of a distraught woman who is barely holding together.*)

CW: (*rises behind desk, and observing the behavior and physical appearance of the client, moves to a chair a comfortable distance and a slight angle from Rita's, sits down, leans forward in an open stance, and with an appearance of concern and inquisitiveness looks directly at Rita*) I'd like to be of help. Where would you like to start?

The crisis worker sees the apprehension in the client and immediately becomes proactive. The crisis worker moves close to the client but does not sit directly in front of her in what could be construed as a confronting stance. The worker inclines forward to focus attention—eyes, ears, brain, and whole body—onto the client's world. The whole posture of the crisis worker is congruent with the verbal message of offering immediate acceptance and willingness to help. In summary, effective attending is unobtrusive, natural, and without pretense. It is a necessary condition for empathic listening.

Verbally Communicating Empathic Understanding. When you can accurately hear and understand the core emotional feelings inside the client and accurately and caringly communicate that understanding to the client, you are demonstrating effective listening. The deeper your level of listening (understanding), the more helpful you will be to your clients. For instance, reflecting a client's message at the interchangeable level is helpful.

Rita: I'm thinking about just walking in and telling Jake I want a divorce—regardless of what Sam is ready to do. I don't think I can go on much longer. My ulcer is beginning to act up, I'm an emotional wreck, and everyone is expecting more of me than I can give.

CW: You sound like you are feeling a sense of urgency because it's adversely affecting your physical and emotional well-being.

A deeper level of listening and communicating empathic understanding to Rita might be expressed thus:

CW: Rita, your sense of urgency is getting to the point where you seem about ready to take a big risk with both Jake and Sam. I sense that your physical and emotional stresses have about reached their limits, and you're realizing that no one else is going to act to give you relief—that you are the one who is going to have to decide and act.

The second response is more helpful because it confirms to Rita a deeper understanding than the first response. Both responses are helpful because they are accurate, and neither adds to nor detracts from the client's verbal, nonverbal, or emotional messages. Whereas the first response is considered minimally helpful, the second response is more facilitative because it lets the client know the worker heard a deeper personal meaning (risk) and a personal ownership of possible action. A word of caution to the worker, however: Beware of reading into the client's statements more than the client is saying, and take care to keep your response as brief as possible.

Reflection of Feelings.   Reflection of feelings is a powerful tool to get at shunted or denied affect. In standard therapy, we constantly hammer at uncovering affect because of client resistance to dealing with threatening and warded off feelings. However, in crisis intervention the desire to uncover feeling is not always the therapeutic best bet. A client who is scoring an 8, 9, or 10 on the Affective Scale of the Triage Assessment Form probably does not need to have a crisis worker attempt to elicit even more feelings. It is not the job of the crisis worker to tell the client what he or she is feeling. The following dialogue moves from a reflection to a judgment and tells the client how she feels.

CW: You are bitter and resentful about being in this dead-end marriage. You can't figure a way out.

Rather, what the crisis worker should do is make an educated guess using conditional statements that allows the client to accept or reject the worker's guess.

CW: It *seems* that you are pretty bitter and resentful about this dead-end marriage and are frustrated that you can't figure a way out.

Effective communication of empathic understanding to the client means focusing on the client's expressed affective and cognitive messages. The worker deals *directly* with the client's concerns and does not veer off into talking *about* the client's concerns or some tangential person or event. That distinction is important.

Rita: I'm afraid Jake might attack me even worse if I tell him I want a divorce.

CW: He did beat you pretty badly. Sam would probably go bananas at that. Your husband Jake has such a violent temper. (*talking about the situation and tangentially focusing on Jake*)

CW: You're feeling some reservations about telling Jake because you really don't want to be beaten up again. (*dealing with Rita's current feelings and concerns*)

The latter response is preferred because it stays on target with Rita's feelings and concerns in the here and now and because it avoids getting off onto Jake, Sam, or any other third party or issue.

The central issue in empathic understanding is to hone in on the client's current core of feelings and concerns and communicate to the client (in the worker's own words) the gist of what the client is experiencing.

Nonverbal Communication.   Empathic understanding means accurately picking up and reflecting more than verbal messages. It involves accurately sensing and reflecting all the unspoken cues, messages, and behaviors the client emits. Nonverbal messages may be transmitted in many ways. The worker should carefully observe body posture, body movement, gestures, grimaces, vocal pitch, movement of eyes, movement of arms and legs, and other body indicators. Clients may transmit emotions such as anger, fear, puzzlement, doubt, rejection, emotional stress, and hopelessness by different body messages. Crisis workers should be keenly aware of whether nonverbal messages are consistent with the client's verbal messages. A part of empathic understanding is the communication of such inconsistency to the client who may not be consciously aware of the difference. For example:

CW: (*observing the way Rita's face lights up whenever she speaks or thinks about Sam*) Rita, I notice you are talking about all the trouble it is for you to keep seeing Sam on the sly. But your body tells me that those are the moments you live for— that right now your only ecstasy is when you're with Sam.

It is important that the crisis worker avoid reading more into body language than it warrants. Communicating empathy in the nonverbal realm is no place for fishing expeditions or long-shot hunches. The crisis worker's main concern with nonverbal communication, however, involves the worker's own messages. All the dynamics of the client's body language apply to the worker as well. Your nonverbal messages must be consistent with your verbal messages. It would not be empathic or helpful if your words were saying to the client, "I understand precisely what you're feeling and desiring," but your body was saying, "I don't care," or "I'm bored," or "My mind isn't fully focused on what you're saying." Your voice, facial expression, posture— even the office arrangement and environment—must say to the client: "I'm fully tuned in to your world while you're with me. I want to give my total mental and emotional energy to understanding your concerns while you're here. I will not be distracted." If your body can communicate such messages so that they are unmistakably understood by the client, then you will have effectively communicated empathy to the client nonverbally, and you will stand a better chance of being helpful.

Silence.   Silence is golden. Beginning crisis workers often feel compelled to initiate talk to fill any void or lapse in the dialogue because they believe they would not be doing their job otherwise. Nothing could be further from the truth. Clients need time to think. To throw out a barrage of questions or engage in a monologue says more about the crisis worker's insecurity in the situation than it does about resolving the crisis. Silence gives the client thinking time—and the crisis worker too.

Indeed, at such times, verbiage from the crisis worker may be intrusive and even unwelcome. Remaining silent but attending closely to the client can convey deep, empathic understanding. Nonverbally, the message comes across: "I understand your struggle trying to put those feelings into words, and it's OK. I know it's tough, but I believe you can handle it. However, I'm right here if you need me."

Rita: The last beating . . . I was so ashamed, yet I couldn't seem to do anything except go back to him.

CW: It hurts you not only to get beaten but also that others might find out—which seems even worse. As a result, you don't see any alternatives.

Rita: (*thinks hard, eyes focused into the distance for more than a minute*) Yes and no! I see alternatives, but I guess until now I haven't had the guts to do anything. I rationalized that something must be wrong with me or that the situation would get better, but it hasn't for five years. It has gotten worse.

CW: (*silence; looks at Rita for some 30 seconds while collecting thoughts*) A couple of things strike me about what you said. First, you've decided to quit blaming yourself. Second, by the fact that you're here now, you've chosen at least one alternative to that five-year merry-go-round of abuse.

In this scene, silence is allowed to work for both the client and the worker. The client needs time to work through her response to the worker, and she is unconditionally allowed to do this. The same is true of the crisis worker. The client's comment is synthesized and processed for its full meaning. By reacting immediately, the crisis worker might make less than a potent response. Taking time to digest both the content and the affect of the client enables the worker to formulate a response that is more likely to be on target and helpful.

Communicating Genuineness

Contrary to the thinking of most beginning human services workers, as evidenced by their behavior, being fully oneself and not some pseudotherapist or mimic of a particular therapist one has heard or seen is an absolutely necessary condition, particularly in crisis intervention. Rogers (1969, p. 228) puts it in clear, simple, and succinct terms:

> When I can accept the fact that I have many deficiencies, many faults, make a lot of mistakes, am often ignorant where I should be knowledgeable, often prejudiced when I should be open-minded, often have feelings which are not justified by the circumstances, then I can be much more real.

Rogers's statement means putting on no false fronts but rather being oneself in the relationship and communicating what "oneself" is to the client. In short, it is being honest.

The advice to be honest is not simply a platitude. To be honest is to be congruent; it means that the crisis worker's awareness of self, feelings, and experience is freely and unconditionally available and communicable, when appropriate, during intervention in a crisis. Egan (1975, 1982, 1986, 1990) has listed essential components of genuineness that would serve the beginning crisis worker well.

1. *Being role free.* The crisis worker is genuine in life as well as in the therapeutic relationship and is congruent in both experiencing and communicating feelings (Egan, 1975, p. 91).
2. *Being spontaneous.* The crisis worker communicates freely, with tact and without constantly gauging what to say, and behaves freely, without being impulsive or inhibited, rule bound or technique bound. Worker behavior is based on a feeling of self-confidence (p. 92).
3. *Being nondefensive.* Crisis workers who behave nondefensively have an excellent understanding of their strengths and weaknesses. Thus, they can be open to negative, even hostile, client expressions without feeling attacked or defensive. The crisis worker who is genuine understands such negative expressions as saying more about the client than the worker and tries to facilitate exploration of such comments rather than defend against them (pp. 92–93).
4. *Being consistent.* People who are genuine have few discrepancies between what they think, feel, and

say and their actual behavior. Crisis workers who are consistent do not think one thing and tell a client another or engage in behavior that is contrary to their values (pp. 93–94).

5. *Being a sharer of self.* When it is appropriate to the situation, people who are genuine engage in self-disclosure, allowing others to know them through open verbal and nonverbal expression of their feelings (p. 94).

The following dialogue between the crisis worker and Rita demonstrates comprehensively the points both Rogers and Egan make.

Rita: Just what the hell gives? Here I am going crazy, and you put it back on my shoulders. You're supposed to help get me out of this mess!

CW: I can see that you're really mad at me because I don't behave the way you think I ought to.

Rita: Well, how can you be such a caring person if you let me hang out there, pushing me to take such risky chances? I could lose everything.

CW: You see me as being a real hypocrite because I'm pushing you to take some action rather than sympathizing with you.

Rita: God knows I could use some . . . and when you act so callously (*cries*) . . . you're like every other damn man!

CW: What would I be doing if I were acting in the most helpful way I possibly could, in your opinion, right now?

Rita: Well, I know you can't solve this for me, but I'd sure as hell like for you to point the way or help me solve this.

CW: So, what you're really wanting is to be able to solve this dilemma on your own, and what you're wanting from me is to help you find your own inner choices that are best for you. What I want to do is to help you find those choices. Let's look at your current options right now.

The dialogue aptly depicts the crisis worker owning feelings, using "I" statements, and focusing on the client's emergent concerns rather than allowing the focus to shift to tangential matters or defensive responses by the worker. Such statements allow the crisis worker to retain integrity, squarely face client hostility without becoming hostile in turn, and model a safe and trusting atmosphere in which clients see that it is all right for them to demonstrate angry feelings and still be accepted by the crisis worker. At the same time, the crisis worker stands by and is consistent with a therapeutic approach without being intimidated by or defensive with the client. The crisis worker above all has the self-confidence and congruence to make such statements in a way that is facilitative for the client.

Communicating Acceptance

The crisis worker who interacts with complete acceptance of clients exudes an unconditional positive regard for clients that transcends clients' personal qualities, beliefs, problems, situations, or crises. The worker is able to prize, care for, and fully accept clients even if they are doing things, saying things, and experiencing situations that are contrary to the worker's personal beliefs and values. The worker is able to put aside personal needs, values, and desires and does not require clients to make specific responses as a condition of full acceptance.

Rita: I hate to bother you with all my problems. I know you're married and have never been divorced. You must think I'm a terribly screwed-up mess.

CW: I hear your concern, and I want you to know that what has happened to you and what you choose to do have nothing to do with my regard for you. What I'm really hoping we can do is to help you arrive at those choices that will best help you get through this crisis and successfully get back in total control of your life.

Rita: I appreciate that very much. But sometimes I wonder whether my running around with Sam doesn't strike you as unwise and immature.

CW: I hope I'm not giving off negative vibes to give you that impression, because your personal preferences have nothing to do with my caring for you. It seems like you really have a concern about my feelings about how you should act.

Rita: Not really. It's just something inside me—that if I were you, I'd be wondering.

CW: So, a source of concern inside you is whether I may evaluate you negatively. What I want you to know is that my esteem for you is not based on what you do.

Even when clients persist in projecting onto the crisis worker negative evaluations or notions such as those expressed by Rita, the worker doesn't have to buy into such notions. If the worker can truly feel an unconditional positive regard for the client, there will be no need for denial, defensiveness, or diversion from the reality of the worker's true feelings. If the worker demonstrates caring and prizing of the client, regardless of the client's situation or status, the client will be more likely to accept and prize him- or herself. That is the essence of acceptance in crisis intervention.

Acting in Crisis Intervention

As shown in Figure 4.1, the crisis worker's level of action and involvement in the client's world, based on a valid and realistic assessment of the client's level of mobility/

Crisis worker is directive.   **Crisis worker is collaborative.**   **Crisis worker is nondirective.**

Client is immobile.   **Client is partially mobile.**   **Client is mobile.**

From the initiating crisis event to resolution, counseling should move from left to right on the directive–nondirective worker continuum as the client moves from immobile to mobile.

Darker shading indicates a more directed approach to counseling when the client is assessed as immobile.

Lighter shading indicates the crisis worker becoming more nondirective and the client becoming more mobile.

FIGURE 4.1 The Directive–Nondirective Action Continuum

immobility, may be anywhere on a continuum ranging from nondirective through collaborative to directive. The appropriateness of alternative coping mechanisms hinges on the client's degree of mobility. Thus assessment of client mobility is a key concept governing the degree of the crisis worker's involvement. One of the first things the worker must determine is what event precipitated the crisis. What brought on the disequilibrium? The answer may not be very clear in the client's complex and rambling story. So the worker may have to ask, early in the interview, "What *one event* brought you to seek counseling today?" When you discover the major precipitating event that took away the client's autonomous coping ability, it will likely signal your primary focus with the client.

Directive Counseling

The directive approach is necessary when the client is assessed as being too immobile to cope with the current crisis. A triage score in the high teens or twenties typically calls for a good deal of directiveness from the worker. The crisis worker is the principal definer of the problem, searcher for alternatives, and developer of an adequate plan, and instructs, leads, or guides the client in the action. Directive counseling is an "I" approach. This is an example of a worker-directed statement: "I want you to try something right now. I want you to draw a deep breath, and while you are doing it, I want you to just focus on your breathing. Don't let any other thoughts enter your mind. Just relax and notice how your tensions begin to subside." By using a very directive stance, the worker takes temporary control, authority, and responsibility for the situation.

Rita: I don't know which way to turn. My whole world has caved in. I don't know what I'll do tonight. It's all so

hopeless. I'm scared to even think about tonight. (*Rita appears stunned and in a state of panic.*) I don't know what to do.

CW: I don't want you to go home in the state you're in now. I'm going to call Domestic Abuse Services, and if they have room for you at their shelter, I want you to consider spending at least one night there. Domestic Abuse Services has offices and a counseling service at one location and a shelter at a different address, which is unlisted. I don't want you to worry. We have a van that can take you to the shelter. In the morning you can leave the shelter and go talk with the Domestic Abuse Services counselors, or you can come back and talk with me; but right now my main concern is that you are safe for today and tonight.

There are many kinds of immobile clients: (1) clients who need immediate hospitalization because of chemical use or organic dysfunction, (2) clients who are suffering from such severe depression that they cannot function, (3) clients who are experiencing a severe psychotic episode, (4) clients who are suffering from severe shock, bereavement, or loss, (5) clients whose anxiety level is temporarily so high that they cannot function until the anxiety subsides, (6) clients who, for any reason, are out of touch with reality, and (7) clients who are currently a danger to themselves or others. Immobile clients are more apt to be suicidal or homicidal than are clients who are ready to respond to collaborative or to nondirective counseling. Or, because of their inability to function effectively, they are more likely to engage in activities that put themselves or others at risk for serious injury. The worker must be able to make a fairly accurate and objective assessment of the client's level of mobility.

However, if the worker makes an error of judgment (believing a client to be immobile when in fact he or she is not), no harm is usually done because the client may simply respond by refusing to accept the worker's direction. In most cases of this sort, the worker can then shift into a collaborative mode and continue the helping session. Many times a worker will begin in a directive mode and then shift into a collaborative mode during the session. For example, with a highly anxious client the worker may begin by directing the client in relaxation exercises, which may lower the client's anxiety level to the point where the worker can make a natural shift into a collaborative mode to continue the counseling.

Collaborative Counseling

The collaborative approach enables the crisis worker to forge a real partnership with the client in evaluating the problem, generating acceptable alternatives, and implementing realistic action steps. When the triage assessment indicates that the client cannot function successfully in a nondirective mode but has enough mobility to be a partner in the crisis intervention process, the worker is collaborative to that degree. When a client has a triage score that is in the high single digits to middle teens, the crisis worker can typically operate in a collaborative mode. Many crisis interventions operate in this mode. Collaborative counseling is a "we" approach, in contrast to the "I" approach of directive counseling and the "you" approach of nondirective counseling. Consider some typical worker statements in the collaborative mode: "What 'they' are going to do sounds overpowering as you say it, but we haven't really considered what 'we' can do if we come up with a plan." "You've come up with a lot of good ideas, but you sound a little confused about which one to act on. Could we put our heads together and make a priority list of alternatives?" The collaborative client is a full partner in identifying the precipitating problem, examining realistic alternatives, planning action steps, and making a commitment to carrying out a realistic plan. The collaborative client is not as self-reliant and autonomous as the fully mobile client, but does have enough ego strength and mobility to participate in resolving the problem. The worker is needed to serve as a temporary catalyst, consultant, facilitator, and support person. Here is an example of a collaborative response to a client.

Rita: I've thought about going to my mother's or going to the battered women's shelter or even calling my school counselor friend for a place to stay tonight.

CW: Let's examine these three choices, and maybe some others available to you that I know of, and we'll see which one will best meet your requirements.

Nondirective Counseling

The nondirective approach is desirable whenever clients are able to initiate and carry out their own action steps. While the crisis worker will want to be as nondirective as possible and give the client as much control as the client can handle, in the initial stage of a crisis the worker is seldom nondirective because of the high level of ratings on the Triage Assessment Form (see Chapter 3). With the "you" approach of nondirective counseling, the worker uses a great amount of active listening and many open-ended questions to help clients clarify what they really want to do and examine what outcomes various choices might produce. These are some possible questions: "What do you wish to have happen?" "What will occur if you choose to do that?" "What people are available now who could and would assist you in this?" "Picture yourself doing that—vividly see yourself choosing that route. Now, how does that image fit with what you're really trying to accomplish?" "What activities did you do in the past that helped you in situations similar to this?" The worker does not manage, manipulate, prescribe, dominate, or control. It is the client who owns the problem, the coping mechanisms, the plan, the action, the commitment, and the outcomes.

The worker is a support person who may listen, encourage, reflect, reinforce, self-disclose, and suggest. Nondirective counseling assists clients in mobilizing what already is inside them—the capacity, ability, and coping strength to solve their own problems in ways that are pretty well known to them already but that are temporarily out of reach. Here is an example of a nondirective response.

Rita: This is it. I've had the last beating I'm going to take from that jerk! I'm simply going to get myself out of this hell!

CW: You've made a decision to choose a different life for yourself, and you've decided that you are the one who is going to start it.

Action Strategies for Crisis Workers

A number of action strategies and considerations may enhance the worker's effectiveness in dealing with clients in crisis. However, before committing to doing anything with the client, consider the following "rules of the road."

Recognize Individual Differences. View and respond to each client and each crisis situation as unique. If you really believe you are multiculturally sensitive, this is the essence of an emic multicultural view. Even for experienced workers, staying attuned to the uniqueness of each person is difficult. Under the pressures of time and exhaustion, and misled by overconfidence in their own expertise, workers find it all too easy to lump problems and clients together and provide pat answers and solutions. Treating clients generically is likely to cost the worker and the client a great deal more in the long run than it saves in time and effort in the short run. Stereotyping, labeling, and taking for granted any aspect of crisis intervention are definite pitfalls.

Assess Yourself. Ongoing self-analysis on the part of the worker is mandatory. At all times, workers must be fully and realistically aware of their own values, limitations, physical and emotional status, and personal readiness to deal objectively with the client and the crisis at hand. Crisis workers need to run continuous perceptual checks to ascertain if they have gotten in over their heads. (See Chapter 16 for a thorough description of the phenomenon called "burnout.") If for any reason the worker is not ready for or capable of dealing with the crisis or the client, the worker must immediately make an appropriate referral.

Show Regard for Client Safety. The worker's style, choices, and strategies must reflect a continuous consideration of the client's physical and psychological safety as well as the safety of others involved. The safety consideration includes the safety of the worker as well as the ethical, legal, and professional requirements mandated in counseling practice. The greatest intervention strategies and tactics are absolutely useless if clients leave the crisis worker and go out and harm themselves or others.

The golden rule is "When in doubt about client safety, get help." If you aren't sure what to do, consult with another crisis worker. Consultation does not mean you are inadequate. What it does mean is that you are a professional practitioner who is seeking a second opinion to validate your own, or you realize that this problem is not an area of your expertise so you are conferring with a person who does have the expertise. Thus, concern for a client's safety may mean appropriate referral interventions, including immediate hospitalization. You need to understand that when you do this, clients may be extremely angry at you; they may say you are unethical, have violated their trust and confidentiality, and even threaten to sue you for unprofessionalism. As hurtful and anxiety provoking as that may be, we will see in Chapter 5, Crisis Case Handling, that such actions are not only ethical but legally mandated.

Provide Client Support. The crisis worker should be available as a support person during the crisis period. Clients may need assistance in developing a list of possible support people, but if no appropriate support person emerges in the examination of alternatives, the worker can serve as a primary support person until the present crisis is over. A warm, empathic, and assertive counseling strategy should be used with clients who are extremely lonely and devoid of supports. For example, "I want you to know that I am very concerned about your safety during this stressful time, and that I'm available to help. I want you to keep this card with you until you're through this crisis, and call me if you feel yourself sliding back into that hopeless feeling again. If you call either of these numbers and don't get an answer or get a busy signal, keep trying until you get me. You *must* make contact with *me*. I will be very disturbed if you are in a seriously threatening situation again without letting me become involved with you. I really want to impress on you my genuine concern for you and the importance of making an agreement or contract to call me whenever your safety is threatened. Will you give me that assurance?"

Define the Problem Clearly. Many clients have complicated and multiple problems. Make sure that each problem is clearly and accurately defined from a practical, problem-solving point of view. Many clients define the crisis as someone else's problem or as some external event or situation that has happened. Attempting to solve the crisis of some third party (who isn't present) is counterproductive. Pinpoint the client's own problem with the event or situation, and keep the focus on the client's central core of concern. Also, attempt to distill multiple problems down into an immediate, workable problem and to concentrate on that problem first. I cannot overemphasize the tenacity with which the worker must avoid being drawn off on tangents by some highly emotional or defensive clients with difficult problems.

Consider these exchanges with Rita's husband, Jake.

Jake: You don't seem to like me much.

CW: Right now, that's not the issue of importance. What I'm trying to do is help you identify the main source of your problem.

Another example:

Jake: Haven't you ever hit your wife too?

CW: No, but that's not what we're working on now. I'm trying to help us figure out a way for you to avoid fighting with her when you first get home each evening.

In both instances the worker stays focused on the client and does not get caught up on side issues such as worker competency, beliefs, and attitudes. Now the worker is ready to work on Task 4, Examining Alternatives.

Consider Alternatives. In most problem situations, the alternatives are infinite. But crisis clients (and sometimes workers) have a limited view of the many options available. By using open-ended questions, elicit the maximum number of choices from the client. Then add your own list of possible alternatives to the client's list. For example, "I get the feeling that it might help if you could get in contact with a counselor at the Credit Counseling Bureau. How would you feel about our adding that to our list?" Examining, analyzing, and listing alternatives to consider should be as collaborative as possible. The best alternatives are ones that the client truly *owns*. Take care to avoid imposing your alternatives on the client.

The alternatives on the list should be workable and realistic. They should represent the right amount of action for the client to undertake now—not too much, not too little. The client will generally express ownership of an option by words such as "I would really like to call him today." Worker-imposed options are usually signaled by the worker's words, such as *"You need to* go to his office and do that right away." Beware of the latter! An important part of the quest for appropriate alternatives is to explore with the client what options have worked before in situations like the present one. Often the client can come up with the best choices, derived from coping mechanisms that have worked well in the past. But the stresses created by the immediate crisis may keep clients from identifying the most obvious and appropriate alternatives for them. Here the crisis worker facilitates the client's examination of alternatives.

CW: Rita, you say you're feeling frightened and trapped right now, and you don't know where to turn. But it sounds like you'd take a step in a positive direction if you could get some of your old zip back. What are some actions you took or some people you sought out in previous situations when you felt frightened or stuck?

Rita: Oh, I don't know that I've been in a mess quite this bad before.

CW: Well, that may be true. But what steps have you taken or what persons have you contacted before in a mess like this, even if it wasn't this bad?

Rita: Hmm . . . Well, a time or two I did go talk to Mr. Jackson, one of my auto mechanics instructors when I was at the Area Vo-Tech School. He's very understanding and helpful. He always seemed to understand me and believe in me.

CW: How would you feel about reestablishing contact with him whenever you're down again?

Plan Action Steps.   After developing a short, doable list of alternatives, the worker needs to move on to making plans. In crisis intervention the worker endeavors to assist the client to develop a short-term plan that will help the client get through the immediate crisis as well as make the transition to long-term coping. The plan should include the client's internal coping mechanisms as well as sources of help in the environment. The coping mechanisms are usually brought to bear on some concrete, positive, constructive action that clients can take to regain better control of their lives. Actions that initially involve some physical movement are preferred. The plan should be realistic in terms of the client's current emotional readiness and environmental supports. It may involve collaboration with the worker until the client can function independently. The effective crisis worker is sensitive to the client's need to function autonomously as soon as feasible.

Rita: Right now I'd like to just be free of the whole mess for a few days . . . just get off this dizzy merry-go-round long enough to collect my thoughts.

CW: It sounds to me like you really mean that. Let's see if together we can examine some options that might get you the freedom and breathing space you need to pull the pieces back together.

Rita: I can't really let go. Too many people are depending on me. That's just wishful thinking. But it would be wonderful to get some relief.

CW: Even though you don't see any way to get it, what you're wanting is some space for yourself right now—away from work, kids, Jake, Sam, and the whole dilemma.

Rita: The only way that would happen is for my doctor to order it—to prescribe it, medically.

CW: How realistic is that? How would that help you?

Rita: It would call a halt to some of the pressures. The treadmill would have to stop, at least temporarily. Yes, I guess that kind of medical reason wouldn't be so bad.

CW: Sounds like consulting your doctor and laying at least part of your cards on the table might be one step toward getting medical help in carving out some breathing space for yourself.

Rita: I think so. Yeah, that's it! That's one thing I could do.

CW: Let's together map out a possible action plan—for contacting your doctor and requesting assistance in temporarily letting go. Let's look at *when* you want to contact your doctor, *what* you're going to say, and *how* you're going to say it—to make sure you get the results you must have right now.

The crisis worker is attempting to work collaboratively with Rita and to facilitate Rita's real ownership of her plan. The worker also implies a view of Rita as competent and responsible.

Use the Client's Coping Strengths. In crisis intervention it is important not to overlook the client's own strengths and coping mechanisms. Often the crisis events temporarily immobilize the individual's usual strengths and coping strategies. If they can be identified, explored, and reinstated, they may make an enormous contribution toward restoring the client's equilibrium and reassuring the client. For example, one woman had previously relieved stress by playing her piano. She told the worker that she was no longer able to play the piano because her piano had been repossessed. The crisis worker was able to explore with her several possible places where she could avail herself of a piano in times of stress.

Use Referral Resources. An integral aspect of crisis intervention is the use of referral resources. A ready list of names and phone numbers of contact people is a necessity. It is also important for the crisis worker to develop skill in making referrals as well as in working with a wide variety of referral agencies. Many clients need to be referred early to sources of help regarding financial matters, legal assistance, long-term individual therapy, family therapy, substance abuse, severe depression, or other personal matters. Here are suggestions we have found to be useful in working with a variety of agencies. Generally, we find that a breakdown in communication with agencies follows our having overlooked a few obvious and simple cautions. So do as we say, not as we sometimes do!

1. Keep a handy, up-to-date list of frequently used agencies. Keep up with personnel changes.
2. In communities that publish a directory of human services, have available the most recent edition.
3. Cultivate a working relationship with key people in agencies you use frequently. Get on community boards, join organizations, and become integrated into the provider system.
4. Identify yourself, your agency, and your purpose when telephoning. Know secretaries and receptionists by name, and use their names when you call. Treat them with dignity, respect, and equality, and thank them for helping you.
5. Follow up on referrals you make—within 24 hours if at all possible.
6. Don't assume that all clients have the skill to get the services they need. Be prepared to assist clients who may be unable to help themselves to avoid runaround and bureaucratic red tape.
7. Whenever necessary, without engendering dependency, go with clients to the referral agencies to assist and to ensure that effective communication takes place.
8. Write thank-you messages (with copies to their bosses) to persons who are particularly helpful to you and your clients.
9. Don't criticize fellow professionals or the agencies they represent, and don't gossip about either workers or agencies.
10. Keep accurate records of referral activities, so you have a paper trail.
11. Know frequently used agencies' hours, basic services, mode of operation, limitations, and, if possible, policies such as insurance and sliding scale fees.
12. Be aware of any agency services the client is already using, so services don't get duplicated.
13. Use courtesy and good human relations skills when dealing with agency personnel. Put yourself in their shoes, and treat them as you would like to be treated.
14. Avoid expecting perfection of other agencies. Give agencies feedback on how they did, and obtain feedback from them.
15. Be aware of sensory impairment in clients, especially in older adults, and make those impairments known in referrals.
16. If the agency has an orientation session, seek to attend and to participate in it.
17. Practice honesty in communicating to referral agencies regarding the status or needs of clients. (Honest and ethical portrayal of the client's needs will build credibility with other agencies.)

Develop and Use Networks. Closely allied with referral is a function called *networking* (Haywood & Leuthe, 1980). Networking, for crisis workers, is having and using personal contacts within a variety of agencies that directly affect our ability to serve clients effectively and efficiently. Although each person in my network is a referral resource, it is the relationship I have with that individual that defines it as a network. Effective crisis workers can't sit behind a desk and wait for assistance to come to them. They must get out into the community and get to know personally the key individuals who can provide the kinds of services their clients require. A personal relationship based on understanding and trust between the worker and vital network people is invaluable in helping the worker cut through bureaucratic red tape, expedite emergency assistance, and personalize many services that might otherwise not be available to clients.

As crisis workers, we do not operate alone in the world. We are interdependent. Networking permits us to spread the responsibilities among other helping professionals. We mean "helping professionals" in the broadest possible context: lawyers, judges, parole officers, ministers, school counselors, federal, state, and local human services workers, directors and key people in crisis agencies, business and civic leaders, medical doctors, dentists, police, and political leaders may play important roles in the networking process. The development and use of effective networking are indispensable functions of the successful worker.

Get a Commitment. A vital part of crisis intervention is getting a commitment from the client to follow through on the action or actions planned. The crisis worker should ask the client to summarize verbally the steps to be taken. This verbal summary helps the worker understand the client's perception of both the plan and the commitment, and gives the worker an opportunity to clear up any distortions. It also provides the worker an opportunity to establish a follow-up checkpoint with the client. The commitment step can serve as a motivational reminder to the client and also encourage and predispose the client to believe that the action steps will succeed. Without a definite and positive commitment on the part of the client, the best of plans may fall short of the objectives that have been worked out by the worker and the client.

CW: So, Rita, it seems to me that what you've decided to do is to reinitiate some kind of meaningful contact with Mr. Jackson. So that we're both very clear on what you've committed yourself to doing, would you please summarize how and when you're going to proceed?

Rita: I'm going straight to my office today and phone him at school. I'll either talk to him or leave a message for him to call me. As soon as I talk to him, I'll set up a definite day and time to meet with him.

CW: And when you've set up . . .

Rita: Oh, yes! And when I've set up my appointment with him, I'm going to phone you and let you know how it went.

CW: Good. And in the meantime, you have my number on the card if you need me—especially if the safety of either you or your children becomes jeopardized.

Rita: That's right, and I'll call if I lose my nerve with Sam. I've got to get some space for myself there—at least some temporary space.

Experienced crisis workers are generally able to sense how far and how fast the client is able to act. Usually the client is encouraged to commit to as much action as feasible. If we cannot get her or him to make a giant leap forward, we'll accept one small step in a positive direction. The main idea is to facilitate some commitment that will result in movement of the client in a constructive direction.

SUMMARY

Crisis intervention from a practitioner's standpoint incorporates a number of fundamental counseling skills that are specifically tailored to crisis intervention. Listening is fundamental to all successful counseling, including crisis intervention, and includes such techniques as restatement, reflection, owning statements, and open- and closed-ended questions. Essential components of effective listening and communication include effective attending, empathy, genuineness, and acceptance. Action skills range across nondirective, collaborative, and directive worker strategies. These strategies may include helping the client focus or expand awareness, providing guidance and information, allowing cathartic release of emotions, providing support and protection, and mobilizing the client to action.

To see some of the concepts discussed in this chapter in action, refer to your *Crisis Intervention in Action* DVD, or see the clips online on the Counseling CourseMate website. To access this site, go to www.cengagebrain.com, where you'll also find an eBook, additional study tools, quizzes, and more. Take another look at the intervention team as they work with Amy. What are the principal listening and responding techniques they use? Do you think they are too nondirective, too directive, or about right? What about their use of intervention strategies? Do they need to get her to focus more? Expand awareness? Give her more information? Let her engage more in catharsis? Provide more support? Push mobilization to action harder?

REFERENCES

Cormier, W. H., & Cormier, L. S. (1991). *Interviewing strategies for helpers: Fundamental skills and cognitive behavioral interventions* (3rd ed.). Pacific Grove, CA: Brooks/Cole.

Egan, G. (1975). *The skilled helper: A model for systematic helping and interpersonal relating.* Pacific Grove, CA: Brooks/Cole.

Egan, G. (1982). *The skilled helper: Model, skills, and methods for effective helping* (2nd ed.). Pacific Grove, CA: Brooks/Cole.

Egan, G. (1986). *The skilled helper: A systematic approach to effective helping* (3rd ed.). Pacific Grove, CA: Brooks/Cole.

Egan, G. (1990). *The skilled helper: Model, skills, and methods for effective helping* (4th ed.). Pacific Grove, CA: Brooks/Cole.

Gilliland, B. E., & James, R. K. (1998). *Theories and strategies in counseling and psychotherapy* (4th ed.). Boston: Allyn & Bacon.

Haywood, C., & Leuthe, J. (1980, September). *Crisis intervention in the 1980s: From networking to social influence.* Paper presented at the annual convention of the American Psychological Association, Montreal.

Myer, R. A., & James, R. K. (2005). *Crisis intervention workbook and CD-ROM.* Belmont, CA: Thomson Brooks/Cole.

Rogers, C. R. (1969). *Freedom to learn: A view of what education might become.* Columbus, OH: Merrill.

Rogers, C. R. (1977). *Carl Rogers on personal power: Inner strength and its revolutionary impact.* New York: Delacorte.

Weiner, M., & Mehrabian, A. (1968). *Language within language.* New York: Appleton-Century-Croft.

CHAPTER 5

Crisis Case Handling

Handling Crisis Cases Versus Long-Term Cases

To understand crisis case handling, we need to distinguish between what crisis interventionists and long-term therapists do, the principles that underlie the two modes, their objectives, client functioning, and assessment procedures. On first glance, typical models for long-term therapy do not look radically different from a crisis intervention model. Our own long-term, eight-step systematic counseling model (James & Gilliland, 2003, pp. 376–381) incorporates predisposition, exploration, examining alternatives, planning courses of action, and obtaining client commitment in much the same operational format as crisis intervention.

What is radically different is that in long-term therapy, defining problems, identifying alternatives, and planning are much broader in scope, more methodological, and rely on continuous feedback loops to check effectiveness of intervention. A typical counseling session with a long-term client reviews progress since the previous session, collaboratively refines the plan of action if needed, processes the content of the session and the client's feelings about it, and then proposes a new homework assignment to be tried out before the next meeting. Crisis intervention models do not operate with such liberal time dimensions or problem scopes. In crisis intervention, exploring the problems, identifying alternatives, planning, and committing to a plan are all much more compressed in time and scope. What in long-term therapy may occur in a rather leisurely fashion over a period of weekly sessions, in crisis intervention may occur in a half-hour to 2 hours.

Whereas in long-term therapy a great deal of background exploration may provide the therapist a panoramic view of client dynamics, the crisis worker's exploration typically is narrow, starting and stopping with the specific presenting crisis. The long-term therapist's view of alternatives and planning a course of action commonly incorporate psychoeducational processes that seek to change residual, repressive, and chronic client modes of thinking, feeling, and acting. In contrast, the crisis worker seeks to quickly determine previous coping skills and environmental resources available to the client and use them in the present situation as a stopgap measure to gain time and provide a modicum of stability in an out-of-control situation. While crisis workers use psychoeducational techniques a great deal, they typically do so to solve immediate short-term problems that evolve from the crisis itself by providing specific information about what is going on with the client, such as PTSD symptoms, or specific information on how to access resources, such as getting help from FEMA for a housing loan after a tornado.

Whereas the long-term therapist would view comprehensive personality change as a necessary part of the therapeutic plan, the crisis worker endeavors to change personality only to the degree necessary for restoring precrisis functioning. A long-term therapist would look toward an evidence-based methodological manipulation of treatment variables, assess those variables on a variety of dimensions, and process the outcomes with the client. A crisis worker often uses a "best guess" based on previous experience with what does and does not work with a particular problem. Protocols for treatment in long-term therapy are typically evidence based and involve many tryouts as the protocol is fine-tuned to the individual's particular needs. Crisis intervention is a good deal more creative. Although it also operates from evidence-based techniques, it adapts and changes quickly as conditions warrant. Paradoxically, it is fairly rigid in that it employs set procedures for moving the client from an immobile to a mobilized state.

Finally, assessment and feedback of outcome measures in long-term therapy typically involve a great deal of processing between client and therapist as to the efficacy of treatment. If treatment outcomes are not as expected, a feedback loop is integrated into the model that will allow a return to any of the previous steps. Feedback and assessment in crisis intervention typically occur on a here-and-now basis, with emphasis on what changes have occurred in the previous minutes and what the client will do in the next few hours.

There are many approaches to long-term therapy. Although Thorne's (1968, pp. 11–13) approach is dated, it is a classic representation of one of the most comprehensive and eclectic systems to be found. To provide a clear delineation between crisis intervention and long-term therapy, we have compared our model of crisis intervention with Thorne's *principles, objectives, client functioning,* and *assessment* of case handling. Tables 5.1, 5.2, 5.3, and 5.4 summarize the contrasts.

Case Handling at Walk-In Crisis Facilities

Types of Presenting Crises

Clients who present themselves for crisis counseling at walk-in facilities generally fall within one of three categories: those who are experiencing (1) chronic mental illness, (2) acute interpersonal problems in their social environment, or (3) a combination of the two. Most clients who avail themselves of community mental health clinics suffer from financial problems that prohibit them from seeking private therapy.

Chronic Crisis.   Since the enactment of the federal Community Mental Health Centers Act of 1963, the major responsibility for treatment of the mentally ill has fallen on community mental health centers. Although in theory the act was designed to deinstitutionalize patients and return those who are able to functional living, in fact the act has placed many people in chronic crisis.

In addition, increased drug abuse, a rise in crime, fragmentation of families, and a host of other societal ills have caused a tremendous upsurge in the need for mental health services. Originally focused on reintegrating long-term hospital patients into the community, mental health centers have tended to assign chronic cases a less-than-priority status. The unspoken reason is that these clients are extremely frustrating to mental health providers because they show little progress and are a constant financial and emotional drain on the resources of the agencies that come in contact

TABLE 5.1 PRINCIPLES COMPARED BETWEEN LONG-TERM THERAPY AND CRISIS INTERVENTION

LONG-TERM THERAPY MODE	CRISIS CASE-HANDLING MODE
1. *Diagnosis:* Complete diagnostic evaluation	1. *Diagnosis:* Rapid triage crisis assessment
2. *Treatment:* Focus on basic underlying causes; on the whole person	2. *Treatment:* Focus on the immediate traumatized component of the person
3. *Plan:* Personalized comprehensive prescription directed toward fulfilling long-term needs	3. *Plan:* Individual problem-specific prescription focused on immediate needs to alleviate the crisis symptoms
4. *Methods:* Knowledge of techniques to systematically effect a wide array of short-term, intermediate-term, and long-term therapeutic gains	4. *Methods:* Knowledge of time-limited brief therapy techniques used for immediate control and containment of the crisis trauma
5. *Evaluation of results:* Behavioral validation of therapeutic outcomes in terms of the client's total functioning	5. *Evaluation of results:* Behavioral validation by client's return to precrisis level of equilibrium

TABLE 5.2 OBJECTIVES COMPARED BETWEEN LONG-TERM THERAPY AND CRISIS INTERVENTION

LONG-TERM THERAPY MODE (LISTED IN NO PARTICULAR ORDER, BUT GLOBAL IN SCOPE)	CRISIS CASE-HANDLING MODE (LISTED IN LINEAR ORDER WITH A CRISIS-SPECIFIC FOCUS)
1. *Prevent problems:* More basic than cure. Use preventive procedures whenever possible. Explore comprehensive future needs based on current assessment of intra- and interpersonal skills and social, vocational, and financial resources.	1. *Ensure client safety:* Always assess client lethality and provide for the physical and psychological safety of the client and significant others.
2. *Correct etiological factors:* Involves comprehensive evidence-based treatment of broad-based psychological and environmental factors in both the past and present.	2. *Predisposition.* Facilitate conditions for client–worker bonding. Reduce threat level.
3. *Provide systematic support:* Comprehensive measures directed toward improvement of the state of psychological and physical health and well-being of the individual.	3. *Define problem:* Clarify in concrete terms the issues that precipitated the crisis.
4. *Facilitate growth:* Treatment should ideally facilitate rather than interfere with natural environmental and developmental processes.	4. *Provide support:* Establish conditions, by either the crisis worker or significant others, whereby the client feels secure and free of threat or abandonment.
5. *Reeducate:* Treatment seeks to reeducate and teach new models of adjustment for lifelong coping.	5. *Examine alternatives:* Provide options for alleviating the immediate situational threat in relation to the crisis.
6. *Express and clarify emotional attitudes:* Major emphasis is on methods of securing emotional release and expression in a permissive and accepting environment.	6. *Develop a plan:* Formulate a stepwise procedure using client coping skills, crisis worker expertise, and systemic measures to energize the client to take action.
7. *Resolve conflict and inconsistencies:* Therapy aims to help the client achieve insight and understanding into the causation and dynamic roots of the behavior and change.	7. *Obtain commitment:* Obtain agreement as to specific time, duration, and number of activities required to stabilize the client and/or crisis situation.
8. *Accept reality:* Help the client to *accept* what cannot be changed. Move forward into new realities and discard problematic histories.	8. *Follow-up.* Short-term follow-up to determine if crisis intervention strategies continue to work.
9. *Reorganize attitudes:* Move the person toward exhibiting a more positive view of life and more effective social integration.	
10. *Maximize intellectual resources:* Improve the functions of sensing, perceiving, remembering, communicating, thinking, behavior management, and self-control.	

TABLE 5.3 CLIENT FUNCTIONING COMPARED BETWEEN LONG-TERM THERAPY AND CRISIS INTERVENTION

LONG-TERM THERAPY MODE	CRISIS CASE-HANDLING MODE
1. Client shows sufficient *affect*; manifests some basis for experiencing and understanding his or her emotional state.	1. *Affectively*, the client is impaired to the extent that there is little understanding of his or her emotional state.
2. Client shows some ability to *cognitively* understand the connection between behavior and consequences—between what is rational and irrational.	2. *Cognitively*, the client shows inability to think linearly and logically and formulate strategies to alleviate the crisis. Irrationality is the norm.
3. There is some modicum of *behavioral* control.	3. *Behaviorally*, the client is out of control and may pose a danger to self or others.

TABLE 5.4 ASSESSMENT COMPARED BETWEEN LONG-TERM THERAPY AND CRISIS INTERVENTION

LONG-TERM THERAPY MODE	CRISIS CASE-HANDLING MODE
1. *Intake data:* Client is stable enough to provide in-depth background regarding the problem. Lengthy intake form may contain details of the client's total history: family, medical history, drug use, education, therapy background, social history. Comprehensive personality and intellectual tests may be given.	1. *Intake data:* Client may not be able to fill out an intake form because of instability or time constraints; a verbal and/or visual evaluation of current maladaptive state may be the only data available.
2. *Safety:* Client safety is not the primary focus unless there are clues pointing toward imminent danger to self or others.	2. *Safety:* Crisis worker's first concern is client and others' safety; determining whether client is suicidal, homicidal, or otherwise a danger or threat to someone by intentional or unintentional acts.
3. *Time:* The therapist has time to procure a variety of assessment data to confirm or contraindicate the hypothesized problem. Total case diagnosis and workups are gathered before the treatment plan is developed. Personality assessment indexes are generally gathered to compare client functioning against norm groups on standard pathology measures.	3. *Time:* Crisis worker has no time for administering formal instruments. Worker must rely on immediate verbal and nonverbal cues emitted by the client to make assessment of degree of pathology.
4. *Reality testing:* The therapist assumes the client is in touch with reality unless assessment data or other clues indicate otherwise.	4. *Reality testing:* Using simple questioning procedures, the crisis worker must determine whether the person is in touch with reality and how effectively the person is functioning in real time.
5. *Referrals:* Referral resources have implications for long-term development. Examples of referrals might be to family services, mental health centers, vocational/educational assistance, and job placement services.	5. *Referrals:* Referral resources have implications of immediacy in terms of getting the client to safety and some degree of stability. Examples of referrals might be to the police, hospital emergency room, psychiatric or medical evaluation, or immediate support people.
6. *Consultation:* Consultants and other backup resources are available as needed. Collaboration is normally initiated after consultation with the client and/or the therapist's supervisor.	6. *Consultation:* Professional consultants who are trained in the diagnosis of pathology may be on call for backup purposes. Police and mobile crisis teams are sometimes available. Most likely the worker is on his or her own.
7. *Drug use:* The therapist relies on data from the intake material and on information developed in the normal course of the therapy to ascertain the level and type of prescription medication or illicit drug or alcohol use.	7. *Drug use:* The crisis worker relies on verbal and visual responses to ascertain the level and type of prescription medication or illicit drug or alcohol use.
8. *Disposition:* Client typically starts and finishes with the same therapist over a course of months. May occasionally be referred to adjunctive therapeutic specialization during the course of therapy. Clients come and go voluntarily and return to home environment.	8. *Disposition:* Client typically starts and stops with the same worker over a course of hours or days. May be referred permanently to long-term treatment with a therapeutic specialization once stabilized. Client may be involuntarily committed, arrested and jailed, or released back to supervised care of custodians, guardians, or significant others.

with them. Many community mental health centers have de-emphasized this role and moved more toward dealing with developmental problems of "normal," more highly functioning people (Slaikeu, 1990, p. 284). Perhaps more ominously, funding cutbacks have forced community mental health centers to look more closely at a client's ability to pay as a precondition for treatment, which means that people who may most need service may be relegated to a waiting list. Furthermore,

because of legal ramifications and funding problems, severely disturbed people who are committed to state hospitals typically have very brief stays and are turnstiled back onto the streets.

The result is that a host of chronically mentally ill people who are poorly functioning, impoverished, homeless, victims or perpetrators of crime, and without support systems of any kind are left to fend for themselves. These people often have multiple problems besides a primary diagnosis of psychopathology. They may be noncompliant with treatment, disregard their medication, abuse alcohol and drugs, have other severe physical problems, and be victimized financially, physically, and psychologically by others (Bender, 1986; Nurius, 1984; Pope, 1991). It is easy to see why such people often wind up in crisis when understaffed and underfunded mental health clinics (Roberts, 1991, p. 31) and other social services agencies cannot care for them. The chronically mentally ill are often on a first-name basis with local police and personnel in emergency rooms, mental health clinics, and social services agencies.

Social/Environmental Crises. People with chronic mental health issues are not the only people who avail themselves of, or are brought to, walk-in facilities. Runaways, addicts, the battered, physically disabled, crime victims, survivors of violent events, the sexually abused, the terminally ill, veterans, the unemployed, and relatives of the chronically physically and mentally ill are some of the many participants in a drama of social crisis that is played out every day and night in mental health clinics, emergency rooms, student counseling centers, social services agencies, and police stations across the country. Many precipitating events may be unexpected and sudden and may have an impact far beyond the individual on families and communities, leaving these systems disorganized and out of control. Crises that are generated in the social environment are some of the most potent for mental health workers because of their ramifications across systems and the heightened emotionality and immediacy that accompany them for both clientele and workers.

Combination of Types. The foregoing crisis types rarely occur as discrete categories. Overlapping among types and problems that face crisis workers is the rule rather than the exception. Attempting to stabilize someone with chronic schizophrenia without providing food and shelter, treating a trauma survivor without first working on a drug addiction, or considering vocational exploration without handling the depression of a middle-aged executive who has just lost her job is a waste of valuable time. Handling multiple crises with the same client is the rule rather than the exception.

Case Handling at a Community Mental Health Clinic

We have chosen Midtown Mental Health Clinic in our hometown of Memphis, Tennessee, as a generic representation of how clients are taken care of who walk into or are brought to a community mental health facility. This clinic's catchment area includes a number of housing projects, the downtown area, the University of Tennessee medical facility, the city hospital, the Memphis Veterans Administration Hospital, the Memphis Mental Health Institute (a state psychiatric hospital), the county jail, several halfway shelters for drug addicts and homeless people, and a variety of other social services agencies. Furthermore, its catchment area has the highest crime rate and incidence of domestic violence in the city, a high percentage of school dropouts, and some of the most impoverished areas of the city.

Entry. Clients may come to the mental health clinic on their own, be brought by relatives or social services agencies, or be taken into custody by the police. At the moment of entry, disposition of the case begins. A person in crisis who walks in or is brought to Midtown may range across the triage scale from mildly to severely disturbed. If the person is severely disturbed, a senior clinician is summoned. An attempt is made to remove the client to an isolated office to reduce environmental stimuli and calm the client so that an assessment can proceed. The clinician tries to obtain a case history. If this is not possible, the clinician makes a visual and verbal assessment in regard to information-processing problems, tangential thinking, hallucinations, disassociation, threats to self or others, or severe drug abuse. If any of these symptoms is present, then a psychiatrist is called to evaluate the client and decide whether hospitalization is warranted.

Commitment. If the client is so mentally fragmented as to be clearly out of touch with reality or deemed an imminent danger to self or others, he or she is committed to an inpatient mental health facility. The person is asked to voluntarily commit to hospitalization. If he or she is unwilling to do so, a physician may write an involuntary commitment order. An officer of the Crisis Intervention Team, a special unit of the Memphis Police Department trained to deal with the mentally ill, is then called to transport the patient. Under no circumstances do mental health workers become involved in transportation, because of safety concerns and the possibility of stigmatizing themselves as punitive agents in the patients' eyes. If patients are financially able, they may be transported to a private psychiatric facility. If they are indigent, they are taken to the city hospital psychiatric emergency unit for evaluation and subsequent placement at the Memphis Mental Health Institute state hospital.

Intake Interview. If the individual is coherent enough to provide verbal and written information, an intake interview is started. Following closely the crisis intervention model in Chapter 3, the intake worker first attempts to assess for client safety, define the problem, and apprise the client of his or her rights. In a patient and methodical manner, the intake worker goes through a standard intake interview sheet. Through open-ended questions and active listening, the worker tries to obtain as comprehensive a picture of the client as possible. The worker also attempts to determine the precipitating problem that brought the client to the clinic. The intake worker must be nonjudgmental, empathic, and caring and must also obtain concrete and specific information from a client who may not be able or willing to reciprocate.

Two critical components are always appraised in this initial assessment: degree of client lethality and drug use. It is a given that crisis situations either involve or have the possibility of acting-out behavior. Therefore, the intake worker evaluates clients in relation to their plans or intent to do harm to themselves or others. Because of the widespread use of prescription and illicit drugs, the worker checks to determine if drugs are involved in the presenting problem. Thus, intake workers need to have a copy of and familiarity with the *Physician's Desk Reference (PDR)*. The intake worker must also have a working knowledge of the side effects of "street drugs" because of the high incidence of their use in the Midtown area.

Disposition. After the intake has been completed, the worker constructs and writes a proposed diagnosis and treatment recommendations. The intake worker discusses the treatment recommendations and possible services with the client. It is then the client's decision to accept or reject services. If services are accepted, the intake worker introduces the client to the therapist who will most likely be in charge of the case. A full clinical team meeting is held to confirm or alter the initial diagnosis and treatment recommendations. At that time a primary therapist is designated and assumes responsibility for the case.

Anchoring. On their initial visit, clients are never left alone. From their intake interview to disposition to a primary therapist, workers help clients feel that a personal interest is being taken in them and their problems. The worker takes and hands over the client to the therapist who will be in charge of the case. The therapist gives the client a verbal orientation about what is going to occur. The idea behind this methodical orientation is to demystify the world of mental health, familiarize clients with what their treatment will be, and provide them with a psychological anchor in the form of a real person who will act as their advocate, support, and contact person. Quickly establishing rapport with the primary therapist is helpful in forestalling future crisis and is extremely important to unstable clients, given the threatening implications of entering a mental health facility, possible loss of freedom, and the bureaucratic maze of the mental health system. It is also designed to immediately empower clients and make them feel they have taken a step in the right direction. In many instances, a compeer volunteer is assigned to the client. Compeers are trained volunteers who act as support and socializing agents for clients who do not have friends or relatives to assist and encourage them.

Short-Term Disposition. Many crises relate to the basic physical necessities of living. If that's the case, the intake worker makes short-term provisions for food, clothing, shelter, and other necessities while setting in motion the wheels of other social services agencies to provide long-term subsistence services. If clients are unable to care for themselves, the Tennessee Department of Family Services is appointed as a conservator to handle their money and look after their basic needs. Thus it is very important that the intake worker and other staff thoroughly understand and can access the local social services network.

Long-Term Disposition. An interdisciplinary team reviews and evaluates the intake worker's diagnosis and recommendations. If the team considers it necessary, a psychiatrist and a pharmacist conduct a psychiatric or pharmacological evaluation of the client. If a psychological evaluation is required, a psychologist evaluates the person on standardized personality and intellectual measures. Depending on the client's needs, people from various specialty units join the team. Once the team is complete, it formulates objectives and goals, and an evidence-based therapeutic plan is put into operation. The team reviews this plan on a regular basis and changes it if necessary.

Twenty-Four-Hour Service. Midtown operates 24 hours a day. After regular working hours, telephone relays are linked into the crisis hotline. Telephone workers there evaluate the call and make a decision on who should handle it. That may be a mobile crisis team or, in the city of Memphis, the Memphis Police Department Crisis Intervention Team, which we will examine at length later in this chapter.

Mobile Crisis Teams.   Mobile crisis teams operate for two distinct reasons. For certain clients, particularly geriatric or physically disabled clients, it may be necessary to make home visits to provide services. In other cases, when a client is out of control and unwilling or unable to go to the clinic, crisis workers go wherever the client is.

The Community Mental Health Act of 1963 mandated that those clinics receiving federal funds must provide 24-hour emergency service. The mobile crisis team has been one answer to that mandate. With the advent of the police department's Crisis Intervention Team, this need has diminished a good deal in Memphis. However, in many other cities these mobile teams are on call and often follow up either along with or after local police departments have contained the situation.

Typically a hotline or 911 mental disturbance call will ask for assistance. Either a police car with a mental health worker riding along will go to the scene, or mental health workers will follow up after police. These teams are typically equipped with sophisticated communication and information retrieval systems that can call up client mental health files or criminal records. In some instances, psychiatric nurses may be members of these teams and can administer psychotropic medication in consultation with psychiatrists (Ligon, 2000).

Depending on state statutes, either the police or licensed mental health workers in these mobile units have the power to take clients into protective custody and transport them to a hospital rather than to jail. There are two problems associated with this approach. First, most such units operate in urban areas; many rural counties in the United States have little provision for such emergency services, in regard to either staff or a mental health facility to transport a client to or the ability to administer on-site crisis intervention (Aron et al., 2009; Bain, 2011; Rouse, 1998; Rural Assistance Center, 2011). Second, no local police jurisdiction is going to transport someone 100 miles if it takes that police officer out of service for any length of time. The bottom line is that the mentally ill wind up in the place most convenient to put them—and that is usually jail, the very last place they need to be.

Police and Crisis Intervention

It may seem odd to many of you reading this section that we are going to spend a lot of time talking about police officers and crisis intervention since crisis workers generally fall into counseling, social work, psychology, nursing, and other medical and social service professions. So why cops? A fat lot they know about empathic responding to people in crisis, right?

Changing Role of the Police

The role of the police is rapidly changing and expanding. In most communities, police departments are being tasked with more and more responsibilities in addition to traditional law enforcement. Increasingly, crisis work with the mentally ill and emotionally disturbed is one of those responsibilities. It is commonly thought that patrol officers concern themselves mainly with *instrumental* crimes such as theft, robbery, and assault. The fact is that police officers deal with a multitude of *expressive* kinds of crime, in which individuals pose a serious threat to themselves or others because of their own anger, fear, vulnerability, depression, or lack of emotional control. Even though police departments do not relish investing much of their time away from providing for public safety and enforcing the law, they have found themselves more and more in a modality of law enforcement/crisis intervention (Borum, 2000; Miller, 2006; Saunders, 2010).

Police and the Mentally Ill/ Mentally Disturbed

The problem has been ongoing and increasing since the advent of the Community Mental Health Act of 1963 and the changes it brought in releasing many mentally ill persons back into the community. Gillig and associates (1990) studied a sample of 309 police officers in Cincinnati and Hamilton County, Ohio, and found that during a 1-month period, almost 60 percent of the officers had responded to at least one call in which a presumably mentally ill person had to be confronted. Almost half of the officers had responded to more than one such call during the 1-month period.

This dilemma puts a heavy responsibility on the shoulders of law enforcement officers, and although many dislike spending their time on crises of a social service nature, they are accepting encounters with the mentally ill as an appropriate aspect of modern police work and are more empathic to their illness (Bahora et al., 2008; Watson et al., 2010). They are also requesting more information, training, and collaboration with mental health and crisis intervention agencies (Compton et al., 2006). The foregoing has highlighted a need to develop training models that include police crisis intervention training with the mentally ill (Compton et al., 2006; Erstling, 2006; Gillig et al., 1990; Luckett & Slaikeu, 1990; Vermette, Pinals, & Applebaum, 2005).

Because of that ongoing need, the Memphis Police Department developed the Crisis Intervention Team (CIT; James, 1994; James & Crews, 2009). CIT was developed specifically to train patrol officers to deal with the mentally ill and emotionally disturbed. The authors of this book were fortunate enough to be involved in that initial, innovative endeavor, which started in Memphis in 1987. Little did we realize at the time that this program, with its humble beginnings attempting to resolve a local problem, would catch fire nationally. Today, the program has come to be known as the Memphis Model for police crisis intervention with the mentally ill. In 2005 the first national convention for Crisis Intervention Team police officers was held in Columbus, Ohio. More than 1,000 police personnel came to that program from all over the country. It is with a good deal of pride that your authors had a hand in training many of those officers who came to Memphis from such diverse jurisdictions as Portland, Oregon; Ft. Lauderdale, Florida; Montgomery County, Maryland; and Hutchinson, Kansas. Currently, all across the United States, law enforcement jurisdictions are establishing CITs, and thousands of police officers are being trained along the lines of what you are about to read in the next few paragraphs (Addy & James, 2005).

The Crisis Intervention Team (CIT) Program

Because budget constraints, economic factors, and social problems have generated enormous numbers of homeless people, dumped-onto-the-streets mental patients who formerly would have been hospitalized as inpatients, many more mentally disturbed people now come into contact with the general public than ever before. Consequently, the Memphis city government, the mental health community, and the police department realized that incidents of police involvement with the mentally ill had resulted in the mentally ill themselves being vulnerable to serious harm and the increased possibility of police officers, untrained in dealing with the mentally ill, getting seriously injured or even killed. Why can't mental health workers take care of the enormous numbers of emotionally out-of-control people

on the streets? Because it is a physical and fiscal impossibility to put enough mental health workers onto the streets to monitor and serve the needs of these out-of-control people and to do so in accordance with the "least restrictive environment" movement in a democratic society.

Spearheaded by the local affiliate of the Alliance for the Mentally Ill, the Memphis Police Department, the mental health community, the city government, and the counselor education and social work departments of two local universities formed a unique and creative alliance for the purpose of developing and implementing proactive and preventive methods of containing emotionally explosive situations in the streets that frequently lead to violence. Because the police were the first and often the only responsible officials on the scene of an out-of-control situation, calling in outside consultants proved unworkable. Therefore, the unique and cohesive alliance of several important community groups determined that highly trained and motivated police officers were the logical personnel to form a frontline defense against the crisis of dangerously expressive, out-of-control persons in the streets. This massive alliance effort resulted in the CIT program's becoming an example of how a successful program can work to accomplish the objectives of public safety and welfare, economic feasibility, and police accountability (James & Crews, 2009).

The Concept.   To comprehend what a difficult and delicate task it has been to bring to fruition a successful and workable CIT program, one must understand how the alliance network functions. If your community does not have such a program, and you think it would be a good idea to get one started, read the following very carefully. The problem of the mentally ill, particularly the homeless mentally ill, is endemic and pervades all jurisdictions that attempt to establish CIT programs. Major Sam Cochran, who was the longtime coordinator of the Memphis CIT program and has been instrumental in helping disseminate the Memphis Model all over the country, puts it very well when he says, "It is not just a program to train police officers to deal with the mentally ill. It is a concept that brings all kinds of interest groups together in a network, and if that concept is not nourished, the program will fail."

The network behind the Memphis CIT program consists of the Memphis city government and the Memphis Police Department (hereafter just referred to as the police); the Alliance for the Mentally Ill; five of the six local community mental health centers; the emergency room components of public hospitals; academic educators from the Department of Counseling, Educational Psychology and Research at the University of Memphis and the School of Social Work at the University of Tennessee; the YWCA Abused Women's Services; the Sexual Assault Resource Center; and several private practice psychologists (hereafter referred to as the mental health community). The power, force, and success of the alliance derive from the process and fundamental working relationship that the police and mental health community have used to both form and maintain the CIT program. The alliance was formed because both the police and the mental health community realized that the problem of crisis in the streets was too severe for either to handle alone and that working together would make life much easier and safer for both as well as provide improved and safer service for clients and the community (James & Crews, 2009).

The alliance conducted a great many collaborative, systematic, and democratic meetings over a period of several months to hammer out a workable CIT blueprint. As a result of these meetings, key individuals from all segments of both police and the mental health community developed effective working relationships with one another and learned a great deal about each other's problems, competencies, rules, and boundaries.

Police were brought into mental health facilities for orientation into the world of mental health. Mental health personnel were brought into the police academy and accompanied police on patrols to learn about the problems, procedures, competencies, roles, and boundaries that law enforcement officers face in their everyday work. Then formal training was developed to ensure that not only the CIT officer selectees but also all supervisory-level police personnel understood the problems, objectives, and operational procedures of the CIT program (James, 1994, p. 187; James & Crews, 2009). The development and training phases provided some essential attitudinal and professional understanding between the police and the mental health community. As a result, CIT officers and their superiors know precisely what training and consultation resources the mental health community can provide. And the mental health professionals know what competencies and resources the police in general and the CIT officers in particular have to offer.

Concomitantly, both sides develop mutual respect, understanding, trust, and cooperation. A CIT officer intervening with a distraught mental patient will likely listen empathically to the patient's feelings and concerns, be familiar with the mental health services available (will possibly know the patient's caseworker personally), and will, within the boundaries of professional ethics, communicate to the patient an understanding of the short-term needs of that person as well as a desire to provide for the immediate safety and referral requirements to contain and stabilize the patient's current crisis. The mental health center caseworker will also understand and have confidence in the CIT officer's ability to be a stabilizing and safe influence on the patient and will, if needed, likely call on the CIT officer for emergency assistance with a particular client. The mental health caseworker may collaborate with the CIT officer in obtaining anecdotal information needed to enhance the patient's treatment plan and prevent the recurrence of that particular patient's crisis in the streets (James, 1994, p. 191).

Based on the trust and confidence built through the powerful and cohesive alliance just described, the police department opted to select experienced police patrol officers to receive training and then serve in the dual role of police officers and crisis intervention team specialists. Volunteers for the program had to have good records as officers, pass personality tests for maturity and mental stability, and be recommended, interviewed, screened, and selected to receive CIT training. The police department committed itself to putting trained CIT officers on duty in every precinct in the city, 24 hours every day. All upper-echelon supervisory officers received formal orientation about the role and function of CIT officers so that whenever any call involving a suspected mentally disturbed person anywhere in the city is received, the CIT officer is the designated responsible law enforcement official at the scene—regardless of rank—and all other officers at the scene serve as backups to the CIT officer who handles the case (James, 1994, p. 194; James, & Crews, 2009).

CIT Training Using Mental Health Experts and Providers.   An integral part of the CIT program is the special preservice training provided for the officers. The importance of effective training by competent, committed, motivated professionals cannot be overemphasized. We also insist that they ride with experienced CIT officers on a Friday or Saturday evening shift prior to the scheduled training of each new group of CIT officers. As Erstling (2006) states, spending 8 hours in a patrol car together goes a long way toward learning to trust and understand one another.

The following topics are covered in the 40 hours of CIT training:

1. Cultural awareness of the mentally ill
2. Substance abuse and co-occurring disorders
3. Developmental disabilities
4. Treatment strategies and mental health resources
5. Patient rights, civil commitment, and legal aspects of crisis intervention
6. Suicide intervention
7. Using the mobile crisis team and community resources
8. Psychotropic medications and their side effects
9. Verbal defusing and de-escalating techniques
10. Borderline and other personality disorders
11. Family and consumer perspectives
12. Fishbowl discussion on-site with mentally ill patients on patient perceptions of the police

While most of these training components are in a lecture-discussion format, two are not. These two components are considered absolutely critical in the training of police officers who do crisis intervention with the mentally ill. They are verbal de-escalation and defusing, and the client fishbowl.

De-escalation and Defusing Techniques. Verbal de-escalation and defusing techniques are taught throughout the weeklong training. These skills are considered so critical that four different trainers are used for 12 hours of training. Basic introductory techniques are taught first. How do you introduce yourself? What is the nonverbal message you convey by your body posture and language? What voice tone do you use? These skills are taught on the second day of training

Next come basic exploratory skills and establishing a relationship. Skills taught include (1) how and when to use open-ended and closed-ended questions, (2) what owning statements are and why they are important, (3) how to keep clients secure without cornering them (see Chapter 14, Violent Behavior in Institutions), (4) officer and client safety, (5) crowd control, (6) when and when not to use reflection of feelings or thinking, and (7) a summary recapping techniques and restatement for client and officer understanding and communication. These skills are taught on the third day of training.

The training is also greatly enhanced if it can skillfully integrate the conceptual with the experiential. Realistic role play, video technology, playback, and discussion are essential. On the fourth day, 4 hours of training are devoted to role plays of actual police–client encounters. Veteran CIT officers role-play clients. These officers bring many valuable firsthand experiences into the learning environment that heighten interest, enhance motivation, and provide realism (James, 1994, p. 187). Trainees are divided into teams of four, and each member of the team is given 4 minutes onstage to attempt to defuse and de-escalate the client. The rest of the trainees (there are usually about 24–30) watch all of the teams perform and hear their critiques. The idea is that by watching others perform, trainees learn from the others' successes and failures. Scenarios range from clients with senile dementia to schizophrenics to diabetic psychosis to enraged jilted lovers. The role players escalate or de-escalate their violent behavior depending on how and what trainees do. Each team segment is videotaped, and after all four trainees have performed the videotape is played back, during which veteran CIT officers comment honestly and objectively on both positive and negative aspects of trainees' performance.

On the fifth day of training, complex CIT scenarios are demonstrated. All of the verbal skills used in preceding sessions are integrated to deal with very difficult clients. Such difficult scenarios as suicidal and severely psychotic clients are demonstrated, and then intervention techniques are broken down and analyzed as to appropriate and inappropriate responses. At the end of the week, trainees are in possession of the basic skills necessary to intervene with the mentally ill. Like most beginners, the new CIT officers are a little unsure of themselves. However, one of our most rewarding experiences in this business has been seeing these officers come back to aid in training, having developed some of the most outstanding crisis intervention skills we have seen in the 40-plus years we have been doing this work.

Fishbowls With Clients. Fishbowl discussions are unique and powerful sessions for CIT trainees. During this component of the training, trainees are brought into a mental health facility to meet in a discussion group circle with selected mental health patients. A mental health professional, who also serves as an instructor in the CIT training program, sits in the center of the circle with the patients surrounded by the CIT trainees. The professional engages in interviews and dialogues with the mental health patients, in the "fishbowl," so to speak. CIT trainees observe and hear what the mental patients have to say about their own personal needs and about their prior interactions, experiences, and perceptions of the police. After the "fishbowl" interview and dialogue, trainees who had been observing the professional–patient dialogue have an opportunity to ask questions and interact directly with the patients. The fishbowl discussion has been described by CIT trainees as profoundly motivational and an essential part of their learning, orientation, and training.

The Success of CIT. In more than two decades since its start in Memphis, CIT has grown exponentially, with training centers now located throughout the country and thousands of police officers trained in its protocols (Saunders, 2010). It is noteworthy that the CIT concept is now international, with its own newsletter and convention. *The Team News*, the newsletter of CIT International, is available at http://www.citinternational.org. CIT programs can now be found across the United States, Canada, Australia, and Sweden. But is there any evidence it really works?

In its first 16 months of operation in 1987–1988, Memphis CIT officers responded to 5,831 mental disturbance calls and transported 3,424 cases to mental health facilities without any patient fatalities. Both calls and transports have increased significantly over the 20-plus years the program has been in operation. This increase in "mental disturbance" service calls happens in other jurisdictions as well (Kisely et al., 2010; Teller et al., 2006) and is most likely attributable to increased awareness by the public of the CIT program. That increased awareness is particularly true of relatives and others responsible for the care and well-being of the mentally ill. Publication and support by the National Alliance on Mental Illness (2011) for CIT officers has led to the belief that caregivers' loved ones will be handled in a sensitive manner and not be killed or injured by the police.

Along with increased calls, there appears to be a reduction in the use of force, more diversion from jail to hospitals (Lamb, Weinberger, & Gross, 2004; Ritter et al., 2011; Skeem & Bibeau, 2008), decreases in time spent on each call, and increased cooperation between mental health service providers and police (Kisely et al., 2010). In a comprehensive review of research outcomes, Compton and associates (2008) found that there was indeed a reduction in the use of force by CIT officers, more sensitivity toward the mentally ill with commensurate diversion instead of arrest, fewer officer injuries, and reduced hostage team callouts. In Memphis it is noteworthy that only two fatalities have occurred to a recipient of service by CIT officers during the more than 20 years the Memphis Police Department CIT has been in operation, and in both of those cases police officers were found to be justified in killing the person.

Suicide by Cop. Indeed, it is extremely significant that the death toll is so low when CIT officers make the scene. A fairly common phenomenon called "suicide by cop" has been well established. In essence, people who do not quite have the courage to kill themselves engage in some activity that gains the attention of the police. Once the police arrive, they engage the police in a threatening manner and succeed in getting themselves shot. In short, the cops complete the suicide (Lindsay & Lester, 2004). Police are highly aware of this dangerous phenomenon and are also very interested in learning how to handle it (Lindsay & Lester, 2004; Vermette, Pinals, & Applebaum, 2005). At least in Memphis we believe the ability of the police to avoid helping complete this suicidal act and to reduce other mortalities is directly attributable to CIT training. Although no figures exist to determine how many persons have been injured while being taken into protective custody during the 20-plus years CIT has been in operation, statistics indicate that injuries to officers have been reduced significantly. Furthermore, barricade situations have also been reduced significantly. The advent of the CIT program has almost put the Memphis Police Department hostage negotiation team out of business because CIT officers arriving on the scene are often able to defuse and control the situation before the hostage team arrives (James, 1994, pp. 189–190).

Why is this so? Compton and his associates (2006) conducted a study of Georgia CIT officers immediately before and after undergoing CIT training. After training, those officers demonstrated much-improved attitudes, more support for treatment, less social distancing, and less stigmatization of aggressive schizophrenics. In summary, besides their increased skill at defusing and de-escalating the violent mentally ill and emotionally disturbed, CIT police officers have become some of the most caring and concerned crisis workers the mentally ill have.

Transcrisis Handling in Long-Term Therapy

Clients in long-term therapy are not immune from crisis. Therapy tends to move in developmental stages with psychological troughs, crests, and plateaus. Even though clients have success in meeting therapeutic goals, each new stage brings with it what are seen in many instances to be even more formidable obstacles. The beginning therapist who has seen a client make excellent progress is often in for a rude awakening when the client's progress comes completely undone and behavior regresses to pretherapeutic functioning—or worse!

Anxiety Reactions

A puzzling aspect of therapy occurs when clients are highly successful in achieving tremendously difficult goals and then are completely undone by a task that to the objective observer does not seem all that difficult. Although it seems cognitively irrational, the fear of failure to achieve this minor goal becomes a self-fulfilling prophecy. The client fears that others will see through her or his sham of competence and irrationally thinks that any real progress is a delusion. At such times, clients engage in various types of flight behavior. Severe anxiety is one way of escaping the threatening situation. Consider Melanie's present dilemma. Melanie has escaped from an alcoholic marriage and subsequently completed 2 years of secretarial science at a community college, but she has fallen apart when faced with an interview for a job she desperately wants.

Melanie: (*extremely anxious and agitated, calling her therapist at 1 A.M.*) I hated to call you, but I'm so scared. I've thrown up twice, and I've got the shakes. This hasn't happened since I walked out on Bill over 3 years ago. God, I can't get a grip, and I need to do my best tomorrow. I know I'll just blow it. I can't think straight, and I can't remember a thing about interviewing. Everything's just running together.

The therapist puts Melanie at a 5 on the triage scale for cognitive and behavioral threat and a 6 for affective anxiety/fear. If the therapist does not help diminish the anxiety, the potential is that Melanie may move upward to 8–9 on these scales by the time she goes for her job interview.

TH: Just do this for a minute, Melanie. Take a deep breath, and let it out slo-o-owly. That's right! Now take another! OK, again. (*Continues in a patient, calm voice for about 2 minutes, taking Melanie through a brief deep-breathing exercise to calm her anxiety attack.*)

After the deep-breathing exercise, when Melanie has regained some semblance of control, the therapist paces with her through the role play they had conducted the previous session, has her write down her blunders and strong points, discusses those with her, determines that her attack is receding, and assesses her as now being between a 2 and a 3 on the subscales. A quick review of the client's other successes reinforces and further buttresses the positive change in current functioning.

TH: Now notice the change in your voice. I'll bet you've also calmed down to where you aren't shaking. Did you notice how much more you're in control now? Remember what you're there for. Although a lot depends on this for you, you've also done even bigger, more threatening and scary things in your life like getting the hell out of that malignant marriage. Remember! You've become very good in secretarial science. They need you as much or more than you need them. I want you to put that up as a big sign-board in your head, in Day-Glo pink: THEY NEED YOU JUST AS MUCH AS YOU NEED THEM!

By role-playing the scene, the therapist puts Melanie back on familiar ground and puts the problem back into context—getting a job as opposed to having a free-floating anxiety attack. By marshaling the client's resources and very specifically and objectively reminding her of what her strengths are, the therapist concretizes the vague dread she feels at having to face the interview. The therapist's exhortation about who needs whom is not placating here. It is realistic. Melanie's ego needs to be reminded of these facts so that she will have a positive mental set toward both her personhood and her skills as she enters the interview. Finally, the therapist offers her the opportunity to have a safety net.

TH: Melanie, I think you're ready to get some sleep and go knock their socks off tomorrow. However, if you wake up tomorrow morning and really have some questions or think you need to role-play that interview once more, give me a call. I've got some free time before your interview, and we can go over it once more. Now go to bed, get some sleep, and dream about that Day-Glo pink billboard.

By leaving her with a positive injunction and making time for her the next day, the therapist continues to provide a support system and a security net for Melanie.

Regression

The risk of taking the next step in therapeutic development may become too overwhelming even though clients have been highly successful in attaining prior goals. When clients are overwhelmed, they may regress in their behavior, retreating to maladaptive but familiar ways of behaving, feeling, and thinking.

Melanie: (*somewhat embarrassed and mumbling in a childlike voice*) I know what you're going to say, but I was thinking I really couldn't cut this, and Bill made that offer even after I got him arrested that he still loved me and was getting help, and I know he doesn't drink much anymore.

TH: (*interpreting the dynamics*) What you're really saying is the prospect of that interview is scaring the hell out of you, and it's so scary that you'd give up 3 years of hard work and sacrifice to go back to a really lousy, not to mention dangerous, way of living, when you're about to get the gold ring. I'm wondering why you've decided to sabotage yourself now.

By interpreting the dependency needs of the client, the therapist welds regressive thinking to the current threat of becoming independent as manifested in the job interview. Although the client's behavior and affect are not blatant, she is moving insidiously higher on the triage cognitive loss subscale. Left alone, that negative self-talk could convince the client to give up her new self-identity and go back to the long-dead and dangerous marriage.

Melanie: Oh, I just knew you'd say that, but I'm not sure I can do this. I mean a big outfit like United Techtronic.

TH: (*in a cool, clear, no-nonsense, but not condemning, voice*) Big or small, United Techtronic is not the question. The question is, Are you going to choose to blow this before you even see if you can cut it? That's one way of never finding out if you're good enough. You can make that choice, although you've now been making a different one for 3 years. I'd hope you wouldn't do that—I believe you are good enough—but then, it's your choice.

This reality-based approach directly confronts the client with the underlying and unwarranted irrational decision she is about to make and vividly points out how she is trying to delude herself into buying back into a dependent status and revictimizing herself.

Problems of Termination

When clients have met their goals for therapy, are fully functioning, and are ready to get back to the business of living their own lives, they may suddenly produce terrible problems that only their therapist can solve. Whatever these problems are, it is an excellent bet that they have been told that it's time to terminate, or they have figured out that termination is about to happen. At such times it is a common occurrence for dependency issues to arise. These problems generally can be resolved by successively approximating the client to termination. For example, instead of every week, the therapist schedules the client every 2 weeks, then once a month, and then for a 6-month follow-up. The other option is to clearly discuss the possibility that this issue will arise.

TH: Melanie, I think it's time we discussed your spreading your wings and flying away from here. You landed that job and . . .

Melanie: (*interrupts*) But I couldn't have done that without you. You give me the courage to try those things. You've been so wonderful. I just couldn't have done any of this without you. And there's still the problem with the kids and . . .

TH: (*gently interrupting*) I appreciate those compliments. They mean a lot to me. Yet although we've worked together on those things, it's been you who's done it, not I. What I want to talk about with you now is some of those fears and really being on your own, like what you just said. That's pretty normal to have those feelings; lots of people do. Sort of like when you left home the first time. I want you to know I'll be here if you need me, but I want you also to know that I think it's time for you to be on your own. I'd like to discuss this with you in today's session.

Crisis in the Therapy Session

One of the scariest times for a therapist occurs when a technique has done its job exceedingly well, and the client gains insight or release from a deeply buried traumatic experience—and then completely loses control. This unexpected turn of events can unsettle the most experienced therapist. As this wellspring of affect emerges, it may go far beyond cathartic insight and leave the client in a severe state of disequilibrium.

At this point it is absolutely mandatory to stay in control of the situation and take a firm and directive stance, no matter how frightening the client's actions or how personally repulsive the uncovered material may be. Our own admonition to students is, "You may feel physically sick, start to break out in a sweat, and wish to be anyplace else but in that room. After the session is over, you can have a world-class anxiety attack if you wish—you probably deserve it—but right now you are the therapist, and you are going to stick with the client." By demonstrating cool levelheadedness to the client, the therapist is modeling behavior that the client can emulate.

TH: I'm just wondering if the reason you ever got into that abusive marriage is that sometimes your father might have abused your mother, and that's what was modeled as the way a marriage ought to be.

Melanie: (*recoils in a shocked state*) He never did have intercourse with me.

TH: (*taken aback*) I'm not quite sure what you said—"intercourse"?

Melanie: (*breaking down and sobbing*) For 12 years that bastard would mess with me and my sister, and Momma knew. She knew and wouldn't do anything about it. (*completely breaks down*) I . . . God . . . he beat us if we didn't do . . . he'd make us masturbate him . . . oh Lord . . . how could he . . . I've kept this secret . . . I can't handle this.

I should have done something . . . killed him . . . (*uncontrolled and wracked sobbing and shaking*).

TH: (*recomposing herself and gently touching Melanie's arm and quietly talking in a consoling and affirming voice*) I am truly sorry for uncovering that old wound, but you *can* handle it. You've finally got it out. You lived with that hell as a child and another hell as an adult. You are a survivor.

Psychotic Breaks

Staying calm and cool is even more important when a person is having a psychotic break with reality. No matter how delusional or dissociative the client becomes, the central thesis is that the client can maintain contact with reality and take constructive action.

Manuel: (*walks into the therapist's office unannounced and unknown*) I need help, and they recommend you. But no telephones, they listen to me through the telephone. (*Picks up the telephone in a threatening manner.*)

TH: (*in a slow, even voice*) I need for you to put that telephone down before we go any further. I will help you, but I want you to put the telephone back on the stand. We've never had the pleasure of meeting. What is your name?

Manuel: It's Manuel. (*hesitates*) I'm just coming apart. They won't leave me alone.

TH: I understand that, but I need you to put the phone down and keep it together, so you can tell me who's after you. Go ahead and sit down and tell me what's bothering you.

Manuel: It's my supervisor. He wants to fire me and catch me stealing, so he listens in on my phone conversations. He's in league with Satan, and he's probably in this room. I can smell the brimstone. (*Starts to become agitated and mumble about Hell.*)

TH: (*calmly but in an assertive voice*) OK! You're having trouble with your supervisor. Now we're getting somewhere. That's good, but stay with me, I personally guarantee Satan is not here. I want to know about your supervisor and how long this has been going on. I also want to get you to a safe place where nobody can hurt you, but to do that I need your help, and I need you to stay in contact, so I can help you.

Manuel: OK. (*Sits down and starts to talk about his supervisor.*)

The therapist immediately seeks to establish contact by obtaining the client's name, while at the same time establishing ground rules for conduct in the therapist's office. When the young man starts to dissociate and talk incoherently, the therapist directively seeks to keep Manuel in contact with reality by focusing discussion on his grievance with his supervisor. While he validates the client's fear, the only acknowledgment he gives to evil spirits is his concern for the client's safety.

The therapist reinforces the client for staying in contact with him and repeats his request to put the telephone down. Because psychotic clients may have difficulty hearing others because of the intrusive hallucinations assailing them, the therapist slowly and clearly repeats his requests for compliance. By staying in control, the therapist turns a potentially violent situation with an unknown client into a satisfactory resolution.

People With Borderline Personality Disorder

Most clients try to manipulate their therapists during the course of therapy, for a variety of reasons. These reasons may range from avoiding engagement in new behaviors to testing the therapist's credibility. Clients with personality disorders are the ultimate test of the therapist's ability to handle manipulative behavior, and can create severe crises for themselves and the therapist if not dealt with in very specific ways (Kocmur & Zavasnik, 1993). In 1938 Adolph Stern, an American psychotherapist, described a group of clients who did not respond well to treatment and in fact generally got worse. He labeled them as a "borderline group" that lay somewhere between neurosis and psychosis (Stern, 1938). While that notion is no longer deemed valid (Paris, 2008, p. 3), no one has yet come up with a better way to describe clients who have some of the most intractable, stubborn character pathology imaginable.

Personality implies stable and enduring patterns of thinking, feeling, and acting across time and situation (Reyes, Elhai, & Ford, 2008). The borderline personality is the antithesis of that construct, and this particular disorder of personality is a handmaiden to many of the crises in this book—particularly if the traumatic event occurred during childhood (Zanarini, 2000). Probably the best way to describe this disorder is through the title of Kreisman and Straus's (2010) classic book for people attempting to live and deal with borderline personalities: *I Hate You—Don't Leave Me*. There is good reason for this ambivalence. Indeed, there is a good deal of evidence that many individuals with border personality disorder have had a rogues' gallery of childhood horrors of physical and sexual abuse and long-term parental neglect (Allen, 2001; Brown, 2009; Herman, Perry, & van der Kolk, 1989; Sroufe et al., 2005; Stalker & Davies, 1995). The rate of childhood sexual assault has been estimated to be a staggering 75% in people with borderline personality disorder (Battle et al., 2004). As a result, they are likely candidates for what many practitioners and researchers refer to as "complex PTSD" (Briere & Scott, 2006; Courtois & Ford, 2009), a concept we will examine in Chapter 7, Posttraumatic Stress Disorder, and Chapter 9, Sexual Assault. So while they are tough customers and can be extremely trying, there are some pretty good reasons that persons with borderline diagnoses act the way they do and are the hallmark of the client who is in transcrisis. Because of these early experiences with trusted others who could not be trusted, the borderline personality has serious attachment problems that can rapidly surface in therapy. There is evidence that these individuals also harbor a deep sense of betrayal (Kaehler & Freyd, 2009). As you can readily see, there is good reason for this mistrust, sense of betrayal, and thus the constant vigilance, testing of the relationship, and paranoia that mark therapy with these individuals.

All-pro, all-star, and all-world therapists have trouble dealing with these individuals, so why in the world are we exposing you rookies to them? First of all, they provide a good example of how manipulative clients can work you over and lead you into being a case example in our chapter on burnout. More important perhaps, they are clients you will run into that manifest many of the crises in this book. Among other maladies, they abuse drugs, become violent, are suicidal, are sexually promiscuous, practice self-mutilation, get raped, have PTSD, and on and on, so here is a snapshot of a client who can blindside you if you are not careful.

The borderline personality type in therapy is an open Pandora's box of crises, in terms of the presenting problems and issues that occur in therapy, as graphically described by numerous researchers, therapists, and family members (Bagge et al., 2004; Beck & Freeman, 1990; Borschmann & Moran, 2011; Brockian, 2002; Chatham, 1989; Drapeau & Perry, 2004; Fonagy, Luyten, & Strathearn, 2011; Freidel, 2004; Kreisman & Straus, 2004; Lachkar, 2011; Lawrence, Allen, & Chanen, 2011; Leichsenring et al., 2011; Paris, 2008; Sansone, Chu, & Wiederman, 2011; Wirth-Cauchon, 2001; Zeigler-Hill & Abraham, 2006) and summarized below.

Presenting Problems. People with borderline personality disorder have problems like no other client has. They include the following:

1. A wide variety of presenting problems that may shift from day to day and week to week
2. Unusual combinations of symptoms ranging across a wide array of neurotic to subpsychotic behaviors

3. Continuous self-destructive and self-punitive behavior ranging from self-mutilation to suicide attempts
4. Impulsive and poorly planned behavior that shifts through infantile, narcissistic, or antisocial behavior
5. Intense emotional reactions out of all proportion to the situation
6. Confusion regarding goals, priorities, feelings, sexual orientation, and so on
7. A constant feeling of emptiness with chronic free-floating anxiety
8. Unstable low self-esteem and high and unstable negative affect
9. Poor academic, work, and social adjustment
10. Extreme approach and avoidance behavior to social relationships
11. Chronic suicidal and/or homicidal ideation
12. Paranoid ideation
13. Depersonalization and hallucinations
14. Drug abuse including alcohol
15. Sexual promiscuity and sexual victimization

Therapeutic Relationship. People with borderline personality disorder do everything in their power to turn the therapeutic relationship upside down. They have:

1. Frequent crises such as suicide threats, abuse of drugs, sexual acting out, financial irresponsibility, and problems with the law
2. Extreme or frequent misinterpretations of the therapist's statements, intentions, or feelings with strong transference issues which can illicit even stronger countertransference issues in the therapist
3. Unusually strong, negative, acting-out reactions to changes in appointment time, room changes, vacations, fees, or termination in therapy
4. Low tolerance for direct eye contact, physical contact, or close proximity in therapy
5. Unusually strong ambivalence on issues
6. Fear of and resistance to change with inability or resistance to carry out therapeutic assignments
7. Frequent phone calls to, spying on, and demands for special attention and treatment from the therapist
8. Inordinate hypersensitivity to significant others including the therapist

People with borderline personality disorder vacillate between autonomy and dependence, view the world in black-and-white terms, are ever vigilant for perceived danger, have chronic tension and anxiety, are guarded in their interpersonal relationships, and are uncomfortable with emotions (Beck & Freeman, 1990, pp. 186–187; Lachkar, 2011; Linehand, 1993; Paris, 2008). Because of these personality traits, they are apt to continuously test the therapeutic relationship to affirm that the therapist, like everybody else, is untrustworthy and not capable of living up to their expectations, while at the same time they desperately crave attention, love, and respect (Brockian, 2002; Freidel, 2004; Kreisman & Straus, 2004; Lachkar, 2011; Linehand, 1993; McHenry, 1994; Paris, 2008; Yeomans, 1993). Do you start to get the picture of why they can become psychological albatrosses around therapists' necks?

When dealing with someone with borderline personality disorder, it is important to set clear limits, structure specific therapeutic goals, provide empathic support, validate the client's actions as understandable, model a safe environment, caringly confront manipulative and maladaptive behavior, and rigorously stick with these guiding principles (Briere & Scott, 2006; Chatham, 1989; Kreisman & Straus, 2004; Lachkar, 2011; Linehand, 1993; Paris, 2008). This is easier said than done because of the dramatic kinds of problems and emotions that these people display. The following dialogue with Tommy, a college student, depicts such problematic behavior.

Tommy: (*calling the therapist at 2 A.M*) I can't take this any longer. Nobody cares about me. I think I'm going crazy again—all these weird voices keep coming into my mind. It'd just be easier if I got a gun and blew myself away.

TH: I can understand the belief that nobody cares about you, considering how you were put in foster care as a kid and how that uncaring attitude of others seems to follow you wherever you go. If that's the case that those abandonment fears are driving you to this point, then I'm concerned enough about your welfare to call 911 and get the police there immediately to take you to the hospital. (*Wise in the ways of people with borderline personality disorder, the therapist immediately confronts Tommy's statement while validating his fears.*) If things are that serious, a phone conversation won't get the job done.

Tommy: Well, I didn't say I was going to kill myself right now! You always jump to conclusions. I just couldn't sleep or study because of all these voices, and I really need to talk about them.

TH: I'm willing to talk for 15 minutes, but if I don't see you calmed down and functional by that time, I'll feel warranted in calling 911.

Setting limits and monitoring client safety is critical (Kreisman & Straus, 2004; Paris 2008). By voicing

legitimate concerns about the client's safety and setting a specific time limit on the conversation, the therapist reaffirms therapeutic control and does not become engaged in a rambling dialogue. The latter would serve nothing other than to reinforce maladaptive client behavior and cause a sleepless therapist to be angry and irritable the next day! No special considerations other than those normally given to any other clients should be given to those with borderline personality disorder.

Tommy: But Dr. James, I really need to change the appointment and see you tomorrow. I've got this research presentation, and my group's meeting during our appointment time. Can't you move somebody else around?

TH: I have an appointment with another client at that time, Tommy. As I told you, to reschedule I need to know 48 hours in advance. It wouldn't be fair to him anymore than it would be fair to you if I did that to your regular time.

Tommy: (*sarcastically*) You just really don't give a damn about me, do you?

TH: The fact is, I do give a damn, and that's why I'm not going to cave in and change the appointment time. We're not talking about rejection here; we're talking about a reasonable policy that I use on everybody. I know lots of times it would be easy for you to believe I'm blowing you off. At times you certainly aren't the easiest client to deal with, but I knew that going in, and I committed to see this through with you. I'll expect you at our regular Thursday time.

The therapist owns both his positive and his negative feelings about the client and directly interprets and confronts the client's underlying fear of rejection (Chatham, 1989). Finally, by reminding the client of his regular appointment, the therapist targets behavior rather than affect. Focusing on behavior is far less problematic than dealing with relational issues, either inside or outside therapy, because of the client's low tolerance for intimacy (Beck & Freeman, 1990; Drapeau & Perry, 2004; Freidel, 2004).

Treatment noncompliance is par for the course with clients with borderline personality disorder.

TH: So how did your assignment go in thought stopping and not arbitrarily categorizing women as saints or prostitutes?

Tommy: Well, I was real busy this week. Besides which, you didn't really make that thought stopping stuff very clear. And then the rubber band reminder on my wrist broke.

TH: (*frustrated, voice raised, and becoming agitated*) This is the sixth week I've gone through this with you. You continuously put women in those one-up or one-down positions. Yet you continuously complain that no females are interested in you. How do you ever expect to have an equitable relationship unless you change your thinking?

Tommy: (*flushed and shouting*) Oh yeah? You're so perfect? I'll bet your supervisor would like to know the way you verbally harass your clients. Screw you! Who needs therapy or bitches, anyway? They're all sluts anyway. (*Storms out of the room and slams the door.*)

Maintaining professional detachment and keeping one's cool are critical and difficult (Kreisman & Straus, 2004). The therapist's frustration may turn to anger if the therapist ascribes malicious intentions to the client's nonperformance, particularly when trying to change the client's black-and-white thinking. Overt frustration often results in reciprocal acting out by the client. The client's passive noncompliance is a balancing act between fear of change and fear of offending the therapist through outright refusal to comply with therapeutic requests. When noncompliance is consistently the normative response, the therapist needs to step back from the situation, seek outside consultation, confront these issues openly, and acknowledge freely the client's right to refuse an assignment rather than doggedly proceeding (Beck & Freeman, 1990).

TH: Tommy, I feel really frustrated right now. We've been going at this one assignment for six sessions. Maybe I'm the problem—pushing too fast. On the other hand, I feel you maybe don't want to make me disappointed, so you go through the motions. You've always got the right to say no to an assignment, and we can certainly discuss the pros and cons of that. What do you want to do about this assignment?

A favorite ploy of people with borderline personality disorder and other dependent types of clients is to externalize and project their problems onto others. They then attempt to get the therapist to intercede for them by acting as an intermediary or otherwise "fixing" the problem.

Tommy: If you could just write my econ professor a note telling him I'm under your care. I've only missed five classes, and he's threatening to flunk me.

TH: School and therapy are separate, and I won't get into that.

Tommy: (*whining and pleading*) But you know how bad off I've been.

TH: If you are sick enough to miss class, perhaps you should consider an academic withdrawal for medical reasons.

Tommy: Well, I'm not that bad off that I need to quit school.

TH: How has getting others to make excuses for you helped in the past?

In refusing to be used by the client, the therapist avoids a pitfall that would invariably lead to more dependent behavior and the continuation of cyclical, self-reinforcing, dependent, and manipulative behavior. Finally, the watchword with people with borderline personality disorders and other clients who consciously or unconsciously seek to manipulate the therapist is: Remain calm throughout therapy, and do not respond to each new crisis as an emergency. The key question therapists must ask themselves is, "Who's doing the majority of work here?" If the answer is, "Not the client!" then there is a good chance the therapist is being manipulated.

Counseling Difficult Clients

Crisis workers must be prepared to deal with many different types of clients, some of whom are "difficult." To assist in coping with such clients, here are some examples of appropriate ground rules as well as suggestions for confronting difficult clients.

Ground Rules for Counseling Difficult Clients

Workers who must deal with difficult clients regularly may wish to print a set of ground rules to place in the hands of clients at the initial session or before the first meeting. The following rules may be used with individuals, couples, or groups:

1. We start on time and quit on time. If couples are involved, both parties must be present; we will not meet unless both parties are present.
2. There will be no physical violence or threats of violence.
3. Everyone speaks for him- or herself.
4. Everyone has a chance to be fully heard.
5. We deal mainly with the here and now; we try to steer clear of getting bogged down in the past and in blaming others.
6. Everyone faces all the issues brought up—nobody gets up and leaves just because the topic is uncomfortable, and everyone stays for the entire session.
7. Everyone gets an opportunity to define the current problems, suggest realistic solutions, and make at least one commitment to do something positive. At least one positive action step is desired from each person present.
8. Limits to graphic descriptions, abusive language, and swearing and cursing need to be clear as to what will and will not be tolerated.

9. Everyone belongs, because he or she is a human being and because he or she is here.
10. The crisis worker will not take sides.
11. There will be no retribution, retaliation, or grudges over what is said in the session. Whatever is said in the session belongs and stays in the session.
12. The time we spend together is for working on the concerns of the person or people in the group—not for playing games, making personal points, diversion, ulterior purposes, or carrying tales or gossip outside the session.
13. When we know things are a certain way, we will not pretend they are another way—we will confront and deal with each other as honestly and objectively as we possibly can.
14. We will not ignore the nonverbal or body messages that are emitted—we will deal with them openly if they occur.
15. If words or messages need to be expressed to clear the air, we will say them either directly or with role playing—we will not put them off until later.
16. We will not expect each other to be perfect.
17. Being drunk or otherwise drug intoxicated is not acceptable in therapy. We do not work with "wet" clients.
18. In the event the ground rules are broken, the consequences will be discussed by the persons involved immediately with the crisis worker. People who comply with the rules will not be denied services because one person disobeys the rules.

The crisis worker may go over the ground rules, in person or over the phone, before the first session. If this is not possible, a brief orientation that includes the ground rules is advisable at the start of the first meeting.

Confronting Difficult Clients

In dealing with difficult clients the worker may have to *confront* such behavior directly. We must be able and ready to use confrontation, assertion, and directive tactics, such as saying, "I will not permit you to violate our ground rules by attacking her that way." There is a possibility that a client may be so difficult that the session may have to be terminated. (This should happen very, very infrequently.) In such a rare case, the worker would openly admit, "We're getting nowhere, so let's adjourn and see if we can figure out a way to try again." Consultation with a professional colleague for suggestions would be one of the first steps the therapist would take after such an adjournment.

Confidentiality in Case Handling

One benchmark of crisis is the dramatic onset of potentially violent behavior. Although we deal extensively with the control and containment of such behavior in Chapter 14, a particular admonition to the crisis interventionist is appropriate here in discussing case handling. That admonition involves the issues of confidentiality and privileged communication.

Confidentiality means an explicit promise to reveal nothing about an individual except under conditions agreed to by the source or the subject (Siegel, 1979). The category of privileged communication is designed to protect confidential information from disclosure in legal proceedings (Dekraii & Sales, 1982). The limits of confidentiality and privileged communication come under scrutiny when a case involves the potential for violent behavior.

Principles Bearing on Confidentiality

Three important principles have a bearing on this issue. Those principles involve the legal, ethical, and moral codes of the helping professions.

Legal Principles.   Legally, the clients of certain professionals have the right of confidentiality through privileged communication. Such professionals include pastors, lawyers, medical doctors, and to a lesser extent licensed psychologists, social workers, and counselors. Depending on the type of setting and the geographic locale in which they practice, human services workers have varying degrees of privileged communication in the eyes of the law. Emphatically, volunteers, no matter what agency they work for, do not have such legal protection unless specifically provided by law.

Ethical Principles.   Ethical standards do not have the weight of law. Although they may closely parallel the law (Thompson, 1983, p. xv), ethical standards are general guiding codes of conduct for a particular profession. Violation of ethical standards may result in censure or loss of license mandated by the profession's ethics board, but it does not necessarily expose the professional to legal problems. Ethics are general guiding principles of conduct for the particular profession, and only that. Professional associations such as the American Psychological Association, the National Association of Social Workers, and the American Counseling Association have specific standards that speak to confidentiality. Certainly, standard professional conduct and reasonable level of care dictate that what is said in confidence remains so; otherwise, the human services worker quickly loses credibility with the clientele.

Moral Principles.   While critics may wrangle over the degree to which a therapist's morals enter into the therapeutic endeavor, they do agree that there is no value-free brand of therapy and thus no morally neutral therapist (Thompson, 1983, p. 3). Although moral precepts may vary widely, when one shares problems of a deeply personal nature, common decency dictates that the recipient should keep the confidence of the individual who shares such information. It is not uncommon that personal moral stands may fly in the face of both ethical and legal considerations. Crisis workers need to carefully consider the consequences of their personal principles when set in opposition to ethical codes and legal statutes.

The Intent to Harm and the Duty to Warn

Given the legal, ethical, and moral principles that uphold a client's right to confidentiality, it's nevertheless true that when the client provides information about the intent to do harm to himself or herself or another person, rules of confidentiality take on an entirely different perspective. The professional is then essentially faced with making a decision about whether to inform the authorities, significant others, or a potential victim of such threats and taking action to ensure the client does not carry them out. It is almost a sure bet, because of the often emotional and highly volatile world of the crisis worker, that a client will eventually appear with such potentially lethal behavior that the crisis worker will have to make a decision about telling someone in order to keep the client or another person safe.

Tarasoff.   The Tarasoff case (*Tarasoff v. Board of Regents of the University of California,* 1976) is the premier example of a therapist, a supervisory staff, and an institution not adequately dealing with a client threat, and it has reconceptualized professional thinking in regard to confidentiality and the duty to warn a potential victim. The Tarasoff case resulted when a male client told his therapist on a university campus that he intended to murder a young woman. Although the intended victim was not specifically identified, the therapist figured out who she was but took no steps to warn her of the client's threats. The therapist wrote a letter to the campus police about the client's homicidal ideation, and the client was

immediately taken into custody for observation. After evaluation, the client was found rational and, having promised to stay away from the woman, was released.

The therapist's supervisor requested that the police return the letter and directed that all copies of it and subsequent notes related to the incident be destroyed. Two months later the client killed the woman (Thompson, 1983, p. 167). The parents of the woman sued the university, and on appeal to the State Supreme Court of California, the court found for the plaintiff. In this precedent-setting case, the court held that when a psychotherapist ascertains that a threat is neither remote nor idle in its content, the public good demands that disclosure of the threat to a third party outweighs the benefits of preserving confidentiality (Cohen, 1978).

This finding appears to hold true whether it involves phone counseling, a private therapy session, or working with someone in crisis on a street corner. Based on the foregoing case, the following points are paramount in guiding the human services worker's actions when a client makes a clear threat of violent behavior toward another person or the client's self.

1. It is a good practice to convey very clearly what you can and cannot hold in confidence and to apprise the client of this before intervention is started (Wilson, 1981). As ridiculous as it may seem, prior to starting a counseling group at a correctional facility, we always warn the participants that we cannot preserve their anonymity if they threaten themselves or others, reveal plans to escape, or attempt to smuggle contraband into or out of the facility. It is noteworthy that we have had to act on this statement more than once!

2. The foregoing concept is particularly problematic when children are the clients. This topic is covered extensively in Chapter 13, Crises in Schools.

3. Planning ahead through consultation with supervisors, fellow professionals, the police, attorneys, and others who are expert and have experience with danger and violence will be invaluable to you when you may have to make split-second decisions. Similarly, developing contingency plans for what you would do, how you would do it, and what you might do given a variety of client reactions is exceedingly important in the fast and furious world of crisis intervention (Costa & Altekruse, 1994).

4. If you are unclear about the implications of a client's threats or unsure about what to do, the cardinal rule is to consult with another professional or an

immediate supervisor and keep notes of the consultation (Wilson, 1981). Consultation is substantiating protection from legal and ethical problems that may arise, particularly when the threat is not clear. If for some reason another professional is not available, the general rule for determining a clear and present danger is that such a danger is present if a client specifies victim identity ("my husband"), motive ("revenge"), means ("gun"), and plan ("I'll wait for him after work") (Thompson, 1983, p. 83). Danger is also present if the client is unable to understand what he or she is contemplating, is incapable of exercising self-control, and is incapable of collaborating with the worker. Corey, Corey, and Callanan (1998) believe if at least two of the foregoing elements are present, the therapist has a duty to warn.

5. If the client does state a concrete threat, then you are bound morally, legally, and ethically to take action. It is your duty to warn the victim if you know who it is (Wilson, 1981), unless a state statute clearly indicates otherwise. Patiently and emphatically explain your concerns to the client, and attempt to get the client calmed enough to get him or her to a place of safety. Tell the client what you are doing to keep him or her safe and why. The client is also far less likely to perceive the crisis worker as another "enemy" and place the worker on a "hit list" (Thompson, 1983, p. 169). Apprise clients in a supportive and empathic manner of your responsibility to protect them, and invite the clients to participate in the process if possible and surrender any weapons they may have. Inform those who need to know, such as your supervisor, the institution's attorney, the police, the psychiatric hospital, and the intended victim (Costa & Altekruse, 1994).

   If the client is vehement or acting out, avoid a confrontation. This has now become a matter for the police or security. If neither is immediately available, then bring in a coworker as a support person to help contain and calm the client until help arrives. In a crisis intervention setting, no worker should ever be alone.

6. Threats of legal reprisal by the client should not dissuade the crisis worker from reporting threats against others (Wilson, 1981). There is no legitimacy in threats of reprisal, given the law in most states. However, to be safe, document in writing that you noted potential danger signs, discussed relevant suicide and violence issues, and were professional and empathic (Costa & Altekruse, 1994).

It is also a good bet to obtain professional liability insurance!

Tarasoff has mandated three conditions that are necessary and sufficient for a duty to warn to occur: (1) there must be a special relationship, such as therapist to client; (2) there must be a reasonable prediction of conduct that constitutes a danger; and (3) there must be a foreseeable victim. But what if there is no malice aforethought or history of violence or any other life-threatening issues except that the client has a fatal and communicable disease?

Crisis intervention with an AIDS client is a classic example of the knotty ethical dilemmas that crisis workers are likely to face. Although on first blush the crisis worker's response would be, "Of course the partner must be told!" the issue is far more complex. What if the partner or partners are anonymous? What if the client had a much more socially acceptable but still potentially lethal disease, such as tuberculosis? Furthermore, to threaten to disclose the client's illness might drive the person away and quite possibly lead to a further spread of the disease by the client. It could be argued that a far more appropriate course of action would be to hold the knowledge of the disease in confidence and counsel the individual regarding abstinence from sexual contact (Stanard & Hazler, 1995).

Cohen (1990) developed a model rule concerning the limits of confidentiality in AIDS cases. The rule states that the counselor has an obligation to disclose if, and only if, there is medical evidence that the person is HIV-positive, the person is in a high-risk relationship, and there is little likelihood of disclosure by the client. Although this rule seems to ease the Solomon-like decision a crisis worker might have to make in warning another, Stanard and Hazler (1995) enjoin the therapist to consider other core issues as well, such as (1) the client's autonomy to choose whom and when to tell, (2) the counselor's doing no harm to the client, (3) the counselor's doing what is beneficial for the client, and (4) the counselor's being just to the client. Breaching confidentiality would undoubtedly do much harm to all those ethical principles and destroy the relationship between the worker and the client.

Clearly, disclosure issues should be dealt with early on by any worker who routinely works with clients who may be HIV-positive by very specifically stating under what circumstances workers might have a duty to warn others. The AIDS client, although representing a particularly thorny ethical problem, is but one among many the crisis worker will face.

Virginia Tech. Seung-Hui Cho's shooting rampage at Virigina Technical University has caused another shift in how potentially violent clients are handled (Myer, James, & Moulton, 2011, pp. 105–123), and it is our prediction that this incident and what the Virginia legislature has done about it (Sharing of Confidential Information, 2008) will be as significant as *Tarasoff* in how institutions handle threats of violence. For facilities that handle mental health problems, particularly in universities, a variety of laws such as the Family Educational Rights and Privacy Act (1974), the Americans with Disabilities Act (1990), and the Health Insurance Portability and Accountability Act (1996) build very strong walls around the ability to transmit information between units, departments, agencies, and institutions with which potentially violent people may come into contact. Such was the case at Virginia Tech, where Seung-Hui Cho's fleeting contacts with mental health facilities both within and without the university were shielded by law and there was no way an increasingly alarmed English department could require him

to get mental health help, or even know if he did. The unintended effect of these laws, which were all meant to protect individuals from various types of personal exposure, discrimination, and potential harassment and exclusion, was to build informational silos so that information could not be transmitted between these entities, and set the conditions for a perfect storm that resulted in Cho's murderous rampage.

What the state of Virginia did, completely overhauling how personal mental health information would be handled, what limits of confidentiality would apply, what universities could do to require counseling, and what sanctions could be applied to students who are not compliant, goes far beyond *Tarasoff* (Inspector General, 2009). At present, such laws apply only in Virginia, but it is certainly foreseeable, with such shootings becoming more commonplace, that other states will move in this direction. Thus, if you are an aspiring professional in this business, it will be extremely important that you know what the laws of confidentiality and privileged communication are in your state.

SUMMARY

Case handling in crisis intervention differs from long-term therapy. Although crisis intervention deals with many of the same components as long-term therapy, crisis work can be differentiated by its emphasis on expediency and efficiency in attempting to stabilize maladaptive client functioning, as opposed to fundamental restructuring of the client's personality. Case handling in crisis intervention emphasizes concern for client safety, brevity in assessment, rapid intervention, compressed treatment time, and termination or referral once equilibrium has been restored. Case handling in crisis intervention can occur both at walk-in facilities and in long-term therapy settings.

Since the Community Mental Health Act of 1963, the major responsibility for treating the mentally ill has fallen on community mental health centers. Such centers, along with a wide variety of other community social services agencies, are on the front lines in dealing with crises of chronic mental illness, severe developmental problems, and social and environmental issues that afflict individuals. Because of the wide variety of clientele seeking services, walk-in facilities must have close linkages with other social services agencies, the legal system, and both short-term and long-term mental

health facilities. Mental health workers who staff such facilities must have a broad background in dealing with a wide variety of psychological problems and be ready and able to deal with whatever crisis walks in the door.

Since the advent of the Community Mental Health Act of 1963, police departments have assumed greater and greater responsibility for initial contact and disposition of the mentally ill. Creation of the Memphis Model of the crisis intervention team (CIT) has resulted in the development and use of regular patrol officers to defuse and de-escalate the mentally ill and other emotionally violent clients. Variations of this model are now in use throughout the United States.

Clients in long-term therapy may also experience crises as they move through the therapeutic process. These crises may be instigated by situational events in the client's environment; by attempts to engage in new, more adaptive behaviors; or by past traumatic material that is uncovered in the therapy session. When such crises occur, therapy may degenerate to the point that clients undergo severe traumatic stress and revert to pretherapeutic functioning levels. At these points in therapy, long-term work must be suspended, and the therapist must concentrate on the emergent crisis until the client has achieved success in overcoming the current stumbling block. The borderline personality disorder is probably the archetype of difficult and crisis-prone clients with which the therapist will work in long-term therapy.

In all crisis work, as indeed in all therapy, client confidentiality is a moral, ethical, and sometimes legal requirement. In many instances, crisis workers are faced with the possibility of violent behavior and the need to ensure the safety of clients and significant others. Therefore, when clients disclose an intent to do harm to either themselves or others, the crisis worker has a moral, ethical, and legal duty to take action, break confidence, and warn intended victims, significant others, or legal authorities.

 To see some of the concepts discussed in this chapter in action, refer to your *Crisis Intervention in Action* DVD, or see the clips online on the Counseling CourseMate website. To access this site, go to www.cengagebrain.com, where you'll also find an eBook, additional study tools, quizzes, and more. Persons with borderline personality disorder are world famous for manipulating their therapists. Chris, the counselor, has his hands full. How do you think he is doing? How do you think you'd do in his place? Do you get a better idea of what we are talking about when we speak of limit setting?

REFERENCES

Addy, C., & James, R. K. (2005, May). *Finding the best CIT practices across the country.* Paper presented at the First Annual National Conference on Crisis Intervention Team Convention, Columbus, Ohio.

Allen, J. G. (2001). *Interpersonal trauma and serious mental disorder.* Chicester, UK: Wiley.

Americans with Disabilities Act. (1990). PL 110-325.

Aron, L., Honberg, R., Duckworth, K., Kimball, A., Edgar, E., Carolla, B., et al. (2009). *Grading the states: A report on America's health care system for adults with serious mental illness.* Arlington, VA: National Alliance for Mental Illness.

Bagge, C., Nickell, A., Stepp, S., Durrett, C., Jackson, K., & Trull, T. J. (2004). Borderline personality disorder features predict negative outcomes 2 years later. *Journal of Abnormal Psychology, 113*(2), 279–288.

Bahora, M., Hanafi, S., Chien, V. H., & Compton, M. T. (2008). Preliminary evidence of effects of crisis intervention team training on self-efficacy and social distance. *Administration and Policy in Mental Health and Mental Health Services Research, 35*(3), 159–167.

Bain, S. F. (2011). Itinerant counseling services for rural communities: A win/win opportunity. *Journal of Rural Community Psychology 13*(1). Retrieved from http://www.marschall.edu/jrcp/current.htlm

Battle, C. L., Shea, M., Johnson, D. M., Yen, S., Zlotnik, C., Zanarini, M. C., et al. (2004). Childhood maltreatment associated with adult personality disorders: Findings from the collaborative longitudinal personality disorders study. *Journal of Personality Disorders, 18,* 193–211.

Beck, A., & Freeman, A. (1990). *Cognitive therapy of personality disorders.* New York: Guilford Press.

Bender, M. G. (1986). Young adult chronic patients: Visibility and style of interaction in treatment. *Hospital and Community Psychiatry, 37,* 265–268.

Borschmann, R., & Moran, P. (2011). Crisis management in borderline personality disorder. *International Journal of Social Psychiatry, 57*(1), 18–20.

Borum, R. (2000). Improving high risk encounters between people with mental illness and the police. *Journal of the American Academy of Law and Psychiatry, 28,* 332–337.

Briere, J., & Scott, C. (2006). *Principles of trauma therapy: A guide to symptoms, evaluation and treatment.* Thousand Oaks, CA: Sage.

Brockian, N. R. (2002*). New hope for people with borderline personality disorder: Your friendly, authoritative guide to the latest in traditional and complementary solutions.* Roseville, CA: Prima Publishing.

Brown, D. (2009). Assessment of attachment and abuse history, and adult attachment style. In C. A. Courtois & J. D. Ford (Eds.), *Treating complex traumatic stress disorders* (pp. 124–144). New York: Guilford Press.

Chatham, P. M. (1989). *Treatment of the borderline personality.* Northvale, NJ: Aronson.

Cohen, E. (1990). Confidentiality, counseling and clients who have AIDS: Ethical foundations of a modern rule. *Journal of Counseling and Development, 66,* 282–286.

Cohen, R. N. (1978). Tarasoff *vs.* Regents of the University of California. The duty to warn: Common law and statutory problems for California psychotherapists. *California Western Law Review, 14,* 153–182.

Compton, M. T., Bahore, M., Watson, A. C., & Oliva, J. R. (2008). A comprehensive review of extant research on CIT programs. *American Academy of Psychiatry & the Law, 36,* 47–55.

Compton, M. T., Esterberg, M. L., McGee, R., Kotwicki, R. J., & Oliva, J. R. (2006). Crisis Intervention Team training: Changes in knowledge, attitudes, and stigma related to schizophrenia. *Psychiatric Services 57*(8), 1199–1202.

Corey, G., Corey, M. S., & Callanan, P. (1998). *Issues and ethics in the helping professions* (5th ed.). Pacific Grove, CA: Brooks/Cole.

Costa, L., & Altekruse, M. (1994). Duty-to-warn guidelines for mental health counselors. *Journal of Counseling and Development, 72,* 346–350.

Courtois, C. A., & Ford, J. D. (2009). *Treating complex traumatic stress disorder.* New York: Guilford Press.

Dekraii, M. B., & Sales, B. C. (1982). Privileged communication of psychologists. *Professional Psychology, 13,* 372–388.

Drapeau, M., & Perry, J. C. (2004). Interpersonal conflicts in borderline personality disorder: An exploratory study using the CCRT-LU. *Swiss Journal of Psychology, 63*(1), 53–57.

Erstling, S. (2006). Police and mental health collaborative outreach. *Psychiatric Services 57*(3), 417–418.

Family Educational Rights and Privacy Act. (1974). PL 93-380.

Fonagy, P., Luyten, P., & Strathearn, L. (2011). Borderline personality disorder, mentalization, and the neurobiology of attachment. *Infant Mental Health Journal, 32,* 47–69.

Freidel, R. O. (2004). *Borderline personality disorder demystified: An essential guide for understanding and living with BPD.* New York: Marlowe & Company.

Gillig, P. M., Dumaine, M., Stammer, J. W., Hillard, J. R., & Grubb, P. (1990). What do police officers really want from the mental health system? *Hospital and Community Psychiatry, 41,* 663–665.

Health Insurance Portability and Accountability Act. (1996). PL 104-1919.

Herman, J. L. Perry, C., & van der Kolk, B. A. (1989). Childhood trauma in borderline personality disorder. *American Journal of Psychiatry, 146,* 490–494.

Inspector General. (2009). *Investigation-Records Virginia Tech Cook Counseling Center, Blacksburg, Virginia. Report #179-09.* Richmond, VA: Office of the Inspector General for Behavioral Health & Developmental Services.

James, R. K. (1994). Commentary to "Dial 911: Schizophrenia and the Police Response." In P. Backlar (Ed.), *The family face of schizophrenia* (pp. 182–200). New York: Jeremy Tarcher/Putnam.

James, R. K., & Crews, W. (2009). Systems consultation: Working with a metropolitan police department. In A. M. Dougherty (Ed.), *Psychological consultation and collaboration in schools and community settings: A casebook* (5th ed., pp. 93–114). Belmont, CA: Brooks/Cole.

James, R. K., & Gilliland, B. E. (2003). *Theories and strategies in counseling and psychotherapy* (5th ed.). Upper Saddle River, NJ: Prentice Hall.

Kaehler, L. A., & Freyd, J. F. (2009). Borderline personality characteristics: A betrayal approach. *Psychological Trauma: Theory, Research, Practice, and Policy, 1*(4), 261–268.

Kisely, S., Campbell, L. A., Peddle, S., Hare, S., Pyche, M., Spicer, D., & Moore, M. (2010). A controlled before-and-after evaluation of a mobile crisis partnership between mental health and police services in Nova Scotia. *Canadian Journal of Psychiatry 55*(10), 662–668.

Kocmur, M., & Zavasnik, A. (1993). Problems with borderline patients in a crisis intervention unit: A case history. *Crisis, 14,* 71–75, 89.

Kreisman, J. J., & Straus, H. (2004). *Sometimes I act crazy: Living with borderline personality disorder.* Hoboken, NJ: John Wiley & Sons.

Kreisman, J. J., & Straus, H. (2010). I hate you—Don't leave me: Understanding the borderline personality (Rev. ed.). New York: Perigee/Penguin Group.

Lachkar, J. (2011). *How to talk to a borderline.* New York: Routledge & Taylor.

Lamb, H. R., Weinberger, L. E., & Gross, B. H. (2004). Mentally ill persons in the criminal justice system: Some perspectives. *Psychiatric Quarterly, 75*(2), 107–126.

Lawrence, K. A., Allen, J., Chanen, A. (2011). A study of maladaptive schema and borderline personality disorder in young people. *Cognitive Therapy and Research, 35*(1), 30–39.

Leichsenring, F., Leibing, E., Kruse, J., New, A., & Leweke, F. (2011). Borderline personality disorder. *Lancet, 377,* 74–84.

Ligon, J. (2000). Mobile crisis units: Frontline community mental health services. In A. R. Roberts (Ed.), *Contemporary perspectives on crisis intervention and prevention* (pp. 357–372). Upper Saddle River, NJ: Prentice Hall.

Lindsay, M., & Lester, D. (2004*). Suicide-by-cop: Committing suicide by provoking police to shoot you.* Amityville, NY: Baywood Publishing.

Linehand, M. (1993). *Dialectical behavior therapy for borderline personality disorder.* New York: Guilford Press.

Luckett, J. B., & Slaikeu, K. A. (1990). Crisis intervention by police. In K. A. Slaikeu (Ed.), *Crisis intervention: A handbook for practice and research* (2nd ed., pp. 227–242). Boston: Allyn & Bacon.

McHenry, S. S. (1994). When the therapist needs therapy: Characterological countertransference issues and failures in the treatment of the borderline personality disorder. *Psychotherapy, 31,* 557–570.

Miller, L. (2006). *Practical police psychology: Stress management and crisis intervention for law enforcement.* Springfield, IL: Charles C Thomas.

Myer, R. A., James, R. K., & Moulton, P. (2011). *This is not a fire drill: Crisis intervention and prevention on college campuses.* Hoboken, NJ: John Wiley & Sons.

National Alliance on Mental Illness. (2011). Crisis Intervention Team resource center. Retrieved from http://www.nami.org/Template.cfm?Section=CIT2

Nurius, P. S. (1984). Stress: A pervasive dilemma in psychiatric emergency care. *Comprehensive Psychiatry, 25,* 345–354.

Paris, J. (2008). *Treatment of borderline personality disorder: A guide to evidence-based practice.* New York: Guilford Press.

Pope, R. (Speaker). (1991). *Crisis counseling of the walk-in.* (Videotape Recording No. 6611-91B). Memphis, TN: Memphis State University, Department of Counseling and Personnel Services.

Reyes, G., Elhai, J. D., & Ford, J. D. (Eds.). (2008). *The encyclopedia of psychological trauma.* Hoboken, NJ: John Wiley & Sons.

Ritter, C., Teller, J., Marcussen, K., Munetz, M., & Teasdale, B. (2011). Crisis Intervention Team officer dispatch, assessment, and disposition: Interactions with individuals with severe illness. *International Journal of Law and Psychiatry, 34*(1), 30–38.

Roberts, A. R. (1991). Crisis intervention units and centers in the United States. In A. R. Roberts (Ed.), *Contemporary perspectives on crisis intervention and prevention* (pp. 18–31). Upper Saddle River, NJ: Prentice Hall.

Rouse, B. A. (1998). *Substance abuse and mental health statistics source book.* Washington, DC: U.S. Government Printing Office.

Rural Assistance Center. (2011). *Health professional shortage area-mental health.* Retrieved March 20, 2011, from http://www.raconlineorg/info_guides/mental_health/#bib

Sansone, R. A., Chu, J., & Wiederman, M. (2011). Sexual behavior and borderline personality disorder among female psychiatric inpatients. *International Journal of Psychiatry in Clinical Practice, 15*(1), 69–73.

Saunders, M. (2010, Summer). CIT statistics. *The Team News.* CIT International. Retrieved March 20, 2011, from http://www.citinternational.org/news-letters/139-citintnewsletters.html

Sharing of Confidential Information. (2008). Virginia Code 38.2-804.

Siegel, M. (1979). Privacy, ethics, and confidentiality. *Professional Psychology, 10,* 249–258.

Skeem, J., & Bibeau, L. (2008). How does violence potential relate to crisis intervention team responses in emergencies? *Psychiatric Services, 59*(2), 201–204.

Slaikeu, K. A. (Ed.). (1990). *Crisis intervention: A handbook for practice and research.* Boston: Allyn & Bacon.

Sroufe, L., Egeland, B., Carlson, E., & Collins, W. (2005). *The development of the person: The Minnesota study of risk and adaptation from birth to adulthood.* New York: Guilford Press.

Stalker, C. A., & Davies, F. (1995). Attachment organization and adaptation in sexually abused women. *Canadian Journal of Psychiatry, 40,* 234–240.

Stanard, R., & Hazler, R. (1995). Legal and ethical implications of HIV and duty-to-warn for counselors: Does *Tarasoff* apply? *Journal of Counseling and Development, 73,* 397–400.

Stern, A. (1938). Psychoanlaytic investigation of and therapy in the borderline group of neuroses. *Psychoanalytic Quarterly, 7,* 467–489.

Tarasoff v. Board of Regents of the University of California, 551 P.2d 334 (1976).

Teller, J. L., Munetz, M. R., Gil, K. M., & Ritter, C. (2006). Crisis intervention team training for police officers responding to mental disturbance calls. *Psychiatric Services, 57*(2), 232–237.

Thompson, A. (1983). *Ethical concerns in psychotherapy and their legal ramification.* Lanham, MD: University Press of America.

Thorne, F. C. (Ed.). (1968). *Psychological case handling: Vol. 1. Establishing the conditions necessary for counseling and psychotherapy.* Brandon, VT: Clinical Psychology Publishing.

Vermette, H. S., Pinals, D. A., & Applebaum, P. S. (2005). Mental health training for law enforcement professionals. *Journal of the American Academy of Psychiatry and the Law, 33*(1), 42–46.

Watson, A. C., Ottai, V. C., Morabito, M., Draine, J., Kerr, A. N., & Angell, B. (2010). Outcomes of police contacts with persons with mental illness: The impact of CIT. *Administration and Policy in Mental Health and Mental Halt Services Research, 37*(4), 302–317.

Wilson, L. (1981). Thoughts on *Tarasoff. Clinical Psychologist, 34,* 37.

Wirth-Cauchon, J. (2001). *Women and borderline personality disorder.* New Brunswick, NJ: Rutgers University Press.

Yeomans, F. (1993). When a therapist overindulges a demanding borderline patient. *Hospital and Community Psychiatry, 44,* 334–336.

Zanarini, M. C. (2000). Childhood experiences associated with the development of borderline personality disorder. *Psychiatric Clinics of North America, 23,* 89–101.

Zeigler-Hill, V., & Abraham, J. (2006). Borderline personality features: Instability of self-esteem and affect. *Journal of Social & Clinical Psychology, 25*(6), 668–687.

CHAPTER 6

Telephone and Online Crisis Counseling

By far and away the vast majority of crisis counseling is now handled by telephone. Most probably the person on the other end of that telephone is a volunteer who does *not* hold a degree in social work, psychiatric nursing, counseling, or psychology. As we move further into the 21st century, the Internet is playing a larger and larger part in real-time crisis counseling. Whether the service provider on the Internet will be a professional with credentials, a well-meaning volunteer with no training, a charlatan out to steal your money or your daughter, or a computer programmed to do crisis intervention is an interesting question (Hsiung, 2002; Gross & Anthony, 2003; James & Gilliland, 2003, pp. 417–428). This chapter is mainly about the large, current venue of telephone use in crisis counseling, but clearly online crisis counseling has arrived, and it is growing at such a staggering rate that books specifically targeted to e-therapy protocol and use are now being written (Adlington, 2009; Anthony & Nagel, 2010; Jones & Stokes, 2009) and an International Society for Mental Health Online has come into existence (https://www.ismho.org/home.asp).

Case Handling on Telephone Crisis Lines

The telephone has long played an integral role in crisis work. The old Bell Telephone advertisement, "Reach out and touch someone!" is a slogan that is particularly appropriate to crisis counseling. As noted in Chapter 1, the first telephone crisis hotline was established in 1906 by the National Save-a-Life League to prevent suicide

(Bloom, 1984). Indeed, the growing suicide prevention movement in the 1950s adopted the telephone as the primary mode of treatment because of its immediacy (Lester & Brockopp, 1973, p. 5), and it remains the most often used method of suicide intervention (Lester, 2001; Mishara et al., 2005; National Suicide Prevention Lifeline, 2011; Seely, 1997a, 1997b; Slaikeu & Leff-Simon, 1990) with dedicated suicide hotlines in many countries, states, provinces, and cities. It is with good reason there are telephones with direct hotlines to crisis intervention call centers on the Golden Gate Bridge, although it appears that they are sometimes out of order (Jacobs, 2010)! But suicidal individuals are not the only callers. People who are lonely, have panic attacks, gamble and drink to excess, abuse relationships, grieve, are depressed, suffer psychotic breaks, are lonely, or experience a whole smorgasbord of crises that could qualify for Ripley's "Believe It or Not" call crisis lines.

Slaikeu (1990, pp. 105–141) refers to emergency telephone help as "first-order intervention" or "psychological first aid." Indeed, the telephone is the most prevalent medium for the initial contact in most crisis service delivery. There are several reasons for the popularity of the telephone in solving psychological problems.

Convenience. Convenience is paramount (Leffert, 2003; Reese, Conoley, & Brossart, 2006). Particularly cell phones have become such an easy way of communicating that calling for psychological assistance is a natural extension of "taking care of business." The tremendous upsurge in the use of cell phones allows a person to call a crisis line from anywhere, including the site of the crisis as it is happening in real time. Further, with the new "smart" phones, not only can clients avail themselves of a crisis hotline or their therapist, they can also access a variety of self-help groups in chat rooms, computer-assisted therapy, and psychoeducational materials (Boschen, 2009; Gross & Anthony, 2003; Preziosa et al., 2009). As in the case of battering, most crises do not occur during normal business hours. When help is needed in a crisis, it is needed immediately, and mobile phones make 24/7 assistance even more available.

Client Anonymity. Guilt, embarrassment, shame, self-blame, and other debilitating emotions make face-to-face encounters with strangers very difficult, particularly in the immediate aftermath of a traumatic event. Opening oneself to another is an act of vulnerability. The ability to hide one's identity may facilitate greater openness and freedom from inhibition (Reese, Conoley, & Brossart, 2006). This is particularly true of adolescents (Christogiorgos et al., 2010; Tolmach, 1985), those who are socially isolated or psychologically desperate, and the relatively stable person who has a one-shot crisis (Lester & Brockopp, 1973, pp. 86–87). Telephone counselors understand that clients have such feelings and are generally not concerned about identifying a client unless a life-threatening emergency is involved. Conversations are usually on a first-name-only basis for both the worker and the client. Thus, a victim of date rape may call a rape hotline and freely discuss her emotions without having to muster the courage to face what may be perceived as a judgmental human services worker.

Control. A great deal of fear, anxiety, and uncertainty occur when a client's life is ruptured by a crisis (Lester & Brockopp, 1973, pp. 81–82). The concept of secondary victimization by institutions (Ochberg, 1988) is well known to victims of a crisis who have sought assistance from a social agency and then been victimized by its bureaucratic callousness. Going for help may be positively humiliating. In telephone counseling, the client decides when and if assistance is to be sought. At any time during a dialogue on a crisis line, the client may terminate the conversation without fear of recrimination. Finally, looks don't matter in phone counseling. Anybody who is self-conscious about how they look finds the phone a wonderful way to obtain counseling (Wark, 1982).

Immediacy of Access. Crisis intervention can occur any place a telephone, or for that matter a computer, is available (Masi & Freedman, 2001). Most institutions and clinics and many private practitioners use pagers. At our own university, a harried residence hall supervisor who is trying to deal with a distraught, suicidal student who is suffering from severe homesickness and academic failure can call campus police. The police will page a member of the staff of the student counseling center who is the after-hours "beeper keeper." The psychologist immediately responds to the request for assistance by checking with the residence hall supervisor on the current mental status of the student and will then come to the residence hall, talk to the student over the phone, or request additional help from the police to transport the student to the city crisis stabilization unit. In case of an imminent threat such as a tornado or the presence of a potential assailant on campus, text and computer messages can go out to all the students and university staff.

Cost Effectiveness. Crisis lines are inexpensive—for both the client and the community (Masi & Freedman, 2001). Clients who cannot pay for private therapy or afford transportation can usually avail themselves of a phone. Most community agency hotlines are staffed by volunteers and are paid for out of United Way or other charitable funds. Reese, Conoley, and Brossert's (2006) study of telephone counseling strongly implies that, for people of limited financial means, face-to-face counseling where money is a factor is not an option as opposed to a free community crisis line.

Therapeutic Effectiveness. Volunteers who staff crisis lines have probably been the single most important discovery in the history of suicide intervention (Dublin, 1969). Volunteers have few pretensions about their "professional role" and are often seen by callers as having more credibility than a paid professional because they "do it out of the goodness of their hearts." Although the idea of obtaining counseling from a volunteer may seem no better or worse than talking to a bartender or hairdresser, and when they receive little training they are probably worse (Derkx et al., 2009), volunteers typically go through a good deal of training in initial point-of-contact mental health counseling. Phipps, Byme, and Deane (2007) found that volunteers who went through training specifically designed to deal with trauma showed significant gain in knowledge and skills from pre- to posttraining. Mishara and his associates (2005) found that less than 0.3 percent of 2,611 calls they monitored at 14 participating call-in centers were found to be blatantly unacceptable in helper responses and could possibly put the lives of the callers at risk.

While there is still a good deal of contempt by professionals for crisis hotlines, research indicates that they are probably as good as other types of face-to-face counseling and are particularly attractive to young people, old people, and people who do not have financial access to professional therapists (Bryant & Harvey, 2000; Day & Schneider, 2002; Evans et al., 1986; Fukkink & Hermanns, 2009; Lester & Brockopp, 1973, p. 86; Reese, Conoley, & Brossart, 2002, 2006; Rohland et al., 2000).

Access to Support Systems.   One of the major reasons people call hotlines is for social support (Watson, McDonald, & Pierce, 2006). Many people who are lonely, anxious, or isolated by physical illness are in need of support (Burgess et al., 2008). Whether you are a shut-in, shy, ugly, recently divorced, widowed, abused, addicted, or you have leprosy, panic attacks, bad thoughts, or any of the issues of problem callers you are about to meet in this chapter, the need for social support and an empathic ear and voice is the common thread that runs through most crisis lines. Beyond the support of the line itself are the telephone and online support systems to which you can be referred or gain access on your own.

Support groups make extensive use of telephone networks (Lester & Brockopp, 1973). From A (Alcoholics Anonymous) to Z (Zen) support groups, telephone support networks provide constant links to group members between organized meetings. A Google search conducted on May 30, 2011, identified 23,800,000 sites for support groups. The bottom line is that if you can't find a support group out there somewhere for your problem, you are probably an alien escapee from Roswell's Area 51 and this book isn't going to be a lot of help to you.

Avoidance of Dependency Issues.   A user of telephone crisis lines can't become dependent on a particular human services worker who may not always be readily available. Standard practice in most crisis lines discourages workers from forming lasting relationships with clients so that dependency issues do not arise (Lester, 2002).

Worker Anonymity.   The fact that workers are anonymous has as many benefits as client anonymity. The absence of body language, facial expressions, and a visual image allows clients to project whatever idealized view they may conjure up of the therapist. By facilitating the development of transference, within limits, the client can make positive changes. The point here is that not only can clients make of the therapist what they will, they can make of them what they need (Lester & Brockopp, 1973, p. 85; Williams & Douds, 2002, pp. 60–61).

Availability of Others for Consultation.   Crisis lines are seldom staffed by one person. When someone encounters a difficult client, other staff at the agency are available for consultation. Furthermore, at least one phone line is reserved for calling support agencies when emergency services are needed.

Availability of an Array of Services.   A vast array of information, guidance, and social services is quickly available via telephone linkages. The specialized services of different agencies and the expertise they offer can provide on-the-spot guidance for emotionally volatile situations. Many an angry mother or father has received "five-minute parenting sessions" from the staff of a metropolitan "parenting line," thus short-circuiting potential child abuse. Any crisis hotline should have readily available a list of phone numbers of specialized agencies to which they can refer callers. The LINC, or Library and Information Network for the Community, is available in most large metropolitan areas and is standard reference for most telephone crisis lines.

Service to Large and Isolated Geographic Areas and Populations.   Many rural areas that have no after-hours mental health facilities or staff are tied in to toll-free crisis lines that cover huge geographic areas. These crisis lines in turn are tied in to emergency service staff such as police, paramedics, and hospital emergency rooms that serve those rural areas and can respond to a crisis line call for assistance that may be 150 miles away. Certainly populations that are homebound, such as the elderly, physically disabled, or agoraphobic, have a lifeline they would not otherwise have (Lester & Brockopp, 1973, p. 82; Williams & Douds, 2002, pp. 59–60).

Telephone Counseling Strategies

Conducting crisis intervention over the telephone is a double-edged sword. Although phone counseling offers the advantages just listed, for generating responses the crisis worker is entirely dependent on the content, voice tone, pitch, speed, and emotional content of the client. Telephone counseling, and Internet counseling for that matter, isn't for everyone, and that includes both clients and interventionists (Eckardt, 2011). For many human services workers, it is unsettling to deal with ambiguous client responses and not be able to link body language to verbal content. Furthermore, the worker depends entirely on his or her own verbal ability to stabilize the client and has little physical control over the situation. It takes only one experience of having a suicidal client hang up on a worker to understand how frustrating and emotionally draining crisis intervention over the telephone can be. Consequently, a great deal of care and effort needs to be taken in responding to clients. The following section outlines some effective telephone counseling strategies.

Making Psychological Contact

First, psychological contact needs to be made, and this endeavor takes precedence over anything else the phone worker does. Psychological contact means that the worker attempts to establish as quickly as possible a nonjudgmental, caring, accepting, and empathic relationship with the client that will give the worker credibility and elicit the client's trust. Therefore, *provide support* becomes the first order of business. It is safe to assume that people who use crisis lines have exhausted or are separated from their support systems. If the client feels no trust in the relationship and hangs up the phone, the crisis worker cannot make an astute dynamic analysis, synthesize material, diagnose the problem, and prescribe a solution! In establishing psychological contact on the phone, providing support is a first priority and is highly integrated with defining the problem through active listening and responding skills.

CW: (*Two A.M. on Monday morning. Phone rings.*) Metro crisis line. This is Chris. Can I help you?

Telephone caller (TC): (*Silence with soft muffled sobs.*)

CW: (*Waits patiently.*) I understand it's pretty hard to talk sometimes, especially when things seem so overwhelming, but if you could, just take a deep breath and then let it out. I wonder if you could just do that?

TC: (*Takes a deep breath and exhales. Sobs less frequently.*)

CW: (*in a soft, modulated, soothing tone*) That's good! Just do that a few more times. Just relax. I'll stay right on the line until you feel like talking. We've got plenty of time.

The phone worker must be able to react in a calm and collected manner. Thus, the worker's voice must be well modulated, steady, low keyed, with an adequate decibel level but not high pitched. Neither should the content of the worker's response be deprecating, cynical, cajoling, or demeaning. Although the foregoing criteria may seem obvious, few people realize how their voice sounds or are aware of what happens to their voice level and pitch when they are caught up in a rapidly escalating and evolving emotional event. Furthermore, when the person on the other end of the line is acting out, angry, intoxicated, or otherwise demanding of the worker to "fix things right now," the worker needs a great deal of self-discipline and emotional security to refrain from becoming caustic, judgmental, and demanding.

Defining the Problem

Once psychological contact is established, the worker attempts to define the problem by gaining an understanding of the events that led to the crisis and by assessing the client's coping mechanisms. Open-ended questions on the *what, how, when, where, who* continuum usually let the worker get a clear picture of the event itself. However, in assessing the coping mechanisms of the client over the phone, it may be hard to get a clear picture of the client's affect. Thus it behooves the worker to become more sensitive to the underlying emotional content and to try to reflect the implied feeling content more than might be required in a face-to-face encounter. Reflecting feelings is a tough job for most beginning mental health workers and is even more difficult on the phone. Yet the worker absolutely must try to reflect feelings, because there is no way to visually assess the client.

One real plus of phone counseling is that the beginning crisis worker can have supportive aids readily at hand without detracting from the counseling session. One useful tactic is to have a reference list of feeling words that cover the gamut of emotions. A second tactic is to have at hand a list of standard questions the counselor can check off to be sure that all areas typically pertinent to the problem are covered. A third tactic is to keep handy a notepad on which the worker can jot down the salient aspects of the events and coping mechanisms the client has used and make a rapid assessment on the triage scale.

TC: (*timorously*) O . . . O . . . O . . . K. I just don't know where to start, it's just an avalanche. I've got no place to turn, so I thought this was my only chance, so I called.

CW: I'm glad you did call. Sounds like right now you're really overwhelmed, so perhaps you could just take it from where you felt like things fell apart and tell me about that. And I want you to take your time. Take plenty of time, and tell me what's going on. We've got all the time in the world, and I'm here to listen until you say everything you need to and we get a real clear picture of what's going on and what needs to happen.

TC: It's Cicily.

The client goes on to explain she has just moved to town from out of state in an attempt to reconcile with her estranged husband. The husband indicated that he wanted nothing more to do with the marriage and was filing for divorce. She indicates that she was pretty much in denial about the failed marriage and had taken a last chance on getting it back together. The denial has now been given a rude reality check. The job that was supposedly waiting for her has also fallen through. She is currently at a friend's house, with her 4-year-old son, with less than $200 and a car on its last legs. She has no relatives or support system besides her friend from college days.

The crisis worker, Chris, listens intently to the client's story. He interrupts only to clarify and summarize what's going on with the client. Chris deeply reflects the feelings of aloneness, hopelessness, and helplessness that wash over the client. The crisis worker allows the client to grieve and ventilate over her failed marriage. When the client's emotional behavior starts to escalate, the crisis worker uses calming techniques such as asking the client to take a deep breath or reinforces the concept that they have plenty of time to work through this problem. As Chris listens to her, he is rapidly jotting notes down and making an assessment on the triage scale. Her predominant emotion is anxiety, which is free-floating into all areas of her life. She is having a lot of difficulty controlling her emotions.

Her score on the Affective Severity scale is 7. She indicates that she has been essentially frozen in time for the last 4 days after her meeting with her estranged husband. Her friend has been taking care of her son while Cicily either has sat paralyzed staring aimlessly at TV or has been hysterically sobbing in bed. Finally, at the urging of her friend, she called the crisis line. Her score on the Behavioral Severity scale is 7 because clearly her daily functioning is impaired. She is immobilized and frozen. As she relates her problems, her thinking seems fairly linear, and she is able to put her story together logically. However, she has been perseverating on the crisis to the exclusion of anything else. There is a lot of wishing and hoping for things to get better and that somehow her husband will have a change of heart. She

is filled with self-doubt and cannot make a decision about what to do. Her score on the Cognitive Severity scale is 8.

Overall her triage scale score is 22. This woman is clearly in crisis and may need more help than the crisis line can provide over the phone. Chris's immediate concern is with a statement Cicily made that "this was my only chance."

Ensuring Safety and Providing Support

During problem definition, the phone worker must be very specific in determining the client's lethality level. If the worker detects the potential for physical injury, then closed-ended questions that obtain information specific to the safety of the client should be asked, not only without hesitation but also with empathic understanding that clearly depicts the worker's overriding concern for and valuing of the client. These questions typically start with *do, have,* and *are,* and in phone dialogues they should be put directly and assertively to the client. (For example, one might ask, "Do you have the pills there with you now?" Or "Are you alone, or is someone there who might help you before you do it?") The phone counselor should check what support systems are available to ensure the client's safety. For many phone clients there will be no support system—the phone counselor is the immediate and sole support system.

CW: I can really hear the hurt and fright in your voice. It's scary being all alone, seeming to have nobody to lean on. I'm concerned about your saying this was your "last chance." Do you mean by that you're thinking of suicide?

TC: (*somewhat emphatically*) I had, but I just couldn't bear to see that bastard and his new girlfriend get custody of Jimmy.

CW: OK. That's good! I needed to check that out. Now you said you were staying with an old college friend, and she asked you to call. Is that where you are now?

TC: Yes, but I hate putting her out like this. But I don't have any other place to go. (*Starts sobbing heavily again.*)

CW: But she's OK with you staying there?

TC: Yesssss. But I hate being a burden on her.

CW: But that's what friends are for. Would you do the same for her if things were reversed?

TC: Well, sure, no question.

CW: So for the time being you've got a roof over your head, something to eat, and are safe?

TC: Yes, I guess so, but I don't know how long this can go on.

CW: What we're going to do is see if we can get some stuff done that will allow you to get back on your own. OK? Are you willing to do that? (*Cicily acknowledges she'll try.*) Good! Although I can't get your husband back, and I know that really left you feeling hopeless and all alone, I can find out about the job problem and perhaps see if we can't do something about that. So let's start with that if it's OK with you. We've got a number of referral sources here that might be able to match your skills, education, and abilities with a job. Would you be willing to tell me a little bit about yourself in that area—education, employment background, desired kind of work? I could pass that on to some of our referral sources and see what we could do. (*Chris listens while Cicily goes through her background, education, and other pieces of pertinent information, reinforcing her for staying on task, mobilizing her thoughts, and keeping her terrifying emotions in control.*)

Looking at Alternatives and Making Plans

Creating alternatives and formulating a plan are integral to one another in any crisis situation but are even more closely tied together in phone counseling. To alleviate the immediate situational threat, the phone counselor needs to jointly explore alternatives that are simple and clear-cut. Without the benefit of an eyewitness view or an in-depth background of the client, the worker needs to be cautious about proposing alternatives that may be difficult to carry out because of logistical or tactical problems of which the worker is unaware. Alternatives need to be explored in a slow, stepwise manner with checks by the worker that the client can do the physical and psychological work necessary to complete the task. Role play, verbal rehearsal, and having the client recapitulate objectives are vital ingredients of a functional plan. No plan should be accepted until the client can reassure the worker that he or she thoroughly understands the plan and has the means and ability to put it into action.

CW: OK! I've got that information. I'll pass it along to the day shift, and they'll pass it along to the JOBS Council and a couple of employment agencies that work with us. I want you to call back to our number tomorrow about 1 P.M. and we'll have some information for you. Can you do that?

TC: Well yes, I can do that. (*Cicily has calmed down and is only occasionally sniffling and lamenting her outcast state. Her triage scale score has moved down to about 15. Chris now approaches other areas of her crisis.*)

CW: I wonder what you did when you got into predicaments beforehand? Maybe there was nothing quite like this, but I'm guessing there were other times when you were overwhelmed.

TC: Well, nothing like this, but I did take care of my mother before she died, kept a job with a printing company, and worked on my degree. Sometimes that was pretty overwhelming.

CW: So what did you do to take care of being overwhelmed?

TC: I'd make a list and set down my goals of what I was going to do and what I had to do. Like Alcoholics Anonymous, one day at a time, you know. It worked pretty well, but I just have got so many things now, I don't know if I can get it all lined out.

CW: But that worked before, and I understand there are lots of things going on like never before, but if it worked then, how's about giving it a try now? (*Chris immediately seizes on her past coping technique and attempts to put it to work. He acknowledges her belief that this is indeed different than before and doesn't discount the fact that it may be tough. He methodically helps her develop a game plan for tomorrow, not the rest of her life.*) So we've got day care for Jimmy taken care of, and you don't really need the car for a while, you can get a bus or streetcar and go anywhere you need to. Even though you've only got 200 bucks cash, you could cash in that $3,000 worth of U.S. savings bonds your mother gave to Jimmy if you had to, until you got back on your feet. You could then repurchase them, so you won't feel like you're robbing your son of his inheritance. So you've written those things down that you can do tomorrow, right? So we're just managing this, like you say, one day at a time, not worrying much beyond that and doing what can be done. Do you feel like we're making progress?

TC: I guess I do. I can do those things.

Obtaining Commitment

Commitment to a plan of action generated over the phone should be simple, specific, and time limited. If at all possible, the worker should try to obtain the client's phone number and call the client back at a preset time to check on the plan or, if the agency accepts walk-in clients, the worker should try to have the person schedule an appointment as soon as possible. If the worker is linking with other agencies, then a phone call should be made to the referral agent to check whether the client has completed the task. Although it is preferable to have the client take the initiative in contacting other agencies so that dependence on the worker is not created, conditions may block the client from doing so. In that case, the worker should have no hesitation in offering to make the call.

CW: So there are three things you're going to do tomorrow. First you're going to call the day care number I gave you and get Jimmy in there. Second, you're going to go to the bank and open an account and cash in the bonds. Third, you're going to call back here at 1 P.M. and ask for the information on the job hunt. Those places I told you about will probably want you to come down, so you'll call them and make an appointment. Will you call back tomorrow night and ask for me? I come on at 11 P.M. I know this has been a pretty upsetting deal, so could you kinda repeat that to me and write down that stuff?

TC: Yes. I've got it. (*Cicily repeats to Chris the steps he has outlined.*) And I'll call back. Thanks a lot. You're a real lifesaver.

CW: You're welcome. Now get a good night's sleep. It's a fresh day tomorrow, and you'll get through it fine with that attitude. (*Chris judges Cicily now to be at a total triage rating of about 8. Affectively she is in control of her emotions. She is thinking clearly enough to help establish a plan in a collaborative manner with the crisis worker and has committed to act on it the next day. Chris judges her to be mobilized enough that he can let her go off the line.*)

The call has taken more than an hour and a half, but in that time a woman who is in a severe developmental and situational crisis has been able to grieve away some of the lost relationship with her husband, work through her terror of being all alone and jobless in a strange city, and start to make specific plans on how she'll get out of the dilemma. She still has many issues and a long road ahead of her, but she has returned to being a functional human again. By any criterion of therapy, the crisis worker has done a good night's work!

Errors and Fallacies

For most of our students who volunteer for crisis line duty, to say that they are scared pea green on their first shift is putting it mildly! Lamb (1973, 2002) has listed a number of irrational ideas that beginners indoctrinate themselves with as they start their careers as phone counselors. We list them here as a way to depropagandize and calm those of you who are about to start on this grand adventure.

First, you are not omnipotent! You are not there to be the instant expert. Your thoughts of "if only I were a psychiatrist, licensed social worker, counseling supercomputer, I could help this person" are doomed to failure. Nobody is an expert on everything that comes into a crisis line. There is no specific piece of information, if found, that will magically transform the caller into a paragon of good mental health.

Second, talking about "it," whatever "it" is, from suicide to getting a hair replacement, will not make it happen, and you will not be the instigator of causing "it" to happen. Callers are resilient and need somebody to talk honestly and openly about "it." Particularly in regard to suicide, tiptoeing around the topic generally indicates to the client that "it" is indeed scaring the daylights out of you too! If you can get an inkling of what "it" is, bring it out into the light of day, specify "it," and talk about "it."

Third, if you feel at times you are being manipulated, you probably are, and that is okay too—within limits. Understand that the caller's need to manipulate you is serving a purpose. As long as that purpose results in restoring the caller to psychological equilibrium without harming anyone, you are doing what you need to do. On the other hand, you are not a doormat to be walked over.

Fourth, all callers are not loving human beings, and you do not have to be Mother Teresa, loving and caring and sharing to all. Many people call exactly because they are *not* loving human beings! They are often overbearing, boring, nasty, insulting, hateful, and a pain in the neck! Having made that assessment, you now know why the caller is facing rejection from others and can directly speak to how his or her actions affect you and reflect on how those actions must be problematic when dealing with others.

By the same token, some callers like to gripe about the incompetence of other agencies, therapists, and significant others who have failed miserably to help them and have made their lives worse. They may be right. Agencies, therapists, and significant others are composed of human beings who get tired of being manipulated and taken advantage of. Questioning your credentials is really more of a question of "Can I really trust you? Can you understand what I am feeling?" Defending yourself and your credentials is pointless. Dr. James, licensed psychologist, licensed professional counselor, National Certified School Counselor, licensed English teacher, licensed school administrator, licensed real estate agent (retired), licensed fisherman, and world-renowned author of crisis textbooks can't! So why should you think you can? Don't get caught up in defending yourself, but rather turn the question back on the caller: "I don't think that is really what you are concerned about, but maybe you are wondering whether you can trust me. Why not run it by me, and let's see?"

Finally, there is the delusion of fixed alternatives. The beginner believes either "If I can't think of it, there must be no answer" or "If that's all I can think of, it must be the only answer." Or, alternatively, "I'll call a consultant. Surely he or she will know." None of these is correct. When you fall under this delusion, crisis intervention is stopped dead in its tracks. Crisis intervention is one part inspiration and nine parts perspiration. You muddle through this together. Solutions are created, not found. Further, you need to understand that you can't palm this caller off on another agency just because the problem is a tough one and you are at a loss as to what to do. Calling the police department Crisis Intervention Team may be appropriate, or it may not. You need to know what other agencies can or cannot do. If you don't know, find out before you embarrass yourself.

What in the world can you do then? You can be yourself. You got into this because you thought you have some pretty good human qualities. You undoubtedly do, so use them. You are there to listen. Few beginners ever believe this, but sometimes, a lot of times in fact, listening is more than enough. You can help the caller come up with alternatives and solutions, or suggest some resources to pursue. You won't know *all* the resources available, but as time goes on you will learn more. You will also learn your own limits and can be honest in owning when you are tired, confused, lacking in knowledge, or downright irritated with the hateful way the caller is acting. You are a pretty good human being doing your best under some trying circumstances. That's it! End of omnipotence!

Regular, Severely Disturbed, and Abusive Callers

The foregoing dialogue is a textbook example of how things ought to go in telephone crisis line work. The problem is that the real world seldom functions in such neat and tidy ways. Many callers use the crisis line for reasons other than its intended use. When this happens, the overriding questions telephone workers must pose to themselves are: What is the person getting out of using the crisis line at this time, and is it helpful to the person? How is this person's use of the crisis line at this time affecting its operation? (McCaskie, Ward, & Rasor, 1990). Crisis lines should not cater to a caller's every whim, fantasy, deviant behavior, or self-indulgence.

Chronic callers can be a plague to crisis lines and devour time and energy of staff, which legitimate callers may desperately need (Peterson & Schoeller, 1991). Chronic callers can also be very frustrating to telephone workers because they do not improve (McCaskie, Ward, & Rasor, 1990). These callers can pose a serious morale problem for the volunteers and staff who receive such calls, particularly when the calls become sexually explicit and the deviant fantasies of callers are directed at the crisis worker (Brockopp & Lester, 2002; Knudson, 1991; Tuttle, 1991).

A counterpoint to this negative view is the approach of the staff at the Lawrence, Kansas, Headquarters Crisis Center, who believe that "chronic" is a negative term and implies that these callers will never improve (Epstein & Carter, 1991). All behavior is purposive. If seen in that light, no matter how aberrant or weird the content of the call, it is important to remember that those who regularly use the crisis line do so for a reason—it helps them make it through the day. For these clients, it becomes part of their lifestyle and method of coping.

Therefore, although the term "chronic" is often used in telephone crisis work, we believe it to be somewhat pejorative and agree with the staff at the Headquarters Crisis Center that "regular" better captures the essence of this clientele. If the caller's dynamics are reframed as lonely, isolated, and reaching out, then the response may be very different from one of mere aggravation (Brockopp & Lester, 2002). By setting limits of 10 to 20 minutes for regular callers, workers acknowledge their needs but also do not become controlled by the regular callers (Lester, 2002).

Understanding the Regular Caller's Agenda

Helping people in crisis is different from being nice to them. The agenda of regular callers places the crisis worker in a dilemma. Although the worker may feel ethically bound to respond to the caller, and the agency's protocol dictates that all calls must be taken, that does not mean that workers need to suffer the abuse and invective leveled at them by such callers. A very real difference exists between what callers may want and what they may need, and helping a caller is generally predicated much more on needs than on wants. Often what these regulars want is a reaffirmation that their problems are unsolvable. Thus they become dependent on the telephone worker to sustain their problem. The worker therefore needs to recognize such patterns and not support them when this blocks progress (McCaskie, Ward, & Rasor, 1990). Telephone workers do themselves and their callers a service when they show that they are not willing to be manipulated or abused and that they value their own needs as highly as they value those of the caller. Generally, if a telephone worker spends more than 15 to 20 minutes with a caller, the client's crisis becomes the worker's crisis (Knudson, 1991).

Given the foregoing admonition, the telephone worker needs to remember that the sameness of the material and the dependency these clients demonstrate day in and day out make it easy to forecast their repetitious behavior and treat them as bothersome, inept, boring, and unimportant clients. Many of these are "Yes, but . . ." callers. Although they seem highly receptive to the suggestions and plans that crisis workers make with them, in the end they find all kinds of excuses and explanations to not follow through on what they promised to do—which makes them extremely exasperating (Waters & Finn, 1995, p. 269).

Regular callers may tend to be placed in a stereotypical catchall category because they represent an aggravation to the crisis line. However, the reasons these people call are diverse. Identifying specific types is at least as important as identifying the specific caller (Peterson & Schoeller, 1991). To this end, McCaskie, Ward, and Rasor (1990) have constructed brief descriptions of some of the more typical personality disorders of regular callers, their outward behavior, inner dynamics, and strategies for counseling them.

Paranoid.   People with paranoia are guarded, secretive, and can be pathologically jealous. They live in logic-tight compartments, and it is difficult if not impossible to shake their persecutory beliefs. They see themselves as victims and expect deceit and trickery from everyone. The counseling focus is to stress their safety needs.

Schizoid.   Those with schizophrenia have extremely restricted emotional expression and experience. They have few social relationships and feel anxious, shy, and self-conscious in social settings. They are guarded, tactless, and often alienate others. The counseling focus is to build a good sense of self-esteem through acceptance, optimism, and support.

Schizotypal.   People with schizotypal behavior have feelings of inadequacy and insecurity. They have strange ideas, behaviors, and appearances. The focus of counseling is to give them reality checks and to promote self-awareness and more socially acceptable behavior in a slow-paced, supportive manner.

Narcissistic.   Narcissists are grandiose, extremely self-centered, and believe they have unique problems that others cannot possibly comprehend. They see themselves as victimized by others and always need to be right. The focus of counseling is to get them to see how their behavior is seen and felt by others, while not engaging in a "no-win" debate or argument with them.

Histrionic.   People with histrionic personality disorder move from crisis to crisis. They have shallow depth of character and are extremely ego-involved. They crave excitement and become quickly bored with routine and mundane tasks and events. They may behave in self-destructive ways and can be demanding and manipulative. The focus of counseling is to stress their ability to survive using resources that have been helpful to them in the past.

Obsessive-Compulsive.   Those with obsessive-compulsive disorder are preoccupied by and fixate on tasks. They expend and waste vast amounts of time and energy on these endeavors. They often do not hear counselors because of futile attempts to obtain self-control over their obsessions. The focus of counseling is to establish the ability to trust others and the use of thought stopping and behavior modification to diminish obsessive thinking and compulsive behavior.

Bipolar (Manic Depressive).   The extreme mood swings of these callers range from "superman/superwoman" ideation when in a manic phase to "born loser" ideation in a depressive stage. If they feel thwarted in their grand plans, they may become very aggressive to those who would stop them. At the other end of the continuum, their depressive "doom, despair, and agony on me" outlook puts them at risk for suicidal behavior. Slowing down and pacing these callers in the manic phase is difficult but needs to be done to put a psychological governor on their runaway behavior. Confrontation about their grandiose plans only alienates them. In the depressive stage, suicide intervention is a primary priority.

Dependent.   People with dependent personality disorder have trouble making decisions and seek to have others do so—often inappropriately. Feelings of worthlessness, insecurity, and fear of abandonment predominate. They are particularly prone to become involved and stay in self-destructive relationships. The focus of counseling is to reinforce strengths and act as a support for their concerns without becoming critical of them or accepting responsibility for their lives.

Self-Defeating.   Those with self-defeating behavior choose people and situations that lead to disappointment, failure, and mistreatment by others. They reject attempts to help them and make sure that such attempts will not succeed. The focus of counseling is stressing talents and the behavioral consequences of sabotaging themselves.

Avoidant. People with avoidant personality disorder are loners who have little ability to establish or maintain social relationships. Their fear of rejection paralyzes their attempts to risk involvement in social relationships. The focus of counseling is encouragement of successive approximations to meaningful relationships through social skills and assertion training.

Passive-Aggressive. Those with passive-aggressive behavior cannot risk rejection by displaying anger in an overt manner. Rather, they engage in covert attempts to manipulate others and believe that control is more important than self-improvement. The focus of counseling is to promote more open, assertive behavior.

Borderline. Borderline personality disorder is so named because such people are chameleon-like and at any given time may resemble any of the foregoing mental disorders. Also, they are always on the "borderline" of being functional and dysfunctional. One of the most problematic of callers, they are dealt with at length in Chapter 5.

Handling the Severely Disturbed Caller

"The behavior of the severely disturbed is primitive, disorganized, disoriented, and disabling. These people are likely to elicit discomfort, anxiety, and outright fear in the observer. These are strange people. These are different people. These are people we lock away in mental institutions, pumping them full of strong drugs that turn the mania into docileness" (Greenwald, 1985b). This stereotypical public view of the mentally disturbed, quoted in the University of Illinois at Chicago's Counseling Center hotline training manual, introduces hotline workers to the mentally disturbed. These are many of the people who call crisis hotlines. On the neophyte phone counselor's first meeting with the disorganized and disjunctive thought processes of the mentally disturbed, all the training the crisis worker has ever received is likely to fall by the wayside.

These callers represent a cornucopia of mental illnesses. They may be delusional and hallucinatory; be unable to remotely test what they are doing, believing, or thinking against reality; be emotionally volcanic or conversely demonstrate the emotionality of a stone; lack insight or judgment about their problems and be unable to relate any linear or logical history of these

problems; be so suspicious in their paranoid ideation that they believe even the phone worker is out to get them; be manipulative, resistant, and openly hostile and noncompliant to the simplest requests; not have the slightest idea of appropriate interpersonal boundaries with significant others or the crisis worker; demonstrate obsessive behavior and compulsive thoughts that they continually harp on to the exclusion of any effective functioning; have no meaningful interpersonal relationships with the possible exception of crisis line workers; impulsively place themselves in problematic and dangerous situations over and over; and present themselves in childlike or even infantile ways (Grunsted, Cisneros, & Belen, 1991). Whether these behaviors are biochemically or psychologically based makes little difference. These people are so distanced from our own reality and so threatening that the beginning phone counselor's immediate reaction is to get off the line! However, if the worker pictures the disturbed client as a person whose developmental processes have gone terribly awry, then the call may take on structure and sense and become less intimidating. No matter how bizarre the call may be, these primary axioms apply to the caller's behavior (Greenwald, 1985a, p. 1):

1. Behavior is always purposeful and serves motives that may be either conscious or unconscious.
2. Behavior is comprehensible and has meaning even though the language used may not.
3. Behavior is characteristic and consistent with personality even though it is exaggerated.
4. Behavior is used to keep a person safe and free of anxiety.

The following rules for dealing with disturbed callers are abstracted from a number of crisis hotlines (Epstein & Carter, 1991; Greenwald, 1985a, 1985b; Knudson, 1991; Lester & Brockopp, 1973; Tuttle, 1991).

Slow Emotions Down. Although disturbed callers have many feelings that have been submerged from awareness, it is not the best strategy to attempt to uncover these feelings. The caller is being besieged by too many feelings and needs to find a way to get them in control. Focusing on here-and-now issues that are concrete and reality oriented is the preferred mode of operation. Do not elicit more feelings with open-ended questions such as "Can you tell me more about that?" Instead, use calming interventions that force the person to order thinking in small, realistic bits of detail.

CW: I understand how scary those thoughts are that keep creeping into your mind and the "things" you think are in the room. What I want you to do right now is look around the room and tell me what is there. Then tell me what happened to start this thinking.

The idea is to slow emotions down. Although the worker may acknowledge the feelings, they are not the focus of attention. By breaking up freewheeling ideation into discrete, manageable pieces, the telephone worker gives the caller a sense of regaining control. The worker may also bring the caller back to reality from a flashback by asking the client what he or she is doing.

CW: You say you're in that alley and he's assaulting you. Were you smoking a cigarette then? I know you just lit a cigarette a minute ago. I want you to slowly inhale, smell that smoke, and tell me where you are. Now blow the smoke out and see where it goes around the room.

Refuse to Share Hallucinations and Delusions. If a caller is hallucinating or delusional, the telephone worker should never side with the psychotic ideation.

Caller: Do you see, hear, smell, feel those things?

CW: No! I'm sorry, I don't. I understand right now you do, and that's terrifying, but what I want to do is get you some help. So stay with me. What is your address so we can get some support for you?

Little if any good ever comes of participating in such thinking, and as the delusion increases, it becomes difficult to extricate oneself from it. Yet grandiose thinking, no matter how bizarre, should not be denied.

CW: (*inappropriate and sarcastic*) Come on, now. The CIA isn't really listening to an auto mechanic by electronic eavesdropping. Certainly they've got better things to do than that. Why do you believe that?

CW: (*appropriate and empathic*) It's pretty clear that you really believe the CIA is listening to you. When did this start?

The worker affirms the paranoid delusion is real without agreeing to its veracity. By asking a *when* question, the worker can start eliciting information that will allow assessment of the scope and extent of the paranoia. A *why* question is never appropriate because of the defensive reaction it may elicit in any caller, especially a paranoid.

Determine Medication Usage. If at all possible, the worker should elicit information as to use of any medication, amount and time of dosage, and particularly, stopping medication without consulting the attending physician. Changing, forgetting, or disregarding medication is one of the most common reasons that people become actively psychotic (Ammar & Burdin, 1991). Furthermore, having this information will give the worker a better idea of the type of mental disturbance the caller is being treated for. Regardless of the reasons or excuses clients give for not taking medicine, the worker should endeavor to get them to their prescribing physician so medication can be adjusted or reinstituted.

CW: Lemuel, I want you to call up your doctor as soon as we get off the phone. I understand that the medicine gives you a bad taste in your mouth and makes you feel queasy. However, your doctor needs to know that, and you need to let her know you're not on your meds.

Becoming familiar with the major tranquilizers, antidepressants, and antipsychotic drugs is important for this work (Pope, 1991). However, given all the different kinds of drugs and their numerous generic and trade names, keeping track of them all is extremely difficult. The *Physician's Desk Reference (PDR)* provides information on what these drugs do, how much is generally given, and what the side effects are. No crisis line office should be without a current edition.

Keep Expectations Realistic. The telephone worker should keep expectations realistic. The caller did not become disturbed overnight. No crisis worker is going to change chronic psychotic behavior during one phone call. The crisis worker is buying time for the caller in a period of high anxiety and attempting to restore a minimum amount of control and contact with reality. If the caller is trying to "milk" the worker through an interminable conversation, confronting the problem in a direct manner will generally determine whether the caller is lonely or is in need of immediate assistance.

CW: It seems as if this can't be solved, and you say you can't wait until tomorrow to go to the clinic. I'm concerned enough that I think we ought to make arrangements to transport you to the hospital right now.

Maintain Professional Distance. Calls from severely disturbed individuals may evoke all kinds of threatening feelings in phone workers, leaving them feeling inadequate, confused, and in crisis themselves! Maintaining professional distance when exceedingly painful and tragic stories are related is difficult for even the most experienced phone worker. When these feelings begin to emerge, it is of utmost importance for workers to make owning statements about their own feelings and get supervision immediately. Passing the line to another worker in no way indicates inadequacy.

CW: Frankly, I'm a bit confused as to what to do. I've done everything I know, and I'm tapped out. I'd like to connect you with Irma, who may have some other ideas, while I talk to our director.

As confused and disoriented as disturbed callers may be, they seem to have a sixth sense about sensitive areas in others. Countertransference (the attributing to clients of the therapist's own problems) is not uncommon, and disturbed callers can sometimes unearth the worker's own hidden agendas and insecurities. A worker's strong reactions, either positive or negative, to these callers should alert the hotline worker that processing and feedback with a coworker or supervisor are needed.

Caller: (*paranoid*) I know who you are, when you work on the hotline, and where you live.

CW: (*inappropriately responding to the threat in a shaky voice*) What have I ever done to you? I'm trying to help you, and you get bent out of shape. I've got a good mind to hang this phone up right now or even call the police. We can trace these calls, you know!

CW: (*appropriately responding to the implication in a clear, firm, but empathic voice*) Jacques, those things are not important to what's going on with you right now. What is important is making you feel safe enough to go back to your apartment tonight and go to the doctor in the morning. I understand why you might get upset over my suggesting you see the doctor, but I also want you to clearly understand it's your safety I'm concerned about. So what's making you angry with me?

By deflecting the caller's paranoia and refocusing the dialogue back on the client's issues, the telephone worker directively forces the caller, in an empathic manner, to respond to his own emotional state.

Avoid Placating. Placating and sympathizing do little to bolster the caller's confidence or to help move the client toward action.

Caller: (*depressed*) I'm just not any good to anybody, much less myself.

CW: (*inappropriately sympathetic*) From all you've told me, you've had a really rocky road. Nobody should have to suffer what you have, but things can only look up.

Rather, by empathically responding and exploring past feelings and coping skills when life was better, the telephone worker not only acknowledges the dilemma but also focuses on the client's strengths.

CW: You do sound pretty hopeless right now, but I wonder how you were feeling when things weren't this way, and what you were doing then that you aren't doing now.

Assess Lethality. Many clients who call crisis lines have active suicidal or homicidal ideation. It may seem puzzling that such people would call a crisis line when they seem so bent on harming themselves or others. Regular callers in particular should be assessed for suicidal or homicidal ideation because they are very prone to underscore the critical nature of their problems and "prove" their need for help by threatening lethal behavior (Brockopp, 2002a). What all suicidal callers are doing is trying to put distance between their thoughts and the actions that might result from those lethal thoughts. As much as the callers may avow intentions of lethality, they are still in enough control of themselves to attempt to place a buffer (the telephone worker) between thinking and acting (McCaskie, Ward, & Rasor, 1990).

Caller: If I can't have him, she sure as hell won't. I'll kill them both, and you, the police, or nobody else can stop me.

CW: Yet you called here, for which I'm glad. Something is holding you back, and I'd like to know what that something is.

Caller: Well, I'm a Christian, but their sins go beyond redemption.

CW: So as a Christian, you probably think the commandment "Thou shalt not kill" is pretty important. What you're saying is you're about to commit sin, just as they did. How will that help you, and how will it look in the eyes of God?

Although it may be construed that the telephone worker is manipulating the spiritual philosophy of the caller to achieve an end, the major goal of the crisis worker is to disrupt the irrational chain of thinking that is propelling the client toward violence. In that regard, when dealing with the disturbed caller, the overriding thesis is "Save the body before the mind" (Grunsted, Cisneros, & Belen, 1991). Crisis intervention over the telephone with those who are severely disturbed is clearly not meant to be curative. It is a stopgap measure designed to be palliative enough to keep action in abeyance until help arrives.

Although no crisis line staff members that we know of would ever instruct their workers to give out their full names or home phone numbers, at times callers can be very seductive in their attempts to extract personal information from crisis line workers. Rookies on the crisis line may be very taken with the heartbreaking stories they hear or feel very gratified by the strokes that dependent callers can give them. Under no circumstances should a crisis line worker ever give out his or her full name or other personal information, nor should the worker ever agree to meet the caller for social or professional reasons. The crisis line's credibility is built on anonymity, and that works both ways. In addition, serious ethical problems may arise when that anonymity is breached. Finally, crisis line workers who do not observe the foregoing run the risk of putting themselves in physical harm's way.

Given all that we have said about severely disturbed callers, our admonition is still to treat these clients not as types, but as individuals with their own idiosyncratic problems. However, those who are severely disturbed are not the only regular or problem callers.

Other Problem Callers

Telephone crisis workers must sometimes deal with covert callers, pranksters, silent callers, manipulators, sexually explicit callers, or even callers presenting legitimate sexual problems. It must be remembered and accepted that every call is an attempt by the caller to fulfill some need or purpose. Following are several types of problem callers and suggestions that should help workers to understand and cope with such callers.

Rappers. Some callers may just wish to "rap," or talk. The question becomes whether time should be spent listening to someone who only wants to talk, with no seemingly pressing issues. However, if "lonely" is tacked onto the description of the person, this may change the telephone worker's perception of the problem. It may also be that the caller is having trouble bringing issues into the open and is testing the waters to get enough courage to jump in. By allowing some leeway in approaching issues, but at the same time gently confronting the caller's loneliness, the worker sets reasonable limits on the conversation and still provides a supportive forum (McCaskie, Ward, & Reasor, 1990).

Covert Callers. Callers who ask for help for another individual may actually be asking for help for themselves. As a result, always assume that the call is about the caller, but never attempt to prove the call is about someone else (Brockopp, 1973a, p. 164; Brockopp, 2002a, pp. 171–175). Other callers may act surprised, "Oh, I thought this was a recording." The response is

to affirm that it is not. "No it isn't. I am Joe, and this is the crisis line. How can I help you this evening?" Yet others may make humorous jests as a test. "You must be really crazy to work there. I'll bet there are some real nuts who call up." The response to these calls is to avoid the "test" and respond empathically by saying, "I wonder if you're concerned that calls are handled seriously here?" These are most likely ways that timid and embarrassed callers have of checking out the crisis line to see what the opening response is and whether it is safe to talk. Intellectual types, on the other hand, tend to be know-it-alls who probably do have more expertise than volunteers. On their own intellectual ground they always "win." In actuality, these callers are often very insecure and unsure of themselves under their self-assured exterior. The key to dealing with intellectualizers is to immediately let them defeat you. "You're right. I am a volunteer here, and I don't know as much as you do about bipolar disorder. What I do know is you sound pretty concerned about it and seem to be looking for some help." Other callers may call and be silent or say they have the wrong number. Particularly at a suicide center, there are no wrong numbers. "May I help you?" or "What number were you calling?" are default responses to "wrong numbers."

Pranksters or Nuisance Callers. Teenagers who are bored at an overnight party may call the line just to bedevil the workers. If the prank call is treated seriously, they will probably hang up and not call back. If they are hung up on, they will continue to call (Brockopp, 1973b; Waters & Finn, 1995, p. 270). Many calls may appear to be of a nuisance nature. However, any person making a nuisance call should be considered to have a problem. Therefore, it is important that calls not be arbitrarily seen as pranks. The crisis line must answer all calls in a straightforward, no-nonsense manner. The crisis line must clearly convey that they are not playing games with people but that callers will be listened to honestly and responded to directly no matter what the purpose (Brockopp, 1973b, pp. 206–210). By so doing, the crisis line builds the perception in the community that the line is serious about what they do (Brockopp, 2002a, pp. 187–190). The teenager who is a prankster one night may be the suicidal teenager another night.

CW: Is it a prank or a dare you're playing or maybe something else that you really do need to talk about?

CW: I do wonder if there is something you might like to talk about. If you do, feel free to call back.

Silent Callers. One of the most frustrating of callers is the person who is silent. Silent callers are ambivalent. Either through embarrassment or hurt they are reticent, or from previous negative experiences they fear rejection and are just plain unable to muster the courage to talk. The worker must overcome his or her initial reaction to hang up, demonstrate acceptance, and attempt to remove any impediment that may keep the person from communicating (Brockopp, 2002b). For the silent caller, an appropriate response would be, "I'll be here when you feel you can talk."

CW: Sometimes it is really difficult to say what you need. Maybe it hurts so much you can't find words. Maybe you are not sure you can trust me. Whatever the reason you feel unable to talk, I am going to wait a little bit before I take another call. Even if you can't talk now, understand that this line is open for you when you need to talk.

If there is still no response, after a minute or so you could say, "I guess it is difficult to talk about this right now. I'll stay on the line for another minute, and then I'll have to go to another call. Call back when you feel ready to talk."

Manipulators. A variety of callers achieve their unmet needs by playing games with telephone workers. Typical manipulative games include questioning the worker's ability, role reversal in which the worker is tricked into sharing details of his or her personal life, and harassment. Redirecting the manipulative ploy and focusing on the unmet needs of manipulators force them to look at the reasons for their manipulative behavior (Brockopp, 2002a, p. 174; Waters & Finn, 1995, p. 269).

CW: You certainly know a great deal more about that subject than I do. How does it feel to be in control like that?

CW: When you question my integrity or try to get me to share intimate details, I wonder if you realize that is trying to meet some of your own needs for control. I wonder if you have considered what those needs to control and manipulate others are getting you.

Sexually Explicit Callers. "Call 1-900-LUST. Cindy's lonely and wants to talk to you!" The proliferation of these ads on late-night television, the Internet, and in porn magazines is a sad testimony to the existence of tens of thousands of men whose sexual insecurities, aberrance, and deviance make "sex talk" a multibillion-dollar business. An even sadder testimony is given by those individuals who use crisis lines for the same purpose. It should not be too amazing that Wark's (1984) interviews with a number of sexually explicit callers found them to be characterized by low self-esteem, feelings of isolation, lack of trust, a sense of being sexually unfulfilled, and little insight into their behavior. The primary purpose of the sexually explicit caller is to masturbate while talking to a female.

The sexually explicit caller is a particular millstone hung on the crisis line because many female volunteers become angry, embarrassed, and afraid and resign out of frustration with frequent sex calls (Baird, Bossett, & Smith, 1994; Brockopp & Lester, 2002, pp. 133–135; Fenelon, 1990). Brockopp and Lester (2002, p. 136) propose staying on the line and tolerating the behavior while attempting to build a more trusting relationship without condoning the behavior itself. That is a very idealistic way of treating the problem, and in the opinion of your authors is a great way to lose a lot of volunteers in a hurry! We will take a stand here and state that the crisis line is just not the place for that behavior to occur. Switching the caller to a same-sex worker and reframing the call in a context suggesting that the caller needs help put a severe damper on such calls.

Callers With Legitimate Sexual Problems. However, many people who have serious sexual or sexually related problems call crisis lines because of the anonymity allowed to frankly discuss their most private issues. These calls may embarrass workers who are not psychologically prepared for such intimate details, feel shocked at what they hear because of the criminal or exploitative nature, or do not have the technical expertise to handle them. Telephone workers must have education in dealing with sexual concerns and training in legal and ethical knowledge about what to do if the caller is a danger to a third party (Horton, 1995, p. 292). The very nature of calls dealing with sexual matters places crisis workers in a potentially value-laden, belief-centered moral and religious arena in which the worker's own opinions come into play. Although in most instances the major role of the worker is to *not* let his or her opinions hold sway and influence clients, avoiding these hot areas may also mean denying the caller much-needed information (Horton, 1995, p. 307). Providing options and information about "responsible" sex is a viable approach, although it should be understood that a very fine line runs between the worker's own biases and providing balanced information and must be monitored carefully.

Even though the preceding types of callers are striving to fulfill their needs, they often pose problems for telephone workers. Following are some techniques to help prepare crisis workers to deal with this sometimes difficult clientele.

Handling the Problem Callers

Pose Open-Ended Questions. Appropriate use of open-ended questions can help defuse the problems generated by frustrated callers (Epstein & Carter, 1991).

TC: You people don't know anything. Everything you've told me is a bunch of crap.

CW: What did you expect to gain from this call, then?

TC: Just to tell you what I think of your lousy service.

CW: If you were me, what would you be doing or saying right now?

These questions refocus the problem back to the caller and force movement toward problem solving rather than keeping the worker subjected to condemnatory statements.

Set Time Limits. When it is apparent that attempts to refocus the problem to the caller are futile, then a time limit should be set (Knudson, 1991).

TC: You ought to be congratulating me on getting my act together, no thanks to you.

CW: I'm glad you've done something positive since you last called. Now we can talk about your current situation for five minutes. Then I'll have to take another call.

Terminate Abuse. When the caller's behavior escalates to what the worker perceives as abusiveness, the call should be terminated in a clear and firm manner (McCaskie, Ward, & Rasor, 1990).

TC: You bitch! Don't you dare hang up this goddamned phone!

CW: (*assertively*) I'm sorry, but that is language we do not tolerate, so I'm going to another caller now. When you can talk appropriately, feel free to call back.

Switch Workers. Particularly with a sexually explicit caller, switching the call to another worker, preferably a male, takes the stimulus thrill out of the situation and makes it very difficult for the caller to bring masturbation to orgasm, which is usually the end goal of such a call (Knudson, 1991).

TC: I'd love to cover you with honey and lick you all over.

CW (female): (*calmly and coolly*) Given your specific problem, I'm going to switch you to Ralph. (*Signals to Ralph.*)

CW (Ralph): (*assertively*) I understand you have a problem. How can I help you?

If a male is not available, the call should be shifted to a supervisor and terminated. The caller should be told that the worker will hang up and that action should be taken immediately (McCaskie, Ward, & Rasor, 1990).

CW (supervisor): (*authoritatively and firmly*) We are *not* here to answer demeaning remarks while you masturbate. You need to know that our calls are taped, and obscene calls and using this service to masturbate are illegal. I am going to hang up. You may call back when you are ready to discuss this problem.

To bait a telephone worker and hold her on the line, sexually explicit callers often externalize their fantasies by reporting some hypothetical significant other's problem in florid detail. When the first hint of this ploy occurs, the worker should interpret the behavior as the caller's own and make the switch (Knudson, 1991).

TC: I'm really worried about my uncle and his 10-year-old daughter. She's a little doll, and he's always giving her these massages in her bedroom and I . . .

CW: (*Interrupts.*) That's out of my area of expertise; please hold the line and let me switch you to our child abuse expert, Ralph.

Use Covert Modeling. Covert modeling or conditioning (Cautela, 1976; Kazdin, 1975) has been used by Baird, Bossett, and Smith (1994) to extinguish repeated calls, particularly by sexually explicit clients. In covert modeling, the client is asked to use mental imagery to picture either reinforcing or extinguishing a particular behavior. The following worker response is abridged from their technique.

CW: As you're talking, I'm wondering if you recognize your real problem and want help with it. I know this would be pretty difficult to give up. But sometime soon, I'm not sure exactly when, as you reach for the phone you'll think to call a therapist instead. And this notion that you'll call a therapist and get help will get stronger every day as you think of it. You'll also start to feel better as you realize the crisis line isn't fulfilling your needs as therapy will. I'm going to hang up now and let you think about getting help with your real problem.

By suggesting that the need to call the therapist will grow, the worker plants the seed for anxiety about the caller's present behavior to grow along with the need to change. Both negative and positive reinforcers are used in the image: the need to seek help and the good feeling that will come from doing so. The worker also speaks of seeking help for the "real problem." This unspecified problem allows the worker to respond emphatically without accusing the caller of terrible, deviant behavior but still clearly states that the caller needs help. The worker does not continue in a dialogue with the client but instead hangs up to let the seed start to grow.

Formulate Administrative Rules. Administratively, crisis lines need to set specific rules to extinguish abusive behavior by doing the following (Knudson, 1991; McCaskie, Ward, & Rasor, 1990):

1. Limiting the number and duration of calls from any single caller
2. Limiting the topics that will be discussed
3. Requiring that only specific workers versed in handling abusive callers take such calls
4. Using speaker phones for on-the-spot consultation
5. Requiring the caller to establish a face-to-face relationship with an outside worker and allow communication between the therapist and crisis line personnel
6. Allowing the staff to prohibit calls for a day, a week, or more, if physical threats are made

The Headquarters Crisis Center of Lawrence, Kansas, uses a tracking log for regular callers that lists their name, phone number, address, style of interaction, major and tangential issues, effective and ineffective response modes, their physician/therapist, medications, support groups, and lethality levels. The log is kept current and available to staff, saving them a great deal of time and energy. This center also has an internal messages notebook labeled "Client Concerns." It contains information about regular callers that workers can quickly read to become updated on the caller's circumstances. It is an effective method to keep staff current and can be used to offer feedback and suggestions to clients (Epstein & Carter, 1991). Staff should be brought together on a regular basis to discuss these callers, plan strategy for them, make suggestions, and voice personal concerns (McCaskie, Ward, & Rasor, 1990). Finally, supervisors need to be acutely aware of the impact that such callers can have on personnel. Crisis center administrators should be ready, willing, and able to process debilitating emotions that such calls often evoke in workers in a caring, empathic, and supportive manner through regularly planned supervision and emergency debriefing sessions when necessary. Crisis intervention over the telephone is tough, grueling work, particularly when clients such as the foregoing emerge. Crisis calls are frequently onetime events with very little

opportunity for positive feedback. Particularly because crisis lines are run chiefly by volunteers, they need to be aware that not everyone can be helped (Waters & Finn, 1995, p. 271).

Hotlines

The tremendous growth of "hotlines" and "warmlines" in number, types of assistance, kinds of problems handled, and geographical coverage attests to the fact that people in crisis avail themselves of telephones to solve a wide variety of personal problems. Picking up the daily newspaper or the telephone directory in any medium-sized city or major metropolitan area, you can quickly find a list of emergency numbers to call for a variety of human services assistance programs. These services may range from generic crisis hotlines to a variety of specialized services such as local "warmlines" for latchkey children to the National Centers for Disease Control AIDS Hotline. There is even a line for a pet loss support group (Turner, 1997). Generic crisis phone lines are typically open 24 hours a day, 365 days a year, whereas more specialized services may operate during regular business hours.

These crisis telephone services may be continuous or time limited. "Warmlines" deal with less-than-life-threatening matters such as homework and are generally continuous or ongoing. "Hotlines" typically deal with problems that can be life threatening or endangering, such as suicide or running away from home. National hotlines are reachable by any phone anywhere in the country, whereas local hotlines serve specific geographic areas.

Time-Limited Hotlines. A time-limited hotline is one that is put into operation for a specified period of time; it is typically used to deal with a specific problem or to engage a special client population, such as immediately before a potential disaster or after a disaster. It may provide brief supportive therapy or serve as an information or referral source.

A particular use of such a hotline was in the wake of 9/11. The New York City Missing Persons Hotline was created to develop a database of missing persons and provide crisis counseling and information services. Counselors were given updated daily resource lists to provide information on everything from practical issues about returning to apartments to air toxicity levels. Lists of hospital admissions were compiled to cross-check against missing persons lists, enabling workers to call back to relatives inquiring about missing persons. However, the primary purpose of the hotline was to help grieving, scared, anxious people work through the trauma. To that end, workers used what would generally be the first four tasks of the model presented in Chapter 3 to provide psychological first aid to the callers.

Continuous National Hotlines. Specialized, toll-free, national hotlines deal with specific topics, such as troubled youth. Although brief supportive therapy may occur on such hotlines, generally the major purpose is to provide information about the geographic location nearest the caller where help can be obtained. These lines are heavily used and cut across all geographic areas, cultural groups, and socioeconomic classes. The two national runaway hotlines not only spend time talking to runaways about their problems, but also encourage them to get off the streets and into the nearest runaway shelter. The national domestic violence hotline is available to any victim of domestic abuse in the United States. Any person with suicidal ideation can call the national suicide hotline. These are a few of the national call centers that specialize in every kind of imaginable human dilemma.

Local Crisis Hotlines.   Local crisis hotlines typically handle all kinds of calls, ranging from suicidal ideation to lost cats (some calls are not as life threatening as others). They are staffed by volunteers from the local community, are listed in the yellow pages, and provide telephone crisis intervention services for a specific geographic locale or a specific population, such as a university student body.

The Internet's Growing Role in Crisis Intervention

Winston Churchill said, "Take change by the hand, because if you don't it will take you by the throat!" Since the advent of the Internet and websites, there has never been any doubt that there would be counseling services on the "net." However, the computer is not only a communication device; it can also function as a simulation device (Wolf, 2003). Both of these applications have great potential for psychotherapy and crisis intervention. So far, however, most professional therapists do not use computer-assisted counseling

or provide online therapy. Various reasons are given, including ethical concerns, commitment to humanistic values that conflict with technology, cost, and the absence of training (Murphy, 2003). Yet, if one reads current writing on the use of technology in counseling (Adlington, 2009; Anthony & Nagel, 2010; Jones & Stokes, 2009), it should be patently clear that the Internet and various forms of electronic communication will become more and more important in the delivery of psychotherapy and particularly crisis intervention.

Although therapists have been slow to adopt this mode of intervention, most consumers have not been—particularly young consumers who are not at all intimidated by the Internet (Calam et al., 2000) and see it as an integral part of their lives. Palfrey and Gasser (2009) identify anyone born after 1980 as a "digital native." Digital natives have access to digital technology networks, use them, and have never known any other way of life—as opposed to "digital settlers," who use digital technology but still rely heavily on analog forms of communication (which would characterize the authors of this book). So about how many natives are out there, and are they restless? About 117 million people sought health care information on the Internet in 2005 ("Number of 'Cyberchondriacs,'" 2005). They logged into chat rooms for support groups by the millions to discuss mental health issues, and chat rooms are only one part of what has come to be known as "behavioral telehealth."

Behavioral Telehealth

Behavioral telehealth is the use of telecommunication and information technology to provide access to behavioral health assessment, intervention, consultation, supervision, education, and information across distance (Nickelson, 1998); it can include e-mail, chat rooms, websites, and Internet video teleconferencing (Barnett & Scheetz, 2003). In some shape or form, all of the foregoing are already being done (Anthony & Nagel, 2010; Deleon, Crimmins, & Wolf, 2003; Jones & Stokes, 2009). Crisis intervention on the web can operate in an asynchronous (time-delayed, such as e-mail and websites) or a synchronous (real-time, such as chat rooms, videoconferencing, Skype, and instant messaging) format. The relevant questions, then, are "How can we ethically and effectively do crisis intervention on the Internet?" and "What crisis intervention services can be ethically and effectively provided on the Internet?" (Ruiz & Lipford-Sanders, 1999, p. 12).

Websites that provide opportunities for net "surfers" to seek emergency help or advice, counseling, or psychological help continue to grow exponentially. Befrienders International is a component of the Samaritans in Cheltenham, England. This group provides an excellent example of a website that offers help to suicidal individuals and other people in crisis. This group has been in the business of helping people for more than 40 years via letter, telephone, and in-person visits. E-mail sent to the Samaritans remains anonymous if the sender desires. Responses are asynchronous but trained volunteers read and reply to e-mail once a day, every day of the year. There are 20 centers around the world, and a trained volunteer with the universal counselor name "Jo" reads all e-mails and answers them within 24 hours (Wilson & Lester, 2002). Their address is jo@samaritans.org. However, many telephone hotlines are also Internet capable and are synchronous. For example, the National Runaway switchboard operates a synchronous live chat room that can be reached at www.1800runaway.org/.

The Appeal of Online Counseling

Clearly, the Internet, websites, e-mail, and other technological, wireless, and online electronic advances are much like the telephone in having the potential to provide a great deal of help to people who are geographically or psychologically isolated from specialized crisis services; are suffering physical or mental disabilities that do not permit them to travel to those services; are shy and do not want to meet face to face; need anonymity; have time management problems; are unavailable during normal working hours; or find it convenient, cost effective, or simply natural to their way of life (Anthony & Nagel, 2010, p. 35; Harris-Bowlsby, 2000; James & Gilliland, 2003, pp. 416–433; Jones & Stokes, 2009, pp. 2–5).

Feedback. When it comes to direct therapeutic intervention, not all aspects of online conversation may be seen as better than face to face, but there are many aspects of it that are. In crisis intervention, continuous and immediate feedback is critical, and synchronous Internet applications can serve this function well. Once the client has regained emotional equilibrium, the therapist can use asynchronous e-mail to check on how well the client is maintaining homeostasis. Feedback several times an hour, day, or week lets the client know the

interventionist is present, listening, and thinking about the client. Clients can initiate contact when they feel the greatest need. Regular and frequent e-mail reports require the client to constantly monitor and report behavior, which is critical in crisis intervention (Castelnuovo et al., 2003). However, as the interventionist, would you really want to sit at your computer all day long, doing instant messaging, or perhaps text message on your cell phone while eating in a restaurant? Of course, if you could turn your counseling computer on and let "HAL" do the counseling, you would have ample free time (James & Gilliland, 2003, pp. 420–428).

Disinhibition. A phenomenon that Suler (2004) named the *disinhibition effect* has appeared in e-therapy. What this effect means is that people tend to open up earlier with more distressing issues then they would normally do in an F2F (net acronym for face-to-face) therapy session. It is not clear why this effect happens, but it may be due to the absence of visual cues that might be perceived as judgmental or merely not having to look the therapist in the eye and tell him or her about the seamier side of one's life. The depersonalization and distance involved seem to make it safer to share intimate information. This appears particularly true for males, who may be reticent to come for face-to-face counseling or even telephone counseling but will use e-mail at least as much as women (Wilson & Lester, 2002).

Whether this phenomenon changes with the increased use of Skype, where there is synchronous F2F, is another interesting e-therapy question. There is also some evidence that there is greater depth of emotional processing when people have to read something as opposed to listening (Hiltz, 1992). There may also be greater depth to cognitive processing, and that includes both client and worker. Certainly it takes a great deal more time and thought to compose a written response; a cursory "hmmmm" probably won't be satisfactory (Wilson & Lester, 2002).

Problems of Online Counseling

Along with this potential, and even some unique advantages over traditional and telephone interventions, some major areas of concern cloud this new electronic horizon. As the flat worlders said to sailors who they thought were going over the edge of the world, "Be wary, there be demons and dragons out there!" While it is one thing to chat casually with another person half a world away, it is quite another to have people providing therapy or interventions about whose credentials you know nothing more than what they tell you. The reverse may also be true for clients who may not be who they say they are. At their most malevolent, clients could attempt to infect the crisis interventionists' computers with viruses or other "malware" that could compromise their files (Maheu, 2001, 2003).

Confidentiality. One of the major issues of therapy on the net is confidentiality. Excellent encryption programs are used by ethical therapists to keep information confidential. However, there is no such guarantee if you are working out of a cybercafé. Even though websites may guarantee anonymity, once a message goes out, there is no absolute guarantee that it cannot be pulled out of the ether by people or agencies you might not be too thrilled to have read your thoughts and pictures. An e-mail message is less like a letter and more like a postcard (Barnett & Scheetz, 2003). So! Do you really want to talk about your sexual inadequacies on a postcard? Additionally, the possibility of violating client confidentiality and the Health Insurance Portability and Accountability Act (HIPAA), which carries severe penalties for doing so, are real concerns for practicing mental health professionals (Fisher & Fried, 2003).

It may also be argued that online therapy is problematic because of identity verification in emergency situations involving homicide, suicide, or other life-threatening events. In most telephone crisis intervention, there is usually some way to access emergency help for the individual. But if the client is in Vilnius, Lithuania, and the crisis interventionist is in Brisbane, Australia, this may be more difficult.

Charlatans. Sad to say, the field is ripe for electronic snake oil salespeople and nefarious individuals who may have somewhat less character and goodness in their hearts than Florence Nightingale. In his review of Internet sites that purport to provide "crisis counseling," Myer (1999) reported that not only are some of the fees exorbitantly high, but based on the questionable claims of their promotional advertisements, people who choose some of these services might be putting themselves at risk for even more traumatization through secondary victimization at the hands of some very incompetent or outright charlatan "service providers." Clearly, although this venue holds much promise, it is a "buyer beware" situation. A cursory review of 1,980,000 hits returned by a search for "crisis intervention therapy" in June 2011

leads us to believe things haven't changed a lot since Myer's study.

Licensing and Insurance. There are other demons that abound in the legal world of the Internet. Do you need to carry professional indemnity insurance even if you are a volunteer at a crisis line (Jones & Stokes, 2009, pp. 141–142)? What happens when you do therapy across state lines or countries? Do you need a license in that state or country, and what can happen if somebody commits suicide or homicide on your watch? Do you know how to be sure your data are encrypted? Do you know how to password protect your files? Do you know how to download files safely, how to keep the downloads secure, how to back them up, and how and where they are stored? Are you familiar with the Online Therapy Institute's Ethical Framework for the Use of Technology in Mental Health (Nagel & Anthony, 2011b) and, for disaster responders, an ethical framework for the use of technology in disasters (Nagel & Anthony 2011a), or other professional ethical standards in your country for the use of technology? If you don't, you have no business doing business on the net.

Learning the Language. If you are going to operate in this world, you not only need to be technologically competent and savvy about the Internet, you also need to know the language. There are now "netizens" among us! Netizens are people who spend a great deal of time in online communities. They operate in what is generally called Web 2.0, which is a way of using the web to develop cultural communities and social networking sites (Anthony & Nagel, 2010, p. 9). These individuals and sites are replete with their own language and "netiquette" (civil and appropriate rules of discourse when operating on the net, particularly in synchronous time with other netizens). Anthony and Nagel (2010, pp. 5–6) contend that real life and online life are not separate but more and more blended, to the point that for millions of people virtual life and real life are one and the same! For many of these netizens, the virtual world they surf through *is* the real world, so it is not hard to see how they would perceive the Internet as the most viable way to access crisis intervention services.

Netiquette

Following are some basic netiquette rules you need to observe if you are working on the net (Anthony & Nagel, 2010; Jones & Stokes, 2009).

1. A typo or two, particularly in synchronous time, is okay. Sloppy writing with lots of typos and grammar problems is not and indicates you don't care much about your client.
2. Emoticons can be helpful in conveying an emotion. They also can be too cute! Check with your client before you use them.
3. Lots of tweeters who use the net have their own expansive set of acronyms. You need to be clear about what those are; don't hesitate to ask if you don't know an abbreviation.
4. Keep your text neutral by using a simple black font; 12-point Times, for example, is easy to read and even bland. Other fonts and colors can get pretty exotic. Your clients can give you a lot of information through what they use.
5. You know what you mean when you write something. But as people read words (a novel is a good example), they attribute their own meaning and subsequent emotional response. So be careful as you construct your responses.
6. Stay cool! Use standard counseling skill responses to do exploratory work. Let the client talk. Brevity in written responses is a good thing.
7. Keep flame wars (intentionally written inflammatory remarks or misinterpreted ones) under control. If you make a mistake, discretely and quickly apologize for it. If you are running a group online, they need to know the limits and that they will be called on their inappropriate behavior.

Congruent with overall netiquette are some basic ways of enhancing text to make it more conversational and add emphasis (Anthony & Nagel, 2010, pp. 51–55). On the negative side, conflict seems to occur more in online than in face-to-face intervention, so it appears that communications need to be constantly clarified so they do not get muddled (Mallen, Day, & Green, 2003). Even when emoticons (keyboard symbols rotated 90 degrees clockwise to look like facial expressions), such as ;) and :(, or emotional bracketing or altered text formats (different type sizes and fonts for emphasis) are used, it may be very difficult to tell when and to what degree emotions are being displayed.

Predispositioning

Because of the nature of online counseling and the great possibility that in a text-only situation miscommunication can occur (Adlington, 2009, pp. 158–159), predispostioning is critical—setting the tone as an empathic,

genuine, caring, unconditionally positive regarding intervener on first contact (Jones & Stokes, 2009, p. 17). It is also important to get across to the client how crisis intervention takes place on the Internet, and how that is different from typical Internet exchanges, tweets, and chat room dialogue.

E-mailer online to crisis center: I'm Featherlite. I've got a problem at home. I'm a 16 year old girl and I need some help with it. I've never done this before. I'm thinking about running away because I can't take much more of my parents climbing my frame because of my boyfriend. So where do we go from here? Can u help?

Dr. J: (*synchronous online in real time*) Featherlite, I'm glad you e-mailed us. Call me Dr. J. Pleased to make your acquaintance, Featherlite. Interesting online name. I am curious. Are you as light as a feather?

While it may seem tangential, the interventionist seeks to establish psychological contact by querying her Internet name.

Featherlite: Pretty much I guess. Especially when I dance. I'm on the modern dance team at my high school. Anyways that what Dad used to say when I was a little kid and he'd pick me up on his shoulders and it kinda stuck. Right now I'd like to pick him up and drop him off the Hernando De Soto Bridge.

Dr. J: Okay. I'd like to read what you have to say. Note I said "read" so that is a bit different from listening. There are some different rules of the road here and I'd like to go over them with you so things don't get messed up. First, we can't see each other so a lot of what passes for nonverbal communication won't happen. Also I can't catch the tone of your voice nor you mine. We might use emoticons to convey an expression, and I use things like brackets and boldface and some other ways of attempting to make clear what I am hearing and asking so there are some ways of using the computer to get meanings across, but there's still room to misread stuff and I don't want that to happen. I'm not going to worry too much about misspells and grammar, although I might ask you to clarify something if I don't understand it and you can do the same with me. I want us to be really clear on what's going on so I won't try to read your mind and misinterpret the issues. So please don't be offended if I ask for clarification, okay? Even though we are working in real time, I may take some time to think about what you are saying. I'll let you know that by using some dots . . . so that you know I haven't stopped and there is more to come. If you like you can do the same. This is a crisis Internet center so it is not long-term therapy. My whole purpose is to get you back on level ground so you can make some good, realistic short-term decisions about your problem and act on it. If you think you need more extensive help down the line we can discuss that. I'll be asking you a lot of questions to get the problem real clear in my mind. I'll probably restate what you say so we are both in agreement on what's going on. To do that I may cut out your words and paste them back into my response in boldface. I'll take some guesses at what you are feeling and thinking. If I am wrong, just tell me so and I'll try again. So this is a no fault deal okay? Now, Featherlite, if you would, think a moment . . . and then tell me the one main thing that caused you to write in tonight. I do see you are pretty **put out with your dad** right now. You said **"it"** and that **"you'd never done this before."** Can you tell me what "it" means and what it is that you haven't done?

This opening statement is designed to give the e-mailer an idea of how online counseling works and to get an idea of what the initiating problem is and the subtext underlying the initial query (Jones & Stokes, 2009, pp. 14–16). This rather long introduction gives the client at least a thumbnail sketch of how the interventionist will operate. A lot of owning statements are used to convey who and what the interventionist is and what he will and will not do. Not engaging in this preliminary discussion is likely to put the intervention in peril from the start, particularly with a client who has never engaged in crisis intervention let alone done so over the Internet. The interventionist's focus is on the immediate precipitating factors that got her to go online.

Featherlite: Well "it" is like my parents y'know. They 4bid me to see my boyfriend, Arley, who is out of high school. They don't like him because they think he is like 2 old for me and they think he does dope and wants me to do it 2 y'know. We really got in it tonight. I'm down at the city library and just serched u up so I haven't done this crisisline thing ever before. I also haven't run way from home, but Arley says we can go to Kentucky and gt married there without my p's consent. I don't want to gt married right now. I want to finish h.s., but I love Arley and don't know how I can go home. I kinda slapped my mom and then my dad really slapped me and I took off.

Dr. J: SO YOU'VE BEEN FIGHTING WITH YOUR P'S BECAUSE THEY THINK YOUR BOYFRIEND IS SUPPLYING YOU WITH DOPE AND YOU'RE SO IN LOVE WITH HIM YOU CAN'T SEE ALL THE FAULTS THEY SEE. RIGHT?

Featherlite: Why are you SHOUTING. You sound like my father. Always critical. YOU THINK I M CRAZY TOO! Am I that bad? Maybe I will run off with him.

Dr. J: Oops $#%$#%%! I accidentally hit the caps lock. Sorry. Not shouting, just old arthritic fingers LOL [laugh out loud]. No I don't think you're crazy. The "right" was just asking if I was on the money not whether you are right or wrong about your feelings.

While lots of shorthand and acronyms get used by clients, the interventionist needs to be careful in this regard. The word "right" in the above example can have many implications. Is our well-intentioned interventionist just seeking acknowledgment, or is he implying somebody is "right," and if so, is it Featherlite, her parents, or somebody else? So it might be a bit better if he were to make things clearer by saying "Am I right?"

Adlington (2009, pp. 8–40) uses a variety of text formats to build rapport with clients. Bracketing and boldfacing serve to indicate that the interventionist is listening closely and thinking about what has been said (pp. 13–14). Adding dots conveys some time spent pondering the issue and that the writer is going to continue with the thought.

Dr. J: Man! That really struck me about comparing me to your dad. Let me think on that a moment. . . .

As in F2F it is easy, perhaps even easier, to get lost in all the verbiage and as a result come back to the client with a whole flock of issues that get the client lost trying to determine which ones are important. A better way is to think of the core issue you want to cover and, as Adlington suggests, direct one central issue back to the client in boldface.

Dr. J: Featherlite, I get the sense this is more than me just sounding like your dad and being critical of your love life that's making you think of running away with Arley. Could you think a bit and tell me some of the long-term issues between you and your parents? I am guessing there may be a bit more than a boyfriend. Although right now **I do understand that the major issue is your wanting to be with Arley and your folks against it and that's what we will work on right now.**

Using the client's own font is one possible way of clearly restating what is being said in the client's own words.

Dr. J: So it seems right now you are so sensitive to your parents constant *criticism* that my goof up puts you on edge and **I sound like your dad.**

It should also be of interest as to what type of font the client uses (Adlington, 2009, p. 15). Would you respond differently if Featherlite were using **Braggadocio**, **𝔉𝔢𝔱𝔱𝔢 𝔉𝔯𝔞𝔨𝔱𝔲𝔯**, or *Edwardian Script* rather than **Comic Sans MS**? Or, for that matter, if the e-mail came with certain words in color (Adlington, 2009, p. 17)? Do you suppose it would make a difference in your interpretation if anger came back in red, purple, blue, or green?

Featherlite: I am so mad [crimson]. They're just jealous [green] because they were never in love like I am with Arley.

Dr. J: OK. I see the feelings. I have a series of questions to ask. They'll come one at a time. First, do you feel safe to go home tonight?

Featherlite: I don't know. The library closes at 11. I don't want to be on the streets then.

Dr. J: Do you have a friend or relative's house you could go to?

Featherlite: Maybe my aunt. Although my p's woud be mad if I went there. Mom doesn't get along with her sister well. Arley would come and take me to his apartment if I called him. He gets off at 11.

Dr. J: You are probably not going to like my response, but right now that might not be your best option. I can get you on the line to Runaway. They would get transportation there, then contact your Ps. That is escalating the situation some because there would have to be a meeting between them and you and your parents and social services would be involved. Right now it is important for you to stay safe. We can continue e-mailing and set some longer term plans up, but I want to see you under cover tonight.

Featherlite: U R probably right. I guess I could call my aunt.

Dr. J: Please do that and then either call into the crisis line phone number or e-mail me back . . . say 10 minutes. OK?

Featherlite: OK. I appreciate u. Pretty kul for an old (((((((gy))))))))) ! ! ! [The brackets denote hugs.]

While this online dialogue is representative of what most crisis interveners would do in any format, there are some notable exceptions. First and foremost, triaging Featherlite is difficult because it is hard to put numbers to her affect or cognition without seeing her facial expressions and hearing her voice. The intervener has to make a best guess based on what he actually knows. Therefore, the default approach is to make best-guess ratings that are generally high. The fact this is a 16-year-old girl about to be on the streets of Memphis alone at night gets her a 9 on the behavioral scale and dictates most of the worker's actions in getting her to a safe place. Second, until practice makes the intervener unconsciously competent with the technology, he will have to be very cognizant of operating and conversing in this new system. Invariably, then, some focus is taken away from the client to deal with system conversance, as is demonstrated by Dr. J's poor fine motor coordination in hitting the caps lock key.

Need for Training

This brief dialogue is meant to give you a snapshot of how crisis intervention works in real time on the net. It is not meant to make you a net competent crisis interventionist. Also, reading this brief section in a book is not going to make you a cyber crisis interventionist. Crisis workers engaging in this work and employing supportive computer programs need to have training beyond standard computer skills to deal with the inevitable technical problems and computer glitches. Understanding how the new medium integrates traditional and cyber counseling is critical (Anthony & Nagel, 2010, pp. 127–141). Further, cultural diversity and linguistic differences make understanding "multiculturalism" as it applies to crisis intervention paramount on the net (Anthony & Nagel, 2010, p. 63).

The worker also needs to be comfortable in the medium. Writing counseling responses using instant messaging or in chat rooms is altogether different from saying them over the telephone or in a face-to-face dialogue. Recognizing when clients are in trouble by their e-mail message content is very different from doing a visual assessment of clients face to face. Knowing how to obtain backup, use referral services, and contact emergency services over vast geographic distances is paramount. Even more important is getting supervision while doing the foregoing (Anthony & Nagel, 2010, pp. 127–141). Finally, the worker needs to educate clients about what cybercounseling can and cannot do for them and gain their informed consent (Castelnuovo et al., 2003; Maheu, 2003; Ragusea & VandeCreek, 2003).

Virtual Reality

Many computer programs available today perform assessment and self-help psychoeducational functions that are seen as effective and reliable. The other great potential use of computer technology in cybercounseling is in simulation and interactive virtual reality. A wide variety of computer programs are being tested for use with panic attacks, phobias, anxiety, depression, obsessive-compulsive disorder, addictions, PTSD, sexual dysfunction, eating disorders, obesity, physical rehabilitation, interpersonal skills deficits, and schizophrenic hallucinations. They are reported to have a high level of acceptance by clients, and outcomes are comparable with those obtained in working with face-to-face therapists (Glantz, Rizzo, & Graap, 2003; Golomb et al., 2011; Meyerbroker & Emmelkamp, 2010; Murphy, 2003; Parsons, 2010; Reger et al., 2011; Rinck et al., 2010; Riva, 2003; Tortella-Feliu et al., 2011; Wuang et al., 2011).

Probably the most intriguing of these approaches is the creation of virtual reality environments in which clients can be exposed to a variety of situations through a computer simulation of reality (Glantz, Rizzo, & Graap, 2003; Riva, 2003). Second Life is a virtual reality community that manifests such adjunctive computer therapy successfully (DeAngelis, 2009; Sutano et al., 2011). Clients can choose their avatar, set up housekeeping, and with assistance and assignments from their cybertherapist, try out new behaviors and see how they work. It does not take a great stretch of the imagination to see how these programs could be used to relax, calm, and defuse crisis clients who are geographically distant from immediate help. Anything you can do in real life you can do in Second Life (Robbins & Bell, 2008), which makes it an excellent medium to safely try out new skills and behaviors.

Legal, Ethical, and Moral Issues of Telephone and Internet Counseling

The bottom line is that there is still much to be done in the way of research and protocol development in behavioral telehealth and cybercounseling. Certainly, any crisis worker or agency moving into this venue needs to know professional ethical standards and state and federal regulations and laws. The technological advances of caller identification, call blocking, and call tracing pose some complex legal and ethical dilemmas for the telephone hotline. Given the ability to screen and identify calls, is it right to deny services to problem clients? Furthermore, given the expectation and the safety callers feel due to the anonymity of call-in services, using these technologies could easily put confidentiality on a collision course with duty to warn. Could other agencies demand the logs of such hotlines when involved in legal proceedings? Would the hotline workers be held civilly or criminally liable for their actions, given knowledge of whom they were working with and what they might have said?

Because most telephone hotline workers are volunteers, they receive minimal training, and the agencies they work for are not bound by state or federal supervision or legislation (Seely, 1997a, 1997b). These issues further compound the problems of how to ethically use these new technologies. There are no clear answers to these dilemmas at present, but they are issues that need to be addressed at every level of government and most certainly within the agencies that provide such services.

With all of these forewarnings, crisis interventionists have one clear ethical responsibility, particularly if that interventionist happens to work in a room that has "School Counselor" on the door: Being knowledgeable about digital technologies is a nonnegotiable ethical responsibility because that's the land your natives inhabit.

Does It Work?

The bottom line for any therapeutic endeavor is how well it works. Doing rigorous controlled-outcome studies is difficult, to say the least, in this anonymous world of electronics. Determining level of expertise and skillful intervention is equally problematic given that the vast number of crisis workers are volunteers. However, a number of studies have been done that sampled users of phone and electronic services (Evans et al., 1986; Mishara et al., 2005; Padach, 1984; Reese, Conoley, & Brossart, 2002, 2006; Rhee et al., 2005; Tolmach, 1985; Wark, 1984). Overall, they consistently rated electronic crisis intervention as helpful, and a number stated they preferred it to face-to-face counseling. The question remains: Does telephone and Internet counseling work? The answer to that, whether it is done by volunteers working crisis lines or professionals working with their own clientele, is pretty much "Yes."

It appears to be particularly true when we look at a sampling of personal issues where crises is almost always present. Controlled studies and meta-analyses that range across suicide (Rhee et al., 2005), cancer (Marcus et al., 2010), depression (Mohr et al., 2008), gambling (Shandley & Moore, 2008), HIV+ (Cook et al., 2009), and incapacitating and debilitating physical disabilities (Dorstyn, Mathias, & Denson, 2011), to name but a few, all indicate generally positive outcomes across a wide range of personality dimensions, coping mechanisms, and positive behavioral adaption and change. Telephone intervention can even help you get off the couch, exercise, eat your veggies, and get your daily dose of fiber (Eakin et al., 2007)!

SUMMARY

Telephone counseling and cybercounseling account for most crisis intervention work done in the world. Typically, local crisis lines field all kinds and varieties of calls while national hotlines field special, problem-specific issues such as runaways. Special crisis lines that are time limited may be set up immediately after major disasters. These services are staffed mainly by volunteers, who are generally seen as effective helpers by the people who call them. However, there are problem callers who can bedevil crisis lines. Some callers may use crisis lines for their own sexual gratification. Others may constantly call and tie up phone lines because of their loneliness.

Cyber crisis counseling will undoubtedly play a larger part in the future of crisis intervention. Many questions about its use and the ethical safeguards that need to be part of it remain unanswered. However, professional associations such as the American Counseling Association, the National Board for Certified Counselors, and the recently formed International Society for Mental Health Online are working hard on many of the birthing pains of this new baby.

Overall, the use of telephone and online services are seen as beneficial by consumers because they are fast, convenient, accessible, cheap, anonymous, and helpful, and there is evidence from empirical studies that supports consumer opinion.

 To see some of the concepts discussed in this chapter in action, refer to your *Crisis Intervention in Action* DVD, or see the clips online on the Counseling Course-Mate website. To access this site, go to www .cengagebrain.com, where you'll also find an eBook, additional study tools, quizzes, and more. So, you are listening in with Brittany as Amy, broken down and alone in Memphis, is trying to decide whether to rob a liquor store. Because of the video you can see Amy, but Brittany cannot. How do you think Brittany is doing without being able to see Amy? How do you feel about your ability to sense what other people are feeling and thinking when you don't have eye contact with them? If you were Brittany and were face to face with Amy, would you do something different? If so, what might that be?

REFERENCES

Adlington, J. (2009). *Online therapy: Reading between the lines*. London: MX Publishing.

Ammar, A., & Burdin, S. (1991, April). *Psychoactive medication: An introduction and overview*. Paper presented at the Fifteenth Annual Convening of Crisis Intervention Personnel, Chicago.

Anthony, K., & Nagel, D. M. (2010). *Therapy online: A practical guide*. London: Sage.

Baird, B. N., Bossett, S. B., & Smith, B. J. (1994). A new technique for handling sexually abusive calls to telephone crisis lines. *Community Mental Health Journal, 30*, 55–60.

Barnett, J., & Scheetz, K. (2003). Technological advances and telehealth: Ethics, law, and the practice of psychotherapy. *Psychotherapy: Theory, Research, Practice, Training, 40*(1/2), 86–93.

Bloom, B. L. (1984). *Community mental health: A general introduction* (2nd ed.). Pacific Grove, CA: Brooks/Cole.

Boschen, M. J. (2009). Mobile telephones and psychotherapy: Capability and applicability. *Behavior Therapist, 32*(8), 168–175.

Brockopp, G. W. (1973a). The covert cry for help. In D. Lester & G. W. Brockopp (Eds.), *Crisis intervention and counseling by telephone* (pp. 193–198). Springfield, IL: Charles C Thomas.

Brockopp, G. W. (1973b). The nuisance caller. In D. Lester & G. W. Brockopp (Eds.), *Crisis intervention and counseling by telephone* (pp. 206–210). Springfield, IL: Charles C Thomas.

Brockopp, G. W. (2002a). The therapeutic management of the chronic caller. In D. Lester & G. W. Brockopp (Eds.), *Crisis intervention and counseling by telephone* (2nd ed., pp. 159–164). Springfield, IL: Charles C Thomas.

Brockopp, G. W. (2002b). Working with the silent caller. In D. Lester & G. W. Brockopp (Eds.), *Crisis intervention and counseling by telephone* (2nd ed., pp. 182–186). Springfield, IL: Charles C Thomas.

Brockopp, G. W., & Lester, D. (2002). The chronic caller. In D. Lester & G. W. Brockopp (Eds.), *Crisis intervention and counseling by telephone* (2nd ed., pp. 154–167). Springfield, IL: Charles C Thomas.

Bryant, R. A., & Harvey, A. G. (2000). Telephone crisis intervention skills: A simulated caller paradigm. *Crisis, 21*(2), 90–94.

Burgess, N., Christensen, H., Leach, L., Farrer, L., & Griffiths, K. (2008). Mental health profile of callers to a telephone counseling service. *Journal of Telemedicine and Telecare, 14*(1), 42–47.

Calam, R., Cox, A., Glasgow, D., Jimmieson, P., & Larsen, S. G. (2000). Assessment and therapy with children: Can computers help? *Clinical Child Psychology & Psychiatry, 5*(3), 329–343.

Castelnuovo, G., Gaggioli, A., Mantovani, F., & Riva, G. (2003). New and old tools in psychotherapy: The use of technology for the integration of traditional clinical treatments. *Psychotherapy: Theory, Research, Practice, Training, 40*(1/2), 33–44.

Cautela, J. R. (1976). The present status of covert modeling. *Journal of Behavior Therapy and Experimental Psychiatry, 6*, 323–326.

Christogiorgos, S., Vassilopoulou, V., Florou, A., Xydou, V., Douvou, M., Vgenopoulou, S., et al. (2010). Telephone counseling with adolescents and counter-transference phenomena: Particularities and challenges. *British Journal of Guidance & Counseling,38*(3), 313–325.

Cook, P. F., McCabe, M., Emiliozzi, S., & Pointer, L. (2009). Telephone nurse counseling improves HIV medication adherence: An effectiveness study. *JANAC: Journal of the Association of Nurses in AIDS care, 20*(4), 316–325.

Day, S. X., & Schneider, P. L. (2002). Psychotherapy using distance technology: A comparison of face-to-face, video, and audio treatment. *Journal of Counseling Psychology, 49*(4), 499–503.

DeAngelis, T. (2009). Can Second Life therapy help with autism? *Monitor on Psychology, 40*(9), 40.

Deleon, P. H., Crimmins, D. B., & Wolf, A. W. (2003). Afterword: The 21st century has arrived. *Psychotherapy: Research, Training, and Practice, 40*(1/2), 164–169.

Derkx, H., Rethans, J., Maiburg, B., Winkens, R., Muitiens, A., van Rooii, H., et al. (2009). Quality of communication during telephone triage at Dutch after-hours centres. *Patient Education and Counseling, 74*(2), 174–178.

Dorstyn, D. S., Mathias, J. L., & Denson, L. A. (2011). Psychosocial outcomes of telephone-based counseling for adults with an acquired physical disability: A meta-analysis. *Rehabilitation Psychology, 56*(1), 1–14).

Dublin, L. I. (1969). Suicide prevention. In E. S. Shneidman (Ed.), *On the nature of suicide.* San Francisco: Jossey-Bass.

Eakin, E. G., Lawler, S., Vanderlanotte, C., & Owen, N. (2007). Telephone interventions for physical activity and dietary behavior change: A systemic review. *American Journal of Preventive Medicine, 32*(5), 419–434.

Eckardt, M. H. (2011). The use of the telephone to extend our therapeutic availability. *Journal of the American Academy of Psychoanalysis Dynamic Psychiatry, 39*(1), 151–154.

Epstein, M., & Carter, L. (1991). *Headquarters training manual.* Lawrence, KS: Headquarters Crisis Center.

Evans, R. L., Smith, K. M., Werkhoven, W. S., Fox, H. R., & Pritzl, D. O. (1986). Cognitive telephone group therapy with physically disabled elderly persons. *Gerontologist, 26*, 8–11.

Fenelon, D. A. (1990, April). *Recognizing and dealing with the bogus sex caller.* Paper presented at the Fourteenth Annual Convening of Crisis Intervention Personnel, Chicago.

Fisher, C. B., & Fried, A. L. (2003). Internet-mediated psychological services and the American Psychological Association Ethics Code. *Psychotherapy: Theory, Research, Practice, Training, 40*(1/2), 86–93.

Fukkink, R., & Hermanns, J. (2009). Counseling children at a helpline: Chatting or calling. *Journal of Community Psychology, 37*(8), 938–948.

Glantz, K., Rizzo, A., & Graap, K. (2003). Virtual reality for psychotherapy: Current reality and future possibilities. *Psychotherapy: Theory, Research, Practice, Training, 40*(1/2), 55–67.

Golomb, M. R., Warden, S. J., Fess, E., Rabin, B., Yonkman, J., Shirley, B., et al. (2011). Maintained hand function and forearm bone health 14 months after an in-home virtual reality videogame hand tele-rehabilitation intervention in an adolescent with hemiplegic cerebral palsy. *Journal of Child Neurology, 26*(3), 389–393.

Greenwald, B. (1985a). *In-Touch Hotline training materials: Coping.* Chicago: University of Illinois at Chicago Circle Campus, Counseling Center.

Greenwald, B. (1985b). *In-Touch Hotline training materials: The disturbed caller.* Chicago: University of Illinois at Chicago Circle Campus, Counseling Center.

Gross, S., & Anthony, K. (Eds.). (2003). *Technology in counseling and psychotherapy: A practitioner's guide.* New York: Palgrave Macmillan.

Grunsted, V. L., Cisneros, M. X., & Belen, D. V. (1991, April). *Working with the disturbed hotline caller.* Paper presented at the Fifteenth Annual Convening of Crisis Intervention Personnel, Chicago.

Harris-Bowlsby, J. (2000). The Internet? Blessing or bane for the counseling profession. In J. W. Bloom & G. R. Walz (Eds.), *Cybercounseling and cyberlearning: Strategies and resources for the millennium.* Alexandria, VA: American Counseling Association.

Hiltz, S. R. (1992). The virtual classroom: Software for collaborative learning. In E. Barrett (Ed.), *Sociomedia: Multimedia, hypermedia, and the social construction of knowledge. Technical communication and information systems* (pp. 347–368). Cambridge, MA: MIT Press.

Horton, A. L. (1995). Sex-related hotline calls. In A. R. Roberts (Ed.), *Crisis intervention and time-related cognitive treatment* (pp. 292–312). Thousand Oaks, CA: Sage.

Hsiung, R. C. (2002). *E-therapy: Case studies, guiding principles, and the clinical potential of the Internet.* New York: W.W. Norton.

Jacobs, J. (2010). Suicide prevention on the Golden Gate Bridge. *American Journal of Psychiatry, 167*(4), 473.

James, R. K., & Gilliland, B. E. (2003). *Theories and strategies in counseling and psychotherapy* (5th ed.). Upper Saddle River, NJ: Prentice Hall.

Jones, G., & Stokes, A. (2009). *Online counseling: A handbook for practitioners.* London: Palgrave Macmillan.

Kazdin, A. E. (1975). Covert modeling, imagery assessment, and assertive behavior. *Journal of Consulting and Clinical Psychology, 43*, 716–724.

Knudson, M. (1991, April). *Chronic and abusive callers: Appropriate responses and interventions.* Paper presented at the Fifteenth Annual Convening of Crisis Intervention Personnel, Chicago.

Lamb, C. W. (1973). Telephone therapy: Some common errors and fallacies. In D. Lester & G. W. Brockopp (Eds.), *Crisis intervention and counseling by telephone* (pp. 105–110). Springfield, IL: Charles C Thomas.

Lamb, C. W. (2002). Telephone therapy: Some common errors and fallacies. In D. Lester (Ed.), *Crisis intervention and counseling by telephone* (2nd ed., pp. 83–87). Springfield, IL: Charles C Thomas.

Leffert, M. (2003). Analysis and psychotherapy by telephone: Twenty years of clinical experience. *Journal of the American Psychoanalytic Association, 51*, 101–130.

Lester, D. (Ed.). (2001). *Suicide prevention: Resources for the millennium.* Philadelphia: Brunner-Routledge.

Lester, D. (2002). When things go wrong. In D. Lester & G. W. Brockopp (Eds.), *Crisis intervention and counseling by telephone* (2nd ed., pp. 167–170). Springfield, IL: Charles C Thomas.

Lester, D., & Brockopp, G. W. (Eds.). (1973). *Crisis intervention and counseling by telephone.* Springfield, IL: Charles C Thomas.

Maheu, M. M. (2001). Practicing psychotherapy on the Internet: Risk management challenges and opportunities. *Register Report, 27,* 23–28.

Maheu, M. M. (2003). The online clinical practice management model. *Psychotherapy: Theory, Research, Practice, Training, 40*(1/2), 20–32.

Mallen, M. J., Day, S. X., & Green, M. A. (2003). Online versus face-to-face conversations: An examination of relational and discourse variables. *Psychotherapy: Theory, Research, Practice, Training, 40*(1/2), 155–163.

Marcus, A. C., Garrett, K. M., Cella, D., Wenzel, L., Brady, M., Fairclough, D., et al. (2010). Can telephone counseling post-treatment improve psychosocial outcomes among early stage breast cancer survivors? *Psycho-Oncology,19*(9), 923–932.

Masi, D., & Freedman, M. (2001). The use of telephone and online technology in assessment, counseling, and therapy. *Employee Assistance Quarterly, 16*(3), 49–63.

McCaskie, M., Ward, S., & Rasor, L. (1990, April). *Short-term crisis counseling and the regular caller.* Paper presented at the Fourteenth Annual Convening of Crisis Intervention Personnel, Chicago.

Meyerbroker, K., & Emmelkamp, P. (2010). Virtual reality exposure therapy in anxiety disorder: A systemic review of process-and-outcome studies. *Depression and Anxiety, 27*(10), 933–944.

Mishara, L. B. L., Chagnon, F., Daigle, M., Balan, B., Raymond, S., Marcous, I., et al. (2005). *A silent monitoring of telephone help provided over the Hopeline network and its short-term effects.* Montreal: Center for Research and Intervention on Suicide and Euthanasia.

Mohr, D. C., Vella, L., Hart, S., Heckman, T., & Simon, G. (2008). The effect of telephone-administered psychotherapy on symptoms of depression and attrition: A meta-analysis. *Clinical Psychology: Science and Practice, 15*(3), 243–253.

Murphy, M. J. (2003). Computer technology for office-based psychological practice: Application and factors affecting adoption. *Psychotherapy: Theory, Research, Practice, Training, 40*(1/2), 10–19.

Myer, R. A. (1999, April). *Crisis intervention using the Internet.* Paper presented at the Twenty-third Annual Convening of Crisis Intervention Personnel, Chicago.

Nagel, D. M., & Anthony, K. (2011a). Ethical framework for the use of technology in disaster mental health. *Online Therapy Institute.* Retrieved from www.onlinetherapyinstitute .com/disaster-mental-health/

Nagel, D. M., & Anthony, K. (2011b). Ethical framework for the use of technology in mental health. *Online Therapy Institute.* Retrieved from www.onlinetherapyinstitute .com/ethical-training

National Suicide Prevention Lifeline. (2011). Retrieved from www.suicidepreventionlifeline.org

Nickelson, D. W. (1998). Telehealth and the evolving health care system: Strategic opportunities for professional psychology. *Professional Psychology: Research and Practice, 29,* 527–535.

Number of "cyberchondriacs"—U.S. adults who go online for health information—increases to estimated 117 million. (2005). *Healthcare News, 5*(8). Retrieved from www .harrisinteractive.com/news/newsletters/healthnews/ HI_HealthCareNews2005Vol5_Iss08.pdf

Ochberg, F. M. (Ed.). (1988). *Post-traumatic therapy and victims of violence.* New York: Brunner/Mazel.

Padach, K. M. (1984). Long-term telephone counseling. In F. W. Kaslow (Ed.), *Counseling with psychotherapists* (pp. 173–190). New York: Haworth Press.

Palfrey, J., & Gasser, U. (2009). *Born digital: Understanding the first generation of digital natives.* New York: Basic Books.

Parsons, T. D. (2010). Virtual environments for clinical psychologists. *Clinical Psychologist, 63*(4), 1–3.

Peterson, B., & Schoeller, B. (1991, April). *Identifying and responding to problem and repeat callers.* Paper presented at the Fifteenth Annual Convening of Crisis Intervention Personnel, Chicago.

Phipps, A., Byrne, M., & Deane, F. (2007). Can volunteer counselors help prevent psychological trauma? A preliminary communication on volunteers' skill using the "Orienting Approach" to trauma counseling. *Stress and Health: Journal of the International Society of the Investigation of Stress, 23*(1), 15–21.

Pope, R. (Speaker). (1991). *Crisis counseling of the walk-in.* (Videotape Recording No. 6611-91B). Memphis, TN: Memphis State University, Department of Counseling and Personnel Services.

Preziosa, A., Grassi, A., Gaggioli, A., & Riva, G. (2009). Therapeutic applications of the mobile phone. *British Journal of Guidance & Counselling, 37*(3), 313–325.

Ragusea, A. S., & VandeCreek, L. (2003). Suggestions for the ethical practice of online psychotherapy. *Psychotherapy: Theory, Research, Practice, Training, 40*(1/2), 94–102.

Reese, R. J., Conoley, C. W., & Brossart, D. F. (2002). Effectiveness of telephone counseling: Field-based investigation. *Journal of Counseling Psychology, 49*(2), 233–242.

Reese, R. J., Conoley, C. W., & Brossart, D. F. (2006). The attractiveness of telephone counseling: An empirical investigation of client perceptions. *Journal of Counseling & Development, 84*(1), 54–60.

Reger, G., Holloway, K., Candy, C., Rothbaum, B., Difede, J., Rizzo, A., & Gahm, G. (2011). Effectiveness of virtual reality exposure therapy for active duty soldiers in a military mental health clinic. *Journal of Traumatic Stress 24*(1), 93–96.

Rhee, W. K., Merbaum, M., Strube, M. J., & Self, S. (2005). Efficacy of brief telephone psychotherapy with callers to a suicide hotline. *Suicide and Life-Threatening Behavior, 35*(3), 317–328.

Rinck, M., Rortgen, T., Lange, W., Dotsch, R., Wigboldus, D., & Becker, E. (2010). Social anxiety predicts avoidance behavior in virtual encounters. *Cognition and Emotion, 24*(7), 1269–1276.

Riva, G. (2003). Virtual environments in clinical psychology. *Psychotherapy: Theory, Research, Practice, Training, 40*(1/2), 68–76.

Robbins, S., & Bell, M. (2008). *Second life for dummies.* Indianapolis, IN: Wiley.

Rohland, B. M., Saleh, S. S., Rohrer, J. E., & Romitti, P. A. (2000). Acceptability of telepsychiatry to a rural population. *Psychiatric Services, 51*(5), 672– 674.

Ruiz, N. J., & Lipford-Sanders, J. A. (1999, October). Online counseling: Further considerations. *Counseling Today, 42*(4), 12, 33.

Seely, M. F. (1997a). The discrete role of the hotline. *Crisis, 18*(2), 53–54.

Seely, M. F. (1997b). The role of hotlines in the prevention of suicide. In R. M. Maris & M. M. Silverman (Eds.), *Review of suicidology* (pp. 251–270). New York: Guilford Press.

Shandley, K., & Moore, S. (2008). Evaluation of Gambler's Helpline: A consumer perspective. *International Gambling Studies, 8*(3), 315–330.

Slaikeu, K. A. (Ed.). (1990). *Crisis intervention: A handbook for practice and research.* Boston: Allyn & Bacon.

Slaikeu, K. A., & Leff-Simon, S. I. (1990). Crisis intervention by telephone. In K. A. Slaikeu (Ed.), *Crisis intervention: A handbook for practice and research* (2nd ed., pp. 319–328). Boston: Allyn & Bacon.

Suler, J. (2004). The online disinhibition effect. *Cyberpsychology and Behavior 7*(3), 321–326.

Sutano, J., Phang, C., Tan, C., & Lu, X. (2011). Dr. Jekyll vis-a-vis Mr. Hyde: Personality variation between virtual and real worlds. *Information and Management, 48*(1), 19–26.

Tolmach, J. (1985). "There ain't nobody on my side." A new day treatment program for black urban youth. *Journal of Clinical Child Psychology, 14*, 214–219.

Tortella-Feliu, M., Botella, C., Llabres, J., Breton-Lopez, J., del Amo, A., Banos, R., et al. (2011). Virtual reality versus computer-aided exposure treatments for fear of flying. *Behavior Modification, 35*(1), 3–30.

Turner, W. (1997). Evaluation of a pet loss support hotline. *Anthrozooes, 10*(4), 225–230.

Tuttle, A. (1991). *Advantages and strategies of telephone crisis counseling* (audiotape). Memphis, TN: The Crisis Center.

Wark, V. (1982). A look at the work of the telephone counseling center. *Personnel and Guidance Journal, 61*, 110–112.

Wark, V. (1984). *The sex caller and the telephone counseling center.* Springfield, IL: Charles C Thomas.

Waters, J., & Finn, E. (1995). Handling crisis effectively on the telephone. In A. R. Roberts (Ed.), *Crisis intervention and time-limited cognitive treatment* (pp. 251–289). Thousand Oaks, CA: Sage.

Watson, R. J., McDonald, J., & Pearce, D. (2006). An exploration of calls to Lifeline Australia: Social support or urgent suicide intervention? *British Journal of Guidance and Counselling, 34*(4), 471–482.

Williams, T., & Douds, J. (2002). The unique contributions of telephone therapy. In D. Lester & G. W. Brockopp (Eds.), *Crisis intervention and counseling by telephone* (2nd ed., pp. 57–63). Springfield, IL: Charles C Thomas.

Wilson, G., & Lester, D. (2002). Crisis intervention by e-mail. In D. Lester & G. W. Brockopp (Eds.), *Crisis intervention and counseling by telephone* (2nd ed., pp. 212–219). Springfield, IL: Charles C Thomas.

Wolf, A. W. (2003). Introduction to the special issue. *Psychotherapy: Theory, Research, Practice, Training, 40*(1/2), 3–7.

Wuang, Y., Chiang, C., Su, C., & Wang, C. (2011). Effectiveness of virtual reality using Wii gaming technology in children with Down syndrome. *Research in Developmental Disabilities, 32*(1), 312–321.

Handling Specific Crises
Going Into the Trenches

Part II focuses on applying intervention strategies to several of the currently most prevalent types of crises in the human experience. The purpose of Part II is to provide crisis workers with information about the background, dynamics, and intervention methodologies needed to effectively help individuals or groups in various kinds of crises.

Part II contains a wide array of crisis case illustrations to enhance descriptions of not only the usual and accepted intervention practices for various type of crises, but also many innovative and cutting-edge strategies for intervention. Indeed, some of these strategies are controversial, but they have gained enough treatment notoriety and preliminary research to be included. Part II examines posttraumatic stress disorder, suicide, sexual assault, domestic violence, substance addiction, personal loss, and crises in schools. Three central themes pervade these chapters:

1. Some crises are *time limited* and some are *transcrisis*, in that the person in crisis may progressively experience severe problems, either deal with or suppress them, and then experience and exhibit repeated responses and symptoms of the same crisis over a period of many years.

2. No one set of theories, assumptions, strategies, or procedures is appropriate for intervening in all crisis situations; rather, a systematic and eclectic approach is recommended and demonstrated as the preferred mode of helping in a broad assortment of crisis problems and settings. The techniques employed in these chapters are "best bets" for the particular kind of client in the particular environment. They are, however, not the only "bets." They are meant to give you a variety of approaches and situations that will start to help you form your own "Gestalt" of an effective crisis worker.

3. Crisis intervention is hallmarked by elastic, fluid situations that change in seconds and minutes and may move from a very benign to a volatile situation in that time. Many of the case illustrations model such dynamics to give you a flavor of what the crisis worker must do to respond quickly and effectively.

CHAPTER 7

Posttraumatic Stress Disorder

Part II's discussion of the more common types of crises that you, as a mental health worker or consumer of mental health care, are likely to encounter opens with posttraumatic stress disorder (PTSD). The reason for beginning here is that many other crises reviewed in this book may be rooted in PTSD. For example, suicide (Chu, 1999; Kramer et al., 1994) and substance abuse (Ouimette, Read, & Brown, 2005; Read, Bollinger, & Sharansky, 2003) may be the end products of attempting to cope with trauma. In contrast, rape, sexual abuse, battering, loss, physical violence, hostage situations, and large-scale natural and human-made disasters may precipitate the disorder (Ackerman et al., 1998; Bigot & Ferrand, 1998; Darves-Bornoz et al., 1998; Davis et al., 2003; Elklit & Brink, 2004; King et al., 2003; Lang et al., 2004; Melhem et al., 2004; North, 2004; Pivar & Field, 2004). Finally, PTSD-like symptoms may appear in the very people who attempt to alleviate the mental and physical suffering of people in crisis (Figley, 2002; Halpern & Tramontin, 2007; Pearlman & Saakvitne, 1995). While acute distress and *acute stress disorder* will be dealt with in other parts of this book, this chapter will deal specifically with the long-term residual effects of trauma on survivors.

We know this is a long chapter and you might need to take a nap or a snack break to get through it. Try as we might to prune it down, we felt that "all this stuff" was critical to giving you the background for understanding not only what PTSD is about, but what occurs in treating the other crisis and transcrisis topics in this book. What we knew about PTSD in the first edition of this book in 1987 and what we know about it now—particularly the neurobiology and just how complex that is in manifesting the various traumatic responses

that occur in humans—is like the difference between writing with a goose quill, inkwell, and papyrus scroll and word processing with an Apple Thunderbolt, OSX Lion operating system, and high-speed printer/scanner/fax. So bear with us! If you nail this chapter down, the other chapters will make a whole lot more sense as to how "all this stuff" goes together.

Background

Psychic trauma is a process initiated by an event that confronts an individual with an acute, overwhelming threat (Freud, 1917/1963). When the event occurs, the inner agency of the mind loses its ability to control the disorganizing effects of the experience, and disequilibrium occurs. The trauma tears up the individual's psychological anchors, which are fixed in a secure sense of what has been in the past and what should be in the present (Erikson, 1968). When a traumatic event occurs that represents nothing like the person's experience of past events, and the individual's mind is unable to effectively answer basic questions of how and why it occurred and what it means, a crisis ensues. The traumatic wake of a crisis event typically includes immediate and vivid reexperiencing, hyperarousal, and avoidance reactions, which are all common to PTSD. The event propels the individual into a traumatic state that lasts as long as the mind needs to reorganize, classify, and make sense of the traumatic event. Then, and only then, does psychic equilibrium return (Furst, 1978). The typical kinds of responses that occur immediately after the crisis may give rise to what are called peritraumatic (around, or like, trauma) symptoms. These are common responses as the mind attempts to reorganize itself and cope with a horrific event. For many people, these responses will slowly disappear after a few days. Most people are amazingly resilient in the aftermath of a crisis and quickly return to mental and physical homeostasis, but if the symptoms continue for a minimum of 2 days and a maximum of 4 weeks and occur within 1 month of the traumatic event, then those time frames will meet the criteria of *acute stress disorder* (American Psychiatric Association, 2000, p. 469). If acute stress disorder symptoms develop, they will typically drop off in 1 to 3 months for most people (Brewin, 2003).

If the person can effectively integrate the trauma into conscious awareness and organize it as a part of the past (as unpleasant as the event may be), then homeostasis returns, the problem is coped with, and the individual continues to travel life's rocky road. If the event is not effectively integrated and is submerged from awareness, then the probability is high that the initiating stressor will continue to assail the person and become chronic PTSD. It may also disappear from conscious awareness and reemerge in a variety of symptomatic forms months or years after the event. When such crisis events are caused by the reemergence of the original unresolved stressor, they fall into the category of delayed PTSD (American Psychiatric Association, 2000, p. 468).

PTSD is a newborn compared with the other crises we will examine, at least in regard to achieving official designation. In 1980, PTSD found its way into the third edition of the American Psychiatric Association's *Diagnostic and Statistical Manual of Mental Disorders (DSM-III)* as a classifiable and valid mental disorder. However, the antecedents of what has been designated as PTSD first came to the attention of the medical establishment in the late 19th and early 20th centuries.

Two events serve as benchmarks. First, with the advent of rail transportation and subsequent train wrecks, physicians and early psychiatrists began to encounter in accident survivors trauma with no identifiable physical basis. Railway accident survivors of this type became so numerous that a medical term, *railway spine*, became an accepted diagnosis. In psychological parlance, the synonymous term *compensation neurosis* came into use for invalidism suffered and compensated by insurers as a result of such accidents (Trimble, 1985, pp. 7–10).

Concomitantly, Sigmund Freud formulated the concept of *hysterical neurosis* to describe trauma cases of young Victorian women with whom he was working. He documented symptoms of warded-off ideas, denial, repression, emotional avoidance, compulsive repetition of trauma-related behavior, and recurrent attacks of trauma-related emotional sensations (Breuer & Freud, 1895/1955). However, what Freud found and reported on the pervasive childhood sexual abuse of these women as the traumatic root of their hysteria was anathema to a puritanical Victorian society, and he was forced to disavow and then reject his findings (Herman, 1997, pp. 13–17).

Second, the advent of modern warfare in World Wars I and II, with powerful artillery and aerial bombardment, generated terms such as *shell shock* and *combat fatigue* to explain the condition of traumatized soldiers who had no apparent physical wounds. As early as the American Civil War, soldiers were diagnosed with "neurasathenia," a state of mental and physical exhaustion. This malady was also termed "soldier's heart" because of the belief that nerves at the base of the heart were somehow affected by combat. The term *nostalgia*, which would be seen as a stress disorder in current terms, was also coined. The thought was that soldiers became nostalgic for home and thus started to manifest a variety of physical symptoms that would relieve them from combat and allow them to go home (Kinzie & Goetz, 1996). Various hypotheses such as the foregoing were proposed to account for such strange maladies (Trimble, 1985, p. 8), but Freud (1919/1959) believed that the term *war neurosis* more aptly characterized what was an emotional disorder that had nothing to do with the prevailing medical notion of neurology-based "shell shock" in World War I.

The U.S. Medical Service Corps came to recognize "combat fatigue" in World War II and the Korean War as a treatable psychological disturbance. The treatment approach was that combat fatigue was invariably acute and that treatment was best conducted as quickly and as close to the battle lines as possible. The idea was to facilitate a quick return to active duty. The prevailing thought was that time heals all wounds and that little concern needed to be given to long-term effects of traumatic stress. Such has not been the case (Archibald et al., 1962). Indeed, a notable proponent of establishing the Vietnam Veterans Centers, Arthur Blank, ruefully commented that when he was an army psychiatrist in Vietnam, he believed there would be no long-term difficulties for veterans (MacPherson, 1984, p. 237).

Although PTSD can and does occur in response to the entire range of natural and human-made catastrophes, it was the Vietnam War that clearly brought PTSD to the awareness of both the human services professions and the public. Through a combination of events and circumstances unparalleled in the military history of the United States, veterans who returned from that conflict began to develop a variety of mental health problems that had little basis for analysis and treatment in the prevailing psychological literature. This combination of events and circumstances had insidious and long-term consequences that were not readily apparent either to the individuals affected or to human services professionals who attempted to treat them. Misdiagnosed, mistreated, and misunderstood, military service personnel became known to a variety of social services agencies that included the police, mental health facilities, and unemployment offices (MacPherson, 1984, pp. 207–330, 651–690).

As the war continued to grind on, more and more veterans started having psychological problems. Rebuffed by the Veterans Administration, these veterans formed self-help groups to try to come to terms with their psychological issues. These "rap" groups rapidly coalesced and became a political force that pushed the federal government to come to grips with their problems. One major result of their lobbying efforts was the establishment of the Vietnam Veterans Centers, where alienated veterans could seek help for a variety of readjustment problems. An informal network of mental health professionals became interested in the veterans and started to classify their symptoms and compare them to the work Kardiner (1941) had done on war neurosis. Their review of clinical records led them to generate 27 of the most common symptoms of the Vietnam veterans' "traumatic neurosis" (van der Kolk, Weisaeth, & van der Hart, 1996, p. 61). Interestingly, many of the physical or somatic complaints resemble those of a large retrospective archival study on the medical records of American Civil War Union veterans (Pizarro, Silver, & Prause, 2006)!

At the same time, researchers in the growing women's movement were looking at psychological problems after domestic violence, rape, and child abuse. What they were finding in the individuals who had suffered from these civilian assaults closely paralleled the problems that Vietnam veterans were experiencing. Their research rediscovered what Freud had found 80 years before and had dismissed: that victims of physical and sexual assault suffered long-term effects of the psychological trauma (Herman, 1997, p. 32). These different research avenues culminated in combining the "Vietnam veterans syndrome," the "rape trauma syndrome," the "abused child syndrome," and the "battered woman syndrome" into one diagnostic category—posttraumatic stress disorder—in the third edition of the American Psychiatric Association's *Diagnostic and Statistical Manual* in 1980 (van der Kolk, Weisaeth, & van der Hart, 1996, p. 61).

Although the Vietnam War may be no more to you than a reference in a high school history book, the wall memorial in Washington, D.C., or your "crazy old Uncle Harold" who continues to wear combat fatigues and a headband with a ponytail, the war's effects are a crucial history lesson in mental health provision (or the lack thereof) that any aspiring mental health worker should learn. For that reason, the psychological lessons learned from the Vietnam War continue to play a major role in the discussion of PTSD in the seventh edition of this book and play a large part of the armed services and Veterans Administration's current treatment programs for it. It should be clearly understood that, even 40 or 50 years after the fact, the events that caused the trauma in many of these approximately 1 million veterans who suffered and suffer from PTSD are as alive for them today as they were then (Price, 2011). What is perhaps even more ominous in regard to the Vietnam veterans is their "graying." Mounting evidence indicates that World War II and Korean War veterans have manifested delayed onset or worsening of posttraumatic complaints as they have grown older. Aging, with its subsequent loss of social supports through death, increased health problems, declining physical and mental capabilities, and economic hardship, appears to put older veterans at increased risk (Aarts & Op den Velde, 1996, pp. 359–374; Hamilton & Workman, 1998). Thus, it would appear that as this population ages, the mental health professions are a long way from being done with the legacy of Vietnam.

Perhaps even more ominous, the current wars in Iraq and Afghanistan have eerily similar parallels to Vietnam. There are no front lines, the enemy fades into the population, everyone in the theater of operations is essentially in combat. As a result, vigilance must be constant, 24/7, throughout one's entire rotation. Degree of combat exposure has been found to be one of the major predictors of PTSD (Miller et al., 2008; Smith et al., 2008).

There are two major differences in these conflicts. So far there is general public support for the troops, whereas in Vietnam there was not. A support group is critical in any crisis, and this is particularly true of troops in an increasingly unpopular war. Lack of support and outright hatred of returning troops was a major contributing factor for PTSD in Vietnam veterans. However, while the armed forces in the current conflicts are all volunteers and not 18-year-old draftees, there are a tremendous number of reserve units in combat action, and there are also huge differences in the number of women involved in direct combat action. Preliminary reports from the Gulf War indicate that British reservists might not be as resilient as regular combat veterans (Hotopf et al., 2006). The question then becomes what the use of reservists and women in combat portends for the onset of PTSD. Preliminary results regarding mental health problems in veterans returning from Iraq and Afghanistan have ranged from 19 to 44 percent of the samples examined (Hoge, Auchterlonie, & Milliken, 2006; Lapierre, Schweigler, & LaBauve, 2007).

Dynamics of PTSD

Diagnostic Categorization

PTSD is a complex and diagnostically troublesome disorder. To be identified as having PTSD, a person must meet the following conditions and symptoms as specified in the *DSM-IV-TR* (American Psychiatric Association, 2000, pp. 463–468). First, the person must have been exposed to a trauma in which he or she was confronted with an event that involved actual or threatened death or serious injury, or a threat to self or others' physical well-being. Examples include but are certainly not limited to military combat, physical or sexual assault, kidnapping, being held hostage, severe vehicle accidents, earthquakes and tornadoes, being a refugee from a war zone, concentration camp detention, and life-threatening illness. The person's response to the trauma was intense fear, helplessness, or horror. As a result, he or she has persistent symptoms of anxiety or arousal that were not evident before the traumatic event.

Second, the person persistently reexperiences the traumatic event in at least one of the following ways:

1. Recurrent and intrusive distressing recollections of the event
2. Recurrent nightmares of the event
3. Flashback episodes, including those that occur on awakening or when intoxicated, that may include all types of sensory hallucinations or illusions that cause the individual to dissociate from the present reality and act or feel as if the event were recurring

4. Intense psychological distress on exposure to internal or external cues that symbolize or resemble an aspect of the traumatic event
5. Physiologic reactivity on exposure to events that symbolize or resemble some aspect of the trauma, such as a person who was in a tornado starting to shake violently at every approaching storm

Third, the person persistently avoids such stimuli in at least three of the following ways:

1. Attempts to avoid thoughts, dialogues, or feelings associated with the trauma
2. Tries to avoid activities, people, or situations that arouse recollections of the trauma
3. Has an inability to recall important aspects of the trauma
4. Has markedly diminished interest in significant activities
5. Feels detached and removed emotionally and socially from others
6. Has a restricted range of affect by numbing feelings
7. Has a sense of a foreshortened future, such as no career, marriage, children, or normal life span

Fourth, the person has persistent symptoms of increased nervous system arousal that were not present before the trauma, as indicated by at least two of the following problems:

1. Difficulty falling or staying asleep
2. Irritability or outbursts of anger
3. Difficulty concentrating on tasks
4. Constantly being on watch for real or imagined threats that have no basis in reality (hypervigilance)
5. Exaggerated startle reactions to minimal or non-threatening stimuli

Fifth, the disturbance causes clinically significant distress or impairment in social, occupational, or other critical areas of living. Examples include not being able to keep a job, having a failed marriage, or becoming a substance abuser. The duration of the foregoing symptoms must be for more than one month.

PTSD is not confined to adults. Children also experience PTSD and manifest symptoms that closely parallel those of adults, with the following notable differences. First, children must experience disorganized or agitated behavior. Children usually do not have a sense they are reliving the past, but rather relive the trauma through repetitive play. Their nightmares of the traumatic event may change to more generalized nightmares of monsters or of rescuing others. A foreshortened future for a child generally involves a belief that they will never reach adulthood. Children may believe they can see into the future and can forecast ominous events. Physical symptoms may appear that include headaches and stomachaches that were not present before the event (American Psychiatric Association, 2000, p. 466).

Complex PTSD

If "catching" PTSD isn't bad enough, the dramatic personality changes that may occur with long-term, intensive trauma have led many respected researchers and practitioners to call for a diagnostic category of "complex PTSD" or "disorders of extreme stress not otherwise specified" (DESNOS) (Briere & Scott, 2006; Courtois & Ford, 2009; Herman, 1997, p. 121; van der Kolk, 1996b, pp. 202–204). The lobbying effort for this diagnostic category has so far fallen short of achieving official recognition, but the three cardinal symptoms are *somatization* (physical problems, associated pain, and functional limitations), *dissociation* (division of the personality into one component that attempts to function in the everyday world and another that regresses and is fixed in the trauma), and *affect dysregulation* (alterations in impulse control, attention and consciousness, self-perception, perception of perpetrators, relationships to significant others, and systems of meaning) (Courtois, Ford, & Cloitre, 2009, pp. 85–86), all of which go beyond the diagnostic criteria of "simple" PTSD.

The DESNOS classification opens a Pandora's box of psychological evils that include the inability to regulate feelings, suicidal and other self-destructive behaviors, impulsive and dangerous risk-taking behaviors, anger management problems, amnesia and dissociation from reality, somatic complaints that take a variety of physical forms, chronic character changes that range from consuming guilt to permanent ineffectiveness in coping with life, adopting distorted and idealized views of perpetrators of the trauma, an inability to trust others, a tendency to victimize or be revictimized, and despair and hopelessness that previously held beliefs about a "fair and just" world are no longer valid. Typical inhabitants of a DESNOS world are persons with long-term exposure to combat service, adult survivors of chronic childhood sexual and physical abuse, and concentration camp survivors. Whether simple or complex, it should be readily apparent that PTSD is an extremely serious condition

and that the *DSM-IV-TR* criteria do not begin to depict all the consequences and effects of the disorder that assail the individual and ripple out to significant others in the individual's life.

Conflicting Diagnoses

Given the wide variety of maladaptive behaviors that characterize the disorder, it is not uncommon for those who suffer from PTSD to have companion diagnoses of anxiety, depressive, organic mental, and substance use disorders (American Psychiatric Association, 2000, p. 427). In fact, it is probably more common to have comorbidity (the presence of two diagnosable disorders such as major depression and substance abuse) (Spinazzola, Blaustein, & van der Kolk, 2005). Further, because of presenting symptoms, PTSD may be confused with adjustment, paranoid, somatic, and personality disorders (Herman, 1997, pp. 116–117; Zanarini et al., 1998; Zlotnick et al., 1999). One of the hallmarks of PTSD is that it is often comorbid—particularly with alcohol abuse (Reynolds et al., 2005; Thaller et al., 2003). That is, the person will have another preliminary mental illness diagnosed in the course of treatment. There are few "pure" cases, and few symptoms are unique to the disorder (Atkinson, Sparr, & Sheff, 1984).

Thus, *no matter what the diagnosis, assessment in crisis intervention should always attempt to determine if there has been exposure to prior trauma,* particularly when the crisis seems to have occurred spontaneously, with no clear, immediate, precipitating stimulus.

The Question of Preexisting Psychopathology

For a variety of political and social reasons, society does not perceive (and has not perceived) being a victim of war, domestic violence, or other types of human cruelty as the equivalent of being mentally ill. Vietnam veterans who early on sought help from Veterans Administration (VA) hospitals were misdiagnosed or thought to have some preexisting psychopathology or character disorder. As a result, they were revictimized by a bureaucratic and rigidly conservative mental health system that added psychic insult to psychic injury (Ochberg, 1988, p. 4). Victims of domestic violence fared no better and were often seen to have a "masochistic" personality that subconsciously enjoyed physical assaults (Herman, 1997, p. 117). Such revictimization and discounting by supposedly "caring" professionals exacerbate the trauma survivor's problems exponentially.

There is evidence of a heritable component to the transmission of PTSD (American Psychiatric Association, 2000, p. 466), and undoubtedly some people, because of a previous psychiatric history, are more predisposed to breaking down under stress than are others (Norris et al., 2002; Ullman & Siegel, 1994). Furthermore, the number and magnitude of the trauma will predict higher potential for PTSD (Norris et al., 2002; Shalev, 1996, p. 86). Exposure to multiple rapes, being held in a concentration camp, extended child abuse, the loss of loved ones, or prolonged frontline combat typically puts the individual at far greater risk for PTSD than a onetime physical assault by a parent or an auto accident in which no one was killed. Additionally, lack of education, low economic status, increased number in family, gender (females are seen as at greater risk), age (younger age at time of event), marital status (not married), and lack of family support systems have all been seen as contributing factors for developing PTSD (Jovanovic et al., 2004; Myers & Wee, 2005; Norris et al., 2002; Suar & Khuntia, 2004; Wilson, Friedman, & Lindy, 2001).

However, no absolute factors guarantee that one person as opposed to another will develop PTSD. Brewin (2005) found that although there are a number of risk factors for PTSD, their effect sizes tend to be small and vary according to the nature of the trauma. Given the right conditions, it appears *anyone can be a candidate*. Several years ago, the collapse of a concrete walkway in a crowded hotel gave us a prime example of how one event may suddenly produce PTSD symptoms. Biographical data gathered following the Kansas City Hyatt Regency skywalk disaster revealed that few survivors had character disorders before the event. Yet 6 months after the event, many were suffering from a variety of presenting symptoms (Wilkinson, 1983). White (1989) found the same result in a study of burn victims suffering PTSD symptoms. The overwhelming majority of these individuals had no previous psychiatric history.

Probably the best summing statement about who will and who will not manifest PTSD was made by Grinker and Spiegel (1945) in their study of World War II veterans. They concluded that no matter how strong, normal, or stable a person might be, if the stress were sufficient to cross that particular individual's threshold, a "war neurosis" would develop. It should also be clearly understood that PTSD is not culture bound. While there are variations on the theme cross-culturally, there is a great deal of evidence that PTSD is a cross-cultural phenomenon common to all people (Brewin, 2003; Marsella et al., 1996). In summary, susceptibility to PTSD is a function of several factors: genetic predisposition, ecological factors, constitution, personality makeup, previous life experiences, state of mind, cultural artifacts, phase of maturational development at onset, spiritual beliefs, social support system before and after the trauma, and content and intensity of the event (Brewin, 2003, 2005; DeVries, 1996; Furst, 1967; Green & Berlin, 1987; Halpern & Tramontin, 2007; Kaniasty & Norris, 1999; Norris et al., 2002; Shalev, 1996; Wilson, Friedman, & Lindy, 2001).

Physiological Responses

In the last 15 years a tremendous number of psychobiological studies have conclusively demonstrated that trauma affects the individual in a variety of physical ways. Researchers have discovered that neurotransmitters, hormones, cortical areas of the brain, and the nervous system play a much greater role in PTSD than was previously suspected (Bremner et al., 1995; Copeland, 2000; Malizia & Nutt, 2000; Rothschild, 2000; van der Kolk, 1996a; Vasterling & Brewin, 2005; Yehuda, 2000). The underlying thesis is that the brain is much more like a "wet" hormonal gland than a "dry" cybernetic computer (Berglund, 1985).

When a person is exposed to severe stress, neurotransmitters, neuromodulators, hormones, endogenous opioids, and specific cortical functions designed to deal with the emergency are activated (Grinker & Speigel, 1945; Santa Ana et al., 2006; Selye, 1976; Siegel, 1995; van der Kolk, 1996a, pp. 215–234; Vermetten & Bremner, 2002). Although cessation of the traumatic event may remove the person from danger and no longer require the body's system to function on an emergency basis, if the stress is prolonged, the nervous system may continue to function in an elevated and energized state as if the emergency were still continuing (Burgess-Watson, Hoffman, & Wilson, 1988; van der Kolk, 1996a, pp. 214–234).

Furthermore, there is evidence that intense and continuous stress can cause permanent physical changes in the brain (Copeland, 2000; Malizia & Nutt, 2000; Vermetten & Bremner, 2002). These changed physiological states are important because they not only cause individuals extreme physical and psychological duress long after the traumatic event but also help explain why people do not "get over" PTSD.

In their study and review of the neuroanatomical correlates of the effects of stress on memory, Bremner and associates (1995, 1997) and Gurvitz, Shenton, and Pittman (1995) found in combat veterans significant decreases in the hippocampal area of the brain where explicit memory encoding, memory consolidation, and organization take place, as did Stein and associates (1994) in women who had experienced severe child sexual abuse. Whether the smaller hippocampus is a causal factor for PTSD or PTSD causes the hippocampus to become smaller is not known. However, Astur and associates' (2006) study of identified PTSD experimental subjects versus non-PTSD controls supports these findings of decreased hippocampal activity.

A great deal of psychophysiological assessment evidence indicates that stimulus presentation to PTSD sufferers of sights, sounds, and smells associated with the long-past traumatic event will immediately send the neuroendocrine system into overdrive and cause physiological responses such as increased heart rate, blood pressure, and triglyceride and cholesterol levels, along with decreased blood flow to the skin and gastrointestinal and renal areas. These psychophysiological responses are not evinced in control subjects who are presented with the same stimuli (Lating & Everly, 1995).

Affective-State-Dependent Retention

There is now very clear evidence that physiological changes occur in the presence of trauma (Briere & Scott, 2006) and are exacerbated when the trauma becomes ongoing and complex (Ford, 2009). Changed physiological functioning due to traumatic stimuli is important as a building block in Bower's (1981) hypothesis of *affective-state-dependent retention*. Bower has proposed that because the traumatic event was stored in memory under completely different physiological (increased heart rate, higher adrenal output) and psychological (extreme fright, shock) circumstances, different mood states markedly interfere with recollecting specific cues of the event. Karl, Malta, and Maercker's (2006) meta-analysis supports the hypothesis that changes in memory processing accompany PTSD. Therefore, the important elements of the memory that need exposure in order to reduce anxiety are not accessible in the unaroused state (Keane et al., 1985, p. 266) and can be remembered only when that approximate state of arousal is reintroduced by cues in the environment (Keane, 1976). Indeed, there is evidence that release of neuromodulators such as norepinephrine when an individual is in a stressful situation leads to pathological response to recall of previous traumatic events for which the individual has no previous memory (Bremner et al., 1995).

To the contrary, the classic dissociative, numbing response and "forgetting" of the traumatic event may be caused by excessive endogenous opioids secreted during prolonged stress (van der Kolk, 1996a, p. 227). Thus the notion that a victim of PTSD can "just forget" or adopt a "better, more positive attitude" does little to effect change in the individual (Keane et al., 1985, p. 266). This proposal has important implications for treatment, particularly with respect to returning the person to as close an approximation of the event as possible. These neurological issues are even more ominously true for children.

Children and Neuropathology

There is a high likelihood for children who experience traumatic events in early childhood to develop neuropathology (Lewis, 2005). If the trauma occurs during early developmental stages, there is a dramatic shift in the brain's functioning from an inquisitive, exploring, learning mode to a reactive, defensive, surviving mode. When the stress response survival systems of the child's brain are operating in overdrive, the learning systems take a back seat. As a result, a wide array of normal developmental activities are placed on hold, with potentially catastrophic consequences across social and educational environments. In plain language, operating systems in the child's brain get damaged.

Damage occurs in three areas: emotional dysregulation, which may be characterized by emotional emptiness or constant distress; dissociation, which manifests as mental disorientation and confusion; and hyperarousal, which physically drains the body to the point of exhaustion. The potential for these devastating outcomes to occur is particularly enhanced if the trauma comes at the hands of a caregiver who is supposed to be nourishing the learning brain of the child rather than activating the survival system (Ford, 2009). You will meet some of the characteristics of these neurological train wrecks later in this chapter and in Chapter 9, Sexual Assault. The foregoing paragraphs should give you a fair idea of why treating childhood PTSD and survivors of extended childhood trauma is so difficult and why transcrisis states are so common with these individuals.

Incidence, Impact, and Trauma Type

Incidence

If PTSD has been with us for so long, what made it finally surface with such profound impact? Epidemiological studies indicate that a lifetime rate of about 8 percent can be expected in the general civilian population of the United States (American Psychiatric Association, 2000, p. 466). So, in the common course of events, the chances of "catching" PTSD are fairly small. The average "catch it" rate for PTSD appears to be about 20 percent after a trauma is experienced (Norris et al., 2002). However, when studies target particular at-risk groups such as adolescents and young adults, people in hazardous occupations, sexual assault victims, severe burn cases, psychiatric cases, and refugees, the incidence of PTSD in these populations is much greater (McFarlane & de Girolamo, 1996, pp. 129–154). The classic at-risk example is the Vietnam veteran. The numbers of returning Vietnam veterans who were having some kind of personality disorder far exceeded what statistics would predict. It is estimated that 26 percent, or 960,000 Vietnam veterans, have had episodes of PTSD (Kukla et al., 1990). This massive number of veterans in severe psychological trouble was simply too large to ignore.

Residual Impact

People's basic assumptions about their belief in the world as a meaningful and comprehensible place, their own personal invulnerability, and their view of themselves in a positive light account to a great extent for their individual manifestations of PTSD (Figley, 1985b, pp. 401–402; Kaniasty & Norris, 1999). Even in the most well-integrated people, who have excellent coping abilities, good rational and cognitive behavior patterns, and positive social support systems, residual effects of traumatizing events may linger. An outstanding example of such residual effects is the experience of a retired Marine captain who had seen extensive field duty as a combat infantryman in Vietnam in 1968. The anecdote he relates typifies the residual effects in an individual who is psychologically well integrated, is securely employed in a professional job, has a tightly knit, extended family support system, and on the whole enjoys life and has a positive outlook on it.

Chris: I had just gotten home from work late one summer evening. The kids had decided to camp out in the woods down by the creek. A thunderstorm was rolling in and I decided I'd better go down and check on them to see if they were packed in for the night. It had started to rain pretty heavily, and there was a lot of thunder and lightning. I pulled on a poncho and got a flashlight, crossed the road, and went into the woods. I don't suppose it was 200 yards to where the kids were camped. Now, I'd grown up running those woods, so I knew it like the back of my hand.

However, once I got into the woods things kinda went haywire. I immediately thought, "Get off the trail, or you'll get the whole platoon zapped." I slipped off the path and became a part of the scenery. Every sense in my body went up to full alert. I was back in Nam again operating with my platoon, and I was on a natural, adrenaline high. Time and place kinda went into suspended animation, and I eased through the woods, kinda like standing off and watching myself do this, knowing it was me, but yet not me too. The last thing I remember before walking into the clearing where the kids had their tent set up was that we could have ambushed the hell out of that place. I don't harp and brood on Nam, put it behind me after I got out of the Corps, but that night sure put me in a different place than central Indiana, July 1984. I just couldn't believe that would ever happen. It's a bit unnerving.

Importance of Trauma Type

Catastrophes, when viewed by the public, tend to fall into one category: bad. However, one of the interesting phenomena around PTSD is that there is a marked distinction between natural and human-made catastrophes. Acts of God create far fewer instances of PTSD than do human-made ones. As an example, the volcanic eruption of Mount St. Helen's incident rate of PTSD was a very low 3 to 4 percent (Shore, Tatum, & Vollmer, 1986).

Human-made acts of trauma create even more instances of PTSD when the trauma directly affects the social support system of the family. Holocaust survivors, hostages, rape victims, children of murdered parents, and victims of incest are all strong potential candidates for PTSD. Survivors of both uncommissioned human-made disasters such as the breaking of the Buffalo Creek dam and commissioned trauma such as the Chowchilla bus kidnapping carry high potential for PTSD. (The Buffalo Creek disaster occurred in 1972 when a coal company retainer dam broke during a series of heavy rainstorms; the resulting flood wiped out the residents of the Buffalo Creek valley in West Virginia. The bus kidnapping occurred in 1976 when a Chowchilla, California, school bus carrying elementary and secondary school children was hijacked at gunpoint. The children were taken from the bus and forced into a truck buried underground; eventually they were able to tunnel out.)

What makes these events so particularly terrible is that they seem to be tragedies that should not have happened, responsibility for them can be readily assigned, and they clearly violate accepted standards of moral conduct (Figley, 1985a, pp. 400–401). As a result, there exists in any human-made catastrophe the likelihood of more severe posttraumatic psychological problems as compared to natural disasters. The problem is that the line between the two is becoming less clear. More and more people look at technology as a means of controlling nature. Thus, for example, Mother Nature makes the rain, but the Army Corps of Engineers builds dikes and opens floodgates (Kaniasty & Norris, 1999), and when things go wrong individuals (and lawyers) start looking for culprits.

Vietnam: The Archetype

In a comparative analysis of PTSD among various trauma survivor groups, Wilson, Smith, and Johnson (1985) isolated 10 variables that were hypothesized as predisposing to PTSD: degree of life threat; degree of bereavement; speed of onset; duration of the trauma; degree of displacement in home continuity; potential for recurrence; degree of exposure to death, dying, and destruction; degree of moral conflict inherent in the situation; role of the person in the trauma; and the proportion of the community affected. They compared these variables in a variety of trauma survivor groups: Vietnam combat veterans as well as victims of rape, auto accident, armed robbery, natural disasters, divorce, life-threatening illness of a loved one, family trauma, death of a significant other, multiple traumas, and a control group.

Veterans were significantly affected in 7 of the 10 dimensions, with rape victims a distant second in terms of number of predisposing variables present. When the data were transformed to fit precise PTSD criteria, all trauma groups were significantly different from the control group (pp. 142–172). In plain words, the data suggest that one could not experience a catastrophic event more likely to produce "complex" PTSD than Vietnam—with one exception. With the advent of women in combat, if sexual assault and combat are combined, such as has occurred in Iraq and Afghanistan, then either women or men who have been in combat and have also been sexually assaulted are one-and-a-half more times likely to be diagnosed with a mental health condition than those who have not been assaulted (Munsey, 2009).

Why did Vietnam mark the birth of what was to become PTSD? Although any war could be construed to produce many PTSD symptoms, the rules of war changed in Vietnam. First, the average age of the soldier in Vietnam was 19.2, compared with 26.0 in World War II (Brende & Parson, 1985, p. 19). A psychologically immature 19-year-old soldier was not mentally prepared for the psychic trauma that awaited him in Vietnam (MacPherson, 1984, pp. 62–63).

Hypervigilance. In Vietnam, there was no front line and no relief from constant vigilance. A 365-day combat tour was exactly that. In comparison to World War II troops, who might be in acute combat situations for a few days or weeks and then be pulled off the line, Vietnam "grunts" spent extended periods of time in the field, and even when they were in a base camp, they had to be alert for rocket attacks and combat assaults on their position. Hypervigilance became an ironclad rule of survival. Listen to Billie Mac, a composite character of many combat veterans I have interviewed.

Billie Mac: I was 18 when the plane set down at Da Nang. The crew chief told us to hit the ground running because Da Nang was under a rocket attack. I was scared stiff. Well, Da Nang was heaven, rockets and all, to what later happened. It got a lot, lot worse than that.

Lack of Goals. No territory was ever "won," so there was no concrete feeling of accomplishment. Combat troops felt betrayed by U.S. politics over a war for which there were no fixed goals for winning and a command structure that was waging a war of attrition, with "body counts" being the primary way of judging whether a mission was successful (Lifton, 1974; MacPherson, 1984, p. 58).

Billie Mac: We swept that one village at least a half dozen times. Sometimes we'd dig in and dare the NVA to hit us, and they did. We lost a half dozen guys in that pesthole. For what? For nothin'. We gave it up, and they moved right back in.

Victim/Victimizer. It further compounded the virulent psychological milieu of Vietnam that veterans, unlike most individuals who suffer from PTSD, played two roles—victim and victimizer. Because both enemies and allies were Vietnamese, a soldier could not distinguish friend from foe, nor could vigilance be relaxed around women or children because of their potential lethality. Also, because the enemy was Asian and had extremely different cultural values from Americans, it was relatively simple to dehumanize killing or maiming them, particularly when troops saw such things done to their comrades. The nasty way guerrilla war is fought brought out brutality on both sides (Lifton, 1974). Shifts of role from victim to aggressor could occur in seconds (Brende & Parson, 1985, p. 96).

Billie Mac: I couldn't imagine killing a kid or woman. That was true until our medic tried to take care of a kid covered with blood. We all thought he was wounded. When John went over to the dink, he opened up his arms and had a grenade. Blew him and the medic away. Kill them after that? You bet!

Bonding, Debriefing, and Guilt. The way the armed services filled units had much to do with lack of a support system within the service itself. Personnel replacements were parceled piecemeal into units, which is a bad idea if you are trying to avoid PTSD. Current research indicates that unit cohesion is a critical buffer against PTSD (Armistead-Jehle et al., 2011). Although this method put rookies with veterans, it was not the best way to bond a unit together. The rotation system also took its psychological toll. Each person did a 365-day tour. The stress of being "short" caused men to become very self-preservative and immobilized. Units as a whole were never moved out of combat, and a man who entered combat singly returned singly without benefit of debriefing time. The war was essentially fought in patrol and platoon actions. It was a loner's war, and the soldier who fought alone went home alone (MacPherson, 1984, pp. 64–65). A man might be sweating out an ambush in the jungle one day, and two days later be sitting on his front porch back home.

It is no great surprise that returning soldiers who had no transition period from Vietnam to the United States were viewed as "different" and "changed" by their relatives (Brende & Parson, 1985, pp. 48–49). Such rapid transitions out of life-threatening situations left many with survivor's guilt (Spiegel, 1981). They were glad to be out of Vietnam, but felt guilty of betrayal for leaving comrades behind; or they took responsibility when they were away from their units and friends were hurt or killed (MacPherson, 1984, p. 237).

Billie Mac: It was inside of a week from jungle to home. My folks thought it was pretty weird because I put my fatigues on and slept in the woods. I just couldn't take being confined in that house. I kept thinking about the guy who took my place as squad leader, Johnson. I knew he was gonna get somebody wasted. I needed to be there, but I sure didn't want to be. I immediately got drunk and stayed that way for a long time.

Civilian Adjustment. The rapid change from intense alertness in order to preserve one's life to trying to readjust to a humdrum society made many question where the "real world" was. Furthermore, the returnee's basic belief system would be quickly jarred when, on his arrival home, he was greeted with insensitivity and hostility for having risked his life for his country (Brende & Parson, 1985, p. 72). Veterans quickly found that for all the ability they had shown in making command decisions of life-or-death importance and the authority they had exercised over expensive equipment in Vietnam, the onus of having been there relegated them to civilian jobs far below their capabilities (MacPherson, 1984, p. 65).

Billie Mac: Any job I could get stunk. They were all menial, and they acted like they were doing me a favor. Hell! I'd made a lot bigger and smarter decisions than anybody I ever had as a boss.

Substance Abuse. The ease with which soldiers could obtain alcohol and drugs to numb themselves and escape mentally from the reality of Vietnam had severe consequences, both in addiction on return and in the public's growing misconception that veterans were all "drug-crazed baby killers," to be shunned as erratic and undependable (Brende & Parson, 1985, p. 72; MacPherson, 1984, pp. 64–65, 221–222).

Billie Mac: Yeah, I drank. Yeah, I shot kids. I drank mainly to try to forget about shooting kids. Anybody who hadn't been there could never understand.

Attitude. The time period during which a vet served in Vietnam seems to be highly correlated with PTSD. Historically the war can be divided into trimesters. Anyone serving in Vietnam during the last two trimesters, from the time of the Tet offensive in 1968 to the U.S. withdrawal in 1973, would have, from a psychological standpoint, a much greater reason to question the purpose of being there than those who had served early on. The prevailing attitude of "Nobody can win, so just concentrate on surviving" cynicism was in direct opposition to the "Save a democracy from the perils of communism" idealism of the first trimester (Laufer, Yager, & Grey-Wouters, 1981).

Antiwar Sentiment. The impact of the antiwar sentiment that veterans met on their return home cannot be minimized. It is unique to the Vietnam War and found its focal point in returnees. Veterans were spurned immediately on their arrival in the United States, suffered prejudice on college campuses as they came back to school, were left out of jobs because of antiwar sentiments, and were disenfranchised from government programs through meager GI Bill benefits and government disavowal of physical problems associated with exposure to the chemical defoliant Agent Orange. Perhaps worst of all were the comparisons their fathers made—men who had fought the "honorable" fight of World War II and could not understand the problems their sons suffered in a war that was not black-and-white but a dirty shade of gray (MacPherson, 1984, pp. 54–58). It is interesting to note that Vietnam combat veterans diagnosed with PTSD whose fathers were also combat veterans are likely to have more severe problems than those Vietnam veterans whose fathers had not seen combat (Rosenheck & Fontana, 1998).

> **Billie Mac:** I tried to talk to my old man about it. He'd been in World War II on Okinawa. Hell, he might as well have been in the Revolutionary War for all he could understand about Nam. He finally got so mad that he told me I was nuts and no damn good. He didn't mean that, but I'll never forget it.

All these factors came together in a sort of witch's brew for veterans trying to make meaning out of a situation that was life-threatening and generally considered pointless (Williams, 1983). To survive such a situation called for imposing psychological defense mechanisms that made a fertile breeding ground for PTSD. When these psychological defense mechanisms go awry, symptoms are typically seen in the three major PTSD diagnostic categories of intrusive thoughts, avoidance, and increased nervous system arousal.

Intrusive-Repetitive Ideation

Intrusive-repetitive thoughts become so problematic for the individual that these thoughts begin to dominate existence. Intrusive thoughts generally take the form of visual images that are sparked by sights, sounds, smells, or tactile reminders that bring the repressed images to awareness (Donaldson & Gardner, 1985, pp. 371–372).

> **Billie Mac:** That day at the village when Al got it keeps coming back. I don't go fishing in the bayou anymore. It smells and looks like Nam, and every time I'd go I'd start thinking about that village, and I'd get the shakes.

Over time, triggers for intrusive thoughts may become associated with subtle and more generalized stimuli that are seemingly irrelevant to the trauma (van der Kolk & McFarlane, 1996, p. 10). These thoughts occur not only in conscious contact with reality but also in the form of flashbacks and nightmares.

> **Billie Mac:** The reason that got me to the vets center is real simple. I was having these awful nightmares about being in a firefight while on a long-range reconnaissance patrol near Laos. The next thing I know, I'm dug into a bunker watching an enemy truck convoy's headlights come down the Ho Chi Minh Trail with my rifle aimed at them. The only problem was that it was on the banks of the Wolf River in Memphis, Tennessee, and it was headlights on I-40. It was also not 1970 but 1988. I knew if I didn't get help I was going to kill somebody.

Denial/Numbing

Accompanying emotions of guilt, sadness, anger, and rage occur as the thoughts continue to intrude into awareness. To keep these disturbing thoughts out of awareness, the individual may resort to self-medication in the form of alcohol or drugs. Self-medication may temporarily relieve depressive, hostile, anxious, and fearful mood states (Horowitz & Solomon, 1975), but what usually occurs is a vicious cycle that alternates between being anesthetized to reality by the narcotic and experiencing elevated intrusion of the trauma with every return to sobriety. The ultimate outcome is increased dependence on the addictive substance as a method of keeping the intrusive thoughts submerged (LaCoursiere, Bodfrey, & Ruby, 1980).

> **Billie Mac:** The drinkin' is no damn good. I know that, but try going without sleep for a week and knowing every time you nod off, that horrible nightmare's gonna come. Then it starts popping up in the daytime and you drink more to keep it pushed back.

As people attempt to cope with catastrophes, they become passive (immobile and paralyzed) or active (able to cope with the situation). Individual reactions fall into three major groupings: momentary freezing, flight reaction, and denial/numbing. In the prolonged stress of a combat situation, denial/numbing is the most common response and allows the soldier to cope and live with the experience in three ways: by believing he is invulnerable to harm, by becoming fatalistic, or by taking matters into his own hands and becoming extremely aggressive. Any of these proactive stances allows the individual to get through the trauma and cope with it without losing complete control (Figley,

1985a, pp. 406–408). Typically, survivors of trauma will let down these defense barriers and will have acute stress disorders immediately after the trauma, but will recover. For those who do not, continued emotional numbing and repression can have severe consequences.

Billie Mac: Looking back on it, I can't believe how callous I have become. SOP [standard operating procedure] was "It don't mean nothin', screw it, drive on." This would be right after a B-40 round had blown your buddy's brains all over you. You had to put it behind you to survive. A guy fell off the construction site I was working on last fall and splattered himself all over the pavement. I sat on a steel beam about 30 feet above the guy and just kept eating my lunch. No big deal!

Submerging emotions out of conscious awareness does not mean that they are summarily discarded. The price is that emotional numbing left in place and not relieved can generalize to other aspects of one's life and result in later psychological difficulties (Wilkinson, 1983). Shunted into the unconscious for a long time, trigger events in the form of everyday stressors can pile up and cause emotional blowouts when the individual is least prepared for them (Figley, 1985a, p. 408).

Increased Nervous Symptom Arousal

Autonomic hyperarousal in people with PTSD causes them to be nondiscriminating to stimuli that may hold no threat to them at all. Acoustic startle response is a cardinal feature of the trauma response (van der Kolk, 1996a, p. 221).

Billie Mac: I can't stand the sound of a chopper. Every time I hear one, I want to run. I get the feeling that every time I hear the 5 o'clock traffic chopper, it's gonna circle in, pick me up, and take me to a hot LZ [landing zone]. One came over the building I was working on. I didn't hear it at first. When I did hear it, I jumped and fell 10 feet and broke my arm.

In the same vein, hypervigilance, when there is no immediate threat, is constantly with the person and causes concentration and attention problems. As these problems distort information processing, the resulting inability to decode messages from the central nervous system causes the person to react to the environment in either exaggerated or inhibited ways (van der Kolk & McFarlane, 1996, pp. 14–15).

Billie Mac: This may sound kinda weird, but I don't ever sit with my back to a door. Matter of fact, I really don't like sitting anywhere where my back might be to somebody else! I get real jumpy.

Dissociation

While dissociation is not listed as a symptom of PTSD, dissociation at the moment of trauma is perhaps the most important long-term predictive variable for PTSD and is invariably connected to "complex" PTSD (Herman, 1997, pp. 118–129; Marmar et al., 1991). Dissociation can range from numbing or lack of emotional responsiveness to the event to derealization ("this is not real; it isn't happening; it's a bad dream") or depersonalization ("I'm out of my body and looking at this from a grandstand") to complete amnesia of the event.

Dissociation splits off the memory from conscious awareness, but that does not mean the noxious stimulus event is extinguished. To the contrary, dissociation can be a last-resort adaptive way of coping with the trauma while it is going on, but the lack of integration of the traumatic event seems to be a leading cause of PTSD. If dissociation continues, it can severely interfere with daily living and breed disconnectedness and isolation (van der Kolk, 1996b, p. 286). At its penultimate, dissociation can become dissociative identity disorder (formerly known as multiple personality disorder).

Billie Mac: It's like a lot of times I'm looking at me doing something sorta through a video camera, maybe. Like I'm smaller than real life, and I sorta know it's me, but it's not like I'm really there. The first time I did that was when we were in that village and my buddy Al got it.

What the person needs most is to bring these thoughts and behaviors into conscious awareness and come to grips with them, so they can be resolved. Yet, rather than confronting the intrusive and threatening material, the person is more likely to deny its existence and use a variety of avoidance responses to escape from the situation (Horowitz et al., 1980). This issue is particularly problematic in therapy and is why those who suffer from PTSD may be particularly resistant and noncompliant to approaches that reexpose them to the feared trauma (Bernstein, 1986).

Family Responses

Natural disasters leave so few emotional scars because such disasters often strike intact social support systems simultaneously (Figley, 1988). In natural disasters that affect the whole community, everyone becomes a survivor. Family members help each other through the horror of the disaster, and there is no blaming the individual (Figley, 1985a, p. 409; Kaniasty & Norris, 1999). One of the keystones for bridging the gap between traumatic events and a return to adequate and wholesome functioning is a strong support system that is most generally based within the family. But when the trauma is intrafamilial and takes the form of child and spouse abuse, those who are most traumatized are most generally the ones who are denied the most social support within the family. Those who should provide the most comfort are the ones who are inflicting the most pain (Figley, 1985a, p. 411).

Further exacerbating family relationships is the ingrained tendency in trauma victims to "not feel." Whereas the individual would like to be able to demonstrate feelings of caring and love, experience has taught him or her that exposure of feelings is foolhardy because it invariably makes one vulnerable to further pain. These concepts strike at the very heart of what sustains family life—trust. The response of family members is to feel misunderstood, unloved, fearful, and angry. The response is reciprocal and plunges all members deeper into a vortex of family discordance.

From a family system perspective, if children, parents, or spouses attempt to regulate the continuing warfare in which the individual is engaging, they will be worn down and out by the effort. The individual may also become so dependent on the stabilizing person (usually the spouse) that the individual's needs breed resentment in anyone else who demands time and effort (usually children). The outcome of this spiral is what the individual may fear most from the support system—rejection. Feelings of guilt, numbing, anger, and loss plague the individual, and the spiral continues ever downward into more inappropriate behavior patterns and ultimate disintegration of the family.

Family members who cannot deal with the trauma may paradoxically turn on the victim. Sadly, this is too often the occurrence in the case of mothers who deny their spouses' abuse of the children, finally are confronted with the issue by children and family services, and then blame the children for the trouble they have caused! The same is true for rape victims who, if children, may have parents who are psychologically unable to provide support for them and indeed revictimize them for having done something that led to the assault in the first place. If adults, rape victims may have a spouse who is unable to respond in supportive ways or who blames the victim for "promiscuous or seductive" behavior that invited the rape or claims the victim "didn't resist enough" (Notman & Nadelson, 1976).

In attempting to deal with a family member who has suffered a traumatic experience, other members may experience the stress to the degree that they become "infected" by it (Figley, 1988). Indeed, if other family members have inadequate coping skills, their own problems may escalate to crisis proportions as the individual's reactions to the trauma create stress within the family. Or, if other members of the family have a hidden agenda of keeping the family in pathological homeostasis, they may engage in enabling the individual's disorder, much as an alcoholic's family may sabotage attempts at recovery. In summary, it should be clear that treating trauma victims also means treating the family (Tarrier & Humphreys, 2003).

Maladaptive Patterns Characteristic of PTSD

Summed dynamically, PTSD involves five common patterns: death imprint, survivor's guilt, desensitization, estrangement, and emotional enmeshment.

Death Imprint.   The traumatic experience provides a clear vision of one's own death in concrete biological terms (Ochberg, 1988, p. 12). Particularly in young individuals, the sense of invulnerability is vanquished and is replaced by rage and anger at one's newfound mortality (Lifton, 1975). For veterans in particular, there is a continuing identity with death. The normal boundary between living and dying is suspended. It is not unusual for veterans to describe themselves as already dead. The only way they have of testing the boundary between life and death is to seek sensation, even if it means danger and physical pain (Brende & Parson, 1985, p. 100). Combined with rage reactions, sensation-seeking behaviors put individuals squarely on a collision path with law enforcement agencies, employers, and families.

Billie Mac: After every law officer in Mississippi started chasing me, I ditched the car and ran into a woods. They even had bloodhounds after me. I slipped through them like they were a sieve. It was crazy, but for one of the few times since I've been back I really felt alive. I'd done that a hundred times on patrol.

Survivor's Guilt.   A second pattern is guilt. Guilt comes in a variety of forms: guilt over surviving when others did not, guilt over not preventing the death of another, guilt over not having somehow been braver under the circumstances, guilt over complaining when others have suffered more, and guilt that the trauma is partly the individual's fault (Frederick, 1980). Most commonly, guilt takes the form of intrusive thoughts such as "I could have done more, and if I had he/she'd still be here," or "If I had just done this or that, it (the trauma) wouldn't have happened." Dynamically, the basis of these thoughts may be relief that the other person was the one to die, or the individual was lucky to get off so lightly (Egendorf, 1975).

Billie Mac: I was the only one in my outfit to get out of the Tet offensive without a scratch. I wonder why. Why me out of all those people? I've screwed my life up since then. Why did I deserve to get out clean when all those other good men didn't? Going to the wall in D.C. last year tore me to pieces. I cried and cried when I saw the names of my buddies up there. Things really got screwed up after that.

For other types of trauma individuals, bereavement is closely allied to survivor's guilt. Facilitating grief includes the expression of affect, reconciliation of the loss of a loved one or a missed part of one's life, the ambivalence of not having shared the same fate as others, and moving on to new and meaningful relationships (Ochberg, 1988, p. 10). Because numbing of affect is a major dynamic response to PTSD, it is extremely difficult for survivors to let loose their emotions and grieve.

Desensitization. A third pattern is desensitizing oneself to totally unacceptable events and then trying to return to a semblance of normalcy in a peaceful world. Feelings of guilt and fear may arise over pleasurable responses to physical violence against others. These feelings may become so acute that the individual conceals firearms for protection against imagined enemies but is simultaneously terrified of the guns and what might happen because of the violence that continuously seethes below the individual's own calm outer appearance. These strong bipolar emotional currents that flow back and forth within the individual lead to hostile, defensive, anxious, depressive, and fearful mood states that find little relief (Horowitz & Solomon, 1975).

Billie Mac: I don't hunt anymore. I hate it. Yet this one guy who was my boss didn't know how close he came to getting killed. I was within one inch of taking him out; I was so hot. It would have been a pleasure; the guy was such an ass.

Estrangement. A fourth pattern is the feeling that any future relationships will be counterfeit, that they mean little or nothing in the great scheme of things. As the person tries to ward off reminders of the experience, severe interpersonal difficulties occur. Because of

the vastly different experiences they have undergone, PTSD individuals become estranged from their peers and truncate social relationships with them because "they don't understand"—and indeed "they" do not. Victimization may also be part of estrangement.

From being victimized in the original trauma, to possible secondary victimization by social services, hospitals, and mental health providers, to revictimization by significant others, the survivor is crushed under the weight of dealing with these initial and secondary assaults (Ochberg, 1988). The result is that the person becomes more isolated from social support systems and develops secondary symptoms that range across diagnostic categories of psychopathology (Horowitz & Solomon, 1975).

Billie Mac: I was sitting at my dad's watching TV when Saigon fell. I went nuts and trashed the house. What the hell was it all for? That really cooked it with my old man. I moved out after that and haven't said anything to him since.

Particularly for victims of sexual abuse, estrangement may take the form of negative intimacy. Invasion of one's personal space and being causes feelings of filthiness and degradation that make reestablishing old relationships or engendering new relationships an extremely difficult ordeal (Ochberg, 1988, pp. 12–13).

Emotional Enmeshment. A fifth pattern is a continuous struggle to move forward in a postholocaust existence but with an inability to find any significance in life (Lifton, 1975). Emotional fixation, particularly for veterans, has disastrous effects on family life. Sent to Vietnam as adolescents and exposed to prolonged trauma that the majority of the population will never experience, these individuals cannot bring themselves to engage in equitable relationships with their families and friends, nor can their families begin to understand their aberrant behavior (Brende & Parson, 1985, pp. 116–117). Depression, anger, avoidance, and alcohol abuse are hallmarks of veterans with PTSD, and these show up in mediating family functioning (Evans et al., 2003). It should not be surprising that those angry feelings are reciprocated by family members and create large fractures in a family structure that is already cracked and breaking.

Billie Mac: I can't believe what I've done to my kids. I love them more than anything in the world. At times, I'm the greatest dad in the world, coach the Little League team, take them everywhere. The next minute I'm all over them.

I've knocked them around in a rage, and that scares the hell out of me. I'm some kind of Jekyll and Hyde, and my kids are afraid of me. My wife hates my guts for it and said if I didn't shape up *now* she was leaving. My solution to that was to go get drunk. When I came home she was gone with the kids. They and me would be better off if I was dead.

Now that you have read the foregoing descriptors of PTSD and Vietnam War veterans, think about current combat theaters in Iraq and Afghanistan. Do you see any similarities? Do you think there will be Billie Macs (or Jenny Lynns) coming home from Iraq or Afghanistan?

The Traumatic Wake of Iraq and Afghanistan

In the previous edition of this book, details on the incidence of PTSD were just starting to be reported on the Iraq and Afghanistan wars. By this writing, more than1.6 million military personnel have cycled through these two theaters. Most of these personnel have been exposed to the petri dish of death, violence, bloodshed, and destruction in which PTSD grows so well. As in Vietnam, there are no front lines; it's hard to tell friend from foe; vigilance must be maintained 24/7 because a firefight, bombardment, or IED can occur at any moment or any place; no territory is "won"; political goals become cloudy; it is increasingly unclear why we are in those places; and termination dates are ill defined.

Further, there is a clear relationship between duration and intensity of specific types of trauma exposure and the number of symptoms of posttraumatic stress disorder (Baker, Risbrough, & Schork, 2008). In contrast to Vietnam, which was a one-year rotation and back to the "world," many veterans have served two or three tours of duty in the Middle Eastern conflicts, which piles stress not only on them but on their families as well. Many combat units are National Guard or reserve units based in hometowns rather than on military bases. These soldiers are both male and female, and they are older and have families and jobs as opposed to their younger counterparts who come from intact regular army regiments and divisions.

About half of service personnel are married and more than 70 percent have children. In real numbers that means 1.85 million children have one or both parents in the military, and 900,000 of those children have had one or both parents deployed one or more times

since 2001 (Chandra et al., 2008). Those deployments cause all kinds of physical, psychological, personal, social, and academic issues with these children (Barnes, Davis, & Treiber, 2007; Engel, Gallagher, & Lyle, 2010; Flake et al., 2009), and that family stress kicks back to soldiers at the front. Combat stress clinics have found the major precipitating factor in homicide/suicide is a stressful relational event that comes from home via e-mail or telephone (Mental Health Advisory Team V, 2008).

Studies so far indicate the PTSD expectancy rate is somewhere between 13 and 25 percent for Middle Eastern war veterans (Milliken, Auchterlonie, & Hoge, 2007; Seal et al., 2007). Even if only 10 percent of service personnel wind up with PTSD, the medical corps and Veterans Administration can expect another 150,000 cases to land on their doorsteps. Now consider the families of these service personnel. Even more ominous perhaps is the service suicide rate, which has increased enough to get national headlines. The grimness of these figures is reflected in a study by Matthews (2009), who asked seniors at West Point whether they believed they would develop PTSD. Only 22 percent thought they "would not" or "most likely would not."

The Department of Defense and the Veterans Administration have been very proactive in designing interventions that range from frontline, in-theater crisis intervention with combat troops through Post-Deployment Health Assessment and Reassessment programs that are designed to detect physical and psychological problems of returning active duty soldiers and veterans and immediately start treating them (Brenner, Vanderploeg, & Terro, 2009). Further, the Veteran Administration has been extremely proactive in providing outreach programs to veterans who cannot easily reach a VA hospital. However, this is a reactive stance, and with the high incidence of mental health problems the Army has initiated the Comprehensive Soldier Fitness (CSF) program, which is an integrated, proactive approach to developing psychological resilience in soldiers, family members, and the Army's civilian workforce (Casey, 2011).

The Comprehensive Solider Fitness Program

The CSF program consists of four components. The Global Assessment Tool, which is used online by soldiers, is confidential, and provides feedback on the following psychological dimensions: positive emotions, negative emotions and depression, optimism, flexible thinking, work engagement, problem-focused coping, character strengths of wisdom, courage, humanity, justice, temperance, and transcendence, social fitness components of trust and friendship, family fitness, and spiritual fitness. This comprehensive psychological fitness exam also comes with self-help modules for each of these areas that soldiers can access independently (Peterson, Park, & Castro, 2011). However, CSF goes far beyond online self-assessment/help. It is also designed to be delivered face to face.

The Master Resilience Trainer course (Reivich, Seligman, & McBride, 2011) is designed to train sergeants who will then teach soldiers in their units. The course has three components. The first, preparation, includes resilience and mental toughness, identifying character strengths, and strengthening relationships. The second is a sustaining component, which focuses on sustaining resilience across the deployment cycle. The third is an enhancement component that uses a lot of the following sport psychology concepts: mental skills foundations, which involves understanding the nature of performance, the relationship between training and trusting mindsets, and identifying the connection between thoughts, emotions, physiological states, and performance; building confidence, which involves learning effective ways to create energy, optimism, and enthusiasm; attention control, which addresses the concentration demands associated with critical military tasks; energy management, which consists of practical skills used to activate, sustain, and restore optimal levels of energy while minimizing the negative effectives of stress; and integrating imagery, which involves ways of creating successful experiences that can enhance aspects of performance. If you start to get the idea of positive psychology at work, you would be right on target.

As we have indicated, support systems are critical in combating PTSD. For the current military, the problem is that while there may be instantaneous communication with family members via cell phone, Skype, Twitter, and other Internet access, they are physically thousands of miles apart with all the stress that brings. The family skills component (Gottman, Gottman, & Atkins, 2011) is designed to educate both service personnel and families on how to alleviate much of this stress. Frontline troops can take relationship enrichment courses along with their families, who are linked via the Internet to access the course materials. Topics include creating and maintaining friendship and intimacy, increasing trust and honesty, managing conflict constructively and gently, de-escalating conflict, practicing cognitive self-soothing, containing cognitive flooding and physical stress responses, soothing and calming one's partner, converting posttraumatic stress to posttraumatic growth through the relationship, building positive relationships and effective discipline with children, and surviving breakups. You don't need a certificate in marriage and family therapy to see that this component of the CFS could be a powerful tool in preventing the critical incidents that according to Mental Health Advisory Team V (2008) turn soldiers' thinking toxic and lethal. In summary, the U.S. Defense Department knows a lot more than it did during the Vietnam War and is now very actively involved in the business of both preventing and alleviating PTSD and its comorbid disorders. It will be very interesting indeed to see the follow-up research on these massive initiatives.

Treatment of Adults

Given the constellation of problems that afflict the person with PTSD, treatment is complex, and the human services worker can expect numerous transcrisis events and crisis points to occur during treatment. The treatment of PTSD has three principal components: (1) processing and coming to terms with the horrifying, overwhelming experience; (2) controlling and mastering physiological and biological stress reactions; and (3) reestablishing secure social connections and interpersonal efficacy (van der Kolk, van der Hart, & Burbridge, 2002). For individuals with complex PTSD, treatment priorities are somewhat different and will be dealt with in Chapter 9, Sexual Assault. Before the worker tackles any of these components, however, comprehensive assessment needs to occur. Assessment is particularly important in PTSD because it is camouflaged by so many other symptoms and problems.

Assessment

Assessment of PTSD should consider at least three goals: First, are symptoms of PTSD present? Although their presence may seem to be a given, length of time from onset may mean that different symptoms are more pronounced at different times. Second, diagnoses of presenting problems such as drug abuse or a variety of personality disorders may mask PTSD unless care is taken to assess for prior trauma. It is highly probable that people in crisis will present with comorbid problems, and PTSD may not be identified as the undergirding problem unless care is taken in assessing for traumatic incidents. Third, because of contextual differences in terms of physical, temporal, social, and political climate, these variables may have a great deal to do with how the event is interpreted (Newman, Kaloupkek, & Keane, 1996, pp. 242–245).

The following examples indicate just how important contextual variables are. A Vietnam veteran with PTSD in the 1970s would be perceived as a crazed baby killer as opposed to a Gulf War, Afghanistan, or Iraq veteran in the 2000s, who would be viewed with compassion because of the dramatic change in the political climate and the social view of men and women who fought in these wars. Likewise, domestic violence, which was formerly seen as a private matter between husband and wife, is now viewed as a societal ill to the extent that the label "battered woman syndrome" has been attached to it. The self-reliant and tightly knit community of Joplin, Missouri, with its extended support system may react to the devastation of a tornado far differently from the way insular and emotionally distant apartment dwellers in New York City react to being forced out of their apartments by the collapse of the World Trade Center towers. Thus, in determining the potential to acquire PTSD or manifest it, one should always take into consideration a thorough background assessment that includes gender, race, socioeconomic class, experience, culture, religion, time components, geographic area, number of incidents of prior exposure to trauma, strength of interpersonal relationships, occupational risk, sociopolitical attitudes, and a host of other contextual variables that may have unforeseen impact on the resiliency of the individual to withstand or fall victim to PTSD. In short, just because you go through a traumatic event doesn't mean you automatically get PTSD or are even a "victim" as opposed to a "survivor" (Gist, Lubin, & Redburn, 1999; Kaniasty & Norris, 1999; Kroll, 2003).

Assessment of PTSD falls into two main categories, structured or semistructured interviews and empirically derived measures.

Structured Interview. If time is available, the structured interview probably remains the best diagnostic device for determining whether a person has PTSD. One of the best structured interviews is the Clinician-Administered PTSD Scale (CAPS-1; Blake et al., 1990). It assesses all the symptoms outlined in the *DSM-IV-TR* as well as eight associated symptoms: guilt over acts committed or omitted, survivor's guilt, homicidality, disillusionment with authority, feelings of hopelessness, memory impairment, sadness and depression, and feelings of being overwhelmed.

It also examines the impact of symptoms on social and occupational functioning, improvement in PTSD symptoms since a previous CAPS-1 assessment, overall response validity, and overall PTSD severity. Current status for all symptoms is assessed first, and if criteria for PTSD are not met, the questions are asked again for a "worst case," 1-month period since traumatic onset. The items also have a QV code, for question validity, when the interviewer has doubts about the truthfulness of the response. The CAPS-1 pays very careful attention to the assessment of lifetime PTSD. Its major drawbacks are the length of time required for administration and its lack of validation with nonveterans (Newman, Kaloupkek, & Keane, 1996, p. 253).

Self-Reports. Self-reports are useful for their efficiency in time, cost, and ease of administration. Because crisis intervention often allows only the most rudimentary assessment, if time is of the essence, we prefer Figley's (1989, 1990) Traumagram Questionnaire, a graphically represented client self-report. It can be self-constructed on the spot. The questionnaire elicits the number of traumatic events, length of time, circumstances, age of client, persons who may have been involved with the events, and self-reported degrees of stress for all previous traumatic experiences and can be easily incorporated into a standard interview format. Clients are then asked to rate their stress level on a 1 (low) to 5 (high) scale at the time of the event, one year later, and in the present. Clients are then asked to consider each traumatic experience, what helped them cope, and what helped them adjust or not to the aftermath of the traumatic event.

Figley's traumagram is also a useful tool in determining the causes of transcrisis. In the course of therapy, at times clients present with symptoms and problems that seem to have no logical basis in reality. They are clearly in crisis. Their symptoms are causing them all kinds of trouble at school, at home, and at work, yet there appears to be nothing in real time that would be causing the problem. This puzzling dilemma is not uncommon when working with people who have been traumatized and have either dismissed the trauma as ancient history or have submerged it from conscious awareness (Shallcross, 2010). At this point we start looking at two distinct possibilities: delayed onset of PTSD or complicated grieving, which we will exam at length in Chapter 12, Personal Loss: Bereavement and Grief. To ferret out these issues, we have modified Charles Figley's (1989) traumagram protocol in the following way. We ask clients to consider not only stressful events in their life but also losses they have suffered. Clients are urged to consider not only loss to death, but also financial loss, job termination, death of a pet, romantic breakup, divorce, geographic moves, and acute onset of a disabling condition either for oneself or a loved one.

By plotting the number of events across the length of time that they were acutely felt on an *x*-axis, and then plotting the degree of stress on the *y*-axis using a scale of 1 (minimum) to 10 (maximum), the interviewer can quickly gain a graphic representation of the total number, type, and duration of traumas and the degree of stress the client has experienced. It gives the interviewer a good picture of what the client feels are the relative power of significant events and also gives the interviewer an opportunity to explore the dimensions of each of these events. It also allows the crisis worker to examine one of the "best bet" indicators for delayed PTSD or the inability to resolve a loss—that is, the

repeated exposure of the subject to traumatic events. Its major weakness is the subjective bias of the individual, but its strength is that clients may have "aha" experiences as events and losses they had submerged from awareness are brought into the light of day.

Dr. James's traumagram in Figure 7.1 presents a graphic description of his life history of trauma and loss over several decades. Seven events are depicted, as listed below. The intensity or level of stress and the duration of the stress for each event vary considerably. In this traumagram, the darker the area under each graph line, the more stresses that have accumulated during that time.

Event #1. Intensity level is 10+. Client is 6 years old on his first overnight camping trip with a summer camp group. After camp counselor sends boys off to bed with "Old Man Pollywog," the story of a creature who lives in the nearby swamp

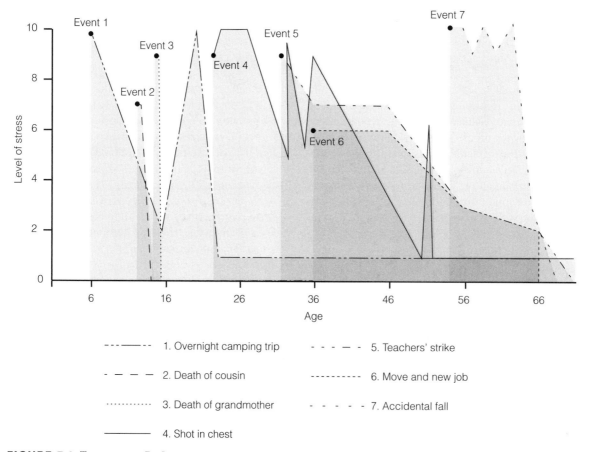

FIGURE 7.1 Traumagram: Dr. James

abducting small boys and carrying them off, the client is somehow locked out of the cabin and forced to sleep on the ground, easy prey for the swamp thing. A terrorizing night that indelibly imprints young Dickie to the point that he does not camp again until he is 23 years of age and canoeing in the Boundary Waters of Quetico Provincial Park in Ontario. The first night out on his canoeing trip Dick has an anxiety attack and is in desperate need of his mommy. Dick becomes desensitized after 14 days in the wilderness, but decides never to camp again if at all possible.

Event #2. Intensity level is 7. Client is 12 years old and is exposed to death for the first time. Traumatic death of 3-year-old cousin due to respiratory paralysis from anesthetic during tonsillectomy. Client is not emotionally close. Onset is acute but quickly resolved over 2-month period.

Event #3. Intensity level is 9. Client is 13 years old. Grandmother dies from cancer. Long-term illness and death expected. Client is emotionally close but reconciled to death. Stress dissipates to zero after 1 month.

Event #4. Intensity level starts at 9, moves to 10+ over a 12-month period. At the age of 21, client is shot in chest while out with girlfriend. Gunshot causes physical problems and what comes to be known 20 years later as PTSD. Client's social relationships plummet. Has anxiety attacks, becomes depressed, socially isolated, and contemplates suicide. After 1 year and 9 months bullet is removed. Client seeks counseling. Intensity drops sharply but is residual at level of 4–5, escalating sharply and acutely for over 3 years in heterosexual relationships until client marries current wife. Intensity level drops to 1 but occasionally spikes during times of severe physical or emotional stress.

Event #5. Intensity level is 9. Client is 32 years old, married father. Caught in the middle of a teachers' strike. Sees nationally validated program he directed disintegrate. Job loss. Complete job change and geographic change of 300 miles. Depression, anxiety attacks, PTSD symptoms resurface. Seeks counseling, makes commitment to job change out of education. Intensity level goes to 7 due to job change and continues for a year and a half, diminishing to level of 2–3 with increasing familiarity in new job in petroleum industry.

Event #6. Intensity level is 6. Client is 34 years old, married, a father. Reenters education with job as university professor. Moves 500 miles. Initial anxiety but mentorship reduces it quickly.

Event #7. Intensity level is 10+. Client is 54, married, father of two. Suffers accidental fall with severe external head trauma and edema while repairing roof on daughter's tree house. Severe pain for approximately 2 months from 300+ stitches and 52 staples in skull to reattach scalp. Self-image issues due to facial scarring. Residual injuries and interventions include plastic surgery on head and herniated C-6 disc operation over following 5 years, with spike levels of 10 and residual levels of 1–3.

(There's more, but this is merely an example and not a soap opera of Dr. James's life.)

After completing the traumagram, we query our clients on their affective, behavioral, and cognitive responses to specific traumas, both at the time they occurred and how those incidents are affecting them now. We are looking not just at specific events but at the overall picture of what is occurring. Is the whole greater than the sum of the individual traumas? Does the person show resiliency and stamina with one particular kind of event and not with another? This dialogue is conducted in a user friendly manner with the admonition, "If some emotions you didn't know were associated with that event pop up, and you get upset and need to take a breather, we'll stop. Just let me know." One of the most critical components of therapy and crisis intervention with a client with PTSD is demonstrating by word and deed that this is a *safe* place to be and that you are a *safe* person to be with (Courtois, Ford, & Cloitre, 2009; Herman, 1992).

As we query our client we are looking for recurrent psychodynamic themes that might give us clues to what is driving current maladaptive behavior. Does the client have continuing anger, regrets, guilt over past experiences? Is there a common affective, behavioral, or cognitive theme running through traumatic events? Do the events seem as potent now as they were then, with the client suddenly flushed and angry as he thinks about a physically abusing father who had the unmitigated gall to go and die on him before he could pay the abuser back? If the client has been fired for insubordinate behavior a number of times, can we trace these incidents back to a primary causal agent?

We are also very interested in how the client reports the events. Recently in class, one of our students was going over her traumagram in a very fluid way with even voice tone and a well-modulated voice level—until she came to event 6, which was about her discovery of a longtime close male friend who lied to her about a sexual assault he perpetrated and was later arrested and convicted of it. Her hesitation, loss of words, and trembling voice clearly indicated that this event was profoundly shocking to her and had caused her to deeply question her ability to gauge and assess people she had come to trust. When the professor reflected on her abrupt change in voice, she was taken aback because she had not recognized how deeply it still affected her. In summary, self-reports can sometimes uncover material that normative, empirical scale tests do not.

Empirically Derived Scales. A variety of empirically derived PTSD instruments have been generated. Of them, the following seem to have reasonable utility in determining if PTSD is present and are reasonably efficient in terms of time and cost to administer. The Mississippi Scale for Combat Related PTSD (Keane, Caddell, & Taylor, 1988) is widely used and has a number of versions for different client populations. The Impact of Events Scale (Horowitz, Wilner, & Alvarez, 1979) is one of the most widely used instruments for detecting PTSD and has been employed with a variety of trauma-related populations. The scale assesses only the extent of avoidance/numbing rather than the full scope of PTSD symptoms that are covered by the other tests mentioned here. The Keane PK scale of the MMPI/MMPI-2 has been formulated for the specific purpose of diagnosing PTSD (Keane, Malloy, & Fairbank, 1984). Because it is embedded in the MMPI/MMPI-2, its score can be compared to the validity scales of the total instrument to determine whether faking or malingering is occurring. Note that some people, such as insurance claimants, malingerers, or incarcerates, may have less than honorable motives in claiming they have PTSD, and their reports may not be valid.

Overview of Assessment. Their responses to questions about social affiliation show a clear distinction between individuals with character disorders and those suffering from PTSD. In general, individuals with PTSD avoid interpersonal relationships, as opposed to the ingratiating gregariousness of a sociopath. Those with PTSD have few close friends, prefer being alone, and discuss few intimate details of their lives. Unexpected contact with other people or stimuli reminiscent of the traumatic event may make these individuals extremely "jumpy" and "edgy" (Keane et al., 1985, p. 270).

The human services worker should never dismiss a report, no matter how trivial it may seem, of involvement in a catastrophic situation or a major loss (Scurfield, 1985, pp. 238–239). Because individuals with PTSD may be very reluctant to talk about the trauma they have been through, human services workers should try to get background information from relatives, coworkers, and any other people who have personal knowledge of the individual. The personal history is particularly important when substance abuse is involved, because if PTSD is not identified, all the efforts of the worker will not ameliorate the substance abuse problem.

Our own and many, many colleagues' clinical experience with depressed and borderline clients has uncovered many who have suffered sexual abuse as children. Until ruled out, PTSD should be suspected as a causative agent. However, getting at it may prove extremely difficult, particularly given the severe social taboos associated with talking about incestuous and abusive relationships. Therefore, in an initial assessment, even though the interviewer may have a strong hunch that repression of a traumatic event is causing the problem, the causative agent should never be exposed, interpreted, or even guessed at until a high degree of trust has been built (Scurfield, 1985, pp. 238–239).

Finally, assessment in treatment of PTSD must be ongoing and overarching, particularly during the course of therapy. The changes that occur in the client vacillate dramatically—sometimes daily or even hourly. Because of the intrusive nature of much of the therapy, it is common to see upsurges in symptoms and problem behaviors (Flack et al., 2002).

Assessment of Billie Mac. In the case of Billie Mac, a CAPS-1 interview showed little if any evidence of traumatic experience prior to Vietnam besides the death of a grandfather, to whom he was quite close. In Vietnam, he was in major battle after major battle, interspersed with patrols and sweeps. He was the only man out of his original company to walk away physically unscathed after the Tet offensive.

After Vietnam, the traumatic wake continued. Violent episodes with his father, his wife, and his children, scrapes with the law, drunken binges, barroom brawls, prolonged bouts of depression interspersed with manic acting out, alcohol addiction treatment, job loss due to nonperformance, suicidal ideation, plus the standard symptoms of PTSD marked his years since Vietnam with almost continuous crises. There were very few months in the 25 years since his return that he would not rank extremely high on the Triage Assessment Scale. Affectively, he goes far beyond what the situation warrants, with large mood swings that cycle through anger, fear, and sadness. He rarely ranks lower than 6 on the Affective Severity scale, and his average is 7.

In the cognitive domain he has suffered physical, psychological, social, and spiritual transgression, threat, and loss. His problem-solving abilities are characterized by self-doubt, confusion, and excessive rumination on Vietnam and his abortive attempts to reacclimatize to the civilian world. His severity rating is consistently an 8 to 9, in the Marked Impairment range.

Billie Mac's behavior invariably makes the situation worse. He either approaches the situation in a hostile-aggressive manner or avoids it for fear of acting out against others. He is immobilized between these two extremes, and significant others report that they feel he is erratic, unpredictable, and dangerous. A most conservative estimate places him at a minimum of 8 on the Behavioral Severity scale. His total scale score is 24, which places him in the lower range of the Marked Impairment category. Perhaps even more ominously, his individual scale scores frequently hit a 10. As he presents for treatment, he is in serious trouble, and at times of stress his triage rating scale score spikes into the lethal Severe Impairment range. He has suicidal thoughts, and at times his behavior verges on homicidal. His CAPS-1 interview ratings indicate a very high frequency and intensity of PTSD symptoms, and the MMPI-2 PK scale confirms his PTSD surely falls into the more complex variety. If he refuses inpatient treatment, he should have closely supervised outpatient treatment.

Phases of Recovery

Brende and Parson (1985, pp. 185–186) have compiled the work of Wilson (1980), Figley (1978), and Horowitz (1976) to construct five phases of recovery in the individual with PTSD. These phases directly parallel treatment approaches, and each has its own crisis stage.

1. *The emergency or outcry phase.* The individual experiences heightened "fight/flight" reactions to the life-threatening situation. This phase lasts as long as the survivor believes the situation to last. Pulse, blood pressure, respiration, and muscle activity are all increased. Concomitant feelings of fear and helplessness predominate. Termination of the event itself is followed by relief and confusion. Questions about why the event happened and what its consequences are dominate the individual's thoughts.

2. *The emotional numbing and denial phase.* The survivor protects psychic well-being by burying the experience in subconscious memory. By avoiding the experience, the individual temporarily reduces anxiety and stress symptoms. Many individuals remain forever at this stage unless they receive professional intervention.

3. *The intrusive-repetitive phase.* The survivor has nightmares, volatile mood swings, intrusive images, and amplified startle responses. Other pathological and antisocial defense mechanisms may be put into place in a futile attempt to rebury the trauma. At this point the delayed stress becomes so overwhelming that the individual is propelled to seek help or becomes so mired in the pathology of the situation that outside intervention is mandated.

4. *The reflective-transition phase.* The survivor develops a larger personal perspective on the traumatic events and becomes positive and constructive, with a forward- rather than backward-looking perspective. The individual comes to grips with the trauma and confronts the problem.

5. *The integration phase.* The survivor successfully integrates the trauma with all other past experiences and restores a sense of continuity to life. The trauma is successfully placed fully in the past.

Neat and orderly progression for the PTSD individual through these stages is the exception rather than the rule. More likely is a precipitating crisis far removed in chronological time from the event itself and then a continuing series of crises that escalate until the individual voluntarily seeks help or is forced to seek it. Once intervention occurs, a cyclic pattern of avoidance, recall, recovery, and more avoidance continues until the core issues that gave birth to PTSD are resolved (Figley, 1985a, pp. 402–404). The human services worker can expect a series of transcrisis events as this process unfolds.

Initiating Intervention Generally, victims of trauma refuse early intervention because they either see the event as too difficult to deal with or believe that people of good character ought to be able to cope with such events on their own without outside intervention. These two faulty assumptions get individuals into the delayed part of the disorder, where most of the treatment population will emerge.

Importance of Acceptance

Given the variety of negative and conflicting emotional baggage the individual brings to the session, it is of paramount importance that the human services worker provide an accepting atmosphere so that the individual can start to recount and encounter the trauma. Disclosure of the trauma is difficult for the PTSD client because recounting what has happened may be horrifying and socially unacceptable. Also, open-minded acceptance of the client's story may be extremely difficult for and repugnant to the human services worker; but if therapeutic progress is to be made, nothing less will do (Brende & Parson, 1985, p. 178).

Billie Mac: (*thinking to himself*) If I tell about killing that kid, what will the counselor think? A baby killer, that's what! Yet, it's bugging the hell out of me. (*Slowly tells the counselor about the incident.*)

Human Services Worker (HSW): (*stating personal feelings*) I can see how hard it was for you to talk about that. A part of me wonders how you or anybody could ever kill a child. However, I understand how scared you were, wondering whether he had a grenade, what a moral quandary that put you in, and the guilt and anguish you feel as you recall the incident.

Therapy with veterans, either individually or in groups, is ideally conducted with veterans as leaders because of the defensiveness and hostility with which most veterans view professionals who have not undergone the experience of combat. The same is true of the firefighters, police officers, and emergency medical technicians (EMTs) you will meet later in the chapter. One could easily extrapolate this notion to group work with other kinds of trauma victims. The problem is that professionals who have also experienced the trauma or the setting within which it occurs are often not readily available. Therefore, the Veterans Center of Memphis published a list of 12 "rules of the road" for establishing the credibility of nonveterans who work therapeutically with veterans (Memphis Vietnam Veterans Center, 1985). These rules should be adapted to any intact group such as police officers, EMTs, and others whose common bond is more than the incidence of PTSD.

1. The client has the experiential knowledge you don't have; you have the clinical and technical knowledge he or she doesn't have. Together you can forge a working alliance.

2. Make your desire to understand come across so that considerable experiential gaps are bridged.

3. Realize that the client wants you to help him or her help you understand. In the process, he or she recreates and reexperiences the sources of the problems, and you, by providing the therapeutic climate, gain an in-depth understanding of the traumatic experience.

4. An opposite-sex therapist serves as a role model—that is, in the case of a male veteran, a woman who can understand and accept the individual for what he is and has done without prejudging him.

5. Clinical experience and expertise are built over time—as your understanding and technical expertise grow, you will be accepted by the individual or the group despite your lack of direct experience.

6. As a nonmember of the "exclusive" group, you can challenge the defense of exclusivity, that one who wasn't there can't understand, thus serving to break through his or her feelings of isolation and "contamination."

7. Your technical naiveté often helps the individual to explore and express him- or herself. In his or her effort to help you understand the technical aspects of combat, emergency medical service, or police tactical procedures, he or she uncovers unknown areas of conflict.

8. At the same time, because of your naiveté, you must guard against becoming too involved in problems and memories, thereby "triggering" situational stress that may need immediate attention and treatment.

9. Realize that moral conflicts will probably be raised for you personally as stories unfold; guard against any display of emotional revulsion to a client who describes atrocities. Be nonjudgmental and objective.

10. Guard against overidentification or hero worship, or you will blunt your problem-solving ability.

11. Expect to need controls and to have to clearly enforce them for your sake and the client's—don't try to do therapy with a client who is drunk or "stoned," refuse to be a party to long tirades on the phone, and bar all weapons and mean it.

12. Heed the signs of burnout: thinking or talking too much about your clients to others, finding yourself having client-specific symptoms such as nightmares, and so on. Step back and evaluate whether you may be too immersed in trying to do too much for too many.

These rules are adaptable to any kind of trauma survivors and the people who work with them *and apply particularly to those who work with adult survivors of childhood sexual abuse.*

One further admonition is necessary for any human services worker who would work with trauma survivors. Frick and Bogart (1982) identified one of the stages that veterans go through as "rage at their counselor." This transference stage (attributing to the human services worker qualities and attributes of significant others in the client's life) is important in coming to terms with the traumatic experience. Human services workers may well become the focal point of all the frustration, grief, fear, lost opportunity, confusion, lack of progress, and attempts at reconciliation with society, family, and friends that mark the trauma survivor's attempt to reintegrate into the social mainstream. Human services workers need to deal with such anger by owning their mistakes in being insensitive to issues, accepting and reflecting the individual's anger while at the same time not being defensive, containing impulsive responses after being attacked, owning their own anger, and not becoming discouraged and giving up.

Risks of Treatment

It is also incumbent on the human services worker to state clearly the risks inherent in treatment. It may be hard to make such statements and to propose a poor prognosis, but probably the individual will have pondered many of the same questions. After the initial crisis has passed and the individual is back to a state of at least semi-equilibrium, the human services worker should convey clearly the following risks, as outlined by Brende and Parson (1985, pp. 168–174):

1. There may be only partial recovery; there are no magical cures for this tenacious and pernicious problem.
2. Because of the continuing nature of the crisis, either long bouts with hospitals or weekly trips to the therapist are required that will play havoc with keeping a job.
3. As catharsis of the event occurs, it is inevitable that the individual gets worse before getting better. Fear of a psychotic breakdown may occur as the individual learns more about the disorder.
4. As the struggle to find oneself goes forward, personality change may put heavy burdens on interpersonal relationships as significant others see a very different person emerge from the therapeutic experience.
5. Psychic pain may become almost intolerable as the individual reexperiences disturbing memories and emotions that, as they are voiced, may cause rejection by friends and professionals alike.
6. Because of the numerous self-constraints placed on volatile emotions, the individual may fear that giving vent to those emotions will lead to uncontrolled anger and result in physical harm to others. Because of the hurt suffered, it will also be very difficult for the individual to give up the idea of revenge on both real and imagined perpetrators of the traumatic event.
7. Because of the compartmentalized and constricted lifestyle that follows the trauma, the individual will safeguard against change and may have extreme difficulty following directions and doing what others may suggest, no matter how reasonable and proper. Giving up such maladaptive self-reliance will put the individual at the mercy of others, a seemingly intolerable situation.
8. A great deal of pain will result from coming to accept the world as it is with all its frailties and injustices. In attempting to gain reentry into such an imperfect world, the individual is in danger of losing patience with it and falling back into the vortex of PTSD.
9. Correlative with accepting the frailties of the world is also the acceptance of one's own set of infirmities; bad memories may return; relationships may not always be excellent; others may obtain better jobs for no legitimate reason.

Acceptance of oneself, including the guilt, sorrow, and regret that go with it, is the sine qua non of getting through PTSD, but it may be an extremely difficult and fearsome task that will call for far more courage than surviving the catastrophe itself.

Multiphasic/Multimodal Treatment

Individual treatment goes hand in hand with group work. From crisis stage to crisis stage, a multimodal therapeutic approach is used with heavy reliance on various combinations of behavioral and cognitive-behavioral therapy (Scurfield, 1985, p. 250). Although cognitive-behavioral approaches have been the generic therapeutic modality with the most successful outcome data to date (Bryant et al., 2003; Ehlers et al., 2005; Grey, Young, & Holmes, 2002; International Society for

Traumatic Stress Studies, 1997; Roemer, Harrington, & Riggs, 2002; Zoellner, Foa, & Fitzgibbons, 2002), various combinations of specific treatment techniques within the realm of cognitive-behavioral therapy have been tailored to deal with specific components of PTSD. Further, because of the idiosyncratic nature of the course of PTSD, various other techniques that employ psychodynamic (Lindy, 1996, pp. 525–536) and humanistic approaches (Turner, McFarlane, & van der Kolk, 1996, pp. 537–558) may also be appropriate. Contextual (Gold, 2009) and contextual behavior therapy (Follette, Iverson, & Ford, 2009) and eclectic experiential and emotion-focused therapy (Fosha et al., 2009) are newer approaches that specifically target complex traumas. Although this may sound like a shotgun approach that aimlessly blasts away at the problem, such is not the case. The complexity of this malady calls for some of the very best in eclectic therapy and eclectic treatment planning. Further, an important component of any psychotherapeutic approach in the treatment of PTSD is the use of psychotropic medication.

Psychotropic Medication

From what is presently known about the biology of PTSD, drugs that regulate neurotransmitters and neuromodulators ought to be helpful in providing at least some palliative relief from the psychophysiological responses that occur with the disorder. Because so many different psychobiological abnormalities may predominate in various PTSD cases, almost every class of psychotropic medication has been prescribed for PTSD clients (Donnelly, 2003; Fichtner, Podding, & deVito, 2000; Filteau, Leblanc, & Bouchard, 2003; Kreidler, Briscoe, & Beech, 2002; Marmar, Neylan, & Schoenfeld, 2002; Sokolski et al., 2003; F. Taylor, 2003; Zullino, Krenz, & Besson, 2003). There is as yet no fixed pharmaceutical regimen for PTSD. The effects of medications for PTSD seem to be so narrow for individuals and specific groups that they are often not generalizable to other populations (Davidson & van der Kolk, 1996, p. 511).

An excellent example is the antidepressant fluoxetine (Prozac), which has been given the highest level of research evidence rating for effectiveness by the International Society for Traumatic Stress Studies in its *Practice Guidelines* (1997). Van der Kolk and his associates (1994) found that fluoxetine did indeed reduce numbing and arousal responses in a clinical treatment group but *did not* in a group of veterans. Further compounding the problem is that one of the side effects of fluoxetine is that while it may reduce numbing and

arousal responses, it can also *increase* startle responses (Davidson & van der Kolk, 1996, p. 512).

Davidson and van der Kolk (1996, p. 521) propose that at early onset of PTSD, drugs such as the benzodiazepines or clonidine that decrease autonomic arousal are the best choice. If PTSD is in place, then antidepressants should be introduced, along with a willingness to use a second drug such as a mood stabilizer, anticonvulsant, or benzodiazepine as adjunctive treatment if the primary drug does not ameliorate symptoms (Davidson & van der Kolk, 1996; International Society for Traumatic Stress Studies, 1997). Because presenting symptoms can seriously interfere with treatment, careful prescription and monitoring of psychotropic medication are critical in allowing PTSD therapy to proceed successfully. Medication for PTSD symptoms should be given by someone who has a great deal of medical expertise with the problem and not by a general practitioner. That medical practitioner should also carefully coordinate medication and monitoring with whoever is doing the "talking" part of the therapy.

Individual Intervention
Emergency/Outcry

In the first phase of recovery, the emergency or outcry phase, the major problem is to get the individual stabilized; this means reducing the anxiety and physical responses associated with the trauma (Meadows & Foa, 1999). Meditation, relaxation, hypnosis, and biofeedback may be used (Evans, 2003; Kolb & Mutalipassi, 1982).

In relaxation training and meditation, the human services worker teaches the client how to relax body muscle groups systematically and to focus calmly on mental images that produce psychic relief of body tensions and stress (Benson, 1976; Wolpe, 1958). Individuals learn how to exercise self-control over many of their stresses and anxieties and dampen debilitating physiological responses.

HSW: OK, Billie Mac. Just imagine that you are lying on the beach with that soft, warm sand, the calm breeze blowing gently over you, the gentle lapping of the cool, crystal-clear water, and just easily focus your attention on that scene. Now just notice the difference in your body too. Notice the difference between how your muscles feel when they are tense and relaxed. Starting with your legs, just tense them up, feel how your muscles tighten up. Now relax them, and just feel that tightness drop away. Notice the difference and the really pleasant feelings that occur when your muscles are just hanging loose and flaccid.

Continue to picture the scene on the beach as you work your way up your body, alternating between tensing and relaxing your muscles. Notice as you continue to do this how you can change the way your body feels and what you can focus on in your mind's eye.

Relaxation alone is helpful in alleviating current symptoms and enabling the individual to regain a measure of emotional and behavioral control, and it is also a preliminary step in tackling the cluster of problems characteristic of PTSD. Through deep relaxation or hypnosis, the client may be regressed back to an image of the traumatic event. Regressing the client in this manner is necessary to elevate bad memories of the traumatic event, and the intrusive images that accompany them, to conscious awareness (Brom, Kleber, & Defares, 1989; Kingsbury, 1988; Spiegel, 1989).

Extinguishing Intrusive Images

Given the previously discussed neuropsychological foundations of PTSD, Ochberg (1988) has concluded that PTSD should be viewed first in terms of autonomic nervous system (ANS) arousal, and any treatment should take into consideration the physiological aspects of the disorder. Thus a standing hypothesis for PTSD treatment has evolved that proposes a return of the client to the original state of elevated psychophysiological arousal in order to affect current maladaptive response sets (Malloy, Fairbank, & Keane, 1983). Once the individual has learned how to relax, other therapeutic strategies such as systematic desensitization, exposure, flooding, implosion, and Gestalt techniques may be employed to create ANS arousal (Cohen, 2002, 2003; Fairbank & Keane, 1982; Feeny, Hembree, & Zoellner, 2003; Foa et al., 2002; Forbes et al., 2003; Hembree, Rauch, & Foa, 2003; Keane & Kaloupek, 1982; Paunovic, 2002, 2003; Paunovic & Ost, 2001).

The human services worker continues to work slowly through the relaxation exercises and the mental imagery, continuously reinforcing the client for being able to shift to calm, relaxed scenes and away from the intrusive, anxiety-producing images. Practice for the individual in this and the other techniques to be covered in individual therapy is important. We recommend that sessions be audiotaped so that the client can practice the procedures at home on a daily basis.

Numbing/Denial

Reexperiencing.   Once the individual has learned how to relax, the second phase of intervention occurs, coincident with the individual's emotional numbing and denial phase of recovery. This phase is concerned with bringing to conscious awareness the traumatic event and the hidden facts and emotions about it that the individual denies (Brende & Parson, 1985, pp. 191–192). In a gentle but forceful way, the human services worker guides the individual, in the here and now of the therapeutic moment, to reexperience in the fullest possible detail what occurred in the traumatic experience so that submerged feelings are uncovered and ultimately expunged (Scurfield, 1985, p. 245). While deeply relaxed, the individual is asked to reexperience the terrible events of the trauma, with the injunction that at any time the memories can be switched off and the individual can return to the pleasant image of the beach.

HSW: Now go back to the village and tell me what is happening.

Billie Mac: (*lying down, relaxed, eyes closed*) The point man all of a sudden comes under fire and gets popped. I see him get hit. He's lying in the open across a ditch about 100 meters from the tree line. It's really getting hot, a lot of fire from concealed bunkers. They're using him as bait. This goes on for about 5 minutes, I guess. All of a sudden I decide to go and get him. Me and some other guys just get up and run across the open field to the ditch. We're getting all kinds of fire and out of five of us, only me and Al make it to the ditch without getting dinged. The point man is only about 5 meters from me, but I can't get at him. (*Billie Mac breaks into a sweat with slight tremors.*) I finally spot where the concealed bunker is that's making it so hot for us. I've got a LAW [light antitank weapon], and I get a bead on the bunker and zap it. At about the same time there's an explosion right next to me, a B-40 grenade, I guess, and that's all I remember until I wake up on the medevac chopper. (*Breaks into profuse sweating and major tremors.*)

HSW: All right, just shift out of that scene and back to the beach, and just relax. Notice the cool water, the warm sand, the gentle breeze, and just let your muscles relax. (*Billie Mac noticeably relaxes and, with continued directives from the human services worker, returns to a calm, relaxed state.*)

Although the account of the combat situation is fearsome in its intensity, the human services worker suspects that it alone is not responsible for the traumatic reaction. Billie Mac was in many such situations, but this village is the focal point of his nightmares and intrusive thoughts. The human services worker suspects that there is more here than what Billie Mac is revealing, and seeks to slowly peel away the psychological walls that defend the trauma from awareness. The human services worker believes that the recounting of the combat situation, despite having psychological value as a defense mechanism, is probably not historically accurate. The individual has left out certain traumatic parts of the story, and the human services worker's job becomes one of trying to fill in the gaps (Horowitz, 1976, pp. 117–118). Having built a very strong rapport and mutual trust with the client (Keane et al., 1985, p. 291), the human services worker probes into the situation and actively seeks to interpret and clarify the content of the client's story with respect to its potentially overwhelming effect (Scurfield, 1985, p. 245).

HSW: Go back to the village and the ditch right before you take out the bunker. What do you see?

Billie Mac: I see the point man. He's alive, but bad off.

HSW: What are you thinking?

Billie Mac: I've got to get him, but I can't. The fire's too heavy.

HSW: What do you feel?

Billie Mac: Scared, I um . . . I can't seem to do anything . . . the rounds are really coming . . .

HSW: What's happening around you?

Billie Mac: Al keeps yelling, "Take the bunker out with the LAW!"

HSW: Then what?

Billie Mac: I . . . can't . . . do it . . . it . . . I'm terrified. (*Starts to shake uncontrollably.*)

HSW: Stay right with that, Billie. I'm right here.

Billie Mac: Al grabs the LAW, stands up and fires it and— Oh, my God! Get down! Oh, Jesus, the B-40 got Al. He's gone. His blood's all over me . . . I killed him. It was my job, and I couldn't do it, and I killed Al. (*Breaks into uncontrollable sobbing and shaking.*)

HSW: It's OK! Just erase that scene from your mind and slide back to that warm, quiet beach. Just put yourself out of the firefight and back to that beach and relax, just focusing that soft sand in your mind.

As the individual breaks through the defenses that have let him numb and shield the actual events from awareness, the full force of the reality of the incident floods over him, along with the overwhelming feelings of fear, guilt, remorse, and terror that accompany the event. As these thoughts come into awareness, they give the human services worker a much clearer picture of the how and why of Billie Mac's phase 2 (denial and numbing) and those of phase 3 (intrusive-repetitive thoughts). The human services worker, using tolerable doses of reminiscence about the event, seeks to push forward into full awareness what the true scene at the event was and not what the individual's mind has fantasized it to be.

HSW: Now shift out of the scene at the beach and go back to the village. The B-40 has just gone off and Al is gone. What happens next?

Billie Mac: I can't remember . . . I don't know . . . I passed out.

HSW: (*gently*) Yes, you can. Just think a moment, and picture the scene. It's scary, but you are there now. Go ahead and just let it come and remember. I am here with you and you can get through this.

The worker gently but forcefully urges Billie Mac forward into the core of his trauma and what he fears most. This is a tightwire the worker walks. Coming to grips with the traumatic core is critical if recovery is to occur. Yet pushed too hard, the client may suffer some severe psychological consequences and lose much of the ground he has gained.

Billie Mac: Oh, God! You've got to get the point man now. You've got to go get him. I'm up and running, the fire is terrible, it's only 20 feet to him, but it's like a mile. I'm so damned scared. (*Breath coming in rapid, ragged gasps.*) I've got him and am dragging him back to the ditch. Bullets are kicking up all around me. I'll be cut in two. He weighs a ton. I get to the ditch and roll him and me into it. I turn him over and . . . Oh, Mother of Mary! He's dead. Why, oh why, didn't I get there sooner? I could have saved him. You puke-faced coward. (*Starts uncontrolled sobbing.*)

HSW: (*very calmly*) You are OK. Just shift out of that scene and back to the beach. Just take all the time you need to relax and erase that scene from your mind. Just let the cool breeze blow over you, smell the clean salt air, and enjoy that feeling of being completely relaxed. (*Time passes, and Billie Mac becomes noticeably more relaxed.*) Now I'm going to count up from 1 to 10, and when I reach 10 you'll be fully alert and refreshed.

The human services worker does this and brings Billie Mac back to present time. The worker then processes the events of the imagery session with Billie Mac.

Interpretation. At this point, the worker uses a more psychodynamic approach, actively intervening in the situation by clarifying and interpreting what the client says. By dynamically integrating the there and then of the trauma with the client's maladaptive attempts to cope and atone in the here and now of the therapeutic moment, the therapist hopes that the client can build a comprehensible picture that will make sense of the memory (Lindy, 1996, p. 534).

HSW: So it's not just that terrible fight at the village, but more what you didn't do. You feel as if you were a coward there, and that cowardice cost the life of your friend. It's almost as if all these years you'd been trying to atone for that in the only way you know how—that is, by doing things that would almost guarantee that you die too. The brushes with the law, the uncontrollable rage that winds up in knockdown, drag-out fights, the DWIs, and the suicide attempt.

Billie Mac: I don't know. (*sobbing*) I feel so terrible about it. How could I have frozen? It would have been better if I had got killed rather than live with this.

HSW: Yet you did act. You went after the man, and you couldn't know whether a minute or two would have saved his life. It seems as if that minute or two of indecision has caused 30 years of terrible retribution that you can never pay off. I'd like to suggest that it has been paid with interest, and now the time has come to pay the balance. Are you willing to do that?

Billie Mac: (*shakily*) I guess . . . although I don't know how much more I can take. You bitch! How could you do this! This really hurts!

HSW: I understand how rough you feel this is and how callous and uncaring I must seem. Remember! We've made it this far. Trust me and yourself. Together we can pull through this.

Even if the human services worker is right on target with her interpretation, getting Billie Mac to integrate the material and also allowing him to reconcile himself to the event are much more difficult. Breaking through the subconscious defenses of the client is not a one-shot deal, and denial is more often the rule than insight and acceptance. Billie Mac's negative reaction to the worker is typical of the client's transference of his or her ills to the worker as the hurtful affect is brought into awareness. At this point it is the worker's primary task to remain as empathic as possible to what is going on with the client (Lindy, 1996, p. 536).

Reflection and Transition

Although it can be extremely traumatic for the client, the human services worker will encourage the client to experience the full range of emotional responses he or she felt at the time of the event, as well as how he or she tried to make sense of it (Donaldson & Gardner, 1985, p. 370). This marks the fourth phase of the crisis, the reflective transition phase (Brende & Parson, 1985, p. 192). The human services worker will help the client by combining behavioral techniques of flooding and thought stopping. The technique of journaling, or having the client write down thoughts as the therapeutic process unfolds, will help the client process the experience.

Flooding/Exposure. Flooding or prolonged exposure is one of the most effective, if controversial, techniques for getting rid of the bad memories of PTSD (Feeny, Hembree, & Zoellner, 2003; Keane et al., 1989; Lyons & Keane, 1989). In flooding and exposure (Stampfl & Levis, 1967), the fear-evoking stimuli are presented continuously. The rationale is that if the individual is literally flooded with anxiety-provoking stimuli, the client will discover that there is no basis for fear. Continuously flooding the client causes the stimuli that are generating the anxiety to diminish; that is, repeating the response without reinforcement diminishes the tendency to perform that response. As the individual reenacts the trauma, the human services worker puts in the missing pieces of the puzzle and ferrets out all conditioned stimuli buried in memory. The result is that no noxious components of memory are left to recondition debilitating responses (Foa et al., 2002; Forbes et al., 2003; Hembree, Rauch, & Foa, 2003; Keane et al., 1985, p. 265; Paunovic, 2002, 2003; Paunovic & Ost, 2001; S. Taylor, 2003). In Chapter 9, Sexual Assault, an even more complex variation of flooding and exposure combined with cognitive restructuring and guided imagery to extinguish intrusive images will be presented. This technique is a very serious therapeutic endeavor and should not be undertaken by neophytes until they have received supervised training.

Thought Stopping. Thought stopping is a simple but powerful device that enables the individual, with help from the crisis worker, to change debilitating, intrusive thoughts to self-enhancing ones. The crisis worker initially sets the scene and builds the images until the fear-evoking stimuli are at maximum arousal, and then shouts "Stop!" and replaces them with positive, self-enhancing thoughts (Williams & Long, 1979, p. 285). The crisis worker tells the individual that at the point when the intrusive scene is most terrifying, the human services worker will slam a book sharply on the table and state in a firm voice, "Stop! Shift back to the beach!" The individual will be passive throughout the procedure, with the human services worker setting and enhancing the scene. A recording of the session is made, and the client is given the assignment of listening to the recording and then using the procedure whenever the intrusive images occur.

HSW: Now erase the beach scene, and come back to the village. You're in the ditch. Smell the stench of that ditch; feel death all around you. You can almost see the grim reaper there. You'd like to run away, but there's nowhere to run. Oh, what a fool you were to ever make the dash out here in no-man's-land! Look back and see your squad members shot up, contorted in pain, with the blood and dirt covering them. Peek over the ditch and see the point man. He's in terrible pain, screaming for help, but there's a blizzard of fire coming from the bunker. It's certain death to stick your head above the dike. Feel the conflict. You want to do something, you know you've got to take the bunker out, but you are paralyzed. You can smell the fear in you, sweating out of your pores. Look at Al. He expects you to do something; you're the squad leader, but you can't. Feel Al's stare. Listen to him yelling, "Take the bunker now, man!" Your fingers are glued to the LAW. Feel Al grab the LAW. Watch him as he stands up in that dreadful hail of death and fires the LAW into the bunker, and in the next instant see the explosion and the dirt fly as the B-40 round hits and Al disappears in the flame and smoke. Smell the smoke of cordite and the sheared copper odor of blood. Enhance those images—hear, smell, feel, see, taste that terrible moment. It's all there now as it really was. (*Billie Mac is writhing in the reclining chair.*) NOW STOP! (*Slams book down on desk.*) Shift away.

Billie Mac: (*screaming*) I can't do it!

HSW: (*in a soft but commanding voice*) Yes, you can! Just slide out of that and into that soft, warm sand. Stay with that beach scene. Smell the salt air, the cool breeze, and know that you can do that any time you want. Notice the difference in how your body feels, what goes through your mind. Just enjoy that feeling of knowing you can move into that scene.

This sequence is repeated over and over until the individual is able to switch volitionally from the intrusive image to the relaxing one with ease. The recording can be taken home to diminish the dissociation and permit externalization of the client's inner dialogue about the event and extinguish the fear that goes with it (Tinnin, Bills, & Gantt, 2002).

Journaling. For PTSD clients, speaking of what has happened to them is extremely difficult. Journaling is an excellent method of opening up affect and allowing nonverbal catharsis to occur. By putting down their thoughts in their own words and then hearing them, individuals place the terrible memories at a safe enough psychological distance that they and the human services worker can analyze them (Cienfuegos & Monelli, 1983). Journal writing gives the human services worker a catalyst for encouraging the kind of free association

necessary to open the crystallized defenses of the individual who might otherwise never explore the traumatic event (Progoff, 1975). One of the veterans who formed the basis of our composite character, Billie Mac, wrote a description of one of those endless nights when no sleep will come or, worse, when the terror comes with sleep.

Where Did B.M. Go?*
What happened to B.M.—the boy from Mississippi—happy-go-lucky, not a care in the world, who loved life, sports, the sunshine, the rain . . . and everything in the used-to-be-beautiful world. Everyone told B.M., "Go to school. Play sports. Go to college." But B.M. decided to do for his country. B.M. wanted to go to war and fight to win . . . to serve his country . . . to make everyone proud of him. B.M. went to war. B.M. killed, massacred, mutilated, burnt, hated—a hate that was like a drunk hate—tore his own heart out a little at a time, time after time.

B.M. fought and survived a war that 127 warriors that went with B.M. didn't.

B.M. looked at everyone around him and wondered why the people hated him.

Why they were scared of him . . . why they feared the warrior from Vietnam who went to a fight they were scared to fight.

B.M. wanted to love . . . to be loved. It seemed like the world was completely different from him and didn't have the same ideals about life and love.

B.M. became a drunk. He drank to forget the war, the brave warriors who had given their lives in Vietnam, to forget the people that he was living around. To these people B.M. was a cold-blooded murdering S.O.B.—a baby-killing M.F.

B.M. had been taught all his life, "Thou shalt not kill, love thine enemy." B.M. lost his morals. B.M. killed his enemies. B.M. cut the heads and ears off some of his enemies. B.M. lost his soul. B.M. is lost to God and can't be forgiven. People can say, "Ask God to forgive you, B.M." But B.M. can't forgive himself and can't ask for forgiveness. B.M. has accepted that feeling like someone took his heart out and stomped it into the ground. There is not a day in his life that he doesn't feel hurt or hurt the ones he loves.

B.M. just wants to be loved . . . to love himself again; to get rid of that hard feeling deep down inside of his heart. B.M. wants to have peace of mind.

---

*Used with permission.

Is it too much for him to ask, to seek, to search for? Is death what it will take for B.M. to finally find peace within himself?

Why can't B.M. get out of all these depressing moods he stays in . . . and cries about nothing when he is driving down the road.

Sometimes B.M. thinks he is a crazy S.O.B. Maybe the people are right. Why can't B.M. keep a job? Because B.M. was a fuck-up after he got back from Vietnam.

His vengeance and his screwed-up attitude keep him in trouble. B.M. would get so much on his mind and B.M. would keep putting it back inside. The more he put it back, the worse his depression would get until it would erupt in a rage of vengeance, which would always wind up hurting himself or the people he loved.

Even the government deceived B.M. They told B.M., "Don't worry, B.M. You go and fight this war for your country and if anything happens we will take care of you." B.M.'s response to this is, "Fine! I will do all I can for my government and my country." But give me my heart and soul back. Make me sleep at night. Make me quit crying. Take this depression away. Help me find a job and help me feel alive again. Give me back what you took from me. B.M. is what you took and I want myself back.

I wish I could give back the lives I have taken from the world, but I know that I can't. I would if I could, and I am the one that will have to live with that in my heart throughout eternity.

B.M. vividly and dramatically illustrates the anguish of PTSD in his writing—anguish from both an intrapersonal and interpersonal standpoint, of guilt he feels within himself for his moral transgressions and rage at the transgressions visited on him by an impersonal government and an uncaring society; anguish over what he was and is and how he is now attempting to resolve and reintegrate these two vastly different people that were and are B.M. Billie Mac continuously uses his initials, pointing over and over to himself, but in the third person. Only in the last paragraph does his plea change clearly to subjective, first-person owning statements. Even these statements are couched in terms of magical thinking—wish fulfillment. The use of Billie Mac's initials as an identifier of what he really perceives himself to be is not happenstance. The initials "B.M." also stand for "bowel movement." Indeed, Billie Mac's self-assessment is that he is mostly worthless "shit" to himself and others. This is typical of the kind of self-condemnation that an individual who is both victim and victimizer experiences.

This excruciating piece of writing is an initiating step in the long process that moves from self-condemnation to what Lifton (1973) calls *animated guilt.* Animated guilt enables the individual to start taking responsibility for past actions and start to experience new degrees of personal liberation. This rather dramatic example of journal writing was done voluntarily, but when clients in a crisis situation will not talk about their experiences, sometimes suggesting that they write down their feelings can be a way of breaking the impasse (James & Gilliland, 2003). Keeping a journal not only can be an extremely effective way of dealing with unbidden feelings and thoughts as they surface, but also can provide the worker and the client with an assessment of how therapy is progressing (Pearsons, 1965). For anyone like Billie Mac who suffers survivor's guilt or victim/victimizer status, journaling may be a particularly effective way to ventilate feelings that the person might otherwise be unable to talk about with the worker.

Integration

The Gestalt technique of reaching into the individual's past and bringing to conscious awareness what Gestalt practitioners call "unfinished business" is particularly helpful in draining the pustulant affect that infects the event (Cohen, 2002, 2003; Scurfield, 1985, p. 246). For Billie Mac this technique will take a different twist and will be the last part of the crisis, that of making atonement, penance, and restitution (Horowitz & Solomon, 1975). A Gestalt technique called the "empty chair" will be used.

HSW: The empty chairs in front of you represent various people. Al, the point man, other members of your squad that got hit on that day in the village. I want you to tell them what you felt about what you did. I may move to one of the chairs or have you take their place. Right now I want you to imagine Al in that chair over there. What are you going to say to him?

Billie Mac: I'm . . . so sorry. I froze. I shouldn't have done that. I killed you, and I can't ever forget that.

HSW: (*takes Al's chair*) Hey, man, what about that time at Chu Lai, and the A Shau valley? You didn't freeze then. You saved my bacon then. Remember how I froze? You didn't say squat. You think you're perfect?

Billie Mac: You were my best friend, and I let that happen. (*Sobs.*)

HSW: (*as Al*) You think you got a corner on the market? Everybody was scared. I just did it. You gave me back my life a half dozen times. I'll never forget that. You did well by me, buddy. I got no regrets.

Billie Mac: Jesus, I miss you. I loved you so damn much.

HSW: (*as Al*) Then remember the good times we had. That R & R in Bangkok, when we took the town apart. Those are the parts I remember. I love you too, buddy, but it's time we were done with that village. It's time for you to say good-bye to me. (*The HSW gets up and goes over and takes Billie Mac into his arms and hugs him. Billie Mac weeps, releasing a flood of emotion.*)

For each man in the squad, the scene is replayed. Sometimes Billie Mac takes the role of the other man, and sometimes the crisis worker does. Each piece of unfinished business is slowly and patiently worked through until Billie Mac has reconciled accounts with each person who was there on that terrible day. Clearly, Billie Mac goes through a painful but necessary grieving process that must take place if he is to put the event behind him (Brende & Parson, 1985, p. 105). As Billie Mac makes atonement for that day long past, and the trauma is expunged, the human services worker seeks to pull him to the present time and help him move forward with his life. Intensive intervention slacks off, and the individual may then go through a series of booster sessions on an "as needed" basis, with a minimum of a booster session once a month for 3 to 4 months (Balson & Dempster, 1980). This point marks the fifth, or integration, phase of the crisis.

Group Treatment

There are two types of treatment groups for people who have been exposed to trauma. The first type is preventive, short term, and typically used for those suffering acute distress. These are generally known as *debriefing groups* and are composed of members who have just survived a common traumatic experience (Mitchell, 1983). Debriefing for acute traumatic stress is discussed in detail in the last chapter of this book. The second type is longer term and is typically composed of class-specific members who have been exposed to the same type of trauma but at different times and under different circumstances. Commonly called a *support group*, this group deals with a variety of transcrisis issues and is the focal point of this chapter's discussion of group work with clients who suffer from PTSD.

Support Groups

Rap or support groups were started for veterans in 1970 by Robert Lifton and Chaim Shatan in New York City. Lifton and Shatan were human services professionals who had become disaffected with the Veterans Administration's constant refusal to acknowledge that many Vietnam veterans were suffering from combat-induced psychological problems. The outcome of this dilemma was that professionals finally came to recognize the success of rap groups and to integrate them into more traditional formats (Walker, 1983).

Emotional attachment and social involvement are basic and important ingredients in armor plating the individual against PTSD. For most of those who suffer from PTSD, social isolation and emotional estrangement are the norm. Thus group work is helpful because of the shared experience, mutual support, sense of community, reduction of stigma, and restoration of self-pride it fosters. The primary task of any group therapy is to help people regain a sense of safety and of mastery because of the shared sense of having gone through the trauma (van der Kolk, McFarlane, & van der Hart, 1996, p. 433). Further, confrontation by peers is more acceptable than confrontation by professionals because it is reality oriented (Scurfield, 1985, pp. 247–248).

Groups also serve to educate clients. The terrifying nature of PTSD calls for clearly delineating what is happening and why. Answers to clients' questions—such as "What are common PTSD symptoms?" "Why do people use drugs?" "How long will it take to get better?" "Am I crazy?" "What do I do in this situation?" "Will I ever be as I was before this happened?"—help build a cognitive anchor for the individual (Brewi, 1986).

We now switch our client emphasis to the men and women who work in police, fire, emergency, and disaster services and who, because of their repeated exposure to trauma, are excellent candidates for PTSD (Bierens-de-Haan, 1998; Corneil et al., 1999; Dreisbach, 2003; Epstein, Fullerton, & Ursano, 1998; Horn, 2002; Tucker et al., 1999; Ursano et al., 1999). We will follow one individual in this group as a generic example of emergency service workers who become at risk for PTSD because of their constant exposure to traumatic events.

The Case of Ryan.   Ryan Sanchez is a 35-year-old who has been a patrolman with the police department for 7 years. In that time he has received numerous commendations and citations for his work. Approximately 1 month ago he was referred to the police psychologist for a rather dramatic deterioration in job performance. He was caught sleeping on the job, had missed several days of work, and was insubordinate to his field commander when confronted with his inadequate performance at a crime scene. That episode culminated in his being hauled away bodily by other patrol officers after he attempted to punch his field supervisor. He was referred for clinical evaluation by his watch commander. An MMPI-2 administered by the police psychologist indicated a high potential for faking good—presenting a better picture of one's personality than one actually feels about it. The PK scale also indicated a good possibility of PTSD. The police psychologist believed that Ryan's initial interview and his MMPI-2 scores were an attempt by Ryan to present a better picture of his mental health than he was actually experiencing.

The psychologist then conducted a CAPS-1 interview and found a variety of problems that reached into both Ryan's job and family. Prior to Ryan's career with the police department, he served as an emergency medical technician (EMT) for 8 years. He decided to leave EMT work because of its stress, but still wanted to work in an "exciting and meaningful" job. He then joined the police department. He has a college degree in biology and a certificate in emergency medical technology. He has been married for 15 years to Mary, a nurse, and has two daughters, Katrina, 12, and Stacey, 8. He has been separated from his wife for 5 months, is currently living with his parents, and sees his daughters on his off-duty days.

He reports that his wife had become progressively more paranoid over other women, accused him of having affairs with them, constantly checked to see if he had perfume or lipstick marks on him after work, and finally attempted to run down, in a mall parking lot, an off-duty female police officer whom she suspected of having an affair with Ryan. That incident resulted in her temporary arrest, but charges were later dropped after she apologized to the female officer.

Ryan reports that at about this time he started suffering a bad case of "nerves." Specifically, he started to experience flashbacks to a series of traumatic events he had experienced as both an EMT and a police officer. He reports a series of instances as an EMT in which he was powerless to save the lives of terminal auto accident victims, a number of them children or adolescents. He reports having become very protective of his daughters as a result and says he wishes "I could put them in a castle with high walls and a moat around it and keep them locked up so nothing could hurt them." His protective view of his children severely strained his relationship with them, and they do not want to go and visit him because of his anger when they are not under his close supervision. He was also an EMT respondent to a natural disaster 11 years ago when a propane truck overturned and blew up, killing more than 30 people. They were charred and burned so badly that rigor had set in, but were still alive. He was relegated to being the mayor's aide de camp and spent most of his time passing information to the mayor about rescue efforts. He felt completely helpless and out of control and was enraged over his assignment. He very much wanted to be in on the rescue efforts, although he paradoxically reports that it was the most horrific scene he had ever witnessed. He reports having had nightmares about it for a number of months after the event. In the last 6 months those nightmares have returned with increasing frequency. He also reports that within the last 6 months he has become severely agitated to the point of a panic attack whenever he is near a propane truck, and will go out of his way to avoid them as well as bulk plants and tank farms where petroleum products are stored.

One other traumatic event is reported as remarkable. This event involved a missing person report while Ryan was a police officer. He and two detectives met the father of a young woman reported missing, at her abandoned apartment. Because they did not have a search warrant, they could not conduct a thorough search of the apartment. Ryan had a hunch that the woman's body was in the apartment buried under a huge mound of bags in a closet, but he was admonished by the detectives that there was nothing they could do. Because it was below freezing in the apartment, there was no foul odor to indicate the presence of a body. Two weeks later he again met the father at the apartment. The father had come in a rental truck and had begun to haul his daughter's belongings out of the apartment when he noticed a foul odor. On his arrival, Ryan immediately knew the odor was that of a dead body. On entering the apartment, he immediately found the woman under the bags of clothing. He reports an indelible picture of the father sitting in the yellow rental truck with a glazed stare that he cannot get out of his mind. He also reported that his uniform smelled like death and repeated washings would not get rid of it. He finally threw his whole uniform out, but lately he believes that somehow his new uniforms have soaked up the smell from his leather uniform jacket. He has never undergone formal debriefings for any of these traumatic events and said that although they bothered him some at the time they happened, he moved on past them—or so he thought.

He does not use alcohol, and that fact is confirmed by his watch commander. He reports he has been taking "tranquilizers" and "sleeping medication" since his separation from his wife. He also reports that things are so bad both on the job and at home that he has recently contemplated killing himself, but he has not formulated a plan because he doesn't want his daughters to be labeled because their dad "was another nutso who blew his brains out." He admits to the psychologist that he clearly has lost control of his life and wonders if he indeed does not have PTSD or is suffering a "breakdown" of some kind.

Ryan's symptoms fit a clear diagnosis for PTSD. He has recurrent, intrusive thoughts and dreams about the traumatic events and experiences severe psychological distress to external cues of the events. He now avoids stimuli that remind him of at least two of the events. He has increased arousal symptoms, hypervigilance over his daughters' safety, difficulty concentrating on his job, and problems falling asleep. The psychologist's diagnosis is posttraumatic stress disorder, with delayed onset. Although delayed onset is relatively uncommon (McFarlane & Yehuda, 1996, p. 159), it is not uncommon for a domino effect to occur in emergency medical workers where one event triggers other supposedly long-forgotten ones (van der Kolk & McFarlane, 1996, p. 9). As his social support system has given way at home, Ryan has become increasingly at risk, and the precipitating event of his wife's vehicular assault on a fellow police officer and his subsequent separation from his family has activated the traumatic memories.

Ryan is referred to a behavioral health maintenance organization for individual treatment and is also referred to an independent support group that is cosponsored by the police, fire, and emergency workers unions and the city and county governments. The police psychologist also makes an antisuicide contract with Ryan and contacts the human services worker who will be attending Ryan, to tell the worker about Ryan's suicidal ideation.

Triage Assessment.   Affectively, Ryan is experiencing extended periods of intense negative moods that are markedly stronger than the situation warrants. Although he has no clear intent or plan for committing suicide, he is agitated and depressed enough to consider it. At times he perceives his negative mood states as not being very controllable. His affective rating is 7 to 8. Cognitively, Ryan's thinking is generally equal to the task of moving forward in day-to-day living. However, his ability to control intrusive thoughts and images about the traumatic events is limited, and

his perception of events, particularly his obsessiveness about his daughters' safety, differs noticeably from the reality of the situation. His cognitive rating is 6 to 7. Behaviorally, Ryan's inability to function at work is noticeably affecting his job performance. His behavioral rating is 6 to 7. Ryan's full-scale triage ranges between 19 and 22. He is in crisis and in need of immediate therapeutic assistance.

Ryan's initial meeting with the human services worker involves carrying forward the antisuicide contract, obtaining a referral to a psychiatrist to review his medication, explaining what individual therapy will entail, and receiving an invitation to join a support group.

HSW: We've got some men and women that meet on Wednesday night to talk about many of the problems you're trying to deal with now. I think you've got a lot in common with them and believe it might be helpful for you to meet them. They've all been or are in the police, fire, or emergency departments and are trying to come to terms with their experiences there. You don't have to talk if you don't want to; that's up to you. You'll probably feel a lot of different emotions, and some of those aren't going to be too pleasant. However, all of the people you'll meet have been feeling a lot of the same kinds of things even though they may have different kinds of problems that brought them into the center. From that standpoint they all know what you're going through, and while it may get tough, they'll support you and not pass judgment. I'd really like to see you come in. You don't have to, but we know that social support is one of the most important ingredients to getting better, and right now it sounds like you could use some of that.

The group meets for an hour and a half each week. The first item is that individuals are asked to introduce themselves by name and unit. This structured event is not just for the purpose of getting into "war stories"; it serves to move men and women psychologically back in time and place to the starting point of their trauma and to cement the "we-ness" of the group. After introductions, anything on anybody's mind is fair game for conversation.

The group is composed of "veterans" who have been through many such sessions and "greenhorns" who are at their first meeting. Command officers are separated from rank-and-file members, so there are no possibilities of recriminations by command staff. Everything said in the group is confidential, and members indicate their willingness to abide by that rule by signing a statement to that effect. The groups are run by independent contractors who are not answerable to the city or county government about personnel decisions or any other matters that could put their clients' jobs at risk. Topics range from problems of day-to-day living to the institutions they work for, issues and questions about PTSD and trauma, replays of how and what they did during traumatic events, family and job issues, and how all these problems affect them.

The leaders of the group are two psychologists who have extensive experience with the police, firefighters, and EMTs. Although they have never served in any of those occupations, they have credibility because of their previous work with these groups, and that is critically important. Distrust and suspicion are strong in the early stage of such groups, and human services workers can be expected to be tested over and over again until they have proved themselves to be congruent and trustworthy (Gressard, 1986).

The leaders are not group therapists in the truest sense of the word. They are more like participatory members who have been endowed with the task of keeping the group within loose guidelines concerning time, monopolizing the group, facilitating support and responses from the other members, and, in a few extreme instances, acting as empathic but firm sergeants-at-arms. As leaders they must be willing to keep a low profile while group members interact. Their leadership role is subtle rather than directive and requires an infinite supply of patience as the group struggles toward resolution of its problems. If therapy in a classical sense of the word is to occur, it happens much later in the game. A clear distinction between the rap/support group and a long-term therapy group is that trauma and the expiation of associated guilt are the main focus, not life adjustment. Life adjustment problems represent another stage in the crisis of this malady and are handled later. The typical support group starts something like this:

HSW: Hi, everybody. We've got some new people here and because they don't know everybody I'd like you all to introduce yourself and your unit. I'm Theo Ewing, a psychologist. I work with the Crisis Intervention Team in the city police department.

Jane: Jane Shore, patrol officer, Delta shift, West Precinct, city. Age 21. (*Rookie on the force, training officer shot in a liquor store holdup. Robbers got away. Feels responsible, nightmares, startle reactions, hypervigilance, some paranoid ideation about abilities.*)

Leann: Leann Sung, EMT, RN, county hospital. Age 50. (*Twenty years' emergency room and ambulance duty, attendant at multiple disasters, catastrophes. Burned out,*

suicide attempt after caught stealing amphetamines from ER pharmacy, peptic ulcer, numbing of affect.)

Alonzo: Alonzo Brown, sheriff's deputy, Able shift, north sector, county. Age 42. (*Shot and killed carjacker after carjacker killed hostage by cutting her throat. First shooting, first violent deaths witnessed, nightmares, intrusive images, high blood pressure, alcohol abuse problem.*)

Lamont: Lamont Evans, paramedic, Life Flight. Age 29. (*Life Flight helicopter crashed and burned. He and other paramedic thrown clear. Everybody else died—including two auto accident victims being lifted to hospital. Survivor's guilt, hypervigilance, startle reactions, nightmares, wife has left, phobic reaction to helicopters since accident.*)

Rachelle: Rachelle Johnson, driver, Engine House 47, county fire department. Age 36. (*Saw wall collapse on two members of her engine company during warehouse fire. Helped pull both dead firefighters from rubble. One was her best friend. Nightmares, survivor's guilt, somatic and general anxiety reactions, eating disorder.*)

Ryan: Ryan Sanchez, patrol officer, Charlie shift, Center Precinct, city. (*Personal data previously given.*)

(*Introductions continue around the group and group welcomes Ryan.*)

HSW: Has anybody got anything that's hot?

Lamont: Well, two things. I haven't had any more helicopters crashing nightmares since last time; I guess that's something. And the wife said she might come back.

(*General congratulations from the group.*)

Rachelle: Man! That's something. I wish I could get rid of the damn things. None of those drugs are doing any good. I can't eat. I can't sleep. I don't know how much longer I can take it.

Jane: Ditto that! I can't get by it, and it seems to get worse.

Lamont: (*gently*) We've all been there and know how tough it is; you knew it'd get worse before it got better; we all told y'all that. It's hell. Y'all been talkin' to your counselors?

Because of the mutual support and resources within the group, lots of suggestions are given about how Rachelle and Jane can grapple with their emotional turmoil. Survivor's guilt is a common thread that runs through emergency, fire, and police personnel. The expectation is that these people are supposed to lay their lives on the line, and when others die or are injured there are always second-guessing and fears of being seen as letting their comrades down. Lamont's comments are therapeutic in that they are accepting and understanding of the guilt both women feel.

Rachelle: Yeah, I been talkin' to her. But it just seems like the more stuff comes up, the worse I feel. Why did they die and not me?

HSW: So it still boils down to the survivor's guilt stuff we've talked about. Lamont, Rachelle, and Jane have all talked about the same issues. (*The group leader takes a few minutes to speak to the typical behavioral dynamics of someone who has survived a trauma when others did not, which is typical of the psychoeducational function that is also a part of support groups.*) Any thoughts?

Jane: I've always wanted to be a cop, and I really thought I'd make a good one, but it's tough being a rookie and a woman at that. I've replayed that robbery a thousand times. I don't know what I could have done differently, and Loren, my training officer, told me I did fine. I'm glad he's gonna be all right, but I still think I screwed up somehow. Maybe I'm paranoid, but I'm not so sure the other cops on my shift trust me. Hell! I'm not so sure I trust myself.

Ryan: Well, I'm new here, so I don't know much, but I heard about that, and it sounded OK to me. What did you think you did wrong?

Jane: Well, that's what's driving me nuts. I don't think I did, but I think the others think I did.

Ryan: Well, if it's because you're a woman, lose that thought. I've got a female for a partner, and she's tops.

HSW: Jane, did you hear what Ryan said?

Jane: Yeah! And thanks.

The leader immediately breaks in so that two people get reinforcement—the newer member of the group for talking and Jane, who can use the affirmation from a male officer who is a veteran.

Alonzo: So what's happened to cause the change in you, Lamont?

Lamont: I'm not blaming myself as much. I still feel bad about the others that died, but I'm getting reconciled to it. I'm really lucky to be alive, and I've got to start working on putting my life back together. And I'm finally realizing that engine failure had nothing to do with Lamont. My counselor calls it *reframing,* kinda lookin' at it from a different viewpoint. I mean both of you were doing what you were supposed to be doing when those things went down. You can't ask more than that.

Alonzo: I wish I could "reframe" my problems that easy. I mean this crackhead carjacks this woman, practically cuts her head off in front of me. I've got no clear shot until he drops her, then I shoot him. Then the shoot team gives me a clouded report. Should have acted sooner, should have had more patience. How the hell do you do both of those at once? I did it all by the book. What that's all about? Then I get a wrongful death suit laid on me by both the victim and the murderer's families. It's not enough I feel bad about both of them, but now I'm the culprit. I'll never get rid of that image. And no damn support from the department. I've been a cop for 19 years, and if I can make it for one more year without having a stroke with this sky-high blood pressure, they can all kiss my ass good-bye. Why shouldn't I drink?

Leann: Yeah well, that's what they do, is use you up. Twenty years at county ER. I've seen it all. When I got caught swiping the speed, I'd been on for four straight shifts through four gun assaults and two knifings, three multiple-injury car accidents, and burn cases of five kids in an apartment fire. I was about to collapse. And I've done that over and over for all these years. And you know what, the ER supervisor who caught me said he could forget it if I could take just the one more shift, said he "knew I needed a pick-me-up." When I said no to that SOB, he turned me in. That's the sum total of my life, no family, a speed freak, a burned-out ER nurse with an ulcer, and a system that uses you up and then dumps you. So tell me why suicide doesn't look like a good career option. (*Starts to weep silently.*)

HSW: Are you still contemplating killing yourself, Leann?

In no uncertain terms, the leader immediately checks out Leann's comment. As she is a past attempter, such comments are never seen as offhand statements.

Leann: No, not really. It just makes me so angry that they'd do that. I told them about that jerk, but they still put me on disciplinary sick leave and didn't do a thing to that blackmailing twerp.

HSW: So it's also the system that you feel betrayed by. It's like after all these years of doing your very best, the system turns its back on you. Not only does it make you madder than hell, but at a deeper level it really hurts to think that somehow an institution that you've given most of your life to would not stick up for you when the chips were down or would even try and blackmail you. (*Leann and Alonzo both nod their heads vigorously in agreement.*)

Although it may appear that the support group has dissolved into a gripe session about uncaring bureaucracies, the stresses put on individuals by notoriously understaffed human services institutions and public safety departments add a great deal to the recipe for posttraumatic stress disorder when emergency situations occur (see Chapter 16, Human Service Workers in Crisis: Burnout, Vicarious Traumatization, and Compassion Fatigue). Expressing emotion is a potent weapon in the arsenal of opening feelings, which is critical in dealing with PTSD (Tarrier & Humphreys, 2003). The group leader reflects these feelings and gives the members a chance at catharsis, but also poses a problem-solving question.

HSW: I wonder what you might do about changing some of that institutional behavior?

Rachelle: I know one thing—if it hadn't been for the union's pushing for this kind of support and now the new debriefing program, we wouldn't be here now. There's got to be more safeguards for people who work in the high-stress jobs we do, and the only way I see that happening is through the union's collective membership. I think I'll talk to my rep about some of that stuff.

Alonzo: That's right! At least they can get all the certifiables in one place and keep an eye on us. (*Group laughs.*) I know how much that hurts, Leann, 'cause I feel the same way. But you gotta think of all you've done and all the lives you saved and the people you've helped. I'm pretty cynical right now, like you, but I had a person stop me the other day and thank me for something I did a long time ago, that he said kept him out of jail. I couldn't really even remember the incident it's been so long ago, but he sure did. It made me feel good. How many people out there do you suppose you've been involved with who wouldn't be alive now if you hadn't been there?

Alonzo, who has been vitriolic in ventilating his feelings, switches roles and becomes a support person to Leann. In mutual help groups such as this, such role shifts are common, and the need to become a helper rather than a beneficiary is extremely important (Silverman, 1986). Theo, the leader of the group, recognizes this shift and wisely lets Alonzo carry the dialogue.

Alonzo: Eh, ah, Ryan. What's happening with you, man?

Ryan: (*Details his problems.*) I mean, I like you guys and all, but I don't know that this group stuff will help much. I mean you can't fix my marriage, and all this other crazy PTSD stuff. I guess the shrink will sort that out. I just don't know.

Rachelle: I understand, Ryan, I haven't been here that long myself, but I'll tell you this much—these people understand what I'm going through. Maybe we can't save your marriage, but we can sure be here for you, 'cause these other folks have sure been here for me.

Rachelle's comment encapsulates the essence of why it is called a *support group*. As the group session closes, each member is given the floor to speak on what has occurred for him or her personally during the meeting. No one else is allowed to respond to his or her comments. Summing statements include both reflections about the impact of the discussion on oneself and reinforcing comments to others. Finally, the group rises, joins hands, and has a silent moment of meditation. The emotionally positive high voltage that flows through the locked hands of some very tough men and women is both touching and powerful, and it conveys far better than words the caring and support each man and woman feel for their comrades.

Evidence suggests that individuals who have suffered other types of catastrophic intrusion into their lives can profit from support groups. Donaldson and Gardner (1985) report that incest victims quickly gain an intense sense of relief in coming together with others in mutual support groups. A typical comment is "No one else understands, but I can come out of the closet here." Defining these groups at a deeper level is Foulkes's (1948) comment that participants in such support groups can reinforce each other's normal reactions and break down each other's pathological reactions because they collectively constitute the very norm from which the individuals deviate. As such, members of a veterans' rap group one of the authors has worked with have what one member called very good "crap detectors": "We can smell it immediately when somebody isn't coming clean with us."

The Life Adjustment Group

PTSD may be seen as having a two-generation, or two-phase, treatment approach. In the first generation, treatment focuses on accessing and working through the trauma and its symptoms. Although this will be difficult, the second generation of treatment may be even more so. In the second generation, treatment moves to the client's attempts to readjust to contemporary society, which will generally not be an easy task (Johnson, Feldman, & Southwick, 1994).

As the guilt and horror of the situation are resolved, clients are moved into the life adjustment group, and another crisis ensues. It is not enough to bring to light hidden traumatic experiences. The key is to integrate past experiences, to find meaning and new ways of coping, to make atonement not only for oneself but for others, and to find new directions in life (Brende & Parson, 1985, pp. 199–201). The group at this point will diminish and absences will increase. The reason is twofold.

First, threatening material will again be covered. Second, action and behavioral change now become mandatory. Moving from the insight gained about what happened in the past to taking that insight and applying it to the present time is a giant step, and one that is guaranteed to be rife with crisis. What is now called for is to get on with the business of living. At this juncture, intervention will take many forms, depending on what the particular problems are that the individual faces. Such problems range from maintaining sobriety to salvaging careers. However, one thread will usually run through the circumstances of all clients at this stage. That thread is of vital importance and must be rewoven into the fabric of their lives. It is their family. Any comprehensive PTSD treatment program should take into consideration the need to reestablish the basic support system of the family, which is of critical importance in helping the survivor move forward in his or her posttraumatic world. Getting family members to open up and express some of their beliefs that influence the client's negative coping behaviors is scary for both the individual and the family; they may believe that discussing their posttraumatic problems would cause so much trouble that the family would disintegrate even though it may presently be in complete chaos (Tarrier & Humphreys, 2003).

Family Treatment

If the trauma is unresolved and chronic, its residue will eventually become enmeshed in the individual's interpersonal network (Figley, 1988, p. 91). As reluctant as the survivor of trauma may be to seek help, often the family is even more unwilling to participate in the recovery process (Solomon, 1986). Even though family members may be suffering terribly because of the individual's actions toward them and their respondent actions toward the individual and each other, they offer much resistance to changing the status quo, even though they adamantly maintain that change is needed. As strange as it may seem, although families may be stressed to the limit in adapting to the PTSD individual, they do try to adapt, at times in pathological ways. As the individual changes, the family may be in for a rude awakening and may not be able to make parallel changes.

Therefore, one of the crisis worker's major tasks is assessing the family's willingness to engage in treatment. The family's ability to resolve the crisis is a function of the nature of the event, the family's definition of the event, the resources they can bring to bear on it, the buildup of stressors that led to the event, and the effectiveness of their past and current coping skills (McCubbin et al., 1980).

Treatment objectives are to develop and implement an intervention program to deal with both the stress disorder of the individual and assorted family dysfunctions that were in place prior to the event or that developed after the event. Learning about the disorder, dealing with the boundary distortions of intimacy and separation caused by it, alleviating psychosomatic results of rage and grief, urging recapitulation of the

trauma, facilitating resolution of the trauma-inducing family conflicts, clarifying insights and correcting distortions by placing blame and credit more objectively, offering new and more positive and accurate perspectives on the trauma, establishing and maintaining new skills and rules of family communication, and initiating new coping and adapting skills as family dynamics change are some of the many tasks the worker will have to tackle (Figley, 1988, pp. 86–88).

The foregoing list of tasks is a major order and is best dealt with by referral to a therapist who specializes in families and conjoint therapy. However, it is practically a must if the family has any hope of survival as a healthy system. The crisis worker should understand that at an early point in the therapeutic process, the family members need to be apprised of their role in the trauma and urged to become proactive in its solution. Finally, for the PTSD individuals, relearning how to be effective members of their families and society calls for the same kind of courage that propelled them into treatment in the first place. However, this time it may be much more difficult, because they will be working with the people they need the most and probably have hurt the most. If outcomes of the family component of the Comprehensive Soldier Fitness program are good, we see no reason why they could not be adapted to other workers in high-risk, high-stress civilian occupations.

Eye Movement Desensitization and Reprocessing (EMDR)
The Controversy Over EMDR

Eye movement desensitization and reprocessing (EMDR) is, to say the least, controversial. The basic technique of EMDR is to have the person picture the traumatic scene in his or her mind or think about the thoughts or feelings associated with the trauma while following the therapist's finger with his or her eyes as it is moved rapidly back in forth in front of the person's face. Newer approaches employ flashing lights that move across the vision field and handheld buzzers that alternate in speed and strength in sending impulses to the client's hands. The procedure is so simplistic and is extolled as so fast and effective in comparison to combinatorial approaches using cognitive behavior and exposure techniques that it has been viewed with skepticism—particularly because PTSD is so intractable that there are as many failures as successes in treating the disorder. However, a number of replicating studies (Carlson et al., 1998; Korn & Leeds, 2002; Lamprecht et al., 2004; Lee et al., 2002; Maxfield, 2002; Scheck, Schaeffer, & Gillette, 1998) do show significant results for EMDR when compared with other treatment modalities. At present there is no clear scientific explanation of what it does to erase trauma. The hypotheses proposed as to why and how it works mainly revolve around dual processing/focus of attention (if you do two things at once you aren't going to be able to pay attention to both nearly as well as one) or distancing (becoming more detached as you try to process the event while keeping some other activity going on) (Bradley et al., 2005; Issacs, 2004; Lee, Taylor, & Drummond, 2006). Other studies (Cahill, Carrigan, & Frueh, 1999; Cusack & Spates, 1999; Devilly & Spence, 1999; Devilly, Spence, & Rapee, 1998; Renfrey & Spates, 1994), however, have not found such stunning results, and reviews of the research on the theory and efficacy of EMDR have been extremely critical (Lee, Gavriel, & Richards, 1996; Muris & Merckelbach, 1999a, 1999b; Rosen, 1999). Even more startling, studies have found that moving one's eyes back and forth, as opposed to doing some other body movement, doesn't really matter (Bériault & Larivée, 2005)!

The controversy that has raged around this technique has been one of the most lively—if not the liveliest—in therapy in the last decade. Gist, Woodall, and Magenheimer (1999) have been particularly vitriolic in their attacks on it and the other "alphabet" therapies such as thought field therapy (TFT), emotional freedom techniques (EFT), and traumatic incident reduction (TIR), naming an article about them "And Then You Do the Hokey Pokey and You Turn Yourself Around . . ." and offering a great deal of support and rationale to make their case that these techniques are nothing more than pseudoscience wrapped in the cloak of postmodernism.

So, then, why use something that a lot of professionals think is snake oil? There are two major reasons. First, it does seem to work with some people, and not just as a placebo! Your authors have used EMDR with some very cynical, objective, hard-nosed, empirically oriented health service professionals, and they have been absolutely incredulous that the intrusive images have changed and the thoughts and feelings surrounding those traumatic images have diminished. Yet with some clients it doesn't work at all!

Second, it is far less intrusive than the cognitive-behavioral therapies that have prolonged exposure as their core treatment element. Bryant and Harvey (2000) warn that exposure therapy should not be used or used with extreme caution when treating clients with anxiety or panic attacks, psychosis, severe depression or suicide risk, substance abuse, borderline personality, marked dissociation, or marked ongoing stressors—which would include most people who have PTSD! At this point, from our experience using it, we agree with Briere & Scott (2006, p. 146) that EMDR appears to be at least as effective in treatment of simple PTSD as the cognitive-behavioral approaches and a lot less noxious, but may run into problems with more complex PTSD. From the standpoint of client welfare, convenience, ease of use, and cost in time and money, it is at least worth a try as a first-order treatment. Given these precautionary statements, here are the basics of EMDR therapy.

EMDR Therapy

Eye movement desensitization (EMD) was developed by Francine Shapiro (1989a, 1989b) at the Mental Research Institute in Palo Alto, California. Shapiro (1991) later added the "R" to the acronym to indicate a reprocessing of information, along with changing to more positive cognitions and desensitization of the traumatic memory. According to Shapiro (1995, pp. 55–73; Shapiro & Maxfield, 2002), there are eight basic treatment components to EMDR: history taking and treatment planning, preparation, assessment, desensitization, installation, body scan, closure, and reevaluation.

History Taking and Treatment Planning.

Initially, clients are evaluated for their ability to handle the high levels of disturbance that may occur with treatment. A comprehensive clinical picture of the client is obtained, and a determination is made of the specific targets to be reprocessed; these targets include past events, current stimuli that trigger symptoms, and positive attitudes and behaviors needed for the future (Shapiro, 1995, p. 68; Shapiro & Maxfield, 2002).

HSW: (*to Ryan*) It appears that at least three events from your past are predominant: the propane truck, the dead body of the missing girl, and the young woman in the auto accident who died in your arms. It also seems that the re-emergence of all these traumatic work events occurred closely after your wife, in a fit of jealous rage, attempted to run down the female officer. The constant theme that emerges from all of these events is that you feel powerless, frustrated, and angry, but were and are paralyzed to do much about these events because of a variety of social and job prohibitions and your own moral stand. It appears that at least three triggers set these flashbacks and anxiety attacks off: propane trucks, yellow rental trucks, and verbal battles with your wife—particularly over custody and safety of your daughters.

Preparation. Preparation for therapy entails explaining to the client what is going to happen, the effects that can be expected, and safety procedures. Shapiro also makes a point of discussing secondary gain issues. That is, if the therapy is successful and the pathology is reduced, what will the client have to give up (Shapiro, 1995, p. 69)? Although this may seem strange, a veteran may not want to lose his or her disability payments or "wounded warrior" status if the PTSD is eradicated.

Assessment. Shapiro (1989a, 1989b, 1995; Shapiro & Maxfield, 2002) proposes that EMDR treats traumatic memory by requiring that the client maintain awareness in one or more of the following: (1) an image of the memory, (2) a negative self-statement or assessment of the trauma, and (3) the physical anxiety response. Once the memory is identified, the client is asked to choose the image that best fits it along with a negative cognition and the chief physical response that goes with it. Although Shapiro (1989a, 1989b, 1995; Shapiro & Maxfield, 2002) proposes that it is optimal when all three conditions are held at the same time, she maintains that the presence of any one is sufficient for desensitization to occur.

Ryan: (*generating images*) I'm standing on the freeway overpass looking down on a scene from Dante's *Inferno*. It looks like a war zone. There are burning wrecks everywhere. I can see blackened bodies. Some are still alive. There are paramedics and firemen and other rescue workers all covered with soot. I can smell burned rubber and flesh. I can hear lots of moans and cries for help and shouting. I can feel the heat coming up out of the freeway on my face and arms. Sometimes when I come upon a propane truck, it all comes back like that. That's why I avoid them if at all possible. (*generating negative self-statements*) I'm powerless. I need to be down there, but I'm not sure I can take it. I've never seen anything like this. I'm a coward. I hate myself for feeling that way. (*generating physical anxiety response*) My skin feels like it's been sandpapered. Every nerve in my body is on fire. I want to run, down there or away, but do something. I can't stand just watching it all.

Anxiety level is assessed by Wolpe's (1982) Subjective Units of Discomfort (SUDs) scale (0 = no anxiety; 10 = highest anxiety possible). Because negative self-cognitions are also part of the disorder, shifts in the client's cognitive view of the traumatic event are also assessed by a Validity of Cognition (VOC) scale that Shapiro (1989a)

developed (1 = the cognition is completely untrue to 7 = the cognition is completely true). Clients are asked to rate themselves on the SUDs and VOC and indicate the physical location of the symptoms (Shapiro, 1989a, 1989b, 1995, p. 70; Shapiro & Maxfield, 2002).

Ryan: The SUDs is way beyond 10. The VOC is 7.

Clients are next asked how they would like to feel and are told to generate a new positive self-statement that reflects the desired feeling (Shapiro, 1989a, 1989b, 1995; Shapiro & Maxfield, 2002).

Ryan: Like I'm in control. I'm not a coward. Not necessarily a hero.

Clients are then asked to judge how true that new statement is (Shapiro, 1989a, 1989b).

Ryan: A generous VOC for that would be 2.

Desensitization. Shapiro (1989b) then gives the client a standard set of instructions designed to diminish performance anxiety and performance demands. She indicates that this step is important because clients may have difficulty accepting the initial changes they feel in themselves. Her instructions are as follows:

What we will be doing is often a physiology check. I need to know from you exactly what is going on, with as clear feedback as possible. Sometimes things will change and sometimes they won't. I may ask you if the picture changes—sometimes it will and sometimes it won't. I may ask if something else comes up—sometimes it will and sometimes it won't. There are no "supposed to's" in this process. So just give as accurate feedback as you can as to what is happening, without judging whether it should be happening or not. Just let whatever happens, happen. (p. 213)

Clients are then told to generate the scene, the negative statements, and their noxious feelings and visually track the human services worker's finger. The therapist's finger is moved rapidly and rhythmically back and forth, about one foot from the client's face, at approximately two back-and-forth movements per second with a sweep of about 12 inches across the client's field of vision. For clients who may have trouble with this approach, Shapiro uses a slightly different format in which the therapist's fingers are to the side of the client's vision field and are alternately moved up and down. The movement is repeated 12 to 24 times for one set. (This is called a *saccade*, which means a sort of pulling or pressing movement.)

After each set of saccades, clients are asked to erase the scene from their minds and take a deep breath. They are then asked to bring up the noxious image again and ascribe a SUDs level to it. If the SUDs level has not changed after two sets of saccades, the client is asked if the picture has changed or if anything new has come into the image. If so, the new image is desensitized before returning to the old image. Periodically, clients are asked to assess the image, cognition, and memory. Their answers are used to determine new insights, perceptions, or alterations.

Ryan: (*after two saccades*) I dunno. It's not as strong now or something. Maybe an 8. It's like it's moving, or I'm moving. I'm not frozen.

HSW: OK. See yourself moving, and put that "I'm not helpless, I'm moving and taking control" billboard under that picture. Can you think of that?

Ryan: Yeah. It's also like I'm frustrated or angry too now.

HSW: That's OK! New images and thoughts come into this. That's normal. We'll work those through too.

The therapist continues to attack the client's image, but this time has him insert the "I'm a coward" billboard into the scene until it too is diminished and changed to a more positive self-statement. The therapist continues eye movements and processes with Ryan until he reports a SUDs level of 1.

Installation. The idea of the installation phase is to install a new, positive cognition of the event. The installation phase starts once the client's SUDs rating has dropped to a 1 or 0. Ryan has changed his image, and the therapist will continue to pursue this until there are no longer additions to the emotional meaning of the image or there is no longer additional positive input.

Ryan: OK! I'm equal to this. I could handle it down there, but my job is up here coordinating things. I'm where I can do my best.

Note that the cognition is not kept in a negative sense, "I'm not a coward," but is put positively and proactively. While the client focuses on the target image and the new positive cognitions, the eye movements are continued until the client can report a VOC for the new positive thoughts at a level of 6 or 7. If the cognition fails to change after two sets of eye movements, there may be a mismatch between the cognition and the image, or vice versa. In each case, both image and cognition must be congruent with one another. If they are not, then one or the other needs to be replaced (Shapiro, 1989a, 1989b, 1995, p. 71).

Body Scan. After the positive cognition has been fully installed, clients are instructed to think of a physical location of anxiety in their body if the SUDs level remains high. They are asked to concentrate on the body sensation while new saccades are given. When the focal point of physical discomfort subsides, clients are asked to return to the original picture of the trauma and the standard EMDR procedure is resumed (Shapiro, 1989a, 1989b). Shapiro believes there is a physical resonance between the body and dysfunctional material. She believes this phase is important because it can uncover new areas of unprocessed or unthought-of material (Shapiro, 1995, p. 730; Shapiro & Maxfield, 2002).

Ryan: I wish I could jump out of my skin, I'm so anxious. It feels like it's burning from the inside out.

HSW: OK, I want you to focus in on your skin. Feel the burning sensation. (*Starts and finishes another saccade.*)

Ryan: (*after two more saccades*) Huh. It's kinda gone now. That's really weird!

Closure. When no new events or negative cognitions are elicited, the EMDR procedure is terminated. The client is never left in a state of emotional disequilibrium, whether reprocessing for the event is done or not. The client is debriefed and reminded that additional intrusive images that may arise after the session are a positive sign of additional processing. Shapiro (1995, p. 73) also recommends that clients keep a journal of their thoughts, situations, dreams, and other information that may come to mind about the memory. This information can be used to target new images at the next session.

Reevaluation. At each new session an assessment is made of the previous targets. The client is asked to reaccess previous reprocessed targets, and the client's journal is examined for any intrusion of the previously examined material.

Ryan: It's weird. That image of the propane truck explosion is just kinda vague or misty or something. I decided to drive by a bulk plant that I always avoid. It's right on my way to my folks' house. Well, I decided to hell with it, let's see. Usually I'd think I was going to have a panic attack the last couple of months if I went near it. But I drove by it, and it was just a bulk plant. Nothing more! Didn't feel a thing! Fancy that!

In subsequent sessions the therapist may successively move through images of the propane truck, the body in the closet, the father of the murdered girl in the rental truck, and the scenes with Ryan's estranged wife. However, if the target and the triggers are well worked out, generalization of effect can occur and positive benefits accrue in other areas of the client's life (Shapiro, 1989a, 1989b, 1995, p. 74; Shapiro & Maxfield, 2002).

Children and PTSD

For a long time prevailing wisdom was that young children were not developmentally mature enough to be affected by trauma and as a result couldn't "catch" PTSD (Bosquet, 2004; Osofsky, 1995). If anything, their reaction to disasters would be fleeting. However, with growing research in the field we now know that is anything but true (Devoe et al., 2011; Osofsky et al., 2010). Of the 74 million children in the United States, 30 to 50 percent will experience at least one traumatic event by their 18th birthday and will probably comprise a substantial proportion of the 2.5 billion people who have suffered some kind of disaster in the last decade (Kazdin, 2008). Trauma for children is also homegrown, with about 1 million cases of substantiated child abuse in the United States reported yearly (deAngelis, 2007).

Of those who experience at least one trauma, somewhere between 3 and 16 percent of girls and between 1 and 6 percent of boys will develop PTSD. What type of trauma children experience makes a big difference. Almost 100 percent of children will get PTSD if they see a parent killed or sexually assaulted. Approximately 90 percent of sexually abused children will develop PTSD. Around 77 percent of children who witness a school shooting experience PTSD, and even witnessing neighborhood violence has a "catch" rate of about 35 percent (National Center for PTSD, 2011).

It shouldn't take a Ph.D. in child psychology to figure out that PTSD and its treatment are different in children by the mere fact of their developmental levels (Saxe, Ellis, & Kapow, 2007). Indeed, PTSD manifests itself very differently in children than in adults in terms of symptoms (DeAngelis, 2007; Terr, 1979, 1981, 1983, 1995) and in how it affects the neurodevelopment of children (Saxe, Ellis, & Kalow, 2007, pp. 23–45). Thus, not only because of their age but also because of how children attempt to cognitively handle trauma, PTSD in children calls for treatment strategies that are very different from those used with adults (Clay, 2010; Cohen, Mannarino, & Deblinger, 2006; Malchiodi, 2008; Saxe, Ellis, & Kaplow, 2007; Webb, 2007).

Therefore, we agree with a number of respected researchers and practitioners that the *DSM-IV-R* criteria for PTSD no longer captures the essence of or fits the criteria of what PTSD, and especially complex PTSD, is in most children. For example, the current *DSM-IV-TR* criterion requiring a verbal description of a subjective mood state makes it an unsound diagnostic criterion for young children due to their developmental inability to verbalize what is happening to them (Scheering & Gaensauer, 2000). A more apt criterion would be that generated by Evangelista and McLellan (2004), who view the reexperiencing and avoidance symptoms more behaviorally through nightmares, developmental regression, and toxic play, along with additional symptom clusters of fears and aggression. In light of some of these issues, Allan Kazdin, former president of the American Psychological Association, appointed a task force to identify what contribution research has made to understanding the effects of PTSD in youth, identify what treatment programs work, and make recommendations on research directions and public policy (Kazdin, 2008).

Support Systems

By now you should clearly understand that support systems are critical in crisis intervention. Supportive family systems are even more critical for children in their attempts to master a trauma (Cohen, Mannarino, & Deblinger, 2006; Courtois & Ford, 2009; Devoe et al., 2011; Saxe, Ellis, & Kapow, 2007; Yule, 1998). Family support systems are important in regard to events both external and internal to the family system. Generally in this chapter we are speaking of family support in the context of a traumatic event that occurs external to the family, such as a hurricane or 9/11. We will speak to family support (or lack thereof) when the trauma is generated within the family, as in child abuse, in Chapter 9, Sexual Assault.

Bowlby's (1982) attachment theory is particularly relevant to traumatized children. In many of the traumas children experience, they are separated from their parents, their homes, and even their communities without warning or preparation. It should come as no surprise that such traumatic separation carries with it a smorgasbord of emotional and personality disturbance. Anxiety disorders, physical maladies, depression, panic attacks, rage reactions, and phobic reactions are common comorbid disorders of childhood PTSD. These are magnified even more when families are rent asunder by a traumatic event and support systems literally disappear in front of the child's eyes (Gordon, Farberow, & Maida, 1999; Halpern & Tramontin, 2007; Norris et al., 2002) and are even more profound when the young child perceives a threat to the caregiver (Devoe et al., 2011). The final ingredient in this witch's brew of pathology is the unresolved grieving that accompanies loss of loved ones when children do not yet have the cognitive ability to understand and resolve their loss (Cohen, Mannarino, & Deblinger, 2006; Gordon, Farberow, & Maida, 1999; Halpern & Tramontin, 2007; Yule, 1998).

Types of Trauma

Childhood trauma is important not only for what it does to children, but also for the aftereffects that carry into adulthood (Morgan et al., 2003). Terr (1995, p. 302) likens childhood trauma to rheumatic fever. Although rheumatic fever is a serious disease of childhood, the damage it causes can later be lethal in adults in a variety of ways. Childhood trauma operates in the same way and can lead to character problems, anxiety disorders, psychotic thinking, dissociation, eating disorders, increased risk of violence by others and by oneself, suicidal ideation and behavior, drug abuse, self-mutilation, and disastrous interpersonal relationships in adulthood (Pynoos, Steinberg, & Goenjian, 1996, pp. 331–352; Terr, 1995).

Terr (1995, p. 303) proposes a division of childhood trauma into two categories: Type I, which is one sudden, distinct traumatic experience; and Type II (analogous to complex PTSD), which is long-standing and comes from repeated traumatic ordeals. Lack of full cognitive and moral development causes distinctive differences in how children react to trauma. It appears that even infants have the capacity to remember traumatic experiences (Courtois & Ford, 2009; Hopkins & King, 1994). Children who suffer from Type I traumas appear to exhibit certain symptoms and signs that differentiate their condition from those that result from more complicated Type II traumas. Type I events are characterized by fully detailed, etched-in memories, omens such as retrospective rumination, cognitive reappraisals, reasons, misperceptions, and mistiming of the event (Terr, 1995, p. 309).

In contrast, Type II traumas result in the psyche's developing defensive and coping strategies to ward off the repeated assaults on its integrity. Massive denial, psychic numbing, repression, dissociation, self-anesthesia, self-hypnosis, identification with the aggressor, and aggression turned against self are prominent. Emotions generated from Type II traumas are an absence of feeling and a sense of rage and/or unremitting sadness. These symptoms may be diagnosed in childhood as conduct disorders, attention-span deficit disorders, depressive disorders, or dissociative disorders (Terr, 1995, pp. 311–312).

Terr's (1983) in-depth, 4-year follow-up on children who were victims of the Chowchilla, California, bus kidnapping is the benchmark study in childhood PTSD. The victims of this trauma were a group of 26 elementary and high school children who were kidnapped together with their school bus driver, were carried about in vans for 11 hours by their kidnappers, and were buried alive in a truck trailer for 18 hours before they dug their way out—a horrific Type I trauma.

Etched Memories

Terr (1983) found that the children still had specific feelings of traumatic anxiety over the event after 4 years. When asked to speak about it, children generalized their anxiety from the event to statements like "I'm afraid of the feeling of being afraid." Unlike combat veterans, who might boast about harrowing experiences, the children were profoundly embarrassed by their experience, were unwilling to talk about the event, and shied away from any publicity. They generally voiced feelings of being humiliated and mortified when asked about their experience. Although 8 of 15 children had overcome their fear of vehicles such as vans and buses, they still reported occasional panic attacks triggered by unexpected sudden confrontation with stimuli such as seeing a van parked across the street from their house and vaguely wondering if some of the kidnappers' friends had come back for them.

Eighteen of the children were found to employ suppression or conscious avoidance of the trauma. Parents often aided them in this endeavor, although the two children whose parents encouraged them to talk about the experience were still not spared its residual effects. Their typical response was that they hated the feeling of helplessness they experienced and needed to feel in control of the situation. All the children could remember almost every second and minute of the event. However, they were able to remember few, if any, of the emotions or behaviors they experienced during the ordeal. This remarkable retrieval of full, precise verbal memories of almost all Type I traumas indicates that these memories are indelibly etched into the psyche, no matter how the child tries to suppress them, and are carried forward into adulthood (Terr, 1995, p. 309).

Memory etching may also come from vicariously viewing trauma. Saylor and associates (2003) found that children who saw images of death or injury from the attacks of 9/11 reported more PTSD symptoms than children who did not. Interestingly, the Internet had a more profound effect than television or print media. No measurable benefit was reported in seeing positive or heroic images of 9/11.

Developmental Issues

Trauma may have severe repercussions on developmental expectations and acquisition of developmental competencies in children (Ford, 2009; Pynoos, Steinberg, & Goenjian, 1996). When traumatic events impact a child in the middle of a developmental stage or in transition from one to the next, regressive behaviors occur (Gordon, Farberow, & Maida, 1999). Eth and Pynoos (1985, p. 44) believe that continuous intrusion of a traumatic event, evolution of a cognitive style of forgetting, and interference with mental processes because of depressed affect very definitely influence school achievement. Children who experience trauma are likely to have problems with "narrative coherence"—the ability to organize material into a beginning, a middle, and an end. This inability to organize a linear story has direct repercussions on reading, writing, and communicative ability (Pynoos, Steinberg, & Goenjian, 1996, p. 342).

Early childhood PTSD is marked by general personality traits that include mood instability, difficulty delaying gratification, withdrawal from or obsessive attention seeking, attention deficit and task completion problems, and oppositional defiance (Manly et al., 2001). Toddlers specifically demonstrate nonverbal attempts to communicate fears and anxiety. Continuous crying, screaming tantrums, excessive clinging, immobility with trembling, frightened expressions, and either running toward the adult or aimless motion. Regression to thumb sucking, bed wetting, loss of bowel and bladder control, a variety of fears, night terrors, sleeping with a light on or an adult present, marked sensitivity to loud noises, speech difficulties, and eating problems may occur (Gordon, Farberow, & Maida, 1999). These symptoms are indicative of the effect survival-threatening stressors can have in rupturing the early attachment bonds that are so critical to development (Ford, 2009, p. 47).

Fears and anxiety continue to predominate in elementary school children, as do the previously mentioned regressive behaviors. School problems also emerge and range from outright refusal to go to school to poor academic performance, fighting, and loss of ability to concentrate (Gordon, Farberow, & Maida, 1999). Trauma may cause anxious attachment to caretakers and separation anxiety. The child regresses socially, which can result in poor affiliation with peers, social isolation, and avoidance of school. Parents may exacerbate this behavior because of their own unresolved fears of the traumatic event, and may become overprotective of the child. Conversely, memories in which the primary caretaker was either unable or unwilling to provide help and succor during the traumatic event do severe harm to the developmental expectation that the caregiver is capable of providing nurturance and security (Pynoos, Steinberg, & Goenjian, 1996, pp. 340–345). A constellation of behavioral problems may appear, such as depression, panic and anxiety attacks, conduct and impulse control disorders, eating and sleep disorders, and sexual identity issues (Cook et al., 2005).

Adolescents who experience trauma invariably find disruption in their peer relationships and their school life. Peers who were not traumatized may shun them because of their "weird" behavior and not know how to offer support. Any outward physical problems may exacerbate their fragile self-concept and ability to fit into the peer group. Behavioral trouble signs include withdrawal and isolation, antisocial behavior, awareness of their own mortality, suicidal ideation, academic failure, alcohol and drug abuse, sleep disturbance, night terrors, depression, mental confusion, school failure, truancy, problems with the legal system, gang involvement, teen pregnancy, and various physical complaints (Ford et al., 2008; Gordon, Farberow, & Maida, 1999; Halpern & Tramontin, 2007).

Other Responses to Type I Trauma

Sense of a Foreshortened Future. Terr (1983) found that intrusive thoughts did not repeatedly enter the children's conscious thoughts; however, sleep brought very different problems. Whereas a few reported daydreams, more children had nightmares through which ran many repetitious themes of death. The children believed these dreams to be highly predictive of the future and made comments such as "I'm 11 now, but I don't think I'll live very long, maybe 12, 'cause somebody will come along and shoot me." Adolescents in particular are brought face to face with their own vulnerability and, in the case of those who have experienced the murder of a parent, report that they will never marry or have children because they fear history will be repeated (Cohen, Mannarino, & Deblinger, 2006, p. 9; Eth & Pynoos, 1985, p. 48; Terr, 1995, p. 308).

Reenactment.   In an attempt to gain mastery over a Type I trauma, children replay the event and develop a reason or purpose for it. Once the reason is found, children often feel intensely guilty about it. "I should have listened to what Mom said and come home right after school!" In Type I traumas the question is, "How could I have avoided that?" as opposed to the question of Type II traumas, "How will I avoid it the next time?" (Terr, 1995, p. 310).

The play of children with PTSD is very distinctive because of its thematic quality, longevity, dangerousness, intensity, contagiousness for siblings, and unconscious linkage to the traumatic event (Maclean, 1977; Terr, 1981). The clearly prevalent dynamic is a continuing reenactment of the children's plight during the trauma (Eth & Pynoos, 1985, p. 42). This thematic play can be characterized as burdened, constricted, and joyless (Wallerstein & Kelly, 1975). Traumatic play is also problematic because it replaces normal developmental play that is a vital component in childhood maturation (Parker & Gottman, 1989). For adolescents, reenactment may take the form of delinquent behavior (Eth & Pynoos, 1985, p. 47), ranging from truancy, sexual activity, and theft to reckless driving, drug abuse, and obtaining weapons (Newman, 1976).

Physical Responses.   Approximately half the children in the Chowchilla kidnapping manifested physical problems that could be construed to be related to the trauma of being held prisoner without food, water, or bathroom access (Terr, 1983). In young children suffering from PTSD, regression may occur and previously learned skills such as toilet training may have to be retaught (Bloch, Silber, & Perry, 1956). Sleep disturbances and severe startle responses can cause a variety of educational and social problems in school (Pynoos, Steinberg, & Goenjian, 1996, p. 350).

Displacement.   In the Chowchilla survivors, a great deal of displacement of affect occurred, with emotions about the event being shifted to a related time, an associated idea, or another person—particularly the interviewing psychiatrist. Prior to the follow-up interviews, children displayed a variety of displaced behaviors, including the belief by one of the children that the psychiatrist had placed notes posing questions about the kidnapping in her school locker (Terr, 1983).

Transposition.   Misperceptions, visual hallucinations, and peculiar time distortions often occur in children who have experienced Type I traumas—as opposed to Type II traumas, in which the perpetrators and events have a long history with the children and are rarely misperceived once the events are brought to awareness (Terr, 1995, p. 311). In the Chowchilla survivors, one of the most profound changes occurred in transposition of events surrounding the trauma. Events that happened after the trauma were remembered as having happened before the trauma (Terr, 1983). Also, there was a general belief that the traumatic events were predictive of what was about to happen to them. Ayalon (1983), in a study of victims of terrorism, found a similar effect in children. Children attempted to resolve their vulnerability and lack of control by saying they should have listened to the omens and "shouldn't have stepped in the bad luck square." In PTSD, such distortions of time become part of the child's developing personality and are attempts to take personal responsibility and even feel guilty for events over which they had no control.

Terr's (1983) study indicates that whereas children behave differently from adults in their attempt to resolve the traumatic event, they are no more flexible or adaptable than adults after a trauma, and it would be erroneous to assume that they "just grow out of the event." Furthermore, these children did not become toughened by their experience, but simply narrowed their sphere of influence in very restrictive ways to control their environment better.

Type II Traumas

Children who have suffered continued physical and sexual abuse and refugee children from war-torn countries are typical victims of Type II traumas. They are poster children for the affective dysregulation that goes with complex PTSD. Massive denial and psychic numbing are primarily associated with Type II traumas. These children avoid talking about themselves, go years without talking about their ordeals, and try to look as normal as they can. If they do tell their stories, they may later deny they did. This aspect is quite different from Type I children, who tell their stories over and over again. Denial may become so complete that Type II children will forget whole spans of their childhood (Terr, 1995, p. 312). Type II children are indifferent to pain, lack empathy, fail to define or acknowledge feelings, and absolutely avoid psychological intimacy. In adulthood, this massive denial cuts across narcissistic, antisocial, borderline, and avoidant personality disorders (Terr, 1995, p. 313). Although self-hypnosis and dissociation in Type II children may take the form of dissociation identity disorders (formerly known as multiple personality disorder) in adulthood, such children most often develop anesthesia to pain and to sex and emotionally distance themselves in the extreme (Terr, 1995, p. 314). That does not mean the rage at what happened to them is not there. Rage includes anger turned inward against the self and outward toward others and can range from self-mutilation to murder. Reenactments of anger occur so frequently in Type II traumas that habitual patterns of aggression are formed, and the seething anger is probably as debilitating as the chronic numbing. Paradoxically, defenses may be formed, whereby the child becomes completely passive or identifies with the aggressor (Terr, 1995, p. 315).

At times crossover changes from Type I to Type II traumas may occur, as when a single event such as an accident that requires long-term hospitalization and many painful operations turns into a Type II trauma. Children who come out of Type I traumas with permanent physical handicaps, disfigurement, long-term pain, or loss of significant others may be forced into adaptational techniques of Type II traumas but still retain clear and vivid memories of the event. Children who are physically injured or disfigured and suffer psychic trauma tend to perpetually mourn their old selves and may employ regression, denial, guilt, shame, and rage over their disabilities (Terr, 1995, p. 316). When traumatic shock interferes with the normal course of bereavement, unresolved grief continues, and the child becomes a candidate for a major depressive disorder (Terr, 1995, pp. 316–317).

A variety of problems that have to do with how a traumatized child looks, acts, feels, and thinks may promote secondary stressors in his or her social milieu (Pynoos, Steinberg, & Goenjian, 1996, p. 341). Communicable disease, altered physical appearance, social distancing, memory impairment, decreased intellectual functioning, guilt, and shame are a few of the problems that can follow in the wake of a trauma. All these problems may present very different before-and-after pictures of the child and alter perceptions by family, peers, and teachers to the detriment of the child.

These negative response patterns are then additive to the initial trauma and present additional psychological burdens to adaptation.

Intervention Strategies

The methods of assessment and therapy used with children are different from those used for adults. Early assessment is critical in determining the potential for trauma (Terr, 1979, 1981, 1983) and should happen as soon as possible after the event (Mowbray, 1988, p. 206). Generally, assessment needs to occur in two complementary areas: trauma-specific issues and generic behavioral issues. While we are interested in isolating specific traumatic events and their effects, focusing on them may miss more general issues of depression or behavior problems.

Interviewing. There is some evidence that allowing children to talk about their experience in an interview format also helps in reducing long-term symptoms of PTSD (Nader, 1997, p. 293). However, parent resistance may be severe, and interviewers should carefully explain to both the parents and the child what the purpose of the interview is and how it is going to be done. Interviewing should involve determining the degree and severity of exposure to trauma and assessing the child's response as it relates to the degree of exposure (Pynoos & Nader, 1988).

Pynoos, Steinberg, and Goenjian (1996, pp. 336–337) suggest that more precise rather than general features of the traumatic experience be elicited, such as hearing unanswered screams for assistance, smelling bad odors, being close to the threat, being trapped, witnessing atrocities, and remembering the degree of brutality and other specific traumatic conditions. Given the targeting of what will probably be very traumatizing material, the crisis worker needs to proceed in as patient, caring, and empathic a way as possible.

Because children's reports may be affected by fear of disclosure, shame, guilt, and other negative attributions, it is also important to get corroboration from parents or other significant adults about the trauma.

Instruments. Because of the need to systematically measure the response of children to trauma, a number of instruments specifically designed for children have been developed. The Trauma Symptom Checklist for Young Children is a caregiver rating for children ages 3–12. It has validity scales and measures a variety of posttraumatic responses plus sexual concerns, anxiety, depression, dissociation, and anger/aggression (Briere, 2005). The Clinician-Administered PTSD Scale for Children (CAPS-C) (Nader et al., 1994) is a comprehensive children's version of the adult CAPS. It measures standard PTSD symptoms plus symptoms of childhood PTSD. It further determines social and scholastic functioning, along with how well the child is coping with the event. The Diagnostic Interview for Children and Adolescents–Revised (DICA-R; Reich, Shayka, & Taibleson, 1991) is a widely used semi-structured interview to assess common psychiatric diagnoses and includes a PTSD subscale. Briere (1996) has also developed a self-report checklist for children, which covers anxiety, depression, anger, posttraumatic stress, sexual concerns, and dissociation. It has an alternate form that leaves out sexual concerns. The Trauma Symptom Inventory (Briere, 1995) is useful for older adolescents who tend to act out their distress. It also has two validity scales that assess under- and overendorsement in rating items. The Child PTSD Symptom Scale has been developed to assess the severity of PTSD in children exposed to trauma (Foa et al., 2001). Finally, the Child Behavior Checklist is a widely used scale that has parents, teacher, and youth self-report forms. This test looks at both external issues such as behavior problems and internal issues such as anxiety and depression, as well as how resilient children are at adapting to stressors (Achenbach, 1991). These and other interview schedules typically use variations of Likert scales (least-to-most numeric ratings) to measure the amount of trauma experienced or currently present.

Projective Techniques. Because children submerge their affect and parents are loath to deal with the trauma until it causes severe repercussions in their lives, children are rarely brought in for counseling until behavior has reached crisis proportions (Mowbray, 1988, p. 206). Triage assessment at this time may not reveal that trauma is the underlying agent. In that regard, the crisis worker who works with children should have a good knowledge of both projective and question-and-answer personality inventories that will ferret out the trauma. A classic example is the artwork of sexually abused children whose drawings are replete with exaggerated genitalia (Kaufman & Wohl, 1992).

Therapy

Treatment of PTSD directed specifically to children falls into two main categories: cognitive-behavioral therapy and play therapy. EMDR may also be used in combination with or exclusive of cognitive-behavioral or play therapy. Also of critical importance is building a caring and supportive social context (Saxe, Ellis, & Kaplow, 2007), as discussed in Chapter 9, Sexual Assault.

Cognitive-Behavioral Therapy. The International Society for Traumatic Stress Studies (1997) proposes cognitive-behavioral therapy as the treatment of choice for children (Amaya-Jackson et al., 2003; Cohen, Mannarino, & Deblinger, 2006; Herpertz-Dahlmann, Hahn, & Hempt, 2005; Meiser-Stedman, 2002; Neubauer, Deblinger, & Sieger, 2007; Silva et al., 2003). Although Saigh (1987) has reported success using flooding techniques with school-age children, it should be strongly emphasized that this is a *hazardous* procedure for children and may exacerbate symptoms. A more benign and controlled approach is the use of desensitization procedures that alternate between relaxing the child and presenting scenes of the trauma that are progressively enhanced to their full florid detail. This is a stepwise procedure that makes small approximations toward exposing the child to the total traumatic event. The key to this approach is that the child can be immediately removed from the noxious image and transferred to a safe, calm, tranquil scene.

Any cognitive-behavioral therapy should give the child a sense of empowerment and control. Relaxation techniques, cognitive restructuring, stress inoculation, anger management, desensitization, and any other behavioral or cognitive-behavioral techniques should be paced *at the child's speed*. A good deal of discussion with the child and the caretakers about what is going to occur, how the child has the power and control over what will be included, and providing adequate time for processing, debriefing, and follow-up should all be a part of the therapeutic regimen (Cohen, Mannarino, & Deblinger, 2006; Deblinger & Heflin, 1996; Gordon, Farberow, & Maida, 1999).

Play Therapy. Creative arts and play therapy have considerable merit and can be efficacious with PTSD in children (Gordon, Farberow, & Maida, 1999; Johnson, 2000b; Malchiodi, 2008; Webb, 2007). Play therapy generally falls into two distinct categories: directive, which is collaborative and interactive between the child and the interventionist; and nondirective, which is child centered and interventionist passive. However, nondirective play therapy may be ill advised because restitutive play becomes increasingly destructive and serves only to increase anxieties that are allowed to go ungoverned (Terr, 1979). We believe a safer approach to reenacting the trauma is to involve the interventionist collaboratively using a variety of play therapy techniques (Gordon, Farberow, & Maida, 1999; Landreth, 1987; Malchiodi, 2008) that include artwork (Drucker, 2001; Loumeau-May, 2008), puppets (Carter, 1987; James & Myer, 1987), sand play (Allan & Berry, 1987; Bethel & Oates, 2007; Vinturella & James, 1987; Zarzaur, 2005), dance (Johnson, 2000a), poetry (Gladding, 1987), writing (Brand, 1987), music (Bowman, 1987; Hilliard, 2008), bibliotherapy (Malchiodi & Ginns-Gruenberg, 2008), computer art (Johnson, 1987), storytelling (White, 2005), and drama (Haen, 2008; Irwin, 1987), as well as drawing the traumatic event and telling a story about it (Chapman et al., 2001; Eth & Pynoos, 1985, p. 37; James, 2003; Schreier et al., 2005). Play therapy is also a nonthreatening way to involve parents in the therapeutic intervention with children who have had trauma exposure (Cattanach, 2008; Haen, 2008; Echterling & Stewart, 2008; Steele & Malchiodi, 2008). All these techniques may be controlled and paced by the therapist in consideration of the psychological safety of the child.

The overarching reason for any of the foregoing techniques is to take the global, nebulous, uncontrollable chaos of the crisis event and make it into a concrete, real object that the child can gain a sense of control over. Play therapy would seem efficacious because it enables the therapist to enter the trauma on the child's cognitive terms, reduce the threat of the trauma, establish trust, and determine the child's current means of coping and ways of defending against the trauma (Gumaer, 1984). Play therapy is a safe exposure technique that allows clients (including adults) to integrate their traumatic memories into active consciousness without the fear of reactivating the sensory trauma demons they are so afraid of letting resurface (Steele & Raider, 2001). Furthermore, as thematic trauma-related play subsides and more socially appropriate play reappears, this is an excellent assessment device for determining how well treatment is proceeding. We will examine three very different cases of how play therapy is used with children in Chapter 9, Sexual Assault; Chapter 13, Crises in Schools; and Chapter 17, Disaster Response.

EMDR. EMDR seems to be effective with children in symptom reduction of PTSD (Adúriz, Bluthgen, & Knopfler, 2011; Chemtob, Nakashima, & Carlson, 2002; Oras, de Ezpeleta, & Ahmad, 2004; Tufnell, 2005). Shapiro (1995, pp. 276–281) indicates a number of special considerations for using EMDR, especially with young children. First, the worker must give special consideration to safety concerns. Although Shapiro does not believe parents should attend the session with the child, she does believe parents should brief the worker with the child present. Then the parent should leave and allow the child to present his or her version. This two-step sequence allows the parents' authority to be transferred to the worker and also gives the child a sense of being special when the worker's attention is focused exclusively on him or her.

For children, average EMDR sessions should be no longer than 45 minutes, with eye movements interspersed with other activities. Because children do not have the cognitive ability to conceptualize SUDs units, more concrete representations of the degree of discomfort need to be devised. Holding a hand close to the floor can represent a "little" hurt, while holding a hand at shoulder height can represent a much "bigger" hurt. Because most children are familiar with the workings of a body thermometer, we have used pictorial representations of a thermometer to let children indicate how much discomfort they are feeling.

Because play is such an integral part of a child's world, eye exercises can be accomplished more easily by drawing puppets on the worker's fingers or using finger puppets to perform the saccades. Creativity in helping the child "bring up the picture" is important, so sound effects such as starting an engine or "blowing up the picture" with a loud explosion can involve the children at their experiential level. Installing new, positive cognitions needs to be simplified. "I'm fine" or "I'm safe" may be highly appropriate because of their simplicity and straightforwardness for young children.

Artwork may also be effective in helping to concretize the memory. Having the child draw the event and then hold the picture in his or her mind while eye exercises are conducted gives the child a concrete way of visualizing the memory. Shapiro (1995) reports that (much as in Gumaer's [1984] method of serial drawing to determine if treatment is effective) when the child is asked to redraw the event after successive eye movements, the intensity of the event as depicted in the drawings is likely to diminish.

Moving Beyond the Trauma

We understand that reading this long introductory chapter into the trench warfare of typical crisis events has been pretty grim and maybe even depressing. Therefore, we want to finish with what we believe is some light at the end of the tunnel. So don't give up! One way survivors move from the tightly wrapped intrapersonal world of agony they have lived in to a more self-actualized and healthy interpersonal focus is to use their experience to help other victims (Lifton, 1973, pp. 99–133). Listen to two Vietnam veterans, one a volunteer and one a professional in the human services field.

Jim: I'm in the group not because of what happened in Nam. I'm pretty much through that. A year's worth of the VA and some excellent help from other people got me over being nuts. I'm here because I owe those folks and maybe, I'm not sure how, to pay some back for what I got.

George: Why did I become a social worker at the vet center? Because I'd been in Nam, hassled with my own stuff, and thought I knew something about it and could help other people. Frankly, I think I've done about all I can here, and I believe I'm ready to start something else professionally. I'm going back to school and would like to concentrate on working with kids.

For both these men, the ghosts of PTSD have been exorcised. They have integrated all aspects of the traumatic experience, both the positive and the negative. They know pretty clearly who they were before, during, and after the event. They have accepted responsibility for their own actions, as imperfect as those actions may have been at the time, and have made atonement for any guilt they carried (Scurfield, 1985, p. 246). They epitomize the full meaning of the Chinese characters for *crisis* that represent both danger and opportunity. Yet, do these two tough and resilient combat veterans represent what really happens to people with PTSD? Do the Chinese characters really represent what happens to most people, or can they ever climb out of the sump hole of PTSD? Tedeschi and Calhoun (1995) believe so and have formulated the concept of posttraumatic growth to characterize the personal positive changes that can come out of individuals' struggle with trauma.

Their evolving model (Tedeschi & McNally, 2011) has five components: First, trauma survivors need to understand the negative aspects of PTSD, especially one's shaken assumptions about oneself, others, and the future. They should also understand that the physiological and psychological responses are *normal* reactions to traumatic experiences. (We take some exception to the use of the word "normal" as a way of toning down the very nasty responses people have to trauma. To our mind, there is nothing remotely "normal" about it. It is about as abnormal as one can get without becoming psychotic. Therefore, we prefer to use the term "common" to denote that it is anything but pleasant, but is about what almost everybody can expect to happen.)

Second, leaning to gain emotional regulation over intrusive thoughts and images allows the sympathetic nervous system to calm down and let people start to engage in effective rumination over the trauma rather than brooding over it. Third is constructive self-disclosure that does not harp on the trauma or its symptoms but, by telling the story to others, unravels the cognitive and emotional tangles that go with the trauma, forms new relationships and bonds, and reconciles the past with the deceased who may have been part of the original trauma.

Fourth is creating a trauma narrative out of self-disclosure that understands the paradoxes of how loss and gain, gaining control and giving up control, and vulnerability and strength are not mutually exclusive. By doing so, individuals begin to build new structures of their personality that are based on personal strength, enhanced relationships with other, spiritual change, appreciation of life, and zest for new opportunities. Finally, Tedeschi and McNally (2011) propose that the end point (or the beginning, for that matter) is to see the trauma as a positive, life-transforming experience that involves becoming more charitable to oneself and others, accepting growth from the traumatic event without guilt, understanding that the experience has transformed oneself in ways others may not be able to comprehend, and becoming a person more in tune and empathic with the human condition and the spiritual aspects that go with it.

Studies are finding that people do indeed grow from traumatic experiences and that positive posttraumatic growth does occur and may even be underestimated (Hefferon, Grealy, & Mutrie, 2009; Lechner & Weaver, 2009; Rosner & Powell, 2006; Smith & Cook, 2004). For those who have PTSD and for those who treat it, that is heartening research.

SUMMARY

Posttraumatic stress disorder (PTSD) has probably been in existence as long as humankind has been rational enough to personalize the disasters that assail us. However, it was the debacle of the Vietnam War that brought PTSD enough publicity to become a classifiable malady. The psychologically virulent milieu that was the Vietnam War became a breeding ground for trauma, which found its way back to the United States in an estimated 960,000 service personnel who have PTSD or related disorders.

PTSD has multiple symptoms and for that reason is often confused with a variety of other disorders. Its basis is maladaptive adjustment to a traumatic event. The disorder is both acute and chronic. In its chronic form it is insidious and may take months or years to appear. Its symptoms include, but are not limited to, anxiety, depression, substance abuse, hypervigilance, eating disorders, intrusive-repetitive thoughts, sleep disturbance, somatic problems, poor social relationships, suicidal ideation, and denial and affective numbing of the traumatic event. Both natural and human-made disasters may be responsible for PTSD, but it is far more likely to occur in individuals who have been exposed to some human-made disaster that should have been prevented and is beyond accepted moral and societal bounds.

Slow to recognize the disorder, human services professionals did little to ameliorate problems returning Vietnam veterans suffered. Self-help groups were started by veterans when they had no other place to turn. Through lobbying efforts by such men, Vietnam Veterans Centers were set up throughout the United States. Along with other mental health professionals who had been grappling with the problems of veterans and other victims of trauma, staffers at the centers began doing research and developing treatment approaches for PTSD. Those research and treatment approaches have spread out to civilian areas of trauma, and much common ground is being found between war-related and civilian-related traumatic events. Recent research on the psychobiological aspects of PTSD is uncovering a great deal of the intricate interplay between traumatic events and the brain's physiological responses to them. Contemporary treatment includes both group and individual intervention that is multimodal and considers psychological, biological, and social bases as equally important. The United States Army is currently putting in place a comprehensive program that attempts to provide psychological fitness to soldiers to inoculate them against PTSD and other emotional disorders that go with combat.

Children are not immune to PTSD, and they do not just "grow out of it." If PTSD has taught the human services one thing, it is that no traumatic experience should ever be dismissed in a cursory manner and that any initial assessment of a crisis client should investigate the possibility of a traumatic event buried somewhere in the client's past. Assessment and intervention are particularly difficult when the traumatic event is of a familial or sexual nature. A great deal of finesse and skill is necessary to uncover and treat such problems because of clients' reluctance to talk about socially taboo subjects or the feeling that a person should have the intestinal fortitude to bear up under the trauma. From what we now know, the latter assumption is patently false; under the right circumstances, anyone can fall victim to PTSD.

There are a couple of books that we think can be helpful to you if you are going to get into or are already in the PTSD business. They are both focused on the military, but could surely be adapted for civilian use. The first is the *Clinician's Guide to Treating Stress After War: Education and Coping Interventions for Veterans* (Whealin, DeCarvalho, & Vega, 2008) and *The Veterans and Active Duty Military Psychotherapy Treatment Planner* (Moore, & Jongsma, 2009). These books have lots of useful tips and worksheets that can be adapted for use with most anyone who has PTSD.

 To see some of the concepts discussed in this chapter in action, refer to your *Crisis Intervention in Action* DVD, or see the clips online on the Counseling CourseMate website. To access this site, go to www.cengagebrain.com, where you'll also find an eBook, additional study tools, quizzes, and more. Put yourself in the place of Paul, the mobile crisis worker. Based on what you now know, and hindsight being 20/20, how might you handle the drunk veteran differently? Once you have him safe and sober, then what?

REFERENCES

Aarts, P. G., & Op den Velde, W. (1996). Prior traumatization and the process of aging. In B. A. van der Kolk, A. C. McFarlane, & L. Weisaeth (Eds.), *Traumatic stress* (pp. 359–377). New York: Guilford Press.

Achenbach, T. M. (1991). *Manual for the Child Behavior Checklist/4-18 and 1991 Profile.* Burlington, VT: University of Vermont, Department of Psychiatry.

Ackerman, P., Newton, J., McPherson, B., Jones, J., & Dykman, R. (1998). Prevalence of posttraumatic stress disorder and other psychiatric diagnoses in three groups of abused children (sexual, physical, and both). *Child Abuse and Neglect, 22*(8), 759–774.

Adúriz, M., Bluthgen, C., & Knopfler, C. (2011). Helping child flood victims using EMDR intervention in Argentina: Treatment outcome and gender differences. *International Perspective in Psychology, Research, Practice, Consultation 1*(S), 58–67.

Allan, J., & Berry, P. (1987). Sandplay. *Elementary School Guidance & Counseling, 21,* 300–306.

Amaya-Jackson, L., Reynolds, V., Murray, M., McCarthy, G., Nelson, A., & Cherney, M., et al. (2003). Cognitive behavioral treatment for pediatric posttraumatic stress disorder: Protocol and application in school and community settings. *Cognitive & Behavioral Practice, 10*(3), 204–213.

American Psychiatric Association. (1980). *Diagnostic and statistical manual of mental disorders* (3rd ed.). Washington, DC: Author.

American Psychiatric Association. (2000). *Diagnostic and statistical manual of mental disorders* (4th ed., Text Revision). Washington, DC: Author.

Archibald, H. C., Long, D. M., Miller, C., & Tuddenham, R. D. (1962). Gross stress reaction in combat—A 15-year follow-up. *American Journal of Psychiatry, 119,* 317–322.

Armistead-Jehle, P., Johnston, S. L., Wade, N. G., & Ecklund, C. J. (2011). Posttraumatic stress in U.S. Marines: The role of unit cohesion and combat exposure. *Journal of Counseling & Development, 89*(1), 81–88.

Astur, R. S., Germain, S., Tolin, D., Ford, J., Russell, D., & Stevens, S. (2006). Hippocampus function predicts severity of post-traumatic stress disorder. *Cyber Psychology & Behavior, 9*(2), 234–240.

Atkinson, R. M., Sparr, L. F., & Sheff, A. G. (1984). Diagnosis of posttraumatic stress disorder in Vietnam veterans: Preliminary findings. *American Journal of Psychiatry, 141,* 694–696.

Ayalon, O. (1983). Coping with terrorism. In D. Meichenbaum & M. Jaremko (Eds.), *Stress reduction and prevention.* New York: Plenum Press.

Baker, D. G., Risbrough, V. B., & Schork, N. J. (2008). Posttraumatic stress disorder: Genetic and environmental risk factors. In B. J. Lukey & V. Tepe (Eds.), *Biobehavioral resilience to stress* (pp. 177–218). Boca Raton, FL: CRC Press, Taylor & Francis Group.

Balson, P., & Dempster, C. (1980). Treatment of war neurosis from Vietnam. *Comprehensive Psychiatry, 21,* 167–176.

Barnes, V. A., Davis, H. M., & Treiber, F. A. (2007). Perceived stress, heart rate, and blood pressure among adolescents with family members deployed in Operation Iraqi Freedom. *Military Medicine, 172,* 40–43.

Benson, H. (1976). *The relaxation response.* New York: Avon.

Berglund, R. (1985). *The fabric of the mind.* Victoria: Penguin Books Australia.

Bériault, M., & Larivée, S. (2005). Guérir avec L'EMDR: Preuves et controverses. *Revue de Psychoéducation 34*(2), 355–396.

Bernstein, A. (1986). The treatment of noncompliance in patients with posttraumatic stress disorder. *Psychosomatic Medicine, 27,* 37–40.

Bethel, B. I., & Oates, J. (2007, March). *The untold story of the Beverly Hillbillies.* Thirty-first Annual Convening of Crisis Intervention Personnel and the CONTACT USA Conference, Chicago.

Bierens de Haan, B. (1998). Le débriefing émotionnel collectif des intervenants humanitaires: L'expérience du CICR. *Schweizer Archiv für Neurologie und Psychiatrie, 149*(5), 218–228.

Bigot, T., & Ferrand, I. (1998). Individualologie de la prise d'otage: Etude auprès de 29 individuelles. *Annales Médico Psychologiques, 156*(1), 22–27.

Blake, D. D., Weathers, F., Nagy, L. M., Kaloupek, D. G., Klauminzer, G., Charney, D. S., et al. (1990). A clinician rating scale for assessing current and lifetime PTSD: The CAPS-1. *Behavior Therapist, 13,* 187–188.

Bloch, D. A., Silber, E., & Perry, S. E. (1956). Some factors in the emotional reaction of children to disaster. *American Journal of Psychiatry, 113,* 416–422.

Bosquet, M. (2004). How research informs clinical work with traumatized young children. In J. D. Osofsky (Ed.), *Young children and trauma: Intervention and treatment* (pp. 301–325). New York: Guilford Press.

Bower, G. H. (1981). Mood and memory. *American Psychologist, 36,* 129–148.

Bowlby, J. (1982). *Attachment and loss: Vol. 1. Attachment* (2nd ed.). New York: Basic Books.

Bowman, R. P. (1987). Approaches for counseling children through music. *Elementary School Guidance & Counseling, 21,* 284–291.

Bradley, R. G., Green, J., Russ, E., Dutra, L., & Westen, D. (2005). A multidimensional analysis of psychotherapy for PTSD. *American Journal of Psychiatry, 162,* 214–227.

Brand, A. G. (1987). Writing as counseling. *Elementary School Guidance & Counseling, 21,* 266–275.

Bremner, J. D., Krystal, J. H., Southwick, S. M., & Charney, D. S. (1995). Functional neuroanatomical correlates of the effects of stress on memory. *Journal of Traumatic Stress, 8,* 527–550.

Bremner, J. D., Randall, P. K., Scott, T. M., Bronen, R. A., Seibyl, J. P., Southwick, S. M., et al. (1997). Magnetic resonance imaging based measurement of hippocampal volume in posttraumatic stress disorder related to childhood physical and sexual abuse: A preliminary report. *Biological Psychiatry, 41*(1), 23–32.

Brende, J. O., & Parson, E. R. (1985). *Vietnam veterans: The road to recovery.* New York: Plenum Press.

Brenner, L. A., Vanderploeg, R. D., & Terro, H. (2009). Assessment and diagnosis of mild traumatic brain injury, posttraumatic stress disorder, and other polytrauma conditions: Burden of adversity hypothesis. *Rehabilitation Psychology, 54*, 239–246.

Breuer, J., & Freud, S. (1955). Studies on hysteria. In J. Strachey (Ed. & Trans.), *The standard edition of the complete psychological works of Sigmund Freud* (Vol. 2, pp. 1–10). London: Hogarth Press. (Original work published 1895)

Brewi, B. (Speaker). (1986). *Crisis intervention with the Vietnam veteran* (Cassette recording No. 9). Memphis, TN: Department of Counseling and Personnel Services, Memphis State University.

Brewin, C. (2003). *Posttraumatic stress disorder: Myth or malady?* New Haven, CT: Yale University Press.

Brewin, C. (2005). Risk factor effect sizes in PTSD: What this means for intervention. *Journal of Trauma & Dissociation, 6*(2), 123–130.

Briere, J. (1995). *Trauma Symptom Inventory.* Odessa, FL: Psychological Assessment Resources.

Briere, J. (1996). *Trauma Checklist for Children.* Odessa, FL: Psychological Assessment Resources.

Briere, J. (2005). *Trauma Checklist for Young Children.* Odessa, FL: Psychological Assessment Resources.

Briere, J., & Scott, C. (2006*). Principles of trauma therapy: A guide to symptoms, evaluation, and treatment.* Thousand Oaks, CA: Sage.

Brom, D., Kleber, R. J., & Defares, P. B. (1989). Brief psychotherapy for posttraumatic stress disorders. *Journal of Consulting and Clinical Psychology, 57*, 607–612.

Bryant, R., & Harvery, A. (2000). *Acute stress disorder: A handbook of theory, assessment and treatment.* Washington, DC: American Psychological Association.

Bryant, R., Moulds, M., Guthrie, R., Dang, S., & Nixon, R. (2003). Imaginal exposure alone and imaginal exposure with cognitive restructuring in treatment of posttraumatic stress disorder. *Journal of Consulting & Clinical Psychology 71*(4), 706–712.

Burgess-Watson, I. P., Hoffman, L., & Wilson, G. V. (1988). The neuropsychiatry of post-traumatic stress disorder. *British Journal of Psychiatry, 152*, 164–173.

Cahill, S., Carrigan, M., & Frueh, C. (1999). Does EMDR work? And if so, why? *Journal of Anxiety Disorders, 13*(1–2), 5–33.

Carlson, J., Chemtob, C., Rusnak, K., Hedlund, L., & Muraoka, M. (1998). Eye movement desensitization and reprocessing (EMDR) treatment for combat-related posttraumatic stress disorder. *Journal of Traumatic Stress, 11*(1), 3–24.

Carter, S. R. (1987). Use of puppets to treat traumatic grief. *Elementary School Guidance & Counseling, 21*, 210–215.

Casey, G. W. (2011). Comprehensive soldier fitness: A vision for psychological resilience in the U.S. Army. *American Psychologist, 66*(1), 1–3.

Cattanach, A. (2008). Working creatively with children and their families after trauma: The storied life. In C. A. Malchiodi (Ed.), *Creative interventions with traumatized children* (pp. 211–225). New York: Guilford Press.

Chandra, A., Burns, R. M., Tanielian, T., Jaycox, L. H., Tanielian, T., & Scott, M. M. (2008). *Understanding the impact of deployment on children and families: Findings from a pilot study of Operation Purple Camp participants* (Working paper). Santa Monica, CA: Rand Corporation.

Chapman, L., Morabito, D., Ladakakos, C., Schreier, H., & Knudson, M. (2001). The effectiveness of art therapy interventions in reducing posttraumatic stress disorder (PTSD) symptoms in pediatric trauma patients. *Art Therapy, 18*(2), 100–104.

Chemtob, C., Nakashima, J., & Carlson, J. (2002). Brief treatment for elementary school children with disaster-related posttraumatic stress disorder: A field study. *Journal of Clinical Psychology, 58*(1), 99–112.

Chu, J. (1999). Trauma and suicide. In D. G. Jacobs (Ed.), *The Harvard Medical School guide to suicide assessment and intervention* (pp. 332–354). San Francisco: Jossey-Bass.

Cienfuegos, A. J., & Monelli, O. (1983). The testimony of political repression as a therapeutic instrument. *American Journal of Orthopsychiatry, 53*, 43–51.

Clay, R. C. (2010). Treating traumatized children. *Monitor on Psychology, 41*(7), 36–39

Cohen, A. (2002). Gestalt therapy and post-traumatic stress disorder: The potential and its (lack of) fulfillment. *Gestalt!, 6*(1), 21–28.

Cohen, A. (2003). Gestalt therapy and post traumatic stress disorder: The irony and the challenge. *Gestalt Review, 7*(1), 42–55.

Cohen, J. L., Mannarino, A. P., & Deblinger, E. (2006). *Treating trauma and traumatic grief in children and adolescents.* New York: Guilford Press.

Cook, S., Pinazzola, J., Ford, J. D., Lanktreee, C., Blaustein, M., Cloitre, M., et al. (2005). Complex trauma in children and adolescents. *Psychiatric Annals, 35*, 390–398.

Copeland, N. J. (2000). Brain mechanisms and neurotransmitters. In D. Nutt, J. Davidson, & J. Zohar (Eds.), *Posttraumatic stress disorder: Diagnosis, management, and treatment* (pp. 69–100). London: Martin Dunitz.

Corneil, W., Beaton, R., Murphy, S., Johnson, C., & Pike, K. (1999). Exposure to traumatic incidents and prevalence of posttraumatic stress symptomatology in urban firefighters in two countries. *Journal of Occupational Health Psychology, 4*(2), 131–141.

Courtois, C. A., & Ford, J. D. (2009). *Treating complex traumatic stress disorders: An evidence-based guide.* New York: Guilford Press.

Courtois, C. A., Ford, J. D., & Cloitre, M. (2009). Best practices in psychotherapy for adults. In C. A. Courtois & J. D. Ford (Eds.), *Treating complex traumatic stress disorders: An evidence-based guide* (pp. 82–101). New York: Guilford Press.

Cusack, K., & Spates, R. (1999). The cognitive dismantling of eye movement desensitization and reprocessing (EMDR) treatment of posttraumatic stress disorder. *Journal of Anxiety Disorders, 13*(1–2), 87–99.

Darves-Bornoz, J. M., Lepine, J. P., Choquet, M., Berger, C., Degiovanni, A., & Gaillard, P. (1998). Predictive factors of chronic post-traumatic stress disorder in rape individuals. *European Psychiatry, 13*, 281–287.

Davidson, J. R., & van der Kolk, B. A. (1996). The psychopharmacological treatment of posttraumatic stress disorder. In B. A. van der Kolk, A. C. McFarlane, & L. Weisaeth (Eds.), *Traumatic stress* (pp. 510–524). New York: Guilford Press.

Davis, J. L., De Arellano, M., Falsetti, S. A., & Resnick, H. S. (2003). Treatment of nightmares related to post-traumatic stress disorder in an adolescent rape individual. *Clinical Case Studies, 2*(4), 283–294.

DeAngelis, T. (2007). A new diagnosis for childhood trauma. *Monitor on Psychology, 38*(3), 32–33.

Deblinger, E., & Heflin, A. H. (1996). *Cognitive behavioral interventions for treating sexually abused children.* Thousand Oaks, CA: Sage.

Devilly, G., & Spence, S. (1999). The relative efficacy and treatment distress of EMDR and a cognitive behavior trauma treatment protocol in the amelioration of posttraumatic stress disorder. *Journal of Anxiety Disorders, 13*(1/2), 131–157.

Devilly, G., Spence, S., & Rapee, R. (1998). Statistical and reliable change with eye movement desensitization and reprocessing: Treating trauma in a veteran population. *Behavior Therapy, 29*(3), 435–455.

Devoe, E. R., Bannon, W., Klein, T., & Miranda-Julian, C. (2011). Young children in the aftermath of the World Trade Center attack. *Psychological Theory, Trauma, Research, Practice, and Policy, 3*(1), 1–7.

DeVries, M. (1996). Trauma in cultural perspective. In B. A. van der Kolk, A. C. McFarlane, & L. Weisaeth (Eds.), *Traumatic stress* (pp. 398–413). New York: Guilford Press.

Donaldson, M. A., & Gardner, R., Jr. (1985). Diagnosis and treatment of traumatic stress among women after childhood incest. In C. R. Figley (Ed.), *Trauma and its wake: The study of post-trauma stress disorder* (pp. 356–377). New York: Brunner/Mazel.

Donnelly, C. (2003). Pharmacologic treatment approaches for children and adolescents with posttraumatic stress disorder. *Child & Adolescent Psychiatric Clinics of North America, 12*(2), 251–269.

Dreisbach, V. (2003). Post-traumatic stress disorder in fire and rescue personnel. *Journal of American Academy of Psychiatry & Law, 31*(1), 120–123.

Drucker, K. (2001). Why can't she control herself? A case study. In J. Murphy (Ed.), *Art therapy with young survivors of sexual abuse: Lost for words* (pp. 101–125). New York: Brunner-Routledge.

Echterling, L. G., & Stewart, A. (2008). Creative crisis intervention techniques with children and families. In C. A. Malchiodi (Ed.), *Creative interventions with traumatized children* (pp. 189–210). New York: Guilford Press.

Egendorf, A. (1975). A Vietnam veteran rap group and themes of post-war life. *Journal of Social Issues, 31*, 111–124.

Ehlers, A., Clark, D., Hackman, A., McManus, F., & Fennel, L. (2005). Cognitive therapy for post-traumatic stress disorder: Development and evaluation. *Behaviour Research and Therapy, 43*(4), 413–431.

Elklit, A., & Brink, O. (2004). Acute stress disorder as a predictor of post-traumatic stress disorder in physical assault individuals. *Journal of Interpersonal Violence 19*(6), 709–726.

Engel, R. C., Gallagher, L. B., & Lyle, D. S. (2010). Military deployments and children's academic achievement: Evidence from Department of Defense education activity schools. *Economics of Education Review, 29*, 73–82.

Epstein, R., Fullerton, C., & Ursano, R. (1998). Posttraumatic stress disorder following an air disaster: A prospective study. *American Journal of Psychiatry, 155*(7), 934–938.

Erikson, E. (1968). *Identity, youth, and crisis.* New York: Norton.

Eth, S., & Pynoos, R. S. (1985). Developmental perspective on psychic trauma in childhood. In C. R. Figley (Ed.), *Trauma and its wake: The study of post-trauma stress disorder* (pp. 36–52). New York: Brunner/Mazel.

Evangelista, N., & McLellan, M. (2004). The zero to three diagnostic system: A framework for considering emotional and behavioral problems in young children. *School Psychology Review, 33*(1), 159–173.

Evans, B. (2003). Hypnosis for post-traumatic stress disorders. *Australian Journal of Clinical & Experimental Hypnosis, 31*(1), 54–73.

Evans, L., McHugh, T., Hopwood, M., & Watt, C. (2003). Chronic posttraumatic stress disorder and family functioning of Vietnam veterans and their partners. *Australian and New Zealand Journal of Psychiatry, 37*(6), 765–772.

Fairbank, J. A., & Keane, T. M. (1982). Flooding for combat-related stress disorders: Assessment of anxiety reduction across traumatic memories. *Behavior Therapy, 13*, 499–510.

Feeny, N., Hembree, E., & Zoellner, L. (2003). Myths regarding exposure therapy for PTSD. *Cognitive & Behavioral Practice, 10*(1), 85–90.

Fichtner, C., Podding, B., & deVito, R. (2000). Posttraumatic stress disorder: Pathophysiological aspects and pharmacological approaches to treatment. In K. Palmer (Ed.), *Pharmacotherapy of anxiety disorders* (pp. 61–92). Hong Kong: Adis International Publications.

Figley, C. R. (Ed.). (1978). *Stress disorder among Vietnam veterans*. New York: Brunner/Mazel.

Figley, C. R. (1985a). From individual to survivor: Social responsibility in the wake of catastrophe. In C. R. Figley (Ed.), *Trauma and its wake: The study of post-trauma stress disorder* (pp. 398–416). New York: Brunner/Mazel.

Figley, C. R. (Ed.). (1985b). *Trauma and its wake: The study of post-trauma stress disorder*. New York: Brunner/Mazel.

Figley, C. R. (1988). Post-traumatic family therapy. In F. M. Ochberg (Ed.), *Posttraumatic therapy and individuals of violence* (pp. 83–113). New York: Brunner/Mazel.

Figley, C. R. (1989) *Helping traumatized families*. San Francisco: Jossey-Bass.

Figley, C. R. (Speaker). (1990). *Posttraumatic stress disorder: Managing bad memories in individuals and family systems* (National teleconference). Tallahassee: Florida State University, School of Social Work.

Figley, C. R. (2002). *Treating compassion fatigue*. New York: Brunner-Routledge.

Filteau, M., Leblanc, J., & Bouchard, R. (2003). Quetiapine reduces flashbacks in chronic posttraumatic stress disorder. *Canadian Journal of Psychiatry, 48*(4), 282–283.

Flack, W., Litz, B., Weathers, F., & Beaudreau, S. (2002). Assessment and diagnosis of PTSD in adults: A comprehensive psychological approach. In M. Williams & J. Sommer (Eds.), *Simple and complex post-traumatic stress disorder: Strategies for comprehensive treatment in clinical practice* (pp. 9–22). Binghamton, NY: Haworth Press.

Flake, E. M., Davis, B. E., Johnson, P. L., & Middleton, L. S. (2009). The psychosocial effects of deployment on military children. *Journal of Developmental and Behavioral Pediatrics, 30*, 271–278.

Foa, E., Johnson, K., Feeny, N., & Treadwell, K. (2001). The Child PTSD Symptom Scale: A preliminary examination of its psychometric properties. *Journal of Clinical Child Psychology, 30*(3), 376–384.

Foa, E., Zoellner, L., Feeny, N., Hembree, E., & Alvarez-Conrad, J. (2002). Does imaginal exposure exacerbate PTSD symptoms? *Journal of Consulting & Clinical Psychology, 70*(4), 1022–1028.

Follette, V. M., Iverson, K. M., & Ford, J. D. (2009). Contextual behavior trauma therapy. In C. A. Courtois & J. D. Ford (Eds.), *Treating complex traumatic stress disorders: An evidence-based guide* (pp. 264–285). New York: Guilford Press.

Forbes, D., Phelps, A., McHugh, A., Debenham, P., Hopwood, M., & Creamer, M. (2003). Imagery rehearsal in the treatment of posttraumatic nightmares in Australian veterans with chronic combat-related PTSD: 12-month follow-up data. *Journal of Traumatic Stress, 16*(5), 509–513.

Ford, J. D. (2009). Neurobiological and developmental research: Clinical implications. In C. A. Courtois & J. D. Ford (Eds.), *Treating complex traumatic stress disorders: An evidence-based guide* (pp. 31–58). New York: Guilford Press.

Ford, J. D., Hartman, J. K., Hawke, J., & Chapman, J. (2008). Traumatic individualization, posttraumatic stress disorder, suicidal ideation, and substance abuse risk among juvenile justice–involved youths. *Journal of Child and Adolescent Trauma, 1*, 72–92.

Fosha, D., Paivio, S. C., Gleiser, K., & Ford, J. D. (2009). Experiential and emotion-focused therapy. In C. A. Courtois & J. D. Ford (Eds.), *Treating complex traumatic stress disorders: An evidence-based guide* (pp. 286–310). New York: Guilford Press.

Foulkes, S. H. (1948). *Introduction to group analytic psychotherapy*. London: Heineman.

Frederick, C. (1980). Effects of natural versus human induced violence upon individuals. *Evaluation and Change* (Special Issue), 71–75.

Freud, S. (1959). Introduction to psychoanalysis and the war neurosis. In J. Strachey (Ed. & Trans.), *The standard edition of the complete psychological works of Sigmund Freud* (Vol. 5). London: Hogarth Press. (Original work published 1919)

Freud, S. (1963). Introductory lectures on psychoanalysis XVII. In J. Strachey (Ed. & Trans.), *The standard edition of the complete psychological works of Sigmund Freud* (Vol. 16). London: Hogarth Press. (Original work published 1917)

Frick, R., & Bogart, M. L. (1982). Transference and countertransference in group therapy with Vietnam veterans. *Bulletin of the Menninger Clinic, 46*, 429–444.

Furst, S. S. (1967). A survey. In S. S. Furst (Ed.), *Psychic trauma* (pp. 23–33). New York: Basic Books.

Furst, S. S. (1978). The stimulus barrier and the pathogenicity of trauma. *International Journal of Psychoanalysis, 59*, 345–352.

Gist, R., Lubin, B., & Redburn, B. (1999). Psychosocial, ecological and community perspectives on disaster response. In R. Gist & B. Lubin (Eds.), *Response to disaster: Psychosocial, community, and ecological approaches* (pp. 1–20). Philadelphia: Brunner/Mazel.

Gist, R., Woodall, J., & Magenheimer, L. K. (1999). "And then you do the hokey pokey and you turn yourself around." In R. Gist & B. Lubin (Eds.), *Response to disaster: Psychosocial, community, and ecological approaches* (pp. 269–290). Philadelphia: Brunner/Mazel.

Gladding, S. T. (1987). Poetic expressions: A counseling art in elementary schools. *Elementary School Guidance & Counseling, 21*, 307–311.

Gold, S. N. (2009). Contextual therapy. In C. A. Courtois & J. D. Ford (Eds.), *Treating complex traumatic stress disorders: An evidence-based guide* (pp. 227–242). New York: Guilford Press.

Gordon, N. S., Farberow, N. L., & Maida, C. A. (1999). *Children and disaster*. Philadelphia: Brunner/Mazel.

Gottman, J. M., Gottman, J. S., & Atkins, C. L. (2011). The Comprehensive Soldier Fitness program: Family skills component. *American Psychologist, 66*(1), 52–57.

Green, M. A., & Berlin, M. A. (1987). Five psychosocial variables related to the existence of post-traumatic stress disorder symptoms. *Journal of Clinical Psychology, 43*, 643–649.

Gressard, C. F. (1986). Self-help groups for Vietnam veterans experiencing post-traumatic stress disorder. *Journal for Specialists in Group Work, 11*, 74–79.

Grey, N., Young, K., & Holmes, E. (2002). Cognitive restructuring within reliving: A treatment of peritraumatic emotional "hotspots" in posttraumatic stress disorder. *Behavioural & Cognitive Psychotherapy, 30*(10), 37–56.

Grinker, R. R., & Spiegel, J. P. (1945). *Men under stress*. Philadelphia: Blakiston.

Gumaer, J. (1984). *Counseling and therapy for children*. New York: Free Press.

Gurvitz, T. V., Shenton, M. E., & Pittman, R. K. (1995). *Reduced hippocampal volume on magnetic resonance imagining in chronic post-traumatic stress disorder*. Paper presented at the International Society for Traumatic Stress Studies, Miami.

Haen, C. (2008). Vanquishing monsters: Drama therapy for treating childhood trauma in the group setting. In C. A. Malchiodi (Ed.), *Creative interventions with traumatized children* (pp. 225–246). New York: Guilford Press.

Halpern, J., & Tramontin, M. (2007). *Disaster mental health: Theory and practice*. Belmont, CA: Brooks/Cole.

Hamilton, J., & Workman, R. (1998). Persistence of combat-related posttraumatic stress symptoms for 75 years. *Journal of Traumatic Stress, 11*(4), 763–768.

Hefferon, K., Grealy, M., & Mutrie, N. (2009). Post-traumatic growth and life threatening physical illness: A systematic review of the qualitative literature. *British Journal of Health Psychology, 14*, 343–378.

Hembree, E., Rauch, S., & Foa, E. (2003). Beyond the manual: The insider's guide to prolonged exposure therapy for PTSD. *Cognitive and Behavioral Practice, 10*(1), 22–30.

Herman, J. L. (1992). *Trauma and recovery: The aftermath of violence—from domestic abuser to political terror*. New York: Basic Books.

Herman, J. L. (1997). *Trauma and recovery*. New York: Basic Books.

Herpertz-Dahlmann, B., Hahn, F., & Hempt, A. (2005). Clinical assessment and therapy of post-traumatic stress disorder in childhood and adolescence: Responsibilities of an outpatient clinic for traumatized children. *Nervenarzt, 76*(5), 546–556.

Hilliard, R. E. (2008). Music and grief work with children. In C. A. Malchiodi (Ed.), *Creative interventions with traumatized children* (pp. 63–80). New York: Guilford Press.

Hoge, C. W., Auchterlonie, J. L, & Milliken, C. S. (2006). Mental health problems, use of mental health services and attrition from military service after returning from deployment to Iraq or Afghanistan. *Journal of the American Medical Association, 295*, 1023–1035.

Hopkins, O., & King, N. (1994). PTSD in children and adolescents. *Behavior Change, 11*, 110–120.

Horn, J. (2002). Law enforcement and trauma. In M. Williams & J. Sommer (Eds.), *Simple and complex post-traumatic stress disorder: Strategies for comprehensive treatment in clinical practice* (pp. 311–323). Binghamton, NY: Haworth Press.

Horowitz, M. J. (1976). *Stress response syndromes*. New York: Aronson.

Horowitz, M. J., & Solomon, G. F. (1975). A prediction of delayed stress response syndromes in Vietnam veterans. *Journal of Social Issues, 31*, 67–80.

Horowitz, M. J., Wilner, N., & Alvarez, W. (1979). Impact of Events Scale: A measure of subjective stress. *Psychosomatic Medicine, 41*, 209–218.

Horowitz, M. J., Wilner, N., Kaltreider, N., & Alvarez, W. (1980). Signs and symptoms of post-trauma stress disorders. *Archives of General Psychiatry, 37*, 85–92.

Hotopf, M., Hull, L., Fear, N., Browne, T., Horn, O., Iversen, A., et al. (2006). The health of UK military personnel who deployed to the 2003 Iraq war: A cohort study. *Lancet, 367*, 1731–1741.

International Society for Traumatic Stress Studies. (1997). *Practice guidelines for the treatment of posttraumatic stress disorder*. Retrieved April 10, 2000, from http://www.istss.org/quick/tg.doc.html

Irwin, E. C. (1987). Drama: The play's the thing. *Elementary School Guidance & Counseling, 21*, 276–283.

Issacs, J. S. (2004). Numerical distraction therapy: Initial assessment of a treatment for posttraumatic stress disorder. *Traumatology, 10*(1), 39–54.

James, R. K. (2003, April). *Drawing out the trauma*. Paper presented at the Twenty-seventh Annual Convening of Crisis Intervention Personnel, Chicago.

James, R. K., & Gilliland, B. E. (2003). *Theories and strategies in counseling and psychotherapy* (5th ed.). Boston: Allyn & Bacon.

James, R. K., & Myer, R. (1987). Puppets: The elementary counselor's right or left arm. *Elementary School Guidance & Counseling, 21*, 292–299.

Johnson, D. R. (2000a). Creative therapies. In E. Foa & T. Keane (Eds.), *Effective treatments for PTSD: Practice guidelines from the International Society for Traumatic Stress Studies* (pp. 356–358). New York: Guilford Press.

Johnson, D. R. (2000b). Creative therapies. In E. Foa & T. Keane (Eds.), *Effective treatments for PTSD: Practice guidelines from the International Society for Traumatic Stress Studies* (pp. 302–314). New York: Guilford Press.

Johnson, D. R., Feldman, S. C., & Southwick, S. M. (1994). The concept of the second-generation program in the treatment of PTSD among Vietnam veterans. *Journal of Traumatic Stress, 7*, 217–235.

Johnson, R. G. (1987). Using computer art in counseling children. *Elementary School Guidance & Counseling, 21*, 262–265.

Jovanovic, A., Aleksandric, B. V., Dunjic, D., & Todorovic, V. (2004). Family hardiness and social support as predictors of post-traumatic stress disorder. *Psychiatry and Law, 11*(2), 263–268.

Kaniasty, K., & Norris, F. (1999). The experience of disaster: Individuals and communities sharing trauma. In R. Gist & B. Lubin (Eds.), *Response to disaster: Psychosocial, community, and ecological approaches* (pp. 25–62). Philadelphia: Brunner/Mazel.

Kardiner, A. (1941). *The traumatic neurosis of war.* New York: Hoeber.

Karl, A., Malta, L. S., & Maercker, A. (2006). Meta-analytic review of event-related potential studies in post-traumatic stress disorder. *Biological Psychology, 71*(2), 123–147.

Kaufman, B., & Wohl, A. (1992). *Casualties of childhood: A developmental perspective on sexual abuse using projective drawings.* New York: Brunner/Mazel.

Kazdin, A. E. (2008). Trauma in children: How can we communicate what we know? *Monitor on Psychology, 39*(9), 5.

Keane, T. M. (1976). *State dependent retention and its relationship to psychopathology.* Unpublished manuscript, State University of New York at Binghamton.

Keane, T. M., Caddell, J., & Taylor, K. (1988). Mississippi Scale for Combat-Related Posttraumatic Stress Disorder: Three studies in reliability and validity. *Journal of Consulting and Clinical Psychology, 56,* 85–90.

Keane, T. M., Fairbank, J. A., Caddell, J. M., & Zimmering, R. T. (1989). Implosive (flooding) therapy reduces symptoms of PTSD in Vietnam veterans. *Behavior Therapy, 20,* 245–260.

Keane, T. M., Fairbank, J. A., Caddell, J. M., Zimmering, R. T., & Bender, M. E. (1985). A behavioral approach to assessing and treating posttrauma stress disorder in Vietnam veterans. In C. R. Figley (Ed.), *Trauma and its wake: The study of post-traumatic stress disorder* (pp. 257–294). New York: Brunner/Mazel.

Keane, T. M., & Kaloupek, D. G. (1982). Imaginal flooding in the treatment of a posttraumatic stress disorder. *Journal of Consulting and Clinical Psychology, 50,* 138–140.

Keane, T. M., Malloy, P. F., & Fairbank, J. A. (1984). Empirical development of an MMPI subscale for the assessment of combat-related posttraumatic stress disorder. *Journal of Consulting and Clinical Psychology, 52,* 888–891.

King, N., Heyne, D., Tonge, B. Mullen, P., Myerson, N., Rollings, S., et al. (2003). Sexually abused children suffering from post-traumatic stress disorder: Assessment and treatment strategies. *Cognitive Behaviour Therapy 32*(1), 2–12.

Kingsbury, S. J. (1988). Hypnosis in the treatment of post-traumatic stress disorder: An isomorphic intervention. *American Journal of Clinical Hypnosis, 31,* 81–90.

Kinzie, J., & Goetz, R. (1996). A century of controversy surrounding posttraumatic stress-spectrum syndromes: The impact of DSM III and DSM IV. *Journal of Traumatic Stress, 9,* 159–179.

Kolb, L. C., & Mutalipassi, L. R. (1982). The conditioned emotional response: A subclass of the chronic and delayed stress disorder. *Psychiatric Annals, 12,* 969–987.

Korn, D., & Leeds, A. (2002). Preliminary evidence of efficacy for EMDR resource development and installation in the stabilization phase of treatment of complex post-traumatic stress disorder. *Journal of Clinical Psychology, 58*(12), 1465–1487.

Kramer, T., Lindy, J., Green, B., & Grace, M. (1994). The co-morbidity of post-traumatic stress disorder and suicidality in Vietnam veterans. *Suicide and Life Threatening Behavior, 24,* 58–67.

Kreidler, M., Briscoe, L., & Beech, R. (2002). Pharmacology for post-traumatic stress disorder related to childhood sexual abuse: A literature review. *Perspectives in Psychiatric Care, 38*(4), 135–145.

Kroll, J. (2003). Posttraumatic symptoms and the complexity of response to trauma. *Journal of the American Medical Association, 290*(5), 667–670.

Kukla, R. A., Schlenger, W. E., Fairbank, J. A., Hough, R. L., Jordan, B. K., & Marmar, C. R. (1990). *Trauma and the Vietnam War generation: Report of findings from the National Vietnam Veterans' Readjustment Study.* New York: Brunner/Mazel.

LaCoursiere, R. B., Bodfrey, K. E., & Ruby, L. M. (1980). Traumatic neurosis in the etiology of alcoholism: Vietnam and other trauma. *American Journal of Psychiatry, 137,* 966–968.

Lamprecht, F., Kohnke, C., Lempa, W., Sack, M., Matzke, M., & Münte, T. (2004). Event-related potentials and EMDR treatment of post-traumatic stress disorder. *Neuroscience Research, 49*(2), 267–272.

Landreth, G. L. (1987). Play therapy: Facilitative use of child's play in elementary school counseling. *Elementary School Guidance & Counseling, 21,* 253–261.

Lang, A. J., Stein, M., Kennedy, C., & Foy, D. W. (2004). Adult psychopathology and intimate partner violence among survivors of childhood maltreatment. *Journal of Interpersonal Violence, 19*(10), 1102–1118.

Lapierre, C. B., Schwegler, A. F., & LaBauve, B. J. (2007). Posttraumatic stress and depression symptoms in solders returning from combat operations in Iraq and Afghanistan. *Journal of Traumatic Stress, 20,* 933–943.

Lating, J. M., & Everly, G. S. (1995). Psychophysiological assessment of PTSD. In G. S. Everly, Jr., & J. M. Lating (Eds.), *Psychotraumatology* (pp. 129–146). New York: Plenum Press.

Laufer, R., Yager, T., & Grey-Wouters, E. (1981). Postwar trauma: Social and psychological problems of Vietnam veterans in the aftermath of the Vietnam War. In A. Egendorf, C. Kadushin, & R. S. Laufer (Eds.), *Legacies of Vietnam* (Vol. 1). Washington, DC: U.S. Government Printing Office.

Lechner, S., & Weaver, K. (2009). Lessons learned about benefit finding among individuals with cancer or HIV/AIDS.

In C. L. Park, S. C. Lechner, M. H. Antoni, & A. L. Stanton (Eds.), *Medical illness and positive life change: Can crisis lead to a personal transformation?* (pp. 107–124). Washington, DC: American Psychological Association.

Lee, C., Gavriel, H., Drummond, P., Richards, J., & Greenwald, R. (2002). Treatment of PTSD: Stress inoculation training with prolonged exposure compared to EMDR. *Journal of Clinical Psychology, 58*(9), 1071–1089.

Lee, C., Gavriel, H., & Richards, J. (1996). Eye movement desensitization: Complexities and future direction. *Australian Psychologist, 31*(3), 168–173.

Lee, C., Taylor, G., & Drummond, P. (2006). The active ingredient of EMDR: Is it traditional exposure or dual focus of attention? *Clinical Psychology & Psychotherapy, 13*(2), 97–107.

Lewis, M. D. (2005). Self-organizing individual differences in brain development. *Developmental Review, 25*, 27–43.

Lifton, R. J. (1973). *Home from the war: Vietnam veterans—neither individuals nor executioners.* New York: Simon & Schuster.

Lifton, R. J. (1974). "Death imprints" on youth in Vietnam. *Journal of Clinical Child Psychology, 3*, 47–49.

Lifton, R. J. (1975). The postwar war. *Journal of Social Issues, 31*, 181–195.

Lindy, J. D. (1996). Psychoanalytic psychotherapy of post-traumatic stress disorder: The nature of the therapeutic relationship. In B. A. van der Kolk, A. C. McFarlane, & L. Weisaeth (Eds.), *Traumatic stress* (pp. 525–536). New York: Guilford Press.

Loumeau-May, L. V. (2008). Grieving in the public eye: Art therapy with children who lost parents in the World Trade Center attacks. In C. A. Malchiodi (Ed.), *Creative interventions with traumatized children* (pp. 112–131). New York: Guilford Press.

Lyons, J. A., & Keane, T. M. (1989). Implosive therapy for the treatment of combat-related PTSD. *Journal of Traumatic Stress, 2*, 137–152.

Maclean, G. (1977). Psychic trauma and traumatic neurosis: Play therapy with a four-year-old boy. *Canadian Psychiatric Association Journal, 22*, 71–76.

MacPherson, M. (1984). *Long time passing: Vietnam and the haunted generation.* New York: Doubleday.

Malchiodi, C. A. (Ed.). (2008). *Creative interventions with traumatized children.* New York: Guilford Press.

Malchiodi, C. A., & Ginns-Gruenberg, D. (2008). Trauma, loss, and bibliotherapy: The healing process of stories. In C. A. Malchiodi (Ed.), *Creative interventions with traumatized children* (pp. 167–188). New York: Guilford Press.

Malizia, A., & Nutt, D. (2000). Human brain imagining and post-traumatic stress disorder. In D. Nutt, J. Davidson, & J. Zohar (Eds.), *Post-traumatic stress disorder: Diagnosis, management, and treatment* (pp. 41–52). London: Martin Dunitz.

Malloy, P. F., Fairbank, J. A., & Keane, T. M. (1983). Validation of a multimodal assessment of posttraumatic stress disorders in Vietnam veterans. *Journal of Consulting and Clinical Psychology, 51*, 488–494.

Manly, J., Kim, J., Rogosch, F., & Cicchetti, D. (2001). Dimensions of child maltreatment and children's adjustment: Contributions of developmental timing and subtype. *Development and Psychopathology, 13*, 759–782.

Marmar, C. R., Neylan, T. C., & Schoenfeld, F. (2002). New directions in the pharmacotherapy of posttraumatic stress disorder. *Psychiatric Quarterly, 73*(4), 2159–2170.

Marmar, C. R., Weiss, D. S., Schlenger, W. E., Fairbank, J. A., Jordan, K., Kulka, R. A., et al. (1991). Peritraumatic dissociation and posttraumatic stress in male Vietnam theater veterans. *American Journal of Psychiatry, 151*, 902–907.

Marsella, A. J., Friedman, M. J., Gerrity, E. T., & Scurfield, R. M. (1996). *Ethnocultural aspects of posttraumatic stress disorder: Issues, research, and clinical applications.* Washington, DC: American Psychological Association.

Matthews, M. D. (2009). *Self-report knowledge of posttraumatic stress disorder and posttraumatic growth among West Point cadets.* Unpublished raw data, United States Military Academy, West Point, NY.

Maxfield, L. (2002). Eye movement desensitization and reprocessing in the treatment of post-traumatic stress disorder. In C. Figley (Ed.), *Brief treatments for the traumatized: A project of the Green Cross Foundation* (pp. 148–169). Westport, CT: Greenwood Press.

McCubbin, H., Joy, C., Cauble, E., Comeau, J., Patterson, J., & Needle, R. (1980). Family stress and coping: A decade review. *Journal of Marriage and Family, 43*, 855–872.

McFarlane, A. C., & de Girolamo, G. (1996). The nature of traumatic stressors and the epidemiology of posttraumatic reactions. In B. A. van der Kolk, A. C. McFarlane, & L. Weisaeth (Eds.), *Traumatic stress* (pp. 129–148). New York: Guilford Press.

McFarlane, A. C., & Yehuda, R. (1996). Resiliency, vulnerability, and the course of posttraumatic reactions. In B. A. van der Kolk, A. C. McFarlane, & L. Weisaeth (Eds.), *Traumatic stress* (pp. 155–181). New York: Guilford Press.

Meadows, E. A., & Foa, E. B. (1999). Cognitive behavioral treatment for traumatized adults. In P. A. Saigh & J. D. Bremner (Eds.), *Posttraumatic stress disorder: A comprehensive text.* Boston: Allyn & Bacon.

Meiser-Stedman, R. (2002). Towards a cognitive-behavioral model of PTSD in children and adolescents. *Clinical Child & Family Psychology Review, 5*(4), 217–232.

Melhem, N., Day, N., Shear, M., Day, R., Reynolds, C., & Brent, D. (2004). Predictors of complicated grief among adolescents exposed to a peer's suicide. *Journal of Loss & Trauma 9*(10), 21–34.

Memphis Vietnam Veterans Center. (1985). *The nonveteran helper* (Pamphlet). Memphis, TN: Author.

Mental Health Advisory Team V. (2008, February 14). *Mental Health Advisory Team (MHAT) V Operation Iraqi Freedom 06-08* (Report chartered by the Office of the Surgeon Multi-National Force-Iraq and the Office of the Surgeon General United States Army Medical Command). Retrieved from http://www.armymedicine.army.mil/reports/mhat/mhat-v/Redacted1-MHATVOIF-4-FEB-2008Report.pdf

Miller, M. W., Wolf, E. J., Martin, E., Kaloupek, D. G., & Keane, T. M. (2008). Structural equation modeling of associations among combat exposure, PTSD symptom factors, and global assessment of functioning, *Journal of Rehabilitation Research and Development, 45*, 359–370.

Milliken, C. S., Auchterlonie, J. L., & Hoge, C. W. (2007). Longitudinal assessment of mental health problems among active and reserve component soldiers returning from the Iraq war. *Journal of the American Medical Association, 298*, 2141–2148.

Mitchell, J. (1983). When disaster strikes: The critical incident stress debriefing process. *Journal of Emergency Medical Services, 8*, 36–39.

Moore, B. A., & Jongsma, A. E. (2009). *The veterans and active duty military psychotherapy treatment planner.* Hoboken, NJ: John Wiley & Sons.

Morgan, L., Scourfield, J., Williams, D., Jasper, A., & Lewis, G. (2003). The Aberfan disaster: 33-year follow-up of survivors. *British Journal of Psychiatry, 182*(6), 532–536.

Mowbray, C. T. (1988). Post-traumatic therapy for children who are victims of violence. In F. M. Ochberg (Ed.), *Post-traumatic therapy and individuals of violence* (pp. 196–212). New York: Brunner/Mazel.

Munsey, C. (2009). Women and war. *Monitor on Psychology, 40*(8), 34–35.

Muris, P., & Merckelbach, H. (1999a). Eye movement desensitization and reprocessing. *Journal of the American Academy of Child and Adolescent Psychiatry, 38*(1), 7–8.

Muris, P., & Merckelbach, H. (1999b). Traumatic memories, eye movement, phobia, and panic: A critical note on the proliferation of EMDR. *Journal of Anxiety Disorders, 13*(1–2), 209–223.

Myers, D., & Wee, D. F. (2005). *Disaster mental health services.* New York: Brunner/Mazel.

Nader, K. O. (1997). Assessing traumatic experiences in children. In J. P. Wilson & T. M. Keane (Eds.), *Assessing psychological trauma and PTSD* (pp. 291–348). New York: Guilford Press.

Nader, K. O., Kreigler, J. A., Blake, D. D., & Pynoos, R. S. (1994). *Clinician Administered PTSD Scale, Child and Adolescent Version (CAPS-C).* White River Junction, VT: National Center for PTSD.

National Center for PTSD. (2011, July). *PTSD in children and teens.* U.S. Department of Veterans Affairs. Available at http/www.ptsd.va.gov/public/pages/ptsd-children-adolecents.asp

Newman, C. J. (1976). Children of disaster: Clinical observations at Buffalo Creek. *American Journal of Psychiatry, 133*, 306–312.

Newman, E., Kaloupkek, D. G., & Keane, T. M. (1996). Assessment of posttraumatic stress disorder in clinical and research settings. In B. A. van der Kolk, A. C. McFarlane, & L. Weisaeth (Eds.), *Traumatic stress* (pp. 242–273). New York: Guilford Press.

Neubauer, F., Deblinger, E., & Sieger, K. (2007). Trauma-focused cognitive-behavioral therapy for child sexual abuse and exposure to domestic violence: Case of Mary, age 6. In N. B. Webb (Ed.), *Play therapy with children in crisis: Individual, group, and family treatment* (3rd ed., pp. 107–132). New York: Guilford Press.

Norris, F., Friedman, M., Watson, P., Byrne, C., Diaz, E., & Kaniasty, K. (2002). 60,000 disaster individuals speak: Part I. An empirical review of the literature, 1981–2001. *Psychiatry: Interpersonal & Biological Process, 65*(3), 207–243.

North, C. S. (2004). Approaching disaster mental health research after the 9/11 World Trade Center terrorist attacks. *Psychiatric Clinics of North America, 27*(3), 589–602.

Notman, M., & Nadelson, C. (1976). The rape individual: Psychodynamic considerations. *American Journal of Psychiatry, 133*, 408–412.

Ochberg, F. M. (Ed.). (1988). *Post-traumatic therapy and individuals of violence.* New York: Brunner/Mazel.

Oras, R., de Ezpeleta, S., & Ahmad, A. (2004). Treatment of traumatized refugee children with Eye Movement Desensitization and Reprocessing in a psychodynamic model. *Nordic Journal of Psychiatry, 58*(3), 199–203.

Osofsky, J. D. (1995). The effects of exposure to violence on young children. *American Psychologist, 50*(9), 781–788.

Osofsky, J. D., Osofsky, H. J., Kronenberg, M., & Hansel, T. C. (2010). The aftermath of Hurricane Katrina: Mental health considerations and lessons learned. In R. P. Kilmer, V. Gil-Rivas, R. G. Tedeschi, & L. G. Calhoun (Eds.), *Helping families and communities recover from disaster: Lessons learned from Hurricane Katrina and its aftermath* (pp. 241–263). Washington, DC: American Psychological Association.

Ouimette, P., Read, J., & Brown, P. J. (2005). Consistency of retrospective reports of DSM-IV Criterion A traumatic stressors among substance use disorder patients. *Journal of Traumatic Stress, 18*(1), 43–51.

Parker, J. G., & Gottman, H. J. M. (1989). Social and emotional development in a relational context. In T. J. Berndt & G. W. Ladd (Eds.), *Peer relationships in child development* (pp. 95–131). New York: Wiley.

Paunovic, N. (2002). Prolonged exposure counterconditioning (PEC) as a treatment for chronic posttraumatic stress disorder and major depression in an adult survivor of repeated child sexual and physical abuse. *Clinical Case Studies, 1*(2), 148–169.

Paunovic, N. (2003). Prolonged exposure counterconditioning as a treatment for chronic posttraumatic stress disorder. *Journal of Anxiety Disorders, 17*(5), 479–499.

Paunovic, N., & Ost, L. (2001). Cognitive-behavior therapy vs. exposure therapy in the treatment of PTSD in refugees. *Behavior Research & Therapy, 39*(10), 1183–1197.

Pearlman, L. A., & Saakvitne, K. W. (1995). *Trauma and the therapist.* New York: Norton.

Pearsons, L. (1965). *The use of written communications in psychotherapy.* Springfield, IL: Charles C Thomas.

Peterson, C., Park, N., Castro, C. A. (2011). Assessment for the U.S. Army Comprehensive Soldier Fitness program: The Global Assessment Tool. *American Psychologist, 66*(1), 10–18.

Pivar, I., & Field, N. P. (2004). Unresolved grief in combat veterans with PTSD. *Journal of Anxiety Disorders, 18*(6), 745–755.

Pizarro, J., Silver, R. C., & Prause, J. (2006). Physical and mental health costs of traumatic war experiences among Civil War veterans. *Archives of General Psychiatry, 63*(2), 193–200.

Price, J. L. (2011). Findings from the National Vietnam Veterans' Readjustment Study. United States Department of Veterans Affairs. Available at www.ptsd.va.gov/professional/pages/Vietnam-vets-study.asp

Progoff, I. (1975). *At a journal workshop.* New York: Dialogue House Library.

Pynoos, R. S., & Nader, K. (1988). Psychological first aid and treatment approach to children exposed to community violence: Research implications. *Journal of Traumatic Stress, 1,* 445–473.

Pynoos, R. S., Steinberg, A. M., & Goenjian, A. (1996). Traumatic stress in childhood and adolescence: Recent developments and current controversies. In B. A. van der Kolk, A. C. McFarlane, & L. Weisaeth (Eds.), *Traumatic stress* (pp. 331–358). New York: Guilford Press.

Read, J., Bollinger, A., & Sharansky, E. (2003). Assessment of comorbid substance abuse disorder and posttraumatic stress disorder. In P. Ouimette & P. Brown (Eds.), *Trauma and substance abuse: Causes, consequences, and treatment of comorbid disorders* (pp. 111–125). Washington, DC: American Psychological Association.

Reich, W., Shayka, J. J., & Taibleson, C. (1991). *Diagnostic Interview for Children and Adolescents (DICA).* St. Louis, MO: Washington University.

Reivich, K. J., Seligman, M. P., & McBride, S. (2011). Master resilience training in the U.S. Army. *American Psychologist, 66*(1), 25–34.

Renfrey, G., & Spates, C. R. (1994). Eye movement desensitization: A partial dismantling study. *Journal of Behavior Therapy and Experimental Psychiatry, 25,* 231–239.

Reynolds, M., Mezey, G., Chapman, M., Wheeler, M. Drummond, C., & Baldacchio, A. (2005). Co-morbid post-traumatic stress disorder in a substance misusing clinical population. *Drug and Alcohol Dependence, 77*(3), 251–258.

Roemer, L., Harrington, N., & Riggs, D. (2002). Behavior/cognitive approaches to post-traumatic stress: Theory-driven, empirically based therapy. In C. Figley (Ed.), *Brief treatments for the traumatized: A project of the Green Cross Foundation* (pp. 59–80). Westport, CT: Greenwood Press.

Rosen, G. (1999). Treatment fidelity and research on eye movement desensitization and reprocessing (EMDR). *Journal of Anxiety Disorders, 13*(1/2), 173–184.

Rosenheck, R., & Fontana, A. (1998). Warrior fathers and warrior sons: Intergenerational aspects of trauma. In Y. Danieli (Ed.), *International handbook of multigenerational legacies of trauma* (pp. 225–242). New York: Plenum Press.

Rosner, R., & Powell, S. (2006). Posttraumatic growth after war. In L. G. Calhoun & R. G. Tedeschi (Eds.), *Handbook of posttraumatic growth after war* (pp. 197–213). Mahwah, NJ: Erlbaum.

Rothschild, B. (2000). *The body remembers: The psychophysiology of trauma and trauma treatment.* New York: Norton.

Saigh, P. A. (1987). In vitro flooding of childhood posttraumatic stress disorders: A systematic replication. *Professional School Psychology, 2,* 135–146.

Santa Ana, E. J., Saladin, M. E., Back, S., Waldrop, A., Spratt, E., McRae, A., et al. (2006). PTSD and the HPA axis: Difference in response to the cold pressor task among individuals with child vs. adult trauma. *Psychoneuroendocrinology, 31*(4), 501–509.

Saxe, G. N., Ellis, B. H., & Kaplow, J. B. (2007). *Collaborative treatment of traumatized children and teens: The trauma system therapy approach.* New York: Guilford Press.

Saylor, C. F., Cowart, B. L., Lipovsky, J. A., Jackson, C., & Finch, A. (2003). Media exposure to September 11: Elementary school students' experiences and posttraumatic symptoms. *American Behavioral Scientist, 46*(12), 1622–1642.

Scheck, M., Schaeffer, J., & Gillette, C. (1998). Brief psychological intervention with traumatized young women: The efficacy of eye movement desensitization and reprocessing. *Journal of Traumatic Stress, 11*(1), 25–44.

Scheering, M. S., & Gaensauer, T. J. (2000). Posttraumatic stress disorder. In C. H. Zeanah, Jr. (Ed.), *Handbook of infant mental health* (2nd ed., pp. 369–381). New York: Guilford Press.

Schreier, H., Ladakakos, C., Morabito, D., Chapman, L., & Knudson, M.(2005). Posttraumatic stress symptoms in children after mild to moderate pediatric trauma: A longitudinal examination of symptom prevalence, correlates, and parent–child symptom reporting. *Journal of Trauma-Injury Infection and Critical Care, 58*(2), 352–363.

Scurfield, R. M. (1985). Post-trauma stress assessment and treatment: Overview and formulations. In C. R. Figley (Ed.), *Trauma and its wake: The study of posttrauma stress disorder* (pp. 219–256). New York: Brunner/Mazel.

Seal, K. J. H., Bertenthal, D. M., Miner, C. R., Saunak, S., & Marmar, C. (2007). Bringing the war back home. *Archives of Internal Medicine, 167,* 476–482.

Selye, H. (1976). *The stress of life.* New York: McGraw-Hill.

Shalev, A. Y. (1996). Stress versus traumatic stress: From acute homeostatic reactions to chronic psychopathology. In B. A. van der Kolk, A. C. McFarlane, & L. Weisaeth (Eds.), *Traumatic stress* (pp. 77–101). New York: Guilford Press.

Shallcross, L. (2010). Treating trauma. *Counseling Today, 52*(10), 26–35.

Shapiro, F. (1989a). Efficacy of the eye movement desensitization procedure in the treatment of traumatic memories. *Journal of Traumatic Stress, 2,* 199–223.

Shapiro, F. (1989b). Eye movement desensitization: A new treatment for posttraumatic stress disorder. *Journal of Behavior Therapy and Experimental Psychiatry, 20,* 211–217.

Shapiro, F. (1991). Eye movement desensitization and reprocessing procedure: From EMD to EMD/R—a new treatment model for anxiety and related traumata. *Behavior Therapist, 14,* 128, 133–135.

Shapiro, F. (1995). *Eye movement desensitization and reprocessing: Basic principles, protocols, and procedures.* New York: Guilford Press.

Shapiro, F., & Maxfield, L. (2002). Eye movement desensitization and reprocessing (EMDR): Information processing in the treatment of trauma. *Journal of Clinical Psychology, 58*(8), 933–946.

Shore, J. H., Tatum, E. L., & Vollmer, W. M. (1986). Evaluation of mental health effects of disaster: Mount St. Helen's eruption. *American Journal of Public Health, 76*(3), 76–86.

Siegel, D. J. (1995). Memory, trauma, and psychotherapy: A cognitive science view. *Journal of Psychotherapy Practice and Research, 4,* 93–122.

Silva, R., Cloitre, M., Davis, L., Levitt, J., Gomez, S., Ngai, I., & Brown, E. (2003). Early intervention with traumatized children. *Psychiatric Quarterly, 74*(4), 333–347.

Silverman, P. R. (1986). The perils of borrowing: Role of the professional in mutual self-help groups. *Journal of Specialists in Group Work, 11,* 68–73.

Smith, S. G., & Cook, S. L. (2004). Are reports of posttraumatic growth positively biased? *Journal of Traumatic Stress, 17*(4), 353–358.

Smith, T. C., Ryan, M. A., Wingard, D. L., Slymen, D. J., Sallis, J. F., & Kritz-Silverstein, D. (2008). New onset and persistent symptoms of post-traumatic stress disorder self reported after deployment and combat exposures: Prospect population based US military cohort study. *British Medical Journal, 336,* 366–371.

Sokolski, K., Denson, T., Lee, R., & Reist, C. (2003). Quetiapine for treatment of refractory symptoms of combat-related post-traumatic stress disorder. *Military Medicine, 168*(6), 486–489.

Solomon, Z. (1986). The effect of combat-related stress disorder on the family. *Psychiatry, 51,* 323–329.

Spiegel, D. (1981). Vietnam grief work under hypnosis. *American Journal of Clinical Hypnosis, 24,* 33–40.

Spiegel, D. (1989). Hypnosis in the treatment of victims of sexual abuse. *Psychiatric Clinics of North America, 12,* 295–305.

Spinazzola, J., Blaustein, M., & van der Kolk, B. A. (2005). Treatment outcome research: The study of unrepresentative samples? *Journal of Traumatic Stress, 18,* 423–436.

Stampfl, T. G., & Levis, D. J. (1967). Essentials of implosive therapy: A learning-theory-based psychodynamic behavioral therapy. *Journal of Abnormal Psychology, 72,* 496–503.

Steele, W., & Malchiodi, C. A. (2008). Interventions for parents of traumatized children. In C. A. Malchiodi (Ed.), *Creative interventions with traumatized children* (pp. 264–284). New York: Guilford Press.

Steele, W., & Raider, M. (2001). *Structured sensory intervention for traumatized children, adolescents, and parents: Strategies to alleviate trauma.* Lewiston, NY: Mellen Press.

Stein, M. B., Hannah, C., Koverola, C., Yehuda, R., Torchia, M., & McClarty, B. (1994, December). *Neuroanatomical and neuroendocrine correlates in adulthood of severe sexual abuse in childhood.* Paper presented at the 33rd Annual Meeting of the American College of Neuropsychopharmacology, San Juan, Puerto Rico.

Suar, D., & Khuntia, R. (2004). Caste, education, family and stress disorders in Orissa Supercyclone. *Psychology and Developing Societies, 16*(1), 77–91.

Tarrier, N., & Humphreys, A. L. (2003). PTSD and the social support of the interpersonal environment: The development of social cognitive behavior therapy. *Journal of Cognitive Psychotherapy, 17*(2), 187–198.

Taylor, F. (2003). Tiagabine for posttraumatic stress disorder: A case series of 7 women. *Journal of Clinical Psychiatry, 64*(12), 1421–1425.

Taylor, S. (2003). Outcome predictors for three PTSD treatments: Exposure therapy, EMDR, and relaxation training. *Journal of Cognitive Psychotherapy, 17*(2), 149–161.

Tedeschi, R. G., & Calhoun, L. G. (1995). *Trauma and transformation: Growing in the aftermath of suffering.* Thousand Oaks, CA: Sage.

Tedeschi, R. G., & McNally, R. J. (2011). Can we facilitate posttraumatic growth in combat veterans? *American Psychologist, 66*(1), 19–24.

Terr, L. C. (1979). Children of Chowchilla: Study of psychic trauma. *Psychoanalytic Study of the Child, 34,* 547–623.

Terr, L. C. (1981). "Forbidden games": Posttraumatic child's play. *Journal of the American Academy of Child Psychiatry, 22,* 221–230.

Terr, L. C. (1983). Chowchilla revisited: The effects of psychic trauma four years after a school-bus kidnapping. *American Journal of Psychiatry, 140,* 1543–1550.

Terr, L. C. (1995). Childhood traumas: An outline and overview. In G. S. Everly, Jr., & J. M. Lating (Eds.),

Psychotraumatology (pp. 301–320). New York: Plenum Press.

Thaller, V., Marusic, S., Katinic, K., Buljan, D., Golik-Gruber, V., & Potkonjak, J. (2003). Biological factors in patients with post-traumatic stress disorder and alcoholism. *European Journal of Psychiatry, 17*(2), 87–98.

Tinnin, L., Bills, L., & Gantt, L. (2002). Short-term treatment of simple and complex PTSD. In M. Williams & J. Sommer (Eds.), *Simple and complex post-traumatic stress disorder: Strategies for comprehensive treatment in clinical practice* (pp. 99–118). Binghamton, NY: Haworth Press.

Trimble, M. R. (1985). Post-traumatic stress disorder: History of a concept. In C. R. Figley (Ed.), *Trauma and its wake: The study of post-trauma stress disorder* (pp. 5–14). New York: Brunner/Mazel.

Tucker, P., Pfefferbaum, B., Nixon, S., & Foy, D. (1999). Trauma and recovery among adults highly exposed to a community disaster. *Psychiatric Annals, 29*(2), 78–83.

Tufnell, G. (2005). Eye movement desensitization and reprocessing in the treatment of pre-adolescent children with post-traumatic symptoms. *Clinical Child Psychology and Psychiatry, 10*(4), 587–600.

Turner, S. W., McFarlane, A. C., & van der Kolk, B. A. (1996). The therapeutic environment and new explorations in the treatment of posttraumatic stress disorder. In B. A. van der Kolk, A. C. McFarlane, & L. Weisaeth (Eds.), *Traumatic stress* (pp. 537–558). New York: Guilford Press.

Ullman, S. E., & Siegel, J. M. (1994). Predictors of exposure to traumatic events and posttraumatic stress sequelae. *Journal of Community Psychology, 22*, 328–338.

Ursano, R., Fullerton, C., Vance, K., & Kao, T. (1999). Posttraumatic stress disorder and identification in disaster workers. *American Journal of Psychiatry, 156*(3), 353–359.

van der Kolk, B. A. (1996a). The body keeps the score: Approaches to the psychobiology of posttraumatic stress disorder. In B. A. van der Kolk, A. C. McFarlane, & L. Weisaeth (Eds.), *Traumatic stress* (pp. 214–241). New York: Guilford Press.

van der Kolk, B. A. (1996b). Trauma and memory. In B. A. van der Kolk, A. C. McFarlane, & L. Weisaeth (Eds.), *Traumatic stress* (pp. 279–297). New York: Guilford Press.

van der Kolk, B. A., Dreyfuss, D., Michaels, M., Shera, D., Berkowitz, B., Fisler, R., et al. (1994). Fluoxetine in posttraumatic stress disorder. *Journal of Clinical Psychiatry, 55*(12), 517–522.

van der Kolk, B. A., & McFarlane, A. C. (1996). The black hole of trauma. In B. A. van der Kolk, A. C. McFarlane, & L. Weisaeth (Eds.), *Traumatic stress* (pp. 3–23). New York: Guilford Press.

van der Kolk, B. A., McFarlane, A. C., & van der Hart, O. (1996). A general approach to treatment of posttraumatic stress disorder. In B. A. van der Kolk, A. C. McFarlane, & L. Weisaeth (Eds.), *Traumatic stress* (pp. 417–440). New York: Guilford Press.

van der Kolk, B. A., van der Hart, O., & Burbridge, J. (2002). In M. Williams & J. Sommer (Eds.), *Simple and complex post-traumatic stress disorder: Strategies for comprehensive treatment in clinical practice* (pp. 23–45). Binghamton, NY: Haworth Press.

van der Kolk, B. A., Weisaeth, L., & van der Hart, O. (1996). History of trauma in psychiatry. In B. A. van der Kolk, A. C. McFarlane, & L. Weisaeth (Eds.), *Traumatic stress* (pp. 47–74). New York: Guilford Press.

Vasterling, J. J., & Brewin, C. R. (Eds.). (2005). *Neuropsychology of PTSD: Biological, cognitive, and clinical perspectives.* New York: Guilford Press.

Vermetten, E., & Bremner, J. (2002). Circuits and systems in stress: II. Applications to neurobiology and treatment in posttraumatic stress disorder. *Depression & Anxiety, 16*(1), 14–38.

Vinturella, L., & James, R. K. (1987). Sand play: A therapeutic medium with children. *Elementary School Guidance & Counseling, 21*, 229–238.

Walker, J. I. (1983). Comparison of "rap" groups with traditional group therapy in the treatment of Vietnam combat veterans. *Group, 7*, 48–57.

Wallerstein, J. S., & Kelly, J. B. (1975). The effects of parental divorce: Experiences of the preschool child. *Journal of the American Academy of Child Psychiatry, 14*, 600–616.

Webb, N. B. (Ed.). (2007). Play therapy with children in crisis: Individual, group, and family treatment (3rd ed.). New York: Guilford Press.

Whealin, J. A., DeCarvalho, L. T., & Vega, E. M. (2008). *Clinician's guide to treating stress after war: Education and coping interventions for veterans.* Hoboken, NJ; John Wiley & Sons.

White, A. C. (1989). Post-traumatic stress. *British Journal of Psychiatry, 154*, 886–887.

White, M. (2005). *An outline of narrative therapy.* Available at www.massey.ac.nz

Wilkinson, C. B. (1983). Aftermath of a disaster: The collapse of the Hyatt Regency steel skywalk. *American Journal of Psychiatry, 140*, 1134–1139.

Williams, C. C. (1983). The mental foxhole: The Vietnam veteran's search for meaning. *American Journal of Orthopsychiatry, 53*, 4–17.

Williams, R. L., & Long, J. D. (1979). *Toward a self-managed life style* (2nd ed.). Boston: Houghton Mifflin.

Wilson, J. P. (1980). Conflict, stress, and growth: Effects of the war on psychosocial development. In C. R. Figley & S. Leventman (Eds.), *Strangers at home.* New York: Praeger.

Wilson J. P., Friedman, M. J., & Lindy, J. D. (2001). *Treating psychological trauma and PTSD.* New York: Guilford Press.

Wilson, J. P., Smith, W. K., & Johnson, S. (1985). A comparative analysis of PTSD among various survivor groups. In C.R. Figley (Ed.), *Trauma and its wake: The study of post-trauma stress disorder* (pp. 142–172). New York: Brunner/Mazel.

Wolpe, J. (1958). *Psychotherapy by reciprocal inhibition.* Stanford, CA: Stanford University Press.

Wolpe, J. (1982). *The practice of behavior therapy.* New York: Pergamon Press.

Yehuda, R. (2000). Neuroendocrinology. In D. Nutt, J. Davidson, & J. Zohar (Eds.), *Post-traumatic stress disorder: Diagnosis, management, and treatment* (pp. 53–68). London: Martin Dunitz.

Yule, W. (1998). PTSD in children. In T. W. Miller (Ed.), *Children of trauma: Stressful life events and their effects on children and adolescents* (pp. 219–244). Madison, CT: International Universities Press.

Zanarini, M., Frankenburg, F., Dubo, E., Sickel, A., Trikha, A., Levin, A., et al. (1998). Axis I comorbidity of borderline personality disorder. *American Journal of Psychiatry, 155*(12), 1733–1739.

Zarzaur, M. (2005, May). *Using a portable sandtray for crisis intervention.* Paper presented at the Twenty-ninth Annual Convening of Crisis Intervention Personnel, Chicago.

Zlotnick, C., Warshaw, M., Shea, M., Allsworth, J., Pearlstein, T., & Keller, M. (1999). Chronicity in posttraumatic stress disorder (PTSD) and predictors of course of comorbid PTSD in patients with anxiety disorders. *Journal of Traumatic Stress, 12*(1), 89–100.

Zoellner, L., Foa, E., & Fitzgibbons, L. (2002). Cognitive-behavior treatment of PTSD. In M. Williams & J. Sommer (Eds.), *Simple and complex posttraumatic stress disorder: Strategies for comprehensive treatment in clinical practice* (pp. 75–98). Binghamton, NY: Haworth Press.

Zullino, D., Krenz, S., & Besson, J. (2003). AMPA blockage may be the mechanism underlying the efficacy of toprimate in PTSD. *Journal of Clinical Psychiatry, 64*(2), 219–220.

CHAPTER 8

Crisis of Lethality

Background

In crisis work the possibility of dealing with suicidal and/or homicidal clients is always present. Thus, in Chapter 3 the importance of the crisis worker's continuous awareness and assessment of risk level for all clients in crisis was emphasized. In this chapter strategies are presented to help crisis workers strengthen their skills in assessing, counseling for, intervening in, and preventing lethal behavior, with the major emphasis on suicide. While this chapter's focus on lethal behavior is mainly concerned with the intent to harm oneself, others may not be exempt from harm. Sometimes an individual in crisis may be homicidal and target a specific victim or random victims. These homicides are not about the criminal who murders a shopkeeper in a holdup or the wife who kills her husband for insurance or to be able to marry another person; those are *instrumental* acts of homicide that occur for some financial or other concrete gain. Rather, a suicidal/homicidal person in this chapter is one who is engaged in an *expressive* act designed to reduce psychological pain. Such suicidal/homicidal people are likely to be emotionally distraught, may feel gravely wronged, depressed, helpless, disempowered, and hopeless, and may attempt to solve their own dilemmas through harm to others and then to themselves.

According to Edwin Shneidman, the founder of suicidology, "Currently in the Western world, suicide is a conscious act of self-induced annihilation, best understood as a multidimensional malaise in a needful individual who defines an issue for which the suicide is perceived as the best solution" (Shneidman, 1999a, p. 155) and who falls into a category of intense and unendurable psychological pain that is caused by unfulfilled psychological needs (Shneidman, 2001, p. 203). To Shneidman's definition should be added "or the murder of significant others."

The Scope of the Suicide Crisis

As with other maladies discussed in this book, suicide has its own mind-numbing statistics. On a worldwide basis, about 1 million people kill themselves each year, or about one every 40 seconds. Worldwide suicide rates have increased about 60 percent in the last 45 years. Eastern European countries, particularly in the Baltic Sea area, are the leaders along with Hungary (World Health Organization, 2011). In the United States, 30,000 to 35,000 people kill themselves every year (Centers for Disease Control and Prevention, 2008; U.S. Department of Health and Human Services, 2003), which translates into about 85 people a day. That number is probably very conservative because many suicides are ruled accidental either due to political, religious, and emotional considerations or because medical examiners just can't say for sure (Granello & Granello, 2007, pp. 3–5). Most official reports indicate that the real numbers of suicide attempts as well as injury caused by suicide attempts are grossly underreported. Experts claim that upward of 60,000 Americans die annually by suicide (Ross, 1999).

Between 300,000 and 600,000 U.S. citizens a year survive a suicide attempt, and about 19,000 of those survivors are permanently disabled as a result of the attempted suicide (Stone, 1999, p. 1; U.S. Department of Health and Human Services, 2003). Suicide ranges from the 10th to 11th leading cause of death in the United States (Centers for Disease Control and Prevention, 2011; National Institute of Mental Health, 2011).

Young people between the ages of 15 and 24 account for the largest increase in suicides during the past 30 years. Men kill themselves at approximately four times the rate for women (Stone, 1999, p. 10). The highest-risk group for many years has been Caucasian men over 35, but the suicide rate among teenagers and young black males has been increasing dramatically since the middle of the 20th century (Fujimura, Weis, & Cochran 1985; National Institute of Mental Health, 2003). Native Americans kill themselves at a rate about 1.5 times the national average (U.S. Department of Health and Human Services, 2003). Even though the elderly make up roughly 10 percent of the total population, 25 percent of all suicides occur in the over-65 population, and rates move up exponentially after age 70 (National Institute of Mental Health, 2011; U.S. Department of Health and Human Services, 2003).

The suicide rate among children and adolescents tripled between 1950 and 1985, and suicide is now the second to third (behind accidents but forging ahead, and in hot competition with murder) leading cause of death among children and teens in the United States and has tended to stay that way (Malley, Kush, & Bogo, 1994; National Institute of Mental Health, 2011; U.S. Department of Health and Human Services, 2003). The bottom line is that a person in the United States is less likely to be murdered than to commit suicide! Granello and Granello's (2007, p. 1) analogy is an excellent one. If an airliner crashed every day and 85 people were killed, there would be national outrage, and the government would be forced to do something about it. Yet the same suicide rate evokes little outcry. Why is that so?

In Goldney's (2005) review of suicide prevention, he noted that as far back as 1993 the World Health Organization laid out six steps for worldwide suicide prevention: comprehensive and follow-up treatment of psychiatric patients, gun-possession control, detoxification of domestic gas and car emissions, and tempering the sensationalism of press reports of suicide. As to specific treatments that could prevent suicide, Goldney's survey found no clear research evidence to indicate what treatments might significantly reduce suicide. Why is that so?

Suicide and the Moral Dilemma

Shneidman's (1980) quote from *Moby Dick*'s opening paragraph, a "damp, drizzly November in my soul," captures the essence of what most suicide is: a dreary, wintry storm of endless life-or-death debate. It is at times low, moaning, and incessant and other times howling and strident in its demands that consciousness must STOP! It is a titanic and reasoned argument that constantly questions and pleads against the continued struggle in the storm of life. It is into this wind-lashed, flat, frozen, forbidding wasteland of the suicide's mind that the crisis interventionist enters. It is neither a simple nor a painless place to be. If you are planning to become a mental health professional, the odds are about 1 in 4 that you will come face to face with a suicide (Granello & Granello, 2007, p. 1).

Of all the crises in this book, it is perhaps the most written about and the most difficult with which to deal. The simple fact is that the worldwide suicide rate hasn't decreased very much in a very long time despite all of the prevention and treatment approaches. Why is that so? First of all, for all its sensationalism, the base rate of completion for any given suicide-prone population is low. So it is difficult to ascertain who are the "few needles in a very large haystack" and study and design treatments that will prevent and stop them from committing suicide. The bottom line is that there are many false positives that are predicted by the conventional risk factors associated with suicide (Goldney, 2005). In other words, lots of people think about suicide, some attempt it, and few complete it. Yet those "few" number in the hundreds of thousands when taken worldwide, and the traumatic wake they leave for survivors numbers in the millions (Granello & Granello, 2007, p. 276).

Perhaps even more problematic for good prevention and intervention outcomes, suicidal ideation and behavior raise complex moral, legal, ethical, and philosophical questions for the crisis interventionist (Stone, 1999, pp. 69–75; Wirth, 1999). Compare your own philosophical view of death to what Everstine (1998, p. 15) has to say about various kinds of deaths: "Death by murder carries no stigma and is seen as a tragedy" (i.e., It is a criminal act and somebody must pay). "Accidental death is fully condoned providing the person didn't do something stupid or careless" (i.e., It is a tragedy—unless they were bungee jumping or sky diving, then it was idiotic). "Death by natural causes and resistance to the end allows grieving without animosity" (i.e., It was a tragedy but he lived a long, good life; or she was too young and heroic to the end). "Less forgivable is natural death by neglect or overindulgence" (i.e., The speeder had it coming; or what did he think drinking would do to his liver?). "The least forgivable death is suicide, for which there is little sympathy and no absolution" (i.e., A sin! A moral flaw! A character deficit! Not up to the task of living).

While in Eastern culture suicide may be seen as a way of removing dishonor, shame, and humiliation from oneself and one's family (Granello & Granello, 2007, p. 17), that has not been so in the Western world. Historically, suicide has been seen as a sin by almost every major religion. It has been seen by civil authority as an abrogation of the citizen's contract to serve the state and for a long time was called "self-murder." Self-murder was often blamed on the instigation of the devil. In the Middle Ages in England, self-murder was an offense against the king and nature, and all of the deceased's lands and goods were forfeit to the crown. Indeed, it was not until 1961 that the common law of felony self-murder was repealed in England. Further, a Christian burial was denied, and suicides were often buried in the middle of a crossroads with a stake driven through the heart (Williams, 1997, p. 12).

Freud's (1916) view that suicide resulted from mental illness has been a double-edged sword. On one side he gave credence to the idea that the suicide was not a person of weak moral fiber "seized by the devil." Yet for the general public a stigma of mental illness that attached to the suicide and the suicide's family has equally negative social attributions.

Euthanasia. Counterpointed against suicide as an act of the devil has been the notion from the Stoic and Epicurean philosophers that suicide could be the right thing to do given terminal illness, unremitting pain, and/or astronomical financial burdens (Williams, 1997, p. 12). Beginning in the latter half of the 20th century, much attention has been paid to *assisted suicide* and *euthanasia* in both the literature and the popular media. The two terms are not synonymous. Stone (1999, pp. 76–89) differentiates between the two by pointing out that in *assisted suicide* someone else provides the means (lethal agent), but the person who is dying administers it. In *euthanasia* someone else administers it.

We live in a time characterized by what Stone (1999, p. 77) calls "prolonged dying." Prior to the 20th century, people typically died fairly young and fairly quickly at home. They generally died as a result of infectious diseases or injury. Today 70 to 80 percent of adults will die in an institution, such as a hospital or nursing home, and probably as a result of degenerative diseases such as heart disease, diabetes, stroke, or cancer. Our deaths may be prolonged, painful, and financially draining for ourselves, our families, and society. Do we have a right to refuse medical treatment, to refuse heroic or artificial interventions to keep us alive when there is no hope of getting better or even of survival?

Further, should a therapist intervene when it is clear that a person wishes to die to end suffering? Every facet of these questions must be examined by our society as we confront the changing human conditions and health care problems in this new millennium (Stone, 1999, pp. 76–82). However, in this chapter, the position is that it is the appropriate role of the crisis worker to intervene and attempt to prevent all suicides and homicides that he or she possibly can.

The Dynamics of Suicide
Psychological Theories
Freudian Inward Aggression. In the Freudian (1916) psychodynamic view, suicide is triggered by an intrapsychic conflict that emerges when a person experiences great psychological stress. Sometimes such stress emerges either as regression to a more primitive ego state or as inhibition of one's hostility toward other people or toward society so that one's aggressive feelings are turned inward toward the self. Freud called this a melancholic state, and it is what we now call depression. In extreme cases, the melancholy becomes so severe that self-destruction or self-punishment is chosen over urges to lash out at others.

Developmental. Developmental psychology views suicide in terms of life stages. Individuals who do not successfully navigate life stages become mistrustful, guilt ridden, isolated, and stagnant (Erikson, 1963) until they are unable to cope any longer and may choose suicide as a way out.

Deficiencies. This model is embedded in the mental illness tradition and proposes that there is some mental deficiency in the suicidal individual as opposed to the nonsuicidal person. These mental deficiencies then become risk factors that can lead to suicide (Rogers, 2001a).

Escape. Escapist suicide is one of flight from a situation sensed by the person as intolerable (Baumeister, 1990).

Hopelessness. The hopelessness theory (Abramson et al., 2000) posits that some individuals believe that highly desired outcomes will not occur or that highly aversive outcomes will occur and that there is nothing they can do to change the situation. The only escape is death. Beck's (Beck et al., 1979) cognitive triad of negative thoughts about self, the world, and the future are at the heart of hopelessness.

Psychache.   *Psychache* is a term coined by the founder of suicidology, Edwin Shneidman (1993). Shneidman's (1987) *Cubic* model combines psychache, perturbation (how disturbed one is and degree of pain), and press (stress increased due to more negative factors piling up); when all three are combined, they create the critical mass necessary to activate a suicide. Psychache refers to the hurt, anguish, soreness, and aching pain of the psyche or mind. It may have to do with guilt, shame, fear of growing old, love lost, or any debilitating cognition or affect. Intolerable psychological pain is the one variable that relates to all suicides. Psychache is tied to frustrated, blocked, and thwarted psychological needs. Suicide thus serves to eliminate the tension related to those blocked needs (Shneidman, 2001).

Sociological Theory

Durkheim's Social Integration.   The most important sociological theory about suicide was originally proposed in 1897 by Emile Durkheim and still holds as the top sociological theory more than a century later. In Durkheim's (1897/1951) approach, societal integration (the degree to which people are bound together in social networks) and social regulation (the degree to which the individual's desires and emotions are regulated by societal norms and customs) are major determinants of suicidal behavior. Durkheim identified four types of suicide: egoistic, anomic, altruistic, and fatalistic (pp. 152–176).

Egoistic suicide is related to one's lack of integration or identification with a group. *Anomic* suicide arises from a perceived or real breakdown in the norms of society, such as the financial and economic ruin of the Great Depression. *Altruistic* suicide is related to perceived or real social solidarity, such as the traditional Japanese *hara-kiri* or, to put it in a current context, the suicide attacks by members of Middle Eastern extremist groups. *Fatalistic* suicide occurs when a person sees no way out of an intolerable or oppressive situation, such as being confined in a concentration camp.

Suicide Trajectory Model.   This model considers the total constellation of risk factors: biological (substance abuse, being male, genetic predisposition to depression); psychological (low self-concept, hopelessness, borderline personality disorder); cognitive (rigid, dogmatic, irrational, black-and-white, all-or-none thinking); and environmental (access to firearms, high-stress occupations, loss, family and job stressors). The more these factors are present and pile up, the greater the potential for suicide (Stillion & McDowell, 1996).

Interpersonal Theory

Joiner and associates (2009) propose that people commit suicide because they can and because they want to kill themselves. This seemingly simplistic, straightforward statement addresses three central components of interpersonal theory. First and foremost, people *acquire suicidal capability* by decreasing their innate fear of death by habituating themselves to the fear and pain of self-injury. Second, they *perceive burdensomeness* to others to the extent that they are so flawed or defective they are beyond repair. They see themselves as such a millstone for themselves, their family, or society that everyone will be better off as a result of their death. Third, *failed belongingness* means that the person has no attachments or value to any other member of society. The theory proposes that while many people consider committing suicide, and large numbers develop the capability, few actually do so because all three ingredients must be present at once to create the critical mass necessary for the act to occur (pp. 5–7).

This theory proposes that those with past suicide attempts will be habituated to pain more than other people because their past attempts help inure them to the potential for pain that accompanies most suicide attempts. Second, those whose job entails exposure to the pain of others will themselves have higher suicide rates than other people because of vicariously experiencing others' pain and thus habituating themselves to it. Indeed, there is a fair amount of research that supports these two notions.

Existential-Constructivist Framework

The existentialist side of the framework comes from Yalom's (1980) work on human pathology and involves what he believes are the four corner posts of existence: *death*, which is unavoidable; *existential isolation*, which means that each of us enters existence alone and leaves it alone; *meaninglessness*, our attempt to make sense out of a universe that is beyond knowing; and *freedom*, the absence of external structure, which means that each person is responsible for making choices, taking actions, and enjoying or suffering the consequences of those decisions. On the other side of the frame, constructivism views death, existential isolation, and meaninglessness as the principal ingredients that provide the motivation for meaning-making activities central to human life (Neimeyer & Mahoney, 1995). As individuals construct their view of self, others, and their relationships, they also construct a worldview where they encounter environmental challenges to which they have to respond. They essentially have three options in response to these challenges. They can retain their original constructions, alter them to build new constructions, or decide that neither response is viable and consider suicide as a final construct. This final construct occurs because trigger events that come from suicide trajectory risk factors (Stillion & McDowell, 1996) combine to form the critical mass that allows the individual to construct a worldview that it is a better choice to no longer view the world at all (Rogers, 2001b). A study of suicide notes' motivational components (Rogers et al., 2007) supports the existential-constructivist model of suicide. The researchers found that suicide notes contained relational, spiritual, somatic, and psychological motivators that are the primary motivational components of the existential-constructivist model.

Other Explanations

Accident.   Individuals who have no real intention of killing themselves may do so by pushing their luck too far. These may range from the teenager who decides in a fit of pique to take "a bunch of pills," passes out, and chokes on her own vomit, to the depressed alcoholic with a blood alcohol content of 0.25 who drives his car into a bridge abutment (Everstine, 1998, pp. 20–21).

Biochemical or Neurochemical Malfunction. This theory proposes that dysfunction in the central nervous system is the primary underlying cause of suicidal/homicidal behavior. Suicide, aggression, and depression are closely related (van Praag, 2001). There is evidence that hyperactivity in the neuroendocrine hypothalamic-pituitary-adrenal axis may have a special relationship to suicidal behavior (Stoff & Mann, 1997, pp. 1–2). It is also now becoming apparent that a serotonin metabolite named 5-HIAA is low (Asberg et al., 1986; Leonard, 2005) in those persons who attempt suicide and that the serotonin transporter 5-HTT gene plays a role in family clustering of depression and suicide (Leonard, 2005; Lopes de Lara et al., 2006). While

these biological differences may be correlates and not causes of suicide, evidence continues to mount that they do play a definite role (Asberg & Forslund, 2000; Chiles & Strosahl, 1995, p. 13; Lester, 1988, 1995, 2000; Stoff & Mann, 1997; van Praag, 2001).

Chaos.   Chaos theory proposes that, paradoxically, unpredictable behavior can occur within predictable systems. Relatively minor events may lead to suicidal behavior or not within the same individual at different points in time (Rogers, 2001a).

Dying With Dignity/Rational Suicide.   This type of suicide is typified by a person's rationally choosing death in the face of a painful, decimating, and incurable illness, or some other major calamity that has no foreseeable positive outcome for a reasonable person. The person has further considered the impact on others and found the action to be more beneficial than harmful. As a result, the person makes a reasoned decision to end his or her life (Fujimura, Weis, & Cochran, 1985; Stone, 1999, pp. 76–93; Wirth, 1999).

Ecological/Integrative.   In seeking to understand suicide, an ecosystemic/integrative theory takes into account that the painful intrapsychic factors within the individual interact with negative interpersonal and societal issues on multiple systemic levels (Leenaars, 1996, 2004; Potter, 2001). Leenaars (2004) proposes that while a person may be highly perturbed and suffer a great deal of psychic pain, lethality must be present for the person to commit suicide. An ecological/integrative theory proposes that both perturbation and lethality, and the resultant contemplation of suicide, can only result from a complex interaction of all these environmental variables with the individual (Potter, 2001).

Interactional.   Everstine's (1998) interactional view of suicide is in direct contrast to Freud's and Durkheim's. Everstine proposes that suicide is not fomented by anger turned inward or social isolation, but by an external rage toward another. It is not at all passive toward the significant other, but is highly aggressive and has a "get even" attitude and revenge as its goal. The suicide's hatred and desire to punish is so consuming that the aggrieved's life or a significant other's life is used as a weapon against the hated other person. The hope is that the survivors have the albatross of guilt over the suicide or homicide hung round their own necks forever.

Ludic. Ludic suicides (Baechler, 1979) relate to the desire to experience an ordeal or a way to prove oneself in gamesmanship. Perhaps the ultimate such game of proving oneself is Russian roulette. Any tribal rite of passage in which death may be an outcome could be considered a ludic suicide.

Oblative. Oblative suicides (Baechler, 1979) are those that are sacrificial in nature and seen to transfigure one to a higher, transcendental plane. Buddhist monks who set themselves on fire and the LSD user who "wants to meet God personally" and overdoses on a smorgasbord of drugs fall into this category.

Overlap Model. The overlap model includes lack of social support, a biological propensity to suicide, the presence of psychiatric disorders, personality issues such as impulsivity, hostility, and depression, and a family history of suicide. The more these areas overlap, the greater the potential for suicide (Blumenthal & Kupfer, 1986).

Parasuicide. Parasuicide (closely resembling suicide) involves commissioned acts which, although not directly lethal, can habituate persons to the pain necessary to kill themselves by inflicting *hesitation* wounds (the idea that it is extremely difficult to kill yourself and people hesitate in their initial attempts to complete the act; Joiner et al., 2009, p. 8). Clients may also engage in self-injurious behavior, such as cutting or burning their bodies, to reconnect to reality from a dissociative state. Or they may indirectly set themselves up to harm themselves by abusing alcohol, driving too fast, combining the two, or engaging in other risky, daredevil behaviors (Jobes, 2006, p. 90). Any one of these acts may end up with the person dead, injured, disabled, disfigured, or maimed.

Suicide by Cop. More a method than a theory or model, suicide by cop (as described in Chapter 5) occurs when a person gets the police to kill him or her by engaging in a threatening act toward the police or someone else, such as in a hostage situation. It is an *indirect* suicide wherein suicidal persons may not have the courage to kill themselves, or they seek to publicize their deaths through the media by "going out in a blaze of glory." Suicide by cop is now so common that many cases get a coroner's verdict of *suicide by legal intervention* (Lindsay & Lester, 2004; Miller, 2006).

Characteristics of People Who Commit Suicide

What is it about a person's inner dynamics that may make suicide or expressive homicide seem sensible? Shneidman formulated 10 common characteristics present in an individual when the act is accomplished. His characteristics are grouped under six aspects (1985, pp. 121–149; italics added throughout):

1. *Situational characteristics:* (1) "The common *stimulus* in suicide is unendurable psychological pain" (p. 124); (2) "The common *stressor* in suicide is frustrated psychological needs" (p. 126).
2. *Motivational characteristics:* (1) "The common *purpose* of suicide is to seek solution" (p. 129); (2) "The common *goal* of suicide is cessation of consciousness" (p. 129).
3. *Affective characteristics:* "The common *emotions* in suicide are hopelessness and helplessness" (p. 131).
4. *Cognitive characteristics:* (1) "The common *cognitive state* in suicide is ambivalence between doing it and wanting to be rescued" (p. 135); (2) "The common *perception* is of constriction such that one's options become very narrowed and the world is seen through tunnel vision so that no alternative thoughts can emerge" (p. 138).
5. *Relational characteristics:* (1) "The common *interpersonal act* in suicide is communication of intention" (letting another person know that one's decision makes sense) (p. 143); (2) "The common *action* in suicide is egression" (the right to exit or go out as one wishes, or the right to autonomously find a way out of one's pain) (p. 144).
6. *Serial characteristic:* "The common *consistency* in suicide is with lifelong coping patterns when deep perturbation, distress, threat, and psychological pain are present" (p. 147).

This list of characteristics points us toward what makes sense to the individual about to embark on suicide. It is not meant to suggest that all suicides are alike. In using the word "common," Shneidman reminds us that suicides, taken together, do reflect similarities. However, he is also careful to note that each suicide is idiosyncratic and that there are no absolutes or universals (1985, pp. 121–122).

Overarching these characteristics and common to all suicides is the individual's sense of perturbation and degree of lethality (Shneidman, 1999a). *Perturbation* is the degree to which the individual is upset.

Perturbation in itself does not lead to suicide. Many of us are upset by events, people, and things a great deal of the time, but we get over being upset. However, when perturbation is combined with how oriented the person is toward death, lethality level rises, and the person becomes more prone to suicide or homicide.

Similarities Between Suicide and Homicide

Often the person who is suicidal is also homicidal. Approximately 30 percent of violent individuals have a history of self-destructive behavior, and 10–20 percent of suicidal persons have a history of violent behavior (Plutchik & van Praag, 1990). West's (1966) study of murderers found that about 30 percent went on to kill themselves after they killed somebody else, and many had long histories of violent behavior and high levels of aggression. That fact is particularly relevant with murder/suicide in elderly couples, domestic violence, infanticide by overwrought parents, and mental illness (Granello & Granello, 2007; Malmquist, 2006; Nock & Marzuk, 2000). The frequency of murder/suicide in American society emphasizes the similarities of motive, sense of hopelessness, opportunity, means, and lethality of method. The 1999 mass murder and suicide witnessed at Columbine High School in Littleton, Colorado, represents a prime example of the parallels of suicide and homicide. However, it should be emphasized that not all suicides or suicidal persons are homicidal. There is a thin line between murder and suicide as an expressive act. According to Everstine (1998, p. 103), suicide is often intended to take the place of homicide and brand the intended victim as the person who is really responsible for the suicide. Given the right circumstances, the choice of homicide or suicide or both may tilt in either or both directions.

Analyzing Suicide/Homicide Notes/Videos

Suicide/homicide notes can provide valuable information, but they do not necessarily provide an open pathway to understanding suicidal/homicidal intention. Contrary to popular opinion, suicide notes are not commonly left. Only about 15–40 percent of completed suicides leave notes (Holmes & Holmes, 2006; Shneidman & Farberow, 1961). Suicide notes typically fall into four categories (Holmes & Holmes, 2006, pp. 82–97; Jacobs, 1967, pp. 67–68). In the first, the writers

beg forgiveness, see their problems as not of their own making but nevertheless overwhelming, and indicate they know what they are doing. Many times financial problems predominate in this type of note. The second category involves an incurable physical or mental illness, and the suicide is tired of putting up with the pain. The third type typically deals with love scorned, and the note is directed toward the significant other who has rejected the suicide. Finally, the fourth type is generally a "last will and testament" with instructions and gives little if any reason for the suicide.

Suicide/homicide notes may generally be characterized by their dichotomous (black-and-white) logic, hostility, and self-blame. As Shneidman (1999c) says, "Suicide notes are testimonials to tortuous life journeys that come to wrecked ends" (p. 277). Many suicide notes are rather mundane, using very specific names, details, and instructions if there are survivors. Interestingly, there tends to be less evidence of how one is thinking and much more about how one is feeling. Hate, disgust, fear, loathing, rejection, shame, disgrace, and failure are constant themes. Rock star Kurt Cobain's suicide note is a classic vitriolic, self-loathing statement about why he ended his life (Shea, 2002, pp. 36–37). As one might suspect, considerable space is given to the various meanings of "love" (Shneidman, 1973).

Unfortunately, a universal, psychodynamic breakthrough in regard to understanding suicide has not occurred after a great deal of research into suicide notes. About the only consistent results found have been that note writers lived alone, were more involved in personal conflicts such as divorce, were less often psychiatrically disturbed, and were less likely to be under medical supervision (Callanan & Davis, 2009; Haines, Williams, & Lester, 2011). Studies examining the degree to which training could improve participants' ability to determine the authenticity of suicide notes have also been conducted. The results indicated that trainees could not accurately discriminate between real and fake notes beyond chance (Bennell, Jones, & Taylor, 2011).

What suicide notes indicate over and over is the idiosyncratic reasons for the suicides and the tunneled, constricted view that there is absolutely no other way out. Paradoxically, while suicide notes are rather barren in themselves, when they are put into context with a detailed life history of the individual they can tell us a great deal about why the individual committed the act (Shneidman, 1999c). An examination of the following suicide/homicide notes graphically illustrates what Shneidman's (1973) research into suicide notes has uncovered.

An Analysis of Seung-hui Cho.   Seung-hui Cho, a student at Virginia Polytechnic Institute and State University, killed 32 people, wounded 14 more, and then took his own life on the Virginia Tech campus. His "note," in the form of a videotape that he sent to NBC News, certainly gives a description of him that fits well into Shneidman's (1985) typology of the classic suicidal person who crosses through a psychological door into becoming homicidal as well. Here again are Shneidman's characteristics, supported by Cho's videotaped statements, as excerpted from the *Memphis Commercial Appeal,* April 19, 2007 (Apuzzo, 2007):

1. *Situational characteristics* of unendurable pain: "You have vandalized my heart and raped my soul." His needs are frustrated: "You forced me in a corner."
2. *Motivational characteristics* directed toward ending his emotional problems and becoming a martyr for all the weak and disenfranchised: "You thought it was one weak boy you were extinguishing. Thanks to you, I die like Jesus Christ to inspire generations of the weak and defenseless."
3. *Affective characteristics* of hopelessness, helplessness, and abandonment: "You loved to crucify me. You loved inducing cancer in my head, terror in my heart, and ripping my soul all this time."
4. *Cognitive characteristics* indicated in his previous history of psychotic behavior and by his tunnel vision of an unjust world, with logic-tight compartments of being persecuted by the rich: "Your Mercedes wasn't enough, you brats. Golden necklaces weren't enough, you snobs." Such statements mark him as a person with paranoid schizophrenia and extremely dangerous to both himself and others.
5. *Relational characteristics* marked by his communication of intention, stating why his rampage across the campus makes absolute sense: "You had a hundred billion chances, but forced me into a corner and gave me no option."
6. *Serial characteristic* discerned in a long history of difficulty in coping, of being different, and of being bullied (see Chapter 13, Crises in Schools). The intended victims are those "who had everything and spit on my face and shoved trash down my throat."

The continuing and unendurable *psychache* (Shneidman, 1993) Cho felt and verbalized in the foregoing statements propels him toward an *egoistic* (Durkheim, 1897/1951) suicidal/homicidal rampage. His alienation, along with a lack of integration into and identification with the group, is both chronic and acute. His isolation and aloneness, manifest in the videotape, are profound, and he broods over real and imagined injustices he has suffered that caused him "to be humiliated and be impaled upon a cross to bleed to death for your amusement." At some point his egoistic suicidal impulses transgress a psychological line to move into Everstine's (1998) *interactional* model of suicide. As with other mass murderers, Cho's depression and pent-up anger turn inside out in a classic Freudian dynamic example of the suicidal and homicidal person (Freud, 1916). At that point the paranoid rage he feels explodes outward and focuses externally on others who have persecuted him. When that occurs and blame is externalized, Seung-hui Cho becomes a candidate to commit mass murder on that large amorphous mass of his tormentors. Why is this so? To the survivors it makes no sense and is the very essence of *chaos* theory (Rogers, 2001a) at work. To Seung-hui Cho, with malice and coldness aforethought, it makes perfect sense to end his pain and air his narcissistic grievances to the world. Why? His martyrlike rationalization to justify his act is: "If not for me, for my children and my brothers and sisters . . . I did it for them." But finally, the real reason very simply is, "I had to."

Myths About Suicide

There are a good many commonly held myths about suicide that the crisis worker should know and take into account when assessing potentially suicidal clients (Bonner, 2001; Duberstein & Witte, 2009; Fujimura, Weis, & Cochran, 1985; Granello & Granello, 2007, pp. 8–11; Kirk, 1993, pp. 1–4; Lester, 1997; McGlothin, 2008; Shneidman, 1999b; Shneidman, Farberow, & Litman, 1976, p. 130; Stack, 2001; Stone, 1999, pp. 51–63; Webb & Griffiths, 1998–1999, p. B42). Some of the myths are as follows:

1. *Discussing suicide will cause the client to move toward doing it.* The opposite is generally true. Discussing it with an empathic person will more likely provide the client with a sense of relief and a desire to buy time to regain control.
2. *Clients who threaten suicide don't do it.* A large percentage of people who kill themselves have previously threatened it or disclosed their intent to others.

3. *Suicide is an irrational act.* Nearly all suicides and suicide attempts make *perfect sense* when viewed from the perspective of the people doing them.

4. *People who commit suicide are insane.* There is evidence of a high degree of association between mental illness and suicide, particularly with chronic depression; schizophrenia; obsessive-compulsive, borderline, schizoid, panic antisocial personality disorder, and panic disorders; and co-occurring substance abuse. However, most suicidal people appear to be normal people who are acutely depressed, lonely, hopeless, helpless, newly aggrieved, shocked, deeply disappointed, jilted, or otherwise overcome by some emotionally charged situation.

5. *Suicide runs in families—it is an inherited tendency.* This may or may not be a myth. Sometimes more than one member of a family does commit suicide. Blood type has been found to be associated with suicide (Lester, 2005). Blood metabolites also appear to play a part in suicide. There is now a great deal of evidence that 5-HIAA, a main serotonin metabolite, is low in people who attempt suicide (Leonard, 2005; Stoff & Mann, 1997) and that the S Tin2 serotonin transporter gene is variant in families that have a history of suicidal behavior (Lopes de Lara et al., 2006). In counterpoint to a purely gene pool theory, self-destructive tendencies may be learned, situational, or linked to depression or other hopeless environmental conditions. The very act of completion in one family member may propel other family members to model that behavior.

6. *Once suicidal, always suicidal.* Many people contemplate suicide at some time during their lives. Most of them recover from the immediate threat, learn appropriate responses and controls, live long, productive lives free of the threat of self-inflicted harm, and never again consider it.

7. *When a person has attempted suicide and pulls out of it, the danger is over.* Most suicides occur within 3 months following the beginning of "improvement." One danger signal is a period of euphoria following a depressed or suicidal episode, which often means the person has everything settled and planned and is at peace with the idea of committing suicide. About 10 percent of those who have previously attemped suicide will go on to kill themselves.

8. *A suicidal person who begins to show generosity and share personal possessions is showing signs of renewal and recovery.* Many suicidal people begin to dispose of their most prized possessions once they experience enough upswing in energy to make a definite plan. Such disposal of personal effects is sometimes tantamount to acting out the last will and testament.

9. *Suicide is always an impulsive act.* There are several types of suicide. Some involve impulsive actions; others are very deliberately planned and carried out.

10. *Suicide strikes only the rich.* Suicide is democratic and strikes at all levels of society. A review of the literature over the past 30 years indicates poor people are generally at greater risk.

11. *Suicide happens without warning.* People invariably give many signs and symptoms of their suicidal intentions.

12. *Suicide is a painless way to die.* It often is not, and many suicide attempts that go awry bring terrible suffering in the form of chronic pain and permanent disfigurement.

13. *Few professional people kill themselves.* Physicians, pharmacists, lawyers, and dentists have high rates of suicide, but who keeps track of truck drivers and laborers?

14. *Christmas season is lethal.* December has the lowest suicide rate of any month.

15. *Women don't use guns to kill themselves because of disfigurement.* Women use guns more often than drugs to kill themselves.

16. *More suicides occur during a full moon.* There is no increased number of suicides during a full moon.

17. *Suicidal people rarely seek medical attention.* Research shows that about 75 percent of people who kill themselves visit a doctor within the month that they kill themselves.

18. *Most elderly people who commit suicide are terminally ill.* While many elderly who attempt suicide may be depressed, they are not terminally ill.

19. *Suicide is limited to the young.* Suicide rates rise with age and reach their highest level among white males in their 70s and 80s.

20. *Suicidal thoughts are relatively rare.* Each year in the United States approximately 8.3 million people (4%) seriously consider suicide. About 1 percent make a plan, and about half of those carry it out.

Assessment
Suicide Clues

The overarching, cardinal rule for *all* crisis workers is this: Workers who deal with *any type* of crisis client should always assess for the presence of clues and risk factors for lethal behavior. Fortunately for the crisis worker, nearly all suicidal/homicidal people reveal some kind of clues or cries for help. According to Shneidman, Farberow, and Litman (1976), no one is 100 percent suicidal. People with the strongest death wishes are invariably ambivalent, confused, and grasping for life (p. 128). Most suicidal clients, feeling high levels of ambivalence or inner conflict, either emit some clues or hints about their serious trouble or call for help in some way (pp. 429–440). The clues may be verbal, behavioral, situational, or syndromatic.

> *Verbal clues* are spoken or written statements, which may be either direct ("I'm going to do it this time—kill myself") or indirect ("I'm of no use to anyone anymore").
> *Behavioral clues* may range from purchasing a grave marker for oneself to slashing one's wrist as a "practice run" or suicidal gesture.
> *Situational clues* might include concerns over a wide array of conditions such as the death of a spouse, divorce, a painful physical injury or terminal illness, sudden bankruptcy, preoccupation with the anniversary of a loved one's death, or other drastic changes in one's life situation.
> *Syndromatic clues* include such constellations of suicidal symptoms as severe depression, loneliness, hopelessness, dependence, and dissatisfaction with life. (Shneidman, Farberow, & Litman, 1976, pp. 431–434)

All of these clues may be considered as cries for help, no matter how subtle or camouflaged they are.

Risk Factors. Let's suppose you fall into some of the foregoing categories and have decided life isn't worth living and you are going to kill yourself. How good a candidate are you to take yourself off this planet? Here are some of the high probability suicide risk categories, so check them off to see how far gone you really are (Cantor, 2000; Cheng & Lee, 2000; Granello & Granello, 2007; Holmes & Holmes, 2006; Joiner et al., 2009; Kerkhof, 2000; Lester, 2001; Lester & Gunn, 2011; Roy et al., 2000; Stenger & Stenger, 2000): You are older than 70 or younger than 20 and a male Caucasian. You have a history of alcoholism, and you abuse other drugs. You have been diagnosed (choose one or more): (a) schizophrenic, (b) bipolar, (c) borderline, (d) anorexic, or you are just plain (e) depressed. You are single, and you don't have a very good job because you lost a really good job just lately. To make up for that you got

drunk, had a hit-and-run accident, were caught, and are now spending your first night in jail. Your spouse has announced he or she is divorcing you, and most of your former friends won't speak to you anymore. This isn't the first time you've tried to kill yourself, and you have thought about it quite a bit since that time. You collect guns and know how to use every one of them and know a nice, quiet wooded area where no one ventures at night. You are a resident of Budapest, Hungary, and have been planning on moving to Latvia if you get out of jail or don't kill yourself first. It is 5 days after Christmas, and the only cards you got were from a lawyer foreclosing your house and the Internal Revenue Service who sent you an audit notice. Meanwhile, your rheumatoid arthritis is really bothering you, the only thing that helped was Vioxx, and it is now off the market. Sadly and ominously, your mother and your mother's father both committed suicide. To top it all off, you originally come from a European country that has a lot of low notes in its national anthem and you think it's pretty gloomy. If this now sounds like a bad country music song and you fit most of these criteria, do not despair or go step in front of a train (all really good country songs must include a train, so that is the way you are going to kill yourself, but you better not do it in Japan or the train company will make your estate pay for the damages since so many people do just that in Japan).

The ability to predict suicide and who will attempt or commit it is problematic, to say the least. While all of the foregoing demographics, personality traits, behaviors, and socioeconomic risk factors can predict incident rates by group and are certainly risk factors, none of them taken singly or collectively predicts very well whether an individual will complete a suicide (Bonner, 2001; Goldney, 2000; Granello & Granello, 2007).

Warning Signs. The American Association of Suicidology (n.d.) has created a list of suicide warning signs with the mnemonic IS PATH WARM:

> I is for ideation
> S is for substance abuse
> P is for purposelessness
> A is for anxiety and agitation
> T is for feeling trapped
> H is for hopelessness
> W is for withdrawal
> A is for anger
> R is for recklessness
> M is for mood fluctuations

Warning signs are different from symptoms. While symptoms can only be described, warning signs are observable.

Assessment Instruments

A variety of instruments have been used in an attempt to identify suicidal ideation and behavior (Joiner et al., 2009; Laux, 2003; McGlothin, 2008; Westefeld et al., 2000). They cover personality characteristics, risk factors, and warning signs. The Minnesota Multiphasic Personality Inventory–2 (Hathaway & McKinley, 1989), the Hopelessness Scale (Beck et al., 1974), the Beck Depression Inventory (Beck & Steer, 1987), and the Psychological Pain Assessment Scale (Shneidman, 1999e) are examples of tests that address personality characteristics associated with suicide.

The Interpersonal Needs Questionnaire (Van Orden et al., 2008) assesses the critical interpersonal issues of burdensomeness to others and lack of belongingness. Along with the Painful and Provocative Events Scale (Bender et al., 2011), which is a self-report of how much the client engages in impulsive, dangerous, pathological, and risk-taking activities, these scales significantly predict high scores on the Acquired Capability for Suicide Scale, which indicates how lethal the client is (Van Orden et al., 2008).

Other instruments such as SAD PERSONS (Patterson et al., 1983) and BASIC (Knight & Kleespies, 1999) are designed to assess manifestations of clinical suicide ideation and empirical factors that have been previously identified as being related to risk for suicide attempts. These scales accumulate data on relevant demographics, symptoms of suicidal behavior, stress, resources outside of self, personal and social history, and historical and situational variables currently identified in the suicide literature as significant predictors of suicide attempts. However, these devices alone have had a notoriously poor track record for prediction. Risk assessment is greatly improved when these instruments are backed up by a clinical interview and third-party collateral information (Rogers, 2001a).

Clinical Interview

The American Association of Suicidology (1997); Battle, Battle, and Tolley (1993); Hazell and Lewin (1993); Jobes (2006); Joiner and associates (2009); Kirk (1993, p. 7); McGlothin (2008); Patterson and associates (1983); Stone (1999, pp. 57–60), and Webb and Griffiths (1998–1999, pp. A44–45) have identified numerous risk factors and warning signs that may help the crisis worker in assessing suicide potential. While there are all kinds of scoring systems for the wide variety of checklists available today, they are rife with the possibility of yielding false positives or, worse yet, false negatives (Sullivan & Bongar, 2006). Here is where science and art commingle and the interview and diagnostic skill of the interventionist comes into play. Whenever a person manifests four or five of these risk factors, it should be an immediate signal for the crisis worker to treat the person as high risk in terms of suicide potential. The client:

1. Exhibits the presence of suicidal or homicidal impulses and serious intent.
2. Has a family history of suicide, threats of harm, and abuse of others.
3. Has a history of previous attempts.
4. Has formulated a specific plan.
5. Has experienced recent loss of a loved one through death, divorce, or separation.
6. Is part of a family that is destabilized as a result of loss, personal abuse, violence, and/or because the client has been sexually abused.
7. Is preoccupied with the anniversary of a particularly traumatic loss.
8. Is psychotic (and may have discontinued taking prescribed medications).
9. Has a history of drug and/or alcohol abuse.
10. Has had recent physical and/or psychological trauma.
11. Has a history of unsuccessful medical treatment, chronic pain, or terminal illness.
12. Is living alone and is cut off from contact with others.
13. Is depressed, is recovering from depression, or has recently been hospitalized for depression.
14. Is giving away prized possessions or putting personal affairs in order.
15. Displays radical shifts in characteristic behaviors or moods, such as apathy, withdrawal, isolation, irritability, panic, or anxiety, or changed social, sleeping, eating, study, dress, grooming, or work habits.
16. Is experiencing a pervasive feeling of hopelessness/helplessness.
17. Is preoccupied and troubled by earlier episodes of experienced physical, emotional, or sexual abuse.
18. Exhibits a profound degree of one or more emotions—such as anger, aggression, loneliness, guilt, hostility, grief, or disappointment—that are

uncharacteristic of the individual's normal emotional behavior.

19. Faces threatened financial loss.
20. Exhibits ideas of persecution.
21. Has difficulty in dealing with sexual orientation.
22. Has an unplanned pregnancy.
23. Has a history of running away or of incarceration.
24. Manifests ideas and themes of depression, death, and suicide in conversation, written essays, reading selections, artwork, or drawings.
25. Makes statements or suggestions that he or she would not be missed if gone.
26. Experiences chronic or acute stressors.

In and of themselves, each of these factors may mean little in regard to suicide. The crisis worker must realize that assessing suicidal or homicidal risk is no simple matter. Indeed, some risk factors such as previous attempts or having a concrete plan are more lethal than others and must be given more weight or attention. There are no direct "if–then" connections. Suicidal risk factors are much more relevant when identifying groups than individuals (Chiles & Strosahl, 1995, p. 8). Yet as these risk factors pile up, the potential for the individual to engage in a lethal act most certainly increases. Therefore, the clinical interview and how it is structured and handled are critical in making on-target assessments of lethality.

CAMS. The Collaborative Assessment and Management of Suicidality (CAMS) is a risk assessment clinical interview framework developed by Jobes (2006). Creation of the therapeutic alliance is critical to this framework, so the emphasis is on collaboration. The Suicide Status Form III is used in this interview to measure psychological pain, self-hatred, hopelessness, stress, and the degree of emotional agitation necessary to take action and end the pain. Clients also give themselves an overall risk of suicide and list reasons for living and dying. Clients self-report their status on these dimensions on a scale of 1 to 5. A rating of 5s across the components signals a clear and imminent danger of suicide.

CASE. Chronological Assessment of Suicide Events (CASE) is a risk assessment clinical interview framework developed by Shea (2002) that has two primary assumptions: first, that people rarely kill themselves without engaging in concrete planning and making plans to do so; and second, that clients may not voluntarily come forward with information about their suicidal thoughts without a lot of rapport building on the part of the interviewer.

RFL. The Reasons for Living scale (RFL; Linehan et al., 1983) is a different kind of suicide assessment tool in that it queries a person's reasons for staying alive by posing 48 questions as to why people would *not* kill themselves. It has a six-point Likert scoring system for each question, and the items can be categorized into six factors: survival and coping beliefs, responsibility to family, child-related concerns, fear of suicide, fear of social disapproval, and moral issues.

SRADT. The Suicide Risk Assessment Decision Tree is a risk assessment clinical interview framework (Cukrowicz et al., 2004; Joiner et al., 1999) that moves through a series of yes-or-no questions to come to a decision about how present and pronounced is the person's acquired capability of killing him- or herself. Interviewers query three domains: previous suicidal behavior, current suicidal symptoms, and empirically related variables that would exacerbate (hopelessness, impulsivity) or diminish (engaging with social supports, stopping drug abuse) suicidal behavior. Completing the decision tree involves obtaining information about the aforementioned areas, inputting the data into the decision tree to determine how high the acquired capability of suicide attempt risk level is, and then using the risk level to determine appropriate intervention. Compelling evidence for a high acquired capability would include multiple suicide attempts or three of the following five symptoms: single suicide attempt, aborted attempt, self-injecting drug use, self-harm practices such as cutting, and frequent exposure to or participation in physical violence (Joiner et al., 2009, pp. 69–70).

Using the Triage Assessment Form in Addressing Lethality

Crisis workers intervening with clients in acute crises should *never* omit an assessment for suicide lethality (McGlothin, 2008; Jobes, 2006; Shea, 2002; Sullivan & Bongar, 2009). The worker must not hesitate to ask questions such as "Are you thinking about killing yourself?" ". . . about killing someone else?" "How?" "When?" "Where?" We absolutely agree with McGlothin (2008, p. 39) that you don't sugarcoat this question for fear of activating suicidal urges in the client or of sounding callous or offensive in broaching such a personal and culturally sensitive topic. Mealymouthed questions such as "Have you . . . considered hurting yourself," "thought about giving up," "felt overwhelmed/really down/strung out/at the end of your rope," along with qualifiers such as "sorta" or "kinda," are not the same as straight questions about "killing yourself" and imply wholly different interpretations that can cause the worker to completely miss lethal ideation.

Asking *the* question about killing oneself or others does not mean doing so in an abrasive, callous manner. As in CAM and CASE interview formats previously mentioned, collaboration and empathy are key components. Asking *the* question about killing oneself or others is a closed-ended question that seeks a yes-or-no response. However, there are varying degrees of "yesness" that range from "Well, not in a long time!" to "I have the 9mm cleaned and loaded and am going out to the state park this afternoon" (McGlothin, 2008, pp. 38–39). Therefore, if you get a positive answer, you need to fully explore the dimensions and degree of that lethality by assessing across affective, behavioral, and cognitive dimensions. McGlothin's (2008, pp. 36–37) acronym SIMPLE STEPS provides a step-by-step method to assess lethality and get a good read on the client's affective, behavioral, and cognitive representation of the dilemma.

Suicidal/homicidal? Are you thinking of killing yourself/someone else?

Ideation: How likely are you to kill yourself/somebody else in the next 72 hours?

Method: How will you kill yourself/somebody else?

Pain: On a scale of 1 to 10, how much psychological pain are you in at the moment? Is there anything you can think of that would make it go higher?

Loss: Have you suffered a loss recently or a significant loss in the past you are not over?

Earlier attempts: Have you ever tried to kill yourself/somebody else before? What happened? What made it not work?

Substance use: Are you currently drinking alcohol or using drugs? What medications are you taking, and are you taking them as prescribed?

Troubleshooting: How tied up in this are your job, family, and so on? And what might change to stop this? Are you willing not to consider killing yourself/somebody? If a miracle happened and you awakened tomorrow and everything were fine, what would that look like?

Emotions/diagnosis: Have you ever been diagnosed with a physical or psychological illness? How are you feeling right now, and have you ever felt this way before? If so, how often? Have you or are you currently seeing a human service worker of any kind for this problem?

Parental/family history: Has anybody in your family thought about or committed suicide or homicide? Have your parents experienced any emotional problems?

Stressors and life events: What is going on in your life that leads you to think that suicide/homicide is a viable option or solution to your problems?

The triage assessment of the client in acute crisis provides for immediate revision of the worker's estimate of crisis severity based on the client's responses to these important and necessary questions or on rapidly elevated TAF ratings due to a sudden change in client feeling, behaving, or thinking about committing suicide or homicide when previously there was no indication of ideation. A client triage profile that may have looked safe before such answers may look quite different a few moments later. If the client is seriously thinking of killing or harming some specific other person, the worker will need to consider the duty-to-warn implications dictated by law developed in the *Tarasoff* case, described in Chapter 5.

Consider the following example. *Before* the lethality questions, the client's presenting problem to a career counselor is job loss due to a plant closing. The counselor identifies the client's depression and frustration over failure to find a suitable replacement job, but the estimated TAF affect value of 3 or 4, cognition score of 6 or 7, and behavior score of 4 or 5 (total TAF of 13 to 16) yields a "low to moderate" severity summary. Such a total score shows no urgent or immediate concern for the client's severity/lethality status.

Nevertheless, the career counselor senses that something is not quite right. The client's voice reveals a hint of verbal euphoria, while the body language seems to contradict the verbal behavior with a slight hint of hopelessness. The worker further knows that job loss, particularly after a lengthy tenure, and suicide are related (Stack, 2001). As a result of the emerging hints and cues (as an example, the client makes a nonchalant side remark implying that he or she will not be around much longer), the counselor probes directly into the client's inner world by asking, "What does that mean?" "How?" "When?" and "Where?" and then rethinks and reframes the TAF assessment.

After the lethality questions—the client's responses, which reflect obvious stress and depression, are "For me, there is no future, no life left. I am too old to retrain, and nobody wants me anyway! I might as well curl up and die," and the client answers "Yes" to the question "Are you thinking of killing yourself because things look so hopeless?"—a second TAF assessment of 9 or 10 on affect, 8 or 9 on cognition, and 8 or 9 on behavior (total of 25 to 28), amounts to a dramatic escalation and would trigger an intervention strategy of immediate hospitalization to ensure the client's safety.

This example of using the TAF as a rapid assessment tool shows how quickly the emotional tone may change in a crisis intervention case. It clearly demonstrates that whenever a crisis worker begins to suspect a higher level of severity or lethality than at first revealed, the worker should not hesitate to directly ask the question and probe deeply into the emotionally charged world of the client. A similar rapid increase in the worker's assessment of lethality is also applicable in cases of homicidal intent or any other situation involving threats of harm to self or others.

Intervention Strategies

This section contains examples of general counseling strategies to use with adults of different ages and different problems. Lethal children will be addressed in Chapter 13, Crises in Schools. Before you even start reading this section, your question might well be, Should one even try, with treatment outcomes so equivocal? While there are no absolutes in suicide treatment, there are some promising approaches (Goldney, 2005; Hawton & Van Heeringen, 2000; Hepp et al., 2004; Jobes, 2006; Lester, 2000; Linehan, & Schmidt, 1995), and it is these that will be considered. Suicide intervention strategies involve "interrupting a suicide attempt that is imminent or in the process of occurring" (Fujimura, Weis, & Cochran, 1985, p. 612). Crisis intervention with suicidal/homicidal clients generally falls into two broad categories, dealing with perturbations and reducing lethality levels.

The Three I's

The major causes of perturbation have to do with the three I's. The person confronts a situation he or she believes to be *inescapable, intolerable,* and *interminable.* The goal of intervention is to change one or more of these I's (Chiles & Strosahl, 1995, p. 74). At the beginning of the interview, the crisis worker must quickly establish a sense of rapport and trust in order to create a working relationship and provide clients with an anchor to life (Michel, 2011). It is also important to begin to reestablish in clients a sense of hope and to diminish their sense of helplessness—to take immediate steps to speak and act on clients' current pain.

The most effective way to do this is to address not the lethality directly but the perturbation the I's are causing. When the perturbation level of the three I's is lowered and some modicum of control and hope is restored in the person's life, lethality will drop below the explosive level. What this means is not just dealing passively with only the intrapersonal issues but actively confronting the interpersonal and environmental issues that afflict and assail the individual (Shneidman, 1999a).

Clients need to be taught to either use existing problem-solving skills or generate new ones so that they can shed the inescapability of unsolvable problems. Clients need to develop self-awareness and self-observation strategies to observe natural fluctuations in pain levels and make associations between doing things a bit differently and feeling better. As a result, they can learn that emotional pain will not be constantly intense and interminable. Clients also need to learn that negative feelings can be tolerated by distancing and distraction skills so that they are seen as a part of life and not something that is overwhelming and interminable (Chiles & Strosahl, 1995, p. 74). Typically, some form of cognitive-behavioral therapy will be used that employs active support for the person; teaches cognitive restructuring, emotional regulation, and learning to balance change and acceptance of how things are and will be; and changes destructive and negative behaviors through psychoeducation and problem solving (Berk et al., 2004; Guthrie et al., 2001; Linehan et al., 2006; Townsend et al., 2001). The following cases demonstrate how a crisis interventionist goes about "dotting the I's."

LeAnn, Age 21. LeAnn was a senior at a large university. During her freshman year at a small liberal arts college, she had experienced an emotional and suicidal breakdown as the anniversary date of her older sister's suicide approached. She had left the small college, returned home, and undergone psychiatric treatment. LeAnn had later enrolled in the university in her hometown, where she lived in a residence hall. She went home frequently but managed to succeed fairly well in her studies and social life. LeAnn was referred to the crisis worker by her mother following a weekend mother–daughter discussion during which

LeAnn disclosed some recurring suicidal thoughts. The mother expressed concern that the fifth anniversary of her sister's suicide seemed to be looming in LeAnn's mind and asked the crisis worker to call LeAnn in for a conference. During the first interview with LeAnn, the worker established that LeAnn did not have a specific, highly lethal plan, but that she did have a lot of suicidal ruminations.

LeAnn: I think Mother thinks I'm crazy. Sometimes I wonder if she's right. (*Long pause.*) I don't seem to handle stress very well, and this is my last semester with my senior thesis due. . . . Sometimes I think I am about to lose it. Do you think I may be going crazy?

CW: No, I certainly don't. What I'm hearing is a lot of confusion and unsettled emotion and a lot of pressure. I'm glad you feel comfortable enough to ask me. I'm wondering what's happening in you to bring up the question. Are you thinking of killing yourself?

LeAnn: Well, I've just been sitting in my room by myself, staring at the wall. I can't get anywhere on that stupid thesis. Not sleeping, not eating, not going out. And I've had this strange sensation of both wanting to run and scream, and to just give up. And I've thought about my sister's death constantly. More than at any time since I was a freshman. It's like I'm destined to go the way she went. Sometimes I think I can't stand it any longer. Then I catch myself and wonder if I *am* nuts. My sister killed herself, and her birthday is coming up. I miss her so much.

CW: Okay, I'm going to ask you a bunch of questions and I've got a couple of forms I want you to fill out. Some of the questions may seem a little intrusive but it's a way of determining where we are going to need to go. When we're done, I'll tell you where I think we need to go.

LeAnn's thoughts and responses are enough to activate the worker to conduct a suicidal assessment process. He first gives her the Suicide Status Form III (Jobes, 2006). Her scores for psychological pain are 3. She reports missing her sister, particularly on the anniversary of her death. Her stress is a 4–5, but she mainly sees her stressors as completing her thesis. Her agitation is low, with no sense of need to take any action that would lead to a suicide. She feels a bit hopeless, but again this has more to do with her senior thesis completion and resulting graduation. She indicates no self-hatred and gives it no score at all. She rates her overall risk of suicide as extremely low. Her reasons for living are graduation, her parents, friends, and a chance to go on to graduate school. She has no reasons for dying, other than she might see her sister in heaven. Her wish to live is "very much" and her wish to die is "not at all." Her

Interpersonal Needs Questionnaire (Van Orden et al., 2008) indicates she does not feel she is a burden and has a very strong sense of belonging to her parents and college sorority sisters. Follow-up questions by the worker using McGlothin's (2008) SIMPLE STEPS indicate few if any of the "hot" cognitions that activate suicidal thinking. The worker relays this information to her in a straightforward, collaborative, and empathic manner.

CW: As you can see, your scale scores are really low, all well within a normal range. I believe that more than anything the anniversary of your sister's death and how much you miss her are contributing to the loneliness and isolation you are feeling. I also think you are pretty normal and reacting pretty normally to school. I wonder if we might talk about those a little and help you make some plans to get out of this rut?

Many people who have suicidal ideation believe they are "going crazy." While some people who are psychotic or suffer from personality disorders are suicidal, suicide is not the first step on the road to "going crazy." The crisis worker positively affirms that LeAnn is not going "nuts" and seeks to normalize the crisis. The crisis worker focuses on the underlying emotional content of the loss of her sister and the upcoming anniversary as likely a key element in decreasing the client's perturbation.

The same is true of getting a handle on a huge source that would perturb most any student—the dreaded senior thesis. While her suicidal ideation is not dismissed out of hand, it is put in perspective as one component of her overall response to the loss of her sister and the other normal stressors she is experiencing at school. For many individuals a suicidal crisis may be a onetime occurrence brought on by acute situational events that, once handled, disappears forever.

Deborah, Age 27.   Deborah had been in therapy, on and off, for 11 years—since she was 16. Deborah (1) had a history of suicide attempts, some of them serious, some of them gestures; (2) had used a wide variety of drugs in her college years—in fact, she had dropped out of college after 2 years because of drug use and resulting poor academic performance; (3) had a history of episodes of severe depression, loneliness, hopelessness, and helplessness followed by mood swings to euphoric and deep religious activity and commitment; (4) had been hospitalized numerous times for psychiatric care; (5) had experienced a great sense of loss and grief at the divorce of her parents when she was 16; (6) had recently gone into self-imposed isolation and remorse—cutting herself off from friends, family, and coworkers; and (7) was feeling a new sense of meaninglessness related to her career—she had been seeking something that she really chose to do (as opposed to working for her father). Deborah, in tears, was trembling and in a state of acute anxiety and standing on the railing of a Mississippi bridge preparing to jump.

The crisis worker is a Crisis Intervention Team police officer, described in Chapter 5, Crisis Case Handling. Police and highway patrol officers have stopped all traffic, and people are out of their cars, watching. The scene is tense, and it appears that at any moment Deborah will jump.

CIT Officer: (*in a clearly audible but confident, soft, caring, and empathic voice*) My name is Mark. Tell me your name.

Deborah: (*hesitantly*) My name . . . is . . . Deborah. What . . . what do you want?

CIT Officer: I want to help you, if I can, Deborah. I can see that you are under some kind of terrible pressure to make you think about jumping off this bridge. I'd like to talk to you and see if there is any way I can be of help to you.

Deborah: I don't know that anybody can help me. (*a little indignantly*) Certainly not a cop! Shrinks haven't helped. How can you?

CIT Officer: Deborah, I'm concerned about your safety and about what's bothering you right now. I'm a cop all right, but I am also a Crisis Intervention Team officer. I deal with all kinds of people in crisis, and that's why they called me. For you to consider jumping, there must be a lot of pain that you can't seem to get relief from. If the shrinks haven't worked, how about giving a cop a chance? What's the harm? We have plenty of time.

The CIT officer immediately seeks to establish rapport with the jumper by establishing a first-name basis of communication. He validates her suicidal actions as a way to relieve emotional pain by matter-of-factly stating what she is doing and seeks to elicit what is causing her to do it. He uses a validation technique from dialectical behavior therapy (DBT; Linehan, 1997) that sets up what at first might seem the exact opposite of what one would do. He promotes the central "dialectic" in DBT, which is that he accepts the client exactly as she is in the moment, with her suicide attempt as being her best problem-solving attempt available, but also simultaneously pushes the client toward changing the maladaptive behavior patterns that have gotten her onto the bridge (Rizvi, 2011). He further acknowledges who he is and what he is capable of doing, without any false promises.

He works very hard to immediately build a trusting, empathic relationship that demonstrates congruence, honesty, and caring. While it may seem like we are harping on this subject, building a therapeutic alliance (and this most certainly includes this police officer on the bridge with this client) is absolutely critical. Michel and Jobes's (2011) book spends more than 400 pages on this topic, providing clinicians with an arsenal of theoretical techniques on how to build the relationship. Michel (2011) quotes a woman whom he met in a support group of people with depression who had attempted suicide. She had the chainsaw scars around her neck to prove the gruesome way she had attempted to kill herself. He asked why these people had not sought help. She said, "We could only have talked to another person we knew would not be afraid of listening, without judging. In a suicidal crisis we could never have trusted a person who would want to talk us out of it" (pp. 5–6).

More than other types of crisis workers, though, the CIT officer's job is dealing with the imminent lethality of the situation. Safety of a suicidal/homicidal client (Rudd, Joiner, & Rajab, 2001, p. 152) is the overriding priority, along with the safety of the officer (Memphis Police Department, 2011).

CIT Officer: With the wind blowing and all the commotion around here, I'm having a difficult time hearing you. I need for you to come down off that railing and come over here to the curb and sit down so we can talk. You look like you could use a friendly ear to listen, and I'll take the time to do just that.

Deborah: I'm not sure talking will do any good. Just go away, and leave me alone. I don't need you here.

CIT Officer: Deborah, do you remember my name? My name is Mark. Let's take some time to talk. We've got time, plenty of time to just sit down together and talk. You do remember my name, don't you?

The crisis worker makes a point to try to establish a first-name mutual communication with Deborah. Whenever a person such as Deborah is emotionally overwhelmed and immobile, one effective way to break through that immobility is to *personalize* the interaction. A good way to personalize a relationship with a client in crisis is to establish a first-name communication as early as possible (Memphis Police Department, 2011). He also attempts to slow the emotionally charged situation by repeating that there is time, plenty of time, to find out what is going on. That tells the client that in this moment, he is committed to the relationship, as transitory as it may be.

Deborah: Your name is Mark. So? How do I know I can trust you, Mark? I don't see how you can make my life any better. I've about had it with this life, with this great big lump of hurt deep inside me that won't go away. I'm really tired of this. Anyway, how do I know you won't just put me in jail or that nuthouse they put me in last time?

CIT Officer: (*in a calm, low-key, confident, reassuring, caring voice tone*) Deborah, what I want to do is to understand what's bothering you, so I can get you some help. What is it that we need to focus on to get you some relief? Right now, all I'm asking you to do for me is just to come over here to the curb, so you and I can take plenty of time to talk, so I can clearly understand just what is upsetting you. I'm certainly *not* here to put you in jail or the nuthouse. What I want to do is to try to find out what part of you is hurting inside so that I can get you to some place to get the help that you deserve. I can see you're carrying such a heavy load to think that the only way of unburdening yourself is jumping off this bridge. I don't want to see you get hurt. So could you at least step off the railing?

Deborah: (*Steps down off the railing and takes a few tentative steps toward the CIT officer.*) It's just so overwhelming and hopeless. Nothing seems to work. Everything I touch turns to crap, school, love life, job, parents. I am tired of it. So tired.

CIT Officer: Okay, thanks for getting off the railing. (*Deborah sits down. Mark slowly moves by her side, sits down, and listens to her story unfold.*) Wow! That *is* a load. No wonder you felt like jumping. I want to take you to a guy I know. He's not a shrink. He's a former police resource officer who works on the mobile crisis team. First I have to take you to the medical center and get you checked out. Is that okay?

Deborah: Will they give me electroshock treatments? I don't want those.

CIT Officer: No, they'll just evaluate you. Look! I want you to ride down there with me. I'll have to put you in handcuffs for the ride there because that's part of the police procedure. That may mean an all-night stay at the medical center, I don't know. But I think I can get them to do the evaluation and then see about getting you out of there pretty quickly to a place and a guy I know about. While they are doing that, I'll call Pete, the guy I told you about. As soon as you are checked out I'll come back and get you and take you to see Pete—with no handcuffs. You ride up front with me. I think you'd like talking to him. I know sometimes I sure do when I'm in a bind. But let's just sit down here and talk awhile, so I can kinda clue Pete in. Would that be okay?

Deborah: What the heck! I've never had my head shrunk by a cop. It can't get any worse. Okay! (*Talks a bit more about what got her here while the CIT officer listens attentively.*)

In this case, the crisis worker was able, in a few minutes' time, to validate himself to Deborah and gain her trust by focusing in on what is disturbing her and exploring her issues (Leenaars, 1994). He establishes rapport by immediately getting her name, giving his, and asking her to repeat his name. Suicidal clients often cannot concentrate, so the crisis worker repeats himself using the broken record technique and continuously seeks to slow things down. He also attempts to get Deborah to a place of safety by asking her to move off the railing. He does not make a promise he cannot keep. As an example, he promises her no electric shock treatments. He can do that because that procedure has not been done in years in his jurisdiction.

CIT officers like Mark have a great deal of discretion in what they can do with emotionally disturbed individuals they take into protective custody. While he might be able to get Deborah off the railing by lying to her about not taking her to jail or the "nuthouse," the next time a police officer was asked to deal with Deborah, she would remember the lie and be much more difficult to work with. Deborah complied with the crisis worker's request and was later taken to the emergency room of a public hospital, where she received medical and psychological evaluations.

The case of Deborah provides a brief example of how some simple verbal techniques, delivered with compassion, caring, and genuineness, can make a dramatic difference in the compliance and survival of many clients who are in acute disequilibrium and actively trying to kill themselves. After being checked out, Deborah meets Pete.

CW: I'm Pete, and you must be Deborah. Mark told me about you. I'm glad to meet you. It sounds like you had a heck of a night, and Mark tells me this isn't the first time you've felt so bad you wanted to kill yourself.

Deborah: He's right. I don't know why I didn't just go ahead. I was as close as I've ever been. I think next time that will be it.

CW: I'd like to do something a little different from what you are maybe used to. Instead of doing crisis intervention, I kinda do crisis management here with the Midtown mobile crisis unit. Are you interested in learning how to manage some of this stuff?

Deborah: Man, if I just could. That would be something else.

Dealing with chronic or episodic suicidal behavior is different from onetime suicide attempts. *Crisis management* refers to the act of planning a response to recurring suicidal behavior in *collaboration* with the client (Chiles & Strosahl, 1995, pp. 125–147; Jobes, 2006). While we are indeed involved in treatment of a lethal behavior, there is an important distinction between treatment and management. Treatment implies an end point "cure." Management implies an ongoing problem that needs a continuous collaborative effort between the client and the worker until such time as the client decides that lethality really is no longer a viable option (Jobes, 2006, p. 69).

The goal is to establish a framework that rewards alternatives to suicidal behavior and minimizes the short-term reinforcements that occur when suicidal ideation and behavior start to develop (Rizvi, 2011; Wenzel, Brown, & Beck, 2009, pp. 173–198). Pete is a member of the mobile crisis team for Midtown Mental Health Unit. He is a retired police officer and still serves as a resource officer for police officers who are experiencing personal and professional difficulties. He will use a collaborative cognitive-behavioral therapy approach (Brown, Wenzel, & Rudd, 2011; Wenzel, Brown, & Beck, 2009) with Deborah. To do that he will need to determine the central cognitive pathway that leads her to consider suicide. He will need answers to the following questions:

1. What about the client's history generates the suicidal behavior?
2. What precipitated this crisis, and is it different from other trigger events?
3. How does the client think about suicide?
4. What does she feel during the crisis?
5. What is she feeling physically?
6. What active or planned suicidal behaviors have occurred or are occurring? (Rudd, 2004, p. 67)

He is straightforward, honest, empathic, supportive, a bit cynical and worldly wise, with little professional psychobabble, one-upmanship, or discounting in his approach. He represents the potential for a perfect match in bonding for a person who has had very few positive attachment figures or trustworthy support persons in her life (Holmes, 2011). Overall, his goals and strategies closely follow Chiles and Strosahl's (1995, p. 85), Jobes's (2006), and Sommers-Flanagan, Sommers-Flanagan, and Lynch's (2001) management plans for continuing treatment of a suicidal client:

1. Destigmatize the suicidal behavior by using an objective, personal (self), scientific approach through teaching self-monitoring and hypothesis testing of behaviors.

2. Objectify the client's suicidal behavior by using reframing and problem solving, validate the emotional pain, move suicidal behavior off center stage, and calmly discuss past, present, and likely future suicidal behavior.
3. Address the likelihood of recurrent suicide behavior by developing agreements with clients about a behavioral crisis protocol and crisis management plan.
4. Activate problem-solving behavior in the client through teaching problem-solving skills, look for spontaneous problem solving, reinforce and enhance skills, and better understand short- and long-term consequences of behavior.
5. Develop emotional pain tolerance by teaching the distinction between just having and getting rid of a feeling, understand that suicide is an emotional cop-out, differentiate between emotional involvement and suffering, impart a contextual approach to negative thoughts and feelings as opposed to a global, pervasive view of negative emotion, and learn how to distance oneself by accepting that negative emotions are merely a part of living and not catastrophic.
6. Develop specific interpersonal problem-solving skills that promote interaction rather than avoidance and isolation.
7. Develop intermediate-term life direction through concrete, positive, initial steps that stress the process of goal striving as opposed to the all-or-none, success-or-failure approach to reaching goals.
8. Stay calm while listening with empathy.
9. Instill hope and confidence while establishing a therapeutic alliance.
10. Establish a treatment plan for living and a backup plan.

CW: Here are some things that I'd like you to think about doing with me. We work together on this, and sometimes other people get involved, but mainly it is you and I. First off, let's just take it as a given that you will probably consider suicide again. That is at present a fact of life. It is not forever, however. What we want to do is take away the reinforcing value of it as a short-term solution and look at the long-term benefits of doing something else. If it happens again, we don't see that as a failure but rather as something to troubleshoot and figure out what we have to do to fine-tune the plan so it is less and less likely to happen. I also want to take a look at when you are having thought disorders and mood symptoms. Those are important to know when they start in, so we can do something about them as opposed to just waiting for them to become a tidal wave of emotions and thought that wash over and drown you. The same is true of booze and drugs. If you are using those, we need to do something about that because they go hand in hand with thinking about killing yourself.

You don't get lectures from me. You choose what it is you want to do about it and I will support you. If you believe AA or other treatment programs are needed, we can work on that. We need to plan activities that substitute for those times when you might drink or get high. We want to think small, specific, and concrete on this plan and just keep it a few days ahead, so it doesn't get too big and cumbersome and hard to do. We want you to see positive, concrete changes in your life and get control back in it. When that happens, suicide behavior won't happen because you won't see the situation as unchangeable. So if I were to ask you if you were to do *something* in the next two days, and you could, would you see that as a sign of progress, and would you be able to tell me exactly what that was and why it was a sign of progress? Those are the things we are looking for in this plan. Things like decreasing social isolation, increasing pleasant and healthful activities, engaging in a work or leisure activity with someone you like. Something that is small to start with, but very concrete. Something you can hang your hat on and say, "See, Pete, that is progress!"

While this is going to be focused on changing behavior and problem solving, we need to remember that suicidal behavior is supported by emotional pain and the feeling that "I can't escape it, and it is intolerable." To that extent we are going to talk about emotions—journal emotions, tape-record emotions—and take them apart and put them back together again. We are going to listen to those emotions and work through them so they don't build up and blow up and become all-encompassing and overwhelming.

Now, if suicidal behavior shows up again, we need to plan for it and be in control. First, I'd like to write down a crisis protocol card, so that you would know exactly what to do. You would be in control of it and not vice versa. On that card we would put the resources you could use and call on, like telephone numbers, e-mail addresses, hours of operation, and so on. We also want to put two or three cues on the card. Things like "Okay, I am starting to feel anxious. I need to take a deep breath and relax, just relax." Or "Whoa! Wait a second. What am I getting into here? If my hands are sweating, that means I need to step back and take a look at this and see what the behavior is getting me." By having these cue cards, lots of times we can spot trouble and stop it before it gets started.

I am going to call you at random to see how you are doing. This is not going to be "snoopervising." It is going to be concern. The calls won't be long, just brief checkups of 2 to 3 minutes. You can do the same with me. Just to keep a check on the plan.

We are also going to talk honestly about when you need to be admitted to a hospital. If that happens, it would be better if you decided to check yourself in for a time-out rather than having me, or somebody like me, involuntarily hospitalize you. I understand that's not real palatable, but it would be you who would be deciding and not somebody else. We are going to do the same thing with medication. What you have been on has not worked very well. I want to look into getting that reevaluated. The whole idea is for you to take more and more control over your decisions. If suicidal behavior should occur, we will see it not as a failure but as an opportunity to troubleshoot what we are doing and change things. The bottom line is that we want to neutralize the reinforcement of suicidal behavior so that it no longer has positive valence, and have other more positive, addicting behaviors and healthful living activities take its place. I will help you manage this, but it is going to be you who will have more and more say in what is to be done. That is a big, long speech. And it sounds like a lot, but we will take it one day and one step at a time. What do you think?

Deborah: It's kinda scary, but kinda thrilling too. I don't know. I kinda feel good for the first time. Maybe like in some control, but that's scary, I've been out of it so long.

The key component in crisis management is normalizing the situation and showing the client that everything comes down to problem solving in a matter-of-fact way. Suicide behavior will invariably recur in a client like Deborah. To keep her from getting discouraged, we treat suicide as an annoying, inconvenient, but important piece of business that is not catastrophic and does not mean she is an abysmal failure. By focusing on problem solving, developing tolerance to emotional distress, changing disturbing self-images, halting impulsive behaviors, creating anger-management skills, and generating better day-to-day functioning at home and work (Michenbaum, 2005), we start to build resiliency and emotional toughness in the chronic, suicidal client. This is not an easy task, but it is one that can be done and can be successful.

CW: We are going to work out a treatment plan for living, but first thing is I'm gonna give you my business card with phone number and e-mail on it. That is for you to call, no ifs, ands, or buts, if things are really starting to go in the toilet. But the important thing is, it is your crisis card and on the back we are going to brainstorm and come up with five activities that when things start to go to hell in a handcart are positive actions that will break that doom-despair thinking and turn off that emotional motor running wild with affective dysregulation, so you don't need to call me but can take control of things yourself. It sounds simplistic but it works. These are positive activities that will require you to get off your rear end and go do something so that you get busy and take your mind off of those inner voices.

Of all the things that don't work in the lethality intervention business, Pete uses a couple of very simple tactics that do work—particularly for those clients who have been hospitalized: follow-up phone calls (Vaiva et al., 2006) and crisis coping cards (Jobes, 2006, pp. 80–82). The phone calls provide follow-up support that says you belong and you are not a burden. The protocol card helps clients to kick-start their crisis management plan, because lots of times it is difficult for clients to initiate problem-solving skills on their own. A bullet point cue card that is concrete gives them specific real-time instructions on recognizing warning signs and instituting coping skills (Brown, Wenzel, & Rudd, 2011).

Simone, Age 36.   Simone was the director of a rape crisis center in a large metropolitan area. She had established a reputation as an effective leader, public relations person, fund-raiser, recruiter, and trainer of volunteer workers for the center. She was tireless, dedicated, popular, and widely known as the leader of one of the best organized and most effective crisis agencies in the community.

Now, after 6 years as director of the center, Simone was approaching burnout. She was also experiencing grief and rage over a broken relationship. Simone was astute enough to finally recognize that she was on the verge of some kind of breakdown and was considering suicide or homicide, so she sought counseling at her agency's employee assistance program (EAP) clinic.

CW: So, Simone, from what I can glean from your intake material and from what you just said, I sense that *you* are fully aware of your vulnerability right now, but are keeping up a good front for the troops.

Simone: (*in a clinical, detached fashion*) That's right. And there's no use in my problems interfering with the work at the center. That's the most important thing. Even so, my issues are affecting me, at least. And, right now, I'm really feeling trapped; no good to them or myself either.

CW: What's the most pressing issue in your entrapment?

Simone: (*Starts to tremble and shake with a tremor in her voice.*) Well, par . . . t of the prob . . . lem is at home. I've had the rug pulled out from under me . . . literally. (*Laughs ironically.*) My partner, Rene, my soul mate for

over 6 years, has taken off. It happened right under my nose. (*Hits her chest in recrimination.*) So stupid! So blind! I didn't see it! She has managed to leave me high and dry with little money and with all the bills. She took most of our furniture, much of which I bought myself. And she took both our dogs too! That cold-hearted bitch! This all happened just when we were getting ready for our one big fund-raising event of the year at the center and just as we were preparing for the accreditation site team to visit the center in a few weeks.

I'm feeling so hurt, so humiliated, and so betrayed that I am overwhelmed with anger, disappointment, and depression. I have scarcely slept or eaten for over a week. I thought our relationship was for keeps. I feel like killing her if I could get my hands on the cheating rat, but I still care about her so much! I want the miserable creep back! I'd kill that little blonde bitch if I could find out where they took off to. Her too! I'm feeling so worthless and undesirable and tired of this nightmare that sometimes I just wish I'd sleep forever.

CW: What you've just said worries me. Now I'm concerned about your safety. Are you feeling so depressed and angry that you might consider suicide—or homicide for that matter?

Simone: I don't know how I feel anymore. I guess I wouldn't go that far. Suicide, that is. I want her back more than anything. But I've even thought to myself, "If I can't have her, then nobody can." But I know that's not realistic either.

CW: Simone. Does that mean that you might consider doing harm to Rene or even to her new girlfriend? Have you thought about how you might hurt them if you were going to?

Simone: When it came right down to it, I don't think so. But I'd certainly feel like it sometimes. No, I'm just distraught and mad as hell right now. I'm really harmless, I guess. I don't know what I need. Some space, maybe. Another job, maybe. I don't know. Just some relief and love and rest and to get over this crushing pain.

Simone continues her catharsis about her romantic betrayal and the deep hurt it has caused her for another 30 minutes. The crisis worker listens intently for signs that she may have the means, access, and availability of acting on her stress and perturbation. During that time she gradually subsides emotionally and regains a good deal of her cognitive ability, to the point the crisis worker rates her affect as 7, behavior as 5, and cognition as 5, for a full scale score of 17. Her Suicide Status Form III (Jobes, 2006) is in the average to above range, with 3's and 4's and an overall rating of 3.5. Her Interpersonal Needs Questionnaire (Van Orden et al., 2008) indicates some feelings of burdensomeness and a lack of belonging in the middle range "as somewhat true." However, she does give "very true" endorsements of people who care about and support her, which is a major plus. More ominous is her Maslach Burnout Scale (Maslach & Jackson, 1981), which indicates an extremely high score on the Emotional Exhaustion and Depersonalization scale and a low score on the Personal Accomplishment scale, indicating she is well on the road to burnout (see Chapter 16, Human Services Workers in Crisis: Burnout, Vicarious Traumatization, and Compassion Fatigue).

Some safety measures will need to be put in place before she walks out the door.

CW: I believe you, but I need a no-harm contract from you, written down and signed before you leave here today. Can I trust you to do that? I also want to institute a treatment plan. Your scores on the two lethality assessments are not in the lethal range, but they are fairly high. The fact that you have considered lethal action is a warning we need to take seriously. You are a smart professional, but even smart professionals don't always know when they are in burnout and your scores on the burnout scale tell me you are, along with what you self-report.

The case of Simone provides one glimpse of a crisis worker inquiring about both the client's suicidal and homicidal potential. The worker has determined that Simone's possible threat to herself and others is in the low-to-moderate range on all dimensions of the TAF. However, she writes an anti-suicide/homicide contract with the client. There is a good deal of divisiveness in regard to "no harm" contracts (Dorrmann, 2005; Granello & Granello, 2007; Joiner et al., 2009, p. 92; Range, 2005). Chiles and Strosahl (1995, pp. 131–132) have criticized the no-harm contract because it specifies what a person *should not* do instead of *should* do, and they question its utility if a person starts to feel guilty about not abiding by it and terminates therapy as a result. Everstine (1998, p. 101) somewhat cynically believes that at least a no-harm contract is protection against a malpractice suit, which Joiner and his associates emphatically refute (2009, p. 92). To that end, the American Psychiatric Association has stated that no-suicide contracts should not be used with patients who are actively suicidal.

Undoubtedly, what we are about to say is going to create some controversy with contemporary suicidologists. However, the Granellos (2007, p. 239) believe that most clients view it as positive and that it communicates a sense of caring and helps build a strong therapeutic relationship. While such contracts have no legal bearing and cannot guarantee the client's or anyone else's safety, your authors have found that clients will rarely if ever go back on their word when asked to commit to such a contract if a commitment to treatment statement is put in place with it. The contract is really a tactical move to buy time. It gives time a chance to operate and ameliorate the hot cognitions that are driving the client's suicidal ideation.

Following are two very different types of no-harm contracts. The first is the more standard type of contract. The stay-alive, no-harm contract is instituted and negotiated in a realistic manner. It is simple and to the point, with no vagueness or wiggle room (Hipple & Cimbolic, 1979, pp. 67–73).

Simone's Stay-Alive, Do-No-Harm Contract

I will not harm myself or anyone else for the next month while I work on my problems.

I will not attempt to kill myself or kill anyone else without talking to you first. If I cannot reach you, that is not an excuse for abrogating the contract. I will call the suicide hotline and talk to them. I will voluntarily check myself into Mid-south Hospital if all else fails.

Date _____ Signature _____

Date _____ Witness _____

A different, somewhat controversial contract has been developed by Everstine (1998, p. 118). Everstine believes that most suicidal/homicidal behavior is caused by our anger toward others. Therefore, his contract focuses on the significant other that the anger is directed toward, but more important, it states that the person's life is important to someone else. Everstine proposes that the self-contract be shown to the beneficiary of it, which will make the contract explicit and change the commitment to a shared one (p. 119). Such a contract fits really well with Simone's anger, so we would attempt to turn her anger and hurt into an asset though the contract.

Simone's Self-Contract

1. The person whom I hate most is: That snake who stole Rene from me. I KNOW THAT THIS HATRED COULD COST ME MY LIFE!
2. If I die, other people who will suffer are: All of the rape victims I could serve and the great staff I have built.
3. I have decided to stay alive because of: The work I do and the possibility of finding another fulfilling relationship.

4. I am also going to commit to a treatment plan that will help with not just my personal issues but professional issues as well, because I need to get a handle on these issues so I can get back to the competent and happy Simone I liked a lot before this happened.

Date _____ Signature _____

Date _____ Witness (Center Staff) _____

Courtois (1991) cautions that antilethality contracts must not be imposed on clients. Rather, such stay-alive contracts must be mutually agreed on by both client and crisis worker. That caution applies also to no-harm homicidal contracts.

Latasha, Age 51. Latasha was an eminent and successful elementary school principal who had devoted her life to children and the teaching profession. She was exceptionally capable, hardworking, conscientious, and efficient. She was also compulsive and a perfectionist in her work and personal habits. At age 51, Latasha faced some life and career decisions that she regarded as catastrophic: (1) She had recently had bypass heart surgery only to discover she had breast cancer, and she could not bear to think about her physician's recommendation to accept early retirement and undergo a mastectomy. (2) She felt trapped between the two perceived unacceptable choices of continuing to hold the principalship in her debilitating physical condition, or becoming the ex-principal who had been forced into early retirement. (3) She was totally unprepared to alter her whole identity, which had included serving the students, faculty, parents, community, school, and the teaching profession. Latasha had no family. She had never married because she had devoted all her energies and talents to education. She came to her longtime friend and colleague, the Jefferson Elementary School counselor, in desperation.

Latasha: (*in tears*) It is so hopeless. Why me? Why has God forsaken me? I have been a good Christian. A good person. A good teacher. A good principal. What have I done to cause me to come to this? I don't think I can bear it. (*Sobs. Pause.*) It's so unfair. I have no choice. (*Sobs.*)

CW: (*reaches out and touches Latasha's arm*) You're feeling hurt, hopeless, and vulnerable—and you're looking for better answers and choices than you've been able to find so far. Because so far there are none.

Latasha: (*still in tears*) For the first time in my life I have no ideas, no options.

CW: I want you to know that I'm glad you have the courage to discuss it. What scares me is the desperation and danger you're feeling. You're feeling that, right now, there are no acceptable choices. That's a really tunnel vision view that's not like you at all.

Latasha: (*Still in tears. Nonverbal clues show that she is experiencing acute fear, anxiety, and hopelessness, and has almost given up.*) None. None at all. There is no future.

CW: Latasha, it sounds to me like you've considered suicide. I want to know your thinking on this subject.

Latasha: (*still in tears*) Oh God! I've thought about that a lot. Toyed with it a lot. And I'll have to admit that it becomes more appealing all the time. I have these pain pills for the cancer treatment. I could take them all at once.

CW: Do you have a plan on how to do it?

Latasha: I would put on some Brahms, get a large glass of Chablis, rip the phone line out so I wouldn't chicken out. No one would be in the office. It'd be June 9th, the day school is out, about 11 in the evening. Everything would be finished up at school, and everybody would be gone. I work late a lot on Friday so security wouldn't bother me. That would give them time to get another principal. I even made some recommendations I have written down. It would be all settled. Actually, I am feeling a little peace with myself as I talk about it. Strange!

Latasha's plan is highly lethal. She has thought carefully about it. She has the means, the method, and the plan is close to irreversible. Her contemplation that she feels at peace is another highly lethal indication that she has settled her affairs. The fact that her colleague and friend is hearing this makes the decision the school counselor is about to make terribly difficult, but it is one that her training has instilled in her. In such instances, it is critical not to match the client's anxiety level. Moralizing, placating, coercion, lecturing, or other attempts to discount the client will only exacerbate the problem (Chiles & Strosahl, 1995, pp. 113–115). The potential for countertransference to arise in such situations is high. Disregarding cries for help because of their threatening nature, denying the facts because of the personal relationship with the client, feeling a lack of expertise because the person is not an "expert" suicidologist but merely a school counselor, and being lulled into a false sense of security by who the client has been as opposed to the state of being the client is now in are serious dangers, and staying in self-control and not becoming vague and tangential are critical to the process of stopping this suicide situation (Leenaars, 1994, pp. 56–57). The *Tarasoff* ruling has just come into play here, and if the school counselor did not assess for suicide and did not take action, she could be held legally accountable as negligent (Granello & Granello, 2007, pp. 266–268).

CW: (*Very clearly, empathically, and emphatically makes the following declaratory and exclamatory statements.*) What you have just said scares the daylights out of me, Latasha. I cannot and will not let you do that! If you won't go to the superintendent with me right now and tell him you need some help, I will call him myself! If I have to, I will call the school resource police officer to contain you until we can get you to a place of safety. I believe that you have become so constricted you see no options. There are options, and you need to stay alive to find them out! I don't think you would have talked to me if you didn't believe there was something left and you needed another view. Well, I am giving you that view. So which do you wish to do? Go with me to the superintendent or have me make the call? You could run right out of here and go swallow all those pills, I suppose, but then we would call an ambulance and they would take you out in front of the kids, which I don't think you would see as real uplifting. So you see there are some choices left, and the first one is, "Do we go now, or do I call now?"

There are no ifs, ands, or buts about this scenario, and there is no need or time to do any kind of written assessment. The TAF puts her clearly in the high 20s. The school counselor is ethically and legally bound to take action (Chiles & Strosahl, 1995, pp. 17–35; Granello & Granello 2007, pp. 266–268; Hipple & Cimbolic, 1979, pp. 94–100; Leenaars, 1994) no matter what the client's protestations about confidentiality, broken friendship, trust, or any other pleas. The school counselor, like any other helping services professional, has a duty to disclose life-threatening behavior. That the client is her boss makes no difference. The counselor also lays a guilt trip on the principal to stop any impulsive attempts by reminding her that it would not be good form or model very good behavior to be hauled off in front of the school in an ambulance or police car. This tactic is one used by Everstine (1998, pp. 113–114) to remind clients that there are many more potential victims than their constricted view of things allows them to see. Latasha's love for the children of her school would be a powerful deterrent to doing anything foolish and precipitous.

While hospitalizing a potential suicide is no guarantee that the person will not kill herself, given the clear intent to do harm to herself, at the very least the crisis worker is removing the principal's immediate access to killing herself (Joiner et al., 2009, pp. 88–89). Whether she goes ahead in the future is another matter, but putting her in the hospital will bring the psychological perturbation she feels into full view of her oncology team who can then step in to deal with that aspect of her cancer.

This example of a close relationship between two colleagues is included here because all too often this is exactly how the discovery of a potential suicide occurs. Close friends should be aware of what they need to do and do it proactively and without guilt. If the worker is not sure about what to do, doesn't feel he or she has the necessary expertise, or is too close to the client personally, the watchword is "consult"! There is no instance in a helping professional's life when consultation with a peer is more important than when dealing with lethality (Leenaars, 1994).

Older Adults

The number of older adults across the world is growing rapidly. As baby boomers age, this fact, combined with the high suicide rate in the elderly, means that a lot more service providers for geriatric populations are going to be needed and those providers are going to need to get into the suicide prevention/intervention business (Erlangsen et al., 2011). Suicide in the elderly is treatable and preventable (LaPierre et al., 2011), yet it is one of the most neglected areas in the entire field of suicidology (Richman, 1994). It is the age of the highest incidence of suicide and, concomitantly, depression, cognitive impairment, isolation, and physical illness (Granello & Granello, 2007, pp. 75–79; Harwood & Jacoby, 2000; Heisel, 2006). Suicide among the elderly is also the most lethal, in that it uses lethal means and is well planned. It is rarely a cry for help or some spontaneous impulsive act (McGlothin, 2008, p. 124). By far and away, it is the male Caucasian in this age group that is at highest risk (Granello & Granello, 2007, p. 79). Research indicates that the percentage of failed attempted suicides decreases with age, and the percentage of completed suicides increases with age (Stone, 1999, pp. 45–50). The same is true for homicide/suicide in the elderly, which occurs at nearly double the rate of young adults. Usually the perpetrator is a male who kills his wife or other intimate and then commits suicide himself (Cohen, 2003).

The worker's assessment brings to the forefront a special consideration for dealing with older people. That assessment should include ego-weakening factors such as chronic and acute physical and mental illness, elder abuse, alcoholism, prolonged stress, failure to respond to medical treatment, and complicated/prolonged grief (for a complete description of this phenomenon see Chapter 12, Personal Loss: Bereavement and Grief). A variety of social factors, such as having fewer friends, living alone, being excluded or living on the periphery of social and family events, and being separated from the family through children leaving, all contribute to the potential for suicide (McGlothin, 2008, p. 124–126). Psychodynamic factors most often include the stress and strain of various losses, such as the loss of a spouse, friends, work roles, and income. Chalking these risk factors up to "just growing old" is to put the elderly at risk for suicide (Richman, 1994).

Roy, Age 68.

Roy had been a farmer all his life. At age 65 he went into semiretirement, turning his land, equipment, buildings, and livestock over to his two sons, who also were career farmers. One year after he began his semiretirement, his wife died. About a year later, he was despondent and could find no purpose in life, even though he was in excellent health and had the good fortune of financial independence. He has been somewhat alienated and estranged from his two sons because of disagreements and arguments over their "newfangled" farming practices that he doesn't always agree with. The foreman of the farm, Juan, came upon Roy standing on a tractor in the hall of the barn. Roy held a rope with a hangman's noose in it, and he was attaching the rope to an overhead crossbeam. Roy, thinking he was completely alone, was surprised at Juan's appearance.

Juan: What on earth are you doing there, man?

Roy: (*Almost falls off the tractor he is so startled.*) Where the hell did you come from? What are you doing here?

Juan: I'll tell you what I'm gonna do right now! I'm taking that rope away from you this minute! You're going to get in my pickup truck this minute. I'm driving you straight to the mental health center. That's where we're going. And I'll tell those boys of yours what you've tried to do too! Don't you know that it'd just kill those boys if you finished what you were planning to do? What the hell did you think you were doing, anyway?

Juan's alert and decisive actions clearly show that one does not have to be a trained human services worker to contain and control a situation in which human life is at risk. The crisis worker at the mental health center knew nothing about Roy's problems, but he recognized that a person of Roy's age, gender, life circumstance, style, and sense of private independence would rarely, if ever, present himself for counseling (Chiles & Strosahl, 1995,

p. 240). In assessing Roy's responses, the worker quickly concluded that he definitely exhibited six of the lethality characteristics that Fujimura, Weis, and Cochran (1985) defined as high-risk factors: (1) the plan was definite and readily accessible, (2) the method was irreversible, (3) there was indication of sleep disruption, (4) support people would not be around, (5) rescue would be improbable, and (6) the most valued possessions had been disposed of. Also, the crisis worker knew that among men Roy's age, there are very few suicide gestures or attempts. Older men are more likely to accomplish the act than to merely attempt it (Shneidman, Farberow, & Litman, 1976; Stone, 1999). The crisis worker immediately suspected loss as a factor in Roy's decision to kill himself. Shea (2002, pp. 27–28) proposes that the elderly are subject to a series of losses, and as they suffer these losses, the potential for lethality rises. They include loss of health, mobility, cognitive functioning, ability for self-care, role with family or society, skills, job or job opportunity, means of self-support, home or cherished possessions, and loved ones including pets.

CW: Roy, lots of times men who have had lots of responsibility find that as they age, their ability to take on those responsibilities becomes more difficult. They also may not feel like they mean much to anyone because they don't have much importance or lose their capabilities—that in fact they are becoming a burden. I'm wondering how you feel about what I just said?

Roy: Well, now there's really nothing else to live for. A man's got to have some purpose. I've got nothing to go to—nothing to get up for in the morning. I just don't know what's gonna happen, and I frankly don't give a tinker's damn. My wife's dead. I can't hardly do anything anymore. The boys don't need me to run the farm, and I damn sure don't need no therapy or no shrink.

CW: (*Thinking to himself: "Wow! He's not fooling! With all this intake information pointing toward suicide lethality, I don't need any more assessment data right now. I'm remembering his age, his male image, his having disposed of all his property, his wife's death—these are potent indicators—and this morning, an aborted self-hanging! It's a wonder he's even here!"*) Roy, what happened this morning is scary indeed. I'm setting up a complete medical evaluation for you today. I have called your family doctor. I have also called your sons, who are on their way in here right now. To say that they are very concerned is putting it mildly. I know you probably hate it that I called them, but we need to get some support systems in place and straighten some things out between you and your family.

While older clients will see their family doctors for a variety of physical complaints, they will seldom, if ever, speak about psychological duress or even consider it as a possibility! Conwell and Heisel (2006) found that up to 75 percent of older adults who committed suicide had been to their family doctor within the previous 30 days. All of Roy's symptoms indicate he has slid, ever so gradually, into being at least demoralized, if not depressed, by life's circumstances. Even though he would appear to have everything to live for, the loss of his wife, when they had grand plans for retirement together, the death of other close friends, and the disintegration of his social network as friends die, go to nursing homes, or move away, all have slowly led Roy to perceive life is no longer worth living.

The benign neglect and estrangement with his sons is another piece of the suicide puzzle that needs to be dealt with. While it might be readily apparent why elderly people would commit suicide if they were physically abused or neglected, more often their adult children are guilty of benign neglect or annoyance at dealing with the foibles and frailties of older people. Grown children have their own lives to lead. They may either believe that their parents have little or no need of them, or become annoyed by their increasing dependence. As a result, they tend to avoid and exclude their parents not only from activities but from decision making.

Social isolation is further compounded by the loss of friends. As a result, one of the key factors in dealing with the elderly is to set up in step-by-step fashion a new set of life supports. Reconnecting with people is paramount. If a person is unable to engage in former leisure or work activities because of a decrease in physical or mental functioning, then new activities that are socially connective and challenging to the client's physical and mental capacity need to be instituted (Richman, 1994).

While at first glance these therapeutic goals may seem a long way from suicide intervention, they are in fact directly related to it! Disengagement (a progressive withdrawal from the wider world), activity (decreased levels of physical, emotional, and cognitive activity), role exit (social usefulness diminishes as work activity ceases), and social exchange (limited ability to engage in new relationships) theories all play a significant part in whether older persons become suicidal (Granello & Granello, 2007, p, 78).

The other compounding problem is medication and neurotransmitter changes. Jacobs (1999) and Wenzel, Brown, and Beck (2009, p. 267) propose that older adults may engage in *chronic or passive suicide* when

they decide to quit taking their medication because of side effects, cost, or the notion that stopping taking it will hasten death. In many instances, forgetting to take medication, misdosage, polymedication administered by different doctors, and bad drug interactions contribute to depression. For this reason, it is paramount that primary care providers be contacted and physical and mental health issues be coordinated (McGlothin, 2008, p. 125). Combined with the effects of alcohol or illicit drugs, the potential for psychological problems becomes exponentially greater in older adults (Chiles & Strosahl, 1995, p. 243). Added to the foregoing is the mounting suspicion that serotonin levels are affected by aging. Thus, the mere fact of getting old may biologically predispose a person to suicide (Granello & Granello, 2007, p. 79; Harwood & Jacoby, 2000).

One of the primary techniques for bringing elderly clients out of suicidal ideation is to remotivate them to live. Chiles and Strosahl (1995) have developed a Reasons for Living Inventory that may be given to clients; it covers survival and coping skills, responsibility to family, child-related concerns, fear of suicide, fear of social disapproval, and moral objections. While clients may naysay many items, there are invariably some they will agree with. The crisis worker may then use these items to combat the suicidal ideation and reinforce the elderly client's desire to live.

CW: (*Two days after Roy has been medically evaluated for an antidepressant and has had an emotional but positive family session with his two sons.*) So, after talking with your boys and taking the inventory, you have said at least these items would be important: not wanting to be seen as a coward or selfish; my sons might not believe I loved them; I do want to watch my grandchildren grow up; others might think I am weak or selfish; I wouldn't want people to think I didn't have control; I have had a love of life; and there are some experiences I haven't had yet. So those are some reasons for living. I further think that the antidepressant the doctor has prescribed will kick in and you will start to feel like your old self. I want to let you know that there is a group of folks that meet at St. Mark's church that I work with. I understand that might be pretty repulsive to you, but I asked Jim Joyner if he wouldn't mind talking to you about our group. I believe you know him. In the meantime, I'd just like to make sure that if you start to feel down, you know you can call me before we meet next week. I have also done a little investigating and I believe the agriculture teacher at the high school would be very interested in your expertise in no-till planting, the top-flight soil conservation you are known for, and working with him on the school ag program.

Roy: Hell, I guess it wouldn't kill me to listen to Jim. It's gut wrenching, but I do appreciate what you're trying to do. I particularly appreciate the head-to-head with Leroy and Ronnie. I couldn't have done that myself. I do take a lot of pride in them and the grandkids. I don't know what got into me. Hmm! The ag teacher said that? Hmmmm! Well, maybe.

CW: Roy, I want you to know that I feel good about your progress and, given I have dealt with a lot of people in a situation like yours, the prognosis for you is good. There are a couple of things I want to do, though. First off, we are going to put together a treatment plan. It isn't a forever plan, and I really believe that it's about 4 to 6 weeks' worth of work. That plan is going to involve coordinating your medication with your primary care doctor; some more meetings with your sons that I want our family therapist here at the clinic to do; getting you back socially involved again; and not just letting all that knowledge you have sit out there and ossify on 1300 County Road 1321 East. I also want you to make a contract for living with me. It is essentially a "I won't kill myself while we are working on this" contract. I believe your word is good, so I am willing to talk through it and get a handshake to seal the deal.

CW: Well you've done okay so far, so I don't see why not. You got my word. (*Leans over and shakes hands.*)

We have spoken to the controversial aspects of no-harm contracting. However, we believe as does Jacobs (1999) that when combined with a treatment plan, a no-harm contract is particularly effective with the elderly because they are excellent at keeping their word and adhering to contracts. Getting Roy involved in a support group with a former friend is a key ingredient in getting a social support group of peers in place. Social support is critical and needs to target the peer groups and pleasurable and stimulating activities with which the elderly are involved (Wenzel, Brown, & Beck, 2009, p. 278). The crisis worker is very directive and active in instigating these interventions because most people who are depressed are going to have a very difficult time initially acting on their own.

CW: (*one week later*) You have a couple of what we call "automatic thoughts" linked with some recently developed core beliefs that have helped kick this depression into high gear. Listening to you, they are very different from what you typically have thought and are really typical of the kind of thing that gets a person depressed. For instance, some of your core beliefs are "I am on a downhill slide and there's no upside. I am a burden and I can't stand that." Some of the automatic thoughts are "It's hopeless and I am helpless to do anything about it. I am a weak old man. I might as well give up. They'd be better off without me."

I am going to give you a cue card with what we call positive counter injunctions on it. For instance, when you are at home sitting alone at night watching TV and all of a sudden one of those thoughts pops up, I want you to pull this card out and read it. It will say something like "That's not true! I am engaged and I am putting my knowledge back to work. I am not a hopeless piece of used junk. I have reestablished my relationships with my family and am enjoying the hell out of helping raise my grandkids. Yes! I miss Helen, but I know she'd want me involved in rearing our grandkids. I don't have a terminal case of 'I-can't-stand-it-itis.' I have withstood a lot of things in life as tough as this. It's inconvenient, all these aches and pains, but I can move and think and I intend to do so and enjoy myself, which is what Helen would want."

These are the positive automatic thoughts I want you to get habituated to. I also have another little program called a Hope Kit I want you to assemble. It consists of a container that holds mementos that will serve as reminders to live and enjoy life. It is not about getting all caught up and getting maudlin about what was, but what symbolizes you and the good life you have lived. I particularly would recommend some photographs or keepsakes of the good times and good memories. But this is definitely not about living in the past; in fact, you just might have some new mementos you want to put in there—like that Future Farmers of America hat you are wearing that I might guess you stole (*both laugh*) from the ag teacher. I want you to use that as a negative thought stopping device, so if you get down in the dumps you can pull it out and start going through it.

As simplistic as it sounds, the Hope Kit (Wenzel, Brown, & Beck, 2009) is extremely effective because it is a concrete reminder of all the positive aspects of the person's life (Jobes, 2006, p. 83). The positive counter injunctions are typical of cognitive-behavioral approaches to stop catastrophic thinking (Beck et al., 1979). Putting these on a crisis card (Rudd, Joiner, & Rajab, 2001) and placing the Hope Kit in a readily accessible place are easily implemented crisis intervention techniques designed to stop negative cognitions in their tracks.

Roy's situation is not unique to older clients. Roy is fortunate in a sense. He is not faced with debilitating financial or health problems, as many of his peers are. These problems further exacerbate the notion that suicide is a viable option. Finally, a compounding problem is that sometimes the problems the elderly face ripple over to spouses or significant other caretakers, who may also come under lethal threat.

Homicide/Suicides of the Elderly. Many people wrongly believe that only unrequited or rejected young love is the reason for homicide/suicide between couples.

Nearly 20 older Americans die each week in homicide/suicides (U.S. Department of Health and Human Services, 2003). These are not "mutual, dying together pacts" but rather acts of desperation, anger, and depression. Nor are they impulsive acts. Cohen (2003) proposes that the perpetrator has thought about the act for months and perhaps years. Cohen has identified three different types of homicide/suicides in the elderly.

1. *Aggressive.* The potential for typical domestic violence homicides most certainly occurs in the elderly. In this situation, there has been a history of marital problems and violence. A pending separation for health, financial, domestic discord, or other reasons will not be tolerated. Death for both is the only answer.
2. *Dependent–protective caregiver.* Here, the couple have been married a long time and are dependent on each other. The man is depressed and fears losing control when the health of one or both changes, or if he merely believes it is changing. Increasing isolation and increasing helplessness in the male caregiver are the primary stimuli.
3. *Symbiotic.* In this case, the husband and wife are usually very old and highly interdependent. Both partners are usually sick. The male has a dominant personality, and the woman is often submissive.

Prevention and intervention with these types of suicide/homicides are no different from any other methods in this chapter except that the interventionist needs to be sensitive to the fact that the many physical impairments that the elderly are likely to suffer call for being patient and understanding and proceeding at a slower pace without being patronizing and condescending. As will be stressed in Chapter 14, Violent Behavior in Institutions, the worker should *never dismiss the elderly client who is in crisis as being harmless.*

Some "Don'ts." A number of authors (Hipple, 1985; Jobes, 2006; Kirk, 1993; Michel, 2011; Neimeyer & Pfeiffer, 1994; Shea, 2002) have identified some "don'ts" of suicide management that serve to supplement the intervention considerations already listed. Our comments are added to each point in the following list. These "don'ts" apply to almost anyone you work with who is suicidal. It's a long list and you don't need to memorize it, but you do need to remember where it is and check it out—particularly when you get those big furry moths flapping around in your stomach making you feel really queasy when you have a hot client in front of you.

1. Don't lecture, blame, give advice, judge, or preach to clients. If that had worked, they wouldn't be with you now.
2. Don't criticize clients or their choices or behaviors. Remember that as "crazy" and "nuts" as it seems, the lethal behavior makes perfect sense to the client.
3. Don't debate the pros and cons of suicide. Philosophy has nothing to do with what is going on in a lethality case.
4. Don't be misled by the client's telling you the crisis is past. Never just take the client's word that things are "settled" and "okay now." Keep checking!
5. Don't deny the client's suicidal ideas. Ideation leads to action. If a person says he or she has lethal intent, even in a joking or offhand way, check it out.
6. Don't try to challenge for shock effects. This is not "Scared Straight" therapy. Challenges may be acted on to show you the client means business.
7. Don't leave the client isolated, unobserved, and disconnected. Provision needs to be made for keeping the client safe and secure, and that means somebody needs to monitor him or her.
8. Don't diagnose and analyze behavior or confront the client with interpretations during the acute phase. Psychodynamic interpretations involving "why" are unimportant at this point.
9. Don't be passive. Suicides are high on the triage scale. You must become active and directive.
10. Don't overreact. Suicidal/homicidal behavior is scary, but it is behavior that can be handled. Stay calm and keep your voice well modulated. That's what this book and chapter are about. You don't have to be a superhero to do this stuff. Just keep calm and practice what you have learned!
11. Don't keep the client's suicidal risk a secret (be trapped in the confidentiality issue) or worry about "snitching" on the client. Whether you are a bosom friend or a professional, this is life-threatening behavior. You need to tell someone in authority who can keep the client safe.
12. Don't get sidetracked on extraneous or external issues or persons. Forget about all the other real and imagined ills and issues. Deal with the lethality. The other stuff can and should be acknowledged as important to the person, but that's it.
13. Don't glamorize, martyrize, glorify, heroize, or deify suicidal behavior in others, past or present. If you want somebody to kill him- or herself or copycat a friend or idol, this is an excellent way to have that happen.

14. Don't become defensive or avoid strong feelings. The possibility for transference is great in lethal behavior. While lethal feelings are scary, they are exactly what need to be discussed and uncovered.

15. Don't hide behind pseudoprofessionalism and clinical objectivity as a way of distancing yourself psychologically from painful and scary material. What you are actually trying to do is insulate yourself from the brutal reality of what is going on, and that is not helpful. You must get into the game and build the relationship.

16. Don't fail to identify the precipitating event. Find what specifically caused the client to decide to become lethal. Global reasons are not helpful. Identify the reason the client got here today, so action plans can be generated to deal with it.

17. Don't terminate the intervention without obtaining some level of positive commitment (you may get sued if you don't). Even if the person later goes ahead and kills him- or herself or somebody else, try as hard as you can to get a commitment from the client to do no harm.

18. Don't forget to follow up (you may get sued if you don't). You must keep track of lethal people until the crisis has passed.

19. Don't forget to document and report (you may get sued if you don't). Keep good records of your assessment of the client and when and what you did with your recommendations.

20. Don't be so embarrassed or vain that you don't consult (you may get sued if you don't). Substantiation by another professional in a difficult case makes good therapeutic and legal sense.

21. Don't fail to make yourself available and accessible (you may get sued if you don't). If you come in contact with a suicidal/homicidal client, you must stay the course, be available, and have backup support.

22. Take your time. Don't be hurried. Things may be frantic and frenetic in the immediate environment, but you are the rock in the middle of the maelstrom. You have time!

23. Watch for countertransference. Shea (2002, p. 122) poses two questions to keep you grounded. "What am I feeling right now?" "Is there any part of me that doesn't want to hear the truth right now?" Those are caution lights and reality checks on your potential loss of objectivity and treatment goals.

24. Don't be blackmailed into caving in to client demands. Set limits and keep them. Clients with borderline personality disorder are especially adept at treatment blackmail. For example, keeping one's guns isn't an option with a highly suicidal client. Refusal to comply with treatment is not an option, nor is maintaining the right to kill oneself during treatment. Refusal to treat this client is not abandonment, but good clinical judgment.

Guidelines for Family, Friends, and Associates

The crisis worker often has to deal with gritty issues that involve family. Getting clients like Roy to come to terms with long-smoldering family issues is not easy. Urging clients to engage in new, resocializing activities is also difficult. However, if they can be done, the quality of life goes up and lethality comes down. Mishara, Houle, and Lavoie (2005) found that direct intervention with families who called into a suicide prevention line resulted in potential suicides' having less suicidal ideation, fewer suicide attempts, and fewer depressive symptoms. Family and friends reported less psychological distress and use of more positive coping mechanisms, and reported that their communication with the suicidal person was more helpful. The family, friends, and associates of the suicidal/homicidal person can do many things to contribute to prevention, especially in the area of correcting the alienated lifestyle that cuts off the at-risk person's connectedness with others.

Crisis workers can serve an important educational role by helping families, friends, and associates learn about and become attuned to the risk factors, cues, and cries for help that suicidal/homicidal people generally display in some way (Hipple & Cimbolic, 1979, pp. 76–78). The crisis worker who talked with Roy's sons focused on including Roy back in their lives both as grandfather and as a wise consultant whose knowledge and skill of farming can complement their own. Families can and should be an integral part of treatment and should be fully informed about the positive role (along with the limits) they can play (Rudd, Joiner, & Rajab, 2001, p. 105). Perhaps the most important component of family involvement is helping the whole family system become aware of how the suicidal member's feelings and actions influence the family and how they are reciprocally influenced by the family members' feelings (Softas-Nall & Francis, 1998, p. 227). To that end, dealing with past issues and recriminations is out of bounds. At least until the suicidal events are resolved, bringing up old psychological baggage does little good. Emphasis is on the present and future and developing new behavioral contracts for positive change in the total family constellation (McLean & Taylor, 1994).

Family, friends, and associates who attend to the many cues that have been described in this chapter can help the suicidal/homicidal person by genuinely and assertively confronting the lethal issues. For instance, they can watch for the lethal person's preoccupation with an anniversary date of a significant loss, such as the death of a loved one, or the resulting depression that a job loss or academic failure generates and intervene in a directive manner if needed (McLean & Taylor, 1994). Significant others can help the survivors cope with suicide/homicide after it happens. On the other hand, if fractures in the family system are severe, discretion may be the better part of valor. Pushing family members together who have long-standing agendas of anger and recrimination is the about the last thing that needs to happen.

When family or other bereaved groups cannot get past the shock of the death and/or exhibit excessive blame or guilt, crisis workers can meet with them and help them deal with their grief (Shneidman, 1975). On a final note, McGlothin (2008, p. 137) believes that all of the family needs to be checked out for suicidal/homicidal ideation because in many families suicide/homicide and violence are operational ways to settle problems

The Psychological Autopsy

Shneidman (1987) developed the psychological autopsy technique for the purpose of compiling detailed postmortem mental histories following suicides or deaths that were equivocal (not sure of cause). Psychological autopsies involve examination of personal demographics such as work, criminal, school, and medical records along with in-depth interviews of friends, relatives, coworkers, and health care professionals to attempt to ascertain the suicide's intent. They also attempt to determine what the trigger events were that might have contributed to the suicide. For instance, normative data from psychological autopsies indicate that an average of 40 percent of suicides had a medical illness and that HIV/AIDS and cancer are two particular illnesses that increase suicidal risk (Kleepies, Hough, & Romeo, 2009). Psychological autopsies also attempt to determine what, if any, psychopathology was present in completed suicides. For example, it appears that between 30 and 40 percent of suicides may meet criteria for personality disorders. Psychological autopsies have determined that besides the big five psychiatric diagnoses of major depressive, bipolar, anorexia nervosa, schizophrenia, and borderline personality disorder

that are precursors to suicide (Joiner et al., 2009), schizoid and antisocial personality disorder also have strong associations with suicidal behavior (Duberstein & Witte, 2009). The autopsy was initially conceived by Schneidman to help clinicians become more cognizant of the warning signs of suicide in cases where intent, reason, and motivation are muddled and unclear.

The following questions seek to flesh out the psychological profile of the decedent's death—indeed, to determine first and foremost whether it was a suicide (Shneidman, 1999d). These questions are posed in an empathic manner to the survivors: Why did the person do it? How did he/she do it? When? That is, why at that particular time? What is the most probable mode of death? Besides details of the death itself, the autopsy seeks to determine the person's personality and lifestyle, typical patterns of reactions to stress, emotional upsets, and periods of disequilibrium, particularly in the recent past. What role did alcohol and/or drugs play in the person's life? What was the nature of his/her interpersonal relationships? What were the person's fantasies, dreams, thoughts, premonitions, or fears relating to death, accident, or suicide? What changes, if any, occurred in the person's habits, hobbies, eating, sexual relations, and other life routines? Information is garnered regarding the person's lifestyle, such as mood up- or downswings, successes, and plans for the future. Not only can these questions help determine whether the death was a suicide, they can also help determine how staff who may have been involved with the client can better prevent suicides (Shneidman, 1999d).

As with many important discoveries, Shneidman (1971) found a serendipitous function of the psychological autopsy. By being empathic and supportive to the survivors in order to elicit more information, the autopsy was therapeutic for the survivors. Thus, the psychological autopsy (Shneidman, 1987) may not only provide information that helps prevent future suicides, but may also represent a postvention method of helping survivors either gain a better understanding of why it happened or feel less guilt and responsibility for the deceased's demise. Indeed, what the psychological autopsy spawned was a variety of postvention strategies to help survivors of a suicide.

Postvention

Emotional Toll. The "real victim" of suicide is said to be not the body in the coffin but the family and other loved ones (Hansen & Frantz, 1984, p. 36). Osterweis, Solomon, and Green (1984) report that survivors of the death of a loved one by suicide are thought to be more vulnerable to physical and mental health problems than are grievers from other causes of death (p. 87). The average suicide leaves 6 to 10 survivors who experience extreme grief (Mitchell et al., 2004). Shneidman (2001, p. 154) puts it eloquently when he says that the person who commits suicide puts his psychological skeleton in the survivors' emotional closet. If that is true, then in the United States alone, with about 4 million survivors, the closet is chock-full of skeletons.

Survivors are faced with guilt, shock, trauma from body discovery, police interrogation, legal issues, shame, sleep difficulties, concentration problems, denial, family relationship problems, and complicated, long-term grief (Granello & Granello, 2007, pp. 281–282). Survivors may also feel double binds of guilt and anger—guilty that they didn't do enough to stop the suicide, and angry that now they are left behind having to raise children alone, struggle with debts, and so on, while the suicide skipped out on his or her responsibilities (Shea, 2002, p. 95).

Survivors of suicidal people generally receive less sympathy and encounter more social isolation, negative cultural messages, and stigmatization than do other bereaved individuals (Moore & Freeman, 1995). Most of us have lost loved ones and been to funerals; we know the routine. Suicide survivors have no such formal guidelines. Survivors frequently sense that they are the objects of gossip and criticism, and they may be right. Bereaved loved ones often blame themselves for the suicide, and more than in any other form of loss, they tend to perceive that they are being neglected by others. Therefore, the loss of a loved one by suicide is doubly stressful (Edelstein, 1984, p. 21; Rando, 1984, p. 150). Grieving loved ones left behind by a suicide may refer to themselves as "victims" because, in addition to the emotional stress of the death itself, the survivors must also deal with burdens such as social stigma, guilt, blame, a search for the cause or meaning, unfinished business, and perceived rejection wrought by the suicide (Rando, 1984, pp. 151–152).

Child Survivors.   The potential for children whose parents have committed suicide to suffer severe pathological problems is extremely high (Cain & Fast, 1966; Sethi & Bhargava, 2003). Psychosomatic disorder, learning disabilities, obesity, running away, tics, delinquency, sleepwalking, fire setting, encopresis, along with social adjustment problems, depression, and PTSD symptoms fly out of a Pandora's box of evil outcomes of a parental suicide. Intervention is particularly important in dealing with children coping with a parent's suicide, who may exhibit shame, denial, and concealment and experience ostracism by their peers. If intervention does not occur, these children may experience a host of feelings that lead them to believe they are bound to suffer the same fate as their parent. Feelings of guilt in the child and distortion in communication between adults and children are constant companions. To neglect such children and assume they'll get over it is an extreme therapeutic error. School counselors, school social workers, and school psychologists are particularly critical in understanding what the suicide of a parent may mean to a child and need to be able to intervene with them and their peers. This kind of traumatic event can cause complicated traumatic grief in children and is absolutely within the purview of crisis workers who operate in school buildings (Cohen & Mannarino, 2011; Webb, 2011).

Parent Survivors.   Parents whose children commit suicide are also likely to suffer severe psychological repercussions as they attempt to come to terms with their loss. Herzog and Resnik (1967) and Lester (2004) have found that the immediate parental response to a child's suicide tends to be hostility toward others, denial of the suicide, and rationalization of the death as accidental. Guilt and depression soon follow, and the likelihood of severe and continuing dysfunction with the surviving family members grows. Getting both children and parents into support groups and keeping them from becoming more isolated with their negative feelings are critical.

Support Groups.   Crisis workers need to be aware of local services that provide such group support. Many organizations, school systems, and communities fail to develop postvention plans for suicide/homicide loss, with the result that survivors have psychological issues that affect those systems (Berkowitz et al., 2011). Baton Rouge, Louisiana, has a model comprehensive program that provides immediate referral for all survivors of suicides from the local coroner. It utilizes an Active Postvention Model that provides trained crisis workers who specialize in the immediate aftermath of a suicide to provide support services to survivors. It provides group support and 24-hour access to services (Campbell, 2011). Communities could not do better than to adopt this model. The following model is fairly representative of what these support groups look like.

Hatton and Valente (1984) conducted a supportive group therapy experience for parents who sought relief from painful grief after the suicide of a child. They held 10 meetings with parents who felt shame, guilt, self-doubt, confusion, and isolation. The first three meetings were spent sharing and ventilating feelings. Four reactions surfaced. First, there was a prohibition of mourning by the parents' social network. The outside world was seen as hostile and incapable of understanding their grief. Second, former coping mechanisms for dealing with grief were useless. Attempting to share the pain even with spouses was impeded by the fear of burdening or depressing the person even further. Third, extreme isolation was felt both from friends and from family. Fourth, parents developed an identity crisis and questioned their ability to parent and maintain self-control.

The next five meetings were spent doing grief work. Sessions focused on giving support and reassurance, looking at adaptive and maladaptive coping mechanisms, gaining a new perspective on the loss, considering the effect of the suicide on their other children, and dealing with the anger they felt at society and the bureaucratic bumbling of authorities. The last 2 weeks were spent reminiscing about the good times, becoming more future oriented, letting go of anger, and sadness at termination of the group.

Transcrisis Postvention.   Resnik (1969) proposes that crisis intervention should occur in three phases. First is *resuscitation*. Within 24 hours, the crisis worker needs to make a supportive visit to assist the survivors in dealing with their initial shock, grief, anger, and most likely self-recrimination, guilt, and blame. This phase may last for several weeks. Survivors should be encouraged to talk about the suicide and experience the full range of feelings associated with it, without feeling ashamed or embarrassed to do so, and tell the story as many times as it needs to be told (Granello & Granello, 2007, p. 283). Phase two involves *resynthesis*. The crisis worker helps the survivors learn new ways of coping with their loss and prevents the development of pathological family responding. Finding a therapist who is experienced with grief work or a self-help group is critical during this time, and this most assuredly holds for children. This second phase may last for several months. The third phase is *renewal*. The crisis worker helps the family reformulate itself in a context of growth and movement beyond the suicide. This process may occur up to a year after the suicide and is usually terminated

on the first anniversary of the suicide. What Resnick proposes in these chronological phases is a vivid example of dealing with transcrisis states.

The Case of Leah.   Leah Nichols, 54-year-old manager of a branch bank, returned home from work Friday evening and discovered her 24-year-old son, Ronnie, dead from a gunshot wound. Ronnie had left a suicide note where he had apparently killed himself in his bedroom. Leah's husband, a college professor, had been dead (of heart failure) about a year, and she and Ronnie lived in the family home. Ronnie's siblings, Brenda, age 31, Richard, age 27, and Larry, age 22, were married and living in cities scattered about the region. Ronnie was a warm, friendly, loving, and lovable person who had never married or dated much. He was very sensitive and was given to mood swings from deep depression to euphoria. He had expressed suicidal ideation since his primary school years and had been under psychiatric care since his adolescent years. But in recent months he had appeared to be gaining in maturity and had gotten off his medication.

Leah's grief had moved progressively toward becoming complicated (see Chapter 12, Personal Loss: Bereavement and Grief, for a complete description of this problem), but she felt she should set a controlled and circumspect image for the three siblings and other friends and relatives. After being admitted to the emergency room and spending 3 days in the hospital for nervous exhaustion, she was referred to the crisis worker.

The following intervention strategy was provided for Leah during the days and weeks immediately following Ronnie's suicide and represents one component of Resnik's (1969) resynthesis phase. The individual follow-up grief work dealt with many issues that are common in suicide work: denial, guilt, bargaining, and depression. The issue of Leah's martyrdom came out during an individual session approximately 3 weeks after Ronnie's funeral.

Leah: My kids think I'm holding back. They say I'm too stoic, too unaffected, or too aloof. They think my lack of showing emotions is not normal—not healthy.

CW: What do you think?

Leah: I don't know. I guess I believe somebody has to keep the lid on—keep a steady head during all this. I haven't wanted to trouble any of them with my problems. Their daddy's death, then Ronnie's. They've had enough without me dumping my grief on them.

CW: What are you saying, at a deep level, below the surface, right now?

Leah: I guess I am saying I'm hurting like hell. I guess my actions have looked pretty cold and strange to them. I guess I've been trying to protect them—to keep them from hurting.

CW: What will it do for you to keep them from hurting?

Leah: Make me a martyr, I guess. I don't know what else it could be.

CW: I wonder if it could keep you from the hurt and anger you have pushed back?

Leah: (*Starts sobbing.*) I . . . I . . . guess . . . I feel so helpless and always have had that feeling for that poor little boy I could not help despite everything I did. (*Weeps while the crisis worker moves over and holds and comforts her.*)

The crisis worker does not attempt to steer Leah to any particular conclusion. Rather, the questioning strategy—a combination of techniques from reality therapy, rational-emotive behavior therapy, and Gestalt therapy—is used to help Leah gain conscious contact with her own inner world. This crisis intervention technique would be ineffective if the worker were trying to analyze or identify pathology in Leah's behavior. Diagnosing, prescribing a cure, and managing Leah's recovery for her would have also been inappropriate. Leah needs to move forward at her own speed and pace to Resnik's (1969) renewal phase.

The Case of Handley. Adults who have been traumatized by the suicide of a close associate, coworker, or friend can profit as well. A brief example of one type of group intervention/psychological autopsy illustrates this point.

Handley, age 27, killed himself by carbon monoxide poisoning. He had had a chaotic and turbulent life, punctuated by a destabilized family, drug and alcohol addiction, and numerous suicide attempts. Despite all his problems, he was a friendly, energetic, charismatic person who worked in a restaurant supply business. He left behind several friends and coworkers who admired him and were surprised at his suicide, even though some of them were aware of his dilemmas and his occasional suicidal ideations.

Several days after Handley's funeral, his coworkers were still in acute grief. Some were emotionally stuck, asking themselves and each other, "Why?" Some were feeling guilty because they did not pick up on the cues and do something to save Handley. The following description is a modified psychological autopsy/group processing that we have developed to aid coworkers affected by a colleague's suicide. It is a variation of a grief debriefing procedure (Mitchell & Wesner, 2011) that is designed to help people share feelings, thoughts, and behaviors both of the deceased's actions and their own responses.

Handley's modified psychological autopsy was convened by a crisis interventionist who met with the group of bereaved coworkers and led them through the following steps:

1. *Introduction.* The worker made a brief introduction, outlining the purposes and structure of the meeting.
2. *Constructing the "why."* The crisis worker helped the group piece together the cues, clues, and signs (pooled from the knowledge contained within the group) that made Handley's suicide more understandable (from Handley's point of view).
3. *Commemorating the positive traits and accomplishments.* The group made a list of Handley's attributes and achievements that they particularly wanted to highlight and remember.
4. *Saying good-bye.* During the second round, each coworker was given an opportunity to take care of unfinished business with Handley and to verbally say good-bye using the "empty chair" strategy. Some members expressed anger as well as love. This was a very emotional and cathartic experience for everyone.
5. *Turning loose.* The crisis worker summarized the material from the preceding three steps and led the group in brainstorming and making another list, gleaned from Handley's case, to help them learn how to detect and prevent future suicides. Further, it allowed the group to turn loose the idea that they might have been in any way responsible or negligent in Handley's death.
6. *Absolving guilt.* The crisis worker obtained a commitment from a member of the group to edit and distribute the psychological autopsy lists to every member of the group. Last, the crisis worker made a statement that essentially (a) expressed appreciation for the group's participation, (b) assured the members that they were not responsible for Handley's death, and (c) gave the group permission to end the acute grieving phase and enter the long-term period of grief.

The crisis worker tapped into the power and cohesiveness of the group to provide stability and equilibrium for individual members. A variation of this group technique would be appropriate with a family, a fraternal group, the employees in a workplace, a school group, or a church group (any group dealing with a loss-related crisis).

Losing a Client to Suicide

Crisis intervention does not always work. Client incidence of suicide among psychologists, social workers, and counselors ranges from 22 to 33 percent (Kleespies & Ponce, 2009). Sometimes even the most skilled professionals and crisis workers cannot succeed. We must remember that if people really intend to kill themselves, despite our best efforts to intervene, they can manage to accomplish the task. The following suggestions have been provided to help workers cope with the loss of clients (Farberow, 2001; Sommers-Flanagan, Sommers-Flanagan, & Lynch, 2001).

Guided debriefings by experts are necessary for workers who have lost a client. Having a client commit suicide or homicide is one of the most stressful events that can occur in the experience of a crisis worker. The guilt, recrimination, rumination, and perseveration may lead to constant second-guessing. The "what ifs," "shoulds," "oughts," and "might have beens" all lead to feelings of owning responsibility. If a client commits suicide or homicide, a psychological autopsy, or debriefing (see the section on critical incident stress debriefing in Chapter 17, Disaster Response), and supervision should be mandatory for the worker.

Indeed, the impact of having failed to save a person who was a client, or a victim of the client, can be overwhelming and can cause the crisis worker to experience what is called *vicarious traumatization* (see the section on vicarious traumatization in Chapter 16, Human Service Workers in Crisis: Burnout, Vicarious Traumatization, and Compassion Fatigue). Such cases call for the utmost of professional expertise to provide intentional and intensive debriefing of the traumatized workers. It is absolutely essential that such workers realistically examine (under the guidance of outside consultants) what happened, learn from the event, and absolve themselves from guilt and responsibility for the regrettable loss.

SUMMARY

The phenomenon of suicide is democratic in that it affects every segment of society and it is everybody's business. Suicide and homicide as expressive problem-solving acts have many similarities and parallels in terms of motive, risk, and assessment of lethality. Suicide is a serious problem that is on the rise among all groups, especially youth, but the highest risk group is, and has remained for many years, Caucasian males over 65. Researchers find few common denominators in their quest to identify suicide/homicide risk types and to predict and prevent suicide/homicide. The two oldest and most prevalent theories of suicide are Freud's notion that suicidal behavior is rage at others turned inward and Durkheim's concept that suicide is tied closely to social pressures and influences. Other theories that have emerged more recently see the basis or cause of suicide as largely accidental, a method of escape, a pervasive sense of hopelessness, interactional and revenge driven, biochemically induced, chaotic, interpersonal, or completely rational in the face of unendurable pain or suffering.

The dynamics of suicide are important because crisis workers who deal with suicidal clients need to know that there are several different types and characteristics of suicide. There are many reasons why people kill or attempt to kill themselves, and there are differing moral and cultural points of view about suicide among various social, ethnic, and age groups. Among the many myths of suicide are two that are particularly salient in impeding crisis work: (1) discussing suicide will cause a person to think about doing it or to act upon it, and (2) people who threaten suicide don't do it. Crisis workers are advised to directly question clients who display any suicidal or homicidal ideation.

Many risk factors have been identified that serve as danger signals and help to determine levels of lethality. Some of the highest risks are the presence of serious intent, a history of prior attempts, and evidence of a specific and lethal plan. These risk factors are important criteria for both assessing and acting in the realm of suicide intervention. Workers who are sensitized to the dynamics find that suicidal people often send out subtle but definite clues and/or cries for help.

Intervention strategies show how crisis workers can be appropriately assertive, directive, and forceful. In work with suicidal clients, workers should not be passive. In suicide intervention, workers must consider many environmental and social factors in addition to attending to client safety (for example, age, gender, social status, availability of supports from family and friends, and community attitudes surrounding the person at risk). Counseling around the issue of suicide/

homicide also involves facilitating the grief and healing of clients who are survivors, as well as the care and debriefing of crisis workers who experience the loss of clients to suicide or homicide. Finally, the psychological autopsy is a primary way of both learning how to prevent suicides and alleviating the guilt and shame of survivors.

If you or someone you know is in a bind and you or they can't get through on your local hotline and can't get help with feelings of lethality, the national suicide hotline is open 24/7 at 1-800-SUICIDE. Across the world, the Samaritans in England answer e-mails at jo@samaritans.org. To find help in a language other than English, e-mail www.befrienders.org.

To see some of the concepts discussed in this chapter in action, refer to your *Crisis Intervention in Action* DVD, or see the clips online on the Counseling CourseMate website. To access this site, go to www.cengagebrain.com, where you'll also find an eBook, additional study tools, quizzes, and more. Consider yourself as one of the team working with Amy. Her life is a mess. As you listen, how soon would you start assessing for suicide? Do you think the team waits too long, or are they too quick, or should they even broach the subject? Now see how good you are at not getting blindsided. Watch Matt working with Ann. Ostensibly the purpose of the counseling session is job outplacement. It turns into something entirely different, though. What are the clues and cues that make Matt start taking the session in an entirely different direction? How do you think career counselor turned crisis interventionist does when he shifts therapeutic gears? How do you think you'd do given the same set of circumstances?

REFERENCES

Abramson, L. Y., Alloy, L. B., Hogan, M. E., Whitehouse, W. G., Gibb, B. E., Hankin, B. L., et al. (2000). The hopelessness theory of suicidality. In T. Joiner & M. D. Rudd (Eds.), *Suicide science: Expanding the boundaries* (pp. 18–32). Boston: Kluwer Academic.

American Association of Suicidology. (1997). *Youth suicide fact sheet* (revised). Washington, DC: Author.

American Association of Suicidology. (n.d.). Understanding and helping the suicidal person: Be aware of the warning signs. Retrieved from www.suicidiology.org/web/web/guest/stats-and-tools/warning signs

Apuzzo, M. (2007, April19). Gunman's goodbye manifesto of murder. *Memphis Commercial Appeal,* pp. 1A, 4A.

Asberg, M., Eriksson, B., Martensson, B., & Traaskman-Bendz, L. (1986). Therapeutic effects of serotonin uptake inhibitors in depression. *Comprehensive Psychiatry, 42,* 70–75.

Asberg, M., & Forslund, K. (2000). Neurobiological aspects of suicidal behavior. *International Review of Psychiatry, 12*(1), 62–74.

Baechler, J. (1979). *Suicides.* New York: Basic Books.

Battle, A. O., Battle, M. V., & Tolley, E. A. (1993). Potential for suicide and aggression in delinquents at juvenile court in a southern city. *Suicide and Life Threatening Behavior, 23*(3), 230–243.

Baumeister, R. F. (1990). *Escaping the self: Alcoholism, spirituality, masochism and flights from the burden of selfhood.* New York: Basic Books.

Beck, A. T., Shaw, A. J., Rush, B. F., & Emery, G. (1979). *Cognitive theory of depression.* New York: Guilford Press.

Beck, A. T., & Steer, R. A. (1987). *BDI, Beck Depression Inventory: Manual.* San Antonio, TX: Psychological Corporation.

Beck, A. T., Weissman, A., Lester, D., & Trexler, L. (1974). The measurement of pessimism: The Hopelessness Scale. *Journal of Consulting and Clinical Psychology, 42,* 861–865.

Bender, T. W., Gordon, K. H., Bresin, K., & Joiner, T. E. (2011). Impulsivity and suicidality: The mediating role of painful experience. *Journal of Affective Disorders, 129*(1-3), 301–307.

Bennell, C., Jones, J., & Taylor, A. (2011). Determining the authenticity of suicide notes: Can training improve judgment? *Criminal Justice and Behavior, 38*(7), 669–689.

Berk, M. S., Henriques, G. R., Warman, D. M., Brown, G. K., & Beck, A. T. (2004). A cognitive therapy intervention for suicide attempters: An overview of the treatment and case example. *Cognitive and Behavior Practice, 11*(3), 265–277.

Berkowitz, L., McCauley, J., Schuurman, D., & Jordan, J. R. (2011). Organizational postvention after suicide death. In J. R. Jordan & J. L. McIntosh (Eds.), *Grief after suicide: Understanding the consequences and caring for the survivors* (pp. 157–168). New York: Routledge/Taylor & Francis Group.

Blumenthal, S., & Kupfer, D. (1986). Generalizable treatment strategies for suicidal behavior. *Annals of the New York Academy of Sciences, 487,* 327–340.

Bonner, R. (2001). Moving suicide risk assessment into the next millennium: Lessons from our past. In D. Lester (Ed.), *Suicide prevention: Resources for the millennium* (pp. 83–102). Philadelphia: Brunner-Routledge.

Brown, G. K., Wenzel, A., & Rudd, M. D. (2011) Cognitive therapy for suicidal patients. In K. Michel & D. A. Jobes

(Eds.), *Building a therapeutic alliance with the suicidal patient.* (pp. 273–292). Washington, DC: American Psychological Association.

Cain, A., & Fast, I. (1966). Children's disturbed reactions to parent suicide. *American Journal of Orthopsychiatry, 36,* 8732.

Callanan, V. J., & Davis, M. S. (2009). A comparison of suicide note writers with suicides who did not leave notes. *Suicide and Life-Threatening Behavior, 39*(5), 558–568.

Campbell, F. R. (2011). Baton Rouge Crisis Intervention Center's LOSS Team Active Postvention Model approach. In J. R. Jordan & J. L. McIntosh (Eds.), *Grief after suicide: Understanding the consequences and caring for the survivors* (pp. 327–332). New York: Routledge/Taylor & Francis Group.

Cantor, C. H. (2000). Suicide in the western world. In K. Hawton & K. Van Heeringen (Eds.), *The international handbook of suicide and attempted suicide* (pp. 9–28). Chichester, England: John Wiley & Sons.

Centers for Disease Control and Prevention. (2008). *Suicide and self-inflicted injury.* Retrieved from www.cdc.gov/nchs/fastats/suicide.html

Cheng, A. T., & Lee, C. (2000). Suicide in Asia and the Far East. In K. Hawton & K. Van Heeringen (Eds.), *The international handbook of suicide and attempted suicide* (pp. 29–48). Chichester, England: John Wiley & Sons.

Chiles, J. A., & Strosahl, K. D. (1995). *The suicidal patient: Principles of assessment, treatment, and case management.* Washington, DC: American Psychiatric Press.

Cohen, D. (2003). Homicide-suicide in older persons: How you can help prevent a tragedy. *Violence & Injury Prevention Program: Homicide/Suicide Prevention & Intervention Resources.* Retrieved November 15, 2003, from http//:www.fmhi.usf.edu/amh/homicide-suicide/art_hs_inolder.html

Cohen, J. A., & Mannarino, A. P. (2011). Supporting children with traumatic grief: What educators need to know. *School Psychology International, 32,* 117–131.

Courtois, C. A. (1991, August 16). *The self-destructive person and the suicidal bind.* Paper presented at the 99th Annual Convention of the American Psychological Association, San Francisco.

Cukrowicz, K. C., Wingate, L. R., Driscoll, K. A., & Joiner, T. E. (2004). A standard of care for the assessment of suicide risk and associated treatment: The Florida State University Psychology Clinic as an example. *Journal of Contemporary Psychotherapy, 34,* 87–100.

Dorrmann, W. (2005). Pros and cons of contracts with patients in acute suicidal crises. *Verhaltenstherapie 15*(1), 39–46.

Duberstein, P., & Witte, T. (2009). Suicide risk in personality disorders: An argument for a public health perspective. In P. M. Kleespies (Ed.), *Behavioral emergencies: An evidence-based resource for evaluating and managing risk of suicide, violence, and victimization* (pp. 257–286). Washington, DC: American Psychological Association.

Durkheim, E. (1951). *Suicide.* New York: Free Press. (Original work published 1897)

Edelstein, L. (1984). *Maternal bereavement: Coping with the unexpected death of a child.* New York: Praeger.

Erikson, E. H. (1963). *Childhood and society.* New York: Norton.

Erlangsen, A., Nordenstoft, J., Conwell, Y., Waern, M., De Leo, D., Lindner, R., et al. (2011). Key considerations to prevent suicide in older adults: Consensus opinion of an expert panel. *Crisis: The Journal of Crisis Intervention and Suicide Prevention, 32*(2), 106–109.

Everstine, L. (1998). *The anatomy of suicide: Silence of the heart.* Springfield, IL: Charles C Thomas.

Farberow, N. (2001). Helping suicide survivors. In D. Lester (Ed.), *Suicide prevention: Resources for the millennium* (pp. 189–212). Philadelphia: Brunner-Routledge.

Freud, S. (1916). Trauer und melancholie. *Gesammelte Werke* (Vol. 10, pp. 427–446). London: Imago.

Fujimura, L. E., Weis, D. M., & Cochran, J. R. (1985). Suicide: Dynamics and implications for counseling. *Journal of Counseling and Development, 63,* 612–615.

Goldney, R. D. (2000). Prediction of suicide and attempted suicide. In K. Hawton & K. Van Heeringen (Eds.), *The international handbook of suicide and attempted suicide* (pp. 85–595). Chichester, England: John Wiley & Sons.

Goldney, R. D. (2005). Suicide prevention: A pragmatic review of recent studies. *Crisis: The Journal of Crisis Intervention and Suicide Prevention, 26*(3), 128–140.

Granello, D. H., & Granello, P. F. (2007). *Suicide: An essential guide for helping professionals and educators.* Boston: Pearson/Allyn and Bacon.

Guthrie, E., Kapur, N., Mackway-Jones, K., Chew-Graham, C., Moorey, J., Mendel, E., et al. (2001). Randomized controlled trial of brief psychological intervention after deliberate self-poisoning. *British Medical Journal, 323,* 135–138.

Haines, J., Williams, C., & Lester, D. (2011). The characteristics of those who do and do not leave suicide notes: Is the method of residuals valid? *Omega: Journal of Death and Dying, 63*(1), 79–94.

Hansen, J. C., & Frantz, T. T. (Eds.). (1984). *Death and grief in the family.* Rockville, MD: Aspen Systems.

Harwood, D., & Jacoby, R. (2000). Suicidal behavior in the elderly. In K. Hawton & K. Van Heeringen (Eds.), *The international handbook of suicide.* New York: John Wiley & Sons.

Hathaway, S., & McKinley, J. (1989). *The MMPI-2.* Minneapolis: University of Minnesota Press.

Hatton, C. L., & Valente, S. M. (1984). Bereavement group for parents who suffered a suicidal loss of a child. In C. L. Hatton & S. M. Valente (Eds.), *Suicide assessment and intervention* (2nd ed., pp. 163–173). East Norwalk, CT: Appleton-Century-Crofts.

Hawton, K., & Van Heeringen, K. (Eds.). (2000). *International handbook of suicide and attempted suicide*. Chichester, England: John Wiley & Sons.

Hazell, P., & Lewin, T. (1993). An evaluation of postvention following adolescent suicide. *Suicide and Life Threatening Behavior, 23*(2), 101–109.

Heisel, M. J. (2006). Suicide and its prevention among older adults. *Canadian Journal of Psychiatry, 51*(3), 143–154.

Hepp, U., Wittman, L., Schnyder, U., & Michel, K. (2004). Psychological and psychosocial interventions after attempted suicide: An overview of treatment studies. *Crisis: The Journal of Crisis Intervention and Suicide Prevention, 25*(3), 108–117.

Herzog, A., & Resnik, K. (1967). A clinical study of parental response to adolescent death by suicide. In N. Farberow (Ed.), *Proceedings of the 4th International Conference on Suicide Prevention*. Los Angeles: Delmar.

Hipple, J. (1985). *Suicide: The preventable tragedy*. Unpublished manuscript, North Texas State University, Denton.

Hipple, J., & Cimbolic, P. (1979). *The counselor and suicidal crisis*. Springfield, IL: Charles C Thomas.

Holmes, J. (2011). Attachment theory and the suicidal patient. In K. Michel & D. A. Jobes (Eds.), *Building a therapeutic alliance with the suicidal patient* (pp. 149–168). Washington, DC: American Psychological Association.

Holmes, R. M., & Holmes, S. T. (2006). *Suicide theory, practice, and investigation*. Thousand Oaks, CA: Sage.

Jacobs, D. G. (Ed.). (1999). *The Harvard Medical School guide to suicide assessment and intervention*. San Francisco: Jossey-Bass.

Jacobs, J. A. (1967). Phenomenological study of suicide notes. *Social Problems, 15*, 60–72.

Jobes, D. A. (2006). *Managing suicidal risk: A collaborative approach*. New York: Guilford Press.

Joiner, T. E. Jr., Van Orden, K., Witte, T. K., & Rudd, D. M. (2009). *The interpersonal theory of suicide: Guidance for working with suicidal clients*. Washington, DC: American Psychological Association.

Joiner, T. E. Jr., Walker, R. L., Rudd, M. D., & Jobes, D. A. (1999). Scientizing and routinizing the assessment of suicidality in outpatient practice. *Professional Psychology: Research and Practice, 30*, 447–453.

Kerkhof, J. F. (2000). Attempted suicide: Patterns and trends. In K. Hawton & K. van Heeringen (Eds.), *The international handbook of suicide and attempted suicide* (pp. 49–64). Chichester, England: John Wiley & Sons.

Kirk, W. G. (1993). *Adolescent suicide: A school-based approach to assessment and intervention*. Champaign, IL: Research Press.

Kleespies, P. M., Hough, S., & Romeo, A. M. (2009). Suicide risk in people with medical and terminal illness. In P. M. Kleespies (Ed.), *Behavioral emergencies: An evidence-based resource for evaluating and managing risk of suicide, violence, and victimization* (pp. 103–122). Washington, DC: American Psychological Association.

Kleespies, P. M., & Ponce, A. N. (2009) The stress and emotional impact of clinical work with the patient at risk. In P. M. Kleespies (Ed.), *Behavioral emergencies: An evidence-based resource for evaluating and managing risk of suicide, violence, and victimization* (pp. 431–448). Washington, DC: American Psychological Association.

Knight, J. A., & Kleespies, P. M. (1999, August 22). *The Boston assessment of suicide ideation correlates (BASIC): Development of a suicide risk assessment for veterans*. Paper presented at the 107th Annual Convention of the American Psychological Association, Boston.

Lapierre, S., Erlanger, A., Waern, M., De Leo, D., Oyama, H., Scocco, P., et al. (2011). A systematic review of elderly suicide prevention programs. *Crisis: The Journal of Crisis Intervention and Suicide Prevention, 32*(2), 88–98.

Laux, J. (2003). A primer on suicidology: Implications for counselors. *Journal of Counseling and Development, 80*, 380–383.

Leenaars, A. A. (1994). Crisis intervention with highly lethal suicidal people. In A. A. Leenaars, J. T. Maltsberger, & R. A. Neimeyer (Eds.), *Treatment of suicidal people* (pp. 45–61). Washington, DC: Taylor & Francis.

Leenaars, A. A. (1996). Suicide: A multidimensional malaise. *Suicide and Life-Threatening Behavior, 26*(3), 221–236.

Leenaars, A. A. (2004). *Psychotherapy and suicidal people: A person-centered approach*. Chichester, England: John Wiley & Sons.

Leonard, B. E. (2005). The biochemistry of suicide. *Journal of Crisis Intervention and Suicide Prevention, 26*(4), 153–156.

Lester, D. (1988). *The biochemical basis of suicide*. Springfield, IL: Charles C Thomas.

Lester, D. (1995). The concentration of neurotransmitter metabolites in the cerebrospinal fluid of suicidal individuals. *Pharmacopsychiatry, 28*, 45–50.

Lester, D. (1997). *Making sense of suicide*. Philadelphia: Charles Press.

Lester, D. (2000). Decades of suicide research: Wherefrom and whereto? In T. Joiner & M. D. Rudd (Eds.), *Suicide science: Expanding the boundaries* (pp. 9–16). Boston: Kluwer Academic.

Lester, D. (2001). The epidemiology of suicide. In D. Lester (Ed.), *Suicide prevention: Resources for the millennium* (pp. 3–16). Philadelphia: Brunner-Routledge.

Lester, D. (2004). Denial in suicide survivors. *Journal of Crisis Intervention and Suicide Prevention, 25*(2), 78–79.

Lester, D. (2005). Blood types and national suicide rates. *Journal of Crisis Intervention and Suicide Prevention, 25*(3), 237–238.

Lester, D., & Gunn, J. F. (2011). National anthems and suicide rates. *Psychological Reports, 108*(1), 43–44.

Lindsay, M., & Lester, D. (2004). *Suicide by cop: Committing suicide by provoking police to shoot you*. Amityville, NY: Baywood.

Linehan, M. M. (1997). Validation and psychotherapy. In A. Bohart & L. Greenberg (Eds.), *Empathy reconsideration:*

New directions in psychotherapy (pp. 353–392). Washington, DC: American Psychological Association.

Linehan, M. M., Comtois, K. A., Murray, A. M., Brown, M. Z., Gallop, R. J., Heard, H. L., et al. (2006). Two-year randomized controlled trial and follow-up of dialectical behavior therapy vs. therapy by experts for suicidal behaviors and borderline personality disorder. *Archives of General Psychiatry, 63*(7), 757–766.

Linehan, M. M., Goodstein, J. L., Nielsen, S. L., & Chiles, J. A. (1983). Reasons for staying alive when you are thinking of killing yourself: The Reasons for Living Inventory. *Journal of Consulting and Clinical Psychology, 51*(2), 276–286.

Linehan, M. M., & Schmidt, H. (1995). The dialectics of effective treatment of borderline personality disorder. In L. Kraneer & W. O'Donohue (Eds.), *Theories of behavior therapy: Exploring behavior change* (pp. 553–584). Washington, DC: American Psychological Association.

Lopes de Lara, C., Dumais, A., Rouleau, G., Lesage, A., Dumont, M., & Chawky, N., et al. (2006). STin2 variant and family history of suicide as significant predictors of suicide completion in major depression. *Biological Psychiatry, 59*(2), 114–120.

Malley, P. B., Kush, F., & Bogo, R. J. (1994). School-based adolescent suicide prevention and intervention programs. *School Counselor, 42*, 130–136.

Malmquist, C. P. (2006). Combined murder-suicide. In R. I. Simon & R. E. Hales (Eds.), *The American Psychiatric Publishing textbook of suicide assessment and management* (pp. 495–509). Washington, DC: American Psychiatric Publishing.

Maslach, C., & Jackson, S. E. (1981). *The Maslach Burnout Inventory.* Palo Alto, CA: Consulting Psychologists Press.

McGlothin, J. M. (2008). *Developing clinical skills in suicide assessment, prevention, and treatment.* Alexandria, VA: American Counseling Association.

McLean, P., & Taylor, S. (1994). Family therapy for suicidal people. In A. A. Leenaars, J. T. Maltsberger, & R. A. Neimeyer (Eds.), *Treatment of suicidal people* (pp. 75–87). Washington, DC: Taylor & Francis.

Memphis Police Department. (2011). Crisis Intervention Team training manual (5th rev.). Memphis, TN: Author.

Michel, K. (2011). General aspects of therapeutic alliance. In K. Michel & D. A. Jobes (Eds.), *Building a therapeutic alliance with the suicidal patient* (pp. 13–28). Washington, DC: American Psychological Association.

Michel, K., & D. A. Jobes, D. A. (Eds.). (2011). *Building a therapeutic alliance with the suicidal patient.* Washington, DC: American Psychological Association.

Michenbaum, D. (2005). Thirty-five years of working with suicidal patients: Lessons learned. *Canadian Psychology, 46*(2), 64–72.

Miller, L. (2006). Suicide by cop: Causes, reactions, and practical intervention strategies. *International Journal of Emergency Mental Health, 8*(3), 165–174.

Mishara, B. L., Houle, J., & Lavoie, B. (2005). Comparison of the effects of four suicide prevention programs for family and friends of high-risk suicidal men who do not seek help themselves. *Suicide and Life-Threatening Behavior, 35*(3), 329–342.

Mitchell, A. M., Kim, Y., Prigerson, H. G., & Mortimer-Stephens, M. (2004). Complicated grief in survivors of suicide. *Crisis, 25*, 12–18.

Mitchell, A. M., & Wesner, S. (2011). A bereavement crisis debriefing intervention for survivors after a suicide. In J. R. Jordan & J. L. McIntosh (Eds.), *Grief after suicide: Understanding the consequences and caring for the survivors* (pp. 397–402). New York: Routledge/Taylor & Francis Group.

Moore, M. M., & Freeman, S. J. (1995). Counseling survivors of suicide: Implications for group postvention. *Journal for Specialists in Group Work, 20*(1), 40–47.

National Institute of Mental Health. (2003). *U.S. suicide rates by age, gender, and racial group.* Bethesda, MD: National Institutes of Health.

National Institute of Mental Health. (2011). *Suicide in the U.S.: Statistics and prevention.* Retrieved from www.nimh.nih.gov/health/publicaitons/suicide-in-the-us-statistics-and-prevention/index.shmtl

Neimeyer, R. A., & Mahoney, M. J. (Eds.). (1995). *Constructivism in psychotherapy.* Washington, DC: American Psychological Association.

Neimeyer, R. A., & Pfeiffer, A. M. (1994). The ten most common errors of suicide interventionists. In A. A. Leenaars, J. T. Maltsberger, & R. A. Neimeyer (Eds.), *Treatment of suicidal people* (pp. 207–219). Washington, DC: Taylor & Francis.

Nock, M. K., & Marzuk, P. M. (2000). Suicide and violence. In K. Hawton & K. Van Heeringen (Eds.), *The international handbook of suicide and attempted suicide* (pp. 437–456). New York: John Wiley & Sons.

Osterweis, M., Solomon, F., & Green, M. (Eds.). (1984). *Bereavement: Reactions, consequences, and care.* Washington, DC: National Academy Press.

Patterson, W. M., Dohn, H. H., Bird, J., & Patterson, G. A. (1983). Evaluation of suicidal patients: The SAD PERSON scale. *Psychosomatics, 24*(4), 343–349.

Plutchik, R., & van Praag, H. M. (1990). Psychosocial correlates of suicide and violence risk. In H. M. van Praag, R. Plutchik, & A. Apter (Eds.), *Violence and suicidality: Perspectives in clinical and psychobiological research* (pp. 76–88). New York: Brunner/ Mazel.

Potter, L. B. (2001). Moving suicide risk assessment into the next millennium: Lessons from our past. In D. Lester (Ed.), *Suicide prevention: Resources for the millennium* (pp. 67–82). Philadelphia: Brunner-Routledge.

Rando, E. T. (1984). *Parental loss of a child.* Champaign, IL: Research Press.

Range, L. M. (2005). No-suicide contracts. In R. I. Yufit & D. Lester (Eds.), *Assessment, treatment, and prevention of suicidal behavior* (pp. 181–203). New York: John Wiley & Sons.

Resnik, H. (1969). Psychological resynthesis: A clinical approach to the survivors of a death by suicide. In E. Shneidman & M. Ortega (Eds.), *Aspects of depression* (pp. 124–148). Boston: Little, Brown.

Richman, J. (1994). Psychotherapy with older suicidal adults. In A. A. Leenaars, J. T. Maltsberger, & R. A. Neimeyer (Eds.), *Treatment of suicidal people* (pp. 101–113). Washington, DC: Taylor & Francis.

Rizvi, S.L. (2011). The therapeutic relationship in dialectical behavior therapy for suicidal individuals. In K. Michel & D. A. Jobes (Eds.), *Building a therapeutic alliance with the suicidal patient* (pp. 255–274). Washington, DC: American Psychological Association.

Rogers, J. R. (2001a). Suicide risk assessment. In E. R. Welfel & R. E. Ingersoll (Eds.), *The mental health desk reference* (pp. 259–263). New York: Wiley.

Rogers, J. R. (2001b). Theoretical grounding: The "missing link" in suicide research. *Journal of Counseling & Development, 79,* 16–25.

Rogers, J. R., Bromley, J. L., Christopher, J., & Lester, D. (2007). Content analysis of suicide notes as a test for the motivational component of the existentialist-constructivist model of suicide. *Journal of Counseling & Development, 85,* 182–188.

Ross, E. B. (1999, April). *After suicide: A ray of hope.* Paper presented at the Twenty-Third Annual Convening of Crisis Intervention Personnel, Chicago.

Roy, A., Nielsen, D., Rylander, G., & Sarchiapone, M. (2000). The genetics of suicidal behavior. In K. Hawton & K. Van Heeringen (Eds.), *The international handbook of suicide and attempted suicide* (pp. 209–222). Chichester, England: John Wiley & Sons.

Rudd, M. D. (2004). Cognitive therapy for suicidality: An integrative, comprehensive, and practical approach to conceptualization. *Journal of Contemporary Psychotherapy, 34,* 59–72.

Rudd, M. D., Joiner, T. E., Jr., & Rajab, M. H. (2001). *Treating suicidal behavior: An effective, time-limited approach.* New York: Guilford Press.

Sethi, S., & Bhargava, S. C. (2003). Child and adolescent survivors of suicide. *Crises, 24,* 4–6.

Shea, S. (2002). *The practical art of suicide assessment: A guide for mental health professionals and substance abuse counselors.* Hoboken, NJ: Wiley

Shneidman, E. S. (1971). Prevention, intervention, and postvention of suicide. *Annals of Internal Medicine, 75,* 453–458.

Shneidman, E. S. (1973). Suicide notes reconsidered. *Psychiatry, 36,* 379–394.

Shneidman, E. S. (1975). Postvention: The care of the bereaved. In R. O. Pasnau (Ed.), *Consultation in liaison psychiatry* (pp. 245–256). New York: Grune & Stratton.

Shneidman, E. S. (1980). *Voices of death.* New York: Harper & Row.

Shneidman, E. S. (1985). *Definition of suicide.* New York: Wiley.

Shneidman, E. S. (1987). A psychological approach to suicide. In G. R. Vandenbos & B. K. Bryant (Eds.), *Cataclysms, crises and catastrophes: Psychology in action* (pp. 147–183) Washington, DC: American Psychological Association.

Shneidman, E. S. (1993). Suicide as psychache. *Journal of Nervous and Mental Disease, 181,* 147–149.

Shneidman, E. S. (1999a). A formal definition with explication. In A. A. Leenaars (Ed.), *Lives and deaths: Selections from the works of E. S. Shneidman* (pp. 154–163). Philadelphia: Brunner/Mazel.

Shneidman, E. S. (1999b). How to prevent suicide. In A. A. Leenaars (Ed.), *Lives and deaths: Selections from the works of E. S. Shneidman* (pp. 154–163). Philadelphia: Brunner/Mazel.

Shneidman, E. S. (1999c). Self-destruction: Suicide notes and tragic lives. In A. A. Leenaars (Ed.), *Lives and deaths: Selections from the works of E. S. Shneidman* (pp. 277–303). Philadelphia: Brunner/Mazel.

Shneidman, E. S. (1999d). The psychological autopsy. In A. A. Leenaars (Ed.), *Lives and deaths: Selections from the works of E. S. Shneidman* (pp. 387–414). Philadelphia: Brunner/Mazel.

Shneidman, E. S. (1999e). The Psychological Pain Assessment Scale. In A. A. Leenaars (Ed.), *Lives and deaths: Selections from the works of E. S. Shneidman* (pp. 41–46). Philadelphia: Brunner/Mazel.

Shneidman, E. S. (2001). *Comprehending suicide: Landmarks in 20th century suicidology.* Washington, DC: American Psychological Association.

Shneidman, E. S., & Farberow, N. L. (1961). Statistical comparisons between committed and attempted suicides. In N. L. Farberow and E. S. Shneidman (Eds.), *The cry for help* (pp. 44–59). New York: McGraw-Hill.

Shneidman, E. S., Farberow, N. L., & Litman, R. E. (1976). *The psychology of suicide.* New York: Aronson.

Softas-Nall, B. C., & Francis, P. C. (1998). A solution-focused approach to a family with a suicidal member. *Family Journal: Counseling and Therapy for Couples and Families, 6,* 227–230.

Sommers-Flanagan, R., Sommers-Flanagan, J., & Lynch, K. (2001). Counseling interventions with suicidal clients. In E. R. Welfel & R. E. Ingersoll (Eds.), *The mental health desk reference* (pp. 264–270). New York: Wiley.

Stack, S. (2001). Sociological research into suicide. In D. Lester (Ed.), *Suicide prevention: Resources for the millennium* (pp. 17–30). Philadelphia: Brunner-Routledge.

Stillion, J. M., & McDowell, E. E. (1996). *Suicide across the live span: Premature exits* (2nd ed.). Washington, DC: Taylor & Francis.

Stoff, D. M., & Mann, J. J. (Eds.). (1997). *Annals of the New York Academy of Sciences: Vol. 836. The neurobiology of suicide: From the bench to the clinic.* New York: New York Academy of Sciences.

Stone, G. (1999). *Suicide and attempted suicide: Methods and consequences.* New York: Carroll & Graf.

Sullivan, G. R., & Bongar, B. (2006). Psychological testing in suicide risk management. In R. I. Simon and R. E. Hales (Eds.), *The American Psychiatric Publishing textbook of suicide assessment and management* (pp. 177–196). Washington, DC: American Psychiatric Publishing.

Sullivan, G. R., & Bongar, B. (2009). Assessing suicide risk in the adult patient. In P. M. Kleespies (Ed.), *Behavioral emergencies: An evidence-based resource for evaluating and managing risk of suicide, violence, and victimization* (pp. 59–78). Washington, DC: American Psychological Association.

Townsend, E., Hawton, K., Altman, D. G., Arensman, E., Gunnell, D., Hazell, P., et al. (2001). The efficacy of problem-solving treatments after deliberate self-harm: Meta-analysis of randomized controlled trials with respect to depression, hopelessness, and improvement in problems. *Psychological Medicine, 31,* 978–988.

U.S. Department of Health and Human Services. (2003). *Suicide in the United States.* Atlanta, GA: Centers for Disease Control and Prevention: National Center for Injury Prevention and Control.

Vaiva, G., Ducrocq, F., Meyer, P., Mathieu, D., Philippe, A., Libersa, C., & Goudemand, M. (2006). Effect of telephone contact on further suicide attempts in patients discharged from an emergency department: Randomised controlled study. *British Medical Journal, 332* (7552), 1241–1245.

Van Orden, K. A., Witte, T. K., Gordon, K. H., Bender, T. W., & Joiner, T. E. (2008). Suicidal desire and the capability for suicide: Tests of the interpersonal psychological theory of suicidal behavior among adults. *Journal of Consulting and Clinical Psychology, 76,* 72–83.

van Praag, H. (2001). Suicide and aggression: Are they biologically two sides of the same coin? In D. Lester (Ed.), *Suicide prevention: Resources for the millennium* (pp. 45–66). Philadelphia: Brunner-Routledge.

Webb, N. B. (2011). Play therapy for bereaved children: Adapting strategies to community, school, and home settings. *School Psychology International, 32*(2), 132–143.

Webb, S. B., & Griffiths, F. (1998–1999). *Young people at risk of suicide: Part A. School facilitators' handbook; Part B. Supplementary resources.* Auckland, New Zealand: College of Education, Massey University.

Wenzel, A., Brown, G. K., & Beck, A. T. (2009). *Cognitive therapy for suicidal patients: Scientific and clinical applications.* Washington, DC: American Psychological Association.

West, D. J. (1966). *Murder followed by suicide.* Cambridge, MA: Harvard University Press.

Westefeld, J. S., Range, L. M., Rogers, J. R., Maples, M. R., Bromley, J. L., & Alcorn, J. (2000). Suicide: An overview. *Counseling Psychologist, 28,* 445–510.

Williams, M. (1997). *Cry of pain: Understanding suicide and self-harm.* London: Penguin Books.

Wirth, J. L. (1999). Introduction to the issue of rational suicide. In J. L. Wirth (Ed.), *Contemporary perspectives on rational suicide* (pp. 1–12). Philadelphia: Brunner/Mazel.

World Health Organization. (2011). *Mental health: Country reports and charts available.* Retrieved from www.who .int/mental_health/prevention/suicide/country_reports/ en/index.html

Yalom, I. D. (1980). *Existential psychotherapy.* New York: Basic books.

CHAPTER 9
Sexual Assault

The Scope of the Problem

Be forewarned: The statistics in this chapter are some of the most controversial and error prone reported in this book! Given the emotional volatility and cultural artifacts that undergird sexual assault, after reading this chapter we hope you'll understand why these statistics may be so error prone. The benchmark National Violence Against Women Survey (National Institute of Justice and Centers for Disease Control, 1998) conducted in 1997 in the United States found that 1 in 6 U.S. women and 1 in 33 U.S. men had experienced an attempted or completed rape as a child and/or as an adult, using a definition of rape that includes forced vaginal, oral, and anal sex. Those statistics are probably very conservative, with other studies ranging from 10 to 15 percent of American men and 15 to 33 percent of American women (Lew, 2004; Rowan, 2006).

Contrary to popular myth, these acts were not all committed by sexual perverts and deviants lurking in big-city dark alleys and nabbing unsuspecting young schoolgirls as they walked by. In 2002, 3 out of 5 sexual assault victims stated the offender was an intimate, relative, friend, or acquaintance (U.S. Department of Justice, 2003). It should not be surprising, then, that rape, sexual assault, and child sexual abuse demographics tend to mimic domestic violence statistics. In short, it is better-than-even odds that someone who knows you will be the one who sexually assaults you.

Further, because most of you reading this book are sitting in a college classroom, be advised that nearly 20 percent of your female classmates will be victims of attempted or actual assault, as will about 6 percent of the men (Krebs et al., 2007). Frazier and her associates

(2009) conducted an online survey that examined the incidence of traumatic events among a large and diverse population of college students. When all of the different types of unwanted sexual contact were combined, they ranked second only to unexpected death in frequency of response to trauma. The really interesting fact in all sexual assault reporting is that a great deal of it doesn't get reported at all, so you can assume that any statistic you see is probably a pretty conservative estimate of what is really happening (Kariane et al., 2005; Weiss, 2010).

This chapter will deal mainly with adult males as perpetrators and women or children as their victims. However, no one should labor under the delusion that adult males are not raped (and this excludes the stereotypes of prison sex or gay sex) (Davis, 2002; Gartner, 2005; Isley & Gehrenbeck-Shim, 1997; Mezey & King, 1998; Scarce, 1997), nor should you believe that women are not capable of some of the most heinous sexual and physical abuse imaginable upon their own children, whether boys or girls (Allen, 1991; Elliot, 1994; Gartner, 2005; Holmes, Holmes, & Unholz, 1993; Lew, 2004; Rosencrans, 1997; U.S. Department of Justice, 2000). Although the majority of assaults are perpetrated on children and females under age 25, sexual assault survivors have been identified among males and females from every segment of the population—children, adolescents, adults, and older adults (U.S. Department of Justice, 1998). An estimated 10 to 20 percent of men are sexually assaulted sometime in their lives (U.S. Department of Justice, 2000). Nor does the United States have a corner on either the rape or child abuse markets (Chen, Dunne, & Wang, 2003; Lalor & McElvaney, 2010; Sanday, 1998; Schwartz-Kenney, McCauley, & Epstein,

2001; Tomoko et al., 2002). About 103,000 children are reported as having been sexually abused in the United States out of 903,000 child maltreatment cases. The true figure is estimated to be between 250,000 and 350,000 (U.S. Department of Health and Human Services, 1997), and Finkelhor and his associates (2005) found in their national survey that 1 in 12 children they surveyed had been sexually victimized in the study year alone! Statistics in nations of Asia, Africa, and Latin America are equally grim (Chen, Dunne, & Wang, 2003; Schwartz-Kenney, McCauley, & Epstein, 2001), and in some cases horrifically worse: Children are sold into thralldom as child prostitutes or indentured servants by their poverty-stricken parents (Rowan, 2006).

Underreporting

The vast majority of crime survey reports do not report sexual abuse of children under the age of 12, yet we certainly see many of those children turnstiling through local child protection centers (Benedict, 1985, pp. 186–192; Brownmiller, 1975, p. 175). The literature consistently estimates that 50 to 90 percent of all rapes or attempted rapes go unreported. Most instances of incest and molestation are never reported. Further, date rapes and even stranger rapes are not reported out of shame, humiliation, guilt, cultural taboos, and the very real fear of secondary victimization at the hands of medical and legal authorities (Cole, 2006; Matsakis, 2003; Weiss, 2010). Beyond the sensationalism of religious cults that practice polygamy with young children (Bottoms et al., 2003) and Catholic priests who sexually abuse young parishioners (McGlone, 2003), it should be very clear that the kinds of sexual assaults this chapter covers are common, are underreported, and the traumatic wake they spread encompasses millions of people.

David Lisek has done seminal research in this area (Lisek & Miller, 2002; Lisek & Roth, 1988). Lisek reports that in 1998 there were 1,687 reported rapes and 526 arrests made in metro Boston. If one multiplies the prevalence number from the National Violence Against Women study (Tjaden & Thoennes, 2000), the true rape incidence for the 1.75 million women living in the Boston metro area was 15,225 rapes. This disparity suggests that only 1 in 9 rapes is actually reported.

The Unique Situation of Sexual Abuse/ Rape Survivors

Abundant evidence suggests that crises resulting from sexual abuse and rape are more intense and differ in nature, intensity, and extent from other forms of crisis (Burgess & Holmstrom, 1985; Finkelhor, 1979, 1984, 1987; Gartner, 2005; Lew, 2004; Matsakis, 2003, Rowan, 2006; Williams & Holmes, 1981). In fact, the psychological traumatic wake of rape both in childhood and adulthood marks it as probably second only to prolonged combat in potential for PTSD, and many of the transcrisis rape treatment approaches closely parallel those of standard PTSD treatment (Cloitre & Rosenberg, 2006; Frazier et al., 2001).

Defining Rape

There are many definitions of rape. Some are based on legal constructs; some are derived from other sources. Brownmiller (1975) distinguishes between most legal definitions and what she refers to as a woman's definition of rape. She sees the legal definition of rape as "the forcible perpetration of an act of sexual intercourse on the body of a woman not one's wife" (p. 380) as much too narrow and protective of male supremacy. Brownmiller's preferred definition from a woman's perspective is that rape is "a sexual invasion of the body by force, an incursion into the private, personal inner space without consent—in short, an internal assault from one of several avenues and by one of several methods [that] constitutes a deliberate violation of emotional, physical, and rational integrity and is a hostile, degrading act of violence" (p. 376). That definition appears to encompass the whole scope of rape, as well as other forms of sexual abuse/misuse/harassment. For the purposes of this chapter, your authors will use Koss and Achilles' (2008) definition of rape as an unwanted act of oral, vaginal, or anal penetration committed though the use of force, threat of force, or when incapacitated; sexual assault refers to a broader range of sexual criminal offenses such as sexual battery and sexual coercion up to and including rape (U.S. Department of Education, 2011).

The Dynamics of Rape

The etiology of rape has roots deeply embedded in the psychosocial and cultural fabric of the particular society in which it occurs (Brownmiller, 1975; Donat & D'Emilio, 1998; Eisler, 1987–1995; Ullman, 1996a, 1996b). According to Brownmiller (1975) and Eisler (1987–1995), the cultural mechanism of male dominance constitutes the driving force in rape in all cultures. The psychosocial, cultural, and personal attitudes and responses of both males and females are important dynamics in considering the phenomenon of rape (Benedict, 1985; Williams & Holmes, 1981).

Social/Cultural Factors

Baron and Straus (1989) characterize rape as a social phenomenon and theorize four different causes: gender inequality, pornography, social disorganization, and legitimization of violence. *Gender inequality* refers to the economic, political, and legal status of women in comparison to men. *Pornography* reduces women to sex objects, promotes male dominance, and encourages or condones sexual violence against women. *Social disorganization* erodes social control and constraints and undermines freedom of individual behavior and self-determination. *Legitimization of violence* is the support the culture gives to violence, as portrayed in the mass media (such as television programming), laws permitting corporal punishment in schools, violent sports, military exploits, and video games.

The notion of male supremacy has its roots deep in our cultural history, which has always equated the property rights of men with access to and control over the bodies of women, children, and others who are perceived as dependents (Brownmiller, 1975). Indeed, Eisler (1987–1995, pp. 153–154) describes rape and sexual assault as one of several threats widely used to ensure the continued domination and control of women. Historically, the crime of rape has been seen not as a crime against the woman but as a crime against her father or her husband (Donat & D'Emilio, 1998).

Brownmiller (1975) and others have documented a part of the history of rape as a psychosocial means by which the victors in wars reward themselves and humiliate their vanquished foes. The wholesale rape and killing of helpless women and children represents the ultimate vulnerability and defeat of a people. It likewise represents the ultimate humiliation and subjugation of a person. Whether it is inflicted on thousands, as reported in war, or on one person, the purpose is quite similar—the use of unrestrained power to force the vanquished into total submission.

Personal and Psychological Factors

Personal and psychological factors unique to men who perpetrate sexual abuse affect both their decision to assault and the way the assault is carried out (Beech, Ward, & Fisher, 2006; Groth & Birnbaum, 1979; Lisek & Miller, 2002; Lisek & Roth, 1988; Williams & Holmes, 1981). The male offender:

1. Acts in a hostile, aggressive, angry, condescending, and domineering manner, and believes he is strong, courageous, and manly even though he often feels weak, anxious, inadequate, threatened, and dependent and believes women are inherently dangerous.
2. Lacks the interpersonal skills to make his point in society and particularly with women.
3. May need to exercise *power* to prove to himself and to the victim that he is powerful, omnipotent, and in total control.
4. May show *sadistic* patterns—the sadistic rapist frequently uses extreme violence and often mutilates or murders the victim in order to attain a feeling of total triumph over the victim.
5. Sees women as primarily sexual objects and has sexual urges that are uncontrollable and all consuming.
6. Holds stereotypical and rigid views of male and female roles with hypermasculine self-views that validate he is a "real man."
7. Harbors chronic feelings of anger, hostility, and fear toward women and seeks to control them by his sexual "conquests."

Feminists, with good historical reason, have attempted to define rape as basically an exercise in power and control. On that basis most rapists have been cast into one of four categories: anger, power exploitative, power reassurance, and sadistic. McCabe and Wauchope (2005) found evidence to support these typologies in two studies, one of men who had only been charged with sexual assault and the other of men who were convicted, but they also found outliers who did not fit the four categories well. A number of researchers (Lisek & Miller; 2002; Lisek & Roth, 1988; Scully & Marolla, 1998; Sussman & Bordwell, 1981) have interviewed convicted rapists and have vividly demonstrated that each rapist's reasons for assault are individual. For example:

1. Some men use rape to punish or exact revenge because a specific woman has "done them wrong." They see all women collectively as responsible for one woman's supposed transgressions. Some negative precipitating event with an intimate causes them to "take it out" on and "get even" with some woman who is a total stranger to them. It doesn't make any difference who it is as long as it is a female— a generic symbol of their lost power, virility, and masculinity that they desperately want back.
2. Criminals who commit rape in the perpetration of a crime often see rape as an added bonus. It's there for the taking, so why not?
3. For some men, rape is attaining the unattainable woman, the woman they would never otherwise

have a chance with. In this instance, sex is the motivating factor.

4. For some men, rape is an impersonal experience and preferred over any demonstrated caring or mutual affection. There is no obligation, and the power, control, and sexual tension release are gratifying.

5. Finally, in its most heinous form, gang rapists see rape as recreation, adventure, and proving they are "macho." These individuals belong to sexually violent subcultures that reflect both the rapist's views of women and the notion that sexual conquest of as many women as possible is a critical measure of manhood. A gang rape is seen as male bonding at its height. While numerous interviewees stated they regretted their actions and were now sorry for them, the immediate impact on them postrape in regard to what they had done was slight. Ominously, if they felt anything, they generally felt good about what they did.

Yet the vast majority of rapes have to do with the power relationships between men and women (Sussman & Bordwell, 1981, p. 12). Somehow the contemporary sociocultural milieu produces some males who feel such absence of power and control in their lives that they develop a need to "take it" (control). These males come to believe that it is their "right" (p. 5) and proceed to rationalize and justify their behavior, even though they have invaded and taken by force another person's life and body.

Myths About Rape

One of the most difficult obstacles that human services workers face in dealing with all forms and aspects of rape and sexual abuse is the abundance of debilitating myths in society (Benedict, 1985; Burt, 1998; Ganas et al., 1999; Matsakis, 2003). For example:

1. *Rape is just rough sex.* The notion that rape equals sex is perhaps the most destructive myth of all. If we believe that rape is sex, then it follows that rape doesn't hurt (physically or psychologically) any more than sex does. We can even believe that the survivor enjoys and is erotically stimulated by its roughness. Rape is violence, torture, and a life-threatening event. It is utterly humiliating, and the joy of "rough sex" has nothing to do with it. However, research indicates that certain types of rapists are aroused by the use of force and violence against victims, and such arousal may be heightened by aggressive resistance of victims (Drieschner & Lange, 1999; Knight, 1999).

2. *Women "cry rape" to gain revenge.* Ganas and associates (1999) hypothesize that this myth permeates our society because such myths (a) provide comfort for our social structure (people don't want to believe that rape really occurred), (b) serve to focus the blame for sexual violence on victims rather than perpetrators, and (c) are easier to believe than the reality of knowing that rape can happen to anyone. As such it is one of the most heated and controversial issues in sexual assault. "Revenge" reports are sometimes heard, and at times the cry of "rape" has been used for secondary gain, such as getting back at a jilted lover, blackmail, job security, or covering up an unwanted pregnancy. A 2 percent rule has been used by the FBI in its training as the percentage of false accusations. Lisek and his associates (2010) found about a 6 percent false accusation rate in their investigation of rape allegations. Yet according to police reports, rapes are no more likely to be falsely reported than other crimes (Lear, 1972).

3. *Rape is motivated by lust.* Eisler (1995) and Scully and Marolla (1998) believe that the motivation for rape is most likely to be domination, power, anger, revenge, control, frustration, or sadism. Benedict (1985, p. 8) and Eisler (1995, pp. 237–239) report that some men may come to associate sex with violence, thereby viewing women not as human beings but as objects of prey and/or domination and viewing sex as an act of power, control, and triumph. However, one counterpoint view, based on studies of the evolutionary theories of rape by Thornhill and Palmer (2000), suggests that the motives of rapists are primarily sexual, with the exercise of power mostly a means to an end. This idea is supported at least in part by Scully and Marolla (1998), who found that some of the rapists they interviewed saw it as the only way to get sexual access to women who were unwilling or "out of their league."

4. *Rapists are weird, psychotic loners.* No such contention can be supported by the research. Rapists come from every walk of life. People who rape and commit other forms of sexual abuse/misuse have been identified in every stratum of society—from judges to messenger boys, from weaklings to bodybuilders, from vagrants to corporate executives, from husbands and fathers to strangers, from partners, known friends, and relatives to unknown intruders (Benedict, 1985, pp. 9–10; Burt, 1998). The idea that rapists were mentally ill held sway for a long time (Groth, 1971) and was seen by feminists as a

particularly odious way of rationalizing the male-dominated societal power and subjugation motives that undergirded and upheld a repressive, patriarchal society. The sheer number of rapes make it statistically impossible that the typical rapist is "mentally ill," given the small number of psychopathic men in the population (Scully & Marolla, 1998).

5. *Victims or survivors of rape provoked the rape or wanted to be raped, so no harm was done.* By acting sexy, wearing sexy clothes or lots of makeup, being at a bar and "coming on" to a man, walking along a road alone at night, or doing laundry or grocery shopping late, somehow or other a woman does something that clearly says "Come rape me!" The bottom line is that through a series of weak inferences and rationalizations, the rapist is able to condone his sexual assault. The rapist is no longer responsible for the way he acted because the woman, by her actions, brought it on herself (Burt, 1998). Although most rapists deny that they are rapists, rationalize that women provoke or want it, or deny that their sexual assaults are rape, there are virtually no documented cases in which women have lured men into raping them. Ganas and associates (1999) and Sussman and Bordwell (1981) have clearly shown that what the survivor does before the rape has little if anything to do with the rapist's decision to assault.

6. *Only bad women are raped.* This myth is one of the most blatant examples of a "blame the victim" attitude (Brownmiller, 1975). This myth is taken to mean that if the woman has a "bad" reputation, the rape is justified. The stereotypical "damaged goods" notion means that a woman who has said "Yes" once can no longer legitimately say "No." She has lost her value (Burt, 1998). For many, the extension of this myth means that prostitutes are so devalued they have no worth at all and therefore cannot be raped (Silbert, 1988). Whether the person is a professional hooker or a minister should make no difference. Neither deserves to be assaulted, and both are entitled to equal protection and treatment.

7. *Real rapes happen only in bad parts of town, at night, in abandoned buildings or lonely fields by strangers who have knives or guns and who engage in brutally beating the victims when they resist heroically—even unto death.* That's pretty much rubbish! While there are rapes that happen that way, remember that half or more of the perpetrators are someone who knows the victim. Most rapes do not involve a weapon or sustaining an injury beyond minor bruises or scratches. And most occur in either the victim's home or the assailant's (Burt, 1998).

8. *If the woman doesn't resist, she must have wanted it.* The old stereotypical notion, which has had some coinage in the courts, is that the woman needs to resist unto death or be so physically drained or hurt that she can't resist any longer. Resisting may get a woman killed, particularly if the assailant is armed and is more physically powerful. Furthermore, there are many psychological obstacles in the way of resisting that have to do with the historical power differential wherein women do submit. Ominously, Kassing and Prietio (2003) found that both male and female counselors in training thought that male rape victims should fight back. There is no conclusive evidence that fighting back or not fighting back is better for the victim (Matsakis, 2003).

It is not easy or simple to eradicate or even to refute the preceding myths in society at large (Ganas et al., 1999). Feminists argue that it is to the advantage of the entire patriarchal society to believe such myths, and it is certainly to the advantage of the rapists (Burt, 1998).

Myths about rape and sexual assault are not the sole domain of females. Here are some of the more prevalent myths about males and sexual assault (Male Survivor, 2011).

1. *Boys and men can't be willing victims.* Let's suppose that a 350-pound NFL noseguard decides to have his way with you. What do you think will happen? Boys and adult males are often physically weaker than their attackers or are threatened with weapons. Or the perpetrator may have power and control over the victim though position, influence, knowledge, and prestige. There is essentially no difference between males and females in regard to this myth.

2. *Homosexuals are usually the perpetrators of sexual abuse of boys.* Pedophiles are pedophiles whether it be boys or girls. They are not gays or lesbians but pedophiles who happen to have different sex and age preferences.

3. *Boys are less traumatized than girls.* While some studies have found boys to be less negatively affected initially, long-term effects are quite damaging, and when the perpetrators are trusted others (which is often the case, as you will read later in this chapter), they become a psychological abattoir for boys.

4. *Boys abused by males will later become homosexual.* How and why adult sexual orientation develops is a complex question. While being sexually assaulted by an adult is almost a guarantee for sexual role confusion, it does not mean one automatically becomes gay as a result. In fact, with males, our own experience is that a number of those who have been victimized by males become homophobic or overcompensate by attempting to prove their manhood by having sex with as many females as possible. The bottom line is, though, that at present this is only one variable in a multitude of variables that influence sexual orientation.

5. *Vampire/zombie syndrome.* The notion is that once you are bitten you become one. This is an especially dangerous myth because it can stereotype victims as perpetrators when the victims desperately need help rather than punishment, ridicule, isolation, and abandonment. Generally, getting psychological help early on is critical to not become a perpetrator later in life.

6. *If a boy (or girl) experiences sexual arousal or organism from abuse, this means he enjoys it.* We are hardwired for sex. Physical stimulation is likely to happen during sex. That does not mean the child wanted the experience, fully participated in it, or "got off" or "wanted it" as many perpetrators try to rationalize.

7. *If the perpetrator is female, the boy just got lucky.* This is a widely held and very, very dangerous stereotype. Some of the most disturbed clients we have seen have been children and adolescent boys abused by females in authority positions and consanguine relationships. The conflict, confusion, rage, and other extremely volatile emotions and thinking they display toward women as adults marks them as threats for harm to females. Above all, these boys should receive treatment immediately after discovery of the assault.

The problem is that, even among "educated" people, these myths have remarkable staying power. Heppner and associates (1995) found that college students believed many myths about rape. That study identified many differences in men's and women's perceptions of rape during and after a session on rape prevention intervention consisting of didactic, video, and question-and-answer discussion. During the intervention, both men's and women's attitudes showed decreased belief in rape myths; at a 2-month follow-up, however, men had regained more of their former beliefs than women had. Research by Varelas and Foley (1998) indicated that both black and white college students who strongly believed rape myths were more tolerant of rapists and less tolerant of victims than those who had weaker beliefs. In addition, women with strong beliefs in the myths were less likely to report sexual assaults or to assist in legal actions against rapists.

Date and Acquaintance Rape

Much of the research reported on date and acquaintance rape deals with sexual assaults on college campuses. Little is known about date rape as it applies to high school students, although at this writing there were 4,000 reported incidents of sexual battery and more than 800 reported rapes and attempted rapes (Robers et al., 2010). According to a 2003 U.S. Department of Justice report, rape is the most common violent crime at U.S. universities. The incidence of rape is 35 per 1,000 female college students per year. However, fewer than 5 percent of these rapes are reported to police. Women may decline to report rape out of shame, self-reproach for drinking too much, or fear of social isolation from the perpetrators and her friends. Ninety percent of the college women who are raped know their assailants, and most rapes occur in a social situation such as partying or studying together in a dorm room (Cole, 2006).

Mills and Granoff (1992) found that 28 percent of college women surveyed acknowledged that they had been victims of rape or attempted rape. In a national survey of college men and women, Koss (1998) found that 8.3 percent of the women felt they had been forced to engage in unwanted sex. Conversely, only 3.4 percent of the men felt they had forced a partner to engage in unwanted sex. Few told anyone about the encounters, although those reporting attempted rape were more likely to tell someone than were those who had actually been raped. A number of male respondents admitted to committing what is legally defined as rape and admitted to continuing to make sexual advances even when their dates had told them "No!"

One of the bigger myths of rape is: *Date rape isn't really rape.* The girl went out with him, didn't she? He probably spent a good deal of money on her. What if she kissed him back and engaged in heavy petting? Then she turned him off? That's a "prick tease"! She deserved it and probably even wanted it even though she said no. Even if it was a boyfriend of long standing, and whatever else may have happened before the rape in terms of sexual foreplay, and no matter how much money was spent, "No!" is "No!" and no one has the right or justification to rape a date.

Date Rape Risk

Date rape survivors in college have been found to be more likely to have experienced stress, maltreatment, and negative home environment/neglect during childhood than were women who reported no date rape experience (Sanders & Moore, 1999). Date rape participants in the Sanders and Moore study were also more likely to have experienced sexual abuse during childhood. Himelein, Vogel, and Wachowiak (1994) suggest that child sexual abuse is an underlying risk factor for both heightened sexual activity and sexual victimization in dating. Shapiro and Chwarz (1997) further suggest that precocious knowledge of sex, confusion about sexual norms, isolation, and neediness might predispose a young abuse survivor to early and frequent sexual activity, which may in turn increase the risk of dating victimization.

Alcohol consumption has also been linked to date and acquaintance rape as a risk factor (Cole 2006; Norris & Cubbins, 1992). A study by Abbey, McAuslan, and Ross (1998) found that the mutual effects of college men's beliefs and experiences with regard to dating, sexuality, and alcohol consumption increased the likelihood that a male would misperceive a female companion's sexual intentions, and that this *misperception* might lead to sexual assault. In contrast, the use of a *date rape drug* (gamma hydroxybutyrate, or GHB) in the commission of a sexual assault constitutes a premeditated and *deliberate* assault (Boyd, 2000). Ullman, Karabatsos, and Koss (1999) found that both victim's and offender's use of alcohol prior to attack was directly associated with more severe victimization of women and that alcohol use played both direct and indirect roles in the outcomes of sexual assaults.

Schwartz and Leggett (1999) found that women who were raped while intoxicated were not less emotionally affected and did not blame themselves any more than women who were raped by force while not intoxicated. It is interesting to note that most of these women did not classify their experiences as rape, although all were victims under criminal law. Norris and Cubbins (1992) found that three-fourths of acquaintance rapes involved drinking and that if both members of a dating couple had been consuming alcohol, the rape was not judged as severely as when only the woman had been drinking. In the latter case, the man was likely to be viewed as taking advantage of a vulnerable woman.

Preventing Date, Acquaintance, and Other Forms of Rape

Mills and Granoff (1992) and Dunn, Vail-Smith, and Knight (1999) suggest that continuing educational and support services (for both men and women) are critically needed to address, in a culturally unbiased manner, the causes and prevention of date and acquaintance rape. Educational programs, especially at the secondary school level, have been recommended as preventive measures in reducing date and acquaintance sexual assaults (Page, 1997). Ullman, Karabatsos, and Koss (1999) recommended that rape and alcohol abuse prevention efforts can benefit from incorporating information about alcohol's role in different sexual assault contexts. It seems reasonable that such prevention initiatives should also address strategies to avoid assaults connected with the use of date rape drugs.

Frazier, Valtinson, and Candell (1994) demonstrated that coeducational and interactive rape prevention programs can succeed in the short run. Their preventive interventions, presented to members of fraternities and sororities, showed that participants endorsed significantly fewer rape-supportive attitudes immediately following the interventions than did control group members. But, like Heppner and colleagues' (1995) participants, experimental and control group members no longer differed after 1 month. Indeed, most studies of rape education programs indicate they do not hold up over time (Garrity, 2011; Vladutiu, Martin, & Macy, 2011). Hillenbrand-Gunn and her associates (2010) have taken a different approach to rape education. They conducted a program for high school students that focused on social norms theory (Perkins & Berkowitz, 1986), which is based on what one thinks one's peers do and believe rather than what the peers actually do and believe. Their program was based on a Men as Allies philosophy and combined it with social norms theory as their theoretical framework. Group psychoeducational/discussion sessions were administered to both male and female high school students through a variety of formats that challenged sexist, coercive, and abusive behavior that is a precursor to thinking that sexual assault is acceptable. Pre- to postprogram results indicated that attitudes changed in the experimental group and not in the control group. The results of this methodologically sound experiment held at a 4-week follow-up for both males and females, suggests that it holds promise as a creative approach focusing on peers, a formidable force for this age group. Clearly, the research indicates that rape prevention programs should be comprehensive and ongoing, rather than programmed as onetime interventions.

Finally, studies by Sawyer, Pinciaro, and Jessell (1998) on the effects of coercion and verbal consent on university students' perception of date rape concluded that, in an act legally defined as rape, male students are generally more prone to deny that a rape occurred unless an assertive or aggressive "No!" is verbalized by the potential victim. The value and effect of profoundly verbalizing "No!" in situations in which women are vulnerable to rape cannot be overestimated.

Perhaps even more disheartening, Kassing and Prietio (2003) found that male counselors in training who had no experience working with sexual assault victims were willing to believe myths about male rape victims, and both male and female counselors in training believed that the male victim should have resisted more. The conclusion with regard to training therapists is clearly that they need to be disabused of some myths about sexual assault!

Intervention Strategies for Rape and Battery: The Case of Melody

Melody Swanson is a 50-year-old teacher. She has been living alone in a small house since the younger of her two children went away to college 2 months ago. Melody was divorced 7 years ago. She had a long weekend off from school and decided to go away to a casino for a mini-vacation. When she returned home from her trip at 9:30 yesterday evening and emerged from her car in her driveway, she was met by a gunman in his middle 20s.

She dropped a small bag of groceries and some items from her purse as she was abducted at gunpoint and forced into the gunman's car, which was parked on the street. Melody was beaten, driven away to an isolated area several miles from her home, raped, beaten again, robbed, and abandoned, bleeding and bruised, with her clothing in shreds. She was weak and dazed, but managed to find her way to the nearest house in the early hours of the morning, where she called for help. It is now 8:30 A.M. and Melody is at the trauma center of a hospital in a large metropolitan city, where she has just

been taken by the police. Melody is experiencing physical and emotional trauma. She personifies a traumatized person. She is in shock, shaking and trembling, has both eyes black, numerous contusions, abrasions, and cuts, and is still in the muddy clothes she was abducted in. She is about to meet what will become a very important person in her life—a crisis worker from the local sexual assault and domestic violence center who specializes in rape cases.

Immediate Aftermath

In most situations the most helpful and appropriate immediate response from a crisis worker is empathy and assurance that the survivor is still alive. Nowhere in crisis intervention is it more important to provide the core facilitative conditions of building trust, displaying unconditional positive regard, using empathic listening and responding, providing concreteness and clarity, and demonstrating patience. The crisis task is predispositioning the client in regard to what she is going to go through, from vaginal examinations to police questioning to the acute stress symptoms that are likely to follow the initial onslaught of emotions she is now experiencing. The worker is going to quickly build what in the psychotherapy trade is called a *working alliance*. Melody's rape is a case in point of how this operates in the immediate aftermath of a trauma. Cloitre and her associates (2004) report that building this alliance is as critical as, if not more important than, mastery of any intervention techniques.

The *impact stage* (Matsakis, 2003, pp. 82–90) occurs during the assault and for approximately 2 weeks following it. During this time a kaleidoscope of emotions, thoughts, and behaviors may occur, or conversely the client may be in a state of shock and dissociation, with both physical pain associated with the sexual assault and dissociation, somatic reactions, hypervigilance, nightmares, and startle responses that are symptomatic of the acute stress disorder that often follows. Stability both from a physical and psychological standpoint are critical at this time (Briere & Scott, 2006, pp. 273). It is the crisis worker's job to do a number of things as soon as the client comes into the hospital or the crisis center.

Some sense of control needs to be restored so the client can go through the physical exam and police report. Paramount is restoring a sense of safety and security to a person whose world has just been turned upside down. To do this, the crisis worker must accurately assess the client's state of mobility and equilibrium and gently but also with assuredness and confidence enter into this upside-down world. The worker needs to gather information while walking a therapeutic tightrope between sensitivity and the need to ask specific behavioral closed-ended questions. Maximum sensitivity means using empathic prefacing statements followed by gathering behavioral information on the assault. To ask for information without voicing sincere concern for the person's trauma is not only callous and insensitive, it will most likely terminate intervention before it starts (McCart et al., 2009). To that end, it is critical that the crisis worker immediately start the Predisposition task of our crisis intervention model. Courtois and Ford (2009) propose the following capstone statement in regard to treating survivors of prolonged complex trauma, but we believe it also fits well here. Your job at this point is to provide relational conditions that encourage the safety of the attachment between the client and the worker (p. 190), and this may be anything but easy for you or the client.

CW: (*talking slowly while she gently picks up Melody's hand in an examining room in the ER*) Hi, Melody, I'm Jolee Mabry. I am a counselor from the Metro Sexual Assault Unit. You have been through a terrible experience, that no one should ever go through, but you survived it. I can't begin to know what it feels like to experience all the feelings and thoughts you are having right now, but I do understand as traumatic as this is you have survived and I am going to be with you while you go through this, if you would like.

Melody: (*looking fearful and struggling for words*) I don't . . . I don't know . . . what to think, do, . . . what will happen? Where is he? Who was he ? Why me? Can he get in here? So many things . . . I . . . I am so cold and it feels like my heart is about to pound through my chest. Is this a nightmare? But I know it's real . . . I think. Where . . . am . . . I? I'm so sorry. I . . . I . . . I don't remember your name. Who are you?

CW: (*Picks up a blanket and gently pulls it around Melody.*) I'm Jolee Mabry. I am a nurse and a counselor at the sexual assault center here. You are safe here. You were brought here by the paramedics and the police. You are in the Elvis Presley Trauma Unit. I'm Jolee Mabry, a counselor here in the trauma unit. You were beaten physically by the man who assaulted you and the paramedics brought you here. You were raped and assaulted, that is very real. That's why you are here to get taken care of, and we do a very good job of taking care of people who have been sexually assaulted. That is my job, to take care of you, steer you through this experience and act as your advocate and just take care of things for you. Do you understand what I just said and know where you are?

Melody: Yes. What's going to happen to me? (*Starts to shake.*)

CW: (*Reaches over and slowly strokes the client's arm with her hand and holds her other hand.*) I can't say it will be pleasant, but the medical staff and police officers who deal with sexual assault here know their business. The nurse who will do the rape kit exam is a specially trained Sexual Assault Nurse Examiner (SANE). She will make it as painless as possible. You will be asked by the police to describe what happened, and there will be a number of medical procedures. As I said, I'll be with you every step of the way, and when they are done I'll be with you to make arrangements to see that you stay safe and do what's necessary to get some stability and control back in your life.

Melody: Absolutely, please stay. (*Grabs Jolee's hand and grips it.*) It was horrible—the rape. I don't know how I came out alive and without any broken bones. He intended to kill me. Part of the time I was in a daze. I don't know what came over me. I must have blacked out. He may have thought I was dead. I don't know how long I lay out there alone after he left me. I certainly didn't fight back or protest. Look at me, I am so dirty. (*Recoils in disgust.*)

CW: Melody, I'm so proud of you for the way you handled it. You did whatever it took to stay alive. You saved yourself, and that took courage. Whatever you did, whether it was blacking out or offering no protests, was right, because it preserved your life, and that's the important thing right now. We are going to get those clothes off of you and get you cleaned up, but we need to get some pictures and take some samples first, so hang in there a bit longer.

Melody: I feel so damn stupid. Always watchful and just let my guard down. So damn angry at me. I'd kill that bastard if I had a chance. Shoot his nuts off! Lord! Did I just say that! I don't say things like that, but that scurrilous low life SOB . . . degrading . . . How can I go back to face my students . . . I feel like I'm in a sort of twilight zone. Maybe part of me did die. I'm feeling so alone and vulnerable. It's like this whole damn thing isn't real. It couldn't be happening to me, but I know it is. I know I keep going back to that and all this whirl . . . I don't know if I can hold it together.

There is no universal response to rape. Melody represents a few of the conflicting emotions that rampage through someone who has been sexually violated. Dissociative responses are a common defense mechanism to try to bring some stability back into the survivor's life as a whirlwind of emotions blow through survivor's mind. The laundry list of responses that follows this dialogue represents a good deal of, but not all of the dirty emotions the client is trying to wash out of her mind. The crisis worker's job is to continuously provide support, safety, and practical assistance. While it may seem to be minimizing and discounting the gravity of the situation to call it *psychological first aid* (National Child Traumatic Stress Network and National Center for PTSD, 2006; National Institute of Mental Health, 2002), that is exactly what the worker is doing. Psychological first aid comprises three primary tasks of our intervention model: predispositioning/bonding, exploration/assessment, and safety. However, how this usually gets done is anything but stepwise. Crisis workers who ply the trade in the field of sexual assault are indeed engaging in a stand-up act where they have to be quick in changing strategies and responses to meet the kaleidoscope of emotions that may range from catatonic-like shock to unbridled rage.

CW: It's really scary, the thought of losing control with all those thoughts and emotions racing around in your head, Melody, but that is common for sexual assault survivors. It may be hard to imagine, but your mind and body are attempting to get order back into what for the past few hours has been complete chaos. It's your mind and body's normal defensive response to a completely abnormal situation. It will pass, and to help move that process along we are going to take this piece by piece, one step at a time, until you get control back.

Melody: I don't know. I guess, but . . . (*Pause, with apprehensive look.*) I'm a teacher, I maintain control, but I just can't seem to get a handle on this . . . (*Starts to breakdown again with muffled sobs.*) I'm so sorry, I'm such a mess, and can't get a grip.

CW: You don't have to be sorry about anything. You are not a mess. Grief is also part of this. You have lost a lot tonight. (*Sits patiently while Melody holds on and sobs quietly with her arm around her.*)

The crisis worker acknowledges her grief, which is a common response to the many losses the client has suffered (Matsakis, 2003, pp. 111–127). She also starts to slowly give her information about the psychological processes occurring within her as a start to developing coping skills and regaining emotional and cognitive control. It is important to start providing basic psychoeducation to clients who are experiencing extreme psychological stress (McCart, 2009). Melody is suffering from what we call peritraumatic stress symptoms. Those are traumalike symptoms that almost all persons would suffer given similar circumstances. Whether these symptoms turn into acute traumatic stress disorder, which we will discuss later in the book, or turns into PTSD will depend a lot on what happens in the next few hours and days. The worker has to be judicious in how much information on psychological coping mechanisms she gives out to avoid cognitive overload.

Indeed, engaging in any formal therapeutic intervention or formal assessment in the next few days is *not* recommended. What is recommended is planning thoroughly for the next few hours and days to keep the client safe, supported, and stabilized. Healing from a rape requires concentration, effort, thought, and time and cannot be rushed (Matsakis, 2003, p. 14).

CW: This whole procedure is going to take about three to four hours to complete. We want you thoroughly checked out in regard to not only your sexual assault but the physical assault as well. The police will interview you. Lt. Lenise Balay is going to do the interview. She and I work together a lot on these cases, and I trust her completely. She is one of the most empathic police officers I know. She will ask you some pretty pointed questions, but understand she wants to get this just right so we can catch who did this to you. You are also going to get a pelvic exam and a rape kit done. Andrea Little is a SANE nurse who specializes in doing this. It won't be pleasant, but again she is a specialist in this business and will be very thorough and gentle. I'll be with you every step of the way. Okay?

This is a brief synopsis of the practical medical and legal information the worker gives the survivor. In rape cases, thoroughly explaining what is going to happen is critical to not secondarily revictimizing the survivor.

CW: (*after the police lieutenant and SANE nurse are done*) Excellent! Dr. Zanzar has gone over all your tests and has okayed your release. You got through that well. Where would you like to go and who would you like to be there with you, someone you really trust?

Melody: Well, my brother, Tom. I'd want him there with me. He's an ex-Marine. Although I don't know how he'd feel about all this and his stupid sister who he's always yapping at to be more vigilant and careful. God! I just feel so ashamed to let him know this happened. But I don't know if I can go back in my driveway or not. That's ridiculous but it still scares me, just the thought of it . . .

CW: I understand how you could feel that way, and the last thing you want to do is tell him about this. Would you like me to call him and get him down here and talk with him? I have done this before and I think I can help you out with that.

Using Support Systems and Stopping Secondary Victimization. In the immediate aftermath of the rape, getting support and safety measures in place is a high priority, as is educating the significant others in the survivor's life to the foregoing dynamics. A critical component is steering the person through the medical and police procedures that can have a high potential for secondary victimization (Howell, 1999; Ochberg, 1988;

Pauwels, 2003). Secondary victim crisis intervention may also be necessary if there are persons in the support system who might either become homicidal or turn on the survivor and blame her (Pauwels, 2003). Particularly husbands, fathers, and boyfriends may need very firm, clear instructions on how they are going to meet the survivor in their first encounter. The difficulty of this initial encounter after the rape cannot be overemphasized. Both from the survivor's and significant others' standpoint, it may be very easy to affix blame as a way of trying to make sense out of what happened. Secondary victimization must not be allowed to occur, so the crisis worker's job will be to educate the significant others on how they can best support the client.

Therefore, it is extremely important that a counselor from a rape crisis or sexual assault unit be contacted immediately, as in the preceding example. A nationwide nursing service called the Sexual Assault Nurse Examiner (SANE) program provides specially trained nurses for first response medical care and crisis intervention. The SANE program provides comprehensive and consistent postrape medical care, such as emergency contraception and sexually transmitted disease prophylaxis, documents forensic evidence accurately, provides expert testimony, promotes psychological recovery, and coordinates multiple service providers to provide comprehensive care for rape survivors (Campbell, Patterson, & Lichty, 2005).

CW: (*Meets brother Tom at the center reception desk.*)

Tom: (*excited, agitated, and loud*) What's this all about? What's going on with my sister? What's she doing at the Rape Crisis Center? Is she in trouble? Did she get raped? WHAT THE HELL IS HAPPENING AND WHERE IS MY SISTER?

CW: Your sister has been beaten and sexually assaulted and . . .

Tom: What the . . . where did it happen ?

CW: In her driveway, about 9:30 last night. She was just coming back from the casino.

Tom: Casino! What the hell was she doing at the casino? Jesus Christ, when I get hold of her . . .

CW: (*Becoming assertive and using a well-modulated but commanding voice, immediately interrupts his ranting.*) I understand that you were in the Marines, so tell me this. Is it the Marine Corps creed if a guy gets wounded to go yell at him and tell him how stupid he has been?

Tom: Well no I . . . um . . . but this is different.

CW: Tell me how so. You took care of your wounded buddies, didn't you? What was your rank anyway?

Tom: Well, uh . . . Master Sergeant. But, uh . . . I don't see what that's got to do with it.

CW: (*well-modulated but clearly assertive*) I'll tell you what, Tom. I didn't get a chance to introduce myself. I am Jolee Mabry, a counselor and nurse with the sexual assault center. I was a nurse in the Gulf War, wore the Eagle, Anchor, and Globe (Marine Corps insignia) myself. First Lieutenant Mabry, USMC retired, at your service. I served in Saudi Arabia and Iraq with mobile surgical units there. If you are as good a marine as I think you are, you retrieved your wounded and did everything possible to keep them alive and safe, did you not? Is that correct, Master Sergeant Swanson?

Tom: (*sort of snaps to attention and in a rather tentative voice*) Yes, ma'am. That is . . . uh . . . affirmative, ma'am.

CW: Good, so you have a wounded sister. You know about PTSD, right? We don't want her going out on a date with that now, do we? What she needs is all the care and support you can give her, don't we now? No blame, no fault finding, don't you agree? No going out hunting the bad guy because your job is taking care of your troop, and your sister is surely that and more, is she not? A lot of care and understanding, compassion and empathy, for the terrible combat experience she has been through, and make no mistake, it is indeed that. So, Master Sergeant Swanson, can you take this mission on, or do I get somebody else?

Tom: Yes, Lieuten . . . uh, er, ma'am. I can certainly do that.

CW: Semper Fi. Now go in there and take care of your sister. Hold her and tell her how much you love her and take her home. Also tell her how brave she was and how smart she was to survive this. You cannot give her too many "way to go's"! Got it? I'll be in touch with both you and her. Here's my card. If you need help, call me. Marines look out for one another. I'll be back with you two after you spend some time together.

Tom: (*sheepishly, wringing his baseball cap in his hands*) I am sorry for my initial behavior, ma'am. I was pretty wound up. I am squared away now. Thank you for straightening me out, I won't mess this up.

Secondary victimization of a rape victim is always close at hand. It is certainly not uncommon for relatives to become angry and blaming of the victim when they are confronted with news of a rape as they seek to get control over what they perceive as an uncontrollable situation. The crisis worker changes her approach as soon as she detects the brother's negative attitude and becomes very directive with lots of "I" assertion statements to get the brother's attention. She lays something of a guilt trip on him to get his attention and change his cognitive sets about what needs to happen. She uses a technique that we would generally be critical of, but works well here. That is, she uses a number of negative interrogative statements ("Don't you think/agree?") that ask for agreement with her point of view. By doing so, she shifts focus to positive rather than negative support for this wounded survivor.

Although you are probably not a marine nor usually would by chance meet a survivor's brother who was, the crisis worker manifests the best of creative and adaptive thinking to create a bond and reframe this in terms he can understand. Although he is not now an active sergeant, she knows that once a marine always a marine and that's why her responses aren't to "Tom" but "Sergeant Swanson." That's an all-star performance which goes to the heart of the adaptability that great crisis workers have.

CW: (*Reenters the room with Melody and Tom.*) You're going to have a lot of different reactions to this. They are not the same for every person, so don't be alarmed if you have some and not others. We will talk about all of this when things settled down. People have lots of different ways of coping with this. The main thing is for you to feel as safe and secure as you can. I am going to give you a number that is on call 24 hours a day. Do not feel guilty about calling. I am going to be your main contact from the Center, so don't be afraid to call me. I will be doing some checking in with you, if that is okay.

The crisis worker's intuition is right when she guesses that the place of safety and comfort for Melody would be her own home but that the frightening part would be getting past the place in her driveway where she was abducted. The crisis worker is also correct in reassuring Melody for her actions, which brought her out alive. Clients will immediately begin second-guessing themselves as to what they should have done and negative emotions of guilt, shame, and embarrassment will start building (Courtois & Ford, 2009, p. 188; Matsakis, 2003, pp.118–119; Weiss, 2010). The crisis worker dispels this notion by clearly and empathically stating that what she did was just right because it got her through the ordeal and out the other side alive. If she is able, the crisis worker immediately starts education in gentle and small doses. Primary education concerns getting the client through the next 24 hours, which are indeed going to be unreal for her. Her brother is a critical support and will need to be given some primary education about rape dynamics.

An important issue for rape survivors is control. Whatever will allow Melody to bring some control back in her life is important to do and is a major goal for the crisis worker. That may or may not be attempting to remember details of the assault. She may want to take a

long, hot shower, or just sleep. Melody has experienced an emotionally draining loss of control to the attacker, and she needs to be reassured that her loss of control is neither total nor permanent. She did what she had to do to survive, and that took courage. It is important to her for others to recognize her and give her credit. There is no wrong way to survive a rape (Howell, 1999)! Nonjudgmentalism and support are critical so that the client immediately starts moving from victim to survivor status (Ganas et al., 1998).

Responses.   Women may exhibit a wide variety of responses to the rape and the subsequent recovery process (Benedict, 1985; Matsakis, 2003, pp. 81–98; Williams & Holmes, 1981). The female who is assaulted:

1. May respond by exhibiting no emotions—appearing unaffected.
2. May feel humiliated, demeaned, and degraded.
3. May suffer immediate physical and psychological injury as well as long-term trauma.
4. May experience impaired sexual functioning.
5. May blame herself and feel guilty.
6. May experience difficulty relating to and trusting others—especially men.
7. May experience fantasies, daydreams, and nightmares—vividly reliving the assault or additional encounters with the assailant—or may have mental images of scenes of revenge.
8. Will never be the same, even though most survivors, over time, develop ways to recover, cope, and go on with their lives.
9. May be fearful of going to the police or a rape crisis center.
10. May be reluctant to discuss the assault with members of her family, friends, and others because of the risk of rejection and embarrassment.
11. May become severely depressed and suicidal.
12. May be extremely angry and revenge seeking to the point of becoming lethal.

The Following Three Months

Rape has high potential for PTSD, depression, suicide, panic attacks, generalized anxiety disorder, social adjustment disorders, sexual dysfunction, eating disorders, dissociation, and more negative worldviews and cognitive distortions. The crisis worker must not let the client regress and retreat into the past. Blaming external factors, self-blaming, and perseverating on why the rape happened are not helpful along with the guilt of "What if-ing?" oneself to death about where one was, what type of clothing one wore, not paying attention to surroundings, and on and on (Frazier et al., 2001; Matsakis, 2003, pp. 81–98;Weiss, 2010).

Follow-up, proactive, and continuous supportive therapy is essential and may include any of the following topics (Ganas et al., 1998, 1999; Howell, 1999; Matsakis, 2003; Pauwels, 2003).

Critical Needs.   During the 3 months following a sexual assault, a survivor such as Melody:

1. May need continuing medical consultation, advice, or treatment; she may experience soreness, pain, itching, nausea, sleeplessness, loss of appetite, and other physical and somatic symptoms.
2. May have difficulty resuming work; the added stress of the sexual assault may create too much stress in the workplace.
3. Needs to have people reach out to her, listen to her, and verbally assure her—not shun her or fear continuing to relate to her.
4. Needs the acceptance and support of family and friends.
5. May have difficulty resuming sexual relations and needs understanding without pressure.
6. May exhibit unusual mood swings and emotional outbursts, which others will need to understand and allow.
7. May experience nightmares, flashbacks, phobias, denial, disbelief, and other unusual effects.
8. May go into depression, which may be accompanied by suicidal ideation or acute traumatic stress disorder.

Critical Supports.   Support people can be of great help during this phase of recovery. In fact, one of the most important things a crisis counselor can do is getting and coordinating support systems in place. The recovery of survivors of sexual assault is enhanced by the empathic help and understanding of the people close to them. Whether the survivor's support people are family, friends, associates, medical or legal personnel, crisis workers, or long-term therapists, the important ingredients in the helping relationship are acceptance, genuineness, empathy, caring, and nonjudgmental understanding (Baker, 1995; Benedict, 1985; Howell, 1999; Remer & Ferguson, 1995). These support people can help survivors of sexual assault by:

1. Understanding and accepting the survivor's changed moods, tantrums, and so on, and allowing her the freedom to act them out.
2. Supporting and being available—but not intruding—while encouraging her to regain control and to recover her life.
3. Ensuring that she doesn't have to go home alone (without overprotecting her).
4. Realizing that recovery takes a long time and lots of hard work.
5. Allowing her to make her own decisions about reporting the rape and prosecuting the assailant.
6. Leaving it up to her to decide whether she wants to change jobs or place of residence.
7. Responding to her in positive ways, so she does not sense that the support person blames her for "letting it happen" or feels she is not capable of taking care of herself.
8. Allowing her to talk about the assault to whomever she wishes, whenever she wishes, but not disclosing the assault to anyone without her prior consent.
9. Showing empathy, concern, and understanding without dominating her.
10. Recognizing that she will likely suffer from low self-esteem and finding ways to show her that she is genuinely valued and respected.
11. Recognizing that her hurt will not end when the physical scratches and bruises are gone—that her emotional healing will take a long time.
12. Finding ways to help her trust men again—assisting male associates (friends, coworkers, brothers, her father) to show tolerance, understanding, and confidence.
13. Encouraging female coworkers, friends, sisters, and her mother to believe in her and not avoid her or avoid talking with her openly about the rape.
14. Including her children, if she has any, in many of the considerations concerning help toward emotional recovery.
15. Referring her to sexual assault support groups for survivors and family members.
16. Recognizing that her husband, partner, or lover may develop symptoms similar to those of the survivor (nightmares, phobias, rage, guilt, self-blame, self-hate, and such) and may need help similar to that needed by the survivor herself.
17. Encouraging her husband or lover to give her time to recover, free from pressure, before resuming sexual activity and to let her know he/she is still interested in her, still desires her, but that former patterns of sex life will be resumed at the survivor's own pace. It is important for a husband or lover to talk this out openly with her, to clear the air for both parties.

The foregoing is not a grocery list to just be handed to support persons. It is something that the interventionist needs to do as part of a psychoeducation program that lets people know what to expect and works with them as they struggle through what will be a period of transcrisis events and points.

PTSD. As previously indicated, rape ranks second only to combat in the potential for PTSD. Because it is a less noxious approach, your authors would first use EMDR as a therapeutic intervention. It is far less intrusive than the cognitive-behavioral approaches generally recommended. If EMDR didn't work, then we would use a combination of the three recommended cognitive-behavioral treatments (Briere & Scott, 2006; Cloitre & Rosenberg, 2006; Courtois, Ford, & Cloitre, 2009; Foa & Rauch, 2004; Frazier et al., 2001):

1. Exposure treatment, which calls for repeated emotional recounting of the traumatic memory
2. Affect regulation, which focuses on teaching clients skills to reduce painful internal emotional states
3. Cognitive therapy, to replace dysfunctional cognitions with new, more adaptive thoughts

These procedures will be demonstrated shortly in this chapter in the case of Heather, an adult survivor of childhood sexual abuse. Two supplementary therapy issues that are specific to rape need to be mentioned. First, there is the fact of opening up the old wound of the rape. Confronting the rape may be painful, but it is absolutely necessary, and the client needs to clearly understand what is going to happen. However, opening this wound, whether it be the recent rape of Melody or the old ones of Heather's adolescent abuse, needs to be done in a carefully gauged manner. To start exposure therapy means pushing away defenses that are in place to keep the client stabilized, although that stability may be anything but healthy (Courtois, Ford, & Cloitre, 2009). However, because these defense systems are being rent asunder, sexual assault survivors have a tendency to go rather blindly in harm's way. While therapy is occurring, they are almost a sure bet to experience transcrisis points as they form new defensive systems and coping mechanisms. As a result, it is not just the psychological safety but the physical safety of the client's with which the worker needs to be concerned.

Adult Survivors of Childhood Sexual Abuse

There is ample evidence that the sexual abuse of children wreaks lasting damage in their lives that continues into adulthood (Briere & Runtz, 1987, 1993; Briere & Scott, 2006; Browne & Finkelhor, 2000; Courtois & Ford, 2009; Kessler & Bieschke, 1999; Mitchell & Morse, 1998; Rosencrans, 1997). If survivors are left untreated, they may experience recurring episodes of revictimization and exhibit debilitating symptoms (transcrisis points) for many years (Briere & Runtz, 1993; Cloitre & Rosenberg, 2006; Davis, Combs-Lane, & Jackson, 2002; Kessler & Bieschke, 1999; Noll et al., 2003; Van Bruggen, Runtz, & Kadlec, 2006).

Psychological Trauma and Sequelae

Effects on Adult Survivors. Histories of adult survivors of childhood sexual abuse show higher incidence of (1) depression, anxiety, shame, and humiliation (Briere & Conte, 1993; Briere & Runtz, 1988; Browne & Finkelhor, 2000); (2) borderline personality disorder, dissociative disorder, and posttraumatic stress disorder (Briere & Runtz, 1993; McLean & Gallop, 2003; Mitchell & Morse, 1998); (3) social stigmatization, alienation, inhibitions, introversion, and interpersonal hypersensitivity (Browne & Finkelhor, 2000; Lundberg-Love et al., 1992); (4) more contacts with medical doctors for somatic complaints including chronic pain problems, such as fibromyalgia and irritable bowel syndrome, and long-term physical health deficits (Kendall-Tackett, 2008; Moeller, Bachmann, & Moeller, 1993; Stevenson, 1999); and (5) negative self-image (Courtois, 1988; Herman, 1981), poor interpersonal relationships and poor parenting skills (Browne & Finkelhor, 2000), and suicide (Ullman & Brecklin, 2002). Yet these are not all of the evil bumblebees that fly out of the Pandora's box of childhood sexual assault.

A long list of studies have found that a significant number of female clients (institutionalized, outpatient, psychiatric patients, and clients in clinics) were sexually abused as children (Briere & Runtz, 1987; Kessler & Bieschke, 1999; Salter, 1995). Adult female survivors consistently demonstrate symptoms similar to those of Vietnam veterans, in addition to compulsive sexual behavior, sadomasochistic sexual fantasy, sexual identity issues, and loss of sexual interest (Briere & Runtz, 1987; Courtois, 1988; Finkelhor, 1979; Herman, 1981; Mitchell & Morse, 1998). And, like combat veterans, child sexual abuse survivors are prone to use alcohol and drugs to submerge bad memories from awareness, as well as to engage in suicidal ideation and attempts (Duncan, 2004; Hien et al., 2009; Rew, 1989; Ullman & Brecklin, 2003).

Male survivors who were abused by adult males fare no better and report essentially the same symptoms, with concomitant sexual orientation ambiguity, mistrust of adult males, homophobia, hypersexuality, poor physical and mental health, lower emotional and social support, reduced activity, and body image disturbances (Choudhary, Coben, & Bossarte, 2010; Gartner, 2005; Lew, 2004; Myers, 1986; Rowan, 2006). Perhaps more important, Monk-Turner and Light's (2010) study of men who had been sexually assaulted and raped found that if actual penetration of a male's body occurred, it was the major variable in *not* seeking treatment.

Revictimization. Many of the foregoing symptoms appear to be even more profound and multiple if women suffered both sexual and physical assault in childhood (Cloitre & Rosenberg, 2006). Early assault is additive, and it appears that the higher the incident rate and the more profound it is, the higher the potential for later problems. If the abuse continues into adolescence, the potential for adult sexual assault also increases (Van Bruggen, Runtz, & Kadlec, 2006). Further, if both sexual and physical abuse occur in childhood and adolescence, the chance for revictimization again increases (Ullman & Brecklin, 2003). Survivors of childhood sexual abuse do not usually experience repetition of their victimization on the conscious level; that is, they do not intentionally precipitate abuse. It may be that revictimization or repetition of the sexual abuse tends to recur through the survivor's reenactment of the physical, sexual, or emotional abuse that was experienced during childhood (Schetky, 1990). Just like their female counterparts, males who were sexually assaulted in childhood are more likely to be assaulted as adults (Aosyed, Long, & Voller, 2011).

Our own feeling from treating such clients is that they have received very few of the typical parental warnings and admonitions that would naturally have been taught to them if they had had a normal childhood. As a result, they tend not to be aware of or reactive to warning signs and cues that would say to most people, "This is not a safe place to be or a safe thing to do or a safe person to be with." They also may respond very much as our combat veterans do by engaging in risky behaviors to achieve adrenaline highs that let

them know they are "still alive and kicking." Because of this, the crisis worker needs to provide psychoeducation on warning signs and cues that may stop survivors from blithely going into dangerous settings and engaging with people who will do them harm.

Child Abuse as a Predictor of PTSD. Child sexual abuse has been shown to predict the development of PTSD in later life (Darves-Bornoz et al., 1998; Kessler & Bieschke, 1999; Pfefferbaum, 1997; Regehr, Cadell, & Jansen, 1999). In a comparison of the prevalence of PTSD and other diagnoses in abused children, Ackerman and associates (1998) studied three groups: sexual abuse (SA) only, physical abuse (PA) only, and both (BOTH). Children in the BOTH group had more diagnoses overall. PTSD was significantly comorbid (disorder or trauma caused by two variables) with most affective disorders. A younger age of onset of SA and coercion to maintain secrecy predicted a higher number of total diagnoses. Also, children had more diagnoses when PA had come from males rather than from females. The research of Darves-Bornoz and associates (1998) indicated that adding physical assault during the rape of children was predictive of chronic PTSD. However, to suppose that PTSD is the only or major pathological outcome of child sexual abuse is to severely underestimate the negative consequences that accrue. Developmental processes associated with affect regulation and interpersonal relational skills may be severely disrupted and pave the way for future assaults (Cloitre & Rosenberg, 2006).

False Memories

The "false memory" concept, applied to work with both adults who were abused as children and perpetrators of abuse, has raised concern and controversy among human services workers (Rubin, 1996). This debate raged in the 1990s, and while it has now subsided you should understand that it still plays a role in criminal defense of accused abusers. The False Memory Syndrome Foundation was created in 1992 by Pamela and Peter Freyd, who had been accused by their daughter of sexual abuse. They propose that false memories occur for three reasons. First is countertransference, in which mental health professionals who have been abused themselves plant the memories to exact revenge and satisfy their own power needs. Second, angry adolescents who are seeking emancipation lash out at their parents by making accusations of sexual abuse. Third is the child who projects her own strong sexual feelings onto the father as his own toward her (Freyd, 1993). The studies of lost and distorted memories of childhood traumas by Bremner (1998) have raised doubts about the degree to which traumatic memories are susceptible to distortion due to misleading and suggestive statements (as may occur during psychotherapy).

The findings also suggest that stress as well as the adult's neuroanatomical conditions can lead to modifications in memory traces. Studies indicate that a significant percentage of women claiming abuse have only foggy memories of the sexual abuse and some have little, if any (Briere & Conte, 1993; Elliot & Briere, 1995; Williams, 1995). Leavitt (2000) confirmed that women who had been sexually abused—both those who had continuous memories and those who had recovered memories of the abuse—produced significantly different Rorschach interpretations compared to those who had not been abused.

Conversely, from their "recovered memory" survey of 154 psychiatrists, Feigon and de Rivera (1998) concluded that the numbers of false accusations of childhood sexual abuse appearing to emerge from the psychotherapy of adults constitute a real problem requiring public acknowledgment as such by the mental health professions. Their study indicates that the specific content of false memories extracted from client interviews depends on the particular interviewer, the way questions are asked, the context in which the interview takes place, and the emotional state of the interviewee. Mitchell and Morse (1998, pp. 67–93) have laid out a clear structure in regard to what kinds of memory systems are involved and how one goes about legitimately retrieving memories. The worker should collect a good psychosocial history and personality assessment but not uncritically accept or confirm suspicions without corroborating evidence. The clinician should avoid leading questions, not endeavor to pull up "repressed" memories, remain neutral, and remember that a particular set of symptoms may not be exclusive to sexual abuse (Courtois, 1999).

Your authors' own experiences indicate that at some unconscious memory level, the sexually abused person almost never forgets at least some of the essential details of the source of the trauma. Knauer (2000, p. xi) supports our own experience, but she works mainly with children who are not as far removed chronologically from the traumatic event. Perhaps more important, we find that when sexual assault survivors are regressed back to the traumatic event, they are not much different from any other kind of PTSD victim in

regard to memory, and they start to fill in the blanks in the same ways.

The debate notwithstanding, psychotherapy with and advocacy of survivors should be done by workers who are highly trained and skilled in dealing with the trauma, the repressed and dissociated memory issues, the risks, and the needs of survivors of child sexual abuse. Similarly, professionals who deal with perpetrators' memories should have a thorough understanding of the complex forms of abuser memory and forgetting that are frequently encountered. The discrepancies, emotions, dissociations, memory blackouts, and discomfort with traumatic memories may affect the way both survivors and perpetrators perceive the past abusive events (Rubin, 1996). To that end, anyone who does this work *absolutely must not* bring their own parental or abuse agendas into therapy. We have witnessed such a happening, and it was extremely destructive for clients and the therapist. Clinicians must strive to neither suggest nor suppress reports of remembered or suspected abuse and trauma. Instead, they must practice from a stance of supportive neutrality (Courtois, 2001).

Intervention Strategies for Adult Survivors: The Case of Heather

Heather was sexually abused by her stepfather regularly from ages 8 through 15. For 20 years she suppressed most memories and emotions related to the sexual abuse, which had included fondling, digital penetration, and intercourse. She has vivid memories of the physical abuse she suffered at both her stepfather's and her mother's hands. It is somewhat ironic that her stepfather was employed as a psychologist at a major university. Now, at age 35, she has regained her memory of the sexual abuse and is experiencing severe symptoms of delayed rape trauma syndrome.

Her marriage is breaking up; her career is in shambles; her communications and relationship with her three children are adversely affected by her personal turmoil; her rage toward her stepfather and her anger toward her mother have robbed her of her self-respect and her affection toward her parents, who live across the state from her. Her only daughter, the middle child, recently had her eighth birthday, and Heather is deeply obsessed with her daughter's safety. Heather feels a great deal of guilt, shame, remorse, and loss of self-esteem. For several years she has been experiencing some suicidal ideation, and since the recovery of her memory of the sexual abuse, this ideation has seriously intensified.

Interventions with Heather included both individual counseling and support group work, in which she willingly participated. In support group meetings, Heather received the encouragement, validation, and information she needed to absolve herself from guilt, shame, and remorse. She also acquired essential advice from support group members on implementing safety measures she could take to ensure that her 8-year-old daughter would not fall prey to the kinds of sexual abuse she herself had suffered. That advice allayed her fears and concerns about her daughter's vulnerability. Often the affirmation and informational resources obtained in support groups are key elements in the emotional healing, fear reduction, enhancement of self-esteem, and rehabilitation of adult survivors of child sexual abuse. It was certainly so with Heather (Mitchell & Morse, 1998, pp. 231–238).

Assessment

Particularly among older women such as Heather who suffered childhood sexual abuse under severe societal and family strictures of secrecy and denial, the abuse will be disguised and repressed. Often such clients will have been under the care of mental health professionals and been diagnosed with a variety of mental illnesses ranging from schizophrenia to depression to borderline personality.

Presenting problems are typically depression, anxiety, dissociation, and compulsive disorders (Courtois, 1988). Although the client may present as competent, responsible, mature, and otherwise capable, these characteristics are a facade for underlying emotional problems. Affectively, behaviorally, and cognitively, abuse victims may present themselves in a bipolar manner, rigidly adhering to one end or the other of the continuum—"I'm great" or "I'm terrible"—or rapidly oscillating between the two (Courtois, 1988).

Triage assessment of these people can be problematic, to say the least. At one moment they present as affectively calm and controlled, perhaps to the point of rigidity. At the next moment, because of some real or imagined slight, particularly in interpersonal relationships, they may become extremely labile (emotionally unstable) with angry tirades or uncontrolled crying and then offer profuse, guilt-ridden apologies for their behavior. It should come as little surprise that many individuals with a diagnosis of borderline personality disorder have suffered from child sexual abuse.

Cognitively, they may present themselves as competent and perceptive thinkers and then, when faced with a stimulus that causes a flashback or intrusive image, completely dissociate themselves from present reality and respond in a confused, disjointed manner. Behaviorally, such individuals may run the gamut of *DSM-IV-TR* (American Psychiatric Association, 2000) diagnostic categories—and then appear perfectly appropriate! If there is any key to making an accurate assessment of adult survivors of childhood sexual abuse, it is their consistent inconsistency across triage dimensions. The astute crisis worker who is struggling to make an assessment in which such inconsistency is displayed should consider childhood sexual abuse as a working hypothesis.

A crisis invariably initiates therapy; as in other forms of delayed PTSD, the crisis may seem unrelated to a past traumatic event. During the intake interview, if some of the common symptoms of PTSD are revealed, then childhood sexual abuse should be suspected as a causative agent and further assessment should target it as a possibility. Construction of a traumagram (Figley, 1985) will often provide clues to the origin of the precipitating event. The crisis worker who suspects PTSD in an adult due to childhood sexual abuse should immediately make plans to refer the client for a comprehensive psychiatric assessment after the initiating crisis is contained.

Heather initially presented at a community mental health center with suicidal thoughts and actions. She had overdosed on sleeping pills, was discovered comatose by a girlfriend, and had been taken to the emergency room, where her stomach was pumped. At intake she showed the counselor cuts she had inflicted on herself with a box cutter. She was dissociative and saw herself "out of her body" as she drew the knife up and down her arms. (Note: Cutting on oneself and other types of bloodletting, as opposed to slashing one's wrists, is not a suicide attempt but rather a tension reduction mechanism, or letting the "bad blood" out. Some cutters save their blood and bandages and find comfort in them. Further, the scar can be a symbol of healing. By doing all this, cutters validate in a very physical way the tremendous emotional pain they feel and have a way of seeing that they really are alive [Mitchell & Morse, 1998].) She had also cut off her parakeet's head (a much more ominous suicidal sign of taking out a prized possession), although she was extremely remorseful about its death and could not imagine why she would have done such a terrible thing. She was currently depressed and saw no reason for living.

The counselor rated her overall on the Triage Assessment Form at 27, set up a stay-alive contract with her, and referred her to a psychiatrist for evaluation and medication for depression. After several false starts and stops at counseling, Heather finally admitted the real issue, that she had been abused sexually and physically as a child by her stepfather from age 8 to 15 and that the abuse had been denied by her mother. Both parents had engaged in physical abuse of Heather during the same time period. At 16 she went to live with her father, who was a functional alcoholic. Those arrangements were chaotic, but no further physical or sexual abuse occurred. That lasted until she moved away to college.

She reports that the behavior that got her to the ER and into counseling has been getting progressively worse and she can no longer keep thoughts of the abuse submerged. She is experiencing severe social estrangement and has very few social relationships—none of which are with males. She wears numerous layers of clothing that hide her female figure, even in very hot weather. She wears no makeup and appears almost unisexual. She is a talented artist and is employed part-time at a graphic design business.

Treatment of Adults

A major component of therapy is to use a posttraumatic stress treatment model that uses some combination of prolonged exposure and cognitive processing or cognitive restructuring (Cloitre & Rosenberg, 2006; Foa & Rauch, 2004; Nishith, Nixon, & Resick, 2005) along with techniques to deal with the severe affective dysregulation (inability to monitor and control one's emotions) that accompanies this form of trauma (Biere & Scott, 2006, pp.76–77; Courtois, Ford, & Cloitre, 2009). However, Finkelhor (1987) proposes that the trauma of childhood sexual abuse goes beyond other causal agents of PTSD because of the unique dynamics of traumatic sexualization, social stigmatization, betrayal of trust by loved ones, and powerlessness of children, so that trust building and affirmation activities are particularly critical.

Discovery and Admission

For survivors of childhood sexual abuse, particular problems arise in the therapeutic process that are absent with victims of other traumatic experiences. If the client is otherwise in crisis and childhood sexual abuse is suspected, do not explore incest material immediately because of the likelihood of compounding the present crisis through decompensation, regression, or dissociation. Client safety is paramount and should always be a primary or conjoint consideration with exploration of the incest (Courtois, 1988, p. 173). At the time the client chooses to own the trauma of incest, the potential for crisis rises exponentially. The worker needs to be very sensitive to the client's admission, gently encouraging the client to disclose the incest and directively and positively affirming the client for doing so. Trust here is critical. Not only have these clients learned that adult caretakers are untrustworthy (Elliot, 1994), but it is more than likely that others in the helping professions have victimized them as well (Ochberg, 1988).

Heather: (*apprehensively*) I don't know what you'll think about this. But I guess I can trust you. I just can't live with this anymore. (*Pauses.*)

CW: (*suspecting from previous indicators what is coming*) Whatever it is, I can see how deeply troubling it is and how difficult it must be. I am here to listen and try to understand. Whatever it is, I want you to know that you will still be the same Heather, and that person is not going to be any different in my eyes. I hope what I've just said makes it easier for you to get it out.

Heather: (*starts sobbing*) This is really bad.

CW: Heather, I am going to reach over and hold your arm, is that okay? (*Heather nods. Counselor softly touches Heather's arm and speaks gently.*) I'm guessing this is about something that somebody did to you or that happened to you, and it's OK, really OK, to talk about it.

Heather: I had sex with my stepfather. (*Relates a long history of sexual and physical torment by her stepfather and mother, with the counselor listening and empathically responding.*)

Heather: (*gently weeping*) I know you're a counselor and all, but you must think I'm horrible.

CW: I understand how terribly difficult that was. I also want you to know that I believe what you said. I don't think you're horrible at all. What I think is that you were a victim and that you are a survivor of those terrible things that shouldn't have happened and did. I want to correct one thing you said. You did not have sex with your stepfather. You were 8 years old and had no choice. He had, and he forced sex on you. That's a big difference. Now I want to give you an idea of what is happening to you, why these bad memories keep coming back, and what they do to disrupt your life.

The crisis worker uses affirming and supportive statements throughout this opening scene. She touches the client only after being given permission because touching can sometimes be construed as anything but supportive by the client.

There are three general phases to this treatment. The first is safety; the second is processing, remembering, and mourning; and the third is reconnecting and reintegration (Courtois, Ford, & Cloitre, 2009; Mitchell & Morse, 1998, pp. 184–195). The first order of business is keeping the client safe and in full knowledge of what is going to occur. There have been far too many secrets in these clients' lives. There are no secrets here.

Psychoeducation. Psychoeducation about the role that PTSD plays in incest trauma is important at this point because it can help allay clients' fears that they are "different," "dirty," or "mentally ill," and it assures them that PTSD is responsive to treatment. Education about PTSD also removes the mystique, confusion, and "craziness," anchoring present maladaptive behavior as purposive and reasonable given the survivor's traumatic history. It also allows the client to believe that something can be done through treatment (Courtois, 1988, p. 173).

CW: (*after an explanation and showing Heather the* DSM-IV-TR *PTSD classification*) So you are not "nuts." Those are the reasons these things are currently happening. We can treat this. It is a long road, and at times it is going to seem as if things are getting worse instead of better. We will have to go back and dig into those memories, and they are going to be painful. I want you to think about this because it is not an easy task. It is something you will need to choose. If you choose to do so, I want you to know that we'll go through this together. (*The counselor then explains what the treatment procedures will be and answers questions the client has about different components of the treatment.*)

Grounding

Grounding refocuses clients' attention onto the immediate therapeutic environment or, when over the phone or Internet, on the physical surroundings they are presently inhabiting as opposed to flashbacks, intrusive thoughts, and dissociative states that are beginning to overwhelm them (Briere & Scott, 2006, pp. 96–97). Briere and Scott propose the following five steps:

1. Attempt to focus the client's attention on the therapist and the therapy. "I am right here. We're together in this room and we are doing exposure therapy. You are not back in the bedroom 20 years ago" are typical verbal responses to a client "going into the wind." At times, gentle touching may also be appropriate.
2. Ask the client to describe the internal experience he or she is presently having. "Describe what's going

on right now." If the client has difficulty or appears frightened or otherwise unequal to the task, then move to step 3.
3. Orient the client to the immediate environment that he or she is in—the room with the worker, where it is, how it looks, what's in it, and how safe it is, and that it is not in the bedroom 20 years in the past.
4. If the client is still indicating stress, start deep breathing and relaxation techniques (which we recommend teaching to these clients).
5. Repeat step 2 and assess the client's ability to return to therapy.

Grounding is a critical component of this therapy, in which clients are taught to literally put their feet on the ground, get physically and psychologically anchored, and stop the fragmentary thought processes and heightened affect that lead to depersonalization, flashbacks, and overpowering emotions (Matsakis, 2003, pp. 57–58; Mitchell & Morse, 1998, p. 198). Sutherland (1993, p. 23) proposes that focusing on gravity in relation to the body starts to make the client aware of the numbness and disowning of various body parts that she uses to dissociate from the trauma. The client is asked to find and identify a "spot of safety" where she can practice grounding. That spot of safety is a place the client can go and feel absolutely safe. One anchor that grounds clients is carrying a talisman with them, something that can literally be touched to connect them with reality. Coins, charms, key chains, totems, worry stones, and so on can all serve this purpose. Your authors use this technique with abused and neglected foster children a lot and see no reason it shouldn't work with adults as well. Matsakis (2003, p. 58) proposes physical grounding, such as holding a familiar or safe item like a teddy bear; emotional grounding by writing oneself an e-mail or leaving a message on one's answering machine and then reading or listening to it; or mental grounding by describing aloud the room one is in, singing, or reading out loud from a magazine.

CW: So the safest place in the house is the bathroom, with you sitting on the commode. Fine! When some of these cues that we've talked about start happening and you start to feel things sliding away, I want you to go into the bathroom, put your feet flat on the floor, and with the toilet lid down, have a seat, pick up a copy of *Car and Driver* (or any other magazine), and say to yourself, "It is 9:15 P.M., Tuesday evening, January 25, 2011. I am sitting on the toilet in my home, reading *Car and Driver*, and I feel a little silly sitting on the toilet lid, but I am quite safe." So just relax and enjoy that. Just notice your eyes scanning over the articles and looking at the pictures.

At times when the client is in crisis and away from the worker, grounding the client over the telephone is critical. This can be done by reassuring her she is safe and asking her to describe what she sees and hears around her. Ask her if she can feel her feet on the floor and if not, press down with her feet and grip something with her hands. Finally, she should keep a list of people she can call and go through the grounding exercise with (Mitchell & Morse, 1998, p. 199).

Validation

As the client starts through the process of therapy, numerous transcrisis points will occur as long-buried trauma is brought back to awareness. In an active, directive, continuous, and reinforcing manner, the human services worker (Courtois, 1988, pp. 167–170; Longdon, 1994; Mitchell & Morse, 1998, pp. 90–91, 184–188):

1. Validates that the incest did happen, despite denial of this fact by significant others; the client is not to blame, it is safe to talk about it, and the worker does not loathe the client for having been a participant.
2. Acts as an advocate who is openly, warmly interested in what happened to the survivor as a child and makes owning statements to that effect but still maintains neutrality and neither advocates for nor dismisses legal action. The worker also understands there is a high potential for transference/countertransference and is clear and consistent in maintaining boundaries.
3. Reinforces the resourcefulness of the victim to become a survivor.
4. Provides a mentor/reparenting role model to help with childhood developmental tasks that were missed.

Extinguishing Trauma

Extinguishing trauma means effecting a psychological extinction—that is, facilitating the reduction or loss of a conditioned response as a result of the absence or withdrawal of reinforcement. In practical terms, this means the reduction or loss of both Heather's negative beliefs about herself and her debilitating behaviors that were responses to her childhood sexual abuse. It also means getting rid of the perpetrator.

When the survivor is in therapy, there are always at least three people there—in Heather's case, there are four

(Mitchell & Morse, 1998, p. 198): the worker, Heather, and the perpetrators—her mother and her stepfather. The crisis worker sought to extinguish Heather's negative beliefs and behaviors by systematically leading her to mentally refute her erroneous perceptions that she was responsible, culpable, or guilty and had her reframe her previous beliefs to help her gain a new insight that she was an innocent victim and can now view herself more realistically as a guilt-free survivor.

When working through traumatic events, the client will experience a dramatic increase in affective and autonomic arousal (Ochberg, 1988). The human services worker must be very careful to provide palatable doses of the traumatic material that do not exceed the client's coping abilities (Courtois, 1988, p. 174) and prompt a crisis within the therapy session. Careful processing with the client before and after each session of extinguishing and reframing traumatic memories is important in preventing such crises.

CW: Let's take a look at what we did today.

Heather: I'm pretty scared. I didn't remember a lot of that stuff until we dug that memory up.

CW: That's pretty typical. Any reasonable person would bury that stuff. If you really start to feel like you're losing it, I want you to call me.

Heather: (*later that evening, calling*) I really hate to disturb you, but I've really got this urge to start cutting myself. I'm also having thoughts about killing my other pet bird. They're starting to get pretty real.

CW: (*very directively*) Do you feel like you're losing it enough that you need to be hospitalized?

Heather: I don't know. Maybe if I just talk this through.

CW: OK. Go get on the toilet seat, put your feet on the ground, and let's talk. (*Heather does so.*) OK, you there? Feet on the ground? OK! Remember what I said about this being rough. What you went through today brought back a lot of old memories and some ugly fresh ones. That's normal. It's nasty, but it is normal. Now I want you to think of how we changed that scene, how you told yourself all those negative things about yourself being dirty and no good, and what the reality of that scene is. (*A dialogue ensues that recaps the day's events. Heather is able to regain control, and after a 20-minute dialogue is able to feel secure enough to relax and go to bed.*)

The worker should be aware that extinguishing one traumatic event does not lessen the fear and trepidation of moving on to other events. This is particularly true in the case of adult survivors of childhood sexual abuse, who may experience increased intrusive behavioral symptoms and regress to former maladaptive behaviors even though they are making good progress in erasing bad memories (Cogdal & James, 1991). Clients may appear to be getting worse instead of better—which is threatening and scary for both client and worker.

The worker should be prepared for this contingency, tell the client of its likelihood, and affirm that it is totally acceptable for the client to check in with the worker if these symptoms and behaviors reemerge between sessions. The worker's role when this happens is to be understanding, affirming, and calming. Constant validation is important because many clients will be discouraged at the length of treatment, afraid and angry over revictimization and extension of the traumatic experience's "life," and flee from therapy (Courtois, 1988, p. 177). The second phase of therapy involves reclaiming the self. It is a painful business to watch, and there is every urge to rescue the client. This must not happen! The work must be done by the survivor, and dependence cannot be allowed to occur (Mitchell & Morse, 1998, p. 190).

Prolonged Exposure/Cognitive Restructuring

Reframing the client's negative and distorted beliefs about him- or herself is critical in allowing the client to separate the fact and fiction of an abusive childhood (Courtois, 1988, p. 181). While imaginally flooding the most abusive childhood scene the client can tolerate, clients paste mental billboards under the scene (Cogdal & James, 1991). These billboards typically deliver all the myths and distorted messages that the abuser gave in addition to the client's own childhood negative self-talk. The image of the assault scene is enhanced though prolonged exposure or flooding by loading all the sights, sounds, smells, and noises as if it were happening in real time to the most distressing level the client can tolerate. The idea is to build the noxious stimuli to such an extent that it finally loses it malignant power over the client and becomes benign.

CW: (*with the client deeply relaxed, eyes closed*) Picture that videotape, the bedroom, the "game," him making you get on him and suck his "peter," almost strangling as you do so. Feel the pain and the disgust. But he makes you keep doing it until he gets off, and the semen is running all over, sticky and wet. Notice the messages underneath that scene. "This is what fathers do to educate their daughters to become women." "You aren't a good daughter if you don't do this." "I'll kill you if you don't keep our secret." Feel the confusion, the fear, and the repulsion as you do

this. Put those messages in big block letters underneath that scene. Do you see them?

Heather: (*eyes closed and body twisting*) Yes!

CW: Freeze that scene and the billboards. Take a snapshot of it. Let it develop. Hold it in your hands.

The client is then asked to destroy the image along with the negative parental injunctions and her own negative self-injunctions (Cogdal & James, 1991).

CW: Now I want you to get rid of that scene. It is in your past, and it is gone, so now get rid of it from your memory also. Do that now, and tell me what is happening.

Heather: I set a match to it. It is burning. It's a huge fire now with yellow, sick-smelling smoke.

CW: Let it burn.

Heather: It's just a crisp cinder now, all gone.

CW: All gone? Is there anything else you want to do with it?

Heather: CRUSH IT!

CW: Do it! What's happening?

Heather: I'm grinding it up with my boot heel. It's nothing; he's nothing.

CW: Fine. Now relax and slip back into that soft, cool mountain glade. Just relax and feel the tranquility, calmness, and peacefulness.

The client then replays the scene, but this time substitutes positive, self-enhancing counterinjunctions based on the facts and not on the fictional messages of the event. The worker guides the image and reframes the stepfather in a truer psychological image (Cogdal & James, 1991).

CW: Go back to the bedroom with him now. Picture the scene, but change it. See him as small, very small, weak. He is a small, selfish, pouting boy, dressed up in a man's pajamas. He looks ridiculous. Put these billboards under the scene. "The only people he has power over are little girls." "It is his fault this is happening." "It is WRONG!" "It is criminal!" "I should have felt confused, fearful. I had the right to feel that way!" "I also have the right to be *angry* about it." "*No*body has the right to do that. *No*body!" Now freeze that picture and snapshot it. Let it develop. Look at it. What are you feeling and thinking?

Heather: (*yelling*) You asshole! You bastard! You are gone from my life, you puke! You lied to me, you scared me to death, and kept at it. You used me because you were afraid of everybody else. I was the only one you could use, you scumbag. You've got no power over me now, you pissant, or my memories. You are history!

CW: I want you to save that picture. Put it someplace else, safe in your memory, and every time that image starts to come back, pull out the picture and look at it. See that scene for what it really is, and see those billboards, flashing. Have you got it?

Heather: Yes. I've got it.

CW: How do you feel?

Heather: Better, relaxed, relieved maybe.

As the client works through a series of traumatic events, each one is set up as it happened with all of the negative distortions and self-talk that accompanied it. These negative self-attributions carry over into the present time and form maladaptive operating schemas for how the client lives. By rooting out these distortions and modifying them into more positive self-enhancing and enabling counterinjunctions, clients are able to compare "old" and "new" schemas and not only modify and rid themselves of the debilitating memories but also begin to incorporate those new schemas into their present-day lives (Cloitre & Rosenberg, 2006).

Relearning Feelings. Like combat veterans, survivors of childhood sexual abuse have developed excellent coping skills to deny and numb feelings. But this is even more problematic for survivors of childhood sexual abuse because learning to differentiate feelings is a skill that develops in childhood. For most of these survivors, their childhood environments were anything but nurturing, and their caretakers may have suffered from severe affective dysregulation, alternating between a flood of feelings and none at all. As a result, a condition called "alexithymia" develops in many survivors of childhood sexual abuse. Alexithymia is the inability to recognize and label feelings. Recognizing and labeling feelings is of utmost importance in helping clients give voice to shunted emotions and warded-off feelings. Heather's bitter and angry emotions are not unlike those of combat veterans as they relive and extinguish bad memories.

Developmentally, clients have to literally relearn and identify their emotional states. Cloitre and Rosenberg (2006) use part of their group format on skills training in affect and interpersonal regulation (STAIR) to teach clients to recognize feelings, monitor emotional intensity levels, learn emotional triggers, and formulate coping/reaction responses. Many of the students in survivor groups have absolutely no idea what the visual cues are that others give them. For example, a professor who gives one of these women a quizzical look after asking a question might well be described as angry or mad by the woman. In work with survivors, one of your authors commonly uses an elementary school classroom guidance technique to train students to recognize feelings. Each student in his survivor groups gets a handout showing faces with different emotions and feeling words attached to them to help the students relabel feelings and discriminate emotional cues from others. Far from seeing this exercise as childish, clients report that they pull out and use these sheets on a daily basis to validate their present emotional state.

Grief Resolution

Beginning to recognize past, buried feelings is to start on the road to acknowledging feelings of anger and rage, as Heather does in the preceding dialogue (Courtois, Ford, & Cloitre, 2009, pp. 93–94). These feelings will ultimately end in sadness and grieving for the loss of a happy childhood, her loss of who she might have been without the trauma, and the loss of a psychologically healthy family instead of the malevolent one she grew up in (Courtois, 1988, p. 181). It is likely to be one of the most painful stages as the client comes to grips with the reality that there is no retrieving the past or changing it and that attempts to do so are fruitless. Only the future holds promise for her, and she can control only that (Hays, 1985). Grieving and resolution, particularly with perpetrators of the abuse, are other transcrisis points in therapy. At this time, the crisis worker will have to move into a grieving and loss mode (see Chapter 12, Personal Loss: Bereavement and Grief).

Heather: I had a call from my mother last night. I wanted to be assertive with her and tell her how I felt, like I had worked out in group. But when it came down to it, I just couldn't. I haven't got the guts. (*Starts crying.*) I'll never get rid of this. Why couldn't she have been different? Why does she still try that stuff of browbeating me? Wasn't what she did enough?

CW: You have every right to feel sad that she wasn't or still isn't what you'd hope a mother might be. I wish she could change, but I have my doubts. So if she won't, what will you do?

Heather: I guess she won't. I guess I'll just kiss her off.

CW: You survived with her battering you, and you've survived for 10 years without her. Perhaps it's time you did say good-bye. (*Patiently lets Heather silently weep.*)

Confrontation. The tremendous push-pull between love and hatred survivors feel for their perpetrators is a difficult issue to resolve. Role-playing with the empty chair technique, writing letters, drawing, and journaling may be ways of mourning the loss. Whether the survivor will ever actually confront the abuser is a question only the survivor can answer. There are a number of reasons it may be good for the survivor to confront the perpetrator, such as empowerment, closure, "setting the record straight," anger, grief, and forgiveness (Cameron, 1994). However, *this must be the survivor's decision*, and the crisis worker must remain scrupulously neutral in this debate. Confronting the abuser is not mandatory for healing (Mitchell & Morse, 1998, p. 162). Further, to believe that the perpetrator will "confess" to the abuse may be very wishful thinking indeed.

The following questions generated by Bass and Davis (1992, p. 134), or some variation of them, need to be asked and processed with the survivor before the decision to confront is made.

1. What is motivating you to do this, and are you prepared to do this?
2. What will you possibly gain, and what will you possibly lose?
3. Could you live with being excluded from family functions and risk losing contact with family members who did not abuse you?
4. Will you be able to handle it if you are labeled "crazy"?
5. Can you handle getting no reaction or denial?

Changing Behavior Through Skill Building and Reconnecting. Although coming to terms with past trauma and stopping maladaptive present behavior are critical to the adult survivor, changing behavior to more self-determining choices is the major end goal of therapy. The vacuum left by the removal of bad memories and the psychic energy previously expended to maintain control of those memories is not easily filled. Pearson (1994) and Mitchell and Morse (1998) recommend using several categories of techniques for skill building, listed earlier in this chapter.

Reeducation is necessary for survivor skill building, and the worker may assume a teaching role in transmitting basic life skills such as communication, decision making, conflict resolution, cognitive restructuring, and boundary setting (Courtois, 1988, pp. 181–182). Herman (1981) likens the survivor to an immigrant who must literally rebuild her life in a culture that is absolutely foreign to what she experienced as a child. From that standpoint, the crisis worker should not be unsettled by the emergence of some rather unusual and personal questions.

Heather: Er, ah, I was just wondering, Dr. James, how you treat your kids. I mean, if they act up do you ground them, or what? What do you talk about at dinner? And do you and your wife ever argue?

Although such questions may be construed as intruding on the private life of the worker or attempts by the client to shift focus from her problems or create dependency, it is important to answer these questions as honestly and succinctly as possible, without shifting the focus away from the client's personal concerns. The client is testing her perceptions against the most valid and stable validity check she currently has—her therapist. For that reason, it is important to urge survivors to join therapy or support groups so that new behaviors can be tested out and discussed with peers. Because many families of survivors such as Heather's are so completely dysfunctional, clients need education on what a functional family is and how it operates. Duncan (2004) has defined the characteristics of a functioning family (not the Hollywood ideal one), and we believe they are well worth spending time on in a support group.

As these survivors reconstruct their lives and start to become interested in developing meaningful relationships, Sheehan (1994) proposes five basic fears that they will have to deal with: abandonment, exposure, merger, attack, and their own destructive behavior. Fear of abandonment comes because there never were protectors in their young lives. Thus they avoid emotional encounters because they vow never to be hurt in the same way again and constantly test whether significant others are really committed to them. Fear of merger means fear of losing control and of losing one's selfhood. Survivors have to learn what personal boundaries are because parent/child boundaries were merged into sexual ones. Fear of attack has to do with real or imagined assault, something quite common in most survivors' backgrounds.

The anger and rage that accompany the traumatic wake can make survivors wonder whether they can control their own destructive impulses and rage toward themselves or others. These are all topics that involve group work and support and can occasion many transcrisis moments for these people.

Support Groups for Adult Survivors

For victims, groups provide a number of potential positive outcomes and help them to move from victim to survivor. Victims may be reluctant to participate, but they should be encouraged to do so, although not all victims may be ready or immediately able to participate in groups. Education as to what the group is about, who the members are, confidentiality issues, what kinds of problems members are working on, and the safety and support of the group format is a critical component in assessing, selecting, motivating, and committing survivors to group work (Courtois, 1988, pp. 253–262).

Courtois (1988, pp. 245–249) lists the following benefits of group treatment for survivors of childhood sexual abuse:

1. The individual's sense of shame, stigmatization, and negative self-image are reduced by meeting other survivors who appear "normal."
2. Commonality of experience raises members' consciousness about incest, so the experience becomes more normalized and may be seen from an interpersonal and sociocultural perspective rather than an "only me" perspective.
3. The group serves as a new "surrogate" family where new behaviors and methods of communicating, interacting, and problem solving can be practiced in a safe, accepting, and nurturing environment.
4. The group allows for safe exploration and ventilation of feelings and beliefs that have been denied and submerged from awareness.
5. Childhood messages and rules that were generated within the abusive environment can be challenged and dissected to determine how they still influence the survivor's maladaptive behavior patterns.

In summary, the case of Heather should make very clear that dealing with an adult survivor of childhood sexual abuse is a complex, tedious, meticulous, and stressful process that is filled with many crisis events. It should come as no surprise that one of the toughest customers a worker will face, the borderline personality disorder, runs rampant in this population. It takes a great deal of expertise, patience, empathy, and personal resiliency to work with such cases. The case of Heather should vividly illustrate why compassion fatigue, vicarious traumatization, and burnout are high probabilities in this kind of work.

Sexual Abuse in Childhood

The first experience of one of your authors with sexual abuse in childhood came as a rookie junior high school counselor in 1967. From the client's report, he made a successful intervention and kept the 14-year-old client from committing suicide. The interesting thing about this anecdote is that he had no idea that sexual abuse was occurring or that he had saved the young woman's life, merely by being a junior high school counselor and listening empathically to her while she discussed other "normal" issues of a teenager, until she told him 30 years after the fact!

While you may now be reconsidering whether one of your authors is an incompetent dolt, consider this: If he had stood up in an Illinois Personnel and Guidance Association convention in 1967 and asked what people were doing about childhood sexual abuse problems, he would probably have been referred for some of that new psychotropic medication to calm him down. In short, people would have thought he was nuts! If he had been a social worker or a psychologist, that would have made little difference. Yet, as evidenced by at least one of his clients, sexual abuse was clearly going on.

While he manifested the very best of Rogerian client-centered therapy with that client (about the extent of his therapeutic expertise at the time), the fact was that he was probably better off not knowing about the sexual abuse. The reason is that he would have been dumbfounded, would have had absolutely no idea what to do about it, would not have known whom to report it to, and would have most likely not been believed if he had, because the perpetrator was the manager of the largest manufacturing facility in that school district. A great deal has changed in 40 years as a variety of nasty family topics that were kept under wraps have emerged from behind closed doors.

The fact is that child sexual abuse has always been with us (DeMause, 1974; McCauley et al., 2001), but a variety of political, social, and cultural factors have kept child abuse—and most particularly, child sexual abuse—behind closed doors in the United States (Costin, Karger, & Stoesz, 1996) and throughout the world (Schwartz-Kenney, McCauley, & Epstein, 2001).

By the time your author was a school counselor in 1966, mandatory reporting laws for physical abuse had been enacted in all 50 states (McCauley et al., 2001)— although there was considerable comment at that time on just how exactly one was to report such abuse and the still unclear question of whether one could get sued or fired for doing so no matter what the law said! (Indeed, no matter what the law says today, you should be aware that when the subject of child physical or sexual abuse rears its ugly head in a school building, there can be and often are repercussions when abusing parents are confronted. For that reason, you should know exactly what you need to do and how to substantiate it when making a report. We believe it is absolutely mandatory to consult with another professional and have him or her bear witness when doing so.)

However, it wasn't until the rise of the women's movement and child advocates in the 1970s and their lobbying efforts to open up the blinds that had been closed on this topic that the public really started to become aware of the extent of the problem. In 1974, the Child Abuse Prevention and Treatment Act was passed in the United States, and its definition of who might be covered under the law included sexual abuse. Just as Leontine Young's book *Wednesday's Children* (1964) raised consciousness levels about the physical abuse of children, David Finkelhor's book *Sexually Victimized Children* (1979) did the same for awareness about child sexual abuse.

Dynamics of Sexual Abuse in Childhood

Manifestations of PTSD do not just spring forth full blown in adulthood (McLeer et al., 1992). Sexually abused children have significantly more specific PTSD symptoms than do physically abused and other psychiatrically hospitalized children (Deblinger et al., 1989; McLeer et al., 1992; Wolfe, Gentile, & Wolfe, 1989). Sexually abused children are at high risk for PTSD and symptoms of posttraumatic stress, anxiety, and depression in the immediate period after disclosure and termination of the abuse (McLeer et al., 1998). PTSD, aggressive behavior, and sexually related problems following sexual assault are greater for boys than for girls (Holmes & Slap, 1998). For example, Kuhn, Charleanea, and Chavez (1998) found that sexually assaulted male adolescents were more emotionally distressed, socially isolated, deviant (for example, lying and stealing), and likely to affiliate with deviant peers than males who did not report sexual assault.

Even when rape and sexual assault on children and adolescents do not later result in full-blown PTSD, the emotional and behavioral fallout is far reaching and destructive. In addition, these children have a wide variety of other problems that include concentration difficulties, poor grades, aggressive behavior, social withdrawing, somatic complaints, overcompliance, depression, antisocial tendencies, behavioral regression, poor body image/self-esteem, eating and sleep disturbances, encopresis and enuresis (loss of bowel and bladder control), hyperactivity, suicidal ideation, and extreme, generalized fears (Conte & Schuerman, 1988; Knauer, 2000; Miller-Perrin, 2001; Sgroi, Porter, & Blick, 1982).

Although the foregoing symptoms may be indicative of many disorders of childhood, the following are not, and are rarely ever found with any stressor other than sexual abuse (Goodwin, 1988; Knauer, 2000, pp. 3–30; McLeer et al., 1992; Miller-Perrin, 2001; Salter, 1988, pp. 230–235). Sexually abused children come to school early, stay late, and are rarely or never absent. They barricade themselves in their rooms or otherwise hide and attempt to seal themselves off from their assailants. They may be "perfect" children to the world and to their teachers.

To the contrary, they may engage in inappropriate and persistent sexual play with peers. They may have a sexually transmitted disease. They will have a detailed and age-inappropriate understanding of sexual behavior. They may have physical and somatic symptoms with overlying sexual content such as vaginal or anal bleeding and odors. Sexual drawings, stories, or dreams are common occurrences. They may suddenly have money or gifts that can't be explained. They may display blatant sexually suggestive poses such as wide-open legs, rubbing of genital areas, and provocative dress. They may engage in excessive, compulsive, and even public masturbation, and may even approach other adults sexually. Small children may act out sexually with real or stuffed animals. Teenagers may run away and engage in prostitution.

They may engage in self-mutilation by either cutting or burning themselves. They may have a sudden dislike for someone or demonstrate inordinate clinging behavior. These behaviors provide a template with which varying patterns of psychopathology seen in adult survivors are drawn.

A particular subset of childhood PTSD are the effects of parental abuse and neglect which often occurs in the course of childhood sexual assault. The differences between how PTSD manifests in abused children with PTSD versus adults with PTSD has become profound enough that a team from the National Child Traumatic Stress network has designated a new disorder called Developmental Trauma Disorder (DTD; DeAngelis, 2007). DTD is characterized by exposure to one or more developmentally adverse interpersonal traumas such as abandonment, betrayal, physical or sexual abuse, and emotional abuse. Emotional outcomes range across rage fear, betrayal, resignation, defeat, and shame. A major marker of DTD is dysregulated development that affects physical health, behavior, cognition, relationships, and self-attribution. Negative expectations about caregivers develop because of their abusive history. As a result, these children stop expecting protection from others and believe future victimization is inevitable (van der Kolk, 2005).

Dynamics of Sexual Abuse in Families

The incestuous family may operate much like an alcoholic or battered family does in developing a series of messages or rules that pivot around denial, duplicity, deceit, role confusion, violence, and social isolation (Courtois, 1988, p. 45). Children receive messages such as:

1. Do not show feelings, especially anger.
2. Be in control at all times; do not ask for help.
3. Deny what is happening, and do not believe your own senses/perceptions.
4. No one is trustworthy.
5. Keep the secret because no one will believe you anyway.
6. Be ashamed of yourself; you are to blame for everything.

Intergenerational Transmission of Sexual Abuse. Typically, there is high potential for intergenerational transmission of sexual abuse in these families. Parents who themselves have been abused often seem to have blind spots for what is occurring in front of them. Further, Knauer (2000, pp. 18–19) proposes that the original attraction to the abuser is because of the familiar traits that the person sees in him that ring true within her own abusive family of origin.

Incestuous fathers display inordinate amounts of jealousy and paranoia over their daughters' dating and relationships with other males and attempt to rigidly control behavior through threats and intimidation, and the same may happen with mothers who abuse their sons (Knauer, 2000, pp. 49–61; Rosencrans, 1997, pp. 69–83; Salter, 1988, p. 237). Abusive fathers are controlling tyrants who erect a facade of respectability in the community and often try to isolate their children and spouses or partners by forbidding them to socialize outside the home and refusing to let them have close friends. However, because of their sensitivity to power, they become meek and contrite when confronted with their abuse (Herman, 1981, p. 178).

Mothers are often oppressed and economically dependent, abused by their mates, and products of incestuous families themselves (Courtois, 1988, pp. 54–55; Herman, 1981, pp. 178–179). Mothers may be physically or mentally disabled, causing the eldest daughter to take on the role of "little mother," which extends

to fulfilling the father's sexual demands (Herman, 1981, p. 179). Although some mothers may confront the abuse once they discover it, many others engage in denial and helplessness, and when confronted with the reality of the situation may revictimize the child by physical or verbal abuse (Salter, 1988, p. 209). In effect, the child becomes the scapegoat for the family's problems (Knauer, 2000, p. 18).

Female Abusers. Females who are abusers are not as much of an anomaly as one might think and are more than likely underreported as sexual abusers. Allen (1991) believes there are about 1.5 million victims in the United States, and Elliot (1994, p. 220) reports a figure of about 500,000 in Canada who have been abused by females. While these numbers may be outrageously high, they also may not be. A study of Latino and European American adolescents who had been sexually abused found that among male high school students, 52.8 percent reported that they had been abused by females (Newcomb, Munoz, & Carmona, 2009).

A few studies have reported on female sexual abusers and the outcomes for their victims (Allen, 1991; Elliot, 1994; Fehrenbach & Monastersky, 1988; Knopp & Lackey, 1987; Mathews, Mathews, & Speltz, 1989; McCarty, 1986; Nathan & Ward, 2001; Rosencrans, 1997). More often they are discovered as coabusers (Elliot, 1994; Rosencrans, 1997). The traumatic wake they leave is generally even more devastating because they are seen as the primary caregivers and the persons in whom most trust and nurturing are placed.

In particular, it is important to disabuse the myth that boys are not troubled by such sexual behavior and "gain experience from older women." The research of Rosencrans (1997, pp. 245–253) indicates quite the opposite. The young man who has sex with an older woman is placed in a double bind. If any part of the experience felt good, the victim may believe it wasn't abusive. If it didn't feel good, then he may have all kinds of recriminations and start to believe that perhaps he is some kind of deviant homosexual (Lew, 2004, p. 61). Lew (2004, p. 61) believes that this causes male survivors to repress memories of abuse by women far more than they do abuse by men. And when those memories do return with a vengeance, they are far more devastating. That outcome is exponentially true when the perpetrator is the victim's mother.

"Motherfucker" is one of the most pejorative, vulgar, and demeaning terms in the English language and has all kinds of negative connotations for boys who might engage in such deviant behavior. That term presupposes the son is the instigator of such illicit sexual contact (Gartner, 2005, pp. 29–30). Research indicates that is anything but true. The Freudian notion of an Oedipal complex wherein the son lusts after the mother has little validity. The social myths and cultural artifacts that mask the true malevolence of female perpetrators on male children minimize this problem in much the same way as the issue of male perpetrators was minimized in the past (Speigel, 2003, p.15). If we turn that term around as "son fucker," does that reframe your thinking on the matter and shed light on who the true aggressor is?

The sexual identity problem that boys face when they have been abused by female caretakers, and particularly mothers, is a psychological abattoir (Elliot, 1994; Mitchell & Morse, 1998; Rosencrans, 1997). Gartner (2005, pp. 106–120) proposes that it can be cataclysmic to the victim to acknowledge he is in an incestuous relationship with his mother. Yet, while the erotic excitement he feels is disturbing, it can also lead to a sense of sexual prowess that can plant the seeds of some very deviant and pathological beliefs about women. This is not a movie plot in which a young man becomes a mature and skillful lover at the hands of an experienced, beautiful, and competent woman. It is sexual abuse at the hands of a woman who is selfish and needy, has failed at marriage, and has severe relationship and pathological problems. Indeed, out of the bad seeds of these relationships may grow some very poisonous adult relationships for these boys. The bottom line is that adult female abuse of boys is extremely serious and can lead to ominous outcomes (Deering & Mellor, 2011).

As an example, the two adult males one of your authors has encountered in his own practice who were sexually abused by their mothers were potentially the most dangerous to women he has ever seen. They had wildly vacillating "madonna–whore" complexes about women they had targeted for their affection that could turn these women from the purest virgin to the sluttiest streetwalker in a moment, all because of some imagined travesty the women had committed. The really scary part of their delusions was that the women had no idea any of this was going on! Rosencrans's (1997, p. 252) informal interview with law enforcement officers tends to confirm that these abused males have a high potential for sexually related crimes.

Our overall knowledge of female sexual abusers probably compares to what we knew about male child abusers 30 years ago. Therefore, the astute crisis worker needs to ask the following when doing an intake interview with a sexual abuse victim who is male.

CW: We have talked about the perpetrator. Did anybody else sexually abuse you? I am wondering if there were any females who ever did those sorts of things to you?

Because of the high incidence of sexual abuse perpetrated on boys and their reluctance to talk about being sexually abused as children, tactful questions should be asked of any age male even when this is not the presenting problem. The plain and simple fact is that we still tend to dismiss sexual acts and the harmful aspects they present in males (Alaggia & Millington, 2008; O'Leary, 2009). A case in point is the filing of criminal charges against abusers of male children. While the cases filed against perpetrators when the child is female are woefully small in relation to the number committed, a study conducted by Edelson and Joa (2010) found that charges are even less likely to be filed against perpetrators when the victim is a male child.

Phases of Child Sexual Abuse

Sgroi (1982) found that the behavior of the abuser can be traced through five phases: (1) engagement, (2) sexual interaction, (3) secrecy, (4) disclosure, and (5) suppression. These phases apply to both intra- and extrafamilial abuse.

Engagement Phase. The abuser's objective in the engagement phase is to get the child involved in sexual activity with the abuser. Both access to the child and opportunity (privacy) are needed if the abuser is to be successful. Therefore, if one were looking for possible instances of unreported abuse, one would identify times and situations when the potential abuser and the child were alone together. One must also look for different strategies that two different types of abusers (child molesters and child rapists) may employ.

Molesters tend to use enticement and entrapment to get the child engaged in sexual activity. *Enticement* may include deceit, trickery, rewards, or the use of adult authority to tell the child in a matter-of-fact way that the child is expected to participate. *Entrapment* is used to manipulate the child into feeling obligated to participate through traps, blackmail, and so forth. Molesters may make pornographic pictures or videotapes and convince the child that there is no choice other than going along with the secret activity, and may also seek to impose guilt by making the child feel responsible for the abuse.

Child rapists use *threat* (particularly the threat of harm) or the imposition of superior physical *force* to engage the child in the abusive activity. Typically, the rapist will threaten to kill or injure the child or someone dear to the child or threaten to commit suicide himself, convincing the child that he or she will be blamed for the rapist's death if the child resists or reports the rape. In using superior force, the rapist may simply overpower the child, restrain the child by tying him or her, give the child drugs or alcohol, or physically brutalize the child into submission.

The vast majority (about 80 percent) of abusers use the first two strategies—enticement and entrapment. Abusers tend to repeat their engagement patterns and show little tendency to move from nonviolent to violent strategies. Molesters are apt to consistently entice or trap children, whereas child rapists tend to use threat or force almost exclusively. The strategy used by the abuser is an important issue in treatment, because survivors typically wonder throughout their lives why they permitted it to occur.

Sexual Interaction Phase. Types of abuse may include (blatant or surreptitious) masturbation (the abuser may masturbate prior to making physical contact with the child), fondling, digital penetration, oral or anal penetration, dry intercourse, intercourse, forcing or coercing the child into touching the abuser's genitals, forced prostitution, and pornography. Children may be coaxed into cooperating, though not consenting, because abusers—as adult authority figures—often command, engage, or enlist cooperation from the child. Children lack the maturity, experience, and age to be able to consent, but they may cooperate because of their subservient status.

Secrecy Phase. Abusers communicate to children that others must not discover the sexual activity. The objective of abusers is to continue the activity. This necessitates avoiding detection and maintaining access to the child while continuing the abuse. The techniques for maintaining the secrecy may involve incorporating "rules" or "games," implicating the child in the activity, and setting the child up to be responsible for keeping the secret.

Disclosure Phase. Sometimes the abuser is discovered accidentally. Other times the abuse is disclosed intentionally by the child or someone else. Intentional disclosure is usually made by the child. Intentional disclosure often enormously complicates the discovery and existence of sexual abuse, because parents and others refuse to face it or believe it. Accidental discovery may occur as a result of such consequences as pregnancy, STDs, sexual acting out, promiscuity, and physical trauma. The way the abuse is disclosed can affect the child's self-esteem and reaction to treatment. For instance, disbelieving adults sometimes respond by blaming and punishing the child—and allow the sexual abuse to continue.

Suppression Phase. The suppression phase may begin as soon as disclosure takes place. Suppression may be attempted by the abuser, the child, the parents, other family members, professionals, the community, or an institution. There are many reasons for suppression: fear of publicity; fear of reprisal; to protect the reputation of a family, an abuser, or an institution; to avoid prosecution; to avoid responsibility; to protect the child; to avoid embarrassment; to avoid the kinds of confrontation and intervention required to deal effectively with the difficult and sensitive situation; and fear of getting involved.

Survival Phase. On the basis of our own experiences and the reports of other writers (Besharov, 1990; Kendrick, 1991), we have added another phase, the survival phase. During this phase, it is important to implement strategies for helping the child and the family respond to and recover from the abuse as much as possible. This phase includes stopping the abuse, providing needed medical and psychological treatment for the child, and helping the significant others close to the child to overcome the trauma, fear, anger, betrayal, and despair caused by the abuse (Benedict, 1985). It also involves preventing further abuse (Bass & Thornton, 1983) and prosecuting and/or getting counseling for the abuser (Benedict, 1985).

Intervention Strategies With Children
Assessment

Assessment includes thorough documentation of the abusive events for possible legal use. Using anatomically correct dolls helps confirm what actually occurred in the abuse. No specific measures currently exist for measuring the effects of psychological abuse in young children, although a complete psychological evaluation may be useful in gauging the child's overall level of functioning (McLeer et al., 1992; Wheeler & Berliner, 1988, p. 235). The previously mentioned behavioral indicators of childhood sexual abuse and PTSD criteria for children are currently the best indicators that sexual abuse has occurred.

Peterson and Hardin (1997) have developed a guide for screening children's art for sexual abuse. The child is asked not to verbally disclose but rather illustrate different subjects and situations. Different indicators of sexual abuse may appear as the child illustrates the requested subject matter—such as a picture of people doing something at home. Assessment includes an analysis of style, treatment of figures, and actions with negative aspects. Point values are awarded for a variety of criteria commonly found in abused children's drawings. Once the point value reaches a certain level, child abuse should be suspected (Peterson & Zamboni, 1998). However, it doesn't take a doctorate in projective techniques to see how different the drawings of children who have been abused are (Kaufman & Wohl, 1992). We would propose that most children do not draw families that are joined by penises and vaginas or have clubs growing out of their arms that are raining blows down on other family members—but sexually and physically abused children do because that's the way their families interact.

Therapeutic Options

Because of the complex nature of child abuse, interventions should comprise multiple components targeting a variety of problem areas (Miller-Perrin, 2001). The first component is play therapy (Gumaer,1984; Malchiodi, 2008; Webb, 2007; White & Allers, 1994). White and Allers (1994) have identified several characteristic behaviors that maltreated children may manifest during play therapy: developmental immaturity, opposition and aggression, withdrawal and passivity, self-deprecation and self-destruction, hypervigilance, inappropriate sexuality, and dissociation.

The second component is cognitive-behavioral therapy that is trauma focused (Cohen, Mannarino, & Deblinger, 2006; Neubauer, Deblinger, & Sieger, 2007). Farrell, Hains, and Davies (1998) found that selected cognitive-behavioral interventions (skills learned through procedures such as relaxation training, positive self-talk, cognitive restructuring, stress inoculation, and emotive imagery) may effectively decrease the anxiety and depression levels in sexually abused children ages 8–10 who exhibit PTSD symptoms.

Deblinger, Thakkar-Kolar, and Ryan (2006) propose a cognitive behavioral approach that involves:

1. Psychoeducation that teaches children about faulty misconceptions they may have and offers new information to help children understand they are not so isolated and alone
2. Behavioral rehearsal and modeling skills that are taught to both children and nonoffending parents to teach them how to regulate emotional expression and develop new cognitive coping skills
3. Relaxation training and graded exposure treatment to the trauma that allows the child to learn that his or her fears and avoidance of the feared situation, object, or person are not nearly as frightening or upsetting as previously thought

The third component is a trauma systems approach (Saxe, Ellis, & Kaplow, 2007). Incorporating an eco-systemic approach that involves not only children and parents, but community systems such as social service agencies, mental health facilities, and schools, increases the chances of stopping emotional and behavioral dysregulation across the entire system where the trauma operates. Saxe and his associates propose that two major components are operating with a traumatized child. First, a traumatized child has difficulty regulating emotional and behavioral states. Second, the social environment and system of care are not able to help the child regulate these emotions and behaviors.

Saxe, Ellis, and Kaplow (2007, pp. 95–108) propose 10 principles of treatment if the system is to be changed.

1. Fix a broken system, not just the identified client. Relentlessly attack the whole trauma system.
2. Put safety first. Nothing takes precedence over safety.
3. Create clear, focused plans that are based on facts and target specific components of the child's emotional dysregulation and the level of instability in the child's environment and system of care.
4. Don't "Go" before being "Ready." Build an alliance with the family, understand logistical problems such as child care and transportation, and create an understanding of what treatment will involve and who will be included.
5. Use resources to gain maximum benefit. Carefully plan and coordinate the tactics and strategy with the system's players for the best possible outcome. Time and money are scarce in the treatment world. Plan carefully so neither gets wasted.

6. Accountability is critical. Accountability has two parts. First is the worker's ability to put words into action and evaluate how well those actions are working and change them if they aren't. Second, and more daunting, is requiring that children, parents, and others in the social ecosystem be accountable as well.

7. Deal with the reality of the situation. If resources aren't there, if family systems are compromised, if children are developmentally delayed, then understand the reality of the situation and adjust goals and expectations to it.

8. Take care of yourself and the treatment team. All the king's horses and all the king's men do not put Humpty-Dumpty back together again if the horses and men are broken themselves. There's a chapter ahead of you in this book on burnout. Guess what one specific area of crisis intervention has high burnout rates? That chapter is the real deal if you are going into this business, so read it carefully.

9. Look for the strengths in the system. The trauma system of the child is rife with pathology and failure. It is easy to find things wrong. Yet there is resiliency and strength within this system. It is your job to keep a positive view of it and make lemonade out of the lemons.

10. Leave a better system. As with all crisis intervention, you are not an adoption agency taking on children and families to raise forever. Teaching families how to take care of themselves is the end goal.

You'll soon meet crisis workers from the Carl Perkins Child Abuse Center, who operate out of Jackson, Tennessee, and cover much of rural west Tennessee. They operationalize all of the foregoing 10 principles and then some! When the entire ecosystem of the child is brought into play, involving all of the players in the treatment using combinations of play and cognitive-behavioral therapy, outcomes for parents include better parenting practices, improvement in depressive symptoms, reduction in abuse-specific emotional distress, and greater support for the child. Children have less externalization of problems, fewer depressive symptoms, reduced behavior problems at home and school, and feel less shame, guilt, depression, and anger due to the abuse. Perhaps even more important, social services, schools, law enforcement, judiciaries, and mental health services all play well together. When this happens, the sum is indeed greater than its parts.

Need for Affirmation and Safety

Initial intervention techniques call for intentionally and positively managing the crisis of disclosure and the resulting fear and anxiety. Affirmation and validation are crucial in regard to what has happened, what is happening, and what will happen to the child, the offender, and significant others. The admonition in the PTSD chapter on *not* using flooding techniques with children holds even more firmly with sexual abuse. If prolonged exposure techniques are to be used, they should be done with gradual and graded exposure to the aversive stimulus, with plenty of time for processing between exposures. Children should also be taught progressive relaxation techniques so that they can learn how to remove themselves from the feared stimuli. Because small children are not fully developed cognitively, most instrumental and operant behavioral techniques that may be used with adult survivors are also not efficacious. Yet anxiety about and fear of the abusive events and the abuser need to be reduced, and this calls for reexposure to the trauma.

Contrary to most popular professional opinions (there are a lot of cognitive behaviorists out there!), your authors believe this work is best accomplished by the use of play therapy, in which the child is given puppets, dolls, and drawing materials to safely distance him- or herself from the trauma. By gently and directively encouraging reenactment and discussion through the safety of the play material, the therapist may enable the child to gradually extinguish fear and anxiety feelings and develop skills in communicating healthy inner feelings and experiences without revictimizing the child (Baker, 1995; Gil & Johnson, 1993; James, 2003; Malchiodi, 2008; Merrick, Allen, & Crase, 1994; Oates et al., 1994; Pifalo, 2002; Sadowski & Loesch, 1993; Webb, 2007).

Regaining a Sense of Control

Anger and grief are emotional by-products for children of sexual abuse. Venting of these feelings should be encouraged, particularly because most adults are not comfortable with them and may attempt to repress such feelings when children exhibit them (Wheeler & Berliner, 1988, p. 237). Drawing, painting, modeling clay, sand play, writing, and learning to verbalize emotions are all therapeutic vehicles to ventilate angry feelings and loss. Play techniques can also give the child a renewed sense of empowerment by allowing play figures to be acted on, thus reducing long-standing feelings of helplessness (James, 2003; Malchiodi, 2008; Sadowski & Loesch, 1993; Webb, 2007). Punching out a Bobo doll or picking up a play telephone and calling the police can give children a sense of control in a situation in which they have little (Salter, 1988, p. 215). Along with relaxation and other stress reduction measures, play techniques such as sand tray therapy can be used to teach the child to control anger when the child constantly acts out with peers or significant others.

Education

Education about adult sex offenders and sex itself is important for children because they will have little if any knowledge of why or what has happened to them. Shame is a predominant feature of the child's response to abuse (Knauer, 2000, pp. 74–82). Children need to know that it is the adult and not the child who made the mistake. Children who have been physically injured need to have these injuries explained and be told that their bodies will be okay. Many children believe that others will be able to tell what happened by looking at them. Children need to know that although they may feel different, sexual abuse does not make them look different.

Understanding developmental stages is critical in what kind of education is provided and how therapy is delivered (Saxe, Ellis, & Kaplow, 2008, pp. 7–12). Cognitively, young children usually have little understanding of sexual functions. Typically they will not initiate questions about sex, but when workers initiate education about sex through slides or books, children will respond with their own questions. Every child who has been sexually assaulted needs some type of sex education and information on what the assault means (Baker, 1995; McLeer et al., 1992; Oates et al., 1994; Salter, 1988, pp. 217–218).

In addition to the play therapy techniques (such as drawing, painting, modeling, and sand play, mentioned earlier), a highly effective means of teaching important social and survival lessons to children is through outreach services into schools, churches, and community centers with professionally developed puppetry programs. One example is the Kids on the Block (1995) system, which uses the unique and dynamic medium of puppetry to educate children and their adult caregivers on how to think about and respond to important and emotionally charged issues that impact children's lives. Trained volunteers perform with puppet characters designed to realistically represent children and the dilemmas they may face.

Through carefully researched and scripted dialogues, these puppets ("children") talk about important issues and then engage in interactive question-and-answer periods with children in the audience, who converse directly with the puppets. This form of puppetry has proved to be an effective strategy for expunging children's myths and misconceptions about physical and sexual abuse and replacing them with facts and sensitivity (Sullivan & Robinson, 1994).

Assertiveness Training

Assertiveness training may be seen as more a preventive measure to keep children out of harm's way than a remedial measure for sexually abused children. Yet, sexually abused children have learned to be compliant to deviant requests and clearly need to learn how to "Just say NO!" (Salter, 1988, p. 219). Because abused children are at greater risk for revictimization, teaching them cues and warning signs and appropriate assertion responses is important so that they can avoid future abuse (Miller-Perrin, 2001; Wheeler & Berliner, 1988, p. 242).

Intervention Strategies for Child Sexual Abuse: The Case of Elizabeth

Elizabeth, age 8, is the middle child in the family. She, her 11-year-old brother, and a 5-year-old sister live with her mother and stepfather, whom her mother married nearly 2 years ago. Elizabeth's mother, Mona, and father divorced when the youngest child was about 1 year old. Elizabeth's stepfather started off by fondling her. This went on for several weeks. Although Elizabeth was bewildered, scared, and intimidated, no one else knew about the abusive activity. Recently, while everyone else was out of the house, her stepfather raped her. He threatened to kill Elizabeth, Mona, and her sister if she told anyone. The following morning Elizabeth confided in her brother, who in turn, told Mona what had happened.

Incredulous over this discovery and paralyzed as to what to do, Mona called the child abuse hotline that she remembered seeing advertised on TV and in the local newspaper. The following dialogue and discussion is representative of what an absolutely outstanding child advocacy agency, the Exchange Club–Carl Perkins Child Abuse Center of Jackson, Tennessee, does.

Disclosure

Mona: (*calling the child advocacy hotline; angry, crying uncontrollably, barely in control*) Hello. Hello! I want to report a (*choke, sob*) rape. He . . . that bastard . . . he raped my baby. That sonofabitch raped my daughter. Oh, how could I have not seen . . . How could I have let this happen? (*Continues ranting and raving in hysterics, beseeching the hotline worker for help and railing at her husband.*)

CW: Okay, I understand you're extremely upset and have every right to be, but I need for you to be in control right now. My name's Delaine. I need to know your name, where you live, and whether you're safe from who did this to your daughter.

Mona: (*Regaining a bit of control, gives her name and address.*) It was my . . . It was . . . my husband . . . Leon. Her asshole stepfather . . . I found her underwear. It was all bloody . . . Oh my God! My baby . . . My poor baby. He's gone in his truck . . . He's headed for Chicago on a run . . . I'll kill him . . . By God! I will kill him if it's the last thing I ever do!

CW: So you are safe, and he's not in the house. How badly hurt is your daughter? Does she need an ambulance and medical attention?

Mona: I don't know. She's kinda in a daze. Just walking around holding on to her teddy bear. Oh, that bastard! I'll castrate that bastard before I kill him!

CW: Mona, I hear how angry and shocked you are, but I need for you to follow me very closely. This is extremely important. I want you not to do anything with Elizabeth. Don't wash her up or change her clothes. I want you to take her to Madison County General Hospital and bring her underwear with you in a plastic baggie. Do you have a way to get to the hospital? Are you OK enough to get to the hospital? (*Gets acknowledgment from the mother that she can get to the hospital.*) There are going to be people at the hospital who are going to want to talk to you and Elizabeth, and we're going to need to do a medical exam of her. This is not going to be easy, but we know how to do this. You did the right thing. I'll meet you at the hospital, and I'll help you get through this. We will get through this! Do you understand? Now tell me what you're going to do and when you'll get to the hospital. (*Mona restates what the crisis worker has told her and assures the worker she can do those things.*)

The initial shock that accompanies discovery and disclosure is invariably highly dramatic and volatile for parents who have been blind to the perpetrator's intent. Because rape is a violent crime, the primary consideration of the crisis worker is to determine if people are now safe from the perpetrator and if they need medical attention. The initiating crisis is multifold. The crisis worker needs to make sure that there is no physical injury to the child and that the out-of-control parent is sufficiently functional to take care of the child and do the things necessary to preserve evidence. She will also need to restore the mother to equilibrium. Exacting revenge by assaulting the perpetrator would put both mother and daughter in jeopardy. The scene at the hospital can be extremely threatening, and the crisis worker does all she can to indicate that the mother has done the right thing and that, as difficult as it may be, the crisis worker will be there with her to the conclusion. The crisis worker's initial job will be to do crisis intervention with the mother by making sure everyone is safe and helping her to get back in control of her emotions and actions (Bottoms, 1999; Knauer, 2000, pp. 31–47).

Immediate Aftermath

In cases where there is physical injury, the survivor will need immediate medical evaluation and care. The crisis worker, after determining that the mother can get herself and her daughter to the hospital, immediately makes other phone calls to the Department of Human Services and the police department. She also calls the hospital and informs them that a child sexual assault victim is on her way and that a sexual assault team needs to be assembled. After making these phone calls, she immediately leaves for the hospital.

Mona: (*at the hospital, in a room with the crisis worker*) All I can think about is that no-good lying creep. He's lucky he's on the road, or he'd be dead now. I'd shoot the asshole's balls right off of him. I've got a .38 Special, and by God . . . as God is my witness . . . I will do it. What's happening to my daughter? They took her away. Is she going to be all right? I've read some stuff on this. It's not just him raping her now, but she'll be scarred for life! How could it happen? How could I be so stupid? What in the hell is wrong with me? He was so nice to her, to all of us! How, oh how could I have been so stupid? (*Starts uncontrolled sobbing and pacing, slamming her purse down again and again.*)

CW: You've certainly been through a lot in the last few hours. And you've done a remarkable job of taking care of Elizabeth. Your concerns about her physical injuries now and her psychological injuries later are certainly justified. I'm not going to sugarcoat this. You're obviously a very good mother who has suddenly been thrust into this—nothing you or Elizabeth did caused it. It was perpetrated on her and you. We are here to assist you in any way we can. We want to provide someone to be with you and Elizabeth during these critical hours, as well as providing aftercare and follow-up counseling.

But right now, even though your husband is away, I'm concerned about your anger. It's certainly justifiable, but what Elizabeth needs is for you to be the best mother you can be right now. If you shoot your husband, how will you be able to support your daughter when she needs you most? You won't! You will be in jail. That's where your husband deserves to be, not you. Let the police handle your husband. What we need to do is handle this and care about Elizabeth. Can you do this? That's really what you want, isn't it, to help your daughter get through this?

Mona: I . . . I . . . I guess so. I appreciate it. Everything happened so fast! I don't know how I managed without falling apart. It's like a wild, awful dream—an ugly nightmare. I don't know how I'll handle it when the dust settles. I'm so mad—I could kill him! I feel like I've been raped too. There's so much on me right now. I don't know if I'm capable of bearing up under all that's got to be done. Damn, damn, damn that man! Excuse me, I shouldn't blow up like that.

CW: That's all right. You have a perfect right to be angry and to say it. It's good that you care enough to be upset, and it's good to see you direct your anger at him—the real cause of Elizabeth's hurt and your anger. Both of you deserve better treatment than he gave you, and no child asks to be raped.

Mona: That's right. I trusted him! And he took advantage of her. She was helpless—a helpless child. I've got to show her where I stand on this. First, I'm going to take good care of her, and then I'm going to send that rotten louse to jail for good!

CW: Mona, I know things are really crazy right now, and you don't know what's happening. I want to take care of that by telling you what's going to happen and how things are going to be done, so you know what's going on and don't feel so out of control. I'll go through each step of what is going to happen today and what we can do to ensure that Elizabeth gets through this in good shape. I'm going to explain what will happen very carefully to you. If you have any questions, stop me. There are no stupid questions about this. I want you to fully understand what's happening, so you can start to get back in control. Mona, the important thing is that you gain control. Right now, I'm being very directive, and will be doing so until you get past this emergency and back on top of things. You have choices, and if, at any time, you feel like making any of the choices yourself, please feel free to do so. You can stop me at any time, and that will be OK. (*The crisis worker patiently goes through all the details of what is going to happen, stopping whenever Mona has questions, and checking to see that she understands what she's being told.*)

The crisis worker permits her to express her anger, isn't threatened by Mona's outburst, encourages her to keep owning and expressing her feelings, and lets her know that neither she nor Elizabeth was to blame for the assault. That strategy is important in letting Mona know that she can be in control and that the worker believes in her, without the worker's jumping in and expressing the anger for her. This is no place for the human services worker who is not calm, cool, and detached in her or his professional demeanor. That the worker must be as solid during a crisis as the rock of Gibraltar is never more true than here. There is probably nothing more heart wrenching and sickening than the aftermath of a severe sexual or physical assault on a child. Intervention here clearly calls for a strong constitution. But more important, if the worker manifests her or his own anger directly at the parent or the perpetrator, then that anger may be misinterpreted as being directed toward the victim.

At times, when the perpetrator is still an immediate threat, the worker must take on the trappings of a crisis worker who deals with battering victims. The family may need to be moved to a safe place until the perpetrator is apprehended. The crisis worker continuously reinforces the mother for doing the right thing and for caring about her daughter. This is an extremely important strategy, because adult caregivers may engage in severe guilt and recrimination because they believe they should have been more vigilant. The crisis worker also must make sure that the mother will not exact revenge on the perpetrator and put herself in jeopardy with the law (Knauer, 2000, p. 46). It will indeed do Elizabeth little good if her mother is facing a charge of assault with intent to commit murder. Finally, the crisis worker patiently educates the parent on what is going to happen. Education about the aftermath of a child assault is critical in giving parents back the sense of control they feel they have lost.

Two components of education are important. First, detailing what the legal proceedings are and what the mother and child need to prepare for allows them to know what is ahead of them and not be blindsided by all the legal, social, and psychological ramifications of a child sexual assault. Second, giving the parent information on how to deal with the child in the immediate aftermath of the discovery is critical in ensuring that the child is not revictimized and that the parent does not feel guilty for doing or saying the wrong thing (Bottoms, 1999). An even more shocking revelation may occur during the initial disclosure and interview. That is, it is not uncommon for the parent to disclose that she was also sexually abused as a child and swore this would never happen to any of her own children.

Mona: (*head in her hands, slumped over*) It's my fault. I let this happen. God knows I should have known. Uncle Ralph did the same thing to me when I was 14. I tried to tell Mom, but she just blew it off 'cause Uncle Ralph helped us out when Mom went through her divorce. And now my own daughter . . . I couldn't even protect her. I'm no better than my mother.

CW: (*reacting coolly, letting Mona talk through her own sexual assault*) There's a big difference. As I hear you say it, your mother didn't follow up because she was afraid and dependent on your uncle. You weren't afraid, and when you found out you took immediate action. See the difference? A big difference! Right now you are being the best mother in the world. Do you see that difference?

The worker, although taken aback, immediately discriminates between what Mona's mother didn't do and what Mona did do. She underscores and reinforces Mona for taking action and reaffirms her as a fit parent.

Prosecuting the Perpetrator
Interviewing the Child

Whenever a child is sexually assaulted, there are two primary concerns. First is taking care of the child and seeing that she or he is safe. Second is obtaining evidence to prosecute the perpetrator. If the child has not been injured or if the discovery is made a good while after the assault, then an interview needs to be conducted that will allow the necessary evidence to be obtained. In the past, report of a child assault would entail numerous interviews with medical staff, police, and social services. The intimidating circumstances and the necessity to repeat the story over and over have a high potential for making the child feel terrorized, guilty, confused, and unequal to the task of meeting the demands of a variety of strange and threatening adults. The potential for revictimizing the child and the parent while going through this procedure is extremely high if not handled appropriately (Bottoms, 1999).

To stop this from happening, the Carl Perkins Center uses an interview procedure that many other child advocacy agencies employ. This approach is a good model for dealing with cases of sexual or severe physical assault on children and is now starting to be instituted across the country. One *trained* forensic interviewer with a listening device in her or his ear conducts the interview and tape-records it at a safe house. Other agencies' staff are behind a one-way mirror. If they need more information on a particular part of the

assault, they transmit that information to the worker in the room via the worker's earpiece. Note here the emphasis on *trained*. Because this is a criminal matter, the worker needs to be able to obtain information without biasing the child's testimony. In other words, the typical mental health worker will not have the expertise to do this. However, the psychological well-being of the child is critical in the aftermath of disclosure, and a typical police interrogation would likely put the child under severe duress. Therefore, whoever does the interview should be skillful not only in obtaining evidence, but also in making the child feel safe while the interview occurs. At Carl Perkins the interview is conducted in a pleasant, child-friendly room by a very caring child-centered forensic worker at the center, not in the stark confines of a police interrogation room (Bottoms, 1999). The worker may also use "good touch–bad touch" with a doll or a figure drawing to have the child indicate where on his or her body (e.g., genitals, mouth) the assault took place. (Note: *Mouth* is included here because oral sex is a common occurrence in child sexual abuse [Knauer, 2000, pp. 5–6].)

If there is no prior knowledge of abuse and the child discloses an assault in a spontaneous manner, then the crisis worker needs to be cool-headed, listen to the child, and be prepared to make an immediate referral. Often the workers at the Carl Perkins Center have staged a Kids on the Block puppet show at a local school. After the presentation on prevention, they invite children who may have been victimized to come down and talk to them about their experiences. At times they have been flooded by children! In that case, the worker needs to write down pertinent information in a calm manner and make an immediate referral to Children and Family Services (Bottoms, 1999).

After the examination, the crisis worker needs to affirm to children that they are okay physically, that some part of their body is not "broken," that they do not now have AIDS, that they will not die, and in the case of a girl, that she is not pregnant (Bottoms, 1999).

CW: (*Very empathic, sits down beside Elizabeth and takes her hand.*) Elizabeth, I'm Delaine from the Carl Perkins Center for Children. I'm guessing some pretty scary things have happened, and you're probably having some pretty scary feelings right now. I want to talk to you about some of those scary things. It's OK to be scared, because it was a pretty scary deal. But you're safe now, and your mom and we are going to make sure you stay safe. So if you'd like, I'll try to answer any questions you have about what happened and what's going to happen.

Elizabeth: (*after the examination and the initial interview by a forensic expert*) When Leon did this to me and he stuck his peter in me, it really hurt. Am I gonna die, 'cause I started bleeding? Will I get pregnant?

CW: No, you're not going to die. It's normal to feel sore after all that and to bleed some. But the doctors said you were OK, and Dr. Ann will be back to see you and tell you you're OK. I checked with the doctor, and you're not old enough to get pregnant yet. Dr. Ann will tell you about all this, so don't worry about that.

It is extremely important for young children who have little information about how their body functions to immediately allay fears of what may happen to their body as a result of the assault. A somewhat controversial issue is whether the initial examination should be done at the child advocacy center, as opposed to a hospital. Many times the child-friendly atmosphere of the center is much more conducive than a hospital for examining victims. The counterargument is that examinations should not be done at the center because the child might associate that frightening procedure with the center's physical environment and generalize it to the staff's subsequent attempts to work there with the child (Bottoms, 1999).

Preparing the Child for Testimony

Sexual assault is a criminal matter, and at some point the child may have to testify in a courtroom. That appearance may be terrifying to a small child who will have to give testimony against a caretaker who may have either been very nice to the child or made threats against the child and his or her family. Depending on the age of the child, the Carl Perkins Center uses puppets, books, and videos to educate the child on what testimony in a courtroom entails. Immediately before the child's appearance in court, a staff member from the center will take the child to the courtroom to acclimate him or her to what may be perceived as a frightening experience. The staff explains about everybody's role and how things will happen. He or she will role-play traffic court so the child gets an idea of how courts operate. Children can explore the courtroom, ask questions, and sit in the judge's and witness chairs, so that they become familiarized with a courtroom and are not terror stricken when they are asked to engage in the real situation.

Another problematic area is time of court appearance. Courts are notorious for not starting on time. Sitting all day on a bench outside a court waiting for it to convene while the perpetrator is seated on an adjacent bench is clearly not conducive to the child's or the family's good mental health. As a result, the Carl Perkins staff keeps the child and the family at the center until a call is received from the courthouse that court is about to convene. Only then are the child and family transported to the courthouse. After the court appearance, the child is brought back to the center and debriefed. Questions such as "How did that feel?" and "What was that like for you?" are posed to alleviate the residual fears of having confronted the perpetrator at close range (Bottoms, 1999).

The span of time from disclosure and discovery of the assault to court appearance may be up to a year, and there will be lots of transcrisis points as time seems to drag on interminably. It is important that each one of these crisis points be met head-on by crisis workers. Thus the Carl Perkins Center staff immediately swings into action in dealing with the child and the family and stays with them in support and therapeutic roles for at least a year after the initial contact is made (Bottoms, 1999).

Aftermath

It should be a given from all you have read in this chapter that any child who has been sexually abused needs counseling (Knauer, 2000, p. 46). Discovery of an incestuous relationship throws the entire family into crisis. The father, and possibly the mother, faces loss of what has become an addictive behavior, possible criminal sanctions, loss of his or her family, and social stigmatization. The nonoffending parent finds her- or himself torn between her or his partner and the assaulted child. The child may find her- or himself discredited, shamed, punished, and still unprotected (Herman, 1981, p. 183). The worker will also face a crisis in deciding what to do and whether or not to believe the child's story. However, discovery of child sexual abuse is no different from discovery of any other physical abuse, and state laws mandate that it must be reported (Sandberg, Crabbs, & Crabbs, 1988). It is a criminal activity and should be dealt with in that manner. For those workers who are unsure of themselves, it may be reassuring to know that fewer than 5 percent of complaints of child sexual abuse are false.

Conversely, it is not uncommon for children to retract their complaints under pressure from the family (Goodwin, 1982). Therefore, until clearly proved otherwise, the child's allegations should be accepted as valid, and the worker's primary consideration should be reporting the abuse to Child Protective Services and obtaining safety for the child (Sandberg, Crabbs, & Crabbs, 1988).

Because the behavior is both criminal and addictive, treating the problem via family therapy is fruitless. What is called for is immediately referring the problem to and cooperating with family services and law enforcement agencies that do not subscribe to a family reunification policy (Sandberg, Crabbs, & Crabbs, 1988). It then becomes much more possible to remove the father from the home through a court order. Removing the child from the home has negative ramifications because it may be construed as banishment and may also serve to strengthen parent bonds against the child. The child needs assurance that she is not to blame for the incest; she should be praised for her courage and clearly told that she is helping, not hurting, her family and will not be abandoned even if she retracts her story (Herman, 1981, pp. 184–185).

Counseling

Aftercare is critically important to prevent a host of maladies from appearing in later childhood and carrying on into adulthood. Universal characteristics such as lying, stealing, fighting, verbal and behavioral oppositional defiance, and promiscuity are typical aftermath behaviors that will assail children who have been sexually victimized.

Boys will typically perpetrate sexual assaults on other children, bully other kids, vandalize property, and generally direct their anger outward. Girls typically turn their anger inward and engage in alcohol and drug abuse, eating disorders, and promiscuity. Reducing problem behavior is important along with dealing with the trauma (Miller-Perrin, 2001). The Carl Perkins Center attempts to deal with these issues before they become major behavioral problems, through play therapy, therapeutic games, and role plays that deal with the inappropriate behavior in both group and individual counseling. The Center follows a variation on the trauma systems approach (Saxe, Ellis, & Kaplow, 2007), including trauma-focused cognitive-behavioral therapy (Neubauer, Deblinger, & Sieger, 2007), play therapy group work (Haen, 2008; Malchiodi, 2008; Nisivoccia & Lynn, 2007), and work with the family, school, and social service systems (Saxe, Ellis, & Kaplow, 2007; Steele & Malchiodi, 2008). This comprehensive approach is all part of the postvention package of a 1-year follow-up (Bottoms, 1999).

Group Counseling

Group counseling is used to normalize the assault and help children understand they are not alone. The group breaks the isolation as children start to share their fears and feelings of shame and guilt. Peer interaction leads to expression of shared feelings, bonding, and higher self-esteem. By validating their experiences, the group helps shift the focus of responsibility off children and onto the perpetrators. Further, the typical parameters of group rules help children learn behavioral limits, identify appropriate interpersonal boundaries with others, and learn to express feelings appropriately (Knauer, 2000; Nisivoccia & Lynn, 2007). Children meet in groups twice a month for a year.

These issues are not sugarcoated. Group leaders discuss these problems in a straightforward manner and teach children how to deal appropriately with the feelings, behaviors, and thoughts that are likely to confront them as they work through the trauma they have experienced. The idea is that if these problems are talked about openly and honestly, then survivors will not be further victimized and will be empowered to start taking control of their lives back (Bottoms, 1999).

The assaulted child may have been told, not only by the perpetrator but also by other family members, that the child him- or herself is the cause of the family's breakup. Constant reinforcement is used to convey to children that the assault wasn't their fault. Workers who are not versed in dealing with sexually abused clients will not understand the importance of driving this point home. The fact is that many, many sexually abused clients will believe it is their fault and that they, and they alone, as a result of their disclosure, have caused all the problems that have occurred for the family (Bottoms, 1999).

Groups are set up in age ranges of 2 to 3 years. Groups are not run for 3- to 5-year-olds because of their short attention span and lack of mature cognitive development. The 3- to 5-year-olds receive only individual counseling. Because of the curriculum and techniques used, groups are also divided into readers and nonreaders. Group participants also receive individual counseling, twice a month on alternate weeks from when groups meet. Different children manifest different problems as they work through the trauma of the abuse. When a child starts to manifest a particular characteristic, such as stealing, then individual counseling is tailored to fit that child's specific needs (Bottoms, 1999). Particularly for younger children, any group therapy should not be entirely devoted to "talking" therapy. Play is the medium that gets the message across; puppets (Webb, 2007), dramatic enactment (Haen, 2007), bibliotherapy (Malchiodi & Ginns-Gruenberg, 2007), sand play (Carey, 2006), art (Malchiodi, 2007), and particularly for older children, board games (Schaefer & Reid, 2001) all provide mediums to get the message of abuse across and teach children cooperative, prosocial behaviors that many of them lack.

Boundary Issues

Boundary issues are endemic to this population. The positive feedback and attention these children receive from engaging in sexual activities with long-term perpetrators transfer over to and generalize to a variety of other situations and people. Thus one of the primary thrusts of counseling at Carl Perkins is to reestablish appropriate personal and interpersonal boundaries.

Sexual assault turns understanding of normal developmental boundaries upside down and children may become erotized, meaning that psychologically the children may believe that the only way to gain attention is to be sexual. Physically, the feeling may have been enjoyable and they do not perceive it as abuse (Knauer, 2000, p. 10). An example of the lack of understanding that sexually assaulted children have of interpersonal boundaries is related by the Assistant Director of the Carl Perkins Center:

Assistant Director: I was on a home visit working with the mother of a young girl who had been sexually abused. My purpose for the visit was to work with the mother in teaching her parenting techniques to use with the daughter. I really wasn't there to deal with the young girl, but she incessantly demanded attention from both me and the mother. Providing her with alternative activities such as coloring books and dolls didn't satisfy her demand for us to attend to her. The little girl left the room and then reappeared with a negligee on and tried to get me to look at her. When that didn't work, the girl got up and sat as close to me as she could. When I still continued to attend to the mother, she climbed in my lap. When I still did not attend to her, she started kissing me, and finally attempted to stick her tongue in my mouth. In her attempt to get my attention and affection, she knew no interpersonal boundaries. It doesn't take a rocket scientist to figure out how that had come to be. Love, attention, and sex are all rolled into one as far as these kids are concerned. I can't tell you the number of times we have discovered these 6-, 7-, and 8-year-olds having sex with other kids when they should be playing with dolls and trucks with those kids. So a lot of time is spent on talking about what appropriate boundaries are.

Group Support Work With Nonoffending Parents

For mothers, the notion of entering a support/therapy group may be very threatening. However, it is quite possibly the only way they will be able to get their families back together. Mothers should be told this fact in plain and simple terms and should be strongly encouraged to join such groups. Groups for spouses of abusers enable members to come to terms with doubts of their own womanhood, regain a sense of control and empowerment in themselves and their families, reduce blame and guilt in themselves, and restore mother–daughter bonds (Brittain & Merriam, 1988; Salter, 1988, p. 211).

Preventing Revictimization

Perhaps most tragic of all the issues that assail a family is revictimization of the child by the nonoffending parent. Often a role reversal occurs whereby the child not only is the sexual object of the perpetrating parent, but also becomes the chief confidant and comfort provider for the nonoffending parent. She or he takes on the role of being the real partner of the nonoffending parent and usurps the nonoffender parent's role. This role reversal may be completed by the nonoffending parent's psychologically taking over the child role.

Therefore, crisis workers spend a good deal of time with nonoffending parents, teaching them to reassume the role as head of household and to stand their ground when the child attempts to reassume her or his pseudo-adult role. Finally, time is spent on talking about the nonoffending parent's not falling into another relationship that has the same outcome, as the parent may be highly likely to do (Bottoms, 1999).

What the Carl Perkins Center does with families who have been involved with sexual abuse is not short-term, brief therapy. The multiple crises that erupt after disclosure should make it readily apparent that there are no quick fixes to this horrific problem. At least a year of continuing crises may be expected as the family attempts to restabilize and reinvent itself, and to be successful, it will need help every step of the way.

Individual Counseling

There are two major purposes in individual counseling following childhood sexual abuse. The first is making it safe enough for the child to discuss the assault. Avoidance is typically a hallmark of a traumatic event for children and children are generally reluctant to discuss it (Webb, 2007, p. 51). Second is reenactment of the trauma and cognitively restructuring it so that it no longer is the axis on which the child's life turns.

Intervention with abused children should never be done in isolation but should include the nonoffending members of the family (Mohl, 2010). Neubauer and her associates (2007) and Saxe and his associates (2007) propose that trauma therapy with children should have parallel parent training and therapy occurring at the same time. Neubauer and her associates propose that individual therapy should progress with the nonoffending parent and child seen separately first. The reason for doing so is to create a safe atmosphere for both the parent and the child to start to openly discuss their thinking and feeling about the abuse, which will not be easy to do under the best of circumstances. Later on, when both the child and the parent have received a good deal of processing and training, they are brought together in conjoint therapy. At this time the child tells the complete story of the abuse, and the parent openly discusses her or his own feelings and reinforces the child's proactive behavior. The end result is that emotional and behavioral dysregulation is first stabilized and then, through the course of therapy, psychoeduction, and parent training, both parent and child can transcend the abuse and move on with their lives (Saxe, Ellis, & Kaplow, 2007).

Session 1: Establishing Safe Ground. In this opening session the worker seeks to establish safe therapeutic ground for the child by asking him or her to talk about something they like or want to do.

CW: Elizabeth, I am pleased to meet you. My name is Delaine Uptown, and I am a counselor here at the center. You and I are going to be spending some time together, so I'd like to get to know you a bit better. I'm wondering if you could tell me a bit about things you really like to do or, in fact, might want to do. Perhaps something you did this weekend or today? Which would you like to choose?

Elizabeth: Well, I mostly stay at home now, but I like to ride my bike and go over to my best friend Cindy's and play in her tree house, it's really neat. We play dolls and stuff up there.

CW: Okay, great, so you've got a good friend and pal that you can depend on and can go play dolls with. I also know that it's a lot easier for kids to sometimes use toys and drawings as ways to express feelings. Take a look around the room, Elizabeth, there are a variety of toys and art supplies here that you can use. There is even a sand tray over here that we can use if you want. The choice is yours, so where would you like to start?

The worker sets the scene with the child in a benign, nonthreatening way. She also introduces Elizabeth to the play materials in the room.

Concurrently the worker will start educating the parent on symptoms and behaviors the child is likely to display as they move through therapy, which will undoubtedly have transcrisis points as the child begins to regulate emotions and behaviors and parents learn new communication and behavior management skills. As the child and the worker begin bonding, the worker will move to trauma.

Session 2: Introducing Traumatic Material

CW: I think you are pretty good at expressing your feelings and ideas about stuff. I think you also are a pretty smart young woman and know that we are here to talk about stuff that happened that doesn't make you or your mom feel good. You know what I mean?

Elizabeth: Like what Leon did to me.

CW: Yes, that's right. We could either talk about it or you could show me what happened. I know you like to draw things.

Elizabeth: Well, he sorta touched me in places where he shouldn't have. (*Takes markers and starts drawing randomly with no apparent meaning or form.*)

CW: Okay. Did he do anything else?

Elizabeth: (*Continues to draw and says nothing.*)

CW: Okay, thank you so much for sharing that with me. So what are you drawing? It looks extremely busy with all those lines.

Elizabeth: Like it's all the lines running everywhere and they don't connect to anything.

CW: Is that perhaps the way maybe you feel sometimes?

Elizabeth: Maybe.

CW: That makes perfect sense to me. Kids who have been abused by people who should take care of them but abuse them would leave anyone pretty jumbled up.

Elizabeth: I guess maybe that's so. The kids in my group talk about that a lot. You wouldn't hurt something you loved like my cat. And my stepfather hurt me.

CW: That is correct, Elizabeth, and that's why he is going to jail. You know I think you ought to write a book about this experience complete with the pictures you have drawn.

This exchange indicates that the worker is moving ever forward in getting Elizabeth to recount and capture the whole episode. Saxe and associates (2007, pp. 269–271) propose that children write a book about the episode that they can then share with their caretakers. Saxe and his associates believe book writing allows the child to narrate in both words and pictures the sequence of the assault. They propose chapter titles like "All About Me," "My Family," "Something Bad Happened to Me," "Things Changed After the Bad Thing Happened," "Some Things Stayed the Same," "People Who Care About Me," "What I Can Do to Protect Myself in the Future," and "Skills I Have Used When My Bad Thoughts Get in the Way." These chapter headings can, in fact, be the topics of counseling sessions. Once recorded, Elizabeth can immediately refer to her chapters so that the behavioral and cognitive sets she will learn—such as deep breathing and relaxation training, sensory and verbal cueing, catching oneself, and setting up cognitive "stop" and "go" signs before things go awry—are readily available and in her own voice rather than the therapist's or what a book says to do.

This initial foray is met with some resistance, but it is a start and the mass of twirling lines apparently do represent a central part of this youngster's thinking. Concurrently the worker has given Mona a homework assignment and discusses her progress in reinforcing Elizabeth and also using natural consequences of actions when she becomes rebellious. The focus here is not on Elizabeth but on Mona's responses.

CW: So, you've gotten through the first part of Becker's *Parents Are Teachers* [Becker, 1972] and have really upped the verbal M&Ms, reinforcing her a lot more than you did. You have even kept a diary. Wow! That is really great. That tells me that you are into changing behavior big time, and not just your kid's. What about timeout when she acts out?

Mona: I'm having some trouble with that. I feel so bad about sending her to her room after all that has happened. I love that girl so much, and it tears me up to have to come down on her and ground her when I know it's all from that no good bastard.

CW: So pick a time last week when things were REALLLLLY good and when they were REALLLLY bad. What were the billboards going through your head that made you continue doing the reinforcement and reading the *Parents Are Teachers* book, and what were the negative ones that made you want to throw in the towel?

Just as she will do with Elizabeth, the worker is not only training Mona in new ways of parenting, she is also teaching her to catch the positive self-enhancing statements she is giving herself and the negative ones that help extinguish attempts at new behavior. In short, she is teaching Mona how to regulate her emotional behavior as well.

The Carl Perkins staff meet with the nonoffending parent twice a month for a year. After the abuse has been discovered, children tend to behave differently. Without knowledge and training, parents are likely to be shocked by these previously unseen behaviors as the child acts out (Knauer, 2000; Miller-Perrin, 2001). Thus, home visits and parent training to educate and normalize the behavioral changes that are likely to occur are critically important. If such training does not occur, then warfare between the parent and the child will create another crisis. Forewarned is forearmed, and if parents start seeing these behaviors, the center staff immediately start tackling these issues with the child. Therefore, center staff keep close contact with the home to catch and stop inappropriate behavior before it gets started (Bottoms, 1999).

A classic example of acting-out behavior is stealing or shoplifting. The immediate knee-jerk reaction of many parents is to use shame as a way of modifying the behavior. Yet using shame to extinguish behavior compounds all kinds of shame-based issues the child may already have. Another example is sexual acting out. A parent who has started to date again after removal of the perpetrator will be horrified when the child attempts to become intimate with this new person. Because of the vacuum left by the removal of the perpetrator, the child's need for love and affection, and her or his confusion over boundaries, the parent's new boyfriend or girlfriend may become a target for the child's commingled notions of how love and sex are intertwined and how she or he can obtain that love through sexual gratification (Bottoms, 1999).

We will speak a good deal about making home visits and their potential for violence in Chapter 14, Violent Behavior in Institutions. However, you should clearly understand that even though one perpetrator has been removed from the home (or thought to be removed) you still need to be cautious and planful when making a home visit, and that plan includes your own personal safety. Saxe and his associates (2007) propose an "On-the-SPOT" decision tree (p. 179) that dictates what you will do if you enter a home that is in crisis and violence boils over. The first question to ask yourself is "Is everything cool and calm here, or is something unusual happening that appears headed toward a crisis?" The very next question is "How safe am I?" If the answer to that question is "I'm not sure" or "Not very," then get out now!

Home intervention also includes many case management activities. Getting ready for court, obtaining an attorney, looking for alternative living arrangements and transportation, dealing with school issues, and applying for victims' compensation and other state support mechanisms for families are but a few of the many support activities that will be needed to help the family restabilize (Bottoms, 1999). As Saxe and his associates propose (2007), this is a systemic effort, and nothing less than dealing with the whole system will do.

Crisis Session.   All of the foregoing sounds swell, but the fact is that the therapy of child sexual abuse rarely progresses in a nice, linear, ever upward, ever onward manner. There are transcrises aplenty with which to reckon.

Elizabeth: (*Tears up the carefully made new family she has been building in the sand tray and breaks down in tears.*) This won't ever come true! Some kids at school said Leon's gonna get out just like their daddies did and will be right back at home. I HATE THIS STUPID SAND TRAY! THIS IS HOPELESS. WE'LL NEVER BE SAFE, AND I HATE THERAPY, AND YOU TOO, MISS DELAINE, so you can just kiss my ass goodbye! (*Stands defiantly as an 8-year-old can, tearfully regarding Delaine with as evil a look as she can muster.*)

CW: (*Says nothing but picks up some modeling clay and popsicle sticks and starts constructing something.*)

Elizabeth: (*Sits over in the corner staring balefully at the worker. Slowly comes over to the worker.*) Whatcha doing with that clay and those stupid popsicle sticks?

CW: I am going to build something I think might help when things are really down. I guess you are so hopeless and helpless right now you couldn't help me.

Elizabeth: I didn't say that. What is it?

CW: (*Sweeps the sand away in the sand tray and parts it to reveal a broad swath of blue board.*) It is a bridge. I am building a bridge over troubled waters. But it has to be a strong bridge with good foundations, strong girders, and support wire because it has to stay solid and mustn't fall in. It carries very important people on it . . . like your mom and you.
    Your stepfather may get out some day, but you will be a grown woman by then. But there are going to be other troubles that will get you down and things that will appear just as hopeless, maybe things you do, or your mom does, or maybe what other people say or do. So it's got to be a strong bridge. I'd like to put this family on the other side with palm trees and beach chairs and sunshine, not on this side with the swamp and all the nasty

swamp things that live in it. But I can't build this alone. It is your bridge.

Elizabeth: (*Grudgingly starts to help mold pillars for the bridge.*) I guess so.

CW: (*after bridge is done*) How do you feel? You see you have a real way to get out of the swamp. I am going to take a picture of this, and I want you to put it in the book. This is very important because it shows that you can get to the other side and you can make your own bridge to get you there. So remember where you have come from. You have indeed crossed over that bridge with all the work we have done. There is no going back, you are across, but every once in a while when things get tough it's good to remember that this bridge we just built really is your bridge, Elizabeth. It is something you now own and can use forever. Now stand over there by the bridge and give me a big cheesy smile!

Drawing or constructing a bridge lets clients concretely fill in gaps when they see little way across "troubled waters." Bridging exercises are mainly used for assessment to determine where people have been and where they are going (Martin, 2008). Here we use bridging as a therapeutic vehicle to get Elizabeth mobilized again and show her where she has been, whence she has come, and where she is going. Here the crisis worker takes action and very actively and directly gets into the game, but as soon as Elizabeth mobilizes herself, the crisis worker assumes a collaborative mode and then becomes nondirective as Elizabeth regains control.

Last Sessions: Transcending.   What Saxe and associates (2007) call the Transcendent phase of intervention occurs when the caregiving parent and abused child are brought together in conjoint therapy. The notion is that both caregiver and child are now able to talk openly and honestly about the abuse. The worker may start these sessions by acting as a game show host and asking both clients questions about sexual abuse (Neubauer, Deblinger, & Sieger, 2007). As survivor and caregiver reaffiliate, the child is encouraged to read passages from her book; Saxe and associates (2007, p. 276) recommend about three chapters per session. As the child reads the chapters, the caregiver expresses his or her own thoughts about what the child has written and gives the child a whole lot of reinforcement for having done such an awesome job of getting her feelings, thoughts, and behaviors about the sexual abuse down on paper (Neubauer, Deblinger, & Sieger, 2007).

SUMMARY

The sexual assault research consistently finds that the incidence of sexual assault is greatly underreported. The majority of reported rapists and other sexual abusers are males, and they come from all walks of life. Most abusers appear to perceive those they attack as objects of prey rather than as people. They usually assault not out of lust or desire for sexual gratification but out of a perceived need to control, exert power over, punish, vanquish, defeat, hurt, destroy, degrade, or humiliate others. Typically, abusers deny, minimize, and/or rationalize their behavior to the extent that they themselves rarely define their attacks as abuse. Instead, they usually claim that the survivor asked for, deserved, seduced, wanted, needed the experience in order to grow up, or somehow caused the abusive activity to occur.

Rape is a complex phenomenon that encompasses and affects the psychosocial, cultural, and personal aspects of society. There are no cause-and-effect formulas that explain why one person sexually assaults another. Consequently, many erroneous assumptions, beliefs, and myths about rape are held by different people, and women and men often differ in their perceptions about rape.

Date and acquaintance rape, especially on college campuses, has become a pressing problem. The problem is exacerbated by the use of drugs and/or alcohol that is usually found to be associated with date rape. One impediment to preventing date and acquaintance rape is the differential perceptions between men and women. The research consistently reveals that men are more tolerant of rape than are women.

Recently, the human services professions have directed a great deal of attention to rape and sexual assault on children. Substantive work has been done in the areas of crisis work, counseling, legal, social, and psychological interventions to help children and to prevent child sexual abuse. Such intervention and prevention have been made even more urgent in light of recent findings that child sexual abuse extends debilitating traumas far into the adulthood of survivors. An enormous amount of research has shown that adult survivors of child sexual abuse often suffer a wide diversity of emotional, physical, psychological, and social pathologies that manifest themselves in various degrees of transcrisis and PTSD symptoms later in adulthood. These findings have produced greater urgency than ever before to help victims of sexual abuse and to stop offenders from assaulting.

Crisis intervention and other human services work in the area of rape and sexual assault of children require unique and specialized knowledge and strategies. Children are vulnerable to many kinds of pressures, and perpetrators of child sexual abuse know all the angles needed to ensnare child victims. The legal, medical, social, mental health, law enforcement, and human services professions as well as the court system are becoming increasingly integrated in attempting to stop the abuse and to work with abused children and their families. There is ominous research on sexual predators' use of the Internet, and that arena will surely deserve even more attention in studies on controlling and containing child sex abuse.

In recent years the public, too, has become increasingly aware of the phenomenon of rape and other forms of sexual abuse, and that new awareness appears to have ushered in a greater sensitivity to and advocacy for the rights and needs of survivors. However, much remains to be done. Society still needs to overcome a number of long-standing myths about rape and other forms of sexual abuse. And survivors' families, friends, and coworkers need to be willing and able to respond to survivors with openness, genuineness, acceptance, understanding, and respect, all of which are key attitudes or conditions for nurturing recovery from the debilitating trauma and effects of sexual assault. Given the high incidence of sexual assault and its underreporting, it is highly likely that a number of you—both male and female—may have experienced this crisis. As a result of reading this chapter, you may experience or be experiencing some of the repercussions this chapter speaks of in people who have been sexually assaulted and abused. We urge you to not be ashamed, embarrassed, or guilty but to understand that this crisis is common to a whole lot of people and to get help! If you don't feel there is help in your community or you are too embarrassed to ask, call the National Office on Violence Against Women's hotlines: the Rape, Abuse, and Incest National Network Hotline at 1-800-656-HOPE (4673), the National Sexual Violence Resource Center at 1-877-739-3895, or the National Teen Dating Abuse Helpline at 1-866-331-9474. If you are attempting to recover on your own from a sexual assault, get Aphrodite Matsakis's *The Rape Recovery Handbook* (2003). It is a step-by-step help program for survivors of sexual assault. It's user friendly, talks straight to you, and has really helpful exercises in it.

To see some of the concepts discussed in this chapter in action, refer to your *Crisis Intervention in Action* DVD, or see the clips online on the Counseling CourseMate website. To access this site, go to www.cengagebrain.com, where you'll also find an eBook, additional study tools, quizzes, and more.

There are two videos with this chapter. One is probably going to amuse you, at least in part; the other will not and may hit pretty close to home if you are a female college student. The college counselor is tasked with taking care of business (doing what is necessary to deal with the physical and legal consequences of the rape) and providing a supportive and caring role (emotional and social support). How well do you think she manages this balancing act? In the adult survivor video, put yourself in the place of both the survivor and the counselor. Would you act the same way as the survivor does? Would you act the same way as the counselor does? Then ask the same questions again, except this time suppose you are indeed a survivor of childhood sexual abuse and suppose that as the counselor you have never experienced someone with this problem and know little about it.

In the second video, ask the same questions. However, if you are the client, also ask yourself if you would even come to the counseling center. It's easy to make a decision if you haven't been assaulted, but if you actually had this happen . . . well? Contrary to what you may think, this chapter isn't about training rape crisis specialists. As the counselor, would you know the procedures and protocols for a rape and how to go through them without absolutely terrorizing and revictimizing the client? The notion here is that if you are working in a high school building, as Paula the counselor in the role play actually does, would you have the basic skills and knowledge to deal with a student rape case as the point of contact?

REFERENCES

Abbey, A., McAuslan, P., & Ross, L. T. (1998). Sexual assault perpetration by college men: The role of alcohol, misperception of sexual intent, and sexual beliefs and experiences. *Journal of Social & Clinical Psychology, 17,* 167–195.

Ackerman, P. T., Newton, J. E. O., McPherson, W. B., Jones, J. G., & Dykman, R. A. (1998). Prevalence of posttraumatic stress disorder and other psychiatric diagnoses in three groups of abused children (sexual, physical, and both). *Child Abuse and Neglect, 22,* 759–774.

Alaggia, R., & Millington, G. (2008). Male child abuse: A phenomenology of betrayal. *Clinical Social Work Journal, 36*(3), 265–275.

Allen, C. M. (1991). *Women and men who sexually abuse children: A comparative analysis.* Orwell, VT: Safer Society Press.

American Psychiatric Association. (2000). *Diagnostic and statistical manual of mental disorders* (4th ed., Text Revision). Washington, DC: Author.

Aosyed, A. C., Long, P., & Voller, E. K. (2011). Sexual revictimzation and adjustment in college men. *Psychology of Men & Masculinity, 12*(3), 285–296.

Baker, D. A. (1995, June). *Talking with young people who have experienced sexual abuse.* Paper presented at the American School Counselor Association Conference and Exposition, New Orleans.

Baron, L., & Straus, M. A. (1989). *Four theories of rape in American society.* New Haven, CT: Yale University Press.

Bass, E., & Davis, L. (1992). *The courage to heal: A guide for women survivors of child sexual abuse.* New York: Harper.

Bass, E., & Thornton, L. (Eds.). (1983). *I never told anyone: Writings by women survivors of child sex abuse.* New York: Harper & Row.

Becker, W. (1972). *Parents are teachers.* Champaign, IL: Research Press.

Beech, A. R., Ward, T., & Fisher, D. (2006). The identification of sexual and violent motivations in men who assault women: Implication for treatment. *Journal of Interpersonal Violence, 21*(12), 1635–1653.

Benedict, H. (1985). *Recovery: How to survive sexual assault—for women, men, teenagers, their friends and families.* Garden City, NY: Doubleday.

Besharov, D. J. (1990). *Recognizing child abuse: A guide for the concerned.* New York: Free Press.

Bottoms, B. L., Nielsen, M., Murray, R., & Filipas, H. (2003). Religion-based related child psychical abuse: Characteristics of psychological outcomes. In J. L. Mullings, J. W. Marquart, & D. J. Hartley (Eds.), *The victimization of children: Emerging issues* (pp. 87–114). Binghamton, NY: Haworth Trauma and Maltreatment Press.

Bottoms, D. (Speaker). (1999, September). *The role of the Exchange Club-Carl Perkins Child Advocacy Center in treating child sexual abuse* (Cassette Recording #7411-99). Memphis, TN: Department of Counseling, Educational Psychology and Research, University of Memphis.

Boyd, T. (2000, April 7). Date-rape drug: GBH means socializing in a new way—even with friends. *Pensacola News Journal,* pp. B1, B3.

Bremner, J. D. (1998). Traumatic memories lost and found: Can memories of abuse be found in the brain? In L. M. Williams & V. L. Banyard (Eds.), *Trauma and memory* (pp. 217–227). Thousand Oaks, CA: Sage.

Briere, J., & Conte, J. (1993). Self-reported amnesia for abuse in adults molested as children. *Journal of Traumatic Stress, 6*, 21–31.

Briere, J., & Runtz, M. (1987). Post sexual abuse trauma: Data and implications for clinical practice. *Journal of Interpersonal Violence, 2*, 367–379.

Briere, J., & Runtz, M. (1988). Symptomatology associated with childhood sexual victimization in a nonclinical adult sample. *Child Abuse and Neglect, 12*, 51–59.

Briere, J., & Runtz, M. (1993). Childhood sexual abuse: Long-term sequelae and implications for psychological assessment. *Journal of Interpersonal Violence, 8*, 312–330.

Briere, J., & Scott, C. (2006). *Principles of trauma therapy: A guide to symptoms, evaluation and treatment.* Thousand Oaks, CA: Sage.

Brittain, D. E., & Merriam, K. (1988). Groups for significant others of survivors of child sexual abuse: A report of methods and findings. *Journal of Interpersonal Violence, 3*, 90–101.

Browne, A., & Finkelhor, D. (2000). Impact of child sexual abuse. In A. C. Donnelly & K. Oates (Eds.), *Classic papers in child abuse* (pp. 217–238). Thousand Oaks, CA: Sage.

Brownmiller, S. (1975). *Against our will: Men, women, and rape.* New York: Simon & Schuster.

Burgess, A. W., & Holmstrom, L. L. (1985). Rape trauma syndrome and post-traumatic stress response. In A. W. Burgess (Ed.), *Rape and sexual assault: A research handbook* (pp. 56–60). New York: Garland.

Burt, M. R. (1998). Rape myths. In M. E. Odem & J. Clay-Warner (Eds.), *Confronting rape and sexual assault* (pp. 93–108). Wilmington, DE: Scholarly Resources.

Cameron, C. (1994). Women survivors confronting their abusers: Issues, decisions, and outcomes. *Journal of Child Sexual Abuse, 3*(1), 7–35.

Campbell, R., Patterson, D., & Lichty, L. F. (2005). The effectiveness of sexual assault nurse examiner (SANE) programs: A review of psychological, medical, legal, and community outcomes. *Trauma, Violence, & Abuse, 6*(4), 313–329.

Carey, L. (Ed.). (2006). *Expressive and creative methods for trauma survivors.* London: Kingsley.

Chen, J., Dunne, M., & Wang, X. (2003). Childhood sexual abuse: An investigation among 239 male high school students. *Chinese Mental Health Journal, 17*(5), 345–347.

Choudhary, E., Coben, J., & Bossarte, R. M. (2010). Adverse health outcomes, perpetrator characteristics, and sexual violence victimization among U.S. adult males. *Journal of Interpersonal Violence, 25*(8), 1523–1541.

Cloitre, M., & Rosenberg, A. (2006). Sexual revictimization: Risk factors and prevention. In V. M. Follette & J. Ruzek (Eds.), *Cognitive behavior therapies for trauma* (pp. 321–361). New York: Guilford Press.

Cloitre, M., Stovall-McClough, K. C., Miranda, R., & Chembtrob, C. M. (2004). Therapeutic alliance, negative mood regulation, and treatment outcome in child abuse–related posttraumatic stress disorder. *Journal of Consulting and Clinical Psychology, 72*(3), 411–416.

Cogdal, P. A., & James, R. K. (1991, August). *Combinatorial technique to treatment of adult incest survivors.* Paper presented at the American Psychological Association convention, San Francisco.

Cohen, J., Mannarino, J. A., & Deblinger, E. (2006). *Treating trauma and traumatic grief in children and adolescents.* New York: Guilford Press.

Cole, T. B. (2006). Rape at US colleges often fueled by alcohol. *Journal of the American Medical Association, 296*(5), 504–505.

Conte, J. R., & Schuerman, J. R. (1988). Research with child victims. In G. E. Wyatt & G. J. Powell (Eds.), *Lasting effects of child sexual abuse* (pp. 157–170). Newbury Park, CA: Sage.

Costin, L. B., Karger, H. J., & Stoesz, D. (1996). *The politics of child abuse in America.* New York: Oxford University Press.

Courtois, C. A. (1988). *Healing the incest wound: Adult survivors in therapy.* New York: Norton.

Courtois, C. A. (1999*). Recollections of sexual abuse: Treatment principles and guidelines.* New York: W. W. Norton & Co.

Courtois, C. A. (2001). Implications of the memory controversy for clinical practice: An overview of treatment recommendations and guidelines. *Journal of Child Sexual Abuse, 9*(3/4), 183–210.

Courtois, C. A., & Ford, J. D. (2009). *Treating complex traumatic stress disorders.* New York: Guilford Press.

Courtois, C. A., Ford, J. D., & Cloitre, M. (2009). Best practices in psychotherapy for adults. In C. A. Courtois & J. D. Ford, *Treating complex traumatic stress disorders* (pp. 82–103). New York: Guilford Press.

Darves-Bornoz, J. M., Lepine, J. P., Choquet, M., Berger, C., Degiovanni, A., & Gaillard, P. (1998). Predictive factors of chronic post-traumatic stress disorder in rape victims. *European Psychiatry, 13*, 281–287.

Davis, J. L., Combs-Lane, A. M., & Jackson, T. L. (2002). Risky behaviors associated with interpersonal victimization: Comparison based on type, number and characteristics of assault incidents. *Journal of Interpersonal Violence, 17*(6), 611–629.

Davis, M. (2002). Male sexual assault victims: A selective review of the literature and implications for support services. *Aggression & Violent Behavior, 7*(3), 203–214.

DeAngelis, T. (2007). A new diagnosis for childhood trauma. *Monitor on Psychology, 38*(3), 32–33.

Deblinger, E., McLeer, S. V., Atkins, M. S., & Ralphe, D. (1989). Posttraumatic stress in sexually abused, physically abused, and nonabused children. *Child Abuse and Neglect, 13*, 403–408.

Deblinger, E., Thakkar-Kolar, R., & Ryan, E. (2006). Trauma in childhood. In V. M. Follette & J. I. Ruzek (Eds.), *Cognitive behavior therapies for trauma* (pp. 405–431). New York: Guilford Press.

Deering, R., & Mellor, D. (2011). An exploratory qualitative study of self-reported impact of female-perpetrated childhood sexual abuse. *Journal of Child Sexual Abuse: Research, Treatment & Program Innovations for Victims, Survivors, & Offenders, 20*(1), 58–76.

DeMause, L. (1974). *The history of childhood.* New York: Psychohistory Press.

Donat, P. L. N., & D'Emilio, J. (1998). A feminist redefinition of rape and sexual assault: Historical foundations and change. In M. E. Odem & J. Clay-Warner (Eds.), *Confronting rape and sexual assault* (pp. 35–49). Wilmington, DE: Scholarly Resources.

Drieschner, K., & Lange, A. (1999). A review of cognitive factors in the etiology of rape: Theories, empirical studies, and implications. *Clinical Psychology Review, 19*(1), 57–77.

Duncan, K. A. (2004). *Healing from the trauma of childhood sexual abuse: The journey for women.* Westport, CT: Praeger.

Dunn, P. C., Vail-Smith, K., & Knight, S. M. (1999). What date/acquaintance rape victims tell others: A study of college student recipients of disclosure. *Journal of American College Health, 47*, 213–219.

Edelson, M. G., & Joa, D. (2010). Difference in legal outcomes for male and female children who have been sexually abused. *Sexual Abuse: Journal of Research and Treatment, 22*(4), 427–442.

Eisler, R. (1987–1995). *The chalice and the blade: Our history, our future.* San Francisco: HarperCollins.

Eisler, R. (1995). *Sacred pleasure: Sex, myth, and the politics of the body.* San Francisco: HarperCollins.

Elliot, D. M., & Briere, J. (1995). Posttraumatic stress associated with delayed recall of sexual abuse: A general population study. *Journal of Traumatic Stress, 8*(4), 629–647.

Elliot, M. (1994). *Female sexual abuse of children.* New York: Guilford Press.

Farrell, S. P., Hains, A. A., & Davies, W. H. (1998). Cognitive behavioral interventions for sexually abused children exhibiting PTSD symptomology. *Behavior Therapy, 29*, 241–255.

Fehrenbach, P., & Monastersky, C. (1988). *A sourcebook on child sexual abuse.* Newbury Park, CA: Sage.

Feigon, E. A., & de Rivera, J. (1998). "Recovered memory" therapy: Profession at a turning point. *Comprehensive Psychiatry, 39*, 338–344.

Figley, C. R. (Ed.). (1985). *Trauma and its wake: The study of post-trauma stress disorder.* New York: Brunner/Mazel.

Finkelhor, D. (1979). *Sexually victimized children.* New York: Free Press.

Finkelhor, D. (1984). *Child sexual abuse: New theory and research.* New York: Free Press.

Finkelhor, D. (1987). The trauma of child sexual abuse: Two models. *Journal of Interpersonal Violence, 2*, 348–366.

Finkelhor, D., Omrod, R., Turner, H., & Hamby, S. L. (2005). The victimization of children and youth: A comprehensive, national survey. *Child Maltreatment, 10*(1), 5–25.

Foa, E. B., & Rauch, S. A. (2004). Cognitive changes during prolonged exposure versus prolonged exposure plus cognitive restructuring in female assault survivors with posttraumatic stress disorder. *Journal of Consulting and Clinical Psychology, 72*(5), 879–884.

Frazier, P. A., Andes, S., Perera, S., Tomich, P., Tennen, H., Park, C., & Tashiro, T. (2009). Traumatic events among undergraduate students: Prevalence and associated symptoms. *Journal of Counseling Psychology, 56*(3), 450–460.

Frazier, P. A., Steward, J., Tashiro, T., & Rosenberger, S. (2001). Responding to survivors of sexual assault. In E. R. Welfel & R. E. Ingersoll (Eds.), *The mental health desk reference* (pp. 252–258). New York: Wiley.

Frazier, P. A., Valtinson, G., & Candell, S. (1994). Evaluation of a coeducational interactive rape prevention program. *Journal of Counseling and Development, 73*, 153–158.

Freyd, J. (1993). Personal perspectives on the delayed memory debate. *Family Violence and Sexual Assault Bulletin, 9*(3), 28–33.

Ganas, K., Sampson, G., Cozzi, C., & Stewart, T. (1999, April). *Exposing our biases: Dealing with a rape survivor in a non-judgmental manner.* Paper presented at the Twenty-third Annual Convening of Crisis Intervention Personnel, Chicago.

Ganas, K., Sampson, G., Vermi, S., & Stewart, T. (1998, April). *Non-judgmentalism in rape crisis.* Paper presented at the Twenty-second Annual Convening of Crisis Intervention Personnel, Chicago.

Garrity, S. E. (2011). Sexual assault prevention programs for college-aged men: A critical evaluation. *Journal of Forensic Nursing, 7*(1), 40–48.

Gartner, R. B. (2005). *Beyond betrayal: Taking charge of your life after boyhood sexual abuse.* Hoboken, NJ: John Wiley & Sons.

Gil, E., & Johnson, T. C. (1993). *Sexualized children: Assessment and treatment of sexualized children and children who molest.* Rockville, MD: Launch Press.

Goodwin, J. (1982). *Sexual abuse: Incest victims and their families.* Boston: John Wright.

Goodwin, J. (1988). Post-traumatic symptoms in abused children. *Journal of Traumatic Stress, 1*, 475–488.

Groth, N. (1971). *Men who rape.* New York: Plenum Press.

Groth, N., & Birnbaum, H. J. (1979). *Men who rape: The psychology of the offender.* New York: Plenum.

Gumaer, J. (1984). *Counseling and therapy for children*. New York: Free Press.

Haen, C. (2008). Vanquishing monsters: Drama therapy for treating childhood trauma in the group setting. In C. A. Malciodi (Ed.), *Creative interventions with traumatized children* (pp. 225–246). New York: Guilford Press.

Hays, K. F. (1985). Electra in mourning: Grief work and the adult incest survivor. *Psychotherapy Patient, 2*, 45–58.

Heppner, M. J., Good, G. E., Hillenbrand-Gunn, T. L., Hawkins, A. K., Hacquard, L. L., Nichols, R. K., et al. (1995). Examining sex difference in altering attitudes about rape: A test of the elaboration likelihood model. *Journal of Counseling and Development, 73*, 640–647.

Herman, J. (1981). *Father–daughter incest*. Cambridge, MA: Harvard University Press.

Hien, D., Litt, L. C., Cohen, L. R., Miele, G. M., & Campbell, A. (2009). *Trauma service for women in substance abuse: An integrated approach*. Washington, DC: American Psychological Association.

Hillenbrand-Gunn, T. L., Heppner, M. J., Mauch, P. A., & Park, H. (2010). Men as allies: The efficacy of a high school rape prevention intervention. *Journal of Counseling & Development, 88*(1),43–51.

Himelein, M. J., Vogel, R. E., & Wachowiak, D. G. (1994). Nonconsensual sexual experiences in precollege women: Prevalence and risk factors. *Journal of Counseling and Development, 72*, 411–415.

Holmes, R. M., Holmes, A. T., & Unholz, J. (1993). Female pedophilia: A hidden abuse. *Law and Order, 41*(8), 77–79.

Holmes, W. C., & Slap, G. B. (1998). Sexual abuse of boys: Definition, prevalence, correlates, sequelae, and management. *Journal of the American Medical Association, 280*, 1855–1862.

Howell, S. (1999). *The Memphis Rape Crisis Center* (Cassette Recording #6760-99). Memphis, TN: Department of Counseling, Educational Psychology and Research, University of Memphis.

Isley, P. J., & Gehrenbeck-Shim, D. (1997). Sexual assault of men in the community. *Journal of Community Psychology, 25*, 159–166.

James, R. (2003, April). *Drawing out the trauma*. Paper presented at the Twenty-seventh Convening of Crisis Intervention Personnel, Chicago.

Kariane, H. M., Fisher, B. F., & Cullen, F. T. (2005, December). *Sexual assault on campus : What colleges and universities are doing about it*. National Institute of Justice. Available at www.ncjrs.gov/pdffiles1/nij/205521.pdf

Kassing, R. L., & Prietio, L. (2003). The rape myth and blame-based beliefs of counselors-in-training toward male victims of rape. *Journal of Counseling and Development, 81*(4), 455–461.

Kaufman, B., & Wohl, A. (1992). *Casualties of childhood: A developmental perspective on sexual abuse using projective drawings*. New York: Brunner/Mazel.

Kendall-Tackett, K. (2008). Chronic pain in adult survivors of childhood abuse. *Trauma Psychology Newsletter, 3*(3), 20–24.

Kendrick, J. M. (1991). Crisis intervention in child abuse: A family treatment approach. In A. R. Roberts (Ed.), *Contemporary perspectives on crisis intervention* (pp. 34–52). Upper Saddle River, NJ: Prentice Hall.

Kessler, B. L., & Bieschke, K. J. (1999). A retrospective analysis of shame, dissociation, and adult victimization in survivors of childhood sexual abuse. *Journal of Counseling Psychology, 46*, 335–341.

Kids on the Block. (1995). *Keeping up with the kids*. Columbia, MD: Author.

Knauer, S. (2000). *No ordinary life: Parenting the sexually abused child and adolescent*. Springfield, IL: Charles C Thomas.

Knight, R. A. (1999). Validation of a typology for rapists. *Journal of Interpersonal Violence, 14*(3), 303–330.

Knopp, F. H., & Lackey, L. B. (1987). *Female sexual abusers: A summary of data from 44 treatment providers*. Orwell, VT: Safer Society Press.

Koss, M. P. (1998). Hidden rape: Sexual aggression and victimization in a national sample of students in higher education. In M. E. Odem & J. Clay-Warner (Eds.), *Confronting rape and sexual assault* (pp. 51–70). Wilmington, DE: Scholarly Resources.

Koss, M. P., & Achilles, M. (2008). *Restorative justice responses to sexual assault*. Harrisburg, PA: VAWnet, a project of the National Resource Center on Domestic Violence/Pennsylvania Coalition Against Domestic Violence. Available at www.vawnet.org

Krebs, C. P., Lindquist, C. H., Warner, T. D., Fisher, B. S., & Martin, S. L. (2007, October). The campus sexual assault study final report xiii, 55. National Criminal Justice Reference Service. Available at www.ncjrs.gov/pdffiles1/nij/grants/221153.pdf

Kuhn, J. A., Charleanea, M., & Chavez, E. L. (1998). Correlates of sexual assault in Mexican-American and White non-Hispanic adolescent males. *Violence and Victims, 13*(1), 11–20.

Lalor, K., & McElvaney, R. (2010). Child sexual abuse, links to later sexual exploitation/high-risk sexual behavior, and prevention/treatment programs. *Trauma, Violence, & Abuse, 11*(4), 159–177.

Lear, M. W. (1972, January 30). Q: If you rape a woman and steal her TV, what can they get you for in New York? A: Stealing her TV. *New York Times Magazine*, pp. 10–11.

Leavitt, F. (2000). Surviving the roots of trauma: Prevalence of silent signs of sex abuse in patients who recover memories of childhood sex abuse as adults. *Journal of Personality Assessment, 74*(2), 311–323.

Lew, M. (2004). *Victims no longer: The classic guide for men recovering from sexual child abuse*. New York: Harper & Collins.

Lisek, D., Gardinier, L., Nicksa, S., & Cole, A. (2010). False allegations of sexual assault: An analysis of ten years of reported cases. *Violence Against Women, 16*(2), 1318–1334.

Lisek, D., & Miller, P. M. (2002). Repeat rape after multiple offending among undetected rapists. *Violence and Victims, 14*, 241–260.

Lisek, D., & Roth, S. (1988). Motivational factors in nonincarcerated sexually aggressive men. *Journal of Personality and Social Psychology, 55*, 795–802.

Longdon, C. (1994). A survivor and therapist's viewpoint. In M. Elliot (Ed.), *Female sexual abuse of children* (pp. 47–56). New York: Guilford Press.

Lundberg-Love, P. K., Marmion, S., Ford, K., & Geffner, R. (1992). The long-term consequences of childhood incestuous victimization upon adult women's psychological symptomatology. *Journal of Child Sexual Abuse, 1*(1), 81–102.

Malchiodi, C. A. (2008). *Creative interventions with traumatized children*. New York: Guilford Press.

Malchiodi, C. A., & Ginns-Gruenberg, D. (2008). Trauma, loss, and bibliotherapy: The healing power of stories. In C. A. Malchiodi (Ed.), *Creative interventions with traumatized children* (pp. 167–188). New York: Guilford Press.

Male Survivor. (2011). *Male sexual victimization and myths*. Available at www.malesurvivor.org/myths.html

Martin, E. S. (2008). Medical art and play therapy. In C. A. Malchiodi (Ed.), *Creative interventions with traumatized children* (pp. 112–131) New York: Guilford Press.

Matsakis, A. (2003). *The rape recovery handbook: Step-by-step help for survivors of sexual assault*. Oakland, CA: New Harbinger.

Matthews, R., Matthews, J., & Speltz, K. (1989). *Female sexual offenders: An exploratory study*. Orwell, VT: Safer Society Press.

McCabe, M. P., & Wauchope, M. (2005). Behavioral characteristics of men accused of rape: Evidence for different types of rapists. *Archives of Sexual Behavior, 34*(2), 241–253.

McCart, M. R., Fitzgerald, M. M., Acierno, R. E., Resnick, H. S., & Kilpatick, D. G. (2009). Evaluation and acute intervention with victims of violence. In P. Kleespies (Ed.), *Behavioral emergencies: An evidence-based resource for evaluating and managing risk of suicide, violence, and victimization* (pp. 167–188). Washington, DC: American Psychological Association.

McCarty, L. (1986). Mother-child incest: Characteristics of the offender. *Child Welfare, 65*, 457–558.

McCauley, M., Schwartz-Kenney, B. M., Epstein, M. A., & Tucker, E. J. (2001). United States. In B. M. Schwartz-Kenney, M. McCauley, & M. A. Epstein (Eds.), *Child abuse: A global view* (pp. 241–255). Westport, CT: Greenwood Press.

McGlone, G. J. (2003). The pedophile and the pious: Towards a new understanding of sexually offending and nonoffending Roman Catholic priests. In J. L. Mullings, J. W. Marquart, & D. J Hartley (Eds.), *The victimization of children: Emerging issues* (pp. 115–132). Binghamton, NY: Haworth Trauma and Maltreatment Press.

McLean, L. M., & Gallop, R. (2003). Implications of childhood sexual abuse for adult borderline personality disorder and complex posttraumatic stress disorder. *American Journal of Psychiatry, 160*(2), 369–371.

McLeer, S. V., Deblinger, E., Henry, D., & Orvaschel, H. (1992). Sexually abused children at high risk for posttraumatic stress disorder. *Journal of the American Academy of Child and Adolescent Psychiatry, 31*(5), 875–978.

McLeer, S. V., Dixon, J. F., Henry, D., Ruggiero, K., Escovitz, K., Niedda, T., & Scholle, R. (1998). Psychopathology in non-clinically referred sexually abused children. *Journal of the American Academy of Child and Adolescent Psychiatry, 37*, 1326–1333.

Merrick, M. V., Allen, B. M., & Crase, S. J. (1994). Variables associated with positive treatment outcomes for children surviving sexual abuse. *Journal of Child Sexual Abuse, 3*(2), 67–87.

Mezey, G., & King, M. (1998). The effects of sexual assault on men: A survey of twenty-two victims. In M. E. Odem & J. Clay-Warner (Eds.), *Confronting rape and sexual assault* (pp. 83–92). Wilmington, DE: Scholarly Resources.

Miller-Perrin, C. L. (2001). Child maltreatment: Treatment of child and adolescent victims. In E. R. Welfel & R. E. Ingersoll (Eds.), *The mental health desk reference* (pp. 169–177). New York: Wiley.

Mills, C. S., & Granoff, B. J. (1992). Date and acquaintance rape among a sample of college students. *Social Work, 37*(6), 504–509.

Moeller, T. P., Bachmann, G. A., & Moeller, J. R. (1993). The combined effects of physical, sexual, and emotional abuse during childhood: Long-term health consequences for women. *Child Abuse and Neglect, 17*(5), 623–640.

Mohl, A. (2010). Sexual abuse of the child: A treatment model for the incestuous family. *Journal of Psychohistory, 38*(2), 168–181.

Monk-Turner, E., & Light, D. (2010). Male sexual assault and rape: Who seeks counseling? *Sexual Abuse: Journal of Research and Treatment, 22*(3), 255–265.

Myers, M. F. (1986). Men sexually assaulted as adults and sexually molested as boys. *Archives of Sexual Behavior, 18*, 203–215.

Nathan, P., & Ward, T. (2001). Females who sexually abuse children: Assessment and treatment issues. *Psychiatry, Psychology, & Law, 8*(1), 44–55.

National Child Traumatic Stress Network and National Center for PTSD. (2006). *Psychological first aid: Field operations guide* (2nd ed.). Available at www.nctsn.org/nctsn_assets/pdfs/pfa/2/PsyFirstAid.pdf

National Institute of Justice and Centers for Disease Control. (1998). *National violence against women survey*. Washington, DC: United States Bureau of Justice.

National Institute of Mental Health. (2002). *Mental health and mass violence: Evidence-based early psychological intervention for victims/survivors of mass violence: A workshop to reach consensus on best practice* (NIH Publication No. 02-5138). Washington, DC: U.S. Government Printing Office.

Neubauer, F., Deblinger, E., & Sieger, K. (2007). Trauma-focused cognitive-behavioral therapy for child sexual abuse and exposure to domestic violence: Case of Mary, Age 6. In N. Webb (Ed.), *Play therapy with children in crisis* (3rd ed., pp. 107–132). New York: Guilford Press.

Newcomb, M. D., Munoz, D. T., Carmona, J. V. (2009). Child sexual abuse consequences in community samples of Latino and European American adolescents. *Child Abuse & Neglect, 33*(8), 533–544.

Nishith, P., Nixon, R., & Resick, P. A. (2005). Resolution of trauma-related guilt following treatment of PTSD in female rape victims: A result of cognitive processing therapy targeting comorbid depression. *Journal of Affective Disorders, 86*(22/23), 259–265.

Nisivoccia, D., & Lynn, M. (2007). Helping forgotten victims: Using activity groups with children who witness violence. In N. Webb (Ed.), *Play therapy with children in crisis* (3rd ed., pp. 294–321). New York: Guilford Press

Noll, J. G., Horowitz, L., Bonanno, G., Trickett, P., & Putnam, F. (2003). Revictimization and self-harm in females who experienced childhood sexual abuse: Results from a prospective study. *Journal of Interpersonal Violence, 18*(12), 1452–1471.

Norris, J., & Cubbins, L. A. (1992). Dating, drinking, and rape. *Psychology of Women Quarterly, 16*, 179–191.

Oates, R. K., O'Toole, B. I., Lynch, D. L., Stern, A., & Cooney, G. (1994). Stability and change in outcomes for sexually abused children. *Journal of the American Academy of Child and Adolescent Psychiatry, 33*, 945–953.

Ochberg, F. M. (Ed.). (1988). *Post-trauma therapy and victims of violence.* New York: Brunner/Mazel.

O'Leary, P. J. (2009). Men who were sexually abused in childhood: Coping strategies and comparison in psychological functioning. *Child Abuse & Neglect, 33*(7), 471–479.

Page, R. M. (1997). Helping adolescents avoid date rape: The role of secondary education. *High School Journal, 80*, 75–80.

Pauwels, S. M. (2003, April). *The scarlet R: Profile of a victim.* Paper presented at the Twenty-seventh Annual Convening of Crisis Intervention Personnel, Chicago.

Pearson, Q. M. (1994). Treatment techniques for adult female survivors of childhood sexual abuse. *Journal of Counseling and Development, 73*, 32–37.

Perkins, H. W., & Berkowitz, A. D. (1986). Perceiving the community norms of alcohol use among students: Some research implications for campus alcohol education programming. *International Journal of Addictions, 21*, 961–976.

Peterson, L. W., & Hardin, M. E. (1997). *Children in distress: A guide for screening children's art.* New York: Norton.

Peterson, L. W., & Zamboni, S. (1998). Quantitative art techniques to evaluate child trauma: A case review. *Clinical Pediatrics, 37*(1), 45–49.

Pfefferbaum, B. (1997). Posttraumatic stress disorder in children: A review of the past 10 years. *Journal of the American Academy of Child & Adolescent Psychiatry, 36*, 1503–1511.

Pifalo, T. (2002). Pulling out the thorns: Art therapy with sexually abused children and adolescents. *Art Therapy, 19*(1), 12–22.

Regehr, C., Cadell, S., & Jansen, K. (1999). Perceptions of control and long-term recovery from rape. *American Journal of Orthopsychiatry, 69*, 110–115.

Remer, R., & Ferguson, R. A. (1995). Becoming a secondary survivor of sexual assault. *Journal of Counseling and Development, 73*, 407–413.

Rew, L. (1989). Long-term effects of childhood sexual exploitation. *Issues in Mental Health Nursing, 10*, 229–244.

Robers, S., Zhang, J., Truman, J., & Snyder, T. D. (2010, November). *Indicators of school crime and safety: 2010.* U.S. Department of Education & U.S. Department of Justice. Available at bjs.ojp.usdoj.gov/content/pub/pdf/iscs10.pdf

Rosencrans, B. (1997). *The last secret: Daughters sexually abused by mothers.* Brandon, VT: Safer Society Press.

Rowan, E. L. (2006). *Understanding child sexual abuse.* Jackson: University of Mississippi Press.

Rubin, L. J. (1996). Childhood sexual abuse: Whose memories are faulty? *Counseling Psychologist, 24*, 140–143.

Sadowski, P. M., & Loesch, L. C. (1993). Using children's drawings to detect potential child sexual abuse. *Elementary School Guidance and Counseling, 28*, 115–123.

Salter, A. C. (1988). *Treating child sex offenders and victims: A practical guide.* Newbury Park, CA: Sage.

Salter, A. C. (1995). *Transforming trauma: A guide to understanding and treating adult survivors of child sexual abuse.* Newbury Park, CA: Sage.

Sanday, P. R. (1998). The socio-cultural context of rape: A cross-cultural study. In M. E. Odem & J. Clay-Warner (Eds.), *Confronting rape and sexual assault* (pp. 93–108). Wilmington, DE: Scholarly Resources.

Sandberg, D. N., Crabbs, S. K., & Crabbs, M. A. (1988). Legal issues in child abuse: Questions and answers for counselors. *Elementary School Guidance and Counseling, 22*, 268–274.

Sanders, B., & Moore, D. L. (1999). Childhood maltreatment and date rape. *Journal of Interpersonal Violence, 14*, 115–124.

Sawyer, R. G., Pinciaro, P. J., & Jessell, J. K. (1998). Effects of coercion and verbal consent on university students' perception of date rape. *American Journal of Health Behavior, 22*, 46–53.

Saxe, G. N., Ellis, B. H., Kaplow, J. B. (2007). *Collaborative treatment of traumatized children and teens: The trauma systems therapy approach.* New York: Guilford Press.

Scarce, M. (1997). Same-sex rape of male college students. *Journal of College Health, 45*(5), 171–173.

Schaefer, C. E., & Reid, S. E. (Eds.). (2001). *Game play* (2nd ed.). New York: Wiley.

Schetky, D. H. (1990). A review of the literature on the long-term effects of childhood sexual abuse. In R. P. Kluft (Ed.), *Incest-related syndromes of adult psychopathology* (pp. 35–54). Washington, DC: American Psychiatric Press.

Schwartz, M. D., & Leggett, M. S. (1999). Bad dates or emotional trauma? The aftermath of campus sexual assault. *Violence Against Women, 5,* 251–271.

Schwartz-Kenney, B. M., McCauley, M., & Epstein, M. A. (Eds.). (2001). *Child abuse: A global view.* Westport, CT: Greenwood Press.

Scully, D., & Marolla, J. (1998). "Riding the bull at Gilley's": Convicted rapists describe the rewards of rape. In M. E. Odem & J. Clay-Warner (Eds.), *Confronting rape and sexual assault* (pp. 109–128). Wilmington, DE: Scholarly Resources.

Sgroi, S. M. (1982). *Handbook of clinical intervention in child sexual abuse.* Lexington, MA: Lexington Books.

Sgroi, S. M., Porter, F. S., & Blick, L. C. (1982). Validation of child sexual abuse. In S. M. Sgroi (Ed.), *Handbook of clinical intervention in child sexual abuse* (pp. 39–79). Lexington, MA: Lexington Books.

Shapiro, B. L., & Chwarz, J. C. (1997). Date rape: Its relationship to trauma symptoms and sexual self-esteem. *Journal of Interpersonal Violence, 12,* 407–419.

Sheehan, P. L. (1994). Treating intimacy issues of traumatized people. In M. B. Williams & J. F. Sommers, Jr. (Eds.), *Handbook of post-traumatic therapy* (pp. 94–105). Westport, CT: Greenwood Press.

Silbert, M. (1988). Compounding factors in the rape of street prostitutes. In A. W. Burgess (Ed.), *Rape and sexual assault* (Vol. II, pp. 75–90). New York: Garland.

Speigel, J. (2003). *Sexual abuse of males: The SAM model of theory and practice.* New York: Brunner-Routledge.

Steele, W., & Malchiodi, C. A. (2008). Interventions for parents of traumatized children. In C. A. Malchiodi (Ed.), *Creative interventions with traumatized children* (pp. 264–281). New York: Guilford Press.

Stevenson, J. (1999). The treatment of long-term sequelae of child abuse. *Journal of Child Psychology & Psychiatry & Allied Disciplines, 40*(1), 89–111.

Sullivan, L. A., & Robinson, S. L. (1994, April). *An evaluation of a preschool child abuse and neglect prevention program: The Kids on the Block go to preschool.* Research report from the University of Alabama at Birmingham, presented at the Conference on Human Development.

Sussman, L., & Bordwell, S. (1981). *The rapist file: Interviews with convicted rapists.* New York: Chelsea House.

Sutherland, S. (1993). Movement therapy: Healing mind and body. *Treating Abuse Today, 3,* 21–24.

Thornhill, R., & Palmer, C. T. (2000). *A natural history of rape: Biological bases of sexual coercion.* Cambridge, MA: MIT Press.

Tjaden, L., & Thoennes, N. (2000). *Full report of the prevalence, incidence and consequences of violence against women* (NCJ 183781). National Institute of Justice, Office of Justice Programs.

Tomoko, I., Asukai, K., Toshilo, I., Inamoto, E., & Kageyama, T. (2002). Mental health effects of child sexual victimization in Japan. *Journal of Mental Health, 48,* 23–28.

Ullman, S. E. (1996a). Correlates and consequences of adult sexual assault disclosure. *Journal of Interpersonal Violence, 11,* 554–571.

Ullman, S. E. (1996b). Social reactions, coping strategies, and self-blame attributions in adjustment to sexual assault. *Psychology of Women Quarterly, 20,* 505–526.

Ullman, S. E., & Brecklin, L. R. (2002). Sexual assault history and suicidal behavior in a national sample of women. *Suicide & Life Threatening Behavior, 32*(2), 117–130.

Ullman, S. E., & Brecklin, L. R. (2003). Sexual assault history and health-related outcomes in a national sample of women. *Psychology of Women Quarterly, 27*(1), 46–57.

Ullman, S. E., Karabatsos, G., & Koss, M. P. (1999). Alcohol and sexual assault in a national sample of college women. *Journal of Interpersonal Violence, 14,* 603–625.

U.S. Department of Education. (2011, April 4). *Dear colleague letter: Sexual violence background, summary, and fast facts.* Available at www.ed.gov/about/offices/list/ocr/docs/dcl-factsheet-201104.html

U.S. Department of Health and Human Services. (1997). *Study findings: Study of national incidence and prevalence of child abuse and neglect: 1988.* Bethesda, MD: U.S. Government Printing Office.

U.S. Department of Justice. (1998). *National violence against women survey.* Washington, DC: Author.

U.S. Department of Justice. (2000, May). Children as victims: 1999 National Report Series. *Juvenile Justice Bulletin.* Washington, DC: Author.

U.S. Department of Justice. (2003). *National crime victimization survey—2002.* Washington, DC: Author.

Van Bruggen, M. L., Runtz, M., & Kadlec, H. (2006). Sexual revictimization: The role of self-esteem and dysfunctional sexual behaviors. *Child Maltreatment, 11*(2), 131–145.

van der Kolk, B. (2005). Developmental trauma disorder in childhood. *Psychiatric Annals, 35*(5), 401–408.

Varelas, N., & Foley, L. A. (1998). Blacks' and Whites' perceptions of interracial and intraracial date rape. *Journal of Social Psychology, 138,* 392–400.

Vladutiu, C. J., Martin, S. L., & Macy, R. J. (2011). College- or university-based sexual assault prevention programs: A review of program outcomes, characteristics, and recommendations. *Trauma, Violence, & Abuse, 12*(2), 67–86.

Webb, N. B. (2007). *Play therapy with children in crisis* (3rd ed.). New York: Guilford Press.

Weiss, K. G. (2010). Too ashamed to report: Deconstructing the shame of sexual victimization. *Feminist Criminology, 5*(3), 145–163.

Wheeler, J. R., & Berliner, L. (1988). Treating the effects of sexual abuse on children. In G. E. Wyatt & G. J. Powell (Eds.), *Lasting effects of child sexual abuse* (pp. 227–247). Newbury Park, CA: Sage.

White, J., & Allers, C. T. (1994). Play therapy with abused children: A review of the literature. *Journal of Counseling and Development, 72*, 390–394.

Williams, J. E., & Holmes, K. A. (1981). *The assault: Rape and public attitudes.* Westport, CT: Greenwood Press.

Williams, L. M. (1995). Recovered memories of abuse in women with documented child sexual victimization histories. *Journal of Traumatic Stress, 8*(4), 649–673.

Wolfe, V. V., Gentile, C., & Wolfe, D. A. (1989). The impact of sexual abuse on children: A PTSD formulation. *Behavior Therapy, 20*, 215–228.

Young, L. (1964). *Wednesday's children.* New York: McGraw-Hill.

CHAPTER **10**

Partner Violence

To anyone who watched television in 1994–1995 and saw the O. J. Simpson trial, the impact of partner violence came full force into the homes of America. Perhaps even more astounding, his major defense lawyer, Johnnie Cochran, had his own physical abuse of his ex-wife detailed in a book written by her (Cochran-Berry, 1995). But O. J. Simpson and Johnnie Cochran, for all their notoriety, are only two grains of sand in a very large beach of domestic violence. The pervasiveness of domestic violence is so great that it cuts across social, economic, religious, ethnic, cultural, racial, and geographical boundaries (Ahrens et al., 2010; Arai, 2004; Archambeau et al., 2010; Browne & Herbert, 1997; Hague & Sardinha, 2010; Haj-Yahia, 2003; Hotaling & Sugarman, 1986, 1990; Kasturirangan & Williams, 2003; Lee, 2002; Levinson, 1989; Maziak & Asfar, 2003; Murdaugh et al., 2004; Robinson, 2003; Santiago, 2002; Sev'er, 1997; Weitzman, 2000; West, Kaufman Kantor, & Jasinski, 1998; Witko, Martinez, & Milda, 2006; Yoshioka et al., 2003; Zanipatin et al., 2005). Indeed, a review of the American Psychological Association abstracts reveals that almost every country the *National Geographic* covers has had a study done on domestic violence. Culture plays a large part in what is defined as domestic violence or if it even exists. Further, if we define culture in terms of the social locations that Laura Brown (2008) speaks so eloquently to, we need to look at being pregnant (Suglia et al., 2010) homeless (Yeater et al., 2011), HIV positive, or a sex worker (prostitute) (Ulibarri et al., 2010) as some of the many locations that lead to physical violence between intimates (Bryant-Davis, 2010).

Certainly, physical abuse in domestic situations is not limited to husband-and-wife relationships. Indeed, single, separated, and divorced women are actually at greater risk for battering than are married women (Stark & Flitcraft, 1987). Furthermore, battering is not confined to heterosexual relationships: lesbians, gays, and bisexuals also batter one another (Kanuha, 2005; Peterman & Dixon, 2003; Randle & Graham, 2011; Ricks, Vaughan, & Dziegielewski, 2002; Stanley et al., 2006; West, 1998). Men are also assaulted by women (Langhinrichsen-Roling, Neidig, & Thorn, 1995; Randle & Graham, 2011; Stets & Straus, 1990; Straus & Gelles, 1990; Wiehe, 1998). Therefore, it should be clearly understood that the concepts discussed in this chapter apply to *all* partners or people involved in any established current or former cohabiting relationship. To further amplify the cross-sectional aspects of battering, the politically correct term has now become *intimate partner violence* (IPV) to encompass all types of couples. Because women form the major target group of severe domestic violence, however, this chapter focuses mainly on crisis intervention with women who are involved in domestic violence and the men who batter them.

The terms *battering*, *abuse*, and *assault* are often used interchangeably in the literature. In this chapter, *battering* indicates any form of physical violence perpetrated by one person on another and typically includes a life-threatening history of injuries and psychosocial problems that entrap a person in a relationship. *Abuse* is a more general term that indicates that physical violence is only one weapon in an armory of coercive weapons. Abuse denotes the unequal power relationship within which the assault occurs and further suggests that a presumption of trust has been violated. *Assaultive behavior* can include not only harmful acts against a person but also both verbal and behavioral threats to significant others, pets, or property. *Domestic violence* subsumes any act of assault by a social partner or relative, regardless of marital status (Stark & Flitcraft, 1988).

The Incidence of Partner Violence

The history of spouse beating in Western society goes as far back as the patriarchal system does. Whereas an assault on or rape of another man's wife caused and still causes immediate and severe legal punishment and moral outrage, abuse by a man of his own wife is quite another story (Pleck, 1987). Common law in the United States early acknowledged the right of a man to chastise his wife for misbehavior without being prosecuted for doing so (*Bradley* v. *State of Mississippi,* 1824). Indeed, the law's attitude toward wife beating to the current day is aptly summarized in the case of the *State of North Carolina* v. *Oliver* in 1874. The court ruled that "if no permanent injury has been inflicted, it is better to draw the curtains, shut out the public eye, and leave the parties to forgive and forget." The implications of such "blind" justice are ominous.

There is no more anxiety-provoking call for a police officer than a domestic disturbance call. Furthermore, domestic disturbance calls far outnumber other types of police calls in which the possibility of violence, injury, and death exists to both civilians and police (Benjamin & Walz, 1983). In the last comprehensive survey on domestic violence, it was estimated that about 1.5 million women and 830,000 men were victims of intimate violence in the United States (Tjaden & Thoennes, 2000). The Centers for Disease Control's report on homicides in the United States from 1981 to 1998 found that approximately one in three murders were intimate partner homicides (Centers for Disease Control, 2001). The good news is that these rates are apparently decreasing (Agency for Healthcare Research and Quality, 2010); however, those most likely to suffer IPV are, like many of you reading this book, women in their 20s to early 30s. A summary of all violent crimes reported that around 500,000 were perpetrated by intimates in 2002, down from the 1.1 million reported to authorities in 1993 (Bureau of Justice Statistics, 2003). Incidence studies report that 25 to 44 percent of women, and about 7.6 percent of men, in the United States have experienced a violent incident with a partner during their adult lifetime (Thompson et al.,

2006; Tjaden & Thoennes, 1998a). The foregoing figures should be viewed as very conservative estimates. Other estimates place the number of domestic violence incidents at anywhere from 4 to 8.7 million! Worldwide, it is estimated that between 8 and 67 percent of women are physically assaulted in their lifetime, with most countries reporting lifetime prevalence rates of 20 percent (Aldarondo & Castro-Fernandez, 2011). These latest figures probably underestimate the magnitude of the problem, for several reasons: cultural norms tolerate and in some instances condone family violence; confidentiality keeps violence a family secret; poor and non-English-speaking women are underreported; women who are institutionalized or hospitalized are often not included; elderly, gay, and lesbian incidents of violence are often not reported; and gender roles based on power differentials that are still sanctioned keep a number of domestic violence cases out of the legal system (Browne & Herbert, 1997; Lee, 2002; Pence & Shepard, 1999; Ricks, Vaughan, & Dziegielewski, 2002; Santiago, 2002; Wiehe, 1998). If there is possibly a worse number in these statistics, it is that an estimated 15.5 million children live in families where violence has occurred and about 7 million have witnessed severe violence (McDonald et al., 2006). What that kind of problem-solving behavior models for children and begets in adulthood should give you an idea why this type of crisis has been so intractable.

One of the major reasons much domestic violence is not reported is that the medical system fails to do so (Hampton, Vandergriff-Avery, & Kim, 1999; Roberts & Roberts, 2002). The American Medical Association, the American College of Obstetricians and Gynecologists, and the American Nurses Association all recommend counseling and screening for domestic violence (Boes & McDermott, 2002). Using a trauma screen to determine how the physical injury has occurred, researchers found that the single most common cause of a female injury brought to medical attention was abuse. In emergency room settings, an estimated 20 to 35 percent of female patients seek treatment for domestic violence, and in family practices, between 25 and 40 percent of women report abuse. However, only 2 to 10 percent of battered women are commonly identified as such by physicians (Hamberger, 1994). The failure of health care professionals to adequately detect partner violence stems from a fear of offending patients, lack of training and knowledge, inability to cure the problem, lack of time, and lack of insurance coverage (Tilden et al., 1994). This failing should not be too surprising because little emphasis on domestic violence has been given in medical schools or nurses' training (Sassetti, 1993). Compounding the problem are state reporting laws that are not nearly as stringent as child abuse laws in requiring health care professionals to report injuries from suspected partner violence (Chalk & King, 1998, p. 173). However, during the 1990s the American Medical Association started an education campaign for its members and started teaching them how to ask appropriate questions to women who appeared to be battered. More recent data suggest that women are more likely to report abuse if they seek out treatment and are asked appropriate questions in an empathic and supportive manner. The problem is that it is still unclear how many women do not seek out treatment (Walker, 2000, p. 31).

Another culprit in the helping professions is the clergy. Many clerics who deal with family violence have a great deal of difficulty with the issue, and a number were found to place the blame on the woman (Wood & McHugh, 1994). However, other human services workers should not feel smug. Research indicates that they, too, may have biases against and stereotypes about abused women that interfere with and hinder treatment (Ross & Glesson, 1991). But it is noteworthy that although crisis workers are not contacted as often by abused women as other professionals are, they were reported to be the most helpful (Hamilton & Coates, 1993).

Emerging Approaches to Partner Violence

Despite the long history of partner abuse, only since 1974 has there been a consistent and planned systematic approach to the problem. Erin Pizzey's book *Scream Quietly or the Neighbors Will Hear* (1974) was responsible for the start of the first women's shelter in England. Subsequently, in the United States, the National Organization for Women, along with grassroots organizations such as the Massachusetts Coalition of Battered Women Service Groups, has come to the forefront in developing funding sources, shelters, support groups, organizing and training manuals, and legislation for battered women. Such increased public awareness and the efforts of feminist and other citizens' groups resulted in the formation of the National Coalition Against Domestic Violence to promote a national power base for battered women (Capps, 1982). This group has exerted a good deal of social and legislative pressure to combat the problem of domestic violence. The Domestic Abuse

Intervention Project in Duluth, Minnesota, has become internationally known as the Duluth model for its integrated approach to the problem (Pence & Shepard, 1999). The Duluth model has become internationally known because of its massive and sustained effort to get every agency that comes in contact with a battering incident—from 911 dispatch that receives the first call to the last judge, probation officer, or therapist who signs off on the batterer as finished with intervention—involved in a systematic and integrated manner so that no battered person or batterer falls through the cracks (Home of the Duluth Model, 2011).

Thus, over the last 30 years, the country's approach to domestic violence has changed dramatically. First, there has been a shift in police procedures, increased prosecution of partner violence, and enhanced legal protection through tougher protective orders and warrantless arrest. In many cities and states, a police call to a domestic dispute in which battering is involved now results in a mandatory arrest; and if convicted, the batterer is mandated by the court to either participate in counseling and a batterer intervention program (BIP) or go to jail (Goodman & Epstein, 2011; Pence & Shepard, 1999; Shupe, Stacey, & Hazlewood, 1987). Second, as a result of lobbying efforts by activists, state legislatures have enacted protection laws with teeth in them that allow judges to tailor-make orders of protections suited to individual cases (Goodman & Epstein, 2011). Third, countywide coordinated community responses on the order of the Duluth model have been formed (Goodman & Epstein, 2011). Fourth, domestic violence units have been formed in police departments, probation and parole offices, states attorneys' offices, and domestic violence courts, which all coordinate efforts to reduce domestic violence (Chalk & King, 1998, p. 172; Pence & Shepard, 1999).

A growing number of women have entered academia in the past 30 years, particularly in the social sciences. Their research on family violence, gender roles, and male dominance has resulted in social activism that has debunked the "safe haven" notion of the family (Jasinski & Williams, 1998, pp. vi–vii). The Violence Against Women Act of 1994 provided $1.2 billion for the improvement of services and community support for domestic violence victims, the criminal justice system's response to violent crimes against women, safety for women in public transit and public parks, assistance to victims of sexual assault, and support for a variety of educational, health, and database services. This bill was reauthorized in 2000 with an increase of $3.3 billion over 5 years to community services to aid survivors of domestic violence, sexual assault, and stalking. It was reauthorized again in 2005 and has received continuous funding. An overview of its many activities can be found at the website of the Department of Justice's Office of Violence Against Women (www.ovw.usdoj.gov).

Media attention about the severity of the problem has raised public consciousness. Television documentaries, newspaper articles, and media coverage have attracted attention, changed public perspectives, and removed some of the cloak of secrecy from domestic violence. Stories such as those of Francine Hughes (subject of the movie *The Burning Bed*), who suffered prolonged and severe beatings by her husband and who finally killed him by pouring kerosene around his bed and setting it on fire, have had an impact on the courts by challenging legal precedents and assumptions about homicide and self-defense (Edwards, 1989). Indeed, psychologist Lenore Walker's (1989) book *Terrifying Love* is a chilling and eye-opening account of her experiences as an expert witness in murder trials of battering victims who have killed their assailants. The result has been the recognition of a history of abuse called the *battered wife syndrome* (Walker, 2000, pp. 160–161) as a valid part of a legal defense for battered women who kill their husbands (Chalk & King, 1998, pp. 171–172).

Once arrested, batterers are required to go through a variety of different educational programs to teach them not to batter (Geffner & Rosenbaum, 2002; Mederos, 1999; Rosenbaum & Kunkel, 2009; Sonkin & Dutton, 2003). Treating batterers has become a big-time business. For example, as of 2006 there were 450 registered batterer programs (BIPs), serving more than 25,000 batterers in California alone (California State Auditor, 2006). All states now have laws on the books that make IPV a crime and domestic violence courts that may mandate sentences ranging from jail time to BIPs (Rosenbaum & Kunkel, 2009).

Although no national register of BIPs exists, Price and Rosenbaum's (2007) survey found 1,750 programs nationwide. That is undoubtedly low because it didn't take into account many of the private programs that exist in addition to those run by local community agencies. It is safe to say that hundreds of thousands of men and women have now gone through some kind of BIP in the United States. In Tennessee, batterers are required to pay for their group treatment from a certified leader. But the philosophy and treatment approaches of these programs vary a great deal, and by no means is there a common, unitary approach.

In their 10-year follow-up study of family violence in 1985, Straus and Gelles (1986) found an overall decline in husband-to-wife violence of 6.6 percent and a decrease in severe husband-to-wife violence (battering) of 26.6 percent. Overall violence reduction has continued to the present, which would lead one to believe that the massive effort by the judiciary, law enforcement, education, social services, and media attention has started to have an impact. However, what was perplexing in their study was that wife-to-husband violence had increased to a rate higher than that of husband-to-wife violence. Other studies support this increase, particularly when courtship is involved (Carrado et al., 1996; Fiebert & Gonzalez, 1997; Morse, 1995). In fact, a number of more recent reports have found comparable levels of female versus male initiated violence (Bowen, 2009; Dutton, 2007; Hines & Douglas, 2011; Randle & Graham, 2011). Needless to say, the veteran feminists who were in the forefront of the fight to get domestic violence out into the light of public scrutiny have hotly disputed these findings.

Clearly, a great deal of violence by women against men is retaliatory, or in self-defense, as opposed to male batterers' attempts to terrorize, control, or intimidate. Also, when women are the victims of assault, it usually means more serious injury than when the opposite occurs. Furthermore, no research places men in the same systematic victimization status of women who are literally terrorized into attempting to escape the relationship (Kaufman Kantor & Jasinski, 1998, pp. 9–10). The apparent statistical decrease in women reporting domestic violence is puzzling given that the number of shelters for abused women has grown from none in 1975 to more than 2,000 shelters in 2002 (Roberts, 2002), and those shelters are constantly beyond capacity and must turn people away.

Dynamics of Partner Violence
Psychosocial and Cultural Dynamics

The overarching dynamic that has held sway over the battering of women is the belief in male supremacy. This belief is the natural result of a long-term sexist, paternalistic social order that rewards aggressive behavior in men but expects women to be passive and submissive (Benjamin & Walz, 1983, p. 65; Pence & Shepard, 1999). This stereotypical and dated view has produced a volatile mix of personality dynamics between the "traditional" male and the female. The flash point of such a mix occurs when the man who lives the traditional male image of chief breadwinner and director of the family perceives himself as losing power in the conjugal relationship.

The question of power is the fuse that ignites this explosive mixture. In this view, the woman's position is to obey, conciliate, perform traditional domestic duties, and, in general, be subservient. Any attempt to establish herself in her own right is likely to be met with punishment for overstepping her bounds (Benjamin & Walz, 1983, pp. 74–77; Pence & Shepard, 1999). Violence, though, is not something that develops only in families. It involves a complex interplay of social, cultural, and psychological factors, and to say that a patriarchal system alone is responsible for battering would seem to fall far short of the mark (Dutton, 1995, pp. 27–62).

The fact is that a great many men who have patriarchal attitudes go through their entire married lives without assaulting their wives, and the sociopolitical beliefs of abusers don't discriminate them from nonabusers (Hotaling & Sugarman, 1986; Straus & Gelles, 1986). So is there one true theory of the abusive/assaultive personality that leads to partner violence? The answer to that question is a resounding "No!"—although most of the following theories have their rabid supporters who would vehemently disagree with that statement. The following theories encapsulate past and present thinking about the causes of battering.

Attachment/Traumatic Bonding Theory. Disruptions of attachment in early life arouse intense anger, grief, sorrow, and anxiety in the child and diminish the child's ability to form mutual and trusting relationships as an adult. High correlations appear among spousal violence, the number of separation-and-loss events abusers and their families of origin experienced, and the erratic caregiving patterns of batterers' parents. Thus, men whose parents were unreliable, abusive, needy, or otherwise unequal to the task of child rearing may be very sensitive to fears of abandonment and enmeshment. The partner may contribute to these fears by her own fears of abandonment. Each partner creates ways to control the other to avoid being abandoned. One of those ways is through violence. Traumatic bonding may explain why some women stay with or return to their abusive partners (Bowlby, 1980; Brewster, 2002; Sonkin & Dutton, 2003).

Coercive Control. Morgan (1982) used the term *conjugal* or *intimate terrorism* to describe a tactic akin to brainwashing and political terrorism, whereby violence

or the threat of violence is used to break the victim's resistance and bend her to the will of the terrorist (batterer). Typical brainwashing and terrorist tools such as social and physical isolation, torture, sleep deprivation, malnourishment, dictating the use of the victim's time, bondage, false confessions, and denouncing and belittling the victim to significant others are all standard operating procedures of abusers to enhance the victim's dependency on them. Johnson (1995) identifies this type of batterer as indeed a terrorist, representative of the type that women who seek out shelters describe. Women who are battered by these men have more injuries, take more painkillers, have more PTSD symptoms, are attacked more frequently, and are less likely to have the violence stop (Johnson & Leone, 2005). This pathological male is very different from the general population of situational batterers and is extremely dangerous.

Cultural Reinforcement. Sociological theories cover a wide gamut of specific theories that are psychosocially and culturally bound. These theories find the roots of violence in institutions ranging from the culture at large down to the family unit. Societal attitudes about the legitimate use of violence to achieve personal ends have their roots in a tradition of perceived "national interest." As a nation, we promote and glorify the controlled use of aggression for protection, law and order, self-defense, and national interest (Benjamin & Walz, 1983, pp. 64–66). Force is a major resource in maintaining the existing social structure and projecting national presence. This notion has been extended to the family by at least implicit permission of the state. For the state, the family is the basic disciplinary agent—family over individual, male over female, adult over child. Control is direct, continuous, personalized, and an efficient way of keeping intact the past social order of the state (Capps, 1982).

Exchange Theory. Exchange theory (Gelles & Cornell, 1985) is a variant of a learning theory approach. It proposes that batterers hit people because they can (Carden, 1994). As long as the costs for being violent do not outweigh the rewards, violence will invariably be used as a method of control (Hampton, Vandergriff-Avery, & Kim, 1999). Particularly when social control agents such as the police, criminal charges, imprisonment, loss of status, and loss of income are not used as negative sanctions that increase the cost of the behavior, batterers will continue to batter. Gender inequality in physical size, financial resources, and social status allows batterers to become violent without fear of retribution. Although there may be loss of status in the larger society for being a child or wife beater, there are certain subcultures in which aggressive and violent behaviors are proof of being a "real man." Finally, exacting "costs" from a partner to pay for her or his supposed "sins and transgressions" is itself satisfying to the batterer (Gelles & Cornell, 1985, pp. 120–125).

Feminist Theory. Feminist theory views social phenomena as determined by the sexist, patriarchal structure of our society and battering as merely one outcome of a structure that allows rape, incest, prostitution, foot binding, and a host of other sexist restrictions to keep women in servile positions (Schechter, 1982; Stark & Flitcraft, 1988). Feminists believe that women have not achieved the political, economic, and social independence that would empower them to leave abusive relationships (Bograd, 1992; Dobash & Dobash, 1992; Pagelow, 1992). They do not believe that a woman has any culpability in promoting or maintaining a violent relationship because the perpetrator alone commits the act; he alone is morally and legally responsible for it and should be the one to suffer the consequences (Avis, 1992; Bograd, 1992). A strict feminist view categorically separates woman battering from other forms of intrafamily violence, or at the most sees the other forms of family violence as a by-product of how women are brutalized (Okun, 1986). The feminist view also holds that until women are seen as other than subservient, compliant victims, little will change. Feminists criticize the mass media for romanticizing violence, male dominance, and female submissiveness (Dines, 1992; Jarvie, 1991). Feminist theory calls for a complete restructuring of society to eradicate the power differential that males enjoy that allows them to batter.

Intraindividual Theory. There is evidence that psychopathology and neurophysiological disorders may play a greater part in some perpetrators of battering than was previously thought. Personality disorders, attention deficit disorder, psychosis, internal head trauma, and substance abuse have been identified as possible contributing factors that lead to aggression and rage reactions (Browne & Herbert, 1997, p. 61; Dutton, 1994, 1995, pp. 26–29; Jasinski & Williams, 1998, p. 42; Stuart et al., 2006). Both male and female adolescents with psychiatric disorders are at greater risk for becoming involved in abusive adult relationships (Ehrensaft, Moffitt, & Caspi, 2006).

Learned Helplessness/Battered Woman Syndrome. Learning theory approaches operate on the principle that both perpetration and acceptance of physical and psychological abuse are conditioned and learned behavior. A great deal of research indicates a strong relationship between being abused by parents and/or witnessing interparental violence as a child and being violent toward a partner as an adult (Astin et al., 1995; Barnett & Hamberger, 1992; Jouriles & Norwood, 1995). Foremost among these theories is Lenore Walker's (1984, 1989, 2000) theory of learned helplessness, which she adapted from animal studies conducted on random, noncontingent punishment.

Applied to battering in particular, the theory proposes that battered women stay in abusive relationships because they have been conditioned to believe they cannot predict their own safety and that nothing they or anyone else does will alter their terrible circumstances. Over time, through continuous conditioning, a battered woman syndrome emerges that causes the woman to lose hope and feel completely incapable of dealing with the situation (Brewster, 2002).

Walker (1984, 1989, 2000) proposed a number of factors in childhood and adulthood that are building blocks for learned helplessness. Childhood factors include witnessing or experiencing battering, sexual abuse, or molestation, health problems or chronic illness, stereotypical sex roles, and rigid tradition. Such experiences teach the child that external, autocratic, and often whimsical forces dictate outcomes. In adulthood, factors that are instigated by the batterer include an emergent pattern of violence, sexual abuse, jealousy, overpossessiveness, intrusiveness and isolation, threat of harm, observed violence toward other people, animals, or things, and alcohol or drug abuse. Given these conditions, the victim cannot escape the noncontingent punishment and thus loses any effectiveness in being able to control what happens to her (Walker, 2000, pp. 10–12).

The term *helplessness* has caused a great deal of furor from feminists because they see this pejorative term as casting women in a victim role with few resources or little empowerment. However, according to Walker (1989), women are not helpless in the standard sense of the term. What learned helplessness means is that battered women choose behavioral responses that have the highest predictability of causing them the least harm in the known situation (pp. 50–52), or what Gondolf and Fisher (1988) call the survivor hypothesis, wherein women become very active and resourceful in protecting themselves and their children (Browne, 1997). Because of the extreme and often lethal violence that occurs when these women attempt to leave, and the lack of social support for making any attempt, it is understandable that a "Better the devil I know!" philosophy predominates for many abused women.

Masochism. Psychoanalytic theory, which has held masochism to be the primary motivating factor in abusive relationships, is now mostly obsolete in the therapeutic community. There is no empirical research to substantiate the notion that erotic enjoyment of pain through battering is a trait found in abused women (Okun, 1986; Stark & Flitcraft, 1988). From a feminist point of view, this theory held sway for a long time because the male-dominated field of psychiatry found it a convenient pigeonhole for a troublesome problem. Until interest in the problem was generated in the 1970s, little research was presented to refute the idea.

Nested Ecological Theory. Because no single factor theory has effectively explained the battering phenomenon, an integrated, multifactor approach may be the best way to understand the complexities of battering (Brewster, 2002). Dutton (1985, 1995) proposed an ecological theory that integrates many of the foregoing theories. Four layers of variables operate within the ecosystem. First is a core of individual experience composed of intrapersonal psychological factors such as shame, denial, and hostility. Second is a family system layer, in which the individual experiences such negative actions as abandonment, neglect, and abuse. Third is a community/peer layer, which inculcates fundamental religious training, alcohol and drug use, and rigid gender role socialization. Finally, in a larger societal context, the individual is exposed to sociopolitical gender inequities, media portrayal of subjugation and violence against women, and racial/ethnic prejudices. As a result, it is not just one but many factors that operate within the individual, in interpersonal relationships, and throughout the larger social environment that are communicated and synthesized to make battering a viable option (Hampton, Vandergriff-Avery, & Kim, 1999).

Psychological Entrapment. Psychological entrapment proposes that the woman does not leave the relationship because she feels she has too much time, energy, and emotion invested in it (Brewster, 2002), or she would feel shame if her terrible secret were found out (Buchbinder & Eisikovits, 2003). She engages in

wishful thinking that some miracle will occur or that she can somehow change the significant other and a nonviolent, intimate, and loving relationship will emerge. For some women, the shame of their battering and the failed relationship is so great that they will do anything to keep it from public view.

Sociobiology. Sociobiology proposes that evolutionary adaptation requires aggression for survival. Thus, there is the inherited tendency to aggress against someone who threatens the chances of survival and, deductively, procreation of the species. If the foregoing is true, then it would be reasonable to expect that males would aggress against other real or imagined males who were trying to take away the female. The question then arises, Why would the male assault the object he wishes to possess instead of other intruding males? The sociobiologists have no clear answer to this question (Dutton, 1995, pp. 29–34).

Stockholm Syndrome. (For a complete description of this syndrome, see Chapter 15, Crisis/Hostage Negotiation.) Akin to being held hostage, the woman is completely isolated and subjugated by her abuser, and her survival is entirely dependent on his whims, desires, or purposes. Because she is shown occasional kindness and is completely isolated from other support systems, she develops a strong emotional bond with the abuser (Brewster, 2002).

System Theory. System theory posits that battering is not attributable to the standard victim–abuser dichotomy. Rather, *conjugal violence* and *battering relationship* are more appropriate terms to depict battering as part of a violence-prone system. The violence is a maladaptive but efficient way to keep the system in homeostasis. Through learning history and rigidly polarized roles for both parties, the system is able to maintain itself (Wiehe, 1998, pp. 87–90).

Although each of the preceding theoretical stances has merit, to this point none has proven able to completely explain the phenomenon of battering. Certainly, there is much to be said for a feminist perspective couched in paternalistic sociocultural terms. If it had not been for the feminist movement's willingness to take on battering as a social issue, it would probably still be "behind drawn shades." There is also clear evidence that at least one factor contributing to our bulging prison population is that certain people will attempt to get away with anything they can with little regard for the cost to others, as long as they believe they can escape the consequences of their actions. Similarly, evidence exists that legions of people with personality disorders would think nothing of manipulating anyone in any manner to satisfy their insatiable narcissistic or dependency needs. There is also clear evidence from a national perspective that Teddy Roosevelt's admonition "Speak softly and carry a big stick!" is extremely effective and has trickled down to the family unit. It doesn't take a doctorate in sociology to figure out that ecological and cultural variations may have profound effects on the kind and incidence of partner violence. Finally, it is hard to argue against the contention that the founding fathers' belief that "a man's home is his castle" has much to do with society's refusal to intervene in the sacrosanct realm of the home.

Psychological Factors

Psychologically, both parties to a battering situation may have certain identifiable characteristics. You should clearly understand that these are not just separate and individual ingredients, but complex forces that interrelate with one another and thus increase the odds of IPV. As an example, Bornstein (2006) has provided an in-depth examination of how emotional dependency in males and economic dependency in females, when combined, become an extremely dangerous mix that can lead to violence.

Men in a battering relationship may:[*]

1. Demonstrate excessive dependency and possessiveness toward their women—although they deny it.
2. Be unable to express any emotion except anger and generally have poor communication skills where emotional issues are concerned.
3. Have unrealistic expectations of their spouses and idealize marriage or the relationship far beyond what realistically may be expected.
4. Have a lack of self-control and, paradoxically, set up rigid family boundaries for everyone else.
5. Be alcohol or drug abusers.
6. Have been abused as children or saw their mothers abused.
7. Deny and minimize problems, particularly battering, that they generate in families.

8. Emotionally cycle from hostility, aggressiveness, and cruelty when they do not get their way, to charm, manipulation, and seductiveness when they do.
9. Be characterized as jealous, denying, impulsive, self-deprecating, depressive, demanding, aggressive, and violent.
10. Feel a lack of comparative power to the woman in economic status, decision making, and communication skills.

Women in a battering relationship may:[†]

1. Have a lack of self-esteem as a result of being told over and over that they are stupid, incompetent, and otherwise inadequate.
2. Experience a lack of control and little confidence in their ability to take any meaningful steps to improve their marriage.
3. Have experienced a history of abuse that leads them to accept their role as victim, or saw their mothers abused and accepted it as their lot.
4. Be so ashamed that they hide their physical and emotional wounds and become socially and emotionally isolated.
5. Lack personal, physical, educational, and financial resources that would allow them to get out of the battering situation.
6. Be extremely dependent and willing to suffer grievous insult and injury to have their needs met.
7. Have an idealized view of what a relationship should be and somehow feel they can "fix" or "change" the man.
8. Not have good communication skills, particularly in regard to asserting their rights and feelings.
9. Have learned stereotyped sex roles and thus feel guilty if they do not adhere to a rigid patriarchal system.
10. Be unable to differentiate between sex and love and believe that love is manifested through intense sexual relationships.

In one way or another, all the concepts just enumerated have to do with power, and all point back to this basic encultured dynamic. If men acted on impulse or some other drive, they would beat up their bosses,

---

[*]This list was derived from Babcock et al., 1993; Barnett et al., 1980; Bornstein, 2006; Ehrensaft et al., 2003; Finkelhor et al., 1983; Gelles & Cornell, 1985; Okun, 1986; Schumacher, Fals-Stewart, & Leonard, 2003; Shupe, Stacey, & Hazlewood, 1987; Walker, 1984, 1989, 2000.

[†]This list was derived from Benjamin & Walz, 1983; Bornstein, 2006; Ehrensaft et al., 2003; Finkelhor et al., 1983; Gelles & Cornell, 1985; Hage, 2006; Ibrahim & Herr, 1987; Okun, 1986; Roberts, 2002; Walker, 1984, 1989, 2000.

secretaries, friends, or neighbors as often as they do their mates and children. Although some sociopaths might fit this category of indiscriminate violence, they are in the minority (Gondolf, 1985; Hastings & Hamberger, 1988; Holtzworth-Munroe & Stuart, 1994). Only in a conjugal relationship do many men generally believe in and exercise their ability to coerce, abuse, and beat women and children (Hart, 1980).

Stressors

If power is the fuse, then stress is the match that lights the fuse. As the idealized image of the relationship breaks down and environmental stresses build up, couples become engaged in an ever-increasing spiral of violent interaction (Barnett et al., 1980). Although they are not generic to all battering, a list of factors that seem to appear over and over in domestic violence follow (Barnett et al., 1980, pp. 7–9; Benjamin & Walz, 1983; Bograd, 2005; Brown, James, & Taylor, 2010; Finkelhor et al., 1983; Gelles & Cornell, 1985; Halbsgut, 2011; Jasinski & Williams, 1998; Koverola & Panchanadeswaran, 2004; Okun, 1986; Parker et al., 1993; Stuart et al., 2006; Walker, 1984, p. 51). These factors may be introduced by the batterer to control the situation, may occur as a product of the relationship itself, or may be environmentally introduced from outside the relationship.

1. *Geographic isolation.* Because of geographic location, the victim has no friends nearby who can provide a support system. A farm woman who cannot drive is an example of the worst case—literally being marooned and held captive by an abusive husband.
2. *Social isolation.* Because of extreme emotional dependence, the woman expects all needs to be met by her partner and has no significant others to turn to when she is assaulted.
3. *Economic stress.* When a woman is unemployed or underemployed, has inadequate housing, is pressured by creditors, and cannot feed and clothe her children by herself, she becomes human chattel to her abusive partner.
4. *Medical problems.* Long-term, chronic medical problems for either spouse or children exact tremendous financial and emotional costs.
5. *Inadequate parenting skills.* A lack of knowledge of parenting skills and conflict over parental roles can lead to situations that start as minor disciplinary problems and escalate into violence in the family.

6. *Pregnancy.* Ranging from heralding an unwanted child through creating anxiety over providing for the new baby to arousing jealousy over a wife's attention to a newborn, pregnancy is an especially acute crisis point for potential abuse.
7. *Family dysfunction.* A veritable kaleidoscope of problems causes dysfunction in the family. Some of these problems are related to age and number of children, presence of stepchildren, loyalty conflicts, death, desertion, and career change.
8. *Alcohol and drug abuse.* Chemical dependence serious enough to cause economic chaos and severe emotional disturbance characterizes addictive families and has spin-offs that commonly include spouse abuse. The insidious problem with alcohol and drugs is that they are often used as an excuse for behavior (battering) that is normally prohibited by societal norms and standards. Interestingly, there appears to be a significant relationship, at least in Australia, between the number and proximity of liquor stores and the incidence of domestic violence (Livingston, 2011).
9. *Educational and/or vocational disparity.* When a female in a relationship has higher educational attainment or higher vocational status than the male, this may raise questions of adequacy and responsibility with both parties. Furthermore, if the man is unemployed and the woman is employed, the man has a great deal of time to brood on his inability to function as the head of household, which males already suffering from feelings of inadequacy may find extremely demeaning. The role of occupational therapy in domestic violence has become important enough that a book has been devoted to that connection (Helfrich, 2001).
10. *Age.* One of the most consistent risk factors of battering is age. Approximately 20 percent of men in the age range of 18 to 25 and 17 percent of men in the age range of 26 to 35 have committed at least one act of violence in the past year.
11. *Disenfranchisement.* Seeking help from the authorities for battering may be very aversive to persons of color, same-sex orientation, minority status, immigrant status, and other marginalized groups because of their previous negative experiences or fear of retribution from the system.
12. *Rejection.* The batterer's perception of rejection is an antecedent to abuse. Men with a family of origin where rejection occurred become extremely

sensitive to any behavior construed as rejection. Their response is likely to be aggressive.

13. *Threat to masculinity.* Some men who perceive themselves as less masculine see their use of battering as affirming their masculinity in comparison to males who have good self-concepts who do not batter.

Myths About Battering

The following myths encapsulate numerous arguments used by those who would submerge, camouflage, and diminish battering (Gelles & Cornell, 1985; Hampton, Vandergriff-Avery, & Kim, 1999; Massachusetts Coalition of Battered Women Service Groups, 1981; Okun, 1986; Roberts, 2002; Stark & Flitcraft, 1988; Straus, Gelles, & Steinmetz, 1980; Weitzman, 2000).

1. *"Battered women overstate the case."* Any person who has contusions, lacerations, and broken bones is not overstating anything. In any other instance, such outcomes are referred to as *assault and battery.*

2. *"Battered women provoke the beating."* Although some women may be classified as the stereotypical "nag," there can certainly be many significant others in a man's life who fit into the "nag" category who are not beaten.

3. *"Battered women are masochists."* If such women did have masochistic tendencies, they would find a variety of ways to suffer pain, not just an abusive mate.

4. *"Battering is a private, family matter."* When beaten women are disenfranchised from their homes and the children of battering relationships learn the pathological roles a battering father models, battering transcends the home and becomes society's problem. All 50 states now have warrantless arrest policies for battering. Battering is anything but private.

5. *"Alcohol abuse is the prime reason for wife abuse."* Although alcohol plays a part in many cases of abuse and is present and used by both men and women who engage in violent relationships, it may be only an excuse for, and not the cause of, violent behavior. There are many violent relationships where alcohol is not present.

6. *"Battering occurs only in problem families."* The dynamic representation of stress factors that assail families shows that any family, at any given point, may be classified as "problem."

7. *"Only low-income and working-class families experience violence."* Members of those socioeconomic classes do come to the attention of the police and welfare agencies to a much greater degree than middle- or upper-class members, but statistics from shelters, police calls, and crisis line calls indicate that battering has no class boundaries.

8. *"The battering cannot be that bad or she would not stay."* The host of personal factors that tie a woman to the relationship militate heavily against simply picking up and leaving.

9. *"A husband has patriarchal rights."* What a man does in his own family is not his own business when the emotional overflow of what he does spills over into the community. No amount or kind of justification from the Bible or any other authority—be it person, institution, or book—can excuse spouse abuse.

10. *"The beaten spouse exaggerates the problem to exact revenge."* Reporting a beating—whether committed by a total stranger or one's spouse—is no exaggeration. If revenge were the motive, there would be a host of ways of going about it that would be far less traumatic than calling or showing up at an abuse shelter.

11. *"Women are too sensitive, especially when they are pregnant."* If a person is too sensitive because she objects to being kicked in the stomach or vagina, thrown down a flight of stairs, or hit in the face with a lamp, then we would suppose that everyone is overly sensitive.

12. *"Battering is rare."* The statistics reported in this chapter clearly indicate otherwise. Family violence is endemic in society.

13. *"Battering is confined to mentally disturbed or 'sick' people."* It appears that less than 10 percent of family violence is caused by mental illness. Although continued physical and psychological abuse may cause many victims to suffer serious emotional distress and posttraumatic stress disorder, they did not enter the relationship "sick." Furthermore, most perpetrators are not mentally ill by any *DSM-IV-TR* definition.

14. *"Violence and love cannot coexist."* Strange as it may seem, members of violent families may still love one another. This paradoxical aspect is most problematic because children in such families grow up believing you hit the people you love.

15. *"Elder abuse between intimates is neither prevalent nor dangerous."* Because of the debilitating factors

that come with aging, the potential for physical abuse becomes greater and more lethal as partners become more frustrated, angry, and depressed over the declining physical and mental capabilities of both themselves and their partners.

Profiling the Batterer

Researchers have examined multiple personality and behavioral typologies of batterers. Dutton (1995), Fowler and Western (2011), Gondolf (1985), Hastings and Hamberger (1988), Holtzworth-Munroe and associates (1994, 1999, 2003), and Saunders (1992) have all developed typologies of batterers based on clusters of demographic, personality, and abuse variables. Holtzworth-Munroe and Stuart (1994) and Holtzworth-Munroe and associates (1999, 2003) have compiled three major groupings—family only, dysphoric (anxious)/borderline, and generally violent/antisocial—and a fourth subgroup, low-level antisocial. Characteristics of the *family only batterer* include high dependency, impulsivity, poor communication skills, and family-of-origin violence. The *dysphoric/borderline* has a history of parental rejection and child abuse, delinquent acts, poor communication and social skills, violence-as-a-solution ideation, extreme fears of abandonment, and low remorse. The *low-level antisocial* has antisocial behavior and moderate levels of domestic and general violence. Fowler and Western's (2011) typologies conform closely to the foregoing types with psychopathic, hostile/controlling, and borderline/dependent. The *generally violent/antisocial batterer* has all the foregoing characteristics, but to a much more profound degree and probably falls into what Jasinski and Williams (1998, p. 1) call the *terroristic* batterer. Such people are extremely aggressive and impulsive, and view violence as appropriate to any provocation inside or outside the home.

The family only batterers are the largest group, and their behavior is consistent with Walker's (1979) cycle of violence. Its members are likely to be contrite and apologetic after battering incidents. Gondolf (1985) reports this group type to be most prevalent, with a 52 percent occurrence rate. The dysphoric/borderline and antisocial types are typical of how women who flee to shelters describe their batterers. They are the most dangerous and according to Gondolf make up about 41 percent and 7 percent of batterers, respectively. Differences in these groups in regard to their level of violence appear to remain somewhat stable over time, and they do not appear to move from one group to the other

(Cavanaugh & Gelles, 2005). Thankfully, not all marital violence escalates nor does it evolve to more dangerous personality types (Holtzworth-Munroe et al., 2003).

There is a good deal of debate over the use of profiling because of the diversity of typologies in battering populations. However, Gibbons, Collins, and Reid (2011) used the Millon Clinical Multiaxial Inventory with a sample of 177 batterers and found that 54 percent fell into a personality disorder category and 37 percent could be characterized as having severe pathology. Taking the foregoing typologies together with an assessment device like the Millon, consider that Eke and associates (2011) found that of their sample of men who had murdered or attempted to murder an intimate partner, 42 percent had previously committed crimes, 18 percent had a psychiatric history, and 15 percent had both. These individuals were given the Ontario Domestic Risk Assault Risk Assessment. Their mean score was in the 80th percentile of "at risk" for domestic violence. The researchers concluded that the use of validated risk assessment data for batterers and indicators of pathology and or criminal behavior would increase the ability to predict who would violently assault an intimate partner and hopefully aid in intervention and prevention of homicidal acts toward intimate partners. We believe some fine-tuning of these instruments, applied to all batterers, would be of some worth in determining their degree of potential lethality and guiding judicial disposition as to what kind of intervention they should receive.

The Cycle of Violence

Barnett and associates (1980) schematically represented the phases leading to the explosion of violence in the family. Walker's (1984) cycle theory of violence— (1) tension building, (2) battering and abuse, (3) contrition and loving respite—closely parallels these phases, and her research supports the theory (p. 95).

> *Phase I. Tranquility prevails.* The relationship may have been characterized as calm to this point, with no previous violent incidents, or a period of calm may follow an earlier violent episode.
>
> *Phase II. Tension starts to build.* A variety of stresses impinge on the relationship. They may come in combination or singly from the common group already mentioned. However, there is no reduction of tension, and the situation grows more strained.
>
> *Phase III. A violent episode occurs.* The episode may range from harsh words to a severe beating. At

this phase, communication has broken down, and the situation is out of control.

Phase IV. The relationship takes on crisis proportions. A variety of options becomes available.

    A. The abuser becomes remorseful and asks forgiveness. Sooner or later the victim forgives the abuser, and calm is restored.

    B. The abuser is not remorseful and feels his control over the situation has been established. The victim gives in and relinquishes control, and calm is restored.

    C. The victim takes new action. Within this option are two possibilities: the abuser negotiates the situation, and, given that the negotiation is agreeable to the victim, calm is restored; or the abuser rejects the new action and a crisis state continues.

It is at this last point, in which no possibility of resolution exists, that the victim is most likely to seek help by contacting an abuse center. Walker found that as the battering continues, the loving contrition phase diminishes and battering becomes more prevalent (2000, p. 128). If effective assessment and intervention do not occur when the violence emerges (Phase III), the likelihood that the violence will recur and will be of greater intensity is dramatically increased (Barnett et al., 1980, p. 34). Dutton (1995, pp. 126–139) has demonstrated that this cycle closely fits that of the borderline personality disorder type of abuser.

Not all battering relationships fit the cycle of violence. Battering between partners may be a once-in-a-lifetime affair. But many women have reported being constantly terrorized and assaulted with no intermittent periods of relief (Dutton & Starzomski, 1993). These are most probably the victims of the antisocial, psychopathic type of batterer, who sees little need for contrition or remorse in his dealing with a partner—or anybody else, for that matter.

Realities for Abused Women

Why, then, do women stay in an abusive relationship? For those who have no experience with violence in a relationship, it is an easy thing to say, "Throw the bum out!" or "I wouldn't tolerate that. I'd call the cops and have him arrested!" or "Forget you, nobody does that to me, I'm leaving!" In actuality, most women who are in battering relationships do leave, and this in itself is a courageous act because it is one of the most dangerous things a woman can do. The batterer tends to do

poorly on his own and would often rather kill or die than be separated from the woman, because he is more terrified of abandonment than violence or punishment (Walker, 1989, p. 65). It is remarkable that a number of women do leave, given their clear understanding that lives hang in the balance—their own, those of their children, and even the batterer's.

The same question could be asked of men. Why do they stay? Henning and Connor-Smith (2011) examined more than 1,000 men who had been adjudicated for battering their partners. More than half said they were planning on staying in the relationship. Their reasons included being older, caring about their children, attributing less blame to the female for the alleged offenses and their arrest, and coming from a family where they saw the same thing as children and regretted modeling their parents' assaultive behavior. Ominously, the researchers also found that some men who were continuing the relationship had low relationship satisfaction predictors: having children, expressing hostile attitudes toward women, being jealous, blaming the victim for the arrest, and describing the victim as being aggressive.

Most women leave a battering relationship an average of three to six times, but do so with varying degrees of permanency (Dobash & Dobash, 1979; Walker, 1979). The following reasons for staying in the relationship have been gleaned from a number of researchers (Benjamin & Walz, 1983; Bograd, 2005; Koverola & Panchanadeswaran, 2004; Okun, 1986; Pagelow, 1981; Walker, 1979, 1984, 1989, 2000), and these realities have nothing to do with the myths listed previously.

1. The woman has a fear of reprisal or of aggravating the attacks even more.
2. Even though the situation may be intolerable for the woman, her children do have food, clothing, and shelter.
3. The woman would suffer shame, embarrassment, humiliation, and even ridicule if her secret got out.
4. Her self-concept is so strongly dependent on the relationship and perceived social approval that leaving would be very destructive to her.
5. Early affection and prior love in the relationship persist and, by staying, the woman hopes to salvage them.
6. If financially well off, the woman is unable to forgo a reduction in her financial freedom.
7. In the cyclic nature of abuse, her mate may not be terrible 24 hours a day, 7 days a week. The victim

may tend to forget the batterings and remember only the good times.

8. Early role models of an abusive parent may lead her to believe that relationships exist in no other way.

9. The woman may hold religious values that strongly militate against separation, divorce, or anything less than filial subjugation to the man's wishes.

10. The woman may be undereducated, have small children to raise, and have no job skills.

11. She may be kept so socially, physically, geographically, and financially isolated that she has no resources of any kind to help her get out.

12. She may be so badly injured that she is unable physically to leave.

13. She may believe the man's promise to reform.

14. She may be concerned for children who are still at home.

15. Love or sorrow at the mate's professed inability to exist without her may impel her to stay.

16. Because of previous negative experiences with the authorities, she may believe she has no options.

17. Due to language barriers or immigration status, she may be unable to communicate her abuse, or she may be afraid to seek help.

Secondary victimization may result by labeling battered women as hysterical, depressed, schizophrenic, alcoholic, or child neglecters and abusers. Such labeling may provide professionals with "reasons" to do things to battered women ranging from overmedication with psychotropic drugs to sending them to jail and removing their children from the home. Any one of the revictimizations by well-meaning or not-so-well-meaning institutions undermines assertiveness and reinforces submissiveness and compliance, which in turn increases vulnerability to abuse (Stark & Flitcraft, 1988; Walker, 1989). It is little wonder that a woman making her first call to an abuse center may be taking only an initial step in a series that sometimes goes on for years before she can make a complete break from the battering relationship.

Intervention Strategies

In the past 35 years the raising of consciousness that domestic violence is epidemic and that it extracts tremendous financial and emotional costs from society has caused an exponential rise in attempts at intervention. To that end, intervention strategies for battering

are different from other types of crises, because they target both victim and victimizer.

Assessment

Assessment in battering and domestic violence is complex and is subject to controversy and many unanswered questions in regard to its precursors, onset, and outcomes for both victims and victimizers. Assessment is also problematic because of the transcrisis nature of battering. Both batterers and those who are battered do not present themselves in a "steady state" that is amenable to stable and consistent measurement.

Personality Measures. Assessment of battered women by personality measures is somewhat confounding and contradictory to what one might logically expect. One never really knows whether the personality factors found in battered women were present before they were battered or are the result of the victimization (Gelles & Cornell, 1985, p. 71). However, Walker (1989, p. 105) reports that as the battering progressively becomes worse, Minnesota Multiphasic Personality Inventory (MMPI) profiles change notably.

The question arises, Are there particular attributes, traits, or psychological profiles that will indicate those women who are potential victims of batterers? In an extensive review of characteristics of battered women, Hotaling and Sugarman (1986) found only one characteristic—having witnessed or been a victim of personal violence as a child—as a consistent characteristic. When they reviewed the responses of 699 women who participated in the first National Violence Study, the researchers could not find even that characteristic (Hotaling & Sugarman, 1990). Thus, there appears to be little empirical evidence that there are any consistent predisposing factors that predict who will and who will not become a victim of abuse.

The Attitude Towards Women Scale (Spence & Helmreich, 1972) measures the traditionality of a woman's attitude about her role as well as her perception of significant others' views of women. Walker found that battered women viewed their father's perception of a woman's role much more traditionally than did a nonbattered control group (2000, p. 105).

The Battered Woman Scale (Schwartz & Mattley, 1993) is used to measure traits that arise as a result of experiences in battering relationships. Overall, battered women present many of the symptoms of posttraumatic stress disorder and can be placed for diagnostic purposes within the PTSD category of the *DSM-IV-TR* (American Psychiatric Association, 2000; Astin, Lawrence, & Foy, 1993). Weaver (1998) found in her study of women who had been either sexually or physically abused as children, raped as adults, or battered that only battering was a common marker for PTSD. Thompson and associates (1999) found that suicide, PTSD symptomology, and physical partner abuse go hand in hand. Women incarcerated for killing or seriously assaulting their partners also show increased levels of PTSD symptomology (Hattendorf, Ottens, & Lomax, 1999; O'Keefe, 1998). Indeed, Walker (1989, pp. 48–49) proposes the battered woman syndrome as a subcategory of PTSD. Therefore, if PTSD symptoms are present, then partner violence should always be suspected.

Clinical Interview.   Probably the best assessment device for partner abuse is a clinical interview. Any family history taking should include questions about hitting, threats, controlling, destruction of property or pets, forced sex, alcohol and drug use, and the partner's hypervigilance and paranoia about the client's actions (Jasinski & Williams, 1998, p. 37).

Walker (1984, p. 122) also has one major rule of assessment that supersedes all others and to which your author strongly subscribes: *When a woman calls or comes in to report a battering, believe her and start intervention immediately.* It is a safe bet that whenever a battered woman seeks help, she is not carrying out the act as some impetuous, hysterical, spur-of-the-moment way to get back at her mate. Battered women refer themselves only after their problems have become exceedingly serious.

Walker (1984, p. 26) found that only 14 percent of battered women surveyed would seek help after a first incident, 22 percent would seek help after a second incident, and 49 percent would seek help only after a series of incidents had taken place. Given the length of time that passes and the degree of severity of the crisis that is typically reached before help is sought, triage assessment of the battered woman should look first and foremost to her safety and the safety of significant others, such as her children. We can assume that a battered woman making an initial call to a crisis line will be at the extremely high end of the assessment scale. She will be behaviorally out of control because of the beating she has just had. She will be affectively out of control because of the trauma she has just suffered and the threat of more to come. Cognitively, she may be just

holding together and may not be far from dissociating from the terrible reality of her situation.

Sadly, many in the helping professions still confuse the effects of domestic abuse with symptoms of other diagnoses. It is extremely important to be aware of these masking symptoms. Compared to women who are not abused, battered women are 5 times more likely to attempt suicide, 15 times more likely to abuse alcohol, 9 times more likely to abuse drugs, 6 times more likely to report child abuse, and 3 times more likely to be diagnosed as psychotic or depressed. It is little wonder that these women experience low self-esteem (Aguilar & Nightingale, 1994).

Crisis workers typically encounter battering victims in the following four settings: in hospital emergency rooms and other medical care settings, on telephone crisis lines, in police follow-up operations on domestic violence calls at crisis centers, and at shelters (discussed later in this chapter). The operational strategy in all of these settings should be twofold. First and foremost: Ask! Ask if the person has been battered, even if the presenting problem appears to have little to do with battering. Chang and associates (2005) advise that workers give a reason for why they are asking about IPV, to reduce women's suspicions and minimize stigma, and that they provide information, support, safety, and access to resources whether or not the woman discloses IPV. By doing so, workers are not seen as trying to diagnose a pathological condition, but communicate compassion, provide valuable information, and open the door for women to self-disclose IPV and consider seeking services.

That show of concern creates increased levels of trust when questions about battering are asked in an empathic manner, confidentiality is discussed, and nonjudgmental and supportive responses and concern for the person's safety are made with offers to provide help, even if IPV is not the basic issue that brings the woman into counseling (Battaglia, Finley, & Liebschutz, 2003). The smorgasbord of symptoms presented in this chapter all come out of battering. While there may be other reasons, one of the biggest mistakes a worker can make is to not empathically query a person about battering and validating their experiences (Day, 2009; Spangaro, Zwi, & Poulus, 2011). When a woman is validated by an external source that she is being battered and that it is unacceptable, that act is a major contributor to her taking action to remove herself from the battering (Day, 2009). Congruent with validation is her sense of support from community resources in providing her with information and supporting her in making the myriad decisions that range from career and geographic moves to religious and moral qualms she has over leaving (McLeod, Hays, & Chang, 2010).

Medical Settings. Contrary to recommendation after recommendation by a variety of medical groups, including the surgeon general of the United States, abuse assessment is still not routine in hospital ERs, maternity wards, obstetrics, and family practices (Boes & McDermott, 2002). Many battered women will not acknowledge abuse no matter how empathic and supportive the medical worker is. Therefore, when physical abuse is suspected, the worker should state that this is just a routine part of any medical examination and that the supportive service information the woman is about to get is also routinely provided. In that way, the woman is given control of the situation, is given support by the worker, and her autonomy is respected (Hamberger, 1994). No one else should be present in the interview for the sake of the patient's safety. The worker needs to ask specific and direct questions while walking a tightrope of not being confrontational or antagonistic.

The following questions are abridged from Snyder's (1994) and Hamberger's (1994) protocols for hospital emergency room staff.

CW: Lots of times people get into arguments, and they get physical with one another. I'm wondering if some of your bruises occurred that way? When you and your husband or boyfriend argue, does he get angry? Do you feel afraid? I'm wondering if he ever loses his temper with the children, and when you step in he loses it with you and maybe winds up hitting you. How does he act with you if he's been drinking or using drugs? Sometimes when people get jealous they overreact and get physical. Did this happen with him? Have you ever been with someone who tried to really control you by hitting you or threatening to hurt you? Are you in one of those relationships now?

By raising the issue of arguing, the worker normalizes the situation and opens the door for the client to talk about the reasons that brought her to the medical facility. By asking about her fears, the worker validates her affective and cognitive bases regarding the situation. These and other questions move from general relationship issues to what Hamberger (1994) calls "funneling" to more behavioral specifics about the abuse, such as number and severity of incidents, types of weapons used, and who did the battering.

Juanita: Well . . . I sorta got hit with a broom handle.

CW: (*empathically but assertively*) A broom handle has to be attached to somebody's hand. Whose hand was it? Is he the man who brought you here?

Specific information about what she can do and what the hospital can do should be given if the patient admits she has been physically abused. Medical staff should be well acquainted with local and state laws governing abuse so they can know what legal obligations they have and what can be done to keep the woman safe. Very specific step-by-step protocols should be formulated and made available to all staff, along with in-service education on domestic violence and its signs. Brasseur (1994) abstracted a typical protocol from Chicago's Rush–Presbyterian–St. Luke's Medical Center to be followed once a battered woman has been identified:

1. Assign a primary nurse.
2. Notify appropriate support services within the hospital.
3. Give a complete physical exam, along with a neurological exam and x-rays.
4. Document statements about who caused the injuries.
5. Make a body map of old and new injuries.
6. Depending on the jurisdiction, make a call to the police, identify the assailant, and have him arrested, if possible.
7. Take photographs of the victim's injuries.
8. Inform the patient of her right to access her medical files and how to do it.
9. Discuss with the woman a posthospital plan that will include shelter or other referral, safety plans if she is not leaving the abusive situation, and community support services.

When a protocol such as the foregoing is followed, identification rates of victims of partner violence go up (McLeer & Anwar, 1989; Olson et al., 1996; Tilden & Shepard, 1987).

Crisis Lines. Of all the dilemmas a crisis telephone worker faces, battering is one of the worst. Women may present emotions that range from icily detached to hysterical to white-hot anger. No matter what the woman's emotional response, the worker's job is to try to help the woman cope with the immediate situation (Roberts & Roberts, 2002). That immediate situation may include the batterer being present while the woman makes the call. The woman may call a crisis line instead of the police in hopes that the police will not have to become involved but the publication of the abuse to an outside agency will make the batterer stop.

At times the woman may ask the worker to talk to the batterer. In almost all cases that is not a wise choice. The woman should be asked if she is in danger and needs police assistance. The focus is on the caller and the caller's safety, not attempting to defuse the batterer. If the batterer truly wants to be defused, then he may call the crisis line. Although the threat of further injury or death to the woman may be extremely high, unless the crisis worker feels danger is imminent and can get the woman to give her name and address so that a 911 call can be made, the best the crisis worker can do is offer short-term assistance to help ease physical pain and calm the emotional state of the client. Duty to warn certainly takes precedence over confidentiality, but deciding whether the danger is sufficiently imminent and lethal to necessitate a call to the police is tricky and has future ramifications. Even then the crisis worker may have raging internal debates about what to do. If the client is helped to a safe place, will that only enrage her mate even more? Is the woman really ready to make such a move? What assets does the battered woman have so that she can leave? What are her debits? That is why the worker should carefully go over each area, making sure that all pertinent information and all possibilities of available action have been carefully considered. No other type of crisis presents as critical a need for comprehensive yet fast assessment.

It is also worth remembering that if the worker calls back a week later, the client may be going through a "honeymoon phase" and may seem not to have a care in the world, only to turn around later at the next battering and beseech the crisis worker to help her. These situations, oscillating from extreme need one day to little if any need the next, can make workers cynical and uncaring if they do not carefully manage their stress levels. Yet such ambivalence is more typical than not as clients slowly come to grips with the risks and realities of leaving the situation or quite possibly facing death there.

Components of Intervention

As a call comes in to the abuse center and the crisis worker picks up the phone, the assessment process begins with active listening. The crisis worker immediately has to be concerned with a variety of roles. The worker must be not only a good listener but also supportive, facilitative, and concerned with the caller's safety and must act as an advocate (Barnett et al., 1980, p. 44).

Listening. Facilitative listening and responding are crucial. The victim must know that the crisis worker understands and accepts her present situation in a nonjudgmental, non-value-laden way. Only then will the battered woman be able to open up and share her feelings about her predicament (Heppner, 1978). The crisis worker also immediately reflects that she understands the difficulty and urgency of the situation by positively reinforcing the battered woman for calling and taking a first step toward resolving her problem.

CW: You did the right thing by calling. No matter how bad it seems and what terrible things have happened, you've made a big step on the road to straightening it out. We're here to help, and we'll stick with it as long as it takes.

Juanita: I . . . I . . . don't know. It's gone on so long. I feel so ashamed. I don't know what to do! It's so confusing.

CW: I understand how you feel and how difficult it was to make this call. The hurt, the fear, the uncertainty of it all. So start anywhere you want. We won't do anything unless *you* decide it's best for you. Right now, I want to listen to what you have to say. I'll listen for as long as it takes, so take your time and tell me what's happened.

Supporting. The caller is given both explicit and implicit permission to ventilate. The free flow of the victim's anger, hurt, fear, guilt, and other debilitating feelings may take from a few minutes to 2 hours to an extended period of months. Supportiveness means empathizing but not sympathizing with the victim. A sense of lack of social support is one of the major factors for battered women (Perrin et al., 1996), and this lack may be particularly severe for immigrants with different cultural backgrounds (Sev'er, 1997, pp. 3–5). Many victims are only partially mobile, and any action steps they take may be months away from happening. Thus, supporting a victim does not mean intervention on a one-shot basis. The crisis worker may have to exert an excruciating amount of patience over a long period of time as the victim slowly moves toward making a decision to take action. No matter how bad the victim's situation looks to the worker, only the victim herself can decide when she is ready to take action to alleviate her traumatic circumstances (Dagastino, 1984).

CW: OK! I understand it's a hard decision to make—getting out. Your marriage has had some good times, and you'd really like to hang onto that part of it, even though the beatings are happening more often. You say you want some time to think about it. That's OK! It's your decision, and we'll help whenever you need us.

Breaking away from a battering relationship is a slow developmental process. The crisis worker cannot move the victim any faster than she is willing to go. The worker must be acutely aware of being manipulated into becoming sympathetic to the victim's needs and attempting to "fix" things for her. Many times the victim will project anger onto the police, a minister, or other significant persons. At some point the victim needs to see that displacement and shifting of responsibility to others are not going to solve the problem. The crisis worker must be aware of this possibility and not get trapped into proposing external remedies.

The victim is actually demonstrating what Heppner (1978) calls the "wishing and hoping syndrome." The victim wishes the situation would change, that her spouse would treat her the way he used to, and hopes the crisis worker can effect a change in her husband. However, cessation of battering by the abuser rarely happens without legal or therapeutic intervention (Dagastino, 1984). Under no circumstances should the crisis worker attempt to rescue the victim by talking to the batterer. It is dangerous and takes responsibility and autonomy away from the victim. Instead, the conversation should be redirected away from what can be done to "fix" the batterer and toward what the victim is now able to do.

CW: Although I hear you wanting me to come and straighten your husband out and make things the way they were, I can't do that. I wish I could, but I'm not a marriage counselor. If you think marriage counseling would work, I can give you some names of people who do that. What I can do is help you make some decisions about what you want to do right now.

A typical response to the crisis worker's refusal to fix the problem is anger.

Juanita: You're no damn help at all. You're just as bad as the rest. You're a horrible counselor. I'm gonna have to go back to him, and he'll kill me, just because you wouldn't do anything.

Because abuse workers do not want to lose clients, such ploys often rub a raw nerve in the workers and propel them to do something they may later regret. The crisis worker should realize that when a victim doubts the worker's ability, she is also doubting her own ability. She is probably looking for a way to resume the relationship and may be displacing her own incompetence

to make changes by blaming the worker (Dagastino, 1984). The best response the crisis worker can make is not to be confrontive but to be empathic, realizing that right now the woman is looking for a way to go back to her mate.

CW: I'm sorry you're angry with me because I won't talk to your husband. I realize the frustration you feel. Yet I'm also not like the others who'll tell you how to act and what to do. I want you to know I'd be happy to work on a plan of action you want to take.

The excerpt typifies the response of a crisis worker who is being supportive yet not taking over for the victim. Usually abuse victims have not been independent to any degree and quickly fall back into a dependent state. If the crisis worker keeps foremost in mind that the woman he or she is now talking to is ultimately going to have to be her own defender and protector, then the crisis worker is not likely to fall into a sympathy trap. The crisis worker who becomes angry or engages in denouncing or criticizing the husband is making a fundamental mistake. The worker may provoke the victim to defend the violent batterer and to attack the crisis worker (Dagastino, 1984).

Facilitating. To facilitate the movement of a victim to action takes a great deal of tenacity and patience. Typically the crisis worker will have to deal with feelings of dependency, ambivalence, and depression, which are all clear-cut signs of the client's immobility. Overarching these immobilizing feelings is the learned helplessness referred to earlier. To generate movement in the victim, the crisis worker strongly reinforces the victim's attempts at rational decision making, self-control, and statements of personal power (Heppner, 1978).

CW: You said that you couldn't do anything, but that's not true. You called here, didn't you? When you first started talking, you were crying uncontrollably, and now you're speaking in a rather level, controlled voice. I also notice a lot of "I" statements, which say to me you're starting to take responsibility. Maybe you don't know it, but those are all signs that you're starting to feel some personal power for the first time in a long while, and I think that's great!

Ambivalence about the situation is predominant in most women who seek help from abuse centers. Ambivalence is particularly strong with regard to the man who, after beating the woman, apologizes, showers her with gifts, and tells her what she wants to hear and what society leads her to believe (Conroy, 1982). To deal with this ambivalent state, the crisis worker cycles between asking open-ended questions and reflecting and clarifying the victim's feelings as an effective means of helping the victim to begin to examine previously denied feelings and thoughts.

CW: What were you thinking and feeling while he was beating you?

Juanita: It was like I was standing off to the side watching a movie of this. It was like this can't really be happening, especially to me.

CW: So that's how you cope with it. Kind of separating yourself from the beating, as if it's happening to someone else.

Juanita: Yes, I guess I've done it that way for a long time. I'd go crazy otherwise.

CW: What is your understanding of why you're being battered?

Juanita: I don't know. I guess I'm just not a good wife.

CW: You're not living up to his expectations, then. How about your own?

Juanita: I'm not sure. I mean, I've never thought of that. It's always been what he wants.

CW: How do you cope with the beating other than just kind of separating yourself from the situation when it happens?

Juanita: I try to do what he wants, but when it starts to build—the tension—I just try to stay out of his way and be nice, although I know sooner or later I'm gonna get it. I dread the waiting. Actually sometimes I push the issue just to get it over with. I know he'll always apologize afterward and treat me nice.

CW: So you do what he wishes even though you know the bottom line is a beating. Yet because of the anxiety you may even push things to get it over with. Seems like you're willing to pay a steep price to get his love back.

Juanita: When you say that, I can't believe I'm letting this happen to me. What a fool . . . a stupid fool!

CW: Then you feel foolish about paying that price. What's keeping you in the relationship?

Juanita: God! I don't know. Love! Honor! Obey! The kids. The good times. Martyrdom. I don't have a job, and I'm pregnant again. I've got to get out. He'll wind up killing me.

Using open-ended questions, restatement, and reflection, the crisis worker relentlessly hammers at the victim's faulty and illogical perception of the abusive situation. Only by looking and listening through the victim's eyes and ears can the crisis worker form an accurate perception of what steps to take and how the crisis worker will operate on the nondirective-to-directive continuum of intervention. Women who have been abused also have in common the feeling of depression. Invariably, once a victim has related the details

of the assault, her affect becomes flat. Depression has taken over. Beneath the depression is a volcano of residual anger that is trying to find an outlet. The crisis worker's job is to help move the victim out of her depressed state and let the angry feelings out (Dagastino, 1984). This is the first step toward taking action.

CW: As you relate the details, it sounds like you're reporting it but not living it. I wonder if that's a typical way you hold it in . . . control it.

Juanita: I guess . . . if I really thought about it, I'd kill the SOB. How could the bastard do this to me?

CW: How does it feel to let some of those angry feelings out?

Juanita: Scary! I'm really scared I would kill him if I got the chance.

CW: That is a legitimate feeling after what you've been through, but that won't get you where you want to go. Let's take a look at some of the alternatives between killing and being killed.

In summarizing the facilitation of the victim's movement from an immobile to a mobile state, the Massachusetts Coalition of Battered Women Service Groups (1981, pp. 25, 67) has made the following recommendations for crisis workers.

1. *Be real.* Don't hide behind a role. You are what you are. To pretend to be something else makes the crisis worker false and discredited in the eyes of the victim.

2. *Set limits.* The crisis worker is not Superman or Superwoman. Owning feelings of puzzlement, anger, stupidity, tiredness, and so forth allows the crisis worker to stay on top of the game. If the worker is tired, is taking on a lot of anger, and cannot work it through with the victim, the worker should own the feelings, ask for time out, and get out of the situation until the problem can be gone over with a fellow professional and a fresh start can be made.

3. *Give the victim space and time to "freak out."* Remember that the victim is experiencing a flood of emotions that have been building over a long period of time. Knowing that anger is one step on the way to becoming her own person can be reassuring and empowering to the victim. Give her time to ventilate before settling down to a plan of action.

4. *Allow the victim to go through the pain, but stay with her.* Your first response may be to become a psychological crutch because the victim is so fragile that she cannot hold together. The crisis worker who remembers that the victim has been down a long road of pain and is just now beginning to experience that

pain will realize that the victim possesses a lot of staying power. Belief in the victim's ability to get out of the mess she is in is of overriding importance.

5. *Maintain eye and ear contact.* Both nonverbal and verbal responses of the victim are important; they tell the crisis worker whether what the victim is saying is congruent with what she is doing. Reading nonverbal responses may be difficult over the phone, but the worker needs to be aware of intonations, pauses, and sighs. How something is said may be as important as what is said. Also, what is not said may be as important as what is said.

6. *Be respectful and nonjudgmental.* The victim's actions must be carefully separated from the victim herself. What the victim does may seem asinine; that does not mean the victim is an ass. That is especially true of the religious and moral issues that go with leaving.

7. *Restate and reflect the victim's thoughts and feelings.* As simple as this sounds, it is often extremely difficult. There is no greater therapeutic help than manifesting these skills.

8. *Set priorities together.* Two heads are better than one. This is why the crisis worker is there. If the victim could handle the problem alone, she would. Likewise, the abuse worker is not in business to run the victim's life for her.

9. *Look at options.* Brainstorming can uncover a variety of previously hidden ideas and actions.

10. *Stay away from "whys."* Asking *why* a person does something like staying in a battering relationship often leads the victim, rightly or wrongly, to assume she is being judged. When a victim feels she is being judged, she is apt to respond in defensive ways that do little to help her or her situation.

11. *Give the victim time to experience catharsis, but do not let her get stuck in self-pity.* The client needs to accomplish movement, and the crisis worker needs to move gently from nurturing emotional release to helping the client start to make plans, however small, concerning her own predicament.

12. *Get back to the victim.* Even if the battered woman says, "I guess I can make it now," get her phone number and call a few days later to make sure she is getting along all right. Many abused women are so embarrassed by their plight and their own self-assessed stupidity that they cannot bring themselves to make another call and admit they have failed again. (Note: It is important to determine when the abuser will *not* be home. Furthermore, it

is important to determine whether the phone has caller ID or call-back features so the victim's safety will not be compromised.)

13. *Peer supervision and feedback are essential for domestic abuse workers.* The intensity of partner abuse is such that few, if any, crisis workers can remain totally objective all the time. Cross-supervision by trusted coprofessionals keeps the worker on track, reduces personal stress, and helps avoid burnout.

Ensuring Safety. The crisis worker's first job is to determine how critical the situation is (Roberts & Roberts, 2002; Walker, 1984, p. 122). Is this a crisis call where danger is imminent or the woman just needs a chance to cathart? All the listening and responding skills known to humanity are of little use if the victim has multiple fractures or if her significant other has threatened to come back and kill her. The crisis worker calmly and cautiously makes an assessment of how bad the situation is. Does the victim need and want medical attention, shelter, a place to send her children, a way out of the house if her husband returns?

All these questions are posed in a measured, deliberate way to avoid adding to the panic the victim already feels. Although the situation may be critical and the best alternative may be for the victim to come directly to the shelter, the crisis worker has to remember that the woman cannot be forced into making that choice. This does not mean, however, that the worker cannot make such a recommendation.

CW: From what you've said, it sounds like the situation is pretty bad. Bad enough that you might consider leaving and coming to the shelter. Do you feel as if you or your children are in danger now? Is he there now? Do you want me to call the police? Do you need medical attention?

Because of a fear of the unknown, the victim may balk at this alternative (Dagastino, 1984). Patiently, the crisis worker explains the role and function of the shelter, answers any questions the victim has, and tries to allay her fears. If, after all this, the victim is still unwilling to make a decision, the worker does not push the issue. In initially reporting the battering, victims often appear to feel that it is an isolated incident and not abuse. They refuse to see it on an ever-escalating continuum. They delude themselves with the belief that "He really does love me, and if I'm a better person, it'll never happen again." As the crisis worker intervenes, he or she should be aware that such incidents are not isolated. Indeed, there is a consistent pattern leading up to the climax of battering (Walker, 1984, p. 24). The crisis worker endeavors to lay that pattern out so that the victim sees it not as isolated but as continuous and predictable. Seeing the pattern is particularly important when the victim is not sure whether to leave or stay. Walker proposes that instead of speaking about the cycle of violence, that the worker lay out the escalating behavior in graphical form. Having the woman draw a graph of the ever-escalating violence and the shorter periods of tranquility can be an eye-opening event that allows her to decide to get out (Walker, 2000, pp. 136–137).

CW: As you tell me about it, I hear a sort of pattern. For about a week he gets surly, starts criticizing the way the house looks, the way you look, the food you cook, and your control over the kids. Those criticisms start out mild but become more severe, until you finally have had enough and say something to the effect that he ought to take more responsibility if he doesn't like things. That winds up with your getting beat up. I wonder if you can look back and see how the situation has repeated itself. Just take a pencil and piece of paper and make a graph back for the past couple of months. Put down the length of time when there has been peace and tranquility. Then put down how many hours or days the tension builds and he gets psychologically abusive, then put down when the fights start and how long they go on before he comes back and says he's sorry.

Juanita: Well, I don't know. I really think it was different this time. I mean this was the first time I needed emergency treatment. He was really sorry afterward. *(Draws out graph.)* Well, maybe it is getting worse. He seems to be getting madder faster.

CW: OK. So you see! What's different is that the pattern seems to be repeating itself more frequently, and it's getting more intense.

Juanita: Damn! I do see! I just don't know, though.

Often the client may be very immobile and may not even hear the question, so the worker may need to pose it again (Dagastino, 1984).

CW: When did he say he'd be back, and what'd he say he'd do?

Juanita: I just don't know whether to take it anymore. I love him, but I'm really scared.

CW: OK, I understand you are afraid, but I need to know how much time we've got and what threats he made.

By gently guiding the victim back to immediate and pressing issues, the crisis worker keeps the session on track but does not deny the emotional hurt and confusion the victim is experiencing.

By the time the battered woman becomes desperate enough to make the call for help, she does not have

time to be analyzed. What she needs is some behavioral action-oriented techniques she can use on a short-term basis (Walker, 1979, pp. 75–77). Just having a plan allows the victim to regain some composure and feel she has obtained some control over the situation. The whole focus of the conversation is to prepare her to get through that one day. At this time, the worker does not worry about tomorrow or any other time. Tomorrow, the worker may call the victim and talk about the next day. If the worker attempts to deal with future events that extend beyond a week, the victim gets lost (Dagastino, 1984).

Because of the flood of critical needs the victim faces, the worker must realistically judge which needs may require immediate action and which ones can be deferred. To help make sense of the heavy flow of information, the crisis worker writes down what the victim tells her so that she can quickly identify and set priorities on the very practical concerns that are pressing at the victim.

Logs that are preprinted and pose a structured set of questions and information ensure that crisis line workers cover critical needs of battered women and provide them with consistent information (Dagastino, 1984; Roberts & Roberts, 2005). Immediate actions and follow-up actions need to be covered and checked. Issues such as getting enough money for the children's lunch the next day may be just as important as taking care of a broken nose, and the worker will need to remember this. By calmly, clearly, and concisely feeding back to the victim her written summary, the crisis worker takes the victim step by step through a review of her most critical needs. By dissecting the crisis in this manner, the worker assures the victim that her problems can be broken down and managed (Dagastino, 1984).

CW: Here are all the things I hear happening to you right now. No wonder you're feeling paralyzed; anyone in that situation would feel the same. You've said you have no job, the children don't want to leave, and that he might kill you. You also indicated that it was against your faith to get a divorce, and particularly coming from Colombia there are some really strong cultural prohibitions. That's a load. Let's take them one at a time and sort through each problem and put them back together.

A careful examination of the woman's fears about these problems, what priorities need to be set on them, and the options she has in dealing with them is extremely important. Until the abused woman can confront such fears openly, she cannot begin developing strategies to deal with her problems (Heppner, 1978).

CW: You're afraid to leave because you feel sure he will come after you when he comes back, and you're not sure what he might do, so that causes tension to build. Yet I really believe if we make a plan right now you'll feel better, even if you don't have to use it.

If the victim states that she does not know what to do, the crisis worker immediately looks at the two basic alternatives—staying and leaving. What has she done before? How is this time different, if at all, from the times before? If so, what different action needs to be taken now? A key ingredient is determining the level of danger at home. Is the abuser really going to act out, or is the fear of his acting out propelling the woman into making the call? To learn what has happened before, the crisis worker asks questions such as "When he's gone out and gotten drunk before, what has he done?" "What have you done?" From the answers, the crisis worker gains a realistic assessment of the danger level of the situation. If the victim is unwilling to leave the house, then the crisis worker role-plays the scene of the drunken abuser returning home.

Assuming the role of the abuser, the worker goes through, in a systematic way, each situation of potential confrontation and then discusses the potential positive and negative outcomes of the victim's attempt to handle the confrontation (Dagastino, 1984).

CW: (*in role*) Hey, honey, come in the bedroom, I need you real bad.

Juanita: (*typical response*) I can't stand having sex with you when you are drunk.

CW: (*as self*) Now, look at how you responded to that. When you shut him off like that, he gets angry, right? What could you do or say differently? How could you change things? How about turning the tables so he had no desire for you at all? What would happen if you had a facial on and your hair up in curlers and had on a frowzy housecoat? Although that might not make you very alluring, would that turn him off?

By looking at options and posing alternative ways of behaving, the worker attempts to provide coping techniques that may defuse the crisis. By the time the worker is done, the victim is feeding back a plan, point by point, either for staying in the house or for moving out. Having an escape plan is critical (Walker, 1984, p. 122).

CW: All right! You've figured out how to get out of the house. You'll keep the back door open. You've given the kids a note to go over to the neighbors. You've got our number, and you know you can get to your car, parked out back, and get to a phone booth and call us.

As indicated in Chapter 6, Telephone and Online Crisis Counseling, computers and electronic technology play a larger and larger role in the lives of young adults. Therefore, the following study would seem to have some potentially important ramifications for younger women who are battered and have access to a computer. A computer program that has been field-tested with a group of battered women currently residing in a shelter holds promise for both keeping women who are abused safer and encouraging them to risk leaving (Glasser et al., 2010). This English/Spanish program was tested on women who had experienced severe threats to their safety. It provides feedback about risk for lethal violence, options for safety, assistance with setting priorities, and a safety plan personalized to the user. From their scores on the Danger Assessment component, 69 percent of the subjects discovered that they were in extreme danger. After using the safety decision aid, the women felt more supported in their decision to leave and had less decisional conflict about doing so.

In summary, both short- and long-term safety depends on helping abused women take action steps rather than remaining immobilized. For many victims, it may not be a question of returning to a precrisis equilibrium. The equilibrium was never there in the first place. Therefore, for many women, taking first, tentative steps toward action is likely to be extremely frightening, confusing, and full of trepidation.

The following points seem worthwhile for crisis workers to know and understand in helping abused women make such decisions and take action (Massachusetts Coalition of Battered Women Service Groups, 1981, pp. 25, 67).

1. Help women think and act on their situation by providing legitimate reinforcement for their efforts.
2. Help women figure out what they want by providing a sounding board for examining ideas and alternatives.
3. Help women identify feelings that prevent them from making decisions.
4. Be honest. The worker cannot tell a person what to do but can clearly state from her own life how the situation would affect her.
5. Help women to do things for themselves, but do not let them become dependent on the worker.
6. Know and offer resources from which battered women can get specific kinds of assistance: Spell out *who*, *what*, *where*, *when*, and *how*.

7. Help women gain a sense of self-confidence and ability to take care of themselves.

8. Be challenging. Support women, but do not be afraid to push them toward a decision-making point.

9. Be open to choices. Each woman has control over her life; the crisis worker must not attempt to assume control for clients.

10. Hear and understand what women have to say, particularly if it does not run parallel to the worker's own beliefs, attitudes, and outlooks.

11. Build on the commonalities that women, particularly battered women, share, but recognize the worth of the individual differences of each person.

12. Assess lethality. "I'm fed up and whipped" may really mean "I'm ready to commit suicide."

The following crisis worker's response to a battered woman, who after two hours of talking on the telephone still could not make up her mind about what to do, aptly illustrates the application of the 12 points just made.

CW: I understand your mixed feelings of wanting to stay and wanting to leave; also the constant fear you live with while waiting for the next time, maybe even wishing it would happen quickly so the tension will ease off. But my guess is that tension reduction only occurs for a short period and then starts to build all over again. I also understand that you feel like you're locked into this, but there are some alternatives, which we have gone over. I want you to pick at least one of those, whichever seems best for you, and do it. I won't take no for an answer. Do something that will make you feel better right now. Go take a hot bath if that'll help, and don't spare the bath oil. I think it would be safer for you to come to the shelter right now, but if you don't really feel you can do that, I understand. However, if you feel the tension start to rise and feel like you just can't take it anymore, I want you to promise to call back here. I won't take no for an answer. I'll call you tomorrow afternoon to see how things are going. What would be a good time?

Advocacy.   Because battered women have been isolated for much of their lives, they generally have little knowledge of alternatives open to them. This is especially true with respect to their rights and options with both legal and welfare systems. Providing court advocates who understand the laws and how to weave through bureaucratic obstacles and how to cut through the red tape that often interferes with someone seeking help from the system is of paramount importance. Weaving one's way through the state employment and welfare system to obtain financial aid and job training requires support and advocacy (Shepard, 1999). The

worker needs to have an excellent networking system to tap into and get immediate help for a variety of problems these women will face.

Transcrisis Perspective.   All the preceding intervention procedures cannot be accomplished in a 20-minute phone call. Even minor crises may require two or three calls to get the client stabilized, in touch with her feelings, and into some semblance of preabuse equilibrium. The crisis worker is not providing a short-term elixir that merely calms the victim and then blithely sends her on her way. What is being provided is a blend that not only deals with the immediate crisis but also has a long-term application. Many battered women need to go through a complete reeducation process about who they are and what they can do. This process should not be hurried even if it takes a year to accomplish this goal.

Indeed, the transcrisis of the battered woman does not end when she gets off the phone and decides to come to the center or go to the shelter. The initiating interview or hotline call is only the first part of the crisis resolution. Other crises will continue to plague the victim. Ibrahim and Herr's (1987) work with battered women who were involved in a group counseling format that concentrated on vocational exploration and economic independence is an excellent example of a transcrisis point. When these women reached the stage of vocational implementation, ready actually to go out into the world of work and test their skills, they experienced all kinds of threatening and anxious feelings and became immobile and paralyzed. The women needed 15 two-hour sessions of intensive support by the group leaders to work through this stage!

Shelters

A center and a shelter are generally two different entities within a domestic abuse program. The center deals with telephone and on-site, short-term crisis intervention and counseling. The shelter is a longer-term facility where women and their families can stay for short or extended periods of time. A comprehensive program will have both a center and a shelter and will be staffed around the clock with a 24-hour hotline and an open door policy for walk-ins (Barnett et al., 1980). Shelters generally provide two other important ingredients, individual counseling and peer support (Hampton, Vandergriff-Avery, & Kim, 1999). There will be tie-ins to other social services agencies: police, free or sliding-scale legal services, hospitals, medical staff and mental health facilities, mobile crisis teams that provide transportation for abuse victims, and direct links to emergency housing facilities with follow-up services (Benjamin & Walz, 1983, p. 83).

The typical shelter is linked to the abuse center and is well publicized, but for security reasons its location may not be made public. For the same reason, it will be well patrolled by the police and will be secure. Staffed by both professionals and volunteers, it will have adequate cooking, sleeping, bath, and child and infant care facilities for a number of families and funds for clothing, food, and transportation (Langley & Levy, 1977). It should also provide a variety of counseling services to help women ventilate feelings, explore alternatives, and make immediate plans for what they will do next (Benjamin & Walz, 1983, p. 84). It should also have comprehensive services for children (Roberts & Roberts, 2005). This ideal shelter is a rarity due to lack of funds, although in the authors' home state of Tennessee, a portion of every marriage license fee goes toward support of shelters.

Counseling Women at Shelters

Women who enter the shelter fit into two categories: those who are unsure about leaving the battering relationship and those who have made a definite commitment to leave it (Dagastino, 1984). Women who fall into the first category need to be monitored on an hour-by-hour basis and are the more critical of the two categories. The crisis worker maintains constant contact with these women and reinforces them for having had the courage to come to the shelter.

CW: I'm glad you made it. I know it took a lot of courage.

CW: (*10 minutes later*) Getting settled in? Come on with me. There are some other women I would like you to meet.

CW: (*2 hours later*) How are things going? Got the kids settled in? They're great-looking children. Want to have a cup of coffee and talk?

Vacillation between going back and staying is characteristic of these women. The longer the women stay at the shelter, the greater the probability is that they will not return to their mates (Hilbert & Hilbert, 1984). However, until women can recover their self-esteem and come to understand that they are not the cause of the abuse, they are at risk to leave and go back (Schutte et al., 1986). The worker does not try to force women to stay at the shelter but does try to get them to take some psychological "time out" to review their situation in a more objective way (Dagastino, 1984). The foregoing is

particularly true of women who have suffered childhood sexual abuse, who are far more likely to return to the batterer because of their emotional attachment (Griffing et al., 2005). Knowing this kind of information is critical to worker intervention and keeping women from leaving before they have a chance to start gaining back their self-esteem.

Juanita: I'm all mixed up. I don't know if I'm wrong or not. I'm Catholic, and I'm Hispanic. Women in my family just don't walk out of a marriage. The church and my family both say we just need to work things out, but I really think he'll kill me.

CW: Let's assume you're taking a 1-day vacation, so you can get some rest before you go back and deal with it. It's fine if you want to go back home, but do this much for me—just take it easy for a while. I can see that you're physically all right and not hurt, and I'm relieved. This is a great time to talk about what you can do if you do or don't go back.

The shelter worker checks repeatedly with the new arrival and reinforces her decision to come. She conveys her concern for the victim and, with the help of other women in the shelter, sees that the victim and her family are settled. The focus is on the here and now. During the first few hours of the victim's separation from her abuser, the worker will probably have to be very directive. Few women at this time have the ego strength to stand on their own, and most need an abundance of support and help. The objective is to keep the victim moving, thinking, and acting so that she is preoccupied and does not have time to let fear, guilt, or any other debilitating and anxiety-ridden emotions overcome her. Domestic chores such as cleaning and cooking seem to be particularly helpful in this regard. In all instances, the worker should be carefully attuned to the victim's needs. Some may find help sitting, talking, or crying with a worker or a group of other women. Others may be so exhausted that they need to go to bed and sleep. Whatever the victim needs, the worker should be adaptable to those needs and flexible enough to change as circumstances demand (Dagastino, 1984).

Shelter Dynamics. A variety of positive dynamics occur at shelters. There is substantial support from other women who have experienced the same kind of trauma. This support enables victims to begin gaining the courage to face people, recovering their lost self-esteem, and learning that the beatings were not their fault (Schechter, 1982, pp. 55–60).

Wife abuse shelters are not vacation spas where one's every whim is catered to. Although an abundance of caring and sharing occurs, women who live in shelters are encouraged to start trusting themselves to make decisions. Part of the decision-making process includes determining what is best for the shelter. This is not an easy task. Limits have to be set with respect to pets, children, cooking, and so on (Schechter, 1982, pp. 63–64). Women get bored, boss each other around, miss their men, miss sex (pp. 55–60), and have problems relating to people from different ethnic and racial backgrounds and sociocultural milieus (Massachusetts Coalition of Battered Women Service Groups, 1981, p. 28).

Shelter user: Getting used to a shelter is overwhelming. You like it, but you don't want to be there, 'cause it isn't home. You've got to put together all your psychological know-how in getting along with different types of people. Wondering if you're going to make it, especially when you see all the pain and confusion and don't know whether it's yours or theirs or what, and hoping nobody finds out you're here. Trying to be understood and feeling like you are a blabbermouth here when you couldn't talk at home. Trying to look forward and all the time wanting to forget . . . wanting to forget . . . wanting to forget (Schechter, 1982, pp. 59–60).

At a shelter, everything is not always as it seems. Many women who come to the shelter are extremely dependent and exceptionally adept at manipulating the workers there (Walker, 1984, p. 126). A statement like "You really understand—you've made my whole life better" is reinforcing to the worker but may actually be manipulation. The woman is using the house and the worker as a security blanket and is not making any progress toward getting out on her own (Dagastino, 1984). The wise shelter worker comes to see the manipulation for what it is, a refusal to take responsibility for oneself and a shift from dependency on an abusive partner to dependency on a caring shelter worker (Weincourt, 1985). Gently but firmly, the worker extinguishes such behavior.

CW: I appreciate what you said, and I appreciate your wanting to cook my dinner and all the other things you want to do for me. Yet I believe your time and mine could be better spent working on getting you set up in an apartment and looking for a job.

Grief.　Besides being dependent, many abused women go through a grief process. Sorrow and depression, guilt and self-blame, and decision-making difficulty are all hallmarks of the grieving process. What would be viewed as normal in a woman who suffered the death of a spouse may be viewed as pathological in an abused woman. However, these responses are just as legitimate for an abused woman who is trying to come to terms

with the loss of a significant relationship, shared parental responsibilities, and a clearly defined role as a wife (Campbell, 1989).

There are a lot of *yes, buts* as workers start to confront abused women with making a new future. As victims shift from a depersonalized view of their situation to depression over it, the process can be extremely frightening to a shelter worker unless she knows that this, too, is another step in the transcrisis that battered women go through (Dagastino, 1984). The woman's grief often puzzles those trying to help her. Many human services workers may be threatened by these feelings and deny the woman's need to mourn by concentrating on dealing with concrete aspects of the woman's dilemma, such as providing food, clothing, and housing.

Her grief can be understood, however, if one asks the question "For what is she mourning?" In most cases, she has defined herself in terms of her relationship with the batterer, and if that relationship ends, she feels as if she has lost everything—including her sense of self (Turner & Shapiro, 1986). She clings quite tightly to the dreams she has for the relationship—including the expectations with which she entered into it. When the relationship ends, she must come to terms with the fact that these dreams will never materialize. Therefore, she is not grieving so much for what was, but for what she hoped could have been (Spanno, 1990). A crisis worker can and should validate that the woman's loss is very real and that she has a legitimate right to mourn and experience the feelings she has over the loss (Russell & Uhlemann, 1994). At this point, the counseling process is little different from grief due to death of a loved one (see Chapter 12, Personal Loss: Bereavement and Grief).

Juanita: I wanted this to work so much. We could have had it so good, but I couldn't take him beating on me and the kids too. What went wrong with that good-looking, happy couple in this picture? He was so handsome and so good to me in the beginning. Then it just slowly went to hell, and now this. (*Weeps while slowly turning over in her hands a wedding picture that she brought with her to the shelter.*)

CW: It's really hard to say good-bye to all those things that were and might have been. It must hurt even more than the beatings to know that all those hopes and dreams won't come to pass.

Juanita: It tears my heart out, but I know I did the right thing. Sooner or later he would have killed me or the kids in one of his rages. It's so weird! I still love that SOB.

CW: The grief you're feeling is as real as if a close friend or a relative had died. Perhaps even more tragic because when this relationship died, a part of you died with it, Juanita. The part of you who struggled out of the barrio, went to college, got an education, made a success of herself, married the perfect man, and then had all those expectations dashed because of the way he treated you and the children.

Juanita: I can't let that stop me. Nothing else did. I made the right decision coming here. I also made the right decision getting a warrant on him. Maybe that last act of love will get him the help he needs or the jolt he needs to wake him up so he doesn't do it to somebody else.

CW: As you say that, I see so much determination coming through the tears. I also see a new, different, stronger person as you say those farewells, as tough as they are.

A woman who has been involved in an abusive relationship needs to grieve and to have her grief validated. The crisis worker does this while reinforcing that although there is now an altered future, it has potential to be a good one. It is through this process that the battered woman can come to see the relationship for what it really was—abusive. The crisis worker will make a very bad therapeutic mistake if she expects the woman to rejoice. If she is expected to be happy for leaving and is discouraged from feeling her sense of loss and expressing it, she may never confront the truth about the relationship. The end result may well be a return to the partner or one just like him (Spanno, 1990).

Depression.   Depression comes in many guises. Many women who come into the shelter sleep much of the time. On first appearance, they may seem to be lazy. Actually, they may be going through a stage of trying to regroup their psychic energy. The worker's task becomes one of trying to help them move past their inactivity, but not by pressuring them or taking them on a guilt trip (Massachusetts Coalition of Battered Women Service Groups, 1981, p. 27).

CW: I've noticed you pretty much sticking to your room and sleeping a lot. I was a little concerned and was wondering how you were feeling. I wonder if you've had a chance to talk to anyone about how you feel since you got here.

Juanita: I feel so guilty. It seems like I have slept ever since I've gotten here, and the other women have been so good to take care of the kids. I'm not really like this. I just don't seem to have any get-up-and-go. I'm really sorry to be so much trouble.

CW: What you are doing is exactly what you should be doing, getting your energy back. You burned up a tremendous amount of it making the decision to get out and get here. The other women have felt the same way, so they understand. In a few days you'll do the same for somebody else.

If you want to talk, we're here. If you want to rest, that's just fine too. The main thing is you're safe, and that's what's important right now.

Terror.   For many women, a stress-related syndrome similar to agoraphobia arises after they have been in the shelter for a while (Massachusetts Coalition of Battered Women Service Groups, 1981, p. 27). They may have extreme and unexplainable attacks of terror that are touched off by seemingly innocuous incidents. These incidents greatly restrict their activities and new freedom. Fear of their mates, fear of their predicament, fear of their separation from a definable past, and fear of an undefinable future can all cause the onset of terror. Under no circumstances should the shelter worker allow it to continue. Victims must be encouraged and helped step by step to pull themselves away from the security blanket of the shelter and out into the real world.

Such progress may take place in very small, slow steps, but the steps must be taken. As women take these steps, they receive very specific, positive reinforcement for what they have accomplished, enabling them not to fall back into learned helplessness but instead to take responsibility for their behavior (Weincourt, 1985). Invariably, victims will not be able to see that they have done much of anything, or they tend to diminish their successes. For women who are faced with leaving a relationship with no means of support, structural change in their economic environment is imperative. Independent housing, job training and opportunities, affordable child care, and social support services are critical. Programs such as the Job Readiness program that is run in a number of Kentucky shelters provide job training to make women employable (Websdale & Johnson, 2005). However, such preparation may bring on its own developmental crises as these women venture into new, unfamiliar territory.

CW: I know you're still scared to death to go down and talk to them at Federal Express about that job. It's a big step, but a week ago you couldn't walk down to the grocery store, and now you're doing that fine. So let's take it a step at a time. Look at what you overcame. We can go through the job interview, play it a step at a time, talk about those steps right here where it's safe, and give you a chance to really become confident about going down there.

Those Who Have Decided to Leave.   The second category of women who come to the shelter are in for a long haul and are not going back to the battering situation. For women who are in for the duration, the crisis worker deals with immediate specifics such as finding a place to live, financial aid, and child care. Emotional support has a low priority because these women are so busy that all they want and need is very practical advice and help. These women are very different from those experiencing acute crisis because they are highly motivated to change their lives. They are much easier to work with, because they have made a decision to get out of their domestic pressure cooker (Dagastino, 1984).

Follow-Up

Once women leave the shelter, they should be provided with follow-up care (Tutty & Rothery, 2002). As immediate demands are relieved, the emotional impact of their decision should be dealt with over the long term. These women are urged to go for counseling with the idea that no one can be beaten even once without suffering some psychological damage. It is not uncommon for a woman to be so busy getting her act together that her emotional reactions are delayed. The victim may be out on her own, well established, and watching television at the time that she experiences a sudden emotional breakdown. The crisis worker apprises the victim of what to expect in the way of emotional aftershocks. Such residual psychological trauma seems to be particularly characteristic of women who initially appear to be very much in control (Dagastino, 1984).

CW: Even though you feel like you've made the break from your husband, don't be surprised if later on you get depressed and really feel like you need and miss him. That's to be expected. We know that, and we're here to help then too!

Indeed, in the worst of scenarios, the victim may become lonely, forget about the terrible abuse she suffered in the past, invite her ex-mate over for dinner, and get beaten up again. Or because of urging from children or the ex-partner, she may feel pressured into reuniting (Tutty & Rothery, 2002). Therefore, in following up with the victim, the crisis worker should understand that there may be relapses and that the victim may fall into old ways of behaving. Or, the victim having made the break, the batterer may seek her out for revenge. Thus, crisis workers not only may have to check up on their clients but also may have to be indirect about it, so the women do not become dependent on them (Dagastino, 1984).

CW: Hello, Juanita. Just called to see if you've been able to make that appointment for counseling at the Human Services Clinic. I know it's hard to get in there at times and thought if you hadn't, I could call the clinic, and we'd have one of the people here drive you down and help you get started.

The crisis worker continues to be a support system until the victim is well connected to a long-term support source (McLeod, Hays, & Chang, 2010), and only then does the crisis worker fade from the victim's life. Long-term support is particularly critical for abused women. Research indicates that women who leave the shelter and strike out on their own continue to undergo emotional changes for at least 6 months after leaving. Therefore, support and advocacy are critical during this time frame. Those who have a support group and advocates who help them access services do significantly better in reaching their goals than do women who lack such services (Sullivan et al., 1994). Support services also build self-esteem, increase locus of control, reduce stress, and enhance feelings of belongingness and support (Tutty, Bidgood, & Rothery, 1993). Follow-up and support are particularly important for women who have little education, few job skills, and minimal financial support (Webersinn, Hollinger, & Delamatre, 1991).

Do the shelter experience and its follow-up services significantly alter a woman's chance of not becoming involved in an abusive relationship again? The data are not clear on this issue. Research indicates that the greater the number of times a woman leaves an abusive relationship, the more likely she is to leave permanently (Schutte, Malouff, & Doyle, 1988). Going to a shelter without benefit of follow-up and other support services may actually *increase* violence (Berk, Newton, & Berk, 1986). Finally, because shelters tend to be based on Western forms of feminism, ethnic minorities with different cultural backgrounds report difficulties in adapting to a shelter environment (Hamby, 1998, p. 238). Clearly, entering a shelter is a major step and not one to be taken lightly. While entering a shelter may be necessary, based on the foregoing it is not necessarily sufficient by itself and is but a first step on a long road (Tutty & Rothery, 2002).

Intervention With Children

There has been a tendency in the battered women's movement to look at children as "secondary" victims (Lehmann & Rabenstein, 2002; Peled, 1997). They are not. Remember that there are an estimated 7 million children who have been exposed to violent abusive conditions in the United States alone (McDonald et al., 2006). First and foremost, children often receive physical abuse along with their mothers (McMahon, Neville-Sorvilles, & Schubert, 1999). Statistics on family violence identify that at least half the homes that suffer domestic violence have children under 12 years of age living in them (Greenfield, Rand, & Craven, 1998). Children are often lost in the shuffle of domestic violence, but that violence has a direct impact on their lives both in the present and in the future (Wolak & Finkelhor, 1998, pp. 73–111).

Lehmann and Rabenstein's (2002) review of research outcomes on children who have witnessed domestic violence indicates a variety of behavioral and emotional problems that range from academic difficulties to approval of violence as a problem-solving method. In adulthood those same children are likely to experience poor interpersonal relationships, use and accept violence as a way to solve problems, have chronic depression and low self-esteem, and engage in criminal behavior. In that light, crisis workers need to be as concerned for children as they are for the women who are immersed in battering relationships.

Of primary concern is the safety of the children, so a lethality assessment should be conducted to determine where the children should reside and who will supervise them during visitation and other occasions on which the perpetrator may be present. For children who are old enough to take action on their own, a safety plan should entail how to determine whether the situation is becoming lethal, how to get away from the perpetrator, and where they can go to be safe. If they are in a shelter, they need to know how to keep the location a secret not only from the perpetrator but also from other relatives and acquaintances. If there is evidence of abuse toward the children, which is highly likely in partner violence, then the crisis worker is mandated to refer the case to a state welfare agency (Wolak & Finkelhor, 1998, pp. 100–101).

Children who have witnessed partner violence or have just fled or been removed from a home can benefit from immediate crisis counseling to stave off typical PTSD symptoms (Lehmann & Rabenstein, 2002) that can follow them into adulthood (Anderson, Danis, & Havig, 2011). (See the sections on children in Chapter 7, Posttraumatic Stress Disorder, and Chapter 9, Sexual Assault, for more detailed assessment and intervention strategies.) Specific immediate intervention with a trained crisis worker should first do a safety assessment, then allow children to recount the events and their feelings about them, correct negative misattributions about self-blame, and work through overwhelming negative feelings (Wolak & Finkelhor, 1998, p. 101). Specific problem-solving strategies need to be developed in which the child's affect is normalized and she or he learns how to anticipate and deal with uncomfortable emotions (Lehmann & Rabenstein, 2002).

There is probably no age too early to start therapy for children who come from abusive home settings. Roberts and Roberts (2005) report that the Jersey Battered Women's Service in Morristown, New Jersey, has developed coloring books that are used during initial contact with the children. The books encourage children to identify feelings, provide assurance of safety, give them information to understand what is happening in their families, provide information to help the children adapt to the shelter setting, and begin to assess the children's needs and concerns.

Therapeutic work done conjointly with caregivers is critical. First, a parental interview should be conducted with the battered parent to determine safety issues, developmental history of the child, a history of the traumatic exposure, what current symptoms are being manifested, and how well the child is handling separation issues, and to provide psychoeducation about children's symptoms as well as hope that things will improve (Weinreb & Groves, 2007). Douglas (1991) used conjoint therapy with mother and child, employing attachment theory to help toddlers ages 15 to 36 months work through traumatic battering events they had witnessed. Hughes's (1982) brief intervention strategy includes intervention with children, mothers, schools, and shelter staff members. Her model is comprehensive in that it provides individual counseling; initiates group meetings for peers, siblings, and family; teaches parenting skills to mothers; establishes a liaison with school personnel; and trains shelter staff members in child advocacy and child development issues.

Malchiodi (2008, p. 254) recommends art and play therapy as a primary therapeutic mode because many children will not want to talk about the violence they have witnessed. Further, children will have difficulty because of their immature cognitive development in verbalizing the complex issues that undergird domestic violence (Weinreb & Groves, 2007).Treatment goals for children and the vicitmized parent include (Malchiodi, 2008; Weinreb & Groves, 2007):

1. Creating an alliance with the parent to help the child heal.
2. Providing psychoeducation to both parent and child about the trauma and therapy.

3. Restoring the parent's self-esteem and confidence to parent.

4. Establishing a safe therapeutic environment for the child to express thoughts and feelings.

5. Relieving the child's symptoms, including difficulty with living transitions, sleeping, nightmares, and other trauma symptoms.

6. Reestablishing the child's previous level of cognitive functioning and strong attachment with the caregiver.

7. Reassurance that what has happened is not the child's fault and the child is not guilty of anything.

8. Helping the child to express thoughts and feelings and regain cognitive and emotional regulation.

9. Providing stress reduction strategies to aid in stopping emotional dysregulation.

Weinreb and Groves (2007) provide an excellent example of why using play therapy is effective with children coming out of domestic violence situations. In this instance a 7-year-old girl had witnessed severe beatings of her mother by her father. She was introduced to therapy by being brought into a play therapy room and invited to play. She used drawing and playing with figurines that represented her violent environment to work through a constellation of conflicted feelings about the traumatic events and separation of the family. She expressed that she was afraid of, yet missed, her father, which are all too common ambivalent feelings about the offending parent. Trying to verbalize these ambivalent, conflicted feelings and integrate them is extremely difficult for an elementary school age child. Working them out through play and anchoring them with drawings, models, and other concrete representations isn't.

Many times group work (Malchiodi, 2008, pp. 252–263) may be used with children; benefits include decreasing isolation, bonding with other victims, and seeing others moving forward from the trauma of the domestic violence they experienced. Malchiodi (2008, pp. 258–261) has adapted Herman's (1992) three-phase trauma recovery model to her groups, which generally meet for 90 minutes for up to 12 sessions. Phase 1 is about establishing safety rules, confidentiality, personal space, and boundaries, which may be put on a colorful poster and signed by the children as part of their behavioral contract. The group engages in activities such as making feeling thermometers; reading about Brave Bart, the traumatized cat who gets into a group of other traumatized cats; creating safety hands

with "safe" adult names and phone numbers on it; learning relaxation and yoga activities; and free drawing and play time. Phase 2 is about telling the trauma story and includes activities such as creating collages of being powerless and powerful, making "how hands can hurt" posters, drawing a picture of "your family," reading therapeutic storybooks, engaging in relaxation and stress reduction activities, practicing scaling techniques with feeling thermometers, learning simple cognitive behavior techniques to reduce negative thinking, and free play and art time. The final phase has to do with returning to the community and reconnecting with significant adults in the child's life who are central to his or her emotional recovery. These caregivers are asked to participate in the final two sessions. Children can share their artwork and have parents engage in reconstructing artwork, cooperatively creating or adding to safety hands to reinforce the child's sense of security and creating past, present, and future collages to show where they have been, where they are now, and the hopeful future they are moving toward.

Outcomes for the children should include the following (Malchiodi, 2008, p. 261):

1. Increased knowledge of the emotional and physical effects of family violence

2. Understanding that violence in the family is not okay and it is not their fault

3. A reduction in stress-related or PTSD symptoms; increased ability to self-regulate emotions

4. Decreased negative self-talk

5. Improved ability to identify feelings, and the ability to communicate those to peers and adults

6. Increased sense of social support

7. Stronger connection with the nonabusive parent

8. Resilience to cope with future crises

Finally, many children are still involved with both parents, and long-term monitoring and intervention are needed. The Duluth Family Visitation Center operates on the premise that this will occur and that parent training is critical for both parents so that children will not be used as messengers, negotiators, or witnesses to further verbal or physical abuse. As such, the Center staff members attempt to remain neutral and to act as advocates for the children with both parents by providing a safe place to exchange children, helping parents develop good parenting relationships with their children, and providing valid information to courts regarding custody and visitation rights (McMahon, Neville-Sorvilles, & Schubert, 1999).

Courtship Violence

To believe that only women who are partners in a conjugal relationship are victims of violence is to be badly mistaken. Studies on courtship violence estimate that it occurs in anywhere from 22 to 67 percent of courtship relationships and cuts across college, high school, and nonschool dating populations (Burcky, Reuterman, & Kopsky, 1988; Henton et al., 1983; Makepeace, 1983). A conservative estimate is that violence occurs in approximately 25 percent of courtship relationships. As simplistic as the following may sound as a predictor of violence, Bergman (1992) found that number of dating partners and dating frequency had the highest positive correlation and that grade point average had the highest negative correlation. As one might expect, adolescents who come out of violent families carry their experiences into their dating behavior. Laporte and associates (2011) found that indeed family of origin violence is a risk factor in dating and aggression. Females who had been victimized by either parent were at greater risk for revictimization but not increased aggression. High-risk males reported being aggressive toward girlfriends, particularly if they had been harshly disciplined by their fathers. For both males and females, but particularly for girls, the extent of their aggression toward their parents predicted their aggression toward partners.

Even more ominous, in a study of high school students by Burcky, Reuterman, and Kopsky (1988), dating violence affected girls as young as 12. These researchers also found that assaultive behavior was not just shoving and pushing. Among those experiencing dating violence, 37.5 percent reported that the minimum assaultive behavior was being punched, and approximately 9 percent reported having been assaulted with a gun or knife! It is noteworthy, and may presage the future of these relationships, that the percentage of violent incidents reported closely parallels that found in samples of married couples and that this violence is reciprocal in nature (Jasinski & Williams, 1998, p. 30; Straus & Gelles, 1986; Straus, Gelles, & Steinmetz, 1980). What is truly astounding is that, in a study by Henton and associates (1983), 25 percent of victims and 30 percent of offenders interviewed interpreted violence in courtship as a sign of love! Research study after research study indicates that violence invariably escalates the longer people are in an abusive relationship. Further, each subsequent year that women experienced violence as adolescents increases their risk for revictimization compared with those who did not have that experience. Across all years, women who are physically assaulted are significantly more likely to be sexually assaulted in that same year (Smith, White, & Holland, 2003). To think that people will give up violent behavior for "love" or any other reason is to think wrong. Worse, to think that one has the power to get a partner to give up an addictive behavior such as battering is patently false!

In that regard, the best directive your authors can offer to anyone who is physically assaulted even once in a dating relationship is, no matter how great the love, how great the good times, how great the sex, how many flowers, apologies, and promises to change are given after an initial assault, *get out of the relationship now!* No battered woman we have met set out with the intention to go with or marry someone who would beat her. However, by letting such behavior occur early in courtship, many battered women unwittingly set the stage for some terrible consequences of their early tolerance.

And if *you* have assaulted someone in a dating relationship, *get help now!* "Assaulted" doesn't necessarily mean that you put the person in the hospital. It may have been a series of hard shakes, a shove or two, or a slap in the heat of an argument or a moment of jealousy. Although you can easily rationalize this behavior away, the chances are good that this behavior will increase in the future. Besides the harm you do to someone you profess to love, the changes in the law and increased judicial sensitivity to battering mean that you will probably spend some time in jail if you are convicted of an assault on your girlfriend or boyfriend. If your school counseling center doesn't conduct anger management groups, there are therapists who do. The section on treating batterers will give you an idea of what you need to look for in a therapist.

Stalking

Epidemiological studies of stalking prevalence range from 8 to 16 percent of women and 2 to 7 percent of men who will be stalked during their lives (Dressing, Kuehner, & Gass, 2006; Tjaden & Thoennes, 2000). Stalking is defined as repeated harassment, following, and/or threats that are committed with the intent of causing the victim emotional distress, fear of bodily harm, and/or actual bodily harm. Fantasy stalkers who typically target movie stars may send out hundreds of e-mails, letters, or phone calls. Most of these stalkers are not targeting their victims for murder, as opposed to stalkers who are strangers to their victims, demonstrate a variety of pathologies, are angry and want power over their victims, and are extremely dangerous sexual predators and murderers (Dressing, Kuehner, & Gass, 2006; Mester, Birger, & Margolin, 2006; Schlesinger, 2006). For the most part, the typical stalker is known to or has had a relationship with his or her victim, as in the case of a broken romance or a divorced spouse (Tjaden & Thoennes, 1998b).

There is probably no more terrifying experience than being stalked. A new phenomenon is stalking over the Internet. Cyberstalking allows the stalker to collect information about the target and then, when communicating with the target, reveal these personal facts. Interestingly, in a study of cyberstalking among college students, Alexy and associates (2005) found that males were more likely to be stalked than females by this method. Stalking targets have many of the same PTSD-like symptoms that battered individuals do and resort to the same kinds of strategies when the stalking becomes intolerable, such as changing one's address, moving away, quitting one's job, changing one's name and appearance, and going underground (Knox & Roberts, 2005).

Stopping stalking can be highly frustrating because the authorities will not likely intervene unless the individual has some proof that she or he is being stalked (Brewster, 2002). Persons who are being stalked need to keep a recorded log of sightings, phone calls, copies of e-mails and letters, and any witnesses to the stalking. The Stalking Behavior Checklist (Coleman, 1997), which is available through many advocacy groups, measures unwanted harassing and pursuit-oriented behavior and can be used to provide excellent documentation. If you are being stalked, you need to call the police now! You need to get in touch with victims' advocacy groups that know how to deal with this problem and have them go with you to the authorities. Federal antistalking legislation was implemented as part of the Violence Against Women Act in 1996, and all 50 states now have laws regarding stalking (Knox & Roberts, 2005). While many jurisdictions have paid little heed to stalking problems in the past, increased awareness has caused the instigation of counterstalking programs like the Nashville Metropolitan Police Department's Counterstalking Plan, which uses a wide array of technology to trap and prosecute stalkers (Roberts & Kurst-Swanger, 2002). Michele Pathé (2002) has written an excellent survival manual for stalking victims.

Gay and Lesbian Violence

Although statistics indicate that same-gendered sexual orientation is prevalent in about 10 percent of the people in the United States (Gebhard, 1997), the attitude of the general public is often highly negative, scornful, and openly hostile to gays and lesbians. This prevailing attitude keeps many same-sex relationships under wraps, so when violence occurs, no report is made. There is also reluctance on the part of same-sex partners to report violence because of the added stigma attached to an already stigmatized perception that gay and lesbian relationships are unhealthy (Bograd, 2005; Elliot, 1996; Kanuha, 2005). Finally, unless they themselves are gay or lesbian, few service providers or researchers have the inclination, resources, or education about same-sex relationships to provide meaningful help (Island & Letellier, 1991; Renzetti, 1996).

Prevalence of Violence

The sparse statistics on gay and lesbian relations indicate that same-sex relationships are no more immune from partner violence than heterosexual ones. What has slowly come to light is that battering is an equal opportunity malady that affects gay men and lesbian women in the same staggering numbers as it does those in heterosexual relationships (Mederos, 1999; Peterman & Dixon, 2003; Ricks, Vaughan, & Dziegielewski, 2002). From 25 to 50 percent of lesbians report being in a battering relationship (Barnes, 1998; Friess, 1997; Lie & Gentlewarrier, 1991; Lockhart et al., 1994; Oatley, 1994). In one study, when all former relationships were considered, the figure moved up to 64 percent (Bologna, Waterman, & Dawson, 1987). In gay relationships, the data are even more sparse. Estimates are that about 10 to 20 percent of males in gay relationships are assaulted each year (Island & Letellier, 1991). When all previous gay relationships are taken into consideration, the figure moves up to 44 percent (Bologna, Waterman, & Dawson, 1987). The bottom line is that it appears that a great deal of violence occurs in such relationships (Bartholomew, 1999; Gillis, 1999; Ristock, 1999; Stanley, 1999). Interestingly enough, in a study by Toro-Alfonso and Rodriguez-Madera (2004), while 48 percent of the gay men interviewed reported emotional abuse, they didn't consider it as interpersonal violence. From your authors' experience of crisis intervention with women and men of same-sex orientations, their presenting problems usually revolve around "outing" (revealing to others, such as parents and employers, of the victim's same-sex orientation), jealousy and mistrust, unwanted breakups, and feelings of loss, grief, and betrayal over dissolved relationships—all of which have the potential for violent confrontations.

Complicating Factors

Although many of the same coercive controls used by heterosexual batterers are employed in the homosexual community, there are differences. Positive HIV status can be used as a coercive control. Failing health or threat of infection may be used to make the partner feel afraid or guilty. If the victim is infected, the coercive partner may refuse to provide support or get medical care for the victim, or double "out" the partner (tell people she or he is both homosexual and HIV positive; West, 1998, p. 170). Indeed, the coercive partner often uses "homophobic" control by threatening to "out" the partner and by constantly reminding the partner that no one in a homophobic world (particularly the police) will believe her or him or will dismiss the violence as inconsequential or what the person may "deserve" (Hart, 1986).

A further complicating factor is that battering may be seen as "mutual." That is, in a same-sex relation there is no clear "identifiable" assailant and victim. Thus, the assaulter can discount the victim's accusations by claiming that both were equally responsible for the violence. The foregoing is particularly true of gays who may be made to feel inadequate for "not taking it like a man" (Stanley et al., 2006; West, 1998, pp. 169–170).

To date, what research there is seems to indicate that many of the factors that influence violence in heterosexual partners are contributors to violence among same-sex partners. Intergenerational transmission of violence, alcohol abuse, dependency, autonomy issues, and power imbalances seem to contribute to same-sex partner abuse (Cruz, 2003; Peterman & Dixon, 2003; Ricks, Vaughan, & Dziegielewski, 2002).

Crisis Intervention Involving Gay and Lesbian Violence

Gay and lesbian battering is no different from heterosexual battering in that power and control are the key motivating factors. Gays and lesbians are also much the same in their reluctance to admit that abuse and violence can occur. However, gay men rank domestic violence third, behind substance abuse and AIDS, as their most pressing health problems (Island & Letellier, 1991). An even more dismal outlook may be forecast for elderly homosexuals, who may be entirely at the economic mercy of their partners and be extremely isolated from other support systems (Peterman & Dixon, 2003).

Sensitivity.   Your authors' own experience indicates a number of issues that make crisis intervention difficult and sensitive with same-sex partners who have engaged in violent acts. First is the person's reluctance to talk about the problem because of trust issues with the crisis worker and the fear that the client will be held in low esteem for his or her sexual orientation. The worker must show a great deal of sensitivity and unconditional positive regard for the client to establish safe ground for the client to talk about such traumatic personal issues. This means that heterosexual workers must acquire knowledge and skills for work with this clientele and not allow their own homophobia to harm clients (Morrow, 2000) by obtaining training in counseling gays and lesbians (Matthews & Lease, 1999).

Precipitating Factors.   Dependency versus autonomy, jealousy, and the perceived balance of power are major precipitating factors in battering in same-sex relationships (Renzetti, 1992). Balancing closeness and attachment with one's partner with independence and autonomy is difficult in any relationship, regardless of sexual orientation. In same-sex relationships, an absence of support outside the relationship may cause couples to turn more intensely to one another. Such dependence on one another may cause major stressors when one partner perceives the other as having become too autonomous, and fears abandonment.

Jealousy is certainly not exclusive to same-sex relationships. However, it may be more pronounced in same-sex relationships because another person of the same sex may pay attention to one partner and not to the other. As a result, such envy and jealousy may promote possessiveness and attempts to restrict and control the freedom of the other person, much as in a heterosexual relationship (Peterman & Dixon, 2003).

Distrust also tends to be much more pronounced in same-sex relationships than in heterosexual ones (Wiehe, 1998, p. 79). This is true because it is not uncommon for former lovers to still be in the support system of same-sex couples (all the same-sex people in a community may constitute each other's support system), whereas it is much easier to terminate those relationships in a heterosexual world (Kurdek, 1994). In summary, Craft and associates (2008) have found that some of the same issues of dependency and attachment theory that are abundant in heterosexual battering are also present in homosexual relations for both gay men and lesbian women. When stressors accumulate and escalate for those who have insecure attachment with their significant other, the threat of violence goes up.

Finally, the term *balance of power* refers to the ability of the person to influence and get others to do what he or she wants. Although heterosexual couples may have a division of labor in regard to household chores divided along stereotypical male–female lines, same-sex couples may have terrible conflicts over such domestic duties because they may perceive an inequity of power in doing these chores (Wiehe, 1998, p. 80)

Specific Issues.   Any exploratory assessment should deal with issues specific to same-sex couples. That is, threats of "outing" the other person's sexual orientation or his or her HIV-positive status, exploration of internalized homophobia, degree of closeting (hiding same-sex orientation from others), and acceptance of sexual orientation are all components that adversely affect gays and lesbians and may be used for coercion.

It should never be assumed that one person is the victim and the other the perpetrator. It is also a myth that same-sex battering is mutual because both partners have equal strength and the ability to fight back (Peterman & Dixon, 2003). Thus, for both the police who respond to the assault and crisis workers who counsel the victims, sorting out the truth is even more complicated than it is in heterosexual battering.

Marrujo and Kreger (1996) found that a third of the lesbian battering relationships they investigated fell into what they call a "participant" category. Although they didn't initiate the aggression, participants did fight back, and once engaged, gave as good as they got. Hopefully, the worker can sort out who did what by the partners' responses. Aggressors may paradoxically propose that they are the real victims, participants may see themselves as righteously justified in retaliating, and victims may express a desire to end the conflict and be safe. Indeed, some lesbian abusers have shown up at shelters claiming to be the abused partner in hopes of finding the person who has left them (Leventhal & Lundy, 1999).

Severity.   By the time a gay man or lesbian woman seeks therapeutic help with a relationship that involves battering, it is likely that a triage rating will put them in the highly impaired range. Interestingly, the person who seeks out therapy in a violent same-sex relationship

may be the *batterer*. He or she may have typical feelings of conjugal paranoia that involve jealousy, betrayal, and fears of abandonment over some new or old partner (Peterman & Dixon, 2003; Ricks, Vaughan, & Dziegielewski, 2002). These feelings may rapidly escalate to guilt, contrition, self-doubt, and self-disparagement as the client attempts to repair the damage to the relationship. The person may be dominated by an "all or none," "If I can't have him/her, nobody will," cognitive set, and be constantly attempting to keep the relationship intact and out of the arms of some other real or imagined threat (Bartholomew, 1999). At this point, lethality becomes a high probability.

Safety and Support.   A major concern is establishing a safety net and a support system because the client will believe that support people or resources are not available to him or her (and in fact they may have few, if any). Locating a support system or a safe place may be very difficult for gay or lesbian clients because a majority report they would not use support groups or go to a shelter and feel they are silenced and isolated when they do try to reach out for help (Lie & Gentlewarrier, 1991; Walters, 2011).

Treatment Issues.   Complex issues revolve around treatment delivery. Although heterosexual battered men have few places to find shelter, there are even fewer places for gay battered men to go—although a few shelters will offer hotel vouchers (Friess, 1997). Lesbians may not be welcomed with open arms by heterosexual women at shelters (Ricks, Vaughan, & Dziegielewski, 2002). Group therapy may be helpful for victims because it reduces feelings of isolation and provides a safe place to work through their issues with empathic others. It may also be helpful for perpetrators, because of the same isolation issues, and it may also offer a place where the peer group can confront the batterer. The problem is that mixing homosexuals with heterosexuals in groups is not recommended (Margolies & Leeder, 1995), and it may be very difficult to generate an intact gay or lesbian group.

Couples therapy, mediation, conflict resolution, or any other approach that brings the two warring parties together is debatable from the standpoint of safety. Further, the abuser may heartily endorse this as a way of keeping the relationship going and shifting blame onto the abused partner (Ricks, Vaughan, & Dziegielewski, 2002). Setting aside the foregoing factors that differentiate homosexual from heterosexual battering relationships, the crisis worker still operates pretty much in the same manner of providing for immediate safety needs, obtaining support, and empowering their clients to leave the relationship (Peterman & Dixon, 2003; Ricks, Vaughan, & Dziegielewski, 2002).

Treating Batterers

During the early 1980s, the Coalition for Justice for Battered Women in San Francisco was instrumental in getting police to redefine how they handle domestic disputes and how the district attorney prosecutes domestic assault cases (Sonkin, Martin, & Walker, 1985, p. 25). Police do not mediate but arrest, and district attorneys do not dismiss but prosecute. In short, batterers need to realize that domestic violence is a punishable crime (Sonkin, Martin, & Walker, 1985, p. 41), and in more and more cities and states it is becoming exactly that.

Although arrest may deter battering while the perpetrator is in jail (Gondolf, 1984; Sherman & Berk, 1984), that same perpetrator will come back to his family, or at least be in close proximity or inevitably form a relationship with another woman. While many believe that "throwing the bum in jail" is justified because of the battering, jail will not have changed the batterer's attitudes and behavior in any way, and he will continue to be a threat (Bent-Goodley et al., 2011).

Many communities and most states have adopted some form of diversion program modeled along the lines of the program the Coalition for Justice for Battered Women in San Francisco and the Domestic Abuse Intervention Program intervention model developed in Duluth, Minnesota (the Duluth model). These are *intervention* models as opposed to *treatment* models. Note the distinction between *intervention* and *treatment*. As with many systemic crises, there are philosophical issues between grassroots activists who organized and lobbied for aggressive intervention with batterers and mental health professionals, who came after them, who focus on the underlying pathology of the batterer and seek to provide treatment to change the personality structures that cause the battering (Rosenbaum & Kunkel, 2009).

Whereas treatment of any psychological issues is generally considered private and confidential, the Duluth model is not concerned with confidentiality and in many ways, according to its critics, goes out of its way to publicize batterers and their issues, in clear violation of the confidentiality rules that all psychological treatment programs we know of abide by. Because it sees battering as a public matter, this stance has invoked the ire of many professionals, who see real ethical dilemmas in approaching treatment of batterers in that manner. They further see the model as based not so much on evidence-based research as on emotion and political pressure (Corvo, Dutton, & Chen, 2009; Dutton, 2007; Dutton & Corvo, 2006, 2007; Rosenbaum & Kunkle, 2009). Supporters of the model, in turn, point to the critics' own research biases and maintain there is psychological theory and criminal justice research that support the Duluth model (Gondolf, 2007). The data are indeed conflicting as to what, if any, good any of these models does in stopping recidivism of batterers.

There is also wide divergence in the length of programs, which range from one meeting a week for 12 weeks up to a full year. There is also wide divergence in the education and training that facilitators must have. In a number of states, no college degree or professional licensure is required, although most states do mandate that some sort of training in domestic violence must be completed. Policies regarding absences and termination for conduct and absenteeism are also extremely variable. The same is true of fees. Many batterers are of lower socioeconomic status and cannot afford the programs, so most states provide for a sliding fee schedule based on income. However, most states do demand that batterers pay some fees so that value is attached to the service (Rosenbaum & Kunkel, 2009).

Intervention Models

These models are feminist based, have highly integrated coordination between a variety of agencies, provide support to survivors of IPV across a range of issues, and provide psychoeducational treatment to batterers. That treatment focuses primarily on power and control issues (Rosenbaum & Kunkle, 2009).

The Duluth model requires a tremendous amount of commitment and integration of community agencies, mental health facilities and institutions, police, and judiciary to provide services for battered women. In Duluth, more than 10 agencies, five distinct levels and types of government, and dozens of workers of those institutions will be involved. As you might well imagine, getting all these agencies and institutions working on the same page is equivalent to herding cats. Lindsay and Brady (2002) acknowledge and discuss some of these issues when such massive integration of services is undertaken. The treatment aspect of the model does have a cognitive-behavioral component to it. However, it also examines the historic separation of roles and power for men and women and seeks to knock down those stereotypes. The program's aim is to give batterers insight into their mistaken beliefs and goals based on these age-old stereotypes about marital roles and functions and to change their belief systems in regard to marriage, relationships, women, masculinity, and the use of aggression to solve problems (Aymer, 2008; Miller, 2010; Pence & McDonnell, 2000).

Treatment Models

Most other models have a cognitive-behavioral basis that focuses on cognitive restructuring of batterers' irrational thinking (Rosenbaum & Kunkle, 2009). Models that emphasize batterer strengths rather than deficits are being tried (Lehmann & Simmons, 2009). Other models provide skill building through self-empowerment strategies. This model works off the notion that targeting self-empowerment can revise and regulate feelings of powerlessness and worthlessness, which are hypothesized as core values that lead to the abuse. In this model, then, abuse is seen as a problem not of the woman, but rather of the abuser's own feelings of inadequacy and failure to develop compassion for loved ones (Stosny, 1995).

From a therapeutic treatment viewpoint, cognitive-behavioral treatments are seen as the preferred mode of operation. Indeed, treatment professionals take umbrage at the notion that this is "anger management training" because they see the issues that batterers are attempting to overcome as far more complex than that. Thus, it will probably come as a surprise to you that most programs and many states prohibit "anger management" as a primary treatment because they see it as an excuse to rationalize a controlled behavior (Rosenbaum & Kunkel, 2009). The fact is that in many instances the Duluth model has been combined with cognitive-behavioral therapy for batterers, so there is a great deal of variance between programs that claim to follow the Duluth model (Bennett & Vincent, 2001; Healy, Smith, & O'Sullivan, 1998).

Hybrid Models

In our own community of Memphis, an adjudicated batterer is given a thorough assessment and diagnostic interview after adjudication. Although specific treatment recommendations such as parent training, drug abuse treatment, and individual mental health counseling are generated for each person, the vast majority will be recommended for anger management. Certainly,

most batterers, particularly those so adjudicated, do not willingly come to a treatment program, nor are they willing to admit that they have problems. People who enter counseling for abuse often manifest outright denial, minimization, or justification and projection of blame to escape owning their abusive behavior (Shupe, Stacey, & Hazlewood, 1987, pp. 26–28).

Denying batterer: I never touched her. Sure, I'd been drinking a little, and we had an argument. She must have fallen, because she was pretty drunk too! (*The complainant had three broken teeth, a fractured jaw, and two broken ribs, plus numerous contusions, cuts, and abrasions.*)

Minimizing batterer: Well, I might have pushed her when we were arguing at the top of the stairs, but I'd never hit her. (*The complainant had a broken nose, a bruised kidney, and two black eyes from the "push."*)

Projecting batterer: Listen, she ain't no rose. She gives as good as she gets. Besides, I got some rights, like dinner when I get home from work, instead of a drunk sittin' in front of the TV suckin' on a drink. She deserved a lesson! She always gets the kids to stick up for her. (*Both the woman and her two children were treated at an emergency room for contusions and lacerations from being whipped with a power cord.*)

Although individual counseling, partner counseling, and partner counseling in groups have been attempted (Shupe, Stacey, & Hazlewood, 1987, pp. 26–27; Stith et al., 2004; Tolman & Bennett, 1990), the prevalent mode of counseling for batterers is court-ordered group counseling. Generally, couples counseling is not recommended until the batterer has made a great deal of progress on anger management and other personality issues, and only if both parties truly wish to reconcile (Hamberger, 1994; Lawson, 2003). Groups provide opportunities for social learning and retraining that would be nearly impossible in individual or couple therapy (Adams & McCormick, 1982). The group also provides a support system for what are typically emotionally isolated individuals and enables these men and women to start to learn how to depend on others in times of stress.

Treatment Goals

Group treatment formats, however they are configured, have four major purposes: (1) ensure the safety of the victimized partner, (2) alter the batterer's attitudes toward violence, (3) increase the batterer's sense of personal responsibility and teach him about equity issues, and (4) help the batterer learn nonviolent alternatives to past behaviors (Edleson & Tolman, 1992; Mederos,

1999). Groups typically use either the Duluth model (Pence & Paymar, 1993), which operates with a power and control focus, or an anger management model, which seeks to understand and control anger (Hamby, 1998, pp. 223–225). There appears to be merit in both approaches.

To accomplish these goals, most groups use a combination of anger management, stress reduction, communication skills, and sex role resocialization components (Dutton, 1995; Gondolf, 1985; Hamby, 1998; Mederos, 1999). Therapeutically, most programs use some form of cognitive-behavioral approach that deals with batterers' irrational thinking and also provides techniques to restructure maladaptive cognitions, overreaction to violent urges, self-sabotage, setting oneself up for violence, and selective forgetting; offers assertiveness training and teaches problem solving; and handles premature "cures" (Dutton, 1995; Hamby, 1998; Hanson, 2002; Lawson, 2003; Mederos, 1999). Programs typically are psychoeducational, structured learning experiences with some time reserved for role play, discussion, and processing concepts and ideas (Edleson & Syers, 1990; Scales & Winter, 1991). Co-leaders are generally used so that they can model together the types of behaviors the batterers need to learn, and any interactions between one leader and a member can be facilitated by the other group leader (Sonkin, Martin, & Walker, 1985, p. 98). Groups typically meet once a week for 2 hours and range from 8 to 32 sessions (Tolman & Bennett, 1990). Before a batterer is inducted into a group, an assessment and intake interview should be conducted to obtain a profile of the battering behavior, incidence of other psychological problems, and motivation to participate in counseling.

Assessment

The Conflict Tactics Scale (Straus, 1979) has been the only instrument used on any wide scale to measure intrafamilial conflict. The scale looks mainly at physical means used to resolve conflicts, does not adequately account for verbal abuse, and entirely ignores the emotional, social, sexual, and economic forms of abuse. It also does not look at power differential—one of the key ingredients in domestic violence (Poynter, 1989). It certainly was not meant to—nor does it—predict who will be violent or who, after being arrested or completing counseling, will recidivate.

One test that should always be given is an alcohol screening test such as the Substance Abuse Subtle Screening Inventory (Miller, 1983), with follow-up interview questions. Determining alcohol abuse is important for two reasons. First, numerous studies have shown *chronic* alcohol abuse to be a strong predictor of more violent behavior (Blount et al., 1994; Heyman, Jouriles, & O'Leary, 1995; Stuart et al., 2006; Tolman & Bennett, 1990). Second, any individual who is under the influence of a mind-altering substance needs to get dried out first.

Probably the worst "bets" for success in anger management and those most likely to recidivate are those individuals who fall into personality disorder categories. Therefore, tests like the Millon Clinical Multiaxial Inventory (Millon, 1987) may be used to determine borderline, narcissistic, depressive, somatoform, antisocial, and other pathological types. If elevated scores on the Millon indicate psychopathology, these individuals may be served better in individual therapy that targets their pathology rather than in a generic anger management group (Hanson, 2002; Lawson, 2003; Mederos, 1999). Dutton (Dutton, 1994, 1995; Dutton & Starzomski, 1993, 1994) has extensively examined borderline personality disorder (BPD) as a unifying personality construct in domestic violence. Dutton's research seems to indicate that the individual who batters looks much more like a full-blown BPD than a normal individual who does not batter. His research presents a strong argument that there are at least some batterers whose major problem is intimacy anxiety and fear of abandonment, hallmarks of the borderline personality, as opposed to the more universal and feminist notion of domestic violence as being an attempt to reinforce male dominance and preserve a patriarchal order (Dutton, 1995, p. 138). This "either/or" view has much to say about how treatment for batterers should be conducted and has bred a great deal of controversy in regard to treatment approaches.

The Intake Interview

The worker should conduct a comprehensive intake interview to assess the batterer's psychological status and motivation and provide information on what may be expected from a counseling group (Sonkin, Martin, & Walker, 1985; Tolman & Bennett, 1990). First, the worker should assess lethality, for both suicidal and homicidal ideation and/or behavior. As paradoxical as it may seem, many batterers are so dependent on their partners that the thought of being without them is worse than death, so suicide and murder may seem viable and realistic options.

There are apparent relationships between lethality and a number of factors common in battering relationships, such as frequency of violent incidents, severity of injuries, threats to kill, suicide threats by the woman, length and incidence of the batterer's drug use, frequency of intoxication, and forced or threatened sexual acts (Sonkin, Martin, & Walker, 1985, p. 73). A fast assessment of the history of the violent relationship would seek details on the first, last, worst, and typical episode to provide a comprehensive profile of the kind, degree, and length of abuse. Assaults and violence on other family members, previous criminal activity, violence outside the home, increased social proximity of victim, attitudes toward violence, life stresses, general mental functioning, physical health, and physical and emotional isolation are important background information on the potential for future violent behavior. The more these indicators appear, the more likely the client is to engage in lethal behavior (Sonkin, Martin, & Walker, 1985, pp. 75–83).

It should be remembered that these men and women are in crisis, and appropriate measures should be taken to ensure everyone's safety. Bodnarchuk and associates (1995) estimate that, based on the National Family Violence Surveys, their domestic violence clients fell into the most dangerous 1 percent of the U.S. population. During intake interviews, such people should be given clear messages about expectations inside and outside the group and what the consequences of inappropriate behavior will be. Finally, there is evidence that clients who are apprised of the procedures, purpose, and goals of the group are less likely to drop out and less likely to recidivate (Tolman & Bennett, 1990).

Motivation

Motivation depends on a number of variables. Men who are younger, are less educated, have lower incomes, were abused as children, and are minorities drop out at a significantly higher rate (Tolman & Bennett, 1990) than do those who are older, have no arrest record, are better educated, are employed, have more children, and witnessed abuse but were not abused themselves as children (Demaris, 1989; Grusznski & Carrillo, 1988). Tolman and Bennett (1990) report that structured groups tend to be more effective, and it appears from the Memphis Family Trouble Center's low attrition rate (10 percent) that the threat of having probation revoked and spending up to a year in jail is a strong external motivator for obtaining the points necessary to complete the program (Winter, 1991).

A Typical 24-Session Anger Management Group

The following profiles the highlights of a typical 24-session group counseling format for batterers. The content of the course is taken from the Memphis Police Department's Family Trouble Center (FTC) anger management program. The counselor dialogue is abstracted from Betty Winter (1991), director of the program and facilitator of numerous anger management groups.

It would be an error to think that only men go through treatment for perpetrating domestic violence. Although better than 90 percent of those who go through the FTC program are men, the percentage of women adjudicated for anger management is increasing. Therefore the generic terms "clients," "members," and "participants" will be used in describing the FTC anger management program because both genders are represented.

Starting the Group. A great deal of anger is ventilated over being arrested and adjudicated to the program. The batterers are mad and hostile about being there. The crisis worker starts the group by sitting in the middle of it and letting the group interview her. She responds to any professional and personal questions she deems appropriate.

CW: (*after giving qualifications*) One of my major credentials is that I get angry a lot, but I've never been arrested for it. Now that I've given you my credentials, I'd like you to give me your credentials, the ones that got you here. I'd like you all to pair off, and I'd like for each pair to share with one another what caused you to get here. Then I'd like each pair to report back to the group.

By putting herself at risk with this group and letting them interview her, the crisis worker turns the tables on these angry clients. It is very difficult for these "macho" clients not to own up to what brought them here when a woman can face up to their angry and caustic interrogation of her and her credentials. The rules of attendance and conduct are reviewed, and positive and negative consequences of appropriate and inappropriate behavior are explained. For many of these individuals, it will be the first structure they have experienced since high school, so they will need to know very clearly what is expected of them. The major purpose of this counseling is corrective and remedial. It is counseling within the criminal justice system. As a result, initially trust is not high, and in these early sessions the therapist meets the issue head on.

CW: I don't expect you to share everything in this group. Take some time to see how safe you feel in here. Although what you say will be held in confidence within the bounds of the legal and ethical standards I've talked about, you're undoubtedly feeling pretty victimized by the system right now. Nobody will force you to say anything you don't want to.

Paradoxically, the admonition to not trust probably does much to establish trust and breaks down some barriers and paranoia about the group.

Making Choices. The group is given an explanation of what taking an anger time-out is and is given a homework assignment of taking practice time-outs at home. Finally, the concept of choices is introduced.

CW: You'll think this is crazy, but you did have a choice in coming here. If you don't like what we're about, you can leave. (*Gets up, walks to the door, and opens it.*) Of course, you will have chosen to violate your probation terms and will probably go to jail.

Batterer: That's no damn choice.

CW: Granted, it's not a good choice, but it is a choice, just like what got you here. Battering was a bad choice, but it was one you made. During the course of the time we're here, we'll be looking at a lot of those choices you make.

Most of the clients do not realize that when they do something, they are making choices. Furthermore, they don't realize the variety of choices open to them. The concept of decision making and choosing wisely will be woven throughout the 24 sessions.

Support and Confrontation. Another key component of the group is instituted in these first sessions: dyadic interaction—"that pairing crap," as participants call it. Clients are immediately paired off and start working with one another in pairs. Pairing off starts to generate closeness and bonding in the group. It also conveys early on that there is interest in hearing their story.

Open-ended questions and reflective responses alone are not conducive to facilitating the start-up phase of a group of hostile and anxious batterers. Therefore, a combination of both open-ended and closed-ended questions and supportive and confrontive statements is needed to break through defense systems, reflect threatening feelings, and reframe irrational thinking (Sonkin, Martin, & Walker, 1985, pp. 64–65).

CW: (*indirectly confrontive*) How did you come to be here?

Batterer: I sorta hit my wife.

CW: (*directly confronting the minimization with a semi-open question*) I don't understand "sorta"! What do you mean?

Batterer: (*projecting and blaming*) I mean she made me mad. She was running her mouth, so I had to hit her.

CW: (*confronting all-or-none thinking*) You say "had to" as if there were no options other than to smack her.

Batterer: Not really—she was really being a bitch!

CW: (*proposing consequences and obtaining facts*) So your choice for stopping her bitching was breaking her jaw. That choice also got you arrested. What happened?

Batterer: She swore out a warrant, and I got sent to jail.

CW: (*confrontive closed question*) Had you ever been in jail before?

Batterer: Lord no!

CW: (*empathically reflecting feeling*) I'm betting that was a scary experience.

Batterer: You better believe it. There were some bad dudes in there. I didn't know if I was gonna get out of there in one piece.

CW: (*reflecting feeling and exploring affect*) So you were feeling pretty alone and helpless. I'm wondering how you're feeling right now?

Batterer: Madder than hell that I got to be here.

CW: (*closed question that seeks to elicit defensive responding*) Do you understand why you're here?

Batterer: (*projecting*) 'Cause she swore out a warrant on me.

CW: (*confronting projection by making client own behavior*) No! You are here because you put your wife in the hospital by beating her. That's criminal assault. The judge gave you a choice, and you are still free to exercise it. You may come here to 24 group sessions for people who have battered. You have the opportunity to learn some things here that may help you with future relationships and that may also keep you out of harm's way in the future. Or you may walk out of here right now.

Batterer: That's not much of a choice.

CW: (*confronting batterer with consequences of his behavior*) Maybe not, but it's more of a choice than you gave your partner.

The responses are typical of a batterer's way of defending himself with denial, externalization of blame, and black-and-white kinds of statements that give little consideration to behavioral options and long-term consequences of behavior. The crisis worker gently but firmly wades into the client's defense system while at the same time attempting to establish rapport. This is not an easy job.

Managing Stress. The time-out assignment is discussed. Participants start looking for physical anger cues, and are asked to write down the signs as warning signals and learn to use those cues to time themselves out of an escalating dialogue that has the potential to turn violent. Basic stress management skills and relaxation techniques are taught and practiced. The worker gives a homework assignment that combines recognizing physical cues of anger with the use of relaxation techniques.

The prevailing pragmatic philosophy of the FTC program is that it is extremely difficult if not impossible to change ideology. Rather, the notion is that the batterer's sex role expectations may differ from his or her partner's and that he or she can be taught how to negotiate those differences. That notion is much more palatable and makes much more sense within clients' social and work environment than attempting to re-indoctrinate them into a more feminist view of role expectations.

Understanding the Cycle of Violence. The idea is to make batterers aware of Walker's (1979) cycle and its commonality to all relationships, both at home and in the workplace, and to help them gain some dynamic insight into their own behavior and that of their partners as they go around in this destructive cycle. Clients are apprised of the difficulty of getting out of the cycle because of how long it has been going on and its familiarity. Anger diaries are started. Anger diaries help to identify instigators of anger and the physical and cognitive responses to it. They also help batterers start to identify feelings that support anger, such as guilt, shame, and depression. The diaries start to condition responsibility, because the person must constantly attend to diaries as he or she monitors anger.

Costs. Few batterers have stopped to think of the costs. Costs vary, but it is not uncommon for a group to average a minimum of $10,000 per person in financing his or her anger.

CW: Add up all the money you've spent on lawyers, work time lost, furniture broken, hospital bills, bail, fines, motel rooms, not to mention divorce proceedings and alimony as a direct or indirect result of violence. What could it have bought you? Wouldn't it be great to never have to spend another dime on your anger? You see, learning to control your anger will make you money. How many of you would be against that?

Time is also spent on the emotional cost to victims. These factors paradoxically start to describe some of the background of batterers because they have also become victims, albeit of their own behavior. Indeed, once they can start to see themselves as victims, they gain insight into how their victims feel. This is the start of empathic understanding for these clients.

CW: Add up all the emotional costs: the guilty, angry, hurt, depressed, dependent, hopeless, helpless feelings. Wouldn't it be great to never have another lousy feeling like that? How does that fit with your partner's notions of being your victim? Is there any difference between how your partner may feel about you after a beating and how you feel about the court system?

Shoulds, Oughts, and Musturbatory Thinking. Members are asked to write down three bad choices and three good choices they have made in their relationships. Anger diaries are used to help the batterers identify the emotional toll that their choice of anger and violence takes on them. The leader introduces the topics of irrational thinking and the maladaptive behavior resulting from it. Cognitive-behavioral techniques from Albert Ellis's (1990) *Anger: How to Live With It and Without It* are illustrated. Specific emphasis is placed on absolutist thinking and *should*, *must*, and *ought* statements. Discussion focuses on how these statements get constructed, what environmental cues set up "*must*urbatory" thinking ("I must have my self-gratification or it will be absolutely intolerable"), and how irrational, self-defeating thoughts and subsequent maladaptive behavior are tied together.

Violence and Families of Origin. A violence and abuse assessment is made of the family of origin. Leaders ask members to respond to such questions as "Did your father hit your mother, or vice versa?" "How were disagreements handled?" "How did you feel about your parents?" "How were you disciplined as a child?" "How do all those events that you learned from early childhood carry over into your present family?" "How do you feel about that?" "How do those irrational beliefs we talked about earlier in the session relate to the behavior that you saw and learned as a child?" Members are given didactic instruction on how transgenerational violence occurs.

Processing the following discussion questions generally results in a shocking and nasty insight, because the very thing the batterers hated most about their own parents they may now be perpetrating on their children. This will be the first time that many of the batterers have ever talked about their childhood experiences with domestic violence, and it is usually a very emotional experience.

CW: What was your feeling as a child in regard to the abuse you saw? How do you suppose your kids are affected by your violent behavior? Do they feel any different from the way you did? Guess at their feelings and what they might be thinking about you and why they might feel and think that way.

The homework assignment is to start changing members' ways of responding to stressful situations by (1) watching out for environmental cues that start *mus*turbatory thinking and (2) using cooler cognitions, such as "It'd be nice, convenient, if XYZ happened, but it doesn't *have* to happen."

Feelings. Participants are asked to list several positive and negative feelings they have. Usually most of them will have a great deal of difficulty with this task, because they have never had to identify any feelings they have. Feelings generally get lumped into two categories, angry and happy. A lecture is given on how males, in particular, are taught at a very early age to "stuff" their feelings and not acknowledge them as real. The anger diaries are used to expand their ability to label and identify the many feelings that support anger.

Outcomes from denying feelings are discussed. Examples are given from Stoop and Arterburn's (1991) *The Angry Man: "Why Does He Act That Way?"* This session is very difficult, because members will be asked to share feelings—a very threatening experience for most of them. Leader statements such as the following are designed to minimize the threat.

CW: Although there are risks when you tell someone how you feel because you become vulnerable, you also become a lot more real. You become much more lovable and find it easier to love when you tell someone how you feel. You need to be prepared for them to do the same and understand that there is the possibility of feeling some pain and hurt from what is said. You don't tell someone your feelings just to get their sympathy. You share your feelings with significant others as a way of taking care of yourself, so you don't have to stuff feelings anymore until they finally boil over and get you in trouble or hurt you.

Outcomes may be very dramatic as clients start to talk about their feelings, relive their experiences as children, and grapple with feelings of guilt, helplessness, dependency, and insecurity that they have had since childhood. It is not uncommon for some highly charged emotional catharsis to occur at this point and, as these feelings emerge, for some strong bonds to form as clients start, for the first time, to share deeply but closely held feelings with another person.

Power and Control. The attempt to convey verbally both positive and negative feelings is discussed and leads into issues of power and control. Power and control are the focus of the session, discussed in relation to faulty belief systems. The stereotypical concept of power in batterers' issues develops out of a mistaken concept of independence: "I've got it, so you don't!" A new way of looking at power is interdependence: "The two of us together are more powerful than any one person!" Questions are posed about how they can form a team with their partner to reduce those powerless feelings. It is interesting that many of these clients who are physically strong may feel extremely powerless and frustrated when they are dealing verbally with others and when they are being "outtalked" in a relationship and may regress to their only way of regaining power and control—violence.

CW: When you allow someone else to push your button, who is in control? How do you use anger as a control tool? Abuse is a last-ditch effort to gain control back in a relationship. Why is that so? Do you believe that you try to get power and control only when you feel you don't have any? If power and control are the bottom line, do abuse, anger, and battering get the job done for you? If they really do get the job done, then why do you still have to rely on them?

Assertion. Closely allied with different ways of obtaining power and control are the concepts of aggressiveness and assertiveness. Because of their inability to use words in powerful ways, most of the participants have difficulty making clear assertions about what their wants and needs are. Furthermore, they have an overriding fear that they will be rejected if they ask for something, and their insecurity does not handle rejection well at all. As a result, they use aggression to meet their needs. The group is taught how to construct assertion statements and given an assignment of using them at home.

The most difficult part of an assertion statement for the group is the "I" or owning part. On the board, the leader puts up "I" or assertion statements and "you" or aggression statements so members know what they sound like, how they differ, and what can happen when each is used. Each member is asked to formulate a problem in terms of "I" and "you" statements and practice with a partner. Using a describe, express, specify, and consequences script (Bower & Bower, 1976), members are asked to identify what behaviors in others bother them, to express how those behaviors make them feel, to specify what new behaviors they want, and to be able to positively reinforce others if those behaviors happen. Careful construction of these clear, precise, and owned assertive statements is practiced through role plays.

Because jealousy is common to most of the stories that have brought members here, time is devoted to members' retelling their original story using the skills they have learned in their first 16 sessions. As these stories are reprocessed, other feelings undergirding the jealousy begin to surface. Hurt, betrayal, insecurity, lack of trust, and dependency are all threatening feelings that are denied and replaced by jealousy, which allows batterers to place blame on their partners for "transgressions," thus providing a face-saving way of not having to deal with their own problems.

Batterer: I hate to admit it, but all that stuff makes sense. Still and all, I don't believe I can trust her.

CW: Maybe you know she can't trust you, so you don't trust her. Could you use some of those "I" statements and discuss it with her, and no matter what she said, not use "you" statements?

The homework is to name a time in their lives when jealousy turned to violence. The members are also asked to mentally substitute a new feeling every time they start to feel jealous and to report back on their experience.

Alcohol and Drug Effects. Because alcohol and drugs play a predominant role in the vast majority of battering incidents, members are educated about how these issues apply to battering—specifically, that alcoholism and drug abuse are not necessarily the cause of battering but release inhibitions enough that batterers can give themselves permission to become violent. Results of the Substance Abuse Subtle Screening Inventory (Miller, 1983) are given to each participant. Participants are shown how alcohol or drugs can be a trigger for violent behavior and an excuse for making violent behavior acceptable.

Sex. Sex is an overriding concern because of all the myths that surround it. Much of the need of the batterer to feel superior, confident, and capable is tied to sex and, particularly for men, their concept of manhood. Many times, particularly with young female leaders, members will say things and use language designed to shock and embarrass the leaders. Although X-rated language just for the sake of X-rated language is not tolerated, some leeway is given for the street vernacular that is commonly used. The ability of group leaders, particularly young women, to weather the language

goes a long way toward establishing their credentials with these men.

Batterer: So she wouldn't give me a blow job, so I smacked her. That's part of earning her keep, to blow my pipes, man!

CW: (*young female graduate student*) So forcing oral sex on her keeps you in control. I wonder if the way you said that isn't designed to shock and embarrass me and kinda control me through verbal sex like you control her physically through sex.

Batterer: Hey, I thought we was supposed to be talking about the real stuff in here.

CW: (*very calmly, with eyes leveled at the batterer, avoiding the taunt*) I'm wondering how you'd like it if Harold (*240-pound ironworker in the group*) were to request oral sex of you, and if you didn't comply, start pounding on you, particularly in your groin. Do you start to get some of the feelings your partner would get? (*The group members nod their heads in agreement.*) I wonder if you can respond to that?

The many myths that hold men up to impossible Hollywood "stud" or women to "love goddess" standards are discussed and debunked. For many of the clients, this will be the first valid information they have ever received about sexual behavior. They will typically experience relief after being told that no man or woman could live up to some of the performance expectations they have self-propagandized for themselves. Homework assignments focus on irrational and negative thoughts clients generate for themselves in their sexual relations. They are asked to watch for and write down some of their unrealistic expectations of themselves. They are also asked to try using assertion statements when asking for sex. Coming to understand that making requests for sex ("I'd like to make love to you") rather than demanding sex ("You get in here and do it") may not only get them sex, but better sex, is a revelation. Finally, the leader asks each member to pick one of the subjects already covered in the group and be prepared to teach a review on it next session.

Summing Up. Amazingly, many of these groups bond. Members express that this is the first time in their lives they have been able to openly express feelings and feel they have been listened to by someone. Participants may actually form friendships as a result of the group.

CW: If you had to tell the judge anything about this program, what would it be? What did you like best and least? What would you like to see changed? What techniques seemed to work for you, and what didn't?

Members then discuss how they are putting their comprehensive anger management plans into action. They also indicate the strengths they now see in themselves and positively reinforce one another for their efforts. Depending on how cohesive the group has become, it is not uncommon for the clients to bring food, exchange phone numbers, and have a graduation party for one another at the last session.

Program Success

Do battering programs work? The results are equivocal. Overall, batterers report that such programs help them gain control of their anger, enable them to communicate better with their partners, and reduce their violence. Shupe, Stacey, and Hazlewood (1987) found that battered women in approximately 7 out of 10 cases reported that physical and sexual violence stopped after their partners went through an anger management program. When violence did recur after the men graduated from these programs, it was almost always remarkably reduced. Relationships were also improved, and many women who had not attended indicated that they had picked up pointers that their partners brought home from the sessions (pp. 113–117). The following have all been found in a variety of studies involving battering groups with different cultural, racial, and socioeconomic backgrounds: increases in self-esteem (Kriner & Waldron, 1988) and assertiveness (Douglas & Perrin, 1987); decreases in depression and anger (Hamberger & Hastings, 1986), in jealousy and negative attitudes toward women (Saunders & Hanusa, 1986), and in overall psychological symptoms (Hawkins & Beauvais, 1985); reduction in both self-reported and corroborated physical and psychological abuse on postcounseling follow-up (Edleson & Syers, 1990; Poynter, 1989); and more cohesive, expressive, and less conflict-ridden family life (Poynter, 1989).

Other researchers have found little evidence to indicate that rates of violence by perpetrators who obtain and complete treatment are very different from those who do not (Rosenfeld, 1992; Tolman & Bennett, 1990). More recent meta-analyses of batterer prevention programs have indicated less than satisfactory results (Babcock, Green, & Robbie, 2004; Stover, Meadows, & Kaufman, 2009). Babcock and associates conducted a comprehensive meta-analysis of battering programs and found small effect size in overall success for programs. They also found little difference between programs that used the Duluth model and those that used CBT programs. What these results mean is that the programs appear to have little impact on recidivism. Stover and her associates found that the recidivism rate for both perpetrator- and partner-focused treatments was about 30 percent after 6 months.

However, there are some important footnotes to these sobering statistics. There are probably as many different programs and different styles of intervention as there are programs. Also, the expertise of individuals providing the treatment may vary a great deal. A critical prerequisite for batterers' not recidivating is the imposition of severe consequences for not completing the program or for battering again. Such consequences are not always enforced. Tracking batterers is difficult. Many of these people are very transient, moving from jurisdiction to jurisdiction, and there is no good way to determine if they have recidivated when they are halfway across the country. Frankly, because of the severity of their pathology, some people do not or cannot profit from group programs.

It appears that close follow-up supervision of batterers makes a large difference in recidivism (Barber & Wright, 2010), so it may be that besides treatment, close follow-up may be a critical variable either from the standpoint of feeling supported or threat of punishment. Where and to whom treatment is rendered also appears to make a difference. Smith (2003) reported that the Duluth model and the Military Family Advocacy Program LEAD model were both effective in reducing domestic violence, with only a 5 percent recidivism rate, in the U.S. Marine Corps. The fact that noncompletion of such a program in the Marine Corps could ruin one's career may be a potent consequence in ensuring completion. Sartin (2005) found differential effects by clustering batterer types. Not surprisingly, family-only batterers were better program completers than antisocial and borderline cluster types. He also found that being employed was the only significant demographic variable predicting program completion. So, keeping a job by not going to jail may be an important motivator.

Another issue is motivation to change. Walker and her associates (2010) developed the Perceived Consequences of Domestic Violence Questionnaire to assess the consequences of intimate partner violence as perceived as the perpetrator. They found that the scale would significantly predict motivation to change and treatment-seeking behavior. Thus, it may be that screening instruments that separate out more pathological types may produce better results in terms of program completion and reduced recidivism. Research indicates that batterers must attend at least 75 percent of the sessions in anger management groups to have a chance of avoiding recidivism (Chen et al., 1989). What is clear is that arrest alone will not change much of anything in a domestic violence situation without concomitant treatment for the batterer (Gelles, 1993; Hirschel, Hutchison, & Dean, 1992).

Although most clients come to battering programs angry and hostile because they are pressured or required to be there, the majority report that they learn from and even come to enjoy the camaraderie of the group (Scales & Winter, 1991). Whether the programs truly change their participants or whether they work in other ways, as graphically described in the following excerpt, clients who complete a battering program are not reported to the police nearly as often as those who have nothing happen to them.

Batterer: Man, I ain't never gonna beat up on a woman again. Nothing will ever make me go through this crap twice! (Shupe, Stacey, & Hazlewood, 1987, p. 103)

Although research indicates that witnessing battering as a child is a primary modeling factor for both the abused and the abuser, as innocuous an event as one's favorite professional football team winning a game (White, Katz, & Scarborough, 1992) or watching World Wrestling Entertainment (Butryn, 2003) may have an impact on battering. Carden (1994) states that "Seventeen years after the founding of the first program designed to eliminate wife abuse by working with the wife abuser, we have only the most primitive notions about what works, why and how it works, or even whether in the long run, it does work" (p. 573). Sadly, after another 17 years and more, we are still only a little further along in our understanding and prevention of domestic violence.

SUMMARY

Battering has deep roots in the psychological, sociological, and cultural makeup of the United States and many other countries that go back to the beginnings of their patriarchal systems. Battering is pervasive through all socioeconomic levels of society and knows no ethnic, racial, or religious boundaries. Same-sex relationships are also not immune from domestic violence. Dynamically, battering may be seen as having much to do with the concept of power. A number of stressors that insinuate themselves into a relationship can escalate relational problems to violence.

A variety of theories have been proposed to explain why battering occurs. However, it is still unclear what propels people into battering relations, why people batter, and what will keep them from battering again. Domestic violence is sequential, developmental, and dynamic. The situation of the battered client is unlike that of many others in crisis in that it is almost always transcrisis in nature; that is, it is cyclic, reaching many peak levels over extended periods of time. For a variety of reasons, it is the rare person who leaves a violent relationship for good after the first battering. Continued and increased violence over a period of years is the typical pattern of battering relationships.

In the last decade, crisis lines, shelters, and programs for battered women and their children have grown exponentially across the United States. Courts and law enforcement agencies have become much more proactive in protecting the rights of these women. However, the number of battered women still far exceeds the capacity of human services to deal with them comprehensively and effectively. One of the most frustrating components of intervention with clients who are victims of domestic violence is their seeming inability to extract themselves from the terrible situations they face.

Providing counseling in such trying circumstances calls for a great deal of empathic understanding. The worker's job is to help keep the client as safe as possible, provide options, and, working patiently with the victim, help her or him explore alternatives and choose a plan of action. Recently, the focus on domestic violence has shifted to include comprehensive and integrated intervention and treatment programs that involve social services agencies, law enforcement, and the judicial system. IBPs operate throughout the country. Typically sent to such groups by court order, batterers learn to understand the factors that lead them to violence, learn to recognize and communicate their feelings, and learn to avoid or stop confrontations that lead them to act out their feelings in violent ways. If you are being battered and don't know what to do, and there don't seem to be resources in your community, call the National Domestic Violence Hotline at 1-800-799-SAFE or

1-800-787-3224 (TTY). If you are suffering from dating abuse, call the Helpline at 1-866-331-9474 or 1-866-331-8453 (TTY). If someone is stalking you, call 1-800-394-2255 or 1800-211-7996 (TTY).

To see some of the concepts discussed in this chapter in action, refer to your *Crisis Intervention in Action* DVD, or see the clips online on the Counseling Course-Mate website. To access this site, go to www.cengagebrain.com, where you'll also find an eBook, additional study tools, quizzes, and more. Being a crisis worker who deals with battering is one of the toughest jobs going and requires infinite amounts of patience. You have three vignettes in the date abuse scenario. Make yourself a frustration scale thermometer, ranging from 1 (no frustration) to 10 (frustration to the max), before you try to reach through the screen and shake the woman to death while yelling "GET OUT!" If you can keep your thermometer below 7 through the third scenario, you are probably cut out for this kind of work. How do you think Becky handles her frustration?

REFERENCES

Adams, D., & McCormick, A. (1982). Men unlearning violence: A group approach based on the collective model. In M. Roy (Ed.), *The abusive partner* (pp. 170–197). New York: Van Nostrand Reinhold.

Agency for Healthcare Research and Quality. (2010). Domestic violence on the decline but young women are at highest risk. *Research activities no. 360*. Washington, DC: U.S. Department of Health and Human Services.

Aguilar, R. J., & Nightingale, N. N. (1994). The impact of specific battering experiences on the self-esteem of abused women. *Journal of Family Violence, 9*, 35–45.

Ahrens, C. E., Rios-Mandel, L. C., Isas, L., & Lopez, A. D. (2010). Talking about interpersonal violence: Cultural influence of Latinas' identification and disclosure of sexual assault and partner violence. *Psychological Trauma: Theory, Research, Practice, and Policy, 2*(4), 273–283.

Aldarondo, E., & Castro-Fernandez, M. (2011). In J. W. White, M. Koss, & A. E. Kazdin (Eds.), *Violence against women and children: Vol.1. Mapping the terrain* (pp. 221–242). Washington, DC: American Psychological Association.

Alexy, E., Burgess, A., Baker, T., & Smoyak, S. (2005). Perceptions of cyberstalking among college students. *Brief Treatment and Crisis Intervention, 5*(3), 279–289.

American Psychiatric Association. (2000). *Diagnostic and statistical manual of mental disorders* (4th ed., Text Rev.). Washington, DC: Author.

Anderson, K., Danis, F., & Havig, K. (2011). Adult daughters of battered women: Recovery and posttraumatic growth following childhood adversity. *Families in Society 92*(2), 154–160.

Arai, M. (2004). Japan. In K. Malley-Morrison (Ed.), *International perspective on family violence and abuse: A cognitive-ecological approach* (pp. 282–299). New York: Erlbaum.

Archambeau, O. G., Frueh, B. C., Deliramich, A. N., Elhai, J. D., Grubaaugh, A. N., Herma, S., & Kim, B. S. (2010). Interpersonal violence and mental health outcomes among Asian American and Native Hawaiian/Other Pacific Islander college students. *Psychological Trauma: Theory, Research, Practice, and Policy, 2*(4), 273–283.

Astin, M. C., Lawrence, K. J., & Foy, D. W. (1993). Posttraumatic stress disorder among battered women: Risk and resiliency factors. *Violence and Victims, 8*, 17–28.

Astin, M. C., Ogland-Hand, S. M., Coleman, E. M., & Foy, D. W. (1995). Posttraumatic stress disorder and childhood abuse in battered women: Comparisons with maritally distressed women. *Journal of Consulting and Clinical Psychology, 63*, 308–312.

Avis, J. M. (1992). Where are all the family therapists? Abuse and violence within families and family therapy's response. *Journal of Marital and Family Therapy, 18*, 225–232.

Aymer, S. R. (2008). Beyond power and control: Clinical interventions with men engaged in partner abuse. *Clinical Social Work Journal, 36*(4), 323–332.

Babcock, J. C., Green, C. E., & Robie, C. (2004). Does batterers' treatment work? A meta-analytic review of domestic violence treatment. *Clinical Psychology Review, 23*, 1023–1053.

Babcock, J. C., Jacobson, N. S., Gottman, J. M., & Waltz, J. (1993). Power and violence: The relationship between communication patterns, power discrepancies, and domestic violence. *Journal of Counseling and Clinical Psychology, 61*, 40–50.

Barber, S. J., & Wright, E. M. (2010). Predictors of completion in a batterer treatment program: The effects of referral source supervision. *Criminal Justice and Behavior, 37*(8), 847–859.

Barnes, P. G. (1998). "It's just a quarrel": Some states offer no domestic violence protection to gays. *ABA Journal, 84*, 24–26.

Barnett, E. R., Pittman, C. R., Ragan, C., & Salus, M. K. (1980). *Family violence: Intervention strategies* (DHHS Publication No. OHD 580-30258). Washington, DC: U.S. Government Printing Office.

Barnett, O. W., & Hamberger, L. K. (1992). The assessment of maritally violent men on the California Personality Inventory. *Violence and Victims, 7*, 15–28.

Bartholomew, K. (1999, August). *Violence in male same-sex relationships: Prevalence, incidence, and injury.* Paper presented at the 107th Annual Convention of the American Psychological Association, Symposium on Outing Same-Sex Partner Abuse—Defining the Issues, Boston.

Battaglia, T., Finley, E., & Liebschutz, J. (2003). Survivors of intimate partner violence speak out: Trust in the patient-provider relationship. *Journal of General Internal Medicine, 18,* 617–623.

Benjamin, L., & Walz, G. R. (1983). *Violence in the family: Child and spouse abuse* (Report No. EDN00001). Washington, DC: National Institute of Education (ERIC Document Reproduction Service No. ED 226-309).

Bennett, L. W., & Vincent, N. V. (2001). Standards for batterer programs: A formative evaluation of the Illinois protocol. *Journal of Aggression, Maltreatment, & Trauma, 5,* 181–197.

Bent-Goodley, T. B., Rice, J., Williams, O., & Pope, M. (2011). Treatment for perpetrators of domestic violence. In M. P. Koss, J. White, & A. Kazdin (Eds.), *Violence against women and children: Vol. 2. Navigating solutions* (pp. 199–213). Washington, DC: American Psychological Association.

Bergman, L. (1992). Dating violence among high school students. *Social Work, 37,* 17–21.

Berk, R. A., Newton, P. J., & Berk, S. (1986). What a difference a day makes: An empirical study of the impact of shelters for battered women. *Journal of Marriage and the Family, 48,* 481–490.

Blount, R. W., Silverman, I. J., Sellers, C. S., & Seese, R. A. (1994). Alcohol and drug use among abused women who kill, abused women who don't, and their abusers. *Journal of Drug Issues, 24,* 165–177.

Bodnarchuk, M., Kropp, R., Ogloff, J., Hart, S., & Dutton, D. (1995). *Predicting cessation of intimate assaultiveness after group treatment* (No. 4887-10-91-106). Ottawa: Health Canada, Family Violence Prevention Division.

Boes, M., & McDermott, V. (2002). Helping battered women: A health care perspective. In A. R. Roberts (Ed.), *Handbook of domestic violence: Intervention strategies* (pp. 255–277). New York: Oxford University Press.

Bograd, M. (1992). Values in conflict: Challenges to family therapists' thinking. *Journal of Marital and Family Therapy, 18,* 245–256.

Bograd, M. (2005). Strengthening domestic violence theories: Intersections of race, class, sexual orientation, and gender. In N. Sololoff & C. Pratt (Eds.), *Domestic violence at the margins: Reading on race, class, gender, and culture* (pp. 25–38). New Brunswick, NJ: Rutgers University Press.

Bologna, M. J., Waterman, C. K., & Dawson, L. J. (1987). *Violence in gay male and lesbian relationships: Implications for practitioners and policy makers.* Paper presented at the Third National Conference for Family Violence Researchers, Durham, NH.

Bornstein, R. F. (2006). The complex relationship between dependency and domestic violence: Converging psychological and social forces. *American Psychologist, 61*(6), 595–606.

Bowen, E. L. (2009). *Domestic violence treatment for abusive women: A treatment manual.* New York: Taylor/Routledge.

Bower, S. A., & Bower, G. H. (1976). *Asserting yourself: A practical guide for positive change.* Reading, MA: Addison-Wesley.

Bowlby, J. (1980). *Attachment and loss: Vol. 3. Loss.* New York: Basic Books.

Bradley v. *State of Mississippi,* 1 Miss. 156 (1824).

Brasseur, J. W. (1994, October). The battered woman: Identification and intervention. *Clinical Reviews, 4,* 45–74.

Brewster, M. P. (2002). Domestic violence theories, research, and practice implications. In A. R. Roberts (Ed.), *Handbook of domestic violence: Intervention strategies* (pp. 23–48). New York: Oxford University Press.

Brown, J., James, K., & Taylor, A. (2010). Caught in the rejection abuse cycle: Are we really treating perpetrators of domestic abuse effectively? *Journal of Family Therapy, 32*(3), 280–307.

Brown, L. (2008). *Cultural competence in trauma therapy.* Washington, DC: American Psychological Association.

Browne, A. (1997). Violence in marriage: Until death do us part? In A. P. Cardarelli (Ed.), *Violence between intimate partners: Patterns, causes, and effects* (pp. 48–69). Needham Heights, MA: Allyn & Bacon.

Browne, K., & Herbert, M. (1997). *Preventing family violence.* Chichester, England: Wiley.

Bryant-Davis, T. (2010). Cultural consideration of trauma: Physical mental and social correlates of intimate partner violence exposure. *Psychological Trauma: Theory, Research, Practice, and Policy, 2*(4), 263–266.

Buchbinder, E., & Eisikovits, Z. (2003). Battered women's entrapment in shame: A phenomenological study. *American Journal of Orthopsychiatry, 73*(4), 355–366.

Burcky, W., Reuterman, N., & Kopsky, S. (1988). Dating violence among high school students. *School Counselor, 35,* 353–358.

Bureau of Justice Statistics. (2003). U.S. Department of Justice. *Crime characteristics 2002.* Washington, DC: U.S. Department of Justice.

Butryn, T. M. (2003). Wrestling with manhood: Boys, bullying, & battering. *Sport Psychologist, 17*(4), 487–489.

California State Auditor. (2006). *Batterer intervention program: County probation departments could improve compliance with state law, but progress in batterer accountability also depends on the courts.* Sacramento, CA: Author.

Campbell, J. C. (1989). A test of two explanatory models of women's responses to battering. *Nursing Research, 38,* 18–24.

Capps, M. (1982, April). *The co-optive and repressive state versus the battered women's movement.* Paper presented at annual meeting of Southern Sociological Society, Memphis, TN.

Carden, A. D. (1994). Wife abuse and the wife abuser: Review and recommendations. *Counseling Psychologist, 22,* 539–582.

Carrado, M., George, M., Loxam, E., Jones, L., & Templar, D. (1996). Aggression in British heterosexual relationships: A descriptive analysis. *Aggressive Behavior, 22,* 401–415.

Cavanaugh, M. M., & Gelles, R. J. (2005). The utility of male domestic violence offender typologies: New directions for research, policy, and practice. *Journal of Interpersonal Violence, 20*(2), 155–165.

Centers for Disease Control. (2001). *Surveillance of homicides among intimate partners—United States, 1981–1998.* Atlanta, GA: Author.

Chalk, R., & King, P. A. (Eds.). (1998). *Violence in families: Assessing prevention and treatment programs.* Washington, DC: National Academy Press.

Chang, J., C., Decker, M. R., Moracco, K. E., Martin, S. L., Petersen, R., & Frasier, P. (2005). Asking about intimate partner violence: Advice from female survivors to healthcare providers. *Patient Education and Counseling, 59,* 141–147.

Chen, H., Bersani, C., Myers, S. C., & Denton, R. (1989). Evaluating the effectiveness of a court sponsored abuser treatment program. *Journal of Family Violence, 4,* 309–322.

Cochran-Berry, B. (1995). *Life after Johnnie Cochran: Why I left the sweetest talking lawyer in L.A.* New York: Basic Books.

Coleman, F. (1997). Stalking behavior and the cycle of domestic violence. *Journal of Interpersonal Violence, 12,* 420–432.

Conroy, K. (1982). Long-term treatment issues with battered women. In J. P. Flanzer & B. Star (Eds.), *The many faces of violence* (pp. 53–75). Springfield, IL: Charles C Thomas.

Corvo, K. M., Dutton, S., & Chen, W. (2009). Do Duluth model interventions with perpetrators of domestic violence violate mental health professional ethics? *Ethics & Behavior, 19*(4), 323–340.

Craft, S. M., Serovich, J. M., McKenry, P. C., & Lim, J. (2008). Stress, attachment style, and partner violence among same sex couples. *Journal of GLBT Family Issues, 4*(1), 57–73.

Cruz, J. M. (2003). "Why doesn't he just leave?" Gay male domestic violence and the reasons victims stay. *Journal of Men's Studies, 11*(3), 309–323.

Dagastino, A. (1984). *Crisis intervention series: Helping abused women in abuse centers and shelters* (Cassette Recording No. 4-1). Memphis, TN: Memphis State University Department of Counseling and Personnel Services.

Day, R. (2009). Counseling victims of intimate partner violence: Listening to the voices of clients—excerpts from a qualitative study. *Trauma Psychology Newsletter, 4*(3), 5–6.

Demaris, A. (1989). Attrition in batterers' counseling: The role of social and demographic factors. *Social Service Review, 63,* 142–154.

Dines, G. (1992). Pornography and the media: Cultural representations of violence against women. *Family Violence and Sexual Assault Bulletin, 8,* 17–20.

Dobash, R. E., & Dobash, R. P. (1979). *Violence against wives.* New York: Free Press.

Dobash, R. E., & Dobash, R. P. (1992). *Women, violence, and change.* London: Routledge.

Douglas, D. (1991). Intervention with male toddlers who have witnessed parental violence. *Journal of Contemporary Human Services, 72,* 515–523.

Douglas, M. A., & Perrin, A. (1987, July). *Recidivism and accuracy of self-reported violence and arrest.* Paper presented at the Third National Conference for Family Violence Researchers, University of New Hampshire, Durham.

Dressing, H., Kuehner, C., & Gass, P. (2006). The epidemiology and characteristics of stalking. *Current Opinion in Psychiatry, 19*(4), 395–399.

Dutton, D. G. (1985). An ecologically nested theory of male violence towards intimates. *International Journal of Women's Studies, 8,* 404–413.

Dutton, D. G. (1994). The origin and structure of the abusive personality. *Journal of Personality Disorders, 8*(3), 181–191.

Dutton, D. G. (1995). *The domestic assault of women.* Vancouver: University of British Columbia Press.

Dutton, D. G. (2007). *The abusive personality: Violence and control in intimate relationships* (2nd ed.). New York: Guilford Press.

Dutton, D. G., & Corvo, K. (2006). Transforming flawed social policy: A call to revive psychology and science in domestic violence research and practice. *Aggression and Violent Behavior, 11*(5), 457–483.

Dutton, D. G., & Corvo, K. (2007). The Duluth model: A data-impervious paradigm and a failed strategy. *Aggression and Violent Behavior, 12*(6), 658–667.

Dutton, D. G., & Starzomski, A. (1993). Borderline personality organization in perpetrators of psychological and physical abuse. *Violence and Victims, 8*(4), 327–338.

Dutton, D. G., & Starzomski, A. (1994). Psychological differences between court-referred and self-referred wife assaulters. *Criminal Justice and Behavior: An International Journal, 21*(2), 203–222.

Edleson, J. L., & Syers, M. (1990). Relative effectiveness of group treatments for men who batter. *Social Work Research and Abstracts, 26,* 10–17.

Edleson, J. L., & Tolman, R. M. (1992). *Intervention for men who batter.* Newbury Park, CA: Sage.

Edwards, S. M. (1989). *Policing domestic violence: Women, the law, and the state.* London: Sage.

Ehrensaft, M. K., Cohen, P., Brown, J., Smailes, E., Chen, H., & Johnson, J. G. (2003). Intergenerational transmission of partner violence: A twenty-year prospective study. *Journal of Consulting & Clinical Psychology, 71*(4), 741–753.

Ehrensaft, M. K., Moffitt, T. E., & Caspi, A. (2006). Is domestic violence followed by an increased risk of psychiatric disorder among women but not among men? A longitudinal study. *American Journal of Psychiatry, 163*(5), 885–892.

Eke, A., Hilton, N. Z, Harris, G. T., Rice, M. E., & Houghton, R. E. (2011). Intimate partner homicide risk assessment and prospects for prediction. *Journal of Family Violence, 26*(3), 211–216.

Elliot, P. (1996). Shattered illusions: Same-sex domestic violence. In C. M. Renzetti (Ed.), *Violence in gay and lesbian domestic relationships* (pp. 1–8). Binghamton, NY: Haworth.

Ellis, A. (1990). *Anger: How to live with it and without it.* New York: Carroll.

Fiebert, M., & Gonzalez, D. (1997). Women who initiate assaults: The reasons offered for such behavior. *Psychological Reports, 80*, 583–590.

Finkelhor, D., Gelles, R. J., Hotaling, G. T., & Straus, A. A. (Eds.). (1983). *The dark side of families.* Newbury Park, CA: Sage.

Fowler, K., & Western, D. (2011). Subtyping perpetrators of intimate partner violence. *Journal of Interpersonal Violence, 26*(4), 607–639.

Friess, S. (1997). Behind closed doors: Domestic violence. *The Advocate, 7*, 48–52.

Gebhard, P. H. (1997). Memorandum on the incidence of homosexuals in the United States. Bloomington: Indiana University, Center for Sex Research.

Geffner, R. A., & Rosenbaum, A. (2002). Domestic violence offenders: Treatment and intervention standards. *Journal of Aggression, Maltreatment, and Trauma, 5*(2), 1–9.

Gelles, R. J. (1993). Constraints against family violence: Do they work? *American Behavioral Scientist, 36*, 575–586.

Gelles, R. J., & Cornell, C. P. (1985). *Intimate violence in families.* Newbury Park, CA: Sage.

Gibbons, P., Collins, M., & Reid, C. (2011). How useful are indices of personality pathology when assessing domestic violence perpetrators? *Psychological Assessment, 23*(1), 164–173.

Gillis, J. R. (1999, August). *Community education and services for same-sex partner abuse.* Paper presented at the 107th Annual Convention of the American Psychological Association, Symposium on Outing Same-Sex Partner Abuse—Defining the Issues, Boston.

Glasser, N., Eden, K. B., Bloom, T., & Perrin, N. (2010). Computerized aid improves safety decision process for survivors of intimate partner violence. *Journal of Interpersonal Violence, 25*(11),1947–1964.

Gondolf, E. (1984). *Men who batter: Why they abuse women and how they stop their abuse.* Indiana, PA: Domestic Violence Study Center, Indiana University of Pennsylvania.

Gondolf, E. (1985). Fighting for control: A clinical assessment of men who batter. *Social Casework, 65*, 48–54.

Gondolf, E. (2007). Theoretical and research support for the Duluth model: A reply to Dutton and Corvo. *Aggression and Violent Behavior, 12*(6), 644–657.

Gondolf, E., & Fisher, E. R. (1988). *Battered women as survivors: An alternative to treating learned helplessness.* Lexington, MA: Lexington Books.

Goodman, L. A., & Epstein, D. (2011). The justice system response to domestic violence. In J. W. White, M. Koss, & A. E. Kazdin (Eds.), *Violence against women and children: Vol.1. Mapping the terrain* (pp. 215–235). Washington, DC: American Psychological Association.

Greenfield, L., Rand, M., & Craven, D. (1998). *Violence by intimates: Analysis of data on crime by current and former spouses, boyfriends, and girlfriends.* Washington, DC: U.S. Department of Justice.

Griffing, S., Ragin, D., Morrison, S., Sage, R., Madry, L., & Primm, B. (2005). Reasons for returning to abusive relationships: Effects of prior victimization. *Journal of Family Violence, 20*(5), 341–348.

Grusznski, R. J., & Carrillo, T. P. (1988). Who completes batterers treatment groups? An empirical investigation. *Journal of Family Violence, 3*(2), 141–150.

Hage, S. M. (2006). Profiles of women survivors: The development of agency in abusive relationships. *Journal of Counseling and Development, 84*(1), 83–93.

Hague, G., & Sardinha, L. (2010). Violence against women: Devastating legacy and transforming services. *Psychiatry, Psychology and Law 17*(4), 503–522.

Haj-Yahia, M. M. (2003). Beliefs about wife beating among Arab men from Israel: The influence of their patriarchal ideology. *Journal of Family Violence, 18*(4), 193–206.

Halbsgut, J. L. (2011). Masculine gender role norms: Understanding the conformity of domestic violence perpetrators. *Dissertation Abstracts International: Section B. The Sciences and Engineering*, 7087.

Hamberger, L. K. (1994). The battered woman: Identification and intervention. *The Female Patient, 19*, 29–30, 32–33.

Hamberger, L. K., & Hastings, J. E. (1986, August). *Skills training for treatment of spouse abusers: An outcome study.* Paper presented at the meeting of the American Psychological Association, Washington, DC.

Hamby, S. L. (1998). Partner violence: Prevention and intervention. In J. L. Jasinski & L. M. Williams (Eds.), *Partner violence: A comprehensive review of 20 years of research* (pp. 210–258). Newbury Park, CA: Sage.

Hamilton, B., & Coates, J. (1993). Perceived helpfulness and use of professional services by abused women. *Journal of Family Violence, 8*, 313–321.

Hampton, R. L., Vandergriff-Avery, M., & Kim, J. (1999). Understanding the origins and incidence of spousal violence in North America. In T. P. Gullotta & S. J. McElhaney (Eds.), *Violence in homes and communities: Prevention, intervention and treatment* (pp. 39–70). Thousand Oaks, CA: Sage.

Hanson, B. (2002). Interventions for batterers: Program approaches, program tensions. In A. R. Roberts (Ed.), *Handbook of domestic violence: Intervention strategies* (pp. 419–450). New York: Oxford University Press.

Hart, B. (1980, June). Testimony at a hearing before the U.S. Commission on Civil Rights, Harrisburg, PA.

Hart, B. (1986). Lesbian battering: An examination. In K. Loebel (Ed.), *Naming the violence: Speaking out about lesbian battering* (pp. 173–189). Seattle, WA: Seal.

Hastings, J. E., & Hamberger, L. K. (1988). Personality characteristics of spouse abusers: A controlled comparison. *Violence and Victims, 3*, 31–47.

Hattendorf, J., Ottens, A., & Lomax, R. (1999). Type and severity of abuse and posttraumatic stress disorder symptoms reported by women who killed abusive partners. *Violence Against Women, 5*(3), 292–312.

Hawkins, R., & Beauvais, C. (1985, August). *Evaluation of group therapy with abusive men: The police record.* Paper presented at the meeting of the American Psychological Association, Los Angeles.

Healy, M. J., Smith, C., & O'Sullivan, C. (1998). *Batterer intervention: Program approaches and criminal justice strategies* (Report No. NCJ 168638). Washington, DC: U.S. Department of Justice.

Helfrich, C. A. (Ed.). (2001). *Domestic abuse across the life span: The role of occupational therapy.* Binghamton, NY: Haworth Press.

Henning, K., & Connor-Smith, J. (2011). Why doesn't he leave? Relationship continuity and satisfaction among male domestic offenders. *Journal of Interpersonal Violence, 26*(7), 1366–1387.

Henton, J., Cate, R., Koval, J., Lloyd, S., & Christopher, S. (1983). Romance and violence in dating relationships. *Journal of Family Issues, 4*, 467–482.

Heppner, M. J. (1978). Counseling the battered wife: Myths, facts, and decisions. *Personnel and Guidance Journal, 56*, 522–525.

Herman, J. (1992). *Trauma and recovery.* New York: Basic Books.

Heyman, R. E., Jouriles, E. N., & O'Leary, K. D. (1995). Alcohol and aggressive personality styles: Potentiator of serious aggression against wives? *Journal of Family Psychology, 9*, 44–57.

Hilbert, J. C., & Hilbert, H. C. (1984). Battered women leaving the shelter: Which way do they go? A discriminate function analysis. *Journal of Applied Social Sciences, 8*, 291–297.

Hines, D. A., & Douglas, E. M. (2011). Symptoms of posttraumatic stress disorder in men who sustain intimate partner violence: A study of help seeking and community samples. *Psychology of Men & Masculinity, 12*(2), 112–127.

Hirschel, J. D., Hutchison, I. W., & Dean, C. W. (1992). The failure of arrest to deter spouse abuse. *Journal of Research in Crime and Delinquency, 29*, 7–33.

Holtzworth-Munroe, A., Meehan, J., Herron, K., Rehman, U., & Stuart, G. (2003). Do subtypes of maritally violent men continue to differ over time? *Journal of Consulting & Clinical Psychology, 71*(4), 728–740.

Holtzworth-Munroe, A., Meehan, J., Herron, K., & Stuart, G. (1999). A typology of batterers: An initial examination. In

X. B. Ariagapa & S. Oskamp (Eds.), *Violence in intimate relationships* (pp. 45–72). Thousand Oaks, CA: Sage.

Holtzworth-Munroe, A., & Stuart, G. L. (1994). Typologies of male batterers: Three subtypes and the differences among them. *Psychological Bulletin, 116*(3), 476–497.

Home of the Duluth Model. (2011). *What is the Duluth Model? Why it works.* Available at www.theduluthmodel.org

Hotaling, G. T., & Sugarman, D. B. (1986). An analysis of risk markers in husband to wife violence: The current state of knowledge. *Violence and Victims, 1*, 101–124.

Hotaling, G. T., & Sugarman, D. B. (1990). A risk marker analysis of assaulted wives. *Journal of Family Violence, 5*, 1–13.

Hughes, H. M. (1982). Brief interventions with children in a battered women's shelter: A model preventive program. *Family Relations, 31*, 495–502.

Ibrahim, F. A., & Herr, E. L. (1987). Battered women: A developmental life-career counseling perspective. *Journal of Counseling and Development, 65*, 244–248.

Island, D., & Letellier, P. (1991). *Men who beat the men who love them: Battered gay men and domestic violence.* New York: Harrington Park.

Jarvie, I. (1991). Pornography and/as degradation. *International Journal of Law and Psychiatry, 14*, 13–27.

Jasinski, J. L., & Williams, L. M. (Eds.). (1998). *Partner violence: A comprehensive review of 20 years of research.* Newbury Park, CA: Sage.

Johnson, M. (1995). Patriarchal terrorism and common couple violence: Two forms of violence against women. *Journal of Marriage and Family, 57*, 283–294.

Johnson, M., & Leone, J. (2005). The differential effects of intimate terrorism and situational couple violence: Findings from the National Violence Against Women Survey. *Journal of Family Issues, 26*(3), 322–349.

Jouriles, E. M., & Norwood, W. D. (1995). Physical aggression toward boys and girls in families characterized by the battering of women. *Journal of Family Psychology, 9*, 69–78.

Kanuha, V. K. (2005). Compounding the triple jeopardy: Battering in lesbian of color relationships. In N. Sololoff & C. Pratt (Eds.), *Domestic violence at the margins: Readings on race, class, gender, and culture* (pp. 71–82). New Brunswick, NJ: Rutgers University Press.

Kasturirangan, A., & Williams, E. N. (2003). Counseling Latina battered women: A qualitative study of the Latina perspective. *Journal of Multicultural Counseling & Development, 31*(3), 162–178.

Kaufman Kantor, G., & Jasinski, J. L. (1998). Dynamics and risk factors in partner violence. In J. L. Jasinski & L. M. Williams (Eds.), *Partner violence: A comprehensive view of twenty years of research* (pp. 1–44). Newbury Park, CA: Sage.

Knox, K., & Roberts, A. R. (2005). Crisis intervention with stalking victims. In A. R. Roberts (Ed.), *Crisis intervention handbook* (3rd ed., pp. 483–498). New York: Oxford University Press.

Koverola, C., & Panchanadeswaran, S. (2004). Domestic violence interventions with women of color: The intersection of victimization and cultural diversity. In K. Kendall-Tackett (Ed.), *Health consequences of abuse in the family: A clinical guide for evidence-based practice. Application and practice in health psychology* (pp. 45–61). Washington, DC: American Psychological Association.

Kriner, L., & Waldron, B. (1988). Group counseling: A treatment modality for batterers. *Journal of Specialists in Group Work, 13*, 110–116.

Kurdek, L. (1994). Areas of conflict for gay, lesbian, and heterosexual couples: What couples argue about influences relationship satisfaction. *Journal of Marriage and the Family, 56*, 923–934.

Langhinrichsen-Roling, J., Neidig, P., & Thorn, G. (1995). Violent marriages: Gender difference in levels of current violence and past abuse. *Journal of Family Violence, 10*(2), 159–176.

Langley, R., & Levy, R. C. (1977). *Wife beating: The silent crisis.* New York: Dutton.

Laporte, L., Jiang, D., Pepler, D., & Chamberland, C. (2011). The relationship between adolescents' experience of family violence and dating. *Youth and Society 43*(1), 3–27.

Lawson, D. M. (2003). Incidence, explanations, and treatment of partner violence. *Journal of Counseling and Development, 81*(1), 19–32.

Lee, M. Y. (2002). Asian battered women: Assessment and treatment. In A. R. Roberts (Ed.), *Handbook of domestic violence: Intervention strategies* (pp. 472–482). New York: Oxford University Press.

Lehmann, P., & Rabenstein, S. (2002). Children exposed to domestic violence: The role of impact, assessment, and treatment. In A. R. Roberts (Ed.), *Handbook of domestic violence: Intervention strategies* (pp. 343–364). New York: Oxford University Press.

Lehmann, P., & Simmons, C. (Eds.). (2009). *Strengths-based batterer intervention: A new paradigm in ending family violence.* New York: Springer.

Leventhal, B. L., & Lundy, S. E. (1999). *Same-sex violence: Strategies for change.* Thousand Oaks, CA: Sage.

Levinson, D. (1989). *Family violence in cross-cultural perspective.* Newbury Park, CA: Sage.

Lie, G. Y., & Gentlewarrier, S. (1991). Intimate violence in lesbian relationships: Discussion of survey findings and practice implication. *Journal of Social Service Research, 15*(1/2), 41–59.

Lindsay, J., & Brady, D. (2002). "Nurturing fragile relationships": Early reflections on working with victims of domestic violence on the National Probation Service's Duluth Pathfinder research programme. *Issues in Forensic Psychology, 3*, 59–71.

Livingston, M. (2011). A longitudinal analysis of alcohol outlet density and domestic violence. *Addiction, 106*(5), 919–925.

Lockhart, L. L., White, B. W., Causby, V., & Isaac, A. (1994). Letting out the secret: Violence in lesbian relationships. *Journal of Interpersonal Violence, 9*(4), 469–492.

Makepeace, J. (1983). Life-events stress and courtship violence. *Family Relations, 32*, 101–109.

Malchiodi, C. A. (2008). *Creative interventions with traumatized children.* New York: Guilford Press.

Margolies, L., & Leeder, E. (1995). Violence at the door: Treatment of lesbian batterers. *Violence Against Women, 1*(2), 129–157.

Margolin, G., & Vickerman, K. A. (2011). Post-traumatic stress in children and adolescents exposed to family violence: I. Overview and issues. *Couple and Family Psychology: Research and Practice, 1*(S), 63–73.

Marrujo, B., & Kreger, M. (1996). Definition of roles in abusive relationships. *Journal of Gay & Lesbian Social Services, 4*(1), 22–32.

Massachusetts Coalition of Battered Women Service Groups. (1981). *For shelter and beyond: An educational manual for working with women who are battered.* Boston: Red Sun Press.

Matthews, C., & Lease, S. H. (1999, August). *Lesbian, gay, and bisexual family.* Paper presented at the 107th Annual Convention of the American Psychological Association, Symposium on Research and Practice with Lesbian, Gay and Bisexual Clients, Boston.

Maziak, W., & Asfar, T. (2003) Physical abuse in low-income women in Aleppo, Syria. *Health Care for Women International, 24*(4), 313–326.

McDonald, R., Jouriles, E., Ramisetty-Mikler, S., Caetano, R., & Green, C. E. (2006). Estimating the number of American children living in partner-violent families. *Journal of Family Psychology, 20*(1), 137–142.

McLeer, S., & Anwar, R. (1989). A study of women presenting in an emergency medical department. *American Journal of Public Health, 79*(1), 65–66.

McLeod, A. L., Hays, D. G., & Chang, C. Y. (2010). Female intimate partner violence survivors' experiences with accessing resources. *Journal of Counseling and Development, 88*(3), 303–310.

McMahon, M., Neville-Sorvilles, J., & Schubert, L. (1999). Undoing harm to children: The Duluth Family Visitation Center. In M. F. Shepard & E. L. Pence (Eds.), *Coordinating community responses to domestic violence: Lessons from Duluth and beyond* (pp. 151–167). Thousand Oaks, CA: Sage.

Mederos, F. (1999). Batterer intervention programs: The past and future prospects. In M. F. Shepard & E. L. Pence (Eds.), *Coordinating community response to domestic violence: Lessons from Duluth and beyond* (pp. 127–150). Thousand Oaks, CA: Sage.

Memphis Police Department. (1999). *Recidivism rates for completers and noncompleters of anger management programs in Shelby County 1997–1999.* Memphis, TN: Author.

Mester, R., Birger, M., & Margolin, J. (2006). Stalking. *Israel Journal of Psychiatry and Related Sciences, 43*(2), 102–111.

Miller, G. (1983). *SASSI: Substance Abuse Subtle Screening Inventory.* Bloomington, IN: SASSI Institute.

Miller, S. (Ed.). (2010). Discussing the Duluth curriculum: Creating a process of change for men who batter. *Violence Against Women,16*(9), 1007–1021.

Millon, T. (1987). *Manual for the Millon Clinical Multiaxial Inventory* (2nd ed.). Minneapolis, MN: National Computer Systems.

Morgan, S. M. (1982). *Conjugal terrorism: A psychological and community treatment model of wife abuse.* Palo Alto, CA: R & E Research Associates.

Morrow, S. L. (2000). First do no harm: Therapist issues in psychotherapy with lesbian, gay, and bisexual clients. In R. M. Perez, K. A. DeBord, & K. A. Bieschke (Eds.), *Handbook of counseling and psychotherapy with lesbian gay and bisexual clients* (pp. 137–156). Washington, DC: American Psychological Association.

Morse, B. (1995). Beyond the Conflict Tactics Scale: Assessing gender difference in partner violence. *Violence and Victims, 10*(4), 251–272.

Murdaugh, C., Hunt, S., Sowell, R., & Santana, I. (2004). Domestic violence in Hispanics in the Southeastern United States: A survey and needs analysis. *Journal of Family Violence, 19*(2), 107–115.

Oatley, A. (1994). Domestic violence doesn't discriminate on the basis of sexual orientation. *Suncoast News*, pp. 19–21.

O'Keefe, M. (1998). Posttraumatic stress disorder among incarcerated battered women: A comparison of battered women who kill their abusers and those incarcerated for other offenses. *Journal of Traumatic Stress, 11*(1), 71–85.

Okun, L. (1986). *Woman abuse: Facts replacing myths.* Albany: State University of New York Press.

Olson, L., Anctil, C., Fullerton, L., Brillman, J., Arbuckle, J., & Sklar, D. (1996). Increasing emergency room physician recognition of domestic violence. *Annals of Emergency Medicine, 27*(6), 741–746.

Pagelow, M. D. (1981). *Woman battering: Victims and their experiences.* Newbury Park, CA: Sage.

Pagelow, M. D. (1992). Adult victims of domestic violence: Battered women. *Journal of Interpersonal Violence, 7*, 87–120.

Parker, B., McFarlane, J., Soeken, K., Torres, T., & Campbell, D. (1993). Physical and emotional abuse in pregnancy: A comparison of adult and teenage women. *Nursing Research, 42*, 173–177.

Pathé, M. (2002). *Surviving stalking.* Cambridge, UK: Cambridge University Press.

Peled, E. (1997). The battered women's movement response to children: A critical analysis. *Violence Against Women, 3*(4), 424–446.

Pence, E. L., & McDonnell, C. (2000). Developing policies and protocols in Duluth, Minnesota. In J. Hanmer & C. Itzin (Eds.), *Home truths about domestic violence: Feminist influences on policy and practice: A reader* (pp. 249–268). New York: Routledge.

Pence, E. L., & Paymar, M. (1993). *Education groups for men who batter: The Duluth model.* New York: Springer.

Pence, E. L., & Shepard, M. F. (1999). An introduction: Developing a coordinated community response. In M. F. Shepard & E. L. Pence (Eds.), *Coordinating community response to domestic violence: Lessons from Duluth and beyond* (pp. 3–24). Thousand Oaks, CA: Sage.

Perrin, S., Van Hasselt, V., Basilio, I., & Hersen, M. (1996). Assessing the effects of violence on women in battering relationships with the Keane MMPI-PTSD Scale. *Journal of Traumatic Stress, 9*(4), 805–816.

Peterman, L. M., & Dixon, C. G. (2003). Domestic violence between same-sex partners: Implications for counseling. *Journal of Counseling and Development, 81*(1), 40–47.

Pizzey, E. (1974). *Scream quietly or the neighbors will hear.* London: Penguin Books.

Pleck, E. (1987). *The making of societal policy against family violence from colonial times to the present.* New York: Oxford University Press.

Poynter, T. L. (1989). An evaluation of a group programme for male perpetrators of domestic violence. *Australian Journal of Sex, Marriage, and Family, 10*, 133–142.

Price, B., & Rosenbaum, A. (2007, July). *A national survey of perpetrator intervention programs.* Paper presented at the International Family Violence and Child Victimization Research Conference, Portsmouth, NH.

Randle, A. A., & Graham, C. A. (2011). A review of the evidence on the effects of intimate partner violence on men. *Psychology of men and masculinity, 12*(2), 97–111.

Renzetti, C. (1992). *Violent betrayal: Partner abuse in lesbian relationships.* Newbury Park, CA: Sage.

Renzetti, C. (1996). The poverty of services for battered lesbians. In C. M. Renzetti & C. H. Miley (Eds.), *Violence in gay and lesbian domestic partnerships* (pp. 61–68). Binghamton, NY: Haworth Press.

Ricks, J. L., Vaughan, C., & Dziegielewski, S. F. (2002). Domestic violence among lesbian couples. In A. R. Roberts (Ed.), *Handbook of domestic violence: Intervention strategies* (pp. 451–463). New York: Oxford University Press.

Ristock, J. L. (1999, August). *Exploring dynamics in abusive lesbian relationships.* Paper presented at the 107th Annual Convention of the American Psychological Association, Symposium on Outing Same-Sex Partner Abuse, Boston.

Roberts, A. R. (2002). Myths, facts, and realities regarding battered women and their children: An overview. In A. R. Roberts (Ed.), *Handbook of domestic violence: Intervention strategies* (pp. 3–22). New York: Oxford University Press.

Roberts, A. R., & Kurst-Swanger, K. (2002). Police responses to battered women: Past, present, and future. In A. R. Roberts (Ed.), *Handbook of domestic violence: Intervention strategies* (pp. 101–126). New York: Oxford University Press.

Roberts, A. R., & Roberts, B. S. (2002). A comprehensive model for crisis intervention with battered women and their children. In A. R. Roberts (Ed.), *Handbook of domestic violence: Intervention strategies* (pp. 365–395). New York: Oxford University Press.

Roberts, A. R., & Roberts, B. S. (2005). A comprehensive model for crisis intervention with battered women and their children. In A. R. Roberts (Ed.), *Crisis intervention handbook* (3rd ed., pp. 441–482). New York: Oxford University Press.

Robinson, G. E. (2003). International perspectives on violence against women: Introduction. *Archives of Women's Mental Health, 6*(3), 155–156.

Rosenbaum, A., & Kunkel, T. S. (2009). Group interventions for intimate partner violence. In K. D. O'Leary & E. Woodin (Eds.), *Psychology and physical aggression in couples: Causes and interventions* (pp. 191–210). Washington, DC: American Psychological Association.

Rosenfeld, B. (1992). Court-ordered treatment of spousal abuse. *Clinical Psychology Review, 12*(2), 205–226.

Ross, M., & Glesson, C. (1991). Bias in social work intervention with battered women. *Journal of Social Services Research, 14*, 79–105.

Russell, B., & Uhlemann, M. R. (1994). Women surviving an abusive relationship: Grief and the process of change. *Journal of Counseling and Development, 72*, 362–367.

Santiago, G. B. (2002). Latina battered women: Barriers to service delivery and cultural considerations. In A. R. Roberts (Ed.), *Handbook of domestic violence: Intervention strategies* (pp. 464–471). New York: Oxford University Press.

Sartin, R. M. (2005). Characteristics associated with domestic violence perpetration: An examination of factors related to response and the utility of a batterer typology. *Dissertation Abstracts International: Section B. The Sciences and Engineering*, 4303.

Sassetti, M. R. (1993). Domestic violence. *Primary Care, 20*, 289–303.

Saunders, D. G. (1992). A typology of men who batter: Three types derived from cluster analysis. *American Journal of Orthopsychiatry, 62*, 264–275.

Saunders, D. G., & Hanusa, D. (1986). Cognitive behavioral treatment of men who batter: The short-term effects of group therapy. *Journal of Family Violence, 1*, 357–372.

Scales, K., & Winter, B. (1991, April). *Anger management for spouse abusers: The interpersonal transaction group.* Paper presented at Crisis Convening XV, Chicago.

Schechter, S. (1982). *Women and male violence.* Boston: South End Press.

Schlesinger, L. B. (2006). Celebrity stalking, homicide, and suicide: A psychological autopsy. *International Journal of Offender Therapy and Comparative Criminology, 50*(1), 39–46.

Schumacher, J. A., Fals-Stewart, W., & Leonard, K. K. (2003). Domestic violence treatment referrals for men seeking alcohol treatment. *Journal of Substance Abuse Treatment, 24*(3), 279–283.

Schutte, N. S., Bouleige, L., Fix, J. L., & Malouff, J. M. (1986). Returning to partner after leaving a crisis shelter: A decision faced by battered women. *Journal of Social Behavior and Personality, 1*, 295–298.

Schutte, N. S., Malouff, J. M., & Doyle, J. S. (1988). The relationship between characteristics of the victim, persuasive techniques of the batterer, and returning to a battering relationship. *Journal of Social Psychology, 128*, 605–610.

Schwartz, M. D., & Mattley, C. (1993). The battered woman scale and gender identities. *Journal of Family Violence, 8*, 277–287.

Sev'er, A. (1997). *A cross-cultural exploration of wife abuse.* Lewiston, NY: Edwin Mellen Press.

Shepard, M. F. (1999). Advocacy for battered women: Implications for a coordinated community response. In M. F. Shepard & E. L. Pence (Eds.), *Coordinating community responses to domestic violence: Lessons from Duluth and beyond* (pp. 115–126). Thousand Oaks, CA: Sage.

Sherman, L. W., & Berk, R. A. (1984). The specific deterrent effects of arrest for domestic assaults. *American Sociological Review, 49*, 1261–1272.

Shupe, A., Stacey, W. A., & Hazlewood, L. R. (1987). *Violent men, violent couples.* Lexington, MA: Lexington Books.

Smith, N. D. (2003). Competing models for reduction of physical spouse abuse in the United States Marine Corps: Which model of treatment is most effective for reducing recidivism in the Marine Corps? *Dissertation Abstracts International: Section B. The Sciences and Engineering*, 4387.

Smith, P. H., White, J. W., & Holland, L. J. (2003). A longitudinal perspective on dating violence among adolescent and college-age women. *American Journal of Public Health, 93*(7), 1104–1109.

Snyder, J. A. (1994). How we do it: Emergency department protocols for domestic violence. *Journal of Emergency Nursing, 20*, 64–68.

Sonkin, D. J., & Dutton, D. (2003). Treating assaultive men from an attachment perspective. *Journal of Aggression, Maltreatment, & Trauma, 7*(1/2), 105–133.

Sonkin, D. J., Martin, D., & Walker, L. E. (1985). *The male batterer: A treatment approach.* New York: Springer.

Spangaro, J. M., Zwi, A. B., & Poulos, R. (2011). "Persist. Persist.": A qualitative study of women's decisions to disclose and their perceptions of the impact of routine screening for intimate partner violence. *Psychology of Violence 1*(2), 150–162.

Spanno, T. K. (1990, April). *Eclipse of the self: The grief of the battered women.* Paper presented at Crisis Convening XIV, Chicago.

Spence, J. T., & Helmreich, R. (1972). The attitude toward women scale: An objective instrument to measure attitudes towards the rights and roles of women in contemporary society. *JSAS, Catalog of Selected Documents in Psychology, 2*(66), 1–51.

Stanley, J. (1999, August). *Exploration of partner violence in male same-sex relationships.* Paper presented at the 107th Annual Convention of the American Psychological Association, Symposium on Outing Same-Sex Partner Abuse, Defining the Issues, Boston.

Stanley, J., Bartholomew, K., Taylor, T., Oram, D., & Landolt, M. (2006). Intimate violence in male same-sex relationships. *Journal of Family Violence, 21*(1), 31–41.

Stark, E., & Flitcraft, A. (1987). Violence among intimates: An epidemiological review. In V. B. Van Hasselt, R. L. Morrison, A. S. Bellack, & M. Hersen (Eds.), *Handbook of family violence.* New York: Plenum.

Stark, E., & Flitcraft, A. (1988). Personal power and institutional victimization: Treating the dual trauma of women battering. In F. M. Ochberg (Ed.), *Posttrauma therapy and victims of violence* (pp. 115–151). New York: Brunner/Mazel.

State of North Carolina v. *Oliver,* 70 N. C. 60, 61–62 (1874).

Stets, J. E., & Straus, M. A. (1990). Gender differences in reporting of marital violence and its medical and psychological consequences. In M. A. Straus & R. J. Gelles (Eds.), *Physical violence in American families: Risk factors and adaptations to violence in 8,145 families* (pp. 151–165). New Brunswick, NJ: Transaction.

Stith, S., Rosen, K., McCollum, E., & Thomsen, C. (2004). Treating intimate partner violence within intact couple relationships: Outcomes of multi-couple versus individual couple therapy. *Journal of Marital & Family Therapy, 30*(3), 305–318.

Stoop, D., & Arterburn, S. (1991). *The angry man: "Why does he act that way?"* Dallas, TX: Word Publishing.

Stosny, S. (1995). *Treating attachment abuse: A compassion approach.* New York: Springer.

Stover, C., Meadows, A., & Kaufman, J. (2009). Interventions for intimate partner violence: Review and implications for evidence-based practice. *Professional Psychology: Research and Practice, 40*(3), 223–233.

Straus, M. A. (1979). Measuring intra-family conflict and violence: The C.T. Scale. *Journal of Marriage and Family, 41*, 75–88.

Straus, M. A., & Gelles, R. J. (1986). Societal change and change in family violence from 1975 to 1985 as revealed by two national surveys. *Journal of Marriage and Family, 48*, 465–479.

Straus, M. A., & Gelles, R. J. (Eds.). (1990). *Physical violence in American families: Risk factors and adaptations to violence in 8,145 families.* New Brunswick, NJ: Transaction.

Straus, M. A., Gelles, R. J., & Steinmetz, S. (1980). *Behind closed doors: Violence in the American family.* Garden City, NY: Anchor/Doubleday.

Stuart, G., Meehan, J., Moore, T., Morean, M., Hellmuth, J., & Follansbee, K. (2006). Examining a conceptual framework of intimate partner violence in men and women arrested for domestic violence. *Journal of Studies on Alcohol, 67*(1), 102–112.

Suglia, S.F., Staudenmayer, J., Cohen, S., Enlow, M., Rice-Edwards, J., & Wright, R. (2010). Cumulative stress and cortisol disruption among Black and Hispanic pregnant women in an urban cohort. *Psychological Trauma: Theory, Research, Practice, and Policy, 2*(4), 326–334.

Sullivan, C. M., Campbell, R., Angelique, H., Eby, K. K., & Davidson, W. S. (1994). An advocacy intervention program for women with abusive partners: Six-month follow-up. *American Journal of Community Psychology, 22*, 101–120.

Thompson, M., Kaslow, N., Kingree, J., Puett, R., Thompson, N., & Meadows, L. (1999). Partner abuse in posttraumatic stress disorder as risk factors for suicide attempts in a sample of low-income, inner-city women. *Journal of Traumatic Stress, 12*(1), 59–72.

Thompson, R. S., Bonomi, A., Anderson, M., Reid, R., Dimer, J., Carrell, D., et al. (2006). Intimate partner violence: Prevalence, types, and chronicity in adult women. *American Journal of Preventive Medicine, 30*(6), 447–457.

Tilden, V. P., Schmidt, T. A., Limandri, B. J., Chiodo, G. T., Garland, M. J., & Loveless, P. A. (1994). Factors that influence clinicians' assessment and management of family violence. *American Journal of Public Health, 84*(4), 628–633.

Tilden, V. P., & Shepard, P. (1987). Increasing the rate of identification of battered women in an emergency department: Use of a nursing protocol. *Research in Nursing and Health, 10*, 209–215.

Tjaden, P., & Thoennes, N. (1998a). Battering in America: Findings from the National Violence Against Women Survey. *Research in brief* (pp. 606–666). Washington, DC: National Institute of Justice, U.S. Department of Justice.

Tjaden, P., & Thoennes, N. (1998b). *Stalking in America: Findings from the National Violence Against Women Survey* (NCJ Report #169592). Washington, DC: National Institute of Justice and Centers for Disease Control and Prevention.

Tjaden, P., & Thoennes, N. (2000). *Extent, nature, and consequences of intimate partner violence.* Washington, DC: National Institute of Justice, and Centers for Disease Control and Prevention.

Tolman, R. M., & Bennett, L. W. (1990). A review of quantitative research on men who batter. *Journal of Interpersonal Violence, 5*, 87–118.

Toro-Alfonso, J., & Rodriguez-Madera, S. (2004). Domestic violence in Puerto Rican gay male couples. *Journal of Interpersonal Violence, 19*, 639–654.

Turner, S. F., & Shapiro, C. H. (1986). Battered women: Mourning the death of a relationship. *Social Work, 31*, 372–376.

Tutty, L. M., Bidgood, B. A., & Rothery, M. A. (1993). Support groups for battered women: Research on their efficacy. *Journal of Family Violence, 8*, 325–343.

Tutty, L. M., & Rothery, M. A. (2002). Beyond shelters: Support groups and community-based advocacy for abused women. In A. R. Roberts (Ed.), *Handbook of domestic violence: Intervention strategies* (pp. 396–418). New York: Oxford University Press.

Ulibarri, M., Strathdee, S., Lozada, R., Maigs-Rodriquez, C., Amaro, H., O'Campo, P., & Pattterson, T. L. (2010). Intimate partner violence among female sex workers in two Mexico-U.S. border cities: Partner characteristics and HIV risk behaviors as correlates of abuse. *Psychological Trauma: Theory, Research, Practice, and Policy, 2*(4), 318–325.

Walker, D., Neighbors, C., Mbilinyi, L., O'Rouke, A., Zegree, J., et al. (2010). Evaluating the impact of intimate partner violence on the perpetrator: The Perceived Consequences of Domestic Violence Questionnaire. *Journal of Interpersonal Violence, 25*(9), 1684–1698.

Walker, L. E. (1979). How battering happens and how to stop it. In D. Moore (Ed.), *Battered women* (pp. 59–78). Newbury Park, CA: Sage.

Walker, L. E. (1984). *The battered woman syndrome.* New York: Springer.

Walker, L. E. (1989). *Terrifying love: Why battered women kill and how society responds.* New York: Harper & Row.

Walker, L. E. (2000). *The battered woman syndrome* (2nd ed.). New York: Springer.

Walters, M. L. (2011). Straighten up and act like a lady: A qualitative study of lesbian survivors of intimate partner violence. *Journal of Gay and Lesbian Social Services, 23*(2), 250–270.

Weaver, T. L. (1998). Method variance and sensitivity of screening for traumatic stressors. *Journal of Traumatic Stress, 11*(1), 181–185.

Webersinn, A. L., Hollinger, C. L., & Delamatre, J. E. (1991). Breaking the cycle of violence: An examination of factors relevant to treatment follow-through. *Psychological Reports, 68,* 231–239.

Websdale, N., & Johnson, B. (2005). Reducing woman battering: The role of structural approaches. In N. Sololoff & C. Pratt (Eds.), *Domestic violence at the margins: Readings on race, class, gender, and culture* (pp. 389–415). New Brunswick, NJ: Rutgers University Press.

Weincourt, R. (1985). Never to be alone: Existential therapy for battered women. *Journal of Psychosocial Nursing, 23,* 24–29.

Weinreb, M., & Groves, B. M. (2007). Child exposure to parental violence: Case of Amanda, age 4. In Nancy Webb (Ed.), *Play therapy with children in crisis: Individual, group, and family treatment* (3rd ed., pp. 73–90). New York: Guilford Press.

Weitzman, S. (2000). *Not to people like us.* New York: Basic Books.

West, C. M. (1998). Leaving a second closet: Outing partner violence in same-sex couples. In J. L. Jasinski & L. M. Williams (Eds.), *Partner violence: A comprehensive review of 20 years of research* (pp. 163–183). Newbury Park, CA: Sage.

West, C. M., Kaufman Kantor, G., & Jasinski, J. L. (1998). Sociodemographic predictors and cultural barriers to help-seeking behavior by Latina and Anglo-American battered women. *Violence and Victims, 13*(4), 361–375.

White, G. F., Katz, J., & Scarborough, K. E. (1992). The impact of professional football games on violent assaults on women. *Violence and Victims, 7,* 157–171.

Wiehe, V. R. (1998). *Understanding family violence.* Thousand Oaks, CA: Sage.

Winter, B. (1991). *The Family Trouble Center anger management program* (Videocassette recording #6781-A-91). Memphis, TN: Memphis State University, Department of Counseling and Personnel Services.

Witko, T., Martinez, R., & Milda, R. (2006). Understanding domestic violence within the urban Indian community. In T. Witko (Ed.), *Mental health care for urban Indians: Clinical insights from native practitioners* (pp. 104–114). Washington, DC: American Psychological Association.

Wolak, J., & Finkelhor, D. (1998). Children exposed to partner violence. In J. L. Jasinski & L. M. Williams (Eds.), *Partner violence: A comprehensive review of 20 years of research* (pp. 73–112). Newbury Park, CA: Sage.

Wood, A. D., & McHugh, M. C. (1994). Woman battering: The response of the clergy. *Pastoral Psychology, 42,* 185–196.

Yeater, E., Austin, J., Green, M., & Smith, J. E. (2011). Coping mediates the relations between posttraumatic stress disorder (PTSD) symptoms and alcohol use in homeless, ethnically diverse women: A preliminary study. *Psychological Trauma: Theory, Research, Practice, and Policy, 2*(4), 307–310.

Yoshioka, M., Gilbert, L., El-Bassel, N., & Baig-Amin, M. (2003). Social support and disclosure of abuse: Comparing South Asian, African American, and Hispanic battered women. *Journal of Family Violence, 18*(3), 171–180.

Zanipatin, J., Welch, S., Yi, J., & Bardina, P. (2005). Immigrant women and domestic violence. In K. Barrett & W. George (Eds.), *Race, culture, psychology, and law* (pp. 375–389). Thousand Oaks, CA: Sage.

CHAPTER 11

Chemical Dependency: The Crisis of Addiction

"Wine is a mocker, strong drink is raging" (Proverbs 20:1). "At the last it biteth like a serpent, and stingeth like an adder" (Proverbs 23:32). These biblical verses depict the continuing saga of drugs and addiction with which humankind has struggled over the ages. Efforts to treat the problem of substance abuse go back at least to the Romans, who attempted aversive conditioning of drunkards by placing spiders in the bottom of wine cups (Smith, 1982, p. 875).

Whole economies have been founded on drug use. The United States has been no shirker in this regard. The discovery that an acre of corn could be made much more salable by turning it into alcohol played a dominant role in developing the economies of colonial New England and the early American frontier. In 1785, nearly everyone in the United States would have thought the idea of abstinence to be ludicrous, but by 1835 a temperance movement "demonizing" alcohol was in full swing (Levine, 1984). Benjamin Rush, the father of American psychiatry, started pushing the notion that alcoholism was a disease as early as the first part of the 19th century. However, early on the evolving words to describe the concept of alcoholism shifted from the morally tinged "intemperance" to the more medical "inebriety" which characterizes the continuing dilemma of naming something a "disease." This contradiction has continuously dogged alcoholism in that it can somewhat hypocritically be both a disease and a moral/spiritual failing at the same time (Tracy, 2007).

The effort to "keep a devil out of the mouth of America" culminated in the Volstead Act and ratification of the Eighteenth Amendment to the Constitution, which brought prohibition to the country in 1920 (Edwards, 1985). This "noble experiment" allowed the rampant growth of organized crime, which provided a thirsty public with bathtub gin, Canadian whiskey, and moonshine. The Twenty-First Amendment repealing prohibition in 1933 stands as a legislative memorial to the futility of trying to prohibit a drug, and from a social perspective it has much to say about what a society believes to be good or evil.

The estimated cost of buying illegal drugs in the United States ranges up to $276 billion a year (Stein, Orlando, & Sturm, 2000). Legal drugs are also big business. Alcohol abuse/addiction is thought to cost about $185 billion a year and tobacco upward of $155 billion a year in the United States alone (Doweiko, 2006, p. 6). But the real costs far exceed mere payment for drugs. If drug-related medical care, lost productivity, murders, fractured families, insurance, suicide, property crime, law enforcement, and treatment are added up, the citizenry of the United States, and the world for that matter, are paying emotional and financial costs far beyond the staggering sums of money spent on the procurement and attempts to control both legal and illegal drugs.

Although alcohol consumption has declined by about 15 percent over the past two decades, the important percentage is this: 10 percent of those who drink consume 50 percent of the alcohol used in the United States. That 10 percent translates into approximately 16 million people who are heavy drinkers, 55 million binge drinkers (drinkers who consume five or more drinks at one sitting), and 18.7 million people abusing or addicted to alcohol who need treatment. Overall about 22.2 million people in the United States abuse legal and illegal drugs enough to need treatment (Office of National Drug Control Policy, 2004; Substance Abuse and Mental Health Services Administration, 2005). *Not* included in the foregoing statistics is the drug that kills more people than all the others combined but generally has no *noticeable* debilitating effects. That is tobacco, used by about 71.5 million people in the United States (Substance Abuse and Mental Health Services Administration, 2005). That's a lot of people!

Some of the most telling statistics come from the National Comorbidity Study (Anthony, Warner, & Kessler, 1997), which provides an excellent statistical profile of the drug-abusing behavior of men and women in the 15- to 54-year-old population of the United States. About 1 in 13 people at some time in their life will have such a problem with a controlled substance that they are dependent on it. About 1 in 6 will have a problem with alcohol such that they are dependent on it. These figures are probably conservative, because the study had no way to consider potential respondents who had already died from the abusive agents they had ingested!

Joseph Stalin, the ruthless dictator of the former Soviet Union, is rumored to have once made a chilling statement to justify his purges and the mass slaughter of millions: "A single auto accident where a family is killed is a tragedy. A million dead is a statistic." The overwhelming statistics that confront the United States and the world as a whole in dealing with the ill effects of both legal and illegal drugs are mind numbing. But for one of your authors, as well as the countless other "statistics," the saga of alcoholism in his family was indeed a tragedy that could never be measured by any statistical yardstick.

Sociocultural Determinants of Substance Abuse

The society and the cultural background of an individual seem to have a great deal to do with what kinds of pharmacological and extrapharmacological effects will occur with use of addictive substances. For example, at a 0.40 percent blood alcohol content (BAC) most people pass out, and that is generally considered the LD-50 level—the level of intoxication at which about half of the people die from an overdose (Goode, 1984, p. 62).

Physiological outcomes are much the same for everyone having that BAC. However, psychological outcomes are very different as the user progresses to a 0.40 percent

BAC level. Whereas one person with a BAC of 0.10 percent may want to fight a whole motorcycle gang, another may be the caricature of the garrulous, happy drunk, and another may sit stone-faced and bother no one.

It is a chemical fallacy that a specific dose of drug Z will invariably cause effect A in a user. What does seem to be true is that set and setting have a great effect on the behavior of the drug user. *Set* can be defined as the mental and emotional state of the user, including expectations, intelligence, personality, feelings, and so on. *Setting* is the social and physical environment of the user at the time of use. It can be defined as immediate surroundings, such as a living room as opposed to a bar, or, in a broader context, can be the legal and religious perspective of the country (Goode, 1984, p. 35).

Set and setting define which situations are considered appropriate for drug use and which are not. Nowhere is this clearer than in the fallacious belief that alcohol automatically releases inhibitions. In a comprehensive study of a number of tribes in southern Africa who have very different beliefs about what is appropriate and inappropriate behavior, MacAndrew and Edgerton (1969) found that people would not automatically lose their inhibitions and violate norms as a result of ingesting alcohol unless the particular culture permitted it.

Furthermore, when a member of one culture was placed in a different cultural setting, that person might act in extraordinary ways when drinking that were very different from his or her own societal norms (Heath, 1985, p. 470). Consider the Hopi and Navajo American Indian tribes who are closely related to one another by blood and geographic vicinity. In a telling cultural study on alcohol consumption, Kunitz and Levy (1974) found that the Navajos thought public drinking was acceptable while solitary drinking was deviant. To the contrary, the Hopis' drinking must be a solitary experience because alcohol consumption is not tolerated in the tribe and those who are caught intoxicated are shunned. Alcohol use and abuse certainly have culture-specific rules, sanctions, prohibitions, admonitions, and permissions. However, to arbitrarily lump ethnic, cultural, racial, or religious groups into stereotypical categories, such as Jewish people drink only for ceremonial occasions, Baptists never drink, or Native Americans can't handle "firewater," is as patently biased as any other kind of racism. There are just too many factors that affect an individual's drug use to make any kind of blanket statement about who will or will not drink, and why (Fisher & Harrison, 2000, pp. 53–82).

Alcohol: Number One Abused Substance

The choice of potential abusive agents available today is much like a cafeteria menu. However, alcohol still seems the best drug to illustrate what happens in the crisis of addiction. Alcohol was found to be the most harmful of all legal and illegal drugs in the United Kingdom, with a score of 72 on a scale of 100. Heroin and crack cocaine came in a distant second and third with scores of 55 and 54 (Nutt, King, & Phillips, 2010). There are several reasons for this choice:

1. *Duration.* No other drug has the longevity, legacy, and history of legislative attempts to control or promote it. From the Whiskey Rebellion of George Washington's era to Carrie Nation and the Women's Christian Temperance Union to Alcoholics Anonymous to the founding of the National Institute on Alcohol Abuse and Alcoholism (NIAAA), alcohol continues to play a great role in how the United States, or any other country in the world, attempts to deal with drug abuse.

2. *Legality.* There are only limited conditions under which one can go to jail for possession or use. Even with stiffer penalties for drunk driving and juvenile possession, social acceptability plays an important part in determining punishment. Some of the worst punishment for DUI (driving under the influence) vehicular homicide barely equals the mandatory time a person might serve when caught with a small amount of crack cocaine.

3. *Widespread use.* Although other drugs receive a great deal of publicity, they are "peanuts" in sheer numbers of users compared to the estimate of more than 16 million people in the United States alone who are directly and indirectly affected by alcoholism (Office of National Drug Control Policy, 2004). About 30 percent of the U.S. population uses alcohol in a way that places them at risk for physical, mental health, and social problems, and 25 percent of that population would meet diagnostic criteria for current abuse or dependence (Mumford, 2005).

4. *Indirect financial costs.* Indirect costs including job absenteeism and firings; family violence and divorce; hospital care; and law enforcement, judicial, and correctional activities related to alcoholism are most likely greater than for any other public health issue, ranging as high as $185 billion (Doweiko, 2006, p. 6).

5. *Psychological costs.* If one believes only part of the literature on the malignancy of codependency and enabling, the bankruptcy of family systems, the physical and sexual assaults on others (Gelles & Straus, 1988), and the legacy that adult children of alcoholics inherit (Hardwick, Hansen, & Bairnsfather, 1995), the mental health costs are truly astounding.

6. *Physical costs.* Although not as shocking in immediate behavior or nearly as sudden in onset as crack, meth, and other mind-altering central nervous system stimulants, the pernicious effects of alcoholism cut a wide physiological path through its victims. The American Medical Association (1993) estimates that 25 to 40 percent of hospitalization in the United States is directly or indirectly related to alcohol, and that does not include nursing home beds that are estimated to hold 15 to 30 percent of alcohol-related illnesses (Schuckit, 2000). Liver and pancreatic disease, Korsakoff's syndrome, reproductive and sexual dysfunction, cancer, heart disease, bone loss, gastrointestinal problems, reduced immunity, malnutrition, brain damage, chronic disease states, and particularly the insidious effects of fetal alcohol syndrome exact a tremendous physical toll on alcohol abusers (Doweiko, 1996, p. 66; Nutt, King, & Phillips, 2010; Ray & Ksir, 2004, pp. 261–267). Piled on top of these long-term effects are the short-term effects of alcohol overdose that consistently earn it between 15 and 20 percent of all emergency room admissions and about the same percentage of emergency room deaths (Beasley, 1987; Mersey, 2003).

7. *Links to crime.* A great deal of publicity is given to "speed freaks" and "crackheads" and the violent crimes they commit, or to the cocaine and heroin addicts who need a "fix" and steal everything they can get their hands on or prostitute themselves for their drug of choice, but alcohol abuse contributes to a majority of the assaults and murders related to drug use in the United States and across the world and has done so for a long time (MacDonald, 1961; National Foundation for Brain Research, 1992; Pernanen, 1976; Ray & Ksir, 2004, pp. 282–283; Shupe, 1953).

8. *Implication in accidents.* The Mothers Against Drunk Driving (MADD) group has good reason for its existence. About 40 to 50 percent of all highway deaths are alcohol related (Blondell, Frierson, & Lippmann, 1996). Death on the highway gets a

lot of notoriety, but drunk boating, drunk home repair, drunk walking into traffic, drunk falling down stairs, drunk hunting, drunk smoking in bed, and drunk swimming are a few of the many ways that a large number of people succeed in killing themselves and others by ingesting alcohol.

9. *Suicide.* The lifetime risk of suicide among alcoholics is approximately 15 percent (Schuckit, 1986). About 200,000 emergency room admissions for suicide attempts in the United States are drug-related (National Institute on Drug Abuse, 2003).

10. *Alcohol is a drug.* Because alcohol can be legally purchased, people forget that it is a drug (Doweiko, 1996, p. 14). There is no biochemical aspect of alcohol use that is different from what most would consider drug use. The important distinction is the arbitrary view of the culture, which generally does not identify a person who drinks one beer as a drug user, whereas a person who smokes one marijuana cigarette is.

11. *Interpersonal relationships.* Alcoholism wrecks families from emotional, physical, and financial standpoints. Alcohol lubricates a great deal of family violence ranging from battering to murder (Centers for Disease Control, 2001; Cohn et al., 2010; Kofler-Westergren, Klof, & Mitterauer, 2010; Taft et al., 2010).

12. *Polyuse.* There are very few pure alcoholics, like the stereotypical street bum or party lush of yore. Far more characteristic is the polyabuser (Doweiko, 1996, p. 6), who lubricates other drugs with alcohol for the cheap, compounding effects it can deliver.

13. *Embroilment in controversy.* Controversy surrounds the issues of both the etiology and treatment of alcoholism. Is it a biological disease or the "disease" with one's ability to cope (Doweiko, 2006, pp. 29–42)? Akin to the disease controversy is the hotly debated topic of total abstinence versus the harm reduction concept. Total abstinence is largely an American drug policy whereas harm reduction is a more European approach that acknowledges use, tolerates it, but seeks to reduce its disastrous effects (Marlatt & Witkiewitz, 2009). Harm reduction makes sense when individuals are willing to reduce substance use but are unwilling to stop or when the user is relapsing and rejects the possibility of immediately starting another cessation attempt (Shadel & Shiffman, 2005). While that may make good sense, it falls on deaf ears for those who believe in total prohibition of alcohol indulgence.

Thus, beliefs are so embedded in the culture and so strongly held that they influence and color funding, research, legislation, theory, and treatment. As a result, a number of models have emerged to explain alcoholism and how it should be treated.

Models of Addiction

Currently no single, clear-cut model or treatment approach based on theory or research holds sway over another (Donovan, 2005). The debate over the efficacy of these models continues and serves to define competing schools of thought rather than facilitate agreement among proponents. Probably at present *no one model is better, and each has usefulness in treatment.* The following brief summary lists each of the major models alphabetically.

Behavioral Learning Model. According to the behavioral learning model, drinking is caused and maintained by the association of alcohol intake with positive rewarding experiences. Habituation is progressively strengthened by repetitive use of alcohol to combat anxiety and alleviate stress (Pattison & Kaufman, 1982, p. 12).

Biopsychosocial Models. As the term implies, addiction is seen as having multiple determinants (Marlatt, 1997, pp. xii–xiii; Donovan, 2005). This is an eclectic model that subsumes many of the other more specific models in this list, giving equal relevance to biological, social, and psychological aspects of addiction. It would appear as more and more research starts to identify the biological underpinnings of addiction that this model will have greater significance (Ray & Ksir, 2004, p. 53).

Cognitive Models. A basic cognitive model operates on the assumption that thoughts or beliefs are the primary causative factors in substance abuse. A negative event such as a serious social, financial, or medical problem does not cause the person to start substance abusing; rather, the core attribution ("I can't stand the nightmares of that automobile wreck and the pain of all that physical rehabilitation") leads to an emotional response ("I feel lousy and depressed") and propels one into addictive beliefs ("Drugs will give me courage and take the pain away") that result in addictive behavior ("I'll go to a bar and stay drunk") (Beck et al., 1993).

Disease Model.   In the disease model of addiction, drug use is seen as an aberrant condition afflicting otherwise healthy people, and exposure to the drug is seen as leading to physiological addiction. Through a sequence of internal events, alcoholics lose control of their drinking behavior (Jellinek, 1946, 1952, 1960). With increased use, more and more alcohol is needed to meet physiological needs. When use ceases or is reduced, the drug reaches too low a level for the tolerance that has been created, the person goes into withdrawal, and physiological craving leads to continued use (Oetting & Beauvais, 1986). The World Health Organization's (1952) and the American Medical Association's (1956) acceptance of a diagnostic framework for alcohol abuse as a disease has lent much credibility to the disease model. The disease model is the foundation on which Alcoholics Anonymous rests and is probably still the most common model used to describe alcoholism.

Final Common Pathway.   Doweiko (2006) uses the term *final common pathway* to suggest that each of the theories of drug addiction contains an element of truth and efficacy. The final common pathway model proposes that substance abuse is not the starting point, but a common end point of different individuals' unique patterns of growth. A variety of different factors, ranging from social forces to psychological conditioning to genetic predisposition (pp. 41–42), may play a part, or not, depending on what life experiences the person has. Neurobiological research on the brain's reward system offers support for this theory in that the arrival of the particular drug of choice sets off a cascade of neurotransmitters in specific parts of the brain that fool it into falsely believing that a wide variety of enhanced abilities and rewards have just been accrued (Reynolds & Bada, 2003). What internal or external factors have to be present to make this happen is not clear.

Gateway Model.   The gateway model proposes an orderly progression from one drug to another and particularly applies to young people as they move into heavier and heavier drug use (Dupont, 1984). The research of Kandel, Yamaguchi, and Chen (1992) lends a great deal of credence to the progression from alcohol and cigarettes to marijuana and inhalants and then on to "hard" drugs.

Genetic Predisposition Model.   The genetic model proposes an inherited and transmitted predisposition

to become a [...] McGee, 200[...] 2001; Vaill[...] netic facto[...] suscepti[...] predispo[...] disease[...] adopted [...] twins of an alco[...] tiproblem families with [...] to five times as likely to beco[...] dren from comparable groups with no [...] ents. Gene (Blum et al., 1990; Noble et al., 19[...] neurotransmitter research (Kranzler & Anton, 1994) has isolated what appear to be distinct biological differences in how alcoholics and nonalcoholics process alcohol and what certain genes have to do with proneness or resistance to alcoholism (Luczak, Glatt, & Wall, 2009).

Lifestyle Model.   In this model's viewpoint, the rewards of living in an altered state of consciousness outweigh all the costs of a destructive, drug-dependent lifestyle. For the people described by the lifestyle model, a drug-free existence is no existence at all (Pattison & Kaufman, 1982, p. 12).

Moral Model.   Addiction is seen as a consequence of personal choice. Individuals make inappropriate decisions regarding alcohol use and can make other choices if they so desire. This model has been adopted by certain religious groups and by the judicial system (Fisher & Harrison, 2000, p. 37). It generally denies the need for any treatment approach other than increasing one's willpower.

Parental Influence Model.   Besides the preponderance of alcohol use by parents, the rise of illicit drug use by parents sets models for children and makes "Do as I say, not as I do!" hypocritical in the extreme. "If my parents use it, why can't I?" is the cynical response seen in national television commercials on the war against drugs (Barnes, Farrell, & Cairns, 1986).

Peer-Cluster Model.   This model links drug use to small groups of people, including pairs such as best friends or boyfriend–girlfriend, who share beliefs, attitudes, values, and a rationale for drug use. Drug use plays an important role in group membership and identification (Oetting & Beauvais, 1986).

PART TWO   Handling[...]
354
Personality Mod[...]
components of [...]
personality pre[...]
prealcoholic [...]
conformist [...]
impulsiv[...]
there is[...]
ident[...]

el. This model posits that certain ...aits and attributes that make up the ...ispose individuals to drug abuse. While ...ersonalities tend to be independent, non-...gregarious, rebellious, thrill seeking, and ... (Ray & Ksir, 2004, p. 53; Slutske et al., 2002), ... no clear set of personality factors that would ...fy one person as a "drug" personality and another ...ot (Renner, 2004; Swendsen et al., 2002).

Prescriptive Model. The prescriptive model suggests that alcoholism begins in self-prescription and physician prescription of alcohol and other drugs as tranquilizing agents to relieve acute or chronic pain symptoms (Blume, 1973).

Problem Behavior Model. The more problematic the behavior of the individual, the more likely the individual is to come into contact with people, places, and instances where drugs are available (Jessor & Jessor, 1977).

Psychoanalytic Model. This model posits that certain pathological personality traits established early in childhood predispose the individual to alcoholism (Zwerling, 1959). Spotts and Shontz (1980) traced the obsession with a particular drug to specific flaws in early development and demonstrated how the action of that drug meshed with the resulting personality.

Psychosocial Model. The psychosocial model proposes that a constellation of factors involving an individual's personality, environment, and behavior are interrelated and organized so as to develop a dynamic state designated as *problem-behavior proneness.* These variables define both the personal problems and the social environments that may underlie involvement with drugs—the greater the level of drug use, the greater the level of deviance (Jessor, Chase, & Donovan, 1980).

Sanctioned-Use Model. The rampant use of Ritalin to diminish the hyperactivity associated with attention deficit disorder has become a double-edged sword (Safer, 1994). The sanctioned and prescribed use of Ritalin by a generation of schoolchildren to keep them calm sends a clear message that it is not only OK to take drugs, it is beneficial. If Ritalin and other prescribed drugs are OK, then why is anything else that makes one feel good considered bad? Amphetamine

use to keep airmen awake during World War II and as late as the Gulf War was profligate, as was its use for depression and weight loss by physicians in the 1960s and 1970s (Emonson & Vanderbeek, 1995). The overprescription and resulting abuse of Valium when it first came on the market are legendary. Given the foregoing, "Just say 'No!' to drugs!" would seem, at a minimum, hypocritical, and at the maximum, ludicrous.

Sociocultural Models. Sociocultural models examine factors external to the individual. The environment is seen as a chief contributing factor; it includes demographic and ethnographic variables such as race, age, socioeconomic status, employment, education, family systems, social norms, religion, crime rates, belief systems, consumption rates, drinking behavior, and so on. In its emphasis on environmental factors, this approach empirically challenges the disease model (Lukoff, 1980).

Stress-Coping Model. The use of drugs is seen as a substitute for effective behavioral and cognitive coping skills when the individual is placed under stress. The less effective the coping skills of the individual, the higher is the likelihood of drug use as a palliative remedy (Wills & Shiffman, 1985).

The major division of thought about the foregoing models of alcoholism distinguishes the disease/genetic/biological models from all the other models, which propose chemical dependency as something other than physiologically based.

Definitions of Commonly Used Terms

Many terms have been coined in an attempt to adequately describe those who get into trouble with drugs. To facilitate understanding this chapter, the following commonly used terms are listed in alphabetical order. As with all the other controversial aspects of chemical dependency, these are not the only definitions for these terms. Rather, they represent *general* definitions. A number of chemical dependency theorists and treatment specialists might disagree with these definitions or even argue the existence of some of the constructs!

> *Abuse.* The chronic, recurrent misuse of chemicals (Lawson, Ellis, & Rivers, 1984, p. 37). Abuse exists when one or more of the following occur in a maladaptive pattern during a 12-month period:

failure to fulfill major role obligations, such as work and school; physical impairment that creates a hazard, such as operating machinery; recurrent legal problems; recurrent social problems, such as physical fights (American Psychiatric Association, 2000).

Addiction. Physically, chemical addiction is a cellular change that occurs with the increased use of most depressant drugs. The primary clinical features are the development of tolerance and the development of withdrawal symptoms on removal of the drug (Lawson, Ellis, & Rivers, 1984, p. 37). Psychologically, it is the compulsion to use drugs regardless of the negative consequences (Fisher & Harrison, 2000, p. 15). It is progressive, potentially fatal, and marked by preoccupation with chemical use and distortion of one's worldview to support continued use, even in the face of its many negative consequences (Doweiko, 1996, p. 4).

Addictive behavior. The term preferred by many psychologists to indicate abuse, dependency, and so forth, because it focuses on behavior rather than fixed categories. Behavior can be changed, while addiction as a chronic, progressive disease cannot. The addition of "behavior" also allows addiction to be broadened beyond substance abuse to include behaviors such as gambling and sex (Marlatt, 1997, pp. xiii–xiv). The concept is problematic. When does a bad habit turn into an addictive behavior? The term is commonly used to refer to so many problem behaviors, such as work, eating, and gambling (Fisher & Harrison, 2000, p. 15), that today any socially unacceptable behavior is likely to be diagnosed as an addiction, whether it be having multiple affairs (love addiction) or spending hours on the computer (Internet addiction) (Schaler, 2000).

Alcoholism. A highly complex condition characterized by preoccupation with alcohol and loss of control over its consumption, so that intoxication results if drinking is begun, by chronicity, by progression, and by a tendency to relapse. It is associated with physical disability and impaired emotional, occupational, and/or social adjustment as a result of persistent use (Shearer, 1968, p. 6).

Chemical dependent. Any person who has a dependence on drugs such that the substance governs his or her life to the extent that it severely impairs the ability to function psychologically and/or physically (Lawson, Ellis, & Rivers, 1984, p. 37). It is used to differentiate chemical addiction from other types such as gambling (Fisher & Harrison, 2000, p. 15).

Codependent/codependency. Reciprocal and complementary in nature, codependency is based on the chemical dependent's need for care to survive and the caretaker's need to control the addict's behavior (O'Brien & Gaborit, 1992). A codependent is any significant person in the chemical dependent's life, such as a spouse, parent, lover, or child, who is enmeshed in the chemical dependency (Maxwell, 1986, p. 7); codependency is characterized by extreme preoccupation with and dependence (emotional, social, and sometimes physical) on a person or object. Eventually this dependence on another person becomes a pathological condition that affects the codependent in all other relationships (Wegscheider-Cruse, 1985, p. 2).

Dependence. As defined by *DSM-IV-TR*, dependence is a cluster of cognitive, behavioral, and physiological symptoms indicating that the individual continues use of the substance despite significant substance-related problems. There is a pattern of repeated self-administration that usually results in physical tolerance, withdrawal, and compulsive drug-taking behavior (American Psychiatric Association, 2000). Psychological dependence occurs in users who have a strong urge to alter their state of consciousness through the use of a chemical. Psychological dependence is the need to use alcohol or other drugs to think, feel, or function "normally" (Fisher & Harrison, 2000, p. 15). This mental state may be the only factor involved, even in cases of the most intense craving and perpetuation of compulsive abuse. These two types of dependence may occur independently or in combination (Lawson, Ellis, & Rivers, 1984, p. 37). Degree of dependency is indicated by the amount and frequency of use and the amount of time spent in drug-seeking behavior (Ray & Ksir, 2004, p. 46).

Drug. A psychoactive substance that has a direct and significant impact on the processes of the mind with respect to thinking, feeling, and acting. The term *drug* is a cultural artifact and a social fabrication because it denotes something that has been arbitrarily defined by certain segments of society as a drug (Goode, 1984, p. 15).

Enabler. Any person who knowingly practices specific behaviors that allow the chemical dependent to continue the abuse/addiction and not be subjected to the full negative consequences of his or her behavior. The enabler may be a family member and may have an overlapping relationship with codependency (Doweiko, 1996, p. 292). Where the relationship is overlapping, maintenance of the relationship is more important than the problem of chemical dependency (Maxwell, 1986, p. 103).

Habituation. The degree to which one is accustomed to taking a certain drug. A habituated user can and will take more of a drug than a first-time experimenter (Goode, 1984, p. 33).

Misuse. Use of a chemical with some adverse physical, psychological, social, or legal consequence (Lawson, Ellis, & Rivers, 1984, p. 37).

Relapse. A simple definition is a return to uncontrolled drinking (Fisher & Harrison, 2000, p. 238). However, since nothing is simple in the abuse and addictions field, it may also be defined as a gradual return to substance use after a period of abstinence; a discrete event that is a return to an initial use of a substance, which may be defined as a "lapse"; or a return to the same intensity of substance use for a defined period of time that requires treatment, also known as "recidivism" (Donovan, 2005).

Slip. An episode of drinking following a period of abstinence (Fisher & Harrison, 2000, p. 238).

Tolerance. The biological ability of the body to transform and excrete the chemical from the body and the increasing insensitivity of the central nervous system to its effects. As a result, more of the drug must be used to achieve the desired effect (Doweiko, 1996, p. 4). Cross-tolerance means the individual also builds up resistance to other drugs from the same pharmacological group (Fisher & Harrison, 2000, p. 16).

Use. The intake of a chemical substance into the body with the goal of altering one's state of consciousness (Lawson, Ellis, & Rivers, 1984, p. 37).

Withdrawal. The production of physical and psychological symptoms by the body on cessation or reduction in use of the drug. Symptoms are variable, depending on length and amount of use, and indicate that tolerance to the chemical has developed (Doweiko, 1996, p. 4).

These definitions do not nearly convey the power that chemical dependence holds over people. The comments of two chemical dependents we knew (both are now dead from the effects of their drugs of choice) paint a striking picture of what being addicted and chemically dependent really means.

Federal correctional incarcerate (polyuser): Think of the best sex you ever had, man! Think how great that feeling was. I mean the best and greatest. Well, that ain't nothin' compared to shovin' that spike in your arm and getting that first rush. That's why I do it.

University professor (recovering alcoholic): When you get stressed out, there may be a number of things you do to get over it. You may go out and jog, pray, meditate, have a fight with your wife, chop wood, and so on. The problem with that is the payoff is variable. It may or may not work. When I get stressed out, I drink. My way works *all* the time and *every* time. It's invariable. I know what will happen before I do it. Beat that!

The Dynamics of Addiction

The dynamics of chemical dependency are complex and sophisticated, and extend beyond the addict into the systems with which he or she interacts.

Defense Mechanisms

Drug abusers offer examples of all the defense mechanisms one might find in a text on abnormal psychology. Gordon, a recovering alcoholic we will follow throughout this chapter, is a composite, displaying the following maladaptive defense mechanisms.

Denial. Alcoholism is often called the "disease of denial" (Lawson, Ellis, & Rivers, 1984, p. 36). Denial is a normal adaptive process for self-protection, but in the alcoholic it becomes rigid and maladaptive. It stops help-seeking behavior, contributes to treatment failure, and sets up relapse (Kearney, 1996). Denial is the emotional refusal to acknowledge a person, situation, condition, or event the way it actually is (Perez, 1985, p. 5).

Gordon: Real men handle their problems. I'll handle mine. I've had a lot of problems lately. Sure I like a drink. Do a lot of business that way. Most of my friends drink. I get loaded every once in a while, but so would you if you had the pressures I do right now.

Displacement. Displacement is the venting of hostility on a person or object, neither of which deserves it (Perez, 1985, p. 6).

Gordon: Yell at my wife? You betcha. Always griping at me for not being at home. Hey! I provided a great living, then when I really needed her support because of the pressure at work, she'd just whine more.

Fantasy.   Alcoholics use fantasy to escape from a variety of threatening circumstances and emotions. They escape boredom with the job, anxiety in coping with relationships, and frustration over career progress by retreating to a drug-induced euphoria. That euphoric state is far more rewarding than the real world and one to which the alcoholic feels compelled to return again and again (Perez, 1985, p. 6).

Gordon: Having a drink takes the edge off. I mean, you can just relax and put it out of your mind for a while—the job, the old lady, everything. I can really get it together and plan the next big project.

Projection.   Alcoholics often attribute motives within themselves to significant others. Sensitivity, suspiciousness, and hostility toward others are outward manifestations of the distancing, estrangement, and lack of communication that characterize the alcoholic (Perez, 1985, p. 6).

Gordon: Amy never did love me. Oh, she loved the house, the club, and the private schools for the kids, and all that. I finally figured that out and told her that straight to her face!

Rationalization.   Alcoholics make all kinds of excuses to support their addiction and their felt inadequacies of acting and behaving (Perez, 1985, p. 6).

Gordon: By God! I had severe back problems from doing the engineering on that sorting machine. Hell! Even the doctor gave me a prescription for the pain. That machine had to get finished. What's wrong with taking a couple of pops at midnight? It made my back quit aching.

Intellectualization.   Alcoholics speak in generalizations or theoretical terms in an impersonal manner and thereby remove themselves from hurtful feelings (Maxwell, 1986, p. 65).

Gordon: They say I drink too much. Well, I've done some extensive reading on the subject, and I certainly don't fit the category of a drunken bum. What do they know, anyway? They're not doctors.

Minimizing.   Alcoholics play down the seriousness of the situation (Maxwell, 1986, p. 64).

Gordon: This is just temporary. I got a little out of line. No problem. I'll just have to watch things a little closer.

Reaction Formation.   Reaction formation occurs as a defense against perceived threat and is one of the most harmful defense mechanisms because it distances dependents from their true feelings. Addicts constantly fear rejection and go out of their way to find it—even when it is not there (Perez, 1985, p. 11).

Gordon: Those kids of mine too. The little ingrates. Gave them everything. Lisa just stares at me. Mark even said I didn't love him because I missed a lousy soccer game. He sure didn't miss his personal computer I got him. No time for the old man 'cause he was too busy himself. That kid never loved me. Always took up for his mom.

Regression.   Alcoholics are often immature and narcissistic, with resulting behavior similar to that of emotional prepubescence. The behavior is intended to manipulate, control, and get one's way. Temper tantrums, sulking, and pouting are all common forms of regression (Perez, 1985, p. 6).

Gordon: There was no use talking to her, so I just clammed up. Wouldn't support me in the business. Me apologize? She's the one who ought to apologize! I'm not saying one word to her until she does.

Repression.   Alcoholics deal with threatening and hurtful events by burying them in unconscious memory (Perez, 1985, p. 7). When sober, alcoholics repress the dependency needs and angry feelings that accompany them, and they remember nothing of the personality and behavior changes that occur when they are intoxicated (Zimberg, 1982, p. 1002).

Gordon: Warnings about my job performance? No way! They just dropped it on me one day. Things were fine up to that point! The same with the family. No warning! No nothing! They just up and leave. I never touched a hair on their heads!

These defense mechanisms are far different from those of the average person. They may be extremely intrusive into others' lives: grossly inconvenient, inexcusable, objectionable, and socially undesirable. The chemical dependent's defenses are primitive and regressive, much like those of an infant. They may personify the alcoholic as a self-centered and dependent person. The two major components of a sociopathic personality—having no conscience and being excessively egocentric—can dominate in the chemical dependent (Perez, 1985, p. 9).

Also enmeshed in the hostile and angry feelings of the alcoholic is depression (Hoffman, 1970). When floods of guilt come pouring through the walls of drug abusers' defenses, they are overwhelmed by an inability to take any kind of reasonable control over their lives and undo the damage they have done to themselves and significant others. The cyclical battering alcoholics take between having no conscience and having an overpowering one is draining and leaves little psychic energy for anything but depression when they start sobering up.

The defense mechanisms of most chemical dependents serve one goal and one goal only: to support, nurture, and help feed the one god in the addict's life, the drug. Nothing else matters. No service is given to anything else until its needs are fulfilled. Feeble attempts to control it are marked by guilt and remorse, but those feelings are miniscule in comparison with the urge to get "fixed" (Stuckey & Harrison, 1982, p. 868).

Gordon: I can't understand how things got this way. We used to have a great family. Yeah! I hate thinking about it. When I get to thinking about it, I feel rotten. Well, you can't function on the job with that kind of cloud hanging over you, so I'd have a drink, and I'd feel better. Four or five and you can forget it all. But what else was I to do under all that?

Enabling and Codependency

The concepts of enabling and codependency are also fraught with controversy. Little empirical research exists to assess the basic assumptions of the concepts (Hands & Dear, 1994). Because alcoholism is typically a male disease (Doweiko, 1996, p. 14), these concepts may be seen as disempowering women, who struggle against terrific odds to keep a family together for a variety of economic, religious, cultural, and safety reasons (Uhle, 1994). Furthermore, many of the personality traits attributed to the codependent can be found in a stereotypical negative personality profile of most women (Cowan & Warren, 1994). In that regard, as may be seen from the chapter on partner violence, a woman in an alcoholic relationship is not altogether different from a woman in a battering relationship. Indeed, alcohol abuse and battering tend to go hand in hand, so it should not be surprising if many of the same dynamics prevail, along with the criticisms that go with them.

Critics also argue that codependents tend to be judged not on their own merits but by the addict's inability to get off drugs. Codependency dictates that the person has some as yet unsubstantiated "disease," "addiction," or "syndrome" of codependency that probably originated in and was "caught" from a dysfunctional family of origin (Trois, 1995). Perhaps most insidious is the notion that once "caught," codependents must admit to their low self-esteem, their enmeshment and powerlessness in a pathological relationship, their inability to withstand rejection, and their avoidance of issues. If individuals are not willing to admit to this prescriptive and pejorative model, then they are clearly in "denial" (Doweiko, 1996, pp. 299–302). Further, the notion of enabling and codependency as real, debilitating constructs is tied to the notion of what *family* means in a white, Protestant, Euro-American sense. These constructs might be seen as positive, strength-promoting qualities in other cultures' definitions of what a family is (Fisher & Harrison, 2000, p. 173).

However, enablers are not just spouses or other family members. Employers and employees may be just as culpable. Whether out of fear of retribution by a union, threat of legal action, or misplaced compassion, an employer may back off confronting an employee about substance abuse. When it is the supervisor who is abusing, any confrontation by employees may wind up getting them fired. Chemical dependents are so good at manipulation they can make enablers feel like they are doing them a favor by:

1. Doing the individual's work
2. "Covering" for poor work performance
3. Accepting excuses or making special arrangements
4. Overlooking frequent absenteeism or tardiness
5. Overlooking evidence of chemical abuse (Doweiko, 1999, p. 323)

It should be understood that codependency and enabling are not necessarily synonymous. Enabling has to do with one's *behavior* toward a chemical dependent. Codependency has to do with one's *relationship* to the chemical dependent (Doweiko, 1999, p. 325). One may be an enabler without being codependent, as in the case of the passerby who gives the street bum a handout. The bum is enabled to buy the wine, but there is no more than a passing relationship.

When a family is enmeshed in addiction, the crisis is compounded, and a strange phenomenon can occur. In an attempt to keep the family in equilibrium, members will first reject and then begin to tolerate the addict. To keep the family in homeostasis, various members unconsciously assume roles that not only keep the system on an even keel but also enable the addict to fall further into the addiction (Ford, 1987, pp. 16–17; Perez,

1985, p. 19). By attempting to maintain the system, even though it is extremely pathological, family members become codependents. They also manifest many of the maladaptive and unconscious defense mechanisms their addicted counterparts have. The responses of Amy, Gordon's wife, illustrate these defenses, which immobilize the family system.

Suppression.   Codependents may suppress the problems the addict brings to the family by maintaining a "stiff upper lip" and not allowing their emotions to surface (Maxwell, 1986, pp. 78–79). This is a defense of quiet desperation and is based on the hope that some miraculous change will occur in the dependent.

> **Amy:** I made a commitment when I got married that it was for keeps. He was probably an alcoholic when we got married, but a contract is a contract. In sickness and health and all that.

Dissociation.   For those who dissociate themselves from the problem and repress it, their perception of events is drastically altered by putting the problem aside. Dissociation means distancing the problem emotionally and sometimes geographically (Maxwell, 1986, p. 80).

> **Amy:** When it got really bad, I'd make sure the kids were busy doing something and then I'd throw myself into the club work. That kept my mind off his problem. The best two weeks of my life every year would be going back home to my parents. I'd take the kids and we could get away.

Repression.   Repression of events takes dissociation a step further. By burying hurtful events in unconscious memory, codependents avoid having to grapple with the terrible feelings that accompany those events (Maxwell, 1986, p. 82).

> **Amy:** I mean he's horrible all the time when he's bombed, but what he actually says I'm not real sure. He's real nasty, but I can't quite put my finger on what he actually does.

Escape to Therapy.   Seeking therapeutic assistance may be another form of escape for codependents. A lot of catharsis may occur in therapy, but little real change is considered because it would also mean that the codependents would have to face reality and make some serious changes away from the maladaptive coping patterns that they have established (Maxwell, 1986, p. 82).

> **Amy:** If somehow he could just change. I don't know, maybe you could talk him into coming here. I know that I at least get a little peace of mind from coming to these sessions.

Intellectualization.   Codependents use intellectualization to keep themselves distanced from the hurtful affect. In attempting to keep the system in balance, they are obsessive-compulsive in planning and attending to details. By compulsively paying attention to the many details of these drinking events, intellectualizers order their outward world but do nothing about their inner turmoil (Maxwell, 1986, pp. 83–84).

> **Amy:** It's exhausting, but I've figured out when he's really going on a bender. So I plan activities down to the last detail to keep everybody busy and out of his way. By putting together a stepwise plan, I can keep it down to a dull roar.

Displacement.   By displacement, a codependent moves feelings off the focal point of the problem, the addict's behavior, and moves them to less frightening and hurtful subject matter (Maxwell, 1986, p. 86).

> **Amy:** I've been reading about this new vitamin therapy, and I'm really concerned Gordon's going to get sick because he's so run down. I've been giving him all kinds of good information on this and even got him an appointment with this M.D. who practices holistic medicine.

Reaction Formation.   As the alcoholic becomes more and more irresponsible, a typical reaction for the codependent is to become more and more responsible. In actuality, this assumed responsibility for the family is focused directly on the alcoholic. Taking over for the alcoholic, codependents "save" the marriage and the family by behaving in ways exactly opposite to their internal feelings about the situation (Maxwell, 1986, pp. 88–90).

> **Amy:** The family has to keep going. That's why I'd take those plans for him when he couldn't make the plane and call in sick for him. I know he said some terrible things to me and the kids, but he really didn't mean them. He wouldn't act that way when he was sober.

Reaction formation overextends the codependent in every conceivable way and can lead to physical or emotional breakdown. In the latter stages of alcoholism, codependents may resort to the very immature defenses of passive aggression and hypochondriasis (Maxwell, 1986, pp. 88–90).

Passive Aggression.   By being late, forgetting, starting arguments and then leaving, overspending, and implying the threat of suicide, the codependent keeps everyone in a state of uproar.

Amy: I don't know what's come over me. I've watched the money so carefully over the years. Gordon's still getting a paycheck, but I just can't seem to get bills paid, and we're getting duns from creditors.

Hypochondriasis. The defense of hypochondriasis converts anger into physical complaints. This is an extremely effective punishment of others because no matter how much consolation they receive, codependents obtain attention by this defense mechanism, and they don't give it up without a struggle (Maxwell, 1986, pp. 94–95).

Amy: (*weeping*) I'm sorry for breaking down like this. It's just with everything else I keep getting these terrible migraines. They knock me flat for a day at a time, and then I get behind and can't handle all the other stuff and wind up bawling.

The typical response to the chemically dependent person is first to reject and then to tolerate the objectionable behavior. This marks a person as an enabler (Maxwell, 1986, p. 103). In the early phases of enabling, there is denial and rationalization that the behavior will improve, and the enabler takes responsibility and assumes guilt for the alcoholic. In the middle phases, the enabler becomes hostile, disgusted, and pitying and becomes preoccupied with protecting and shielding the alcoholic. In advanced phases, the enabler's feelings of extreme hostility, withdrawal, and suspicion become generalized to the total environment. In the final phases, responsibility for and quarreling with the alcoholic become all encompassing. Outside interests and maintenance of self are disregarded in all-consuming and obsessive attempts to keep the system and the alcoholic stabilized (Kaufman & Pattison, 1982b, pp. 1022–1024).

In the final phase of enabling, all the foregoing defense mechanisms are evidenced as variations on the following three enabler roles characterized by Ellis and associates (1988), and may be immediately recognized by the crisis worker and called to account: (1) the *silent sufferer* achieves pathological satisfaction by being a martyr to the cause of maintaining the relationship; (2) the *messiah* condemns the drug use and appears to fight the addiction vigorously to save the addict, but never pushes the issue enough so the addict will have to face the consequences of his or her actions; and (3) the *joiner* subsidizes and attempts to control the chemical dependent by doing drugs with the chemical dependent or doling out money for drugs.

Children in Alcoholic Families

Children raised in homes where open communication is practiced and consistency of lifestyles is the norm usually have the ability to adopt a variety of roles, depending on the situation. Children growing up in alcoholic homes seldom learn the combinations of roles that mold healthy personalities. They become locked into roles based on their perception of what they need to do to survive and bring some stability to their lives in a chaotic family (Black, 1981, p. 14). The following generic roles of children who live in alcoholic families have been profiled by Black (1981) and Wegscheider-Cruse (1989). Again, it bears mentioning that these are roles based on clinical *impressions* of a Euro-American population and may not be representative of other cultures at all. Although these roles are stereotypical and no child can be so neatly categorized, they do seem to represent common themes of personality patterns in such families.

The Scapegoat. The scapegoat is the stereotypical troubled child of an alcoholic family. This acting-out child is the one who comes to the attention of school administrators, police, and social services. These children have extremely poor self-images and attempt to enhance themselves by rebellious, attention-seeking behavior. Acting-out children use unacceptable forms of behavior to say "Care about me" or "I can't cope." Socially, these children generally gravitate toward peers who have equally low self-esteem and are prone to engage in delinquent behavior. They fill correctional facilities, mental health institutions, and chemical dependency units in hospitals. Termed "scapegoats" by Wegscheider-Cruse (1989), they enable the addiction by becoming another stressor that can serve as an excuse for substance abuse and by focusing the family's anger and energy away from the addict and onto themselves (Black, 1981, pp. 25–27).

The Hero. The oldest child is most likely to be a very sophisticated child or family hero (Wegscheider-Cruse, 1989). This is the little adult who takes care of the alcoholic, the spouse, and the other children. In attempting to care for the family, the responsible child enables the alcoholic by giving her or him more time to drink. Not only are such children highly responsible to the family, they are also highly responsible in their academic and extracurricular endeavors. Outwardly, they appear as stalwart and outstanding young men and women who are successful in much that they do. Heroes learn to rely completely on themselves, because adults neither can be depended on nor are astute or sensitive enough to provide direction (Black, 1981, pp. 17–20).

The Lost Child.   This is usually a middle or younger child. Called "the lost child" by Wegscheider-Cruse (1989), this child follows directions, handles whatever has to be handled, and adjusts to the circumstances, however dysfunctional they may be. The lost child outwardly appears to be more flexible, spontaneous, and somewhat more selfish than others in the home. These children don't feel, question, get upset, or act in any way to draw attention to themselves. They enable the alcoholic by not being a "bother." Typically, the lost child is academically average in school. Socially, this child doesn't take leadership roles and is generally a loner (Black, 1981, pp. 21–23).

The Family Mascot.   The family mascot is usually the youngest child, who placates and comforts everybody in the family and makes them feel better (Wegscheider-Cruse, 1989). This child thinks that by making family members feel better, he or she can divert attention from the problem, and it will subside or go away. This placating child may operate in three distinctive patterns. First, the mascot may act the clown and distract the family through humorous antics. Socially, these people may be the life of the party but have few close friends because they discount everybody's feelings as a stress reduction mechanism. In school, if mascots defuse stress by humor, such antics may land them in trouble with their teachers (George, 1990, pp. 72–76). (One of your authors landed in trouble with many teachers from grade school through graduate school for his humorous antics. Do you suppose he sometimes experiences it now?)

Second, the mascot may assume a role of sympathetic counselor to the rest of the family. Highly sensitive to the needs of others, this child may be the apologist for the family's behavior and attempt to apply psychological balm to the emotional wounds other members of the family suffer. Such sensitive characteristics are well rewarded at school, where such children are praised for their compliant, helpful, and sharing qualities. The mascot abets the alcoholic by distracting the family from being forced to come to grips with the constant conflicts they are engaged in (Black, 1981, pp. 23–25).

Third, the mascot may assume the "sick" role in the family by manifesting continuous and sometimes severe psychosomatic illnesses. This overprotected child becomes the illness focal point for the family, and enables the chemical dependency by deflecting the family focus on sickness away from the addict (George, 1990, p. 76).

To keep the foregoing dysfunctional family roles operational, ironclad family rules must be followed, as discussed in the next section.

Family Rules in Alcoholic Families

There is a clear method to the madness of the foregoing roles, and to survive, members of addictive families learn unspoken rules very quickly. In the parlance of substance abuse programs, families of addicts have a metaphorical pink elephant sitting in the living room that everybody sees, that everybody walks around, and that nobody acknowledges. The presence of this elephant makes children think there is something wrong with them, because nobody else seems to be much concerned with the elephant (the addictive behavior) or at least isn't acknowledging it. What is even more disconcerting is that these children tend to believe that everyone else lives in an idyllic Cleaver or Huxtable family. Yet this is certainly not the Bill Cosby show, and to make things livable in the grim reality of addictive families, children have to adopt the following rules to survive (McGowan, 1991).

Don't Talk/Don't Have Problems.   Because of the denial of alcoholism in an alcoholic family, seldom are any of the children's problems recognized, and the family problem—alcoholism—is never discussed. In the alcoholic family, parents make clear injunctions, "We don't have that problem here, and you better not talk about it" (Doweiko, 1999, p. 337). If one does talk about it, then bad things happen (Black, 1981, pp. 33–37).

Lisa: Early on, Dad would be throwing up in the sink in the morning. Mom would just say he was sick. It scared me 'cause I thought he had, like, cancer or something, and he was gonna die. Every time I'd ask a question about it, she'd just blow me off or get mad at me.

Don't Trust.   The single most important ingredient in a nurturing relationship is honesty. No child can trust or be expected to trust unless those around him or her are also open and honest about their own feelings. One should never trust that parents will be there emotionally, psychologically, or even physically for a member of an addictive family (Doweiko, 1999, pp. 338–339). Children not only cannot depend on the alcoholic, but they also may not be able to depend on the other enabling parent because he or she is so busy trying to meet the alcoholic's needs and will minimize, rationalize, or blatantly deny that certain events are taking place (Black, 1981, pp. 39–45).

Mark: Even though it's a long way to the ballpark, I always plan on riding my bike. Dad says he'll take me, but he works late a lot and can't get home on time. Sometimes Mom has to take care of him when he's sick, or she doesn't feel well herself. So I just always plan on getting myself there for practice and the games.

Don't Feel. Members of addictive families have a well-developed denial system in regard to feelings—particularly one's own feelings. Members quickly learn that vocalizing feelings of fear, guilt, anger, sadness, embarrassment, and other hurtful feelings just brings more pain to the family. Although these feelings are shunted aside and submerged in the maladaptive roles family members assume, they are experienced over and over in addictive families and do not go away when one gains adulthood and leaves the addictive family of origin (Black, 1981, pp. 45–49).

Mark: I really wish Dad and Mom could have been there to see me get most valuable player, but Lisa was, and my coach told me how proud he was of me, and then the whole team went to his house for ice cream. Well, it wasn't that big a thing anyway . . . just a Little League championship.

Don't Behave Differently. Any attempt to shift roles within the family is not allowed because this would turn the system topsy-turvy. If role vacancies do occur, they must be quickly filled by other members of the family (George, 1990, p. 79).

Lisa: Oh yeah! I tried to be Little Miss Goody Two-Shoes, the perfect kid. Got good grades in school, went out for the volleyball team, dated "nice" guys, and was a "nice" girl. But I got yelled at even more for not doing good enough. It's never good enough for Dad. So forget that. I might as well get yelled at for having fun like before.

Don't Blame Chemical Dependency. Assigning blame to people, things, and situations outside the family is typical of the denial of personal responsibility for one's actions that pervades a chemically dependent family. Although the addict may receive some severe judgment by the rest of the family, family members believe that it is fate that keeps an iron grip on the family's misery (Doweiko, 2006, pp. 332–333).

Amy: I know he can be such an SOB, but it's been the lot of the O'Leary women to marry that kind of guy for three generations now. I swear my younger sister married a clone of Gordon. It just runs in the family, I guess.

Do Behave As I Want. The family must behave as the alcoholic wants, so the drinking behavior can continue. For those who don't comply, various sanctions and threats are applied. They include "I won't love you"; "I won't support you with money or my presence"; "I'll go out and get drunk"; or "I'll abuse you physically" (Doweiko, 1996, p. 304).

Gordon: (*shouting*) All I'm good for is to bring home a paycheck. We haven't got the money to go to Disney World! The only time you little parasites love me is when I'm giving you money. If you don't shut up, I'll shut you up with the back of my hand. (*Takes another long drink from his highball and stares sullenly at the TV.*)

Do Be Better and More Responsible No matter what the family attempts to do to compensate for the alcoholic, it will never be good enough. As all the defense mechanisms of the alcoholic so clearly indicate, blame is projected onto significant others to compensate for the alcoholic's slide into failure (Doweiko, 1996, pp. 306–307).

Mark: Here's my report card. I made the honor roll!

Gordon: (*Blearily staring at Mark's report card, drunk on martinis.*) Yeah, well, thoze AAAsss er OK, but whash that goddamn C in mashmaticks? Yule nevr get inna collash tha' waye. Wy the hell didn' you get the yard cut 'n raked like I tole ya? Now, get your tail out there 'n get on it!

Don't Have Fun "Fun" is drinking. Broken promises because of hangovers and benders in regard to vacations, recital attendance, going to ball games, and so on, and angry recriminations keep "fun" out of the family. Not inviting friends overnight or for birthday parties because of the unpredictability of the alcoholic's temper keeps "fun" out of such households. Finally, family members are so busy working to keep the system in some semblance of equilibrium, they are too tired to have fun (Doweiko, 1996, pp. 306–307).

Mark: Hey, Lisa. Are you going to invite all your cool girlfriends over for a slumber party on your birthday?

Lisa: (*with eyes downcast and a look of disappointment*) Well, I wanted to, and asked Mom, but she said Dad wouldn't like it. And you know how he gets.

Mark: (*angrily and kicking the wastebasket with his foot*) Yeah. I know.

Certainly, the trauma experienced by children who live and survive in chemically dependent families would seem bitter enough. However, the trauma and the crises of childhood in a chemically dependent family do not end with an escape from home or maturation into adulthood. The traumatic wake of being reared in a chemically dependent family often ripples into adulthood in the form of a variety of transcrisis events that might seem on first glance to have little reason for being and no discernible links to one's family of origin.

Adult Children of Alcoholics

In the 1980s a new phenomenon gained a great deal of publicity and attention in therapeutic settings and became a darling of the media talk shows. In the past, the primary focus of treatment of alcoholism was on the addicted person. Rarely were family members seen as the primary recipients of treatment for their own codependent and personal problems arising from the addiction (Schaef, 1986, p. 6). As a best-guess estimate, there are about 28 million adult children of alcoholics in the United States (Collette, 1990; Mathew et al., 1993), so it is not difficult to understand why a treatment approach that focuses on codependents would quickly gain a great deal of notoriety and credibility.

The zealotry that sometimes assails the chemical dependency field is not missing here. As reported by Schaef (1986) in her review of the codependency literature, Wegscheider-Cruse (1984) believes that 96 percent of the population of the United States is codependent! In the popular self-help literature, almost every problem of identity development or impulse control has been associated with codependency (Hogg & Frank, 1992).

The whole concept of the Adult Children of Alcoholics (ACOA) movement is based on a "damaged goods" model (Wolin & Wolin, 1995) that sees people as essentially passive victims of their environment with few compensatory resources. Such "victim" status may give people who come into treatment lots of excuses for not doing what they need to do to move on with their lives. But research studies indicate that this victim status is simply not universally true (D'Andrea, Fisher, & Harrison, 1994; Senchak et al., 1995), because numerous ACOAs have had the resilience to have lived in an alcoholic family and then do as well with their adult lives as anybody else (Lyon & Seefeldt, 1995). Further, many of the characteristics attributed to ACOAs are not necessarily unique to them. When ACOAs are compared to adults who come out of severely dysfunctional homes where no alcoholism was present, there

is little difference between the two groups (Hardwick, Hansen, & Bairnsfather, 1995).

Finally, Doweiko (1999, p. 345) points out that the ACOA movement is also essentially a white, middle-class invention. Virtually nothing is known about children from other cultures with different family systems whose parents do other kinds of drugs. What they may or may not become as adults is virtually anybody's guess. It is with these qualifiers that you are introduced to the ACOA, who may well be proceeding out of the transcrisis of the family of origin's alcoholism into his or her own crisis.

Facts. There is clear evidence that the following three facts relate to ACOAs (Kerr & Hill, 1992; Mathew et al., 1993; Sher et al., 1991):

1. Alcoholism runs in families. Rarely is a case seen in isolation. There may be generational skips, but alcoholism is invariably found in the extended family of the alcoholic.
2. Children of alcoholics run a higher risk of developing alcoholism than do children in the mainstream of the population. Males are four times as likely and females are three times as likely as their peers from nonalcoholic families to become alcoholic.
3. Children of alcoholics tend to marry alcoholics. Rarely do they go into the marriage with that knowledge, but the phenomenon occurs over and over.

Much like sufferers of PTSD and submerged trauma, ACOAs may present themselves in transcrisis with problems that bear little resemblance to the instigating issues of familial alcoholism. Thus, the astute crisis worker would do well to assess the client's family of origin for amount and duration of drug use before making a triage assessment decision.

Feelings. On reaching adulthood, the majority of children of alcoholics continue to experience problems related to trust, dependency, control, identification, and expression of feelings. They have difficulty saying no and may be manipulated by others and extend themselves beyond any reasonable human capacity (Brabant & Martof, 1993). ACOAs often experience an overwhelming sense of fear. In particular, the fear of abandonment is predominant and intensifies after childhood. These fears are episodic in that extreme high and low mood swings are experienced and are manifested by either clinging behavior or an inability to form meaningful relationships. Because they have learned to stifle feelings so well as children, ACOAs have a fear of confrontation and seldom argue or fight, even when their emotions are boiling over. Fear results in a tendency for ACOAs to discount their own perceptions and not have the courage to check out other people's perceptions (Black, 1981, p. 116).

Anger is seldom acknowledged by the ACOA. Because the ACOA as a child was seldom if ever allowed to acknowledge or display anger, it is a feeling that is often repressed, twisted, and distorted in the ACOA. This feeling is invariably denied, yet it manifests itself in a variety of mental and physical health problems that include psychosomatic illnesses, phobias, depression, narcissism, anxiety, panic, and eating disorders (Hibbard, 1993; Mathew et al., 1993). Behaviorally, anger is most often manifested as passive-aggressive behavior toward others. Particularly for females, anger seldom comes out in confrontive ways but rather continuously seethes in a chronic state. Attachment and individuation problems cause ACOA females to be highly sensitive to real or imagined criticism. In contrast, ACOA males tend to have higher rates of state (periodic or situational) anger, and when they lose control, they lose it in a hurry. However, for both sexes, anger's bedfellow is guilt (Black, 1981, p. 115; George, 1990, p. 86).

Guilt is a tenacious feeling that ACOAs may hold onto for 10, 30, or even 60 years. The guilt may be over a range of things, from wishing parents would die to not doing enough for the family to running away from the problem. If no resolution with or confrontation of a parent occurs before the parent's death, the guilt may lead to more severe disturbances (Black, 1981, p. 120; George, 1990, p. 86) and turn into unresolved grieving problems.

Effects of Childhood Roles. Dynamically, the adaptive roles ACOAs take on in childhood may follow them into adulthood. Heroes become extremely responsible adults who are scared to death of losing control. Heroic ACOAs had little fun as children, and they have little ability to enjoy life as adults. Heroes have to be in charge, stay in one-up positions, and allow no room for equal relationships. For the responsible ACOA, alcohol can remove the stress and anxiety of always retaining rigid control (Black, 1981, p. 123; George, 1990, p. 89).

For the ACOA lost child, life is a perpetual roller coaster. These adults perceive themselves as having few alternatives because, when forced to make commitments based on logical and linear thinking, they have few mental resources to call on. They have never learned that choices are available to them, because they

have never had to make a decision; they have merely adjusted to changing conditions. They find mates who are chaotic representatives of their former childhood experiences. The problem is that these relationships are insubstantial because no one takes responsibility for making decisions. The result is a person who is lonely, depressed, and isolated socially. Alcohol can give these people a false sense of power and control (Black, 1981, p. 85; George, 1990, p. 89).

Placaters or family mascots are experienced by others as nice people because of their attempts to please others. They are adept at diverting attention from themselves; otherwise they'd have to deal with their own pain (Black, 1981, pp. 23–25). These ACOAs have always been so responsible for others that they have lost the ability to take care of themselves and their own needs. Chemical dependents are perfect marriage partners for these individuals because they can continue the loving and supportive role that they perfected in their alcoholic family of origin. The comic placater as an adult is the life of every party but of no use in an emotional maelstrom. The psychosomatic version of the placater draws sympathy and attention but never focuses on any issues of change that would allow for a more fulfilling and productive life. Finally, the placater who is always sensitive to and supportive of others actually does little to help others confront the dilemmas they face. As a result, placaters make excellent enablers (Black, 1981, pp. 59–61; George, 1990, p. 90).

Finally, acting-out children may experience life as adults in two operating modes. First, they may continue to rebel, but in more sophisticated and dramatic ways. Their rebellion extends out from the family into society. They lack education and job skills, have anger control problems, marry early, and produce illegitimate children. In law enforcement terms, they graduate from misdemeanors to felonies. They are prime candidates for having severe addiction problems and also suffer from mental health problems. They are the stereotypical bad apples that live on the edge of society or are outcast from it (Black, 1981, pp. 62–63; George, 1990, p. 89). If the acting-out child assumes the scapegoat role, as ACOAs they become everyone's doormat because they are incapable of standing up for themselves. They allow themselves to be used and abused by others. Indeed, they become excellent candidates to marry into or work in abusive relationships. Their low self-concept makes them prime candidates for chemical dependency because of the false sense of well-being it provides (George, 1990, p. 89).

Whether one believes that ACOAs are doomed to suffer the sins of the fathers being revisited on them, or that they merely use their ACOA status to rationalize less-than-adequate coping skills as adults, one thing is sure: There are a lot of us out there. ACOAs make up approximately 60 percent of all patients in chemical dependency programs (Liepman, White, & Nirenberg, 1986, p. 39).

Treatment Approaches
Alcoholics Anonymous (AA)

AA is the most widely known and used treatment model in the world, with more than 2 million members in 100,800 groups. Its founder, Bill W. (Wilson), started AA in 1934 out of desperation, because there was little if any intervention or long-term treatment for alcoholism available other than expensive inpatient sanatoriums. AA started as a support group of outcast individuals who came together and admitted that they couldn't control their drinking. AA believes that alcoholism is a disease much like diabetes. Thus, abstinence is the guiding treatment principle, and everything else AA does is focused on staying sober and NOT drinking. To that end, abstinence anniversaries are big occasions for celebration.

Probably the two best-known components of AA are its anonymous group meetings that offer support to people in recovery and its Twelve Step program. The famous opening line of its meetings is a person voluntarily standing up and saying, "Hi! I'm Dick (no last names, please) and I'm an alcoholic!" to which the group's bonding response is, "Hi, Dick!" New members are given sponsors who are their emergency crisis support system. So while AA meetings are the primary tool for obtaining support for abstinence, sponsors are the fail-safe support that may get a call in the middle of the night: "Steve, this is Dick, and my wife just left, I am devastated, and I am thinking of solving that problem by getting a bottle of whiskey and drinking it right now. I'm sorry to call you so late, but I need to talk."

A sponsor is a more experienced person in recovery who guides the less experienced aspirant ("sponsee," or "sponsoree") through the program. New members in twelve-step programs are encouraged to secure a relationship with at least one sponsor. Publications from twelve-step fellowships emphasize that sponsorship is a "one-on-one" relationship of shared experiences focused on working the Twelve Steps. According to Narcotics Anonymous (2004), sponsors share their experience, strength, and hope with their sponsees. A sponsor's role is not that of a legal adviser, a banker, a parent, a marriage counselor, or a social worker, nor is a sponsor a therapist offering some sort of professional advice. A sponsor is simply another addict in recovery who is willing to share his or her journey through the Twelve Steps. As in most crisis situations, support is critical to keeping psychological equilibrium and, in substance abuse, staying clean. Research by Johnson, Finney, and Moos (2006) and Kingree and Thompson (2011) has found that having a close sponsor makes a significant difference in long-term abstinence.

Twelve-step programs address how to live a life that has a past filled with alcohol and a future that isn't. The Twelve Steps were originally published in 1939, in *Alcoholics Anonymous: The Story of How More Than One Hundred Men Have Recovered from Alcoholism* (Alcoholics Anonymous, 2001). These are the original Twelve Steps as published by AA (2001):

1. We admitted we were powerless over alcohol—that our lives had become unmanageable.
2. Came to believe that a Power greater than ourselves could restore us to sanity.
3. Made a decision to turn our will and our lives over to the care of God *as we understood Him.*
4. Made a searching and fearless moral inventory of ourselves.
5. Admitted to God, to ourselves, and to another human being the exact nature of our wrongs.
6. Were entirely ready to have God remove all these defects of character.
7. Humbly asked Him to remove our shortcomings.
8. Made a list of all persons we had harmed, and became willing to make amends to them all.
9. Made direct amends to such people wherever possible, except when to do so would injure them or others.
10. Continued to take personal inventory and when we were wrong promptly admitted it.
11. Sought through prayer and meditation to improve our conscious contact with God *as we understood Him*, praying only for knowledge of His will for us and the power to carry that out.
12. Having had a spiritual awakening as the result of these steps, we tried to carry this message to alcoholics, and to practice these principles in all our affairs.

The spiritual component of AA can be clearly seen in the Twelve Steps. That component has heaped both praise and scorn on AA's faith-based approach and "giving oneself over to a higher power." The fact is, though, that the spirituality component of dealing with addiction appears to be a powerful factor in getting and staying sober. A number of researchers (Dreup, Johnson, & Bindl, 2011; Kelly et al., 2011; Miller & Saunders, 2011; Robinson et al., 2011) have found that those individuals who see improvement in spiritual and religious functioning over the course of treatment are more likely to experience improvement in drinking behavior and alcohol-related problems after treatment has stopped.

As treatment models have evolved and all the trappings of a professional field of study such as therapist licensure, institutional certification, and government bureaucracies have come into being to study and treat alcoholism, AA has fought hard, and at times bitter and divisive, battles to maintain its stature in the treatment field. It has not been without criticism for its spiritual emphasis, its labeling of persons with alcoholism as deviant, problems with self-diagnosis, and the alcohol-as-disease concept (Fry, 1985; Trice & Staudenmeier, 1989; Young, 2011).

AA's standing and political clout, though, remain strong thanks to its huge participant base and those who believe they have gotten clean by using it. The fact that it costs nothing more than the time to find a meeting, and the ability to stand up and say "Hi! I'm Dick and I'm an alcoholic," gives it huge appeal for people who cannot afford treatment. Its potency as a political force can be seen in the fact that, unlike any other area of psychotherapy, in most states it requires only a high school diploma (and a ton of experience working in the field) to get a license as an addictions therapist. The reason is specifically that many therapists in the field are recovering alcoholics or other substance abusers who do not have college degrees but do have a lot of seat time in AA meetings.

Besides the AA *Big Book* (2011), which is now available online, there are a variety of self-help and resource books describing how to work the program (Fennell, 2006; Gorski, 1989; Kettelhack, 1992). Add to those resources the fact that almost every small town in the United States has an AA meeting every week, and that somewhere in the world there is an AA meeting going on as you read these words, and you should understand that AA is an extremely powerful treatment approach that works for people (Majer et al., 2011) and has shown a lot of staying power. In that regard, while it may not be for everyone, millions of people have benefited from it, and we believe it should be, at the very least, considered as part of any treatment program and most particularly as part of any *crisis* treatment where substance abuse is involved.

Cognitive-Behavioral Therapy (CBT)

Standard cognitive-behavioral techniques are used to treat the "stinkin' thinking" that goes with alcoholism. The central thesis of a CBT approach is disrupting the automatic thoughts and the entrenched beliefs that are triggers for starting to drink (Beck et al., 1993). CBT is also highly effective with the depression that often accompanies alcoholism (Emmelkamp, 2004). Teaching clients to become aware of these triggers and replace them with positive counterinjunctions is a critical component of relapse prevention (Meichenbaum, 1977, 1985).

Beck and associates (1993) believe there are three basic styles of beliefs that propel the drug abuser to use. Anticipatory beliefs focus on the expectation of reinforcement; relief-oriented symptoms focus on reduction of negative psychological or physical symptoms; and permissive beliefs refer to the belief that it is OK to use drugs. Disputation of these beliefs through evidence-gathering questions such as "How do you explain those lost weekends as being relaxing"? is a primary initiating technique. Developing control beliefs is critical to recognizing and stopping automatic thoughts by become observant of personal and environmental cues that lead to drinking behavior (Beck et al., 1993; Meichenbaum, 1977) and then manufacturing and implementing positive coping statements and specific thought-stopping and positive counterinjunctions to change stinkin' thinkin'.

At a deeper philosophical level, alcoholics get caught up in all-or-none, black-and-white thinking about their general functioning and living status. That thinking turns into behavioral "shoulds," "oughts," and "musts" about themselves, others, and the world in general that, when not met, are a great rationalization to go drink or drug (Ellis et al., 1988). Alcoholics' use of all the defense mechanisms indicated earlier in the chapter, and particularly their use of regression, makes it important to dispute and disrupt their absolutistic cognitions about drinking and how it affects them. CBT and operant behavioral therapies have typically been the main counterpoint therapy to AA. Cognitive-behavioral approaches appear to work both for substance abuse alone (Brook, 2011; Kiluk et al., 2010; Moyers & Houck, 2011; Sobell & Sobell, 2011; Sudak, 2011) and for substance abuse with co-occurring disorders (Cornelius et al., 2011; Granholm, 2011).

Inpatient Treatment: The Minnesota Model

The Minnesota model has long been the most widely used inpatient treatment format for chemical dependents (Doweiko, 2006, pp. 367–369). It has two major components. The first is its comprehensive treatment team that uses experts from a wide variety of disciplines to evaluate and implement treatment procedures in whatever parts of the client's life are needed. The second is the inpatient, 28-day treatment regimen, which has become an industry standard. The Alcoholics Anonymous (AA) approach and philosophy are highly integrated with this model. Unfortunately, there is little evidence to support the efficacy of the 28-day program over any other program as far as rehabilitation is concerned, and no evidence to indicate that forced compliance with AA works (Doweiko, 2006, p. 369). Furthermore, the model tends to "cookie-cutter" all clients through the same daily regimen, and there is ample evidence to indicate that chemical dependents are far less likely to relapse when programs are individually tailored (Beutler et al., 1993; DiClemente et al., 1994; Donovan et al., 1994; Donovan & Mattson, 1994; McKay & Maisto, 1993).

What is clear is that the 28-day inpatient program is a lot more expensive than an outpatient treatment program. As a result, health-care providers have balked at the expense and the model's inability to show that its inpatient timeline does any better than any other inpatient timeline or outpatient approach (Doweiko, 1996, pp. 341–343). Paradoxically, if outpatient treatment is warranted and the insurance company will only pay for inpatient, residential treatment, guess where the client is going? Thus, there has been a rapid movement away from the time frame of the model to either very brief stays in the hospital or no admission at all (Knack & Murray, 1996).

Outpatient Programs

The primary notion of an addiction program is to keep individuals from relapsing. The track record of most intervention programs in regard to relapse has never been great and is sometimes poor. Given the tremendous expense of inpatient treatment using the 28-day model and the hard-nosed economics of insurances companies' refusal to pay for such programs, the industry standard today has become some form of outpatient treatment.

DWI schools are short-term outpatient programs to educate drunk drivers about the dangers of drinking and driving. *Short-term outpatient programs* (STOP) include several variations on a theme of individual and group therapy that is combined with psychoeducational materials, reading assignments, and support groups such as AA. They usually meet once or twice a week for up to 2 months. More intensive forms of STOP programs for moderate to severe substance abuse meet four or five times a week for up to 6 months. AA and family therapy sessions are often included along with individual and group sessions for the client. *Intensive long-term outpatient treatment* (ILTOT), which may last up to 18 months, is used for clients who have relapsed numerous times and would stand little chance of success without long-term care. Intensive and extensive individual and group counseling sessions are planned along with specific support programs to help the client move through the early stages of recovery (Doweiko, 2006, pp. 375–376).

A great deal of criticism has been leveled at outpatient programs mandated by many health-care providers. The two main criticisms have been that many patients are just too sick to be treated on an outpatient basis and should be treated in a hospital setting until they can be stabilized, and the more cynical criticism that health-care providers are trying to "get by on the cheap." It doesn't take an addictions specialist or medical doctor to know that a person admitted to an inpatient treatment program with a severe addiction problem is not going to come out of it 3 days later physically clean, not to mention psychologically clean.

On the positive side, outpatient treatment is not financially ruinous, clients can continue to stay in their home environment and assume more responsibility for their recovery, the treatment can be extended over a much longer time period, it is much more flexible (meetings and therapy sessions may be held during the day, evenings, or on weekends) and allows clients to continue working, and noncompliance can be easily monitored by random urine checks (Doweiko, 1996, pp. 349–350).

What *generally* (note the emphasis on "generally") appears to be true is that longer rather than shorter inpatient treatment (Arbour, Hambley, & Ho, 2011; Nordfjaern, 2011), along with intensified and prolonged aftercare booster sessions (Emmelkamp & Vedel, 2006; Matheson, Dohery, & Grant, 2011; Nordfjaern, 2011; Tuten et al., 2012; Witkiewitz & Marlatt, 2009), appears to work better in relapse prevention or at least extend abstinence. Type, kind, and duration of aftercare and the ability to stick with it appear to be particularly important if inpatient therapy is briefer.

Contingency Management (CM)

Contingency management is used for both inpatient and outpatient therapy. It is based on vintage Skinnerian operant conditioning principles that have been around for more than 60 years and have been used for a long time in contingency contracting. Simply put, based on completing a task (drug-free urine test, zero breathalyzer check), the client is rewarded with a tangible reinforcer (coupon for a #4 at the Golden Arches) (Higgins, Silverman, & Heil, 2008). Contingency management is pretty standard operating procedure in inpatient settings of all types, with rewards (visitor passes, extra recreation time) based on a point/token system for performance and compliance. Using a CM model depends on having enough staff and constant supervision to adequately monitor behavior, which works well in an inpatient setting but not so well in outpatient settings where supervision and monitoring of compliance are less frequent (Petry, 2012, p. 10).

The major sea change in CM has been its adaption to outpatient treatment. There are three basic principles to CM (Petry, 2012, pp. 11–12): (1) The behavior to be changed is monitored frequently. This does not mean once a week or on a random basis over a month, as is typically the case, but rather two to three times a week. (2) Abstinence is immediately reinforced with positive, tangible reinforcers such as vouchers, gift certificates, chances to win prizes such as lottery tickets, or even money. (3) When the behavior doesn't occur, the positive reinforcers are withheld. There is no punishment, but there is also no reinforcement. The idea is that while alcohol is a potent reinforcer, behavior can be altered by using contingent scheduling of alternate reinforcers that are powerful enough to substitute for and extinguish alcohol use (Wong, Silverman, & Bigelow, 2008).

CM works, but it takes careful preparation and thoroughness on the part of clinicians. Petry and her associates (2000) used prize drawings and continuous toxicology screens on 42 alcohol dependent clients and compared the results to those obtained through standard care consisting of twelve-step sessions, daily planning activities, life skills training, health education, and cognitive-behavioral skills training treatment. The CM clients also received the same standard care package. Those clients on CM were 69 percent abstinent at the end of treatment, compared to 39 percent in the standard care only group. Further, only 26 percent in the CM group, compared to 61 percent in the standard

group, relapsed to heavy alcohol use. These positive outcomes appear over and over, not only with alcohol abusers but with cocaine and polydrug abusers as well (Bryne & Petry, 2011; Litt et al., 2007; Schumacher et al., 2007; Walker et al., 2010; Wong, Silverman, & Bigelow, 2008). So why is this silver bullet of a treatment approach not pervasive? There is institutional and therapist resistance to its use because of the intensive and constant monitoring required. It also costs money, because payoffs need to increase and they need to be constant (Petry, 2012, pp. 23–24). It is also seen by many as a form of bribery.

One of the major historical criticisms of all contingency contracting (Homme, 1971) and management programs, whether it be for sixth graders doing their homework for TV time and getting money for good grades or cocaine addicts giving drug-free urine samples, has been that it's bribery. That is not so. Bribery happens when Mom buys a toy first if a screaming child promises to pipe down in a store. The reward comes before the task is completed. Bribery occurs when an official is paid off to look the other way so an illegal act can occur (Becker, 1970).

If you read this book carefully, underline passages, take notes, study hard, and get an A on a test, you have essentially been on a contingency contract. You do good work, and you get rewarded. You have to perform to get the reinforcement. That's CM! Your professor didn't tell you that you would get an A if you just showed up and kept quiet in her class and didn't bother her. That's bribery! The long and short of it is that CM works, and it works well with and boosts the effectiveness of other kinds of treatment programs for substance abuse (Bryne & Petry, 2011; Litt et al., 2007; Schumacher et al., 2007).

Community Reinforcement Approach (CRA)

CRA is a comprehensive behavioral program that crosscuts all of the ecosystems of the individual in an attempt to rein in substance abuse (Meyers & Smith, 1995). Started in the 1970s, CRA is somewhat eclectic in its approach in that it may use Antabuse (a drug that will make you very sick if you ingest alcohol) or Naltrexone, an opioid antagonist, which can reduce binges. It may also include communication skills training, behavioral skills training, and job skills training. It may use therapy groups that focus on what it means to have friendships and social activities that revolve around drinking and replacing them with activities that don't. It may have variations on CM in that it awards prizes for attendance, for meeting performance goals, for target date compliance, and so on, besides extensive and intensive individual counseling sessions when treatment is first started (Meyers & Squires, n.d.).

Its main focus, though, is on systemic behavioral intervention in all of the environments the client inhabits, from recreational to work to home. The overall goal is to increase satisfaction and payoffs in nondrinking areas. To do that, it creates a treatment plan that includes a Happiness Scale that asks the client to rate current happiness in the following categories: drinking, job, money management, social life, personal habits, family relationships, legal issues, emotional life, communication, and general happiness. Following clients' assessment of how happy they are in each of these areas, a counseling goals plan is collaboratively formulated for each of these areas (Meyers & Smith, 1995; Meyers & Squires, n.d.).

CRA is a no punishment approach that continuously reinforces proactive, prosocial, and drug abstinence behavior. CRA is a "weness" approach in which the interventionist seeks to form a collaborative relationship with the client. Its treatment goals are brief, positive, and specific enough to measure. It is dogged in its attempts to conduct a functional analysis to find both external environmental triggers (associates, settings, times) and internal (thoughts, physical sensations, feeling states) that are the triggers to drink. Along with sobriety sampling, functional analysis of what leads to drinking is a key component of treatment (Meyers & Smith, 1995; Meyers & Squires, n.d.).

It may also have a family therapy component, called Community Reinforcement Approach and Family Training (CRAFT). CRAFT is not about getting drinkers to stop or doing therapy with the family, but rather teaching family members how they can change the social environment so that they are aware of and can change inadvertent reinforcers that can trigger drinking, along with reinforcing behaviors that are related to abstinence (Meyers & Smith, 1997). Its use of operant behavioral principles to reinforce substitute behaviors for drinking has been highly effective for more than 35 years (Abbot, 2009; Azrin, 1976; Garner et al., 2009; Gianini, Lundy, & Smith, 2009; Godley et al., 2009; Lange, Reker, & Driessen, 2008; Smith, Meyers, & Delaney, 1998).

Reinforcement-Based Treatment (RBT)

RBT is sort of a combination of CM and CRA on steroids. It is an intensive outpatient treatment program/combination of interventions with a conceptual basis of operant conditioning that employs components of both CA and CRA. In addition, it emphasizes a positive, supportive, consumer-oriented approach to abusers, incorporates motivational intervention techniques, emphasizes recreational activities that are substitutes for drug-related ones, and also believes that a critical ingredient is providing safe, drug-free housing for its clients. Along with motivational interviewing, initial treatment is intensive in that it takes up a lot of the time the individual would otherwise spend procuring drugs. Barriers to treatment are vigorously eliminated so that problems such as child care and lack of transportation do not become issues in getting to treatment (Tuten et al., 2012, pp. 10–17).

The operational hypothesis of this approach is that behaviors are learned and maintained as a result of environmental stimuli and reinforcers that result in negative consequences for the abuser. However, through massive doses of reinforcement and alteration of environmental settings and setting events (known as *triggers*), change can occur, including long-term abstinence from the addictive substance. Treatment is highly individualized and is nonjudgmental, nonconfrontational, and strengths based. Clients are treated much as businesses would treat customers. Each client has an employment or educational goal and receives extensive support in meeting this goal. Besides the tangible reinforcers given to clients for abstinence, a great deal of positive social reinforcement is given for accomplishments along with participation in a Social Club, which is a weekly group meeting where goals and activities for the weekend (weekends can be troublesome with too much idle time available to start ruminating on getting high) are reviewed and certificates are presented for numbers of days in attendance with much peer social reinforcement occurring at meetings. Finally, RBT graphically portrays client progress to give clients concrete, visual representations of what they are doing and how they are succeeding (Tuten et al., 2012, pp. 18–19). Tuten and her associates report positive outcomes using RBT (Gruber, Chutuape, & Stitzer, 2000; Jones et al., 2005) in regard to postintervention abstinence.

So, while all of these approaches can recount successes, none of them is a panacea and each faces barriers when they are put to work in the real world

(Amodeo et al., 2011). With that major qualifier, let's see how components of these approaches might operate in the alcoholic world of Gordon Brand.

Inpatient or Outpatient?

When a decision has to be made for inpatient versus outpatient status, monetary costs are (one hopes) not the only consideration. For Gordon, the decision ideally is based on the following five criteria (Group for the Advancement of Psychiatry, 1990).

1. *Is the client's condition associated with significant medical or mental health problems?* Gordon comes to the hospital in bad shape physically and has been warned by his doctor of the physical effects alcohol is having on him.
2. *Is the client's withdrawal going to be severe?* Although Gordon isn't quite to the delirium tremens stage, he is going to go through a tough time withdrawing and will need medical supervision to do it.
3. *What is the severity of the client's addiction and polyuse?* Gordon has a long history of alcohol abuse and a shorter history of polyuse with Xanax. From his physical symptoms and medical problems, he is severely addicted to alcohol and abusing tranquilizers.
4. *Have there been multiple failed attempts at outpatient treatment?* Gordon has never had any kind of treatment for chemical dependence.
5. *How are the client's support systems?* Gordon's support systems are questionable. His wife and children are fed up with his behavior. Whether they would willingly participate in treatment or sabotage it is open to question. His employer is also fed up, but both indicate support if treatment occurs.

Given the mixed bag of responses to the foregoing questions, Gordon will receive a combination of both inpatient and outpatient treatment, which is the least restrictive treatment necessary for his present condition.

Contemporary Model

Knack and Murray (1996) describe a principles-of-treatment approach that is different from the traditional Minnesota model of treating chemically dependent patients. This model is buttressed with components of CM (Higgin, Silverman, & Heil, 2008; Petry, 2012), CRA (Meyers & Smith, 1997), and RBT (Tuten et al., 2012). The fundamental principles are contained in the following statements:

1. There is a simultaneous treatment of addictions and psychiatric disorders.
2. Case management styles have moved away from the 28-day model of treatments toward a longer continuum of holistic and total care based on the assessed needs and circumstances of each patient.
3. Weekly reviews of each patient's progress enable treatment managers to assign and rapidly move patients from one level of a treatment continuum to other levels as appropriate.
4. Computer-based quantitative admissions assessment protocol and follow-ups provide treatment managers with the information and flexibility needed to move patients among different levels of treatment and least restrictive environments and to validate patient progress and program outcomes.
5. Outpatient aftercare programs such as the RBT social club on Friday evenings provide for group support, including family therapy, and both social and material reinforcement for abstinence along with drug screens. They are a key component of treatment for those patients who have significant family connections.
6. Patient autonomy and responsibility are the main driving forces governing treatment decisions. Success is viewed as a succession of progressive, incremental, and intentional levels of functioning.
7. Failure to maintain sobriety may result in the patient's being reassigned to a different level or intensity of treatment, but not being kicked out of the program. Plans fail, people don't.
8. Scientific evidence indicates that chemical dependency has a biological basis. Treatment regimens must take into account that genetics and biological background are important factors to be considered.
9. A viable treatment program must be holistic. Patients are evaluated and treated in a comprehensive way, including their psychiatric, addiction, medical, family, housing, and other needs. The variety of professionals who may participate in a coordinated way to provide such holistic treatment includes counselors, social workers, staff psychologists, addiction therapists, psychiatrists, internal medicine physicians, nurses, physicians' assistants, occupational therapists, recreation therapists, educational therapists, and physical therapists.
10. Gender issues are an important factor in chemical dependency treatment. Women and men have different biological and emotional needs and responses to treatment strategies.

11. Multicultural issues are essential in the educational component of chemical dependency treatment programs. The world represents a pluralistic environment, and patients need to develop understanding and tolerance of diversity in order to function adequately in the social environment as well as the workplace.

Multivariate Diagnosis
Matching Treatment to Client

A great deal of work has been done in the last two decades in attempting to match specific treatment with the individual. Not only do setting events contribute to how treatment is carried out, but also the particular personality constellation, demographics, learning history, ethnicity, social support systems, term of abuse, sex, age, and drinking systems determine the behaviors of the alcoholic and dictate specific treatment (Marlatt & Witkiewitz, 2009; McCrady, 1982, p. 682; Petry, 2012; Tuten et al., 2012). It appears that factoring in all of the foregoing variables in tailoring intervention to specific client needs has a better chance of success as far as program completion and relapse are concerned (Longabaugh et al., 1997; McLellan et al., 1997; Nielsen, Nielsen, & Wraae, 1998; Tuten et al., 2012).

While all of this sounds ideal, it should be stated that in a less-than-perfect world, treatment facilities often have almost identical treatment plans for all individuals, the only difference being the type of addictive drug used. Also, the construction of the treatment plan may have more to do with the philosophy of the institution than the individual's needs. As such, if the treatment philosophy revolves around a disease model, it is almost guaranteed that will be the treatment plan for everyone (Fisher & Harrison, 2000, pp. 129, 149).

Dual Diagnosis

It has only been in the past two decades that human services professionals have come to understand that many chemically dependent clients also may have underlying mental health problems (Doweiko, 1996, pp. 259–267) and use alcohol to self-medicate other psychological issues such as depression, personality disorders, and psychosis (Marlatt & Witkiewitz, 2009; Schmidt, Hesse, & Lykke, 2011). Estimates vary, but it appears that up to 50 percent of all alcohol and substance abuse problems mask other psychiatric problems (Brown et al., 1989; Carey, 1989; Hobbs et al., 2011).

One classic example of this problem has been the attempt to treat PTSD sufferers for their chemical dependency problems only. They may be dried out for a while, but the nightmares and sleeplessness that PTSD causes will invariably drive them back to self-medicating to get some sleep (Drapkin et al., 2011). Treating a battered woman or a rape survivor for alcoholism alone is akin to pouring sand down a rat hole—it never fills up and treatment is never finished because clients give up. The woman drinks to relieve both physical and emotional pain. Until battering stops, there is little reason for the drinking to stop, and many reasons for it to continue. Similarly, until treatment for the PTSD the rape survivor is experiencing takes effect, there is little reason for the drinking to stop and many reasons for it to continue (Hien et al., 2009).

The concurrent issues of a mental illness and drug and alcohol abuse pose a big problem. It has been found that drug abuse is 7 times and alcohol abuse is 10 times as prevalent in the mentally ill as in the general population (Kivlahan et al., 1991). The major issue with concurrent drug or alcohol abuse with a mental disorder is that, contrary to the individual's self-medication plan to ease the pain of the disorder or desire to experience the drug's effects, research shows that such drug use almost invariably *aggravates* the disorder, because the mentally ill seem to be especially sensitive to the drugs' effects. The crisis worker should be acutely aware of these people because they are disproportionately high users of emergency medical and mental health services (Doweiko, 1996, pp. 270–275).

The dual diagnosed client composes a high percentage of the potentially violent mentally ill that the Memphis Police Department Crisis Intervention Team officers deal with on our city streets, and reports from other police jurisdictions tend to support that high percentage. They go off their medication for the mental illness, start abusing drugs for their enjoyment or sense of expanded control, become psychotic, violent, or physically ill, and wind up in emergency rooms or in confrontations with authorities over and over again. Therefore, crisis workers on emergency call or admission should always consider a dual diagnosis as a distinct possibility when a drug-abusing client calls or shows up.

For a long time in the addictions treatment business the emphasis on treatment for dual diagnosed clients was exclusionary. Psychological symptoms were seen as off limits because of the fear of aggravating substance abuse (Hien et al., 2009, p. 3). These clients get passed back and forth between treatment professionals, "Your depression is causing you to drink excessively!" and "Your drinking is aggravating your depression!" and as a result of this double bind drop out of treatment (Marlatt & Witkiewitz, 2009). Yet meta-analyses of treatment approaches that tackle both substance abuse and psychological disorders show them to be effective (Hobbs et al., 2011; Kelly, Daley, & Douaihy, 2012). Thus, there is a strong need to tie together both sides of the issue into a unified treatment approach (Hien et al., 2009; Marlatt & Witkiewitz, 2009).

Intervention Strategies

The theoretical approach of this chapter, backed by a great deal of reported research (Beck et al., 1993; Doweiko, 2006, pp. 386–396; Emmelkamp & Vedel, 2006; Hien et al., 2009; Marlatt & Witkiewitz, 2009; Pattison & Kaufman, 1982), is that alcoholism is a multivariate construct, which implies the following:

1. Multiple interactive etiological variables combine to produce a particular individual pattern of alcoholism.
2. Treatment interventions must be multimodal to correspond to a specific person's particular pattern of alcoholism.
3. Treatment outcomes will vary in accordance with specific alcoholism patterns, persons, cultural background, social contexts, treatment processes, posttreatment adjustment patterns, and the interaction of all these factors.
4. Treatment of other life problems can improve outcomes in people with alcohol problems.

Crisis in a substance abuser's life rarely manifests itself as a onetime occurrence. The abuser's life is characterized by both a transcrisis state and transcrisis points. A transcrisis state is related to the whole process of addiction, with all the economic, social, physical, and psychological problems that chemical dependency entails. *Transcrisis points* are related to the recurrent crises in the chemical dependent's everyday life that seem to erupt in spontaneous ways whenever the person encounters stressors and that are rarely identified as being rooted in the greater underlying transcrisis of addiction. These transcrisis points continue through the course of withdrawal, therapy, and follow-up and apply not only to the alcoholic but also to those support persons who experience fallout from the crises.

Motivation and Stages of Change

You will soon meet two experienced alcohol and drug therapists. Among the many things these therapists are good at is motivating clients to change who may be anything but ready to change their drinking habits. Prochaska and associates (DiClemente & Prochaska, 1998; Prochaska, DiClemente, & Norcross, 1992) developed a *motivation to change* model that is based on the hypothesis that persons going through recovery go through very definite stages and will experience different kinds of characteristics and crises at each stage. Prochaska's stages of change, like most stage models as they evolve, have recently moved from being held as absolute truth and beauty to experiencing some critical rebuke. However, what they have most certainly done is provide therapists with baselines and benchmarks that can guide their intervention strategies. Following are a description of those stages (Prochaska, DiClemente, & Norcross, 1992) and briefly what treatment implications they have for the therapist.

Precontemplation. The person does not recognize a problem exists and still uses drugs. The therapist gives the client a thorough assessment and then relays the information to the client in a helpful, empathic way that attempts to enhance the motivation to change by trying to make contact and bond in a therapeutic alliance with the client through acceptance, support, and empathic understanding (Miller, 1995; Yeager & Gregoire, 2006). While persons may have moments of clarity as to the issues the drugs are causing, they generally continue their use, don't see it as a problem, and really aren't thinking much about stopping (Tuten et al., 2012, p. 64).

Contemplation. The person is still using drugs, but has some ambivalence about continuing and starts to entertain thoughts of quitting. About 40 percent of alcohol abusers may be found in this stage at any given time (DiClemente & Prochaska, 1998). Abusers may be dissatisfied with what drugs are doing to them, but may go on for years in this stage before moving forward, if ever. The therapist's job is now to enhance motivation to change by pointing out what is occurring with the client as a result of drug abuse and looking for positive exceptions and resilience in the muck and mire of the client's drug life (Miller, 1998; Yeager & Gregoire, 2006).

Determination/Preparation. The person has made a decision to quit in the near future. While they are starting to take action to stop their drug use, they aren't really sure what they need to do (Tuten et al., 2012, p. 64). The therapist's job is to actuate the decision by offering encouragement and support, provide empathic listening, gentle confrontation, humor, and reflection of hopes and fears, and use scaling questions to determine degree of current pain and commitment to a future drug-free life. Miracle questions are used to determine what one would look and feel like drug free. The therapist starts to cooperatively generate plans on controlling the abuse with the client as soon as he or she is able (Miller, 1998; Yeager & Gregoire, 2006).

Action.   Only about 20 percent of addicted persons can be found in the last three stages (DiClemente & Prochaska, 1998). The person starts to take active steps, such as entering treatment to change addictive behaviors. The therapist accentuates positive coping skills, helps the client monitor for relapse triggers and cues, minimizes slips as minor exceptions to progress, and tracks and reinforces success (Miller, 1998; Yeager & Gregoire, 2006).

Maintenance.   At about 6 months, the person has made the behavior change and controlled drug use. The person continues to work on behaviors that will keep changes operative with no relapse and few, if any, slips. The therapist helps identify and deal with personal and environmental issues that affect recovery and cause relapse or slips, and provides feedback and continuing support along with empowerment for success (Miller, 1998; Yeager & Gregoire, 2006).

Termination.   At about 5 years, the person has made cognitive and emotional changes necessary to support continuing control of the drug abuse. Social support systems, such as family or AA, are firmly in place to help the client over humps and around potholes that may lead to relapse. Evaluation takes the form of continued assessment of success in living drug free.

Motivational Interviewing.   Miller (1995, 1998; Miller & Rollnick, 2002) has developed a *motivational interviewing* (MI) technique that our therapists will use with Gordon that coincides nicely with the Prochaska stages of the motivation to change model. Motivational interviewing has become the gold standard in initiating interaction with substance abusers and indeed appears to have an impact on drug abusers' decision to change (Burke, Arkowitz, & Menchola, 2003).

When combined with CM, CRA, or especially RBT, the interventionist takes on the role of a trusted, objective, significant other who helps the client debate the merits of seeking treatment, but also verbally reinforces the client for at least thinking about abstinence. Early on in treatment at either the Precontemplation or Contemplation stage, *client feedback* may be given, which is an individualized summary of the client's history of drug and alcohol use based on standardized tests and personal data. Feedback is both a verbal discussion and an objective report that may be extremely sobering (no pun intended), but is also supportive (Tuten et al., 2012, p. 59).

Motivational stance is critical to the worker's interview and is composed of three specific behaviors: (1) affirming clients for having the courage to even contemplate changing, and acknowledging the difficulty of doing so; (2) developing clients' awareness of discrepancies in their current situation and getting them to start making value judgments about how well their substance abuse is serving their interests; (3) accurately summarizing the clients' situation and feelings without injecting the worker's value judgments (Tuten et al., 2012, p. 65). If you have just had the stunning insight that these sound very much like some of the basic tools of the crisis intervention trade illustrated in Chapter 4, you are on the proverbial ball!

Overall, motivational interviewing puts the ball in the client's court. The basic question starts with "It's your decision. No one can force you to stop drinking. What do you want to do?" When the question is posed this way, the person is not put on the defensive and backed into a psychological corner. Pantalon (2011) proposes that the worker ask permission to pose the following six questions. By asking permission, the worker gives the client a further sense of autonomy and freedom of choice, which is a critical ingredient in moving along the stages of change. The worker (Ray) poses these six questions to Gordon.

Ray: (*Question 1*) Why might you do this?

Gordon: So I wouldn't land up here again.

Ray: That's certainly true. What else might be some reasons?

The worker does not accept a one-shot answer, but rather uses an open lead to get the client to consider what other positive outcomes could occur.

Ray: (*Question 2*) How ready are you to do this? Put your readiness on a scale of 1 to 10, with 1 being "not at all" and 10 being "absolutely." Where are you?

Gordon: Maybe a 3 or 4.

Ray (*Question 3*) Why didn't you pick a lower number? Hmm, you could have picked a 1, but you didn't. You picked a 3 or 4, which indicates you have some desire to do this.

Gordon: Well, maybe I have got some problems that I could use some help with that I'm not sure how to fix.

Once the client gives a number other than 1, then the worker immediately notes that there is some positive inclination to move forward and reinforces the client. If the client says "1," then the worker can respond with "I get that you're not quite ready to do this right now, but what would it take for you to change that up to, say, a 3 or 4?"

Ray: (*Question 4*) Imagine that you already did this. What would the positive outcomes be?

Gordon: Hell, I don't see anything. You tell me?

Ray: Right now it is awfully hard to see anything that could come out of this mess. Let's suppose I could tell you there was some blue sky and sunshine out there, what might I be saying to you and what might that look like?

Gordon: Well, the family would be back together again and my kids would respect me, I guess. I wouldn't be about to be fired but back on good terms with my boss.

The worker frames the question as if it were already done, so that instead of being confronted with the awesome task ahead and the possibility of failure, the client can get a picture of success. This future-oriented, task-completed question allows people to be optimistic and excited about taking the task on.

Ray: (*Question 5*) Why would those outcomes be important to you?

Gordon: Well, duh! Everything would be back to normal, and I could get on with living my life and enjoying it.

Ray: OK, so enlighten me a bit. Could you be a bit more specific? Why would those things be important to you? What would those things look like? What would "normal" look like? It sure sounds like you want to get back on good terms with your kids again. I can see you are really proud of them and would like to be there for them. Tell me what "being there for them" would look like?

The idea here is to push clients toward specificity so that they are not just vague, nebulous goals, but ones that are clear and measurable, let the client know when they are accomplished, and have personal meaning.

Ray: (*Question 6*) So what's your next step, if any? It is your choice.

Gordon: Well, hell! I guess I'm in for treatment. How do I get started?

Ray: Excellent! Just excellent! I am really pleased and proud I am going to be working with you on this. You bring a lot of skills into the equation, based on your abilities, accomplishments, and education. This has all the appearances of being a great journey, and I'm glad to be a part of it. That's the first step on a big journey, but it's a giant step.

The last question asks for a specific short-term goal to get to the long-term mega-goal. By stating what he is going to do in the short term, the client is linking motivation to action. The worker reinforces him for this decision and sets the stage for a collaborative working relationship. The "if any" tacked on the end of the sentence is used to increase client autonomy and give the client the feeling that he is making a decision and not being forced into anything (Pantalon, 2011, pp. 8–9).

As the worker poses these questions, he is empathic but continuously develops discrepancies by highlighting the differences in the client's goals as opposed to current behavior. The worker also rolls with any resistance and does not debate or argue with the client. The worker is not an oak tree standing in the middle of a hurricane to be blown down, but rather a willow that bends with the resistance. Finally, motivational interviewing seeks to support the client's self-efficacy, the sense that change is possible on the basis of the client's abilities and past successes (Tuten et al., 2012).

Motivational interviewing may be used alone or in combination with the other approaches in this chapter. Motivational interviewing has proven to be so effective that it has become the seminal approach both to initiating intervention and in follow-up for relapse prevention (Burke, 2011; Driessen & Hollon, 2011; Feldstein Ewing et al., 2011; Jensen et al., 2011; Mason et al., 2011; Martin, Christopher, Houck, & Moyers,; Moyers & Houck, 2011; Söderlund, 2011).

To Drink or Not to Drink

One of the major problems with substance abuse is that it stubbornly refuses to proceed in a neat linear model of stepwise stages. It would be better described as cyclical (Doweiko, 2006, p. 388). Indeed, linear progress would be the exception. Relapses and slips happen so frequently that they should be thought of as part of the process of quitting rather than a failure to maintain sobriety. In that statement lies another of the controversies that continue to rage between adherents of disease models and other models of addiction. Can one engage in controlled drinking and maintain sobriety? Adherents of the disease model and AA would say absolutely not! However, this all-or-none view, given the tremendous number of abusers who relapse, almost guarantees a failure identity that they will never be able to attain sobriety in getting the monkey off their back. For some time in Europe, the end goal of substance abuse has been drinking that is more controlled rather than total abstinence, and there is mounting evidence that this can be accomplished (Coldwell & Heather, 2006; McMurran, 2006).

To put it mildly, that idea has not been as well received in the United States (Sobell & Sobell, 2006). Essentially, controlled drinking is seen as a harm reduction approach, much like a nicotine patch for those trying to quit tobacco. Certainly, every alcoholic in the world would like to think that he or she could be part of the group that can engage in controlled drinking. For some people it may not be an option, but for others it may well be, and the disease model adherents need to come to grips with controlled drinking as a viable treatment model for some substance abusers (Coldwell & Heather, 2006; Hodgins, 2005). On the other side of the issue, Doweiko (2006, p. 404) makes a cogent and articulate argument, backed up with research, that perhaps *abusers* can be taught *controlled drinking* but moderately or severely *addicted* individuals quickly return to *abusive past drinking* patterns.

Assessment

Assessing chemical dependency is a complex task and is critical for formulating differential diagnoses, specific outcome goals, and valid treatment modalities (Kaufman & Pattison, 1982b, p. 1091). Although a biochemical test is a fairly reliable and valid indicator of the presence or amount of drugs in a person's system—breathalyzers being one familiar assessment device—it will not indicate whether a person is an occasional user, an abuser, or a full-blown addict. Let us turn, then, to the old standby of assessment techniques, the paper-and-pencil test. The Addictions Research Institute at the University of Texas–Austin (2011) has done a really nice job of listing 173 assessment instruments from the National Institute of Alcohol Abuse and Alcoholism and the Center on Alcoholism and Substance Abuse and Addictions, and another 58 counseling forms and supportive materials courtesy of Texas Christian University. That does not include commercially available instruments, so it should be apparent that there is no shortage of ways to measure most facets of drug use/abuse, treatment, and relapse.

Personality Inventories.   A wide variety of personality tests have been used in attempts to characterize an alcoholic personality (Knox, 1976). A prototype is the MacAndrew Alcoholism Scale, from the Minnesota Multiphasic Personality Inventory (MMPI). The MacAndrew has been fairly successful in predicting alcoholism and a general tendency toward addiction (Greene, 1980; Knox, 1980). However, the MacAndrew scale appears to have a cultural bias (African Americans tend to score higher than Caucasians) and categorizes clients who suffer blackouts for *any* reason, who are exhibitionistic or extroverted, who are assertive, or who enjoy risk taking as chemically dependent when they may not be (Doweiko, 1999, p. 350; Isenhart & Silversmith, 1997).

Another self-report inventory that specifically targets substance abuse but is camouflaged as to its purpose is the Substance Abuse Subtle Screening Inventory (SASSI). It has subscales that allow the examiner to use a series of decision rules to determine whether the individual is a chemical abuser (Miller, 1983).

A major problem with these and other personality tests, though, is that they are unstable over time. The alcoholic may have very different scores and configurations prior to and after detoxification (Knox, 1976), and even the MMPI is subject to subterfuge by addicts who may not be straightforward, are defensive, or minimize or exaggerate their addiction for a variety of less-than-honorable reasons (McDermott et al., 1997).

Direct Measures.   Direct psychometric methods are related to alcoholic behavior and use. Prototypical is the Michigan Alcohol Screening Test (MAST; Selzer, 1971), which asks questions about alcohol consumption and problematic drinking behavior. This often used test is a 25-item questionnaire that asks such questions as "Does your spouse or other family member complain about your drinking?" (No = 0, Yes = 1) and "Have you been arrested more than once for driving under the influence?" (No = 0, Yes = 5). The maximum score is 53, but a score as low as 5–6 is considered as "having a problem with alcohol," 7–9 as "alcoholism," 10–20 as "moderate alcoholism," and above 20 as "severe alcoholism." That minimal score is problematic because it can trigger false positives for alcohol abuse that can range up to 31 percent (Jacobson, 1989). Our own experience is that almost every student who came to our college counseling center who drank at all would test as "having a problem."

The Alcadd Test (Manson, 1949) is composed of 60 items designed to reveal five characteristics of the alcoholic addict: (1) regularity of drinking, (2) preference for drinking over other activities, (3) lack of controlled drinking, (4) rationalization of drinking, and (5) excessive emotionality. The revised edition assesses extent of alcoholic addiction, measures specific areas of maladjustment, and yields an Alcoholic Probability Index, which tells you how likely it is that the individual taking the test is a member of an alcoholic population (Ornstein, 1976).

The CAGE is a simple four-item questionnaire about one's drinking history. Answering "Yes" to any two of the questions would indicate problems with alcohol use (Ewing, 1984). The four questions are:

1. Have you ever tried to **C**ut down on your drinking?
2. Have you ever become **A**nnoyed with people criticizing your drinking?
3. Have you ever felt **G**uilty about your drinking?
4. Have you ever started the day off with an **E**ye-opener to steady your nerves or get rid of a hangover?

Parsimony.   *Parsimony* is a fancy word that means being thrifty, even stingy, in practicing economy in the use of a means to an end. For busy practitioners, particularly medical personnel, administering lengthy assessment instruments doesn't cut it. Therefore, for adults, the National Institute on Alcohol Abuse and Alcoholism (NAIAA) has come up with the most parsimonious of screening devices: one question. That question is, "Has any heavy drinking occurred in the prior 12 months?" since virtually all those who have alcohol-related disorders would answer that question positively (Mumford, 2005).

The NAIAA (2011) has a little more complicated screening device for youth. It involves two questions. The first is, "Do you have any friends who have drunk beer, wine, or any drink containing alcohol in the past year?" A "Yes" to this question puts children in the moderate risk category. The second question is, "How about you—have you ever had more than a few sips of any drink containing alcohol?" A "Yes" to this question puts children in the severe risk category. The NAIAA has a risk grid with number of days of drinking and child's age as its *x* and *y* axes. Suffice it to say that an elementary school child who reports 1–5 days' drinking is immediately at highest risk. If you think that posing this question to an 11-year-old is going a bit overboard and being paranoid about alcohol abuse, consider that the NAIAA (2011) research indicates that 1 in 3 children starts drinking by the eighth grade, and half of those report being drunk. If you are working with children, the NAIAA has a really handy pocket version of their youth screening device that you can download or order from www.niaaa.nih.gov/YouthGuide or by calling 301-443-3860.

Computer-Administered Direct Measures.   The Addiction Severity Index (ASI) (McLellan et al., 1980, 1992) asks clients to respond to problems they have experienced in the past 30 days and over their lifetime. It covers seven domains—medical, employment, drug, alcohol, legal, family/social, and psychiatric issues—and rates problems on a scale of 0 (no real problem; treatment not indicated) to 9 (extreme problem; treatment absolutely indicated). The final score is based on a mathematical formula and not clinician judgment alone. It is one of the most widely used measures of problem severity in substance abuse programs and has been translated into 13 languages and expanded to cover such specialized populations as Native Americans, prisoners, dual-diagnosed clients, and antisocial personality-disordered persons (Budman, Portnoy, & Villapiano, 2003). It is also heartily disliked by a great many clinicians because it is time consuming, boringly repetitive, and expensive to administer (Butler et al., 2001).

As a result, the ASI-MV has been created (Budman, Portnoy, & Villapiano, 2003). Clients self-report on the ASI-MV on a computer while being queried by a different virtual reality interviewer in each of the seven domains. It has excellent reliability and validity and produces a comprehensive report into which counselors can easily insert their clinical impressions (Butler et al., 1998, 2001). In fact, computer programs are now emerging for both diagnosis and treatment of substance abuse. They appear to increase client motivation, be less threatening than face-to-face meetings with therapists, and reduce alcohol-related harm through skill-building exercises, and it appears that clients may be more forthcoming about socially embarrassing issues such as drug abuse (Gerbert et al., 1999; Hester & Miller, 2006). It also appears that the web version of commonly used instruments in addictions assessment are as reliable as paper-and-pencil versions (Miller et al., 2009).

The Problem Is ...   A major problem with these self-report questionnaires is that deception is easy, and what drug abusers have to say about their chemical dependency should be always highly suspect (Knox, 1980,

p. 58). The general rule of thumb, that whatever a person reports drinking should be doubled, hasn't had any validity studies done on it, but it is not an unfair hypothesis. Thus, these inventories should always be part of a comprehensive assessment and be corroborated by significant others, and should never be used as a standalone assessment for alcoholism (Fisher & Harrison, 2000, p. 95).

Motivation to Change. Because motivation to change has become such a central issue in substance abuse treatment, instruments have been developed to determine not only how motivated clients are, but also where they are in terms of Prochaska and DiClemente's (1982) motivation to change stages. The Stages of Change Readiness Scale and Treatment Eagerness Scale (SOCRATES; Miller & Tonigan 1996) yield three factorially derived scale scores: Recognition (Re), Ambivalence (Am), and Taking Steps (Ts). Scoring is accomplished by transferring to the SOCRATES Scoring Form the numbers circled by the respondent for each item. The sum of each column yields the three scale scores. Besides a 19-item drug/alcohol questionnaire for clients, there is a 32-item alcohol questionnaire for significant others of males and a parallel form for females. The parallel forms for significant others are designed to assess the motivation for change of those significant others, not to obtain collateral estimates of the client's motivation.

McConnaughy, Prochaska, and Velicer (1983) have developed a more general stages-of-change measure known as the University of Rhode Island Change Assessment (URICA). The URICA is a 32-item self-report that includes four subscales measuring the stages of change: precontemplation, contemplation, action, and maintenance. Cluster analyses yielded five stages among adult outpatients at the time of entering alcoholism treatment: precontemplation, ambivalent, participation, uninvolved, and contemplation. In addition, motivation for change may be assessed using a second-order factor called Readiness to Change that seems useful at pretreatment. Clinicians may use the URICA to evaluate an individual's level of motivation for change and use this information to help guide treatment approaches. Subscale scores can be used to track shifts in attitudes related to the specific stages of change. The URICA differs from the SOCRATES in that SOCRATES poses questions specifically about alcohol or other drug use, whereas URICA asks about the client's "problem" and change in a more general manner.

The Readiness Ruler (Center for Substance Abuse Treatment, 1995) operates on a 1–10 continuum for readiness to change, with anchor points "not ready to change," "unsure," "ready to change," and "trying to change." Finally, the staging "algorithm" classifies an individual into one of five stages of change: precontemplation, contemplation, preparation, action, or maintenance (Prochaska, DiClemente, & Norcross, 1992). All of these scales appear to have good predictive validity, with the Taking Steps component of the SOCRATES being a better predictor of percentage days absent and drinks per drinking day at 6 and 12 months (Maisto et al., 2011; Willoughby & Edens, 1996).

Intake Assessment. An initiating interview should assume that the defense mechanisms of the chemical dependent person will be granite hard, and the worker must be aware that these defenses will do all they can to safeguard the abuser's secret. Analysis starts by monitoring the client's verbal defenses. Hedging, minimizing, seduction, changing the subject, projecting onto significant others, and refusal to speak directly about oneself in the here and now are defenses all clients may manifest. However, these are extremely pronounced in the alcoholic. For example, ruminating on past drinking episodes and drinking friends should not be viewed as innocent, idle nostalgia; rather, it suggests that the person has not learned to fill the social void in his or her life left by giving up the abusing agent, and that physically detoxified is not psychologically detoxified (Perez, 1985, pp. 34–37).

Behavioral assessment includes such simple procedures as noticing whether there is alcohol on the client's breath. Chewing peppermint or gum and heavy use of cologne or perfume may be attempts to mask alcoholic odors. The physical appearance of an alcoholic may include facial puffiness, a red nose, sudden weight gain, a glazed look or a hunted, fearful aspect, shaking, rigid attending and listening, or a very casual, laid-back guise (Perez, 1985, pp. 34–37).

Assessment of Spirituality. A major component of triage assessment for chemical dependency is a careful analysis of the individual's spiritual resources. This analysis has little to do with religion. The assessment should focus on the despair and hopelessness addicts feel and the emptiness in their lives that they attempt to fill through their addiction. Diagnosis and treatment goals should routinely incorporate spirituality in program planning.

Triage Assessment. In any assessment of chemical dependents, the crisis worker should follow two rules proposed by Doweiko (1990, p. 214) that should probably be chiseled in granite. First, always seek collateral information. A spouse's or an employer's response to a MAST may be very different from the alcoholic's. Second, until proven otherwise, always assume deception.

Until chemical dependents have hit rock bottom, they will cover their figurative and literal drug tracks affectively, behaviorally, and cognitively in self-defeating efforts to deny to themselves and to others the control that the drug exercises over them. Many of our colleagues in chemical dependent treatment programs use the following standard measure in interviews about consumption of alcohol: Whatever an alcoholic reports as the amount consumed should be doubled to arrive at a very conservative estimate of the real amount used! Although Doweiko (2006, p. 347) reports that alcohol abusers as a group will generally honestly report the amount they drink, and your authors' experience with college students is that they often exaggerate the amount they drink, many abusers will minimize the amount they drink, particularly if they are facing legal or job sanctions. Therefore, an absolute, ironclad rule in assessment of substance abuse is to gather collateral information from family, employers, and anyone else who knows the client's drinking history (Juhnke, 2002).

Diagnostic Intake. In a tailor-made treatment program that will probably be done on an outpatient basis, it is absolutely critical to obtain as comprehensive and complete a clinical assessment of the individual as possible. Combined with a complete medical workup and psychometric measures, the profile should provide circumstances for referral, drug and alcohol use patterns, legal history, military record, educational and vocational history, developmental and family history, psychiatric and medical records, sexual health, motivation, social-recreational-community involvement, and previous treatment history (Doweiko, 1996, pp. 320–324; Poley, Lea, & Vibe, 1979).

The Continuous Data Questionnaire (CDQ) is such an intake format (Poley, Lea, & Vibe, 1979), and when combined with the ASI-MV it can generate a very precise treatment program. The CDQ accomplishes a number of important tasks. First, it monitors a client at many points in the treatment process. Second, it is not concerned with drug issues to the exclusion of other problems. Its comprehensiveness allows the worker to obtain information on a variety of areas that may need remediation. Third,

the CDQ's historical perspective provides an excellent analysis of what treatment goals need to be established and how those goals are being met.

An Example: Intake Analysis and Summary of Gordon Brand. Gordon Brand was seen after initial admission for polydrug overdose. Stage of treatment is initial assessment. The client is a 42-year-old male Caucasian who was brought to St. Polymorpheus by the paramedics for treatment of a drug overdose. BAC was 0.37 percent on admission, with evidence of Xanax ingestion. Gordon was semicomatose on entry and was in intensive care for 24 hours.

Chemical use. Preferential drug is alcohol. Over the past 3 months, Gordon reports consuming a bit less than a pint of whiskey per day, although this quantity is subject to scrutiny because of client's defensive responses. Drinking is continuous, and Gordon does not remember when he was last abstinent. Drinking has been with peers from work and alone at home. Lately drinking has been mostly by himself. Xanax was prescribed by Gordon's family physician for "stress," and Gordon has used it rather extensively for a number of years, especially when he was trying to "cut down" alcohol use.

Educational and vocational background. Gordon is a college graduate with a degree in mechanical engineering and a master's in business administration. He is employed as director of internal operations by United Tectonics. His income is approximately $150,000 a year, with numerous perquisites. He reports no absences from work due to alcohol- or drug-related problems, but does report he has missed approximately 20 days of work in the last 2 months due to "intestinal problems" and generally feeling "unwell." His best estimate of being late to work is 10 times during the last month. He indicates he is moderately satisfied with his job, but says he would be extremely satisfied if the company president "would get off his back and leave him alone." He rates his job performance as quite good and says it would be excellent if he were not currently ill. He is not sure how much money he owes at present because "that was always his wife's job." Cost of drinking is "peanuts." He vaguely remembers his wife saying something about bills being overdue.

Family status. Gordon currently resides with his wife and children in an upper-middle-class subdivision and has lived there for the past 8 years. He relates that he used to love his wife a great deal, but now gets along poorly with her. He maintains that he gets along moderately well with his children, Lisa and Mark, although "they side with their mother on most things." Prior to the last 2 months, he often (several times a week) did things with his family. He believes his family is very important to him but is extremely angry that his wife is not more supportive. He also feels he is extremely important to his family but states this in economic terms: "All I'm good for is to bring home a paycheck." He does not handle arguments with his wife well and "clams up" after initial exchanges. His dealings with his children are much the same, and he reports, "They don't listen to me and are rebellious."

Social involvement.   He reports having many business acquaintances, but no real friends. Gordon has been involved with a number of charitable and service organizations in the community until the last couple of years when he got so involved in work that he could not do those things anymore. He enjoyed service activities, particularly with the Boys' Club. His recreational pursuits are "tinkering" in his shop at home, fishing and hunting, and reading military history. He used to play tennis and golf with his wife and go kayaking with a group, but that "has been years ago."

Judicial involvement.   Aside from being found by the police passed out in his car, he has no prior arrest record. He reported one domestic disturbance call when he and his wife were arguing, but smoothed that over with the officer who responded to the call.

Health.   His physical and mental health has been average to poor. He last saw a doctor about 6 months ago and was told that he had the beginning of major health problems, "something to do with my guts and stress." He has been taking antacid for the problem. He has "fallen down" on his eating habits because of both stress and a nervous stomach and only occasionally eats regular, well-balanced meals. He averages about 5 or 6 hours' sleep a night and uses alcohol and Xanax to help him get to sleep, particularly when he is under stress. He has never been in the hospital for other than minor medical problems. He has never considered suicide, but states it is not the worst thing in the world. His sexual health is poor. He has not had or cared to have sex in a long time.

Gordon presents the appearance of a man coming out from addiction. After he was stabilized for his overdose, he slept for almost 24 hours. His withdrawal symptoms were severe enough that he was given benzodiazepines to ease the pain of withdrawal. His appearance is sallow and wan. He is overweight, and his muscle tone is poor, with his flesh sagging over his body. He has a hunted look to his eyes and is constantly wringing his hands. His agitation is further demonstrated by pitched-up and accelerated speech patterns.

Personality profile.   His personality and emotional development are rated moderately low in responsibility to self and others, very low in self-worth and general feeling of well-being, and high on anxiety and depression. He is more tense than relaxed, more critical than tolerant, more depressed than happy, more nervous than calm, more unfriendly than friendly, more unforgiving than forgiving, and much more sickly than healthy. The MMPI supports this self-analysis and also indicates he is depressed. His validity scale scores indicate he is attempting to present a better picture of himself than what he is. The SASSI scores confirm he is a heavy alcohol abuser.

Motivation.   His URICA and SOCRATES scores indicate he is generally ambivalent about changing, although he is contemplating it. While he can articulate goals, they are generally nonspecific, such as "straightening things out at home and work." His rating of present attempts to accomplish these tasks is that they are very unsuccessful, and he rates as moderately important a goal to stop abusing alcohol "for a while." His most desirable use of alcohol would be to drink socially, "because drinking alone really isn't all that good and probably helped get me here in the first place." He believes no one is interested in his problems "except to get on my back."

Corroboration.   Follow-up includes checking with Gordon's employer, wife, and doctor. Their story is a good deal different from what Gordon reports. Mr. Fredricks, the president of United, indicates that Gordon was one of his best employees until about 3 years ago, when his drinking got steadily worse and his performance declined. At first, Mr. Fredricks said nothing about the drinking because Gordon still had a performance rating that was superior to those of most other members of the staff—drunk or sober. Later, Mr. Fredricks gave him some fatherly advice about his problem, which Gordon ignored. Three months ago, the advice turned into a warning about absences and poor performance. Mr. Fredricks now feels that unless Gordon dries out and takes care of his problem, termination is imminent. Mr. Fredricks also agreed that Gordon had been such a valuable employee that the company would pick up any cost for treatment that insurance did not cover. The employer agreed to support and coordinate efforts with the hospital. Analysis of employer cooperation in regard to chemical dependency treatment is excellent.

Gordon's wife, Amy, supports his employer's analysis of the problem. His drinking has steadily escalated to the point that the family has become completely dysfunctional. She and the children are terrified of Gordon when he is drunk, which is most of the time. He has become an isolate from his family and relates to them only when he wants something. Any mention of his drinking causes severe arguments and then a period of sullen hostility. Amy also reports serious financial problems, saying that they are behind on the house and car notes and owe credit card accounts of $17,000.

Two months ago Gordon got drunk, became violent, and threatened her. The police intervened in the situation, and Gordon left the house. Amy threatened to obtain a restraining order on Gordon but relented after he promised to remain sober and be the husband and father he used to be. He kept his vow for 2 weeks, then he started drinking even more heavily. She states that she is near a nervous breakdown and has a number of physical complaints that are probably due to the stress of trying to deal with Gordon for so many years. She is "sick" of it and is thinking of filing for divorce. She did agree to come to the hospital for an interview if Gordon agreed to treatment. General analysis of the home situation is that it is extremely poor and may not be redeemable.

Gordon's doctor indicated that he had given Gordon a severe upbraiding 6 months ago about his drinking and stated that he would no longer give him prescriptions for Xanax. He had recommended at that time that Gordon seek immediate treatment for severe alcohol abuse. He also told Gordon that he was having liver, pancreas, and intestinal problems due to alcohol and that if he kept drinking he was going to be in critical trouble in short order. Gordon became hostile and told his family doctor of 15 years that he wasn't much good if he couldn't give him some tranquilizers for the stress he was experiencing.

Spirituality.   Gordon was reared in a strict fundamentalist church, but left it during college because they were "real bluenoses who never had any fun." He later tried a more liberal church, attending fairly regularly with his wife in the early years of their marriage, but quit attending that church because they were "pretentious asses." Aside from his nonattendance of any organized religious services, Gordon is spiritually bankrupt—with the exception of the spirits he drinks. Any relationship that presently exists between him and a higher power is in name only: "Well, sure, I believe in God." He is alone, helpless, and hopeless in a hostile world.

Functional assessment.   A functional assessment (Tuten et al., 2012, p. 43) was conducted on Gordon and included the following:

1. Details of the client's longest period of abstinence: Gordon can't remember the last time he didn't drink.
2. What antecedents and consequences follow drug use? He gets uptight when pressure escalates on the job, but drinking takes the edge off. He now realizes that he almost died, but believes it was because he accidently ingested too much Xanax and not the high BAC of .37 that almost killed him.
3. Which drugs are being used, and in what order and quantity? Gordon is unclear as to quantity due to memory loss or denial, but uses vodka, whiskey, and beer regularly and in quantity, with one or sometimes two .5 mg Xanax to get to sleep.
4. When are drugs being used? No drugs are used before or at work. After work is a different story. Typically drinks with coworkers and then continues drinking at home. Xanax is used almost every night, and alcohol use is daily with increased use on the weekends. Weekends are sometimes lost, as was the last one when he got in trouble. He has little memory of it.
5. With whom does substance use occur? Alone at home and in the company of office mates after work.
6. Where does substance use occur? Both at home and in various bars but particularly a watering hole near work, the Olde English Inn.
7. What motivated the client to seek treatment? Brought to the emergency room by paramedics due to drug overdose.

Total triage assessment.   The total triage assessment of Gordon is 28. He is in the lethal range and needs to be in a place where he can be safe. Affectively, his rating is 9. He is angry and depressed, with many of the standard defensive affective responses characteristic of full-blown addiction. Behaviorally, he is out of control in regard to his chemical dependency. His BAC level was approaching LD-50 on admission. Overlaid with tranquilizers, he is lucky to be alive. He obtains a behavioral rating of 10 without even considering how he acts in regard to his work or family. Cognitively, he is deeply rooted in denial about his addiction and has paranoid ideation about his family and his employer. His perception of the events leading up to his admission to the emergency room is radically different from the view of others who know him. His periods of memory loss and obsessive-compulsive thoughts about drinking mark him at a 9.

Conclusions. General analysis of interviews with Gordon, his boss, his wife, and his doctor indicates that Gordon shows clear signs of chemical dependency (alcohol) and abuse (tranquilizers) across physical, psychological, and social components of his life. He denies that he has a problem with alcohol and has put in place strong defense mechanisms to shield him from the reality of the situation. He is in extreme peril of losing his job, his family, and quite possibly his life. His ASI-MV score and profile analysis confirm he is in need of immediate treatment.

Recommendations after case staffing with the chemical dependency unit were as follows: Gordon must fully experience the crisis he is in, and workers should gain his agreement to undergo treatment first in the chemical dependency unit and later on an outpatient basis. If Gordon agrees to undergo treatment, his family should be contacted with the proposal that they also undergo treatment as codependents. If he agrees to treatment, specific goals should be established for a comprehensive rehabilitation plan. Controlled drinking is not an option because of the seriousness of his physical problems, his job and marriage being in jeopardy, and the failure of his previous self-managed attempts to quit.

Crisis Points in Chemical Dependency Treatment

Clients who are addicted will have used drugs to shield themselves from all kinds of hurtful feelings, thoughts, and behaviors. Once this shield is taken away, all the problems will tend to converge like an accordion, and clients will be assailed from all sides at once. The very reasons that the alcoholic drank in the first place will return in condensed, magnified, and more powerful ways. Each instance will present a crisis point for

clients. As a result, the whole therapeutic inpatient treatment program may be seen as transcrisis. Successfully jumping one hurdle generally means getting ready immediately for the next one and the next one after that.

The first crisis to be dealt with is getting the client motivated to dry out. Working with a "wet" person is impossible, because all the person is interested in is getting "fixed" (Parker, 1986). To get the person to detoxify means creating enough of a crisis that the person becomes aware of the problem and voluntarily agrees to stay. The best way to do this is by examining the client's vulnerable points. For Gordon, there are two: his job and his health.

The Counselors. Gordon is about to meet two chemical dependency counselors, Carolyn and Ray. They are both certified drug counselors. Carolyn is a licensed professional counselor (LPC) and Ray is a licensed clinical social worker (LCSW). Carolyn is a recovering alcoholic who tends to be direct, assertive, and confrontive. At times she uses self-disclosure about her own dependency so that the client can't get away with saying, "Nobody knows the trouble I've seen." She has a high degree of credibility. She is also a good model. The alcoholic can look at her as a peer and say, "Here is a tough, competent person who has been where I am, and if that's true, then there's hope for me" (Graham, 1986).

Ray is more nondirective and unconditionally accepting. His stock in trade is the basic skills of empathic listening and responding. His job is to build a healthy, trusting relationship, to focus on the client's positive attributes, to promote faith in the client, and to help the client come to his or her own self-realizations about the problem. Ray is also a model in that he is a professional who is not an alcoholic. Clients cannot reject treatment on the basis that "they're just a bunch of burned-out boozers here." Another reason that Carolyn and Ray operate as a team is that drug users may con one person, but they will have a much more difficult time conning two people. Teaming is also a support mechanism for the workers. Working with drug addicts is one of the toughest jobs in therapy (Parker, 1986). They are going to do their best to make Gordon aware of the serious trouble he is in with drugs.

Counselor Attributes. For many years, the notion was that addiction had to be directly and actively confronted, and indeed, because of the denial inherent in the problem, the person almost had to be destructed and put back together again. However, there is a good deal of evidence to indicate that this confrontational approach doesn't really work with most substance abusers (Doweiko, 2006, pp. 366–369; Fisher & Harrison, 2000, pp. 119–123; Miller et al., 1993). What does work is professionals who have strong interpersonal skills and who are able to form a strong therapeutic alliance with clients by being collaborative, nonjudgmental, objective, genuine, congruent, positive, reinforcing, and empathic. Such alliances have the most positive outcomes for clients, including staying in treatment, increasing motivation, and feeling satisfaction with the treatment process (Doweiko, 2006, pp. 366–367; Hser et al., 2004; Ilgen et al., 2006; Meier et al., 2006; Petry, 2012; Tuten et al., 2012). This does not mean that confrontation is not used, but when it is, as demonstrated here by Carolyn, it is done with caring and concern (Ramsay & Newman, 2000), with the idea of bringing denied and warded-off thoughts, feelings, and behaviors into conscious awareness without shaming, belittling, or discounting the person.

Carolyn: Hello, Gordon. I'm Carolyn, and this is Ray. We're from the chemical dependency unit here at the hospital, and we'd like to talk with you.

Gordon: Well, that's fine, but I don't know why you're talking to me. I made a dumb mistake and took some pills I shouldn't have, but that won't ever happen again.

Carolyn: Maybe not. But from your intake interview, test results, and the problem that got you here, we think you might need to consider coming into treatment.

Gordon: I really need to get out of here and get back to my job. It's hanging by a thread as it is.

Ray: We understand how concerned you are about your job. We've talked to your employer, Mr. Fredricks, and he understands the situation. He's willing to support you if you go into treatment.

Gordon: (*angrily*) I'll bet! That SOB used to be my best friend. He'll use me being a drunk to give me the axe. That's all the excuse he'd need.

Carolyn: He may be the biggest SOB in the state. But he cares about you and has offered you a choice. He believes that if you don't seek help from us, then you're not going to have a job at all. He also said you'll have your same job when you finish treatment. I have him outside, and I want you to hear it with your own ears. (*After a lengthy conversation, Mr. Fredricks leaves.*)

Gordon: He really means it. My God! No job. What'll I do?

Ray: Look at it this way. You know you've got some pretty severe physical problems. What difference will a few days make? You meet your commitment to your boss, and

you're also someplace where your physical problems can be monitored. It's a no-lose deal. On a scale of 1 to 10, 10 being worst, how sick would you say you are right now?

Gordon: I'm no drunken bum! But I'd say maybe an 8.

Ray: We understand that, but I'm wondering if this statement rings true: that drinking at times produces results you dislike, and right now you are an 8. If you think back to when you were really doing well and had not been drinking so much or using Xanax, what would you have rated yourself then?

Gordon: Well, probably a 2 or 3, but that was a while ago.

Ray: If things were like they were when you were at a 2 or 3 and a miracle happened and you woke up tomorrow, what would you be?

Gordon: Well, maybe not a 2 or 3, not that great, but probably a 4 or 5.

Ray: So if we could help you get back to that 4 or 5, it seems like it would be worth your time to find out a bit more about how to do that, wouldn't it? What's a few days' difference one way or the other?

Gordon: Sure! But going into a dry-out ward. It's like I can't handle my problems.

Ray: I'd guess that going into treatment would seem like a sign of weakness, but I'd like to point out that if anything else was wrong with you, it would be a sign of mature and healthy thinking to get it taken care of, wouldn't it? You have a serious illness here that needs help.

Carolyn: If you had cancer, would you try to do surgery on yourself? You do want to get better in regard to your health problems, don't you? The doctor told you how serious your physical problems are, didn't he? That you have liver, pancreas, and severe intestinal problems and that if they're not taken care of, you will most likely die. This isn't "Scared straight!" Gordon, you are a bright, capable man in an executive position with a major company, so you are smart too. We are concerned about you, as are a number of other people in your life, including your family doctor. Do you believe he's putting you on, or is that what you want? You might notice your hands right now. They're shaking so hard, I'm guessing you couldn't hold a pencil and write your name.

Gordon: I can too.

Carolyn: Go ahead and do it then. (*Hands Gordon the pencil and paper.*)

Gordon: (*Attempts to write his name and produces an illegible scrawl that wobbles across the page.*)

Carolyn: In all honesty, is that your typical signature?

Gordon: (*Voice breaks.*) I . . . no, it isn't. I'm . . . I'm sick. Crap! I guess maybe I am a 10.

Carolyn: Yes, you are sick! That's why we're concerned about you and want you to come into the program. We have what is called a client feedback summary on what we know to date about your drug issues. If you would like, we can give you that information now and discuss what it means and see what you think about it.

Gordon: Well, I don't guess that would hurt. Always good to know the facts.

Carolyn relates his lethal blood alcohol level on admission, a MAST test score of 21 that put him in the serious addiction range, URICA and SOCRATES motivation to change scores that place him in the contemplation range, and a Beck Depression Scale score that indeed shows Gordon is clinically depressed. She explains the stages of change model and where he currently is on it. Carolyn relates these scores while Ray uses open-ended leads to solicit Gordon's opinion and start to pull him into a collaborative partnership with them. Carolyn then gives him some psychoeducational information on the typical kinds of occurrences and outcomes for Gordon's substance abuse behavior given his age, sex, gender, and other demographic factors that affect outcomes, and what the potential up- and downsides are, as a way to start him having an inner debate and moving him from the contemplation to the determination stage.

Gordon: Man oh man! I can't believe that. How the hell did I get here? Jesus Christ! What a loser. What in the world am I gonna do?

Ray: No wonder you are feeling anxious about doing this. Anybody that is feeling as bad as you are would. It speaks highly of you that you were so honest and forthright on your tests. This is a big, difficult decision to make, but you have reached that point, and I am betting, based on your engineering background and your tenacity in getting the job done, you will make the decision to go ahead with treatment.

Gordon: (*downcast but still defiant*) OK. I'll give it a try, but I'm not promising anything. I don' t know where this is going to go. I guess I don't have a choice but to try it. I've been drinking a long time. To give it up completely . . . man! If I don't like it, I guess I can leave.

Ray: That's all we ask. Now let us tell you in general what your treatment is going to be. We want you to know what's going to happen, so you can help us plan what'll be most effective for you.

Creating a Crisis for Gordon. Very few clients are self-motivated to change their abusing behavior (Lawson, Ellis, & Rivers, 1984, p. 67). Outside motivation must often be used. In this case, it is Gordon's job

and his health. For most male alcoholics, their job is critical, and it is the last part of their environment to suffer. There are two major reasons for this. First, a job is at the core of one's self-esteem, and to lose that is to admit that the chemical dependent has hit rock bottom. Second, without a job, there is no money to keep up one's supply of the addictive substance (Trice & Beyer, 1982, pp. 955–956).

Carolyn's confrontations are not based on some personal agenda, nor are they directed at the client's global attributes. Rather, they are targeted at specific behaviors, thoughts, and affects the client uses to deny the problem or to support a return to drinking. Empathic understanding of a chemical dependent does not mean being permissive, does not mean shielding the client from the natural consequences of his or her actions, and does not mean avoiding appropriate confrontation when chemical dependents seek to lie and delude themselves and others.

Balancing confrontation about poor job performance is an empathic and genuine concern for Gordon's health that specifically tells him that someone now cares what happens to him. Ray uses two of solution-focused brief therapy's primary motivational techniques (Campbell et al., 1999). He normalizes the experience by indicating that anybody would have feelings of trepidation if they were as sick as Gordon is. Normalizing is not discounting the problem but rather emphasizing that others have experienced similar problems and are not crazy, wrong, or a failure for being in that situation. He also restructures the impasse of seeking or not seeking treatment by emphasizing Gordon's strong points and ability to make good decisions. By alternating between the two approaches, the workers seek to set the stage for Gordon through a combination of fear for his life and hope through treatment. They are creating a therapeutic alliance with Gordon.

While creating the crisis, the workers avoid directly confronting or accusing Gordon of being an alcoholic. Early attempts to make clients confess to their addiction will likely lead to very defensive behavior. Although the word *manipulate* has an ugly connotation, in a sense all therapists manipulate their clients to positively increase the chances of successful therapy (Lawson, Ellis, & Rivers, 1984, p. 77). The first few days of treatment are going to be the most difficult, and throughout this time one of the workers' major tasks will be to keep Gordon from leaving against medical advice (Parker, 1986). Gordon is in Prochaska's (Prochaska,

DiClemente, & Norcross, 1992) contemplation stage. He perceives he has some problems with drinking but is certainly not ready to give it up. Brief motivational interviewing such as Ray and Carolyn just conducted has been found to be effective in getting clients to commit to treatment (Vasilaki, Hosier, & Cox, 2006) and also stay in it (Longshore & Teruya, 2006). Ray's use of scaling is a standard solution-focused brief therapy (SFBT) approach that uses a miracle question (de Shazer, 1985) to get the client started thinking about positive outcomes for his drinking behavior.

Using Family Intervention to Create a Crisis. Whereas Gordon's case is clearly one of "hitting bottom," in addiction parlance, for those chemical dependents who have not "bottomed out" Vernon Johnson (1980, 1986) and the Johnson Institute (1972) have developed a family intervention model that involves carefully coaching family and friends in a supportive group confrontation of the chemical dependent in language he or she clearly understands. The purpose is to break through the denial and other defense systems of the alcoholic by confronting the individual with the crises he or she has caused. It is hoped that the intervention process will "raise the bottom" before death or other catastrophic loss occurs (Fisher & Harrison, 2000, p. 111). This creates a severe crisis for the chemical dependent and the family. It is not something that is done on the spur of the moment, out of frustration, or with malice and intent to punish the chemical dependent's transgressions (Doweiko, 1996, p. 331).

The ingredients for creating such a crisis must be planned and rehearsed beforehand with a professional in the chemical dependence field who is well versed in such interventions. As many family members and significant others as possible should be present to combat the denial, bargaining, and promises to change that are sure to be a part of the addict's defense system. At a very minimum, at least two or more caring people—four or more would be ideal—who are willing to be honest about what they see in the addict's behavior should be present. Significant others such as a boss, a minister, coworkers, and close friends should be involved to support the family with their factual presentations (Fisher & Harrison, 2000, p. 112). Each of the interveners should be willing to undergo formal training and education about the illness of addiction. They should also be willing to accumulate and write down specific data about the self-destructive behavior of the addict, rehearse with a professional what facts they will report

and how they will report them, and then commit to caringly confront the addict with these facts (Johnson, 1986). Confrontation is not judgmental, generalized, or self-serving. Facts are reported objectively and specifically. Significant others caringly confront the addict with fact after specific fact.

Individual confrontation with addicts is futile because of their superior ability to deny, threaten, cajole, plead, and otherwise subvert attempts to interfere with pursuit of their addiction. Therefore, support and corroboration of accounts are important in pinning the addict down. Very clear consequences of separation and detachment from the addict are specified and followed through on if the offered treatment is refused. This is neither an attempt to bluff the addict into treatment nor an empty threat that may have been used before. Logical consequences of actions and the commitment to follow through on those actions should be calmly and specifically described (Johnson, 1986). The human services worker's role in this endeavor is first to provide support and educate family members about how the crisis setting is created. The worker then helps the family assemble the most powerful and influential people in the addict's life and teaches them how to collect facts of the addict's behavior and how to confront the addict with those facts in a caring manner. The worker also handles the logistics of arranging who will talk, what will be said, in what order it will occur, how and where the client will be transported, and what treatment arrangements will be made (Fisher & Harrison, 2000, p. 114).

During the intervention, the worker acts as a facilitator by coordinating each person's intervention, gently confronts the addict with his or her attempts to defend himself or herself, provides a point-by-point listing of the symptoms of addiction that the intervention has brought out, and then confronts the addict with the choice of undergoing treatment or having the family and friends detached from the addict. If the addict agrees, then the worker indicates what the treatment options are, that the addict's bags are packed, and that a car is waiting to take him or her to the treatment center. If the foregoing is not done in a coordinated and united manner, the prospects for successful intervention are minimal (Doweiko, 1990, pp. 233–234; Johnson, 1986; Wegscheider-Cruse, 1985). In no instance do we believe that a family should attempt this intervention without first consulting a professional substance abuse worker.

While this approach may appear to be extremely coercive, coercion works with clients who believe they have a great deal to lose. In that regard, such an intervention probably works best with people of the age and social and economic status of Gordon. A family intervention with a 19-year-old college student who is polyusing alcohol and marijuana would likely be less successful (Fisher & Harrison, 2000, p. 114).

Detoxification

Detoxification is a very serious medical process, depending on how badly addicted the alcoholic is. Although the procedure may seem to run counter to the goal of detoxification, Gordon is given benzodiazepines (tranquilizers) to control the tremors, hyperactivity, convulsions, and anxiety attacks that accompany alcohol withdrawal (Schuckit, 1995, p. 105). Gordon's detoxification is monitored very closely because alcohol and barbiturate withdrawal can be lethal. During the process, Gordon is allowed to watch television and is encouraged to sleep as much as possible and eat a well-balanced diet. If he is up to it, other clients who have gone through detoxification will come in and talk with him. The other patients do not come to proselytize but to let him know that, as tough as it is, they made it through this preliminary crisis stage, and so will he (Parker, 1986). This is another attempt to use SFBT to normalize a tough situation and show the addict that there is a way out and others have done it (Campbell et al., 1999).

Henry (*another patient*): Hi! My name's Henry Schultz. I'm another patient here. Ray thought you might be up for some company.

Gordon: Man, I'm glad to talk to somebody. This is tough. I guess I was strung out.

Henry: It *is* tough! I went through it 3 weeks ago. I guess you could use a drink, huh?

Gordon: Brother, could I!

Henry: Yeah, I know. That's not gonna get easier for a while, either. They make you come face up to it here. It's no piece of cake, but they really care about you. I just wanted to tell you I'm here if you want to talk. I'm getting into AA in a big way, and it's really helping.

Gordon: I don't know about that, spilling your guts and all. I don't think I could do that.

Henry: I thought the same thing. Lay my soul bare in front of a bunch of drunks, no way! But it's easier than you think. Especially when you meet the people. Hell! There's all kinds of people in it, some big shots, little shots, but all of us are not-so-hot shots when it comes to drinking. (*The conversation continues for a good bit, with Gordon asking all kinds of questions about treatment and about Henry's drinking problems, and guardedly discussing himself.*)

This initial dialogue with one of the other clients is important because it safely lets Gordon consider what the possibilities for recovery are, provides a peer as a resource, gives him a role model, and establishes at least one relationship within the therapeutic community (Parker, 1986). The point of this is that detoxification alone is pretty much futile in cleaning the addict up. Detoxing without treatment results in a 95 percent relapse rate (Craig, 2004).

Principles of Treatment
Treatment Techniques

To bolster and enhance motivation, our treatment team will use some solution-focused brief therapy (SFBT) approaches (de Shazer, 1985) as they are applied to addictions (Berg & Miller, 1992; Yeager & Gregoire, 2006), twelve-step adjunctive support based on the Alcoholics Anonymous model, rational-emotive behavior therapy (Ellis et al., 1988), cognitive behavior therapy (Meichenbaum, 1977, 1985), and reinforcement-based therapy (Tuten et al., 2012).

Treatment Goals

After Gordon's assessment and detoxification, but prior to going into treatment, Carolyn and Ray carefully go over treatment goals with Gordon. His treatment plan contains a comprehensive set of goals. Each was developed from his assessment plan, which identifies a specific debilitating condition, a goal to alleviate that condition, and a set of specific objectives for attaining the goal. Here are two sample goals.

1. Gordon's Drinking Goal

Condition: Excessive consumption of alcohol. Gordon has difficulty meeting the demands of his work and social responsibilities without drinking.

Goal: Eliminate the consumption of alcohol.

Objectives: Gordon will

a. Eliminate the intake of alcohol both during working hours and after working hours every day, including the weekend.
b. Express his feelings and choose positive coping behaviors, which he will employ to deal with stress-producing persons, events, or situations.
c. Demonstrate, for the appropriate length of treatment time called for in Gordon's assessment protocol and aftercare, that he is able to cope successfully

with people, events, and situations at work and at home that trigger anxiety and avoid the use of alcohol to reduce that anxiety.

d. Use the group and St. Polymorpheus's staff as a source of support and strength in attaining the goal of eliminating alcohol consumption by actively participating in group, helping other people attain their goals, and committing himself to accepting help and support from others in working on his own goals.

2. Gordon's Emotional and Social Goal

Condition: Gordon either withdraws from interaction or inappropriately acts out with others, including his own family, when he is stressed.

Goal: Emit appropriate emotional and social responses while in the presence of others who may produce stress, including his own family.

Objectives: Gordon will

e. Engage in nondrug conversation with a staff member at least twice each day and with a peer at least three times each day during inpatient treatment.

f. Carry on at least one nonargumentative discussion with each family member (Amy, Mark, Lisa) during each visit during inpatient treatment.

g. During aftercare, carry on at least two nonargumentative discussions per day with Amy and at least one such discussion per day with both Mark and Lisa.

h. Engage in a minimum of one social activity (game room, gym, horseshoe pit, lake area, dancing, or such) during inpatient treatment.

i. Engage in a minimum of two social activities (in the absence of alcohol) with his family during 6 months of aftercare—activities to be planned by the family as a group.

Formulating comprehensive treatment goals reflects a multimodal approach that recognizes and addresses biological, psychological, and social aspects of addiction (Frances, 1988). Multimodal treatment at St. Polymorpheus is based on a variation of the therapeutic community model, which emphasizes both abstaining from alcohol and addressing emotional factors of drug use. It also includes individual therapy sessions that focus on cognitive and behavioral approaches that target the irrational thoughts ("stinkin thinkin"), setting events, urges and cravings, and triggers and

cues that sets up the client for relapse. There is a great deal of evidence that cognitive-behavioral treatment techniques are effective in changing thinking and behavior so that relapse does not occur (Beck et al., 1993; Ellis et al., 1988; Kaminer & Slesnick, 2005; Toneatto, 2005). Motivational enhancement therapy (Longshore & Teruya, 2006; UKATT Research Team, 2005; Vasilaki, Hosier, & Cox, 2006) flavored with solution-focused brief therapy (de Shazer, 1985; Yeager & Gregoire, 2006) will also be used to enhance the client's self-efficacy and continued reinforcement of positive outcome expectancies. The therapeutic community perspective views drug abuse as a disorder of the whole person reflecting problems in conduct, attitudes, values, moods, and emotional management across environments and people (De Leon, 1989). As such, family intervention will be an integral part of the treatment plan (Copello, Templeton, & Velleman, 2006; Kaminer & Slesnick, 2005).

At the center of the therapeutic community is involvement with one's peer group. Through involvement with each other, chemical dependents learn how to manage emotional issues effectively, practice new and more adaptable behaviors, confront and support each other appropriately, and take responsibility for themselves (Polcin, 1992). The therapeutic community's goals are global lifestyle change, abstinence from drugs, elimination of antisocial behavior, enhanced education and constructive employment, and development of prosocial attitudes and values (Center for Substance Abuse Treatment, 1995, p. 51).

Treatment Protocol

Gordon's crisis treatment schedule contains a systematic and integrated set of components tailored to fit his needs. His inpatient status lasts only long enough to get him through detoxification and stabilization to the point where he can be a responsible participant in his treatment. After that, the bulk of his treatment will be on an outpatient basis.

Gordon's outpatient treatment components will consist of (1) individual therapy, (2) group counseling and group education, (3) family counseling, (4) participation in an AA group, and (5) prescription of naltrexone to inhibit drinking urges and cravings. All these treatment components will be closely monitored by the St. Polymorpheus staff, and changes in level of intensity of treatment, medications, therapy, and counseling formats may be made anytime his program evaluations indicate such changes are needed.

Gordon's protocol is monitored via computerized tracking. At each individual therapy session, both Gordon and the therapist examine via the computer screen his assessed progress, medical and psychological status, goals, and projected need of and change in level and intensity of treatment. There are no secrets. Gordon is in a collaborative and participative role in his own therapy. The therapist walks a fine line between overprescription and insufficient direction as she lays out the program (Miller & Rollnick, 2002, p. 129). While she takes Gordon's thoughts about what will work into consideration, she ultimately has to make the final decision about treatment plans. At this point it is probably equal parts art and science, and a good deal of experience on Carolyn's part lies behind the "art."

Individual Therapy

The individualized therapy for Gordon will include both inpatient and outpatient formats. It should be emphasized here that only those aspects of treatment that impact the *crisis* stage of his progress toward recovery are covered. Gordon's ultimate goal will be reaching a state of autonomy and equilibrium in handling his own drug-free functioning. After detoxification and stabilization on an inpatient basis, Gordon will meet with Carolyn regularly on an outpatient basis, and concurrently meet with his AA group in the evenings and with his family counseling group in the late afternoons.

Carolyn: (*sitting with Gordon in front of the computer screen in the private counseling room*) I've edited the contract you made yesterday. Take a look at it and tell me if we've left anything out. Also, tell me if you think the behavioral components are within your capacity to attain and if you're ready to make a firm commitment to accomplish these stated incremental goals.

Gordon: (*scanning the screen*) Yeah. That looks OK. I wonder if I can get a copy of this to take to group this afternoon?

Carolyn: Sure. That's fine. Now, let's do a little more work on where we left off yesterday on those processes we called "stress inoculation" and "emotive imagery." You remember that, to get the most benefit out of this procedure, we do it in a very relaxed manner.

Gordon: Yeah. That was pretty good. I never thought I could be that relaxed, but it worked really well. I've thought about it and practiced it since we did it yesterday. I believe it really helps, though I don't understand why.

Carolyn: The important thing is that you know it works for you, because this kind of technique gives you the power and control to do it without me or anyone else, and that's the ultimate goal.

Carolyn proceeds to carry Gordon through the steps of stress inoculation. She uses relaxation techniques and emotive imagery to empower Gordon to attain the ability to retrieve those vivid and powerful internal images and messages and to give himself the appropriate positive inoculative self-talk (Meichenbaum, 1985) to get him over the rough shoals and reefs that will invariably beset him as he embarks on a new and chemical-free existence. Emotive imagery pairs specific emotions with the vividly described and verbalized images that, during the process of stress inoculation (Cormier & Cormier, 1991), Carolyn asks Gordon to visualize in his mind's eye.

Carolyn: (*during the middle of an individual session, while Gordon is relaxed with his eyes closed*) As vividly as you can, just see and feel the stresses at the office today. You've had it! In your mind's eye, you can see the inviting and familiar neon sign as you approach the Olde English Inn. In your mind's nose, you can whiff the aroma of the beverages being served up in the Inn. In your mind's ears, you can hear the low and familiar drone around the pub. As you perceive these images, noises, and aromas, notice that, because of your commitments to stay off the stuff, you are both drawn toward and scared of the conflicting feelings you're having right now. (*Silence and a time of processing what has been presented ensue.*) Now, vividly perceive yourself as you fortify yourself, ahead of time, against any similar conflict.

Perhaps you're saying to yourself, "I know that a drink might relax me, but I know that the consequences would rob me of the progress I've made. I can see the neon sign and pass it by and still feel relaxed, comfortable, empowered, centered, and in control. I am the master of me! And I feel energized knowing that my future, my family, my job, and my reputation are more important than caving in to that Inn. Just relish and appreciate the power of that moment when you feel triumphant and in complete control of the situation. (*Long pause.*)

Gordon: (*after a long period of thoughtful and thoroughly relaxed silence*) I can feel the conflict. It isn't easy. But I *can* see myself doing those things. I *can* smell the booze! I *can* hear the sounds. And I *can* feel the urge to go into that Inn. But I can also feel and enjoy the power and control that are building within me. I won't lie about it. The smell of that pub is inviting. But, right now, the feeling of power and control and even the joy of winning this battle are important to me. I am in control of me!

Carolyn: Excellent! Open your eyes up now. On a 1 to 10 scale, 10 being tops, how well did you have that image fixed in your mind?

Gordon: (*Chuckles.*) I'll be darned. Pretty good, really, like an 8 or maybe a 9. I think I am getting a handle on it.

Carolyn: (*Leans over and pats Gordon on the back.*) By golly, Ollie, I think you are. I may have to make you my show-and-tell guy in group.

I want you to see something else here, Gordon. I have been struck by the fact that you never had an "eye-opener" before going to work, or snuck a drink during work, and in fact were pretty adamant about not having a three martini lunch and didn't tolerate any of your supervisees that did. The point I am making here is that for at least eight hours out of every day, and longer when you were working overtime which was a lot, you didn't drink at all. I think that is awesome and shows a great deal of determination in focusing on a goal. I'd like to think that. How were you able to do that? That's pretty amazing, given the off-duty time drinking.

Gordon: Booze is for recreating, getting loose, chilling out. The job is different. No fooling around. You are alert and on your toes. If you screw up, you can hurt people with engineering mistakes. You're known for your work, and I never ever wanted my name associated with junk, and the company sure as hell expected the same.

Carolyn: I wonder if you ever looked at your drinking as the exception rather than the rule. Seems to me most of the time you could stay sober when it made sense to do so. Ever think about it that way?

Gordon: Er, hmmm, well no, now that you mention it, I didn't ever take a drop when a job had to be done.

Carolyn: Sooooo . . . That's a huge exception! How about this current job? It appears if you decide to not drink it is certainly within your capacity to do so, and in fact you did it quite a lot beforehand.

Here, Carolyn and Gordon have shown only one thumbnail sketch of how stress inoculation may be enhanced when used with relaxation therapy and emotive imagery (Meichenbaum, 1985). Other cognitive-behavioral techniques (Beck et al., 1993) are appropriately used to further enhance Gordon's progress toward overcoming the crisis, and they are demonstrated in the section on the treatment group. Carolyn also reinforces Gordon and does some SFBT cheerleading (Sklare, 1997, p. 49) about his newfound ability and notes the huge amount of time he spent not drinking so there were large exceptions to his drunken state (Berg & Miller, 1992).

Gordon has moved to the *action* stage of Prochaska's (Prochaska, DiClemente, & Norcross, 1992) model. According to Miller and Rollnick (2002, p. 127) the client is committed to change when there is decreased resistance, a willingness to discuss problems, and resolve to do something, and when there are talk and questions about change and experimentation with change.

The Treatment Group

There are a number of reasons groups are effective in treating addiction. First and foremost, the relationship skills of chemical dependents are typically wretched. Chemical dependents desperately need positive social interaction to replace isolated self-involvement with their chemical seducer (Lawson, Ellis, & Rivers, 1984, p. 122; UKATT Research Team, 2005). Belonging, acceptance, affection, social interaction, nonuniqueness, equality, and development of a new self-concept are all relationship needs that can best be met by the treatment group (Dinkmeyer & Muro, 1979). The group format offers opportunities for peers to successfully confront clients in ways that the individual therapist can rarely, if ever, do. It allows them to learn more effective social skills, self-disclose threatening issues, and try out new behaviors in a safe environment, increase focus on here-and-now activities rather than past events, emotionally invest in others as well as themselves, produce tension that promotes change, instill hope, and regain a sense of humor (George & Dustin, 1988; Knack & Murray, 1996; Ohlsen, 1970).

Crisis treatment at St. Polymorpheus consists of several kinds of group work: group therapy, group education, multiple-family therapy, and AA group meetings. Usually there are from 6 to 10 members in the therapy group, representing a heterogeneous mix of sex, age, and race. This mix occurs by design because the staff wants the unique problems of each member to surface. Addicts have severe blind spots for their own defenses but not necessarily for each other's. Thus the members' diversity should allow them to be able to see through their peers' defense mechanisms, confront these blind spots, and help their peers accomplish treatment goals (Ohlsen, 1970, pp. 109–110). For brevity's sake, four representative members of Gordon's group will be introduced.

Alice is a 55-year-old Caucasian housewife who had been finishing off her afternoon in an alcoholic haze of martinis. Her children have left, and she is now an "empty nester." Her husband and children had denied her drinking until she was involved in an auto accident, left the scene, and was picked up driving while intoxicated. She was remanded to St. Polymorpheus by a judge.

Liz is a 35-year-old African American nurse. She was in charge of an intensive care unit. She burned out on the job and was caught raiding the pharmaceutical cabinet. She yo-yos between depressants (alcohol and pills) to take the pain of the job away and amphetamines to get her "up" for her job. She is on suspension and in danger of losing her job and her license.

Manuel is a 24-year-old suspended bank guard whose father died an alcoholic when Manuel was 11. His Chicano background invites a macho image that says "I take care of and handle everything," including alcohol and pills—which he did not handle. He is single and has used alcohol and pills since he was a teenager.

Ruth is a 41-year-old Caucasian who was repeatedly sexually abused by her father when she was a teenager. She married at 18, had two children, and was divorced at 23. She has worked as a bookkeeper for a construction company for the past 10 years. She has had several short, fruitless liaisons with men. She has been an alcohol abuser since her teenage years. Recently, she got drunk, took some sleeping pills, and turned on the gas in her apartment. The paramedics brought her to St. Polymorpheus.

Learning Relationship Skills

Relationship skills occupy center stage in the first few meetings of a group. As Brill (1981, p. 129) indicates, during the initial phases of a group, the group leader should provide support and structure, setting the stage for group members to develop trust and cohesiveness. Videotaping is important to this endeavor. The use of videotaping is a powerful tool for assessment, feedback, and therapeutic purposes, catching in pictures and words the dysfunctional defense systems the clients build for themselves (Brill, 1981; Sobell & Sobell, 1978).

During session 2 with his group, Gordon's poor relationship skills are evident. Despite Gordon's stated desire and willingness to interact positively with other clients and to work on his own addiction in the group, this initial dialogue shows typical difficulties during early developmental phases of the group. Gordon's long history of denial and lack of communication of feelings, trust, and personal needs carries over into the early group sessions.

Gordon: Nothing against the rest of you here, but I really don't understand the reason for putting me in here with such heavy abusers.

Ray: You don't see yourself fitting in?

Liz: Yeah, Gordon, you think your boozing's different from ours? Looks to me like you're Mr. High-and-Mighty, and we're a bunch of gutter bums.

Alice: Afraid we've got your number? Still denying what you are? Boy, have you got something to learn.

Carolyn: What I see happening here is basically a lack of trust in this group. That's not only an important issue for

here but for outside as well. What I want to do is turn on the video and go back over the introductions and the individual goals you'd all set for yourself that we did in our first session. They may help us all begin to see this group as a unified whole with common needs.

Accepting Responsibility

Clients learn to retake control over their lives, but this is not always easily done. Listen to Gordon as he confronts responsibility during session 3.

Gordon: What gripes me is they treat you like kids around here. Do this, go here, learn that!

Alice: Do you know why we're supposed to do that? It's because we need to know those things if we're going to be any good when we finish our treatment.

Gordon: That's fine, but I'm an adult, and I can read this on my own.

Liz: Have you? And if you did, could you get anything out of it?

Gordon: I don't know who you are to talk about responsibility. They nailed you for raiding the pharmacy cabinet, didn't they?

Carolyn: When you unload on Liz, that's a neat way of getting the load off your back. If you could make us as angry at you as you feel toward everybody else, then you'd be justified in telling us all to buzz off.

Gordon: She asked for it. We're talking about all the Mickey Mouse stuff like cleaning up your room and so forth. If that's helping me with my drinking problem, I'll kiss your foot.

Manuel (*Gordon's roommate*)**:** Maybe if you'd paid more attention to the Mickey Mouse stuff and not the booze you wouldn't be here now. Every morning I got to say something about living in a pigsty. If you were that sloppy, I'm surprised you still got that big bucks job.

Gordon: Oh! Now it's my work. I'll have you know I carried my load at work, and I sure as hell don't see what making my bed's got to do with getting back on track.

Ray: When the others say those things to you, it's hard to believe you aren't responsible. Hence, you react angrily to them. Although you were highly responsible and capable in the past, it's tough and hurts to be confronted with the fact that you're having trouble keeping up now.

Gordon: That's not right, I . . .

Ruth: Then what is right, Gordon? Sure, it's not fun. It's not supposed to be a vacation. You've got as many days here as is needed, and no more, to prove that you can be responsible. You haven't been responsible for a long time is what the others are saying, and now you pull the same thing with us. (*angrily*) How easy do you think it is for me to take responsibility and move forward living with the fact that my God damn father was fucking me for six years and I tried to solve that by finally trying to kill myself after busted marriages and drinking a trainload of booze. I am sick of your pissing and whining. (*Tears up and storms out of the room. Carolyn quickly follows.*)

Gordon: (*somewhat taken aback by Ruth's outburst and departure*) What do you want from me? Jeez! You all sound just like my wife. Maybe Ruth's got the right idea. Leave!

Ray: It's the same old tune you're hearing from them, and it makes you angry when you have to take on responsibility, so you'll show them.

Manuel: *If* he can't even get his bed made, he's not showing me much.

Gordon: I'll show you all!

Ray: It's not a question of showing them anything. It's a question, I think, of having the courage to show yourself.

Gordon: I don't know. It scares the hell out of me. I'm not sure what I can do anymore.

Ray: When you say it that way, I think we all understand. It's not just the simple things like making a bed or reading the assignment. It's the scary feeling of doing something you haven't done for a long time and wondering whether you'll fail again.

If Gordon can find enough fault with the treatment center, the staff, or their practices and get them to respond in the same manner, he will be "justified" in his stance and also justified in returning to alcohol. This rebellious attitude is met by the therapist with empathy and some interpretation. Confrontation would be inappropriate and would place the locus of control too far outside the client—it would put control of his sobriety into the hands of someone else (Wallace, 1978, p. 38).

When Gordon answers the other group members in caustic ways, the workers respond empathically to the people attacked, and when Gordon is attacked, the workers respond in supportive ways to him, casting hypotheses about how he feels now and how it may generalize to others who have attacked him (Ohlsen, 1970, pp. 116–129). By not reinforcing such dependent behavior but reinforcing Gordon when he takes responsibility on his own shoulders, the workers provide a model for reassuming independence (Blume, 1978, p. 71).

Treatment groups for substance abusers are not all tea and crumpets. Bringing out all the dirty laundry that goes with substance abuse can be extremely emotion provoking. That's why it is important to have two leaders, one to facilitate and the other to engage in monitoring the group. Further, if a member needs to leave there is no disruption, as one leader can immediately move to the person in crisis and remove her from the group (Hien et al., 2009, pp. 180–181).

Two days later.

Ruth: (*weeping*) I know it sounds silly, but that damn wood sculpture I've been working on in art therapy is terrible. I can't get it right. It's just like everything else in my life.

Gordon: Ah, look, Ruth. I used to do that as a hobby. If you wouldn't mind, I could maybe give you a hand. I know how frustrating it can be.

Manuel: Hey, man! That's the first time you ever said you'd do anything for anybody. You feelin' OK?

Gordon: It's no big deal.

Ray: Yet I think Manuel's got a point. It's good to see you care about Ruth. Offering to help her says you're taking on responsibility for someone else, something you haven't been able to do in a long time. (*Professes and feigns amazement.*) How in the world did that happen? Now if we can just get you to make Manuel's bed. (*General laughter, Gordon included.*)

Ray reinforces Manuel's response to motivate Gordon to socially rejoin the community, an important step that moves him outside his own encapsulated ego and self-involvement. He also uses humor and an SFBT technique called positive blame, which notes exceptions to the problem behavior.

Getting Past Denial

In adults a rigid, nonmodifiable, and repeated use of denial is a defense that is usually associated with psychotic disorders and addiction. As long as it is intact, the client cannot feel concern with doing anything constructive about his or her illness (Maxwell, 1986, p. 176). The most difficult task of the worker is to lessen the denial and encourage increased self-awareness and disclosure while at the same time keeping anxiety at minimal levels (Wallace, 1978, p. 32).

In the treatment of alcoholism, two levels of denial exist. The first is the denial of the presence and magnitude of a drinking problem (Blume, 1978, pp. 68–69). Continued denial specifically associated with drinking is a poor prognosis, and the chemical dependent who continues to use denial is not likely to stay sober. The second level is denial of long-standing life problems. Although it may sound antithetical to recovery, denial of serious life problems other than drinking is an appropriate defense mechanism early on in treatment. This is so because those are the stressors that probably triggered drug use in the first place. To break down defenses in these areas would put more stress on the system, increase anxiety, and set the client up for failure (Chalmers & Wallace, 1978, p. 262). Breznitz (1988) has described seven types of denial that progressively escalate as more information becomes available to the denier and more questions are raised regarding the threatening situation. See how Gordon Brand uses each of these stages of denial.

1. Is there information about the problem? You woke up in the hospital, close to delirium tremens, and can't remember anything as to how you got here. That certainly appears to be a problem.

   Nah! There must have been some kind of accident is all, and I was unlucky enough to be in it.

2. Is it threatening? You were told you were near death from an alcohol and other drug overdose.

   Well, that was an accident because I took an extra Xanax to get to sleep. That'll never happen again.

3. To me? Because of this your boss is threatening to fire you, your family is threatening to leave, and you are in severe financial straits besides the physical crisis you are going through as you withdraw from alcohol.

   That's their problem, not mine. It just goes to show they all are uncaring selfish people who don't care about me other than what they can suck out of me. I will have to cut back on my drinking a little and maybe get off Xanax.

4. Now? You are in the hospital, brought in half-dead by the paramedics, and you are suffering withdrawal symptoms from alcohol abuse. You need to get some serious help now for an addiction problem.

   I don't think that it is all that urgent. Just a onetime mistake. Never happened before, won't happen again.

5. Can I cope? You are vulnerable across social, family, vocational, physical, and financial environments. You, and nobody else, got yourself into this mess, so it is your responsibility to get out of it.

   Hey! I can get back on my feet if I just get a little rest and recuperation. It's everyone else who is sucking the life out of me.

6. Am I anxious? You are scared to death, and you don't have a clue as to what to do other than use all those defense mechanisms you are so good at.

   I just have to get back in control, and a drink would sure help about now.

7. Is my anxiety relevant? You bet your sweet bippy it is. If you don't get this straightened out, and soon, you are looking at a dirt nap and pushing up daisies in short order.

   I really need a drink now as this is really making me start to have an anxiety attack, so a Xanax or two would help as well.

An objective outsider looking at this example would typically react, "That's nuts. This guy is blind as a bat to what's happening to him. He's in deep trouble. He needs to shape up now!" The problem is that these defense systems have been in place for so long and have become so highly sophisticated and make such perfect sense that they are not willingly going to vacate the client's psyche on request. However, as new information comes into his system, it becomes more and more alarming, and increased defense systems need to be erected to keep reality at bay. Hopefully, at some point the increasing urgency of the situation and the client's escalating vulnerability to it will cause a crisis to occur and denial will break down to make way for more proactive, rather than reactive, regressive coping mechanisms as the client is confronted with the true reality of the situation.

Confrontation

When heavy denial and its defensive consorts are encountered, which is the case for most addicts, confrontation is probably the most potent and dangerous weapon the worker has (Lawson, Ellis, & Rivers, 1984, p. 125). The use of confrontation as a therapeutic technique needs to be carefully considered. Putting a resisting and denying client in the "hot seat" is a questionable practice for a variety of reasons. First, other clients may viciously attack the client and in the process force compliance or make a scapegoat of the client. Second, focusing only on the one client may permit other members in the group to become less involved (Ohlsen, 1970, pp. 127, 168).

The purpose of confrontation is not to vent personal frustration, impose belief systems contrary to those of the client, or act in punitive ways (Lawson, Ellis, & Rivers, 1984, p. 101). Confrontation is simply a matter of pointing out that there is a discrepancy between what the client says and how he or she acts (Ivey, Bradford-Ivey, & Simek-Morgan, 1993). Critical to the confrontation is the worker's emotional astuteness and competence in determining the correct moment to confront (Perez, 1985, p. 164).

A principal characteristic of confrontation is its challenge. The challenge is embedded in a question so that an immediate feeling response is evoked. A second characteristic of confrontation is that it is direct and action oriented. The client is constantly placed in new roles and situations calling for a response. Explored in a sensitive, perceptive manner, these new roles and situations enable a client to be aware of discrepancies between behaviors and intentions, feelings and messages, and insights and actions (Dinkmeyer, Pew, & Dinkmeyer, 1979, p. 110).

Confrontive statements can be hooked to reflective and interpretive statements. They also are generally connected with an owning statement, one that says clearly that "I, the crisis worker, own this." If the client denies the statement, then the confrontation is redirected: "OK, if that's not you, then what is you?" Confrontations are generally made in the form of a demand and are linked to alternatives. Confrontation catches a client in a contradiction and asks the client why he or she behaves in such a contradictory manner. Used judiciously and altered to fit the dilemma, confrontation can be extremely helpful in jarring clients out of old response patterns (Shulman, 1973, p. 198).

There are five major areas of confrontation:

1. *Experiential:* a response to any discrepancy by the client.
2. *Strength:* focused on the client's resources, especially if the client does not recognize them.
3. *Weakness:* focused on the client's liabilities or pathology.
4. *Didactic:* clarification of misinformation or lack of information.
5. *Encouragement to action:* pressing the client to act on his or her world in a constructive manner and discouraging a passive attitude toward life.

Experiential, strength, didactic, and encouragement should be used most frequently, with much less reliance on exploiting the client's weaknesses (Lawson, Ellis, & Rivers, 1984, p. 103). Confrontation is always used in relation to behaviors and never used to attack a client's personhood. Many confrontations will be paradoxical, will be enlarged to farcical dimensions, and will have humor attached so that the client can clearly see the ridiculousness of the behavior called into question. For example, during session 5 with his group, Gordon is confronted by both workers and group members as a way of cracking his denial.

Gordon: It's easy for you to say I shouldn't go drinking with the guys after work. You just can't do that and stay on the inside track.

Carolyn: (*catching the discrepancy*) So if you don't do what they want, you're out. Yet the very act of continuing to drink has almost put you out. Do you see the discrepancy there?

Gordon: Yes, but I've got to be a team player. Can't let those young sharks get ahead.

Manuel: (*calling the question*) Ahead of what?

Carolyn: (*creating an exaggerated image*) Picture this, Gordon. You're a little minnow swimming around in a martini glass with all these big hungry fish circling you, but you're so goofy from that vodka ocean that you swim right into their jaws. How does that fit? It certainly is your decision, but I wonder how that picture fits with who you would like to think you are.

Gordon: (*Chuckles.*) OK. I'll accept that. If only there was some way to get out of that double bind.

Ray: (*proposing action*) What would happen if you did exactly the opposite of what you've been doing? That is, just turn that after-work happy hour down. Become one of the sober sharks instead of the drunken minnows? What would you get out of that?

Gordon: I don't know. (*lamely*) Then I wouldn't be a regular guy.

Ruth: (*drawing the paradox*) Yeah. You've been a regular guy, all right. That's with a four Manhattan drink dinner. Why don't you put a half-dozen down? Then you'd be Superman. I thought I was Superwoman when I did that crap, and you see me now.

Gordon: (*sullenly*) Now, wait a second! I didn't mean that. (*Turns to Carolyn.*) That's not true. How can she say that? We're supposed to be helping each other. How can you let her attack me?

Carolyn: (*redirecting*) Then what did you mean? (*replacing a demand with a reflection*) I understand how that hurts, but I also believe that when you try to get me to support you and imply that I'm a lousy counselor if I don't, I'd just be playing into that game of "poor me." What will you do instead? (*proposing alternatives*) You have some choices. You can sit and sulk, you can be dependent and ask me to take your part, or you can use your considerable strength and make a clear assertive statement back. Which will it be?

Alice: (*creating an image*) See how you get yourself? You want to be so darn independent, yet you continuously say, "Come and hold me, look what a poor child am I." I get this picture of a big baby in a crib, and it's full of empty bourbon bottles and you nestled in there.

Gordon: By God, that isn't true. I'm not a baby. Life's been a bitch.

Carolyn: (*commiserating overbearingly*) Yep! Life's that way. It's rotten, cruel, and unusual punishment. Wouldn't it be wonderful to make everybody responsible for your drinking put on hair shirts and roll around in cinders? That would pay them back for all the harm they've done to you.

Gordon: People just don't understand me, and that includes all of you. I'm gonna leave this stinkin' place.

Carolyn: (*avoiding a trap*) I'd not like to see that happen, but what they're doing is confronting your own ways of fooling yourself and attempting to get you to see the strengths you've got. If I get them off your back, you don't have to be responsible. If I don't, you leave and I'm at fault. Either way you'd have an excuse for continuing to blame somebody else. (*attributing the projection*) It seems as if you'd like me to get into the same kinds of double binds you put yourself in. (*owning*) So if you believe I'm not much of a counselor because of that, it's certainly your privilege. All that to avoid taking the risk to see what strengths you really might have, but being too scared to try. (*interpreting the externalization of blame and encouraging new behavior*) Earlier in this session you asked for help. Why did you want that if you are getting nothing out of being helped?

Gordon: (*Rocks back in chair.*) I do that? Damn! I guess maybe I do.

Some of the responses may seem to put Gordon in the hot seat, but the other members are willing to own that they too have been where Gordon is now. The confrontations are exhortations to action. The group is pushing Gordon to make changes in his life, particularly in regard to the way he denies and defends his drinking behavior.

Limit Testing

Dependability and consistency apply to the enforcement of rules of the program and are critical to getting better. Clients often test the limits to determine consistency in the therapist's treatment approach by missing appointments, disobeying treatment rules, and taking drugs (Doweiko, 1996, p. 360). Stability and consistency in what is expected from the chemical dependent are the hallmarks of good treatment. As a result, deviancy from the ground rules should be immediately confronted by the crisis worker.

Gordon: Sorry I'm late, I was talking with Ruth and forgot the time.

Carolyn: I may sound really picky here, but that's an excuse for not taking care of business. I wonder how many times you've used that before to not be on time and excuse your drinking. On a scale of 1 to 10, right now how ready are you to change?

Gordon: (*sarcastically*) Yeah, I stopped and got a Manhattan at the nurse's station. Maybe a 5. I dunno.

Carolyn: What you did was take a little step toward excusing your behavior, and that little minidecision can lead to bigger, bad decisions when you get out of here. I want you to recognize and be aware of those little decisions and where they can lead. A 5 tells me that there is at least half of you that is committed to this, how 'bout let's see that half and what he would look like. I'm curious as to why you didn't pick a lower number if you didn't want to do anything.

Gordon: Well I do want to do something.

By making Gordon scale his motivation, Carolyn gets him to admit that some part of him is open to the idea of change, and that's the part she immediately reinforces.

Treatment Secrets

Chemical dependents sometimes attempt to co-opt the treatment by telling "secrets" to staff members—usually to a neophyte. The chemical dependent confesses a rules infraction to the staff member but asks the staff person not to tell the other staff members. If the client can get the staff member to go along, the chemical dependent can later blackmail the staff member by threatening to tell his or her supervisors.

Gordon: (*Calls Sheila, a counseling intern, to the side after the group outpatient meeting.*) Errh, ahh, I need to talk to you . . . I think I can trust you . . . ahh . . . with something I don't want Carolyn to know 'cause she'd chew my ass. Well . . . one of my friends came by and while we were talking in the car he pulled out a beer from a cooler . . . and well, doggone it . . . I had one . . . only one . . . I feel bad about it and just had to tell somebody. But please don't tell her.

Sheila: (*in a kind, but assertive voice*) I'm glad you told me about what you did, Gordon. I want to now encourage you to go to Carolyn and tell her and also tell the group at our next meeting. I don't keep secrets about drug use. If I did, I'd be no different from all the other people who have enabled your drinking. So you decide. Do you tell her now, or do I bring it up in the team meeting?

Besides an immediate confrontation with the "secret," Doweiko (1996, p. 360) suggests that the staffer immediately write down what the client told him or her about the "secret" and refer it to the treatment team. Contrary to what some might assume, that Gordon has "fallen off the wagon" after having a beer and will soon be in total relapse, Carolyn calls it a "slip" and takes immediate action. The conflict, guilt, and shame that can arise from a slip can undermine self-efficacy and increase expectations of continued failure (Annis, 1990, p. 121).

Gordon: I screwed up for sure. Pretty much proves the point I am a loser.

Carolyn: I want to look at this as an exception to twenty-two days of sobriety. We have talked about slips. They are troublesome, but we know they happen. This slip is not a catastrophe and not an excuse to drink either. You chose to stop before this and you can certainly choose now. I am going to write that down on a card. I want you to put that card in your wallet. If you get in a situation like that again, take it out and read it. You are in control.

Doweiko (2006, p. 398) makes a valid point that in almost all other medical problems, treatment noncompliance is not seen as a failure as it often is in substance abuse treatment. Carolyn has to tread a slippery slope here. Crisis workers must be careful not to appear to condone slips, but on the other hand they must deal with the reality that slips are more likely to occur than not and plan for and deal with them (Fisher & Harrison, 2000, p. 251).

Disrupting Irrational Mental Sets

According to Ellis (1987), it is not an event itself but our belief about that event that causes us to feel and act in certain irrational ways. By starting to think "insane" thoughts about what people or events "should," "ought," "must" do or be to make it a perfect world, chemical dependents become victims of their irrational thoughts about the events. By putting such irrational statements up on the billboard of their minds, chemical dependents can easily fall back into hurt, rejected feelings and can manifest these feelings in behavior designed to pay back the people or events that intrude into their self-centered universe. It is extremely important to catch chemical dependents as they begin to build these billboards, because this kind of thinking is what starts a chain of events that can ultimately build up to another drinking episode. The key to stopping this "insane" thinking is teaching the person to recognize the cues that appear antecedent to the negative feelings and subsequent bad behavioral outcomes. Once these cues are picked up, new, rational statements can be manufactured to replace the old, debilitating ones that underlie beliefs.

For example, in Gordon's treatment, a videotape of session 6 was used as the focus for group therapy in session 7. Session 6 had examined the events and behaviors that brought each client to St. Polymorpheus. The group viewed excerpts of session 6 that were selected by the group leaders to vividly re-create and model each individual's unique addictive situation and to stimulate and uncover each member's defense mechanisms. Clients first portrayed themselves; then members exchanged roles and attempted to model what the other's defenses appeared to be.

Manuel: Man, those were tough. Liz played me to a tee! I also thought Alice really hit Gordon's nail on the head too!

Ray: How he first rationalizes, and then when things really get hot, regresses.

Gordon: Before I saw that videotape, I would never have believed it! But there I was. Rationalizing my drinking by telling myself I was "sick" when I couldn't make it to work because I was hung over or still smashed. Boy, was that sad! It made me sick to watch that. What a jerk!

Ruth: What about that preadolescent stuff, "I'll take my ball and go home," see how Liz did that with the doctor routine? It was just like yesterday with the family therapy. I didn't know whether that was your mother or wife, the way you were manipulating her and sulking like a kid who didn't get any candy.

Gordon: (*angrily*) What do you mean, acting like a kid? Why don't we take a look at how you act around that teenager of yours?

Liz: Look at what you just did, Gordon. You're regressing right now!

Alice: That videotape didn't lie. Don't you see how you get into that?

Carolyn: Remember the work we did on cueing in our verbal and nonverbal behavior the other day. Notice what feelings you get when your defense mechanisms kick in and what thoughts go through your head to get that going. (*Gordon looks at videotape again.*)

Gordon: (*sheepishly*) Maybe I *was* acting like a kid. Maybe I wasn't connecting that stuff you call cueing to my real life.

Carolyn: Right here we have a good example of how you might begin to use that cueing. When Ruth confronted you just a minute ago, what messages went through your mind to cause you to react angrily and then attack her—rather than looking at yourself?

Gordon: The first thing that flashed through my mind was "You're just like my wife." She's always implying I'm not capable of acting like an adult. She makes me crazy when she does that.

Carolyn: Using Gordon as an example, what cues did we teach you all to recognize, and what did we learn to do to counteract our irrational thinking as well as our behavior?

Ruth: First off, Gordon needs to recognize that as one of those stop signs you were talking about. Anytime that he relates to the old ways he behaved toward Amy and hears, "I'm not good enough," he needs to see that as a warning sign that he's kicking in a lot of that old dependent putdown crap.

Manuel: He also could change "she" to "I," 'cause it's really him and his beliefs about what she said. He allows that to happen.

Alice: He could make an assertive statement out of it, like, "I understand how you might feel that way, but right now

I'm feeling like I'm behaving pretty straight with you, and it hurts me that you'd feel I haven't changed."

Cueing provides Gordon with psychological stop signs. These are not easy to see, especially when, in the heat of the moment, it is all too easy to revert to years' worth of programmed thinking. Cueing is like any other new skill and will take much practice and feedback before the client is able to "rewire" his or her thinking.

Carolyn: I want you all to list out your cues for those predicaments that make you crazy, angry, depressed, and so on, in your logs. Then let's work on building new belief statements. Monitor yourself as we work together, and see if you can catch yourself before others do. If you feel a bit odd when you put those new statements in and say them, then you're on the right track.

If clients cannot catch the insane messages they send themselves, then other physiological or affective responses may work as cues. Sweating hands, a lump in the throat, and a palpitating heart may be good physical cues. The flush of anger, the chagrin of embarrassment, and the gloom of despair may be good affective cues.

Overcoming Environmental Cues That Lead to Drinking

Subtly but surely, settings and the events that occur within them provide powerful cues to respond in particular ways. Returning to a world that is filled with potent environmental cues to drink or take drugs strains the recovering addict's newfound coping skills to the limit and can create another crisis point (Sobell & Sobell, 1978).

Putting chemical dependents in role plays and imaginal sets in groups helps them recognize and manipulate environments that powerfully reinforce their chemical dependency. By learning how to use cognitive restructuring (McMullin & Giles, 1981), imaging (Neisser, 1976), coping thoughts (Cormier & Hackney, 1987), emotive imagery and covert modeling (Cormier & Cormier, 1985), stress inoculation (Meichenbaum, 1985), and node-link mapping (Collier et al., 2001; Czuchry & Dansereau, 2003), clients can arm themselves against the negative setting events that they will inevitably encounter. In session 10 of Gordon's treatment group, the group constructs and role-plays a setting event that portrays Gordon getting into his car after a very stressful day at work, which has been interrupted by phone calls from home saying that Mark has been suspended from school because he was found

with a marijuana cigarette in his possession. A guided node-link map (Collier et al., 2001; Dansereau & Dees, 2002) has been put up on the wall that outlines the steps that Gordon would need to take in dealing with such a problem. Gordon watches as Manuel plays the part.

Manuel: (*as Gordon, talking to himself as he guns the car out of the company lot*) Jesus Christ! Everything was supposed to be better. If this is better, screw it! Work sucks! The president is on my back again. Produce! Produce! Produce! That's all I hear. And now Mark! I suppose that's my fault too. Amy sure laid that one on me while going nuts over the phone. That's what I got to look forward to when I hit the door. Hey, there's the Olde English Inn coming up over the hill. My favorite watering hole. Man, do they make a mean Manhattan in there. I'll bet some of the old crowd's still there too, and Roxie, my favorite bartender. They sure never gave me any flak. It's happy hour too! Two for the price of one. To hell with it. I'll just have one and go. It'll take the edge off before I hit the door and have to deal with Amy and Mark. (*Manuel turns the car into the inn parking lot.*)

Ray: OK! The world isn't perfect, and you're going to run into problems like that, feel those lousy emotions, and those tempting places like the Olde English Inn are going to be there just waiting for a day like that. What are you going to do, Gordon? Look at the way we have mapped that out on the overhead. That is your map. Let's see how well you can read it.

Gordon's map (Collier et al., 2001; Czuchry & Dansereau, 2003; Dansereau & Dees, 2002) lays out in schematic form:

What his goal is: "Not use stressful situations at work to decide to drink."

Problems he might encounter: "Combination of stressors at work and at home."

Why he wants to reach the goal: "Do not set myself up for relapse by making excuses to drink."

What supports he has to reach his goal: "His AA sponsor, his family to talk to if necessary, and his own skills at using the foregoing cognitive behavioral techniques."

What steps he should take and ways to deal with the problem: "Pull off the road and call AA sponsor, start relaxation techniques, and institute positive self-enhancing and coping statements."

Gordon: All right. Let me put my plan into action. My positive self-statements will be "I don't care how rough it's been at work, I did a helluva job today. The boss always gripes like that around the end of the month, so don't take it personally." My stress inoculates will be a number of things.

First, I'll put Mozart on the tape deck; that's calming and reminds me of being on the banks of Lake Zurich just watching the sailboats glide by. Behaviorally, I can practice my breathing skills, just taking deep, easy breaths, and letting all that stress flow right out my nose. While I'm doing that, I can see my jogging shoes and sweats waiting for me by the back door at home. I can replace my negative thoughts about home by saying, "I would have come in and blustered and stormed around and grilled Mark, generally raised hell and then sulked. That didn't do a damn bit of good except get me stressed out even more. I know I can think clearer and more rationally after I've worked out. I can feel the sweat pouring out of my body, cleaning it out. That'll feel good."

Now here comes the inn over the hill. I'm starting to think how easy it'd be to just turn in there. I can feel my hands getting sweaty, and my throat's dry. I put my thought stopping into gear, "STOP THAT! Switch. Think what your sagging, pulpy body was after you got through with a bout in there, turkey! You couldn't stumble to the john without gasping for air. God, were you ever a sorry sucker." To cue myself on how good I now feel, I'll flex my leg and feel that hard thigh muscle, a great tactile cue to remind me how far I've come, and I'm not giving that up. Reviewing my self-talk, I can say, "Yeah, Roxie and the inn were a great place to get quietly smashed, but that was then. Looking at the place in broad daylight, it's shopworn, and I've got real oak in my study instead of that fiberboard, ersatz stuff in there. Ha! I'll bet the boys look a little shopworn too after today. Further, I never really liked that sweet smell of a Manhattan, always covered it with a cigarette. I don't want that crap. It's a bitch about Mark, but I don't need to catastrophize over it. I can handle that, and I'll take the time to handle it. My family's the most important thing in the world to me, and I'm not just paying lip service to it, I'm living it! If I have to I can also call Hal, my AA sponsor. Press the accelerator down and go on by with no regrets."

By taping and practicing these new mental images over and over with the assistance of the workers and the group, Gordon learns how to use a wide variety of positive coping mechanisms to get by this potentially dangerous environmental set (Ahsen, 1993). This is not a one-shot exercise. It will take Gordon a great deal of practice to reprogram himself to ignore those old cues that set him up to drink. The node-link map on the overhead shows graphically what a client needs to do and the pathway to follow. It is especially effective with low-verbal individuals who may have trouble grasping complex treatment plans (Czuchry & Dansereau, 2003). These exercises are all part of armor-plating the addict against relapse.

Treating the Family

The attitudes, structure, and function of the family system have been shown to be perhaps the most important variables in the outcome of treatment (Copello, Templeton, & Velleman, 2006; Fisher & Harrison, 2000, pp. 189–195; Kaminer & Slesnick, 2005). Barnett (2003) conducted an extensive review of research, literature, and Internet-based resources. The conclusion was that alcohol dependency flourishes within the social context of the family system and is one of the leading causes of family dysfunction. She proposes that it is imperative that the family be recognized as the unit of treatment and be included in the treatment plan. Family intervention generally falls within two areas of intervention, systems and behavioral therapies (Seneviratne & Daeppen, 2009).

Two important factors need to be considered in family counseling with alcoholics. First, a very important consideration in any family therapy is the cultural background of that family, and that is never more true than in addiction counseling. Terms such as "enmeshment," "enabling," and "codependency" that may be construed as pathological in a Euro-American family may be anything but that in families with different cultural backgrounds (Fisher & Harrison, 2000, pp. 172–173, 182–183). Second, stepfamilies of the "yours," "mine," "ours," and even "theirs" variety may have very different boundaries, bonds, and decision-making processes from intact nuclear families (Anderson, 1992, pp. 172–174), which will need to be considered in deciding how to conduct therapy.

If the system changes from enabling to more adaptive behavior, it may sustain improvement and change in the alcoholic (Kaufman & Pattison, 1982a, p. 669). However, this is easier said than done because, paradoxically, if the alcoholic makes a commitment to stop drinking, the maladaptive family may become threatened enough to try to reinstitute the perceived homeostasis of alcoholism. Family homeostasis is the natural tendency of the members to attempt to maintain structure, balance, and stability in the face of change (Jackson, 1957); even though that structure may be terribly maladaptive, it is "the devil they know."

In Gordon's case, supportive counseling required all members, including Gordon, to view the situation as far more than simply Gordon's stopping drinking. Family counseling uses drinking cessation only as a starting point to confront the fundamental problems driving the dependency, and each member of the family is seen as having a key role in solving the problems afflicting each other and in building a strong, healthy, and supportive family system.

There are three major advantages to family therapy when it is conducted with a view to helping the whole family. First, the family can confront the chemical dependent's addiction and can support his or her attempt to move into recovery. For example, RBT (Tuten et al., 2012) uses a family sponsor, which is much like an AA sponsor, only a family member. The family sponsor meets with the worker and client periodically, receives updates on the client's progress including drug testing, provides praise and reinforcement for remaining abstinent and for meeting recreational and job goals, receives phone calls and visits from the client at times when the client needs additional emotional support to stay clean, provides instrumental support such as transportation to job interviews, provides contingent rewards such as going to a concert if drug free, and speaks positively to other family members about the client (pp. 152–153).

Behavioral couples therapy (Emmelkamp & Vedel, 2006; O'Farrell, 2011; O'Farrell et al., 2010; Powers, Vedel, & Emmelkamp, 2008) focuses on maintaining self-control and coping skills to stay abstinent, improve relational functioning, and improve functioning in other social systems within which the couple is involved, along with improving the significant other's coping with drinking-related situations. To do the foregoing, couples may engage in a *daily sobriety trust contract*. This contract is the only time during the day when substance abuse is discussed. It is brief and ends with a positive statement to one another. An Antabuse contract adds on daily Antabuse ingestion in the presence of the partner. An additional component to the standard functional analysis is the potential relationship factors that function as an antecedent or consequence of substance abuse. Attention bias is used to stop focusing on negative behaviors and start focusing on positive ones by writing down positive or pleasant behaviors they have observed in one another, along with increasing positive interaction behaviors by increasing caring and pleasant behaviors. Training in communication and problem solving is given to help couples work on relationship issues and relapse prevention plans (Emmelkamp & Vedel, 2006, pp. 70–71).

Second, the family learns how substance abuse is related to other patterns of family life, such as roles, rules, and patterns of communication, and may become aware of how they play a part in keeping others in

the system in thrall to it (Cable, Noel, & Swanson, 1986, pp. 73–74). One of the toughest issues for the family to come to grips with is the notion that they indeed play a part in enabling the alcoholism to continue. It is easy to point to the identified patient (the alcoholic) as the person to be treated and "cured," but the fact of the matter is, if one believes in the family as a system, it is the whole family that needs to be considered as the client.

For example, in Transactional Analysis theory, enabling and codependency are depicted graphically in the Karpman Drama Triangle (Karpman, 2007), which has a persecutor, rescuer, and victim at each apex of an equilateral triangle. As long as all three positions are in place, the sides of the triangle support a very strong codependent and enabling relationship. Of these roles, the "rescuer" is not a person who comes to someone's aid in an emergency, but rather someone with a covert motive who gets a payoff for appearing to be heroic, as in the long-suffering spouse who covers for her alcoholic husband and gets a great deal of sympathy and admiration "for putting up with so much" from her church circle.

Interestingly, family members do not always keep the same roles but, according to the payoffs involved, may move around on the triangle. Thus, for example, the rescuer heroically tried and having failed over and over, becomes the victim. So also may the persecutor and the victim move around on the triangle. As a result of these dynamics, each person moves from role to role, unconsciously, habitually, and frustratingly in perpetual, albeit very unhealthy, motion. However, when a family member decides to no longer assume one of those roles, a side is removed and the triangle is in danger of collapsing. Thus, a crisis is created because the enabling and codependency stop, and the pathological homeostasis the family has been in comes to a screeching halt.

Third, and perhaps most important, the children can be educated as to the part they play in the dysfunctional system (Liepman, White, & Nirenberg, 1986, pp. 56–57).

However it is conducted, family therapy provides a supportive and safe place to tackle such big family issues as the need to change lifestyle, individual members' perfectionism, power imbalances in the family, rivalries, and various ways members jockey for leadership. Many families are not consciously aware of the influence these dynamic factors play in the family. Even if both codependents and dependent agree to change, there should not be explicit or implicit assumptions that family ties will be fully reconstituted. Avoidance of enabling behavior and assumption of responsibility are difficult, as Gordon's first family therapy session shows.

Family Therapy Session. The primary task of the worker is to detect and penetrate the defense systems the addictive family has set up to keep things stable. As we discussed earlier in this chapter, there are three rules that govern almost all alcoholic families: "Don't talk!" "Don't trust!" and "Don't feel!" (Black, 1981). Almost without exception, the alcoholic family members will have real trouble expressing feelings and communicating with one another (Maxwell, 1986, pp. 205–206). There will also be an "identified patient" (Reilly, 1992). In Gordon's family, it is Gordon. However, to keep the family together it may as easily be some other family member who not only gains power from being the patient, but also serves to keep the family defocused from the alcoholism and still stay together (Fisher & Harrison, 2000, p. 189).

By keeping a low profile in the beginning, the worker lets the pathology of the family emerge (Parker, 1986). As Carolyn sits quietly, Gordon, Amy, Lisa, and Mark exchange stilted pleasantries and defensive comments, punctuated by long, awkward silences. As soon as the worker obtains an adequate assessment of the family's dynamic interaction, she becomes involved.

Amy: Now, I don't want you to worry about anything. I talked to your boss, and he assured me the company is behind you 100 percent.

Gordon: That's great!

Carolyn: Amy, I'd like you to notice what you just did. You decided to take care of Gordon. What about your own feelings about carrying the load?

Amy: I just didn't want him to worry about his job. I know how much he's put into it.

Carolyn: Yes, but what about your feelings?

Amy: It just seems to me that Gordon should concentrate his efforts on getting better, don't you think?

Carolyn: Do you see what you're doing? I've asked you twice to speak to your feelings. Yet each time, you take responsibility for Gordon. You talk about him and not yourself. You pose a question that asks for my agreement. And you shift to events rather than dealing with your feelings. How does that strike you, Gordon?

Gordon: Er, I don't know. I guess Amy ought to express how she feels.

Carolyn: How do you feel?

Gordon: I think we probably don't do enough talking about our feelings.

Carolyn: That's right, but how do you feel?

This short exchange graphically demonstrates the tremendous difficulty the two adults have in expressing feelings to one another. They adroitly shift off this topic in a variety of ways. One very subtle way to avoid direct confrontation about feelings is to send a messenger. Of course, the messenger has to be very careful about how the news is delivered; otherwise, he or she may get psychologically murdered in completing the task.

Amy: Lisa, tell your father what Grandpa and Grandma had to say.

Lisa: Ah, they said they were real sorry they didn't get to see you, and hoped you get well. They'd have really liked to stay and come here today, but Grandpa had to get back to Chicago for a meeting.

Carolyn: I wonder why you asked Lisa to tell Gordon that. My guess is that's a touchy subject about his parents leaving. Does your mom often ask you to do that?

Lisa: You bet! You do that all the time, Mom. Whenever you've got something you think'll cause a ruckus, you always send me to tell Dad 'cause you think he'll take it from me. Then I'm the bad guy. I hate it!

Carolyn: So you see, there's another way of getting around dealing with feelings. Send somebody else and let them deal with it, because feelings are risky, scary, and hard to handle.

Amy: Lisa has always been the apple of her dad's eye. She's always had a way with him.

Carolyn: Excuse me for picking on you right now, Amy, but what were you just doing?

Amy: I was talking about Lisa and her relationship with her dad.

Carolyn: That's right! You were talking *about* her, not *to* her. What would happen if you said that straight out? You might risk getting a feeling response back.

Lisa: Mom, you wouldn't like that. You always tell me to bear up when I try to talk to you about my feelings, and that goes for you too, Dad!

Carolyn: Great, Lisa! Lisa's raised some pretty hot issues. Any feelings about them?

Gordon: (*looking at Carolyn*) I guess I just didn't realize I wasn't being the father I could be to her. I didn't realize I was doing that. I'm sorry.

Carolyn: Gordon, do you want me to be your messenger to Lisa?

Gordon: No!

Carolyn: Then don't tell me, but tell her that.

Amy: Well, I just know Mark doesn't feel that way. He's kept a stiff upper lip through all this, kept up his grades and done everything around the house, plus made his own spending money mowing yards.

Carolyn: Amy, it is interesting that you find it difficult to feel for yourself, yet can tell others how they feel and even answer for them. What I'd like to do now is give each one of you an assignment for next time that specifically gets at what problems I see with communication in this group. Mark, since you didn't say anything today, I want you to write a letter to each member in the family telling each how you feel about him or her. Lisa, I'd like you to wear a big paper heart next time, and every time somebody doesn't respond directly to you or speak to their feelings, I'd like you to tear a piece of your heart off. Amy, in the codependency group I want you to solicit direct, feeling responses from people. I'll give you the questions to ask. Gordon, I want you to write down some of the feelings you had in here today into a script, and then take it back to the group and we'll role-play it on the videotape.

The major task is to teach all the family members to express their feelings in an open and honest way. Debilitating communication patterns are pointed out over and over to all family members who engage in disruptive communications. It is noteworthy that no one mentions Gordon's drinking. This conspiracy of silence still continues even after Gordon is in a chemical treatment unit and the whole family is in therapy for the problem. As Parker (1986) says, "There's a big, pet, pink elephant [alcoholism] sitting there in the middle of the family, but everybody circles around it as if it didn't even exist, and it just keeps getting bigger and bigger and taking up more space." This problem will need to be reflected by the worker, for the sooner the alcoholism is brought into the open, the quicker the family can start building a new communication system.

Another issue is Mark, who has remained silent throughout the session. Invariably there is someone who can be extremely helpful in changing the system (Kaufman & Pattison, 1982b, p. 1031). Mark may have a great deal to do with changing the family network. Lisa is also a potent member of this system. The worker early on acknowledges her strength and reinforces her for clear, directional feeling responses—a rarity in this family. Finally, to facilitate communication, tasks may be assigned within the session as homework.

Therapy for the Children. Whenever therapeutic assistance is sought or recommended for the family, it should not be surprising if children are resistant. They will feel it is the chemically dependent parent who needs help, not them. The therapist's legitimate and sincere explanation is that although this is the chemical dependent's problem, it is also a family problem, and the children in particular deserve special attention (Black, 1981, p. 102). Cable, Noel, and Swanson (1986, p. 69) have listed several treatment goals for children who experience crisis because of parental chemical dependency:

1. Providing emotional support for the children
2. Providing accurate, nonjudgmental information about alcoholism and the disease concept
3. Correcting the children's inaccurate and guilty perceptions that they are the cause or reason for their parent's drinking
4. Helping the children focus on their own behavior by giving them a sense of control and the perception of being able to make responsible choices and, if necessary, helping them learn how to have fun
5. Helping the children learn how to cope with real situations that may arise because of the parent's alcohol abuse—for example, if the parent passes out
6. Reducing the children's isolation and helping them to share their dilemma with other children in similar situations
7. Reducing the children's risk of developing substance abuse or, alternatively, treating the children's substance abuse

For children going through the crisis of a family member's addiction or recovery, Alateen, family therapy, or specialized counseling groups for codependent children are critical treatment components that provide information and emotional support. Children learn that there are alternative ways to cope with their problems other than the maladaptive ones taught by their families (Liepman, White, & Nirenberg, 1986, pp. 56–57). However, there is a good deal of evidence that children do not wish to be identified as members of an alcoholic family because of negative stereotypes (DiCicco et al., 1984), and indeed that view is held by peers and even mental health workers (Sher, 1991, p. 169). As such, children, particularly in school settings, should never be labeled as being in "alcoholic" or "drug" groups. The bottom line is that the emotional issues of *all* children raised in chemically dependent homes need to be addressed because *all* children are affected.

Aftercare and Relapse Prevention

If Gordon stays sober a year into recovery, he will be in the 20 percent minority of substance addicts to do so (DiClemente & Prochaska, 1998). He will certainly be at the action stage of Prochaska's motivation to change model. Yet his most critical challenge is to get to the maintenance stage and hold his gains (Prochaska, DiClemente, & Norcross, 1992). There is clear evidence that extended aftercare treatment, whether by phone or face to face, combats relapse. Further, these findings tend to hold whether aftercare is offered by itself or in combination with support groups, continued behavioral or family therapy, and pharmacotherapy (McKay, 2005). The first 90 days following discharge from treatment are a period of special vulnerability. Sadly, statistics for abstinence-based programs indicate that 90 percent of those discharged will have a drink within the first 90 days after discharge, and 45 to 50 percent revert to pretreatment drinking after one year (Polivy & Herman, 2002). At St. Polymorpheus, the aftercare program requires that the client attend meetings following dismissal from inpatient treatment and that aftercare checkups continue for 6 months with constant drug screens.

Gordon will inevitably encounter several crisis points. The percentages of people who relapse have been calculated to be as high as 45 to 50 percent in the first year (Polivy & Herman, 2002) and up to 90 percent over time (Svanum & McAdoo, 1989). A number of issues need to be monitored very carefully during this critical time period. Stress, negative emotional states, interpersonal pressure, euphoria, social and environmental drug-related cues, medication noncompliance, and use of other substances are traps that can cause the chemical dependent to relapse (DeJong, 1994). Marlatt and Gordon (1985) discuss relapse as issuing out of a series of minidecisions that form a chain of high-risk cognitions and behaviors; relapse is most likely when the individual is in a negative emotional or physical state or under social pressure.

According to Chiauzzi (1990), there are four elements common to relapse:

1. *Long-standing personality traits* such as narcissism or dependency resurface. The chemical dependent either can't admit weakness or attempts to please others and starts to drink again.
2. *Symptom substitution* is another danger signal for relapse. Symptom substitution can range from obsessive work habits to immediately falling in love to binge eating. Symptom substitution is the hallmark of the "dry drunk," the person who is still practicing the addictive behavior except that alcohol happens not to be part of the current behavioral repertoire.

3. *Tunnel vision* of the recovery process is also designed to get the recovering chemical dependent set up to drink again. Religiously going to AA meetings is only one part of the overall personality and behavioral change the recovering dependent will have to make to stay sober. Without working on the global issues that led to the addiction in the first place, the chemical dependent will slowly drift back into addiction.
4. *Warning signals* begin flashing when recovering dependents start to rationalize thoughts, feelings, and behaviors that set them up to drink again. Examples are going back to the neighborhood bar to "just watch the football game with my buddies" or continuing to buy lottery tickets at the liquor store. The "using" dream is a phenomenon that is frequently encountered by those in recovery. The using dream is so intense and real that the abuser wakes up thinking he or she has been under the influence. These dreams are dangerous triggers, and the reason for their existence is not known. Clients should be warned that these using dreams are a very real possibility and should not be dismissed as idle nightmares (Doweiko, 2006, p. 403).

To increase Gordon's odds of not relapsing, work will be done on both high-risk situations such as driving by the Olde English Inn and overall lifestyle changes. Addicts who have just come off drugs have a huge vacuum in their lives. They need to relearn how to use leisure time wisely, reconnect to support systems, continue work on social and communication skills, and reestablish personal good hygiene, physical well-being, personal grooming and clothing habits, and good financial planning and budgeting. If this sounds like a tall order, it is, and it is no small wonder that any addict doesn't relapse given the general life issues they face besides physically and psychologically craving their drug of choice. To address the issues of codependency and enabling activities, workers try to ensure that all significant family members also participate in aftercare. The objectives of aftercare are:

1. To provide ongoing education and information needed to maintain sobriety
2. To create an environment in which natural and healthy patterns of social influence reinforce positive behaviors and self-esteem
3. To establish an ongoing group of caring, accepting, empathic, genuine, trusting individuals who serve

as an extended family, among whom the individual can always feel safe and understood

4. To serve as the first line of safety anytime a crisis occurs

Gordon's aftercare will extend for a minimum of 6 months on a regular basis. During that time he will have weekly meetings with Carolyn to discuss how well he is following and meeting his aftercare objectives and goals in regard to his work, his family, his physical health, and his mental health.

Cognitive-Behavioral Boosters. Gordon will continuously practice the cognitive-behavioral techniques he has learned through a self-help method called Rational Recovery (Schmidt, 1996; Schmidt, Carns, & Chandler, 2001), a variation of rational-emotive behavior therapy (Ellis et al., 1988). In particular, Gordon will constantly monitor his addictive voice, the one that tells him, "There should, must be, perfect solutions, at work and at home, and if there aren't it is terrible and catastrophic, and the only solution is to get drunk." He will immediately recognize that voice when it starts talking to him and will have a variety of positive counterinjunctions he and Carolyn have created to stop it dead in its tracks. On his last day in treatment, Carolyn has this terminating interview. She uses an SFBT technique called "writing the message" (de Shazer 1991, pp. 143–144) that will hopefully give Gordon a huge reinforcing boost for exiting the program and will also give him an anchor to hold onto when crises arise.

Carolyn: You have done a good job here, Gordon. It has not been easy. You know there are going to be tough times ahead. I have taken my case notes and written you a message. It is yours to keep and look at from time to time when things get tough. (*reading the message*) You said in your initial interview that you wanted to get to a 4 or 5 on that scale of life adjustment. I have been impressed by your tenacity to change your life while you have been here. By being in the group and being supportive and open to others' comments and criticisms, you have shown me your ability to take risks that could be hurtful—and to learn and grow from doing so. Your ability to dig into and practice the cognitive-behavioral and emotive imagery assignments tells me you are serious about this and will use those skills as soon as you start feeling anxious about drinking again. Perhaps the most impressive part of what you have done is starting to come to grips and deal honestly, forthrightly, and openly with your family. That tells me you do love them and care very much that you salvage your family. Because you have done these things, I believe

you can retain your sobriety. I believe you can continue to develop relationships with your family and not seek solace or refuge in a bottle. I believe you can retain that 4 or 5 rating you have now and move toward even a 2 or 3 in the next 6 months.

Writing the SFBT message means generating at least three compliments that are legitimate and behavior based. Those compliments are then hooked to desired future outcomes and bridged with a *because* statement. The statement is particularly critical because it links from the compliment to what has to be done (Sklare, 1997, pp. 57–59). Carolyn reminds Gordon of his original scaling statement to show him that he has reached his original goal and now can move to an even better rating.

Pharmacology. Until recently the only drug that had any effect on stopping an alcoholic from drinking was disulfiram (Antabuse). This drug causes a violent physical reaction if the abuser ingests alcohol. However, it is a dangerous drug that can cause severe side effects and even be lethal if not monitored, so it is generally no longer recommended (Schuckit, 1995, pp. 316–317), although recent studies have indicated it may be more useful when combined with the following drugs that reduce alcohol craving (Suh et al., 2006) or when used in tightly controlled and monitored outpatient programs such as RBT.

Naltrexone, nalmefene, and acamprosate, and even an extract of one of the most noxious weeds in the southern United States, kudzu, are opioid antagonists that seem to hold some promise in stopping alcohol craving (Feeney et al., 2006; Hunt, 2002; Kranzler, 2006; Lukas et al., 2005; Roozen et al., 2006). Whether an aftercare drug regimen is indicated is the decision of the physician on the treatment team, but besides antidrinking drugs, Gordon may well also be prescribed an antidepressant, given his long-standing depression that is a constant handmaiden of alcoholism.

Euphoria. The aftercare safety line may need to extend to one of the most difficult crises the drug dependent faces—the euphoria that often accompanies recovery and the distrust and cynicism of family members—in the new and strange home that no longer has the pink elephant of drug addiction sitting in the living room. Maxwell (1986, p. 229) refers to recovery euphoria as a reaction formation. Gordon used euphoria as a highly sophisticated defense to replace the immature defenses that he had used during his active chemical dependency. Almost immediately after he left inpatient treatment, Gordon changed to a rabid proselyte. His life revolved around AA and being the completely responsible parent and husband. Although he was overbearing, his family was so afraid that confronting his behavior would send him back to drinking that they walked on eggshells. In fact, when such reaction formations occur, family members may resent the dependent's sober behavior so much that they secretly wish he or she would return to drinking.

Carolyn: Gordon, a moment ago you described how frustrated you have been because Mark clams up and withdraws from you, and you also spoke to the fact that now Lisa seems to be even more resentful of you than when you were drinking. Notice how Mark is slumped back in his chair and Lisa is sitting with arms and legs crossed as you discuss how exasperated you are.

Gordon: I can't understand it. Dinner is supposed to be our time together. Right after I got out of inpatient treatment, we were really communicating. But that's all changed lately. They've started shutting me out again. I love them, and I want what's best for them. I just want to make it up to them for being the lousy dad and husband I was for so long.

Carolyn: Mark, what are your feelings as your dad is relating his frustration?

Mark: (*shedding tears*) I'm mad at him . . . because nothing I say is right, and everything I do is either wrong or not good enough.

Lisa: Yeah. I wish sometimes you were drinking again. At least then you left us alone.

Amy: Gordon, the kids are finally saying what we've all been feeling at home. Your personality is so overpowering since you quit drinking that none of us can come up to your standards. And AA, as good as it is, has become the center of our universe. We're worn out. We just need a normal life. We don't need you as Superman.

Gordon: I don't know what to say. I just wanted to make things up to you. I don't know what to do!

Carolyn: This whole thing you're experiencing is not uncommon. As problematic as it is, it's a good sign and sort of a stage of development on the road to recovery. Understand it for that, and we can work on it just like we have the other hot spots that have come up.

Such euphoric responses should be carefully monitored in aftercare settings because they may literally drive significant others to return to enabling behavior.

AA's Role in Aftercare. Gordon will also have as a goal a minimum of three AA meetings a week. Zealous immersion in programs such as AA is also fraught with peril. The premise is that the recovering alcoholic now knows all the answers and will gladly tell them to anyone who will listen. Having said that, the very last thing Gordon needs to do is stop going to AA. AA meetings provide a format for alcoholics to socialize and stay away from the isolation that can set a recovering alcoholic up to drink. AA also helps members to understand that their problems are not unique and allows people to be accepted and restore their self-esteem. Finally, it offers predictability and consistency, which have pretty much gone from the alcoholic's life (Doweiko, 1999, pp. 480–481).

To summarize the major task of aftercare, if the chemical dependent, aside from performing his or her jobs inside and outside the home, is concentrating almost solely on maintaining chemical freedom, he or she is doing about all that needs to be done. If codependents, aside from jobs inside and outside the home, are focusing on themselves rather than on the dependent, then they are doing all that needs to be done (Maxwell, 1986, p. 234).

Gordon: (*in family therapy session, 6 months after inpatient treatment*) The truth is I am still scared to death. I'll probably always need AA, and while that bugs me at times, I know there are things that bug everybody else, and that's OK. I guess I'd rate myself as an average father and husband. We still have problems, and I guess that doesn't make me much different from any other guy. And the best part about that is it feels just fine.

SUMMARY

The crisis of addiction is unique among all crisis categories. It is full of complexities, controversies, and contradictions. In no other crisis does culture play a greater role than in alcoholism. The prognosis for cure is poor because the condition is beset with multiple transcrisis points. A person may appear to be cured, only to relapse later into a drug episode more severe than before.

There are several hypothesized models of addiction that attribute the problem to inherited, environmental, social, biological, chemical, or psychological causative factors. The major historical model sees alcoholism as a disease, but there are many critics of this notion and combativeness between these two divergent factions is the norm rather than the exception. In terms of dynamics, it seems that there are many types and degrees of addiction.

The most prevalent and puzzling dynamic revolves around the concepts of psychological denial and enabling. The chemical dependent tends to deny adamantly that there is addiction and to deny that any problem exists related to the addictive behavior. The treatment and rehabilitation of clients are enormously complicated when significant others such as family, friends, and even bosses reinforce the narcissistic and sociopathic behavior of the chemical dependent by enabling the dependency.

In the early 1980s a new phenomenon appeared in the identification of a group called ACOAs (adult children of alcoholics). It is hypothesized that what ACOAs suffered as children growing up in alcoholic families dogs them into adult life. Being an ACOA has the potential to lead to a wide variety of pathological behaviors based on the childhood roles the ACOA was forced to play to keep the family in some sort of homeostasis.

The stabilization of an addictive crisis is difficult in that it usually requires, first, that the dependent become aware that he or she needs help, and second, that the person have some motivation to seek help. To that end, reasoning with the dependent about the problem is generally useless. Most often, direct confrontation and the generation of a crisis of significant proportions by some significant other such as an employer or spouse are the only ways to propel a drug abuser to treatment.

Clearly, addicted people need a multimodal approach to get through the crisis. Competent medical supervision and counseling are needed from the detoxification phase through aftercare. Group counseling is a primary operating mode because peers who are themselves recovering addicts are highly effective in breaking down denial systems of fellow chemical dependents. Extensive use is made of family, friends, employers, and support groups such as Alcoholics Anonymous to supplement what professional caregivers can do for clients. In the 21st century, the Minnesota model of inpatient hospital care has largely been replaced by a variety of outpatient treatment models. Outpatient models such as contingency management (CM), the community reinforcement approach (CRA), and reinforcement-based treatment (RBT) rely on operant conditioning with intensive and extensive supervision of clients; they appear to be at least as outcome effective as inpatient treatment approaches and are generally more cost effective.

Currently a combination of treatment modalities seems to be the most effective way of treating alcoholism. These modalities include group therapy to provide and enhance social support; individual cognitive-behavioral therapy to change and restructure maladaptive thinking; motivational enhancement therapy to provide encouragement and treatment adherence; operant conditioning models that reinforce drug abstinence and seek to replace drug activities with job, social, and recreational substitutes; AA to provide social and spiritual support; family therapy to combat enabling and codependency; and medicinal treatment to reduce drug craving. When all is said and done, however, the sobering fact is that relapse rates are extremely high.

 To see some of the concepts discussed in this chapter in action, refer to your *Crisis Intervention in Action* DVD, or see the clips online on the Counseling Course-Mate website. To access this site, go to www.cengagebrain.com, where you'll also find an eBook, additional study tools, quizzes, and more. You are now dealing with Egyptian royalty, otherwise known in the addictions business as the King or Queen of De-nial (pun intended). How do you like being in the position of the addictions counselor and chasing Tanya around and around the merry-go-round as she denies her problem? Would you like to reach through the screen and ring her neck? Do you see why it is extremely frustrating to deal with substance abusers? Do you also think you have the patience, empathy, and unconditional positive regard to use RBT, CM, or CRA on these folks?

REFERENCES

Abbot, P. J. (2009). A review of the community reinforcement approach in the treatment of opioid dependence. *Journal of Psychoactive Drugs, 41*(4), 379–385.

Addictions Research Institute at the University of Texas–Austin. (2011). *Alcohol and substance abuse measurement instrument collection.* Available at www.utexas.edu/research/cswr/nida/instrumentListing.html

Ahsen, A. (1993). Imagery treatment of alcoholism and drug abuse: A new methodology for treatment and research. *Journal of Mental Imagery, 17,* 1–60.

Alcoholics Anonymous. (2001). *Alcoholics Anonymous* (4th ed.). New York: Alcoholics Anonymous World Services.

Alcoholics Anonymous. (2011). *The big book online* (4th ed.). New York: Alcoholics Anonymous World Services. Available at www.aa.org/bigbookonline

American Medical Association. (1956). Hospitalization of patients with alcoholism. *Journal of the American Medical Association, 162*, 750.

American Medical Association. (1993). *Factors contributing to the health care cost problem.* Chicago: Author.

American Psychiatric Association. (2000). *Diagnostic and statistical manual of mental disorders* (4th ed., Text Rev.). Washington, DC: Author.

Amodeo, M., Lundgren, L., Cohen, A., Rose, D., Chassler, D., Beltrame, C., et al. (2011). Barriers to implementing evidence-based practices in addiction treatment programs: Comparing staff reports on Motivational Interviewing, Adolescent Community Reinforcement Approach, Assertive Community Treatment, and Cognitive-Behavioral Therapy. *Evaluation and Program Planning, 34*(4), 382–389.

Anderson, J. Z. (1992). Stepfamilies and substance abuse: Unique treatment considerations. In E. Kaufman & P. Kaufman (Eds.), *Family therapy of drug and alcohol abuse* (2nd ed., pp. 172–189). Boston: Allyn & Bacon.

Annis, H. M. (1990). Relapse to substance abuse: Empirical finding within a cognitive–social learning approach. *Journal of Psychoactive Drugs, 22*, 117–124.

Anthony, J. C., Warner, L. A., & Kessler, R. C. (1997). Comparative epidemiology of dependence on tobacco, alcohol, controlled substances, and inhalants: Basic findings from the National Comorbidity Survey. In G. A. Marlatt & G. R. VandenBos (Eds.), *Addictive behaviors: Readings on etiology, prevention, and treatment* (pp. 3–40). Washington, DC: American Psychological Association.

Arbour, S., Hambley, J., & Ho, V. (2011). Predictors and outcomes of aftercare participation of alcohol and drug users completing residential treatment. *Substance Use & Misuse, 46*(10), 1275–1287.

Azrin, N. H. (1976). Improvements in the community reinforcement approach to alcoholism. *Behaviour Research and Therapy, 14*, 339–348.

Barnes, G. M., Farrell, M. P., & Cairns, A. (1986). Parental socialization factors and adolescent drinking behaviors. *Journal of Marriage and the Family, 48*, 27–36.

Barnett, M. A. (2003). All in the family: Resources and referrals for alcoholism. *Journal of American Academy Nurse Practitioners, 15*(10), 467–472.

Beasley, J. D. (1987). *Wrong diagnosis, wrong treatment: The plight of the alcoholic in America.* New York: Creative Infomatics.

Beck, A. T., Wright, F. D., Newman, C. F., & Liese, B. S. (1993). *Cognitive therapy of substance abuse.* New York: Guilford Press.

Becker, W. C. (1970). *Parents are teachers.* Champaign, IL: Research Press.

Berg, I. K., & Miller, S. D. (1992). Working with the problem drinker: *A solution-focused approach.* New York: Norton.

Beutler, L. E., Patterson, K. M., Jacob, T., & Shoham, V. (1993). Matching treatment to alcoholism subtypes. *Psychotherapy, 30*, 463–472.

Black, C. (1981). *It will never happen to me.* Denver, CO: M.A.C.

Blondell, R. D., Frierson, R. L., & Lippmann, S. B. (1996). Alcoholism. *Postgraduate Medicine, 100*, 69–72.

Blum, K., Noble, E., Sheridan, P., Montgomery, A., Ritchie, T., Jagadeeswaran, P., et al. (1990). Allelic association of human dopamine D2 receptor gene in alcoholism. *Journal of the American Medical Association, 263*(15), 2055–2060.

Blume, S. B. (1973). Iatrogenic alcoholism. *Quarterly Journal of Studies on Alcohol, 34*, 1348–1352.

Blume, S. B. (1978). Group psychotherapy in the treatment of alcoholism. In S. Zimberg, J. Wallace, & S. B. Blume (Eds.), *Practical approaches to alcoholism psychotherapy* (pp. 63–76). New York: Plenum.

Brabant, S., & Martof, M. (1993). Childhood experiences and complicated grief: A study of adult children of alcoholics. *International Journal of the Addictions, 28*, 1111–1125.

Breznitz, S. (1988). The seven kinds of denial. In P. B. Defares (Ed.), *Stress and anxiety* (pp. 73–90). New York: Harper and Row.

Brill, L. (1981). *The clinical treatment of substance abusers.* New York: Free Press.

Brook, D. W. (2011). Cognitive behavior therapies. In M. Galanter (Ed.), *Psychotherapy for the treatment of substance abuse* (pp. 175–192). Arlington, VA: American Psychiatric Press.

Brown, V. B., Ridgely, M. S., Pepper, B., Levine, I. S., & Ryglewicz, H. (1989). The dual crisis: Mental illness and substance abuse. *American Psychologist, 44*, 565–569.

Bryne, S., & Petry, N. M. (2011). Concurrent alcohol dependence among methadone-maintained cocaine abuser is associated with greater abstinence. *Experimental and Clinical Psychophamacology, 19*(2), 116–122.

Budman, S. H., Portnoy, D., & Villapiano, A. J. (2003). How to get technology innovation used in behavioral health care: Build it and they still might not come. *Psychotherapy: Theory, Research, Practice, Training, 40*(1/2), 45–54.

Burke, B. L. (2011). What can motivational interviewing tell us? *Cognitive and Behavioral Practice, 18*(1), 74–81.

Burke, B. L., Arkowitz, H., & Menchola, C. (2003). The efficacy of motivational interviewing: A meta-analysis of controlled clinical trials. *Journal of Consulting and Clinical Psychology, 71*, 843–861.

Butler, S. F., Budman, S. H., Goldman, R. J., Newman, F. L., Beckley, K. E., Trottier, D., et al. (2001). Initial validation of a computer-administered Addiction Severity Index: The ASI-MV. *Psychology of Addictive Behaviors, 15*, 4–12.

Butler, S. F., Newman, F. L., Cacciola, J. S., Frank, A., Budman, S. H., McLellan, A. T., et al. (1998). Predicting Addiction Severity Index (ASI) interviewer severity ratings for a computer-administered ASI. *Psychological Assessment, 10*, 399–407.

Cable, L. C., Noel, N. E., & Swanson, S. C. (1986). Clinical intervention with children of alcohol abusers. In D. C. Lewis & C. N. Williams (Eds.), *Providing care for children of alcoholics: Clinical and research perspectives* (pp. 65–80). Pompano Beach, FL: Health Communications.

Campbell, J. Elder, J., Gallagher, D., Simon, J., & Taylor, A. (1999). Crafting the "tap on the shoulder": A complement template for solution-focused therapy. *American Journal of Family Therapy, 27*, 35–47.

Carey, K. B. (1989). Emerging treatment guidelines for mentally ill chemical abusers. *Hospital and Community Psychiatry, 40*, 341–342, 349.

Center for Substance Abuse Treatment. (1995). *Planning for alcohol and other drug abuse treatment for adults in the criminal justice system* (Treatment Improvement Protocol #17). Rockville, MD: Author.

Centers for Disease Control. (2001). *Surveillance of homicides among intimate partners—United States, 1981–1998.* Atlanta, GA: Author.

Chalmers, D. K., & Wallace, J. (1978). Evaluation of patient progress. In S. Zimberg, J. Wallace, & S. B. Blume (Eds.), *Practical approaches to alcoholism psychotherapy* (pp. 255–279). New York: Plenum.

Chiauzzi, E. (1990). Breaking the patterns that lead to relapse. *Psychology Today, 23*(12), 18–19.

Cohn, A. M., McCrady, B. S., Epstein, E. E., & Cook, S. M. (2010). Men's avoidance and female partner's drinking behavior: A high-risk context for partner violence? *Journal of Family Violence, 25*(7), 679–687.

Coldwell, B., & Heather, N. (2006). Introduction to the special issue. *Addiction Research and Theory, 14*(1), 1–5.

Collette, L. (1990). After the anger, what then? *Family Therapy Networker, 14*, 22–31.

Collier, C. R., Czuchry, M., Dansereau, D. F., & Pitre, U. (2001). The use of node-link mapping in the chemical dependency treatment of adolescents. *Journal of Drug Education, 31*(3), 305–317.

Copello, A. G., Templeton, L., & Velleman, R. (2006). Family interventions for drug and alcohol misuse: Is there a best practice? *Current Opinion in Psychiatry, 19*(3), 271–276.

Cormier, L. S., & Hackney, H. (1987). *The professional counselor: A process guide to helping.* Upper Saddle River, NJ: Prentice Hall.

Cormier, W. H., & Cormier, L. S. (1985). *Interviewing strategies for helpers: Fundamental skills and cognitive behavioral interventions* (2nd ed.). Pacific Grove, CA: Brooks/Cole.

Cormier, W. H., & Cormier, L. S. (1991). *Interviewing strategies for helpers: Fundamental skills and cognitive behavioral interventions* (3rd ed.). Pacific Grove, CA: Brooks/Cole.

Cornelius, J. R., Douaihy, A., Bukstein, O. G., Daley, D. C., Wood, S. D., Kelly, T. M., et al. (2011). Evaluation of cognitive behavioral therapy/motivational enhancement therapy (CBT/MET) in a treatment trial for comorbid MDD/AUD adolescents. *Addictive Behaviors, 36*(8), 843–848.

Cowan, G., & Warren, L. M. (1994). Codependency and gender stereotyped traits. *Sex Roles, 30*, 631–645.

Craig, R. J. (2004). *Counseling the alcohol and drug dependent client.* New York: Allyn & Bacon.

Czuchry, M., & Dansereau, D. F. (2003). A model of the effects of node-link mapping on drug abuse counseling. *Addictive Behaviors, 28*(3), 537–549.

D'Andrea, L. M., Fisher, G. L., & Harrison, T. C. (1994). Cluster analysis of adult children of alcoholics. *International Journal of the Addictions, 29*, 565–582.

Dansereau, D. F., & Dees, S. M. (2002). Mapping training: The transfer of a cognitive technology for improving counseling. *Journal of Substance Abuse, 22*(4), 219–230.

DeJong, W. (1994). Relapse prevention: An emerging technology for promoting long-term abstinence. *International Journal of the Addictions, 29*, 681–785.

De Leon, G. (1989). Psychopathology and substance abuse: What is being learned from research in therapeutic communities. *Journal of Psychoactive Drugs, 21*, 177–188.

de Shazer, S. (1985). *Keys to solution in brief therapy.* New York: Norton.

de Shazer, S. (1991). *Putting difference to work.* New York: Norton.

DiCicco, L., Davis, R. B., Hogan, J., MacLean, A., & Orenstein, A. (1984). Group experiences for children of alcoholics. *Alcohol Health and Research World, 8*, 20–24.

DiClemente, C. C., Carroll, K. M., Connors, G. J., & Kadden, R. M. (1994). Process assessment in treatment matching research. *Journal of Studies on Alcohol, 12*(December Suppl.), 156–162.

DiClemente, C. C., & Prochaska, J. O. (1998). Toward a comprehensive transtheoretical model of change. In W. R. Miller & N. Heather (Eds.), *Treating addictive behaviors* (2nd ed., pp. 79–96). New York: Plenum Press.

Dinkmeyer, D. C., & Muro, J. (1979). *Group counseling: Theory and practice.* Itasca, IL: F. E. Peacock.

Dinkmeyer, D. C., Pew, W. L., & Dinkmeyer, D. C., Jr. (1979). *Adlerian counseling and psychotherapy.* Pacific Grove, CA: Brooks/Cole.

Donovan, D. M (2005). Assessment of addictive behaviors for relapse prevention. In D. M. Donovan & G. A. Marlatt (Eds.), *Assessment of addictive behaviors* (2nd ed.) (pp. 1–48). New York: Guilford Press.

Donovan, D. M., Kadden, R. M., DiClemente, C. C., & Carroll, K. M. (1994). Issues in the selection and development of therapies in alcoholism treatment matching research. *Journal of Studies on Alcohol, 12*(December Suppl.), 138–148.

Donovan, D. M., & Mattson, M. E. (1994). Alcoholism treatment matching research: Methodological and clinical approaches. *Journal of Studies on Alcohol, 12*(December Suppl.), 5–14.

Doweiko, H. E. (1990). *Concepts of chemical dependency.* Pacific Grove, CA: Brooks/Cole.

Doweiko, H. E. (1996). *Concepts of chemical dependency* (3rd ed.). Pacific Grove, CA: Brooks/Cole.

Doweiko, H. E. (1999). *Concepts of chemical dependency* (4th ed.). Pacific Grove, CA: Brooks/Cole.

Doweiko, H. E. (2006). *Concepts of chemical dependency* (6th ed.). Belmont, CA: Thomson Brooks/Cole.

Drapkin, M., Yusko, D., Yasinski, C., Oslin, D., Hembree, E. A., & Foa, E. B. (2011). Baseline functioning among individuals with posttraumatic stress disorder and alcohol dependence. *Journal of Substance Abuse Treatment, 41*(2), 186–192.

Dreup, M. L., Johnson, T. J., & Bindl, S. (2011). Mediators of the relationship between religiousness/spirituality and alcohol problems in an adult community sample. *Addictive Behaviors, 36*(12), 1317–1320.

Driessen, W. E., & Hollon, S. D. (2011). Motivational interviewing from a cognitive behavioral perspective. *Cognitive and Behavioral Practice, 18*(1), 70–73.

Dupont, R. L. (1984). *Getting tough on gateway drugs.* Washington, DC: American Psychiatric Press.

Edwards, G. T. (1985). Appalachia: The effects of cultural values on the consumption of alcohol. In L. A. Bennett & G. M. Ames (Eds.), *The American experience with alcohol* (pp. 131–146). New York: Plenum Press.

Ellis, A. (1987, January). *Employee assistance training workshop: A rational-emotive approach.* New York: Institute for Rational-Emotive Therapy.

Ellis, A., McInerney, J. F., DiGiuseppe, R., & Yeager, R. J. (1988). *Rational-emotive therapy with alcoholics and substance abusers.* New York: Pergamon Press.

Emmelkamp, P. M. G. (2004). Behavior therapy with adults. In S. Garfield & A. Bergin (Eds.), *Handbook of psychotherapy and behavior change* (3rd ed., pp. 383–442). New York: Wiley.

Emmelkamp, P. M. G., & Vedel, E. (2006). *Evidence-based treatment for alcohol and drug abuse: A practitioner's guide to theory, methods, and research.* New York: Routledge/Taylor & Francis Group.

Emonson, D., & Vanderbeek, R. (1995). The use of amphetamines in the U.S. Air Force tactical operations during Desert Shield and Storm. *Aviation, Space, and Environmental Medicine, 66*(3), 260–263.

Ewing, J. A. (1984). Detecting alcoholism: The CAGE questionnaire. *JAMA, 252,* 1905–1907.

Feeney, G. F., Connor, J., Young, R., Tucker, J., & McPherson, A. (2006). Combined acamposate and naltrexone with cognitive behavioural therapy is superior to either medication alone for alcohol abstinence: A single centre's experience with pharmacotherapy. *Alcohol and Alcoholism, 41*(3), 321–327.

Feldstein Ewing, S. W., Filbey, F. M., Sabbineni, A., Chandler, L. D., & Hutchison, K. E. (2011). How psychosocial alcohol interventions work: A preliminary look at what fMRI can tell us. *Alcoholism: Clinical and Experimental Research, 35*(4), 643–651.

Fennell, F. (2006). *Stake your claim to happiness: An in-depth analysis of how the Twelve Steps will help anyone find serenity.* Pleasant Prairie, WI: Vision Press.

Fisher, G. L., & Harrison, T. C. (2000). *Substance abuse* (2nd ed.). Boston: Allyn & Bacon.

Ford, B. (1987). *Betty: A glad awakening.* New York: Doubleday.

Frances, R. J. (1988). Update on alcohol and drug disorder treatment. *Journal of Clinical Psychiatry, 49,* 13–17.

Fry, L. J. (1985). Social thought, social movement, and alcoholism: Some implications for AA's linkage with other entities. *Journal of Drug Issues, 15*(1), 135–146.

Garner, B. R., Godley, S. H., Funk, R. R., Dennis, M. L., Smith, J. E., & Godley, M. D. (2009). Exposure to adolescent community reinforcement approach treatment procedures as a mediator of the relationship between adolescent substance abuse treatment retention and outcome. *Journal of Substance Abuse Treatment, 36*(3), 252–264.

Gelles, R. J., & Straus, M. A. (1988). *Intimate violence: The definitive study of the causes and consequences of abuse in the American family.* New York: Simon & Schuster.

George, R. L. (1990). *Counseling the chemically dependent: Theory and practice.* Upper Saddle River, NJ: Prentice Hall.

George, R. L., & Dustin, D. (1988). *Group counseling: Theory and practice.* Upper Saddle River, NJ: Prentice Hall.

Gerbert, B., Bronstone, A., Pantiliat, S., McPhee, S., Allerton, M., & Moe, J. (1999). When asked, patients tell: Disclosure of sensitive health-risk behaviors. *Medical Care 37*(1), 104–111.

Gianini, L., Lundy, S., & Smith, J. E. (2009). Community Reinforcement Approach: CRA and CRAFT programs. In L. M. Cohen, F. L. Collins, A. M. Young, D. E. McChargue, T. R. Leffingwell, & K. L. Cook (Eds.), *Pharmacology and treatment of substance abuse: Evidence- and outcome-based perspectives* (pp. 197–219). New York: Routledge/Taylor & Francis Group.

Godley, S. H., Smith, J. E., Meyers, R. J., & Godley, M. D. (2009). Adolescent Community Reinforcement Approach (A-CRA). In D. W. Springer & A. Rubin (Eds.), *Substance abuse treatment for youth and adults: Clinician's guide to evidence-based practice* (pp. 109–201). Hoboken, NJ: John Wiley & Sons.

Goode, E. (1984). *Drugs in American society.* New York: Knopf.

Gorski, T. T. (1989). *Understanding the Twelve Steps: An interpretation and guide for recovering people.* New York: Simon & Schuster.

Gorski, T. T., & Miller, M. (1986). *Staying sober: A guide for relapse prevention.* Independence, MO: Herald House/Independence Press.

Graham, D. (Speaker). (1986). *Denial, dependency, and codependency in drug treatment programs* (Cassette Recording No. 8–1). Memphis, TN: Department of Counseling and Personnel Services, Memphis State University.

Granholm, E., Tate, S. R., Link, P.C., Lydecker, K. P., Cummins, K. M., McQuaid, J., et al. (2011). Neuropsychological functioning and outcomes of treatment for co-occurring depression and substance use disorders. *American Journal of Drug and Alcohol Abuse, 37*(4), 240–249.

Greene, R. L. (1980). *The MMPI: An interpretative manual.* New York: Grune & Stratton.

Group for the Advancement of Psychiatry. (1990). Substance abuse disorders: A psychiatric priority. *American Journal of Psychiatry, 148,* 1291–1300.

Gruber, K., Chutuape, M. A., & Stitzer, M. L. (2005). Reinforcement-based intensive outpatient treatment for inner city opiate abuser: A short-term evaluation. *Drug and Alcohol Dependence, 57,* 211–223.

Hands, M., & Dear, G. (1994). Codependency: A critical review. *Drug and Alcohol Review, 13,* 437–445.

Hardwick, C. J., Hansen, N. D., & Bairnsfather, L. (1995). Are adult children of alcoholics unique? A study of object relations and reality testing. *International Journal of the Addictions, 30,* 525–539.

Heath, D. B. (1985). American experience with alcohol: Commonalities and contrasts. In L. A. Bennett & G. M. Ames (Eds.), *The American experience with alcohol: Contrasting cultural experiences* (pp. 461–480). New York: Plenum Press.

Hester, R. K., & Miller, J. H. (2006). Economic perspective: Screening and intervention: Computer-based tools for diagnosis and treatment of alcohol problems. *Alcohol Research & Health, 29*(1), 36–40.

Hibbard, S. (1993). Adult children of alcoholics: Narcissism, shame, and the differential effects of paternal and maternal alcoholism. *Psychiatry: Interpersonal and Biological Processes, 56,* 153–162.

Hien, D., Litt, L. C., Cohen, L. R., Miele, G. M., & Campbell, A. (2009). *Trauma services for women in substance abuse treatment: An integrated approach.* Washington, DC: American Psychological Association.

Higgins, S., Silverman, K., & Heil, S. H. (Eds.). (2008). *Contingency management in substance abuse treatment.* New York: Guilford Press.

Hobbs, J. D., Kushner, M. G., Kee, S., Reardon, S. M., & Mauer, E. W. (2011). Meta-analysis of supplemental treatment for depressive and anxiety disorder in patients being treated for alcohol dependence. *American Journal on Addictions, 20*(4), 319–329.

Hodgins, D. (2005). Can patients with alcohol use disorders return to social drinking? Yes, so what should we do about it? *Canadian Journal of Psychiatry, 50*(5), 264–265.

Hoffman, H. (1970). Depression and defensiveness in self-descriptive moods of alcoholics. *Psychological Reports, 26,* 23–26.

Hogg, J. A., & Frank, M. L. (1992). Toward an interpersonal model of codependence and contradependence. *Journal of Counseling and Development, 70,* 371–375.

Holt, M. P. (Ed.).(2006). *Alcohol: A social and cultural history.* New York: Oxford Press.

Homme, L. (1971). *How to use contingency contracting in the classroom.* Champaign, IL: Research Press.

Hser, Y., Evans, E., Huang, D., & Anglin, M. (2004). Relationship between drug treatment services, retention, and outcomes. *Psychiatric Services, 55,* 767–774.

Hunt, R. R. (2002). How effective are pharmacological agents for alcoholism? *Journal of Family Practice, 5*(6), 577.

Iacono, W. G., Malone, S. M., & McGee, M. (2003). Substance use disorders, externalizing psychopathologies and P300 event–related amplitude. *International Journal of Psychophysiology, 48,* 147–178.

Ilgen, M. A., McKellar, J., Moos, R., & Finney, J. (2006). Therapeutic alliance and the relationship between motivation and treatment outcomes in patients with alcohol use disorder. *Journal of Substance Abuse Treatment, 31*(2), 157–162.

Isenhart, C., & Silversmith, D. (1997). MMPI-2 response styles: Generalization to alcoholism assessment. In G. A. Marlatt & G. R. VandenBos (Eds.), *Addictive behaviors: Readings on etiology, prevention, and treatment* (pp. 340–354). Washington, DC: American Psychological Association.

Ivey, A. E., Bradford-Ivey, M., & Simek-Morgan, L. (1993). *Counseling and psychotherapy: A multicultural perspective* (3rd ed.). Boston: Allyn & Bacon.

Jackson, D. D. (1957). The question of family homeostasis. *Psychiatric Quarterly Supplement, 31,* 79–90.

Jacobson, G. R. (1989). A comprehensive approach to pretreatment evaluation: I. Detection, assessment, and diagnosis of alcoholism. In R. K. Hester & W. R. Miller (Eds.), *Handbook of alcoholism treatment approaches: Effective alternatives* (pp. 17–43). Elmsford, NY: Pergamon Press.

Jellinek, E. M. (1946). Phases in the drinking history of alcoholics. *Quarterly Journal of Studies on Alcohol, 7,* 1–88.

Jellinek, E. M. (1952). Phases of alcohol addiction. *Quarterly Journal of Studies on Alcohol, 13,* 673–684.

Jellinek, E. M. (1960). *The disease concept of alcoholism.* New Haven, CT: Hillhouse Press.

Jensen, C. D., Cushing, C. C., Aylward, B. S., Craig, J. T., Sorell, D. M., & Steele, R. G. (2011). Effectiveness of motivational interviewing intentions for adolescent substance use behavior change: A meta-analytic review. *Journal of Consulting and Clinical Psychology, 79*(4), 433–440.

Jessor, R., Chase, J. D., & Donovan, J. E. (1980). Psychosocial correlates of marijuana use and problem drinking in a national sample of adolescents. *American Journal of Public Health, 70,* 604–613.

Jessor, R., & Jessor, S. L. (1977). *Problem behavior and psychosocial development: A longitudinal study of youth.* New York: Academic Press.

Johnson, J. E., Finney, J. W., & Moos, R. H. (2006). End-of-treatment outcomes in cognitive-behavioral treatment and 12-step substance use treatment programs: Do they differ and do they predict 1-year outcomes? *Journal of Substance Abuse Treatment, 31*, 41–50.

Johnson, V. E. (1980). *I'll quit tomorrow.* Minneapolis, MN: Johnson Institute.

Johnson, V. E. (1986). *Intervention: A professional guide.* Minneapolis, MN: Johnson Institute.

Johnson Institute. (1972). *Alcoholism: A treatable disease.* Minneapolis, MN: Author.

Jones, H. E., Wong, C. J., Tuten, M., & Stitzer, M. L. (2005). Reinforcement-based therapy: 12-month evaluation of an outpatient drug-free treatment for heroin users. *Drug and Alcohol Dependence, 79*, 119–128.

Juhnke, G. A. (2002). *Substance abuse assessment and diagnoses.* New York: Brunner-Routledge.

Kaminer, Y., & Slesnick, N. (2005). Evidence-based cognitive behavioral and family therapies for adolescent alcohol and other substance abusers. In M. Galanter (Ed.), *Recent developments in alcoholism: Vol. 17. Alcohol problems in adolescents and young adults* (pp. 385–405). New York: Plenum Press.

Kandel, D. B., Yamaguchi, K., & Chen, K. (1992). Stages of progression in drug involvement from adolescence to adulthood: Further evidence for the gateway theory. *Journal of Studies on Alcohol, 53*, 447–458.

Karpman, S. B. (2007, August). *The new drama triangle.* USATAA/ITAA Conference. Retrieved from www.KarpmanDramaTriangle.com

Kaufman, E., & Pattison, E. M. (1982a). The family and alcoholism. In E. M. Pattison & E. Kaufman (Eds.), *Encyclopedic handbook of alcoholism* (pp. 662–672). New York: Gardner Press.

Kaufman, E., & Pattison, E. M. (1982b). The family and network therapy in alcoholism. In E. M. Pattison & E. Kaufman (Eds.), *Encyclopedic handbook of alcoholism* (pp. 1022–1032). New York: Gardner Press.

Kearney, R. J. (1996). *Within the wall of denial: Conquering addictive behaviors.* New York: Norton.

Kelly, J. F., Stout, R. L., Magill, M., Tonigan, J. S., & Pagano, M. E. (2011). Spirituality in recovery: A lagged meditational analysis of Alcoholics Anonymous' principal theoretical mechanism of behavior change. *Alcoholism: Clinical and Experimental Research, 35*(3), 454–463.

Kelly, T. M., Daley, D. C., & Douaihy, A. B. (2012). Treatment of substance abusing patients with comorbid psychiatric disorder. *Addictive Behaviors, 37*(1), 11–24.

Kerr, A. S., & Hill, E. W. (1992). An exploratory study comparing ACOAs to non-ACOAs on current family relationships. *Alcoholism Treatment Quarterly, 9*, 23–38.

Kettelhack, G. (1992). *First year sobriety: When all that changes is everything.* Center City, MN: Hazelden.

Kiluk, B. D., Nich, C., Babuscio, T., & Carroll, K. M. (2010). Quality versus quantity: Acquisition of coping skills following computerized cognitive behavior therapy of substance abuse disorders. *Addiction, 105*(12), 2120–2127.

Kingree, J. B., & Thompson, M. (2011). Participation in Alcoholics Anonymous and post-treatment abstinence from alcohol and other drugs. *Addictive Behaviors, 36*(8), 882–885.

Kivlahan, D. R., Heiman, J. R., Wright, R. C., Mundt, J. W., & Shupe, J. A. (1991). Treatment cost and rehospitalization rate in schizophrenic outpatients with a history of substance abuse. *Hospital and Community Psychiatry, 41*, 609–614.

Knack, M. A., & Murray, R. (Speakers). (1996). *Chemical dependency treatment issues* (Cassette Recording No. 8-02-08-96-A). Memphis, TN: Memphis Veterans Administration Medical Center/University of Memphis Department of Counseling, Educational Psychology and Research.

Knox, W. J. (1976). Objective psychological measurement and alcoholism: Review of the literature, 1971–72. *Psychological Reports, 38*(Monograph Suppl. 1-V38), 1023–1050.

Knox, W. J. (1980). Objective psychological measurement and alcoholism: Survey of the literature, 1974. *Psychological Reports, 47*(Monograph Suppl. 1-V47), 51–68.

Kofler-Westergren, B., Klof, J. & Mitterauer, B. (2010). Juvenile delinquency: Father absence, conduct disorder, and substance abuse as risk factor triad. *International Journal of Forensic Mental Health, 9*(1), 33–43.

Kranzler, H. (2006). Medications to treat heavy drinking: Are we there yet? *Addiction, 101*(2), 153–154.

Kranzler, H., & Anton, R. (1994). Implications of recent neuropharmacologic research for understanding the etiology and development of alcoholism. *Journal of Consulting and Clinical Psychology, 62*, 1116–1126.

Kunitz, S. J., & Levy, J. E. (1974). Changing ideas of alcohol use among Navaho Indians. *Quarterly Journal of Studies on Alcohol, 46*, 953–960.

Lange, W., Reker, M., & Driessen, M. (2008). Community Reinforcement Approach: A review of an integrative approach to substance abuse treatment. *Sucht: Zeitschrift für Wissenschaft und Praxis, 54*(1), 123–223.

Lawson, G. W., Ellis, D. C., & Rivers, P. C. (Eds.). (1984). *Essentials of chemical dependency counseling.* Rockville, MD: Aspen Systems.

Levine, H. (1984). The alcohol problem in America: From temperance to alcoholism. *British Journal of Addiction, 79*, 109–119.

Liepman, M., White, W. T., & Nirenberg, T. D. (1986). Children in alcoholic families. In D. C. Lewis & C. N. Williams (Eds.), *Providing care for children of alcoholics: Clinical and research perspectives* (pp. 39–64). Pompano Beach, FL: Health Communications.

Litt, M. D., Kadden, R. M., Kebela-Comier, E., & Petry, N. (2007). Changing network support for drinking: Initial findings from the Network Support Project. *Journal of Consulting and Clinical Psychology, 75*(4), 542–555.

Longabaugh, R., Wirtz, P. W., Beattie, M., Noel, N., & Stout, R. (1997). Matching treatment focus to patient social investment and support: Eighteen month follow-up results. In G. Marlatt & G. VanderBos (Eds.), *Addictive behaviors: Readings on etiology, prevention, and treatment* (pp. 602–628). Washington, DC: American Psychological Association.

Longshore, D., & Teruya, C. (2006). Treatment motivation in drug users: A theory-based analysis. *Drug and Alcohol Dependence 81*(2), 179–188.

Luczak, S. B., Glatt, S. J., & Wall, T. L. (2009). Meta-analyses of ALDH2 and ADH1B with alcohol dependence in Asians. In G. A. Marlatt & K. Witkiewitz (Eds.), *Addictive behaviors: New readings on etiology, prevention, and treatment* (pp. 677–712). Washington, DC: American Psychological Association.

Lukas, S. E., Penetar, D., Berko, J., Vicens, L., Palmer, C., & Mallya, G. (2005). An extract of the Chinese herbal root kudzu reduces alcohol drinking by heavy drinkers in a naturalistic setting. *Alcoholism: Clinical and Experimental Research, 29*(5), 756–762.

Lukoff, I. F. (1980). Toward a sociology of drug use. In D. J. Lettieri, M. Sayers, & H. W. Pearson (Eds.), *Theories on drug abuse: Selected contemporary perspectives* (NIDA Research Monograph No. 30). Rockville, MD: National Institute on Drug Abuse.

Lyon, M. A., & Seefeldt, R. W. (1995). Failure to validate personality characteristics of adult children of alcoholics: A replication and extension. *Alcoholism Treatment Quarterly, 12*, 69–85.

MacAndrew, C., & Edgerton, R. B. (1969). *Drunken comportment.* Chicago: Aldine.

MacDonald, J. (1961). *The murderer and his victim.* Springfield, IL: Charles C Thomas.

Majer, J. M., Jason, L. A., Ferrari, J. R., & Miller, S. A. (2011). 12-step involvement among a U.S. national sample of Oxford House residents. *Journal of Substance Abuse Treatment 41*(1), 37–44.

Maisto, S. A., Krenek, M., Chung, T., Martin, C. S., Clark, D., & Cornelius, J. (2011). A comparison of the concurrent and predictive validity of three measures of readiness to change alcohol use in a clinical sample of adolescents. *Journal of Studies on Alcohol and Drugs, 72*(4), 592–601.

Manson, M. D. (1949). A psychometric determination of alcohol addiction. *American Journal of Psychiatry, 106*(3), 199–205.

Marlatt, G. A. (1997). Introduction. In G. A. Marlatt & G. R. VandenBos (Eds.), *Addictive behaviors: Readings on etiology, prevention, and treatment* (pp. xi–xxv). Washington, DC: American Psychological Association.

Marlatt, G. A., & Gordon, J. R. (Eds.). (1985). *Relapse prevention.* New York: Guilford Press.

Marlatt, G. A., & Witkiewitz, K. (2009). Introduction. In G. A. Marlatt & K. Witkiewitz (Eds.), *Addictive behaviors: New readings on etiology, prevention, and treatment* (pp. 3–16) Washington, DC: American Psychological Association.

Martin, T., Christopher, P. J., Houck, J. M., & Moyers, T. B. (2011). The structure of client language and drinking outcomes in project match. *Psychology of Addictive Behaviors, 25*(3), 439–445.

Mason, M., Pate, P., Drapkin, M., & Sozino, K. (2011). Motivational interviewing integrated with social network counseling for female adolescents: A randomized pilot study in urban primary care. *Journal of Substance Abuse Treatment, 41*(2), 148–155.

Matheson, F. I., Doherty, S., & Grant, B. A. (2011). Substance abuse aftercare prevents recidivism among women on parole. *Clinician's Research Digest, 29*, 9.

Mathew, R. D., Wilson, W. H., Blazer, D. G., & George, L. K. (1993). Psychiatric disorders in adult children of alcoholics: Data from the epidemiologic catchment area project. *American Journal of Psychiatry, 150*, 793–800.

Maxwell, R. (1986). *Breakthrough: What to do when alcoholism or chemical dependency hits close to home.* New York: Ballantine.

McConnaughy, E. A., Prochaska, J. O., & Velicer, W. F. (1983). Stages of change in psychotherapy: Measurement and sample profiles. *Psychotherapy: Theory, Research, and Practice, 20*, 368–375.

McCrady, B. S. (1982). Marital dysfunction: Alcoholism and marriage. In E. M. Pattison & E. Kaufman (Eds.), *Encyclopedic handbook of alcoholism* (pp. 673–685). New York: Gardner Press.

McDermott, P., Alterman, A., Brown, L., Zaballero, A., Snider, E., & McKay, J. (1997). Construct refinement and confirmation for the Addiction Severity Index. In G. A. Marlatt & G. R. VandenBos (Eds.), *Addictive behaviors: Readings on etiology, prevention, and treatment* (pp. 323–339). Washington, DC: American Psychological Association.

McGowan, S. (1991, October). Effects of parental alcoholism. *AACD Guidepost*, pp. 1, 8, 10.

McKay, J. R. (2005). Is there a case for extended interventions for alcohol and drug use disorders? *Addiction, 100*(11), 1594–1610.

McKay, J. R., & Maisto, S. A. (1993). An overview and critique of advances in the treatment of alcohol use disorders. *Drugs and Society, 8*, 1–29.

McLellan, A. T., Grissom, G., Zanis, D., & Randall, M. (1997). Problem-service matching in addiction treatment: A prospective study in four programs. *Archives of General Psychiatry, 54*(8), 730–735.

McLellan, A. T., Kushiner, H., Metzger, D., Peters, R., Smith, I., & Grisson, G. (1992). The fifth edition of the Addiction Severity Index. *Journal of Substance Treatment, 9*, 199–213.

McLellan, A. T., Luborsky, L., O'Brien, C. P., & Woody, G. E. (1980). An improved diagnostic instrument for substance abuse patients: The Addiction Severity Index. *Journal of Nervous and Mental Diseases, 168*, 26–33.

McMullin, R. E., & Giles, T. R. (1981). *Cognitive behavior therapy: A restructuring approach*. New York: Grune & Stratton.

McMurran, M. (2006). Controlled drinking for offenders. *Addiction Research and Theory, 14*(1), 59–65.

Meichenbaum, D. (1977). *Cognitive behavior modification: An integrative approach*. New York: Plenum Press.

Meichenbaum, D. (1985). *Stress-inoculation training*. New York: Pergamon Press.

Meier, P. S., Donmall, M., McElduff, P., Barrowclough, C., & Heller, R. (2006). The role of the early therapeutic alliance in predicting drug treatment dropout. *Drug and Alcohol Dependence, 83*(1), 57–64.

Mersey, D. J. (2003). Recognition of alcohol and substance abuse. *American Family Physician, 67*, 1529–1536.

Meyers, R. J., & Smith, J. E. (1995). *Clinical guide to alcohol treatment: The community reinforcement approach*. New York: Guilford Press.

Meyers, R. J., & Smith, J. E. (1997). Getting off the fence: Procedures to engage treatment resistant drinkers. *Journal of Substance Abuse Treatment, 14*, 467–472.

Meyers, R. J., & Squires, D. D. (n.d.). *The community reinforcement approach: A guideline developed for the Behavioral Health Recovery Management project*. Springfield: Illinois Department of Human Services' Office of Alcoholism and Substance Abuse.

Miller, E. T., Neal, D. J., Roberts, L. J., Baer, J. S., Cressler, S. O., Metrik, J., et al. (2009). Test–retest reliability of alcohol measures: Is there a difference between Internet-based assessment and traditional methods? In G. A. Marlatt & K. Witkiewitz (Eds.), *Addictive behaviors: New readings on etiology, prevention, and treatment* (pp. 323–342). Washington, DC: American Psychological Association.

Miller, G. (1983). *SASSI: Substance Abuse Subtle Screening Inventory*. Bloomington, IN: SASSI Institute.

Miller, M. L., & Saunders, S. M. (2011). A naturalistic study of the associations between changes in alcohol problems, spiritual functioning, and psychiatric symptoms. *Psychology of Addictive Behaviors, 25*(3), 455–461.

Miller, W. R. (1995). Increasing motivation for change. In R. K. Hester & W. R. Miller (Eds.), *Handbook of alcoholism treatment approaches* (pp. 45–63). New York: Allyn & Bacon.

Miller, W. R. (1998). Enhancing motivation for change. In W. R. Miller & N. Heather (Eds.), *Treating addictive behaviors* (2nd ed., pp. 135–147). New York: Plenum Press.

Miller, W. R., & Rollnick, S. (2002). *Motivational interviewing* (2nd ed.). New York: Guilford Press.

Miller, W. R., & Tonigan, J. S. (1996). Assessing drinkers' readiness to change: The Stages of Change Readiness Scale and Treatment of Eagerness Scale (SOCRATES). *Psychology of Addictive Behaviors, 10*, 81–89.

Moyers, T. B., & Houck, J. (2011). Combining motivational interviewing with cognitive-behavioral treatments for substance abuse: Lessons learned from the Combine research project. *Cognitive and Behavior Practice 18*(1), 38–45.

Mumford, G. (2005). One drink too many. *Monitor on Psychology, 36*(8), 62–63.

Narcotics Anonymous. (2004). *Sponsorship, revised: What does a sponsor do?* Van Nuys, CA: Author. Available at www.na.org/?ID=litfiles/us_english/IP/EN3111.pdf

National Foundation for Brain Research. (1992). *The cost of disorders of the brain*. Washington, DC: Author.

National Institute on Alcohol Abuse and Alcoholism (NIAAA). (2011). *Alcohol screening and brief intervention for youth*. National Institute of Health. Available at www.niaaa.nih.gov/Publications/EducationTrainingMaterials/YouthGuide

National Institute on Drug Abuse. (2003, June 25). *NIDA info facts*. Retrieved September 26, 2003, from www.nida.nih.gov/Infoax/treatmenttrends.html

Neisser, U. (1976). *Cognition and reality: Principles and implications of cognitive psychology*. San Francisco: Freeman.

Nielsen, B., Nielsen, A., & Wraae, O. (1998). Patient treatment matching improves compliance of alcoholics in outpatient treatment. *Journal of Nervous and Mental Disease, 186*(12), 752–760.

Noble, E., Blum, K., Ritchie, T., Montgomery, A., & Sheridan, P. (1991). Allelic association of the D2 dopamine receptor gene with receptor-binding characteristics in alcoholism. *Archives of General Psychiatry, 48*, 648–654.

Nordfjaern, T. (2011). Relapse patterns among patients with substance use disorders. *Journal of Substance Use, 16*(4), 313–329.

Nutt, D. J., King, L. A., & Phillips, L. D. (2010). Drug harms in the UK: A multi-criteria decision analysis. *Lancet, 376*(9752), 1558–1665.

O'Brien, P. E., & Gaborit, M. (1992). Codependency: A disorder separate from chemical dependency. *Journal of Clinical Psychology, 48*, 129–136.

Oetting, E. R., & Beauvais, F. (1986). Peer cluster theory: Drugs and the adolescent. *Journal of Counseling and Development, 65*, 17–22.

O'Farrell, T. J. (2011). Family therapy. In M. Galanter & H. D. Kleber (Eds.), *Psychotherapy for the treatment of drug abuse* (pp. 329–350). Arlington, VA: American Psychiatric Publishing.

O'Farrell, T. J., Murphy, M., Alter, J., & Fals-Stewart, W. (2010). Behavioral family counseling for substance abuse: A treatment development pilot study. *Addictive Behaviors, 35*(1), 1–6.

Office of National Drug Control Policy. (2004). *National drug control strategy*. Washington, DC: U.S. Government Printing Office.

Ohlsen, M. (1970). *Group counseling.* New York: Holt, Rinehart & Winston.

Ornstein, P. (1976). The Alcadd Test as a predictor of post-hospital drinking behavior. *Psychological Reports, 43,* 611–617.

Pantalon, M. V. (2011, October 1). How to get anyone to say yes fast. *Bottom Line, 32*(19), 8–9.

Parker, C. (Speaker). (1986). *Alcoholic inpatient treatment* (Cassette Recording No. 8-2). Memphis, TN: Department of Counseling and Personnel Services, Memphis State University.

Pattison, E. M., & Kaufman, E. (1982). The alcoholism syndrome: Definitions and models. In E. M. Pattison & E. Kaufman (Eds.), *Encyclopedic handbook of alcoholism* (pp. 3–30). New York: Gardner Press.

Perez, J. F. (1985). *Counseling the alcoholic.* Muncie, IN: Accelerated Development.

Pernanen, K. (1976). The biology of alcoholism. In B. Kissin & H. Begleiter (Eds.), *Social aspects of alcoholism* (Vol. 4, pp. 42–57). New York: Plenum Press.

Petry, N. M. (2012). *Contingency management for substance abuse treatment: A guide to implementing evidence-based practice.* New York: Routledge/Taylor & Francis Group.

Petry, N. M., Martin, B., Cooney, J. L., & Kranzler, H. R. (2000). Give them prizes and they will come: Contingency management for treatment of alcohol dependence. *Journal of Consulting and Clinical Psychology, 68*(2), 250–257.

Polcin, D. L. (1992). A comprehensive model for adolescent chemical dependency treatment. *Journal of Counseling and Development, 70,* 376–382.

Poley, W., Lea, G., & Vibe, G. (1979). *Alcoholism: A treatment manual.* New York: Gardner Press.

Polivy, J., & Herman, C. P. (2002). If at first you don't succeed. *American Psychologist, 57,* 677–689.

Powers, M. B., Vedel, E., & Emmelkamp, P. G. (2008). Behavioral couples therapy (BET) for alcohol and drug use disorders: A meta-analysis. *Clinical Psychology Review, 28*(6), 952–962.

Price, M. (2008). Genes matter in addiction. *Monitor on Psychology, 38*(6), 16.

Prochaska, J. O., & DiClemente, C. C. (1982). Transtheoretical therapy: Toward a more integrative model of change. *Psychotherapy: Theory, Research, & Practice, 19,* 276–288.

Prochaska, J. O., DiClemente, C. C., & Norcross, J. C. (1992). In search of how people change. *American Psychologist, 47,* 1102–1114.

Ramsay, J. R., & Newman, C. F. (2000). Substance abuse. In F. M. Dattilo & A. Freeman (Eds.), *Cognitive-behavioral strategies in crisis intervention* (2nd ed., pp. 137–156). New York: Guilford Press.

Ray, O., & Ksir, C. (2004). *Drugs, society and human behavior* (10th ed.). New York: McGraw-Hill.

Reilly, D. M. (1992). Drug abusing families: Interfamilial dynamics and brief triphasic treatment. In E. Kaufman & P. Kaufman (Eds.), *Family theory of drug and alcohol abuse* (pp. 105–119). Boston: Allyn & Bacon.

Renner, J. A. (2004). Alcoholism and alcohol abuse. In T. A. Stern & J. B. Herman (Eds.), *Massachusetts General Hospital psychiatry update and board preparation* (2nd ed., pp. 230–252). New York: McGraw-Hill.

Reynolds, E. W., & Bada, H. S. (2003). Pharmacology of drugs of abuse. *Obstetrics and Gynecological Clinics of North America, 30,* 501–522.

Robinson, E., Krentzman, A. R., Webb, J. R., & Brower, K. J. (2011). Six-month changes in spirituality and religiousness in alcoholics predict drinking outcomes at nine months. *Journal of Studies on Alcohol and Drugs, 72*(4), 660–668.

Roozen, H. G., de Waart, R., van der Windt, D., van den Brink, W., de Jong, C., & Kerkhof, J. (2006). A systematic review of the effectiveness of naltrexone in the maintenance treatment of opioid and alcohol dependence. *European Neuropsychopharmacology, 16*(5), 311–323.

Safer, D. J. (1994). The impact of recent lawsuits on methylphenidate sales. *Clinical Pediatrics, 33,* 166–168.

Schaef, A. W. (1986). *Co-dependence: Misunderstood—mistreated.* San Francisco: Harper & Row.

Schaler, J. A. (2000). *Addiction is a choice.* Chicago: Open Court.

Schmidt, E. (1996). Rational recovery: Finding an alternative for addiction treatment. *Alcoholism Treatment Quarterly, 14*(4), 47–57.

Schmidt, E. A., Carns, A., & Chandler, C. (2001). Assessing the efficacy of rational recovery in the treatment of alcohol/drug dependency. *Alcoholism Treatment Quarterly, 19*(1), 97–106.

Schmidt, L. M., Hesse, M., & Lykke, J. (2011). The impact of substance use disorders on the course of schizophrenia—a 15-year follow-up study: Dual diagnosis over 15 years. *Schizophrenia Research, 130*(1–3), 228–233.

Schuckit, M. A. (1986). Primary men alcoholics with histories of suicide attempts. *Journal of Studies on Alcohol, 47,* 78–81.

Schuckit, M. A. (1994). Low level of response to alcohol as a predictor of future alcoholism. *American Journal of Psychiatry, 151*(2), 184–189.

Schuckit, M. A. (1995). *Drug and alcohol abuse: A clinical guide to diagnosis and treatment* (4th ed.). New York: Plenum Press.

Schuckit, M. A. (1998). Biological, psychological, and environmental predictors of the alcoholism risks: A longitudinal study. *Journal of Studies on Alcohol, 59*(5), 485–494.

Schuckit, M. A. (2000). *Drug and alcohol abuse: A clinical guide to diagnosis and treatment* (5th ed.). New York: Plenum Press.

Schuckit, M. A., Edenberg, H. J., Kalmijn, J., Flurry, L., Smith, T. L., Reich, T., et al. (2001). A genome-wide search for genes that relate to a low level of response to alcohol.

Alcoholism: Clinical and Experimental Research, 25(3), 323–329.

Schumacher, J. E., Milby, J. B., Wallace, D., Meehan, D. C., Kertesz, S., Vuchinich, R., et al. (2007). Meta-analysis of day treatment and contingency-management dismantling research: Birmingham Homeless Cocaine Studies (1990–2006). *Journal of Consulting and Clinical Psychology, 75*(5), 823–828.

Selzer, M. L. (1971). The Michigan Alcoholism Screening Test (MAST): The quest for a new diagnostic instrument. *American Journal of Psychiatry, 3,* 176–181.

Senchak, M., Leonard, K., Greene, B., & Carroll, A. (1995). Comparisons of adult children of alcoholics, divorced, and control parents in four outcome domains. *Psychology of Addictive Behaviors, 9*(3), 147–156.

Seneviratne, A., & Daeppen, J. (2009). Implications of the family in the treatment of alcohol dependencies: A review of the literature. *Alcoologie et Addictologie, 31*(4), 283–293.

Shadel, W. G., & Shiffman, S. (2005). Assessment of smoking behavior. In D. M. Donovan & G. A. Marlatt (Eds.), *Assessment of addictive behaviors* (2nd ed., pp. 113–154). New York: Guilford Press.

Shearer, R. J. (1968). *Manual of alcoholism of the American Medical Association.* Washington, DC: American Medical Association.

Sher, K. J. (1991). *Children of alcoholics: A critical appraisal of theory and research.* Chicago: University of Chicago Press.

Sher, K. J., Walitzer, K. S., Wood, P. K., & Brent, E. E. (1991). Characteristics of children of alcoholics: Putative risk factors, substance abuse, and psychopathology. *Journal of Abnormal Psychology, 100,* 427–448.

Shulman, B. (1973). *Contributions to individual psychology: Selected papers of Bernard Shulman.* Chicago: Alfred Adler Institute.

Shupe, L. (1953). Alcohol and crime. *Journal of Criminal Law and Criminal Political Science, 44,* 661–664.

Sklare, G. (1997). *Brief counseling works: A solution-focused approach for school counselors.* Thousand Oaks, CA: Corwin Press.

Slutske, W. S., Heath, A. C., Madden, P. A., Bucholz, K., Statham, D., & Martin, N. (2002). Personality and the genetic risk for alcohol dependence. *Journal of Abnormal Psychology, 111,* 124–133.

Smith, J. E., Meyers, R. J., & Delaney, H. D. (1998). The community reinforcement approach with homeless alcohol-dependent individuals. *Journal of Consulting and Clinical Psychology, 66,* 541–548.

Smith, J. W. (1982). Treatment of alcoholism in aversion conditioning hospitals. In E. M. Pattison & E. Kaufman (Eds.), *Encyclopedic handbook of alcoholism* (pp. 874–884). New York: Gardner Press.

Sobell, M. B., & Sobell, L. C. (1978). *Behavioral treatment of alcohol problems: Individualized therapy and controlled drinking.* New York: Plenum Press.

Sobell, M. B., & Sobell, L. C. (2006). Obstacles to the adoption of low risk drinking goals in the treatment of alcohol problems in the United States: A commentary. *Addiction Research and Theory, 14*(1), 19–24.

Sobell, M. B., & Sobell, L. C. (2011). *Group therapy for substance use disorders: A motivational cognitive-behavioral approach.* New York: Guilford Press.

Söderlund, L. L., Madson, M. B., Rubak, S., & Nilsen, P. (2011). A systematic review of motivational interviewing training for general health care practitioners. *Patient Education and Counseling, 84*(1), 16–26.

Spotts, J. V., & Shontz, F. C. (1980). A life theme of chronic drug abuse. In D. J. Lettieri, M. Sayers, & H. W. Pearson (Eds.), *Theories on drug abuse: Selected contemporary perspectives* (NIDA Research Monograph No. 30, pp. 59–70). Rockville, MD: National Institute on Drug Abuse.

Stein, B., Orland, M., & Sturm, R. (2000). The effect of copayments on drug and alcohol treatment following inpatient detoxification under managed care. *Psychiatric Services, 51,* 195–198.

Stuckey, R. F., & Harrison, J. S. (1982). The alcoholism rehabilitation center. In E. M. Pattison & E. Kaufman (Eds.), *Encyclopedic handbook of alcoholism* (pp. 865–873). New York: Gardner Press.

Substance Abuse and Mental Health Services Administration. (2005). *Results from the 2005 National Survey on Drug Use and Health: National findings.* Retrieved April 3, 2007, from http://oas.samhsa.gov/nsduh/2k5nsduh/2k5results.htm

Sudak, D. M. (2011). *Combining CBT and medication: An evidence-based approach.* Hoboken, NJ: John Wiley & Sons.

Suh, J. J., Pettinati, H., Kampman, K., & Obrien, C. (2006). The status of disulfiram: A half century later. *Journal of Clinical Psychopharmacology, 26*(3), 290–302.

Svanum, S., & McAdoo, W. B. (1989). Predicting rapid relapse following treatment for chemical dependence: A matched subject design. *Journal of Consulting and Clinical Psychology, 34,* 1027–1030.

Swendsen, J. D., Conway, K., Rounsaville, B., & Merikas, K. (2002). Are personality traits familial risk factors for substance use disorder? Results of a controlled family study. *American Journal of Psychiatry, 159,* 1760–1766.

Taft, C. T., O'Farrell, T. J., Doron-Lamarca, S., Panuzio, J., Suvak, M. K., Gagnon, D. R., et al. (2010). Longitudinal risk factors for intimate partner violence among men in treatment for alcohol use disorders. *Journal of Consulting and Clinical Psychology, 78*(6), 924–935.

Toneatto, T. (2005). Cognitive versus behavioral treatment of concurrent alcohol dependence and agoraphobia: A pilot study. *Addictive Behaviors, 30*(1), 115–125.

Tracy, S. W. (2007). *Alcoholism in America: From reconstruction to prohibition.* Baltimore, MD: Johns Hopkins Press.

Trice, H. M., & Beyer, J. M. (1982). Job-based alcoholism programs: Motivating problem drinkers to rehabilitation. In E. M. Pattison & E. Kaufman (Eds.), *Encyclopedic handbook of alcoholism* (pp. 954–978). New York: Gardner Press.

Trice, H. M., & Staudenmeier, W. J., Jr. (1989). A sociocultural history of Alcoholics Anonymous. In M. Galanter (Ed.), *Recent developments in alcoholism: Vol. 7. Treatment research* (pp. 11–35). New York: Plenum Press.

Trois, F. P. (1995). An examination of Cermak's conceptualization of codependency as personality disorder. *Alcoholism Treatment Quarterly, 12*, 1–15.

Tuten, L. M., Jones, H. E., Schaffer, C. M., & Stitzer, M. L. (2012). *Reinforcement-based treatment for substance abuse disorders: A comprehensive behavioral approach.* Washington, DC: American Psychological Association.

Uhle, S. M. (1994). Codependence: Contextual variables in the language of social pathology. *Issues in Mental Health Nursing, 15*, 307–313.

UKATT Research Team. (2005). Effectiveness of treatment for alcohol problems: Findings of the randomized UK alcohol treatment trial. *British Medical Journal, 331*, 331–339.

Vaillant, G. E., & Milofsky, E. (1982). The etiology of alcoholism: A prospective viewpoint. *American Psychologist, 37*, 494–503.

Vasilaki, E. I., Hosier, S. G., & Cox, W. M. (2006). The efficacy of motivational interviewing as a brief intervention for excessive drinking: A meta-analytic review. *Alcohol and Alcoholism, 41*(3), 328–335.

Walker, R., Rosvall, T., Field, C. A., Allen, S., McDonald, D., Salim, Z., et al. (2010). Disseminating contingency management to increase attendance in two community substance abuse treatment centers: Lessons learned. *Journal of Substance Abuse Treatment, 39*(3), 202–209.

Wallace, J. (1978). Critical issues in alcoholism therapy. In S. Zimberg, J. Wallace, & S. B. Blume (Eds.), *Practical approaches to alcoholism psychotherapy* (pp. 31–46). New York: Plenum Press.

Wegscheider-Cruse, S. (1984). Codependency: The therapeutic void. In *Codependency: An emerging issue* (pp. 1–19). Pompano Beach, FL: Health Communications.

Wegscheider-Cruse, S. (1985). *Choice-making for codependents, adult children, and spirituality seekers.* Pompano Beach, FL: Health Communications.

Wegscheider-Cruse, S. (1989). *Another chance: Hope and health for the alcoholic family* (2nd ed.). Palo Alto, CA: Science and Behavior Books.

Willoughby, F. W., & Edens, J. F. (1996). Construct validity and predictive utility of the Stages of Change Scale for alcoholics. *Journal of Substance Abuse, 8*, 275–291.

Wills, T. A., & Shiffman, S. (1985). Coping and substance abuse: A conceptual framework. In S. Shiffman & T. A. Wills (Eds.), *Coping and substance abuse* (pp. 3–24). Orlando, FL: Academic Press.

Witkiewitz, K., & Marlatt, G. A. (2009). Relapse prevention for alcohol and drug problems: That was Zen, this is Tao. In G. A. Marlatt & K. Witkiewitz (Eds.), *Addictive behaviors: New readings on etiology, prevention, and treatment* (pp. 403–428). Washington, DC: American Psychological Association.

Wolin, S. J., & Wolin, S. (1995). Resilience among youth growing up in substance abusing families. *Pediatric Clinics of North America, 42*, 415–429.

Wong, C. J., Silverman, K., & Bigelow, G. E. (2008). Alcohol. In S. T. Higgins, M. K. Silverman, & S. H. Heil (Eds.), *Contingency management in substance abuse* (pp. 120–139). New York: Guilford Press.

World Health Organization (WHO). (1952). Expert Committee on Mental Health, Alcoholism Subcommittee: Second report (World Health Organization Technical Service Report No. 48). In H. Milt (Ed.), *Basic handbook on alcoholism* (pp. 121–135). Fairhaven, NJ: Scientific Aids.

Yeager, K. R., & Gregoire, T. K. (2006). Crisis intervention application of brief solution-focused therapy in addictions. In A. Roberts (Ed.), *Crisis Intervention Handbook* (3rd ed., pp. 566–601). New York: Oxford University Press.

Young, L. B. (2011). Joe Sixpack: Normality, deviance, and the disease model of alcoholism. *Culture & Psychology, 17*(3), 378–397.

Zimberg, S. (1982). Psychotherapy in the treatment of alcoholism. In E. M. Pattison & E. Kaufman (Eds.), *Encyclopedic handbook of alcoholism* (pp. 999–1010). New York: Gardner Press.

Zwerling, I. (1959). Psychiatric findings in an interdisciplinary study of 46 alcoholic patients. *Quarterly Journal of Studies on Alcohol, 20*, 543–554.

CHAPTER **12**

Personal Loss: Bereavement and Grief

One of your authors is about to fill his gas tank at a self-serve when he notices an elderly woman struggling to fill her tank. It becomes apparent to your knight-in-shining-armor that he needs to render assistance to this clearly distraught and frustrated woman. He does so and immediately gets into a grief counseling session as the woman has an emotional come-apart at the gas pump. Her husband, you see, took care of all the "mechanical" issues in their lives, including filling the car with gas, for 50 years of marriage. After he dropped dead from a heart attack 2 months ago, this woman's world turned from a very secure, knowable, and predictable life into a fairly good working analysis of what we describe in Chapter 1 as chaos theory. A hour-and-a-half later your chivalric, somewhat disheveled author, now late for a meeting with the dean, who, while sitting in a car in a strip mall parking lot, has experienced a range of emotions from his unintended client that range from hysterical grief to rage against her husband's chauvinism that has left her helpless with things "mechanical," gets her somewhat stabilized after a cell phone call to a friend of the woman to come and take her home and a commitment from this bereaved and grief-stricken woman to go to a church in town that has workshops and counseling for the newly widowed.

Your author is not a good one-trial learner. A number of years ago when he was a junior high school counselor who had become a self-styled expert in parent training (subject of his doctoral dissertation), he decided to really show how astute he was at ferreting out parenting issues after he invited a school psychologist over to see how his revolutionary communications/behavior management parenting class (it was 1971)

worked. A mother was talking about her seventh-grade daughter who was acting rebellious and oppositionally defiant since her father passed away more than a year ago. It was about 8:30 P.M. with another half hour to go in the meeting. Dr. Freud decided to make an astute interpretation of the mother's complaints and reflected to her that it appeared it was not just the daughter, but she who had not gotten over the death of her husband. That keen insight started a delayed grieving process that was not the highlight of the evening for the other parents, who would have rather been almost anywhere than the teacher's lounge of Jefferson Junior High School at that point in time. The ending of this story occurred at about 10:30 P.M. when your now thoroughly ego-deflated and wrung-out author drove the parent back to her home in a small rural community 15 miles from school and had to listen to his school psychologist friend, who had to follow him out to her farm, needling him about his therapeutic insight on the ride back to town. This is a trilogy, as most tales of wisdom are, so there is one anecdote more to go.

At one point in his life, your self-same author was thoroughly burned out with education and counseling and decided to get into the oil business. He ran a bulk petroleum products plant in Wisconsin. In that capacity he served a number of dairy farmers by making home deliveries of gas and diesel fuel in his tank delivery truck. One farmer in particular was a jovial if somewhat rowdy individual who had a reputation for wrecking bars when he got a little too much beer in his system. As a result, this robust young dairy farmer had a good deal of respect and some bit of fear from his neighbors. One spring day he was gearing up to

414

cultivate for spring planting. His 5-year-old son was badgering him to ride on the tractor, but dad thought it too dangerous so he was sent back into the yard to play. Somehow the 5-year-old was able to get over the locked gate into the feed lot. There, he turned on the automatic feeding system, got caught on an auger and was chewed to pieces. This was a horribly traumatic death with a closed casket. Empty words or no words of condolence could be said to the devastated parents. Your author had a Ph.D. in counseling psychology, but had little experience in grief work, as the previous anecdote would indicate. No one knew what to say, or indeed was afraid to say anything to attempt to assuage his grief and self-blame for his son's death. Finally, after watching this desolated and isolated young man for a month after the funeral, your author sucked up his courage, made plans to finish his route early, walked into the milking parlor, and told the aggrieved farmer that in another life he had been a counselor and was willing to talk and listen to him about his son's death and the circumstances surrounding it. That conversation went on for 2 hours. It was one of the toughest counseling sessions your author ever had. It was also a turning point, because it convinced him that he didn't want to be a millionaire oil baron, but needed to get back into the business of counseling. So the point of this long-winded opening is . . .

To be human in the world as we know it is to experience loss. While you may, if you are really lucky, never experience any of the other crises in this book, you are going to experience loss. Almost every chapter in this book has statistics about the chapter's affliction in it. This one doesn't, because sooner or later you are all going to experience at least one loss—your own! Besides that ultimate loss, you will also experience loss in two other ways. First, you will lose something near and dear to you. Second, and just as important, if you go into the human service business, you are also going to experience dealing with clients who have experienced loss. Actually, you are going to deal with it a lot more than you think because it's not just death you are dealing with, but almost any other kind of loss you can think of having. Therefore, this chapter on loss is indeed about you, and perhaps your denial and fear of it.

Of all the tough issues that crisis workers face, probably none is more difficult than dealing with individuals who have suffered a traumatic loss. The Dyregrovs (2008) capture the essence of this in a father's response to the traumatic death of his child: "We are taught to handle most situations, but whenever sudden, traumatic death occurs, we are completely helpless both in terms of handling it personally and giving others support" (p. 47).

Our students, who are required to do "volunteer" work, avoid hospice like the plague for the most part. However, the unlucky few whose schedule won't fit other programs are practically gang-pressed into it. Scared pea green going in, they invariably come out changed and report it is one of the most positive, life-changing experiences they have had. So while you might enjoy a root canal more than reading this chapter, know full well that you will need it, and perhaps, like others, you will come to find satisfaction in doing a job few others care to do or in fact can do very well.

It is not uncommon as you read and discuss this chapter to experience some potent feelings regarding loss that you thought were pretty much buried. As we indicated in Chapter 7, Posttraumatic Stress Disorder, when we use Charles Figley's (1985) traumagram we always ask people to graph their losses as well as their traumas. Lots of times when we are absolutely perplexed as to the reasons people are manifesting the problems they do, the reason lies with an unreconciled loss. So understand that what you read here may well cause some of the same feelings to arise in you. For that reason, our course syllabus in crisis intervention specifically states that if you have suffered a recent or unreconciled loss, this is probably not the best time for you to take this course. That being said, if you are experiencing discomfort in reading this chapter, we urge you to talk to your professor or supervisor to find a grief counselor and talk though your loss.

Recovery from major *primary* losses, such as the death of a friend, child, parent, or spouse, may require several years, and the traumatic event may have a profoundly lasting effect on the remainder of one's life (Costa & Holliday, 1994; Finkbeiner, 1998; Lerner, 2000; McCown & Davies, 1995; Morse, 2000; Pearlman, Schwalbe, & Cloitre, 2010). Although generally not as catastrophic as death, other loss events—job loss, bankruptcy, physical paralysis, job disability, a forced move to a different residence, chronic illness (both physical and mental), geographic and school change, limb amputation, divorce, or loss of one's home or possessions from flood or fire—can have many or all of the same ramifications (Colgrove, Bloomfield, & McWilliams, 1991, p. 2; Farina, 2000; Lerner, 2000; McCown & Davies, 1995; Michaels, 2009; Morse, 2000; Schliebner & Peregoy, 1994).

Terms Critical to Understanding Loss

The objective of this chapter is to provide a general survey of ways in which crisis workers may help clients understand and cope with losses without attempting to deal with the infinite ways in which loss occurs and clients attempt to resolve it. To that end, it is important to understand a number of terms that coexist with crisis intervention involving loss.

Bereavement is a period of sorrow following the death of a significant other (Humphrey, 2009, p. 6). It is an objective state or condition of deprivation that is especially caused by death and is then followed or accompanied by grief (Pine, 1996). In Rubin's (1999) two-track model of bereavement, the first track is the individual's own adjustment (or lack thereof) in overall biopsychosocial functioning—affective, behavioral, cognitive, social, somatic, and meaning-making systems. The second track involves the individual's affective-cognitive relationship to the deceased and how that is reconciled over time.

Uncomplicated bereavement is the process that occurs as the bereaved individual works through a variety of tasks to integrate the reality of moving forward in life without the person who died (Cohen et al., 2002, p. 309). Those tasks include (1) moving from an interactive, living relationship to memories that establish continuing bonds with the deceased; (2) coming to terms with the reality of death; (3) experiencing and working though the painful, negative emotions associated with the loss; (4) finding meaning in the loved one's death; (5) adjusting to life without the loved one and forming new relationships with other peers; (6) becoming open to the possibility of changing negative attitudes such as fear, sadness, anger, and bitterness about life and one's loss into joy and happiness as new opportunities, relationships, and transformations evolve and develop (Cohen, Mannarino, & Knudsen, 2004; Van Praagh, 2000; Worden, 1991).

Grief is a psychic state or condition of mental anguish or emotional suffering and a result or anticipation of the bereavement (Pine, 1996). Grief is highly unique and multidimensional; a person's affective, behavioral, and cognitive makeup and the contextual and ecosystemic influences that operate on it dictate what the grief experience will be. Grief and grieving may apply to both primary and secondary losses. Although grief is a universal experience, there is no universal agreement on what it is, and considerable controversy exists over its "normal" duration (Howarth, 2011).

Complicated grief and *prolonged grief* are interchangeable terms, although the latter term now seems to be prevalent and has achieved such status that it is being proposed as a personality disorder in the new DSM-V (Kersting & Kroker, 2010; Prigerson, Vanderwerker, & Maciejewski, 2008). The majority of people who suffer loss and grieve do not manifest complicated or prolonged grief. While grief itself is not a sign of mental illness, prolonged grief is if we define it as a personality disorder, which many researchers and practitioners hope will happen, although some critics argue that it is only grief along the extreme end of the continuum of grieving (Humphrey, 2009, p. 12). Persons suffering from complicated or prolonged grief are preoccupied with the deceased and may have recurrent, intrusive images or thoughts of the death. People with complicated grief experience prolonged grieving that causes distress and impairment that can affect both physical and mental health (Shear & Mulhare, 2008).

Traumatic grief is generally subsumed under complicated or prolonged grief, with the additional requirement that the person witnessed or was in close proximity to the violent sudden, unexpected, horrifying death of a loved one (Cohen, Mannarino, & Deblinger, 2006, p. 15). In such cases, PTSD symptoms generally go hand in hand with the grief.

Disenfranchised grief occurs when a person has experienced a deep and meaningful attachment, experienced loss, and cannot openly acknowledge or grieve the loss or have it validated by others (Doka, 1989; Stroebe et al., 2008). It might be erroneously thought that disenfranchised grief occurs only in clandestine relationships involving gay or lesbian lovers who have not come out or two married people carrying on an affair. However, cultural and societal norms may also forbid—or at least not sanction—displays of grief between coworkers, men, various types of professionals such as medical doctors, and other people who should "keep it together" or "not care all that much."

Further, individuals may feel ashamed about the relationship, be afraid that an overt display of emotion could hurt them professionally, or just experience emotions that inhibit the grieving process (Doka, 1989). Many people would believe it "silly and overemotional" to grieve over a pet. They may keep their feelings of grief closely to themselves unless they feel they are absolutely safe in sharing them. Yet to act as if the death means nothing for the sake of "having a stiff upper lip" can be a harmful variation of disenfranchised grief—particularly for children and older adults (Doka, 1994).

Loss is a universal human phenomenon, but people respond to it with varying degrees of grief and mourning (Howarth, 2011). Any loss is some form of death. Death of a loved one, death of a relationship through the breakup of a marriage or a friendship, leaving a job, putting down a pet, repossession of a home, geographic moving away from friends and family, even the loss of precious keepsakes can constitute a loss that becomes a crisis. All losses produce some degree of grieving (Giunta & Giunta, 2002, p. 4).

Primary loss is a significant event such as a death. *Secondary loss* is a consequence of a primary loss. Death of a spouse may cause loss of status, social contacts, financial security, and sexual intimacy, which are secondary losses. Primary loss of a job may cause financial insecurity, reduced self-esteem as family provider, and lack of self-confidence in vocational ability, which are secondary losses (Humphrey, 2009, p. 20).

Ambiguous loss is of two types. The first is when a person is physically absent but psychologically present, as in the case of a missing person. The second is when a person is physically present but psychologically absent, as in the case of dementia or schizophrenia (Boss, 2006).

Mourning is a social or cultural state or condition expressing grief or feeling because of bereavement (Pine, 1996). Mourning is a communal rather than an individual reaction to loss, generally prescribed by cultural protocol and the time frame in which it occurs (Bedikian, 2008; Humphrey, 2009, p. 5; Morgan & Laungani, 2002; Stroebe et al., 2008). The public appearances one makes, the clothing one wears, the music one listens to, the religious rituals one performs, even the food one eats, are many of the artifacts prescribed for mourning. Mourning can apply to both death and nondeath losses (Humphrey, 2009, p. 10).

Thus, when dealing with the crisis of personal loss, crisis workers are likely to encounter a variety of issues. First are the individuals suffering the loss, which may range from a terminal illness to the breakup of a teenage romance to the loss of a job to the loss of a pet—all of which may be perceived as intolerable and catastrophic. Second are their caregivers, who must provide help and succor not only for those experiencing the loss but also for themselves (Allen et al., 2006; Okun & Nowinski, 2011). Third are survivors who may be experiencing problems that range from shame, sorrow, guilt, and anger to prolonged grief, depression, substance abuse, serious physical illness, and suicidal behavior (Boelen & Prigerson, 2007; Giunta & Giunta, 2002; Parkes & Prigerson, 2010; Rosenblatt, 2010; Wakefield, Schmitz, & Baer, 2011).

Further complicating the issues that confront workers who are dealing with grieving individuals are the cultural contexts within which their clients operate.

Dynamics of Bereavement
Cultural Dynamics

No area of crisis intervention is quite so culturally sensitive as mourning and bereavement after a loss. While grief responses are largely biological and common across all societies, mourning and bereavement are culturally based and vary greatly from society to society (Morgan & Laugani, 2002, 2003, 2004a, 2004b; Morgan, Laungani, & Palmer, 2009; Stroebe et al., 2008; Weiss, 1998). Humphrey (2009, pp. 8–9) exhorts us to recognize that loss and grief occur in the multiple and fluid context of personal, familial, social, cultural, and historical influences. Humphrey proposes that an individual's grieving is a continuous negotiation process among a wide array of sociocultural influences specific to the person and the environment in which he or she lives. These influences range from beliefs and values about meaning, to rules and conduct for behaving, to support networks to religious practices and healers, to an individual or collectivist society, to traditions and rituals, to communication style, to levels of acculturation and assimilation, to ethnicity (p. 8). Suffice it to say that Brown's (2008) social locations you read about in Chapter 2 play a huge role and act in infinite ways to form the individual's response to loss.

Consider the term *culture* in the broadest possible context. Race, religion, gender, geographic region, sexual orientation, disabling condition, socioeconomic class, and temporal context all factor in multiple ways into the loss experience (Doka & Davidson, 1998). The manner in which humans grieve differs from culture to culture and from time to time. As Bedikian (2008) suggests, the ecosystem within which we operate has a great deal to do with how we mourn and grieve. The prolonged grief that Queen Victoria felt for Prince Albert in late-19th-century Great Britain translated into rigid rules of mourning for women that included heavy black costumes and black crepe veils for up to 4 years after the dearly beloved's demise to show their grief. The advent of World War I brought that practice to a screeching halt because women went to work in factories and formal mourning etiquette gave way to the necessity of showing up for work in work clothes. That somber and extended approach to mourning has given way to wearing a dark dress or suit to a visitation or memorial service of a half hour and going back to work that afternoon.

Thus, each culture develops its own beliefs, mores, norms, standards, and attitudes toward death, and these can change over time to meet changing conditions (Dutro, 1994). Further, groups from differing backgrounds within a particular culture may have vastly divergent attitudes and perceptions about death (Dutro, 1994), and individuals within that group may further differ dramatically in how they construct and make meaning from the loss (Neimeyer, 2001).

Rando (1984) stated that "for all societies there seem to be three general patterns of response: *death accepting, death defying,* or *death denying*" (p. 51, italics added). Joffrion and Douglas (1994) characterize modern Western society as a death-defying culture. Kübler-Ross (1975) writes that in our culture "death has become a dreaded and unspeakable issue to be avoided by every means possible," noting "that death reminds us of our human vulnerability in spite of our technological advances" (p. 5). Do you suppose that is why there are drive-by funeral homes in California where you can view the body from your car without ever having to get out? Ramshaw (2010) proposes that while postmodern Euro-American Protestant funerals have become highly impersonal, there still exists a desire and a need to personalize rituals as a celebration of the person's life.

Contrast that drive-by visitation to being in the second line at a New Orleans funeral procession (the mourners following the funeral band) as the body is carried to the cemetery. Do you believe you would see a very different view of how death is dealt with in Louisiana and how emotionally involved you were in it? Let's suppose you were the main object of attention. Would you prefer the drive-by visitation (barely in sight, quickly out of mind) or an African American family's 2-hour funeral ritual in Kentucky that was full of reverence, respect, open grief, and spiritualism for the departed plus a lot of singing, music, and dinner on the church grounds (Collins & Doolittle, 2006)?

Contrast that last image with what Westerners view as utterly incomprehensible—Muslim suicide bombers, who are seen as martyrs absolutely merged with God and God's will in their own willingness to sacrifice themselves. Indeed, for Muslims in general, prolonged public mourning and expression of grief are discouraged because of the great value placed on acceptance of God's will with restraint and understanding. While Muslims may cherish memories of the departed and

grieve mightily in private, their return to public functioning after a loss is strongly encouraged (Rubin & Yasien-Esmael, 2004).

Contrast that notion again to Mexican American families as they handle traumatic grief. Perhaps because of the mingling of Aztec and Catholic beliefs about death as a way into a new life and beginning, along with the strong family bonding that predominates in the Mexican culture, death plays a prominent role. Besides the famous Day of the Dead, when parades and festivities honor deceased family members, living family members honor and maintain a strong bond to the deceased through storytelling, dreams, keepsakes, ongoing faith-based altars at home, and rituals through church (Doran & Hansen, 2006).

Finally, consider how two very different cultures half a world apart process grief. Bonanno and his associates (2005) measured grief processing and deliberate grief avoidance in the United States and the People's Republic of China. How people in both cultures grieved initially predicted how they would process their grief later on. However, contrary to how those in the United States fared, continued grief processing or avoidance did not predict negative psychological consequences for the Chinese.

What needs to happen as far as grieving is concerned and what the culture expects to happen often butt heads. Van der Heijden and Swartz (2010) investigated a peer-led HIV/AIDS prevention strategy in South Africa for vulnerable children who had lost parents to the disease. The intervention ran into trouble because attempts to talk about death and elicit memories of loved ones ran counter to the cultural practice of maintaining silence about the deceased and protecting children from unpleasantness. What all of the foregoing boils down to is that loss and its reconciliation consitute one of the most culturally sensitive areas into which a crisis interventionist ventures. To say that one must tread lightly here and be very observant when dealing with cross-cultural loss is one of the bigger understatements made in this book!

Sociocultural Mores

Schoenberg (1980) describes how societal mores and attitudes toward life, death, and dying in the United States have changed over the years. As the country has shifted from a rural to an urban orientation and lifestyle, there has been a shift from a death-defying culture to a death-denying culture (pp. 51–56). Whereas farm families usually came in contact with birth, life, and death of animals as well as of people, city dwellers rarely encountered dead animals or dead people. People in rural communities cared for their own dying relatives and friends. They prepared the corpses for burial and dug the graves by hand. They laid out the bodies of the dead in the parlor and commemorated the lives of the departed; then they buried them in the family or community cemetery. That's quite a contrast to the way dying, death, grieving in public, and funerals are carried out in most communities in the United States today. Death in modern Western societies has been sanitized and generally removed from the context of everyday life (Crase, 1994; Joffrion & Douglas, 1994; Morgan & Laungani, 2003; Schoenberg, 1980).

The social organization of bereavement and the social reaction to the loss of loved ones have changed partly because of shifts in age-specific mortality patterns (Osterweis, Solomon, & Green, 1984). In former times, adult life expectancy was short and infant mortality was high. Epidemics and famines frequently wiped out large numbers of people. Communities were small and close-knit. Death was taken personally by everyone in the community, and mourning rituals were community-wide events (pp. 199–200). People saw death every day, and fiery sermons about hell, death, and eternal damnation made people acutely aware that they were always one step away from the grave. Changes in families, geographic mobility, urbanization, information technology, aging patterns, the job market, birth control and child-rearing practices, medical and nutritional improvements and advances, and information dissemination and processing have greatly affected the way society views and deals with death, loss, and grief (Green, 2008; Morgan & Laungani, 2003, 2004a).

In modern times, the bereavement process has tended to become standardized by laws, regulations, and the development of specialists who carry out the laws and regulations. Death usually occurs in a hospital or nursing home. Frequently, the deceased are older people who have been out of the mainstream of community activity for a number of years; as a result, they are not as widely known as they were in their younger years. Mourning has tended to move out of the home and into funeral parlors and hospital chapels. Laws affecting the role of funeral directors and the policies of employers have influenced the ways society mourns. Workplaces have established rules governing the time employees can take off from work following the death of a close family member or loved one. Many institutional constraints on behavior have tended to impose

social uniformity on the previously diverse patterns of grief and bereavement (Green, 2008; Morgan & Laungani, 2003, 2004a).

Grief that follows a death has become much more institutionalized (Osterweis, Solomon, & Green, 1984, pp. 201–202), but such institutionalization is not necessarily negative. For example, some funeral homes offer professional grief counseling programs for their clientele and communities (Riordan & Allen, 1989). Thus, the sociocultural changes that occurred between 1900 and 2000 brought about important changes in reliance on such helpers as physicians, nurses, psychologists, social workers, counselors, rehabilitation specialists, hospice workers, and caregivers for survivors of loss (Dershimer, 1990, pp. 14–36; Huber, 1993; Schneider, 1984, p. ix). Indeed, Morgan and Laungani's (2002, 2003, 2004a, 2004b) multivolume set on a global perspective of death and bereavement looks like a Dictionary of Occupational Titles search in regard to the wide array of occupations that are represented in the contributing authors.

Spirituality and Religion

One of the major reasons religion exists is to make meaning of and understand death (Walsh, 2009). Whether you believe in Zeus, Odin, God, Buddha, Isis, Allah, the Great Spirit, or Charlie Brown's Great Pumpkin, the human quest for meaning in life and death has looked to some deity to provide the answers. Whether you believe in Valhalla, heaven, Nirvana, paradise, reincarnation, that great NASCAR racetrack-in-the-sky, or anything else that means a secure, happy, peaceful place in the hereafter, humans have continuously attempted to cheat the finality of death by creating an afterlife and making sense of why bad things happen to good people and why the good die young (Drescher & Foy, 2010; Giunta & Giunta, 2002; Green, 2008; Walsh, 2009). Faith, beliefs, and religious practices are the foundation stones for dealing with life's end and the loss of loved ones. They offer comfort, hope, support, and connection when one feels hopeless, unsupported, and disconnected. Spiritual resources provide guidance to family members and friends in how to honor the deceased and mourn their loss, across the world and through the millennia (Walsh, 2009). To that end, Kaut (2006) proposes that any end-of-life assessment and counseling should include a bio-psycho-social-spiritual network.

However, religion, spirituality, and supreme beings are a double-edged sword. What they bequeath as far as hope is concerned, they can also snatch away. One of the biggest problems people face when faced with loss is making meaning structures that work and help them move through the grief. That's fairly easy in a just and equitable world, but in the world of crisis intervention, as you should know by now, very often it is anything but fair and equitable. That can put people out of sorts with their particular deity of choice when their beliefs, attitudes, assumptions, values, and everything else they hold dear to make sense of the world become ruptured, disjointed, and chaotic (Gillies & Neimeyer, 2006). If the Great Pumpkin continues to dash Charlie Brown's hopes for a meeting, then it may challenge one of his deepest held beliefs and then lead him to question whether this whole "spiritual" thing is just one giant house of cards and he needs to find another vegetable deity or just go worship Lucy!

So it should become clear that attempting to make sense and meaning of a loss can challenge one's most deeply held religious and spiritual beliefs (Humphrey, 2009, p. 26). On the other edge of this spiritual sword, the Giuntas (2002) are among a multitude of authors who spend a great many pages of print hooking all of the many facets of grief up with why God has not left the building with Elvis and is still a shoulder to lean on. The process of making sense or meaning out of loss, then, involves examining those constructs that help make sense out of life up to the point of the loss and then renewing, redefining, or revising them to restore homeostasis and equilibrium (Humphrey, 2009, p. 26).

In that regard, in the areas of death and major losses, a significant proportion of people (in all societies, including ours), perhaps a majority, find faith to be their most important resource for coping, recovery, and growth. Crisis workers must be comfortable in allowing grieving clients to find healing in their faith and spirituality (Culliford, 2002). This stand does not, of course, mean that crisis workers should inject or impose their own religious beliefs on their grieving clients.

Conceptual Approaches to Bereavement

There are a variety of models, ranging from psychodynamic to constructivist to cognitive-behavioral approaches, that seek to deal with loss (Bowlby, 1969, 1973, 1980; Cohen, Mannarino, & Deblinger, 2006; Gillies & Neimeyer, 2006; Neimeyer & Levitt, 2000;

Osterweis, Solomon, & Green, 1984; Powers & Griffith, 1987; Raphael, 1983). Historically, stage/phase models (Bowlby, 1969, 1973, 1980; Kübler-Ross, 1969; Kübler-Ross & Kessler, 2005) have achieved a great deal of fame and notoriety.

Stage/Phase Models

Kübler-Ross's Stages. Probably the loss model best known to the general public is that of Elisabeth Kübler-Ross (1969), which views loss as a series of five stages—denial, anger, bargaining, depression, and acceptance—that people go through as they come to grips with their own imminent death. She later used these five stages to describe grief and the grieving process (Kübler-Ross & Kessler, 2005). While never intended as a strictly linear, stepwise model, it has come to be perceived as such. As popular and valid as this model has become in the general public's mind, there is little research to substantiate its validity (Konigsberg, 2011). Thus, while its simplicity gives it a lot of curb appeal to the public, there is little empirical evidence to substantiate its use and it causes problems when people stubbornly refuse to move though its stages as Kübler-Ross proposed. No matter how much people want a neat ribbon-wrapped package that sets out simple rules and stages for grief, there are simply no stages of grief that fit all persons (Friedman & James, 2009). As a result, Kübler-Ross's and most other stage models have been pretty much consigned to history's dustbin.

Bowlby's Attachment Theory. Probably most widely known in the therapy field is Bowlby's attachment theory (1969, 1973, 1980), which was generated from his studies of separation and reunion of young children with their parents. Attachment theory is a linear phase model that focuses on the nature of the griever's relationship to the deceased. The breaking of affective bonds and the disruption caused by the loss require grieving. Failure to grieve intensely is seen as problematic in not coming to terms with the loss of the object. The need to emotionally turn loose or "detach" from the person or object is the end goal of the grief process. This phase model also has its share of controversy and criticism. Grief may not follow a prescribed set of stages the way Bowlby proposes. Moreover, failing to grieve intensely may be a sign of resilience rather than pathologically avoidant suppression of feelings. Finally, detachment may not necessarily be preferable to continuing to keep bonds and memories of the lost object (Shaver & Fraley, 2008).

Schneider's Growth Model. We feel that one of the better stage/phase models is Schneider's (1984) eight-stage process model of loss. It is a holistic, growth-promoting model designed to nurture as much personal growth as possible within a context of stress, loss, and grief (p. x). Its focus on growth from loss is currently attracting a great deal of attention in the study of the potential positive aspects for growth in the wake of a trauma (Cann at al., 2011a, 2011b; Triplett et al., 2011).

The model includes the following stages (Schneider, 1984, pp. 104–226): (1) initial awareness of a loss, which is generally a significant stressor; (2) attempts to limit awareness of the loss, holding on by means of concentrating one's thoughts and emotional energy, for a period of time, on whatever positive aspects of the loss one can recognize and making use of whatever inner resources one has to immediately stave off immobility and disequilibrium; (3) attempts at limiting awareness by letting go, which involves recognizing one's personal limits with regard to the loss and letting go of unrealistic goals, unwarranted assumptions, and unnecessary illusions; (4) awareness of the extent of the loss, recognizable as mourning—the most painful, lonely, helpless, and hopeless phase through which the loss sufferer goes; (5) gaining perspective on the loss, reaching a point of accepting that what is done is done and providing time to make peace with the past; (6) resolving the loss, which occurs when the bereaved can see and pursue activities unconnected with the loss without its being a reaction against (letting go) or identifying with (holding on) the lost person or object; (7) reformulating loss in a context of growth, which involves discovering potential rather than limits, seeing problems as challenges, being curious again, and seeking a balance between the different aspects of self; (8) transforming loss into new levels of attainment, which involves an integration of the physical, emotional, cognitive, behavioral, and spiritual aspects of the person and is an integral part of the process of reformulation to higher levels of understanding and acceptance of the loss.

A Counterpoint to Traditional Models

Dutro (1994) has described how our concepts of grief and loss have become more dynamic, moving from the medical or pathology theories to more interactive models. Dutro's comprehensive and dynamic model views grief and loss from the perspective that each individual experiences loss according to psychophysiological, affective, and cognitive-behavioral factors, such as the mode of death, relationship of the deceased, prior losses

experienced, and dominant subcultural norms. These factors figure into a dynamic structural model of grief that, according to Dutro, is in sync with sociocultural life in the 21st century. His and others' dynamic, individualistic grief models (Dyregrov & Dyregrov, 2008; Humphrey, 2009; Konigsberg, 2011; Neimeyer, 2000; Worden, 2002) refute many ideas about grief that have been associated with older stage theories:

1. The common assumptions concerning "stages" of grief are not supported.
2. Placing time limitations on grief is inappropriate.
3. The withholding or suppression of sadness in response to bereavement is not necessarily pathological.
4. Insistence on severing ties or detaching oneself from lost objects denies lifelong bonding and usefulness of positive memories.
5. One-size-fits-all models don't work because each individual griever's experience is unique. Grief is not a unitary phenomenon but rather a multidimensional, interactive, individual experience for every bereaved person, based on a complex set of interwoven variables.
6. There are no fixed beginning and ending points in grieving.
7. While grief does not end, it does change.

From that standpoint two current models, the dual process model (Stroebe & Schut, 2001; Stroebe et al., 2008) and the adaptive grieving model (Martin & Doka, 2000), seem to best represent current thinking (Doughty, 2009) on the fluid, idiosyncratic nature of grief and grieving and how the crisis worker should consider approaching them.

The Dual Process Model. The dual process model may be characterized as an approach–avoidance model that has two components: loss orientation and restoration orientation. *Loss orientation* stressors are associated with the loss itself, which may be experienced in ruminating about it and having behavioral, emotional, and cognitive reactions to it that oscillate between avoiding and confronting the disrupted bond with the object of the loss (Stroebe & Schut, 2001; Stroebe et al., 2008). Stroebe and Schut see this process as a normal and natural process of loss adaptation. For instance, a college athlete may feel sadness and anger over the loss of a girlfriend (confronting the stressors), but redouble workouts and increase his study time (avoiding the stressors) in efforts to put lost love out of his mind.

As the loss recedes in time, and in line with how processing models are supposed to operate, a restoration orientation begins.

Restoration orientation occurs when grievers start to come to grips with the consequences of the loss and begin to form new roles and identities, develop new relationships, make life changes, and engage in new activities that distract their grief. The newly aggrieved widow we met at the gas pump at the beginning of this chapter may start to engage in restoration orientation by alternately avoiding her confrontation with loneliness by sitting in front of the TV for hours on end and deciding to confront it by joining a church renewal group that her newly met crisis counselor and pump jockey told her about. One of the major advantages of this model is that it recognizes that grief is not static, but is a series of waves with crests and troughs that ebb and flow at their own pace but gradually move into more quiet, placid, and calm affective, behavioral, and cognitive waters that nourish growth. However—and this is a big "however" —these researchers propose that the griever can get into hot water and move into prolonged grief if this ebb and flow does not occur (Stroebe et al., 2008). So the crisis worker who uses this model should understand that it will make absolute sense when the griever bounces back and forth between a loss and a restoration orientation that operates on an approach–avoidance continuum and get the worker's undivided attention when it does not. If you understand this model, then, it is not upsetting but rather understandable that people are not static or stable as they grieve, but move back and forth as they attempt to bring equilibrium and homeostasis back into their lives.

The Adaptive Model. Martin and Doka (2000) identify grieving as three basic styles that operate along a continuum, with *intuitive* grieving on one end, *instrumental* grieving on the other, and an infinite number of variations between the two. Intuitive grievers respond to loss mainly in terms of emotion, while instrumental grievers think through their grief and/or act on it. Most people, Martin and Doka believe, operate somewhere in the middle and have a blended style. The other component of the adaptive model targets the preferred affective, behavioral, cognitive, and spiritual strategies that grievers use to adapt to the loss. Martin and Doka place a heavy emphasis on spiritual components because of the model's strong theoretical basis in Jungian psychology and the fact that many people place a great deal of emphasis on the spiritual aspects of adaptive grieving.

It is important to note that adaptive strategies are a good deal more than, and different from, coping strategies. Coping implies "getting along" or "bearing up," while adaptation means engaging in behavior that will result in change. Interestingly, the same adaptive strategies may be used by persons at both ends of the intuitive–instrumental continuum but for entirely different reasons. For example, the common practice of going through a photo album of the deceased and reminiscing about happier times may be used by both intuitive and instrumental grievers. For intuitive grievers, it is a cathartic release of emotions as memoires flood conscious awareness and are relived. For the instrumental griever, the photo album may be a way of remembering, organizing, and planning activities. So for the intuitive griever, pictures of riding horses on the family farm bring back memories of Sunday afternoon rides, picnics by the river, the smell of horses and harness leather, and grandfather's wide-brimmed Stetson cowboy hat bobbing along in front on his horse Whiplash. For the instrumental griever, the same photos may remind him or her that the upcoming sale of the farm equipment needs to be inventoried and favorite items parceled out according to requests from brothers and sisters.

It should be clearly understood that adaptive styles do not necessarily mean a rose-covered remembrance path down memory lane. Adaptive styles that are useful in the short term may be counterproductive in the long run. Emotional catharsis verging on hysteria may be fine at the funeral, but level-headed business sense is called for when the family farm is put on the auction block. Also, if primary grievers have different grieving styles, they may butt heads. An instrumental griever who throws herself back into her work may be confounded by a husband who continues to emote at any small remembrance of a daughter who has died in an auto accident. Likewise, he may be appalled that she is so callous and cold as to start packing their beloved daughter's clothing to give to Goodwill 6 months after the funeral. While they are both using adaptive strategies that serve them well, the interpersonal divisiveness that may occur is something else to behold.

It should become readily apparent to you as the crisis worker that being able to ferret out and understand these styles can be critical in helping grieving individuals move through grief and, even more important, in helping significant others understand that the bereaved's grief is not some weird, aberrant pathology but a highly functional, idiosyncratic adaptive measure that works for him or her.

Assessment Tools

The Texas Revised Inventory of Grief (TRIG).   The TRIG (Faschingbauer, Zisook, & DeVaul, 1987) is probably the most widely used inventory to measure grief. It has two scales, Current Grief and Past Disruption. Because of their temporal nature, the two scales allow the worker to determine what kind of progress in grief resolution has been made. The inventory asks respondents to rate themselves on a Likert scale (1 = completely false to 5 = completely true) in response to 8 questions about past behavior at the time the person died (I felt a need to do things the deceased had wanted to do; I was angry at the person; I found it hard to sleep) and 13 questions about how the person presently feels about the person's death (still cry when I think of the person who died; I cannot accept this person's death; I hide my tears when I think of the person who died). It has few validity studies, and some of the items ("crying") are replicated while other well-known concepts such as guilt are left out. Yet it has been used with a wide variety of groups, providing good cross comparisons and a wealth of normative data.

Grief Experience Inventory (GEI).   The GEI (Sanders, Mauger, & Strong, 1985) assesses the longitudinal course of grief. Self-descriptive items that are answered true/false compromise the inventory. Nine clinical scales cover Despair, Anger/Hostility, Guilt, Social Isolation, Loss of Control, Rumination, Depersonalization, Somatization, and Death Anxiety; six research scales include Sleep Disturbance, Appetite, Loss of Vigor, Physical Symptoms, Optimism–Despair, and Dependency; and three validity scales cover Denial, Atypical Response, and Social Desirability.

Hogan Grief Reaction Checklist (HGRC).   The HGRC (Hogan, Greenfield, & Schmidt, 2001) is designed to discriminate grief reactions from depression or anxiety. Its 61 items target categories of Despair, Panic, Blame/Anger, Disorganization, Detachment, and Personal Growth. It can discriminate variability in the grieving process as a function of cause of death and time elapsed since death.

Inventory of Complicated Grief (ICG).   The ICG (Prigerson et al., 1995) specifically targets symptoms of grief that are distinct from bereavement-related depression and anxiety, and predicts long-term functional impairments. Its items are rated on a Likert scale from "never" to "always." Items target long-term grief, such

as not accepting the death, feeling anger or disbelief, avoidance, and auditory and visual hallucinations of the person.

Types of Loss

People may encounter many different types of loss that produce stress, trauma, and/or grief. Following are several types of loss that crisis workers may encounter. It is not the purpose of this text to provide crisis intervention techniques for dealing with every specific type of loss. What is shown here is that loss covers a broad scope, and that certain fundamental helping skills and strategies apply in a generic way to helping individuals who are suffering from loss.

Death of a Spouse

An unimaginable, indescribable loss has taken place and the numbness and excruciating pain is so deep because someone you love has died and it is unmatched for its emptiness and profound sadness (Kübler-Ross & Kessler, 2005, p. 29; Parkes & Prigerson, 2010). The death of a spouse is one of the most emotionally stressful and disruptive events in life (Cramer, Keitel, & Zevon, 1990; Daggett, 2002; Leahy, 1993). Camelley and associates (2006) studied the long-term effects of widowhood. They found that the widows continued to talk, think, and feel emotions about their lost spouse decades later. Twenty years post-loss, they would still reminiscence about their spouse every week or two and had a conversation about their spouse once a month on average. Twelve and a half years post-loss they reported still feeling upset between "sometimes" and "rarely" when thinking about their dead spouse.

Based on this research, does it surprise you when at the end of a year your surviving parent is not "over it"? Losing a mate is in a way as if part of yourself has died. You are now alone when you need your significant other the most, and you are stricken to think that what you have built over your entire life is now pretty meaningless (Van Praagh, 2000, p. 96). As James Van Praagh states, "On the day my mother died my father was not the man I had known all my life" (p. 97). That simple statement is as well put as we can find and pretty much encapsulates what is going to take place as the widow/widower attempts to put life back together. Van Praagh's statement makes two points. First is clearly what will happen with dad and how he will come to grips with his loss. The other component is not only how the family will handle their grief over the loss of mom but how they will handle dad. This issue becomes even more critical if dad is now responsible for raising young children alone (Glazer et al., 2010).

There are more women survivors (widows) than men (widowers), and the bereaved spouse typically faces a number of problems and stages of bereavement alone (Kübler-Ross, 1969; Kübler-Ross & Kessler, 2005). In addition to the immediate shock and stress, many survivors face serious personal, physical, emotional, economic, social, career, family, and community problems (Buckley et al., 2010; Johnson, 1977; Khosravan et al., 2010; Osterweis, Solomon, & Green, 1984, pp. 71–75; Pizzetti & Manfredini, 2008; Rando, 1984, pp. 144–149; Vahtera et al., 2006). More ominous for the elderly, the death of a spouse increases the mortality rate for the surviving spouse (Elwert & Christakis, 2008; Hart et al., 2007).

It appears that other variables intrude into mortality rates of surviving spouses as well. Elwert and Christakis (2006) found that race played a significant role in mortality rates of surviving spouses, with Caucasians suffering a large and enduring effect of mortality while African Americans did not suffer a detectable effect. Religion may also affect how long people live after a spouse dies. Abei and Kruger (2009) found that Catholic men lived 2.2 years longer than Jewish men after a wife died and Catholic women lived 1.5 years longer after their husbands died than Jewish women.

So should you be calmed if you are an African American Catholic and anxious if you are a Caucasian Jew? Not necessarily, but you should understand as a crisis worker that a multitude of variables go into survivorship and realize that some pretty mundane demographics go into what you need to be observant of when dealing with grief and bereavement. Further, while some may argue that bereavement and grief should not be classified as mental illness, an abundance of research indicates that there is a Pandora's box of evil hornets that can sting some survivors in multiple ways, and if some of those survivors do not have good immune systems, it can hasten their deaths. Therefore, it would appear important that crisis workers and medical health care workers in particular be aware of the part bereavement and grief play in physical health issues.

Loss Due to Caregiving

Caregiving is a major issue for spouses and parents. Long-term care causes radical changes not only in attitudes toward the receiver, but in the provider as well. You might stereotypically think in terms of someone in this category as providing heroic years-on-end efforts in caring for a bedridden individual with some terminal disease or chronic disability. Think also about the parents of a 28-year-old son with schizophrenia who has delusions of persecution to the extent that he is on a first name basis with the local CIT, goes off his medication, and becomes dangerous to the extent that his parents sleep in watches and have a heavy-duty reinforced deadbolt on their steel bedroom door. In other words, there are many brands of caretakers, there are a lot of them, and there are going to be even more as the Baby Boomer generation ages and continuing advances in medical science prolong more lives, saving those who otherwise might have died but are profoundly and severely mentally and physically disabled.

Grief and bereavement over lost relationships are compounded by frustration over the ambiguousness of the loss. The receiver of care is alive but not there for the caregiver either mentally, physically, or both, so that former behavioral duties (who takes care of the taxes, bills, car, kids' lunches), affective relationships (emotional support, sexual activity), and cognitive abilities (figuring out job moves, college decisions, buying a house) are no longer functional (Betz & Thorngren, 2006). Caregivers often report a sense of loss of their identity (Dickson et al., 2010)—for example, from former spouse and lover to caregiver and nurse—as they move farther and deeper into caretaker roles.

Bad things happen to good caretakers who take care of individuals with spinal cord injuries, internal head trauma, multiple sclerosis, end stage cancer, renal disease, Alzheimer's, dementia, the profoundly mentally and physically challenged, the mentally ill, and others who are so incapacitated by their maladies that they require constant care and or vigilance. Those who wound up having complicated grief reported that there were more intense end-of-life family conflict and problems dealing with other family members who refused to accept the illness or manner of care (Kramer et al., 2010).

Caregivers reported a kaleidoscope of problems. They suffer depression, sadness, anger, guilt, worry, isolation, resentment, financial difficulties, frustration, relational deprivation, loss of employability, worry about the future of the person they care for if they are older, and have their own physical health problems that are often exacerbated by the constant physical and psychological stress of caregiving (Adams, 2006; Morgan, 2009; Ott, Sanders, & Kelber, 2007; Taylor et al., 2008). Length of time in dying also has an effect on the surviving caregiver. Keene and Prokos (2008) found that compared to spouses who were non- or short-term caregivers, long-term caregivers reported more relief and less depressive symptoms than their counterparts. As coldhearted as it may seem, relief from long-term care of the terminally ill seems to allow caregivers to cope with their loss better.

It is a safe bet that the caregiver population is going to grow in the United States as the Baby Boomer population ages into degenerative disease territory. Other countries provide supportive services at the national level; how well these programs are working is still an open question. In the United States, this population is underserved and depends on charitable organizations such as the Alliance for the Mentally Ill, the Alzheimer's Association, and other malady-specific support groups. Most caregivers constantly live in subtranscrisis or transcrisis states due to the ever-present threat of medical or financial crises for the disabled person and their own continual stress in caring for them.

These caregivers and the people they care for often come to the attention of first responders such as CIT officers. Helping these individuals find support groups, get relief through time off/out programs, plan for future events, obtain psychological first aid or supportive psychotherapy, normalize negative feelings, find outside help, obtain financial, medical, and legal advice, acquire psychoeducation about caregiver issues, and develop meaningful narratives about their losses are all program components that crisis workers might well provide (Adams, 2006; Dillenburger & McKerr, 2009; Haley et al., 2008; Morgan, 2009).

Death of a Child

Regardless of the ages of parents or children, the death of a child is always a major loss (Edelstein, 1984; Finkbeiner, 1998; Kübler-Ross, 1983; Rando, 1986; Romanoff, 1993; Silverman, 2000). The death of a child is perhaps the ultimate loss for a person to endure. Parents are left to deal with the incomprehensible fact that their child died before they did, and often feel enormous guilt that they should have done something differently to have prevented it (Van Praagh, 2000, pp. 154–155). Death of a child is another type of loss that survivors don't "get over" quickly. McCarthy and associates (2010) studied parents whose children had died from cancer. While few of the parents suffered from complicated/prolonged grief disorder or depression, after an average of 4½ years they still reported significant separation

distress associated with persistent longing and yearning for their children.

Every parent is unique in terms of needs, history, personality, coping style, relationship to others, social concerns, family situation, and sense of meaning regarding the death of a child (Braun & Berg, 1994; Finkbeiner, 1998; Romanoff, 1993). Therefore, every parent suffers the loss of a child somewhat differently. The death of a child is traumatic for parents, whether it occurs as stillbirth or sudden infant death syndrome (SIDS) or follows accident or illness in adolescence or young adulthood (Osterweis, Solomon, & Green, 1984, pp. 75–79). It is equally traumatic for aged parents to lose their children who may be middle aged or older.

Ann Finkbeiner (1998, pp. xxi, 37, 44, 54), after several years of grief and healing, shared her deep personal meanings regarding the loss of her only child, an 18-year-old son who was killed in a train accident. Her comments cut to the core of what it means to lose a child.

> I learned two things about the long-term effects of losing a child. One is that a child's death is disorienting. The human mind is wired to find patterns and attach meanings, to associate things that are alike, to generalize from one example to another, in short, to make sense of things. Your mind could no more consciously stop this than your heart could consciously stop beating. But children's deaths make no sense, have no precedents, are part of no pattern; their deaths are unnatural and wrong. So parents fight against their wiring, change their perspectives, and adjust to a reality that makes little sense.
>
> The other thing I learned is that letting go of a child is impossible. One of my earliest and most persistent reactions to T.C.'s death was surprise. I had no idea whatever how much he had meant to me. All I knew was that I hadn't wanted to think about it. Our children are in our blood; the bond with them doesn't seem to break, and the parents find subtle and apparently unconscious ways of preserving that bond.

Bereavement in Childhood

Children who experience the death of a parent or sibling may show overt signs of bereavement, but sometimes their grief may be covert, leading caregivers to assume that the children are not affected by the loss. Norris-Shortle, Young, and Williams (1993) have documented the fact that *young children do grieve*. Most children who experience loss of a loved one go through mourning as a normal process and do not necessarily end up with pathological responses (Glazer, 2010). However, the death of a parent, the death of a sibling, or the death of a friend can bring about disenfranchised, traumatic, and complicated/prolonged grief (Cohen & Mannarino, 2011; Cohen, Mannarino, & Deblinger, 2006, pp. 199–203; Cowan, 2010; Crenshaw & Lee, 2010; Howarth, 2011). Because the majority of time that children spend outside of the home is at school, it necessarily follows that strengthening school support systems that can deal with traumatic grief in childhood is important (Cohen & Mannarino, 2011; Heath & Hudnall, 2011; see Chapter 13, Crises in Schools), particularly in supporting caregivers who may be having their own difficulties resolving grief issues.

Studies by Gudas (1990) suggest that signs and symptoms of behavioral and psychological difficulty occur differently between bereaved preschool and school-age children. Older children, with concepts of permanence of death and personalization of their own mortality, experience more anxiety, depression, and somatic symptoms than do younger children (p. 7). Depending on the age and cognitive development of the child, his or her understanding about death may be very different and unsettling. From a Piagetian standpoint, the preoperational child's egocentric view of death may be laced with magical thinking and fantasy with no clear view as to death's finality (Brown, 1988, pp. 70–74). Children at the concrete operational stage may understand the "why" of death as a specific cause-and-effect event, whereas children at the formal operational stage can understand the finality and irreversibility of death and have all kinds of questions concerning the "whys" (Brown, 1988, pp. 7–81; Matter & Matter, 1982).

Toddlers.   Toddlers ages 18 months to 3 years do not understand how death differs from going away. Because they live in an egocentric world, they may well assume that they caused the death to occur. While death does not have meaning as such for them, they do understand when something is lost, and that loss may be very distressing. They may exhibit high levels of anxiety, seen in agitated/restless behavior, excessive crying, thumb sucking, biting, and tantrums. While it is unlikely they will retain a strong memory of the traumatic event of the person's passing, they may have some physical memoires (Giunta & Giunta, 2002, p. 244).

Preschoolers.   Children ages 3 to 5 also experience profound reactions to loss and may display feelings of

sadness, anger, crying spells, feelings of remorse and guilt, somatization, and separation anxiety (Gudas, 1990, pp. 1–2). At about age 4, children have a limited and unclear understanding of death. Because they are still ego centered, they may believe they caused the death. They are not yet able, for the most part, to understand the permanency of death (Webb, 2007). While they are much clearer about who died and the sense of loss in their lives, they are usually quite literal about their interpretation of what it means to go to heaven, perhaps wondering "Does Bobbie get to have pizza and birthday cake and other little angels over to his house on his birthday?" Because of their egocentric stage of development, they also may feel that they caused the death (Webb, 2011) "Bobby gets everything, mommy and daddy love him most, and I wish he was dead."

At this age, children will start to play the event out, often to the dismay of parents who, horrified and distressed from their own grief, forbid children to do so. There is likely to be severe separation anxiety from caretakers, including excessive clinging and crying on separation, needing to be held, and not wanting to sleep alone. Children this age may see a change in daily routine as a threat and feel angry and rejected for no apparent reason. They may become mute and withdrawn, with extended periods of sadness. There may be noticeable regression in physical independence such as inability to dress themselves, tie shoes, go to the bathroom, or eat with utensils. Bed-wetting and night terrors may occur (Giunta & Giunta, 2002, p. 245). Because their vocabulary is still very limited, when preschoolers hear such words such as "passed," "lost," "gone over," and other euphemisms for death, these words will be taken quite literally (Webb, 2011), so if dad is "lost" it is the family's or police's duty to go find him.

Primary School Age.   At about age 6 or 7, most children understand the universality and irreversibility of death. Death is now more specific, precise, and factual. Elementary school–age children operate in the concrete stage of development. As such, they may report matter-of-factly the gory details of a pet getting run over and thus be seen by adults as cold and uncaring (Gudas, 1990.) Conversely, because of their sensitivity to pain, they may become quite agitated if they hear the gory details about how mutilated the body was and will attempt to avoid such conversations (Webb, 2011). They may also be able to run a balance sheet and see that while their sister's death is a sad thing, their parents will now be able to spend more time and money on them.

Play is used extensively to attempt to work though the trauma. If play becomes both extensive and intensive and is focused on the trauma, it has now moved into traumatic childhood grief (Terr, 1981; see Chapter 7, Posttraumatic Stress Disorder). At this point there will be difficulty concentrating in school, with commensurate behavior and/or academic problems. Numerous somatic complaints may arise (headaches, stomachaches, dizziness, unspecified malaise with numerous school absences). Primary school–age children may have increased difficulty controlling their own behavior and may exhibit radical changes from quiet and shy to verbally aggressive and acting out, or vice versa (Cohen & Mannarino, 2011; Guinta & Giunta, 2002, p. 245).

Intermediate/Middle School Age. While children at this age will generally understand the permanence of death, they may exhibit a good deal of anger and rage at the unfairness of it. They may develop a sense of foreboding and doom about a foreshortened future and see their existence as now pretty meaningless. They may alternately feel euphoria and excitement at having survived, then guilty feelings for having survived when others didn't. Such mood swings may occur often and dramatically as they attempt to cope with emotional dysregulation. They may become highly judgmental about their own and others' behavior, particularly in regard to the deceased or the handling of events surrounding the trauma (Cohen & Mannirino, 2011; Guinta & Guinta, 2002, p. 246; Webb, 2011).

However, to suppose that a child's concept of death progresses in an orderly chronological manner is to suppose wrongly. Life experiences have much to do with a child's perspective and understanding of what death is (Silverman, 2000, pp. 47–53). One can only imagine the difference in perspective and view of death between the average 6-year-old in Baghdad, Iraq, and an average 6-year-old in Des Moines, Iowa.

Intervention and Treatment. Children's affective, behavioral, and cognitive responses must be approached not in terms of adult perspectives but in terms of each child's understanding and developmental stage (Rando, 1984, pp. 157–162). Children are especially vulnerable during periods of major loss because their inexperience and their undeveloped personalities can easily lead to confusion and misinterpretation of events and lack of grieving (Schoenberg, 1980, p. 200). Because children's personalities are growing and absorbing social stimuli

at a very rapid and concentrated rate, care must be taken to provide reassurance and support during family bereavement (Schonfeld, 1989). They may ask the same questions over and over about the loss, not so much for the factual information, but for reassurance that the adult view is consistent, that the story has not changed, and that the grieving adults and children are safe. Children need to hear, over and over again, the simple, truthful, reassuring words of adults who are relatively secure and who show genuine concern for the children's feelings (Osterweis, Solomon, & Green, 1984, p. 100).

Some people believe that children should be shielded and protected from exposure to death and loss. Sugarcoating death, such as daddy having gone away, should not happen. While death is indeed a dirty word in contemporary society, it is one that needs to be used to honestly convey what has happened. The research suggests very strongly that bereaved children will make healthier adjustments to loss if they are informed about the loss truthfully and permitted to participate actively in mourning (Osterweis, Solomon, & Green, 1984, pp. 99–127; Rando, 1984, p. 155; Schoenberg, 1980, pp. 151–154). Even though children may exhibit behavioral responses during the bereavement process that adults may interpret as "not caring" or "not understanding," children should be permitted to proceed with mourning at a level and pace appropriate to their development. Children should not be forced to participate in activities when they decline to do so, but should be included when they request to do so.

Cohen and Mannarino (2011) indicate that treatment models should include five tasks that incorporate *gradual* exposure to the loss and the traumatic grief:

1. Resilience-building stress management skills help children re-regulate feelings, behaviors, and thoughts related to the traumatic death. Techniques include use of positive reinforcement, encouragement, and selective attention for positive behaviors by both parents and teachers, and teaching relaxation skills such as focused breathing and muscle relaxation to stop and reverse physical manifestations of stress.

2. Affective expression skills development helps children and parents accurately label and express different feelings without passing judgment on negative feeling states. Children should be encouraged to share feelings rather than deny them. At times both parents and children may be terrified at the variety and intensity of their feelings, so it is

important to teach both parents and children affective modulation skills so that they feel confident of not only speaking to their feelings, but also controlling them as well.

3. Cognitive coping skills aid both children and parents in hooking up connections among thoughts, feelings, and behaviors. Children and parents learn how to assess how their thinking is adaptive or maladaptive and to change maladaptive thinking through thought stopping, reframing, and cognitive restructuring techniques.

4. Trauma-specific interventions focus on building a trauma narrative, which is usually started after resiliency skills have been developed in children and parents. This narrative may take several forms, including stories, poems, artwork, and play. The purpose of the narrative is to decrease avoidance behavior, directly confront the feared trauma, make sense of it, and put it in the past. Concomitant with exposure to the feared trauma, safety issues may be dealt with if the traumatic event involved violence in which the child was involved or an observer.

5. Grief-focused interviews help children and parents develop more adaptive grieving processes and include many of the conflicting and ambivalent emotions they may have about the deceased.

Webb (2007) recommends directed play therapy as a vital adjunct to cognitive restructuring (Cohen, Mannarino, & Deblinger, 2006) of the traumatic event in tackling the issue of avoidance. Webb lists the following reasons for doing so:

1. Play therapy provides cathartic relief from tensions and anxiety.

2. It provides ways for the child to symbolically review in play what happened, and build armor plate against the feared feelings of the traumatic event in concrete form through manipulating the play media. Through manipulation of the play material, the child and therapist can safely rehearse plans, problem-solve, and gain resolution.

3. It permits role rehearsal to strengthen the child's feeling of competence in handling the future.

4. It can provide a restorative function and transformative experience that moves the child from despair, hopelessness, and lack of self-confidence to reconciliation, hope, and self-confidence. (p. 48)

It is also critically important to carry out intervention in a team approach that integrates home and school

(Cohen & Marinnarino, 2011). Teachers, school counselors, psychologists, and social workers can all serve as supportive personnel that aid and abet therapeutic endeavors by knowing what is occurring at home and in therapy and by providing backup or indeed serving as the primary therapeutic agent.

Bereavement in Adolescence

Kandt (1994) cites research indicating that 90 percent of middle and high school students have experienced a loss associated with death. Almost half have experienced the death of a friend, and one out of five has witnessed a death. Adolescents today are encountering death and loss more frequently than ever before, and this presents a challenge to both adolescents and their caregivers. Other crises such as destabilized families and parents' job loss create in adolescents feelings of pessimism, futurelessness, confusion, depression, and isolation (Schliebner & Peregoy, 1994). A peer death can be a particularly traumatic experience for an adolescent because it is a nonnormative experience that shouldn't happen, often is violent, and may be seen as preventable. Peer deaths can foster school problems, depression, substance abuse, suicidal ideation, and delayed developmental processes (Balk & Corr, 2001; Balk, Zaengle, & Corr, 2011; Malone, 2011).

Value of Connectedness. Hansen and Frantz (1984, pp. 36–47, 62–72) describe adolescents who are in bereavement as needing to be included (involved) in the family's grief, while at the same time needing periods of privacy. Often the adolescent may feel excluded, for example, at the sudden death of a grandparent. Bereaved adult family members may erroneously assume that the adolescent's perceptions of events are the same as theirs. At such times, adolescents may not know how to behave because they do not have a sufficient understanding of death, the circumstances surrounding it, the appropriate mourning role, or life experience in general (Brown, 1988, p. 77–79).

Adolescents may feel a deep sense of pain, fear, anger, guilt, helplessness, confusion, loneliness, and grief (Balk, 2009), yet they may not know how to express or feel comfortable in expressing these emotions. They need opportunities to be included in discussions, planning, mourning, and funeral and commemorative activities (Hansen & Frantz, 1984, pp. 62–67). Guerriero-Austrom and Fleming (1990), researching the effects of sibling bereavement on adolescents, found that physical and emotional symptoms fluctuate over time, showing the most severity at 6 to 12 months following the sibling death and emerging again at 18 to 24 months. Females exhibited more death anxiety and health-related problems than did males. Adolescent grief reactions were documented as long as 3 years following the death of the sibling (p. 11). The problem with these reactions is that death brings a stark reality to an already cynical teenager who may act out his or her anger and depression in dangerous, life-threatening ways (Brown, 1988, pp. 79–81).

Intervention and Treatment. One of the key components in promoting resiliency to a parent's death has been positive parenting (Sandler et al., 2003; Worden, 1996). While adolescents reported themselves as fearful and anxious over a parent's death (Worden, 1996), they also reported themselves as more mature when assuming parental responsibilities and grew up faster. Effective parenting cannot be done in hindsight, but interventions that include parents individually or in treatment groups can be effective in supporting both adolescents and surviving parents in moving forward.

While less is known about the effect of good parenting practices on adolescents when a peer dies, it is important that parents understand and acknowledge the importance of that loss and avoid discounting the loss and turning it into disenfranchised grief. Oftentimes the traumatic death of peers comes from making typically dumb teenage decisions: the daredevil stunt that goes horribly awry and results in a broken neck and quadriplegia; alcohol, fast driving, and a victory celebration over an archrival that end in vehicular homicide and injury to friends; any of a variety of videotaped we'll-put-it-on-YouTube stunts that go wrong, causing injury, death, and lawsuits; the aftermath of the accident leading to the instigator's depression and suicide. These classic examples of immature adolescent behavior resulting in accidental deaths are vilified by parents.

Parents need to be cautious about knee-jerk critical reactions about the stupid behavior of their children's peers or the inconsequential nature of their children's loss. When parents dismiss or criticize adolescent peer friendships, first loves, and high school bonds as transitory and insubstantial, they are essentially telling adolescents their friendships don't mean much and their feelings don't count for much either (Balk, Zaengle, & Corr, 2011). Nothing could be further from the truth, and wise parents will react sensitively to their adolescents' grieving over lost friends and relationships.

Finally, school is a major source of support for adolescents (Balk, Zaengle, & Corr, 2011). Chapter 13, Crises in Schools, provides a good deal of information on the part that schools play in helping adolescents move through the loss of a peer.

Bereavement in Elderly People

The literature is rife with studies on the issues of grief and older folks. As of October 2011, the American Psychological Association database (psycINFO®) contained more than 700 studies conducted in the 21st century. The fact is that older adults may experience considerable difficulties with bereavement (Hansson & Stroebe, 2007; Hinrichsen & Clougherty, 2006). As medical advances extend life and retirement becomes prolonged, commensurate issues arise involving finances, health, cognitive difficulties, and social support systems that often include loss of independence. Independence is a precious commodity and older adults do not lose their desire for it (Langer, 2011), as most children become aware when they deal with aging parents who become obstinate and rebellious over suggestions about quitting driving or going to a retirement center. For older adults, losses of friends are a continual degradation of their support system, and as these losses pile up, when ultimate loss—the death of a spouse—arrives, the potential for loss to cascade into prolonged grief and bereavement increases exponentially. Indeed, the most profound and devastating loss older people may encounter is the loss of a spouse (Schoenberg, 1980, pp. 211–214). Demographic data indicate that the elderly population, age 65 and older, is growing at an increasing rate. It is predicted that by 2030 there will be about 70 million older adults, more than double the number now, and that number will represent 20 percent of the U.S. population (Schwiebert, Myers, & Dice, 2000, p. 123), so it is clear that this potential problem is going to grow . . . a lot!

From a developmental standpoint, bereavement among elderly people is compounded by decreases in sensory acuity, general decline in health, and reduced mobility. Having a lower income and fewer support people available to them than in their younger years also represent changes that are detrimental to their psychological well-being. Elderly people generally experience more losses than do their younger counterparts: loss of relatives and friends; loss of job, status, and money; loss of bodily functions and abilities; and loss of independence and self-respect (Freeman, 1978,

p. 116). It appears that advancing age tends to correlate with a decrease in coping strategies, but it is not known whether this decrease is related to one's greater awareness of impending death, decrease in physical stamina and function, or other factors (Schoenberg, 1980, pp. 221–223).

Schoenberg (1980, p. 230) summarizes four conclusions that may be drawn from the literature on bereavement and age:

1. Elderly people present more somatic problems than psychological problems.
2. There is no indication that the intensity of grief varies significantly with age of the elderly person.
3. Evidence suggests that grief among older people may be more prolonged than among younger people.
4. Elderly people tend to be lonelier and to have far longer periods of loneliness than do their younger counterparts.

Crase (1994) found that the ways the older generation generally deals with loss fall into the following three broad categories.

1. One group totally ignores the inevitability of death and makes no preparation for it. People—especially men—in this category engage in little or no open discussion of death. By ignoring death issues, these elderly individuals attempt to avoid negative feelings, using denial as a defense mechanism. They are vulnerable to being unprepared when struck by disabling disease, crisis, disaster, or the death of their spouse.
2. A second group thinks about death and dying excessively and makes unusual preparations for death's inevitability. These individuals go overboard in making meticulous plans for every detail of their decline, death, and funeral.
3. A third group demonstrates a healthier balance. They are attuned to the developmental implications of total loss, making appropriate plans and decisions, and going on with their normal lives.

The realization of disease, suffering, and eventual loss of life should foster the motivation to look ahead to our death with intelligent preparation, just as we would prepare for any of life's major stages or events (Kaplan & Gallagher-Thompson, 1995). When we don't do this, it is an open invitation for the crisis worker to enter the picture.

HIV/AIDS

Since the 1980s, acquired immune deficiency syndrome (AIDS) and the human immunodeficiency virus (HIV) that precedes and accompanies AIDS have become pandemic. What HIV/AIDS has shown us is that health epidemics are rarely, if ever, just about disease. The psychological milieu that accompanies an epidemic is different from that of other diseases, and HIV/AIDS is different from other epidemics. While a person with AIDS may have many terrifying, uncontrollable physical problems and psychological issues similar to those of cancer patients, the complex sociocultural aspects of HIV and its transmission set it apart from any other modern-day disease (Hoffman, 1996). The worker must be prepared to consider a variety of the client's secondary losses, such as stigmatization, personal rejection, prejudice, religious rejection, job loss, economic deprivation, discrimination, legal oppression, fear of contagion, guilt, shame, and loss of self-esteem.

The AIDS pandemic affects millions of victims and their families and is the epitome of the multiple ways that a pernicious disease can bring loss and grief to its victims, significant others, and families (Morgan, Laungani, & Palmer, 2009). Shelby (1995) and Miller (1990, pp. 189–195) have noted that emotional trauma commences when the client first receives notification of seropositivity (HIV-positive status). Typically expected clinical reactions include disorganization of self, particularly in the initial weeks after notification of results, episodic periods of anxiety, depression, self-blame, shock, denial, suicidal ideation, demoralization, psychosomatic symptoms, low self-esteem, exacerbation of premorbid relational conflicts, and social withdrawal in the months following discovery.

Diagnosis results in immediate and powerful emotional responses, often long before any physical symptoms occur. Victims may feel emotional and physical abandonment, romantic betrayal, and face medical treatment issues that spread a sense of loss and grief across multiple dimensions of their lives (Mphande-Finn & Sommers-Flanagan, 2007). The HIV-positive person may experience any number of severe physical and emotional manifestations such as nausea, panic attacks, diarrhea, dizziness, skin rashes, lethargy, tremors, visual disturbances, sweating, depression, and sleeplessness. It is difficult to distinguish whether and to what extent these symptoms are related to the HIV infection itself or to its cognitive effects on clients (Miller, 1990, p. 190).

Further, HIV/AIDS clients have many legitimate reasons for developing anxieties as the disease manifests itself in physical symptoms. Their short- and long-term medical prognosis may be grim. HIV/AIDS clients are particularly at risk of infection as well as being subject to the burden of stigmatization, marginalization, and social, occupational, domestic, and sexual hostility. They face potential abandonment, isolation, and physical pain (Nord, 1997, pp. 43–64). HIV-infected people may feel it is impossible for them to alter their circumstances. It is difficult for them to maximize their future health prospects, and they have little control over helping loved ones and family members to cope. Adequate medical, dental, and welfare assistance may be very difficult to obtain. They may face negative social pressures and ostracism because they have been identified as homosexuals, drug users, prostitutes, or unfaithful. Further, Theuninck and associates (2011) found that when gay men start to experience symptoms, see others die from AIDS, and undergo the rigors of medical treatment, they became excellent candidates for traumatic grief and PTSD.

AIDS squarely impacts the families and support system of its victims (Duggan, 2007). The epidemic of AIDs in Africa has caused the disintegration of families and turned children and grandparents into major providers and caretakers for HIV-infected parents, with all the inherent crises, grief, and loss that entails (Boon et al., 2010; Nkomo, Freeman, & Skinner, 2009; Van der Heijden & Swartz, 2010; Wood, Chase, & Aggleton, 2006).

The HIV-positive person may also suffer from lack of privacy and confidentiality, feel the loss of dignity with increasing physical dependency, experience sexual unacceptability, and lose physical and financial independence (Nord, 1997, pp. 43–64). All these factors militate against clients' coping mechanisms and are fertile fields in which crises may develop. Kübler-Ross (1987), Miller (1990), Ostrow (1990), Hoffman (1996), Shelby (1995), and Sikkema and associates (2003) have documented a variety of difficult psychological as well as physical obstacles that people with HIV diagnoses face. They may view their entire physical being as transformed and obsessively search for new bodily evidence of the disease progression; they may relentlessly pursue fads related to health and diet regimens; and they may become preoccupied with illness, death, and avoidance of new infections.

Compounding the problem, AIDS strikes a disproportionate percentage of people who have fewer resources to combat it. In the United States, the poor, minorities (especially African Americans and Hispanics), women (especially women of color), youth, gay and bisexual men, drug addicts, and people who are homeless or mentally disabled are all at higher risk (Britton, 2001; Meris, 2001).

The unique issues related to AIDS define it as a disease of crisis events. The stigma associated with it cannot be dismissed because it colors every facet of the client's life. The isolation caused by the disease can result in extreme problems in maintaining intimate relationships—both sexual and platonic. Its unpredictability makes decision making—concerning such things as jobs, relationships, and even planning for one's end—a hellish emotional roller-coaster ride. While a 75-year-old may have a pretty fair psychological reconciliation with his or her coming demise, a 25-year-old who is grappling with career and other life-planning issues is ill prepared to be faced with the grim news of being HIV positive (Britton, 2001).

Whether or not one's view of AIDS is biased by a moralistic judgment about its victims' sexual or other "sinful" habits, HIV infection drains intrapersonal, interpersonal, and material resources and cannot be thought of as a single stressful life event (Kalichman, 1995, p. 1). It is unremitting, with an uncertain course, and is a transcrisis of pervasive loss in every sense of the word. There is probably no other crisis work that is more important, challenging, or necessary than that done with the AIDS/HIV-positive clientele, a group that is growing throughout the world. The special knowledge, training, and attitudes of workers who counsel and help people in this underserved population deserve special consideration and commendation, and these workers have a high potential for countertransference and burnout (Gueritault-Chalvin et al., Kalichman, Demi, & Peterson, 2000; Kuhn, 2008; van Dyk, 2007).

Job Loss

We are pretty much defined by our jobs. If you don't believe that, consider the first question you generally ask a stranger at a party after you find out the person's name. We would wager that it's something on the order of "What do you do for a living?" Jobs and one's identity with a job have far more than work and wage ramifications. Besides the fact that jobs determine how much money we will make and what our earning potential may be, jobs structure our day and delineate a regular and required set of activities as we prepare for, go to, and finish our day's work. Our jobs account for our status and identity, our sense of participation and purpose, and the social interaction and network that work brings (Jahoda, Lazarfield, & Zeisel, 1933/1971). While losing one's job under any circumstances can certainly be a crisis, losing one's job for no reason, or one that has nothing to do with job performance, absolutely is. For those it happens to, what they experience looks and feels very much like grief (Vickers, 2009).

Technological progress and a free market economy have changed the American workplace dramatically. A major ramification of that change has been the loss of millions of well-paying white- and blue-collar jobs that provided a wage earner with income, job security, and the hallowed, and much aspired to, middle-class existence (Lerner, 2000). In the new economic millennium, the possibility of economic restructuring and job loss is ever present no matter how diligent and faithful employees are (Newman, 1993).

The ripple effects stretch out to the families of those employees and result in a variety of pathological reactions as the primary breadwinner comes to realize that he or she is now downwardly mobile, with little chance of regaining his or her former job status. Alcoholism, drug use, battering, child abuse, divorce, suicide, and murder are but a few of the family handmaidens of job loss. On a personal basis, depression, anger, blame, projection, loss of self-esteem, loss of personal identity, lower self-concept, loss of social support systems, stigmatization, loss of control, disintegration of ego integrity, and overall negative mental health are emotional outcomes for someone who may now also suffer secondary victimization not unlike rape or other assault victims (Price, Friedland, & Vinokur, 1998).

That victimization may occur at the hands of others who need to rationalize that the person is somehow incompetent, lazy, or otherwise unequal to the job. To acknowledge otherwise would put themselves in peril and say very clearly that they had no control over their own destinies any more than the coworker who was let go (Reichle, Schneider, & Montada, 1998). Further compounding the problem, the victim often reacts in the same way as the victimizers, casting about in a futile attempt to make sense out of what has happened (Lerner, 2000). When whole industries shut down, outsource, or downsize, entire towns are put at risk, and we now have a systemic crisis.

The negative effects of unemployment on both physiological and psychological well-being are well documented, while job loss as it pertains to grief is relatively new and unknown. Much like those bereaved who suffer traumatic loss due to death, the assumptive world of the newly unemployed is shattered, their view of a just world is challenged, and views of themselves as valuable and worthy are invalidated (Harris & Isneor, 2011). Brewington and associates (2004) studied factors hypothesized to relate to job loss grief. Grief scores correlated positively with time since job loss and number of dependents and negatively with length of notice of termination. Income loss and lack of perceived reemployment prospects related positively to grief subscales. Donahue (2010) compared a job loss group to a bereaved group. The job loss group demonstrated similar levels of hopelessness, tension, stress, confusion, and physical symptoms and had higher degrees of irritation, guilt, withdrawal from social responsibility, oversensitivity, and brooding than the bereaved group.

Therefore, to say that career counseling is a dull and humdrum job when dealing with job loss is to have one's head stuck in the sand. Vocational outplacement counselors often have to dance between helping individuals look for work and engaging in crisis support therapy for grief, anxiety, depression, and stress (Harris & Isenor, 2011). The ramifications of job loss can be far-reaching and devastating. As we saw in the lethality chapter in the example of the outplacement job counseling that turns into a suicide intervention, the potential for crisis when job loss occurs is ever present and often blindsides the unwary human service worker.

Another issue that is often overlooked is how grief is handled in the workplace. Sooner or later, people who lose significant others need to go back to work. Generally it is sooner; there is nothing like a pregnancy leave of absence for grief-stricken workers. Grieving workers can make poor business decisions, miss business opportunities, have accidents, and cause financial losses (Hazen, 2009). For all these reasons, it is in the best interests of management to pay attention to the human reality of death and bereavement in the workplace (Charles-Edwards, 2009). With increased knowledge about the negative effects of complicated/prolonged grief, it should be apparent that businesses need to look beyond the obligatory floral arrangement for the deceased in making provisions for valued employees who have suffered the loss of a loved one.

Separation and Divorce

Almost 50 percent of all marriages in the United States end in divorce, and this statistic has held steady for quite a while (National Center for Health Statistics, 2003). It is devastating to adults and children alike when the relationship dies but the person is still living (Harris, 2011). It doesn't take an expert in marriage and family counseling or a grief specialist to understand the heartache, sense of loss, and all of the accompanying bad emotions that go with a divorce. The crisis of separation and divorce followed by acrimonious custody fights often places children in untenable positions, causing them to feel confused, insecure, fearful, trapped, angry, unloved, and guilty (Karkazis & Lazaneo, 2000). Bruce and Kim (1992) found that major depression is prevalent among both men and women experiencing marital disruption. According to Johnson (1977), the most common experience that marriage partners have regarding separation is intense and disturbing fear and emotional turmoil.

Almost all separations produce negative feelings and outcomes that were not anticipated by either party. Even when the separation is desired and sought, it precipitates a sense of frustration, failure, loss, and mourning. Schneider (1984) reports that people suffering from loss due to divorce or widowhood "show significant and consistently higher vulnerability to almost every major physical and mental disorder, particularly to heart disease" (p. 19). Colgrove and associates (1991) advise that surviving and healing following such loss begin by recognizing and facing the loss immediately and doing the mourning now (pp. 1–2).

Death of a Pet

It is estimated that in the United States there are 57 million dogs and 62 million cats kept as pets (to say nothing of other pets such as horses, snakes, gerbils, and so on). As many as 63 percent of American households have pets. There are good reasons for pet cemeteries and the expense to which pet owners will go to keep a dying pet alive. The human–animal bond is now recognized as an integral part of pet owners' lives, and it is important for us to recognize and validate the grief that pet owners experience when their beloved companion animals die (Lagoni, Butler, & Hetts, 1994; Nieburg & Fischer, 1982; Planchon et al., 2002). Weisman (1990–1991) and Reitmeyer (2000) compared bereavement following the death of a companion animal to the experience of the loss of another human.

Smith (2009) speaks of individuals who have suffered the loss of a pet as manifesting profound grief and depression. Smith notes, somewhat tongue-in-cheek, that there is good reason for such severe reactions. Unlike humans, dogs are absolutely loyal, they keep our secrets, they don't complain, clearly communicate

their needs, and are pretty patient unless they have to relieve themselves and need to go out or haven't been fed all day.

When pets die or suffer terminal illness and have to be "put to sleep," the owners may suffer grief, guilt, and other emotional reactions similar to those experienced at the death of human family members. Hsu (2010) found that pet owners she examined could be partitioned into high and low grief groups. High grief groups were distressed by dreams of their pets, were distressed by fond memories, kept their pets' belongings, erected shrines and memorials, and felt more social constraints, feelings of alienation, and lack of support for their grief. Low grief participants, on the other hand, were comforted by dreams of their pets, gave their pets' belongings away, and were comforted by fond memories of their pets. These feelings and responses may be especially acute in the elderly whose main object of affection is a pet (Brooks & Martinez, 1999) or those who live alone (McCutcheon & Fleming, 2001–2002).

The death of a pet may provide a naturally occurring opportunity for adults in the family to introduce children to the concept and experience of death and dying (Koocher, 1975; Nieburg & Fischer, 1982; Schoenberg, 1980, pp. 203–204). Recently, pet loss counseling has become widespread in the United States. The Delta Society publishes a national directory of pet loss counselors. These counselors are a legitimate and growing occupation and are now affiliated with schools of veterinary medicine, local humane societies, and private practices (Reitmeyer, 2000).

Complicated/Prolonged Grief, Bereavement, and Mourning Reaction

When a person is unable to mourn a loss and move on in a context of renewal and growth, the possibility of delayed or chronic grief arises (Middleton et al., 1998; Raphael & Minkov, 1999). These are the precursors to a complicated or prolonged grief, bereavement, and mourning reaction, which involves continuous distressed yearnings, pangs of severe separation anxiety, intense intrusive thoughts, feelings of increased aloneness and emptiness, excessive avoidance of tasks related to the deceased, loss of interest in personal activities, and disturbances in sleeping, eating, and other daily living patterns present more than a year after the loss (Horowitz et al., 1997). Complicated/prolonged grief is persistent and does not tend to go away (Ott, 2003). There is a continued and increased sense of and binding to the deceased that hampers the griever's ability to function in a normal social and occupational manner (Rando, 1993, p. 175).

Kersting and colleagues (2011) found that the incidence of complicated/prolonged grief in a representative sample (N = 2,520) was about 3.7 percent in the general population and the potential for developing it after major bereavement was 6.7 percent. High-risk predictors for developing it were female gender, low income, older age, having lost a child or spouse, or cancer as the cause of death, although there appear to be limitations to these particular subsets due to small cell sample sizes.

Some people don't begin to have complicated/prolonged grief symptoms until 6 months after the loss. Others experience acute symptoms immediately that continue for a year or more. They also tend to experience co-occurring disorders such as major depression, posttraumatic stress disorder, and generalized anxiety, although researchers contend that prolonged grief is distinguishable from those disorders (Boelen et al., 2010; Horowitz et al., 1997; Prigerson & Jacobs, 2001). People in both time frames do have a higher risk for a major depressive disorder, PTSD, or generalized anxiety disorder than those whose grief runs a more conventional course or who are treated (Kersting & Kroker, 2010; Prigerson, Vanderwerker, & Maciejewski, 2008; Shear & Mulhare, 2008). More ominously, they have a higher incidence of suicidal ideation and risk of suicide (Shear & Mulhare, 2008). Indeed, people with complicated/prolonged grief appear to have an incidence rate of these disorders and behaviors that is equal to or higher than psychiatric outpatients with other known disorders, those bereaved by suicide, survivors of disaster events, caregivers of people with dementia, and older adults (Piper et al., 2011).

In all complicated or prolonged grief, two dynamics predominate and do not allow the individual to move forward. First, the person denies, represses, or avoids aspects of the loss, its pain, and the full realization of its implications for the mourner. Second, the individual holds onto and avoids relinquishing the lost loved one (Rando, 1996). The contrast with normal grief reactions and typical bereavement patterns, in terms of period and intensity of mourning, is so pronounced that practitioners and researchers have proposed including distinct diagnostic criteria in the forthcoming fifth edition of the American Psychiatric Association's *Diagnostic and Statistical Manual* (Shear et al., 2011).

Proposed criteria for prolonged grief as a personality disorder in the new DSM-V include distressed yearning to be reunited to the extent that it causes physical or emotional suffering, preoccupation with the deceased, intrusive recurrent images or thoughts of the death, as well as a number of the following symptoms still being experienced 6 months or more after the loss: (1) emotional numbness; (2) a stunned, dazed, or shocked feeling; (3) a feeling that life is meaningless; (4) bitterness or anger over the loss; (5) estrangement from and mistrust of others; (6) difficulty accepting the loss; (7) avoidance of reminders of the deceased; (8) difficulty moving on with life; (9) a feeling that part of oneself has died; (10) excessive avoidance of tasks reminiscent of the deceased; (11) unusual sleep disturbances; (12) loss of interest in usual activities; (13) hallucinations of the deceased (Forstmeier & Maercker, 2007; Horowitz et al., 1997; Prigerson, Vanderwerker, & Maciejewski, 2008; Simon et al., 2011).

Traumatic Death/Traumatic Grief. When death occurs by traumatic means, such as a vehicle accident, murder, or natural or human-made disaster, the potential for complicated mourning increases exponentially (Figley, 1996; Lord, 1996; Rando, 1996; Redmon, 1996). The degree of trauma is increased by (1) the suddenness and lack of anticipation, (2) violence, mutilation, and destruction, (3) preventability and/or randomness, (4) multiple deaths, and (5) the mourner's own confrontation with death or witnessing of violence or mutilation (Rando, 1996, p. 143). Besides type and degree of violence in the death, the relationship, both in regard to kinship and emotional connection, and what social support systems are available are external variables that play a large role in how and whether traumatic grief will turn into complicated/prolonged grief (Hibberd, Elwood, & Galovski, 2010).

Survivors who have not initiated or finished grieving for their lost ones are vulnerable to suffering from residual trauma, transcrisis, impaired functioning, or worse. It is not uncommon in traumatic deaths for the griever to be reexposed over and over to the traumatic death if the legal system becomes involved through either civil or criminal actions (Rynearson, 2010). The differentiating factor between traumatic grief and complicated/prolonged grief appears to be that complicated/prolonged grief is a function of one's degree of emotional relationship with the loss object, whereas in traumatic grief the degree of distress has more to do with situational factors such as degree of violence, extent of maiming of the body, and physical proximity to and witnessing of the death (Holland & Neimeyer, 2011). If the foregoing is now starting to remind you of PTSD stimuli, you are right! In fact, when a complicated/prolonged grief reaction occurs, they may be considered co-occurring disorders and treatment for PTSD is generally recommended concurrent with bereavement counseling (Figley, 1996; Rando, 1996).

Clues for Identifying Complicated Grief Reaction. Rando (1996) and Worden (1991) have constructed clues for identifying complicated/prolonged grief reaction that may prove useful to crisis workers in cases in which survivors of loss are in serious denial. Examples might be a parent who has experienced the loss of a child and refuses to face the fact that the child is gone, keeping the child's room just as it was years after the death; a spouse or partner whose mate has either died or left for good, and the survivor carries on as if the partner has simply stepped out to the corner convenience store and will return shortly; or an adult child angry over the death of a parent with whom he had unfinished business that cannot now be resolved who projects his rage onto everyone else. Rando's (1996, pp. 145–146) and Worden's (1991, pp. 75–77) list of clues may help crisis workers identify and offer help to people who manifest such severe denial or other debilitating reactions.

Crisis workers and other caregivers should take note of and attend to clients when:

1. The person cannot speak of the deceased without experiencing intense and fresh grief.
2. Some relatively minor event triggers an intense grief reaction.
3. The survivor cannot remove material possessions or belongings of the deceased.
4. Loss themes continually come up during interviews.
5. The griever manifests the same physical symptoms as those the deceased had.
6. The individual exhibits radical changes in lifestyle following the death or excludes family, friends, activities, or visitation of places associated with the deceased.
7. The person experiences a long history of depression following loss, often marked by persistent guilt and lowered self-esteem.
8. There is a compulsion to imitate the dead person.
9. The person exhibits self-destructive impulses or suicidal ideation.

10. There is unaccountable sadness at certain times of the year.
11. The person has phobias about illness or death.
12. There is definite avoidance of death-related rituals or activities.
13. There is obsessive reconstruction of events surrounding the death.
14. The person focuses on what was happening in the relationship at the time of death (usually negative) to the exclusion of the complete span of the relationship (more positive).
15. Secondary losses, such as the loss of a house or savings due to a lack of planning, impetuous spending, or vulnerability to scams, occur and cause financial problems.
16. There are compulsive and obsessive attempts to fix blame and assign responsibility if the death was caused by humans.

Workers are reminded that relatively few grievers display all of the clues on the list. The value of this list lies in the fact that such grievers are encountered more often than one might think and workers need to be prepared, and not show surprise, when faced with such behavior in grievers whom they counsel (Worden, 1991, pp. 65–78). Indeed, many times clients who have complicated grief reactions have submerged the loss experience from conscious awareness or summarily dismissed it as "part of life." When you are faced with a client who is in crisis for no apparent legitimate reason, you should always assess for unresolved grief and loss issues. These issues may not necessarily have to do with unreconciled loss and sadness over a loved one; they may involve anger over unfinished business with the deceased, the departed lover, or the lost job. Under circumstances in which parting was anything but sweet sorrow, the aggrieved individual must be able to forgive and let go, which is not an easy task (De Moss, 2003).

Intervention Strategies

If we believe the current research that tells us the stage theories that have held sway for so long in the field of loss and grieving are not very workable, then we are faced with the business of tailor-making and custom fitting an intervention for every person who has a grieving problem. Further, when we dichotomize normal against complicated/prolonged grief, we are faced with another dilemma because they are essentially two different constructs. So how in the world do we go forward? Even though a huge volume of research has been done on the concepts underlying this chapter and on demographics such as age, race, and sex in describing grieving characteristics, the actual testing of interventions as to how effective they are is pretty sparse.

To complicate matters even further, it appears that what is presently being done in the field of grieving and bereavement isn't working very well. Meta-analyses of outcome studies have consistently shown that, in general, grief intervention outcomes don't measure up to outcomes for most other psychotherapy issues. Essentially, most people with grieving problems don't get better as a result of intervention and in fact may get worse (Allumbaugh & Hoyt, 1999; Currier, Holland, & Neimeyer, 2007; Currier, Neimeyer, & Berman, 2008; Kato & Mann, 1999; Neimeyer, 2000; Rosner, Kruse, & Hagl, 2010).

There is a caveat to these findings. While intervention with normal grief reactions is generally unproductive, individuals with complicated/prolonged grief may indeed derive some benefits equivalent to other areas of psychotherapeutic intervention. It also appears that when individuals self-select for intervention they do much better than do those selected by the researchers (Currier, Neimeyer, & Berman, 2008; Rossner, Kruse, & Hagi, 2010). That finding seems to resonate pretty clearly with the entire area of loss; that is, you can't push grieving people into action until they are ready to do something about it.

What we do know about the business of counseling, though, is that more than anything else, the quality of the relationship between a client and a counselor is probably the best basis for determining how effective the counseling is going to be. From that standpoint, we believe that Altmaier's (2011) view of best practices in grief work that focuses on the relationship has a great deal to say about how effective workers can be in dealing with normal grief.

Being There for Grievers: A Worker Imperative

Particularly as the news of a death is received, "being there" is as important as anything the crisis worker does. Being there manifests the qualities *of empathic presence, gentle conversation, providing available space*, and *eliciting trust* (Altmaier, 2011).

Empathic presence involves listening, silence, and support through accepting and encouraging the expression of feelings, allowing pain to be expressed, and responding in a noncritical, nonjudgmental manner in allowing the grief-stricken to tell their story (Altmaier,

2011). Above all else in grief work, empathic listening to the bereaved and their families appears to be the single most useful skill or strategy available to crisis workers (Rando, 1984). Studies by Balk (1990) confirm the value of empathic listening. He found that bereaved college students identify "attentive listening and presence" as being the most helpful to grievers and "avoidance" as being the least helpful.

Gentle conversation avoids clichés and easy answers (Altmaier, 2011). "She's in a better place." "It was God's will." "The good die young." "He's at home now." "There's no more pain." "God loves those who suffer most." "Better days are ahead." All these pat phrases are discounting at best and demeaning at worst. They are clichés that people use who are absolutely confounded as to what to say to the griever. What they really mean is, "I haven't a clue as to how to help you assuage this grief and am really embarrassed to try, but I'll mumble this and maybe I'll feel better and can get out of this uncomfortable situation." Gentle conversation allows for memory sharing, telling and retelling stories, and owning statements from the worker such as "I am sorry. I don't have words to begin to touch the feelings you must have, but I am here, and I will stay here and listen if you care to talk."

Providing available space has to do with what contemporary research and practice in the field of loss keep harping about—that is, helping the client find support, doing things clients can't do for themselves right now (pumping gas), but letting them tell us what they can and can't do so they have at least a modicum of control in their lives. Providing available space also has to do with time. Since each client's grieving process marches to its own drummer, patience is a huge virtue for the worker (Altmaier, 2011).

Eliciting trust is a keystone that communicates that clients have the ability to get through tough times, recover, and grow (Altmaier, 2011). It is not cheerleading, but it is gentle encouragement and trust that the client can engage the grief and not avoid it. Hughes (1988) believes that grieving clients' expectations of the worker's abilities are crucial in facilitating the healing process. Hughes stated that the worker's expectations are always communicated directly or subtly to the client and that clients heal when they are "informed" by the worker that they are never helpless victims, but instead are powerful and capable of healing themselves (p. 77).

We agree that by being there, the crisis worker is an empathic, nonjudgmental pillar of support who provides emotional understanding and allows the client to feel *felt* (Wylie, 2004, p. 33). As odd as that sounds, "feeling felt" ribbon-wraps the total package of "being there." As Schuurman and De Cristofaro (2007) state, "It is that simple, and that complex" (p. 174).

We also believe that a critical component that does much to lend the worker credibility is much like intervention in a disaster area; that is, one builds up sweat equity with clients by doing some very pedestrian and mundane activities. These may include calling relatives, helping make arrangements for organ donation, contacting funeral homes and flower shops, finding legal papers, contacting charitable organizations, and attending to other basic necessities that go with the death of a loved one. If no relatives or friends are present or capable of doing this, it is reasonable and proper for the workers to offer their services in that regard.

Fitting Technique to Style of Grief

The Dual Process Model. When workers operate with contemporary grief models, they are going to have to be nimble, fluid, and adaptable as clients oscillate back and forth between a loss orientation and a restoration orientation. In Stroebe and associates' (2005) dual process model, the griever sometimes confronts and sometimes avoids the stressors of both orientations (Humphrey, 2009, p. 49). In fact, one of the primary jobs of the worker is not only to tolerate but to encourage such oscillation (Stroebe & Schut, 1999). Humphrey (2009, p. 51) lists the following recommendations for using the dual process model:

1. Identify and explore both loss and restoration stressors and the specific avoidance and confrontation responses the client uses.
2. Keep in mind that an initial period when the client is fixed in a loss orientation is normal. Identify evidence (or lack thereof) of oscillation as time moves forward.
3. Normalize and validate the dual process model by explaining how it works and why it applies to the client's particular situation.
4. Address problematic avoidance such as excessive alcohol/drug use, extreme denial, suppression of emotion, or acting out.
5. Do not push clients toward restoration. Let the oscillation work.

To Humphrey's recommendations we would add another, which we feel is critical to effective resolution of any situation where families or significant others are interwoven in the fabric of the grief. That

recommendation is psychoeducation with family and other support systems as to how this model works. Otherwise, there may be some very frustrated and unhappy significant others who, on the surface, see little progress and indeed regression. In that regard, we feel it is highly important to include significant others in progress assessments and support meetings that reinforce them for "sticking in there."

The Adaptive Grieving Model. The same flexibility and ability to operate in a fluid manner is called for from the worker in Martin and Doka's (2000) adaptive model. In our experience, clients seldom remain fixed at one point on the model's intuitive–instrumental continuum. In our opinion, this model calls for a fairly high degree of ability and skill to operate in an eclectic manner across a wide array of therapeutic modalities to fit with affective, behavioral, cognitive, and spiritual reactions of clients. Note the addition of *spiritual* to the usual triad of intervention strategies. While we don't necessarily believe you have to be able to quote directly from the Bible, Talmud, Koran, or any other spiritual source, we do believe you had better know something about this area and be able to work in it. To not know about spirituality and faith when working with loss, grief, and bereavement or, worse yet, discounting them is akin to not knowing or discounting any of the affective–behavioral–cognitive triad modalities when involved in other therapeutic endeavors. Given the foregoing admonition, the following strategies from Martin and Doka (2000) can serve as starting points:

Affective strategies should initially allow for emotional catharsis through a range of what may be construed as negative emotions from crying to angry swearing. Because emotional dysregulation is seen as a major problem in problematic grieving, setting the stage for emotional exposure is important in regaining regulating abilities. Successive approximation to full emotional regulation through carefully graded, stepwise exposure to experiencing painful feelings is important. Likewise, carefully planning and choosing times, places, and people with whom to field-test affective interaction with others moves the grief from the counseling session into the real world. Assessment and revision of these field experiments is important in determining abilities, skills, and limits and also reinforces the idea that plans fail but people don't.

Behavioral strategies involve a variety of actions that may include substituting a range of positive addicting behaviors, such as running, quilting, fishing, gardening, singing, biking, or building something, for static behaviors such as sitting trancelike, watching television for hours on end, and ruminating about the loss. Making plans that deal with current problems and tasks, such as disposing of the deceased's belongings, locating a retirement center, starting a job search, and reviewing financial plans, are all examples of concrete, forward-looking behavioral strategies. Confronting and motivating new adaptive behaviors that deal with negative addictions such as alcohol and drug abuse, overeating, anorexic tendencies, or gambling are also part of the behavioral game plan for the crisis worker.

Cognitive strategies deal with changing maladaptive thinking. Workers help clients create positive counter-injunctions and positive mental billboards in place of negative self-defeating thoughts. Workers aid clients in reframing and restructuring hot, all-or-none, intolerable, catastrophic thinking into cooler, less absolutistic, more preferable and tolerable thoughts. They also caringly confront clients on cognitive avoidance, denial, minimizing or discounting the impact of the loss.

Spiritual strategies are about transcending the loss through faith-based activities. This is a sensitive and tricky area to operate in because of each person's idiosyncratic interpretation of the part that spirituality and faith play in both the loss and its resolution. This is so because a secondary loss may indeed be a loss of faith over the perceived injustice or the uncaring of God in the primary loss. The worker needs to be extremely sensitive in regard to what will help the client deepen, renew, or discover new or old spiritual wellsprings. So whether through prayer, meditation, reading scripture with a group or on one's own, burning incense at an altar, hugging a large Douglas fir tree, or spending time stargazing, the idea is to activate spiritual resources. The worker does not have to be an ordained minister to do this.

Perhaps the best prototype for this area is the work of the Christian Stephen ministry, which trains laypeople to administer spiritual psychological first aid to persons who are experiencing all kinds of trouble. Named after Saint Stephen, the first Christian martyr who cared for the poor, they provide a complete system of training and equipping laypeople to provide quality Christian care to hurting people (Stephen Ministries, 2011). We think the analogy of them being the spiritual equivalent of community emergency response workers (CERTs; see Chapter 17, Disaster Response) is an apt one, and crisis workers who do not have in-depth spiritual training might do well to go through the Stephen Ministry's workshop or its equivalent with other religions. Barring that, we heavily endorse forming a relationship with a trusted cleric with whom the worker can coordinate this facet of grief recovery.

Cognitive-Behavioral Approaches

Cognitive-behavioral therapies, which focus on changing maladaptive thinking, are the most commonly used therapies for those who suffer from complicated/prolonged grief (Cohen, Mannarino, & Deblinger, 2006; Humphrey, 2009; Shear & Frank, 2006). Cognitive-behavioral strategies are used in dealing with both loss and restoration orientations (Shear & Frank, 2006). A variety of cognitive-behavioral techniques, including relaxation training, desensitization, thought stopping, cognitive restructuring, depropagandizing and disputing irrational beliefs, guided imagery, and in vivo imagery, are used to deal with the emotional dysrgulation, behavioral dysfunction, maladaptive cognitions, and avoidance issues that are characteristic of complicated/prolonged grief.

Added to basic cognitive-behavioral therapy are the postmodernist constructivist therapies (Neimeyer, 2001, 2010b; Neimeyer et al., 2007) that focus on one of the major tasks of complicated/prolonged grief counseling—meaning making. Meaning making has to do with one's interpretation of reality and truth as the central process of one's life (Humphrey, 2009, p. 62). Certainly one of the core issues of loss is making sense of it in such a way as to reformulate one's life, develop a new sense of purpose, and move from the past to the future.

Narrative Therapy

Narrative therapy is a postmodern social constructivist approach that emphasizes the stories or narratives of people's lives (Monk et al., 1997; White, 1989). Narrative therapy is particularly important in grief work because it involves the telling and retelling of stories that thematically represent the meaning of the loss in the person's life. It brings to light and helps clients challenge the underlying beliefs and assumptions of dominant, maladaptive narratives that they have created in an attempt to make sense and meaning of the loss and challenges negative descriptions of themselves as guilty, weak, ruined, wasted, broken, guilty, shamed, cowardly and so on, that are often a complicating factor in loss adaption (Humphrey, 2009, p. 175). Narrative therapy also helps reconstruct, rather than relinquish, the relationship of the deceased and gives voice to the unspeakable thoughts and feelings that dog grievers' attempts to reclaim their lives and make meaning of them (Neimeyer, 2010a).

Attachment Theory and Therapy

Attachment theory is one of the oldest theories to deal with grief. While it has origins as a phase theory, it still has a great deal of utility and is a basic premise of grief and loss. Attachment creates bonds that are rooted in the core of our existence, and when those attachments are broken, severe fractures and breaks can occur in the personality. Attachment theory emphasizes separation anxiety arising from the griever's attachment to the deceased, the breaking of bonds of affection, and the need to emotionally detach from the lost object. Attachment theory proposes that human beings form close affiliation bonds (emotional attachments) from birth because close attachment between parent and child is an evolutionary adaption that keeps infants secure and safe, and the resulting close physical contact with the parent enhances physical, emotional, and cognitive development (Bowlby, 1969, 1980, 1988).

The key component in understanding attachment theory comes from Main's (1996, 2000) research on "coherent narrative," which is the way parents told the stories of their lives. It was the most potent predictor of whether their own children would be securely attached to them. In other words, it wasn't what actually happened to them as children, but how they made sense of what happened to them. Thus, making meaning of one's childhood, regardless of the actual event, corresponded positively with emotional integration and better parenting (Schuurman & De Cristofaro, 2007). When Bowlby's and Main's research is translated to loss and grief, it is thus not how one actually lived with the deceased, but how one *thought* about how one had lived with the deceased that really matters. As such, how the narrative of that thought process unfolds has a great deal to do with whether one moves through the loss and grief well or not. If the narrative is maladaptive, then it follows that the griever will be maladaptive as well. At that point, narrative therapy's ability to change the story comes into the therapeutic picture. Thus, attachment theory can blend well with narrative therapy (Dallos & Vetere, 2009).

Dealing With Loss
Sudden Death of a Spouse

Stuart Wynn, a 44-year-old machinist, his wife Kate, a 42-year-old bookkeeper, and daughter, Anne, an 18-year-old high school senior, were a stable, middle-class family living in a quiet neighborhood in a large city. On her way to work one morning aboard a commuter train, Kate Wynn suffered a severe stroke and was taken by ambulance to a hospital emergency room, where she died. As far as Stuart knew, Kate had been in good health and had had no medical history to indicate that she might have had a health problem.

Sudden deaths have their own constellation of problems, and survivors' ability to use adaptive coping mechanisms is often overwhelmed (Redmon, 1996). The sudden death is often violent, which means that authorities, autopsies, inquests, identification and return of remains, and a variety of other state and legal activities will often be involved. The news media and the criminal justice system can be intrusive and dramatic in clients' lives. Survivor reactions may be equally dramatic (Cummock, 1996). Cognitive dissonance in sudden—and, in particular, violent—death is almost always high. The death makes no sense, and the mind cannot comprehend the reality of it. Emotions and many times behaviors are completely out of control because of the blame, accusation, and fault finding that the aggrieved erroneously believes will somehow make sense out of this impossible event (Redmon, 1996).

On the Triage Assessment Form, the worker mentally computed Stuart's profile: affective, 5 (emotionally shocked but substantially under control); behavioral, 8 (minimally able to perform tasks relevant to his wife's death); cognitive, 3 (thought processes affected by the crisis but under volitional control and congruent with reality); total, 16 (moderate impairment). Stuart's actions are not atypical in a situation involving sudden death by heart attack or stroke (Hersh, 1996). Despite the immediate disequilibrium following the sudden death of his wife, at that moment Stuart was maintaining psychological equilibrium; only later would the impact of the loss catch up with him and would he experience severe affective, behavioral, and cognitive impairment. But for the moment he could cope, even though the help of a crisis interventionist was needed and welcomed.

His daughter, Anne, was triaged as being much more substantially out of control. Her affect was rated as 10. She was decompensating and highly agitated and could not keep her emotions under volitional control. Behaviorally, she was erratic and unpredictable. She had accused the ER staff of not keeping her mother alive and had to be contained by security. Her behavioral rating was also 10. Her problem-solving skills were barely adequate to the situation. She could barely contain herself after the intervention of security. Her cognitive rating was 8, for a full-scale score of 28. The attending physician suggested that Stuart might wish to have his daughter kept in the hospital overnight and that she be given medication to deescalate her extreme agitation. It was also recommended that a staff psychiatrist evaluate her due to her extreme agitation and the fact that her triage assessment put her in the potentially lethal range. While Anne is certainly a critical part of the case, here the focus will be specifically on Stuart as the surviving spouse. The case of a surviving child and the problems he or she may encounter will be dealt with later in the chapter.

The first intervention session was a very brief meeting that included only the crisis worker and Stuart. The second meeting, approximately 20 minutes later, was also a short-term intervention session that featured a meeting between Stuart and his daughter and a multidisciplinary care team consisting of the crisis worker, the attending physician, a psychiatric nurse, and the hospital chaplain.

Care teams are important because they are a response to complex biological, psychological, and social problems in sudden death situations that call for experts from more than one profession (Larson, 1993, p. 199). These initial short-term sessions were aimed at providing the following:

1. Empathic understanding and acknowledgement of the special problems related to Kate's sudden death
2. Assurance to Stuart and Anne that all appropriate emergency medical measures had been attempted in efforts to save Kate
3. Emotional support for both Stuart and Anne by the worker and by the other members of the multidisciplinary team
4. Assurance that Stuart and Anne would have time alone with Kate's body prior to its being picked up for autopsy
5. Referral resources that Stuart needed immediately to make arrangements for the funeral, notification of kin, and other matters
6. Information about autopsy rights and procedures, in case Stuart requested it (which he did)

7. Contact with the family minister, at Stuart's request
8. Immediate medical and psychological assistance for Anne

The care team laid out a long-term treatment plan that included the following intervention strategies to be provided during the initial hours and days immediately following Kate's death. Under no circumstances should you suggest that the person immediately seek out a survivors' group or grapple his or her way through stage models of loss and bereavement. These activities will occur on the person's own mourning timeline and not some "hypothetical" or "scientific" timeline (Humphrey, 2009, p. 6; Shallcross, 2009).

1. *Immediate crisis intervention.* Dealing with the immediate practical necessities of Kate's death, such as autopsies, organ donation, funeral arrangements, contacting her employer, contacting family members. Continued assessment of Stuart's coping ability. Provision of support persons from the hospital, church, family, and friends. Discussion and recommendation to Stuart of immediate temporary hospitalization for Anne due to assessed potential to do injury to herself or others.

2. *Transcrisis individual counseling and intervention.* Identification of Stuart's grieving style on the adaptive model intuitive–instrumental continuum and tailoring intervention to that style (Martin & Doka, 2000). Issues of loneliness and bereavement related to Kate's absence (Giunta & Giunta, 2002, pp. 125–146). Implications for regaining equilibrium and going on with his life. Identification of functions and roles in the family that were previously carried out by Kate and that must be reevaluated or reassigned. Grief work regarding Stuart's new identity without Kate: "I, Stuart," instead of "We, Stuart and Kate" (Van Praagh, 2000, pp. 95–153). Identifying and dealing with Stuart's areas of vulnerability created by Kate's death. Assessment of ways to remember and use the positive strengths of Kate's life in a healthy and growth-promoting way for both himself and Anne through the use of attachment theory and constructivist meaning-making strategies.

3. *Spouse-survivor support group work.* Assessment of overall implications of Stuart's widowhood, such as loss of social connections. Suggested referral to a support group, when Stuart and Anne are ready. Group-generated alternatives available to Stuart and others who had recently experienced the death

of a spouse. Suggestions from the support group on Stuart's responses to his new single-parent role with his daughter. Group focus on ways to cope with the loneliness and other emotions brought on by the absence of one's spouse. Use of narrative therapy to help tell their stories and make sense of Kate's death (Monk, Drewery, & Winslade, 2005).

4. *Conjoint child–parent sessions.* Given Anne's extremely agitated reaction, she is most likely going to have some severe problems working through from a loss to a restoration orientation. Different family members grieve differently, and they are going to need to negotiate and understand that each person's grieving style needs to be recognized and honored. Differential family member grief, if not dealt with after a traumatic death, can cause severe family problems as the family attempts to reorganize and redefine itself (Humphrey, 2009, pp. 52–53). Both parent's and child's reorientation may prove to be difficult as they come to grips with a new family system that does not include a wife and mother. To that end, each is going to need to develop loss narratives that move deceased mother and wife from active presence to bonded memory. While father and daughter may develop their loss narrative individually, at some point they need to come together in conjoint therapy and compare those narratives (Cohen, Mannarino, & Deblinger, 2006, pp. 153–156).

On the afternoon of Kate's sudden death, the crisis worker met individually with Stuart. The following segment illustrates a part of that first intervention session.

CW: (*holding Stuart's hand*) Stuart, I realize your wife's death has been sudden and overwhelming to you. I want you to know that I am here to help you with whatever you need done. (*Silence. Still holding Stuart's hand.*) I'll be with you and assist you in whatever way I can. (*Silence. Still holding Stuart's hand.*)

The crisis worker's assessment is that Stuart's emotional status is one of shock, denial, or disbelief.

Stuart: (*After a long pause, during which the worker waits patiently, Stuart gathers himself and responds.*) This is so unreal! I just can't believe she's gone. It's such a sudden blow to me. Right now all I can think about is Anne, my daughter, and how she is. My God! What will I tell her? My sister-in-law just brought her here.

CW: I will be there with you for as long as you need me. Certainly we both can talk to Anne and your sister-in-law. We have a whole team that will help you now.

Stuart: I want to be with Kate—to be alone with her some before they take her away. Anne, too, if she wants. Can you arrange for us to do that?

CW: Yes, we'll arrange for that right now.

Stuart: I'm afraid I'm going to be in pretty bad shape after I've seen her. Her sister will be too. I just don't know about Anne. Could you arrange for us to sit in the chapel a while after we get back? And is there a chaplain around who could be with us for a few moments? I left a message with our minister at the church, but I don't know when he can get here.

CW: I'll phone Chaplain Myer again. He's aware of Kate's death, and he said he'd be available anytime, if you want him. I'll go with you and leave you alone with Kate's body and then, when you're ready, I'll go with you to the chapel.

The work with Stuart was immediate and intense. Such a cascade of events, problems, and emotions is typical in a sudden death. Particularly seeing and/or touching the body is important to verify that the loved one is actually dead (Hersh, 1996). Stuart manifests very well the initial impact of Stroebe and Schut's (2001) dual process model of an initial loss orientation. Thus, the worker's primary goal was to help Stuart deal with rapidly emerging needs an hour at a time or a day at a time.

The worker kept in mind that as time evolved Stuart and his daughter would need to start moving toward restoration. But for the moment, the short-term intervention focused on Stuart's need to deal with his initial shock. The worker was also sensitive to allowing Stuart to become aware of his own loss. The worker never tried to or considered trying to manage, defer, speed up, or otherwise intrude on Stuart's grief process. Note the patience and use of respectful silence as a primary intervention tactic and the worker's ability to model strength and acceptance of the client's emotionally distraught state. From that standpoint, while the worker assumed a *facilitator* role in helping make immediate post-death arrangements, the worker provided only the degree of structure necessary and appropriate to client needs, goals, and preferences. The worker's main function at this time was to serve in a *witness* role to observe, listen, and not do anything other than "be with" the client and allow the client to feel "felt" (Humphrey, 2009, pp. 213–214; Wylie, 2004, p. 33).

About 2 weeks later, after initially taking the death in stride, Stuart was hit with the full impact of Kate's loss. Stuart's grief and his feeling of helplessness regarding emotional support for his daughter were reflected in a rapid escalation of his observed triage assessment scores: affective, 8; behavioral, 7; cognitive, 8; total, 23. This later assessment prompted an immediate referral of Stuart to a long-term therapist for grief work. Such a rapid escalation is a frequent occurrence among clients who have experienced the sudden loss of a loved one.

Traumatic Death of a Child

Brad Drake, age 34, a farmer, and his wife Helen, age 30, had twin sons, Gene and Jerome, age 6. Late one afternoon, while Brad was doing the chores at the barn behind their house and Helen was preparing supper, Gene tried to cross the highway in front of their house to catch a runaway goat and was struck by a grain truck. Gene was airlifted to a regional trauma unit hospital 52 miles away, but was pronounced dead on arrival. The death of Gene left his parents feeling a soul-deep sense of shock, grief, hurt, bewilderment, guilt, powerlessness, psychological immobility, and vulnerability, and searching for answers and meaning.

The death was ruled accidental; the driver of the grain truck that struck Gene was a local farmer, a friend who was as grief stricken as the Drakes. Approximately 2 weeks after Gene's burial, Brad and Helen together sought counseling. The crisis worker saw them immediately following the intake interview. The worker decided that crisis intervention could do four interrelated but equally important things: (1) facilitate the release of their grief energy, (2) reassure them that their feelings were normal, (3) put them into communication with other grieving parents, and (4) assess for posttraumatic stress disorder and complicated grieving and mourning reactions. These goals of intervention, described by Hansen and Frantz (1984, pp. 21–22), Cable (1996), Redmon (1996), and Rando (1996), formed the basis for starting grief work with Brad and Helen Drake.

This case is an example of long-term intervention. The following strategies were provided and issues explored with Brad and Helen during the days and weeks following Gene's burial.

1. *Assessment for posttraumatic stress disorder (PTSD).* Gene's death fit several of Rando's (1996) criteria for traumatic death. It was sudden, it involved a child, there was traumatic and disfiguring physical injury, and it was preventable. These are excellent growing conditions for Horowitz's (1986) stress response syndrome. A very grave mistake in loss counseling is to not deal with the potential for PTSD that arises out of stress response syndrome and overlays mourning. When this occurs, full-scale intervention for PTSD must be instituted before mourning can even begin (Rando, 1996). Thus, assessment for PTSD, as described in Chapter 7, Posttraumatic Stress Disorder, should be considered.

2. *Couple counseling and intervention.* The situation surrounding Gene's death made it a good bet that one or both parents would blame themselves (Redmon, 1996). Also, the impact of the death on the twin brother, Jerome, would require appropriate parental handling so that Jerome would not be neglected as they grieved, or overprotected because they feared he would also die (Brown, 1988, pp. 66–68; Silverman, 2000, p. 159). Brad and Helen were reassured that they were not going crazy, because for many couples suffering the traumatic loss of a child, the recrimination, guilt, questioning, vulnerability, and incomprehensibility will make them think they are (Redmon, 1996). They received affirmation that they were the best parents they could be and that their parenting should not be blamed for the accident.

3. *Assessment of family problems and potentials.* This included assessment of marital and family systems relationships following Gene's death and exploration of ways to cope with the effects of the bereavement on the marriage and family. When a child dies, there is a high probability there will be serious marital problems within months following the death (Brown, 1988, pp. 57–65). Parents may attempt to support each other by telling the other person that he or she was not at fault, only to have the other parent even *more* sure that the spouse is merely attempting to assuage his or her own feelings and placate them. Or, if blame is assigned, the whole system will deteriorate (Redmon, 1996). A good deal of psychoeducation was conducted with both parents and Jerome. Brad and Helen were reassured that the grief and pain would continue for a long time and that this is normal; that they'll always have memories of the loss; that they will, in time, let go of the pattern of holding onto their grief and move on; and that there is no set timetable for them to finish their grieving.

4. *Parent survivor and support group work.* Brad and Helen became involved in a group whose common focus is the loss of a child. Social support is critical in traumatic loss and needs to remain in place long after the funeral (Pine, 1996). Putting the parents in touch with intervention supports such as parental self-help bereavement groups (Bordow,

1982; Dickens, 1985) is an important social support. Group-supported talk, reminiscence, sharing, grief, and tears will help the Drakes bond with members who have had similar experiences. It will also give them a point of reference as they see older group members making progress and newer members struggling with issues they have already overcome (Cable, 1996).

5. *Reading and media material.* The Drakes were provided with books, other reading materials, CDs, and videos about bereavement in children and youth, as well as in parents.

First Crisis Session Three Months After Gene's Death

The first crisis intervention session with Brad and Helen took place when both were still in a stage of denial, isolation, and depressed. They were clearly stuck in a loss orientation and were regressing even further into it. They were given the Texas Revised Grief Inventory, which showed that both had not moved past their initial response to the loss.

Helen: But my words are nothing compared to my thinking since this happened. I'm thinking I may be going insane or something. I keep going to Gene's side of the bedroom and cleaning it up. I got on Jerome for going over there and messing with Gene's stuff the other day

CW: Helen, you're not going insane. You're responding in a way that makes perfect sense to me. You have both lost the most important and precious gift a mother and father can lose. It is natural and typical for you to experience unusual feelings and grief. You're doing a very good thing by talking openly about your thoughts and feelings. That's why I'm glad you came and reached out to me today. Nobody can erase your hurt or bring your son back, but I will help as best I can.

Brad: I don't know anything anymore. Everything I knew about dealing with problems doesn't even begin to deal with this.

CW: First of all, there is nothing to compare with the tragedy of Gene's death that you have encountered. As bad and terrible as your feelings are, they are absolutely typical for parents I have dealt with who are going through what you are. You are not going insane, and there are things we can do that can help you get unstuck, because the inventory you took tells me that you are, in fact, stuck. I want to take some time and let you both tell me the events that got you from Gene's death three months ago to my office today. I may ask some questions from time to time, but mainly I am going to listen and understand the emotions, thoughts, and behaviors you are dealing with right now. I want to take time to understand this, so start where you would like.

The crisis worker reaffirms that the abnormality they are experiencing is to be expected. The death of a child has been likened to an amputation. A part of the parent has been cut off much like an amputated limb, and the missing part will always be missed and mourned (Klass, 1995). The worker acknowledges this terrible and everlasting hurt and in the same breath issues the parents an offer of her help. Later in the same session, the crisis worker facilitated their release of grief energy and suggested that they contact an ongoing support group, the local chapter of Compassionate Friends, a national organization for parents who have lost a child.

The worker uses basic client-centered therapy. By demonstrating empathy, acceptance, unconditional positive regard, congruence, and concreteness, the worker provides a nurturing, trusting, and safe environment. That environment is particularly important when the griever's reactions are still very strong and he or she feels anything but safe and in control (Cable, 1996).

The crisis worker noted that they exhibited signs of being physically and emotionally drained; they vacillated between moping and benign circumspection but showed no indication of movement from a loss orientation to a restoration orientation. The crisis worker's goal was not to push them; rather, the aim was to understand their current inner concerns and to provide them with opportunities to identify and express their immediate and deep feelings openly. Narrative therapy calls this listening to the *problem-saturated* story (Humphrey, 2009, p. 180).

CW: (*after listening for half an hour to the Drakes' story*) I get the sense that you are both feeling drained of your emotional energy—like you're stuck there and cannot seem to move on after Gene's death.

Brad: Yes, *stuck* is the word. I don't want to talk about this, just get on with it. Helen talks all the time about it and I can't stand that. But just sucking it up isn't doing me any good either. (*Awkward silence.*) It's like a fog that won't let up that chills you to the bone. It physically hurts, and hurts terribly.

CW: So you are hamstrung, Brad. You don't want to hear about Gene's death, but trying to shut it out isn't working either. Where are you with the problem?

Helen: We've just about stopped talking about it. We've become two lonely recluses in the same house. That scares me and hurts almost as much as the accident. I never, ever thought about us ever getting a divorce, but we can't go on like this. This is almost as bad as Gene's death. At least we could put him to rest. We can't seem to do that with this. It just grows and grows.

CW: Helen, what would you like to be doing right now, instead of being stuck and isolated?

Helen: I'd like to be more open. I'd like to know what's going on with Brad, and I'd like to be able to share feelings—even though they may be sad. I have this need to talk about it, but Brad doesn't seem to want to.

CW: If we were to give the problem both of you are having a name, almost as if it were an invasive weed that had come onto your farm, what would it be?

Helen: Paralyzed.

Brad: Mired.

CW: Okay, Mired and Paralyzed. How has that kept you from doing something?

Brad: Every time I go out, I seem to just go through the motions. Not getting anywhere or anything much done.

Helen: I get up and do pretty much the same thing every day. Go through the motions. Go to bed. Can't think of anything in between. Neither one of us sleeps much. I know it's bad for Jerome. He has his own problems, he feels guilty over letting the goat get out, but I can't seem to talk to him about it. Whenever I do, he just takes off. (*Starts to sob.*)

CW: (*Hands Helen a tissue.*) So what do Mired and Paralyzed do for you?

Brad: Nothing. We have never been like that. Always faced hard times, drought, floods, hail, wind, insect invasions, you name it. Put your shoulder to the wheel and git 'r done.

Helen: Yes. Nose to the grindstone. Even though it hurts, you move through it, knowing there will be better times. That has always seen us through until now.

CW: I wonder if that's the problem, that you are putting your shoulder to the wheel and nose to the grindstone but it's a pretty immovable object and something you can't sharpen and get an edge on. So how are Mired and Paralyzed causing you to be motionless? I want you to picture Mired and Paralyzed. What would they look like?

Brad: Just gumbo earth like I can't get though in the south 40 acres. I track the stuff around, can't get it off my boots.

Helen: It's like I have a 100-pound backpack on.

CW: Those are really good examples. Could you see those boots and backpack sitting in the foyer? I'd like you to imagine taking both things off for a minute and just sitting there. How would that feel?

Brad: Different. I dunno. You mean just setting it aside.

CW: Gene will never be out of your life, and I feel like you are trying to slug your way through this and keep him in it in a way that can't be anymore, when it might be OK to just set the Mire and the Paralysis in the foyer. I wonder if you both could go home and just literally say to one another, boots off here, backpack off here. You might even want to get a backpack and muddy boots to really make those feeling concrete. If you need to pick them up and wear

them tomorrow, OK, but right now they are off. What do you think?

Brad and Helen: (*in unison*) Like it was a dead weight off of us.

The worker's opening statement uses the most profane of contemporary words—"death." Using this word, as opposed to "passed," "went to his reward," or other analogies that deny and soft-pedal the death, acknowledges exactly what has happened (Cable, 1996). The grievers must learn to deal with the painful aspects of the loss, and supposedly kinder, gentler words are a trap the worker must not fall into.

Initially, the worker is attempting to respond in a way that would give both parents the autonomy to experience their current state of bereavement and, at the same time, encourage them to open up and provide mutual support for one another. The worker is also using a series of narrative therapy strategies to help this couple start to oscillate from loss to restoration. After the worker listens to the problem-saturated story, he *externalizes* the problem and gives it substance by having the couple give names to it (Winslade & Monk, 1999). In most counseling the last thing we want is to externalize the problem, as in the drug addict who complains that "The crack does this to me" and take no responsibility for his use of crack cocaine. With the Drakes' grief, however, they are so enmeshed in the problem they need to separate from it. By naming the problem and giving it substance, such as muddy boots or a rock-filled backpack, it is something that can be set down. The crisis worker does not get rid of it, because grief is not abnormal nor something to be eliminated (Humphrey, 2009, p. 181). By attaching a name to it, it can be put in its proper perspective as a problem, but one that can be set down as well. Notice that the worker says they may choose to put those emotions back on, but they can indeed take them off too.

The worker also uses a constructivist narrative technique by using client-generated metaphors. Metaphors are helpful because they reduce resistance and provide a safe way of talking about threatening material (Romig & Grunenke, 1991). The worker uses the client metaphors of how they have lived their lives and hooks it to how they continue to strive mightily against the Mire and Paralysis of their grief but sinker deeper in it. What the worker does is explore the metaphors with the clients and attempt to extend them (Humphrey, 2009, pp. 132–133) by changing the metaphors to their antonyms.

CW: I am going to give you a DVD to watch that we can talk about, and a couple of books as well. *Always* (Spielberg, 1989) is about grieving and processing of bonds. It may be difficult to watch, but I think it is worth seeing and talking about to get this process started. I also think it is critical you get in a support group. There is not one here in Brighton, but there is one in Memphis called Compassionate Friends. There are chapters all over the country and you can google it up to see what they are about, but above all else the research shows that a support system is critical to your getting through Gene's death, and as tough as it may be, you need to talk about this with other people who have gone through trauma.

Brad: I'm glad we came today. We would like to come in again. The group of parents you spoke about is a good idea. I think we need that now, and we are going to need it more.

Helen: We didn't know about Compassionate Friends. I'll call them this afternoon. It's good to know that such a group exists. It sounds like a wonderful thing.

CW: I think you will both be glad you discovered Compassionate Friends. I'm truly glad you came, and I look forward to seeing you again.

Compassionate Friends has more than 650 chapters in the United States and Puerto Rico. It exists to support bereaved parents, siblings, and family members in the positive resolution of their grief and to foster physical and emotional health. The Compassionate Friends' credo suggests the unifying sense that bereaved parents can gain from joining a support group: "We reach out to each other with love, with understanding and with hope. Our children have died at all ages and from many different causes, but our love of our children unites us. Whatever pain we bring to this gathering of the Compassionate Friends, it is pain we will share just as we share with each other our love for our children. We need not walk alone" (Compassionate Friends, 2011).

The worker also gave Brad and Helen *After the Death of a Child: Living With Loss Through the Years* by Ann K. Finkbeiner (1998), one of the best your authors know in regard to loss of a child, and Harold Kushner's (1983) paperback *When Bad Things Happen to Good People*, which is a classic in the field and a best seller. The two books together represent comprehensive guidelines for surviving the death of a loved one. The crisis worker was employing a strategy of grief bibliotherapy (Becvar, 2001, pp. 237–239), which is an effective way of providing information, reinforcement, and support through reading and other media that can be used to help clients on the path to restoration.

Second Crisis Session One Week Later

CW: How are things going?

Brad: It's strange. I did get an old pair of boots and we got one of Gene's old backpacks and set it on the back porch. With mud on the boots and rocks in the backpack. Jerome thinks we have really gone nuts. We finally told him what we were doing. Lo and behold, the goat collar and rope appeared out there yesterday. We didn't ask him why and he didn't tell us, but clearly he is trying to set something down too.

CW: So how does it feel to merely set that Mire and Paralysis down and watch the world go by and just let things happen?

Helen: You know we went back home and did that after dinner. We went back into the living room and sat down, looked at each other, and sorta goofily smiled at one another.

Brad: Yeah, then we laughed cause we both thought Gene and Jerome would be shocked that we just set the stuff down and didn't work our tails off. We both talked some, did a little reminiscing, and then started to talk a little bit about establishing a scholarship with the Future Farmers of America in Gene's name. Helen knows I want to do that and listened to me. That instrumental thing you talked about, I guess.

Helen: I cried some at the thought, but it is something Gene wanted to be in when he got to high school. I suppose we are getting to understand each other's style of grieving a bit more after what you told us. I do feel like maybe we have started into the restoration part of this wretched business. I slept pretty good that night, and I know Brad did from his snoring. (*Smiles at Brad.*)

It is not uncommon for two parents to have entirely different views and coping mechanisms (Brown, 1988, pp. 58–59). Helen's need to continuously talk about the accident and weeping at a moment's notice is a common example of catharsis (Lord, 1996). She personifies a largely intuitive grieving style, while Brad's "git 'r done" attitude operates more from an instrumental style. Getting Brad and Helen to understand that they use these different styles is an important issue, so the worker spends time giving them information about adaptive and dual model processes. The change in this session may be considered in terms of the narrative therapy steps of mapping. Mapping the influence of the problem on the person lets clients understand how the problem has been affecting them. The turning point from a complete loss orientation to one that oscillates between loss and restoration is reversing the mapping to focus on the influence of the person on the problem (Humphrey, 2009, pp. 182–184).

CW: So how did all that happen? I mean, I am good but not *that* good. (*A little self-deprecation and humor when clients are able to handle it is never a bad thing, in our opinion.*)

Helen: Well, I was filling the backpack with rocks and it really felt like I was taking the damn thing off my back, and I dunno. . . . Then Brad said he didn't feel so mired down, and so we decided to go for a walk back to the river, which we used to do a lot, but it kinda reminded us of taking the boys back fishing and we stopped doing that, and we just sorta decided to get out, and I dunno. . . . It just sorta happened.

CW: So taking some time to be with one another, and that hasn't happened for a long time. How did that feel? What was different?

Brad: It felt pretty good, and we talked some going down to the river. Like old times, talking about crops, neighbors, and stuff. Once we got to the river, maybe we put the back-pack on and boots on for a while remembering, but we did make the walk, which was impossible before that, and (*smiles sheepishly*) we did hold hands on the way back.

CW: I would really like to have you take those instances apart so you know really clearly what the alternative story line you are now writing it is and can continue to build on it. It's called *deconstructing.* Deconstructing means taking apart those disrupted meanings you have created since Gene's death that get in the way of some of the core values you have had up to that time. As for instance, when you started to put the boots and backpack on down at the river, you took them off on the way home. I am interested in your holding hands. Could that be a cue that might allow you to refocus when the problem arises and you want to put the boots and backpack on again? Maybe you could think of a new name for yourselves, too, as you work through Mired and Paralyzed.

Here the worker uses constructivist strategies by taking apart (deconstructing) the disruptive meanings and attempting to use refocusing (Malkinson, 2007) from the symbols of the disrupted meanings (boots and backpack) to older core meanings (holding hands)—starting to realize that when they put the disrupted meanings back on, they can use that as a cue to stop the disruption and substitute an old positive behavior. The worker also attempts to install a positive external name for their efforts to readapt.

Third Crisis Session a Week Later

Helen: We have a new name for us. Peace and Harmony.

CW: Wow, that is different! So Peace and Harmony is now in charge. What will that look like in a month? Six months? What would people at your church say about Peace and Harmony as opposed to what they are saying now about Mired and Paralyzed?

Working out the alternative story is not easy. One way of reinforcing the new story line is to create a support system of significant others to bear witness to the change or to create an imaginary audience to give voice to their efforts at restoration. Indeed, at some point in the future, Brad and Helen may invite witnesses to bear testimony to their change (Humphrey, 2009, pp. 188–189).

Testing One's Faith.   Faith, or the absence of it, is of critical concern in most traumatic deaths. Trauma survivors who run into trouble with their faith generally fall into Fowler's (1991) faith development model stages of *mythical literal*, which is a one-dimensional view of God as an entity that doles out rewards and punishment based on how rigorously one practices one's faith and follows its commandments, and *synthetic-conventional*, which conforms to the community's basic cultural standard of moral behavior, normative beliefs, values, and religious practices. When losses occur, people in these stages may do three things. They may adhere to these stages and do nothing but pray harder and accept God's will that they are sinners and must atone by hard sacrifices, as their recent loss illustrates. Alternately, they may reject any and all faith, feel that their religion and their God have abandoned them, and become embittered at their faith and the community that supports it. Finally, they may conduct a critical examination of their religious faith, move into progressively higher stages of introspection, and become even more grounded in their faith.

Brad: We just don't know where to turn. We take our religion seriously, and we've talked to our minister. That doesn't seem to help us. I keep on asking, "Why, why, why?"

Helen: We know the story of Job and such as that. We know tragedy strikes anywhere and anybody. Still, we don't know—we can't see—that a God of love or a God of justice can condone or permit the life of a good and innocent child like that to be snuffed out. I'm amazed at myself for talking like that. There is no justice, no fairness in this. No just God allows a sweet child like Gene to die so horribly.

Attempting to find meaning in the tragic accidental death or murder of a child tests the most dedicated believer. The notion that a life lived according to one's religious precepts, particularly that of a child, is seemingly for naught causes a tremendous amount of anger at God and can cause a severe secondary loss in regard to the person's religious beliefs (Becvar, 2001, p. 235). Religion is not an insurance policy against the outrageous slings and arrows of death, nor does it preclude suffering. Doubting is part of the cycle of faith (Grollman, 1996).

It is not the worker's job to move people from one developmental stage to the next (Humphrey, 2009, p. 30). What discussion of their faith does is allow the worker to assess another significant component of the clients' story and determine whether faith is part of the problem saturation.

CW: I don't begin to have answers, and I would submit that no one but you does have the answers to what part God and your faith play in this tragedy and if you can find solace in your faith. What I might ask you to do as part of the narrative you are creating is to write down your thoughts on these questions that Chaplain Ray Guinta, who is well known for his work in a variety of traumatic events, has posed. You can discuss them with me or your minister or just consider them and talk with one another. At the least, writing this out will allow you to get your thoughts out in the open. These are the questions (Guinta & Guinta, 2002, pp. 13–14):

Think about the loss you have experienced. If you listen to your heart, why did it happen and who is to blame?

What do you think your head might be telling you about your perspective that your grieving heart might not be able to hear?

How do you think God is seeing you in your loss?

How do you see God right now? Do you see him as raising his hand against you or as a loving Father with arms wide open wanting to help your hurt?

Pastoral counselors, in particular, must be very careful how they use their religion and spiritual beliefs to deal with grieving. "It's God's will" or "She is in a better place now" may be very little consolation to a mother whose heart is breaking because she so badly wants to hold her dead 7-year-old daughter again and sit down to tea with her after school. It follows, then, that rather than attempting to provide spiritual answers (which the authors of this book most certainly do not have), our goal must be to find ways of providing encouragement and support in searching for meaning (Wheeler, 2001). Given the foregoing qualifiers, it still appears that there is a tremendous amount of power and healing in prayer, religious ritual, religious ideation, and spiritual faith (Walsh et al., 2002). Your authors firmly believe bereaved individuals should be encouraged to explore this as one of their options.

Bereavement in Childhood

Thadeus and Latoya Kirk, ages 36 and 38 respectively, were spending all the time, energy, and money they could in their attempts to cope with the terminal illness of their son, Charles, 5 years old. They spent 2 years in and out of the children's research hospital, and the family was exhausted physically and emotionally by the time Charles died. Their only other child, Makeena, age 7, felt sad, bewildered, lonely, and neglected. The whole family was consumed with grief the day Charles died. In addition to grief, Makeena suffered from guilt. She felt guilty because for several months she had dared to wish that Charles's illness would just end and get it over.

Somehow Makeena believed that her wish had contributed to the death of her brother (Brown, 1988, p. 85). She also felt guilty because she was alive and didn't deserve to live as much as Charles. She was also afraid because she was sure she would "catch" the cancer her brother had. Overridden by guilt and fear that she was now an "endangered species" (Becvar, 2001, p. 129), Makeena became isolated both at home and at school, and her grades plummeted. She also started to have physical symptoms similar to what her dead brother had, which is not an uncommon occurrence (Bernstein, 1997). The school counselor, who had a good deal of experience in workshops for trauma and grieving children, was asked to intervene with Makeena.

Little attention has been given to siblings, who often get lost in the shuffle—both during the illness and afterward in the parents' grief—to the point that the siblings may feel abandoned (Brown, 1988, p. 67). Parents may also establish rules that prohibit talking about the deceased sibling because it is too painful. Relatives may ask siblings how well their parents are holding up and completely neglect how the sibling is feeling. Family discipline may disintegrate, leaving the surviving children with the sense that they really don't count for anything because nobody cares what they do.

Further, if they are afraid they will suffer the same fate as the deceased sibling, they may become paranoid or obsessive in their behavior to "not step on a crack and break my back." Finally, siblings may fear that their parents are too vulnerable and are not able to bear the burden of the surviving child. As a result, they may act out or attempt to become perfect (Becvar, 2001, pp. 129–135). These feelings will almost always be present in such instances. Siblings may have big problems if those feelings are not dealt with in a timely manner, and those feelings may follow them throughout their lives.

The following intervention strategies were provided and issues explored with the Kirk family during the days and weeks immediately prior to and following Charles's death.

1. *Individual counseling and intervention.* Assessment of Makeena's concept of death. Ensuring that Makeena has opportunities to participate actively and learn the medical facts relating to Charles's terminal illness in a truthful and realistic manner (Griffith, 2003). Use of child-centered play therapy counseling approaches in helping Makeena deal with and refute her guilt feelings related to her brother's death. Assessment of the impact of Charles's death on both parents and Makeena. Including Makeena in the funeral plans and commemorative activities. Providing opportunities for each family member to release grief energy. Assessment of the impact of Charles's illness and death on the marriage and provision of individual therapy for Thadeus and Latoya as needed.

2. *Family systems therapy.* Assessment of the family's stress level and coping resources. A variety of toxic responses can come as a result of a prolonged illness of a family member—particularly when it is a child. Scapegoating, stonewalling, detachment, guilt, and masochism are a few of the defensive responses that can occur (Johnson, 1987). Provision of opportunities for the family together to explore the important issues related to Charles's death: the meaning, the good times and memories, guilt, blame, anger, rejection, unfinished business, and new family alignments (Brown, 1988, pp. 74–77; Silverman, 2000, p. 161). Focus on Makeena: ensuring that she knows that she is loved and that the time and energy that Thadeus and Latoya have devoted to Charles in no way diminished their love and devotion to Makeena. Discussion of feelings openly and honestly, keeping in mind the developmental capacity of Makeena (Brown, 1988, pp. 74–77). Ensuring that all family members have permission to mourn openly. Assuming that Charles's death will have a lasting impact on Makeena and will be manifested through her play, her fantasy life, and her relationship to both Thadeus and Latoya.

Using puppets in crisis counseling with Makeena, the worker was able to help her dispute her irrational and magical belief that her covert wish had caused her brother's death. During two previous sessions with the crisis worker, Makeena had developed a great deal of trust in the worker and considerable facility and ease in using the raggedy puppets. At the third session, there were five puppets: Raggedy Ann, Raggedy Billy (Raggedy Ann's dying brother), Raggedy Mom, Raggedy Dad, and Raggedy Doctor.

CW: (*holding Raggedy Billy and Raggedy Mom—Raggedy Billy speaking*) Mommy, Mommy, Ann said I'm dying because she had bad thoughts—she wished I would die so you and Daddy could leave the hospital and come back home.

CW: (*holding Raggedy Billy and Raggedy Mom—Raggedy Mom speaking*) Oh, Billy! Wishing someone is dead can *never, never* make it happen! Your sister, Ann, has a perfect right to wish for this hurting and sickness to end. She is so lonesome for Mommy and Daddy and for you, too. It's normal for her to wish this sickness were ending. But Ann should never feel bad or guilty just because she wished something. Remember, *wishing* doesn't make it happen!

CW: (*holding Raggedy Billy and Raggedy Mom—Raggedy Billy speaking*) Mommy, I wish I could see my sister, Ann. I'd like to tell her it's OK.

CW: (*holding Raggedy Billy and Raggedy Mom—Raggedy Mom speaking*) Oh, Billy, my dear son! (*Raggedy Mom kisses Raggedy Billy.*) I love you, and I love Ann. Here comes your sister now. Why don't you talk to her? She's in the hospital to visit you.

CW: (*holding Raggedy Billy and Raggedy Mom—turning toward Makeena, Raggedy Billy speaking*) Hi, sister Ann. I'm glad you came to the hospital to see me. I wanted to tell you how much I love you and how much I will miss you when I die. I want you to know that you should not worry about the wishes and thoughts you had. My disease is making me die. Your thoughts cannot make me or anyone else die. I want you to know it's all right. I love you, Mom loves you, and Daddy loves you. We will always love you.

Makeena: (*holding Raggedy Ann and Raggedy Dad—Raggedy Ann speaking*) I'm sorry. I wish you wouldn't die. I'm very, very sorry. I hope you don't die.

CW: (*holding Raggedy Billy and Raggedy Mom—Raggedy Mom speaking*) Oh, Ann, we all hope he doesn't die. But I'm afraid he will. Then we will all be sad together. We will miss him. But we will have to learn to live without Billy when he's gone. We will still love him. But we will have each other and love each other. We will never blame you or ourselves for his death. His death will be caused by his sickness, not by your thoughts or wishes, nor by my thoughts or wishes.

Makeena: But then Raggedy Ann could catch what Raggedy Billy caught, and she could die. (*Lays Raggedy Ann out as if in a casket.*)

CW: (*Takes Raggedy Doctor out, who picks up Raggedy Ann and gives her back to Makeena.*) No she can't, and I know because I'm Doctor Feelgood. Raggedy Ann could catch some different kinds of bugs and get sick all right, but Raggedy Billy didn't have a bug. He had cancer. You can't catch cancer, so Raggedy Ann shouldn't worry about that. Raggedy Ann could never catch what Raggedy Billy had.

Makeena: (*looking wistfully at Raggedy Ann*) Well, maybe.

CW: (*looking at the doctor puppet*) Dr. Feelgood, do you suppose we could talk to that other doctor, who is a real cancer expert? He is a friend of yours, Dr. Degrott. He takes care of lots of kids who have cancer at St. Jude's.

Makeena: (*Smiles and hops up.*) Yes! Let's do that. He took care of my brother. I know him.

CW: OK! I'll go make a phone call and see if we can do that.

Although the segment cannot reveal all the preparatory work and dialogue that preceded and followed this brief encounter, it provides some idea of how versatile and effective puppetry can be. The crisis worker uses directive play therapy, as opposed to the nondirective approach used with most child therapy. The reason is that with the kind of traumatic material being dealt with here, the child may be very reticent to venture into this forbidding territory, and once there have no idea what to do. Directive, crisis/trauma-focused therapy can help a child to process anxious feelings and to learn methods to cope with these terrifying "bad" thoughts (Webb, 2007, pp. 50–51). The crisis worker is focusing here on only two dimensions of bereavement during childhood: Makeena's guilt feelings and her fear of dying from what her brother had.

Once the worker has moved though "forbidden" territory, the child can move forward and grieve the loss. Makeena's grief work could have been processed with equal effectiveness by a crisis worker skilled in using artwork, dolls, storytelling, modeling clay, sand play, or psychodrama (Brown, 1999; Corr & Corr, 1996, pp. 258–261; Johnson, 1987).

CW: (*Two pieces of poster board have large word balloons already colored in. A ground line is drawn, with some balloons anchored to the ground and others floating away.*) Makeena, I would like you to draw a picture of you and Charles doing something together that was fun for both of you. We can talk about that and other fun things you two did together. When you get done, we are going to put some words in the balloons. The balloons up in the air represent things you have lost with your brother. The balloons anchored to the ground represent all the things you still have of Charles, including your memories.

Makeena: (*Draws herself and Charles fishing.*) I like fishing, and Charles would always put the worm on and take the fish off.

CW: So that is something you remember that's really positive. Can you put that in one of the balloons floating away. I wonder, do you remember how Charles did that?

Makeena: Yes. He threaded the worm just on its head and let the rest of the worm dangle. He also pushed down and back on the hook while holding the fish's top fin down so it wouldn't stick him.

CW: So that is something you have learned. You can keep that right here in this balloon that is anchored right by the pier.

The whole purpose of the balloon activity is to contrast what has been and what is: while memories of the positive relationship remain, the real-life experiences of the past are now gone (Stubenbort et al., 2001). From a cognitive-behavioral standpoint, this work is necessary in mentally reworking or cognitively restructuring the loss (Cohen, Mannarino, & Deblinger, 2006). From a narrative therapy standpoint, it is part of the *restorying* (Zimmerman & Dickerson, 1996) process of creating a new storyline that she feels best about instead of the problem-saturated story she carried into therapy.

We are very big on "anchoring" those positive thoughts in the person's brain with an associated stimulus that is readily available to retrieve memories.

CW: Makeena, you can take this really nice drawing home and hang it up in your bedroom. Now I want you to put these balloons in an imaginary file drawer in your brain that you can pull out whenever you need to remember the good things and times you and Charles had before he died. So, picture a file drawer right up here in your head. Show me where it is. (*Makeena points to a spot behind her right ear.*) OK, that's where it is from the side. Where is it from the top? (*Mekeena points to the left side of the center of her head*). Excellent, so I am going to take both your fingers from the top and the side and point directly where it is. (*Makeena points so there is an imaginary bisected line in her brain*). Excellent! You have it right there, and every time you need it you can pull it out. OK, now just shut your eyes and try it. (*Mekeena smiles and nods her head.*) Good! I believe Charles would be very proud of you the next time you go fishing with your family, because you can go right there and get those instructions and tell them Charles showed you how to do it.

Separation and Divorce

When Eric Ishitani, age 32, an automobile salesman, came home and announced to Nancy, age 30, a very successful lumber wholesale manager, that he was in love with another woman and wanted a divorce, it shattered Nancy's world. The marriage had been going downhill for a long time, and during the preceding months Eric had been staying out nights. Nevertheless, Nancy wanted to patch things up and to have a child. But Eric was adamant, and left. Nancy was extremely distraught, with feelings of grief, guilt, worthlessness, and failure. She felt her life was meaningless. She didn't want to face life alone; she was stuck in grief and felt that she was doomed to live the remainder of her life unfulfilled, without a husband or a child. She felt like a complete failure and blamed herself for not succeeding in the marriage. Nancy found herself frozen in a state of grief, remorse, guilt, depression, and self-pity.

The following intervention strategies were provided and issues explored with Nancy during the days and weeks immediately following Eric's announcement that he wanted a divorce.

1. *Individual counseling and intervention.* Assessment of Nancy's lethality level. Assessment of her coping skills and resources. Provision of a safe atmosphere for her to talk her grief out and ventilate her emotions. Assessment of available support people. Consideration of her feelings of worthlessness, fear, failure, guilt, anger, depression, self-pity, and lack of self-efficacy and self-confidence. Use of rational-emotive behavior therapy (Ellis & Grieger, 1978) and behavioral modalities (Williams & Long, 1983) to help Nancy identify and successfully refute her negative and self-defeating beliefs and self-statements and start modifying her maladaptive behavior. Reprogramming her internal sentences and developing positive action steps that she can own, practice, and carry out independently of a helping person. Develop a new restoration narrative that no longer includes her ex-husband.

2. *Support group work.* Identification of divorce self-help groups for Nancy to use as supports. Assessment of her social needs on a time continuum from the present forward for several years. Use of the self-help group to assist her in making realistic plans for her personal and social adjustment to her new situation.

3. *Referral resources.* Assessment of Nancy's need for legal, vocational, and financial assistance. If necessary, identification of specific referral people for her to contact immediately. While interviewing her, careful assessment of statements reflecting her present autonomy and ability to attain her goals. For example, depending on her husband's attorney, banker, or accountant may not serve her best interests. Many newly estranged wives find that they need a different attorney, banker, and accountant from the ones used by their spouses. They also may need to find employment or training to enable them to become economically self-sufficient. Often this

is a sudden and difficult switch. The worker must be sensitive, supportive, realistic, and assertive, because Nancy is so vulnerable during this phase of her separation.

The abrupt termination of a relationship by separation is frequently accompanied by emotional responses that are as traumatic as after the death of a loved one. People who experience the loss of separation may exhibit shock, disbelief, denial, anger, withdrawal, guilt, and depression. Attachment theory indicates that separation and the subsequent feelings of loss can occur in many ways (Bowlby, 1969, 1973, 1980), and emotional reactions to a divorce may be very similar to those to a death of a partner. Each person responds in unique ways. Some will cry for several days. Some will verbally ventilate for days on end—to anyone who will listen. Some will go into a state of withdrawal, described by one person like this: "When he came in and told me he was leaving, packed his clothes, and left, I got in the bed and didn't move. I intended to stay there until I died." The loss by separation may be the result of severance of a marriage, a heterosexual, gay, or lesbian love relationship, a long-term friendship, a business partnership, or any other close personal attachment.

Helping people overcome the emotional and behavioral results of the loss of a relationship requires crisis intervention skills similar to those needed in other types of grief and bereavement. In Nancy's case, the client presented herself for crisis intervention several days after she had stayed in bed with the intention of crying and grieving herself to death. Nancy truly wanted to die after Eric told her he was leaving permanently. At first her denial was so profound that she thought to herself, "This can never be. I will never be a divorcée. My parents must never know. My friends must never find out." Nancy did not talk to anyone about Eric's leaving for several days. There was denial: "He really isn't leaving for good. He will be back. We will work things out." There was guilt: "What did I do to cause this? I must have been a terrible wife. I shouldn't have been so blind to his needs. If I just died in an accident, he could go on and marry the other woman and no one would ever have to know." There was anger: "I've got a good mind to find her and pay her back for all the misery she's caused me." Nancy experienced a flood of negative emotions before she brought herself to the point of presenting her problem to the crisis worker, who was a marriage and family therapist. As she presents herself, her thinking is full of all-or-none, catastrophic thinking. Her sentences start and end with words like "should," "ought," and "must." She believes that the activating event, Eric's request for a divorce, is causing the consequences of her depressed, angry, abandoned behavior, when in fact it is her irrational beliefs and automatic thoughts about the event that are causing her distress (Dryden & Neenan, 2004; Ellis, 1973; Ellis & Dryden, 1977; Liese, 1994; Malkinson, 2007).

CW: Well, Nancy, what brings you to see me today?

Nancy: My whole life is a wreck. It's really a mess. The main thing is that my marriage is breaking up. Well, I guess it has broken up. My husband's gone. Been gone for over three weeks. I have just got to get him back. That's all there is to it. I am nothing without him. We were high school sweethearts and this is supposed to be forever.

CW: You're feeling pretty hopeless about the marriage, but you don't want to give up on it. What has happened today, in relation to your marriage breakup, to impel you to come in right now?

Nancy: Well, I was tired of lying around feeling sorry for myself—thinking about killing myself or harming my husband's girlfriend. My intuition told me that neither one of those acts would solve anything, so I've come in here looking for better answers. There should be an answer to this, and I have absolutely got to have some answers to this or I'll go nuts or wind up alone in some old folks home with no one.

CW: Nancy, I'm really glad you decided to come today. What I want to find out first is whether you are in danger of suicide or homicide now. Is your intuition still keeping you safe? Do you have a means at hand to do it? And how close are you to suicide or homicide now?

The crisis worker's first concern was Nancy's immediate safety. It appeared from her verbal and nonverbal cues that she was hopeful and stable enough to have some mobility. The fact that she came to present her problem was another positive factor. However, the crisis worker still checked out her lethality level. Then, when Nancy told the worker that she didn't have a definite plan or a definite means to kill herself, the worker proceeded with other steps in the crisis interview. At one point, Nancy appeared to be in a stage of "holding on," which Schneider (1984) describes as having elements of anger, bargaining, and denial, some of the primary stages of Kübler-Ross's stage theory (1969) of loss.

Nancy: I just can't believe this is happening to me. My whole world has caved in on me. This is simply horrible. I just can't stand it. I just don't know what I'm going to do without him. I must be a total loser. I haven't told anybody, but

I think everybody in the sales department knows because my sales are way down. Christ! I probably have LOSER tattooed on my forehead. And I am so ashamed to tell my mother, although I think she knows something's amiss. My God! I am so pitiful, I just want to crawl in a hole and never come out.

CW: I want to do a couple things that I think will help you get a handle on the situation. I want to tape-record our session, and I am going to give you a homework assignment that involves some more taping. I think this is a good assignment because I want you to hear what I call *automatic thoughts*. In just the few minutes you have been here I have heard a dumpster load of them, and those can get you in the kind of hot water you seem to be in now. Automatic thoughts result from people's underlying assumptions and beliefs. The most common type of automatic thoughts involve all-or-none statements like you're making. *Telling yourself* that you can't stand it and *believing* that it's horrible and that you're terrible seem to be exaggerations that are getting in the way. If you listen to all those "musts" and "shoulds," those are also indicators that your belief system is out of sync with what you need to do and is contributing to what I am going to call a problem-saturated narrative you have been building that won't allow you any leniency from all those self-condemning statements your belief system is making. That is different from telling yourself that it is bad, you don't like it, you wish it weren't happening, but that you didn't cause it and that it isn't the end of the world—even though it may make your life very difficult for a while. I want you to see where your catastrophizing, exaggerating, and awfulizing color your thinking and get in the way of your clearly and objectively assessing not only what has happened but also what your real options are. Don't you?

Nancy: Well, I don't know if that's right. I mean, I am pretty logical and linear and rational. I didn't get to be sales manager of one of the biggest wholesale hardwood lumber companies in the world by being a witless twit.

CW: I understand that, but would it be fair to say this is a little different than a sales campaign and the outcomes are a bit different? I have a little exercise I'd like you to do. I'd like you to make a loss and grief map.

Nancy: Well, yes, but . . . OK, I guess that'll be interesting.

CW: Draw a circle in the middle of the page and put your primary loss in it. Think of all your thoughts and feelings associated with it and write them down around the circle. [See Figure 12.1.] Focus on the thoughts, the billboards that pop up when you think about the word D-I-V-O-R-C-E. Once you have the thoughts down, put the feelings down that go with it. Go back and look at feelings. As you think about them, see if others don't bubble up. Lots of times we have a feeling about a feeling. For example, "stupid" might lead to "regret."

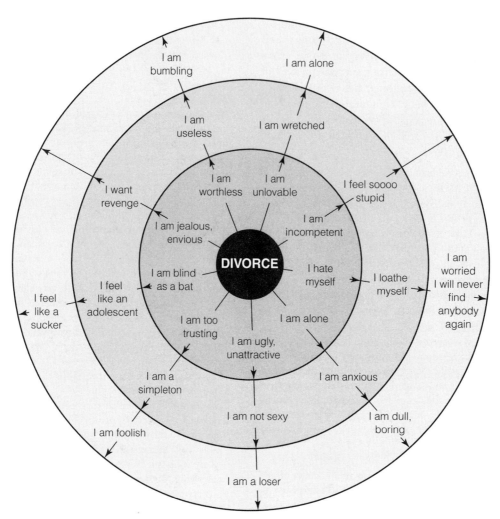

FIGURE 12.1 Nancy's Divorce Map

Nancy: Yes. I see it. That's pretty bad. I guess I have come down harder on myself and on the problem than is necessary. I know it isn't the end of the world, but I feel, at the time, that it's horrible and awful.

CW: Then your *believing* it's horrible and awful is the real culprit, isn't it? There is a difference between your beliefs and how things really are.

Nancy: You're right! It helps just to look at it differently, even though it doesn't solve my big mess.

CW: You're right. It doesn't solve it. But we can objectively examine it and together begin to figure out options you can choose if we know on the front end, even though you're grieving over your hurt, that we are not dealing with a world-shattering catastrophe.

The crisis worker was intervening by using elements of rational-emotive behavior therapy (REBT) and cognitive-behavioral therapy. The worker was attempting to dispute the client's irrational beliefs about the separation and help her begin to direct her emotional energy toward the real issues. Nancy was an intelligent person who quickly responded to the rational ideas presented. But, as is typical in such cases dealing with the emotional state during loss, the worker knew that repetition, practice, support, and encouragement would be needed. A person in Nancy's state must have far more than just a one-shot session using REBT to get her beyond crisis and back to a state of equilibrium.

In addition to using REBT as a crisis intervention strategy, the crisis worker also used a self-managed behavioral technique (Williams & Long, 1983) to help Nancy expend her grief energy over a period of several weeks. What Nancy did was to make a series of audiotapes—alone, at home—in a sequential and systematic manner. The purposes for making the tapes were (1) to serve as a mechanism for self-catharsis; (2) to present to both her and the crisis worker her full story and form the basis for changing it from a problem-saturated story line to a restoration narrative; (3) to clarify, in her own mind, the loss and movement toward restoration she was going through; and (4) to document her progress in controlling her automatic thoughts and catching her "shoulds," "oughts," and other mustrabatory statements about love, marriage, and her self-concept.

The loss and grief map (Greenspan, 2003) is a concrete representation of all the absolutist, negative, irrational beliefs she has about herself and the divorce. Once she has those in conscious awareness, she and the worker will start working on positive counterinjunctions that cool these hot cognitions off. The worker will also set up a self-managed behavior model with her that will allow frequency counts of the number of times she makes those statement to herself in a day. He will use a thought-stopping procedure and cueing (Dr. James's magical rubber band-on-the-wrist-thought-stopper) to cue her to shift from those all-or-none irrational thoughts to cooler, more positive, self-enhancing counterinjunctions that are designed to start changing her narrative to one of restoration.

The audio recordings were quite useful to the crisis worker in verbally journaling her changing narrative as she worked her cognitive behavioral plan. But the main value of the behavioral plan was providing Nancy the purpose and the experience of doing it. She described in detail her thoughts, feelings, and actions throughout several stages: shock and disbelief, denial, anger, withdrawal, guilt, depression, searching, and resolution. Nancy made eight cassette tapes. She reported that the most valuable and helpful aspect of the activity was listening to her own tapes, which she found herself doing over and over. Nancy kept the cassettes with the stated intention of continuing to listen to them. But she later reported that after her crisis subsided, she didn't need to listen to them anymore.

Nancy also contracted with the worker to go to a divorce support group at a local church. Such groups provide crisis support, role models for survival, adaptation pathways, and new social networks (Raphael & Dobson, 2000). You will note that over and over we advocate the use of these groups as part of a comprehensive crisis and transcrisis intervention treatment model. They are an important part of the response to bereavement, and there is evidence that they are effective as a social and healing process (Kitzman & Gaylord, 2001; Raphael & Dobson, 2000).

Death of a Pet

The Thompsons—Hollis, age 36, Faye, age 33, and their adopted daughter, Dawn, age 5—were grieving over the death of Tincup, their aged terrier. Tincup had been like a member of the family. He had been a faithful companion to the Thompsons since they were newlyweds; he had been the affectionate and protective playmate of Dawn from the day the Thompsons got her through the adoption agency. Lately he had developed severe health problems, and the veterinarian had finally told the Thompsons that Tincup's medical condition made it necessary to terminate his life. After making the painful decision, the Thompsons decided that they would all be present at his euthanasia.

While on a first reading, this may seem horrific for a small child, Butler and Lagoni (1996) make an excellent case that an honest discussion of the pet's condition and the need to put it to death is important. Children respond well to straightforward and concrete explanations. Note that we do not use the more palliative "put to sleep." As Butler and Lagoni (1996) suggest, small children may think that because they go to sleep every night, they may be "put to sleep" if they are bad and never wake up.

The following intervention strategies were provided and issues were explored with the Thompson family during the days and weeks immediately following the death of their pet.

1. *Individual counseling and intervention.* Assessment of the levels of grief, guilt, and stress in each—Hollis, Faye, and Dawn. Assessment of Dawn's understanding of the death of the pet. Provision of a period to grieve and release grief energy. Follow-up play therapy and ceremonial events as outlets for Dawn (Schoenberg, 1980, pp. 203–204) and display of meaningful objects that link Dawn to her deceased pet (Lagoni, Butler, & Hetts, 1994, p. 265).

2. *Group work.* Providing an opportunity for the family to talk about Tincup's death in a realistic, factual, and honest manner. Using the pet's death to help Dawn begin to develop her concept of death,

free of misinformation. Providing opportunities and activities for the family to commemorate the pet's life and to reformulate the death within a context of growth.

3. *Bibliotherapy* about bonding with pets and coping with crisis and loss.

The pet counselor from the veterinary clinic met with the family 3 days after Tincup's death.

Dawn: I was a little scared at first, but Dr. Hobbs explained exactly what they were going to do to Tincup and how it wouldn't hurt. I really wanted Tincup to stay alive, but he would yelp every time I tried to pick him up, and I didn't want him to hurt anymore. I helped Dr. Hobbs get Tincup ready, and my parents did too. He just sorta relaxed, and I petted him while they put the medicine in him. It was all done in a minute or so, and my parents and I petted Tincup for a while and then we took him home. He is buried out in the backyard, and I go visit him every day. I think I may want a new puppy for my birthday, but right now I just want to go visit Tincup.

As Butler and Lagoni (1996) suggest, getting new pets immediately is not always a good idea. Children, and for that matter adults, need time to grieve the loss of their pets just as they need time to grieve any other important loss. Schoenberg (1980) suggested that families use ceremonial events to help deal with their grief following the death of a pet (pp. 203–204). The Thompsons used a ceremonial event of pet burial to help open up opportunities for discussion, sharing of feelings, and explaining death to their daughter.

Faye: We had a small funeral in the backyard. I helped Dawn invite a few of her close friends to the funeral, and our next-door neighbors mailed us a sympathy card. Hollis and Dawn dug Tincup's grave, and we had a simple but beautiful graveside service. There were flowers and friends, and we paid tribute and said good-bye to him. It was a good thing for our family and for the friends who came. We even had another small ceremony when we put Tincup's collar on the bulletin board in Dawn's room. We're still grieving somewhat over his death, but it has been a learning experience for all of us, and I think Dawn will have a more realistic and healthy view of death, loss, and grief as a result of these activities.

We also got *Zach and His Dog* (Meagher, 2009), which is a story about pet loss and bonding with children. We read that together and had some tears, but it helped put things in perspective too. So Dawn still touches Tincup's collar before she goes to bed, but I think probably by Christmas there may be a new puppy under the tree Christmas morning.

The strategies used in dealing with the loss of pets are aimed at the same goals as those used in any human loss: helping the grievers work through their various stages of grief in healthy and growth-promoting ways. Rituals for pets may seem a bit over the top, but their purpose for children as well as adults is to keep them from getting stuck (Reeves, 2011). It is recommended that people who work with clients who have lost pets read from sources such as *The Human–Animal Bond and Grief* (Lagoni, Butler, & Hetts, 1994) and *Pet Loss and Human Bereavement* (Kay et al., 1984).

Bereavement in Elderly People

Lenore and Robert Kizer, ages 82 and 85 respectively, had been living in a nursing home for 4 years. Robert had been there more than a year when Lenore had to join him. Their three living children resided in other states and were busy with their own families, so Lenore placed Robert in the nursing home when he was 80 and she was no longer able to care for him because he required 24-hour nursing care. Lenore was in the dining room eating breakfast when one of the medical staff members came and requested that she come to Robert's room because they couldn't rouse him. When Lenore arrived at the room, a staff physician met her and informed her that Robert had apparently died in his sleep. The following intervention strategies were provided and issues explored with Lenore during the days and weeks immediately following Robert's death.

1. *Individual counseling and intervention.* Assessing Lenore's level of grief and coping ability. Providing opportunities for Lenore to release her grief energy. Assessing Lenore's physical and mental capacities to cope. Assessing her children's ability to help. Examining her economic, medical, and legal needs. Using therapeutic strategies such as cognitive/spiritual, reminiscence, and constructive/narrative therapy to help Lenore revalidate herself as a worthwhile person separate from Robert.

2. *Group work.* Groups within the nursing home. Social groups outside the nursing home.

3. *Referrals.* Medical, religious organizations, legal assistance, Lenore's church, her children, senior citizens' agencies.

Lenore Kizer continued to live in the nursing home following Robert's death. Lenore had several assets, which the crisis worker, a pastoral counselor, used to validate her life as it had been lived and revalidate what her new life would be without Robert. She was physically mobile, she had lots of friends in the nursing home and in the community, she was an outgoing person with an optimistic outlook on life, and her children were supportive. Even with the positive factors she had going for her, Lenore experienced periods of denial, isolation, loneliness, fear, anger, bargaining, and depression that were profound. The crisis worker's goal was to help Lenore achieve a satisfactory degree of reconciliation with and acceptance of Robert's death, and to begin to reorient her postcrisis life as a worthwhile person who was not identified as Robert's wife or Robert's widow. He did this by first tapping into her strong faith. He used cognitive restructuring (Meichenbaum, 1985) and existential therapy (Frankl, 1969) to reinvest her socially and inject new meaning into her life. Finally, he attempted to change her negative interpretations of the event by using a narrative/constructionist approach (Neimeyer & Levitt, 2000).

Lenore: Sometimes I feel it is terrible that I am so alone.

CW: I wonder if you might look back on your strong faith and say that a little differently, Lenore. Something like, "Robert is indeed gone, but God is still with me and so are my friends and my children."

Lenore: I know, and sometimes I forget that. God is always here. If I stop and pray a minute, God generally gives me a way to go. I get so moping around I forget that.

By reframing and proposing follow-through actions, the crisis worker attempts to cut through the ever-deepening vortex of isolation and despair that assails the grief-stricken when a longtime partner has died. Particularly with the elderly, creating resiliency and finding new meaning in life are critical. Many therapists are skittish about bringing spirituality into therapy. However, combining cognitive therapy with spiritual therapy can be extremely powerful (Ramsey & Blieszner, 2000).

Lenore: A lot of times I just mope around. Some of the time I get to feeling sorry for myself. Then sometimes I forget and find myself walking down to Robert's room before I remember that he isn't there anymore. My life seems so meaningless without him.

CW: You're really missing him, and you're also having trouble remembering. What would you like to recall most, and when your life is better, how will it be like that? It's certainly fine to do that reminiscing, but also thinking about how you two worked through things together and how you can use his memories to do that.

While the worker uses reminiscing (described in detail in Chapter 14, Violent Behavior in Institutions),

the focus is on marshaling positive assets Lenore has used in the past to cope with the present and the future. Together, the crisis worker and the client rewrite the client's story line by deconstructing reality (Humphrey, 2009, pp. 184–185) into more positive self-descriptions that are much closer to her life, as opposed to the terrible exception she now faces (Ramsey & Blieszner, 2000).

Lenore: We were very active politically and socially conscious. We were also very active in our church.

CW: So if you were to write those down as the major narratives of your life, and have a conversation with the Lord about it, what do you suppose might come of that?

Lenore: Well, it isn't actually in the Bible, but it is a good saying. "The Lord helps those who help themselves." Robert used to say that, and I think it is true. I need to get off my rear end and help myself.

CW: So, suppose a miracle happened and indeed the Lord came down and in a vision tonight said, "Lenore, I am about to make a miracle happen with you. Tomorrow you will be as you were before. Robert will not be there, but you will be. What will I see happening, Lenore?"

Lenore: Well, you would see an old woman, but still full of a zest for living, taking the retirement van down to the church and going in the church van out to visit the shut-ins. I suppose you would see me also down at the local Republican Party headquarters doing some things there. I also haven't gone to my quilting group in a while, and I want to make every one of the grandchildren a quilt to remember me by. I have been putting that off, but time is flying by. I guess that is kinda egotistical, huh, Lord? (*A wry smile crosses her face.*)

CW: So, could you do that? And I wonder if you might relate what you have said with the women's group next week.

Lenore: Well, I expect I could do that.

The crisis worker uses the miracle question (de Shazer, 1985) in a spiritual format to help Lenore recognize and reinforce the many positive attributes she has had and still has. By having Lenore look at this period in her life as the exception rather than the rule, the crisis worker reframes the loss narrative and seeks to reconstruct her view of life and its meaning. When life stories are rendered chaotic by narrative disruption due to the loss of a lifelong mate, reframing that narrative in more positive terms can foster healing (Neimeyer & Levitt, 2000). That healing may be made much more powerful by helping the client form or reform a spiritual foundation.

It may be argued that the foregoing is a "goody-two-shoes" approach to pacify and mollify the aggrieved and that no real change will occur. Further, it may be patently ridiculous to assume that disheartened old people who are only waiting for the grim reaper to appear could be uplifted by reviewing and hearing encouraging and joyous stories. We propose that this view is as negatively stereotypical of the elderly as one can be. Reconstruction of one's self-concept as a primary task of adaptation to spousal loss is a primary task no matter how old or young one is (Lopata, 1996), and research suggests that allowing older persons to discuss their thoughts and feelings (Segal et al., 2001) helps reduce a variety of negative effects. Further, the elderly are not helpless; they have the capacity to adapt and learn new coping responses even after suffering the loss of a mate (Hanson & Hayslip, 2000).

Bereavement in an HIV-Infected Client

Clint's partner of 6 years died of AIDS 18 months ago. Last week Clint lost his job as a bank loan officer and desperately needs a job. He is somewhat paranoid and suspects that the people at the bank found out that he tested positive for HIV last May, although his job performance had deteriorated considerably and his absences from work did not help. Normally, Clint is an intelligent, enthusiastic, energetic, outgoing, friendly, and positive individual. He is an exceptionally competent employee whom the bank was grooming for management work. Now he presents himself as unsure of himself, depressed, angry, nervous, and anxious. He is riddled with various somatic complaints, none of which has so far proven to be an actual AIDS-related illness. Besides the primary loss of his partner, he has suffered a secondary loss of his job and is further suffering from *stigmatized* loss, which often jeopardizes or even prohibits the use of support systems (Humphrey, 2009, p. 22).

Clint: On top of everything else, I have never come out to my parents. I wouldn't mind telling my mom, but I would have real trouble revealing to my dad that I'm gay. I also worry that telling him that I've tested positive will be too much for his heart, because he's had two bypasses already. I may have to find a cheaper place to live, too. I have too many things to deal with right now. Not to mention the physical problems.

CW: Clint, I'm really glad you came in here today. I can see that you are feeling really depressed today. Are you to the point of thinking about killing yourself?

The first thing the crisis worker does is to explore Clint's lethality level. Because clients may be experiencing an enormous array of situational, medical, and environmental problems, workers must be diligent in defining the total scope of problems, ensuring physical and psychological safety, and providing emotional supports. Crisis intervention with HIV-infected clients must start with sensitive and empathic listening.

CW: I'm happy to know that you're safe for now. Clint, what do we most need to work on right now?

Clint: I just don't see how I can handle everything, how I can make plans, so much is happening.

CW: You're overwhelmed with all the issues you are facing, and you're needing some help, understanding, and supports right now.

Clint: It's been hard enough since my partner died. I still miss him terribly, and now I've lost my job—I have to tell my parents I'm gay—God! Gay and HIV positive, too! Sometimes I think I am going crazy, or then I worry, is it the onset of AIDS-related dementia? Then I wonder if I am not a sinner in the hands of an angry God, and I am getting my just desserts.

CW: Clint, all that would be overwhelming to anyone. I don't want to minimize this at all, but what I do want to do is see if we can't get a handle on this and start to manage these problems. You do not have an execution date, even though it may seem that way. Your HIV can be managed, like any other life-threatening disease. The question is, How do you wish to use your time while you are fighting it? I want to break this down into manageable components. You had huge responsibilities in the bank, so I know you can break complex issues down and plan what to do. This is an exception to what you are normally capable of doing, and I want you to see it that way. So let's use those considerable talents and brainstorm a list of the possible actions you can take, when they'll be done, and what resources and assets you have.

First, though, I want to get you into a support group of people who are HIV positive. This will do two things. It will give you good information and feedback for what is going on medically and how people cope with the physical problems. Second, it will get you out of the social isolation and all of the bad things that go with that.

The crisis worker acknowledges the continued losses Clint has faced, as well as the problem of revealing to his parents his HIV status and the difficulty he will face in the future. Concomitantly, the crisis worker begins to think about what concrete actions Clint will need to take immediately: employment counseling, support groups to help Clint regain a sense of control over his life, and medical services. He challenges the client in a typical REBT therapy manner to stop catastrophic thinking and start problem solving (Ellis & Abrahms, 1978); he also uses a solution-focused technique of cheerleading and pointing out that this is an exception to otherwise very competent behavior (de Shazer, 1985), stressing his abilities to solve complex problems. At this point the worker makes a decision that has more to do with crisis intervention than loss reorientation. He makes an assessment that Clint needs to divide his crisis into manageable pieces and seeks to break the multiple problems down into manageable issues.

Research by Williams and Stafford (1991) indicates that a fundamental form of intervention with partners and adult family members of persons with HIV/AIDS is the use of peer groups to break down the prevalent feelings of isolation, enhance sharing of personal grief, and promote healing (pp. 425–426). Support groups are absolutely critical in educating the person about the disease, sharing intense emotions, observing how others cope (effectively and ineffectively), coming to terms with the disease and its "dreaded" issues, and receiving help from and giving help to others (Hoffman, 1996, p. 72; Nord, 1997, pp. 233–235). They are also critical in helping those individuals who have stigmatized grief find a safe, supportive place to ventilate and get suggestions.

Clint agreed and was referred to an existing group at the Aid to End AIDS Center that could provide the help he needed in an environment of warmth, acceptance, professional competence, and healing. The crisis worker followed up by contacting the center director to make sure that Clint obtained the services he needed. The crisis worker also needed to break down the tidal wave of emotions that was rolling over Clint by validating the intensity of those emotions. The crisis worker attempts to reframe the cognitions about the disease by getting Clint to see that a good life and a long life are not inextricably linked (Hoffman, 1996, p. 80).

CW: So what's the first priority?

Clint: I would like to get clear with my parents. I would also like to do some things to honor my partner, Mark. I did nothing when his parents buried him. They don't want to talk to me. I was cutthroat ambitious in the bank business—the original Scrooge. I want to get another banking job, but I want to do it in a kinder, gentler way, perhaps doing finance work for Habitat for Humanity.

CW: So how do you want to plan on doing those things? I might suggest we role-play that conversation, both to give you practice and be sure how you want to get that over to your dad without upsetting him.

The worker assumes a collaborative role to get the client mobilized. Motivating HIV-positive clients to set goals and challenging them to achieve a meaningful quality of life are extremely important parts of counseling those clients. The crisis worker must not shy away from doing so out of fear that the client will not be up to the task (Hoffman, 1996, pp. 92–94).

Two other critical crisis issues need to be confronted. First is safe sex and general health-promoting practices. Stopping the spread of the disease is critical, and one of the major ethical dilemmas a crisis counselor faces is getting an infected client to practice safe sex. Whether clients are heterosexual or homosexual, the central issue is educating them about safe sex and disclosing their status to their partners or potential partners (Hoffman, 1996, pp. 100–112). Because of revenge, pride, ego, shame, loneliness, or sexual drive, getting a client to practice safe sex is not an easy issue. The psychological implications embedded in the destruction of the client's assumptive world have everything to do with the reason why some people continue to engage in risky behaviors and why public education campaigns to discourage risky behavior have been only marginally effective (Nord, 1997, p. 249). The last thing most young men want to do is admit to a potential sexual partner that they are infected.

CW: Sex may be the last thing on your mind right now, but it will come up. I am ethically and morally bound to say something about this because you would be putting another at lethal risk. I can't stop you from having sex, but I can help you to educate yourself about how to have sex and explore some of the reasons you might not feel you ought to tell somebody else. I want to refer you to Pete Endicott, a counselor at Aid to End AIDS. He can help you make some good decisions about sexual relations.

The complex and multiple loss issues that surround HIV infection and AIDS make it a horrific crisis. Initial crisis intervention generally means bringing runaway emotions to a halt and breaking the multiple issues of loss into discrete, manageable components. At the same time, the crisis worker is also tasked with dealing with clients' larger issues of attempting to find meaning from the disease and its effects, while living as good a life as they can.

Complicated Grief: Death of a Mother

These case examples end with the most difficult type of grief and loss issue—complicated grief reaction (Rando, 1993). Ann Marie is a 38-year-old legal secretary who went one-on-one with a bridge abutment and lost. Her car was totaled. She was unconscious and taken to the hospital for an examination. Luckily, her only injury was a concussion. However, her blood alcohol content was found to be 0.17—twice the legal limit. She was charged with a DUI and was ordered by the court to see an addiction counselor.

However, Ann Marie's case is not about addiction to alcohol but about a complicated and chronic grief reaction to the sudden death of her mother after a long bout with lupus. The problem is that neither she nor the crisis worker is aware of that at the moment. The crisis worker is a licensed addiction counselor who has also worked in bereavement.

CW: So what was going on before you had the wreck?

Ann Marie: I was angry at my father, and I finally decided to get out of the house and go out to a club with my girlfriend.

CW: Angry! How?

Ann Marie: (*Starts weeping.*) Look at me. I am 38 and taking care of my father. I never go out. I haven't had a date in forever. I don't know what got into me. I generally don't drink very much at all.

CW: What do you suppose *did* get into you to make you to decide to go drinking and driving? As I look at your record, this is your first offense. You don't have so much as a speeding ticket.

Ann Marie: I work all day. I come home at night and cook, wash, fetch, clean, sew for my dad and my brother Ralphie, who is 36 and living at home. I do everything for them. Ever since Mom died, they've expected me to take her place. I even moved back home from Phoenix, and now here I am. It is useless. I am useless.

CW: When you say "useless," I don't like the sound of that. You sound so down and out I am wondering if getting into that car and slamming into that bridge abutment was not a way of attempting to kill yourself without the stigma of suicide attached to it.

While it may appear that your authors continuously harp on this issue and you are tired of being nagged about assessing for suicide with every client, many suicides are accomplished by automobile. Mustering enough courage to do it by getting intoxicated is another common feature of suicide by automobile. Further, suicidal ideation is one of the markers for a complicated grief reaction. The addiction counselor immediately picks up on Ann Marie's hopelessness and helplessness, and pursues it. The addiction counselor has now shifted to crisis mode. Suicidal behavior is one of Worden's (1991, p. 76) complicated grief clues.

Ann Marie: (*cynical laugh*) If I was really serious about that, I'd have knocked Ralphie in the head and stuck him on the front of the hood. Kill myself? Not yet. Drink too much and do something stupid cause I feel sorry for myself? Yes!

CW: Okay. I needed to check that out. You mentioned Phoenix. What was that like and how is this different in Pittsburgh?

Ann Marie: I had a great job with a great law firm in Phoenix 4 years ago. I had a great boyfriend there. I had a great life. I was going to get married. I just got a promotion to executive secretary. Then Mom got sick. She had always waited on Dad hand and foot. He was useless without her (*laughs cynically*), about like me now. I started flying home to help out, but the lupus got worse and Mom went to a wheelchair and then to a nursing home. I got a job out here. The boyfriend said I had to choose. I did. A helluva choice. A dependent father and shiftless brother and a third-rate job. Maybe I did try to drive myself into that abutment. I don't think so, but I don't know anymore. I don't see much of a life for me anymore.

The client's losses are large and many. There is no rule that says grieving and bereavement must be over a death. The sacrifices the client has made careerwise and in her relationships are profound. The isolation, loneliness, depression, anger, and sadness encapsulate all of the first five of McKenna's (1999) components of survivor grief.

CW: So you have sacrificed your life for your parents. What you have gotten from that is a smorgasbord of bad feelings and bad outcomes.

Ann Marie: (*Continues weeping softly.*) My mother died last year. Worked herself to death for them. (*Clinches her fist and pounds it into her hand.*) Christ! I wish she were back here. I miss her, but I would give her a piece of my mind for not standing up to those two jerks I am taking care of and make them grow up.

CW: How do you feel about your mother's death?

Ann Marie: Why . . . why . . . what do you mean? Terrible, of course. I loved her. We used to talk at least twice a week when I was in Phoenix.

CW: I am just wondering. You indicated your dad and brother were pretty dependent on her, and now they seem to be that way on you.

Ann Marie: Oh, Dad says he'll get a housekeeper. He's been saying that since Mom got sick, but he won't when he's got his daughter for an indentured servant. And that failure-to-launch brother of mine. "Yeah, I'll pitch in, Sis, right after I get back from the game. Say, mind washing my work clothes? I forgot and don't have any clean for Monday."

The crisis worker's content query moves immediately to the deceased mother. He is well aware that what clients say about their dead loved ones may be very different from how they feel. Unfinished business (Attig, 2000, pp. 112–117) can be a major problem in grief counseling. This is particularly true when the death is sudden (Cummock, 1996). Whether that unfinished business is guilt over having or not having done something, or having or not having said something, unfinished business is a common issue that is particularly problematic because of prohibitions against "speaking ill of the dead" or, indeed, the inability to speak to them at all.

In a very odd way, but anything but uncommon, what the client is manifesting is *disenfranchised grief*. It also has characteristics of rational-emotive behavior therapy's mustrabatory behavior (Ellis & Grieger, 1977) in that the client is duty bound and "must" absolutely take over for her mother no matter the cost to her because that is what "good daughters" do. This mustrabatory behavior segues into and goes a good deal beyond the client's primary loss of her mother to secondary losses of a love life, career, and her independence. When these are piled one on top of the other, they are an excellent recipe for complicated/prolonged grief. Ann Marie meets the proposed criteria (Prigerson, Vanderwerker, & Maciejewski, 2008; Zhang, el-Jawahri, & Prigerson, 2006) for complicated/prolonged grief in the following ways:

Criterion A: Yearning, pining, and longing for the deceased to a distressing degree (although she hasn't verbally acknowledged it yet because of her anger).

Criterion B: Experiencing four of the following in the last month as marked, overwhelming, and extreme: (1) trouble accepting the death; (2) inability to trust others since the death; (3) excessive bitterness or anger over the death; (4) feeling uneasy about moving on with one's life; (5) feeling emotionally numb or detached from others since the death; (6) feeling life is empty or meaningless without the deceased; (7) feeling the future holds no meaning or prospect of fulfillment without the deceased; (8) feeling agitated, jumpy, or on edge since the death. Ann Marie clearly meets Criterion B.

Criterion C: The above symptoms and disturbances cause marked dysfunction in social, occupational, or other important domains. Ann Marie's social and work life have been seriously impaired by the death.

Criterion D: The above symptoms and disturbances must last at least 6 months. A period of 4 years definitely meets this criterion.

Ann Marie: (*pounding her fist into her hand*) I told Mom again and again to make them be independent. She'd just say, "Oh, you know your dad, he likes to be taken care of, and your brother's had tough luck."

CW: But now it is you who is taking care of them. If you could speak to your mother about what you are now feeling, what would you say to her?

Ann Marie: That's crazy. She's dead. I can't speak to her.

CW: Do you visit her gravesite or memorial?

Ann Marie: I go there every morning and pray in the mausoleum. I am a good Catholic. I also light a candle at Mass. My old girlfriend from high school says I am going too much and can't get over it. It has been almost a year now. She was the one I went drinking with the other night. The only friend I've got . . . from high school! My God, but I am pitiful!

CW: I understand you care very deeply for your mother, but sometimes there are things that are left unsaid or undone. If your mother were sitting right here right now, what might you say to her?

The crisis worker uses a tried-and-true Gestalt therapy technique of the "empty chair" to attempt to allow some of the client's powerful and buried affect about the predicament her mother has left her in to come out (Cable, 1996; Humphrey, 2009, pp. 154–166). While it may seem this technique is used in a lot of situations in this book, it is one of the best for objectifying emotions—and many, many seemingly intractable crises call for just that.

Ann Marie: (*tentatively*) I guess . . . like always, that I loved her.

CW: Speak to her as if she were here right now in that chair over there!

Ann Marie: I love you, Mom. I wish you were still here. I miss you so much sometimes.

CW: What would you tell her about the situation with your dad?

Ann Marie: Not much, I guess, just I am bearing up.

The crisis worker gently reflects and confronts the buried anger he guesses she is feeling and calls her on her behavior.

CW: I sense some anger about that, not just your dad's demands and needs and your own lack of a life. Bearing up under her load. A load she left you with. Did she ask you to do that?

Ann Marie: Well, sorta. She never asked me to come back home, but she asked me to look after Dad.

The crisis worker now makes an owning statement targeted directly at the anger in an attempt to get the client to speak to the affect. This is not a one-step process; it calls for repeated attempts to uncover the pent-up emotion. This process may take considerable time—or perhaps never happen with some clients who are so deeply mired in it.

CW: If it were me, I might feel a great deal of resentment. I wouldn't quite know how to deal with it, but I would surely feel it. I might even be afraid of some of those feelings that would not seem right, forbidden even. It wouldn't be right to be angry with my mother who died heroically trying to take care of my father, yet I would be angry about the predicament I was in and the loss of my own life—love life, career goals, a chance for a family. I would be very angry about that. If you were that angry, what might you tell her? I have an assignment, if you are up to it. I want you to go back to the mausoleum, and I want you to tell her how you feel. I will go with you if you want, but you need to do this.

Many times people will go out of their way to avoid returning to the gravesite or memorial site because of the fear of their inability to control their feelings. Or alternatively, their feelings will be so out of control that they practically deify the gravesite, they are there so often. The client should be willing to make the visit and should never be forced. Having an agenda such as Ann Marie's is important. When the grief is complicated, it is important that the crisis worker be willing to go with the client. While there, the client may write a letter and burn it, or put a message in a helium balloon and let it fly away. After the gravesite visit, it is helpful if the client does something positive, rests, and is reinforced for the accomplishment of the visit. The summation of this visit is to literally put the body to rest and bring closure (Johnson, 1987, p. 181).

Ann Marie: (*7 A.M. at the mausoleum by her mother's crypt*) I feel so stupid. I . . . I can't . . . I don't know what to say.

CW: Just say what is in your heart.

Ann Marie: (*Struggles with long pauses.*) I miss you. I . . . love you. I wish . . . you wouldn't have let Daddy and Ralphie be so dependent on you because they are on me, and I don't know how . . . what to do. I am kinda angry with you about that. . . . In fact, I am VERY ANGRY WITH YOU! How could you have done this? You always encouraged me to go out and be independent. To seek my own life, and I did . . . but then you hooked me and reeled me back in. Damn it! How could you! How could you do that! (*Leans against the crypt and wails while the crisis worker holds her.*)

CW: (*very gently while holding his arm around Ann Marie's shoulders.*) Is it possible that underneath that anger is a lot

of loneliness for your mom? That the real anger is that she left you without your main support, her wisdom, and the talks you had about your hopes and dreams? I wonder if you can forgive her for that.

Ann Marie: (*sobbing*) Oh, Momma, I do miss you, and not just for having to take care of Daddy and Ralphie. For always encouraging me and supporting me. I feel so selfish. I do forgive you and hope you can forgive me.

Forgiveness is a difficult thing to do. The anger that overlays her frustration also overlays her fears of now being on her own, of her deep personal insecurity now that her main support system is no longer there. Forgiveness is critical to letting go. By understanding and getting past the subtle fears that prevent forgiveness of real or imagined past indiscretions, injustices, hurts, failures, and insults, clients are finally able to move forward (De Moss, 2003).

CW: (*Waits for her emotions to pour out.*) Your mother wanted you to be independent. What do you suppose she might say to you about exerting some of that independence with your dad and Ralphie?

Ann Marie: (*regaining some composure*) I guess . . . I . . . guessss . . . maybe . . . she would . . . say, "Ann Marie, you know good and well that is not what I meant. You must lead your own life. Now you sit down with them and tell them there are going to be some new rules. I took care of your dad and Ralphie, but I wasn't a babysitter for them. You know I didn't mean for you to do that either." (*Continues dialogue with her mother.*)

CW: I would like you to write up a list of "new rules" for your dad and Ralphie, and describe how you are going to behave toward them. I would like you to come and visit your mom tomorrow and discuss those rules with her.

While it may seem strange to have a conversation with a dead person who most assuredly will not answer, the fact is that clients may well have a fruitful dialogue and begin to concretize diffuse and abstract feelings that were heretofore unreachable.

We can objectify unfinished business in many ways, such as writing letters, having dialogues, playing music, drawing and painting pictures, creating scrapbooks, sculpting, or creating other symbolic ways to relieve our hurt and anger with the unfinished business (Attig, 2000, p. 116). By doing so, Ann Marie was able to start letting go of the complicated grief reaction she had developed, and forgive her mother for dying on her so suddenly and leaving her with two dependent men.

While prayer can be positive and helpful in many circumstances, prayer in this case served only to punch back the real feelings Ann Marie was holding toward her mother for having the audacity to leave her with a very dependent father. Until she was able to express her feelings and vent her anger, Ann Marie would continue to have transcrises in her own life, which could indeed become lethal for her. Ann Marie is representative of many people we see in crisis who appear to have one kind of crisis, yet have a different one underlying it. This underlying crisis is often complicated grief and unreconciled bereavement.

Indeed, while Ann Marie's DUI is most assuredly a problem, and her drinking may be a problem as well, the undergirding crisis is her sense of loss—loss of a job, loss of a romantic relationship, loss of her independence, and finally loss of a parent—none of which she had adequately grieved but over which she had instead built up a tremendous amount of unconscious resentment. Complicated grief is a delicate, sensitive, and troublesome issue that is surrounded by emotional minefields and taboo cultural totems (Rando, 1993). Yet if a crisis worker suspects an unresolved grief problem, much as our addiction counselor did, then this is the very place that intervention must go. If you do not feel comfortable in doing this, and even we "experts" sometimes don't, then refer the client.

Ann Marie was able to move forward and confront her father and brother. She was also able to engage some effective support systems to help her father and brother become more independent. None of these steps was fast or easy. She no longer visited her mother every day, but still remembered her by lighting a candle for her at Mass once a week. She completed her DUI course and got her driver's license reinstated. At last report she was actively engaged in a number of community activities and hobbies, and had moved to another, larger law firm with more responsibility. Although she has yet to find true romance, she has accomplished a great deal. She has mourned the loss of her mother, removed the unresolved grief that was an emotional anchor around her neck, regained some of her independence, and started to reinvent and reinvigorate her life.

The Crisis Worker's Own Grief

Before workers engage in grief work with others, they must first take care of themselves. This means becoming proactive in maintaining their own vitality. Failure to do so can result in the phenomenon known as *vicarious traumatization* or *compassion fatigue* (see Chapter 16, Human Services Workers in Crisis). Indeed, working with loss and bereavement has high potential for burnout.

Schneider (1984) reminds us that "it is not possible to be a facilitator of the growth aspects of bereavement if the helper is not also experiencing growth in relation to personal losses" (p. 270). The knowledge and perspective gained from one's own growth following grief should serve as a quiet reservoir of strength for workers. But the worker's own grief experience should not be projected or imposed on clients. Both Rando (1984) and Schoenberg (1980) challenge caregivers to come to grips with their own personal and professional attitudes toward death, grief, and bereavement before venturing into helping relationships with clients who are in grief. According to Rando (1984), there are several reasons why caregivers should ensure that their own grief and attitudes about grief are not allowed to intrude on their strength and vitality for helping others (pp. 430–435).

1. *Emotional investment in the client.* A certain degree of emotional investment in clients is normal and needed. Overinvestment in those whom they help may require crisis workers to expend an inordinate amount of energy on their own grief responses in cases of dying and bereaved clients.

2. *Bereavement overload.* If the worker forms close bonds with several clients, the emotional load may involve too many risks and grief responses on the part of the worker. Workers can deal with their own bereavement overload provided that they are aware of it while it is happening to them and that they act on their internal signals to get help and/or take steps to effect their own renewal before several client losses get them down.

3. *Countertransference.* Sometimes crisis workers engaged in grief work with others find that such work awakens their own feelings, thoughts, memories, and fantasies about losses in their own lives. Solomon, Neria, and Ram (1998) report on the tremendous countertransference issues that Israeli mental health workers had in dealing with Holocaust survivors and the equally tremendous problems that caused for them and their clients. Workers who experience such countertransference will be severely impaired in helping others. To deal with countertransference, caregivers who regularly work with loss-related clients should be involved in peer supervision, case staffing, psychological autopsies, and debriefing groups for reducing emotional overload caused by constant involvement with client grief.

4. *Emotional replenishment.* Caregivers in the area of grief and bereavement work must take special care

to minister to their own emotional needs. Caregivers need support systems to provide for their physical, emotional, and psychological wellness. Emotional replenishment involves both taking care of oneself internally and having environmental supports from significant others—a supervisor, friends, family, colleagues—and meaningful physical and emotional activities that take the person completely away from loss and back into a positive emotional and physical state.

5. *Facing one's own mortality.* One of the important aspects of loss work is that it may arouse existential anxiety over one's own death. Support groups, supervision, inservice training, and reading are suggested coping mechanisms. Spiritual growth activities are worthwhile alternatives for many caregivers.

6. *Sense of power.* Caregivers, like all other people, need a sense of power or control. Working with clients in dying, grief, and bereavement may cause workers to identify vicariously with the losses of their clients. Such identification may result in a sense of loss of power or control on the part of workers. Strategies for preventing feelings of loss of power are essentially the same as those recommended for dealing with countertransference.

7. *Tendency to rescue.* It is essential that workers relinquish the rescue fantasy, especially when dealing with grief and bereavement, because rescuing someone who has experienced or is about to suffer loss is to deny the inevitability of the loss.

The seven proactive points just noted are good starting points for worker vigilance in preventing vicarious trauma, compassion fatigue, and burnout in themselves. It is highly recommended that you thoroughly read Chapter 16, Human Services Workers in Crisis, for further coping strategies if you are going to do this work.

Humphrey (2009, pp. 218–219) has posed some hard questions for professionals in human service interested in doing this work. They are abridged, encapsulated, and stated here with our own additions. Think carefully about them and see what your answers are!

1. Can I see the differences between my own grief experiences and those of my clients?
2. Am I aware of my own unresolved issues of loss, do I have unfinished business with them, and do they spill over into my work?
3. Do I rescue clients from their grief because it is too terrifying for me or I can't handle their pain?

4. Do I have to expend so much of my energy controlling my own emotions that I am ineffective with my clients?
5. Do I avoid, deny, or otherwise sidestep certain grief-related issues because of my own issues with them?
6. Am I unwilling to let my clients experience the pain of grief because I don't believe they can handle such emotion-laden topics?
7. Does the mere mention of the topic of death or dying make me apprehensive or anxious and start dreading the counseling session?
8. Are my own losses so new and raw as to not allow me to work effectively with someone else's loss?

Is There Any Lemonade in All These Sour Lemons?

Of all the chapters in this book, Personal Loss: Bereavement and Grief is one of the most difficult and depressing, at times, to write. The question becomes, Given the overwhelming nature of most losses, can we hope for anything better than just getting back to some level of homeostasis and equilibrium? And if so, then what? Richard Tedeschi and Lawrence Calhoun are two researchers in particular who have been working on this problem for more than 15 years (Calhoun & Tedeschi, 2001; Tedeschi & Calhoun, 1995, 2003, 2004, 2006, 2009; Tedeschi, Park, & Calhoun, 1998). Here's the good news: It doesn't happen to everybody, but overall there is a fair amount of research to indicate that people can grow out of trauma and bereavement and do so for the better (Armstrong & Shakespeare-Finch, 2011; Caserta e al., 2009; Cryder et al., 2006). They do better than just adapt, but indeed experience positive growth beyond what and where they were before their losses and the ensuing crises. What is probably most interesting is that the more severe the loss reported, the higher the levels of growth (Armstrong & Shakespeare-Finch, 2011). So take heart! There is lemonade!

It also appears that crisis workers can experience positive growth out of dealing with trauma and loss (Arnold et al., 2005). So we end this chapter by finishing the horrific story of the Wisconsin dairyman you met at the beginning of the chapter. The whole community pitched in to take care of the farm so our dairyman could take his family and get away for a vacation (very hard to do when one milks twice a day and shovels a lot of fertilizer in between). That in and of itself was extremely moving and growth promoting for the whole community. One farmer told your author while the two were shoveling fertilizer at the dairyman's farm, "We used to do this a lot. It's the right thing to do and by God, we did it for Lutherans, Catholics, and even that Methodist family! It didn't make any difference. We helped people when they were down and hurting, no matter who. I personally feel damn good about this, and my guess is everybody else does too."

The dairyman took his family to Disney World, where his deceased son had wanted to go. A week after they returned, your author pulled his truck into the farm lot on his regular Friday route. The dairyman came out of the milking parlor and said, "Ah, come on inside, I got something for you. It isn't much but it just, umh, ah, my way of, I guess, well, umh, sorta saying thanks for listening to me. It helped a lot." With that he gave your author a cigarette lighter from Disney World. Your author doesn't smoke anymore, but he still has that lighter and that was in 1976.

But he got more than that from going into the jaws of this terrible death. He made a decision to get back in the business of counseling, which ultimately led to the University of Memphis, helping give birth to the CIT program that has become international in scope and the gold standard for police training for crisis intervention with the mentally ill; training more than 3,000 counselors, and writing a seventh edition of this crisis book that we humbly believe has affected thousands and thousands of students and, in turn, hopefully has helped them deal effectively with thousands more clients. So from the dread of walking into that milk house 35 years ago, it is safe to say one of your authors grew more than he could have possibly imagined.

SUMMARY

The stages models of death, dying, grief, and bereavement have become outdated due to a lack of research to prove their viability. Newer models of loss picture grief as highly individualist and not progressing neatly through linear stages. The adaptive model proposes that grieving over loss occurs along a continuum of styles and that no particular style is the one, right, true path to resolution. The dual process model promotes grieving as oscillating back and forth between a loss orientation and a restoration orientation over an extended period of time.

Several different types of loss typify the kinds of human events or tragedies that might bring crisis workers into contact with persons experiencing grief. All of these losses are the same in that they may strike individuals with grief and all that grief entails. Examples of such losses are (1) the death of a spouse, (2) the death of a child, (3) bereavement in childhood, (4) job loss, (5) separation and divorce, (6) the death of a pet, (7) bereavement in elderly people, and (8) the trauma associated with HIV and AIDS. However, loss is also different in that persons may suffer from a primary loss, secondary loss, multiple loss, ambiguous loss, and stigmatized loss.

Every human being will, at one time or another, suffer personal loss. During our lives most of us will encounter numerous people who are experiencing bereavement or grief as a result of some personal loss. What may be clearly perceived as a personal loss ranges from a devastating occurrence, such as the death of a spouse or a child, to what many people might view as a minor loss, such as that of a pet or a family heirloom. In any event, it is an important loss if the individual perceives it as such, and workers must treat each client's loss with empathy, caring, and sensitivity. Although the bereaved can never forget the loss and return to a state of complete precrisis equilibrium, he or she can be helped to reformulate the loss within a context of growth and hope.

Most loss is resolved by grieving and mourning that help the person place the loss in memory and move forward with living. Complicated/prolonged grief is a manifestation of loss that has not been resolved, grief that has gone unreconciled, mourning that hadn't been completed, and as a result is now floregenic and pathologic. Complicated/prolonged grief may occur after an extended period of time in regard to a nontraumatic loss and have coexisting disorders such as depression and anxiety. It may also result from a traumatic loss and be classified as traumatic grief with the possible coexistence of PTSD. Complicated/prolonged grief is transcrisis in nature and, if not dealt with, can cause serious to lethal physical and psychological problems for the individual suffering from it.

Intervention strategies, techniques, and skills that crisis workers need for helping people in these categories of grief are focused on cognitive-behavioral and constructivist approaches, but may be highly eclectic when interventions are tailor made to fit the idiosyncratic needs of the individual's grief process.

Crisis workers who work with grieving clients, and particularly clients with complicated/prolonged grief who do not take care of themselves emotionally, physically, and spiritually, become vulnerable to vicarious traumatization and compassion fatigue, particularly if they have not resolved their own losses.

 To see some of the concepts discussed in this chapter in action, refer to your *Crisis Intervention in Action* DVD, or see the clips online on the Counseling CourseMate website. To access this site, go to www.cengagebrain.com, where you'll also find an eBook, additional study tools, quizzes, and more. When we think about loss, most often it has to do with death. However, the fact is that most "loss" that workers encounter may not have to do with physical death but rather the death of a relationship, be it with another person or institution. Put yourself in the outplacement counseling session with Ann. Would you be blindsided by her dramatic shift from an outplacement counseling session to potential lethality? Would you see that underlying all that anger is a grief issue about loss of a relationship and a secondary loss of self-efficacy?

REFERENCES

Abei, E., & Kruger, M. L. (2009). The widowhood effect: A comparison of Jews and Catholics. *Omega: Journal of Death and Dying 59*(4), 325–337.

Adams, K. B. (2006). The transition to caregiving: The experience of family members embarking on the dementia caregiving career. *Journal of Gerontological Social Work, 47*(3/4), 3–29.

Allen, R. S., Haley, E., Roff, L. L., Schmid, B., & Bergman, E. J. (2006). Responding to the needs of caregivers near the end of life: Enhancing benefits and minimizing burdens. In J. L. Werrh & D. Blevins (Eds.), *Psychosocial issues near the end of life: A resource for professional care providers* (pp. 183–201). Washington, DC: American Psychological Association.

Allumbaugh, D. L., & Hoyt, W. T. (1999). Effectiveness of grief therapy: A meta-analysis. *Journal of Counseling Psychology, 46*(3), 370–388.

Altmaier, E. M. (2011). Best practices in counseling grief and loss: Finding benefit from trauma. *Journal of Mental Health Counseling, 33*(1), 33–42.

Armstrong, D., & Shakespeare-Finch, J. (0211). Relationship to the bereaved and perceptions of severity of trauma differentiate elements of posttraumatic growth. *Omega: Journal of Death and Dying, 63*(2), 125–140.

Arnold, D., Calhoun, L. G., Tedeschi, R., & Cann, A. (2005). Vicarious posttraumatic growth in psychotherapy. *Journal of Humanistic Psychology, 45*(2), 239–263.

Attig, T. (2000). *The heart of grief: Death and the search for lasting love.* New York: Oxford University Press.

Balk, D. E. (1990, August). *The many faces of bereavement on the college campus.* Paper presented at the annual meeting of the American Psychological Association, Boston.

Balk, D. E. (2009). Adolescent development: The back story to adolescent encounters with death and bereavement. In D. E. Balk & C. A. Corr (Eds.), *Adolescent encounters with death, bereavement, and coping* (pp. 3–20). New York: Springer.

Balk, D. E., & Corr, C. A. (2001). Bereavement during adolescence: A review of research. In M. S. Stroebe, R. O. Hansson, H. Schut, & W. Stroebe (Eds.), *Handbook of bereavement research: Consequences, coping and care* (pp. 199–218). Washington, DC: American Psychological Association.

Balk, D. E., Zaengle, D., & Corr, C. A. (2011). Strengthening grief support for adolescents coping with a peer's death. *School Psychology International, 32*(2), 144–162.

Becvar, D. S. (2001). *In the presence of grief.* New York: Guilford Press.

Bedikian, S. (2008). The death of mourning: From Victorian crepe to the little black dress. *Omega: Journal of Death and Dying, 57*(1), 35–52.

Bernstein, J. R. (1997). *When the bough breaks: Forever after the death of a son or daughter.* Kansas City, MO: Andrews & McKeel.

Betz, G., & Thorngren, J. M. (2006). Ambiguous loss and the family grieving process. *Family Journal, 14*(4), 359–365.

Boelen, P. A, & Prigerson, H. G. (2007). The influence of symptoms of prolonged grief disorder, depression, and anxiety on quality of life among bereaved adults: A prospective study. *European Archives of Psychiatry and Clinical Neuroscience, 257*(8), 442–452.

Boelen, P. A., van de Schoot, R., van den Hout, M. A., de Keijser, J., & van den Bout, J. (2010). Prolonged grief disorder, depression, and posttraumatic stress disorder are distinguishable syndromes. *Journal of Affective Disorders, 125*(1–3), 374–378.

Bonanno, G. A., Papa, A., Lalande, K., Zhang, N., & Noll, J. G. (2005). Grief processing and deliberate grief avoidance: A prospective comparison of bereaved spouses and parents in the United States and the People's Republic of China. *Journal of Consulting and Clinical Psychology, 73*(1), 86–98.

Boon, H., Ruiter, R. A., James S., van den Borne, B., Williams, E., & Reddy, P. (2010). Correlates of grief among older adults caring for children and grandchildren as a consequence of HIV & AIDS in South Africa. *Journal of Aging and Health, 22*(1), 48–67.

Bordow, J. (1982). *The ultimate loss: Coping with the death of a child.* New York: Beaufort Books.

Boss, P. (2006). *Loss, trauma, and resilience.* New York: Norton.

Bowlby, J. (1969). *Attachment and loss: Vol. 1. Attachment.* London: Hogarth/New York: Basic Books.

Bowlby, J. (1973). *Attachment and loss: Vol. 2. Separation, anxiety, and anger.* London: Hogarth/New York: Basic Books.

Bowlby, J. (1980). *Attachment and loss: Vol. 3. Loss, sadness, and depression.* London: Hogarth/New York: Basic Books.

Bowlby, J. (1988). *A secure base: Parent–child attachment and healthy human development.* New York: Basic Books.

Braun, M. J., & Berg, D. H. (1994). Meaning reconstruction in the experience of parental bereavement. *Death Studies, 18*, 105–129.

Brewington, J. O., Nassar-McMillan, S., Flowers, C. P., & Furr, S. R. (2004). A preliminary investigation of factors associated with job loss grief. *Career Development Quarterly, 53*(1), 78–83.

Britton, P. J. (2001). Guidelines for counseling clients with HIV spectrum disorders. In E. R. Welfel & R. E. Ingersoll (Eds.), *The mental health desk reference* (pp. 60–66). New York: Wiley.

Brooks, J. D., & Martinez, C. (1999). Animals as neglected members of the family in studies of death and dying. In B. De Vries (Ed.), *End of life issues: Interdisciplinary and multidimensional perspectives* (pp. 167–179). New York: Springer.

Brown, E. B. (1988). *Sunrise tomorrow: Coping with a child's death.* Grand Rapids, MI: Baker Bookhouse.

Brown, E. B (1999). *Loss, change and grief: An educational perspective.* London: David Fulton.

Brown, L. (2008). *Cultural competence in trauma therapy: Beyond the flashback.* Washington, DC: American Psychological Association.

Bruce, M. L., & Kim, K. M. (1992). Differences in the effects of divorce on major depression in men and women. *American Journal of Psychiatry, 149*, 914–917.

Buckley, T., McKinley, S., Tofler, G., & Bartrop, R. (2010). Cardiovascular risk in early bereavement: A literature review and proposed mechanisms. *International Journal of Nursing Studies, 47*(2), 229–238.

Butler, C. S., & Lagoni, L. S. (1996). Children and pet loss. In C. A. Corr & D. M. Corr (Eds.), *Handbook of childhood death and bereavement* (pp. 179–200). New York: Springer.

Cable, D. G. (1996). Grief counseling for survivors of traumatic loss. In K. J. Doka (Ed.), *Living with grief after sudden loss: Suicide, homicide, accident, heart attack, stroke* (pp. 117–126). Washington, DC: Hospice Foundation of America.

Calhoun, L. G., & Tedeschi, R. G. (2001). Posttraumatic growth: The positive lessons of loss. In R. A. Neimeyer (Ed.), *Meaning reconstruction & the experience of loss* (pp. 157–172). Washington, DC: American Psychological Association.

Camelley, K. B., Wortman, C. B., Bolger, N., & Burke, D. T. (2006). The time course of grief reactions to spousal loss: Evidence from a national probability sample. *Journal of Personality and Social Psychology. 91*(3), 476–492.

Cann, A., Calhoun, L., Tedeschi, R. Taku, K., Vishnevsky, T., Triplett, K., et al. (2011a). A short form of the Posttraumatic Growth Inventory. *Anxiety, Stress, & Coping: An International Journal, 23*(2), 127–137.

Cann, A., Calhoun, L., Tedeschi, R., Triplett, K., Vishnevsky, T., & Lindstrom, C. (2011b). Assessing posttraumatic cognitive processes: The Event-Related Rumination Inventory. *Anxiety, Stress, & Coping: An International Journal, 24*(2), 137–156.

Caserta, M., Lund, D., Utz, R., & de Vries, B. (2009). Stress-related growth among the recently bereaved. *Aging & Mental Health, 13*(3), 463–476.

Charles-Edwards, D. (2009). Introduction to the special section on death, loss, and work. *Death Studies, 33*(5), 399–401.

Cohen, J. A., & Mannarino, A. P. (2011). Supporting children with traumatic grief: What educators need to know. *School Psychology International, 32*(2), 117–131.

Cohen, J. A., Mannarino, A. P., & Deblinger, E. (2006). *Treating trauma and traumatic grief in children and adolescents.* New York: Guilford Press.

Cohen, J. A., Mannarino, A. P., Greenberg, T., Padlo, S., & Shipley, C. (2002). Childhood trauma and grief: Concepts and controversies. *Trauma, Violence, & Abuse, 3*, 307–327.

Cohen, J. A., Mannarino, A. P., & Knudsen, K. (2004). Treating childhood traumatic grief: A pilot study. *Journal of the American Academy of Child and Adolescent Psychiatry, 43*, 1225–1233.

Colgrove, M., Bloomfield, H. H., & McWilliams, P. (1991). *How to survive the loss of a love.* Los Angeles: Prelude Press.

Collins, W. L., & Doolittle, A. (2006). Personal reflections of funeral rituals and spirituality in a Kentucky African American family. *Death Studies, 30*(10), 957–969.

Corr, C. A., & Corr, D. M. (1996). *Handbook of childhood death and bereavement.* New York: Springer.

Costa, L., & Holliday, D. (1994). Helping children cope with the death of a parent. *Elementary School Guidance & Counseling, 28*, 206–213.

Cowan, D. S. (2010). Death of a friend during childhood. In C. A. Corr, D. E. Balk (Eds.), *Children's encounters with death, bereavement, and coping* (pp. 219–236). New York: Springer.

Cramer, S. H., Keitel, M. A., & Zevon, M. A. (1990). Spouses of cancer patients: A review of the literature. *Journal of Counseling and Development, 69*, 163–166.

Crase, D. (1994). Important consumer issues surrounding death. *Thanatos, 19*(1), 22–26.

Crenshaw, D. A., & Lee, J. (2010). The disenfranchised grief of children. In N. B. Webb (Ed.). *Helping bereaved children: A handbook for practitioners* (3rd ed., pp. 91–108). New York: Guilford Press.

Cryder, C. H., Kilmer, R. P., Tedeschi, R. G., & Calhoun, L. G. (2006). An exploratory study of posttraumatic growth in children following a natural disaster. *American Journal of Orthopsychiatry, 76*(1), 65–69.

Culliford, L. (2002). Spirituality and clinical care. *British Medical Journal, 325*, 1413–1435.

Cummock, V. (1996). Journey of a young widow. In K. J. Doka (Ed.), *Living with grief after sudden loss: Suicide, homicide, accident, heart attack, stroke* (pp. 1–10). Washington, DC: Hospice Foundation of America.

Currier, J. M., Holland, J.M., & Neimeyer, R.A. (2007). The effectiveness of bereavement interventions with children: A meta-analytic review of controlled outcome research. *Journal of Clinical Child and Adolescent Psychology, 36*(2), 253– 259.

Currier, J. M., Neimeyer, R. A., & Berman, J. S. (2008). The effectiveness of psychotherapeutic interventions for bereaved persons: A comprehensive quantitative review. *Psychological Bulletin, 134*(5), 648–661.

Daggett, L. M. (2002). Living with loss: Middle-aged men face spousal bereavement. *Qualitative Health Research, 12*(5), 625–639.

Dallos, R., & Vetere, A. (2009). *Systemic therapy and attachment narrative: Applications in a range of clinical settings.* New York: Routledge/Taylor & Francis Group.

De Moss, C. (2003, April). *Forgiveness—What's the secret?* Twenty-Seventh Convening of Crisis Intervention Personnel, Chicago.

Dershimer, R. A. (1990). *Counseling the bereaved.* New York: Pergamon Press.

de Shazer, S. (1985). *Keys to solutions in brief therapy.* New York: Norton.

Dickens, M. (1985). *Miracles of courage: How families meet the challenge of a child's critical illness.* New York: Dodd, Mead.

Dickson, A., O'Brien, G., Ward, R., Allan, D., & O'Carroll, R. (2010). The impact of assuming the primary caregiver role following traumatic spinal cord injury: An interpretative phenomenological analysis of the spouse's experience. *Psychology & Health, 25*(9), 1101–1120.

Dillenburger, K., & McKerr, L. (2009). "40 years is an awful long time": Parents caring for adult sons and daughters with disabilities. *Behavior and Social Issues, 18*, 155–174.

Doka, K. J. (1989). *Disenfranchised grief: Recognizing hidden sorrow.* Lexington, MA: D. C. Heath.

Doka, K. J. (1994). Disenfranchised grief. In L. A. DeSpelder & A. L. Strickland (Eds.), *The path ahead* (pp. 271–275). San Francisco: Mayfield.

Doka, K. J., & Davidson, J. D. (Eds.). (1998). *Living with grief: Who we are, how we grieve.* Washington, DC: Hospice Foundation of America.

Donahue, M. (2010). Investigating the grief process related to job loss. *Dissertation Abstracts International: Section B. The Sciences and Engineering, 7850.*

Doran, G., & Hansen, N. D. (2006). Constructions of Mexican American family grief after the death of a child: An exploratory study. *Cultural Diversity and Ethnic Minority Psychology, 12*(2), 199–211.

Doughty, E. A. (2009). Investigating adaptive grieving styles: A Delphi study. *Death Studies, 33*(5), 462–480.

Drescher, K., & Foy, D. W. (2010). When horror and loss intersect: Traumatic experience and traumatic bereavement. *Pastoral Psychology, 59*(2), 147–158.

Dryden, W., & Neenan, W. M. (2004). *Counselling individuals: A rational emotive behavioural handbook* (4th ed.). London: Wiley.

Duggan, D. (2007). Children and young people affected by AIDS. In S. Books (Ed.), *Invisible children in the society and its schools* (3rd ed., pp. 235–261). Mahwah, NJ: Erlbaum.

Dutro, K. R. (1994, April). *A dynamic, structural model of grief.* Paper presented at the Eighteenth Annual Convening of Crisis Intervention Personnel, Chicago.

Dyregrov, K., & Dyregrov, A. (2008). *Effective grief and bereavement support: Friends, colleagues, schools, and support professionals.* Philadelphia: Jessica Kingsley.

Edelstein, L. (1984). *Maternal bereavement: Coping with the unexpected death of a child.* New York: Praeger.

Ellis, A. (1973). Humanistic psychotherapy: The rational-emotive approach. New York: McGraw-Hill.

Ellis, A., & Abrahms, E. (1978). *Brief psychotherapy in medical and health practice.* New York: Springer.

Ellis, A., & Dryden, W. (1977). *The practice of rational emotive behavior therapy.* New York: Springer

Elwert, F., & Christakis, N. A. (2006). Widowhood and race. *American Sociological Review, 71*(1), 16–41.

Elwert, F., & Christakis, N. A. (2008). The effect of widowhood on mortality by the causes of death of both spouses. *American Journal of Public Health, 98*(11), 2092–2098.

Farina, A. (2000). The few gains and many losses for those stigmatized by psychiatric disorder. In J. H. Harvey & E. D. Miller (Eds.), *Loss and trauma: General and close relationship perspectives* (pp. 183–207). Philadelphia: Brunner-Routledge.

Faschingbauer, T., Zisook, S., & DeVaul, R. (1987). *The Texas Revised Inventory of Grief.* In S. Zisook (Ed.), *Biopsychosocial aspects of bereavement* (pp. 111–124). Washington, DC: American Psychiatric Press.

Figley, C. R. (Ed.). (1985). *Trauma and its wake: The study of post-trauma stress disorder.* New York: Brunner/Mazel.

Figley, C. R. (1996). Traumatic death: Treatment implications. In K. J. Doka (Ed.), *Living with grief after sudden loss: Suicide, homicide, accident, heart attack, stroke* (pp. 91–102). Washington, DC: Hospice Foundation of America.

Finkbeiner, A. K. (1998). *After the death of a child: Living with loss through the years.* Baltimore, MD: Johns Hopkins University Press.

Forstmeier, S., & Maercker, A. (2007). Comparison of two diagnostic systems for complicated grief. *Journal of Affective Disorders, 99*(1–3), 203–211.

Fowler, J. W. (1991). Stages in faith consciousness. *New Directions for Child Development, 52,* 27–45.

Frankl, V. (1969). *The will to meaning: Foundations and applications of logotherapy.* New York: World.

Freeman, L. (1978). *The sorrow and the fury: Overcoming hurt and loss from childhood to old age.* Upper Saddle River, NJ: Prentice Hall.

Friedman, R., & James, J. W. (2009, March). The myth of the stages of grieving, death, and grief. *Counseling Today,* 48–52.

Gillies, J., & Neimeyer, R. A. (2006). Loss, grief, and the search for significance: Toward a model of meaning reconstruction in bereavement. *Journal of Constructivist Psychology, 19,* 31–65.

Giunta, R., & Giunta, C. (2002). *Grief recovery workbook.* Brentwood, TN: Integrity Publishers.

Glazer, H. R. (2010). Filial play therapy for grieving preschool children. In C. E. Schaefer (Ed.), *Play therapy for preschool children* (pp. 89–105). Washington, DC: American Psychological Association.

Glazer, H. R., Clark, M. D., Thomas, R., & Haxton, H. (2010). Parenting after the death of a spouse. *American Journal of Hospice & Palliative Medicine, 27*(8), 532–536.

Green, J. W. (2008). *Beyond the good death: The anthropology of modern dying.* Philadelphia: University of Pennsylvania Press.

Greenspan, M. (2003). *Healing through the dark emotions: The wisdom of grief, fear, and despair.* Boston: Shambhala.

Griffith, T. (2003). Assisting with the "big hurts, little tears" of the youngest grievers: Working with three-, four-, and five-year-olds who have experienced loss and grief because of death. *Illness, Crisis, & Loss, 11*(3), 217–225.

Grollman, E. A. (1996). Spiritual support after a sudden loss. In K. J. Doka (Ed.), *Living with grief after sudden loss: Suicide, homicide, accident, heart attack, stroke* (pp. 185–188). Washington, DC: Hospice Foundation of America.

Gudas, L. (1990, August). *Children's reactions to bereavement: A developmental perspective.* Paper presented at the annual meeting of the American Psychological Association, Boston.

Gueritault-Chalvin, V., Kalichman, S. C., Demi, A., & Peterson, J. L. (2000). Work-related stress and occupational burnout in AIDS caregivers: Test of a coping model with nurses providing AIDS care. *AIDS Care, 12*(2), 149–161.

Guerriero-Austrom, M. G., & Fleming, S. J. (1990, August). *Effects of sibling death on adolescents' physical and emotional well-being: A longitudinal study.* Paper presented at the annual meeting of the American Psychological Association, Boston.

Haley, W. E., Bergman, E. J., Roth, D. L., McVie, T., Gaugler, J., & Mittleman, M. S. (2008). Long-term effects of bereavement and caregiver intervention on dementia caregiver depressive symptoms. *Gerontologist, 48*(6), 732–740.

Hansen, J. C., & Frantz, T. T. (Eds.). (1984). *Death and grief in the family.* Rockville, MD: Aspen Systems.

Hanson, R. O., & Hayslip, B. (2000). Widowhood in later life. In J. H. Harvey & E. D. Miller (Eds.), *Loss and trauma: General and close relationship perspectives* (pp. 345–354). Philadelphia: Brunner-Routledge.

Hansson, R. O., & Stroebe, M. S. (2007). *Bereavement in late life: Coping, adaptation, and developmental influences.* Washington, DC: American Psychological Association.

Harris, D. L. (2011). Navigating intimate relationship loss: When the relationship dies but the person is still living. In D. L. Harris (Ed.), *Counting our losses: Reflecting on change, loss, and transition in everyday life* (pp. 65–74). New York: Routledge/Taylor & Francis Group.

Harris, D. L., & Isenor, J. (2011). Loss of employment. In D. L. Harris (Ed.), *Counting our losses: Reflecting on change, loss, and transition in everyday life* (pp. 163–170). New York: Routledge/Taylor & Francis Group.

Hart, C. L., Hole, D. J., Lawlor, D. A., Smith, G., & Lever, T. F. (2007). Effect of conjugal bereavement on mortality of the bereaved spouse in participants of the Renfrew/Paisley study. *Journal of Epidemiology and Community Health 61*(5), 455–460.

Hazen, M. (2009). Recognizing and responding to workplace grief. *Organizational Dynamics, 38*(4), 290–296.

Heath, M. A., & Hudnall, G. (2011). Special issue on strengthening school-based support for bereaved students: Editors' introduction. *School Psychology International, 32*(2), 115–117.

Hersh, S. P. (1996). After heart attack and stroke. In K. J. Doka (Ed.), *Living with grief after sudden loss: Suicide, homicide, accident, heart attack, stroke* (pp. 17–24). Washington, DC: Hospice Foundation of America.

Hibberd, R., Elwood, L. S., & Galovski, T. E. (2010). Risk and protective factors for posttraumatic stress disorder, prolonged grief and depression in survivors of the violent death of a loved one. *Journal of Loss and Trauma, 15*(5), 426–447.

Hinrichsen, G. A., & Clougherty, K. F. (2006). *Interpersonal psychotherapy for depressed older adults.* Washington, DC: American Psychological Association.

Hoffman, M. A. (1996). *Counseling clients with HIV disease: Assessment, intervention, and prevention.* New York: Guilford Press.

Hogan, N. S., Greenfield, D. B., & Schmidt, L. A. (2001). Development and validation of the Hogan Grief Reaction Checklist. *Death Studies 25*(1), 1–32.

Holland, J. M., & Neimeyer, R. A. (2011). Separation and traumatic distress in prolonged grief: The role of cause of death and relationship to the deceased. *Journal of Psychopathology and Behavioral Assessment, 33*(2), 254–263.

Horowitz, M. J. (1986). *Stress response syndromes* (2nd ed.). Northvale, NJ: Jason Aronson.

Horowitz, M. J., Siegel, B., Holen, A., Bonnanno, G., Milbrath, C., & Stinson, C. H. (1997). Diagnostic criteria for complicated grief disorder. *American Journal of Psychiatry, 154*(7), 904–910.

Howarth, R. A. (2011). Promoting the adjustment of parentally bereaved children. *Journal of Mental Health Counseling, 33*(1), 21–32.

Hsu, M. V. (2010). Continuing bonds expressions in pet bereavement. *Dissertation Abstracts International: Section B. The Sciences and Engineering*, 2049.

Huber, J. T. (1993). Death and AIDS: A review of the medico-legal literature. *Death Studies, 17*, 225–232.

Hughes, R. B. (1988). Grief counseling: Facilitating the healing process. *Journal of Counseling and Development, 67*, 77.

Humphrey, N. M. (2009). Counseling strategies for loss and grief. Alexandria, VA: American Counseling Association.

Jahoda, M., Lazarfield, P. F., & Zeisel, H. (1971). *"Marrienthal": The sociography of an unemployed community.* Chicago: Aldine. (Original work published 1933)

Joffrion, L. P., & Douglas, D. (1994). Grief resolution: Facilitating transcendence in the bereaved. *Journal of Psychosocial Nursing and Mental Health Services, 32*(3), 13–19.

Johnson, R. G. (1987). Using computer art in counseling children. *Elementary School Guidance & Counseling, 21*, 262–265.

Johnson, S. M. (1977). *First person singular: Living the good life alone.* Philadelphia: Lippincott.

Kalichman, S. C. (1995.) *Understanding AIDS: A guide for mental health professionals.* Washington, DC: American Psychological Association.

Kandt, V. E. (1994). Adolescent bereavement: Turning a fragile time into acceptance and peace. *School Counselor, 41*, 203–211.

Kaplan, C. P., & Gallagher-Thompson, D. (1995). Treatment of clinical depression in caregivers of spouses with dementia. *Journal of Cognitive Psychotherapy, 9*, 35–44.

Karkazis, J. L., & Lazaneo, S. L. (2000). Unyielding custody disputes: Tempering loss and courting disaster. In J. H. Harvey & E. D. Miller (Eds.), *Loss and trauma* (pp. 375–385). Philadelphia: Brunner/Mazel.

Kato, P. M, & Mann, T. (1999). A synthesis of psychological interventions for the bereaved. *Clinical Psychology Review, 19*(3), 275–296.

Kaut, K. P. (2006). End-of-life assessment within a holistic bio-psycho-social-spiritual framework. In J. L. Werth & D. Blevins (Eds.). *Psychosocial issues near the end of life: A resource for professional care providers* (pp. 111–135). Washington, DC: American Psychological Association.

Kay, W. J., Neiburg, H. A., Kutscher, A. H., Grey, R. M., & Fudin, C. E. (Eds.). (1984). *Pet loss and human bereavement.* Ames: Iowa State University Press.

Keene, J. R., Prokos, A. H. (2008). Widowhood and the end of spousal caregiving: Relief or wear and tear? *Ageing & Society, 28*(4), 551–570.

Kersting, A., Brahler, E., Glaesmer, H., & Wagner, B. (2011). Prevalence of complicated grief in a representative population-based sample. *Journal of Affective Disorders, 131*(13), 339–343.

Kersting, A., & Kroker, K. (2010). Prolonged grief as a distinct disorder, specifically affecting female health. *Archives of Women's Mental Health, 13*(1), 27–28.

Khosravan, S., Salehi, S., Ahmadi, F., Sharif, F., & Zamani, A. (2010). Experiences of widows with children: A qualitative study about spousal death in Iran. *Nursing & Health Sciences, 12*(2), 205–211.

Kitzman, K. M., & Gaylord, N. K. (2001). Divorce counseling. In E. R. Welfel & R. E. Ingersoll (Eds.), *The mental health desk reference* (pp. 32–37). New York: Wiley.

Klass, D. (1995). Spiritual aspect of the resolution of grief. In H. Wass & R. A. Neimeyer (Eds.), *Dying: Facing the facts* (pp. 243–268). Washington, DC: Taylor & Francis.

Konigsberg, R. D. (2011). *The truth about grief: The myth of its five stages and the new science of loss.* New York: Simon & Schuster.

Koocher, G. (1975). Why isn't the gerbil moving? Discussing death in the classroom. *Children Today, 4*, 18–36.

Kramer, B. J., Kavanaugh, M., Trentham-Dietz, A., Walsh, M., & Yonker, J. A. (2010). Complicated grief symptoms in caregiver of persons with lung cancer: The role of family conflict, intrapsychic strains, and hospice utilization. *Omega: Journal of Death and Dying, 62*(3), 210–220.

Kübler-Ross, E. (1969). *On death and dying.* New York: Macmillan.

Kübler-Ross, E. (1975). *Death: The final stage of growth.* Upper Saddle River, NJ: Prentice Hall.

Kübler-Ross, E. (1983). *On children and death.* New York: Macmillan.

Kübler-Ross, E. (1987). *AIDS: The ultimate challenge.* New York: Macmillan.

Kübler-Ross, E., & Kessler, D. (2005). *On grief and grieving: Finding the meaning of grief through the five stages of loss.* New York: Scribner.

Kuhn, J. (2008). Countertransference reactions in psychotherapy group work with HIV positive children. *Psychoanalytic Psychotherapy in South Africa, 16*(1), 33–60.

Kushner, H. S. (1983). *When bad things happen to good people.* New York: Avon.

Lagoni, L., Butler, C., & Hetts, S. (1994). *The human–animal bond and grief.* Philadelphia: Saunders.

Langer, N. (2011). Who did you *used* to be? Loss for older adults. In D. L. Harris (Ed.), *Counting our losses: Reflecting on change, loss, and transition in everyday life* (pp. 215–221). New York: Routledge/Taylor & Francis Group.

Larson, D. G. (1993). *The helper's journey: Working with people facing grief, loss, and life-threatening illness.* Champaign, IL: Research Press.

Leahy, M. J. (1993). A comparison of depression in women bereaved of a spouse, child, or parent. *Omega: Journal of Death and Dying, 26*(3), 207–215.

Lerner, M. J. (2000). The human cost of organizational downsizing: The irrational effects of the justice motive on managers, dismissed workers, and survivors. In J. H. Harvey & E. D. Miller (Eds.), *Loss and trauma: General and close relationship perspectives* (pp. 208–224). Philadelphia: Brunner-Routledge.

Liese, B. S. (1994). Brief therapy, crisis intervention, and the cognitive therapy of substance abuse. *Crisis Intervention, 1,* 11–29.

Lopata, H. Z. (1996). *Current widowhood: Myths and realities.* Thousand Oaks, CA: Sage.

Lord, J. H. (1996). America's number one killer: Vehicle crashes. In K. J. Doka (Ed.), *Living with grief after sudden loss: Suicide, homicide, accident, heart attack, stroke* (pp. 25–41). Washington, DC: Hospice Foundation of America.

Main, M. (1996). Introduction to the special section on attachment and psychopathology: Overview of the field of attachment. *Journal of Consulting and Clinical Psychology, 64*(2), 237–243.

Main, M. (2000). Attachment theory. In A. Kazdin (Ed.), *Encyclopedia of Psychology* (Vol. 1, pp. 289–293). Washington, DC: American Psychological Association.

Malkinson, R. (2007). *Cognitive grief therapy: Constructing a rational meaning to life following loss.* New York: Norton.

Malone, P. (2011). The impact of peer death on adolescent girls: An efficacy study of the adolescent grief and loss group. *Dissertation Abstracts International Section A: Humanities and Social Sciences,* 4568.

Martin, T., & Doka, K. (2000). *Men don't cry . . . Women do: Transcending gender stereotypes of grief.* Philadelphia: Brunner/Mazel.

Matter, D., & Matter, R. (1982). Developmental sequences in children's understanding of death with implications for counselors. *Elementary School Guidance and Counseling, 17,* 112–118.

McCarthy, M. C., Clarke, N., Ting, C., Conroy, R., Anderson, V., & Heath, J. (2010). Prevalence and predictors of parental grief and depression after the death of a child from cancer. *Journal of Palliative Medicine, 13*(11), 1321–1326.

McCown, D. E., & Davies, B. (1995). Patterns of grief in young children following the death of a sibling. *Death Studies, 19,* 41–53.

McCutcheon, K. A., & Fleming, S. J. (2001–2002). Grief resulting from euthanasia and natural death of companion animals. *Omega: Journal of Death & Dying, 44*(2), 169–188.

McKenna, S. (1999, September 28). *Stages of grieving.* Retrieved May 13, 2003, from www.thirdage.com/features/family/alone/sb01.html

Meagher, D. K. (2009). *Zach and his dog: A story of bonding, love, and loss for children and adults to share together.* Bloomington, IN: Authorhouse.

Meichenbaum, D. (1985, May). Cognitive behavior modification: Perspectives, techniques, and applications. Two-day workshop, St. Louis, MO, presented by Evaluation Research Associates (Syracuse, NY).

Meris, D. (2001). Responding to the mental health and grief concerns of homeless HIV-infected gay men. *Journal of Gay & Lesbian Social Services: Issue in Practice, Policy, & Research, 13*(4), 103–112.

Michaels, K. (2009, November). Recession depression: Coping and survival techniques. *Counseling Today,* 48–50.

Middleton, W., Raphael, B., Burnett, P., & Martinek, N. (1998). A longitudinal study comparing bereavement phenomena in recently bereaved spouses, adult children and parents. *Australian & New Zealand Journal of Psychiatry, 32,* 235–241.

Miller, D. (1990). Diagnosis and treatment of acute psychological problems related to HIV infection and disease. In D. G. Ostrow (Ed.), *Behavioral aspects of AIDS* (pp. 187–206). New York: Plenum Press.

Monk, G., Drewery, W., & Winslade, J. (2005). Using narrative ideas in group work: A new perspective. *Counseling and Human Development, 38*(1), 1–13.

Monk,, G., Winslade, J., Crocket, K., & Epston, D. (Eds.). (1997). *Narrative therapy in practice: The archeology of hope.* San Francisco: Jossey-Bass.

Morgan, J. D., & Laungani, L. (Eds.). (2002). *Death and bereavement around the world* (Vol. 1). Amityville, NY: Baywood.

Morgan, J. D., & Laungani, L. (Eds.). (2003). *Death and bereavement around the world* (Vol. 2). Amityville, NY: Baywood.

Morgan, J. D., & Laungani, L. (Eds.). (2004a). *Death and bereavement around the world* (Vol. 3). Amityville, NY: Baywood.

Morgan, J. D., & Laungani, L. (Eds.). (2004b). *Death and bereavement around the world* (Vol. 4). Amityville, NY: Baywood.

Morgan, J. D., & Laungani, L., & Palmer, S. (Eds.). (2009). *Death and bereavement around the world* (Vol. 5). Amityville, NY: Baywood.

Morgan, M. C. (2009). The impact of traumatic brain injury in the survivor's partner or spouse: Implications for treatment. *Dissertation Abstracts International: Section B: The Sciences and Engineering,* 3180.

Morse, G. A. (2000). On being homeless and mentally ill: A multitude of losses and the possibility of recovery. In J. H. Harvey & E. D. Miller (Eds.), *Loss and trauma: General and close relationship perspectives* (pp. 249–262). Philadelphia: Brunner-Routledge.

Mphande-Finn, J., & Sommers-Flanagan, J. (2007). The experience of HIV/AIDS among rural women in the Northwestern United States: A qualitative analysis. *Journal of Community Psychology, 35*(1), 3–11.

National Center for Health Statistics. (2003). *Divorce rates for 2002.* Retrieved April 16, 2003, from www.cdc.gov/nchs/fastats/divorce.htm

Neimeyer, R. A. (2000). Searching for the meaning of meaning: Grief therapy and the process of reconstruction. *Death Studies, 24,* 541–558.

Neimeyer, R. A. (Ed.). (2001). *Meaning reconstruction and the experience of loss.* Washington, DC: American Psychological Association.

Neimeyer, R. A. (2010a). Reconstructing the continuing bond: A constructivist approach to grief therapy. In J. D. Raskin, S. K. Bridges, & R. Neimeyer (Eds.), *Studies in meaning 4: Constructivist perspective on theory, practice, and social justice* (pp. 65–91). New York: Pace University Press.

Neimeyer, R. A. (2010b). Reconstructing life out of loss: Reorganizing the continuing bond. In M. Kerman (Ed.), *Clinical pearls of wisdom: Twenty-one leading therapists offer their key insights* (pp. 104–117). New York: Norton.

Neimeyer, R. A., Holland, J. M., Currier, J. M., & Mehta, T. (2007). Meaning reconstruction in later life: Toward a cognitive-constructivist approach to grief therapy. In D. Gallagher-Thompson, A. M. Steffen, & L. W. Thompson (Eds.). *Handbook of behavioral and cognitive therapies with older adults* (pp. 264–277). New York: Springer.

Neimeyer, R. A., & Levitt, H. M. (2000). What's narrative got to do with it? Construction and coherence in accounts of loss. In J. H. Harvey & E. D. Miller (Eds.), *Loss and trauma: General and close relationship perspectives* (pp. 401–413). Philadelphia: Brunner-Routledge.

Newman, K. S. (1993). *Declining fortunes: The withering of the American dream.* New York: Basic Books.

Nieburg, H. A., & Fischer, A. (1982). *Pet loss: A thoughtful guide for adults and children.* New York: Harper & Row.

Nkomo, N., Freeman, M., & Skinner, D. (2009). Experiences of children heading households in the wake of the human immunodeficiency virus/acquired immune deficiency syndrome (HIV/AIDS) epidemic in South Africa. *Vulnerable Children and Youth Studies, 4*(3), 255–263.

Nord, D. (1997). *Multiple AIDS-related loss: A handbook for understanding and surviving a perpetual fall.* Washington, DC: Taylor & Francis.

Norris-Shortle, C., Young, P. A., & Williams, M. A. (1993). Understanding death and grief for children three and younger. *Social Work, 38,* 736–741.

Okun, B., & Nowinski, J. (2011). *Saying goodbye: How families can find renewal through loss.* New York: Berkley Books/Penguin Group.

Osterweis, M., Solomon, F., & Green, M. (Eds.). (1984). *Bereavement: Reactions, consequences, and care.* Washington, DC: National Academy Press.

Ostrow, D. G. (Ed.). (1990). *Behavioral aspects of AIDS.* New York: Plenum Medical.

Ott, C. H. (2003). The impact of complicated grief on mental and physical health at various points in the bereavement process. *Death Studies, 27*(3), 249–272.

Ott, C. H., Sanders, S., & Kelber, S. T. (2007). Grief and personal growth experience of spouses and adult-child caregivers of individuals with Alzheimer's disease and related dementias. *Gerontologist, 47*(6), 798–809.

Parkes, C., & Prigerson, H. A. (2010). *Bereavement: Studies of grief in adult life* (4th ed.). New York: Routledge/Taylor-Francis Group.

Pearlman, M. Y., Schwalbe, K. D., & Cloitre, M. (2010). *Grief in childhood: Fundamentals of treatment in clinical practice.* Washington, DC: American Psychological Association.

Pine, V. R. (1996). Social psychological aspects of disaster death. In K. J. Doka (Ed.), *Living with grief after sudden loss: Suicide, homicide, accident, heart attack, stroke* (pp. 103–116). Washington, DC: Hospice Foundation of America.

Piper, W. E., Ogrodniczuk, J. S., Joyce, S. S., & Weideman, R. (2011). Risk factors for complicated grief. In W. E. Piper, J. S. Ogrodniczuk, S. S. Joyce, & R. Weideman (Eds.), *Short-term group therapies for complicated grief: Two research-based models* (pp. 193–202). Washington, DC: American Psychological Association.

Pizzetti, P., & Manfredini, M. (2008). "The shock of widowhood": Evidence from an Italian population (Parma 1989–2000). *Social Indictors Research, 85*(3), 499–513.

Planchon, L. A., Templer, D. I., Stokes, S., & Keller, J. (2002). Death of a companion cat or dog and human bereavement. *Society & Animals, 10*(3), 327.

Powers, R., & Griffith, J. (1987). *Understanding life-style: The psycho-clarity process.* Chicago: American Institute of Adlerian Studies.

Price, R. H., Friedland, D. S., & Vinokur, A. D. (1998). Job loss: Hard times and eroded identity. In J. H. Harvey (Ed.), *Perspective on loss: A sourcebook* (pp. 303–316). Philadelphia: Brunner/Mazel.

Prigerson, H. G., & Jacobs, S. (2001). Traumatic grief as a distinct disorder: A rationale, consensus criteria, and a preliminary empirical test. In M. S. Stroebe, R. O. Hansson, & H. Schut (Eds.), *Handbook of bereavement research and practice: Consequences, coping, and caring* (pp. 613–641). Washington, DC: American Psychological Association.

Prigerson, H. G., Maciewjewski, P. K., Reynolds, C. F., Bierhals, A. J., Newsom, J. T., Fasiczka, A., et al. (1995).

Inventory of Complicated Grief: A scale to measure maladaptive symptoms of loss. *Psychiatry Research* 59(1/2), 65–79

Prigerson, H. G., Vanderwerker, L. C., & Maciejewski, P. K. (2008). A case for inclusion of prolonged grief disorder in DSM-V. In M. S. Stroebe, R. O. Hansson, H. Schut, & W. Stroebe (Eds.), *Handbook of bereavement research and practice: Advances in theory and intervention.* (pp. 165–186). Washington, DC: American Psychological Association.

Ramsey, J. L., & Blieszner, R. (2000). Transcending a lifetime of losses: The importance of spirituality in old age. In J. H. Harvey & E. D. Miller (Eds.), *Loss and trauma: General and close relationship perspectives* (pp. 225–236). Philadelphia: Brunner-Routledge.

Ramshaw, E. J. (2010). The personalization of postmodern post-mortem rituals. *Pastoral Psychology, 59*(2), 171–178.

Rando, T. A. (1984). *Grief, dying, and death: Clinical interventions for caregivers.* Champaign, IL: Research Press.

Rando, T. A. (Ed.). (1986). *Parental loss of a child.* Champaign, IL: Research Press.

Rando, T. A. (1993). *Treatment of complicated mourning.* Champaign, IL: Research Press.

Rando, T. A. (1996). Complications in mourning traumatic death. In K. J. Doka (Ed.), *Living with grief after sudden loss: Suicide, homicide, accident, heart attack, stroke* (pp. 139–160). Washington, DC: Hospice Foundation of America.

Raphael, B. (1983). *The anatomy of bereavement.* New York: Harper & Row/Basic Books.

Raphael, B., & Dobson, M. (2000). Bereavement. In J. H. Harvey & E. D. Miller (Eds.), *Loss and trauma: General and close relationship perspectives* (pp. 45–61). Philadelphia: Brunner-Routledge.

Raphael, B., & Minkov, C. (1999). Abnormal grief. *Current Opinion in Psychiatry, 12*, 99–102.

Redmon, L. M. (1996). Sudden violent death. In K. J. Doka (Ed.), *Living with grief after sudden loss: Suicide, homicide, accident, heart attack, stroke* (pp. 53–72). Washington, DC: Hospice Foundation of America.

Reeves, N. C. (2011). Death acceptance through ritual. *Death Studies, 35*(5), 408–419.

Reichle, B., Schneider, A., & Montada, L. (1998). How do observers of victimization preserve their belief in a just world cognitively or actionally? Findings from a longitudinal study. In L. Montanda & J. Lerner (Eds.), *Responses to victimizations and belief in a just world* (pp. 55–87). New York: Plenum Press.

Reitmeyer, R. (2000). Dog gone? From cats to snakes, counselors help heal human hearts following a pet loss. *Counseling Today, 42*(9), 1, 26–27.

Riordan, R. J., & Allen, L. (1989). Grief counseling: A funeral home–based model. *Journal of Counseling and Development, 67*, 424–425.

Romanoff, B. (1993). When a child dies: Special consideration for providing mental health counseling for bereaved parents. *Journal of Mental Health Counseling, 15*, 384–393.

Romig, C. A., & Gruenke, C. (1991). The use of metaphor to overcome inmate resistance to mental health counseling. *Journal of Counseling & Development, 69*(4), 414–418.

Rosenblatt, P. C. (2010). Shame and death in cultural context. In J. Kauffman (Ed.), *The shame of death, grief, and trauma* (pp. 113–137). New York: Routledge/Taylor & Francis Group.

Rosner, R., Kruse, J., & Hagl, M. (2010). A meta-analysis of interventions for bereaved children and adolescents. *Death Studies, 34*(2), 99–136.

Rubin, S. (1999). The two-track model of bereavement: Overview, retrospect and prospect. *Death Studies, 23*(8), 681–714.

Rubin, S., & Yasien-Esmael, H. (2004). Loss and bereavement among Israel's Muslims: Acceptance of God's will, grief, and the relationship of the deceased. *Omega: Journal of Death and Dying, 49*(2), 149–162.

Rynearson, E. K. (2010). The clergy, the clinician, and the narrative of violent death. *Pastoral Psychology, 59*(2), 179–189.

Sanders, C. M., Mauger, P. A., & Strong, P. N. (1985). *A manual for the Grief Experience Inventory.* Palo Alto, CA: Consulting Psychologists Press.

Sandler, I. N., Ayers, T. S., Wolchik, S. A., Tein, J. Y., Kwok, O. M., Haine, R., et al. (2003). The Family Bereavement Program: Efficacy evaluation of a theory-based prevention program for parentally bereaved children and adolescents. *Journal of Consulting and Clinical Psychology, 71*(3), 587–600.

Schliebner, C. T., & Peregoy, J. J. (1994). Unemployment effects on the family and the child: Interventions for counselors. *Journal of Counseling and Development, 72*, 368–372.

Schneider, J. (1984). *Stress, loss, and grief: Understanding their origins and growth potential.* Baltimore, MD: University Park Press.

Schoenberg, B. M. (Ed.). (1980). *Bereavement counseling: A multidisciplinary handbook.* Westport, CT: Greenwood Press.

Schonfeld, D. J. (1989). Crisis intervention for bereavement support: A model of intervention in the children's school. *Clinical Pediatrics, 28*, 27–33.

Schuurman, D. L., & DeCristofaro, J. (2007). After a parent's death: Group, family, and individual therapy to help children. In N. B. Webb (Ed.), *Play therapy with children in crisis* (pp. 173–196). New York: Guilford Press.

Schwiebert, V. L., Myers, J. E., & Dice, C. (2000). Ethical guidelines for counselors working with older adults. *Journal of Counseling & Development, 78*, 123–129.

Segal, D. L., Chatman, C., Bogaards, J. A., & Becker, L. A. (2001). One-year follow-up of an emotional expression intervention for bereaved older adults. *Journal of Mental Health & Aging, 7*(4), 465–472.

Shallcross, L. (2009, September). Rewriting the "rules" of grief. *Counseling Today*, 28–31.

Shaver, P. R., & Fraley, R. C. (2008). Attachment, loss, and grief: Bowlby's views and current controversies. In J. Cassidy & P. Shaver (Eds.), *Handbook of attachment: Theory, research, and clinical applications* (2nd ed., pp. 48–77). New York: Guilford Press.

Shear, K., & Frank, E. (2006). Treatment of complicated grief: Integrating cognitive-behavioral methods with other treatment approaches. In V. M. Follette & J. I Ruzek (Eds.), *Cognitive-behavioral therapies for trauma* (2nd ed., pp. 290–320). New York: Guilford Press.

Shear, M. K., & Mulhare, E. (2008). Complicated grief. *Psychiatric Annals, 38*(10), 662–670.

Shear, M. K., Simon, N., Wall, M., Zisook, S., Neimeyer, R., Duan, N., et al. (2011). Complicated grief and related bereavement issues for DSM-5. *Depression and Anxiety, 28*(2), 103–117.

Shelby, R. D. (1995). *People with HIV and those who help them: Challenges, integration, intervention.* Binghamton, NY: Hayworth Press.

Sikkema, K. J., Kochman, A., DiFranceiso, W., Kelly, J., & Hoffman, R. G. (2003). AIDS-related grief and coping with loss among HIV-positive men and women. *Journal of Behavioral Medicine, 26*(2), 165–181.

Silverman, P. R. (2000). *Never too young to know: Death in children's lives.* New York: Oxford University Press.

Simon, N. M., Wall, M. M., Keshaviah, A., Dryman, M. T., LeBlanc, N. J., & Shear, M. K. (2011). Informing the symptom profile of complicated grief. *Depression and Anxiety, 28*(2), 118–126.

Smith, S. (2009, September). Why does it hurt so much? Grieving the loss of a pet. *Your Mind Your Body.* American Psychological Association. Retrieved at www.yourmindyourbody.org/about-2

Solomon, Z., Neria, Y., & Ram, A. (1998). Mental health professionals' responses to loss and trauma of holocaust survivors. In J. H. Harvey (Ed.), *Perspective on loss: A sourcebook* (pp. 221–231). Philadelphia: Brunner/Mazel.

Spielberg, S. (Director). (1989). *Always* [Motion picture]. Los Angeles: United Artists.

Stephen Ministries, Saint Louis. (2011). *Transforming lives and equipping the saints for ministry since 1975.* Available at stephenministries.org

Stroebe, M. S., Hansson, R. O., Schut, H., & Stroebe, W. (Eds.). (2008). *Handbook of bereavement research and practice: Advances in theory and intervention.* Washington, DC: American Psychological Association.

Stroebe, W., & Schut, H. (1999). The dual process model of coping with bereavement: Rationale and description. *Death Studies, 23*, 197–224.

Stroebe, W., & Schut, H. (2001). Making meaning in the dual process model of coping with bereavement. In R. A. Neimeyer (Ed.), *Meaning reconstruction and the experience of loss* (pp. 55–69). Washington, DC: American Psychological Association.

Stroebe, M., Schut, H., & Stroebe, W. (2005). Attachment in coping with bereavement: A theoretical integration. *Review of General Psychology, 9*, 48–66.

Stubenbort, K. M., Donnelly, G. R., & Cohen, J. (2001). Cognitive-behavioral group therapy for bereaved adults and children following an air disaster. *Group Dynamics: Theory, Research, and Practice, 5*, 261–176.

Taylor, D. H., Kuchibhatia, M., Østbye, T., Plassman, B. L., & Clipp, E. C. (2008). The effect of spousal caregiving and bereavement on depressive symptoms. *Aging & Mental Health, 12*(1), 100–107.

Tedeschi, R. G., & Calhoun, L. G. (1995). *Trauma & transformation: Growing in the aftermath of suffering.* Thousand Oaks, CA; Sage.

Tedeschi, R. G., & Calhoun, L. G. (2003). Routes to posttraumatic growth through cognitive processing. In D. Paton, J. M. Volanti, & L. M. Smith (Eds.), *Promoting capabilities to manage posttraumatic stress: Perspective on resilience* (pp. 12–26). Springfield, IL: Charles C Thomas.

Tedeschi, R. G., & Calhoun, L. G. (2004). Posttraumatic growth: Conceptual foundations and empirical evidence. *Psychological Inquiry, 15*(1), 1–18.

Tedeschi, R. G., & Calhoun, L. G. (2006). Time of change? The spiritual challenges of bereavement and loss. *Omega: Journal of Death and Dying, 53*(1/2), 105–116.

Tedeschi, R. G., & Calhoun, L. G. (2009). The clinician as expert companion. In C. L. Park, S. C. Lechner, M. H. Antoni, & A. Stanton (Eds.), *Medical illness and positive life change: Can crisis lead to personal transformation?* (pp. 215–235). Washington, DC: American Psychological Association.

Tedeschi, R. G., Park, C. L., & Calhoun, L. G. (Eds.). (1998). *Posttraumatic growth: Positive changes in the aftermath of crisis.* Mahwah, NJ: Erlbaum.

Terr, L. C. (1981). "Forbidden games": Posttraumatic child's play. *Journal of the American Academy of Child Psychiatry, 22*, 221–230.

Theuninck, A. C., Lake, N., & Gibson, S. (2010). HIV-related posttraumatic stress disorder: Investigating the traumatic stress. *AIDS patient care and STDS, 24*(8), 458–491.

Triplett, K., Tedeschi, R., Cann, A., Calhoun, L., & Reeve, C. (2011). Posttraumatic growth, meaning in life, and life satisfaction in response to trauma. *Psychological Trauma: Theory, Research, Practice, and Policy, 14*, 35–68.

Vahtera, J., Kivimäki, M., Väänägen, A., Linna, A., Pentti, J., Helenius, H., et al. (2006). Sex differences in health effects of family death or illness: Are women more vulnerable than men? *Psychosomatic Medicine, 68*(2), 283–291.

Van der Heijden, I., & Swartz, S. (2010). Bereavement, silence, and culture within a peer-led HIV/AIDS-prevention strategy for vulnerable children in South Africa. *African Journal of AIDS Research, 9*(1), 41–50.

Van Dyk, A. C. (2007). Occupational stress experienced by caregivers working in the HIV/AIDS field in South Africa. *African Journal of AIDS Research, 6*(1), 49–66.

Van Praagh, J. (2000). *Healing grief: Reclaiming life after any loss.* New York: Random House.

Vickers, M. H. (2009). Journeys into grief: Exploring redundancy for a new understanding of workplace grief. *Journal of Loss and Trauma, 14*(5), 401–419.

Wakefield, J. C., Schmitz, M. F., & Baer, J. C. (2011). Did narrowing the major depression bereavement exclusion from DSM-III-R to DSM-IV increase validity? Evidence from a national comorbidity study. *Journal of Nervous and Mental Disease, 199*(2), 66–73.

Walsh, F. (2009). Spiritual resources in family adaptation to death and loss. In F. Walsh (Ed.), *Spiritual resources in family therapy* (2nd ed., pp. 81–102). New York: Guilford Press.

Walsh, K., King, M., Jones, L., Tookman, A., & Blizard, R. (2002). Spiritual beliefs may affect outcome of bereavement: Prospective study. *British Medical Journal, 324*(7353), 1551.

Webb, N. B. (2007). Sudden death of a parent in a terrorist attack: Crisis intervention conjoint therapy with a preschool boy and his mother. In N. B. Webb (Ed.), *Play therapy with children in crisis: Individual, group, and family treatment* (pp. 389–407). New York: Guilford Press.

Webb, N. B. (2011). Play therapy for bereaved children: Adapting strategies to community, school, and home settings. *School Psychology International, 32*(2), 132–143.

Weisman, A. D. (1990–1991). Bereavement and companion animals. *Omega: Journal of Death and Dying, 22,* 241–248.

Weiss, R. S. (1998). Issues in the study of loss and grief. In J. H. Harvery (Ed.), *Perspectives on loss: A sourcebook* (pp. 343–353). Philadelphia: Brunner/Mazel.

Wheeler, I. (2001). Parental bereavement: The crisis of meaning. *Death Studies, 25*(1), 51–66.

White, M. (1989). *Selected papers.* Adelaide, Australia: Dulwich Centre.

Williams, R. J., & Stafford, W. B. (1991). Silent casualties: Partners, families, and spouses of persons with AIDS. *Journal of Counseling and Development, 69,* 423–427.

Williams, R. L., & Long, J. D. (1983). *Toward a self-managed life style* (3rd ed.). Boston: Houghton Mifflin.

Winslade, M. J., & Monk, F. (1999). *Narrative counseling in schools: Powerful and brief.* Thousand Oaks, CA: Corwin Press.

Wood, K., Chase, E., & Aggleton, P. (2006). "Telling the truth is the best thing": Teenage orphans' experiences of parental AIDS-related illness and bereavement in Zimbabwe. *Social Sciences & Medicine, 63*(7), 1923–1933.

Worden, J. W. (1991). *Grief counseling and grief therapy: A handbook for the mental health practitioner* (2nd ed.). New York: Springer.

Worden, J. W. (1996). *Children and grief: When a parent dies.* New York: Guilford Press.

Worden, J. W. (2002). *Grief counseling and grief therapy: A handbook for the mental health practitioner* (3rd ed.). New York: Springer.

Wylie, M. S. (2004, September–October). Mindsight. *Psychotherapy Networker,* 29–39.

Zhang, B., El-Jawahri, A., & Prigerson, H. (2006). Update on bereavement research: Evidence-based guidelines for the diagnosis and treatment of complicated bereavement. *Journal of Palliative Medicine, 9,* 1188–1202.

Zimmerman, J. L., & Dickerson, V. C. (1996). *If problems talked: Narrative therapy in action.* New York: Guilford Press.

CHAPTER 13

Crises in Schools

The New-Millennium, Violence-Proof School Building

Welcome to the (pretty much) violence-proof school building of the new millennium. We are not spending any money on landscaping, because people can hide behind shrubbery and we want every square inch of the exterior in plain view of security vehicles that will patrol the perimeter on a 24-hour basis, 7 days a week. We really don't want taggers making their artistic statements on the school or common juvenile delinquents vandalizing it, so we have floodlit the whole facade and built a 10-foot chain-link security fence around the grounds. We maintain a vehicle path around the perimeter so that security vehicles or police cars can easily keep surveillance on the building.

We prefer that all students come to school in buses equipped with video monitors and two-way radios. For those few who drive, the student parking lot is enclosed by a 10-foot chain-link fence with razor wire on top. The lot is gated, so all student drivers need passes and hanger tags to get in. A security guard will check all students and parents who come into the parking lot. We also have concrete median dividers angled so that there can be no straight-on assault by individuals intent on drive-by shootings or school bombings.

We have only one student entrance into the school where all students must go through a metal detector. Only see-through backpacks are allowed and will be run through an x-ray machine. School uniforms are mandatory. Once students are in the building, all entry and hall doors will be electronically locked down.

Teachers have swipe cards so they can move through the building. Closed-circuit TV and a call box at the front entrance enable parents to gain access.

Although uniforms are mandatory, you can have your choice of school colors—as long as those colors are not used by any known gangs operating in or around the school. All students must have holographic ID cards attached to their uniforms, as must the faculty. Students also must have GPS locaters, either carried or skin-implanted. All faculty are equipped with panic alarms and carry cell phones with speed-dial numbers preset to call security.

Kevlar bulletproof vests in the school colors will be issued to all staff. The building itself has almost no windows; the few, very small windows are made of bulletproof glass. Walls are double-brick thick (newer munitions can fairly easily penetrate a single-brick thickness). A central monitoring station is capable of visual, auditory, and motion surveillance of the entire school building—both inside and out. All classroom doors are equipped with timed electronic locks that can be operated only through a computer program or be overridden from the central monitoring station. Hallways also have locked electronic doors at strategic locations for crowd control and isolation of intruders.

The real savings is in building architecture. First, we have downsized the gymnasium. We don't need bleachers, because crowds are hazardous. Any pep assemblies, sporting events, plays, or pageants will be piped back into classrooms via TV monitors. Athletic events will be played on isolated fields, and spectators can watch via community cable television. As a result, we do not need showers or locker areas. In addition, we have also cut the width of hallways, because there are no lockers in this school—lockers are conducive to hiding contraband. There is no need for a cafeteria. Lunches can be either microwaved in classrooms or hot-packed from a central food preparation facility. Cafeterias are places where students congregate, and a congregation of students provides a setting for dangerous behavior. Thus, cafeterias are becoming as extinct as the little red schoolhouse.

There are no faculty bathrooms. Student bathrooms are dangerous settings and must be policed. So while faculty are relieving themselves, they can also watch students. Finally, the administrative area is now a command-and-control center that is target hardened with maximum security measures for its protection as the school's nerve center. Because most interaction between administrators and students and teachers is by video, there is little if any need for students or teachers to access this area. Therefore, only staff who require access to the administrative area have electronic card keys. The central staff are a little different from the staff of schools in the last millennium. Besides the administrative staff, secretaries, and support personnel such as crisis workers, four school police officers specially trained in dealing with school violence operate from a police-ready room. A central communications staff is in charge of all electronic surveillance and media from the central monitoring station.

The principal in this new-millennium school plays a somewhat secondary role. The coadministrator is the chief of security. She has a criminal justice degree and experience in law enforcement, as well as a thorough understanding of computer and security systems. In any emergency, she is the primary decision-making authority. This will happen because the principal does not have the necessary expertise to coordinate security, any more than he would have the ability to operate a nuclear power plant! If you are having trouble picturing exactly what this new-millennium school looks like, a reasonable facsimile would be any correctional facility built in the past 10 years.

Universities will change also in the 21st century. Because campuses are spread out over many buildings, the preferred method of security will be a large compound with carefully guarded entrances and high, blast-proof walls topped with razor wire running along the entire perimeter. Access will be carefully controlled; students not only will have to show IDs, but they will also be subjected to iris, handprint, or voice recognition checks. No part of the university campus will be without surveillance cameras, which will be linked to

a central command post. If any suspicious activity is spotted, a blue light will start flashing in that area and heavily armed police will be dispatched. Students will also have GPS transmitters that will immediately give their location anywhere on campus to central security (optional at the university level but definitely required in K–12). Students will be required to carry cell phones, and those cell phones must be turned on and keyed to a university threat and warning system that will automatically page the entire student body if a threat is imminent, followed by text message information telling students what to do. Faculty will not like this safety feature, because students' cell phones will often ring in class when students forget to put them in vibrate mode. Loudspeakers and intercoms all over campus will ensure that every person will hear warnings and evacuation instructions. All buildings will have electronic locking systems, which can be activated immediately upon a threat announcement. All faculty and residence hall staff will be trained to recognize any early danger signs and threats of violence. There will be few commuter students because of the hassle of getting through the checkpoints at the school compound entrances. Most students who do not live on campus will take courses by distance learning or online. Indeed, cars will be parked at least a quarter mile away from university buildings to reduce the threat from car bombs. The campus police chief will be much higher up in the chain of command and will operate out of a hardened command center with a number of technologists to keep all the security apparatus running.

Are you appalled at the idea of a school that is in effect a penitentiary? Although we have not seen a school with every one of the attributes just described, we *have* seen each component just mentioned in at least one school building in the United States. In fact, many experts in school safety have recommended the foregoing features (Astor, 1999; Blauvelt, 1998; Brock, Sandoval, & Lewis, 1996; Dorn & Dorn, 2005; Giduck, 2005; Haynes & Henderson, 2001; Jimerson & Furlong, 2006; Nadel, 2004; Poland, 1999).

The National Center for Education Statistics (2010) reports that between the 1999–2000 and 2007–08 school years, there was an increase in the percentage of public schools reporting the use of the following safety and security measures: controlled access to the building during school hours (from 75 percent to 90 percent); controlled access to school grounds during school hours (from 34 percent to 43 percent); students required to wear badges or picture IDs (from 4 percent to 8 percent); faculty required to wear badges or picture IDs (from 25 percent to 58 percent); the use of one or more security cameras to monitor school (from 19 percent to 55 percent); the provision of telephones in most classrooms (from 45 percent to 72 percent); and the requirement that students wear uniforms (from 12 percent to 18 percent). Between the 2003–04 and 2007–08 school years, there was also an increase in the percentage of public schools reporting the use of drug testing for student athletes (from 4 percent to 6 percent), as well as for students in other extracurricular activities (from 3 percent to 4 percent). During the 2007–08 school year, 43 percent of public schools reported that they had an electronic notification system for a schoolwide emergency, and 31 percent of public schools reported that they had a structured, anonymous threat-reporting system.

Our somewhat tongue-in-cheek new-millennium school building or college campus may seem patently ludicrous in Carmi, Illinois; Red Lake, Ontario; Truth or Consequences, New Mexico; or your own hometown or university. But to say that such a school building or college campus will never be built is to be so unaware of school violence in the United States that one would believe you have been living off-planet for the past 20 years. The violence that has arisen in schools is the reason many of these building modifications and security measures are being deemed necessary by more and more school districts and universities. In part, that is what this chapter is about.

School systems are generally able to deal with developmental crises because they are squarely in the middle of one of the greatest developmental crises of all, growing up! But they have not been prepared to deal with situational crises that arise unexpectedly and violently. Why is this so? First, it has simply not been deemed cost expedient to provide all the material and human support needed (Pitcher & Poland, 1992). Our new-millennium, violence-proof school building is not cheap, and the support personnel to staff it will not be cheap either!

Conflicting Statistics

The Clery Act requires colleges and universities to report all the crime that happens on their campus, so you might suppose we would have pretty good statistics on what happens in K–12 schools as well. Unhappily, that is not the case because police jurisdictions around the United States do not report crime to the FBI in the same way, nor should you believe that K–12 school administrations, fearful of bad publicity, necessarily report

all the crimes that occur in their buildings, nor do students report those crimes out of fear for their own safety. A great deal of debate occurs around whether crime is going up or going down in the more than 90,000 schools in the United States with nearly 50 million students in attendance (National Center for Education Statistics, 2005b).

Some research indicates there has been an increase in school violence; a study from the School Violence Resource Center, for example, showed that the percentage of high school students who were threatened or injured with a weapon increased from 1993 to 2001 (School Violence Resource Center, 2003). Other research, however, notes decreases in student victimization rates for both violent and nonviolent crimes during a similar time period (1992–2002; National Center for Education Statistics, 2004). Perhaps more problematic is that the sensational crimes, such as those at Columbine and Virginia Tech, get far more attention than the tens of thousands of mini-aggressions that occur every day and create a climate of fear and hostility in schools (National Center for Education Statistics, 2005a; National Institute of Justice, 1998).

Violent Crime Rates.   In summary, the FBI's comprehensive study of crimes in schools and colleges over a 5-year period (Noonan & Vavra, 2007) found that 3.3 percent of all incidents reported through the National Incident-Based Reporting System involved school locations. The following statistics represent the latest report from the National Center for Education Statistics (2010). Preliminary data on the 2008–09 school year show that there were 38 student, staff, and school-associated nonstudent violent deaths from July 1, 2008, through June 30, 2009, of which 24 were homicides and 14 were suicides. In 2008, among students ages 12–18, there were about 1.2 million nonfatal crimes at school, including 619,000 thefts and 629,800 violent crimes (from simple assault to serious violent crime). In 2009, 8 percent of students reported being threatened or injured with a weapon, such as a gun, knife, or club, on school property; 10 percent of male students in grades 9–12 reported being threatened or injured with a weapon in the past year, compared to 5 percent of female students (National Center for Education Statistics, 2010).

Incidents of Crime.   During the 2007–08 school year, 85 percent of public schools recorded that one or more incidents of crime had taken place at school, amounting to an estimated 2 million crimes. This figure translates to a rate of 43 crimes per 1,000 public school students enrolled in 2007–08 (National Center for Education Statistics, 2010).

Eleven percent of public schools reported that student acts of disrespect for teachers other than verbal abuse took place on a daily or weekly basis. With regard to other discipline problems reported as occurring at least once a week, 6 percent of public schools reported student verbal abuse of teachers, 4 percent reported widespread disorder in the classroom, 4 percent reported student racial/ethnic tensions, and 3 percent reported student sexual harassment of other students. Interestingly, the percentage of students in grades 9–12 who reported that drugs had been offered, sold, or given to them decreased from 32 percent in 1995 to 23 percent in 2009 (National Center for Education Statistics, 2010).

In 2009, 31 percent of students in grades 9–12 reported they had been in a physical fight at least once during the previous 12 months, and 11 percent said they had been in a fight on school property. Between 1993 and 2009, the percentage of students who reported carrying a weapon at least one day anywhere during the past 30 days declined from 22 percent to 17 percent, and the percentage who reported carrying a weapon at least one day on school property also declined, from 12 percent to 6 percent (National Center for Education Statistics, 2010).

Fear and Avoidance.   In 2007, approximately 5 percent of students ages 12–18 reported that they were afraid of attack or harm at school, and 3 percent reported that they were afraid of attack or harm away from school. Smaller percentages of white students (4 percent) and Asian students (2 percent) reported being afraid of attack or harm at school than their black (9 percent) and Hispanic (7 percent) peers. Seven percent of students ages 12–18 reported that they had avoided a school activity or one or more places in school in the previous 6 months because of fear of attack or harm (National Center for Education Statistics, 2010).

Threats to Teachers.   During the 2007–08 school year, a greater percentage of teachers in city schools (10 percent) reported being threatened with injury than teachers in town schools (7 percent) or suburban or rural schools (6 percent each). A greater percentage of teachers in city schools (5 percent) and suburban schools (4 percent) reported being physically attacked, compared to teachers in rural schools (3 percent). A

greater percentage of secondary school teachers (8 percent) reported being threatened with injury by a student than elementary school teachers (7 percent). However, a greater percentage of elementary school teachers (6 percent) reported being physically attacked than secondary school teachers (2 percent) (National Center for Education Statistics, 2010)

Disciplinary Action.   Forty-six percent of public schools (approximately 38,500 schools) took at least one serious disciplinary action against a student during the 2007–08 school year. Of the 767,900 serious disciplinary actions taken, 76 percent were suspensions for 5 days or more, 19 percent were transfers to specialized schools, and 5 percent were removals with no services for the remainder of the school year. Although the overall percentage of public schools taking a serious disciplinary action declined between 1999–2000 (54 percent) and 2003–04 (46 percent), there has been no measurable change since then (National Center for Education Statistics, 2010).

While those are big numbers, in comparison to the 90 million children going to school over that 5-year span it really isn't a lot—unless, of course, you or your child was one of those statistics or was subject to a microaggression that was never reported. Schools have long been prepared for disasters such as tornadoes and fires, but preparing for these kinds of disasters is relatively simple. The situational crisis that involves violence perpetrated by others on students or teachers is not. Schools are relatively safe places as far as lethality is concerned, with school-associated violent deaths representing less than 1 percent of all homicides that occur among school-age children (Anderson, Kaufman, & Simon, 2001). However, that does not mean schools are absolutely safe havens for learning. Assaults, threats, intimidation, property destruction, bullying, and physical injury occur, and they occur fairly often. They do occur more often in large urban schools, and perhaps more alarmingly they occur more often in middle schools (Kaufman, Chen, & Choy, 2002), but they also occur in rural and suburban schools, and when the media portray those incidents the public is shocked and alarmed that such things could happen (Stewart & MacNeil, 2005).

It is not enough that schools must be prepared to deal with the direct effects of a crisis such as a suicide or homicide. School staff must also be prepared for a variety of ripple effects. How to deal with huge numbers of other students affected by the crisis? How to deal with critical and concerned parents? How to keep the school safe without trampling on the rights of individuals who may be under suspicion or alleged to have committed violent acts? How to deal with the media that may descend vulturelike on the school in the event of a crisis? In short, few if any institutions have as many issues to deal with when subjected to such a crisis as a school district does.

This chapter will not deal with the potential for terrorist attacks on a school or the effects of a terrorist attack on a community, but you should certainly not disabuse yourself of that notion. The parents, teachers, and students of School Number One in Beslan, Russia, know all too well what the ramifications are, and crisis interveners in the United States have certainly been thinking and planning for just such an occurrence (Dorn & Dorn, 2005; Giduck, 2005; Jimerson & Furlong, 2006; Thompson, 2004; Webber, Bass, & Yep, 2005).

The opening of this chapter sounds more like an introductory course in criminology than in crisis intervention. However, you are going to meet some principal players in school crisis intervention who don't look anything like your U.S. history teacher or school counselor, or at least have very different roles than teaching you about government branches or filling out course schedules.

Violence and Youth

Why have today's youth become more violent? Poor parenting practices, an ineffective welfare system, marginalization of minorities and other disenfranchised students, availability of high-powered automatic weapons, racism, the growth of gangs, violence in homes, bullying, lack of male role models, hate crimes, physical abuse, and drug involvement are but a few of the ills that spill over into schools (Blauvelt, 1998; Collier, 1999; Goldstein, 1991; Goldstein & Kodluboy, 1998; Grossman, 1995; Hazler, 1996; Miller, Martin, & Schamess, 2003; Pledge, 2003; Poland, 1994; Soriano, Soriano, & Jimenez, 1994).

Media Violence.   Perhaps the most chilling reasons, though, are proposed by David Grossman in his book, *On Killing* (1995, pp. 302–305). He proposes that there are three learning theories at work: Classical conditioning is at work when one sits comfortably in front of a movie or television screen watching mayhem and carnage while eating popcorn and drinking a soda. Operant conditioning thrives at video arcades, which provide immediate feedback and rewards for killing and maiming. Social learning enters the scene when a whole new

series of role models, such as Freddy Krueger, do not end up saving the girl and kissing the horse, but slash the girl's throat and the horse's, too. Glorification of a thug culture interlaced with weapons, women as sexual objects, and drug use are cornerstones of contemporary music and media that cater to youth. Even the movie and television heroes are antiheroes and operate outside the law because the justice system is seen as weak and powerless.

It doesn't take a great deal of imagination after reading Grossman's book to understand why Westside Middle School in Jonesboro, Arkansas, and Columbine High School in Littleton, Colorado, became killing fields, and why drive-by shootings occur at any number of other schools across the United States. There is a continuing debate on how much influence experiencing vicarious violence via television and video games has on the manifesting of that violence in children (Azar, 2010). We believe there shouldn't be. Brain imaging studies show a clear relationship between brain areas that regulate and govern emotion and images of violence (Bailey, West, & Anderson, 2011; Brummert-Lennings & Warburton 2011; Englehardt et al., 2011; Hummer et al., 2010); Krahe & Moller, 2011; Krahe et al., 2011; Sestir & Bartholow, 2010). A large meta-analysis of violent media and aggression research by Anderson and his associates (2010) strongly suggest that exposure to violent video games is a causal risk factor for increased aggressive behavior. However, there are enough detractors (Ferguson, 2011; Ferguson et al., 2011; Ferguson & Kilburn, 2009, 2010) that the American Psychological Association reversed its 2005 (Price, 2007) stand that the research strongly suggested a link between violent media and aggressive behavior (Azar, 2010). As this chapter is being written, the powerful entertainment lobbies have essentially won out with a U.S. Supreme Court decision overturning a California law that prohibited selling M(mature)-rated video games to minors. It may be that there are mediating factors such as family domestic violence, competition, and different degrees of exposure (Zhao & Jiang, 2010), and older adolescents may not have as much reaction as younger ones (Bucolo, 2011), but the preponderance of research shows that the two correlate and almost any elementary school teacher can tell when students have been watching *South Park* the night before. In summary, while it cannot be said that media violence causes school shootings, Langman's (2009) in-depth examination of school shooters found that they often have a fascination with violent media and become obsessed with it (p. 8).

Modeling.   Modeling is an extremely effective way to reinforce behavior. The field of counseling is a great example. Dr. James wants his students to understand empathic understanding. He first lectures his students on various techniques such as open-ended questions and reflection of feelings. The students ask questions, and a classroom discussion ensues. However, empathic understanding and the techniques that facilitate it have only been talked about, not demonstrated. So Dr. James models these techniques in real time in front of the students. The students watch him, ask questions, and then are turned loose to try the techniques out for themselves under his watchful eyes and tuned-in ears in the classroom. Modeling also facilitates violence. Peggy Noonan, columnist for the *Wall Street Journal*, put it well when she wrote, after watching the video of Seung-hui Cho, the Virginia Tech murderer, "We'll be seeing more of that from thousands of disaffected teenagers who watched and thought, 'Wow! I could do that! Boy, would that teach them a lesson. Everybody would know me then!'" (Noonan, 2007).

Cho's role models were Dylan Klebold and Eric Harris of Columbine High School infamy. Who will see Cho as a role model to emulate? The showing of Cho's tape by NBC and other networks over and over in the view of millions of children set him up as a role model for those children. Playing a violent video game such as *Grand Theft Auto*, putting "gangsta" pictures on MySpace, or watching videos of school shooters or slasher movies does not automatically make a child a schoolyard shooter. If that were true, every kid who played *Grand Theft Auto* would go on a murder spree. However, along with other contributing variables discussed later in this chapter, the potential for violence can grow until those biological, sociological, and psychological factors coalesce into a homicidal gestalt, and little Eddie Haskell turns into Freddy Krueger.

The lethality issues to be dealt with in this chapter include potential physical assault by gang members, bullies, the estranged violent student, and suicidal children. However, targeted violence against specific students is not the only crisis that schools face. In addition, natural disasters, terrorist assaults, drug abuse, physical and sexual abuse, medical emergencies, and classmate, parent, and teacher deaths are all seen as crises. Crisis in the context of a school, although similar to the definition in Chapter 1, has unique features because of the social structure of the school and the sense of community within the school (Allen et al., 2002). As such, a crisis affects more than one student. It has ripple effects

that can tear at the very fabric of the school to the point of destabilizing it (Johnson, 2000, p. 18). Therefore, this chapter will also provide the basic elements of what a school crisis plan should entail as a best bet for prevention, intervention, and postvention, who the players are in that plan, and what their roles are when a crisis of any type strikes a school.

Gangs
Types of Gangs

Of all the other contributors to violent behavior, none appears to have the predictive validity and potential for violent behavior in high school as do gangs (Rainone et al., 2006). The 2009 FBI Gang Assessment reported about 20,000 gangs of different types in the United States with a total of more than 1 million members. They are not just the stereotypical Mafia or Hispanic drug cartels, and they operate from the inner city to the suburbs to rural areas to Indian Reservations ("Gang Threat," 2009). Twenty percent of public schools reported that gang activities had happened during 2007–08, and 3 percent reported that cult or extremist activities had happened during that school year (National Center for Education Statistics, 2010). There are basically five types of gangs that human services workers in school districts are likely to encounter.

Homegrown Copycats/Wannabes.   There is more than enough media representation of gang members to let every student in the United States who has access to cable TV, movies, magazines, music, or the Internet set up a stereotypical Vicelords, Gangster Disciples, Crips, or Latin Kings–type gang (Goldstein & Kodluboy, 1998, p. 5; U.S. Office of Juvenile Justice and Delinquency Prevention, 1995). "Wannabe" status may make them more dangerous in their attempts to prove how tough and cool they are. Generally they are short-lived. Makeup is composed of any ethnic group resident in the population.

Homegrown Survivalist, Aryan Nation, Neo-Nazi, Extreme Right-Wingers.   These gangs are based on political/religious philosophies inculcated by adults and in response to the perceived "browning" of America and the supposed threat that entails. They are often supported both financially and/or morally as "youth corps" by both local and national organizations. Members are typically related to or are friends of adults who espouse such views. They may be transitory or stable in terms of membership, depending on adult support available. They specifically target ethnic/racial minority groups for violence. They are almost always Caucasian and "Christian" (Goldstein, 1991, p. 24; Goldstein & Kodluboy, 1998, p. 7; U.S. Office of Juvenile Justice and Delinquency Prevention, 1995).

Transients From Megagangs. Offshoots of megagangs are started by gang members moved to supposedly "safe" rural havens by parents seeking to escape the problems of big-city crime or feeling extreme pressure from law enforcement agencies in their city of origin (Goldstein & Kodluboy, 1998, p. 7; U.S. Office of Juvenile Justice and Delinquency Prevention, 1995). Their children are already members of the gangs they try to escape. These transported gang members start their own gangs. Indian reservations receiving families out of big cities are a prime example of this transient population. Racial/ethnic makeup may be mixed, but these gangs are typically ethnic group or race based.

Megagangs Opening New Territory. Increased competition in large metropolitan areas forces gangs to seek new territory to sell their wares (mainly drugs). Interstate arteries and towns adjacent to them are primary targets because of ease of access (Goldstein, 1991, pp. 20–21; Goldstein & Kodluboy, 1998, p. 7). This is the most formidable type of gang organization. It has older adults who may derive their livelihood from its criminal enterprise. It has a clear hierarchy of members, sophisticated organizational plan and operating rules, large numbers, recruitment programs, financial backing, and the will to be very violent in pursuit of its interests. Racial/ethnic makeup of these gangs is predominately African American or Hispanic in the Midwest, but may be a variety of nationalities on the East or West Coasts. This is the stereotypical street gang of the media (U.S. Office of Juvenile Justice and Delinquency Prevention, 1995).

Smorgasbord Home Boys. Some small gangs are started for a variety of reasons, ranging from instrumental criminal behavior such as theft to expressive behavior such as hate crimes or responses to being perceived as social outcasts. The organizing themes of these gangs range from skinhead neo-Nazism to demonology and devil worship to auto theft to retaliation for perceived social injustices perpetrated on them. This gang type generally is transitory and short-lived, with small numbers of members. Depending on the type, it may avoid violence if theft is its major activity or may be extremely violent and sadistic if it is into racism, Satanism, or a response to social ostracism. It is mostly Caucasian in makeup (Goldstein, 1991, pp. 20–24; Goldstein & Kodluboy, 1998, p. 7; U.S. Office of Juvenile Justice and Delinquency Prevention, 1995).

Emergence of Suburban and Rural Gangs

Why have gangs or the threat of gang formation become problematic for suburban and rural areas? A variety of trends have emerged that make gang formation a probability for Opie in Mayberry, rural America. The development of diverse, multicultural communities in the United States will proceed at an accelerated rate in the 21st century, particularly in historically white farming communities of the Midwest (Goldstein & Kodluboy, 1998, pp. 63–91). We have generally not had a stellar history in welcoming and integrating newcomers in the United States who don't look, talk, act, and think like us, as witnessed by the contemporary debate over illegal immigrants. Cable television, the Internet, and other electronic information systems make the most pristine and rustic rural area a part of the global community. Glorification of violence and gangs through electronic media sends children who feel powerless against the world messages about how they can be powerful (Goldstein & Kodluboy, 1998, p. 7).

Chat rooms, websites, and e-mail provide gangs plenty of opportunity to talk to Opie. If Opie is feeling alone and powerless out on 1300 Country Road East, he is likely to talk back. All of the ills that assail dysfunctional families are as characteristic of suburban and rural families as they are of urban ones. Gang leaders are highly sensitive to these parentless, throwaway kids and, like Fagan in *Oliver Twist,* recruit them. The gang becomes a surrogate family (Grossman, 1995, pp. 303–305; Melton, 2001).

Gang Intervention/Prevention Programs

Although this book is about crisis intervention, the fact is that when dealing with gangs, prevention is far more likely to be effective than intervention. After a gang has taken root and grown, fear and intimidation become huge obstacles to constructive change. Changing gang members' attitudes about gang membership is anything but easy. Gang members typically fall into what are called "at-risk" student categories. By definition, "at risk" means that a young person is liable to be an academic or social failure when the potential for becoming a responsible and productive adult is limited by barriers at home, at school, or in the community (Fusick & Bordeau, 2004). At-risk students are truant; have trouble with the legal system; are characterized by impulsive behavior, self-doubts, anxiety, depression, drug use, and suicidal ideation; are poor learners; and have few bonds with the culture of the school. They are what Melton (2001) calls "phantom students" because, much like the Phantom of the Opera, they wear tough masks to hide their emotional scars and largely remain in the shadows of the school culture.

Because of the publicized school shootings in recent years, a great deal of interest has been generated in what are believed to be two of its root causes—at-risk students and bullying or being bullied. While not all at-risk students are gang members, many gang members are at-risk students, lost between the cracks and dropping out of school. Not all bullies are gang members, but the reverse is generally true, because bullies and gangs both gain power and control over others by fear, threat, and intimidation. Therefore, in discussing intervention methods with "gang" members, the same characteristics and procedures also apply to at-risk students and bullies. Violence prevention approaches are legion; they range from teaching students warning signs of impending student violence (Alvarez, 1999) to teaching body movement exercises for self-control (Kornblum, 2002). The following approaches have all been tried, with varying degrees of success, with children who make up the bulk of gang membership.

Counseling. Counseling, in the sense of having a continuing, person-centered, nonevaluative, nonjudgmental dialogue with a gang member, is one of the least effective intervention strategies (Lipsey, 1992). Given their past experiences with uncaring and punitive adults, alienated and disenfranchised gang members are suspicious and do not establish relationships easily. They are ultrasensitive to perceived threats and insults, and they are manipulative and reluctant to share information (Melton, 2001). John and Rita Sommers-Flanagan (1997) propose that challenging such kids is an excellent way to start establishing rapport and trust.

CW: So you don't want to be in here getting this counseling "crap." Is that about right?

Gangbanger: Yeah, that's right. I'm outta here.

CW: Okay. I'll just call your probation officer, and he can make the arrangements for you to go to the Wilder Youth Facility if you don't want to do this. Now, you are

adjudicated here for 12 sessions, but since you don't want to be here, I can see us doing this in, say, 6 sessions, if you are smart enough to catch onto this stuff and not give me a bunch of "crap," as you say, and work hard to get through this stuff. What's your choice?

Counseling that uses reality therapy (Glasser, 1965, 2000) and targets behavior and consequences of actions is more likely to be successful when gangbangers are constantly confronted with their actions and given choices as to what they want to do (Loeber et al., 1998; Sandhu, 2000). The same is true of victims.

Victim: (*Lucinda has been absent from school the last 3 days and is talking to the school counselor about her absences. Finally she breaks down sobbing and tells the counselor why.*) This is the fifth time the Rosebuds have taken my lunch money in the past two weeks, but they threatened to break my legs, and they can do that. I've seen Tina do that with a ball bat. She's crazy and scares me to death. They also told me not to snitch or they would hurt my little sister.

School Counselor: Lucinda, I'd really like to get Officer Bates in on this and have you tell him. It is not your fault that you are being mugged. You didn't ask for it, and you don't deserve it. It isn't normal, and it isn't okay. You don't have to face this on your own. I and other people will help you.

Victim: No way! No cops! I could get killed.

School Counselor: I understand that it's scary, and there are some real risks. We will keep this confidential, and no one will know but the three of us. But you are not the only one who is getting mugged. You can make a choice about helping to stop this. I have an idea you are pretty tired of getting assaulted. School should be a place to come and have fun with your friends and learn. It is not a place you should be afraid to come to. Officer Bates and I are working with a lot of teachers and other kids. If enough kids like you say "That's enough!" we can stop this. I won't force you to see the school police officer or even tell him. I think your parents need to know about this. If you want to have your parents come in and talk, we can do that too. The choice is yours.

The counselor acknowledges the danger to Lucinda as real. Attempts to coerce a student into informing are fraught with ethical peril and quite literally can be dangerous to the student if a great deal of care is not taken to keep the information confidential until the school and law enforcement are ready to act. However, if the counselor feels that the threat to Lucinda is high (see the definitions of low, medium, and high threats later in the chapter), her parents should be informed and so should the police.

School Resource Officer. The crisis worker attempts to bring the school resource police officer (SRO) into the crisis because multidisciplinary school pupil personnel service teams that involve the SRO are critically important to stopping threatening and intimidating behavior (James, Logan, & Davis, 2011; O'Toole, 2003; Welsh & Domitrovich, 2006). Police in the schools can do much more than direct after-school traffic and monitor ball games. SROs go through a good deal of training beyond the initial police academy (National Association of School Resource Officers, 2011). Coordinating intelligence between the police department and the school, working conjointly with school human services workers in gang prevention programs, helping students problem-solve, finding resources and making referrals, deterring violence, obtaining information about illegal activities, role modeling, and mentoring are proactive measures that integrate police officers into the fabric of the school (Dogutas, 2008; Finn, 2006; Finn et al., 2005; Italiano, 2001; James, Logan, & Davis, 2011; Petersen, 2008; Vancleave, 2008).

If you read any of the statistics at the beginning of this chapter, it should be apparent why SROs are in school buildings. They are there not only to preserve the peace, but also to provide support to troubled students by building rapport with them, serving as empathic listeners, and eliciting information. As such they are excellent conduits to provide information to school officials that might not otherwise be forthcoming (James, Logan, & Davis, 2011). Because many SROs, such as officer Davis whom you are about to meet, have Crisis Intervention Team training to deal with the mentally ill and emotionally disturbed, they make excellent first-line interventionists—particularly when the presence of an authority figure is needed with out-of-control students (James, Logan, & Davis, 2011). We strongly urge that human service workers and school administrators incorporate these police officers as part of a comprehensive pupil personnel services team that deals with violent and potentially violent students, because what they do works (Johnson, 1999).

Meet School Resource and Crisis Intervention Team (CIT) officer Scott Davis of the Montgomery County, Maryland, Police Department (S. Davis, personal communication, February 18, 2007). Officer Davis is responsible for policing a high school, a middle school, and three elementary schools. Officer Davis's day starts with roll call at 6 A.M. He patrols the neighborhood and keeps an eye out for people or activities that don't belong and other potential problems. This past month one of those problems included a very large gang fight that brought a number of police officers to the scene to break up the melee. Because those involved are "his kids," he takes a personal interest in the incident. He follows up with those who were arrested and looks for any others who might have been involved. Occasionally during the day he will hop in his cruiser and look for truants. He spends about 75 percent of his time at the high school and 20 percent at the middle school, with drop-in visits to his three elementary schools. His first task of the day is to meet with the high school principal in the morning, go over any potential problems that might be occurring before school, and greet the students as they come in the front door. Parents come to his office to talk about problems their kids are having. During the day he checks out a number of students who have been having problems and promotes his Boy Scout Police Explorer program.

At first glance his job appears pretty humdrum, but what isn't apparent is that Officer Davis is putting his considerable CIT skills to use every day with "humdrum" stuff and using the same skills when things are boiling over. Laura is 17 years old and a runaway. A social worker has been called to the school and is attempting to take her back to a bad home situation. Officer Davis has personal knowledge of the home because he has responded to a disturbance call there. Laura's mother is a drug addict and long gone from the home. Laura tried to hit her father with a brick in one argument, so it is clear that home is not workable. As Officer Davis makes the scene, tensions are rising between Laura and the social worker, who is threatening to have Laura arrested.

Officer Davis: (*in a calm but authoritative voice*) All right, let's just everybody cool off! First off, you can't have her arrested for a status offense. It's clear home isn't working real well, so Laura, let's you and me go to my office and talk about what's going on and what you think needs to happen.

As Laura explains her situation, Officer Davis asks numerous open-ended questions to allow her to ventilate. He finds out she has a drinking problem, but only occasionally uses others drugs. Home is intolerable, but she does come to school. He also finds out she is bipolar but not taking her medication because of the side effects.

Officer Davis: Okay, let's try this. How about going to the crisis center with me. I've got some friends there who might be able to help both in regard to the medication and a place to stay. It may not be exactly what you want, but it beats going home and running away again, 'cause that doesn't seem to be working real well for you. I'll stay there with you and see what they can do. How about it?

Laura: Hey! You're kinda different. Most cops push people around. Okay.

Officer Davis takes her to the crisis center, where she is evaluated and indeed prescribed different medication. She is also placed in a short-term foster home until her medication can be regulated.

Laura: *(A month later, in school, waves to Officer Davis.)* Hey! Remember me?

Officer Davis: Sure, Laura. How are things going?

Laura: Not real great, but I'm getting by. I went back home. The old man and I are sorta getting along.

Officer Davis: Hey! You're here, aren't you! Best place you can be! Here you've got options. The more you're here, the less you're at home. Thought about any after-school activities or sports? Get your grades up, and pretty soon the only time you are at home is to eat and sleep.

Officer Davis enthusiastically reinforces Laura for making it to school. Laura may not be a huge success story, but at least she is in school, has made contact with somebody, and feels like somebody is really interested in her. These are little victories in the everyday grind of working in a school, but added up they can win wars for hearts and minds in working with troubled kids. But Officer Davis's life is about to take an exciting turn, and we will return to him later in the chapter.

Guidance Programs. Passive, lecture-based guidance programs that target fear arousal, moral appeal, and self-esteem building have not proven to be highly effective (Gottfredson, Gottfredson, & Skroban, 1998) in dealing with gangs or bullying. Active guidance programs that provide direct student involvement through modeling, role play, and behavioral rehearsal in areas such as anger management, bullying, conflict resolution, and peer mediation are more helpful in tackling gang and bullying issues (Beane, 1999; Coloroso, 2003; Davis & Davis, 2003; DuRant et al., 1996; Embry et al., 1996; Feindler & Scalley, 1998; Gottfredson, Gottfredson, & Skroban, 1998; Hausman, Pierce, & Briggs, 1996; Hazler, 1996; Horne, Bartolomucci, & Newman-Carson, 2003; Larson, 1994; Lupton-Smith et al., 1996; Sexton-Radek, 2004). To be effective, these programs must not be a one-shot session but should have continuous behavioral rehearsal and feedback sessions built into them. They must also have clear, easily implemented

practices, be intense, and continue long enough with follow-up sessions to reinforce and change some very resistant behaviors in both victims and victimizers (Gottfredson, Gottfredson, & Skroban, 1998; Sullivan, 2011; Willard, 2007; Zins et al., 1994).

Peer Counseling/Peer Mediation. One of the very *worst* approaches is to use peer crisis workers who are gang members or bullies, or for the crisis worker to attempt to run homogeneous counseling groups composed entirely of gang members or bullies (Goldstein & Kodluboy, 1998, pp. 107–110). The gang members or bullies will take over the group. However, there is some evidence that heterogeneous counseling groups, those in which students are chosen from a representative cross-section of the ethnic, social, and economic strata of the school, are useful in helping gang members look at alternative solutions and develop new behaviors. There is also some evidence that a peer counseling/leader program that provides mentoring, tutoring, and support functions keeps at-risk and marginalized students out of trouble and in school (Allen, 1996; Cohen, Kulik, & Kulik, 1982; Fatum & Hoyle, 1996; Scruggs, Mastropieri, & Richter, 1985).

Peer mediation (Cassinerio & Lane-Garon, 2006; Day-Vines et al., 1996; Schrumpf, Crawford, & Bodine, 1997) is another approach that uses students to deal with other students who have anger problems. While it may seem that the last thing a gang member or bully would be willing to submit to is peer mediation, it should be remembered that peer pressure and the need to conform exert a tremendous amount of pressure on all students.

Further, if a student is unwilling to submit to peer mediation, he or she is ratcheting up the consequences by essentially saying, "I am not willing to try to work this out." Institutional use of these programs should start in elementary schools and be continuously carried through middle and high schools so there is a clear, consistent, and longitudinal approach to providing support to alienated, angry, and disenfranchised students. In fact, elementary schools are the best place to stop bullying, harassment, prejudice, and other forms of problem behavior.

Anger Management. A variety of anger management techniques have been developed to work with adolescents and children (Davis, 2004; Feindler & Weisner, 2006; Nelson, Finch, & Ghee, 2006; Smith, Larson, & Nuckles, 2006). Most of these approaches involve skill training and behavior rehearsal in prosocial behaviors and teaching students cognitive techniques that cool off their hot cognitions about stressful situations. While anger management approaches are effective in reducing abusive verbal and physical responses (Humphrey & Brooks, 2006; Rosenberg, 2004; Sharp & McCallum, 2005; Smith, Larson, & Nuckles, 2006), the problem is their pervasiveness and the environmental variables from both the home and the street that oftentimes see control of anger as weakness instead of strength.

After-School and Community Outreach Programs. As Goldstein and Kodluboy (1998, p. 126) state, "Playing on a basketball team means you are not stealing a car while you're at the game, but it does not prevent you from stealing a car before or after the game." Research indicates that although such after-school programs may have recreational value, they are not highly effective in delinquency reduction. However, programs such as the Boys and Girls Clubs of America that have a comprehensive curriculum integrating recreation with academic and social skill building, and career and personal counseling, do have high potential for stopping delinquency and reducing gang activity (Sherman et al., 1997).

Schools. Schools and school districts are not without culpability in the growth and development of gangs, bullying, and violence. Megaschools and megadistricts limit many students' participation in the academic and extracurricular activities of the school; because of the large numbers of students and the criteria that restrict who can participate, relatively few students in very large schools do take part in such activities as band or sports or even the chess team (Goldstein & Kodluboy, 1998, pp. 21–22). Schools can play an active role in the prevention and intervention of gang activity. Schools need to set a number one priority of inclusiveness, nurturance, school as community, and the philosophy that no student is left behind either academically and socially (Cypress & Green, 2002). This concept is particularly important in schools where heterogeneity (diversity) of race and culture is the norm. Fairness and consistency for everybody, with open communication among stakeholders, are essential.

Communication flows not only outward from the administration but inward to them. There must be fair rules and clear sanctions that are enforced evenly in school (Goldstein & Kodluboy, 1998, p. 22). There should be an expectation of success. The total philosophy of the system, starting in kindergarten and working its way up through high school, should not be "If you graduate," but "When you graduate" (Allen, 1996).

Gangs grow in a vacuum. A school is asking for trouble if it has unmonitored areas, such as parking lots and bathrooms; dismisses rumors about planned violence or weapons, drugs, or other contraband brought onto school grounds; excuses the violent behavior of "good kids"; or sees intervention in any of the foregoing areas as "not my job" (Dykeman, 1999; Remboldt, 1994). A school reduces violence when its staff and teachers have high expectations, care about and are involved with their students in inclusive ways, enforce rules and procedures, maintain buildings and keep classrooms neat and clean, and believe it's everyone's job to do so (Stephens, 1997).

School safety goes beyond high-tech security systems. School safety is a sense of not only physical well-being but psychological well-being as well. Schools can maintain or take back their turf when they cooperatively develop mission statements, share decisions about school policies, maintain buildings and remove graffiti, organize gang awareness and prevention programs, promote parental and student involvement, allow zero tolerance of bullying, harassment, or gang recruitment, and have school authorities that declare, "This is our turf, not yours" (Blauvelt, 1998; Brock, Sandoval, & Lewis, 1996). Instead of asking, "How do I know which students will shoot next?" the question might be, "What is the faculty doing to build quality relationships with students and open lines of communication, and to develop the type of climate that will foster a wholesome sense of self in each individual as well as respect for others?" (Cypress & Green, 2002). But preventing gang growth and violence is a task that is much too great for a single school counselor, social worker, psychologist, teacher, or principal—or even a school system.

The Community. It takes everybody in the community working as a team to combat gangs. Cooperation with other agencies such as the courts, corrections, probation, parole, mental health, public assistance, and housing is crucial. Civic and religious organizations must provide personnel and financial support. City and county government must be willing to put in place ordinances that say there is zero tolerance for this kind of behavior and back it up with law and code enforcement (Bemak & Keys, 2000; Miller, Martin, & Schamess, 2003; Schaefer-Schiumo & Ginsberg, 2003).

Louvre (2008) makes a compelling argument for integrating community action in school crises. She is puzzled why there is so little outrage over the 97 percent of child murders that occur outside of school walls every year. Louvre argues persuasively that rebuilding trust and a sense of community in a school after a crisis requires the total participation of the community. That is what SARA (scanning, analysis, response, and assessment; Eck & Spelman, 1987), the Justice Department's model for combating gangs, is about. SARA is not about getting rid of gangs in one day. It is about little victories, such as getting loiterers off school property and cleaning up graffiti. It gets all of the stakeholders in having a safe community involved in continuous and ongoing linkages that set goals and generate plans to achieve the continuous little victories that make SARA so effective. Turf guarding and political boundaries have no place in a fight to eradicate gangs (Roth, 2000). This approach benefits communities by not letting gangs gain a further foothold in the community, resulting in improved performance by students who went to school in fear each day; decreased teacher stress and burnout; decreased need for security staff/equipment; fewer injuries and lives lost; and most important, renewed freedom in the school and the community. You can find further information about SARA on this book's website (www.cengage.com/counseling/james).

Bullying

Probably no other topic has received as much attention in the school counseling literature and at conferences in the past 10 years as face-to-face bullying and, more recently, cyberbullying (Burnham, Wright, & Houser, 2010; Chamberlin, 2006; Holladay, 2010; Paterson, 2010; Sabella, 2010; Suniti Bhat, Chang, & Linscott, 2010)—its causes (Crothers & Levinson, 2004; Espelage, Bosworth, & Simon, 2000), effects (Carney, 2008; Sullivan, 2011; Willard, 2007), and intervention strategies (Bauman, 2011; Burnham, 2011; Burrow-Sanchez et al., 2011; Leo, 2010; Newman, Horne, & Bartolomucci, 2000; Paterson, 2011; Ratts, Ayers, & Bright, 2009; Saufler, 2010; Sullivan, 2011; Willard, 2007). That is particularly true with regard to gay, lesbian, bisexual, and transgendered (LGBT) students (Callahan, 2001; Jackson & Harding, 2010; Jones Farrelly & Robles-Fernandez, 2011; McCollum, 2010; Windmeyer, 2009), who have little power or support systems in most K–12 buildings.

The crisis dimensions this problem has taken on culminated in a White House Conference on Bullying in March 2011. That conference sought to establish replicable training and intervention programs that were cost effective and time manageable for teachers already stretched thin (Munsey, 2011). The fact that a number of elementary, middle, and high school students have committed suicide because of bullying and cyberbullying in the past few years has gotten the attention of the federal government and caused the Department of Education to assist in bully prevention. In December 2010 a technical assistance best practice memo highlighting comprehensive state antibullying laws was sent to state school officers and governors. The Office for Civil Rights at the Department of Education and the Department of Justice are working together and will vigorously pursue complaints of bullying and harassment. This information and much more is available at www.stopbullyng. Finally, the Office of Safe and Drug-Free Schools will offer competitive grants to measure safety by surveying students and then providing federal funds those schools identified through as having the greatest need of intervention. Schools will also be required to make the "safety scores" public so they can be held accountable for performance in providing a safe environment (Jennings, 2011).

Bullying and intimidation affect large numbers of students. One study that found that 77 percent of junior and senior high school students in a Midwestern United States school survey reported being a victim of bullies (Espelage & Swearer, 2003). In 2007, 32 percent of U.S. students ages 12–18 reported having been bullied at school that year. In this survey, 21 percent of students said they had been made fun of; 18 percent reported being the subject of rumors; 11 percent said they were pushed, shoved, tripped, or spit on; 6 percent said they were threatened with harm; 5 percent said they were excluded from activities on purpose; and 4 percent each said that someone had tried to make them do things they did not want to do or that their property had been destroyed on purpose (National Center for Education Statistics, 2010).

Bullying has been around for a long time. Why has it now taken on such a preeminent place in the media and the minds of the public? Bullying behavior can affect the physical and psychological health of those who are frequently bullied and those students who bully their peers at an early age (Batsche & Knoff, 1994). It can be direct, such as hitting, kicking, or pushing a person. It can be verbal, such as malicious teasing, threatening, or

taunting. It can be indirect or relational, where the idea is to damage relationships or social standing through exclusion (Bauman, 2011, p. 18). Langman (2009) defines bullying as having three components: First, the bully has more power than the victim, because of larger size, greater strength, or greater numbers (clique or gang). Second, bullying involves intimidation through threats, to the point that victims are made to fear for their safety. Third, bullying involves a pattern of behavior, not a onetime push (p. 12).

Bullies are proactive aggressors who use aggression methodically, subtly, and with increasing intensity until they achieve their desired goal of personal gain of some kind. Bullying is preplanned and calculated to instill fear and gain control over others with little remorse for its effects on them (Hubbard et al., 2001; McAdams & Schmidt, 2007; Vitaro & Brendgen, 2005; Vitaro, Brendgen, & Tremblay, 2002). An entire school can be affected by systematic bullying behaviors. If left unchecked, an atmosphere of fear, mistrust, and low morale, along with the academic and behavioral problems that go with a hostile work environment, can create a negative atmosphere for all students (Hoover & Hazler, 1991). Finally, if left unchecked, bullying as a form of aggression can lead to lethal behavior from either the bully or the bullied.

Cyberbullying

Cyberbulling, simply defined, means using technology to harass, humiliate, or threaten someone (Holladay, 2010). Cyberbullying is different from face-to face bullying. In face-to-face bullying the effects are immediately known, and the victim knows who the bully is and who his or her supporters are. Cyberbullying can be far more insidious because the bully can remain unknown. Effects can also be more disastrous because the messages can go to an audience literally in the millions (Bauman, 2011, p. 19).

There are eight types of cyberbullying (Bauman, 2011, p. 57; Willard, 2007, p. 2):

Flaming refers to angry offensive language. "You are a shit-brained hootchy mama slut."

Harassment is the technology version of discriminatory or hostile behavior toward someone based on gender, race, religion, disability, or sexual orientation. "Jay is a limp-wristed fag gimpy Yid."

Denigration is sending or posting defaming information about someone. "Jennifer Sonstegarrd is screwing every boy on the hockey team . . . and the coach too!"

Masquerading is using someone else's identity to send messages that are rude and inappropriate. "Leslie, you stink! Literally! Get some feminine hygiene products. Signed Phewwwie! Joey" (a guy Leslie is interested in, but so is Devonne who actually sent the e-mail).

Outing or *trickery* is a way of getting people to reveal personal information that might then be used against them. "Leslie, I really have been thinking you're the fox of the history class. I wonder if you'd like to go out for a pizza and movie Saturday night. INTERESTED A LOT, JOEY." When Leslie replies, Devonne then puts it out on the net: "Leslie thinks Joey is going out with HER on Saturday night. How delirious and out of touch with reality is she?

Social exclusion is a means of deliberately excluding someone from a buddy list, chat room, discussion board, or game. "How many of you want Leslie off the discussion board and out of the game? Everybody who does, vote "aye."

Cyberstalking is the electronic version of pursuing a person who is not interested in the personal attention he or she is receiving, but receiving it anyway. "Don't think I don't know when you come on the discussion board because I do, and I am going to be here watching and listening."

Cyberthreats are clearly meant to evoke fear and imply that danger is imminent. "It'll be dark by the time you get out of cheerleader practice and this is the night you always walk home. Have a nice night . . . and . . . oh . . . I'll be watching . . . and waiting."

The crisis worker's intervention with these bullies is difficult and fraught with legal and ethical issues. Some school counselors and other human service workers in schools have set up websites where students can contact them to deal with bullying and other personal issues in the virtual world that students inhabit. However, because of fear of sexual predators, the Missouri legislature attempted to make it illegal for any person employed by a school to have an individual dialogue with a student over the net. A judge ruled against the law as unconstitutional, but it is a slippery slope and workers can put themselves at risk legally and professionally. The better road to follow, at least at this point, is having clear district policies in place in regard to the use of the Internet

(Willard, 2007). Those policies should include the following (pp. 195–265):

1. A cyberbullying/cyberthreat and face-to-face-review policy for threatening materials sent over the Internet or hard copies found at school
2. School actions and options that are taken in regard to misuse of the Internet by students
3. Incident and report forms that track and record behavior so that a chain of continuity can be built (see the TASSLE form later in this chapter)
4. A comprehensive district plan to assess cyber use and misuse
5. Student needs assessment
6. Teacher needs assessment
7. District use policy for the Internet and agreement signed by students and parents that includes netiquette guidelines, to be given to and discussed with both students and parents

To sum this up, just doing this and calling it "done" won't work. There has to be initiative across the board within the whole community. The school's philosophy and policy have to fit with their antibullying efforts or it is useless. There also has to be regular evaluation of the program and updating of it or it will wither and die (Burnham, 2011; Sullivan, 2011).

Individual Intervention

Intervention with bullies first and foremost should include a strict policy against harassment and intimidation (Kerr, 2009, p. 112) and that policy should be clearly spelled out with no loopholes (McAdams & Schmidt, 2007; Willard, 2007). Once a bully has been identified, Sullivan (2011) proposes three approaches to remediation. First is punishment, which can range from dealing with the criminal justice system to expulsion, detention, or other disciplinary procedures. We believe that should be a last resort because it essentially has no remediation but is used solely to maintain the safety and integrity of the affected students. Second is a consequences approach. Bullies are generally masters of manipulation and rationalization, so the worker needs to be wary of getting into debates with them or accepting excuses for their aggressive behavior. Bullies don't change overnight, so positive reinforcement needs to be used cautiously and only when prosocial behavior has started to occur consistently (McAdams & Schmidt, 2007). While negative sanctions are involved, they are more educative than punitive in nature. Consequences may be attending an anger management

group or working with special education students if that was the target population of the bully; behavioral contracting social skills training can be used (Burnham, 2011). Third is a feelings approach that focuses on stopping the dehumanization and discounting of target individuals and focuses on building empathy for one's fellow students. Bullies may develop considerable skill in avoiding the consequences of their actions, but have much more trouble when the focus is on feelings generated by their hurtful behaviors, so that bullies begin to comprehend that there may be consequences when others feel victimized (McAdams & Schmidt, 2007).

Joy Burnham and her associates (2010) have developed an innovative virtual world program model that the worker can use with both bullies and bullied students. Scenarios can be set up to teach different kinds of responding skills, hopefully making the bully aware that there are better alternatives and also teaching the bullied student how to respond more assertively.

Bauman (2011) believes that with minor bullying cases brief solution-focused counseling can help both victims and bullies. This approach looks at bullying events as exceptions rather than the norm. It builds on both the victim's and the bully's self-identified strengths and develops strategies for similar situations in the future. For more severe cases she believes support groups can be effective. Supporters of the victim, other individuals involved in the incident, and the main perpetrator can come together to agree on a support plan for the victim. Bauman proposes for the most serious cases that a restorative justice program be undertaken. First the victim is allowed to express how he or she can be helped. Then the bully has the option of coming up with a plan to meet the victim's needs in trying to make amends. There is a prescribed procedure and a very formalized structure as to what and when things are done, which most likely takes some additional training.

Glasser (1969) believes that classroom meetings that target real-time school and peer problems are an excellent vehicle for bringing a great deal of peer consensus and pressure into play on problems such as the Rosebuds' strong-arm tactics. Once the majority of students in a school or a classroom decide that a particular behavior is "uncool," it tends to diminish very quickly. The major problem with bullying is that bystanders do not speak up. Mobilizing the masses stops bullying and intimidation in their tracks (Charach, Pepler, & Zeigler, 1995). Further, by using the democratic, participatory process of Glasser's classroom meetings to problem-solve, students come to feel empowered and are able to stand up to bullying and intimidating behaviors (Glasser, 1969). Having students write out experiences with bullying can help make it safe for them to start talking about it.

School Counselor: (*Starting a classroom meeting with a sixth-grade class. The objective is to start shining a very bright light on the strong-arm tactics of the Rosebuds, but the counselor does not specifically mention them by name. Indeed, there are two probable gang members in the room.*) I want you all to write down four stories about bullying, using the following instructions.

1. Describe a time when someone's words or behavior hurt you.
2. Describe a time when you said or did something to hurt another person.
3. Describe a time when you saw or heard bullying but didn't do anything about it.
4. Describe a time when you saw or heard bullying and either got help or tried to stop it.

After the students finish writing their stories and share them with the group, the school counselor opens up a discussion centered on how students felt as they heard different stories. What did they think about what they heard? What would they do? And what would the consequences be if they did do something or changed what they did (Beane, 1999, p. 22)? Once students have started openly discussing threatening and intimidating behaviors, the counselor can use the hallmark of the classroom meeting and reality therapy, making a commitment (Glasser, 1969) to make their school a safer and more friendly place by pledging to do so and writing down specifically how that is going to happen (Newman, Horne, & Bartolomucci, 2000, p. 123). There are a number of effective antibullying programs, and if handled correctly, they can cut bullying and the potential violence that goes with it.

Finally, Paterson (2011) summarizes a number of researchers and practitioners in advocating for bullies to get counseling. Many of these bullies have themselves been bullied and need empathy and support as they themselves struggle with the effects of bullying. It may also be that while bullies see their approach as making them powerful, their thinking is distorted and will invariably get them in deeper trouble. As such, cognitive interventions that reframe their distorted notions of how they obtain and hold power over others may be effective. The problem is that for both offender and victim, if things don't straighten out and get better they run the risk of falling into the next section—and those are the lethal students who make headlines.

The Estranged Violent Juvenile Offender

The U.S. Department of Education (Dwyer, Osher, & Warger, 1998) has an excellent booklet that deals with safe schools in a general way. The booklet specifically mentions the school counselor as one of the lead professionals in helping prevent violence but says little about the specifics of the counselor's role, or the role of any other human services worker for that matter. Although gang violence is a major component of violence perpetrated by and among school-age children and is a major contributor to violence perpetrated by what Loeber and associates (1998) call the serious violent juvenile offender (SVJO), recent school shootings and subsequent homicides and injuries have been perpetrated by juveniles who do not typically fall into the "gang" SVJO category. The purpose of this section is to examine these different, potentially violent juveniles in regard to their psychological profile, screening mechanisms to detect them, and counseling methods to uncover their violent thoughts before those thoughts turn into action.

Peter Langman (2009) has written an excellent in-depth book on school shooters. He believes that most school shooters share some psychological symptoms. He further believes they fall within three general trait categories: psychopathic, psychotic, or traumatized. We believe that these three categories encompass what we call the EVJO. The term *estranged* violent juvenile offenders (EVJOs) is chosen because these juveniles typically are separated from their peers in distinctive ways and harbor a great deal of enmity toward their peers or the school system. We believe these individuals are distinct from their equally lethal SVJO counterparts. In contrast to a gang culture, in which violence is generated in order to bind its members together in perpetuation of the gang's growth and stature, the EVJO is typically isolated and has no allegiances unless to a very few others who are also experiencing the same estrangement. EVJOs can be partitioned into two major categories, those who are mentally ill and those who are not. Langman's (2009) two categories of psychopathic and psychotic shooter would most nearly fall under our mentally ill EVJO category and his traumatized shooter would fall under our not mentally ill EVJO category. Although it could be argued that anyone who would shoot a number of his fellow students is "crazy," that does not necessarily make him mentally ill under the American Psychiatric Association's (2000) *DSM-IV-TR* classification system. Therefore, it is also important to discriminate between EVJOs who are and are not mentally ill because of differences in profiles, screening, and intervention. Although we do not arbitrarily exclude the potential for females in this group, the preponderance of offenders will be male. As a result, we will use the male gender to describe the potential offender.

A Comparison of Traits, Characteristics, and Behaviors of SVJOs and EVJOs

The following traits, characteristics, and behaviors have been compiled from a number of published sources and interviews with human services workers who deal with both the SVJO and EVJO (Batsche & Knoff, 1994; Busch et al., 1990; Carney et al., 1999; Corder et al., 1976; Cunningham & Davis, 1999; Duncan & Duncan, 1971; Dwyer, Osher, & Warger, 1998; Fein et al., 2002; Galatzen-Levy, 1993; Hardwick & Rowton-Lee, 1996; James & Dorner, 1999; Lempp, 1990; Levis, 1992; Loeber, 1990; Marohn et al., 1982; Myers & Mutch, 1992; National School Safety Center, 1998; O'Toole, 2003; Sage & Dietz, 1994; Sloan, 1988; Vossekuil et al., 2002; Webster & Wilson, 1994; Zagar et al., 1990). These characteristics fall within what the FBI's Critical Incident Response Group and the National Center for the Analysis of Violent Crime call the four-pronged assessment model that evaluates the likelihood of carrying out a threat of violence. The four-pronged assessment model considers the personality of the student, family dynamics, school dynamics, and social dynamics (O'Toole, 2003).

Understand that there are serious moral, ethical, and legal implications of attempting to label potentially violent students (Simmons, 2000). A heated debate rages on whether an accurate profile of a school shooter exists. There is a belief that such profiles are overinclusive, biased, stigmatizing, and can potentially violate the student's constitutional rights (Bailey, 2001; Reddy et al., 2001; Vossekuil et al., 2000; 2002). Mulvey and Cauffman (2001) argue that such profiling is not only unproven, but has limited usefulness and often does more harm than good, particularly when a false positive identification is made and the student becomes labeled as a "homicidal maniac."

Langman's (2009) profiling of infamous school shooters in the last 15 years is an eye-opener in regard to some of the stereotypical myths that make for good media sound bites. While the characteristics that follow may be present to some degree in all school shooters, it would be a severe mistake to suppose that any one factor, such as bullying, being a loner, or having a fascination with violence and guns, is *the* factor that causes students to become homicidal, nor is it very likely that the student will have all of the characteristics that profile the school shooter. It is much more reasonable to say that each school shooter has a mix of these potentially lethal ingredients that, when combined in the right amounts and cooked for the right amount of time in the right ecosystem, turn into a recipe for lethality.

Thus, there seems to be enough evidence that when these traits and characteristics are combined with specific behaviors that indicate an increased threat level, they are at least a preliminary screening device that crisis workers can employ if reasonable judgment and care are used. On the other side of the dilemma, to not recognize that there is a potential threat is also professionally unethical and morally indefensible. More ominously, there are growing legal opinions that unanticipated acts of violence in schools can be anticipated and courts will expect schools to have prevention programs in place (Capuzzi, 2002).

Summarizing these characteristics of the potentially violent juvenile, your authors would emphatically echo the U.S. Department of Education's *Early Warning, Timely Response: A Guide to Safe Schools* (Dwyer, Osher, & Warger, 1998, p. 3) and the Federal Bureau of Investigation's *The School Shooter: A Threat Assessment Perspective* (O'Toole, 2003, p. 30) in their warning that it is important to avoid inappropriate labeling, stereotyping, or stigmatizing individuals based on the following categories. None of the categories by themselves or in combination can absolutely predict who will become violent and who will not. However, if the child fits into multiple categories, the crisis worker should be aware that the *potential* for violence increases and that this is an extremely troubled person. What we are more interested in when conducting a threat assessment are the demonstrated behaviors and communications that are likely to indicate intent (Fein et al., 2002; Langman, 2009). Therefore, when reading the following categories, focus not so much on the categories themselves but on what behaviors are being manifested by the individual in his actions and communications. As these behaviors and communications stack up, the potential for violence increases.

Abusive Childhood. Sexual, psychological, and physical abuses in childhood are fertile fields in which the SVJO and EVJO take root and grow. Exposure to violent role models at home, maternal or paternal deprivation, frequent moves, loss of a parent, inconsistent and punitive discipline, and rejection are characteristics of both. There is little parental control or supervision of curfews, Internet access, or television. Both SVJO and EVJO may rule the roost at home, and parents may be intimidated and afraid of the child. For the EVJO who does have a positive and supportive family, his sense of integration into the family likely will be weak and alienated. He will express contempt for his parents and dismiss their role in his life. He will insist on an inordinate degree of privacy, and his parents will have little information about his activities, friends, or school life. Such alienation may be particularly true for the mentally ill EVJO, even though he has an extremely supportive family situation and has received a great deal of nurturing and care. Parents may be in a great deal of denial about the potential for violence in either type.

Academic Problems. The SVJO will probably have a history of school problems that includes truancy, poor grades, discipline problems, and trouble with teachers. A combination of ADHD and conduct disorder is a high predictor of future violent behavior for the SVJO. In contrast, the EVJO will likely be passively compliant in school and may even do well academically. Unless some traumatic incident causes him to act out, he may well go unnoticed, or even be respected by his teachers. Both may have mild to severe language disorders that, when they are placed under stress, will cause them to be more likely to act than talk. The mentally ill EVJO will be likely to experience many academic problems because of his difficulty in maintaining contact with the reality and demands of the classroom.

Altered States of Consciousness. Even if psychoactive substances are not ingested, their cognitive processes lead both the SVJO and the EVJO to limited reality testing. Typical reports after a violent incident include derealization, decompensation, and depersonalization. Statements such as "I was just seeing red and sort of blanking out," or "It's like I wasn't there, sorta watching a videotape, so it was like me but really not me," are characteristic of both the SVJO and the EVJO. The mentally ill EVJO may operate in a continued state of altered consciousness and have minimum contact with the reality of the situation if not controlled by medication. Abuse of street or prescription psychotropic drugs increases the potential for violent behavior.

Anger/Low Frustration Tolerance. Both types react to stress in self-defeating ways. The SVJO is likely to have a "short fuse" and immediately aggress in a stressful situation, whereas the EVJO typically will flee the situation or act in a more passive way. The low frustration tolerance of the SVJO is much more immediate and seen in highly observable ways. In contrast, the EVJO may have less observable behavioral manifestations because his anger is turned inward and sublimated. He may be erroneously seen to have a high frustration tolerance. In contrast, the mentally ill EVJO may have a very low frustration tolerance because of his tenuous grip on reality.

Bully/Bullied. The SVJO is the stereotypical bully. A bully at school, he is most probably a victim at home. The EVJO is the stereotypical bullied child. He may fall into one of two categories, the passive victim or the aggressive victim. The aggressive victim may be hot tempered and attempt to retaliate when attacked. Paradoxically, the aggressive victim may also be seen as a bully. Whereas the passive bullied child is depicted as lonely and socially isolated at school, the aggressive victim is one of the most disliked and notorious members of his peer group. Although the passive bullied child may be much slower to act than his aggressive counterpart, both may bring weapons to school to counterbalance their perceived inferiority to their tormentors.

Chemical and Substance Abuse. Both types may alter consciousness by using psychoactive substances and freeing themselves of psychological restraints to commit violent acts. With the mentally ill EVJO, discontinued use of prescribed psychotropic medication combined with illicit drug use has a high likelihood of precipitating a violent episode. Substance abuse markedly increases the potential for violence.

Criminal Behavior. In contrast to the gang member, who probably has a long history of contacts with the police and juvenile authorities, the EVJO most likely does not. The EVJO is as likely as not to be seen as a good and compliant student by his teachers. Comments from his neighbors are typically, "He's a real quiet, polite boy." He may have excellent church attendance and belong to the Boy Scouts or other socially appropriate organizations. If the EVJO has any contacts with the police, it will most likely be of a petty misdemeanor nature and involve passive acts against objects rather than aggressive acts against people. If the

EVJO is mentally ill, he may have had contacts with the authorities through domestic disturbance or "mentally ill" calls. He will be on some type of antipsychotic medication and will likely have quit taking it because he doesn't like the side effects.

Delayed Cognitive and Affective Development. Both types may not have reached Piaget's formal operational or even concrete stage of development. Linear and logical thinking is stunted, and short-term emotional gratification overrules long-term behavioral consequences. Their notion of the finality of death or the realness and pain of bodily injury may be very much like a game of cops and robbers in which they are shot and killed over and over in the course of an afternoon. They may not relate their violent actions to any negative emotional outcomes for either their victims or themselves.

Emotional Lability/Depression. Whereas the SVJO demonstrates a quick temper, "short fuse," and rapid mood swings, the EVJO may show depressive characteristics in which anger is turned inward. The EVJO may be serious to the point of sullenness, and see little humor in his world, particularly if he has been the object of derisive humor by his peers or significant others in his life. The severely depressed EVJO may see the end point of retaliation against his tormentors as also the end point for himself and may see suicide as a viable option after he has exacted revenge. The mentally ill EVJO may have bizarre thoughts and emotions with correlative mood swings that range from rage to fear. He also may have suicidal ideation, depending on his emotional state and particular mental illness.

External Locus of Control. Fate, God, "The Man," and other external entities play a large part in the behavior of the SVJO and the EVJO. The SVJO may view himself as both the victimizer as a way of gaining power, and the victim because of his circumstances. The EVJO clearly assumes a victim status. Both blame others for their outcast state. The EVJO's external locus is tied to a low self-concept that is constantly reaffirmed as being inadequate by the world around him. The mentally ill EVJO may receive "messages" from "voices" that tell him to act against others.

History and Threats of Violence. One of the best predictors of violence is past violence. Particularly when threats of violence are coupled with a past history of

violence, the probability of violence increases. Whereas the SVJO will more likely be clear, immediate, and direct with his threats, the EVJO's threats are likely to be more implied, conditional, and veiled for a longer period of time. The mentally ill EVJO may make threats that commingle reality with fantasy such that specific individuals may be symbolized as "monsters" or other objects that are threatening to him.

Hypersensitivity. Both the SVJO and EVJO are hypersensitive to criticism and real or perceived slights and threats. They will both be suspicious, fearful, distrustful, and paranoid in their worldview. Whereas the SVJO will be more overt in his manifestation of these characteristics through name-calling, swearing, and angry outbursts, the EVJO will be more passive. Both are overly sensitive to what they believe others think, feel, and act toward them. They are "injustice collectors"; they harbor resentment over past wrongs and will not forget them or the people believed to be responsible. The mentally ill EVJO will be exponentially more hypersensitive to imagined threats to his well-being and react angrily to them. Paradoxically, both may have little sensitivity or empathy for others.

Impulsivity. The SVJO is quick to act and wants immediate gratification. He has little consideration for the consequences of his actions, lacks insight, has poor judgment, and has little understanding of how his belief system filters actions and resulting consequences. He habitually makes violent threats when angry. In contrast, the EVJO may be slow to act. He may be hypersensitive as a result of past negative experiences that have been socially and emotionally punitive. His belief system will turn to a "them against me" view that continues to build until his frustration spills out and he aggresses against his real or imagined tormentors. The mentally ill EVJO may fall along a continuum of high to low impulsivity depending on the disorder from which he suffers.

Mental Illness. Hospitalization for mental illness alone is not an indicator of potential violence. However, when hospitalization of the mentally ill SVJO or EVJO is preceded by a history of violent offenses, it is an indicator. Violence potential is further exacerbated when psychotropic medication is stopped because of its side effects, the inability to obtain it, or inadequate supervision in administering it.

Negative Role Models.   For the SVJO, local and nationally known gangbangers and movie and music "gangstas" may be role models. The EVJO may be drawn to malevolent historical figures such as Hitler, religious figures such as Satan, and antiheroes in books, videos, and game simulations. The mentally ill EVJO may create his own alter ego who tells him to do violent things.

Odd/Bizarre Beliefs.   Odd or bizarre beliefs fall into two categories. Schizophrenic-type mental illnesses and personality disorders are defined by odd and bizarre beliefs and behaviors, which would characterize the mentally ill EVJO. The second category more closely typifies the EVJO without mental illness. His thoughts and behaviors may range from an interest in demonology, magical thinking, and satanic cults to extremely rigid political and religious views that promote violent solutions to society's problems, which he knows little about. He disregards facts, logic, and reasoning that might challenge these opinions. Joining splinter groups that advocate such views is a way of achieving the affiliation, status, and power that the EVJO craves.

Pathology and Deviance.   A psychological smorgasbord of problems may be exhibited by both types of juvenile offenders. Fire setting, cruelty to animals, defacing and destroying property, temper tantrums, running away from home, and oppositional defiance to authority are some examples. When these behaviors have a long history, they are probably more characteristic of the SVJO. When they seem to occur spontaneously with no prior history, or are kept under wraps by parents who are in denial and concerned about the social stigma attached to these behaviors, they more aptly characterize the EVJO. Parents of both groups may be passive in regard to what most parents would find very disturbing and abnormal behavior. If contacted by school officials or law enforcement, parents may respond defensively and minimize or reject reports of obvious misconduct.

Physical Problems.   Particularly for the EVJO, physical problems that range from stuttering to severe acne to delayed physical development may contribute to a poor body image and feelings of inferiority. Internal head injuries, congenital brain damage, and a variety of neurological problems may contribute to the potential for violence in the mentally ill EVJO.

Preoccupation With Violent Themes.   Both the SVJO and the EVJO may become fixated on movies, books, television shows, videos, and music that glamorize violence. Interest in violent pornography, weapons collections, sadomasochistic paraphernalia, and instruments of torture allow the powerless EVJO, and particularly the mentally ill EVJO who is paranoid, to fantasize about dominance over his persecutors and plot very meticulously how to get rid of them.

Social Status.   The SVJO may be ostentatious and gregarious in his social relations as a means of gaining status. He sees females as providers of "goods and services" and tends to use them for his own self-gratification. He may display a pathological need for attention, and have an overall attitude of superiority and an exaggerated sense of entitlement. A social assessment of the EVJO would generally depict him as a social isolate from the majority of his peers with affiliations that place him in outlier groups. However, there are EVJOs who are popular, participate in extracurricular activities, and would generally be seen as involved in the school community. If asked, his classmates might characterize the EVJO in terms such as "geek," "Goth," "nerd," "freak," "weird," and other terms that clearly set him apart from the social mainstream. His attempts to form relationships with the opposite sex will generally be clumsy and fraught with failure. Females who try to be kind to him may well have their kindness misinterpreted. When the EVJO makes attempts to move beyond "kindness" in the relationship and his romantic overtures are rejected, the isolation he feels is further compounded. Because of his bizarre behavior, the mentally ill EVJO will be extremely socially isolated from his peers and labeled as "nuts," "mental," or "crazy."

Suicidal Ideation.   Both the SVJO and EVJO may have severe depressive episodes with significant mood swings. The result may be angry outbursts against others or self, with concomitant threats or attempts of suicide. Such threats or attempts may occur particularly after a real or perceived personal loss. The mentally ill EVJO may consider suicide a very viable option to get the demons out of his head or as a way to keep "them" from getting him and further persecuting him after he does away with his enemies.

Weapons.   Both the SVJO and the EVJO may have an undue fascination with and knowledge of weapons. The family may keep guns or other weapons accessible in the home, or the SVJO or EVJO may have easy means of obtaining them on the street. Parents or significant role models may have a casual attitude toward weapons and see them as a useful or normal means of settling disputes. The SVJO may commonly carry or have access to a weapon for both "protection" and "revenge" against other gang members. When the EVJO carries a weapon to school, he is most likely getting ready to act out against his tormentors. The mentally ill EVJO may be much like the SVJO in carrying weapons for both protection and revenge against his imagined enemies.

Case Study: Seung-hui Cho

Now consider Seung-hui Cho at Virginia Tech in April 2007. How well do you think he fits the foregoing behaviors and characteristics?

Seung-hui Cho, the Virginia Tech mass murderer and suicide, is the personification of the mentally ill EVJO. The following behaviors, characteristics, and traits are gleaned from the video he sent to NBC and from a report by Michael Ruane (2007), who interviewed Cho's former suite mate, Andy Koch.

Cho clearly had altered states of consciousness as exemplified by his imaginary supermodel girlfriend "Jelly," whom he claimed he was making out with in his locked room. He had severe ego identity problems, as indicated by his alter ego, Ismail Ax, a name written in red ink on his arm, and by his signature "?" on a class role, which earned him the nickname of the "Question Mark Kid." Claiming to vacation with Russia's president, Vladimir Putin, and to live in the ominous room "666" when his hall had only five floors, boosted his weak self-concept and gave him power. Like most EVJOs he had no apparent history of direct threats to anyone, but his behavior was most certainly threatening to all around him. His plays were so dark, twisted, and threatening that they caught the attention of his English professors. They are characteristic of the commingling of reality and fantasy for a person with paranoid schizophrenia and cannot be passed off as the works of "another Stephen King in the making." Cho's stalking behavior, scrawling of scary lines from Shakespeare on a girl's residence hall door, and other antisocial and bizarre behaviors over an extended period of time were precursors of his ultimate acts of violence; those oblique threats would slowly grow and finally take form in the direct and methodical act of mass murder. His hypersensitivities to external threats were legion and ranged from girls to the "rich snobs." He had been involuntarily hospitalized, was found to be depressed but

not a threat to anyone else, and was released. Numerous complaints brought the police to his door. His antiheroes Eric Harris and Dylan Klebold, the mass murderers at Columbine High School, were ideal role models for the rampage he was contemplating. Most likely another role model, Ismail Ax, his imaginary alter ego, urged him along.

Cho's physical problems included not being able to speak well, being small of stature, and being different, although at this writing it is unclear whether "being different" related to being Korean, bullied, a loner, or some other factor or constellation of factors that set him apart. His writings and Facebook illustration of himself as a Zorro-like figure with only a large question mark in an otherwise blank face portray the graphic images of the violence he was contemplating. Finally and tragically, these characteristics were known to numerous people, from his roommate to professors to the police. The psychological leakage that characterizes a potentially violent student was a veritable flood for Seung-hui Cho.

In summary, if you now look back through the traits, behaviors, characteristics, and screening factors for the mentally ill EVJO and compare them to Cho, they should scream at you, "Do something!" However, "doing something" in the case of a college student, even one whose behavior is as blatant as Cho's, is not so easily accomplished, as we shall see in this chapter's section on legal and ethical issues of potentially violent behavior.

Screening the EVJO

Langman (2009) emphasizes that the key is early detection and prevention because once an armed suicidal/homicidal student sets foot on the school ground with a plan of action, all the metal detectors in the world are not going to stop him from carrying out his intended plan. The problem with profiling the estranged violent juvenile offender who is not mentally ill is that any staff member in a school could probably identify at least 20 percent of the male population who might fit the foregoing profile and have many of the characteristics described in the foregoing section. How, then, can this population be screened for those students who might have such characteristics and, more important, the intent to carry out a violent act?

Leakage. Leakage occurs when a student intentionally or unintentionally reveals feelings, thoughts, fantasies, attitudes, or intentions that signal a violent act. They can be delivered through stories, diaries, essays, poems, drawings, doodles, songs, tattoos, videos, or other media that make boasts, threats, predictions, or ultimatums. Another form of leakage occurs when unwitting friends and classmates are coerced or deceived into helping in preparations for violent acts. Leakage can be cries for help, signs of inner conflict, or boasts that may presage a serious threat. Leakage is considered one of the most important clues that precede a violent act (O'Toole, 2003). Being aware of and acting on threats are critical in the prevention of a violent act (Wattendorf, 2002).

Writings, Drawings, Pictures, Videos, and E-Mails.
The writings, drawings, homemade pictures, and videos of EVJOs are often an open pathway into their troubled minds. In cases of potential violent behavior, artwork may make the point more vividly than a verbal description. Graphic themes of violence that pervade the writings, drawings, photographs, videos, and e-mails of EVJOs are a tip-off that the student may be contemplating violent action against school staff or fellow students. These hard-copy emotional messages should be taken very seriously when previous incidents of violent behavior have occurred and when such graphic displays of violent ideation are issuing from the "quiet kid" who has no history of disruption in the school. School crisis workers need to apprise teachers of these indicators of predisposition to violence, and such student-generated work should be passed on to the crisis worker (Duncan & Duncan, 1971; Hammond & Gantt, 1998; James & Dorner, 1999).

Peer Referral.
There are very, very few instances in which the EVJO does not give some warning of his intentions to harm himself or others. Invariably, in psychological postmortems of situations that resulted in injury or death due to violence by an EVJO, students had heard statements or seen notes from the student indicating his intent to do harm but had generally dismissed them as just "talk" (Hardwick & Rowton-Lee, 1996; James & Dorner, 1999).

However, the problem with peer referral is twofold. First, other students are afraid of and repelled by the notion of "narking" or "snitching" on another student. This reticence to inform on another is particularly true when the student in question may be so threatening that other students fear for their own safety or dismiss the threat of a student they have known for years and in their opinion is absolutely harmless. Students need to feel safe in providing information about a potentially dangerous situation (Dwyer, Osher, & Warger, 1998, p. 4; Stewart & MacNeil, 2005).

One of the best ways to screen for potentially violent students is through a peer referral and notification system run by peers and coordinated by school crisis workers (Allen, 1996). Conflict resolution, peer mediation, peer leadership, and peer counseling are all programs that allow students to legitimately notify faculty of potentially violent students without becoming informers. Whatever type of peer program is offered should not be operated from the standpoint that its only purpose is to "catch bad kids." The primary purpose of peer programs should be to help other students resolve conflicts, mediate disputes, and provide support, help, and referral for common maturational problems associated with adolescence and acclimation to school. However, when in the course of providing such peer helping services, peer helpers gain information about fellow students in crisis who may be planning to commit violent acts, it is clearly appropriate for them to apprise the crisis worker of the information they have received (James & Dorner, 1999).

Peer helpers need to be carefully trained, monitored, and supervised by crisis workers lest they exceed their limits (Allen, 1996). Peer helpers should be selected from a broad cross-section of the school population (Day-Vines et al., 1996). It has been your authors' experience that students who represent the full spectrum of the student population are much more effective in reaching their peers and being accepted by them. That does not mean that there are lowered expectations of peer helpers either academically or morally. The best peer helpers have been able to demonstrate a willingness to work with and help all of their fellow students. Their very diversity allows the program to reach a broader constellation of students than it otherwise might (Allen, 1996).

Threat Assessment Team.
The other major step is establishing a threat assessment team much like those that now exist on many college campuses (Myer, James, & Moulton, 2011) and in some K–12 school systems. The team should be composed of at least an administrator, a counselor, an SRO, and enough teachers spread across all grades and all sections of the school to ensure that at least one team member has direct contact with each student. Currently Dr. Rick Myer of Duquesne University is working on a K–12 TASSLE form, a simplified version of the Triage Assessment Form (R. Myer, personal communication, April 2011) that you will read about later in this chapter.

Interviewing the Potential EVJO

When interviewing the potential EVJO, the first two tasks of the crisis intervention/prevention model, Pre-dispositioning and Problem Exploration, along with the default task of Safety, are particularly critical in getting the EVJO to start talking about a violent act. The third task, Providing Support, and the default task of Safety are critical in assuring the student that the overriding concern is the student's own safety and well-being and that the issues that brought him to this point are not going to be shoved in a file drawer and never see the light of day. Coordinated with these preliminary tasks is the three-level threat assessment model provided in *The School Shooter: A Threat Assessment Perspective* (O'Toole, 2003, pp. 8–9).

Low threat is one that poses a minimal risk to the proposed victim. The threat is vague and indirect. The information is inconsistent and implausible, lacks detail, or is unrealistic. The content suggests it is unlikely to be carried out. *Medium threat* is one that could be carried out, although it may appear to be unrealistic. It is more direct than a low-level threat. Wording indicates that some thought has been given to how it will be carried out. There is a general indication of possible place and time. There is little indication the threatener has taken preparatory steps or made solid plans. There may be a specific statement seeking to convey the threat is real, as in "I'm serious, and I mean it!" *High threat* poses an imminent and serious danger to the safety of others. The threat is direct, specific, and plausible. Concrete steps have been taken toward carrying it out, and there is a solid plan with means, opportunity, knowledge, and lethal methodology to carry it out.

Problem Definition.   The school crisis worker who interviews a potential EVJO initially needs to proceed with basic listening and responding skills that deeply reflect the student's feelings and allow him to ventilate his angry feelings. It should be understood that other negative emotions are undergirding and supporting the anger the student feels. Suspicion, betrayal, embarrassment, grief, anxiety, inadequacy, threat, insecurity, and particularly, hopelessness and frustration, are but a few of the negative feelings that may be pushing the student toward violence. As indicated in Chapter 15, Crisis/Hostage Negotiation, when an individual is contemplating an expressive crime, empathic listening with open-ended leads and deep reflections of thinking and feeling will allow vitriolic feelings to emerge.

Case of John.   John is a 14-year-old high school freshman who was referred to the school counselor by a teacher who had screened out John's theme after she had been through a workshop on profiling potentially violent students. The counselor has read John's theme, which is filled with angry and violent threats about a group of girls who have been teasing him.

CW: John, I've read your theme Mrs. Smith sent to me. You seem really angry. Would you like to tell me about what's making you so angry right now?

John: I'm sick of the Tri-Beta Club. Particularly the girls. They ask me to do stuff, and I do it, but then they make fun of me.

CW: Sounds like you're not only angry but hurt too. How do they hurt you?

These feelings and their antecedent causes need to be fully explored by the crisis worker to make a clear determination of what is going on and with whom it is occurring. Exploration is important for two reasons. First, by allowing the student to ventilate, the crisis worker does much toward defusing the potentially violent situation and can start to help the student develop alternative coping and problem-solving strategies. The crisis worker wants to establish an open and trusting relationship with this troubled student. Hearing the student and affirming him, through summary clarification and restatement of the content of his problem and reflection of his feelings, go a long way toward doing that.

John: Yeah. I want to be friends, but I don't think they really want me for a friend. When they need somebody to build a float or put up posters, I'm just fine. But when I asked Sally Johnson if she wanted to go get a soda after the float was done, she laughed at me, said I was a loser, and then told the other girls, and they laughed too. I hate them!

CW: So they really put you down and embarrassed you when you did everything they wanted you to do.

Second, by adequately exploring the affective, behavioral, and cognitive dimensions of the student's problem, the crisis worker may gain valuable information about the *who, what, where, when,* and *how* of the student's proposed course of action. The worker stays away from *why* questions because of their interrogatory nature. John is already defensive, and the crisis worker does not wish to do anything that will further alienate him.

CW: John, it sounds like you'd really like to get back at them for the way they've treated you. How might you do that?

Ensuring Safety.   Assessment of lethality is primary in any crisis intervention. Contrary to exploring issues by using open-ended questions, we subsequently assess the potential for suicidal or homicidal behavior by asking specific, closed-ended questions that are designed to get direct answers about the student's threat level. The questions we ask could come straight from a detective's homicide manual and fall within the following areas:

1. Is there a motive?
2. Is there opportunity?
3. What is the method or plan?
4. What are the means?

Most people in psychological crisis who have suicidal or homicidal ideation will talk about what they are going to do, and talking about their plan does not, contrary to popular myth, make them more likely to carry it out. Even though they may believe they have exhausted all other possibilities, their willingness to talk about their thoughts and contemplated actions is a positive sign and an indication that at least some part of them believes there is an alternative. The potential EVJO, in particular, fits this pattern because of his feelings of anger, hopelessness, and frustration and his need to vent those feelings. If questions are asked in an empathic, nonjudgmental way, he will be willing to talk about the four points just listed. There is one major exception, and that is the mentally ill EVJO who is paranoid about the behavior of others toward him. He is highly unlikely to voluntarily come to counseling or think that he needs it. After all, he believes it is the others who are all wrong and messed up—not him! Persuading him to talk may best be accomplished by eliciting talk about "them" and displaying a good deal of empathy in regard to injustices perpetrated on him.

As motive, opportunity, method, and means are covered, the threat assessment goes up as each becomes more concrete. The motive of the EVJO is often unclear, or muddled, and therefore may be dismissed as inconsequential. It would be a mistake to dismiss such ideation, however, because it is not just the motive itself but the intensity and the lability with which it is discussed that are important. The more emotive the EVJO is about the injustices done him, the more he clarifies and elaborates on his plan and the opportunity to carry it out, and the more lethal his means, the higher the threat assessment (O'Toole, 2003, p. 9).

It should be abundantly clear that if the potential EVJO has access to firearms or other weapons and knows how to use them, the threat becomes critical, and there is increased risk for violence (Dwyer, Osher, & Warger, 1998, p. 10; Langman 2009, p. 182). Thus the crisis worker should not hesitate to ask the student what he knows about firearms and if he has access to them. If the crisis worker does not know about types and use of firearms, the SRO should be consulted.

The following two scenarios, using John as an example, depict low versus high levels of threat.

Scenario 1

John: I wish they were all dead. It'd serve them right!

CW: So if they were dead, it'd pay them back for what they've done to you. How might that happen?

John: Well, I don't know for sure. I'd wish they'd get some incurable disease and really suffer a lot.

CW: So you'd like to see them hurt as much as they've hurt you. How might that happen?

John: Yeah. Well, I dunno for sure. Maybe they'd get that bird flu or food poisoning from the cafeteria.

Here, the student's wish for the death of his tormentors is couched in fantasy with no clear means or method for carrying out his plan. This fantasized revenge would not carry a high lethality level, but would certainly indicate that this student is in need of support and continued work with the crisis worker.

Scenario 2

John: I wish they were all dead. It'd serve them right.

CW: So if they were dead, it'd pay them back for what they've done to you. How might that happen?

John: It'd be easy. I'd wait for them after school. When they go out to work on the homecoming float at the bus barn, I'd be behind the incinerator. I could shoot them real easy.

CW: John, do you know how to use a gun?

John: Sure. My dad's got a 9 mm pistol. He showed me how to use it. He says I'm pretty good with it.

CW: Can you get your dad's gun?

John: Well, he's got it locked up in the gun safe, but I know the combination.

CW: John, when are you planning on doing this?

John: I don't know, but if they make fun of me one more time, soon.

In this second scenario, the student's motive, method, opportunity, and access to lethal means are much clearer and better defined. Such a response would indicate a much higher threat level and would call for clear and immediate action on the part of the crisis worker.

Providing Support. In any case in which a student's lethality level is high, we need to provide clear owning statements about what we will need to do to keep the client and others he may intend to harm safe. Parents must be informed, and a clear line of communication needs to be established with the school administration, law enforcement, and other agencies that may become involved (Dwyer, Osher, & Warger, 1998, p. 11).

CW: (*responding to scenario 2*) John, what you have said really concerns me. It sounds like you've really worked out the details, and if you carry this out, I'm afraid for you and the other students. I understand you're really angry and hurt by what they've done to you, I can certainly understand how you could feel that way, but I don't want to see you get hurt any more, either by the other students in what they say and do to you, or by the police. I don't want you to shoot anybody, and I don't want the police to shoot you. I need to get some help for you right now, and I need to be sure you're safe. I want you to stay with me until I can make sure you are safe. I need to talk to your parents because I'm sure they would be concerned for you. I also need to talk to the principal to make sure that she understands what's going on, so she can make sure that you stay safe. I understand that you might be upset with me for doing this, but I'm really concerned about you right now, John. I understand that right now you think this is the only solution you've got, but I believe there are other ways to handle this, and I want you to understand that I'll help you to figure some of those out. I'll stay with you and work with you until we do get things worked out and you are safe.

Many clients will not be happy when they are informed about what is going to happen to them. One of the best responses the crisis worker can make when this happens is to use a combination of what are called "I understand" statements and the "broken record" technique, which continuously and repeatedly acknowledges the client's unhappiness about our decision, but also reaffirms our concern and caring for him. If the student becomes angry or enraged over the worker's insistence that help is required, and becomes threatening, the worker needs to acknowledge the anger, but also set limits.

John: Hey, everything is supposed to be confidential in here. You tricked me. No way you tell my parents, my old man would beat me to death. Screw this. (*Jumps up with fists clenched.*)

CW: (*Immediately rises from her chair as a safety precaution.*) No, I did not trick you, John. You heard what I said about confidentiality when we talked about harming yourself or others. John, I totally get what you say, but don't you want some respect, don't you want to feel better about coming

to school? Don't you not want to be tricked and made fun of anymore? These things can happen because you have not acted on that angry notion. So please sit down and let me go to work for you. Nothing has happened so far that says we can't get some more positive results. So please sit down and let me do my job to help you out.

The worker first acknowledges his anger and sense of betrayal. She then uses a series of negative interrogative questions that ask for agreement and attempt to reframe his present cognitive and emotional state to what he desires to have happen. She also uses "these" things to gain psychological closeness as opposed to "that" notion which she wishes to distance psychologically. Finally, she also uses Fauteux's (2010) technique of showing there is still time because nothing has happened yet that would destroy the possibility of John's getting what he wants other than revenge.

If these techniques do not get John to calm down, then the worker needs to consider her own safety and follow our recommendations in Chapter 14, Violent Behavior in Institutions, to get out of the room and/or get help.

At other times, what may at first seem to be a high threat situation may not be and, in fact, may mask other crisis issues. Return now to Officer Davis whom you met earlier in the chapter, and see how his day is going to become very interesting indeed.

Officer Davis receives a call from the school secretary at his home (S. Davis, personal communication, February 17, 2007). She is very distressed. The school has received a phone call from some kind of a psychotherapist in California who has been communicating with and working with a student via the Internet, a Goth 16-year-old white male. The therapist is very concerned because the student indicates he is tired of being bullied and is making a bomb to blow up the school. She calls long distance and tells the school secretary this information after the school day is over and the students are gone. The student has put that information on MySpace and indicated he is going to blow up something or somebody. Through some good detective work on the part of the school secretary, she has determined that the boy is Paul Jones. Officer Davis discretely meets the boy at school the next morning and pulls him into his office.

Officer Davis: Talk to me, Paul. What's going on? You seem kinda depressed.

Paul: Not really. Some kids trash talking me is all, and I'm tired of getting bullied by them.

Officer Davis: Look, you're not in any trouble okay, but I gotta check this out. It looks like you put some stuff on the net about making a bomb. Want to show me what it was?

Paul: Well yeah! I put some of that stuff on there, but I'm not really making one.

Paul shows him what he put on the net. Officer Davis e-mails this information to the local bomb squad, who are sitting in unmarked cars outside Paul's house. They get very excited over the information and immediately want to search Paul's house for bomb-making material. Officer Davis calls the parents and informs them of what is occurring. A search of the house is quietly conducted, and nothing is found in the way of explosive devices, much to the relief of the parents and everyone else. However, Officer Davis's CIT training kicks in, and he feels something more is going on with this troubled young man. He continues to explore Paul's feelings with him.

Officer Davis: Look, I've done a lot of this stuff, Paul, and I get a good sense when things are really troubling people. You seem really down or maybe something else. I think it's more than getting trash talk for being Goth. You sure you don't want to talk to me about it?

Paul: Okay. Look, this is weird. Like I have spiders crawling all over my arms right now. And there is a waterfall right in back of you. Plus my dad talks to me a lot in class, but like he's at work and not really there, but nevertheless, he is talking to me, and it really is distracting and scary. See I scratch my arms, but the spiders still come back.

Officer Davis: (*thinking to himself, "Holy mackerel! This kid is having schizophrenic episodes!"*) Paul, that certainly concerns me. Have you told your parents?

Paul: No, I'm too embarrassed. I don't want them to know. I keep thinking they'll go away. They don't come often, but when they do, it's pretty scary. That waterfall behind you right now is pretty real.

Officer Davis: I don't see or hear it. I know you do, and that needs to get taken care of. I've got a friend at the crisis center who deals with this stuff. I believe after I talk with your parents you need to meet him.

Officer Davis now calls the parents, who are at their home with the bomb disposal unit, and informs them of their son's hallucinating episodes. To say that this is a day they would like to soon forget is putting it mildly. However, Officer Davis calmly talks them though the problem and then drives Paul to the crisis center, where the parents meet him. Whenever Officer Davis has to take someone to the crisis center, he stays to make sure

the person is being seen and treated before he leaves. This is particularly true of students, who need a friendly face when they are taken to a mental health facility and are under emotional duress. This tactic allows students to know that he is not abandoning them and pays off down the road when he encounters them again. They know they can trust him and that he really is interested in them as people.

It may be argued that a school counselor, psychologist, or social worker might be the best person to handle this situation. However, when a school resource officer like Scott Davis is also CIT trained, the fact that this is a potentially lethal situation with disaster ramifications makes him the very best qualified person to deal with Paul. You may wonder whether this is a rose-colored picture of a police officer. With the spread of CIT training across the United States, officers like Scott Davis are becoming more and more common and are, in every sense of the definition, crisis interventionists. Further, they certainly have ample opportunity to ply their trade in 21st-century schools (James, Logan, & Davis, 2011).

Acting

How the crisis worker acts depends on a continuous assessment of the student. If the crisis worker determines that the student is indeed a threat, then the worker's response should be to make an immediate referral and notify parents, administrators, and, if necessary, law enforcement personnel. If the crisis worker determines that the student's lethality level is not high, then the worker can move forward in the model to examining alternatives, making plans, and obtaining a commitment to work on positive actions that will help him become less alienated and angry. An investigation might indicate that the behavior was merely a "throwaway" statement that had no meaning other than ordinary misguided playfulness or a momentary pique of anger. Even then, it would be a proper educative and counseling activity to teach the student not to play this game. However, in today's school environment, threats against others should not automatically be discounted. Thus, the crisis worker needs to keep a record of the encounter and follow up with the student to ensure that those threats do not escalate into action (James & Crawford, 2002).

Punishment by expulsion is not the answer and in fact does at least two things we don't want to have happen. First, it likely increases the student's grudge against the school or those in it he feels are responsible for his misery. Second, it is likely to leave the student unsupervised at home and give him free license to plan and assemble the necessary weaponry to pay the school back (Langman, 2009, p. 186). What needs to happen is that the student is evaluated for psychiatric and/or behavioral problems, medicated if necessary, provided counseling, and placed in an alternative school that is well supervised.

A primary consideration is what to do if the student is carrying a weapon. If the crisis worker feels the relationship with the student is positive enough and the student indicates that he has a weapon in his possession, then the crisis worker may ask for it for safekeeping. In taking a weapon, the crisis worker should always be sure it is handed over butt first or, if a knife, haft (handle) first. If the crisis worker is unsure of the student's intent or if the student is resistant, the crisis worker should *immediately seek help and get out of the room.* If the student indicates he has a weapon in his locker or some other hiding place, the crisis worker should have another person go with him or her to the hiding place. *In no instance should the crisis worker attempt to be a hero and attempt to forcibly take a weapon away from a student* (Crews, 1998). There is no known formula for determining whether to attempt to get the weapon away from the student or leave the premises to get help. Probably the best rule to follow is whatever the crisis worker believes will be the safest course of action for both the crisis worker and the student.

School-Based Suicide Prevention and Intervention

Because adolescence is the most volatile period of transition in the human cycle of development, factors involving youth who are at risk for suicide are dramatically different from those affecting adults who kill themselves (Berman, Jobes, & Silverman, 2006; Maples et al., 2005; Pfeffer, 2006). Suicide ranks third (12 percent) behind homicide (15 percent) and vehicle accidents (31 percent) as one of the leading causes of death in adolescents. From 1952 to 1995, the incidence of suicide among adolescents rose 300 percent. From 1980 to 1997, the rate of suicide among persons aged 10–14 rose 109 percent (Centers for Disease Control, 2002). Factoring in that there are about 6,000 to 7,000 completed suicides among children and adolescents per year, and that for every one completed suicide there are between 100 and 200 youths who attempt it (National Center for Health Statistics, 1992), there is an average likelihood that every year, every teacher in every high school classroom in the United States can expect two girls and one boy to seriously contemplate or attempt suicide (King, 2000), and every principal in the average American high school can expect one completed suicide every 5 years and 170 attempts in any given year, although most certainly most of these will never come to the school's attention (Brock, Sandoval, & Hart, 2006). Suicide is a problem that is far more prevalent and far more lethal than all the school assaults combined—even though school shootings get far more publicity.

From these figures it would seem apparent that crisis response programs in schools should incorporate suicide prevention, intervention, and postvention components that are comprehensive and systematic (Austin, 2003; Capuzzi, 2002; Kalafat, 2003; Komar, 1994; Malley, Kush, & Bogo, 1994; Reis & Cornell, 2008; Webb & Griffiths, 1998–1999). If a school system does not have a written formal policy, the board and the community should require that suicide prevention/intervention/postvention procedures be developed and implemented (Malley, Kush, & Bogo, 1994, p. 135). School-based child and adolescent suicide prevention/intervention/postvention should include (Capuzzi, 2002; Kerr, 2009; Malley, Kush, & Bogo, 1994, p. 131; Maples et al., 2005; Thompson, 2004):

1. A written, formal suicide policy statement
2. Written procedures to address and ensure the safety of at-risk students
3. Faculty and staff inservice orientation and training in warning signs and referral of at-risk students
4. Identification and training of mental health professionals on-site or readily available crisis teams
5. Prevention materials for distribution to students, parents, and the community, and for classroom discussion
6. Procedures for psychological screening, identification, and counseling of at-risk students
7. Preplanned postvention responses and strategies that occur following any completed suicide
8. Written criteria for crisis workers to assess lethality of a potential student suicide
9. Written policies on how the school-based child and adolescent suicide prevention/intervention/postvention program is evaluated

Kerr (2009, pp. 24–26) has taken these general procedures a step further and outlined what the response should be to a suicide threat, a suicide attempt on school grounds, a suicide attempt off school grounds or during a school-sponsored activity and reported to an employee, and a completed or suspected completed suicide.

Risk Factors/Predictors/Cues

Almost all adolescent suicide victims have experienced some form of psychiatric illness. These range across affective, conduct, and attention deficit disorders (Shaffer, 1988) to antisocial personality, substance abuse, and depressive disorders (Guida, 2001; Hacker et al., 2006; Shaffer, 1988). Adolescents who have questions about their sexual identity, have recently experienced a loss, suffered humiliation at school or home, been bullied or cyberbullied, had an interpersonal conflict with a romantic partner or a parent, a dramatic change such as the death of a friend, or a pregnancy, are heavily into alcohol or drug use, have been traumatized by sexual or physical assault, are depressed, have a physical illness, have made a major geographic move to a new school, engage in risky behaviors (parasuicidal), or are petulantly angry and impulsively act out are all candidates for suicidal ideation, threats, and acting (Capuzzi, 2002; Guida, 2001; Nelson & Galas, 1994). When faced with these conflicts, it appears that lack of family or peer support is a precipitating factor in generating suicidal ideation (Mazza & Reynolds, 1998). Interestingly, giftedness may also be a contributing factor (Nelson & Galas, 1994). The individual who comes from a home where suicide has been attempted or has had a close friend who has attempted suicide may be at greater risk (Capuzzi, 2002; Nelson & Galas, 1994). But probably the best single predictor is a previous suicide attempt (Nelson & Galas, 1994; Shaffer et al., 1988).

The clues and behaviors that are commonly found in the suicide indicators in Chapter 8, Crisis of Lethality, would hold true for most adolescents and children. For children and adolescents, however, warning signs also include a sudden change in friends or dress habits, cutting hair or changing hairstyles, difficulty concentrating, persistent boredom, sudden or increased promiscuity, reversal of valuation of prized objects, use of drugs or alcohol, and a decline in school achievement (Capuzzi, 2002; Greene, 1994; Maples et al., 2005; Nelson & Galas, 1994). Copycat suicides are particularly problematic for adolescents, particularly if the adolescents believe there will be notoriety for them. This phenomenon occurs after a suicide when peers, who may have had similar thoughts, also attempt suicide

(Austin, 2003). Although most adolescents give cues to their attempts, not all do. Adolescents may verbally indicate their decision to kill themselves in clear terms, or they may be far less direct with such statements as "I wonder what death is like" or "I'm tired of all of this."

Preadolescent Suicide

There is a prevailing notion that young children do not commit suicide. Have a conversation with any elementary school counselor, social worker, or school psychologist who has been in the business for any length of time and you will be quickly disabused of that faulty notion. The problem is that while a ton of work has been done with adolescents, relatively little has been done with young children. Price (2010), in a brief overview, pointed this out. The experts he queried indicated that most young children who commit suicide have some kind of mental disorder and are likely to have been victims of physical or sexual abuse. However, that is certainly not true of every child.

The other major issue is that when children are found to be suicidal they tend to be treated as miniature adults rather than in terms of the cognitive and developmental stage they are in. Indeed, because of their level of cognitive development, many young children's thought processes that lead to suicide would not generally be considered reasons to kill themselves if they were adults. But, as with all suicidal persons, it makes perfect sense to them. Consider the following reasons: wanting to meet a friend or relative who died; feeling guilty that they are the cause of parents' getting a divorce; avoiding punishment or embarrassment they believe is worse than death; wanting to punish someone else (although this can certainly happen with adolescents and adults); believing they will be martyrs for some cause; and escape from an intolerable situation such as an abusive home or a concentrated cyberbully attack (Muro & Kottman, 1995, pp. 324–325).

Further, parents and teachers tend to dismiss clues that are common to suicidal ideation. Indeed, it is interesting that most child counseling and therapy books tend to lump a lot of what is known about adolescent suicide into their recommendations and counseling techniques for elementary age children. The bottom line is that young children who emit suicidal clues should be taken seriously, and the child counseling procedures that are depicted in other parts of this chapter and book should be used with them along with the general suicide prevention and intervention techniques that are used with adults. To that end, our own state of Tennessee mandates by law training for all school personnel in suicide prevention, and we believe that it should be part of the policy of every elementary school that parents are educated about suicide prevention.

Child and Adolescent Cases of Suicidal Ideation

Here are some strategies and suggestions (Capuzzi, 2002; Fujimura, Weis, & Cochran, 1985; Nelson & Galas, 1994) for anyone (crisis worker or layperson) who comes into contact with a child or adolescent suspected of being suicidal:

1. Trust your suspicions that the young person may be self-destructive.
2. Tell the person you're worried about him or her; then listen to the person in a nonjudgmental, supportive way.
3. Ask direct questions, including whether the youngster is thinking about suicide and, if so, whether he or she has a plan.
4. Don't act shocked at what the youngster tells you. Don't debate whether suicide is right or wrong, or counsel the person yourself if you're not qualified. Don't promise to keep the youngster's intentions a secret. Be calm and supportive and reinforce the person for talking about it.
5. Don't leave the youngster alone if you think the risk of suicide is immediate.
6. Do not be embarrassed or reticent about getting help from a competent counselor, therapist, or other responsible adult.
7. Ensure that the youngster is safe and that the appropriate adults responsible for the youngster are notified and become actively involved with the youngster.
8. Assure the youngster that something is being done, that the youngster's suicidal urges are not being discounted, and that, in time, the emergency will most likely pass. Apprise the youngster that survival is a step-by-step, day-to-day process; that help is at hand; and that calling for help in a direct manner is necessary whenever the suicidal urge gets strong.
9. Assume an active and authoritarian role as needed to protect the child at risk. This is a crisis and calls for applied, directive guidance and management. After the youngster has apparently resolved the high-risk crisis, monitor progress very closely. Many persons have been known to suddenly commit suicide after they seemed to be renewed and strong.
10. Actively acknowledge the reality of suicide as a choice, but do not "normalize" suicide as a good choice.
11. Consider hospitalization if parents are not cooperating, if the youth is highly agitated, or if the student has not been eating, is exhausted or dehydrated, or has some other exacerbating physical condition.
12. Refuse to allow the youth to return to school without an assessment and release by a qualified mental health professional. This assures that the youth will receive the necessary treatment and also protects the school from liability if a suicide attempt or completion takes place.

The following scenarios incorporate many of the suggestions just given.

Billy, Age 11. In a group counseling session, children ages 9 to 12 (including Billy) were engaged in relaxation training, emotive imagery, and self-esteem building. The children were taking turns disclosing a positive image each was experiencing. Billy had been rather quiet and complacent in previous counseling sessions.

Billy: I see myself beside the highway. There's a big 18-wheeler—going fast. I'm feeling like I'm gonna die. I want to die. I see myself jumping in front of it.

CW: Billy, that concerns me to hear you say that! Could you and I talk about that after the others leave? And Billy, I want you to know that I'm glad you didn't keep that image a secret from us.

The crisis worker was shaken and surprised at Billy's sudden description of his images. The worker assessed the suicide risk to be high because of the content and the context of the disclosure (the group activity had been clearly structured to facilitate sharing only positive, growth-promoting images, which other members of the group had done).

Billy's nonverbal body posture and profoundly serious facial expression communicated that he was not fooling. The crisis worker did not deny, refute, or admonish Billy. Recognizing that Billy was taking a great risk by disclosing his death wish, the worker responded by assuring Billy that he had received the message as sent and conveying to members of the group the worker's willingness to attend to and answer Billy's cry for help.

Lester, Age 14. Lester was an intelligent youngster who made good grades in school and had a reputation for being quiet, cooperative, and well behaved.

Following his parents' bitter divorce, while living with his mother and a younger sister and brother, Lester began to get into trouble in school because of his overt acting out and belligerent behavior. He lost interest in his studies and school activities, and his grades began to tumble. He became rebellious with his mother, and his appetite decreased to the degree that he just picked at his food. He became very withdrawn—seldom leaving his room—in contrast to his previous behavior of being actively engaged in outside activities whenever possible.

Lester's mother and the school counselor decided to place him in a student support group consisting of male and female middle school students, all of whom were experiencing severe difficulty following the separation and/or divorce of their parents. At the conclusion of one of the group sessions, Lester asked to speak with the crisis worker.

CW: Lester, sounds like something happened in the group today that got pretty close to you.

Lester: (*hesitant, looking down, nervous*) I . . . I've been feeling weird lately. Strange. Like I'm somewhere else.

CW: You mean like you're outside your own body observing yourself?

Lester: Yeah. Even at night. I don't understand it. I've even thought I might be going crazy.

CW: (*closely observing Lester's body language*) Lester, it sounds like this is so serious you may have even been wishing you were dead.

Lester: Yeah. I've been scared. I've just thought about how it would be to just go to sleep and not wake up.

CW: Have you thought about making that happen? Killing yourself, so that you'd never wake up?

Lester: Thought about it, yeah. Thought about it more lately.

The crisis worker had sensed prior to the interview that Lester might be suicidal. At least six indicators on the risk assessment checklist pointed to the conclusion that Lester was at a high risk level: his changing family life, his changing behavior and attitudes, his body language, his eating habits, his social habits, and his grades. Any one of these would have been an important lethality signal (Curran, 1987, pp. 111–118).

Crisis workers and other adults who work with suicidal youngsters must pay careful attention to clues indicating that suicidal ideation is present. Hunt, Osten, and Teague (1991, pp. 20–21) found that classroom teachers who are sensitive to the emotional changes in and have a close relationship with their students can be primary identification, support, and referral sources for youth who are suicidal.

Lester's science teacher, Mr. Birch, overheard Lester talking to a classmate about giving him his "boom box" and some CDs. Lester had also taken a pair of scissors and chopped off his long hair. He had gotten in a shouting match with a girl in class and almost come to blows with her before the teacher intervened.

These behaviors were clearly uncharacteristic of Lester. Mr. Birch also knew from a staffing meeting with Lester's teachers that Lester had thoughts of killing himself. The teacher had a list of warning signs he had received at an inservice training on suicide (Maples et al., 2005). After he became suspicious of Lester's behavior, he looked over the warning signs and made an immediate referral for Lester to the crisis worker. The crisis worker called Lester's mother, who confirmed Mr. Birch's suspicions. The assistant principal also indicated that Lester had had two disciplinary referrals for fighting after school in the last 2 weeks.

CW: (*three months after the initial intervention*) Lester, I asked for this conference because I'm worried about you again. I thought you were doing great! But now, frankly, I'm scared to death for you. Mr. Birch and your mom are worried too and asked me to see you.

Lester: Oh, I'm OK. Things are going great.

CW: (*in a calm, soft, caring, empathic voice—not a lecturing or agitated tone*) They may seem OK to you, but what concerns me right now is what you've been doing lately. Your mother is very upset and puzzled because you've given your CD player to a friend, and the principal is livid because you've picked two fights on the way home from school this week. I've noticed that the last two days in the hallways and cafeteria you've been like an entirely different person. If these things say what they appear to say, I don't think I can leave here today until I can be sure you're safe. I don't want to wake up in the morning and hear that you're dead!

Lester: It's really not anything you should feel worried about. I'm OK, really I am.

CW: (*soft, empathic vocal tone continued*) Fine, then you can help me feel OK by discussing with me what's going on. I just want you to know that the clues I'm picking up spell danger and that I'm as concerned for you as I've ever been. And I need to know that you're safe, even though you say you're OK. I really care about you.

The crisis worker was confrontive and persistent even though it would have been desirable and comforting to believe that Lester was OK. As it turned out, Lester was indeed on the threshold of suicide again. The important thing was that the worker interpreted Lester's unusual actions as clues that called for help— whether Lester overtly called for help or not.

Suicide of Impulsivity. One particular type of suicidal ideation is particularly characteristic of children and adolescents, and on the face of it, seems absolutely "crazy." Yet, as in all suicides, a suicide of impulsivity makes perfect sense to the individual contemplating it. Even though they have reached the formal operational stage of cognitive development, most teenagers believe they are immortal and really don't personalize the finality and irreversibility of their own death. When children and adolescents are enraged at some perceived injustice, one way to get back at their alleged persecutors is to plan to kill themselves. Their egocentrism that others are as obsessed by the adolescent's behavior as they are themselves is legendary. At times their impulsiveness leads them to believe that a perfect way of punishing somebody else or eliciting care and concern for real or imagined transgressions and injustices would be to kill themselves (Maples et al., 2005). They believe they will die as martyrs and everybody will feel guilty and sorry for the terrible injustices they have done to them. In a fit of pique, they are sometimes able to do just what they intended.

The following aversive use of emotive imagery (Cormier & Cormier, 1998, pp. 317–341; Lazarus, 1977) is designed to be shocking and confront the client with his or her irrational thinking about what the true consequences of a suicide are. By flooding the client with vivid pictures of death and decay and counterpointing them with the rest of his or her family living, growing, and changing, it is designed to show the client that his or her "payback" will be short lived. It is constructed to help the client reframe his or her thinking about what the real consequences of suicide are and is used as a vehicle to offer the client ways to adapt and change his or her lifestyle to a more positive approach that has options other than an impulsive suicide attempt.

A few words of caution in using this technique: This type of aversive imagery should be used only when the crisis worker is sure that suicidal ideation and attempts are impulsive, angry acts intended to pay back others or get attention without consideration of what the finality of death is all about. It should never be used with a clinically depressed client who may well see the peace and quiet and "dust to dust" images as a highly desirable option. When used with minors, this technique should be very carefully explained to parents so that they fully understand what is going to happen and why it is going to be used. Consent forms that spell out what the treatment regimen will be should be signed by both parents. If you are getting the idea that this is a radical procedure, you are right. Be forewarned! What you are about to read may be very unsettling.

Ivana, Age 14. Ivana is a pretty, popular, and petulant 14-year-old freshman cheerleader. She has an older sister, Charlotte, 18, and a brother, Bill, who is 16. The operative term to describe her would be "spoiled." She was referred to the crisis worker after a teacher found her attempting to slice her wrists in the ninth-grade girls' restroom.

Ivana was not hurt too badly and received first aid at the local emergency room. Her aborted attempt caused quite a stir, and everybody in the school is talking about her. She seems to like the attention and in an angry tirade with her parents told them she hated them and was sorry she was alive. Her parents were shocked to think their wonderful daughter would even think of suicide, much less attempt it. Her reasons for attempting the suicide were twofold. She was mad at her boyfriend for not doing what she wanted to do on their last date, and she was mad at her parents for not permitting her to go on an unchaperoned weekend trip with some male and female college cheerleaders.

After a consultation with her parents, the crisis worker explained the following technique to them and why it would be used. They signed a consent agreement, and the crisis worker went to work with Ivana.

CW: Would you like to tell me what caused you to consider killing yourself?

Ivana: (*quickly angry and defiantly gesturing in a loud, demanding voice*) I'll tell you why for sure. It's, like, my rotten parents and my rotten boyfriend, you know. Like really! They never let me do anything, and it's always what he wants to do, not what I want to do, you know. I'll just kill myself. Then they'll all be, like, sorry. Like really sad and sorry. It'll serve them right, you know. And I'll do it too. Next time I'll get some pills or turn the gas on in the kitchen or whatever. Like, you know, that would be awesome. Do it at home. Then they'd find me themselves, like, really. That would really, like, hurt them bad, you know! And the other girls in this school, like, in my crowd, suck, really. They never do what I want, you know. And the school sucks too, like, really sucks, man. I hate this place, really! You know!

After listening to this defiant and impulsive adolescent's diatribe against her parents, her boyfriend, the school, her friends, and the world in general, the crisis worker decides that the impulsive and angry teenager she has in front of her needs a dose of reality in regard to what death is. Her assessment is that this young woman's threats and gestures are more theatrical and attention seeking than intentional. However, the possibility that Ivana might accidentally kill herself is real, and no threat should ever be dismissed as inconsequential.

As a result, the crisis worker will use guided imagery to aversively give her as graphic a picture as possible about what killing herself will really mean.

CW: (*controlling her distaste for Ivana's petulant behavior and responding empathically*) I understand how mad and disappointed you are that everybody seems to be against you. So I wonder if you'd like to picture what killing yourself would really mean to all these people, particularly your family. Would you like an idea of how they would pay for that the rest of their lives?

Ivana: You bet, like really, that'd be cool.

CW: Ivana, I want you to close your eyes and picture the following scenes in your mind. Picture yourself now dead. (*Ivana has a little difficulty in complying. The crisis worker, in a methodical, soft, soothing voice, offers a few words of guidance and reassurance and coaches her in relaxing. Ivana is able to close her eyes and image the scene.*) You are in the funeral home, there are lots of beautiful flowers around you, and the room is full of your friends. Your family is in the front row. They are all red-eyed and teary. Your favorite music is being played. You are in a beautiful rosewood and silver casket in your beautiful pink dress. You look just like Sleeping Beauty. You are so lovely. As you look at the scene, it is just so perfect.

Your boyfriend is almost in pieces, he is feeling so bad. They all feel so bad and guilty that they didn't do what you wanted. (*A flicker of a sly smile crosses Ivana's face as she contemplates the scene.*) Now the pastor gives the eulogy and everyone files by the casket and your beautiful body to say good-bye. Your family is last, and they are crying. It serves them right for how badly they treated you. After the room empties, the funeral home director comes over and shuts the lid on the casket and screws the clamps down. Now it is absolutely dark and absolutely quiet. You feel your body being lifted up, and then suddenly you feel a slight bump. Then you feel yourself moving. You are in the hearse headed for the cemetery. After about 15 minutes you feel the hearse stop. You then feel yourself being lifted up and then abruptly put down. You hear some muffled sounds, and then it is absolutely quiet and absolutely dark. Suddenly you feel a short drop, and then you start to hear muffled thuds. You have been put in the grave and they are now burying you. It is absolutely dark and absolutely quiet, and that is because you are DEAD!

Now, Ivana, I want you to erase that scene from your mind and move forward a year. You're looking in at your family's house. Your picture is up on the mantle. It's the anniversary of your death. Your mom has been teary-eyed

all day, and it's a somber family that sits down to dinner. But after dinner, your brother, Bill, has a ball game, and your sister, Charlotte, has a recital, so the family is off and running. Now erase that scene. Picture this in your mind. You are in your casket, it is absolutely dark and absolutely quiet. Water has started to leak through the vault and your pink dress is starting to mildew. The coffin worms have found their way to your body and thousands of them are wiggling and crawling throughout your body as they feast on your decaying flesh. The elasticity on your skin has shrunk back against your bones as the worms eat the flesh away from your once beautiful body. You have, in fact, really started to be nothing but skin and bones because you are DEAD!

Now erase that scene and move forward 5 years. It is the anniversary of your suicide. Look in on your home. There is your picture on the mantle, but there are other new pictures there too. There is a picture of your brother in the baseball uniform of State University. There's your sister—in a wedding dress—with a really great-looking guy you don't know. Your dad sits at the table and looks at your picture and wonders aloud what you might have become if you had lived. He sets your picture back on the mantle and goes back to reading his paper. Your mother is getting a package ready. It looks like a care package for your brother she's going to send to State U. You'd always wanted to go there. Now erase that scene from your mind. Picture the cemetery and go down into your grave. Your rosewood casket is starting to rot through, and what the worms didn't get, the water and bacteria will. Your pink dress is in tatters, with large blotches of mildew all over it. Your skin has pulled tight around your bones and is like parchment. You can see patches of your skull where the skin has peeled away and bones are starting to stick through your skin. Your eyes have sunken in and the eyelids are just covering your sockets. There is no flesh left since the worms have long finished their job. It is absolutely dark and absolutely quiet because you are DEAD!

Ivana: (*twisting uncomfortably in her chair with a grimace on her face*) I . . . I don't think I want to do any more of this.

CW: One more time and we are finished. It is now 10 years after your suicide. Picture your house in your mind. There are new pictures on the mantle. It's your brother and he's in a military uniform, standing beside an airplane. He must be a pilot. Wow! And there's your sister, but there are also pictures of three cute children there. They must be hers. Your picture is now in the back, covered with dust and the varnish on the frame starting to peel. Of course, it has not changed. It never will. As your gaze moves through the house you see your mother and father packing. They are talking. What's this! They're taking all of your old school stuff and clothes, teddy bears, and games, and there's your cheerleader uniform. They're packing it in boxes. They're GOING TO GIVE IT TO GOODWILL!

As they talk your mother goes over your stuff lovingly, as she packs it up. But your parents are planning on moving to a retirement community, so they really don't have room for all the stuff in the attic. All that ever was of you that could have enjoyed life is now reduced to one dusty picture on the back of the mantel and memories, because you chose death instead of life by committing suicide.

Now go back to the cemetery. Your beautiful rosewood casket is decayed and riddled from termites. It has collapsed in on what is left of your body. There are a few scraps of bones left, but the gophers are chewing those up for the minerals. Your teeth and fillings are still attached to your skull, but barely. Earth and water have leaked into the vault and now what is mostly left is mud, which of course is what it should be since your body has gone back to the earth. It is absolutely dark and absolutely quiet, because you are DEAD.

You can open up your eyes when you want.

Ivana: (*agitated, shaking, and sweating*) That was, like, really terrible! How could you do that? You're supposed to help people.

CW: Do what? Is that not what you wanted, to kill yourself? To show your parents and everybody else. I gave you a picture of what it is like to live and move on with your life or be dead and not. What did you expect?

Ivana: That's not what I meant at all. That's gruesome. I don't want to be like that.

CW: Ivana, neither I nor your parents nor anyone else wants that for you. But you need to understand that death is final and irreversible. You cannot come back from it like Sleeping Beauty. I think we can do some things that will help you get a more positive outlook about why life is worth living. But you must choose. Nobody else can do that for you. I think you really do want to live and have a great life, but if you continue to act on your anger by attempting suicide, you may well succeed. Then that is the true picture of what your life (or death) will be. It's like Charles Dickens's *A Christmas Carol* and Scrooge. You have the power to change that if you want.

Ivana: Well, maybe I would like to talk to you some about some stuff, like, maybe I do get a little pushy and demanding, but sometimes I just don't know what to do and get really frustrated and angry and then get my feelings hurt, and I just want to lash back, like, you know?

CW: Fine. I'd be glad to talk with you about that, and I believe we can plan some things that will deal with some of those angry hurt feelings. Do we have a deal? If so, I'd like your handshake on it, and also your promise that you're not going to try committing suicide while we do this.

Ivana: OK, I can shake on that, but I don't think I want to go through one of those image things again, you know.

CW: I know, and it's a deal.

Finally, use of this intrusive, aversive technique should be closely monitored in aftercare so that the client is not traumatized by it to the extent that we now have replaced a suicide of impulse with PTSD. Even though Ivana seems to have gotten a wake-up call, the crisis worker still institutes an antisuicide agreement as part of a transcrisis treatment plan. Until Ivana has a good deal more control over her impulsive behavior, the crisis worker, her parents, and her teachers will need to be vigilant about knee-jerk reactions about killing herself. Teaching Ivana behavioral alternatives to her angry, petulant outbursts as a reaction to her insecurity about her typical adolescent identity crisis and ego involvement is a high priority.

Group work with peers who give her honest feedback about her selfish behaviors and what that does to destroy relationships will help her to learn more equitable and amicable behavior toward her peers. Working with her parents to provide logical and natural consequences of behavior without feeling guilty that they may be driving her to suicide is also a vital piece of a comprehensive aftercare treatment that will decrease her impulsivity and make her suicide proof.

Many of the suicide intervention techniques in Chapter 8, Crisis of Lethality, fit equally well for children and adolescents. Counselors write behavioral contracts all the time with very young students. Thus, writing an anti-suicide contract using the child's language and verbal comprehension level will work as well with them as it will with adults. What is particularly helpful for them is decreasing their feelings of isolation and marginalization (Berman, Jobes, & Silverman, 2006). Including suicidal children and adolescents in support groups and other activities that make them feel like valued and contributing members to their school and peer group is an important part of moving them away from suicidal thinking and behaving. Berman and Jobes (1994) found that suicidal adolescents particularly need empathic therapeutic alliances to help them feel affirmed, valued, and understood.

Postvention

Clustering of Suicides. Cluster or contagion suicides occur when more than one suicide attempt or completion happens within a proximate geographic area, giving the appearance that these events are related (Gould & Shaffer, 1986; Kirk, 1993, p. 15; Webb & Griffiths, 1998–1999, pp. B43–48). There is evidence that publicity about child and adolescent suicide completions and media programs depicting factual or fictional suicides have been associated with suicide attempts and completions in geographic areas reached by the publicity (Austin, 2003; Kalafat, 1990, p. 364).

Kirk (1993, pp. 15–16) likens such clustering to the infectious disease concept; that is, when a pathogen is introduced into a vulnerable population, the probability of infection is spontaneously increased. Similarly, when an adolescent suicide occurs and is sensationally reported or somehow glorified, other adolescents who may already be in a state of despair, helplessness, or hopelessness may be influenced toward terminating their lives or see it as an excellent way to get a great deal of attention.

Contagion. Sandy Austin (2003) reported on a series of four suicides at her school in an 8-month period. The school crisis response team immediately responded to the suicides in the following manner. After each suicide, faculty were called and informed of a meeting the next morning where they were briefed. District mental health personnel were contacted for support. The principal, counselor, and SRO visited the deceased's family members and asked if a memo could be read that stated the student "took his own life" instead of "committed suicide" to convey the finality of the act and decrease the "glory" of it. Memos were drafted and read in each class. At the end of the day, faculty met for a debriefing to determine how students were doing. Students were invited to come into the counseling office for one-on-one or group counseling or just to come to a "safe room." Parent/community meetings were hosted with an expert to address the suicide issue. The media were asked to construct their stories in a "signs to look for" manner and "how to help someone access resources" to address the contagion effect.

The crisis team was then confronted with another problem. Instead of dealing in typical teenager fashion with the ruts and potholes of adolescence, the students started talking about suicide as a viable option for taking care of problems. The counselor and student representatives visited each English class and asked students to be observant and tell someone if a friend started talking about suicide or showed warning signs. Posters were created on the subject of getting help and watching for clues and placed throughout the community. Crisis line phone numbers were put on cards and passed out. Austin reported that for the rest of the school year there was at least one tip a day on a potential suicide. The toll went beyond the suicides and the grief felt for their loss. Two peer counselors

became suicidal, and one school counselor had to take a month's sick leave due to stress. Thus, you should get a pretty clear notion that vicarious trauma, which you will read about in Chapter 16, is real.

The school district did everything by the book. They did everything they could possibly do and generally did it right, but still the suicides continued. Shaffer, Vieland, and Garland (1990) reported that among adolescent suicide attempters, "talking about suicide in the classroom makes some kids more likely to try to kill themselves" (pp. 3153–3155). Thus, "postvention" classroom programs designed for suicide education and prevention may be appropriate for the majority of adolescents who are not currently at risk, but may not be appropriate for the at-risk population. Or at least a massive effort will be needed to get all of the student body involved and willing to tell an adult about a peer's suicidal thoughts or threats without fear of being labeled a snitch.

Publicity and Contagion. Kirk (1993, p. 17), in his investigation about media effects on adolescent suicide, makes three interesting observations: (1) The more sensational the reporting of the suicide, the greater was the increase in suicides within the reporting area. (2) There was a significant increase in auto accidents involving teenagers following media reports of youth suicides. (3) There was an increase in adolescent suicides following certain made-for-television motion pictures that focused on episodes showing suicides in the lives of troubled and suicidal adolescents. That's why it is critically important for the media liaison to work closely with the media, as in the case of Sandy Austin's school district.

Imperatives for SCRTs in Suicides. School crisis response teams (SCRTs) must be knowledgeable about suicide postvention so that clustering does not occur. Crises of suicide are different from other crises because of the self-instigating behavior that goes with them and because so many different emotional evaluations are placed on suicide. If SCRT members do not know about the dynamics of suicidal behavior, they need to get outside consultation that does, and they need to have it available immediately. The worst possible scenario is an insecure SCRT that does not want to "look bad" because it needs outside help to handle the crisis. In our own experience, we have witnessed an SCRT that did not know what it was doing and wound up with three more completed suicides and two attempts on its hands in the space of 2 months in the same high school! Thus, it is critical that parents, teachers, and students be given notification and information regarding warning signs of suicide—particularly after a completion (Maples et al., 2005).

Jennifer, Age 17. Jennifer was terrified. Although she had suffered from depression, loneliness, and low self-esteem for several years, she had managed to have a satisfactory social life, maintain average grades in school, and regain her equilibrium following each depressive episode. Several stressors during the past year had combined to complicate and disrupt her life. Indeed, one of the major contributors to child and adolescent suicide is the role of the family (Berman, Jobes, & Silverman, 2006; Wagner, 1997). Her parents' separation and divorce were unexpected and bitter. Her maternal grandmother, to whom she had been very close, died from rapidly progressing intestinal cancer. Jennifer was living with her mother and two younger sisters. The mother began dating a single man and permitted him to move in with them. Jennifer changed schools during the middle of the year when her parents' original home was sold. Because of her lack of social adjustment and academic achievement in the new school, Jennifer was placed in a support group at the school and was also seen regularly by an individual counselor.

Following a weekend episode of trauma over the suicide of a friend who attended another school, Jennifer showed signs of being upset, severely depressed, exhausted, and withdrawn. The crisis worker had been notified that Jennifer had missed school on Friday to attend her friend's funeral. Being wary of *contagion suicide*, sometimes called *copycat suicide* (Gould & Shaffer, 1986), the crisis worker knew that Jennifer's risk level was probably elevated because of her trauma over her friend's suicide, in addition to her already stressful family situation.

CW: Jennifer, it frightens me to see you this way. What's happening to cause you so much pain right now?

The crisis worker could see the physical and emotional devastation Jennifer was feeling. It was important to communicate to Jennifer the worker's affective concern and to provide a direct and open opportunity for Jennifer to feel safe and to respond (Patros & Shamoo, 1989, pp. 126–128).

Jennifer: (*after a long pause, in a very low, subdued voice*) I . . . I've never been this scared before in my life. (*Pause.*) All weekend I've been at the end of my rope. I've just thought, there's no use going on anymore. And ever since

last Friday at Etta's funeral, I've wondered if it wouldn't be better if I just went like she did. They said such nice things about her. She and I were so close. It was so sad but so comforting to hear all the wonderful things they said about her.

CW: Jennifer, I'm glad you're here now. I can see how the death of Etta and her eulogy really affected you. What frightens me right now is what you just said, that it would be better if you joined her. Does this mean that you're planning to kill yourself over this?

The crisis worker's questioning was aimed at swiftly making an assessment of Jennifer's lethality and quickly heading off the idea of contagion suicide. The answer to such a question drastically impacts and changes what the crisis worker does. Even though Jennifer's destabilized family situation would have been signal enough to inquire into any suicidal thoughts and plans she might have, the hint of contagion suicide served as a red flag, alerting the crisis worker to be assertive and direct in asking the suicide question.

The concept of contagion suicide is controversial. Skeptics and critics claim that there is little scientific proof of clustering and copycatting because it is difficult to prove that one suicide attempt or completion directly causes another. But according to Kirk (1993, pp. 16–17), there is too much evidence of recent contagion suicides in the United States to ignore or dismiss claims of clustering. We agree with his conclusions and believe from our own experience that it is extremely important for school crisis response teams that go into a school after a suicide to know that this phenomenon has a possibility of being activated if postvention is not handled correctly.

There is evidence that providing peer support such as a professionally led peer counseling group can help suicidal teenagers (King et al., 2006). One of the major support systems in schools to prevent initial and contagion suicides is a peer counseling system such as Allen's (1996) peer leader program. Allen's peer counselors meet weekly to talk about issues and problems that are occurring in their high school. They are the eyes and ears of the counselor and are privy to information of a far wider and current scope than school staff will ever be. By relaying information to the school counselor about peers who are severely affected by a school trauma, they enable intervention to happen much more effectively and quickly. As Allen says, "I have no idea what types of drugs or alcohol are currently hot. I don't know who is depressed because he broke up with his girlfriend, but my peer leaders do, and they are not seen as snitches for telling me. It is okay because the rest of the kids see it as the peer leaders' job."

Grief and Mourning After Adolescent Suicide.

Kirk (1993, pp. 112–115) found that suicides of adolescents and other youth represent a type of death that severely complicates survivors' mourning and adjustment. He cited the following reasons:

1. The adolescent suicide is generally unexpected.
2. The death of a young person is harder to accept than that of an older person who has lived a full life.
3. To many people, suicide is incomprehensible and perhaps even morally wrong.
4. The suicide completer's family and friends are left with guilt, anger, and a sense of unfinished business with the deceased, which mourners must work through.
5. There is less social support for a suicide completer's family than there may be for other bereaved families because people tend to unjustly ascribe blame to the family.

Kirk also stated that when a suicide occurs in a school setting, grief reaction is often further complicated by the group response of classmates and school personnel. Educators, school crisis response teams, parents, and others involved in designing prevention, intervention, and postvention procedures should be sensitive to the unique grief factors just mentioned. A suicide absolutely must not be glorified or made heroic. However, that doesn't mean that feelings are ignored or questions concerning the deceased are not answered as truthfully and honestly as possible. Empathic understanding of concerns of other students or faculty is of primary importance, and no questions or comments should be summarily dismissed (Capuzzi, 2002).

As with other traumatic events, a room for counseling students should be set up, factual information should be disseminated, and an SCRT meeting should be held to determine whether other students may be at risk. Maples and her associates (2005) describe an adaption of a four-stage model (Brammer, Abrego, & Shostrom, 1993) that can be used to work with teenage survivors of a suicide. In *stage 1* there will be *shock* and *disorganization*. Typical responses are "It couldn't happen," and "No, not possible!" Initial intervention follows along the lines of the intervention responses described in Chapter 12, Personal Loss: Bereavement and Grief, and uses basic nonjudgmental listening and responding skills. *Stage 2* is the most potentially

volatile stage of this particular grieving process. It involves feelings of *anguish*, *remorse*, and *guilt* over not having done something to prevent the suicide. "Why didn't I see this coming?" "I could have stopped it!" are common themes of recrimination. Besides conducting a psychological autopsy on the order of the one in Chapter 8, Crisis of Lethality, using cognitive-behavioral strategies such as thought stopping and positive mental videotapes may be effective in helping students control their feelings.

Heather: (*16-year-old best friend of a suicide starting to shake uncontrollably and with tears streaming down her face*) I think I am going crazy. Every time I pass Sally's locker I come apart. We had been best friends since first grade. I could have, should have stopped this, and I didn't even know it. That's some kind of friend.

CW: Remember what we said in the psychological autopsy. It made perfect sense to her. It is a terrible tragedy, but neither you nor I nor anyone else can be, or should be, responsible for her suicide. You have that pink memory band on your arm. Every time you pass where her locker was [note crisis worker's movement to past tense], tap the band and say "STOP!" when those feelings start to flood over you, and remember that one great moment you said when the two of you won the sixth-grade talent show. Smile and remember how deliriously happy and goofy you looked in your Raggedy Ann and Andy costumes. Then move on. You need to do this every time you go by the locker. Don't avoid the locker like you have been, but just make it part of your normal routine. We are going to get that mental image squarely in your mind, so lean back, close your eyes, and let's practice that.

Stage 3 has to do with *reconciliation of the loss*. When faced with traumatic death for the first time, teenagers may struggle with existential questions such as the meaning of life or the futility of everyday living. "What's it all about?" and "Why bother with school?" are topics for group grief work that help students reconcile and move on with their lives. Spiritual components of these questions should be considered, and working alliances and referrals to pastoral counseling are good options.

Stage 4 has to do with *emergence of new goals* for survivors. Recommitment to established friendships or dedication to a worthy cause or a sport season are ways of helping teenagers move past the suicide. Typically this stage will mark the passing of the friend and recommitment to living by the surviving teenagers.

Suicide of a popular student or teacher is one of the most difficult challenges human service workers in schools face. The potential for interventions to go terribly awry is high, and thus interventions must be thought through and carefully applied. One of your authors witnessed one instance in which the faculty of a school assembled after school to engage in a debriefing with the SCRT of the district. The teachers had all sorts of questions and emotions to deal with concerning the suicide of a fellow teacher the previous night. They were told, "If you are having problems with your fellow teacher's death, we suggest you call your behavioral health service provider and talk with them." Then the SCRT leader dismissed the group, leaving the principal and school counselor to deal with more than 50 enraged and frustrated faculty members.

As in any crisis, being at the school of the completed suicide as soon as possible after notification is critical for planning and for making assessments about the emotional state of faculty and students, quelling rumors, assessing for other possible suicides, and depropagandizing and deglorifying the suicide by debriefing faculty and students. It is fruitless and damaging for the SCRT to come straggling in late in the afternoon or the next day. Such dilatory behavior lets rumor and chaos run wild, and makes a statement that there is not a great deal of concern about the health and well-being of the school.

The following points are recommended when the death of a student or teacher is due to suicide (American Association of Suicidology, 1991, 1998):

1. Don't dismiss school or encourage funeral attendance during school hours.
2. Don't hold a large-scale memorial to the deceased or dismiss school to do so.
3. Do provide individual and group counseling.
4. Verify the facts, and do treat the death as a suicide.
5. Do emphasize that no one thing or person is to blame for the suicide.
6. Do emphasize that help is available, that suicide is preventable, and that everyone has a role to play in prevention.
7. Don't build a tangible memorial such as a bench or a tree with a marker or dedicate a yearbook to the suicide.
8. Do not release information in large groups such as an assembly. Work by classroom or in small groups.

Do suicide prevention programs work? Zenere and Lazarus (1997) studied a comprehensive suicide prevention and intervention program in a large, urban, culturally diverse school district. Students were tracked over a 5-year period. What they found was that although

suicidal ideation remained stable, the rate of attempts and completions was dramatically reduced. Although prevention programs may not be able to stop a student from thinking about committing suicide, an effective program can stop the act!

Legal and Ethical Issues of Potentially Violent Behavior
Confidentiality and Duty to Warn

While the overriding ethical consideration of any counseling session in the past was confidentiality, we have now ventured into *Tarasoff* legal territory (*Tarasoff v. Board of Regents of the University of California,* 1976) about the duty to warn. Indeed, ethical standards of the American School Counseling Association (the major professional organization of human services workers in schools) mandate that when a student's behavior is a clear and present danger to others, the appropriate authorities must be warned (American School Counselor Association, 1998, § A.7).

School officials have a legal obligation to take action when students pose a danger to other students (Bailey, 2001) or themselves (Maples et al., 2005). To this date, though, courts have been reluctant to find school authorities liable in school violence cases (Hermann & Remley, 2000), with some notable exceptions. The primary legal concern related to providing services for students prior to, during, or after a crisis is negligence. Although we are mainly speaking of intent to harm others, negligence can occur in any crisis situation. School districts become liable in a suicide case (as do professional staff) when there is foreseeability and negligence. An example of foreseeability would occur when a student note indicating a potential homicide or suicide was intercepted, but was dismissed as harmless. Negligence would occur if a violent act occurred and no intervention or planning for that act had been made or attempted. These legal concepts come into play when there is a lack of preparation by the school and due diligence by staff (Maples et al., 2005). Thus, the school district would be well advised to make a written policy statement that details its procedures for all crisis situations as an initial step in avoiding liable suits (Brock, Sandoval, & Lewis, 1996, p. 42). Part of that policy is that parents are always notified if suicide or violence is suspected, even if the child denies it (*Eisel* v. *Board of Education of Montgomery County,* 1991). Kerr (2009, p. 28) makes the important point that not having a policy in place prior to procedures can waste valuable time and cause all kinds of problems. A crisis is not the time to debate policy but rather to have it in place and know what it is.

Once a policy is generated, it needs to be followed (Hermann & Finn, 2002). Courts have found school personnel negligent when they failed to follow a policy designed to keep students safe (*Garcia* v. *City of New York,* 1996), particularly if the violence was foreseeable by "true" threats that were backed up by past episodes of violence (Hermann & Remley, 2000). A "true" threat may be considered as one in which a reasonable person in the same circumstances would find the utterance to be a serious and unambiguous expression of intent to do harm based on the language and context of the threat (Hermann & Finn, 2002).

A decision must be made about duty to warn. This is not a simple decision, particularly when we are dealing with juveniles, and can create a difficult dilemma for a crisis worker. The worker has to weigh two alternatives that may both be unattractive.

On the one hand, by informing the student's parents and bringing authorities into the case, we run the risk of compromising our credibility with the student population and making the parents extremely angry because they will believe the school has labeled their son or daughter a "homicidal maniac" or "suicidal nut case" to the whole community. Regarding the first scenario for John in this chapter, informing the cheerleaders' parents that John is out to "get" them is unwarranted, because it is not based on clear intent, method, or any other substantiating evidence other than his vague, fantasized notions of revenge. It would probably cause a panic and might well invite a lawsuit. We do not wish to take any action that would have the effect of labeling the student as violence prone or use other negative terms that might cause embarrassment to the child or the child's family without substantiating evidence. However, even with his vague threats, John's parents should be brought in and told about his problems in an empathic, nonaccusatory, problem-solving manner. The question is not "Should the parents be called?" because that is a given, but rather what to say to parents and how to elicit a supportive reaction from them (Poland, 1989). Although Poland speaks specifically to suicidal ideation, there is no reason that what he says should not apply to homicidal ideation as well.

On the other hand, if the crisis worker does not warn others, he or she puts at risk the lives of the student and others who may be in harm's way, and the crisis

worker may suffer civil liability as a result. In cases of suicide and homicide, growing case law indicates that school systems are liable if they do not have plans in place to prevent acts of lethality from happening. The issue is not whether the school might have caused it, but whether they attempted to prevent it (Poland, 1994). The second scenario in which John details the intent, the method, and the means provides sufficient reason to label the act as lethal and warn both the parents of the child and the parents of the intended victims.

Although most state statutes do not give clear guidance on this point, it is likely that existing law will support any warning that is based on specific behavior indicating an obvious and unequivocal danger (*Lavine* v. *Blaine School District,* 2001; *Lovell* v. *Poway Unified School District,* 1996). Even though parents may object violently and sue the district and school personnel, courts have viewed the contemporary scene of school violence as one in which officials can suspend students until trained mental health professionals have determined they are not a danger to themselves or others (Hermann & Finn, 2002). Such obvious and unequivocal danger is best determined by focusing on specific behaviors. Although it may be easy for complaining parents to dispute the meaning of a particular behavior, it is more difficult to deny the behavior itself.

The *in loco parentis* status of the schools (being in the position of a parent to the child in the absence of the parent) is reason enough to take action, if based on concrete behaviors or a reasonable suspicion and if the action follows the school district's plan as to what to do about a possible lethal act (James, 1994; James & Crawford, 2002). Thus, any school safety issue is tied to the concept of reasonableness, the intent of educators to promote a safe learning environment, and what the educator knows or objectively suspects about a student (James, 1994).

Keeping Records.   Taking clear and precise notes is of the utmost importance in substantiating the duty to warn. These notes should include date, time, parties involved, specific behaviors observed, statements made, and procedures followed. Mere intuition or "gut feelings" are not sufficient to explain why a particular intervention was made. It is necessary to articulate and record the behaviors, subtle though they may have been, that led to the intervention (James & Crawford, 2002).

Consultation.   It is also of critical importance that the crisis worker immediately consult with another trusted professional in the field, receive validation that his or her analysis of the situation is correct, and keep clear and concise notes about when, why, and with whom the crisis worker sought consultation (Capuzzi, 2002; James & Crawford, 2002). The ethical standards of most human services professions promote consultation with other trusted professionals as a reasonable part of providing a good standard of care and preventing violence (American Counseling Association, 1995, § B.1.c; American School Counselor Association, 1998, § A.7).

School officials have been very cautious about transmitting data to other individuals or institutions because of the Family Educational Rights and Privacy Act regulations (James, 1997). However, when the student demonstrates behaviors that may have lethal intent, or the crisis worker has reasonable grounds to believe those behaviors are lethal, then there should be little question about sharing data and information. To do otherwise would be unethical and might invite a lawsuit (James & Crawford, 2002). Given agreement between professionals, it would seem reasonable to assume that any reports that were supported by others in the field would go a long way toward insulating crisis workers and school systems from legal liability.

Consistency of Intervention

Inconsistent actions invite complaints of bad faith or individual prejudice; consistent actions indicate that the interventions are based on behaviors and not on the attributes of any one individual. When exceptions occur, they should be explainable as mere mistakes or lapses of judgment rather than decisions to intervene differently from time to time in a capricious manner. It is only partly in jest that our former colleague, Dr. Robert Crawford, who is a lawyer, counselor, educator, and legal and ethical scholar, states that it is better to be consistently wrong than inconsistently right. That is why establishing a set safety plan and applying its procedures universally are legally critical (James & Crawford, 2002; Langman, 2009, p. 180).

Zero Tolerance.   When we speak of consistency of intervention, we are not advocating a strict zero tolerance policy. Such policies have become the predominant operational mode of schools frightened of legal liability and accusations that they are prejudiced, arbitrary, and capricious in their decision making, as in the case of 15-year-old Oregon school shooter Kip Kinkel because his parents were teachers in the district. The negative

side of a zero tolerance policy has proved acrimonious and put districts at odds with parents because of its unreasonableness in not deviating from ironclad policies and rules—for example, suspending an elementary age child for 60 days for bringing nail clippers to school.

The American Psychological Association Zero Tolerance Task Force (2008) studied this problem and found little substantive data to justify the approach. The sparse data that did exist showed that it was mostly ineffective. It causes alienation of both students and parents and tends to focus on minorities and students with disabilities. Zero tolerance often serves as a pipeline into the juvenile justice system when in fact most cases could have been handled at school.

The task force made a number of recommendations that cut across practice and policy when zero tolerance is applied. They recommended giving teachers more discretion as first-line providers, carefully defining infractions as to whether they are major or minor, training staff in regard to how to handle them, and changing policy so that zero tolerance is reserved for the most severe infractions. The task force also recommended alternatives to zero tolerance, including using threat assessment procedures, implementing measures to improve school climate for at-risk students, providing a variety of options other than expulsion, and increasing training for teachers in culturally responsive classroom behavior management and instruction. Finally, they called for organized research efforts in looking at both zero tolerance and alternatives to it. All in all the recommendations are sound, but they are difficult and expensive to carry out, whereas zero tolerance is not.

In summary, it absolutely behooves crisis workers who work in schools to keep up to date on legal and ethical mandates related to school violence (Hermann & Finn, 2002). While the foregoing techniques and procedures may seem difficult, unwieldy, and fraught with peril and legal liability for a school district, now try transferring the foregoing scenarios into a university setting.

The Problem of "Doing Something" in a University Setting

Although this chapter is mainly concerned with K–12 school systems and the minors who inhabit those academic worlds, there have been some long-festering issues in institutions of higher education in regard to violent students, which surfaced with the Virginia Tech massacre in April 2007.

The first, knee-jerk reaction to such violence is to put tighter controls on gun purchases, because the ability to purchase firearms is seen as the cause of, or at least the factor that allowed, this rampage. Everything Seung-hui Cho did in purchasing his guns in Virginia and some of his ammunition online was perfectly legal. Short of barring the possession of guns—and indeed, the state of Virginia bars all firearms on any state school campus—no gun control law on earth could have stopped the Virginia Tech massacre. What allowed the Virginia Tech massacre to happen is a perfect storm of laws that are designed to protect individuals, particularly individuals who have handicapping conditions. When applied in a university setting, these laws can tie the institution's "hands" legally so that the individual cannot be dismissed from school, be suspended from classes, or even tossed out of a residence hall for bad behavior, and a parent or other adult cannot even be informed that the student is having problems.

In Chapter 14, Violent Behavior in Institutions, we will discuss some of the factors that have led to the violent environment now being experienced in the human services field. One of those factors has been the closing down of large state mental health hospitals and the consequent release of thousands of mentally ill back into society. Seung-hui Cho was taken into custody on a psychiatric hold for a mental evaluation in December 2005. The special justice found Cho to be a threat to himself but not to others and decided that involuntary hospitalization was not necessary (Shute, 2007). Before you decide to tar and feather the special justice, consider that there was most likely no place to put Cho other than jail, and he had not done anything illegal to this point. The simple fact is that in every state in the union there are far too many mentally ill for the beds available in state or private hospitals. Health insurance usually runs out long before the disorder is under control, and at that point, unless the patient is very rich, neither a hospital bed nor the therapy to go with it is available.

Another issue in "doing something" in a university setting is whether outpatient counseling, inpatient psychotherapy, prescribing psychotropic medication, or even seeing a residence hall counselor as opposed to a psychiatrist can be mandated by the university. Unless ordered by a court, no one can be required to get counseling of any kind, and a university can only suggest it. Nor can parents play much of a part in providing support, removing a son or daughter for psychiatric help, or for that matter even being made aware that their child is in psychological or academic hot water unless the children themselves inform the parents. Once an individual turns 18, the Family Educational Rights and Privacy Act of 1974 comes into force. Among other provisions designed to protect the individual's privacy rights, this act forbids the transmittal of any kind of personal information from an institution of higher learning without the express written consent of the student. The Health Insurance Portability and Accountability Act of 1996 added further restrictions on the transmittal of information. The result is an iron curtain pulled down between any mental health activities on campus and other agencies. That includes notification of parents if any counseling is needed or is occurring or what that counseling may be about. Thus, it may be that parents have absolutely no idea that their child is in academic or psychological trouble (Myer, James, & Moulton, 2011).

Now add two other laws to the mix. The Rehabilitation Act of 1973 and its subsequent amendments in 1974, along with further amendments to that law in the Americans With Disabilities Act of 1990, prohibit discrimination based on a physical or mental disability or drug addiction. The discrimination section 504 of the Rehabilitation Act has become so famous that such complaints or cases are commonly known as "504s." These laws effectively prohibit discrimination against students based on any disabling condition. While the foregoing is the spirit and intent of the laws, these laws also effectively hamstring institutions when they seek to remove a student (for example, a student whose handicapping condition is mental illness) because that individual causes disruption to the educational process and is infringing on the rights of other students (Myer, James, & Moulton, 2011).

Any institution seeking to dismiss a student for cause must first deal with section 504. That means that removal of a student must be done through a hearing process in which the student has the right to appeal the university's decision. Any other attempt to remove the student will be viewed as arbitrary and capricious and invite a lawsuit that the university is likely to lose. If the student believes that the university is discriminating against him or her, then the student may ask the U.S. Office of Civil Rights to investigate. Once the Office of Civil Rights enters the fray, it will look at one thing only in determining whether the student should be removed: Does that student constitute a threat to self or others, and was that determination based on an individualized and objective assessment of the student's ability to safely participate in the institution's program, based on a reasonable medical judgment relying on the most current medical knowledge or the best available objective evidence? Furthermore, the assessment must determine the nature, duration, and severity of the risk, the probability that the potentially threatening injury will actually occur, and whether reasonable modifications of policies, practice, or procedures will sufficiently mitigate the risk (Gallager, 2005).

The foregoing is a tall order indeed, and it should come as no surprise that it is very difficult for a university to succeed in expelling a student or removing that student from a community living situation once 504 comes into effect. The facts that Seung-hui Cho was bothersome, weird, bizarre, and threatening in a varieties of ways, and that he fit multiple indicators when screening for an estranged violent juvenile offender, were insufficient because he did not specifically engage in a threatening act that had a definite plan, motive, or means. The bottom line is that fear of litigation and the poor track records of universities in lawsuits that have sought to overturn dismissals make universities reluctant to attempt to remove such students (Myer, James, & Mouton, 2011).

Compounding the legal issues are issues of philosophy, morals, and worldview as well as pragmatic, logistical considerations of keeping disruptive students in communal living arrangements. Residence hall directors are tasked with one of the most difficult jobs in the world. They are responsible for keeping safe people like many of you reading this book. They need to do this in some kind of civilized group living arrangement that is conducive to the pursuit of an education. That's a formidable undertaking with recently emancipated teenagers who may become very disruptive to the learning environment as they experiment with alternate lifestyles in their newfound freedom. Add to that the pressures on the students to succeed in school and, for many, to cope with being away from home for the first time. Now further add to this new and potentially threatening environment, for some, a history of mental illness or severe psychological disturbance. It is small wonder that depression rates, anxiety attacks, and suicidal ideation skyrocket among college students.

Indeed, most schizophrenias and bipolar disorders typically first make their appearance at about the age of admission to college. In addition, because of the Americans With Disability Act of 1990 and the Rehabilitation Act of 1973, the number of students with mental illness who come to college campuses is growing. If those students experience severe pressures, and pressures are certainly legion in a university environment, then the stage is set for a psychotic episode. Furthermore, if a student with a diagnosed mental illness is on medication and either forgets, runs out, or decides not to take the psychotropic medication, then a rapid slide back into psychotic behavior will occur.

If you do not believe that the Virginia Tech massacre has made students in every university in the United States hypervigilant in regard to the "kooks," "weirdos," and "psychos" they know in their residence halls and classes, you would be very mistaken. Now factor in hundreds of thousands of anxious parents, and you start to imagine the pressure that residence hall directors are under to get these "psycho killers" out of the dormitory or that administrators feel to get the "crazies" out of the university. Thus, age-old biases and fears about "insane homicidal maniacs" take hold in a fertile field. As indicated in Chapter 14, Violent Behavior in Institutions, very few people with mental illnesses become violent. However, those who are mentally ill with a *prior* history of violence are indeed people to be monitored closely for lethal behavior. Thus, for very pragmatic reasons, residence hall coordinators need to remove emotionally unstable people who should not be in a community learning environment until they are mentally stable (Myer, James, & Moulton, 2011).

On the other side of the issue are the counseling centers and student disability services personnel who are tasked with dealing with mentally ill individuals. They rightfully stand up for these students and believe that they need to advocate for them because these students are different and are easily discriminated against, and such discrimination will probably increase after the Virginia Tech shootings. Their view is that accommodating diversity is paramount and that all students must learn to live with and accommodate one another. In that regard, the counselors and human services workers are generally loath to support the removal or dismissal of a student based on a fulminating psychological disturbance unless there is clear, concrete evidence that the student intends to harm someone else or him- or herself (Myer, James, & Moulton, 2011).

This issue is truly a classic conundrum that pits the rights of the individual (no matter how "deviant" that individual is) against the rights of the many (no matter how "normal" they may be). In our opinion, the mass murders at Virginia Tech are going to cause this issue to move along the judicial lines that resulted in the *Tarasoff* "duty to warn" decision (see Chapter 5, Crisis Case Handling) and other K–12 schools' safety decisions discussed later in this chapter. Somehow, protection of the mentally ill individual must be balanced against the needs of society and, in particular, the learning environment when the individual's behavior becomes disruptive to other students—and that balance should be achieved long before the individual's behavior becomes lethal. If that is to happen, federal law will have to be changed to give institutions of higher learning the power to act on individuals when early, serious warning signs appear.

TASSLE. Given the legal and ethical issues that emerge when the possibility of violence arises in universities, and particularly when a student is becoming disruptive to the learning environment in a residence hall, what can be done? The Triage Assessment System for Students in Learning Environments (TASSLE; Myer et al., 2007) is a simplified version of the TAF that can be used by student affairs staff on university campuses to make on-the-scene decisions about critical incidents. The TASSLE provides assistance in determining the amount of support and supervision a student requires. It also gives the ability to monitor the effectiveness of strategies used in defusing and deescalating a crisis situation. The TASSLE can be used as a single incident assessment or as a cumulative record to track a student's problematic behaviors and to make decisions about how to provide assistance for the student and what is best for the learning environment.

With the TASSLE, residence hall staff are required to complete a one-day training session including video simulations of a wide range of out-of-control residents with problems ranging from romantic breakups to psychotic episodes. These simulations allow residence hall staff to practice assessing types of individuals they are likely to encounter. Professional crisis interventionists conduct the training sessions.

Figure 13.1 is the front page of the TASSLE form. When a residence hall director or resident assistant is informed about a problem student and contact is made with the student, the TASSLE form may be used to summarize the contact. The columns allow the rater to simply check off observed behaviors. Behaviors with one asterisk generally denote that the student should not be left alone until there is assurance that the behavior has stabilized. Descriptors with three asterisks indicate that the potential for lethality either to self or others is high and precautions should be taken to move the student to a place of safety where the individual's physical and mental health can be monitored.

Immediately below the descriptors are the feelings, behavioral, and thinking scales. These scales each have two ratings: an "X" for an initial assessment and an "O" for a terminal assessment, thus allowing both a pre- and a post-assessment. From start to finish of an incident, ratings may change significantly. The ratings may change because the intervention of the resident hall staff has calmed and defused the situation. Alternatively, the arrival of the police or other authorities may cause the individual to temporarily suspend problem behavior. The two ratings are also meant to diminish a rater bias of generalization. In essence, a generalization bias might lead the rater to give a global rating that was based more on a high initial score when in fact the ending rating was much lower, or vice versa. The three scores (feelings, behaviors, thoughts) are then combined, and the traditional TAF scoring system is used, with single-digit summed scores indicating that the individual is free to go, scores in the teens indicating that more supervision and support are needed, and scores in the 20s indicating that intervention and transport to a safe place away from the residence hall are required. Although one episode does not necessarily brand the individual as lethal, a continuing record of high TASSLE scores gives a clear behavioral analysis of the individual and is a concrete behavioral record that warrants intervention. Furthermore, when in addition to the residence hall staff the campus police and counseling center staff are also trained in the use of the TASSLE, the coordination of intervention activities among these three entities should be much smoother.

Threat Assessment Team. It is absolutely imperative that information such as TASSLE ratings and incident reports be gathered in one central repository so that incidents can be cross-referenced and students rated on their potential for violence. This assessment will occur with what most universities call a Threat Assessment Team. The team is composed of a variety of individuals, much as in a K–12 school, that are likely to come in contact with disturbed students. That team will surely have representatives from housing, recreation, food services, counseling center, police department, maintenance, administration, health services, student judiciary, media relations, legal office, fire department, presidential liaison, and a cross section of faculty members. This team will be the one who makes a decision on what action is to be taken, and that action will be based on an accumulation of factual behaviors not conjecture (Myer, James, & Moulton, 2011).

Staff Member: _____

Date: _____ Incident Type: _____ Location: _____

Times: Contacted: _____ On Scene: _____ Cleared: _____

Complaint Information _____

_____

Student Name: _____ DOB: _____
            (Last)   (First)   (Middle)

Race: _____ Gender: ___ Male ___ Female

Observations   (Check as many that apply)

___ off medication*
___ hallucinating*** (__ smells __sights __sounds __touch)
___ bizarre behavior/appearance
___ poor hygiene
___ absurd, illogical, nonsensical speech
___ paranoid/suspicious thoughts
___ flashbacks, loss of reality contact*
___ intoxicated/drugged*
___ harassment
___ coercion/intimidation

___ aggressive gestures
___ self injurious behavior*
___ physically violent***
___ verbal threats to self or others
___ suicidal/homicidal thinking/verbalizing*
___ suicidal/homicidal gestures/behaviors***
___ suicidal/homicidal plan clear***
___ uncooperative
___ absence of emotion/affect

___ impulsivity
___ hysterical*
___ confusion*
___ unable to follow simple directions*
___ unable to control emotions*
___ cannot recall personal information (phone, address)*
___ situation perceived as unreal (spectator)
___ nonresponsive*

*support services recommended   ***removal from housing recommended

---

Triage Assessment (X = Initial Assessment / O = Terminal Assessment)

Feelings
__ Anger __ Fear __ Sadness

1 2 3 4 5 6 7 8 9 10

Behavioral
__Approach __Avoidance __Immobile

1 2 3 4 5 6 7 8 9 10

Thinking
__Transgression __Threat __Loss

1 2 3 4 5 6 7 8 9 10

Initial Total Score: _____   **Terminal Total Score:** _____

FIGURE 13.1 Triage Assessment System for Students in Learning Environments (TASSLE). Source: © CIP-Solutions, July 2006. All Rights Reserved. Reprinted with permission of Crisis Intervention Prevention and Solutions, Inc.

Planning for a Crisis

A crisis plan for a school system is not done overnight. It takes a great deal of planning and commitment by the school district and the staff (Brock, Sandoval, & Lewis, 1996; Kerr, 2009; Luna & Hoffman, 1999; Maples et al., 2005; Montano & Dowdall-Thomae, 2003; Newgass & Schonfeld, 2005; Petersen, 1999; Petersen & Straub, 1992; Rubin, 1999; Stephens, 1997). Crisis plans are both generic and idiosyncratic. Crisis plans of other schools and consultants can be extremely helpful in making a skeletal outline for what needs to be covered in containing a crisis. No matter whether the crisis occurs in Brooklyn, New York, or Brooklyn, Mississippi, many of the same needs and responses generic to all crises of lethality will be applicable to each. When a disaster hits schools the federal government encourages schools to follow the National Incident Management System (2011), which standardizes how a crisis response is organized. That's all well and good, but the professional responders will leave after the emergency is over and guess who gets to carry on? Also, they won't be there in the first few minutes or hours of the crisis when the Chaos theory you vaguely remember in Chapter 1 is running rampant.

Further, each school district and each school building has its own peculiarities in regard to its physical plant, its staffing, its student population, and its community makeup. Each of these variables plays a critical part in how specific planning for a crisis will be conducted. To think that a crisis plan for the Los Angeles school district can be taken wholesale and applied to Waterloo, Iowa, would be misguided, to say the least. A crisis response in a school needs a delivery system. The chief components of any service delivery system are the written policy of what to do when a crisis occurs, the physical resources to carry out the policy, and the trained personnel to implement the service (Nelson & Slaikeu, 1990, p. 339). A crisis plan must cover safety and security; obtaining, verifying, and providing accurate information to the various constituencies of the school; and also deal with the emotional needs of those constituencies. If these three areas are not addressed concurrently as the crisis unfolds, none will be addressed effectively (Newgass & Schonfeld, 2005).

The Crisis Response Planning Committee

Initial planning should use a crisis response planning committee (Brock, Sandoval, & Lewis, 1996; Kerr, 2009; Montano & Dowdall-Thomae, 2003; Newgass & Schonfeld, 2005; Petersen, 1999; Petersen & Straub, 1992; Poland, 1999; Rubin, 1999; Stephens, 1997). A decision needs to be made on the size of the committee. If it's too large, it becomes unwieldy. If it's too small, it's not viable enough to meet a large crisis. The ideal is probably a two-tiered team if the district is large enough to support it and a super-tier regional team outside the district. The first-tier team is a districtwide effort that deals with the big picture of crises. This team should be composed of a wide variety of individuals representing a cross section of social services and government

institutions that will have to respond to the crisis. The second tier is a building response team that is familiar with its physical plant and its constituency. These individuals represent the teaching staff and administration, the parents, and most important, the support staff (failure to include the custodian might mean that nobody knows how to shut off the gas or electricity in the building) (Brock, Sandoval, & Lewis, 1996, p. 31). One of the critical ingredients is coordination between these two tiers. If these two levels operate at cross-purposes, not only will they hinder crisis resolution, they can make it worse. Coordination should be systemic and integrate partnerships among a variety of stakeholders that work with adolescents (Lubell & Vetter, 2006).

A needs assessment should be conducted to determine what the school staff needs in the way of training and, even more important, whether the constituency believes in and is willing to support the effort (Davis & Salasin, 1975). One might suppose that few people would be opposed to implementing a full-scale crisis prevention and intervention program in a school given the current publicity about school violence. That supposition may not be true when it comes to the reality of passing a bond issue, providing release time for staff, or disrupting ease of access to school buildings. Therefore, fully apprising the community and determining their resistance or acceptance are critical to implementing an effective plan (Davis & Salasin, 1975).

A clear system for dealing with a major school crisis should be established long before the need for intervention. It should ensure that all personnel are clear as to what is going to happen, when it will happen, who will be responsible for each component, how a report is made, who is to make the report, and subsequent follow-up action.

Such planning should include all the school staff and administration. Furthermore, because such interventions will undoubtedly involve law enforcement and perhaps other mental health agencies, they too should be involved in planning for violence intervention and know what part they are to play in it (Blauvelt, 1998; Brock, Sandoval, & Lewis, 1996, pp. 33–37; Montano & Dowdall-Thomae, 2003; Newgass & Schonfeld, 2005).

Your authors have seen a number of voluminous crisis plans developed by school systems that are quite impressive. One plan has 29 different leaders, directors, officers, and chiefs, with very detailed roles and functions for each! These plans are gathering dust on the principal's and superintendent's bookshelf. Any crisis plan should be usable, and it should be simple enough that everybody knows his or her role in implementing it (Blauvelt, 1998; Goldstein & Kodluboy, 1998, pp. 170–171). From that standpoint, while no school district goes without a tornado, earthquake, or fire drill on a regular basis, very few schools have drills regarding armed intruders or other kinds of crises. If staff is not trained to implement the plan, and if a school crisis plan is not practiced, evaluated, critiqued, reviewed, and updated on a regular basis (Brock, Sandoval, & Lewis, 1996, pp. 243–248; Poland, 1999, p. 4), it is pretty much useless.

The School Crisis Response Team (SCRT)

When a crisis is of such magnitude that local staff are overwhelmed or emotionally devastated because of personal involvement, then outside help should be summoned. Mobilizing this regional tier should be planned for a long time before the crisis occurs. In small rural school districts where the labor power and expertise for the following positions are beyond the district's capabilities, it is absolutely mandatory that linkages be established between districts and support personnel. It is even more important for these small districts that they have close linkages between countywide, state, and federal disaster management teams that compose this super tier.

If the crisis can be handled with help from within the district, the community generally will be better served because these people will be familiar with the setting and their clientele and the district will know what level of expertise these people have (Brock, Sandoval, & Lewis, 1996, p. 61; Rubin, 1999). Not everyone is cut out to do crisis intervention work. Just because a person is a counselor, a social worker, a school psychologist, or a caring teacher or administrator does not automatically make her or him the best person to be involved with the team. Careful consideration should be given to team composition, and people who feel that they might not be capable of handling a severe crisis should not be discriminated against because they are truthful about their trepidation (Kerr, 2009, p. 35).

The following roles make up what would be a competent SCRT. There should be redundancy in these roles (Brock, Sandoval, & Lewis, 1996, pp. 74–75; Kerr, 2009, pp. 36–45; Poland, 2004). If the crisis response coordinator is a principal who is being held hostage, or the intervention coordinator is a school counselor who is injured in an explosion, there needs to be someone else familiar enough with that role to take over.

Poland (1999, p. 4) speaks of three waves in the aftermath of a disaster. The first wave is the medical personnel and police. The second wave is the media. The third wave is the parents. Therefore, it is not just the victims and survivors that a school must be concerned with, but a host of other problems as well. Therefore, an SCRT will need to have a number of other people on it who may not have any expertise at all in crisis intervention but do have the expertise to allow the SCRT to handle the crisis effectively.

Crisis Response Coordinator. This person should be someone with decision-making capability, most likely a school administrator who is knowledgeable about the school district and staff. He or she is highly knowledgeable about the crisis plan and has good communication links within and outside the system. This person is in charge of coordinating, implementing, and evaluating crisis response plans (Brock, Sandoval, & Lewis, 1996, pp. 67–68; Rubin, 1999). This role is different from that of the person who would actually coordinate the intervention.

Crisis Intervention Coordinator. This person is responsible for implementing and carrying out the crisis plan. The intervention coordinator should have a thorough understanding of crisis intervention techniques and strategies. He or she should have a clear understanding of the objectives and methods of the crisis intervention plan and should be able to deal with a multiplicity of crises that range from individual suicides to natural and human-made disasters. This person also needs to be a good administrator and delegator who can coordinate a number of activities and people under very stressful and chaotic conditions (Brock, Sandoval, & Lewis, 1996, pp. 68–69; Petersen, 1999). It should be readily apparent that time should be allocated for the crisis intervention coordinator to plan and coordinate for crisis events, and not just have these "added on" as a supplementary task.

Media Liaison. It is one thing to deal with the local news crew that the SCRT leaders may have developed close personal relationships with over the course of time; it is quite another to deal with national news media. Imagine yourself as a school counselor in Anytown Middle School who has been designated as the SCRT coordinator. An assault at 8:30 A.M. by a person with paranoid schizophrenia leaves six children and two teachers dead, the school principal seriously wounded, and nine other children in the hospital with severe gunshot injuries. A panic ensues as frantic parents come to the school to get their children. You are attempting to get information out about who is hurt and dead, trying to coordinate psychological triage of survivors who witnessed the carnage, giving information to law enforcement personnel who are looking for the still-at-large perpetrator, attempting to reunite distraught students with equally distraught parents, plus a myriad of other tasks, when at 10 A.M. the first national news helicopter lands on the football field and is quickly followed at around noon by a convoy of national news trucks with satellite uplink capability. There is a horde of reporters attempting to interview anybody they can get their hands on. They are particularly interested in getting any school personnel to comment on who is responsible, why it happened, why the school didn't prevent this from happening, what the school is now doing, who the dead and survivors are, and how you personally feel about this, among other intrusive and invasive questions to which they are clamoring for answers.

It should become very clear from the foregoing scenario that dealing with the media is a major responsibility and should be the sole responsibility of one person specially designated and trained for the job. Such a person should be able to keep relationships with the media positive, but should also be able to effectively control them by determining how and what information should be shared with them through well-thought-out and well-prepared statements (Brock, Sandoval, & Lewis, 1996, pp. 69–70). One of the worst scenarios in a school crisis is to allow anybody and everybody to talk to the media. The repercussions from the innuendo, rumor, half-truths, and incomplete data can be extremely severe for survivors and further exacerbate the psychological trauma. Media need to be given press releases that indicate how the media can best help and be least disruptive to students. The media liaison provides written notification to parents on what happened as quickly and currently and with as much factual information as possible and also provides helpful literature and directories of support services to deal with the traumatic repercussions of the event (Newgass & Schonfeld, 2005). Kerr (2009, p. 74) has generated a list of media questions that are designed to obtain information that may well be used to cast the district in a negative light. She has also generated a list of "dos" and "don'ts" in regard to those questions that any media representative would do well to learn (p. 75).

Security Liaison. The security liaison should have close links with local law enforcement agencies and would coordinate responses to single events such as a bus accident or recurring events such as gang-initiated drive-by shootings. One of the major preventive tasks of the security liaison is training staff in implementing safety procedures across a wide array of potential crisis scenarios (Brock, Sandoval, & Lewis, 1996, p. 71).

Community/Medical Liaison. The medical liaison should have established close links between the local emergency, fire, medical, and mental health systems and the school. A critical component of her or his role is planning for medical triage of victims of a school crisis and communicating to parents and staff the medical condition of those involved in the crisis (Brock, Sandoval, & Lewis, 1996, pp. 71–72; Rubin, 1999). If there is a local emergency management agency, the liaison should have a seat on its board so that he or she knows whom to contact and what kinds of resources are available in a disaster.

Parent Liaison. The parent liaison's job is dealing with parents, period! Keeping parents calm, providing them with information, and furnishing them support are critical in the containment of a crisis. This person works closely with the media liaison in determining what information, about the event itself and support services, is disseminated to parents and how it gets to them. Where part of the community is not fluent in English, provision will have to be made for translators, both oral and for all written information that goes out to parents. Because parents may need the services of other components of the team, this school official must have a good working knowledge of each member's role (Rubin, 1999).

Community Liaison. This person or persons needs to be the direct link to community resources (Kerr, 2009, p. 37). An ideal member may be the Local Emergency Management Agency director, the mayor's community action officer, or a high-ranking member of the police or fire department.

Crisis Interveners. While direct service crisis interventionists are most likely to come from the ranks of school counselors, psychologists, social workers, and nurses, it is important to obtain interventionists who are directly linked to children. Thus, it is helpful to include teachers who have direct contact with a broad sample of the students who might be affected. In an elementary school, at least one primary and one intermediate teacher should be on the team, and in middle and senior high schools, teachers who represent many different subject matter areas or curriculum tracks should be part of the team (Brock, Sandoval, & Lewis, 1996, p. 72).

The school and district unit should be capable of handling a small crisis such as the suicide of a teacher or a gang shooting. In a large crisis such as a bus–train wreck, backup workers from the local mental health system should be available, and in a very large crisis such as the Columbine shooting, the crisis interventionists would be an even larger integrated team of school, local, state, and national interventionists. Incorporating students into the team is also a good idea. They can act as messengers, help identify which students are missing, provide information about the status of other students, and function as peer counselors (Rubin, 1999).

Resource/Facilities Person. This member will need to know where a variety of available supplies are and how to get them from point A to point B in a hurry. Depending on the size and type of the crisis, the resource person may need to know how to obtain everything from pencils and paper to a backup diesel generator. This is not a menial job. If the material supplies are not available, including provision of food and drink when a crisis is going full tilt, then everything grinds to a halt (Rubin, 1999). This person also has a working knowledge of building plans and the systems that operate them. Knowing how to shut off gas lines, knowing the location of electrical junction boxes, and being able to show others the opening to steam tunnels can be critical in a crisis where knowledge of building structures is involved (Kerr, 2009, p. 37).

Implementing the Crisis Plan

The following minimum requirements are critical to a school crisis plan (Brock, Sandoval, & Lewis, 1996, pp. 75–76; Brown & Bobrow, 2004; Conoley & Goldstein, 2004; Gerler, 2004; Montano & Dowdall-Thomae, 2003; Petersen & Straub, 1992; Rubin, 1999; Williams, 2004).

Physical Requirements

Counseling Locations. As many locations as possible need to be identified for crisis counseling offices. Crisis counseling will involve a wide variety of activities that will require different accommodations. Auditorium-size rooms will be needed to handle large groups of people for briefings of factual information about the crisis as it unfolds and psychoeducational information about what people can expect and need to do in the aftermath of the crisis. Classrooms will need to be designated to administer psychological first aid. Offices will be needed to perform psychological triage and provide individual counseling. If school is in session, a great deal of rescheduling and shuffling of rooms and assignments will be necessary and should be planned for ahead of time, or alternate buildings such as churches will need to be used.

Operations/Communications Center. In a very large crisis, a room that will become the nerve center for a crisis needs to be designated and equipped. All necessary equipment—additional phone lines, supplies, and furniture for additional staff, computers with Internet capability, emergency equipment such as portable phones, citizen band and police band radios, and portable generators—should be available here. This nerve center will become the key component of an efficient crisis operation. In it, people will monitor procedures to determine what staff is available, establish procedures for getting written messages to staff, screen outsiders, and disseminate and coordinate media releases and crisis intervention procedures.

Break Room. A place that is private and will allow workers time to relax, eat, and rest, it may also double as a debriefing room for SCRT members and other crisis personnel.

Information Center. A room large enough to handle a number of media personnel, it should be equipped with a sound system and other visual media equipment. It may also double as an information dissemination or briefing room for parents.

First-Aid Room. This room should be stocked with first-aid supplies for minor physical problems.

Logistics

On-Site Communications. Message boards, computers linked to central files, dedicated telephone lines, citizen and police band radios, and walkie-talkies should be accessible. Because telephone lines may be jammed or otherwise inoperable, a central message board should be available for announcements, bulletins, student lists, and other personal information. If possible, dedicated phone lines with the numbers known only to officials and staff responsible for handling the crisis should be available. Because there may be little or no communication on-site, walkie-talkies are vital. Portable "to go boxes" provide vital hard-copy data such as updated attendance lists, release cards, emergency numbers, parent/guardian names, and so on, and can be moved to an alternate site to check off names of students. All teachers should have a "to go box" in addition to a master main office "to go box."

Establishing a Phone Tree Among All Staff. In any size crisis, a redundant phone tree is absolutely imperative. All staff members of a school building need to be informed of a crisis event as soon as there is knowledge of it. The phone tree is critical so that all staff members can begin to operate in a crisis mode and assume preplanned positions and duties. Messages about the crisis should be written down by each person on the tree. Relying on memory and verbal transmission will guarantee that facts get commingled with fiction. One of the worst mistakes that can be made is for staff not to be aware of what is happening and go blundering into an ongoing crisis. We have experienced such lack of communication firsthand, and it is, to say the least, a nightmare.

Procedural Checklist. Although it may seem time wasteful to go through a procedural checklist when a crisis is in full swing, not to do so in a chaotic situation is asking for trouble. It is too easy to overlook a critical component of the intervention plan and assume it has been taken care of by somebody else.

Building Plans. Building plans are vital to emergency personnel and police. Blueprints of every building in the district should be quickly available. Someone with knowledge of the building should be available to interpret the plans to emergency personnel.

Provisions. Because crisis personnel may be involved for extended periods of time, food and drink should be provided or be delivered on-site.

Responding to the Crisis

The following points, in linear order, indicate what needs to occur in a crisis response (Brock, Sandoval, & Lewis, 1996, pp. 80–104; Gerler, 2004; Kerr, 2009; Petersen, 1999; Petersen & Straub, 1992; Poland, 2004; Poland & McCormick, 1999; Rubin, 1999). Kerr has an

operational acronym that should be a general overall operating guide to all responders called BE CALM. It stands for:

> **Be**fore you act be sure you have the facts.
> **C**all for help, communicate instructions, and collaborate with other responders.
> **A**nticipate what could happen next and adjust the plan.
> **L**isten to your audience and learn what they need.
> **M**anage the crisis and maintain the responders with food, rest, water, debriefing, etc., and modify the plan as needed. (p. 9)

Getting the Facts. The ability to quash the rumor mill that invariably starts up in a crisis is critical to calming fears and anxiety of the public and also to providing valid information to crisis workers on how many and which students were affected, what level of response will be required, what information needs to be disseminated, and to whom it will be given. Facts need to be checked and rechecked. Getting a team member to the scene of a crisis to make a factual report is critical. Distraught parents and hysterical children make for extremely unreliable sources of information. Especially in the case of a suicide, getting verification from the medical examiner is a must.

Impact Assessment. As soon as the facts are known, an SCRT meeting should be held and an assessment should be made of the impact the crisis will have on the school. Considerations in assessing the impact are popularity of the victim, degree of exposure by staff and students, history and recency of similar crises, resources currently available, and timing (a crisis during vacation is likely to be less traumatic than one during school time). At that time, a decision will have to be made as to the degree of mobilization of internal staff and what, if any, outside assistance will be needed.

Triage Assessment. Once the facts are determined and the possible impact of the crisis event is gauged, a triage assessment needs to be conducted to determine those individuals most affected by the crisis. The SCRT needs to compile a list of those who may be directly and indirectly affected and determine who is most in need of acute intervention and who may need less immediate, intensive attention. Once this list is compiled, interviews and paper-and-pencil tests such as those described in the chapter on PTSD may be used to further divide individuals into primary- and secondary-care groups.

It should not be assumed that relatives, survivors, witnesses to the event, and close friends within the school are the only people needing immediate and intensive attention. Siblings and close friends in other schools may be just as traumatized, and efforts should be made to assess these individuals as well. Individuals who are known to be at risk due to other factors and students whose reactions are out of proportion to their involvement should also be considered as high risk.

Parents and teachers need to be given checklists and warning signs that will let them know whether their children are starting to develop the symptoms of acute or posttraumatic stress disorder and referral sheets and phone numbers that will enable them to refer those students who may have been missed by the SCRT. Embedded within these referrals should be questions on lethality. Any student who is expressing thoughts about harming him- or herself or others should immediately be assessed as high risk and in need of immediate crisis intervention.

Psychological First Aid. Psychological first aid (Aguileria, 1997; Slaikeu, 1990, pp. 105–129) is a first-order response that deals with all of the affected individuals no matter what their degree of involvement. The components of psychological first aid are making psychological contact, exploring dimensions of the problem, examining possible solutions, gaining assistance in taking action, and offering follow-up services. Psychological first aid is intended as a method to provide support, furnish a platform to be heard and valued, dispel rumors, allow catharsis and ventilation of emotions, reactivate problem-solving abilities, reduce potential lethality, and restore general stability to the school. It is probably most easily done in classroom meetings with teachers who are trained and supported by the SCRT. Such classroom meetings are an excellent vehicle for providing factual information about the event, giving students information about the psychological effects they may encounter, and dealing with personal issues and problems students may have as they come to grips with and attempt to resolve the crisis.

The NOVA Model. For older students, the National Organization for Victim Assistance (NOVA; 1997) group crisis intervention model may be used. This model operates along the lines of the critical incidents stress debriefing (CISD) program of Mitchell and Everly (1995). However, it is not as tightly structured as CISD, and the facilitator is a great deal more interactive with participants.

These groups meet for usually no more than 2 hours. The session has a brief introduction detailing safety and security for the participants. Time is then spent on reviewing physical sensory perceptions, going over emotional reactions of shock and disbelief, and giving opportunity for ventilation and validation of these reactions. Typical questions posed are "Where were you when it happened? Who were you with? What did you see, hear, smell, taste, or touch at the time? What did you do? How did you react?" Time is then taken to review the emotional turmoil that has been experienced and to allow ventilation and validation of these feelings.

Questions are asked in regard to the aftermath of the event. "What are some of the memories that stand out in your mind? What has happened in the last 48 hours? What do you remember seeing or hearing during that time? How have you reacted?" The facilitator validates the thoughts and feelings of the group members. No judgments are made as to right or wrong. Where applicable, the facilitator draws comparisons between members to create a common bond and normalize thoughts and feelings that go with the abnormal event (National Organization for Victim Assistance, 1997, pp. 8–10).

Questions are then posed to elicit expectations about the future, what coping strategies can be used, and help predict and prepare the group for what may happen over the near future. "After all that you've been through, what do you think will happen at school in the next few days and weeks? Do you think your family has been or will be affected? How do you believe you might deal with the problems and issues that have been raised?" As the members identify positive coping strategies, they are reinforced and given alternative strategies if they are generating negative coping methods. Referrals for more in-depth help are suggested. These components are then followed by a summary recapitulation to validate what has been said and reaffirm the validity of the participants' experiences. A postgroup session of about 30 minutes is used to distribute handouts, answer individual questions, and say good-bye (National Organization for Victim Assistance, 1997, pp. 9–10).

Conducting a large assembly of all the school to do this is not recommended. Although a large assembly may be deemed efficient and expedient, it does not begin to address the many personal questions and issues that students may have. Psychological first aid is a two-way street and, to be effective, should allow an interchange of information between staff and students. In and of itself, psychological first aid may be an excellent way of determining who may be in need of more in-depth crisis intervention by observing reactions of students as they talk about the crisis. This admonition is particularly important in the case of suicide where other students may have "caught" the contagion and need to be identified.

Crisis Intervention. Any student who is assessed as needing more than psychological first aid should be given a complete screening interview (Aronin & Ransdell, 1994). That interview should consider what the student's exposure and recollection of the events are, whether the event is persistently reexperienced, whether there are attempts to avoid reminders of the event, increased levels of physical and mental arousal, feelings of survivors' guilt, failure of previous coping skills to ameliorate problems, somatic complaints, self-destructive or impulsive behaviors, and pre- and postevent comparisons on effectiveness of daily functioning. In short, the screening interview should look at the diagnostic criteria set forth by the *DSM-IV-TR* (American Psychiatric Association, 2000) for the onset of traumatic stress disorder.

It is important to take the time necessary to completely discuss the crisis, and attempts to immediately reintroduce the academic regimen should be held in abeyance until this task can be completed. Although getting back to the standard humdrum schedule of school is important in normalizing the situation, very few students are going to be academically able to do so if they are struggling with attempts to resolve the crisis.

Classroom meetings can help students move from reaction to proaction. That is, students can move from talking about the event to planning how they can take action to solve the residual effects of the event. By moving to a proactive stance, students can begin to attain a feeling of empowerment and reinstitute control in their lives. They can also gain closure on the event by cooperatively planning memorials and memorial services (note the previously mentioned exception of memorializing suicide).

The worker should be especially watchful for client reports that perseverate on special details, worst moments, and violence or physical mutilation. These will be extremely potent points in the crisis and need to be thoroughly worked through and controlled (Pynoos & Eth, 1986, p. 309). If there are perpetrators involved in the crisis, one of the greatest fears of children is that the perpetrators "will get them." Whether these perpetrators are caught and punished or are still at large makes little difference. The worker needs to take time to clarify

what happened to the perpetrators or what is being done to catch them. Feeling of self-blame for not having done enough and an inability to take action, desires to retaliate and punish the perpetrators, and fear that they will be revictimized need to be explored and worked through (Brock, Sandoval, & Lewis, 1996, p. 168).

Briefing and Debriefing. Each morning of the aftermath of the crisis, a morning briefing and planning session needs to be held to obtain updated information, review responsibilities, assign tasks, and plan interventions. At the end of each day, actions need to be reviewed, weaknesses and strengths need to be examined, and reviews of referred students, staff, and parents need to made. Plans are then made for the next day and what staff and resources will be needed to accomplish the goals. Additionally, a nightly debriefing should be held to give the SCRT a chance to exchange information, obtain reassurance, and ventilate feelings (Berman & Jobes, 1991; Rubin, 1999; Williams, 2006). The Missouri School Counselor Association's (2002) *Crisis Manual* makes the following points for SCRT members:

1. Keep your life in balance.
   a. Eat well-balanced meals and get plenty of exercise.
   b. Balance work and rest.
   c. Stick to a schedule as much as you can. It provides stability and the comfort of a normal routine when your feelings are out of control.
   d. Avoid new major projects or decisions.
2. Be realistic about what you can do.
3. Recognize and acknowledge your own feelings of loss and grief. Give yourself permission to mourn. No matter what the nature of your relationship, there is loss. Give yourself the same latitude you give your students. Meet with fellow SCRT members and be supportive of each other or form a support group.
4. Be kind to yourself. You don't have to get it all together right away. You don't have to do it all, be strong for everyone, or take care of everything. Treat yourself with the same gentleness and understanding you would anybody else.

Demobilizing. Demobilizing occurs when the crisis is finished. It allows the SCRT to integrate the experience into their lives and go back to their regular jobs. An overall evaluation is conducted by the crisis response coordinator with the SCRT. The crisis intervention co-ordinator writes an after-action report that includes a description of the crisis event and the interventions conducted, an evaluation of the effectiveness of the intervention, and recommendations for future events. As such it provides the SCRT with a potent learning tool. Furthermore, if questions are raised in the future about what was done or not done, this report documents what happened (Brock, Sandoval, & Lewis, 1996, p. 100).

Bereavement in Schools

The sudden death of a student, teacher, or other school personnel may precipitate a bereavement crisis for an entire school or school community, which can lead to posttraumatic stress disorder, high-intensity grief, and complicated mourning. The closer the friendship to the deceased, the more the foregoing is likely to occur. As such it is important to have a grief resolution program in place (Poijula et al., 2001). Many children will be dealing with the reality of death for the first time. They will also be struggling with the significance of the loss and grappling with the idea that life is no longer predictable or fair. Further, they may have no idea how to grieve and may receive little help if their parents are also grief stricken (Kraft, 2003). Many of the bereavement procedures in Chapter 12, Personal Loss: Bereavement and Grief, are appropriate for working with children and adolescents. However, because of the social community and culture of schools, there are some specific actions that need to occur when a member of the school community dies.

Individually or in groups, team members may focus on the grief of a specific grade level, provide group discussion for particular subgroups, temporarily relieve bereaved teachers of classroom responsibilities, staff mini-counseling centers, or work with parents. Two SCRT members may follow a deceased student's schedule. One member will talk with each class, provide factual information, answer questions, clarify misinformation, provide support, provide information on funeral arrangements, explain what funerals and visitations are like and what to expect, suggest what types of things can be said to family members, and encourage students to talk about their memories of the deceased student. While this class discussion is taking place, the other member can assess and identify students who are not coping well and escort them to a support room (Missouri School Counselor Association, 2002).

Assessing students' needs prior to returning to school may help lessen anxiety. A home visit or a phone call that empathically responds to the student's progress can be made. Questions might include "How are you feeling about coming back to school? What is the most difficult thing for you about returning? Is there something you would like me to do to help you? Are you worried about what other students will think?" All these questions are designed to allow the student to talk about his or her fears and trepidation and allow the SCRT member to help him or her start to feel less anxious. After the student has been back to school a few days, the crisis worker may discuss with the child how she or he is doing with questions such as "Now that you are back at school, what has been the hardest thing for you? What has been on your mind the most? How has the death affected you at school?" These questions allow the worker to determine how well the child is making the transition back into school (Rubin, 1999).

Kandt (1994, p. 207) suggests that school human services personnel working with grieving adolescents should (1) educate themselves about the grief process; (2) give permission to grieve; (3) allow time to grieve; (4) listen, listen, listen; (5) understand that reminiscing is essential; (6) give support for a variety of feelings; (7) know they can't "fix" the pain; (8) draw the adolescents out, keep in touch, and don't abandon them; (9) design a support group; and (10) let them know that they are not alone.

Swihart, Silliman, and McNeil (1992) surveyed grieving students and listed the following issues that caregivers should be sensitive to:

1. Many students were affected by the loss, even students who were not close to the deceased; therefore, they were reminded of their own mortality.
2. Teachers should not expect peak performance from students who are still too numb the first week following the death.
3. Teachers should be allowed to express their own grief to students who are willing to simply listen.
4. Students should be allowed to grieve in different ways—some in groups, some in their individual ways.
5. After-school activities should be provided for students to work off their grief by expending physical energy.
6. Students should be brought together in commemorative activities so that students who were not very close to the deceased one are not excluded.

7. Students should be permitted to discuss grief issues; denial of the opportunity to openly discuss their thoughts and feelings may cut the teenagers off from an open forum of support.

8. School administrators should be cognizant of the deceased student's role in the school; if the deceased was in a leadership role, the school will need to have administrative leadership in filling the role vacated by the deceased.

9. The school should be prepared to respond to the loss for a considerable length of time.

Group Work

An accident following the prom in early May resulted in the deaths of four Cedar Grove High School students: Phil, age 16, the driver of the car; Jerry, age 17; LaTara, age 16; and Tracey, age 17. A group of seven classmates at school, representing the four youngsters' closest friends, appeared to be stuck in their grief. Keena, Lee, Samantha, and Rashid, all 17, and Eddie, Amber, and Tarunda, all 16, requested the help of the school counselor in reaching some understanding and resolution of their feelings of anguish and grief.

The following intervention strategies were provided and issues explored with these adolescents by the school counselor during the days and weeks immediately following the burial of the four teenagers who died.

1. *Individual counseling and intervention.* Assessment of individual stress levels. Providing individuals a safe place to release stress energy. Helping adolescents feel comfortable in expressing how they feel. Providing death education for adolescents.

2. *Group grief work.* Providing an atmosphere for the seven adolescents as a group to deal with the deaths of their four classmates in particular, and with the area of death and dying in general. Providing for group sessions and projects that commemorate the deceased classmates. Group exploration of unfinished business through written or role-playing exercises. Provision for students to deal with the deaths outside the group within the school environment through peer support groups. (Samide & Stockton, 2002)

Gray (1988) reported that bereaved teens in support groups found peers to be "most helpful," compared to other school-related workers, and that bereaved adolescents did not want to be singled out or treated in special ways (pp. 187–188). In cases of sudden death, grief, and bereavement among adolescents, a great deal of shock, vulnerability, remorse, and other emotions quickly emerge. Because most adolescents lack experience dealing with the death of their peers and because social influence is powerful and pervasive in a setting such as a high school, the use of adolescent group grief work is an ideal strategy for controlling distortions and rumors and for helping young people release grief energy and begin to resolve their feelings of loss.

The counselor, meeting with the group in the group guidance room, served as the crisis worker. She met with several grief work groups during the days immediately following the deaths of the four students. The counselor set the tone by introducing the topic and encouraging members to share their emotional responses to the loss. Later during the session, after the release of students' grief energy, the counselor began to use structured techniques to help them sharpen their memories and focus on reality.

CW: I really appreciate all the expressions of your feelings you've given so freely. Before the session begins today, I asked Samantha to go by the yearbook office and pick up a copy of this year's *Wildcat*. I also asked her to pick up some leftover photographs that the yearbook staff did not use. Samantha, would you like to share some of them with the group?

Samantha: I put filing cards in the pages of the annual that I thought we'd like to look at. Oh, and I've got some great shots of LaTara, Jerry, and Tracey. I only found one of Phil, and that was in a group. But Phil's class picture is in there (*pointing toward the yearbook*), and all four of them look so real and alive and so happy in the activities section.

The students in the group showed a great deal of interest and released a great amount of stress energy while examining the photographs of the deceased students. Later in the session, the group discussed death in general, the impact of death on the living, and their own deaths. The counselor then used a technique called Memory Moments. Students finished off sentences such as "When I heard you died, I . . . ," "Our last conversation was . . . ," "My head feels . . . ," "My heart feels . . . ," "I wish I had said. . . ." All of these sentence stems allow students to openly speak to the wide range of emotions they are carrying (Counce & Sommer, 2003).

The counselor was able to use another technique that is sometimes effective in group grief work—the epitaph exercise. Each group member was given four index cards and was instructed: "If you were given the responsibility for writing the epitaphs for Phil, Jerry,

LaTara, and Tracey, write down the exact words on the cards that would appear on their gravestones." The group shared their epitaphs and discussed them.

Eddie: I thought Tarunda's was really good when she wrote— about Jerry—"Here lies the Martin Luther King of Cedar Grove," because he really did like and care for everybody. (*Students nod in agreement.*)

Keena: I *almost* cried when I wrote Tracey's, and then I *did* when Amber read LaTara's. I just felt like I couldn't stand it. It's so true. I'm really going to miss that girl. (*Students nod in agreement. Long period of silence; thoughtful look on all faces.*)

CW: I think what we've done is to write down, in the briefest form, what we want to remember most about each of our beloved classmates.

Before the session ended, the counselor led the group in identifying the positive contributions that each of the deceased students had made and in verbalizing their good-byes to each of their departed classmates. The counselor was attempting to use the power and social influence of the group setting to enhance the emotional impact on each member and to prepare each member to say good-bye, let go of the deceased, and begin to get ready to go on living.

Defining the Boundaries

Probably one of the toughest jobs of an SCRT and the school administration is to discourage parents, students, or various other interest groups in the community from honoring the death by conducting a commemorative service or other memorial at the school. Unequivocally, suicidal students should not be formally memorialized by the school because of possible copycats (Capuzzi, 2002). It cannot be overemphasized that the school administration and the SCRT should be the ones to make decisions about the response to school tragedies in which deaths occur. Overall, it is probably best for the school not to memorialize any kind of deaths in any fashion—assemblies, yearbooks, trees planted, rooms or fields named, and so on—because of the perception of differential treatment.

Bluntly stated, schools are in the education business not in the funeral home or memorial business (Trotter, 2003). Trotter recommends that after the funeral, all of the drawings and other eulogies and epitaphs be collected and given to the family and not kept on display in the school. She also recommends that the student's chair be left alone until the day after the funeral, but then all chairs in the room need to be rearranged. She

proposes that immediately upon notification, a member of the SCRT should go to the student's locker and collect all personal items when students are not present and prevent memorializing the locker.

The student's locker should be left vacant for the remainder of the year, but then be merged into the standard locker assignment for next year's class. Louvre (2002) believes that with younger children, the desk should be left in the room until the other students want it moved out. She further proposes that a suitable memorial be constructed by the children such as positive epitaphs or a signed teddy bear that the class might give to the parents when they come to school to collect the dead child's things.

Transcrisis Intervention

For those children who are in need of assistance beyond psychological first aid, transcrisis intervention uses many of the approaches detailed in the chapters on PTSD and sexual assault. Use of drawings, modeling clay, and other manipulative play materials is particularly helpful in empowering children to take control of a situation that may seem beyond their ability to do so. Initially, the child should be allowed to use the materials to construct whatever he or she desires. The crisis interventionist uses this time to build trust and rapport.

Invariably the crisis will be manifested in the child's play and will provide clues to the source of the child's anxiety and means of coping (Pynoos & Eth, 1986, p. 307). At some time during the process, a child who has been numbing and repressing the crisis event is going to have an emotional release that may be shocking and unsettling to the crisis worker (Pynoos & Eth, 1986, p. 308). At that point, the worker must be calm, cool, and collected and be able to psychologically and physically comfort the child.

The use of guided imagery and the employment of superheroes as helpers in those images (Lazarus, 1977), conscious dreaming to help stop recurring nightmares (Garfield, 1984), and relaxation and desensitization techniques to teach anxiety control (Thompson & Rudolph, 1992, p. 173) are all potent ways of helping children empower themselves and take back control over their feelings, thoughts, and behaviors.

The Case of Josh

Josh is a 7-year-old second grader who has just recovered from a bite from a brown recluse spider (one of the most poisonous spiders in North America). Josh was bitten in the leg, and the necrosis that developed required reconstructive surgery. He now walks with a cane and a limp. He is embarrassed by his disability and feels his classmates are making fun of him behind his back. For a time, it was feared that Josh might lose his leg. What has compounded the problem is that recently thousands of brown recluses were discovered in the steam tunnels of Josh's school. This discovery set off a panic, because the children had seen what happened to Josh and had also viewed news items on television about the brown recluses' movement into their geographic area. Although the school district immediately hired exterminators to rid the school of the spiders, the children's fears were not allayed.

Josh is now hypervigilant in regard to any insects, is afraid to sleep in his own bed, has developed school phobia, and shrieks and screams in terror at going to school. He has recurrent nightmares about hoards of huge, hairy spiders covering his body. He is very sure he is going to die from a spider bite. His academic achievement has fallen, and he is in danger of failing second grade. His parents have talked to him about switching schools, but he is sure that all schools now contain brown recluses. Most of his conversation is centered on insects. He avoids outdoor activities for fear of getting bitten. The duration of his symptoms is now into its sixth week. After an interview with the school psychologist, Josh is given a diagnosis of acute traumatic stress disorder.

Because many other children at the school are manifesting symptoms of traumatic stress due to the brown recluse infestation, the SCRT has a meeting and determines that intervention is necessary with both the student population as a whole and Josh individually. Josh's parents are called, and they agree to individual intervention. The team's media person prepares a number of press releases and goes on radio and television news shows to explain what is being done to control the situation. In coordination with the parent liaison, bulletins are also sent home to all parents.

The medical liaison has classroom meetings with every homeroom in the school. She provides detailed information about what brown recluse bites look like and what medical care is needed, and answers the students' questions in a truthful, no-nonsense manner. Another classroom meeting is held with the high school biology teacher, who shows the students what the spider looks like, describes its habits, and also indicates to them that although the brown recluse is poisonous, it is a very shy spider that tries to avoid contact with people. Question-and-answer sessions follow, and students get a good idea of what they need to do at both school and home to avoid being bitten.

Parents are invited to a special parent–teacher meeting where all the SCRT staff are present to provide information about helping children cope with the sudden siege of arachnophobia (fear of spiders and similar creatures). After completing the psychological first aid program, the SCRT staff poll the teachers, who indicate the students seem to have conquered their fears of spiders. But Josh has not!

The crisis worker goes to Josh's home and, after making Josh's acquaintance, sets up the following exercise:

CW: I want you to draw me the feeling of what "scared" looks like, Josh.

Josh: (*Takes markers and poster board and draws a picture of a very large tarantula-like spider with huge dripping fangs about to pounce on a small boy cowering in a corner. While drawing, Josh gives the crisis worker a blow-by-blow gruesome description of what the spider is going to do to the little boy.*)

CW: Boy! that's scary all right. I wonder what we could do to make that big nasty spider run away and hide?

Josh: I dunno. Nothin', I think.

CW: Well, that is pretty tough with a spider that big, but you know, I've got an idea. It takes a spider to catch a spider. And I've got just the guy to do it. (*Pulls out a Spider-Man comic book.*) Have you ever read a Spider-Man comic? He is way cool.

Josh: (*Eyes light up and takes the comic book and starts looking at it.*) Yeah, and I've seen him in the movie. He is cool!

CW: So let's get him to help us. Takes a Spider-Man to catch a spider, right?

Josh: Well, I guess that's right.

CW: All right! Let's jump Spider-Man off the comic book and onto your poster board. Can you draw him on there and tell me what's happening?

Josh: Well, OK. (*Draws Spider-Man casting a big net over the spider.*) Spider-Man throws this big net over him, see, and the spider doesn't like it. But the more it struggles, the more it gets tangled up. Ha! Ha! Caught in a spider net. That's cool! He can't get out, but he's still there, though. I don't like him right there.

CW: OK! How could we get rid of him?

Josh: Well we could take him to the bug-man, and let him douse him with bug juice.

CW: Fine. Go ahead and do that. (*Gives Josh another piece of poster board.*)

Josh: (*Continues to draw Spider-Man pulling the spider over to an exterminator who looks very much like Josh.*)

CW: Now what?

Josh: I'm gonna douse him good.

CW: Good! Do that! What does that spider look like now?

Josh: He's gonna shrivel up and blow away. (*Continues to draw the spider all shriveled up; he and Spider-Man triumphantly hold the spider up as a trophy.*)

Over the course of the next several sessions, the crisis worker continues to use modeling clay and drawing to give Josh and Spider-Man increasing control over his environment (Webb, 2007). The crisis worker uses the superhero to help empower this frightened and traumatized little boy. The crisis worker now moves further to help Josh regain control over more of his environment by taking him outside to the backyard. Although Josh is somewhat timid about going outside, he goes with the crisis worker, one hand clutching the worker's hand and the other clutching a Spider-Man figurine.

CW: Boy! We're outside here. How do you feel?

Josh: Yeah, I think the backyard is where I got bit.

CW: And you're back out here. That's pretty courageous, almost like Spider-Man.

Josh: Well, it's OK 'cause Spider-Man's here with me . . . and well . . . you too.

CW: Josh, I wonder if Spider-Man could help us with those nightmares too. What I'd like you to do is just sort of have a daydream, you know like let your mind wander like there was sort of nothing to do and you were just kind of relaxing, and just shut your eyes and instead of having a nightmare, just imagine yourself and Spider-Man. Just you and Spider-Man out on patrol, saving the world from those huge spiders. Can you picture yourself and Spider-Man like that? Now just lie back and listen to me and just let yourself relax. (*The crisis worker deeply relaxes Josh and then helps him create an image of him and Spider-Man.*)

The crisis worker uses a combination of relaxation training and guided imagery to decrease Josh's anxiety and help him build a mental image of himself and his powerful friend taking control of the nighttime environment.

Josh: (*with his eyes closed.*) Yeah, me and Spider-Man are scaling up a tall building, looking for big old hairy spiders. (*Josh goes on to explain how they are out on patrol catching all kinds of spiders.*)

The crisis worker helps keep Josh on track, and when he gets stuck trying to catch a really huge, fast, fluorescent chartreuse spider, the crisis worker gives him a can of superstrong glue, and Josh and Spider-Man spread it out and get the spider stuck in it.

CW: Good. Now what I want you to do is get that image real clear in your mind. You and Spider-Man giving each other high-fives for catching that really monstrous spider. If you start to have that same old nightmare tonight, I want you to change that nightmare, and do just what you and Spider-Man did. That's what I want you to dream. I'll bet you can do that! (*Gives and returns a high-five from Josh.*)

The power of suggestion and use of guided imagery to enable a child to change his dreams may seem far-fetched, but it must be remembered that children work out their problems through fantasy and play. As the crisis worker continuously reinforces Josh for getting back in control of his environment through the help of the superhero, Josh can start to feel safe not only in his backyard, but also in his sleep.

Finally, to expedite Josh's return to school, the crisis worker sets up a classroom meeting with his classmates. Josh tells his classmates about his real spider bite and all the things that happened to him in the hospital. The rest of the children are very curious about all this and ask him many questions. Josh has been embarrassed about his scar and his limp, but now he's in the limelight and eagerly starts to tell them what went on while he was in the hospital and doesn't hesitate to tell them some of the more gruesome details with accompanying "Oohs," "Aahs," and "Ughs" from the class. He also shows them the pictures he drew and tells them, with the help of the crisis worker, how he's "not afraid of any darned old spiders anymore." An examination of Josh's drawings indicates just how potent serial drawing can be (Gumaer, 1984). Over a series of sessions, the spiders get smaller and smaller, and Josh and Spider-Man get bigger and bigger until the spider is in realistic proportion to Josh in the drawings, no more than a spot on the poster board. In the course of 8 weeks, Josh was able to return to school, his nightmares of spiders went away, and he was able to resume the life of a normal 7-year-old boy.

Epilogue

If you are planning on being a school counselor and are reading this book in a formal graduate class, you are probably ahead of most of your peers. That statement probably holds as well for social workers and school psychologists. There is a reason that the Council on Accreditation of Counseling and Educationally Related Programs (CACREP) is mandating crisis intervention in its new standards for school counseling. Wachter (2007) has done a comprehensive study on school counselors and crisis, and what she found is sobering. Although school psychologists, school social workers, police officers, other in-school staff, and community mental health workers may well be involved in crisis intervention, the typical first responder in a school will be a school counselor. Particularly in a school shooting, school counselors are most likely to become the leaders in their school building. Many are unprepared to take on such a task, but they get it anyway when a building or district has not done the preplanning it needs to do (Fein, Carlisle, & Issacson, 2008).

Wachter found that more than half the school counselors (53.1 percent) reported dealing with all the crises discussed in this chapter plus sexual and physical abuse. About a fifth of the counselors (21.7 percent) reported that they had received no training at all during their master's degree program for any kind of crisis intervention. Forty-four percent reported that after obtaining a master's degree they had picked up training in areas such as suicide intervention and critical incident stress debriefing on their own. Interestingly, these counselors perceived their on-site staff and resources to be more helpful than external sources of support. The school counselors identified assessment for suicidal and homicidal ideation and the provision of support for students who are at risk for both as critical knowledge components.

Crisis and burnout go hand in hand. Fein and his associates (2008) found that indeed school counselors suffered from the stress of being leaders in an unknown and chaotic situation where they had to make fast decisions. They learned how to do debriefing on the fly, which would be unthinkable for emergency responders such as police, EMTs, or firefighters. They also engaged in decisions they had never figured they would be involved in doing and suffered traumatic symptoms as a result. While Wachter found no significant difference in burnout symptoms and individual exposure to crisis, she did find significance in higher burnout rates

when physical abuse was the precipitating crisis event. Wachter also determined that master's level training in the kind of course you are now taking with this book is significantly related to *reducing* burnout rates in school counselors. Finally, Wachter noted that building internal support systems and getting continuing education in crisis intervention is helpful in preventing burnout.

While every school district in the United States most likely has at least some kind of crisis plan that goes beyond fire, tornado, and earthquake drills, and some of those school districts may go to great lengths to detail how crisis teams will operate in large-scale disasters, the simple fact is that school personnel who deal with the day-in and day-out grinding crises that afflict many students don't have a lot of resources to help them (Heath & Sheen, 2005). So if you are a school counselor or other school professional taking this course, you may find that Heath and Sheen's (2005) book, *School-Based Crisis Intervention: Preparing All Personnel to Assist*, and Kerr's (2009) book, *School Crisis Prevention and Intervention*, would be very helpful in training the people you most likely will have to count on, your fellow professionals. Heath and Sheen's book goes into specific detail about the basic, hands-on crisis intervention skills and activities that teachers, secretaries, custodians, and bus drivers will need to help you out. Kerr's book has more to do with laying out the larger operational picture. Along with Scott Poland's (1999) book, *Coping with Crisis: Lessons Learned*, which deals with the logistical, tactical, and strategic problems of a crisis, it is especially appropriate for administrators. And make no mistake about it, you will need their help. Going it alone in a school building when dealing with the kinds of "stuff" this chapter is about will make you an odds-on favorite to be what the burnout in this book is about. So, if you are an aspiring school counselor, be assured that what's in this book is "stuff" you are going to need. The question is absolutely not "If" but "When?"

SUMMARY

The rise of school violence perpetrated by the estranged violent student has caused a great deal of public concern and received widespread media coverage because of its perceived senselessness and its occurrence in communities where residents previously thought they were immune from such horrific events. Although the focus has been on the tragedy of estranged students who act out their frustration and anger in lethal ways, the growth and spread of gang-initiated violence in urban, suburban, and rural communities far exceed the tragedies the estranged juvenile has perpetrated.

Homicides are not the only lethal malady to afflict schools and cause crises. The suicide rate has risen to epidemic proportions among children and adolescents. School personnel face a wide variety of crises that reach far beyond the normal developmental issues and crises of childhood and adolescence. Schools have been called upon to develop wide-ranging prevention strategies for profiling, screening, and preventing acts of violence both to oneself and to others. Contemporary crisis strategies in schools deal not only with prevention, but with intervention and postvention as well. Crisis workers interact with students, faculty, and parents who have been associated with, witnessed, or suffered from traumatic events originating within the school or with students.

Although no known intervention plan will guarantee that tragedies will not take place, there are approaches that hold promise in dealing with a variety of crises that can afflict schools. These approaches call for everyone—community service organizations, child welfare agencies, mental health facilities, local, state, and national governments, the courts, law enforcement agencies, and all of the staff in schools—to work cooperatively in developing and implementing crisis intervention plans. Most important, no school should be without a crisis plan and a well-trained crisis response team.

 To see some of the concepts discussed in this chapter in action, refer to your *Crisis Intervention in Action* DVD, or see the Counseling CourseMate website. To access this site, go to www.cengagebrain.com, where you'll also find an eBook, additional study tools, quizzes, and more. There you will meet a high school senior who is being ostracized by his former teammates. As his story unfolds, what do you gauge his threat level to be: low, medium, high? What part does his language play in your decision? Should it? Overall, do you think the counselor follows the protocol outlined in this chapter? Oh, and by the way, you now are the school counselor hearing this. What do you want to do?

REFERENCES

Aguileria, D. C. (1997). *Crisis intervention: Theory and methodology* (8th ed.). St. Louis, MO: Mosby.

Allen, M., Burt, K., Rashid, E., Carter, D., Orsi, R., & Durkan, L. (2002). School counselors' preparation for and participation in crisis intervention. *Professional School Counseling, 6*(2), 96–103.

Allen, S. (1996, November). *The rural school counselor.* Paper presented at the Tennessee Counseling Association Convention, Memphis, TN.

Alvarez, T. (1999). APA and MTV launch youth anti-violence initiate. *Practitioner Focus. May–June 1999.* Washington, DC: American Psychological Association, Public Relations and Communications Practice Directorate.

American Association of Suicidology. (1991). *Postvention guidelines for the schools.* Denver, CO: Author.

American Association of Suicidology. (1998, Fall). *News Link 24*(3), 126–128.

American Counseling Association. (1995). *Code of ethics and standards of practice.* Alexandria, VA: Author.

American Psychiatric Association. (2000). *Diagnostic and statistical manual of mental disorders* (4th ed., Text Rev.). Washington, DC: Author.

American Psychological Association Zero Tolerance Task Force. (2008). Are zero tolerance policies effective in schools? *American Psychologist, 63*(9), 852–862.

American School Counselor Association. (1998). *Ethical standards for school counselors.* Alexandria, VA: Author.

Anderson, C. A., Shibuya, A., Ihori, N., Swing, E., Bushman, B., Sakamoto, A., et al. (2010). Violent video game effects on aggression, empathy, and prosocial behavior in Eastern and Western countries: A meta-analytic review. *Psychological Bulletin, 136*(2), 151–173.

Anderson, M. A., Kaufman, J., & Simon, T. R. (2001). School-associated violent deaths in the United States, 1994–1999. *Journal of the American Medical Association, 286,* 2695–2702.

Aronin, L., & Ransdell, J. (1994). *A handbook for crisis intervention.* Reseda, CA: Los Angeles Unified School District.

Astor, R. (1999). Unknown places and times. *American Educational Research Journal, 36,* 3–42.

Austin, S. (2003). Multiple lessons from multiple suicides. *ASCA School Counselor, 41*(2), 22–27.

Azar, B. (2010). Virtual violence. *Monitor on Psychology. 41*(11), 36–39.

Bailey, K. A. (2001). Legal implications of profiling students for violence. *Psychology in the Schools, 38,* 141–155.

Bailey, K. A., West, R., & Anderson, C. A. (2011). The association between chronic exposure to video game violence and affective picture processing: An ERP study. *Cognitive, Affective, & Behavioral Neuroscience, 11*(2), 259–276.

Batsche, G. M., & Knoff, H. M. (1994). Bullies and their victims: Understanding a pervasive problem in the schools. *School Psychology Review, 23*(2), 165–174.

Bauman, S. (2011). *Cyberbullying: What counselors need to know.* Alexandria, VA: American Counseling Association.

Beane, A. L. (1999). *Bully-free classroom.* Minneapolis, MN: Free Spirit Press.

Bemak, F., & Keys, S. (2000). *Violent and aggressive youth: Intervention and prevention strategies for changing times.* Thousand Oaks, CA: Sage.

Berman, A. L., & Jobes, D. A. (1991). *Adolescent suicide: Assessment and intervention.* Washington, DC: American Psychological Association.

Berman, A. L., & Jobes, D. A. (1994). Treatment of the suicidal adolescent [Special Issue: Suicide assessment and intervention]. *Death Studies, 18*, 375–389.

Berman, A. L., Jobes, D. A., & Silverman, M. M. (Eds.). (2006). *Adolescent suicide: Assessment and intervention* (2nd ed.). Washington, DC: American Psychological Association.

Blauvelt, P. D. (1998). *Blauvelt . . . on making our schools safe* (2nd rev. ed.). College Park, MD: National Alliance for Safe Schools.

Brammer, L. M., Abrego, P., & Shostrom, E. (1993). *Therapeutic counseling and psychotherapy* (6th ed.). Upper Saddle River, NJ: Prentice Hall.

Brock, S. E., Sandoval, J., & Hart, S. (2006). Suicidal ideation and behaviors. In G. Bear & K. Minke (Eds.), *Children's needs III: Development, prevention and intervention* (pp. 225–238). Washington, DC: National Association of School Psychologists.

Brock, S. E., Sandoval, J., & Lewis, S. (1996). *Preparing for crisis in the schools.* Brandon, VT: Clinical Psychology.

Brown, E. J., & Bobrow, A. L. (2004). School entry after a community-wide trauma: Challenges and lessons learned from September 11, 2001. *Clinical Child and Family Psychology Review, 7*(4), 211–221.

Brummert-Lennings, H., & Warburton, W. A. (2011). The effect of auditory versus visual violent media exposure on aggressive behavior. *Journal of Experimental Social Psychology, 47*(4), 794–799.

Bucolo, D. (2011). Violent video game exposure and physical aggression in adolescence: Test of the general aggression model. *Dissertation Abstracts International: Section B The Sciences and Engineering,* 5180.

Burnham, B. (2011). Schoolwide bully prevention. *ASCA School Counselor, 48*(6), 13 –17.

Burnham, J., Wright, V., & Houser, R. (2010, July). *Reduce cyberbullying with virtual world scenarios.* American School Counselor Conference, Boston.

Burrow-Sanchez, J. J., Call, M. E., Zheng, R., & Drew, C. (2011). How school counselors can prevent online victimization. *Journal of Counseling & Development, 89*(1), 3–10.

Busch, K. G., Zagar, R., Hughes, J. R., Arbit, J., & Bussell, R. E. (1990). Adolescents who kill. *Journal of Clinical Psychology, 46*(4), 472–485.

Callahan, C. J. (2001). Protecting and counseling gay and lesbian students. *Journal of Humanistic Counseling, Education and Development 40*(1), 5–10.

Capuzzi, D. (2002). Legal and ethical challenges in counseling suicidal students. *Professional School Counselor, 6*(1), 36–45.

Carney, J. (2008). Perceptions of bullying and associated trauma in adolescence. *Professional School Counseling 11*(3), 179–187.

Carney, J., Hazler, R., Higgins, J., & Danser, S. (1999, April). *Peer-on-peer violence.* Poster session at the American Counseling Association World Conference, San Diego, CA.

Cassinerio, C., & Lane-Garon, P. (2006). Changing school climate one mediator at a time: Year-one analysis of a school-based mediation program. *Conflict Resolution Quarterly, 23*(4), 447–460.

Centers for Disease Control. (2002). *Adolescent health survey.* Atlanta, GA: U.S. Department of Health and Human Services, Public Health Service.

Chamberlin, J. (2006). Cyberbullies increasingly target peers online. *Monitor on Psychology, 37*(9), 17.

Charach, A., Pepler, D., & Zeigler, S. (1995). Bullying at school—A Canadian perspective: A survey of problems and suggestions for intervention. *Education Canada, 35*(1), 12–18.

Cohen, P. A., Kulik, J. A., & Kulik, C. C. (1982). Educational outcomes of tutoring. A meta-analysis of findings. *American Educational Research Journal, 19,* 237–248.

Collier, C. (1999). *School violence: Facts, causes and recommendations.* Poster session at the American Counseling Association World Conference, San Diego, CA.

Coloroso, B. (2003). *The bully, the bullied, and the bystander.* New York: HarperCollins.

Conoley, J. C., & Goldstein, A. P. (Eds.). (2004). *School violence intervention: A practical handbook* (2nd ed.). New York: Guilford Press.

Corder, B. F., Ball, B. C., Haizlip, T. M., Rollins, R., & Beaumont, R. (1976). Adolescent paracide: A comparison with other adolescent murder. *American Journal of Psychiatry, 133*(8), 957–961.

Cormier, S., & Cormier, B. (1998). *Interviewing strategies for helpers: Fundamental skills and cognitive behavioral interventions* (4th ed.). Pacific Grove, CA: Brooks/Cole.

Counce, C., & Sommer, L. (2003, June). *Gentle guidance eases grief.* Paper presented at the American School Counselor Conference, St. Louis, MO.

Crews, W. (1998). *Memphis Police Department procedures manual for school police officers.* Memphis, TN.

Crothers, L. M., & Levinson, E. M. (2004). Assessment of bullying. *Journal of Counseling and Development, 82*(4), 496–503.

Cunningham, N. J., & Davis, B. (1999, April). *A study of middle school bullying using a framework for violence prevention.* Poster session at the American Counseling Association World Conference, San Diego, CA.

Curran, D. K. (1987). *Adolescent suicidal behavior.* New York: Hemisphere.

Cypress, S., & Green, R. (2002). Preventing fatal shooting attacks in schools. *Global Visions for Counseling Professionals, 6*(1), 43–49.

Davis, D. L. (2004). *Your angry child: A guide for parents.* Binghamton, NY: Haworth Press.

Davis, H. T., & Salasin, S. E. (1975). The utilization of evaluation. In E. L. Struening & M. Guttentag (Eds.), *Handbook of evaluation research* (Vol. 1, pp. 621–666). Beverly Hills, CA: Sage.

Davis, S., & Davis, L. (2003). *Schools where everyone belongs: Practical strategies for reducing bullying.* Wayne, ME: Stop Bullying Now.

Day-Vines, N., Day-Hairston, B. O., Carruthers, W. L., Wall, J. A., & Lupton-Smith, H. (1996). Conflict resolution: The value of diversity in the recruitment, selection, and training of peer mediators. *School Counselor, 43,* 393–410.

Dogutas, C. (2008). Reactive vs. proactive strategies the effectiveness of school resource officers to prevent violence in schools. *Section A: Humanities and Social Sciences 68*(10-A), 4470.

Dorn, M., & Dorn, C. (2005). *Innocent targets when terrorism comes to school.* Macon, GA: Safe Haven International.

Duncan, J. W., & Duncan, G. M. (1971). Murder in the family: A study of some homicidal adolescents. *American Journal of Psychiatry, 127*(11), 74–78.

DuRant, R. H., Treiber, F., Getts, A., McCloud, K., Linder, C. W., & Woods, E. R. (1996). Comparison of two violence prevention curricula for middle school adolescents. *Journal of Adolescent Health, 19,* 111–117.

Dwyer, K., Osher, D., & Warger, C. (1998). *Early warning, timely response: A guide to safe schools.* Washington, DC: U.S. Department of Education.

Dykeman, C. (1999, June). *Preventing school-based violence: Practical steps for school counselors.* Paper presented at the American School Counselor Association Convention, Phoenix, AZ.

Eck, J. E., & Spelman, W. (1987). *Problem-solving: Problem oriented policing in Newport News.* Washington, DC: Police Executive Research Forum.

Eisel v. Board of Education of Montgomery County, 597A. 2d 447 (Maryland, 1991).

Embry, D. L., Flannery, D. J., Vazsonyi, A. T., Powell, K. B., & Atha, H. (1996). Peacebuilders: A theoretically driven, school-based model for early violence prevention. *American Journal of Preventive Medicine, 12*(5), 91–100.

Englehardt, C. R., Bartholow, B. D., Kerr, G., & Bushman, B. (2011). This is your brain on violent video games: Neural desensitization to violence predicts increased aggression following violent video game exposure. *Journal of Experimental Social Psychology, 31*(4), 35–47.

Espelage, D., Bosworth, K., & Simon, T. R. (2000). Examining the social context of bullying behaviors in early adolescence. *Journal of Counseling & Development, 78*(3), 326–333.

Espelage, D., & Swearer, S. (2003). Research on school bullying and victimization: What have we learned and where do we go from here? *School Psychology Review, 32*(3), 365–384.

Fatum, W. R., & Hoyle, J. C. (1996). Is it violence? School violence from the student perspective: Trends and interventions. *School Counselor, 44*(1), 28–34.

Fauteux, K. (2010). De-escalating angry and violent clients. *American Journal of Psychotherapy, 64*(2), 195–213.

Fein, A. H., Carlisle, C. S., & Issacson, N. S. (2008). School shootings and counselor leadership: Four lessons from the field. *Professional School Counseling, 11*(4), 246–252.

Fein, R. A., Vossekuil, B., Pollack, W. S., Borum, M., Modzeleski, W., & Reddy, M. (2002). *Threat assessment in schools: A guide to managing threatening situations and creating safe school climates.* Washington, DC: U.S. Secret Service and U.S. Department of Education.

Feindler, E. L., & Scalley, M. (1998). Adolescent anger management for violence reduction. In K. C. Stoiber & T. R. Kratochwill (Eds.), *Handbook of group intervention for children and families* (pp. 100–119). Boston: Allyn & Bacon.

Feindler, E. L., & Weisner, S. (2006). Youth anger management treatments for school violence prevention. In S. R. Jimerson & M. Furlong (Eds.), *Handbook of school violence and school safety: From research to practice* (pp. 353–363). Mahwah, NJ: Erlbaum.

Ferguson, C. J. (2011). Video games and youth violence: A prospective analysis in adolescents. *Journal of Youth and Adolescence 40*(4), 377–391.

Ferguson, C. J., Colwell, J., Mlacic, B., Milas, G., & Miklousic, I. (2011). Personality and media influences on violence and depression in a cross-national sample of young adults: Data from Mexican-Americans, English and Croatians. *Computers in Human Behavior, 27*(3), 1195–1200.

Ferguson, C. J., & Kilburn, J. (2009). The public health risks of media violence: A meta-analytic review. *Journal of Pediatrics, 154*(5), 759–763.

Ferguson, C. J., & Kilburn, J (2010). Much ado about nothing: The misestimation and overinterpretation of violent video game effects in Eastern and Western nations: Comment on Anderson et al., 2010. *Psychological Bulletin, 136*(2), 174–178.

Finn, P. (2006). School resource officer programs: Finding the funding, reaping the benefits. *Law Enforcement Bulletin 75*(8), 1–7.

Finn, P., Townsend, M., Shively, M., & Rich, T. (2005). *A guide to developing, maintaining, and succeeding with your school resource officer program: Practices from the field for law enforcement and school administration.* A report submitted to the U.S. Department of Justice Office of Community Oriented Policing Services. Cambridge MA: Abt Associates.

Fujimura, L. E., Weis, D. M., & Cochran, J. R. (1985). Suicide: Dynamics and implication for counseling. *Journal of Counseling and Development, 63,* 612–615.

Fusick, L., & Bordeau, W. (2004). Counseling at-risk Afro-American youth: An examination of contemporary issues and effective school-based strategies. *Professional School Counseling, 8*(2), 102–115.

Galatzen-Levy, A. (1993). Adolescent violence and the adolescent self. *Adolescent Psychiatry, 19,* 418–441.

Gallager, M. (2005, March 18). *Letter to the president of Marietta College.* Cleveland, OH: United States Department of Education Office of Civil Rights.

The gang threat. (2009, February 6). *Federal Bureau of Investigation.* Available at www.fbi.gov/news/stories/2009/february/ngta_020609

Garcia v. City of New York, 646 N.Y.S. 2d 508 (App. Div., 1996).

Garfield, P. (1984). *Your child's dreams.* New York: Ballantine Books.

Gerler, E. R., Jr. (Ed.). (2004). *Handbook of school violence.* New York: Haworth Press.

Giduck, J. (2005). *Terror at Beslan.* Golden, CO: Archangel Group.

Glasser, W. (1965). *Reality therapy.* New York: Harper & Row.

Glasser, W. (1969). *Schools without failure.* New York: Harper & Row.

Glasser, W. (2000, May 28). Invited address at the Evolution of Psychotherapy Conference, Anaheim, CA. Retrieved August 14, 2002, from www.wglasser.com

Goldstein, A. P. (1991). *Delinquent gangs: A psychological perspective.* Champaign, IL: Research Press.

Goldstein, A. P., & Kodluboy, D. W. (1998). *Gangs in schools: Signs, symbols, and solutions.* Champaign, IL: Research Press.

Gottfredson, D. C., Gottfredson, G. D., & Skroban, S. (1998). Can prevention work where it is needed most? *Evaluation Review, 22*(3), 315–340.

Gould, M., & Shaffer, D. (1986). The impact of suicide in television movies: Evidence of imitation. *New England Journal of Medicine, 315,* 690–693.

Gray, R. E. (1988). The role of the school counselor with bereaved teenagers: With and without peer support groups. *School Counselor, 35,* 185–192.

Greene, D. B. (1994). Childhood suicide and myths surrounding it. *Social Work, 39,* 230–233.

Grossman, D. (1995). *On killing: The psychological cost of learning to kill in war and society.* Boston: Little, Brown.

Guida, A. (2001). Depression . . . or just the blues? *ASCA School Counselor, 39*(2), 10–13.

Gumaer, J. (1984). *Counseling and therapy for children.* New York: Free Press.

Hacker, K., Suglia, S., Fried, L., Rappaport, N., & Cabral, H. (2006). Developmental differences in risk factors for suicide attempts between ninth and eleventh graders. *Suicide and Life-Threatening Behavior, 36*(2), 154–166.

Hammond, L. C., & Gantt, L. (1998). Using art in counseling: Ethical considerations. *Journal of Counseling and Development, 76,* 271–275.

Hardwick, P. J., & Rowton-Lee, M. A. (1996). Adolescent homicide: Toward assessment of risk. *Journal of Adolescence, 19*(3), 263–276.

Hausman, A., Pierce, G., & Briggs, L. (1996). School-based violence prevention education. *Journal of Adolescent Health, 19*(2), 104–110.

Haynes, R. A., & Henderson, C. L. (2001). *Essential strategies for school security: A practical guide for teachers and school administrators.* Springfield, IL: Charles C Thomas.

Hazler, R. J. (1996). *Breaking the cycle of violence: Interventions for bullying and victimization.* Washington, DC: Accelerated Development.

Heath, M. A., & Sheen, D. (2005). *School-based crisis intervention: Preparing all personnel to assist.* New York: Guilford Press.

Hermann, M. A., & Finn, A. (2002). An ethical and legal perspective on the role of school counselors in preventing violence in schools. *Professional School Counselor, 6*(1), 46–54.

Hermann, M. A., & Remley, T. P., Jr. (2000). Guns, violence, and schools: The results of school violence litigation against educators and students shedding more constitutional rights at the school house gate. *Loyola Law Review, 46,* 389–439.

Holladay, J. (2010, Fall). Cyberbullying. *Teaching Tolerance,* 43–46.

Hoover, J. H., & Hazler, R. J. (1991). Bullies and victims. *Elementary School Guidance & Counseling, 25,* 212–219.

Horne, A. M., Bartolomucci, C. L., & Newman-Carson, D. (2003). *Bully busters: A teacher's manual for helping bullies, victims, and bystanders.* Champaign, IL: Research Press.

Hubbard, J. A., Dodge, K. A., Cillessen, A. H. N., Coie, J. D., & Schwartz, D. (2001). The dyadic nature of social information processing in boys' reactive and proactive aggression. *Journal of Personality and Social Psychology, 80,* 268–280.

Hummer, G. A., Wang, Y., Kronenberger, W., Mosier, K., Kalnin, A., Dunn, D., et al. (2010). Short-term violent video game play by adolescents alters prefrontal activity during cognitive inhibition. *Media Psychology, 13*(2), 136–154.

Humphrey, N., & Brooks, A. (2006). An evaluation of a short cognitive-behavioural anger management intervention for pupils at risk of exclusion. *Emotional & Behavioural Difficulties, 11*(1), 5–23.

Hunt, R. D., Osten, C., & Teague, S. (1991). Youth suicide: Teachers should know. . . *Tennessee Teacher, 91,* 16–21, 29.

Italiano, F. (2001). Listening and learning at North Arlington High School. *Police Chief, 68*(9), 53–55.

Jackson, K., & Harding, M. (2010, July). *Advocating for LGBTQ students.* American School Counselor Conference, Boston.

James, B. (1994). School violence and the law: The search for suitable tools. *School Psychology Review, 23*(2), 190–203.

James, B. (1997). FERPA and school violence: The silence that kills. In A. P. Goldstein & J. C. Conoley (Eds.), *School violence prevention: A practical handbook* (pp. 460–489). New York: Guilford Press.

James, R., & Crawford, R. (2002). The estranged, violent, juvenile offender: Profiling, screening, intervention, and legal considerations. *Global Visions for Counseling Professionals, 6*(1), 1–14.

James, R., & Dorner, K. (1999, June). *Profiling, screening, and counseling the estranged juvenile violent offender.* Paper presented at the American School Counselor Association Convention, Phoenix, AZ.

James, R., Logan, J., & Davis, S. (2011). Including school resource officers in school-based crisis intervention: Strengthening student support. *School Psychology International, 32*(2), 210–224.

Jennings, K. (2011). Federal action to stop bullying. *ASCA School Counselor, 48*(6), 14–15.

Jimerson, S. R., & Furlong, M. J. (Eds.). (2006). *Handbook of school violence and school safety: From research to practice.* Mahwah, NJ: Erlbaum.

Johnson, I. M. (1999). School violence: The effectiveness of a school resource officer program in a southern city. *Journal of Criminal Justice, 27*(2), 173–192.

Johnson, K. (2000). *School crisis management: A hands-on guide to training crisis response teams* (2nd ed.). Alameda, CA: Hunter House.

Jones Farrelly, M., & Robles-Fernandez, R. (2011, April). *Counseling skills and issues in gay straight alliance advisement and LGBTQ youth.* Paper presented at the American Counseling Association Conference, New Orleans.

Kalafat, J. (1990). Adolescent suicide and the implications for school response programs. *School Counselor, 37,* 359–369.

Kalafat, J. (2003). School approaches to youth suicide prevention. *American Behavioral Scientist, 46*(9), 1211–1223.

Kandt, V. E. (1994). Adolescent bereavement: Turning a fragile time into acceptance and peace. *School Counselor, 41,* 203–211.

Kaufman, P., Chen, X., & Choy, S. P. (2002). Indicators of school crime and safety: 2001 (NCES 2002.113/NCJ-190075). Washington, DC: U.S. Departments of Justice and Education.

Kerr, M. M. (2009). *School crisis prevention and intervention.* Upper Saddle River, NJ: Pearson.

King, C. A., Kramer, A., Preuss, L., Kerr, D., Weisse, L., & Venkataraman, S. (2006). Youth-nominated support team for suicidal adolescents (Version 1): A randomized controlled test. *Journal of Consulting and Clinical Psychology, 74*(1), 199–206.

King, K. A. (2000). Preventing adolescent suicide: Do high school counselors know the risk factors? *Professional School Counseling, 3,* 255–263.

Kirk, W. (1993). *Adolescent suicide: A school-based approach to assessment and intervention.* Champaign, IL: Research Press.

Komar, A. A. (1994). Adolescent school crises: Structures, issues, and techniques for postventions. *International Journal of Adolescence and Youth, 5*(1/2), 35–46.

Kornblum, R. (2002). *Disarming the playground: Violence prevention through movement and prosocial skills.* Oklahoma City: Woods and Barnes.

Kraft, S. G. (2003). Sudden unexpected deaths create unique challenges when counseling children. *Counseling Today, 46*(1), 12.

Krahe, B., & Moller, I. (2011). Links between self-reported media violence exposure and teacher ratings of aggression and prosocial behavior among German adolescents. *Journal of Adolescence, 34*(2), 279–287.

Krahe, B., Moller, I., Huesmann, L., Kirwil, L., Felber, J., & Berger, A. (2011). Desensitization to media violence: Links with habitual media violence exposure, aggressive cognitions, and aggressive behavior. *Journal of Personality and Social Psychology, 100*(4), 630–646.

Langman, P. (2009). *Why kids kill: Inside the minds of school shooters.* New York: Palgrave MacMillan.

Larson, J. (1994). Violence prevention in the schools: A review of selected programs and procedures. *School Psychology Review, 23*(2), 151–164.

Lavine v. Blaine School District, 257 F.3d 981 (9th Cir. 2001).

Lazarus, A. (1977). *In the mind's eye: The powers of imagery for personal enrichment.* New York: Guilford Press.

Lempp, R. C. (1990). To the diagnostic of "incomprehensible" offenses of adolescents and juveniles. *Acta Paedopsychiatrica, 53,* 173–175.

Leo, J. (2010, Fall). Let the hot air out of bullies! *Teaching Tolerance, 12.*

Levis, D. O. (1992). From abuse to violence: Psychophysiological consequences of maltreatment. *Journal of American Academy Child and Adolescent Psychiatry, 142*(10), 1161–1166.

Lipsey, M. W. (1992). Juvenile delinquency treatment: A meta-analytic inquiry into the variability of effects. In T. D. Cook (Ed.), *Meta-analysis for explanation* (pp. 67–89). Beverly Hills, CA: Sage.

Loeber, R. (1990). Development and risk factors of juvenile antisocial behavior and delinquency. *Clinical Psychology Review, 10,* 1–41.

Loeber, R., Farrington, D. P., Rumsey, C. A., & Allen-Hagen, B. (1998, May). Serious and violent juvenile offenders. *Juvenile Justice Bulletin.* Washington, DC: U.S. Department of Justice.

Louvre, C. (2002). Helping students grieve a friend's death. *School Counselor, 39*(5), 10–11.

Louvre, C. (2008). Weaving the community tapestry. *School Counselor, 45*(5), 28–31.

Lovell v. Poway Unified School District, 90 F.3d. 367 (9th Cir. 1996).

Lubell, K. M., & Vetter, J. B. (2006). Suicide and youth-violence prevention: The promise of an integrated approach. *Aggression and Violent Behavior, 11*(2), 167–175.

Luna, J. T., & Hoffman, R. M. (1999, June). *The counselor as catalyst: Forming partnerships for school violence reduction.* Paper presented at the American School Counselor Convention, Phoenix, AZ.

Lupton-Smith, H., Carruthers, W. L., Flythe, R., Goette, E., & Modest, K. H. (1996). Conflict resolution as peer mediation: Programs for elementary, middle, and high school students. *School Counselor, 43,* 375–391.

Malley, P. B., Kush, F., & Bogo, R. J. (1994). School-based adolescent suicide prevention and intervention programs. *School Counselor, 42*(2), 1301–1336.

Maples, M. F., Packman, J., Abney, P., Daughtery, R., Casey, J., & Pirtle, L. (2005). Suicide by teenagers in middle school: A postvention team approach. *Journal of Counseling & Development, 83*(4), 397–405.

Marohn, R., Locke, E., Rosenthal, R., & Curtis, G. (1982). Juvenile delinquents and violent deaths. *Adolescent Psychiatry, 10,* 147–170.

Mazza, J., & Reynolds, W. M. (1998). A longitudinal investigation of depression, hopelessness, social support, and major and minor life events and their relation to suicidal ideation in adolescents. *Journal of Suicide and Life-Threatening Behavior, 28,* 358–374.

McAdams, C. R., & Schmidt, C. (2007). How to help a bully: Recommendation for counseling the proactive aggressor. *Professional School Counseling, 11*(2), 121–127.

McCollum, S. (2010, Fall). Country outposts. *Teaching Tolerance, 33*–35.

Melton, B. (2001). Seeing the unseen. *ASCA School Counselor, 39,* 21–25.

Miller, J., Martin, I., & Schamess, G. (2003). *School violence and children in crisis: Community and school interventions for social workers and counselors.* Denver, CO: Love Publishing.

Missouri School Counselor Association. (2002). *Crisis manual.* Hamilton, MO: Author.

Mitchell, J. T., & Everly, G. S., Jr. (1995). *Advanced critical incidents stress debriefing.* Ellicott City, MD: International Critical Incidents Stress Foundation.

Montano, R., & Dowdall-Thomae, C. (2003, June). *Are you ready for the crisis?* Paper presented at the American School Counselor Association Convention, St. Louis, MO.

Mulvey, E. P., & Cauffman, E. (2001). The inherent limits of predicting school violence. *American Psychologist, 56*(10), 797–802.

Munsey, C. (2011). APA is front and center at White House bullying conference. *Monitor on Psychology, 42*(5), 18–19.

Muro, J. J., & Kottman, T. (1995). *Guidance and counseling in the elementary and middle schools.* Dubuque, IA: William C. Brown Communications.

Myer, R. A., James, R. K., & Moulton, P. (2011). *This is not a fire drill: Crisis intervention and prevention on college campuses.* Hoboken, NJ: Wiley.

Myer, R. A., Rice, D., Moulton, P., Cogdal, P., Allen, S., & James, R. (2007). *Triage assessment system for students in learning environments.* Pittsburgh, PA: Crisis Intervention and Prevention Solutions.

Myers, W. C., & Mutch, P. J. (1992). Language disorders in disruptive behavior-disordered homicidal youth. *Journal of Forensic Sciences, 37*(3), 919–992.

Nadel, B. (2004). *Security: Handbook for architectural planning and design.* New York: McGraw-Hill.

National Association of School Resource Officers. (2011). *NASRO Training.* Available at www.nasro.org/mc/page .do?sitePageId=114191&orgId=naasrp

National Center for Education Statistics. (2004). *Indicators of School Crime and Safety: 2004.* Available at http://nces .ed.gov/pubsearch/pubsinfo.asp?pubid=2005002

National Center for Education Statistics. (2005a). *Indicators of School Crime and Safety: 2005.* Available at http://nces .ed.gov/pubs2006/2006001.pdf

National Center for Education Statistics (2005b). *Public Elementary and Secondary Students, Staff, Schools, and School Districts: School Year 2002–03.* Available at http:// nces.ed.gov/pubsearch/pubsinfo.asp?pubid=2005314

National Center for Education Statistics. (2010). *Indicators of School Crime and Safety: 2010.* Available at http://nces.ed .gov/programs/crimeindicators/crimeindicators2010/ key.asp

National Center for Health Statistics. (1992). Advance report of final mortality statistics. *NCHS Monthly Vital Statistics Report, 45*(Suppl. 3). Hyattsville, MD: Author.

National Incident Management System. (2011*). About the National Incident Management System.* Available at www.fema.gov/emergency/nims/AboutNIMS.shtm

National Institute of Justice. (1998). *Crime in the schools: A problem-solving approach.* (Summary of a Presentation by Dennis Kenney, Police Executive Research Forum), Washington, DC: Author.

National Organization for Victim Assistance. (1997). *Community crisis response team training manual* (2nd ed.). Washington, DC: Author.

National School Safety Center. (1998). *Checklist of characteristics of youth who have caused school-associated violent deaths.* Westlake Village, CA: Author.

Nelson, E. R., & Slaikeu, K. A. (1990). Crisis intervention in schools. In K. A. Slaikeu (Ed.), *Crisis intervention: A handbook for research and practice* (2nd ed., pp. 329–347). Boston: Allyn & Bacon.

Nelson, R. E., & Galas, J. (1994). *The power to prevent suicide: A guide to helping teens.* Minneapolis, MN: Free Spirit.

Nelson, W. M., Finch, A., & Ghee, A. (2006). Anger management with children and adolescents: Cognitive-behavior therapy. In P. C. Kendall (Ed.), *Child and adolescent therapy: Cognitive-behavioral procedures* (3rd ed., pp. 114–165). New York: Guilford Press.

Newgass, S., & Schonfeld, D. J. (2005). School crisis intervention, crisis prevention, and crisis response. In A. R. Roberts (Ed.), *Crisis intervention handbook* (pp. 499–518). New York: Oxford University Press.

Newman, D. A., Horne, A. M., & Bartolomucci, C. L. (2000). *Bully busters: A teacher's manual for helping bullies, victims, and bystanders, grades 6–8.* Champaign, IL: Research Press.

Noonan, J. H., & Vavra, M. C. (2007). *Crime in schools and colleges: A study of offenders and arrestees reported via national incident-based reporting system data.* Available at http://www.fbi.gov/about-us/cjis/ucr/nibrs/crime-in-schools-and-colleges-pdf

Noonan, P. (2007, April 21–22). Cold standard. *Wall Street Journal,* p. 16.

O'Reilly, J. T., Hagan, P., & de la Cruz, P. (2001). *Environmental and workplace safety: A guide for university, hospital, and school management.* New York: Wiley.

O'Toole, M. E. (2003). *The school shooter: A threat assessment perspective.* Quantico, VA: Federal Bureau of Investigation.

Paterson, J. (2010). Bullies with byte. *Counseling Today, 53*(12), 44–47.

Paterson, J. (2011). Young and depressed. *Counseling Today, 54*(1), 32–35.

Patros, P. G., & Shamoo, T. K. (1989). *Depression and suicide in children and adolescents: Prevention, intervention, and postvention.* Boston: Allyn & Bacon.

Petersen, J. V. (2008). The role of the Chandler Police Department resource officers as law-related educational leaders. *Dissertation Abstracts International, 69*(6-A), 2078.

Petersen, S. (1999, April). *School crisis planning.* Workshop at the American Counseling Association World Conference, San Diego, CA.

Petersen, S., & Straub, R. L. (1992). *School crisis survival guide: Management techniques and materials for counselosr and administrators.* West Nyack, NY: Center for Applied Research in Education.

Pfeffer, C. R. (2006). Suicide and suicidality. In M. K. Dulcan & J. M. Wiener (Eds.), *Essentials of child and adolescent psychiatry* (pp. 621–632). Washington, DC: American Psychiatric Publishing.

Pitcher, G. D., & Poland, S. (1992). *Crisis intervention in the schools.* New York: Guilford Press.

Pledge, D. S. (2003). *When something feels wrong: A survival guide about abuse.* Minneapolis, MN: Free Spirit.

Poijula, S., Dyregrov, A., Wahleberg, K., & Jokelainen, J. (2001). Reactions to adolescent suicide and crisis intervention in three secondary schools. *International Journal of Emergency Mental Health, 3*(2), 97–106.

Poland, S. (1989). *Suicide intervention in the schools.* New York: Guilford Press.

Poland, S. (1994). The role of school crisis intervention team to prevent and reduce school violence and trauma. *School Psychology Review, 239*(2), 175–189.

Poland, S. (1999). *School crisis & youth violence: Lessons learned.* Houston, TX: Cypress-Fairbanks Independent School District, Department of Psychological Services.

Poland, S. (2004). School crisis teams. In J. Conoley & A. P. Goldstein (Eds.), *School violence intervention: A practical handbook* (2nd ed., pp. 131–163). New York: Guilford Press.

Poland, S., & McCormick, J. S. (1999). *Coping with crisis: Lessons learned.* Longmont, CO: Sopris West.

Price, M. (2007). TV violence harms children, APA member testifies to Congress. *Monitor on Psychology, 38*(8), 16.

Price, M. (2010). Suicide among preadolescents. *Monitor on Psychology, 41*(9), 52–53.

Pynoos, R. S., & Eth, S. (1986). Witness to violence: The child interview. *Journal of the American Academy of Child Psychiatry, 25*(3), 306–319.

Rainone, G. A., Schmeidler, J., Frank, B., & Smith, R. (2006). Violent behavior, substance use, and other delinquent behaviors among middle and high school students. *Youth Violence and Juvenile Justice, 4*(3), 247–265.

Ratts, M., Ayers, L., & Bright, M. (2009). Sticks and stones. *ASCA School Counselor, 47*(1), 20–25.

Reddy, M., Borum, R., Berglund, J., Vossekuil, B., Fen, R., & Modzeleski, W. (2001). Evaluating risk for targeted violence in schools: Comparing risk assessment, threat assessment, and other approaches. *Psychology in the Schools, 38,* 157–173.

Reis, C., & Cornell, D. (2008). An evaluation of suicide gatekeeper training for school counselors and teachers. *Professional School Counseling, 11*(6), 386–394.

Remboldt, C. (1994). *Violence in schools: The enabling factor.* Minneapolis, MN: Johnson Institute.

Rosenberg, S. (2004). Inoculation effect in prevention of increased verbal aggression in schools. *Psychological Reports, 95*(2), 1219–1226.

Roth, L. (2000, April). *Preventing school violence through community organization.* Proceedings of the Twenty-Fourth Annual Convening of Crisis Intervention Personnel, Chicago.

Ruane, M. E. (2007, April 22). Cho's bizarre behavior alarmed suite mate. *Memphis Commercial Appeal,* pp. 1A, 5A.

Rubin, R. (1999, June). *Crisis intervention.* Paper presented at the American School Counselor Association Convention, Phoenix, AZ.

Sabella, R. A. (2010, July). *Cyberbullying.* Paper presented at the American School Counselor Conference, Boston.

Sage, R., & Dietz, W. (1994). Television viewing and violence in children: The pediatrician's agent for change. *Paediatrics, 94*(4), 600–607.

Samide, L. L., & Stockton, R. (2002). Letting go of grief: Bereavement groups for children in the school setting. *Journal of Specialists in Group Work, 27*(2), 192–204.

Sandhu, D. S. (2000, June). *Psycho-cultural profiles of violent students: Implications for counseling and therapy.* Paper presented at the American School Counselor Association Convention, Cherry Hill, NJ.

Saufler, C. (2010, July). *Bringing the brain to bullying prevention.* Paper presented at the American School Counselor Conference, Boston.

Schaefer-Schiumo, K., & Ginsberg, A. (2003). The effectiveness of the warning signs program in high school youth about violence prevention: A study with urban high school students. *Professional School Counseling, 7*(1), 1–8.

School Violence Resource Center. (2003). *Weapons and schools: II. Fact sheet.* Fayetteville: University of Arkansas System.

Schrumpf, F., Crawford, D. K., & Bodine, R. J. (1997). *Peer mediation: Conflict resolution in schools: Student manual* (Rev. ed.). Champaign, IL: Research Press.

Scruggs, T. E., Mastropieri, M. A., & Richter, L. (1985). Peer tutoring with behaviorally disordered students: Social and academic benefits. *Behavioral Disorders, 10,* 283–294.

Sestir, M. A., & Bartholow, B. (2010). Violent and nonviolent video games produce opposing effects on aggressive and prosocial outcomes. *Journal of Experimental Social Psychology, 46*(6), 934–942.

Sexton-Radek, K. (Ed.). (2004). *Violence in schools: Issues, consequences, and expressions.* Westport, CT: Praeger.

Shaffer, D. (1988). The epidemiology of teen suicide: An examination of risk factors. *Journal of Clinical Psychiatry, 49,* 36–41.

Shaffer, D., Garland, A., Gould, M., Fisher, P., & Tratuman, P. (1988). Preventing teen suicide: A critical review. *Journal of the American Academy of Child and Adolescent Psychiatry, 27,* 675–687.

Shaffer, D., Vieland, V., & Garland, A. (1990). Adolescent suicide attempters: Response to suicide prevention programs. *Journal of the American Medical Association, 264,* 3151–3155.

Sharp, S. R., & McCallum, R. (2005). A rational emotive behavior approach to improve anger management and reduce office referrals in middle school children: A formative investigation and evaluation. *Journal of Applied School Psychology, 21*(1), 39–66.

Sherman, L. W., Gottfredson, D., MacKenzie, D., Eck, J., Reuter, P., & Bushway, S. (1997). *Preventing crime: What works, what doesn't, what's promising* (Report to the United States Congress). Baltimore: University of Maryland, Department of Criminology and Criminal Justice, Office of Justice Program.

Shute, N. (2007, April 30). What went wrong? *U.S. News and World Report,* pp. 42–46.

Simmons, J. (2000, October). FBI release study aimed at identifying dangerous students. *Counseling Today, 43*(4), 1, 22.

Slaikeu, K. A. (1990). *Crisis intervention: A handbook for practice and research* (2nd ed.). Boston: Allyn & Bacon.

Sloan, J. H. (1988). Handgun regulations, crime, assaults, and homicide. *New England Journal of Medicine, 319,* 1256–1262.

Smith, D. C., Larson, J., & Nuckles, D. (2006). A critical analysis of school-based anger management programs for youth. In S. R. Jimerson & M. Furlong (Eds.), *Handbook of school violence and school safety: From research to practice* (pp. 365–382). Mahwah, NJ: Erlbaum.

Sommers-Flanagan, J., & Sommers-Flanagan, R. S. (1997). *Tough kids, cool counseling: User-friendly approaches with challenging youth.* Alexandria, VA: American Counseling Association.

Soriano, M., Soriano, F., & Jimenez, E. (1994). School violence among culturally diverse populations: Sociocultural and institutional considerations. *School Psychology Review, 23*(2), 216–235.

Stephens, R. D. (1997). National trends in school violence: Statistics and prevention strategies. In A. P. Goldstein & J. C. Conoley (Eds.), *School violence prevention: A practical handbook* (pp. 72–90). New York: Guilford Press.

Stewart, C., & MacNeil, G. (2005). Crisis intervention with chronic school violence and volatile situations. In A. R. Roberts (Ed.), *Crisis intervention handbook* (3rd ed., pp. 519–540). New York: Oxford University Press.

Sullivan, K. (2011). *The anti-bullying handbook.* Thousand Oaks, CA: Sage.

Suniti Bhat, C., Chang, S. H., & Linscott, J. A. (2010). Bullying as a media literacy issue. *New Horizons in Education, 58*(3), 44–57.

Swihart, J., Silliman, B., & McNeil, J. (1992). Death of a student: Implications for secondary school counselors. *School Counselor, 40,* 55–58.

Tarasoff v. *Board of Regents of the University of California,* 551 P.2d 334 (1976).

Thompson, C. L., & Rudolph, L. B. (1992). *Counseling children.* Pacific Grove, CA: Brooks/Cole.

Thompson, R. A. (2004). *Crisis intervention and crisis management: Strategies that work in schools and communities.* New York: Brunner-Rutledge.

Trotter, S. (2003, June). *Handling a crisis at school.* Paper presented at the American School Counselor Association Conference, St. Louis, MO.

U.S. Office of Juvenile Justice and Delinquency Prevention. (1995). *A comprehensive response to America's youth gang problem.* Washington, DC: Author.

Vancleave, J. A. (2008). School resource officers: What high school teachers consider to be the most important tasks. *Dissertations Abstracts International: Section A. Humanities and Social Sciences, 69*(1-A), 389.

Vitaro, F., & Brendgen, M. (2005). Proactive and reactive aggression: A developmental perspective. In R. E. Tremblay, W. W. Hartup, & J. Archer (Eds.), *Developmental origins of aggression* (pp. 178–201). New York: Guilford Press.

Vitaro, F., Brendgen, M., & Tremblay, R. E. (2002). Reactively and proactively aggressive children: Antecedent and subsequent characteristics. *Journal of Child Psychology and Psychiatry, 43,* 495–505.

Vossekuil, B., Fein, R. A., Reddy, M., Borum, R., & Modzelski, W. (2002). *The final report and findings on the safe school initiative: Implications for the prevention of school attacks in the United States.* Washington, DC: U.S. Secret Service and U.S. Department of Education.

Vossekuil, B., Reddy, M., Fein, R., Borum, R., & Modzeleski, W. (2000). *U.S. Safe School Initiative: An interim report on the prevention of targeted violence in schools.* Washington, DC: U.S. Secret Service, National Threat Assessment Center.

Wachter, C. A. (2007, March). *Crisis in the schools: Crisis, crisis intervention training, and school counselor burnout.* Paper presented at the American Counseling Association Convention, Detroit.

Wagner, B. (1997). Family risk factors for child and adolescent suicidal behavior. *Psychological Bulletin, 121,* 246–298.

Wattendorf, G. E. (2002). School threat decision demonstrates support for early action. *Police Chief, 69*(3), 11–12.

Webb, N. (Ed.). (2007). Play therapy with children in crisis. New York: Guilford Press.

Webb, S. B., & Griffiths, F. (1998–1999). *Young people at risk of suicide: Part A. School facilitators' handbook; Part B. Supplementary resources.* Palmerston North, New Zealand: College of Education, Massey University.

Webber, J., Bass, D., & Yep, R. (Eds.). (2005). *Terrorism, trauma, and tragedies: A counselor's guide to preparing and responding.* Alexandria, VA: American Counseling Association.

Webster, D. W., & Wilson, M. (1994). Gun violence, angry youth and the pediatrician's role in primary prevention. *Paediatrics, 94*(4), 617–622.

Welsh, J. A., & Domitrovich, C. (2006). Safe schools, healthy students initiative in rural Pennsylvania. In S. R. Jimerson & M. Furlong (Eds.), *Handbook of school violence and school safety: From research to practice* (pp. 511–524). Mahwah, NJ: Erlbaum.

Willard, N. (2007). *Cyberbullying and cyberthreats: Responding to the challenge of online social aggression, threats, and distress.* Champaign, IL: Research Press.

Williams, M. B. (2004). How schools respond to traumatic events: Debriefing interventions and beyond. In N. B. Webb (Ed.), *Mass trauma and violence: Helping families and children cope* (pp. 120–141). New York: Guilford Press.

Williams, M. B. (2006). How schools respond to traumatic events: Debriefing interventions and beyond. *Journal of Aggression, Maltreatment & Trauma, 12*(1), 57–81.

Windmeyer, S. (2009). Helping LGBTQ & ally students find the right college fit. *ASCA School Counselor, 47*(1), 24.

Zagar, R., Arbit, J., Sylvies, R., Busch, K., & Hughes, J. (1990). Homicidal adolescent: A replication. *Psychological Reports, 67,* 1235–1242.

Zenere, F. J., & Lazarus, P. J. (1997). The decline of youth suicidal behavior in an urban, multicultural public school system following the introduction of a suicide prevention and intervention program. *Suicide and Life-Threatening Behavior, 27*(4), 387–403.

Zhao, L., & Jiang, G. (2010). Exposure to violent games: A research about aggression in middle school students. *Chinese Journal of Clinical Psychology, 18*(6), 765–768.

Zins, J. E., Travis, L., Brown, M., & Knighton, A. (1994). Schools and the prevention of interpersonal violence: Mobilizing and coordinating community resources. *Special Services in the Schools, 8*(2), 1–19.

PART III

On the Home Front

Crisis in the Human Services Workplace

Part III deals with helping the crisis worker cope with crises that might occur in the human services workplace. The world in which we live and in which crisis workers function is becoming increasingly dangerous and violent for clients as well as for human services professionals. Chapter 14, on violent behavior in institutions, provides information and techniques to help workers better understand and deal with both the volatile environment and the dilemmas of clients who strive to cope within that environment. Hostage taking is another phenomenon of the contemporary human services setting that has become increasingly prevalent. Chapter 15, on hostage negotiation, discusses concepts and strategies that could save the lives of both crisis workers and their clients. Chapter 16 deals with human services worker burnout, vicarious traumatization, and compassion fatigue. These are major crises that directly affect the crisis worker.

CHAPTER 14
Violent Behavior in Institutions

There have not been a lot of statistics published lately on what kinds of violent assaults human services workers experience, and happily overall violent crime in the United States is down in the last 5 years. Of 13,636 murders in the United States in 2009, only 10 occurred in institutions, according to the FBI's 2009 Uniform Crime Report. Good news indeed, except to the 10 people who were murdered and their loved ones and the thousands of others who were assaulted. Thus, to think that violence against caring and sharing human service workers has never existed or doesn't still exist is to be gravely mistaken (Flannery, 2009; Gabe & Elston, 2009; Slovenko, 2006).

From 1996 to 2000 there were 69 homicides in the health services industry in the United States, and none of these people were killed at the post office! However, the vast majority of workplace violence is composed of nonfatal assaults. In 2000, 48 percent of all nonfatal injuries from occupational assaults in the United States occurred in health care and social services (U.S. Department of Labor, Bureau of Labor Statistics, 2001, 2002). For mental health workers in particular, the average number of assaults was 68.2 per 1000 (U.S. Department of Justice, Bureau of Justice Statistics, 2001). These results were chilling enough that the Federal Bureau of Investigation sponsored a workplace symposium on violence in 2002. (To put those statistics in terms that tell you how dangerous the mental health services can be, you would be as likely to be assaulted as if you worked in a convenience/liquor store (68.4/1000). Besides law enforcement and corrections occupations, only bartending is more likely to get you assaulted (91.3/1000) (U.S. Department of Justice, Bureau of Justice Statistics, 1998)! A best estimate is that the chance of human services workers being assaulted on the job during their lifetime is approximately 50 percent (Turns & Blumenreich, 1993, p. 5). Newhill's (2003, pp. 35–54) comprehensive review of violence studies on social workers in the United States found that between 20 and 50 percent of the professionals studied reported that they had been assaulted. Other countries such as the United Kingdom (Brown, Bute, & Ford, 1986; Leadbetter, 1993; Rowett, 1986), Canada (MacDonald & Sirotich, 2001), Israel (Guterman, Jayaratme, & Bargal, 1996), and Australia (Koritsas, Coles, & Boyle, 2010) confirm a high incidence of violence and threatened violence against human service workers.

Perhaps more ominous is the notion of threat. Newell found in her own study that social workers who do not suffer an assault may experience destruction of property or verbal threats. Those threats are not taken lightly given the violent histories of many of the clients with whom they are dealing (Newhill, 2003, pp. 46–47). Constantly wondering whether an emotionally disturbed or mentally ill client will make good on his or her threats every time a human service worker walks out of the office is not the way to have a fulfilling and rewarding work experience.

In summary, the foregoing statistics should tell you one thing: Although you may believe that you are some combination of Jane Addams, Carl Rogers, and Mother Teresa ministering charitably and caringly to the disenfranchised and outcast, your clients may have a different idea (Newhill, 2003, p. 206)! Why is this so?

Precipitating Factors

A variety of hazards now put human services professionals more at risk of being victims of violent behavior than they have been in the past. This problem has become so pervasive that the American Psychological Association formed a task force to report on education and training in dealing with behavioral emergencies (American Psychological Association, 2000). They found in a survey of the literature that between 35 and 50 percent of psychologists in clinical practice had reported being assaulted. The threat has become so compelling that the American Psychological Association (2002) incorporated in their ethical standards a section to specifically address psychologists' freedom to terminate therapy if they feel threatened or endangered.

The social work profession has become very interested in violence because social workers are invariably in the line of fire as frontline workers attempting to deal with some of the most economically, socially, and emotionally disenfranchised individuals in the human service business. Interestingly, the counseling profession has not seemed as concerned, although high school counselors in particular are in the line of fire with one of the most volatile and violence-prone age groups there is. The amount of violence that now occurs in K–12 schools in the United States is approaching epidemic levels.

Substance Abuse.   Probably the most noteworthy trend in the upsurge of violence has been the increasing numbers of substance abuse clients (Blumenreich, 1993b, pp. 23–24; Occupational Safety and Health Administration, 2003; Monahan et al., 2001; Turns & Blumenreich, 1993, p. 7). Intoxication's disinhibiting effect (McNeil, 2009) appears to directly influence violence, particularly in those individuals who are aggressive and impulsive (Chermack, Fuller, & Blow, 2000) and those with diagnosed major mental disorders (RachBeisel, Scott, & Dixon, 1099).

Deinstitutionalization.   Since the "least restrictive environment" movement and subsequent deinstitutionalization of patients in the 1970s, day care centers, halfway houses, and shelters have filled the gap left when the warehousing facilities of state mental institutions were emptied. Lack of facilities for transients, shortage of staff, lack of follow-up care, and inability to monitor medication closely have created a fertile breeding ground for clients to regress to their previous pathological states (Occupational Safety and Health Administration, 2003; Weinger, 2001, p. 4).

Mental Illness.   The role of mental illness in violent behavior has been hotly debated. To say that all mentally ill people will become violent is patently ludicrous. However, there is some clear evidence that a subset of mentally ill people will and do become violent (McNeil, 2009; Newhill, 2003, pp. 96–104). Delusions (schizophrenics), hallucinations (multiple disorders), and violent fantasies (sex offenders, multiple murderers) are all cues to possible violence in the mentally ill. Organic issues such as internal head injuries, brain diseases, and dementia all have the potential for increased violence (McNeil, 2009; Monahan et al., 2001; Tardiff, 2003). The personality disorders are rife with the kinds of mental disorders that may become violent. Many of the personality disorders are marked by anger control issues, impulsivity, and inability to regulate or control emotions (Newhill, 2003, pp. 99–104). Most particularly, those persons diagnosed with antisocial personality disorders and those with explosive personality disorders are prime candidates for acute onset of anger and violence (McNeil, 2009).

Furthermore, because society and the judicial system have become increasingly aware of the role that mental illness plays in crime, a number of people who would formerly have been incarcerated are now remanded to mental health facilities (Occupational Safety and Health Administration, 2003). Also, because of prison overcrowding, potentially violent people are released on early parole. Farmed out to halfway houses that are also understaffed, and assigned to parole officers who have tremendous caseloads, parolees do not always get the follow-up care and supervision they need. Police now routinely use hospitals for criminal holds on acutely disturbed, violent individuals. Thus, human services workers are now being asked to deal with a wider variety of felons than before (Hartel, 1993; Occupational Safety and Health Administration, 2003; Walker & Seifert, 1994).

Gender.   The stereotypical notion that males are more aggressive is becoming dated (Weinger, 2001, p. 7). While young males account for the majority of assaults, women are catching up. In regard to equal opportunity violence, Lam, McNeil, and Binder (2000) found that females were as likely to assault staff on a locked inpatient unit as were their male counterparts. Ryan and her associates (2004) found in their study of assaults on staff by youths that gender did not differentiate between who would and would not assault staff.

Gangs. Gang violence can be found in settings ranging from emergency rooms to juvenile detention facilities. Gang members' extreme violence, either as a rite of passage into the gang or in retaliation for offenses against them, is without fear or remorse regarding any person, time, or place (Kinney, 1995, pp. 168–169; Occupational Safety and Health Administration, 2003).

Required Reporting. The development of child and elder abuse reporting laws and domestic violence laws have made human service workers into something other than Florence Nightingale in the eyes of those who come into conflict with the social services and legal systems. Most of the time field staff such as social workers for human service agencies and school counselors and school psychologists become the objects of offenders' ire (Weinger, 2001, p. 5).

Elderly. The increase in the number of elderly people now institutionalized in nursing homes and hospitals has created a whole new population of potentially violent individuals. Casually dismissed as infirm and incapable of rendering harm to anyone, geriatric patients commit a disproportionate percentage of violent behavior against human services workers. The assumption that elderly clients are passive recipients of care is misguided. Study after study indicates this clientele to be at risk for behaving violently (Astroem et al., 2002; Daugherty et al., 1992; Gates, Fitzwater, & Succop, 2005; Hillman et al., 2005; Mentes & Ferrario, 1989; Ochitill & Kreiger, 1982; Petrie, 1984, p. 107; Petrie, Lawson, & Hollender, 1982; Snyder, Chen, & Vacha-Haase, 2007; Weinstock et al., 2008).

Institutional Culpability

By their very nature, most care providers are readily accessible to clientele and have minimal security checks. Often unrestricted movement throughout a facility may be gained by agitated and distraught family members, gang members, boyfriends and girlfriends, and clients who are frustrated over long waits and seeming lack of service. Care providers are also easy prey to anyone who walks in off the street with intentions other than seeking services and may believe drugs or money is readily available (Occupational Safety and Health Administration, 2003; Turner, 1984, pp. v–vi).

Security training and security devices cost time and money. Administrators trained solely in handling the financial, logistical, and personnel functions of institutions with the responsibility of maintaining adequate patient care are unaware of what it takes to provide an adequately secure environment for their staff (Dyer, Murrell, & Wright, 1984). Physical features of mental health facilities built to deemphasize security and confinement as a reaction to the "snake pit" mental hospitals of old have paradoxically put the human services workers at greater risk (Turns, 1993). Emotionally "cold and uncaring" settings, unclear staff roles, poorly structured activities, downsizing of staff, and unpredictable schedules are all stress elevators for the potentially violent client (Blumenreich, 1993a, pp. 38–39; Occupational Safety and Health Administration, 2003).

Assessment of potential for violent behavior should be mandatory in institutions and clinical facilities that deal with the mentally ill and emotionally disturbed (McNeil, 2009). Instruments are now available that, combined with clinical judgment, do a good job of predicting violent behavior if—and that is a big if—institutions will use them.

Universities and Their Counseling Centers

We have been particularly concerned with safety issues at many university counseling centers we have toured and two we have worked in. In an effort to be open, warm, and accessible, the university counseling center typically has no choke point that controls access to counseling offices. Students are free to roam about the center. Yet many of the offices are separated from the reception area and are extremely isolated. Even if there are visual, sound, and code alarms, the reaction time for help to arrive will be slow, giving a perpetrator time and ease of egress to escape. Career counseling, academic advising, and personal counseling clients in the university counseling center may all be mixed together in a very egalitarian environment, but it is a situation that has security risks. As evidenced by Seung-hui Cho's rampage at Virginia Tech in April 2007, some of the individuals who frequent the university counseling center may not be there just because they are homesick (Grayson & Meilman, 2006; Myer, James, & Moulton, 2011).

Numerous studies indicate that university counseling centers are dealing with more severe psychopathology than they have in the past (Benton et al., 2003; Bishop, 2006; Erdur-Baker et al., 2006; Pledge et al., 1998) and that more students are on psychotropic medication (Schwartz, 2006). More than 1 in 10 students sought counseling center services in 2009, which is the highest percentage ever found in the long-running National Survey of Counseling Center Directors. Further, about 48 percent of the students seen in those counseling centers has severe psychological problems (Munsey, 2010). Those shifts appear to be true not only in the United States but in the United Kingdom as well (Waller et al., 2005). Are those changes due to the general population in the United States becoming more pathological, or is the on-campus population changing because of the Rehabilitation Act of 1973 and the Americans With Disabilities Act of 1990, which made college campuses more receptive and accommodating to people with existing mental illnesses? This question has become so important that the *Journal of College Counseling* devoted its Fall 2005 issue to the topic of severe and persistent mental illness on college campuses (Beamish, 2005).

The implications for safety issues overall in the university as an institution are sobering. One recent study (Kelly & Torres, 2006) found that women students felt a "chilly campus climate" that had nothing to do with the weather and everything to do with their perception of being unsafe on campus. This issue is even more compelling in regard to "chilly" safety considerations in university counseling centers. It is interesting to note that extended searches for any studies analyzing safety issues in university counseling centers turned up no hits.

Rudd's (2004) summary analysis of why college counseling centers are looking more and more like community mental health clinics is sobering. Counseling centers and universities that do not become proactive in tightening their security, notification, and oversight procedures will put their general populations at risk. Rudd contends that if university administrations have not already identified a risk management officer to place in the counseling center, they will soon have to do so.

In 40 years of counseling in some tough public schools, a state mental hospital, and a federal penitentiary, and meeting lots of disgruntled and unhappy customers with Memphis Police Department Crisis Intervention Team officers, we have yet to meet more severely mentally ill and emotionally disturbed individuals who were not incarcerated for their own safety than we have in a university counseling center. The only three colleagues we have known who were killed in the line of duty died from assaults inflicted on them by clients at the college counseling centers where they

worked. Given our history and background, we may clearly have a bias. However, we do not think the murderous assault at Virginia Tech in April 2007 was happenstance. Subjective evidence tells us that many of our colleagues in counseling centers around the country still wear rose-colored glasses when it comes to truly appreciating the potentially dangerous people who find their way to a college counseling center and the lack of security that characterizes those centers. Combining those two variables results in a lethal formula.

Denial

Because of the negative publicity that accrues from violent incidents, institutions are loath to admit that they occur (Lanza, 1985), and it appears that such episodes go largely unreported (California Occupational Safety and Health Administration, 1998, p. 3; Hartel, 1993; Occupational Safety and Health Administration, 2003). Indeed, the reticence of colleges and universities to report campus crime for fear of bad publicity was in large part responsible for the Crime Awareness and Campus Security Act of 1990, known as the Clery Act for Jeanne Clery, a 19-year-old Lehigh University freshman who was raped and murdered in her campus residence hall in 1986. A recent study conducted to determine whether parents were aware of the Clery Act and how to find information on crime statistics found their knowledge of the act to be low (Janosik, 2004). It seems somewhat ironic that the study was carried out at Virginia Tech. One can only wonder if the results of that study would be different today.

Understaffing, overwork, poorly maintained physical environment, poorly educated nonprofessional staff, high staff turnover, absenteeism, on-the-job accidents, poor or incomplete communication between administration and staff, lack of staff training in recognizing and managing escalating hostile and assaultive behavior, and lack of a unifying treatment philosophy allow frustration to build within the staff and disrupt the treatment routine. As the staff transfer their frustration to the clients, the clients in turn become more threatened and start testing the limits of what will be tolerated. When staff attempt to impose behavioral limits under these erratic conditions, the outcome is often violent behavior by clients (Blair, 1991; Jensen & Absher, 1994; Occupational Safety and Health Administration, 2003; Piercy, 1984, pp. 141–142).

Finally, secondary victimization occurs when, after an injury by an assaultive client, there is the underlying belief that "It wasn't handled right by the worker"

(Turns, 1993, p. 131). Thus, not only does the human services worker suffer physical assault and all the psychological ramifications that go with it, but he or she also becomes a scapegoat for an administration unable to handle the increased violence (Newhill, 2003, p. 209).

Staff Culpability

Staff members are also culpable. A prevailing philosophy is that because human services workers are caring, well-intentioned people, recipients of their services will act in reciprocal ways toward them (Newhill, 2003, p. 13; Turner, 1984, p. vii). The ostrichlike assumption that "It can't happen to me, and besides, there are so few violent incidents that I really don't need to be concerned" is fallacious (Dyer, Murrell, & Wright, 1984, p. 1). Madden, Lion, and Penna (1976) interviewed psychiatrists who had been assaulted and found that more than half could have predicted the assault if they had not been in denial and thought themselves immune from the threat.

From the client's viewpoint, becoming violent is invariably seen as a consequence of being provoked by the worker in some way (Rada, 1981; Ryan et al., 2004). Paradoxically, most staff members have little idea what they or the institution do that is provocative. For many clients, treatment may be perceived as coercive, threatening, or frightening. When a client feels little control over treatment conducted by an authoritarian staff, the client may feel the only option is to aggressively act out (Blair, 1991). Furthermore, if the staff treatment philosophy includes limit setting such as use of restraints, seclusion, medication, locked units, and assaults as "part of the territory" (Occupational Safety and Health Administration, 2003), then a self-fulfilling prophecy is likely to develop, with violent acting out as the norm and the only way to get attention. Conversely, a staff's failure to set limits in regard to appropriate behavior in a positive, firm, fair, and empathic manner, as opposed to dictatorially taking away privileges without defining how those might be lost or explaining how they can be regained, increases the potential for violence (Blair & New, 1991). The attitude of staff toward clients also plays a part in who gets assaulted. Staff members who are burned out are more likely to be assaulted than those who are not (Isaksson et al., 2008).

Experience also makes a difference. The great majority of assaults occur to people like you who are reading this sentence—that is, rookies in the field who don't know the lay of the land (Flannery et al., 2011). Guy,

Brown, and Poelstra (1990) found, in a national study of psychologists who had been assaulted, that 46 percent of all assaults involved students or trainees and that the incidence of assaults decreased the more years of experience workers had. So, you might want to personalize the contents of this chapter a little more than usual.

Legal Liability

Although health-care providers may be the victims of assaults, they may also become legally liable for their actions, no matter how well intended those actions may be (Monahan, 1984). Such liability extends to the institutions and directors of those institutions, who may fall under a heading of "vicarious" civil and criminal liability (Dyer, Murrell, & Wright, 1984, p. 23). As paradoxical as it may seem, assaultive clients have held institutions and their employees liable for failure of "duty of care owed" to those selfsame clients (Belak & Busse, 1993, pp. 137–143). Numerous successful lawsuits also have been brought against health-care providers for failure to properly diagnose, treat, and control violent clients or protect third parties from assaultive behavior (Felthous, 1987).

Workplace violence has become so serious that the Centers for Disease Control has declared workplace violence a national health problem (National Institute for Occupational Safety and Health, 1992), and the federal Occupational Safety and Health Administration (OSHA) has come to the conclusion that workplace violence can no longer be tolerated (California Occupational Safety and Health Administration, 1998, p. 5). OSHA has recently started issuing citations to employers who fail to adequately protect their employees from violence in the workplace.

One of the better predictors of who will or will not be at risk to become violent is the pooled clinical judgment of human services workers who have come into contact with the clients (Douglas, Ogloff, & Hart, 2003; Durivage, 1989; Werner et al., 1989). One of the primary reasons that cases have been decided in favor of the plaintiff is the failure of one clinician to communicate with another clinician that a client has a history of violence and might present a future danger (Beck, 1988; Belak & Busse, 1993, p. 147). From that standpoint, the institution and worker who wish to avoid a court appearance would do well to flag records of violent acts or ideation and relay that information to other members of the treatment team for feedback and possible action (Blair, 1991; Martin et al., 1991).

Dynamics of Violence in Human Services Settings

The dynamics of violence in human services settings is complex. It involves not only the clients themselves, but also the human services workers and the institution. The ability to predict who will be violent, when, and under what conditions has been notoriously unreliable (American Psychiatric Association, 1974; Kirk, 1989; Monahan, 1988; Mulvey & Lidz, 1984; Palmstierna & Wistedt, 1990; Sloore, 1988). Predictions are especially likely to be wrong when crisis workers have little background information on clients and may not have time to make more than an "eyeball" assessment of the situation before they have to act. Yet data do exist to present general profiles of clients who are more likely than others to become violent, given the right constellation of conditions. To that end, accurate behavioral information is the central core in assessment for violent behavior. Cawood and Corcoran (2009, p. 17) propose that the depth and accuracy of behavioral information obtained are directly correlated to the quality and accuracy of assessment of who may become violent, where, and under what conditions.

Violence Potential Assessment Instruments

The HCR-20 (Webster et al., 1997) is a violence risk assessment rating device that asks clinicians to rate clients on 20 variables based on a variety of questions concerning clients' history of violence, clinical mental health status, self-management, and degree of risk upon return to society. The ratings show good reliability in predicting who among forensic psychiatric clients will become violent both in the long term (Douglas, Ogloff, & Hart, 2003) and in the short term (McNeil et al., 2003), although it fared poorly when assessing incarcerated females in regard to who might commit a violent crime and had an inverse ability to predict which females had been convicted for murder (Warren et al., 2005)!

The Violence Screening Checklist–Revised (VSC-R) includes checkoff items that review history of physical attacks and fear-inducing/threat behavior during the first 2 weeks of hospital admission, presence or absence of suicidal behavior, schizophrenic or manic diagnosis, and male gender (McNeil & Binder, 1994). This instrument appears to be highly reliable, particularly in regard to the first few days of hospital admission (McNeil et al., 2003).

The Broset Violence Checklist (BVC; Linaker & Busch-Iversen, 1995) checks for the presence or absence of six factors that are frequently seen as a prelude to violent incidents on acute psychiatric wards: confusion, irritability, boisterous acting out, verbal threats, physical threats, and attacks on objects. This device has been shown to have good predictive validity during 24-hour follow-ups if two or more of these items are checked. A large-scale study of geriatric patients who were violent as opposed to those who were not found the BVC to be a good predictor of violent episodes and a good discriminator between those who would and would not become violent (Almvik, Woods, & Rasmussen, 2007).

The Dynamic Appraisal of Situational Aggression (DYAS) checks for immediate risk of violence and is also a treatment plan aid that helps in reducing the risk of violence. When combined with professional observation, the DYAS was found to be a better predictor than clinical judgments alone (Ogloff & Daffern, 2006).

While all of these instruments would seem to do a good job of predicting both short- and long-term violence risk in psychiatric populations, the problem is still predicting when it is happening "RIGHT NOW!" and doing something about it. From that standpoint, knowing the verbal and physical cues and using interocular and auditory analysis (eyeballing and listening) are still the best bet for staying out of harm's way.

Bases for Violence

Keeping in mind the terms "general profiles" and "right conditions," the following bases for profiling violence are "best bet" predictors of "RIGHT NOW!"

There are biological, psychological, and social bases for violence. Biologically, low intelligence, hormonal imbalances, organic brain disorders, neurological and systemic changes of a psychiatric nature, disease, chemicals, intense and chronic pain, or traumatic head injury may lead to more violence-prone behavior (Fishbain et al., 2000; Hamstra, 1986; Heilbrun, 1990; Heilbrun & Heilbrun, 1989; McNeil, 2009; Newhill, 2003, pp. 107–108). Psychologically, specific situational problems, certain functional psychoses, and character disorders are predisposing to violence (Greenfield, McNeil, & Binder, 1989; Heilbrun, 1990; Heilbrun & Heilbrun, 1989; Klassen & O'Connor, 1988; McNeil, 2009; Newhill, 2003, pp. 94–106). Socially, modeling the violent behavioral norms of family, peers, homelessness, lack of social support, relationship with potential victims, and the milieu within which one lives can exacerbate violent tendencies (McNeil, 2009; Nisbett, 1993; Tardiff, 1984a, p. 45; Wood & Khuri, 1984, p. 60).

Finally, specific on-site physical environmental stressors such as heat, bad lighting and décor, crowding, noise, conflict, and poor communication can trigger violence (Anderson, 2001; Jensen & Absher, 1994; Newhill, 2003, p. 190; Vaaler, Morken, & Linaker, 2005). When all these ingredients are mixed together, the results start to resemble the kinds of people and environments with which the crisis worker is likely to come in contact (Tardiff, 1984a, p. 45).

Age.   Males between the ages of 15 and 30 tend to be the most violent subgroup (Blumenreich, 1993a, p. 36; Fareta, 1981; Kroll & Mackenzie, 1983; Shah, Fineberg, & James, 1991). Next come elderly clients, who are disproportionately represented in the population that may become violent (Astroem et al., 2002; Hindley & Gordon, 2000; Petrie, 1984, p. 107). Crisis workers tend to dismiss this group as being harmless, but in a study of 200 cases of assault at the Cincinnati Veterans Administration Medical Center, Jones (1985) discovered that 58.5 percent of the assaults took place in the geriatric facility. This statistic is noteworthy because the institution also had a large psychotic and substance-abusing population.

Substance Abuse.   There is probably no psychotropic drug, either legal or illegal, that does not correlate with violence when it is abused. Whether the abuser is going on a meth high, coming off Valium, or experiencing the withdrawal of heroin, violence and drug use have a strong relationship (Blumenreich, 1993b, p. 24; Piercy, 1984, pp. 131–135; Rada, 1981; Simonds & Kashani, 1980). The foregoing statement most certainly includes alcohol. Alcohol has been associated with more than half of reported cases of violence in emergency rooms and one-fourth of reported cases in psychiatric institutions (Bach y Rita, Lion, & Climent, 1971). The potential for violence is further increased when individuals who have a history of psychosis engage in alcohol or drug use (Klassen & O'Connor, 1988; Yesavage & Zarcone, 1983).

Predisposing History of Violence.   A history of serious violence, homicide, sexual attacks, assault, or threat of assault with a deadly weapon is one of the best predictors of future violence (California Occupational Safety and Health Administration, 1998, p. 3; Fareta, 1981; Monahan, 1981). Any background that includes

contact with the criminal justice system for aggravated felonies, weapons possession, threats against prospective victims, or a history of assaultive behavior while hospitalized should automatically put the human services worker on notice to be extremely cautious with the client (Blumenreich, 1993a, p. 37; Klassen & O'Connor, 1988). Of all the predisposing clues for violent behavior, probably there is none better than being brought to a facility for violent behavior as a part of emotional disturbance or mental illness.

Psychological Disturbance.   A variety of mental disorders may be predisposing to violence: the antisocial personality type who has a history of violent behavior, emotional callousness, impulsivity, and manipulative behavior; the borderline personality who lacks adequate ego strength to control intense emotional drives and repeatedly exhibits emotional outbursts; the paranoid who is on guard against and constantly anticipating external threat; the manic who has elevated moods, hyperactivity, and excessive involvement in activities that may have painful consequences; the explosive personality who has sudden escalating periods of anger; the schizophrenic who is actively hallucinating and has bizarre or grandiose delusions; the panic attack victim who is fearful, dissociative, and has extreme fight-or-flight reactions; and the depressed suicidal ideator who is hopeless, agitated, and acting out suicidal plans (Blumenreich, 1993b, pp. 21–22; Grassi et al., 2001; Greenfield, McNeil, & Binder, 1989; Heilbrun, 1990; Heilbrun & Heilbrun, 1989; Klassen & O'Connor, 1988; McNeil, 2009; Murdach, 1993; Newhill, 2003, pp. 96–104).

Social Stressors.   Loss of a job, job stress, breakup of a relationship, a past history of physical or sexual abuse, and financial reversals are a few of the social stressors that cause acute frustration and rage in an out-of-control social environment that leads to violence (Blumenreich, 1993a, p. 370; Munoz et al., 2000).

Family History.   A history of violence within the family is often carried into other environments. An early childhood characterized by an unstable and violent home is an excellent model for future violence (Wood & Khuri, 1984, pp. 65–66). A history of social isolation or lack of family and environmental support also may heighten the potential for violence (Heilbrun & Heilbrun, 1989; Munoz et al., 2000). A nasty predictor of future criminal and violent behavior is cruelty to animals (Felthous & Kellert, 1986; Hellman &

Blackman, 1966). It doesn't take too much imagination to predict that children who set cats on fire or do other cruel things to pets are capable of a lot of violence as they become adults. Predisposing family histories of witnessing family violence, being abused, enduring excessive physical punishment, abandonment, deprivation, and neglect, as explicated in the chapter on partner abuse, are all predisposing to adult aggression (Eddy, 1998).

Work History. A history of fractiousness and problems at a worksite is another correlate with violence (Newhill, 2003, pp. 110–111). Being fired at the post office is not the only situation in which workers exact revenge. Job loss and economic instability easily translate into paranoid "they did me wrong" thinking, which can then transfer over to social workers in unemployment offices and vocational counselors at employment services.

Time. In relation to a person's admission and tenure in a facility, time is critical. Admission on Friday or Saturday night during "party hours" significantly increases the potential for violence. In geriatric and mental hospitals, the evening hours, with the onset of darkness, change of shift, and decrease in staff, often lead to client disorientation and states of confusion (Occupational Safety and Health Administration, 2003). The effects of this time period have become so notorious that they have been labeled the *sundown syndrome* (Piercy, 1984, p. 139). Mealtime, toileting, and bathing are also prime times for violent outbursts (Barrick et al., 2008; Jones, 1985). Patients in both general and forensic psychiatric hospitals are more likely to be violent immediately after admission to the hospital (McNeil et al., 1991). McNeil, Binder, and Greenfield (1988) found that recent violent acts in the community are highly associated with violent acts in the first 72 hours of inpatient care. For most patients committed involuntarily, the possibility of assault is significantly increased during the first 10 to 20 days after admission, and for paranoids it remains high during their first 45 days (Rofman, Askinazi, & Fant, 1980).

Presence of Interactive Participants. Violent behavior may be contingent on those who bring the person to the institution (Occupational Safety and Health Administration, 2003). Family members or friends who bring patients in for treatment often interact in a volatile manner with admitting staff, particularly if the

staff are seen as abrasive and callous (Ruben, Wolkon, & Yamamoto, 1980) and treat either the patient or support persons in a curt or uncaring manner (Wood & Khuri, 1984, p. 58). Arguments that may occur between the client and support persons are easily transferred to staff. Furthermore, when admonitions by distraught or intoxicated supporters to "fix" the client are not given immediate attention, they or the client may express grievances against the institution and staff by acting out. Any client who is accompanied to the institution by a police officer should be viewed as potentially violent (Kurlowicz, 1990; McNeil et al., 1991; Piercy, 1984, pp. 140–141).

Motoric Cues. Close observation by the human services worker of physical cues will often give clues to emergent states predisposing to physical violence (Kurlowicz, 1990; Petrie, 1984, p. 115; Weinger, 2001, p. 24). Early warning signs include tense muscles; bulging, darting eye movements; staring or completely avoiding eye contact; closed, defensive body posture; twitching muscles, fingers, and eyelids; body tremors; and disheveled appearance (Tardiff, 1989, p. 98; Wood & Khuri, 1984, p. 77). If the client is pacing back and forth, alternately approaching and then retreating from the worker, this may be a sign that the individual is gathering courage for an assault (Dang, 1990). The agitated client may have an expanded sense of personal space up to 8 feet in radius, instead of 3 to 4 feet, and may be extremely sensitive to any intrusion into that space (Moran, 1984, pp. 244–246).

A number of verbal cues are precursors to violent action by the client. Heightened voice pitch, volume, and rapidity of speech may occur, particularly if the client has been using amphetamines or other psychostimulants. Confused speech content can reflect confused thought and psychotic breaks. Clients may use profanity or verbally threaten significant others, the worker, or the world in general. Note that there is a high correlation between threats of violence and acting on those threats. The more specific the threat is to the person, method, and time, the more seriously the threat should be taken (Blumenreich, 1993a, p. 37; Tardiff, 1989, p. 99).

Multiple Indicators. The more the foregoing indicators are combined, the higher the potential for violence becomes (Klassen & O'Connor, 1988). Tardiff (1989) indicates that, if possible, the human services worker should attempt to assess all these factors; if they are present, the worker should clearly note the potential for violence on an intake form (p. 97) or on one of the violence prediction instruments previously mentioned. Tardiff further proposes that whether or not this information is available, one of the better verbal assessment techniques is to ask, "Have you ever lost your temper [in a violent manner]?" If the answer is "Yes!" the worker should proceed to ask how, when, and where this happened, and then perform an assessment much like that for suicide (p. 98). If any of the foregoing factors are apparent or are stated by the client, no matter how calm the client may appear to be, then a triage assessment of 10 on the interpersonal behavioral dimension should be made, the client's record should be flagged, and caution should be used in regard to the potential of the client to harm self or others. Does this mean you should not go into the human services business and go into something less stressful, like hauling explosives? Your authors would propose not, because about 85 to 90 percent of violence is preventable (Mack et al., 1988). The rest of this chapter will attempt to demonstrate how that percentage can be achieved.

Intervention Strategies

Because the institution itself plays such a large part in the who, what, why, how, and when of treatment, it may be viewed as an equal and contributing partner in resolving problems with clients disposed to becoming physically and verbally assaultive. No two institutions are alike with respect to a number of variables that affect what the institution can do about the problem of violence. Yet when confronting clients who may be distraught, angry, fearful, and experiencing disequilibrium, all institutions have a common core of problems. Given the financial, legal, treatment, organizational, and philosophical limits idiosyncratic to each setting, the following intervention strategies should be viewed as a best "general" approach.

Security Planning

No antiviolence program can be accomplished without the commitment and involvement of top management such that everybody in the institution or agency understands that preventing violence is an absolute top priority (Barret, Riggar, & Flowers, 1997; California Occupational Safety and Health Administration, 1998, p. 6; Newhill, 2003; Weinger, 2001). The five main components of any effective safety and health program also apply to the prevention of workplace violence.

These components are management commitment and employee involvement, worksite analysis, hazard prevention and control, safety and health training, and record keeping and program evaluation (Occupational Safety and Health Administration, 2003).

Commitment and Involvement

One of the first steps in preventing violence is understanding what precautions the institution has taken to ensure the safety of clients and staff. Management commitment and employee involvement in a safe workplace are critical (Occupational Safety and Health Administration, 2003). The institution should have a zero tolerance policy for violence for both clients and providers. It should assign clear responsibility to all staff members so that they know what is expected of them, along with adequate resources to carry out those responsibilities and make them accountable for doing so.

Certain precautions can be taken to ensure that workers are not put at extreme risk by their clientele. First and foremost, management should conduct a security management analysis with experts in the security field (Ishimoto, 1984, p. 211; Kinney, 1995, pp. 47–50). Kinney (1995) urges that management recognize that the people with the most knowledge are the frontline workers who deal with the institution's clientele on a day-in, day-out basis, even though management may not want to hear from these workers for fear of what they might say. There should be channels for employees to bring their concerns to management and receive feedback without fear of reprisal or censure (Occupational Safety and Health Administration, 2003).

Worksite Analysis

A worksite analysis involves taking a step-by-step approach to addressing potential hazards, focusing on areas in which they may develop, and reviewing procedures put in place to curtail violence (Occupational Safety and Health Administration, 2003). There is a condensed security analysis questionnaire from Kinney (1995, pp. 211–216) and Ishimoto (1984, pp. 211–216) in the website exercises for this chapter, and you are invited to peruse the rather lengthy list of questions. This questionnaire analyzes and tracks records, generates screening surveys, and reviews workplace security (Occupational Safety and Health Administration, 2003). If such a survey is not taken, not only does the facility risk outbreaks of violence but the staff will perceive management as not being greatly concerned about what happens to them (Lewellyn, 1985). Once the results of the survey are compiled, the organization should institute planning in hazard prevention and control.

Hazard Prevention and Control

All staff should have input into these questions, and a comprehensive security plan should be worked out and disseminated (California Occupational Safety and Health Administration, 1998, p. 8; Occupational Safety and Health Administration, 2003). Such a plan should be comprehensive and simple, detailing who is responsible for what, under which conditions. The plan should cover the entire domain of the institution, starting with the parking lot, moving through the front door to admissions, and proceeding through the building to encompass day treatment facilities, staff offices, food services, pharmaceutical dispensaries, and client rooms (Ishimoto, 1984, pp. 209–223). Although the administration may view the initial costs in time and money for this service as burdensome, net cost will be minimal if this action avoids just one lawsuit by a client or staff member (Moran, 1984, p. 249).

Threat Assessment Teams. While consultants with different areas of expertise in violence containment may be helpful, planning should start by forming a threat team composed of a cross section of the staff and by naming a violence prevention coordinator. The duties of this team and coordinator will be to (1) outline the scope and activities of a threat management policy; (2) issue a clear and publicized statement against violence, even if the statement simply says, "This organization will not tolerate violence and aggression either from within or from outside the organization"; (3) identify a location and person for reporting threats; (4) determine when threats are serious enough to convene the team; (5) set training for all staff; and (6) establish a protocol for violence reduction that addresses unacceptable types of behavior as well as appropriate sanctions for that behavior (Kinney, 1995, pp. 73–80; Myer, James, & Moulton, 2011; Newhill, 2003, pp. 189–199; Nicoletti & Spooner, 1996; Weinger, 2001, p. 53).

Establishment of a threat assessment team is particularly critical on a college campus (Myer, James, & Moulton, 2011, pp. 256–267). Virginia Tech is a classic example where, for various political, logistical, legal, and ethical reasons, a silo mentality occurred and critical information was kept in separate units and never shared. It should be clearly understood that Virginia Tech was no different from any other institution in regard to the barriers erected and communication channels that were effectively blocked that could perhaps have mitigated the effects of a mass murderer before he got to the tipping point. In fact, thanks to changes in Virginia law, institutions of higher education and mental health facilities in Virginia are now better able to communicate and exert sanctions and exclusions on individuals who fail to cooperate in assessment and treatment programs than in most other states (Mandatory Treatment of Mental Health Patients, 2007; Threat Assessment Team Formation, 2008; Threat of Violence, 2008).

An individual such as Seung-hui Cho may come to the attention of a variety of individuals, entities, and departments but never be so blatant and labile that he or she comes to the attention of anyone and nothing is done to proactively contain the person until a tragedy occurs. That's why a cross section of campus representatives from housing, recreation, food services, academic departments, the counseling center, and law enforcement all need to be part of a threat assessment team that meets regularly and sifts through all incident reports that occur on campus. That threat assessment team also needs a common language such as TASSLE (Myer et al., 2007), discussed in Chapters 3 and 13, so that they have a common set of terms and behavioral anchors to use in making dispositions of individuals that come to their attention (Myer, James, & Moulton, 2011, pp. 233–270).

Precautions in Dealing With the Physical Setting. Safety precautions should be taken that deal with the physical settings of the institution in which staff members are most likely to become involved in potentially violent situations with clients. Two critical areas important to all crisis workers are the admissions area and the worker's office. The reception area or waiting room should offer a television set, reading material, and accessibility to snack areas. Availability of entertainment and food and drink gives clients and visitors an opportunity to engage in a pleasurable activity that can offset the hostile feelings that may be engendered by the problems they are facing and can defuse the stressful situation of admission (Wood & Khuri, 1984, pp. 79–80). One admonition is necessary with regard to food and drink: Clients who are extremely rebellious about entering the institution may attempt to choke themselves on food or even swallow pull tabs from metal cans. The admissions staff should carefully monitor clients if they are allowed to eat or drink (McCown, 1986).

The admissions area should be clean and well kept, with furniture, carpet, and wall coverings well maintained. First impressions are lasting. If the client's first impression of a facility is that staff have little regard or respect for the facility, the client will have little reason to respect what goes on there either (Marohn, 1982). Suffice it to say that fire engine red paint is not a decorating choice. Bright, cheery, energizing decorations should not be used any more than the somber and depressing institutional grays and greens of many mental institutions and prisons one of your authors has worked in and visited (Newhill, 2003, p. 190; Vaaler, Morken, & Linaker, 2005). Subdued painting and decorating and comfortable, relaxing furniture do a lot to alleviate anger, tension, and pent-up agitated feelings and thoughts. No sharp, movable objects, including furniture, should be available as potential weapons (McCown, 1986). Clients should be given lockers in which to put their belongings (Munsey, 2008).

The area should be set up so that it is a choke point: only one way into the rest of the facility should be available from the admissions area. Video surveillance should be kept on this area to record everybody who comes in and out, along with a sign-in sheet that records everyone coming in and is checked to make sure that everyone has gone out (Annis, McClaren, & Baker, 1984, p. 30). There should, however, be another way out for workers, and a panic room where workers could secure themselves from intruders is not a bad idea (Munsey, 2008). Depending on how much security is needed, the reception area may also have electronically locked doors that separate it from the rest of the facility, identity check procedures, curved mirrors, and metal detectors (California Occupational Safety and Health Administration, 1998, p. 10; Munsey, 2008). Clients who are waiting for service should be treated in a courteous and friendly manner and updated on interview delays. Waits should be kept to a minimum (Weinger, 2001, p. 53). In that regard, is it any wonder that people become agitated and enraged in most hospital emergency rooms?

The admissions worker will make the first contact with the client and will engage the person during one of the most potentially violent moments the institution is likely to encounter. The admissions worker should be highly skilled in crisis intervention techniques and should have one primary job—*staying with and attending to the client being admitted*! Under no circumstances should a secretary, receptionist, or any other support person who is not professionally well versed in

crisis intervention or who has other tasks to perform, such as typing letters or answering the telephone, be delegated to handle this important assignment. The admissions worker should not leave the client until all admitting procedures have been accomplished and the client is safely settled (McCown, 1986).

The admissions worker should also never be left in a position of isolation from the rest of the staff (Turnbull et al., 1990). Security support equipment such as a body alarm (a button-activated device that when triggered will automatically send an alarm and position fix to security), an automatic dialer preset to in-house security and 911, convex mirrors to monitor the whole waiting area, panic buttons, closed-circuit television monitoring equipment, button locks on elevators, and a metal detector at the entrance should be available. Initial interviews are critical in setting the tone for what will occur behaviorally. Therefore, the interview area should be open, yet afford privacy. At times, if the client is very agitated, other staff or indeed a police officer may need to be present (Doms, 1984, pp. 225–229; Jones, 1984; McCown, 1986; Weinger, 2001, p. 53; Wood & Khuri, 1984, pp. 79–80).

Now a word about what you need to look like. The following admonition is probably politically incorrect, and we are going to sound like your overprotective father to many of you young women reading this, because we are now going to tell you what you need to wear. Low-cut necklines are all the rage right now. This is not the setting to be a slave to fashion! Some clients have real boundary problems (Newhill, 2003, p. 191), and here is not the place for their impulsivity to take over and you to wind up being sexually or physically assaulted. Put on professional work clothes that say, "I am here to help you, but I mean business!" And if you are a guy and you are into grunge and you think that looking like a punk rocker will help you relate to your clients, you probably need to go into a street ministry. Conversely, you don't need to look as though you stepped out of *GQ* or *Vogue* magazine, but not looking like a professional conveys the impression that you aren't. It is called *face validity*. If clients don't believe you look as though you know what you are doing, you will probably not get the chance to demonstrate that you do.

Personal work environments should also be safe. Desks should be set up so that they allow for separation of client and worker, even though communicating across a desk is not the most desirable counseling setup. Furniture should be heavy and difficult to move. Space should be arranged to permit both the worker and the client clear access to the door and to allow the worker to leave the room without having to confront the client or cross the client's personal space. No potential weapons such as paperweights, letter openers, and sharpened pencils should be openly displayed or within easy reach of the client. The same personal warning devices and procedures recommended for the reception area should also be in place in workers' offices (Jensen & Absher, 1994, 1998; Tardiff, 1984a, p. 50).

The receptionist or others in the building need to be able to warn the worker if danger is imminent, and vice versa. There should be a common code word that is understood to mean a summons for immediate help. A panic button and a telephone that the worker can use to get in touch with the outside world should be available. These last two points are particularly critical because of the typical isolation of the human services worker with a client in a therapeutic setting (Jensen & Absher, 1994, 1998; Tardiff, 1984a, p. 50).

Training

Planning is of little consequence if no training follows. Staff who have been trained in the appropriate methods, techniques, and procedures have increased confidence in their ability to deescalate violence and have reduced assaultive behavior (Thomas, Kitchen, & Smith, 2005; Turnbull et al., 1990). Training should include both knowledge and skill building and should be ongoing, with immediate training for new members of the treatment team and continuing education for veterans (Dyer, Murrell, & Wright, 1984, pp. 12–15; Newhill, 2003, p. 207; Turnbull et al., 1990; Weinger, 2001, pp. 52–53). Every employee should understand that violence should be expected but can be avoided or reduced through preparation (Newhill, 2003, p. 206; Occupational Safety and Health Administration, 2003).

Training should begin with the crisis intervention skills listed in Chapters 3 and 4 and additionally cover legal aspects, theories of aggression, reporting and recording of incidents, assessment of contextual and environmental variables, verbal defusing techniques, triggers of aggression, warning signs, use of safety and alarm devices, self-defense and restraint techniques, behavioral observation, consultation, follow-up staffing procedures, and debriefing (Blair, 1991; Kinney, 1995; Murray & Snyder, 1991; Occupational Safety and Health Administration, 2003; Turnbull et al., 1990). A critical component of training is not just talking about problems but gaining practice in solving them. There is no better way of doing this than in role-play and incident simulation situations, which can be videotaped for analysis and feedback by instructors and peers (Forster, 1994; Turnbull et al., 1990). Training should also include the people who need it most—the clients!

Anti-Violence Intervention. Most approaches to anti-violence prevention involve the use of behavioral (token economies, shaping, modeling contingency contracting) or cognitive-behavioral intervention methods (reframing negative attributions, thought stopping, relaxation training, positive counterinjunctions) (Douglas, Nicholls, & Brink, 2009). The risk-needs-responsivity (RNR) model is a procedure that is taken from the corrections field. The risk component proposes that high-risk individuals get more targeted, specific, and tailored therapeutic inputs before they go critical. The needs component focuses on the dynamic risk factors that when changed reduce recidivism. This procedure has been applied to anti-violence programs with the severely mentally ill and severely emotionally disturbed. RNR usually incorporates cognitive-behavioral therapy, social skills training, anger management, and behavioral techniques that apply role rehearsal, modeling, and shaping to prosocial behavior (Douglas, Nicholls, & Brink, 2009). While not perfect by any stretch of the imagination, it appears that RNR is at least somewhat effective with severely mentally ill and severely emotionally disturbed individuals (Lovell et al., 2001; van den Brink et al., 2010; Wong, Gordon, & Gu, 2008; Yates et al., 2005) who present with very tough, intractable, and chronic issues that are generally resistant to change.

Assumptions. Adequate training should endow the crisis worker with the ability to make certain assumptions and take certain precautions when dealing with potentially violent clients (Newhill, 2003, pp. 121–165; Turnbull et al., 1990; Weinger, 2001, p. 45; Zold & Schilt, 1984, pp. 98–99).

1. Assume the need to set limits and provide clear instructions with options that define what positive and negative consequences will occur.
2. Assume the client feels a number of debilitating emotions such as fear, depression, anxiety, helplessness, anger, rejection, and hopelessness, and demonstrate concern by encouraging verbal ventilation through *how* and *when* questions, showing empathic concern by restatement and reflection of the client's feelings, and reinforcing appropriate behavior and communication of feelings.

3. Assume frustration of normal activity and boredom when the client is in residence, and provide activities to keep the client fruitfully busy.

4. Assume a threat to the client's self-esteem, independence, and self-control, and provide choices and opportunities to help in carrying out medical and psychological activities.

5. Assume tension and arousal, and provide a calm and relaxing atmosphere, particularly in high-tension periods, by manipulating environmental variables and using a cooperative "we" approach.

6. Assume that there will be confusion, and provide a careful explanation of all procedures to be employed, being particularly sure that all staff are operating from the same frame of reference.

7. Assume responsibility, and provide for one primary staff member to act as chief caretaker and advocate of each client.

8. Assume disconnectedness and rootlessness if the client is to be institutionalized for any length of time, and provide familiarity and psychologically calming anchors associated with pleasant memories.

Precautions.   While providing support through the preceding proactive behaviors, the wise human services worker should observe a number of precautionary measures (Blair, 1991; Forster, 1994; Greenstone & Leviton, 1993; Moran, 1984, p. 244; Piercy, 1984, p. 143; Turnbull et al., 1990; Weinger, 2001, pp. 33–48; Wood & Khuri, 1984, p. 69).

1. Don't deny the possibility of violence when early signs of agitation are first noticed in the client.

2. Don't dismiss warnings from records, family and peers, authorities, or fellow workers that the client is violent.

3. Don't become isolated with potentially violent clients unless you have made sure that enough security precautions have been taken to prevent or limit a violent outburst.

4. Don't engage in certain behaviors that may be interpreted as aggressive, such as moving too close, staring directly into the client's eyes for extended periods of time, pointing fingers, or displaying facial expressions and body movements that would appear threatening.

5. Don't allow a number of the institution's workers to interact simultaneously with the client in confusing multiple dialogues.

6. Don't make promises that cannot be kept.

7. Don't allow feelings of fear, anger, or hostility to interfere with self-control and professional understanding of the client's circumstances.

8. Don't argue, give orders, or disagree when not absolutely necessary.

9. Don't be placating by giving in and agreeing to all the real and imagined ills the client is suffering at the hands of the institution.

10. Don't become condescending by using childish responses that are cynical, satirical, or otherwise designed to denigrate the client.

11. Don't let self-talk about your own importance be acted out in an officious and "know-it-all" manner.

12. Don't raise your voice, put a sharp edge on responses, or use threats to gain compliance.

13. Conversely, don't mumble, speak hesitantly, or use a tone of voice so low that the client has trouble understanding what you are saying.

14. Don't argue over small points, given strong opposition from the client.

15. Don't attempt to reason with any client who is under the influence of a mind-altering substance.

16. Don't attempt to gain compliance based on the assumption that the client is as reasonable about things as you are.

17. Don't keep the client waiting or leave a potentially violent client alone with freedom to move about.

18. Don't allow a crowd to congregate as spectators to an altercation.

19. Don't use *why* and *what* questions that put the client on the defensive.

20. Don't allow the client to get between you and an exit.

21. Don't dismiss increasingly vociferous client demands as merely attention-seeking, petulant, or narcissistic behavior.

22. Don't enter a room ahead of unknown clients. Stay behind and visually "frisk" them as you go into the room.

23. Don't remain after hours with a potentially violent client unless proper security is available.

24. Don't fail to make contingency plans for violent incidents. Take your personal safety seriously by playing "what if this happens" scenarios in your mind and with others.

25. Most important, *don't attempt to be a hero.*

Outreach Precautions.   In the rapidly changing world of mental health, much crisis intervention now occurs on-site (see Chapter 17, Disaster Response).

Although outreach and "mobile go-out" teams give the crisis interventionist far more mobility and rapid response capability, on-site intervention also has the potential to put crisis workers in extreme danger as they operate in violent neighborhoods and households (Burry, 2002). Besides the foregoing warnings given for in-house operation, the following injunctions generated by your authors and a variety of others (Cawood & Corcoran, 2009; Greenstone & Leviton, 1993, pp. 31–33; Jensen and Absher, 1998; Newhill, 2003, pp. 199–204; Weinger, 2001, pp. 56–59) should be added to the repertoire of the crisis worker who operates outside the walls of the institution.

1. If at all possible, go with a partner, or at least have a cell phone or other means of communication to get help in a hurry.
2. Let someone else in the office know where you are going and when you will be back.
3. Check out your surroundings. Although time is of the essence in most crisis intervention, move into the situation slowly and carefully, and be fully aware of what is going on in the environment around you.
4. Plan what you are going to do before you go. Take time to gather in-depth and accurate behavioral information on the client and family. Note any incidents of violence, drug abuse, or other potentially threatening behaviors in the client's folder before the visit. Our Crisis Intervention Team officers for the Memphis Police Department rendezvous and plan who is going to do what before they enter a hazardous situation whenever possible. You should do the same.
5. Don't park directly in front of the place where the crisis is occurring. Check out the area as you drive by, and park just beyond it. If you have to leave in a hurry, this position allows you to leave without crossing the line of sight of a person who may be able to harm you.
6. Before knocking on a door or entering a building, listen carefully for a few seconds for clues as to what may be going on inside.
7. Never stand directly in front of a door. Knock and, as the police do, stand aside, so you are not assaulted or shot through the door. If the client hesitates in opening the door, be very wary of going inside. If you think that something is happening that is suspicious or that could be hazardous to your health, politely terminate the appointment and leave.

8. Consider what you are wearing from a safety viewpoint. A tie or a choke chain may make you look more professional, but it can also get you strangled. High heels are elegant, but you can't run in them. Loose-fitting, mobile, and nonflashy clothing is the watchword.
9. Once the door is open, immediately scan the room to determine who is in it and where they are. Compare these visual data to information you may have received previously on the situation. Don't take anyone for granted, particularly elderly people who may look harmless. Ask if there are other people in the house and who and where they are. If they are not supposed to be there, politely postpone the appointment and leave.
10. Monitor the verbal and nonverbal behavior of all the people in the room. What are they doing, and what must you do to stabilize the situation? If there are intoxicated people present, politely postpone the appointment and leave.
11. Enter the room only a short distance so that you can first assess what's going on and can get out quickly if you have to.
12. Don't let a crowd of bystanders gather or let neighbors "drop in" to see what's going on. Politely ask them to leave. If they won't leave or refuse to disperse, get out or get the police!
13. Alert the client you are coming to visit, find out who else will be there, or if you are in a housing project, alert the building captain or housing authority police.
14. If a verbal dispute is going on, first and foremost consider your own safety. If necessary, leave and call the police. If you believe you can control the situation or don't seem to have any other choice, attempt to take control as quickly as possible. Separate disputants and have them sit down. Stay calm, and make clear, concise, assertive statements about what you want them to do. If that doesn't work, get their attention by making a tangential request: "Stop that! I need to use the telephone to call in." If all else fails, a police whistle gets everybody's attention.
15. Sit in a chair where you can observe what's going on. Seat yourself so you're leaning forward and can easily get out of the chair quickly! If you sense that the situation is deteriorating, leave. *Don't be a hero!*
16. Leave your credit cards, purse, jewelry (except your wedding band, which can be a deterrent to sexual advances), and most cash at the office. Carry only

your identification and driver's license. You don't want to get mugged.

17. Stay out of kitchens. They have knives and other things that can hurt you. Interview in the living room.

18. Remember that you are not on your own turf, and the unexpected can happen at any time. Stay alert from the moment you enter the neighborhood until the moment you leave the neighborhood.

These injunctions are not a recipe for avoiding violent confrontations, but they are general working procedures that will help the human services worker move adroitly with the client through the intervention stages.

Record Keeping and Program Evaluation

Employees follow a procedure that provides for reporting *all* incidents, with or without injury. They participate in a safety and health committee that receives information and reports on security problems, makes facility inspections, analyzes reports, and makes recommendations for corrections. Regular case conference meetings are used to identify potentially violent clients and discuss safe ways of handling them (California Occupational Safety and Health Administration, 1998, p. 7; Newhill, 2003, pp. 205–213; Occupational Safety and Health Administration, 2003; Weinger, 2001, pp. 49–55). Most important, good records allow for program evaluation.

Stages of Intervention

There are three primary levels of intervention (dos Reis et al., 2003). At level 1, the primary objective is to prevent further escalation. Level 2 intervention aims to reduce the target symptoms. Level 3 intervention maintains the safety of the clients and staff. Within these three broad levels, management of potentially violent situations should proceed in a sequential manner, based on a nine-stage model developed by Piercy (1984, pp. 147–148). The stages are (1) education, (2) avoidance of conflict, (3) appeasement, (4) deflection, (5) time-out, (6) show of force, (7) seclusion, (8) restraints, and (9) sedation. The cardinal rule for all of these stages, as stated by Larry Chavez (1999)—a noted authority on violence prevention in the workplace—is "Never, ever deprive another human being of personal dignity, respect, or hope nor allow anyone else under your control to do so." For each of these stages, personal responsibility is paramount. Furthermore, whether by circumstance or design, the first person who comes in contact with the

problem is the one most likely to be the agitated client's focus of attention (Moran, 1984, pp. 233–234).

Stages 1 through 5 all rely heavily on talking instead of acting, in accordance with one of the primary goals of crisis intervention with violence-prone individuals: getting them to talk out rather than act out. This approach may seem obvious, but it is difficult to achieve. The agitated client clearly has a limited ability to talk and think through problems, as opposed to acting on them and giving little thought to the consequences (Tardiff, 1984a, p. 52). While the immediate goal is to defuse and de-escalate clients' rapid movement toward violence, the overall end goals are to alter violent clients' motivation so that they can utilize nonviolent ways to reestablish their lost sense of control; monitor them and preempt their reengagement of violence; and model for and assure significant others such as peers, family, fellow patients, and staff that calmness and serenity will prevail and violence will not be tolerated (Cawood & Corcoran, 2009, p. 8).

As we move through the nine stages, we will follow Jason, a 15-year-old white male client, and Carol, a therapist who by most standards is an old pro. She has been at Seashore Village, a comprehensive mental health inpatient treatment facility, for 4 years. Jason is new to the business of institutions. However, he is not new to being angry, which he is right now as he sits with a deputy sheriff in the reception area waiting for Carol to come through the door.

Jason's teen years have been filled with petty larceny, truancy, conduct problems at school, alcohol and drug use, and parents who have gotten him out of one scrape after another. He is impulsive, has anger management problems, and has difficulty controlling his emotions. His latest escapade of stealing a car landed him in front of a juvenile court, and he was sent to Seashore as an alternative to the state juvenile correction system. His father, fed up with Jason's behavior and over the objections of Jason's mother, has pushed for this placement. Jason feels betrayed and is extremely angry at his father for doing so.

Seashore itself is representative of a broad sample of institutions. It is neither the best nor the worst in terms of clients, staff, resources, and security measures. The endeavor here is to paint as representative a picture as possible, so please withhold judgments about the efficacy and appropriateness of these strategies in every institution. Our hope is that the procedures used in the case of Jason will make you think carefully about your own present or future role in an institution, compare the ideas proposed here with the requirements imposed on you, analyze the procedures used, and thoughtfully compare these techniques and the real world within which you operate.

Jason: (*thinking to himself, hands sweating, slight tremors racing through his body*) Man, this place is scaring the hell out of me. How'd I ever get in this fix? What are they gonna do to me? I'll be at the mercy of the rest of the crazies in here. I'll really go nuts if I stay here. I gotta get out of this place if it's the last thing I ever do.

Jason is extremely angry and anxious about what will happen to him, frustrated that he has lost control of his life and that what he has considered to be normal activity is going to be severely curtailed. He also feels extremely vulnerable, confused, bewildered, and alone. Jason's feelings are typical of those of a client who is being introduced to a long-term treatment facility for the first time (Blair, 1991; Zold & Schilt, 1984, p. 96). Anger generally comes out of frustration or hurt and is one way of creating an emotional wall that protects us from being vulnerable (Fauteux, 2010). To say that Jason is feeling very vulnerable right now is a big understatement.

As soon as Jason enters Seashore, someone from admissions immediately calls the adolescent unit. Carol comes quickly to the reception area and meets Jason. As she enters the room, she makes a fast visual assessment of Jason's verbal and nonverbal behavior and monitors Jason closely to see what his reaction to her initial query will be.

Carol: (*thinking to herself*) What's going on with this kid? Any signs he is agitated? Yes! He's pacing around, eyes darting to and fro, keeps cracking his knuckles, looking at the door and the cop. He'll run if he gets the chance! Muttering to himself. Who brought him in? Nobody else here but that cop over there. He keeps watching him. Must be an adjudication. If a cop brought him here, be careful.

Carol picks up the file the deputy has brought, quickly looks it over, and finds the boy's name and rap sheet. A fast review tells her that Jason has been in a series of escalating scrapes with the law, that his parents are fed up with his behavior and feel he's out of control, and that he has been involved in fights when his explosive personality got out of control. Carol then talks briefly with the deputy and finds out what kind of a trip Jason had from the juvenile detention center.

Carol: (*thinking to herself*) OK! Check him out and see how stabilized he is, and let him find out what's going to happen to him.

Stage 1: Education. Clients need to be educated about what is happening to them, and why and how it is happening, through reasoning and reassurance. One way of doing this is to assume the role of the client's advocate (Pisarick, 1981).

Owning statements that indicate concern over the client's welfare are a good opening gambit. It must be assumed that in this new, strange, and alien environment the primary feeling of the client will be fear and anger (Rada, 1981). Open-ended questions and reflection of the client's feelings are crucial to conveying that the client's feelings count for something and are being taken into consideration (Turnbull et al., 1990).

Carol: Hi! My name's Carol, and you must be Jason. I'm the person who'll be working with you.

Jason: (*Gives a menacing look.*) Yeah! So what? (*Points to officer.*) The cop got me in here, but I ain't gonna go any farther.

Carol: I understand how you feel. Most people who come here feel about the same way. Seems like everybody's against you, telling you what to do. I'd be angry too! I want you to know, though, that here at Seashore you're going to have some options about what happens.

Jason: Screw your options. I ain't stayin' here. (*Makes a menacing move toward Carol.*)

Carol: (*Senses move and moves back and a little to Jason's left, giving him some increased space.*) One of your immediate options is that I'd like you to come with me and meet some of the other kids here and have them tell you what's going on and see if what they have to say fits with what you're about. On the other hand, the court sent you here, and if you don't like the first option and want to fight it out, you could be carried back to the unit, and we can wait until you've got yourself together. I understand you're angry, and I'd be angry too, but I'd like to know if you feel that fighting or running is gonna make it better for you and improve your situation rather than checking things out. So you've got a choice. I think you might be interested in meeting some of the other kids, but you'll have to show me you can handle that, starting right now.

In this initial meeting, the worker uses the technique of providing options (Newhill, 2003, p. 158; Turnbull et al., 1990). This opening statement includes acknowledging the client's feelings but also conveys expectations that the client can control himself. By doing so, Carol sets the tone for what the behavioral expectations are in a clear and caring, yet firm, way (Steveson, 1991). She is letting the client have some semblance of control of the situation but is also clearly outlining what the consequences of his choices are. As soon as possible, she is going to model option therapy (McCown, 1986). Option therapy, in simple terms, says, "You always have a choice. You need to start deciding as soon as possible who's going to have control over those choices, you or us."

Jason: Well . . . all right . . . lady, I'll give it a look-see, but I ain't promisin' nothin' after that.

Carol: I don't expect any more than that at the moment. What I want most for you is to see what's going on here and what some of the other kids think about what we do before you make any kind of promises. We don't lie, and we don't make promises we can't keep.

The worker has to make a quick judgment about how directive or nondirective to be. Telling Jason he needs to calm down is not an option. How do you react when you are upset and somebody tells you "Just calm down"? Doesn't work very well, does it, and probably upsets you even more, and goodness knows you handle your emotions pretty well. That statement would be telling the client he is not in control but someone else is, which affirms for him that he isn't in control so the behavior escalates even more (Fauteux, 2010). Carol is directive only to the extent of setting boundaries equivalent to how out of control the client is. Her other mission is to establish rapport and credibility with the client. She does this by accepting and acknowledging the client where he is and in turn stating the same from the institution's perspective. She offers no platitudes or false promises (Turnbull et al., 1990). Her technique of letting the client talk to other people on the unit is designed to let the client hear and see with his own ears and eyes what is going on without feeling he is getting a lot of propaganda. However, she will not provide a forum for him to act out, and if in her judgment Jason is not controlled enough to make a tour with her, she will summon assistance, and Jason will be escorted to an observation room (McCown, 1986).

Carol: We have a lot of activities, so if you don't clearly understand what's happening or you want to know some more about it, just ask. (*Carol outlines Jason's schedule.*)

Very little free time is available. For most people who enter a facility such as Seashore, a major problem has been too much free time and the inability to handle it well. Structuring the environment brings some badly needed discipline back into their lives. Particularly for adolescents, burning up energy in constructive ways is of paramount importance. Furthermore, too much free time is a fertile breeding ground for acting out behavior (Jensen & Absher, 1994).

Seashore is also on a behavior management program that makes use of levels. Part of that behavior management program is a risk-need-responsibility component that will be used to help Jason to learn how to control his emotions. Jason will start at entry level. Depending on how Jason operates in his environment, he will go up or down on the level system and will concomitantly receive more or fewer privileges. At an entry level, he will have few privileges—early bedtime, no passes—and will be under fairly close supervision. By conducting himself in a responsible manner, he may increase his level designation and gain access to a broader array of recreational activities, later bedtime, ground privileges, and weekend passes. The system is explained to Jason in a careful and clear manner, with emphasis on the fact that whether or not he moves to higher levels is his responsibility.

Educating a client about what is to happen medically and psychologically needs to be done slowly, methodically, and in nontechnical terms with numerous perceptual checks. Keeping explanations simple and helping the client gain understanding ameliorate the situation, whereas complexity only increases the chance for violent behavior to occur (Jensen & Absher, 1994; Moran, 1984, p. 234).

Jason: (*somewhat belligerently*) Like, what's this group meeting?

Carol: The group meets every day. The group decides how to tackle a community problem and then collectively makes a commitment to do something about it. Second, when problems between people arise, we all put our heads together and see how those problems can be solved. You don't necessarily have to accept an idea, but you must listen to what's being said.

Jason: I don't think I got anything to say to these nerds.

Carol: Maybe you don't. However, a lot of kids here do. You're not going to be here forever. Therefore, we look pretty hard at what's going on with you right now as you deal with other people here, how that behavior may or may not cause you problems, and what's down the road for you if you do decide to change some things in your life and what's likely if you don't. We don't ask you to love everybody here, but we do ask you to respect what they're trying to do, just as we ask them to respect you.

The human services worker's responses are from Glasser's reality therapy (1965, 1969) and focus on the issues of becoming involved, looking at alternatives, making value judgments, accepting no excuses, and assuming responsibility and consequences for one's actions. In this manner Carol goes over the entire schedule with Jason. While she explains the content of the program, she also makes sure to assess and reflect the emotional content of Jason's responses, again and again reinforcing the idea of options, responsibilities, and commitments.

Stage 2: Avoidance of Conflict. Conflict and confrontation are avoided whenever possible. Matching threat for threat is likely to obtain for the human services worker exactly the opposite of control and containment of the situation (Dubin, 1981; Fauteux, 2010). Workers who delight in continuously pushing and escalating issues are not practicing good therapeutic intervention techniques and are clearly asking for trouble (Blair, 1991). One week has elapsed since Jason's admission.

Jason: (*standing in the hallway, shouting, shaking, and trembling, face flushed*) If you think you or anybody else can make me stay in my room or in this place, you're crazier than I am. I just wanted a drink of water, and Mr. Richardson started yelling at me that it was past quiet time. Just try stopping me and see what happens.

Carol: (*quietly and calmly*) Jason, OK, sounds like you feel he put you down, but if it's a drink you want, then return to your room, I'll bring you a cup of water. Please go into your room. You can have your drink, and we can talk about it.

The worker reflects his feelings, which have now probably become more important than the drink he was going to get. However, by offering to get him a drink if he complies, the worker is giving him an honorable way out, reinforcing prosocial behavior, and also offering to listen to his concerns (Fauteux, 2010). If the client is fast approaching a point of no return, let him or her ventilate feelings. Although shouting, cursing, and yelling are not pleasant, they are better than hand-to-hand combat (McCown, 1986; Vinick, 1986). The worker should attempt to remove the agitated client from the vicinity of other residents, who may aggravate the situation (Chavez, 1999; Turnbull et al., 1990). This is best done by immediately asking the client to go to an area that is away from the other residents (McCown, 1986). If the client retains some semblance of control, the client's own room may be an appropriate place. If the client is fast losing control and cannot calm down, a better choice is a room devoid of stimuli. Such a place should be specifically prepared and reserved for this sort of occurrence.

Carol: What are you angry about?

Jason: (*still standing in the hallway, quite agitated*) He was treating me just like my old man, just making me feel like a baby.

Carol: And what were you doing?

Jason: Hey, I was just going to get a drink of water. I still had 2 minutes until quiet time. He made me so mad I wanted to pick up a chair and bust him. I still feel like going after that jerk.

Carol: What will that accomplish?

Jason: It'll show him he can't push me around like my old man does.

Carol: If you do that, it'll just confirm that you need to be here, that you can't control yourself. Is that what you want?

Jason: Maybe I just don't care.

Carol does not display anger or fear, even though the situation is potentially volatile. She speaks in a calm, controlled voice, lower and slower than Jason. She is setting the example and controlling the dialogue (Chavez, 1999). For those clients who do not respond to verbal attempts to defuse the situation, the next step for the human services worker is to give assurance that violent behavior by anybody, including both staff and clients, is unacceptable, and then to indicate what the person's choices and consequences will become if the behavior persists (Kinney, 1995, p. 49; Wood & Khuri, 1984, pp. 67–68).

Carol: You can choose to pick up a chair, Jason, but that'll mean a number of things will happen. First, nobody is allowed to hit anybody else here, and that goes for both staff and kids. If it comes to that, we will restrain you, something I'd not like to see happen. Second, if you choose to do that, no one else will get to hear your side of it, and we won't have a chance to work your problem out with Mr. Richardson. Another choice would be to go back to your room and then ask for a drink. If you do that, I will get Mr. Richardson and we'll all sit down and work this through. Would you be willing to do that?

Carol is absolutely truthful with what will happen to the client. At this stage, loss of credibility would be catastrophic (Chavez, 1999). Clients should be confronted with their inappropriate behavior, but in a caring, supportive, and problem-solving way that is not tinged with sarcasm or challenge. If the situation is deteriorating so rapidly that the worker no longer feels that communication can be maintained, it may be fruitful to have someone else enter the scene whom the client will perceive as a neutral party (Lakeside Hospital, 1988). This tactic is risky and involves a judgment call on the worker's part. Allowing clients to be rewarded for acting out by getting other people to come to the scene may reinforce inappropriate behavior and lead clients to believe that they and not the institution control the situation. Carol uses a combination of confrontation and empathy. She also provides options for Jason and sets limits as to what will be tolerated (Newhill, 2003, p. 158).

Jason: It ain't just Richardson. This whole place sucks. They won't let me do nothin'. And you don't understand either. Chaplain Gentry's the only guy who I can really talk to.

Carol: I understand that you're really disappointed and mad that you couldn't get a drink. I also know you're pretty angry at me and everybody else right now, and about the last thing you want to do is go peacefully back to your room. I know that you and Chaplain Gentry are pretty close. Would you be willing to go to your room and wait quietly while I get him?

If the client does not choose this option, then the worker will have to move the client to a safe place, which will be a time-out room. A show of force may be necessary to send a clear message: "If you can't handle yourself, we will."

Carol: Jason, I want you to go down to observation for 15 minutes and think this out. (*speaking to technicians*) Bob and Jerry, will you see that Jason gets to observation? In 15 minutes I'll be down to see if you're ready to talk this through.

Stage 3: Appeasement.   Stages 3 and 4 are probably most appropriate in emergency situations in which the worker has little basis to judge the client's aggressiveness and violence and is unable to obtain immediate assistance. Appeasement is not applicable in a number of settings under ordinary circumstances, and if Jason had reached the point of being removed to involuntary time-out, appeasement or deflection of feelings (Stage 4) would be highly inappropriate and run counter to good therapeutic practice.

However, generally it is better in all situations to err on the side of humility than to project a "tough guy" image, regardless of the client's verbal barbs, threats, and exhortations. This recommendation does not mean that the human services worker should become a doormat to be walked all over by the client. It does mean that by operating in an empathic mode we can see just how frightening and alarming the situation is to the client. The reason threats are made is mostly because clients are scared, frustrated, and at a loss as to what to do over situations they can't control (Newhill, 2003,

p. 175). Any attempts by the workers to counter threat with threat in an emergency situation are likely to confirm the client's suspicions that bad things are going to happen.

Appeasement can be attempted if the client's demands are simple and reasonable, even if those demands are made in a bellicose manner. Early on it is better to grant demands and to defer until later worry about what "lessons" need to be taught (Piercy, 1984, p. 148). This approach may be difficult for some human services workers to accept, because it is based on the idea that there is no winner or loser in a potentially violent confrontation between an agitated client and the institution (Moran, 1984, p. 234). In Jason's case, when he feels that his use of anger to make his point is ignored, that makes him more aggressive and his anger moves up to hostility and threat.

Jason: (*Barges into the human services worker's office, fists clenched, and starts shouting in an agitated, high-pitched voice.*) Listen, big shot! I wanted to mail this letter to my girl. She doesn't know what's happened to me, and that jerk Richardson won't give me a stamp. I could bust all yer heads!

Carol: (*in a calm, collected voice*) He's going by the rules, but I understand your being hot under the collar. Please sit down at the table here, and I'll see what can be done about getting a stamp.

The human services worker meets this demand because it is easily done and does not seriously conflict with institutional rules. She is also alone with an extremely agitated client who may or may not act out. There may be a discussion afterward with the other worker who gave the original order, but there needs to be a clear understanding among all workers that in emergencies, judgment calls may bend the rules a bit or countermand orders of others.

Stage 4: Deflection.   Deflection of angry feelings is attempted by shifting to other, less threatening topics. This may be done in a variety of ways. Asking the client to take a physically less threatening position shifts the focus away from agitated motor activity to problem solving (Wood & Khuri, 1984, p. 68).

Carol: (*repeating her statement patiently, firmly, and respectfully*) Jason, I understand how important it is for you to be able to write to your girlfriend, and how it frustrates you when things don't seem to go your way, but getting in my face won't get you what you want. Please sit down. Then I'll get you a stamp and see if we can iron out this problem.

The human services worker literally and figuratively gets the client off his feet and in a less threatening operating mode (Epstein & Carter, 1988). The worker is also quietly but firmly setting limits by asking the client to sit. When clients engage in bullying behavior, it is important for the worker not to threaten the person's critical need to get control, but it is equally important to let the client know you will not be intimidated by it (Fauteux, 2010). Because agitated people seldom listen closely to requests for compliance, Carol acknowledges Jason's feeling state and then uses the broken record routine (Canter & Canter, 1982) of repeating her request. She is also employing another behavior management technique: By making a reward contingent on a compliant behavior, Carol is using "Grandma's law" (Becker, 1971), which basically states, "First you eat your spinach, and then you get your ice cream." By using problem-solving techniques, no matter how small the real or imagined injustice is, the human services worker conveys to the client an interest in the client as an individual and not just another name in the institutional computer (Wood & Khuri, 1984, p. 71). Parceling out the problems into workable pieces, the worker removes them from the realm of the enormous and makes them solvable (Weinger, 2001, p. 45).

Jason: I can't get nothin' done here. Everything's screwed up. School, home, people, the food, my freedom. It's a concentration camp.

Carol: OK. There seem to be at least three things that are really bugging you right now. Not being able to get a pass yet, the way your dad got angry in family therapy, and your problem with the math assignment yesterday. Together, I can see how it'd become overwhelming. Let's take them one at a time and see what can be done about each. Let me take some notes, so I can keep all this straight. (*Jason goes into a long-winded explanation while Carol listens and takes notes.*)

Until absolutely sure what the problem is, the human services worker should never make promises about what can or cannot be done when attempting to calm an agitated client (Newhill, 2003, p. 210; Wood & Khuri, 1984, p. 71). By allowing Jason to ventilate and by taking notes, Carol affirms that what he has to say is important and plays up rather than down the client's concerns (Chavez, 1999).

Carol: I know that weekend pass is really important. A pass is based on good behavior and your level status. If you feel like you've gotten jerked around, griping about it won't help much. Very specifically, write down why you think you deserve the pass. I'll take it to the staffing this afternoon.

Having the client write down problems also defuses angry feelings and acting out. In many instances, the client may just be testing limits. Testing limits is a given with a client such as Jason, and the human services worker can be expected to be tested over and over again (Poliks, 1999). To write down clearly and logically what the problem is calls for time and effort, which very few clients will invest if the problem is not important (Epstein & Carter, 1988). Writing down the particulars of the problem is also cathartic for clients, allowing them to gain some emotional distance from it and view the situation in a more objective light (McCown, 1986).

When other, more overt ploys are ineffective, the client may use manipulation and threat to obtain demands.

Jason: If you don't get that pass for me, you ain't much of a counselor, and they'll be real sorry they didn't give it to me.

Carol: When you try and lay that guilt trip on me and make threats about what you'll do if you don't get your way, that's a pretty good indication that the staff's judgment was right and makes it even more difficult to act as your advocate. It's not so much any of the demands that you want, but more like pushing the limits to see how far you can get by manipulating and threatening me.

The response the human services worker makes is one from Adlerian psychotherapy called "avoiding the tar baby" (Dinkmeyer, Pew, & Dinkmeyer, 1979, p. 118). By responding directly to the client, the human services worker does not allow herself to be caught up in the manipulative trap the client lays for her. Although the response is confrontive, it is exceedingly effective with manipulative individuals because it deflects them from their game plan and causes them to consider the consequences of their actions (Wood & Khuri, 1984, p. 71).

When clients become agitated, deflecting anger through physical activity can be helpful. Clients can take out their frustrations through activities that range from pounding on a heavy bag (Vinick, 1986) to tearing up telephone directories (McCown, 1986). At the same time, the human services worker can reinforce the client for acting in more appropriate ways (Jensen & Absher, 1994). Although teaching anger management skills may be more effective in the long run (LeCroy, 1988), appropriate and safe physical exertion to burn up angry feelings is an effective short-term solution.

Jason: (*tearing up the Yellow Pages*) Umphf! I . . . get so mad . . . I . . . Arggh! I . . . wish this phone book was that no-good SOB's face.

Carol: But in fact you haven't torn anybody's face off. You've made a good choice. Much better than when you were going around clobbering people. You don't have to pay any consequences at all for tearing up the phone book. You get it out of your system and get back in control.

Jason: (*Continues ventilating, until finally he runs out of energy and lets his arms hang limply at his side.*)

Carol: (*Continues to reinforce Jason for acting appropriately and within limits.*) Look at what you could have done. You could have swung a chair at Mr. Richardson, which would have gotten you into hot water. The very kinds of thing that got you here in the first place. But you didn't do that. What you did was perfectly acceptable and within the limits here.

Stage 5: Time-Out. When clients cannot contend with the emotion of the moment, they are asked to go to a reduced-stimulus environment, to be alone and think things out. A clear assessment of how agitated the client is needs to be made at this point. Is the client able and willing to leave a high-stimulus situation for a few minutes to rest and think things over? If the client is not overly reactive, then the worker may ask the client to take a minimal time-out in living quarters.

Jason: I don't want to sit, talk, or be reasonable. I want this scumbag place to do something!

Carol: Right now I can see there's no way this is going to get solved. You can go to your room and think things over. Go for 15 minutes. If you can come back and show me you're in control, that's it, no reduction in level, no write-ups, and it's forgotten.

When a clear threat is made, there is still a possibility of reducing the tension by telling the client that threats will not work, but the client has still not done anything wrong so there is still time to work things out (Fauteux, 2010). However, if the client can't calm down and start to work on the problem constructively, then time-out is the next option (Vinick, 1986).

Carol: I've tried to work this through with you, and you clearly don't want to hear it. When you continue to make threats, you're saying to me you're not willing to abide by the rules and are choosing to have rules enforced. I want you to go to the observation room for 30 minutes right now. At the end of that time I'll be around to see you. If you don't feel like talking, you don't have to, but you can go back in the room for another 30 minutes. You can continue to do that until you're willing to talk to me about how you think you've been treated unfairly.

The human services worker states these conditions in a matter-of-fact manner and does not press the issue (Vinick, 1986). If the client is so agitated as to be beyond the grasp of reality and is unwilling to be compliant with the human services worker's request, then the worker needs help to contain the situation.

Stage 6: Show of Force. If the client is unable to proceed to time-out or is otherwise noncompliant or acting out, then a show of force is needed (Piercy, 1984, p. 148). If the client is already agitated enough to warn the human services workers that help may be warranted, the interview should be carried out in an open hallway or large meeting room where the participants are in plain view of other staff members and the client can be restrained easily (Viner, 1982). The show of force indicates that any display of violence or threat of violence will not be tolerated and often helps disorganized clients regain control of themselves (Wood & Khuri, 1984, p. 68). If this stage is reached, the potential for violence is high, and the worker should not attempt to deal with the client alone. Either by paging help through an emergency code or by having assistance readily available, the worker needs to be able to summon enough help to demonstrate that compliance is now required (Lakeside Hospital, 1988).

However, there are times when, through no fault of the worker, potentially violent situations occur when the worker is alone and not immediately able to call for assistance. The following procedures may keep the worker out of harm's way (Chavez, 1999; Epstein & Carter, 1988; Lakeside Hospital, 1988; Moran, 1984, pp. 238–248; Morrison, 1993, pp. 79–100; Thackrey, 1987; Turnbull et al., 1990).

1. *Stay calm and relaxed.* Tensing of muscles and agitated movement only fuel the situation and cause the client to expect that something bad (for the client) is about to happen. Relaxation techniques such as simple deep breathing are extremely helpful, allowing one to stay loose, anticipate client responses, and move quickly.

2. *Practice positive self-talk.* Even in the worst situations, running positive "billboards" through the mind's eye will help keep control of the situation.

3. *Do not stare at the client.* Keep casual eye contact because the eyes of the individual will typically move to where a blow might be struck. Focus on an imaginary spot on the client's upper chest, about where the first button on a shirt would be, occasionally glancing at the eyes and other parts of the individual's body. Keeping focus on the centerline

of the client's body will also let the human services worker avoid being faked out by extremity movements.

4. *Stay an arm's length away or more.* Make a judgment about how long the client's arms are, and stay an arm's length and a bit more away. Remember that agitated clients generally have an expanded sense of personal space and feel threatened when that space is entered.

5. *Stay on the client's dominant side.* Know which of the client's hands is dominant and stay close to the client's dominant side. Especially on males, the watch hand typically indicates the client's weak side. If you cannot determine this for sure, stay on the client's right side since most people are right-handed. In an aggressive stance, a person invariably places the foot of the weak side forward. If the worker keeps to the dominant, or right, side of an assailant, any blow aimed by the assailant is likely to have less power and be a glancing one, because the assailant will have to pivot to get the worker back on his or her left in order to hit the worker more easily. Staying on the right, or dominant, side means the assailant will have to take time to move into a more favorable position and will not be able to use his or her strength as effectively.

6. *Keep arms at sides and hands open.* Folded arms or hands on hips are bad for two reasons. They imply hostility or authority, and they put the worker at a distinct disadvantage because of the time it takes to unfold them and defend oneself.

7. *Assume a defensive posture.* Stand with feet slightly spread, face to face with the client but tending a bit to the client's weak side. Move the dominant leg slightly to the rear with the knee locked ready to pivot and run. Move the other leg slightly forward of the body and bent slightly at the knee. This position will allow the worker the best chance to stay upright, and staying upright is the best safeguard against being hurt.

8. *Avoid cornering.* When the client is placed in an angle formed by two walls or other objects, with the human services worker directly in front of the client, the only way out is through the worker.

9. *Avoid ordering.* When a client is threatening violence, attempting to order or command a client to do something is likely to aggravate the situation further. Staying with the basic empathic listening and responding skills used throughout this book is far more likely to lead to satisfactory results.

10. *Do perceptual checks.* Ask for the client's help. If current verbal responses are merely agitating the situation, ask the client what solutions or techniques might calm things down.

11. *Admit mistakes.* If you've made an error in judgment, admit it and make an apology. If things have gone this far, do not be afraid to lose face.

12. *Do nothing.* If doing something will make matters worse, do nothing. If the client is determined to leave and help is not immediately available, let the client go. *Never* attempt to touch a client under these circumstances without first indicating what you are about to do and getting the client's agreement to do so.

13. *Give validation.* In a sincere and empathic manner, acknowledge that the person has a good reason for feeling that way and let him or her leave.

All human services providers and especially crisis workers should undergo training in simple self-defense and takedown procedures (Blair, 1991; Morrison, 1993, pp. 79–100; Thackrey, 1987; Turnbull et al., 1990). Gately and Stabb (2005) found restrain and defensive training topics least attended to by training programs. Numerous facilities provide such training for little or no charge. Local YMCAs or YWCAs and college continuing education courses may offer such instruction, or the local high school wrestling coach may even be prevailed on. Instruction should be a priority of the institution, and *all* personnel should receive training. The organization should certainly provide self-defense training. If it doesn't, and you have decided to work there, you absolutely need to get training yourself.

Stage 7: Seclusion. Seclusion may be generally differentiated from time-out by its length, its setting, and its involuntary nature. Seclusion is a severe type of limit setting for the client in a safe and secure environment where the client can reorganize thinking, feeling, and behavior (Mattson & Sacks, 1978). When seclusion or physical or chemical restraints are used, federal and state guidelines must be followed. They should be used only when there is imminent danger to the client or others and no safer or more effective alternatives are available (dos Reis et al., 2003). There is a great deal of controversy as to whether seclusion or restraints should be used, given the potential for physical and psychological harm (Glezer & Weintrab, 2010; Kumble & McSherry, 2010; Mohr, 2010). However, in some cases there is no other option if self-harm or harm to others is imminent.

There are a number of reasons for seclusion: (1) the client is agitated, hyperactive, verbally threatening, or damaging property; (2) the client is impulsive or intrusive and does not respond to limit setting; (3) the client is making suicidal gestures and is unable or unwilling to make a verbal contract about controlling behavior; or (4) the client must be protected from possible harm by others (Baradell, 1985; Lewis, 1993, p. 105). This intervention still allows the client some control over mobility, thinking, and autonomy. Seclusion may be of greater benefit to clients who are overstimulated by social contact (dos Reis et al., 2003).

Negative emotions such as anger, guilt, confusion, helplessness, and loss of control are typical client responses to seclusion (Outlaw & Lowery, 1992). Given these negative feelings, it is more than likely that the client may not willingly go to seclusion. In the confrontation with Jason, a response team has been called and is ready to take Jason to seclusion.

Carol: I'd really like you to go on your own down to time-out. It's up to you. You can go on your own right now, or the technicians will take you to seclusion.

Even at this late hour, the worker is still attempting to allow Jason to exercise options and make choices (Baradell, 1985).

Jason: I ain't gonna go nowhere 'ceptin' outta here.

Carol backs away, and the response team moves in. On a predetermined signal by the leader, they quickly take Jason down. One member holds his head, and the other four carry him to seclusion. Once placed in seclusion, the client is oriented to what is going to occur, and a staff member is assigned to monitor the client. Checks are made at 15-, 30-, or 60-minute intervals, depending on the client's mental status. Copies of nursing and general care orders are given to both staff and the client. Seclusion has a low level of sensory input—no radio or television, no visitors—and emphasis is on biological needs. "Low level" does not mean that the client is sensorially deprived; it is important to prevent feelings of abandonment. The client is shown acceptance by the human services worker and reassured that seclusion is necessary and temporary and that the client can return to normal routine when behavior calms down (Baradell, 1985).

Carol: I'm sorry you chose to go to seclusion, Jason. You decided to exercise that option, but when you can agree to not make threats, control your behavior to the point you can talk this through, and make a written contract as to what you will do, you can come back out.

In an acute stage of agitation such as Jason has just experienced, it is no longer appropriate to explore conflicts or feelings (Ruesch, 1973). Carol's communication with the client is brief, direct, concrete, but kind. Given the client's sensory overload, sleep is an excellent therapeutic modality, and the client should be allowed to use it (Baradell, 1985).

One negative footnote is appropriate here: A few clients may use seclusion as a way of achieving notoriety and a macho image (Gutheil, 1978). If such a hidden agenda is suspected, the human services worker should thoroughly discuss this problem with the other residents and obtain their help in being nonresponsive to the client's "tough guy" behavior.

Stage 8: Restraints. Restraints are most often employed in psychiatric facilities and are used in conjunction with a request from the nursing staff and backed by a doctor's order. When a client is placed in restraints, close observation is absolutely necessary. Under no circumstances should clients be restrained without such guidelines and available professional medical staff. If the client is acting out and will not go to seclusion, restraints will have to be used. Restraints might be either physical or chemical. Restraints are controversial, and their use is closely regulated in both a legal and an ethical sense (dos Reis et al., 2003). Restraints are employed when it is evident that the client may be harmful to self or others (Stilling, 1992; Tardiff, 1984a, p. 48). If the client is to be restrained, then adequate staff should be available, consisting of at least one person for each limb and another person who serves as leader, for a total of five members. Written guidelines and constant rehearsal of procedures with observation and critique should be used to keep the team's skills well honed (Tardiff, 1984b).

Seclusion and restraints should *never* be used as a way of controlling clients, making life "easier" for the custodians, or as punishment. These are truly last-resort measures, because their use can cause a host of other problems for the client (Morrison, 1993, p. 105). If at all possible, the crisis worker should not be involved in the episode, because involvement may erect barriers to future therapeutic endeavors.

Stage 9: Sedation. If all else fails, the client needs to be chemically restrained by a doctor's order (dos Reis et al., 2003). The problem now becomes clearly medical, and until the medical staff believes that medication is no longer necessary, there is little the human services worker can do. If sedation is needed with Jason, it does not mean the end of Jason's story. Stage 9 is essentially a complete time-out for both Jason and the staff. For Jason, it will allow the sensory overload he is experiencing to diminish and return to normal limits. It will give the staff members time to reorganize their thoughts on how best to deal with this highly agitated adolescent. When Jason comes out of sedation, the staff will start down the treatment road with him again and will have developed a new plan to deal with this angry young man.

The Violent Geriatric Client

Although medical science has been able to prolong the lives of Americans, treatment for neuropsychiatric disorders concomitant with increased longevity remains beyond the reach of medical science at present. Accompanying the neuropsychiatric problems of the geriatric client are reduced judgment and increased impulsivity, limited mobility, drug dependency, multiple personal loss, financial problems, and limited social supports, which all potentially contribute to violent behavior (Mentes & Ferrario, 1989; Petrie, 1984, p. 107). Nursing home staff are at high risk for assault by patients, and they need to be trained to be aware of and respond to potential threats of physical assault (Gates, Fitzwater, & Succop, 2005; Hillman et al., 2005; Newhill, 2003, pp. 91–92; Tardiff, 1989).

The case of Cliff demonstrates how the agitated and mildly disoriented elderly client can be stabilized without medication. Reality orientation (Osborn, 1991; Taulbee & Folsom, 1966), reminiscence (Butler, 1963), and remotivation (Garber, 1965) techniques are workable options for the mildly disoriented elderly client. The case of Grace shows how validation therapy (Feil, 1982) may be used with the severely disoriented elderly. These cases illustrate that psychologically infirm elderly clients need not always spend this final stage of their lives in chemically induced compliance.

Mild Disorientation: The Case of Cliff

Cliff Hastings has lived a full and eventful life, but now, at the age of 74, he is a resident of a skilled nursing care facility. He was a strapping man who had worked all over the world on big construction projects until he was 72. He invented many engineering techniques in steam fitting and chilled water cooling systems. He lost his wife to cancer 10 years ago but submerged himself in his work and lived a highly productive life as a widower.

He has had excellent relationships with his two children, Jan and Robert. Although they and their families live geographically distant from Cliff, they love their father very much and are very concerned about him.

At age 73, Cliff got up one morning, prepared to go to work, and fell flat on his face with a stroke. Although he recovered to the extent that he was able to shuffle around the house, lung complications set in. He was diagnosed as having emphysema and went on oxygen. Six months later, he was no longer able to take care of himself physically, was starting to have memory lapses, and was moved to Hursthaven Nursing Home by his children. At Hursthaven, he has become progressively more confused about people, places, and times, and when asked to do something has been either rebellious or passively resistant.

A crisis was precipitated when he knocked over an oxygen tank in the middle of the night because the "Arabs were after him" and broke the nose of a male attendant who tried to calm him down as he attempted to struggle out of his bed. Cliff is about to meet Marilyn, a gerontological counselor. She has just been retained by Hursthaven to deal with crisis situations such as Cliff's.

Assessment. Marilyn has thoroughly reviewed Cliff's chart and has discussed his case with the medical and primary care staff. Many of the primary care staff members maintain that Cliff is noncompliant, badly disoriented, and dangerous, and they would like to keep him heavily sedated. Cliff's stroke, his unplanned aggressive outburst, his hostile and uncooperative behavior, his fear of the medical equipment, and his depression, plus the fact that his outburst occurred at night, all support the staff's contention that little but chemical restraint is left for Cliff.

Marilyn decides to conduct her own assessment by interviewing Cliff. She has three purposes in mind: (1) to determine Cliff's degree of disorientation and agitation, (2) to use her therapeutic skills to reduce his disruptive behavior and help him return to a state of equilibrium with as little reliance on medication as possible, and (3) to help Cliff use whatever resources he has to live this final stage of his life as fully as he is able.

Marilyn: Hello, I'm Marilyn. I don't believe I've met you. You seem pretty angry about something.

Cliff: (*suspiciously*) Who the hell are you?

Marilyn: I'm new here, part of the staff, and I'm getting around meeting all the residents. Sorry you're so angry. What can I do to help?

Cliff: I'm Cliff Hastings, and I'm mad as hell. Look at what those SOBs have done to me. I pay $6,000 a month for this place to strap me down. I'll kill the bastards if I get a chance. Can you get me out of here?

Marilyn: (*speaking in a strong but soft and empathic voice, while pulling up a chair and sitting down directly in his line of sight*) No! I can't right now. I guess I'd be mad too if I were strapped in like that. Do you know where you are?

Cliff: I'm in Hell, and these people are all devils.

Marilyn: It may feel like that right now, but this is Hursthaven Nursing Home. Do you know that?

Cliff: Too damn well.

Marilyn: Do you know what day it is?

Cliff: Who cares? They're all the same in here.

Marilyn assesses Cliff's degree of contact with reality by determining how well oriented he is to person, place, and time. Although he does not give specific, concrete responses, his retorts indicate that he is fairly well in touch with reality, given his present agitated state.

Marilyn: I'm sorry you're feeling so angry. Can I get you a drink of water?

Eliciting Trust.   Offering clients food or drink tends to defuse the situation and make them more accepting of initiating overtures the worker may tender (Wood & Khuri, 1984, p. 67). Marilyn also sits down by Cliff and meets him at eye level. She places herself on his physical level and in his direct line of sight. Standing over a client who is confused tends to distort the caregiver's image in grotesque ways and may be very threatening (Wolanin & Phillips, 1981, p. 106).

Cliff: (*Takes a sip of water from cup Marilyn offers.*) Yeah, that's the least somebody around this place could do for the money I pay to be doped up and trussed up like a pig.

Marilyn: How do you feel?

Cliff: How the hell do you think I feel, young lady?

Marilyn: I guess I'd not only feel like a pig all trussed up, but mad as a wildcat in a gunnysack. How did this happen?

Marilyn matches the vernacular of the client and interjects a bit of humor (Tomine, 1986). She is interested in knowing what happened, but her major concern is to continue posing open-ended questions to assess how much in touch with reality Cliff is and to let him know she is interested in and concerned about him. Marilyn manages to gain a working rapport with Cliff and explores last night's incident.

Marilyn: So what happened last night that got you in that fix?

Cliff: The Arab, he was after me. He was gonna strangle me, but nobody believes me. (*Points to attendant.*) That guy said it was one of the guys that work here at night. Said I busted his nose. Well, it was the Arabs.

Marilyn: Why do you think it was the Arabs?

Reality Orientation.   Marilyn is taking a first step in attempting to relieve Cliff's confusion by using reality orientation (Taulbee & Folsom, 1966). Reality orientation focuses on anchoring clients to who they are, where they are, and why they are there. When a client's response or behavior is out of touch with reality, the worker asks the client a *why* question, in an approach contrary to that of most therapeutic interventions (Taulbee, 1978, p. 207). Marilyn does this because she is trying to find out the reason for the behavior. Once she knows that, she can start to reorient Cliff.

Cliff: I spent a lot of time in Arabia, you know. Worked in construction. Put up a lot of refrigeration plants and steam systems. Hard to believe you'd need steam in that hothouse. Sometimes I wish I was back in Arabia. But that doesn't mean any damn Arab terrorist can come in here in the middle of the night and kill me.

Marilyn: (*genuinely interested*) Hey! That sounds pretty exciting. I've hardly been out of the Midwest. I'll bet you've seen some pretty hair-raising things, and I can guess how you might think somebody was an Arab, being in a strange place like this.

Cliff rambles on for quite a while about his experiences there, with Marilyn listening and responding using person-centered techniques of attending, affirming, restating for clarification, reflecting feelings, and asking open-ended questions.

Pacing.   Cliff's response about working in Arabia gives Marilyn a clue about the image Cliff saw attacking him in the night. However, she does not try to change his mind about what happened. She keeps pace with Cliff. She lets him tell his story without hurrying or trying to persuade him that he was mistaken last night. Patience is of maximum benefit in gaining the trust she will need if she is to accomplish anything with him (Taulbee, 1978, p. 210).

Reminiscence Therapy.   Marilyn's approach in urging Cliff to talk about his past is contradictory to most standard operating procedures and generally accepted counseling techniques. Most therapeutic systems try very hard to keep clients in present time and view trips to the past as counterproductive to changing real-time problems. However, allowing geriatric clients to ruminate about past experiences can be therapeutically effective (Brooker & Duce, 2000; Buchanan et al., 2002; Cully, LaVoie, & Gfeller, 2001; Ebersole, 1978a, p. 145; Hsieh & Wang, 2003; Hyer et al., 2002).

Reminiscence therapy (Butler, 1963; Osborn, 1991) is a nonthreatening experience that allows older clients to reflect on their lives and restore credibility to them (Miller, 1986). Reminiscence therapy has become one of the standard treatments for the depressed elderly and has been successfully used worldwide in both individual and group formats (Ando, 2005; Cappeliez & Watt, 2005; Haber, 2006; McKee et al., 2005; Spar & La Rue, 2006; Van Puyenbroeck & Maes, 2006; Wang, 2005). Memory dysfunction and personality disorganization are central to Cliff's current crisis and confusion. Reminiscence helps in personality reorganization and increases self-confidence because it draws on aspects of long-term memory that have been imprinted and can be recalled easily (Singer, Tracz, & Dworkin, 1991). Reminiscence can be therapeutic and healing for the client; it is a simple, enjoyable sharing of anecdotes that allows the worker to form a close affiliation with the client (Ebersole, 1978a, p. 145).

Individuals may use reminiscing to reconcile and put to rest bitter memories, reconstruct and enjoy pleasant memories, reduce boredom, and prepare for death (Cully, LaVoie, & Gfeller, 2001). Further, if reminiscence is used in groups, interpersonal bonds can be increased as clients relate to historical benchmarks, personal achievements, objects, locations, and people. Older clients regain a sense of empowerment as the "experts" on the times they have lived in. Self-esteem is enhanced through recall of past achievements in the face of declining physical capacities (McMahon & Rhudick, 1964, pp. 292–298). "Unfinished business" from the past may be identified and handled (O'Leary & Nieuwstraten, 2001). It also offers the opportunity for physical contact and validation for what the elderly have done with their lives (Baker, 1985) and helps them cope with grief and depression through social interaction and renewed social skills (Hsieh & Wang, 2003; Singer, Tracz, & Dworkin, 1991).

Cliff: Yeah . . . (*Voice trails off.*) . . . I used to be hot stuff . . . but I'm not so hot now. Hell, half the time I don't even know who, what, or where I am.

Marilyn: (*Touches client's arm lightly with her hand.*) It sounds like that's pretty scary, having run things most of your life, and now things are out of control.

Cliff: I hate to admit it, but that's right. Now I got to have help getting to the john! How'd you like that? It embarrasses the hell out of me. They treat me like a 2-year-old.

Marilyn: So being embarrassed and not being treated like a man are the worst parts of being here. I wonder what we might do to change that?

Anchoring. Marilyn uses a reflective statement of feeling to integrate Cliff's past with his present. By bringing up past incidents and hooking them to the present, she attempts to reinforce and help Cliff reassert his competence. Marilyn also uses touch to anchor him psychologically to someone in the institution (Wolanin & Phillips, 1981, pp. 105–106). Prior to the assault, a kind but sterile atmosphere had existed for Cliff at Hursthaven.

Like most human beings, Cliff has not responded well to living in an emotional vacuum. Since the attack, the atmosphere between Cliff and the staff has become adversarial in nature. Marilyn needs to change Cliff's view of the staff as being against him and the staff's view that Cliff is to be avoided. Staff members who have hands-on contact with Cliff on a regular basis need to be given training in the approaches Marilyn is using. Staffing and case review are particularly important for coordinating the different staff members who will deal with Cliff in a 24-hour period. All staff members who come in contact with him during the course of the day will introduce themselves, call Cliff by name, state the date, give a short preview of the next few hours' activities, and also explain any procedures, medical or otherwise, that they are carrying out. By consistently orienting the client, the staff takes a first step in treating confusion (Taulbee, 1978, p. 209).

Marilyn also picks up on Cliff's fear of losing control. Being wildly out of control is completely out of character for clients like Cliff, who are frightened at the prospect of losing their minds. Even more fears are generated when elderly clients sense someone is afraid of them or avoiding them because of fear of violence (Lion & Pasternak, 1973). Marilyn engages in a number of activities in this dialogue. The most important is that she has made a small but significant change in the interactional system that currently exists between Cliff and the staff by representing herself as an empathic, caring spokesperson for the institution and as an advocate for him (Fisch, Weakland, & Segal, 1983). Second, she reflects Cliff's anger, fear, and loss of control. She acknowledges and validates his experiences, but she is not just mouthing platitudes. She knows that the more he lacks current orientation, the more the staff will tend to avoid him. The more he is avoided, the less contact he has with people, and the more out of touch and disoriented he is likely to become (Petrie, 1984, pp. 114–115). The cycle can become deeper and deeper if uninterrupted and may cause even more disorientation and aggressive acts in the future (Miller, 1986).

Distinguishing Between Illusions and Hallucinations

Marilyn understands that what agitated Cliff was probably not a hallucination, as the staff thinks, but more than likely an illusion. While piecing together the tale of the night before, she determines that one of the Sisters of Charity who works at the nursing home made rounds about the time Cliff became agitated. The sister's habit may have made her look like an Arab in the dim light. Thus, what Cliff saw was probably an illusion based in fact, not fiction.

By proposing an explanation of the event, Marilyn allows Cliff to understand that he was not delusional but was misperceiving reality. The two problems are very different, and the difference is of great significance in calming Cliff. Although this conclusion may sound very pat, such happenings are all too common among mildly confused and disoriented clients. Very definite, concrete stimuli often create illusions that disrupt peace of mind for geriatric clients, leaving them to doubt their own perceptions. It is extremely important for the worker to relate such a hypothesis to mildly confused clients such as Cliff who are very much concerned about keeping in touch with reality (Wolanin & Phillips, 1981, p. 107).

Marilyn: (*Relates her hypothesis to Cliff.*) So I believe that you weren't really crazy last night, but actually saw Sister Lucy making rounds. If you think about it, it makes sense.

Cliff: I don't know. I still really believe there was an Arab in here.

Marilyn: From all you've told me about your experiences there, I can understand that. But I also know that when you're zonked out in a strange place with the medical equipment around and strangers passing to and fro, suddenly waking up and seeing things differently is not uncommon and doesn't mean you're nuts. I'll bet if you think about it, it has happened before. I know it has happened to me. There's a big difference between misunderstanding what you see and seeing something that isn't there.

Sundown Syndrome. Because the event happened in the early evening, the sundown syndrome must be considered. Events that accompany the end of the day

in an institution are strange and unsettling to residents who have been used to a regimen of activities based on their own time and the security of their own home. Unmet toilet needs, absence of a snack, staff members' attitudes, different noises, decreased light, effects of sedatives, and presence of fewer personnel all add up to fear and strangeness without the support of another human being. These conditions can lead the client to act out (Blair & New, 1991; Stilling, 1992; Wolanin & Phillips, 1981, p. 107). Given the need to further assure Cliff about the reality of the situation, Marilyn relates the problems that occur with the approach of evening in the institution and makes some suggestions about how things might be changed to make this time less threatening.

Marilyn: If you could make things here a bit more like home, what would they be?

Cliff: Well, I used to put my earphones on and listen to some country music and have a beer before I hit the hay. I don't know much else, just watch TV and stuff. No special furniture or anything. I lived in apartments and hotels most of my life.

Marilyn: I notice that there's not much of you in this room. It looks like a hospital room instead of Cliff's room. You mentioned a lot of items you collected over the years and picture albums of all your travels. Where are they?

Cliff: Oh, my kids just stored them away.

Marilyn: I'd like to see if we couldn't get some of those in here, dress the place up a bit, so when people come by they'd know it was Cliff Hastings, world-class engineer, who lives here.

Security Blankets. Marilyn proposes that articles familiar to Cliff be brought into the room for two reasons. First, creating a familiar environment may go a long way toward creating a basis in reality for the fact that this is now Cliff's home and reconciling him to this stage in his life (Petrie, 1984, p. 116). Second, suddenly awakening in a medical environment with a variety of strange machines and tubes running in and out of one's body is extremely threatening because such foreign objects alter a person's body images and surroundings in a very negative way (Wolanin & Phillips, 1981, p. 106). Having familiar objects immediately visible can help Cliff reorient without becoming agitated in the process. Marilyn will check with administrative staff to see whether Cliff's stereo equipment can be brought into his room. She will also check with medical staff to see whether a bottle of beer in the evening will confound his medication. If possible, providing these amenities will further approximate Cliff's routine at home and provide orientation and security (Miller, 1986).

Remotivation.   Finally, Marilyn will attempt to involve Cliff in the activities of the institution. It is important to involve clients interpersonally and have them become physically and psychologically active in their environment. For people like Cliff who have been highly active throughout their lives, it is critical to fill idle time in meaningful ways to keep such clients from drifting into depression (Donahue, 1965). This does not mean forcing and cajoling clients into doing something contrary to what interests them. Playing bingo might be fun for many people, but forcing a person to engage in such an activity is inappropriate (Miller, 1986). After listening to Cliff, Marilyn makes a proposal designed to reinvolve him with other humans.

> **Marilyn:** I'd like you to consider a proposition I have to make. Hursthaven has an alliance with St. Peter's Orphanage. None of those kids have anybody to care about them. I have a couple of boys in mind that I think you could do some good with. You've got some great stories that they'd love and probably some wisdom that could be helpful to those guys. They just mainly need a man to talk to, and I wonder if you'd be willing to help out.

Marilyn's agenda is twofold. She is truthful in what she tells Cliff. She also knows that the two boys will have a positive effect on Cliff in turn. Older people seem particularly interested in sharing their experiences with the young (Ebersole, 1978b, p. 241). Cliff's candidness, wisdom, and trove of stories are likely to have a positive effect on two boys who are as anchorless as Cliff. She focuses on Cliff from a strength perspective (Newhill, 2003, pp. 160–161). Rather than focusing on what is wrong with the client, she capitalizes on the client's strong points, positive qualities, and overall potential for controlling his behavior.

Remotivation therapy is a technique used to stimulate and revitalize people who are no longer interested in the present or the future (Dennis, 1978, p. 219). It is based on a combination of reminiscence and reality orientation. Remotivation attempts to persuade the client that he or she is accepted by others as an individual who has unique and important traits that make him distinguishable from everyone else (Garber, 1965). Reminiscing about one's experiences with the concrete world and identifying and asserting one's experiences through interactions with others often lead to strengthening the concept of reality. Being encouraged to describe oneself concretely as a person with roles and specific social functions and speaking accurately about past and present experiences give a person strength (Dennis, 1978, p. 220).

Severe Disorientation: The Case of Grace

The standard regimen for working with geriatric clients has been to attempt to "reality orient" them to the present. Such an approach becomes problematic for moderately confused clients and profoundly so for those who have almost entirely retreated from the reality of the present. Attempts to orient moderately to severely confused, very old clients to person, place, and time are generally futile. For many of these clients, nothing could be less worthwhile, for there is clearly not much in the present worth remembering (Miller, 1986). Seizing on this notion, Naomi Feil developed validation therapy (Feil, 1982). Her thesis is to acknowledge the feelings of the person, no matter how irrational they may seem to be. By dignifying feelings, the worker validates the person. To deny the client's feelings is to deny past existence and thus deny the personhood of the individual.

Feil also believes that validating early memories enables clients to resolve the past and justify their role in old age. Positive outcomes from using the approach are restoring self-worth, reducing stress, justifying life, resolving unfinished conflicts, and establishing a better and more secure feeling for the client (Feil, 1982, p. 1). The worker continuously validates the client as a first step in restoring self-worth and affirming that at least one person is interested and concerned enough to listen to what the client's life has been. Anyone overhearing a dialogue between a worker and a client who has severely regressed into an irrational past would probably wonder at first whether the worker had also become senile. For validation therapy to be effective, the worker must have some creative insight into the verbal meanderings and repetitive behaviors of the client (Miller, 1986).

Listen to Marilyn as she attempts to convince an 83-year-old woman to go to dinner. Grace is standing in the hallway refusing to be moved. She is engaging in a rocking motion with her arms and softly humming to herself. Staff's efforts to get her to go to dinner have been fruitless, and she is becoming increasingly agitated and threatening as a number of staff members are attempting to orient her and get her to comply with their requests. Marilyn enters this scene and asks the rest of the staff to leave them.

Grace: There, there! Don't you cry.

Marilyn: I see you're really concerned about your baby.

Grace: Yes, I've been up all night with Ellen. She must have colic, but I can't seem to get her to settle down. I need to get Dr. Heinz, he's our family doctor, but I don't have anyone to drive me to town.

Marilyn: It really worries you that Ellen doesn't seem to be getting any better. You must be awfully tired and hungry!

Grace: Even though Ellen's cranky, she's no bother. She's really a beautiful baby. It's just that her father isn't around much. He works on the railroad, and I could use some help sometimes.

Marilyn: You must love her very much. Maybe we could go down to dinner together, and you could tell me some more about her.

Grace: She's got to have quiet to get to sleep. It's too noisy there.

Marilyn: It's important to you that she gets to sleep. Perhaps we could have dinner served in your room. It'd be quiet there.

Grace: Well, I suppose, if you'd really like to.

In this short exchange the worker demonstrates two critical components of validation therapy. The client may well have lost the ability to comprehend and reason with any degree of complexity. By keeping communication short and simple, the worker avoids losing the client in a variety of ideas that may rapidly become overwhelming. The worker also responds directly and continuously to Grace's feelings, validating to her that the symbolic act she is engaging in is highly important (Miller, 1986). Although the purpose of validation therapy is not to manipulate the client, the worker's approach is far better than forcibly taking the client to the dining room, where she will probably be so distraught over having to neglect her baby that she will not eat anyway.

Whether Grace has ever had a baby named Ellen, or whether she is trying to resolve some shortcoming she has long felt in regard to mothering, is of little concern in the present moment. What is of concern is that the worker treat the situation as if it were real and of importance to the client and acknowledge the client's scattered thoughts and feelings in a congruent, empathic manner. Feil (Feil & Altman, 2004) is adamant that validation therapy is not a "therapeutic lie," as some propose, that is meant only to humor those with dementia. Feil proposes that all people with dementia deserve to be treated with dignity and respect, and to listen to them is an excellent way of doing so. She believes it is absolutely normal for the aged to return to the past to attempt to resolve unfinished business before they die. When these emotions are expressed and someone listens with empathy and unconditional positive regard, frustrations are eased.

Validation therapy is not intended to return the client to reality. However, for the human services worker who has to intervene in a crisis situation with the severely disoriented elderly, it does have the potential to calm them down, avoid situations conducive to acting out, and provide an effective therapeutic technique in an area where few have been found (Miller, 1986). Even though Grace appears to be a pathetic, senile, frail, and confused woman who is easily handled by the crisis worker, don't be misled. The very person Grace represents, if thwarted and frustrated, is the reason that assaults against geriatric workers who discount the Graces are so high.

Follow-up With Staff Victims

Follow-up after an assault is critical to both the person assaulted and the rest of the staff (Kleespies & Ponce, 2009). Workers may brush off assaults as just part of the business and then find out that the psychological ramifications are far greater than they imagined (Fauteux, 2010). Workers who are victims of violent attacks by clients may have emotional responses that include hypervigilance, startle responses, intrusive thoughts, unresolved anger, and poorer overall mental health and anger control (Lenehan & Turner, 1984, p. 256; Wykes & Whittington, 1998). They may look much like the victims of PTSD (California Occupational Safety and Health Administration, 1998, p. 17; Murray & Snyder, 1991).

Practitioners who experience assault feel disempowered, anxious, depressed, and fearful (Littlechild, 2002). Their job performance suffers as they lose confidence to carry out their work roles, question their competence, feel less caring and attachment to clients, and experience self-blame, guilt, and anger about the incident. Further, they fear for their future safety, fear reporting future episodes that would label them as incompetent, and fear that their fellow employees and managers will not see them as dependable (Flannery et al., 2001; Littlechild, 1995).

Bard and Sangrey (1986) found that workers go through three stages of trauma resolution after a physical assault. First they experience a *disorganization of self* that includes feelings of shock. They may dissociate from the experience as unreal, as if it didn't happen or they viewed it as a video of themselves. They may blame themselves and start having peritraumatic stress disorder symptoms involving sleep disturbances and emotional outbursts. The second stage, *period of struggle*, is characterized by anxiety attacks, intrusive thoughts, hypervigilance, and psychosomatic symptoms, which are characteristic of acute stress disorder. The third stage is *readjustment of self*. If the worker is able to move forward, then the incident is integrated into the self and the worker becomes the wiser for it, comes to see that clients can be dangerous, and takes more precautions. However, if the worker does not integrate the incident, then the possibility of PTSD looms large.

Lanza (1984) found that nurses who had experienced such attacks had negative emotional, cognitive, and behavioral reactions up to a year afterward. It is extremely important to work through the aftermath of violent behavior suffered by staff, for two reasons: first, so that the victim does not become debilitated personally and professionally by the incident, and second, because other members of the staff will perceive that the institution takes such events very seriously and is concerned for their safety as well.

After an attack, staff members initially may ascribe blame to the victim to ease their own fear and trepidation about the possibility that it could happen to them. Under no circumstances should this be allowed to happen. Sympathy and support for the victim are vital. Pity, condescension, or subtle implications about provoking the assault should be avoided. There should be acknowledgment that the attack occurred and crisis intervention should be started immediately. Normalizing the situation is imperative and lets the worker know that others would feel the same way that he or she is feeling.

Psychoeducation should be conducted with workers to familiarize them with some of the psychological reactions they may have and what strategies they may use to alleviate them (Weinger, 2001, pp. 66–67). Institutional support groups for victims of violence should be available (Stortch, 1991), and staff should be prepared to give immediate help with problem solving and decision making, such as determining injuries, providing medical transportation, staying with the victim, providing moral support, and helping with medical, legal, and police reports (Lenehan & Turner, 1984, pp. 255–256). Unit staff should also receive counseling to prevent "a blame the victim attitude" from developing (California Occupational Safety and Health Administration, 1998, p. 17).

As soon as the victim is able, a psychological autopsy should be performed on the incident. A psychological autopsy examines in detail the situation that led to the violent episode. (See Chapter 8, Crisis of Lethality, for a complete description of this procedure.) Having the worker and others write a report as soon as they are able may be helpful in allowing workers an emotional outlet and to further understand and conceptualize the incident. *This report should not be seen as a scapegoating or blame-fixing exercise and should be clearly stated as such by the administrative head.*

All staff members who are involved with the client should attend the autopsy. It dissects what the staff and the client did behaviorally before, during, and after the incident. *It is also not about fixing blame, but finding out what caused the incident to happen so that it won't happen again.* Further attention should be given to the environmental setting to determine whether it played a role in instigating the aggressive behavior. Hopefully, the autopsy will provide clues as to the *why's, how's,* and *what's* of the incident, so it does not recur. The victim's opinions should be solicited and should be used as expert testimony. Staff should gather to discuss what happened, work through feelings about the event, and generate options for preventing a recurrence. Reviewing the traumatic experience also enables the victim to deal with feelings of loss of security and control (Lenehan & Turner, 1984, pp. 254–259).

In the past, mental health institutions have left worker recovery from a client assault pretty much to chance, with a "Suck it up; it's part of the job!" approach. That is now patently unacceptable. Some form of debriefing should be conducted simultaneously with the psychological autopsy in helping the assaulted human services worker attain precrisis equilibrium and homeostasis (California Occupational Safety and Health Administration, 1998, p. 17; Fauteux, 2010; Kinney, 1995; Mitchell & Everly, 1995; Spitzer & Burke, 1993; Spitzer & Neely, 1992; Vandenberg, 1992). Debriefing seeks to alleviate the acute stress crisis that workers experience when they are traumatized by an event such as a physical assault on them. Generally, debriefing should occur as soon after the event as is reasonably possible, but it should also take into consideration the worker's ability to go through it. Dr. James Cavanaugh of the Isaac Ray Center for Rush–Presbyterian–St. Luke's, a pioneer in development of debriefing critical incidents such as assaults on staff, cites compelling evidence that immediate posttrauma care can be very effective in helping both individuals and organizations become stabilized after a crisis (Kinney, 1995, p. 188).

The Assaulted Staff Action Program (Flannery et al., 1991) is a combination of the foregoing. When an assault occurs, a staff member responds to offer support, basic psychological first aid, and determine whether additional medical or psychological care is necessary. The responding ASAP member queries the victim as to whether he or she feels able to manage his or her feelings and whether he or she is able to return to work. The ASAP member keeps up with how the member is doing for up to 2 weeks post-incident. ASAP also offers support groups for assaulted staff members.

Finally, Gately and Stabb's (2005) survey of doctoral-level counseling and clinical psychology students should serve as a bellwether. Students overwhelmingly reported that their training to deal with violent clients was inadequate and their confidence in working with these clients was low. Since it is beginning practitioners who are most likely to be assaulted, it is your authors' considered opinion that to not train human services students to understand and deal with violent clients, given the degree and knowledge we have today of violence in the human service workplace, is unethical and immoral.

SUMMARY

Violence in the human services setting has increased exponentially in the past three decades. Increased abuse of drugs, the closing down of large state mental hospitals, child and adult abuse reporting laws, gang violence, increased adjudication of felons to mental health facilities, and increases in the geriatric population have been major contributors to this phenomenon. The problem pervades all parts of human services, and institutions as well as workers may be culpable in allowing violence against staff to proliferate. Both service providers and their staffs have largely looked the other way, and when violence against staff has occurred, either it has been seen as going with the territory or the victim has been blamed for being incompetent, stupid, and careless.

Human services statistics indicate a strong likelihood that sometime during the worker's career he or she will become a victim of violence. Given that high probability, it would seem mandatory that both workers in the field and students in human services should be educated about the potential for violence and taught defusing and deescalating skills to be used with potentially violent clients. Techniques ranging from option therapy to validation therapy are intended not only to help the client stabilize but also to prevent the human services worker from being the object of an assault.

Finally, the worker who has been assaulted should be given immediate support from the administration and fellow workers. Critical incident stress debriefing and psychological autopsies should be mandatory after every assault on staff.

To see some of the concepts discussed in this chapter in action, refer to your *Crisis Intervention in Action* DVD, or see the clips online on the Counseling CourseMate website. To access this site, go to www.cengagebrain.com, where you'll also find an eBook, additional study tools, quizzes, and more. As you watch Demarcus deal with the irate student, don't just listen to his words as he attempts to defuse her rage at being flunked. Watch his body language. Most of us don't have a good idea of what our body language is. In confronting a violent client, it is critical that your body language be congruent with what is coming out of your mouth. One of our major exercises in this chapter is role-playing dealing with angry clients. The task is to get them to sit down. Your instructor may give you this task. If so, it will be really important to monitor your body as to how close you get, how you move in relation to the client, where your hands and arms are, and what your facial expression conveys. If you can get a videotape of yourself in this role play you may be surprised at what you see.

REFERENCES

Almvik, R., Woods, P., & Rasmussen, K. (2007). Assessing risk for imminent violence in the elderly: The Brøset Violence Checklist. *International Journal of Geriatric Psychiatry, 22*(9), 862–867.

American Psychiatric Association. (1974). *Clinical aspects of the violent individual.* Washington, DC: American Psychiatric Association Press.

American Psychological Association. (2000). *Division 12, section VII report on education and training in behavioral emergencies.* Retrieved February 20, 2003, from www.apa.org/divisions/div12/sections/div12/sections/section7/tfreport.html

American Psychological Association. (2002). Ethical principles of psychologists and code of conduct. *American Psychologist, 57,* 1060–1073.

Anderson, C. A. (2001). Heat and violence. *Current Directions in Psychological Science, 10*(1), 33–38.

Ando, M. (2005). A case study of usefulness of cognitive therapy based on reminiscence method for cancer patient. *Japanese Journal of Health Psychology, 18*(2), 53–64.

Annis, L. V., McClaren, H. A., & Baker, C. A. (1984). Who kills us? In J. T. Turner (Ed.), *Violence in the medical care setting: A survival guide* (pp. 19–31). Rockville, MD: Aspen Systems.

Astroem, S., Bucht, G., Eisemann, M., Norberg, A., & Saveman, B. (2002). Incidence of violence towards staff caring for the elderly. *Scandinavian Journal of Caring Services, 16*(1), 66–72.

Bach y Rita, G., Lion, J. R., & Climent, C. E. (1971). Episodic dyscontrol: A study of 630 violent patients. *American Journal of Psychiatry, 128,* 1473–1478.

Baker, N. J. (1985). Reminiscing in group therapy for self-worth. *Journal of Gerontological Nursing, 11,* 21–24.

Baradell, J. G. (1985, February). Humanistic care of the patient in seclusion. *Journal of Psychosocial Nursing and Mental Health Services, 23,* 9–14.

Bard, M., & Sangrey, D. (1986). *The crime victim's book* (2nd ed.). New York: Brunner/Mazel.

Barret, K. E., Riggar, T. F., & Flowers, C. R. (1997). Violence in the workplace. Preparing for the age of rage. *Journal of Rehabilitation Administration, 21*(3), 171–188.

Barrick, A. L., Rader, J., Hoeffer, B., Sloane, P. D., & Biddle, S. (2008). General guidelines for bathing persons with dementia. In A. L. Barrick, J. Rader, J. B. Hoeffer, P. D. Sloane, & S. Biddle (Eds.), *Bathing without a battle: Person-directed care of individuals with dementia* (2nd ed., pp. 17–21). New York: Springer.

Beamish, P. M. (2005). Introduction to the special section—severe and persistent mental illness on college campuses: Consideration for service provision. *Journal of College Counseling, 8*(2), 138–139.

Beck, J. C. (1988). The therapist's legal duty when the patient may be violent. *Psychiatric Clinics of North America, 11,* 665–679.

Becker, W. C. (1971). *Parents are teachers.* Champaign, IL: Research Press.

Belak, A. G., & Busse, D. (1993). Legal issues. In P. E. Blumenreich & S. Lewis (Eds.), *Managing the violent patient: A clinician's guide* (pp. 137–149). New York: Brunner-Mazel.

Benton, S. A., Robertson, J. M., Tseng, W., Newton, F., & Benton, S. L. (2003). Changes in counseling center client problems across 13 years. *Professional Psychology: Research and Practice, 34*(1), 66–72.

Bishop, J. B. (2006). College and university counseling centers: Questions in search of answers. *Journal of College Counseling, 9*(1), 6–19.

Blair, D. T. (1991). Assaultive behavior: Does provocation begin in the front office? *Journal of Psychosocial Nursing and Mental Health Services, 29,* 21–24.

Blair, D. T., & New, S. A. (1991). Assaultive behavior: Know the risks. *Journal of Psychosocial Nursing and Mental Health Services, 29,* 25–29.

Blumenreich, P. E. (1993a). Assessment. In P. E. Blumenreich & S. Lewis (Eds.), *Managing the violent patient: A clinician's guide* (pp. 35–40). New York: Brunner/Mazel.

Blumenreich, P. E. (1993b). Etiology. In P. E. Blumenreich & S. Lewis (Eds.), *Managing the violent patient: A clinician's guide* (pp. 21–33). New York: Brunner/Mazel.

Brooker, D., & Duce, L. (2000). Well-being and activity in dementia: A comparison of group reminiscence therapy, structured goal-directed group activity and unstructured time. *Aging & Mental Health, 4*(4), 354–358.

Brown, R., Bute, S., & Ford, P. (1986). *Social workers at risk: Management of violence.* London: Macmillan.

Buchanan, D., Moorhouse, A., Cabaico, L., Krock, M., Campbell, H., & Spevakow, D. (2002). A critical review and synthesis of literature on reminiscing with older adults. *Canadian Journal of Nursing Research/Revue, 34*(3), 123–139.

Burry, C. L. (2002). Working with potentially violent clients in their homes: What child welfare professionals need to know. *Clinical Supervisor, 21*(1), 145–153.

Butler, R. (1963). The life review: An interpretation of reminiscence in the aged. *Psychiatry, 26,* 65–76.

California Occupational Safety and Health Administration. (1998). *Guidelines of security and safety of health care and community service workers.* Sacramento, CA: Author.

Canter, L., & Canter, E. (1982). *Assertive discipline for parents.* Santa Monica, CA: Canter Associates.

Cappeliez, P., & Watt, L. (2005). L'integrazione della retrospettiva di vita e della terapia cognitiva della depressione con le persone anziane. *Piscioterpaia Cognitiva e Comportamentale, 11*(2), 151–164.

Cawood, J. S., & Corcoran, M. H. (2009). *Violence assessment and intervention: The practitioner's handbook* (2nd ed.). Boca Raton, FL: CRC Press/Taylor & Francis. Chavez, L. (1999). *Workplace violence awareness for managers and supervisors.* Internet course. Retrieved May 3, 2003, from members.aol.com/hrtrainer/ defuse.html

Chermack, S. T., Fuller, B., & Blow, F. (2000). Predictors of expressed partner and non-partner violence among patients in substance abuse treatment. *Drug and Alcohol Dependence, 58*(1–2), 43–54.

Cully, J., LaVoie, D., & Gfeller, J. D. (2001). Reminiscence, personality, and psychological functioning in older adults. *Gerontologist, 41*(1), 89–95.

Dang, S. (1990). When the patient is out of control. *RN, 59,* 57–58.

Daugherty, L. M., Bolger, J. P., Preston, D. G., Jones, S. S., & Paynes, H. C. (1992). Effects of exposure to aggressive behavior on job satisfaction of healthcare staff. *Journal of Applied Gerontology, 11,* 160–172.

Dennis, H. (1978). Remotivation therapy groups. In I. M. Burnside (Ed.), *Working with the elderly: Group process and techniques* (pp. 219–235). North Scituate, MA: Duxbury Press.

Dinkmeyer, D. C., Pew, W. L., & Dinkmeyer, D. C., Jr. (1979). *Adlerian counseling and psychotherapy.* Pacific Grove, CA: Brooks/Cole.

Doms, R. W. (1984). Personal distress devices for health care personnel. In J. T. Turner (Ed.), *Violence in the medical care setting: A survival guide* (pp. 225–229). Rockville, MD: Aspen Systems.

Donahue, H. H. (1965). Expanding the program. *Hospital and Community Psychiatry, 17,* 117–118.

dos Reis, S., Barnett, S. R., Love, L. C., Riddle, M. A., & Maryland Youth Practice Improvement Committee. (2003). A guide for managing acute aggression among youths. *Psychiatric Services, 54*(10), 1357–1363.

Douglas, K. S., Nicholls, T. L., & Brink, J. (2009). Reducing the risk of violence among people with serious mental illness: A critical analysis of treatment approaches. In P. M. Kleespies (Ed.), *Behavioral emergencies: An evidence-based resource for evaluating and managing risk of suicide, violence, and victimization.* (pp. 351–376). Washington, DC: American Psychological Association.

Douglas, K. S., Ogloff, J. R., & Hart, S. D. (2003). Evaluation of a model of violence risk assessment among forensic psychiatric patients. *Psychiatric Services, 54*(10), 1372–1379.

Dubin, W. R. (1981). Evaluating and managing the violent patient. *Annals of Emergency Medicine, 10,* 481–484.

Durivage, A. (1989). Assaultive behavior: Before it happens. *Canadian Journal of Psychiatry, 34,* 393–397.

Dyer, W. O., Murrell, D. S., & Wright, D. (1984). Training for hospital security: An alternative to training negligence suits. In J. T. Turner (Ed.), *Violence in the medical care setting: A survival guide* (pp. 1–18). Rockville, MD: Aspen Systems.

Ebersole, P. P. (1978a). A theoretical approach to the use of reminiscence. In I. M. Burnside (Ed.), *Working with the elderly: Group process and techniques* (pp. 139–154). North Scituate, MA: Duxbury Press.

Ebersole, P. P. (1978b). Establishing reminiscence groups. In I. M. Burnside (Ed.), *Working with the elderly: Group process and techniques* (pp. 236–254). North Scituate, MA: Duxbury Press.

Eddy, S. (1998). Risk management with the violent patient. In P. M. Kleespies (Ed.), *Emergencies in mental health practice: Evaluation and management* (pp. 217–231). New York: Guilford Press.

Epstein, M., & Carter, L. (1988). *Training manual for Headquarters staff.* Lawrence, KS: Headquarters.

Erdur-Baker, O., Aberson, C., Barrow, J., & Draper, M. (2006). Nature and severity of college students' psychological concerns: A comparison of clinical and nonclinical national samples. *Professional Psychology: Research and Practice, 37*(3), 317–323.

Fareta, G. (1981). A profile of aggression from adolescence to adulthood: An 18-year follow-up of psychiatrically disturbed and violent adolescents. *American Journal of Orthopsychiatry, 51,* 439–453.

Fauteux, K. (2010). De-escalating angry and violent clients. *American Journal of Psychotherapy, 64*(2), 195–213.

Federal Bureau of Investigation. (2002, June). *Workplace violence symposium.* Landover, MD. Available at www.fbi .gov/stats-services/publications/workplace-violence

Feil, N. (1982). *Validation: The Feil method.* Cleveland, OH: Edward Feil Productions.

Feil, N., & Altman, R. (2004). Validation theory and the myth of the therapeutic lie. *American Journal of Alzheimer's Disease and Other Dementias, 19*(2), 77–78.

Felthous, A. R. (1987). Liability of treaters for injuries to others: Erosion of three immunities. *Bulletin of the American Academy of Psychiatry and the Law, 15,* 115–125.

Felthous, A. R., & Kellert, S. (1986). Violence against animals and people: Is aggression against living creatures generalized? *Bulletin of the American Academy of Psychiatry and Law, 14*(1), 55–69.

Fisch, R., Weakland, J. H., & Segal, L. (1983). *The tactics of change.* San Francisco: Jossey-Bass.

Fishbain, D. A., Cutler, R. B., Rosomoff, H. L., & Steele-Rosomoff, R. (2000). Risk for violent behavior in patients with chronic pain: Evaluation and management in the pain facility setting. *Pain Medicine, 1*(2), 140–155.

Flannery, R. (2009). *The violent person: Professional risk management strategies for safety and care.* Riverdale, NY: American Mental Health Foundation Books.

Flannery, R., Fulton, P., Tausch, J. M., & DeLoffi, A.(1991). A program to help staff cope with psychological sequelae of assaults by patients. *Hospital and Community Psychiatry, 42,* 935–938.

Flannery, R., Le Vitre, V., Rego, S., & Walker, P. (2011). Characteristics of staff victims of psychiatric patient assaults: 20-year analysis of the Assaulted Staff Action Program. *Psychiatric Quarterly, 82*(1), 11–21.

Flannery, R., Stone, P., Rego, S., &Walker, A. (2001). Characteristics of staff victims of patient assault: Ten year analysis of the Assaulted Staff Action Program (ASAP). *Psychiatric Quarterly, 72,* 237–248.

Forster, J. (1994). The psychiatric emergency: Heading off trouble. *Patient Care, 28,* 130.

Gabe, J., & Elston, M. (2009). "We don't have time to take this." Zero tolerance of violence against health care workers in a time of insecurity. D. Denney (Ed.), *Living in dangerous time: Fear, insecurity, risk and social policy* (pp. 131–149), London, GB: Wiley-Blackwell.

Garber, R. S. (1965). A psychiatrist's view of remotivation. *Mental Hospitals, 16*, 219–221.

Gately, L. A., & Stabb, S. D. (2005). Psychology students' training in the management of potentially violent clients. *Professional Psychology: Research and Practice, 36*(6), 681–687.

Gates, D., Fitzwater, E., & Succop, P. (2005). Reducing assaults against nursing home caregivers. *Nursing Research, 54*(2), 119–127.

Glasser, W. (1965). *Reality therapy.* New York: Harper & Row.

Glasser, W. (1969). *Schools without failure.* New York: Harper & Row.

Glezer, A., & Brendel, R. W. (2010). Beyond emergencies: The use of physical restraints in medical and psychiatric settings. *Harvard Review of Psychiatry, 18*(6), 353–358.

Grassi, L., Peron, L., Mafangoni, C., Zanchi, P., & Vanni, A. (2001). Characteristics of violent behavior in acute psychiatric in-patients: A 5-year Italian study. *Acta Psychiatrica Scandinavica, 104*(4), 273–279.

Grayson, P. A., & Meilman, M. W. (Eds.). (2006). *College mental health practice.* New York: Routledge.

Greenfield, T. K., McNeil, D. E., & Binder, R. L. (1989). Violent behavior and length of psychiatric hospitalization. *Hospital and Community Psychiatry, 40*, 809–814.

Greenstone, J. L., & Leviton, S. C. (1993). *Elements of crisis intervention.* Pacific Grove, CA: Brooks/Cole.

Guterman, N. B., Jayaratme, S., & Bargal, D. (1996). Workplace violence and victimization experienced by social workers: A cross-national study of Americans and Israelis. In G. R. VandenBos & E. Q. Bulatao (Eds.), *Violence on the job: Identifying risks and developing solutions* (pp. 175–188). Washington, DC: American Psychological Association.

Gutheil, T. G. (1978). Observation on the theoretical basis for seclusion of the psychiatric inpatient. *American Journal of Psychiatry, 135*, 325–328.

Guy, J. D., Brown, C. K., & Poelstra, P. L. (1990). Who gets attacked? A national survey of patient violence directed at psychologists in clinical practice. *Professional Psychology: Research and Practice, 21*, 493–495.

Haber, D. (2006). Life review: Implementation, theory, research, and therapy. *International Journal of Aging & Human Development, 63*(2), 153–171.

Hamstra, B. (1986). Neurobiological substrates of violence: An overview for forensic clinicians. *Journal of Psychiatry and Law, 14*, 349–374.

Hartel, J. A. (1993). The prosecution of assaultive clients. *Perspectives in Psychiatric Care, 29*, 7–14.

Heilbrun, A. B. (1990). The measurement of criminal dangerousness as a personality construct: Further validation of a research index. *Journal of Personality Assessment, 54*, 141–148.

Heilbrun, A. B., & Heilbrun, M. R. (1989). Dangerousness and legal insanity. *Journal of Psychiatry and Law, 17*, 39–53.

Hellman, D. S., & Blackman, S. (1966). Enuresis, fire setting, and cruelty to animals: A triad predictive of adult crime. *American Journal of Psychiatry, 122*, 1431–1435.

Hillman, J., Flicker, S., LeGendre, L., & Traczuk, K. (2005). The pervasiveness of patient aggression among elderly residents in long-term care: Implications for intervention and prevention. In J. P. Morgan (Ed.), *Psychology of aggression* (pp. 69–85). New York: Nova Science Publishers.

Hindley, N., & Gordon, H. (2000). The elderly, dementia, aggression and risk management. *International Journal of Geriatric Psychiatry, 15*(3), 254–259.

Hsieh, H., & Wang, J. (2003). Effect of reminiscence therapy on depression in older adults: A systematic review. *International Journal of Nursing Studies, 40*(4), 335–345.

Hyer, L., Sohnle, S., Mehan, D., & Ragan, A. (2002). Use of positive core memories in LTC: A review. *Clinical Gerontologist, 25*(1/2), 51–90.

Isaksson, U., Graneheim, U. H., Ricter, J., Eisenmann, M., & Astrom, S. (2008). Exposure to violence in relation to personality traits, coping abilities and burnout among caregivers in nursing homes: A case-control approach. *Scandinavian Journal of Caring Sciences, 22*(4), 551–559.

Ishimoto, W. (1984). Security management for health care administrators. In J. T. Turner (Ed.), *Violence in the medical care setting: A survival guide* (pp. 209–223). Rockville, MD: Aspen Systems.

Janosik, S. M. (2004). Parents' views on the Clery Act and campus safety. *Journal of College Student Development, 45*(1), 43–56.

Jensen, D., & Absher, J. (1994, April). *Assaultive behavior, the crisis is over: Preventing another crisis.* Paper presented at the Eighteenth Annual Convening of Crisis Intervention Personnel, Chicago.

Jensen, D., & Absher, J. (1998, April). *Predicting/managing violence in crisis situations: Ensuring provider safety.* Paper presented at the Twenty-Second Annual Convening of Crisis Intervention Personnel, Chicago.

Jones, J. (1984). *Counseling in correctional settings* (Cassette Recording No. 25-6611). Memphis, TN: Memphis State University, Department of Counseling and Personnel Services.

Jones, M. K. (1985, June). Patient violence: Report of 200 incidents. *Journal of Psychosocial Nursing and Mental Health, 23*, 12–17.

Kelly, B., & Torres, A. (2006). Campus safety: Perceptions and experiences of women students. *Journal of College Student Development, 47*(1), 20–36.

Kinney, J. A. (1995). *Violence at work.* Upper Saddle River, NJ: Prentice Hall.

Kirk, A. (1989). The prediction of violent behavior during short-term civil commitment. *Bulletin of the American Academy of Psychiatry and the Law, 17,* 345–353.

Klassen, D., & O'Connor, W. A. (1988). A prospective study of predictors of violence in adult male mental health admissions. *Law and Human Behavior, 12,* 143–158.

Kleespies, P. M., & Ponce, A. N. (2009). The stress and emotional impact of clinical work with the patient at risk. In P. Kleespies (Ed.), *Behavioral emergencies: An evidence-based resource for evaluating and managing risk of suicide, violence and victimization* (pp. 431–448). Washington, DC: American Psychological Association.

Koritsas, S., Coles, J., & Boyle, M. (2010). Workplace violence towards social workers: The Australian experience. *British Journal of Social Work, 40*(10), 257–271.

Kroll, J., & Mackenzie, T. B. (1983). When psychiatrists are liable: Risk management and violent patients. *Hospital and Community Psychiatry, 34,* 29–37.

Kumble, S., & McSherry, B. (2010). Seclusion and restraint: Rethinking regulation from a human rights perspective. *Psychiatry, Psychology and Law, 17*(4), 551–561.

Kurlowicz, L. H. (1990). Violence in the emergency department. *American Journal of Nursing, 90,* 35–40.

Lakeside Hospital. (1988). *Verbal techniques for deescalating violent behavior.* Memphis, TN: Author.

Lam, J., McNeil, D. E., & Binder, R. L. (2000). The relationship between patients' gender and violence leading to staff injuries. *Psychiatric Services, 51*(9), 1167–1170.

Lanza, M. L. (1984). A follow-up study of nurses' reactions to physical assault. *Hospital and Community Psychiatry, 35,* 492–494.

Lanza, M. L. (1985, June). How nurses react to patient assault. *Journal of Psychosocial Nursing and Mental Health, 23,* 6–11.

Leadbetter, D. (1993). Trends in assault on social work staff: The experience of one Scottish department. *British Journal of Social Work, 23,* 613–628.

LeCroy, C. W. (1988). Anger management or anger expression: Which is most effective? *Residential Treatment for Children and Youth, 5,* 29–39.

Lenehan, G. P., & Turner, J. T. (1984). Treatment of staff victims of violence. In J. T. Turner (Ed.), *Violence in the medical care setting: A survival guide* (pp. 251–260). Rockville, MD: Aspen Systems.

Lewellyn, A. (1985). *Counseling emotionally disturbed high school students: The Mattoon, Illinois, TLC program* (Cassette Recording No. 12-6611). Memphis, TN: Memphis State University, Department of Counseling and Personnel Services.

Lewis, S. (1993). Restraint and seclusion. In P. E. Blumenreich & S. Lewis (Eds.), *Managing the violent patient: A clinician's guide* (pp. 101–109). New York: Brunner-Mazel.

Linaker, O. M., & Busch-Iversen, H. (1995). Predictors of imminent violence in psychiatric inpatients. *Acta Psychiatrica Scandinavica, 92*(4), 250–254.

Lion, J. R., & Pasternak, S. A. (1973). Countertransference reactions to violent patients. *American Journal of Psychiatry, 130,* 207–210.

Littlechild, B. (1995). Violence against social workers. *Journal of Interpersonal Violence, 10,* 123–131.

Littlechild, B. (2002). The effects of client violence on child protection networks. *Trauma, Violence, & Abuse, 3,* 144–158.

Lovell, D., Allen, D., Johnson, C., & Jemelka, R. (2001). Evaluating the effectiveness of residential treatment for prisoners with mental illness. *Criminal Justice and Behavior, 28,* 83–104.

MacDonald, G., & Sirotich, F. (2001). Reporting client violence. *Social Work, 46,* 107–114.

Mack, D. A., Shannon, C., Quick, J. D., & Quick, J. C. (1988). Stress and the preventative management of workplace violence. In R. W. Griffin & A. O'Leary-Kelly (Eds.), *Dysfunctional behavior in organizations: Violent and deviant behavior. Monographs in organizational behavior and industrial relations, 23,* Parts A & B (pp. 119–141). Stamford, CT: Jai Press.

Madden, D. J., Lion, J. R., & Penna, M. W. (1976). Assaults on psychiatrists by patients. *American Journal of Psychiatry, 133,* 422–425.

Mandatory Treatment of Mental Health Patients. (2007). Virginia Codes 37.2-817.1 through 37.2-817.3.

Marohn, R. C. (1982). Adolescent violence: Causes and treatment. *Journal of the American Academy of Child Psychiatry, 21,* 354–360.

Martin, L., Francisco, E., Nichol, C., & Schweiger, J. L. (1991). A hospital-wide approach to crisis control: One inner-city hospital's experience. *Journal of Emergency Nursing, 17,* 395–401.

Mattson, M. R., & Sacks, M. H. (1978). Seclusion: Uses and implications. *American Journal of Psychiatry, 135,* 1210–1212.

McCown, C. (1986). *Counseling in an adolescent psychiatric treatment facility* (Cassette Recording No. 7). Memphis, TN: Memphis State University, Department of Counseling and Personnel Services.

McKee, K. J., Wilson, F., Chung, M., Hinchliff, S., Goudie, F., Elford, H., et al. (2005). Reminiscence, regrets and activity in older people in residential care: Associations with psychological health. *British Journal of Clinical Psychology, 44*(4), 543–561.

McMahon, A., & Rhudick, P. (1964). Reminiscing: Adaptational significance in the aged. *Archives of General Psychiatry, 10,* 292–298.

McNeil, D. (2009). Assessment and management of acute risk of violence in adult patients. In P. M. Kleespies (Ed.), *Behavioral emergencies: An evidence-based resource for evaluating and managing risk of suicide, violence, and victimization.* (pp. 125–146). Washington, DC: American Psychological Association.

McNeil, D., & Binder, R. L. (1994). The relationship between acute psychiatric symptoms, diagnosis, and short-term risk of violence. *Hospital and Community Psychiatry, 45*, 133–137.

McNeil, D. E., Binder, M. R., & Greenfield, T. L. (1988). Predictors of violence in civilly committed acute psychiatric patients. *American Journal of Psychiatry, 8*, 965–970.

McNeil, D. E., Gregory, A. L., Lam, J. L. M., Binder, R. L., & Sullivan, G. R. (2003). Utility of decision support tools for assessing acute risk of violence. *Journal of Consulting and Clinical Psychology, 71*, 945–953.

McNeil, D. E., Hatcher, C., Zeiner, H., Wolfe, H. L., & Myers, R. S. (1991). Characteristics of persons referred by police to the psychiatric emergency room. *Hospital and Community Psychiatry, 42*, 425–427.

Mentes, J. C., & Ferrario, J. (1989). Calming aggressive reactions: A prevention program. *Journal of Gerontological Nursing, 15*, 22–27.

Miller, M. (1986). *Counseling geriatric clients* (Cassette Recording No. 14). Memphis, TN: Memphis State University, Department of Counseling and Personnel Services.

Mitchell, J. T., & Everly, G. S., Jr. (1995). *Critical incidents stress debriefing: The basic course workbook.* Ellicott City, MD: International Critical Incidents Stress Foundation.

Mohr, W. K. (2010). Restraints and the code of ethics: An uneasy fit. *Archives of Psychiatric Nursing, 24*(1), 3–14.

Monahan, J. (1981). *The clinical prediction of violent behavior.* Rockville, MD: National Institute of Mental Health.

Monahan, J. (1984). The prediction of violent behavior: Toward a second generation of theory and policy. *American Journal of Psychiatry, 141*, 10–15.

Monahan, J. (1988). Risk assessment of violence among the mentally disordered: Generating useful knowledge. *International Journal of Law and Psychiatry, 11*, 249–257.

Monahan, J., Steadmam, H. J., Silver, E., Applebaum, P. S., Robbins, P. C., Mulvey, E. P., et al. (2001). *Rethinking risk assessment: The McArthur Study of mental disorder and violence.* New York: Oxford University Press.

Moran, J. F. (1984). Teaching the management of violent behavior to nursing staff: A health care model. In J. T. Turner (Ed.), *Violence in the medical care setting: A survival guide* (pp. 231–250). Rockville, MD: Aspen Systems.

Morrison, J. M. (1993). Physical techniques. In P. E. Blumenreich & S. Lewis (Eds.), *Managing the violent patient: A clinician's guide* (pp. 79–100). New York: Brunner-Mazel.

Mulvey, E. P., & Lidz, C. W. (1984). Clinical considerations on the prediction of dangerous mental patients. *Clinical Psychology Review, 4*, 379–401.

Munoz, M., Joaquin, C., Noval, D., Moringo, A., & Garcia de la Concha, J. A. (2000). Factores predictores de agresividad en esquizofrenicos hospitalizados. *Actas Espanolas de Psiquiatria, 28*(3), 151–155.

Munsey, C. (2008). Stay safe in practice. *Monitor on Psychology 39*(4), 37–39.

Munsey, C. (2010). More students with serious psychological issues are showing up at campus counseling centers. *Monitor on Psychology 41*(4), 10–11.

Murdach, A. D. (1993). Working with potentially assaultive clients. *Health and Social Work, 18*, 307–312.

Murray, G., & Snyder, J. C. (1991). When staff are assaulted. *Journal of Psychosocial Nursing, 29*, 24–29.

Myer, R. A., James, R. K., & Moulton, P. (2011). *This is not a fire drill: Crisis intervention and prevention on college campuses.* New York: Wiley.

Myer, R. A., Moulton, P., Cogdal, P. C., Rice, N. D., James, R. K., & Allen, S. (2007). *Triage Assessment System Training Manual: Higher education: Instructor's manual.* Pittsburgh, PA: CIPS-Solutions Inc.

National Institute for Occupational Safety and Health. (1992, October). *Epidemiology of workplace violence.* Atlanta, GA: Centers for Disease Control.

Newhill, C. E. (2003). *Client violence in social work practice; Prevention, intervention, and research.* New York: Guilford Press.

Nicoletti, J., & Spooner, K. (1996). Violence in the workplace: Response and intervention strategies. In G. R. VandenBos & E. Q. Bulatao (Eds.), *Violence on the job: Identifying risks and developing solutions* (pp. 267–282). Washington, DC: American Psychological Association.

Nisbett, R. E. (1993). Violence and U.S. regional culture. *American Psychologist, 48*, 441–449.

Occupational Safety and Health Administration. (2003). *Guidelines for preventing workplace violence for healthcare and social service workers.* OSHA 3148. Washington, DC: U.S. Department of Labor.

Ochitill, H. N., & Kreiger, M. (1982). Violent behavior among hospitalized medical and surgical patients. *Southern Medical Journal, 75*, 151–155.

Ogloff, J. R., & Daffern, M. (2006). The Dynamic Appraisal of Situational Aggression: An instrument to assess risk for imminent aggression in psychiatric inpatients. *Behavioral Sciences & the Law, 24*, 799–813.

O'Leary, E., & Nieuwstraten, I. M. (2001). The exploration of memories in Gestalt reminiscence therapy. *Counselling Psychology Quarterly, 14*(2), 165–180.

Osborn, C. L. (1991). Reminiscence: When the past eases the present. *Journal of Gerontological Nursing, 15*, 6–11.

Outlaw, F. H., & Lowery, B. J. (1992). Seclusion: The nursing challenge. *Journal of Psychosocial Nursing, 30*, 13–17.

Palmstierna, T., & Wistedt, B. (1990). Risk factors for aggressive behaviour are of limited value in predicting the violent behaviour of acute involuntarily admitted patients. *Acta Psychiatrica Scandinavica, 81*, 152–155.

Petrie, W. M. (1984). Violence: The geriatric patient. In J. T. Turner (Ed.), *Violence in the medical care setting: A survival guide* (pp. 107–122). Rockville, MD: Aspen Systems.

Petrie, W. M., Lawson, E. C., & Hollender, M. H. (1982). Violence in geriatric patients. *Journal of the American Medical Association, 248*, 443–444.

Piercy, D. (1984). Violence: The drug and alcohol patient. In J. T. Turner (Ed.), *Violence in the medical care setting: A survival guide* (pp. 123–152). Rockville, MD: Aspen Systems.

Pisarick, G. (1981, September). The violent patient. *Nursing,* pp. 63–65.

Pledge, D. S., Lapan, R., Heppner, P., Kivlighan, D., & Roehlke, H. (1998). Stability and severity of presenting problems at a university counseling center: A 6-year analysis. *Professional Psychology: Research and Practice, 29*(4), 386–389.

Poliks, O. (1999, April). *The noble victim: Survival, self-care and spirituality.* Paper presented at the Twenty-Third Annual Convening of Crisis Intervention Personnel, Chicago.

RachBeisel, J. M., Scott, J., & Dixon, L. (1999). Co-occurring severe mental illness and substance use disorders: A review of recent research. *Psychiatric Services, 50,* 1427–1434.

Rada, R. T. (1981). The violent patient: Rapid assessment and management. *Psychosomatics, 22,* 101–109.

Rofman, E. S., Askinazi, C., & Fant, E. (1980). The prediction of dangerous behavior in emergency civil commitment. *American Journal of Psychiatry, 137,* 1061–1064.

Rowett, C. (1986). *Violence in social work.* Cambridge, MA: Institute of Criminology.

Ruben, I., Wolkon, G., & Yamamoto, J. (1980). Physical attacks on psychiatric residents by patients. *Journal of Nervous and Mental Disease, 168,* 243–245.

Rudd, M. D. (2004). University counseling centers: Looking more and more like community clinics. *Professional Psychology: Research and Practice, 35*(3), 316–317.

Ruesch, J. (1973). *Therapeutic communication.* New York: Norton.

Ryan, E. P., Hart, V., Messick, D., Jeffrey, A., & Burnette, M. (2004). A prospective study of assault against staff by youths in a state psychiatric hospital. *Psychiatric Services, 55*(6), 665–670.

Schwartz, A. J. (2006). Are college students more disturbed today? Stability in the acuity and qualitative character of psychopathology of college counseling center clients: 1992–1993 through 2001–2002. *Journal of American College Health, 54*(6), 327–337.

Shah, A. K., Fineberg, N. A., & James, D. V. (1991). Violence among psychiatric in-patients. *Acta Psychiatrica Scandinavica, 84,* 305–309.

Simonds, J. F., & Kashani, J. (1980). Specific drug use and violence in delinquent boys. *American Journal of Drug and Alcohol Abuse, 7,* 305–322.

Singer, V. I., Tracz, S. M., & Dworkin, S. H. (1991). Reminiscence group therapy: A treatment modality for older adults. *Journal for Specialists in Group Work, 16,* 167–171.

Sloore, H. (1988). Use of the MMPI in the prediction of dangerous behavior. *Acta Psychiatrica Belgica, 88,* 42–51.

Slovenko, R. (2006). Violent attacks in psychiatric and other hospitals. *Journal of Psychiatry & Law, 34*(2), 249–268.

Snyder, L. A., Chen, P., & Vacha-Haase, T. (2007). The underreporting gap in aggressive incidents from geriatric patients against certified nursing assistants. *Violence and Victims, 22*(3), 367–379.

Spar, J., & La Rue, A. (2006). *Clinical manual of geriatric psychiatry.* Washington, DC: American Psychiatric Publishing.

Spitzer, W. J., & Burke, L. (1993). A critical-incident stress debriefing program for hospital-based health care personnel. *Health & Social Work, 18*(2), pp. 149–156.

Spitzer, W. J., & Neely, K. (1992). The role of hospital-based social work in developing a statewide intervention system for first responders delivering emergency services. *Social Work in Health Care, 18,* 39–58.

Steveson, S. (1991). Heading off violence with verbal deescalation. *Journal of Psychosocial Nursing, 29,* 7–10.

Stilling, L. (1992). The pros and cons of physical restraints and behavior controls. *Journal of Psychosocial Nursing, 30,* 18–20.

Stortch, D. D. (1991). Starting an in-hospital support group for victims of violence in the psychiatric hospital. *Psychiatric Hospital, 22,* 5–9.

Tardiff, K. (1984a). Violence: The psychiatric patient. In J. T. Turner (Ed.), *Violence in the medical care setting: A survival guide* (pp. 33–55). Rockville, MD: Aspen Systems.

Tardiff, K. (1984b). *The psychiatric uses of seclusion and restraint.* Washington, DC: American Psychiatric Association Press.

Tardiff, K. (1989). *Assessment and management of violent patients.* Washington, DC: American Psychiatric Association Press.

Tardiff, K. (2003). Violence. In R. E. Hales, S. C. Yudofsky, & J. A. Talbot (Eds.), *Textbook of clinical psychiatry* (4th ed., pp. 1489–1509). Washington, DC: American Psychiatric Press.

Taulbee, L. R. (1978). Reality orientation: A therapeutic group activity for elderly persons. In I. M. Burnside (Ed.), *Working with the elderly: Group process and techniques* (pp. 206–218). North Scituate, MA: Duxbury Press.

Taulbee, L. R., & Folsom, J. C. (1966). Reality orientation for geriatric patients. *Hospital and Community Psychiatry, 17,* 133–135.

Thackrey, M. (1987). *Therapeutics for aggression.* New York: Human Sciences Press.

Thomas, C., Kitchen, D., & Smith, A. (2005). The management of aggression care plans: Implementation and efficacy in a forensic learning disability service. *British Journal of Forensic Science, 7*(2), 3–9.

Threat assessment team formation. (2008). Virginia Code 23-31 9.2:3C.

Threat of violence. (2008). Virginia Code 23-31 92:10.

Tomine, S. (1986). Private practice in gerontological counseling. *Journal of Counseling and Development, 68,* 406–409.

Turnbull, J., Aitken, I., Black, L., & Patterson, B. (1990, June). Turn it around: Short-term management for aggression and anger. *Journal of Psychosocial Nursing and Mental Health Services, 28*, 7–13.

Turner, J. (Ed.). (1984). *Violence in the medical care setting: A survival guide*. Rockville, MD: Aspen Systems.

Turns, D. M. (1993). Institutional response to violent incidents. In P. E. Blumenreich & S. Lewis (Eds.), *Managing the violent patient: A clinician's guide* (pp. 131–135). New York: Brunner-Mazel.

Turns, D. M., & Blumenreich, P. E. (1993). Epidemiology. In P. E. Blumenreich & S. Lewis (Eds.), *Managing the violent patient: A clinician's guide* (pp. 5–20). New York: Brunner-Mazel.

U.S. Department of Justice, Bureau of Justice Statistics. (1998). *Data from the National Crime Victimization Survey 1992–1996*. Washington, DC: Author.

U.S. Department of Justice, Bureau of Justice Statistics. (2001). *Data from the National Crime Victimization Survey 1993–1999*. Washington, DC: Author.

U.S. Department of Labor, Bureau of Labor Statistics. (2001). *Survey of occupational injuries and illnesses, 2000*. Washington, DC: Author.

U.S. Department of Labor, Bureau of Labor Statistics. (2002). *Census of fatal occupational injuries and illnesses, 2000*. Washington, DC: Author.

Vaaler, A. E., Morken, G., & Linaker, O. (2005). Effects of different interior decorations in the seclusion area of a psychiatric acute ward. *Nordic Journal of Psychiatry, 59*(1), 19–24.

Vandenberg, N. (1992). Using critical incidents and debriefing to mediate organizational crisis, change, and loss. *Employee Assistance Quarterly, 8*, 35–55.

van den Brink, R. H., Hooijschuur, A., van Os, T. W., Savenije, W., & Wiersma, D. (2010). Routine violence risk assessment in community forensic mental healthcare. *Behavioral Sciences & the Law, 28*(3), 396–410.

Van Puyenbroeck, J., & Maes, B. (2006). Program development of reminiscence group work for ageing people with intellectual disabilities. *Journal of Intellectual & Developmental Disability, 31*(3), 139–147.

Viner, J. (1982). Toward more skillful handling of acutely psychotic patients: Part I. Evaluation. *Emergency Room Report, 3*, 125–130.

Vinick, B. (1986). *Counseling in a state mental hospital* (Cassette Recording No. 13). Memphis, TN: Memphis State University, Department of Counseling and Personnel Services.

Walker, Z., & Seifert, R. (1994). Violent incidents in a psychiatric intensive care unit. *British Journal of Psychiatry, 164*, 826–828.

Waller, R., Mahmood, T., Gandi, R., Delves, S., Humphrys, N., & Smith, D. (2005). Student mental health: How can psychiatrists better support the work of university medical centre and university counseling services? *British Journal of Guidance & Counseling, 33*(1), 117–128.

Wang, J. (2005). The effects of reminiscence on depressive symptoms and mood status of older institutionalized adults in Taiwan. *International Journal of Geriatric Psychiatry, 20*(1), 57–62.

Warren, J. I., South, S., Burnette, M., Rogers, A., Friend, R., Bale, R., et al. (2005). Understanding the risk factors for violence and criminality in women: The concurrent validity of the PCL-R and the HCR-20. *International Journal of Law and Psychiatry, 28*(3), 269–289.

Webster, C. D., Douglas, K. S., Eaves, D., & Hart S. D. (1997). *HCR-20: Assessing risk of violence*. Burnaby, BC: Simon Fraser University.

Weinger, S. (2001). *Security risk: Preventing client violence against social workers*. Washington, DC: National Association of Social Workers Press.

Weinstock, R., Read, S., Leong, G. B., & Silvia, J. (2008). The elderly. In R. I. Simon & K. Tardiff (Eds.), *Textbook of violence assessment and management* (pp. 381–406). Arlington, VA: American Psychiatric Publishing.

Werner, P. D., Rose, T. L., Murdach, A. D., & Yesavage, J. A. (1989). Social workers' decision making about the violent client. *Social Work Research and Abstracts, 25*, 17–20.

Wolanin, M. O., & Phillips, L. R. (1981). *Confusion: Prevention and care*. St. Louis, MO: Mosby.

Wong, S., Gordon, A., & Gu, D. (2007). Assessment and treatment of violence-prone forensic clients: An integrated approach. *British Journal of Psychiatry, 190*(49), 66–74.

Wood, K. A., & Khuri, R. (1984). Violence: The emergency room patient. In J. T. Turner (Ed.), *Violence in the medical care setting: A survival guide* (pp. 57–84). Rockville, MD: Aspen Systems.

Wykes, T., & Whittington, R. (1998). Prevalence and predictors of early traumatic stress reactions in assaulted psychiatric nurses. *Journal of Forensic Psychiatry, 9*(3), 643–658.

Yates, K., Kunz, M., Czobar, P., Rabinowitz, S., Lindenmayer, J. P., & Volavka, J. (2005). A cognitive, behaviorally based program for patients with persistent mental illness and a history of aggression, crime, or both: Structure and correlates of completers of the program. *Journal of the American Academy of Psychiatry and the Law, 33*, 214–222.

Yesavage, J. A., & Zarcone, V. (1983). History of drug abuse and dangerous behavior in inpatient schizophrenics. *Journal of Clinical Psychiatry, 44*, 259–261.

Zold, A. C., & Schilt, S. C. (1984). Violence: The child and the adolescent patient. In J. T. Turner (Ed.), *Violence in the medical care setting: A survival guide* (pp. 85–106). Rockville, MD: Aspen Systems.

CHAPTER **15**

Crisis/Hostage Negotiation

It may seem strange to have a chapter on hostage nego- tiation in a crisis book. There are several reasons this chapter is included, and they all pertain to your gen- eral health, well-being, and indeed, ability to do crisis intervention of the most harrowing kind under emer- gency conditions. First, the name of this chapter has been changed to include crisis negotiation. The Federal Bureau of Investigation found that only about 12 per- cent of all incidents in which a perpetrator is barricaded and refuses to surrender involve hostages. Most crises involving barricade situations occur in the home, are unplanned, and involve males who are enraged by do- mestic disputes (Roush, 2002; Strentz, 2006), which is clearly a population with whom many readers of this book will deal. Many more crisis interventionists are now either employed by or work with law enforcement agencies in a consultant capacity (Hatcher et al., 1998; Slatkin, 2000). Because police officers such as those of the Memphis Crisis Intervention Team routinely inte- grate hostage negotiation skills with crisis intervention techniques in a wide variety of crisis situations, the term "crisis negotiation" is a more apt and descriptive term.

Second, the chilling accounts of hostage takings that occur a continent away by terrorists make sensational headlines. Most of us assume that being taken hostage would happen to "the other guy" but not to us. Yet if you are a school counselor, a mental health worker, or even a medical staff member at a world-famous hospi- tal such as St. Jude's Children's Research Hospital in Memphis, Tennessee, you might be "the other guy." About 52 percent of all hostage takings are instigated by mentally ill or emotionally disturbed individuals (Blau, 1994, p. 257). This statistic should indicate that

human services providers are not insulated from the potential for being taken hostage.

The third reason for this chapter is that because vio- lence is rising in the workplace (Kein, 1999; Runyan, Zakocs, & Zwerling, 2000) and acts of hostage taking occur there, it is likely that crisis interventionists will be involved in debriefing the hostages or serendipi- tously doing the negotiation because they are on the premises (McWhirter & Linzer, 1994).

The fourth reason is that crisis intervention is the core of hostage negotiation. Donohue, Ramesh, and Borchgrevink (1991) call hostage negotiation "crisis bargaining," which they define as negotiation aimed at coercing another person to comply with some course of action. All the elements of a crisis are present: Disequi- librium and stress, dysfunctional behavior, poor cogni- tion, heightened emotionality, and the traumatic wake that occurs after the resolution of the event are all part and parcel of a hostage situation.

A crisis negotiation happens, according to Hammer (2007, p. 32), because five conditions that characterize a crisis are almost always present. First, a decision- making point is present such that severe negative outcomes can occur if the "wrong" decision is made. Second, the element of surprise is present and is invari- ably not pleasant. Third, the event is unexpected; it has a low probability of happening and high negative con- sequences when it does. Fourth, the situation is highly unstable and time appears extremely limited. Fifth, it is characterized by extreme stress, emotional arousal, anxiety, and fear. Further complicating matters, while the event itself is occurring the interventionist is deal- ing with the perpetrator, not the victims. There is probably no other crisis situation in which an intervener will need to be so skillful in handling a variety of difficult problems in rapidly changing circumstances under such dangerous conditions.

The fifth reason for this chapter is that the psychological dynamics of people who survive being held hostage are not unlike those of victims of battering, coerced prostitutes, and abused children, which can give you a new perspective on what it means to go through those traumas essentially as a hostage (Herman, 1995, p. 92). Therefore, many of these skills you will learn from using this book are the foundation on which crisis negotiation interactions are built (Hammer, 2007; McMains & Mullins, 2010; Noesner, 2010; Strentz, 2006).

Sixth, a number of potential suicides and domestic violence situations end up as barricade or hostage situations. At times, individuals who are bent on killing themselves and do not quite have the courage will enlist the help of the police, who will indeed shoot back when shot at. Lord and Sloop (2010) examined data from the national Hostage Barricade Data System (HOBAS; Federal Bureau of Investigation Crisis Management Unit, 2008) that designate death as a Suicide-by-Cop (SbC) event and compared them to general self-inflicted suicides. Their model predicted a 97.9 hit rate for those suicides as SbCs. So it is clear that there are suicidal persons who use the police to expedite their departure from this world. In regard to the part domestic violence plays in barricade/hostage situations, 46 percent of the incidents reported by the HOBAS system involved spouse/ex-spouse, family members, or significant others.

Finally, more than 95 percent of crisis/hostage situations are resolved peacefully without shots being fired, and this is due to the purposeful use of crisis intervention theory and techniques (Slatkin, 2005; Strentz, 1995, p. 134). Recent HOBAS data confirm that negotiation is effective, with 57 percent of negotiations resolved by verbal techniques only. In 80 percent of the situations hostages were not killed or injured, and in 82 percent the hostage taker was not killed or injured (Federal Bureau of Investigation Crisis Management Unit, 2008).

To bring the issue "up close and personal," the human services worker is likely to meet people who have had their lives radically altered in what they may feel are very negative ways by human services agencies. The rise of the American health-care system as a bureaucratic institution has led people to feel uncared

for and ignored in times of emotional stress, particularly when they do not seem able to find coping mechanisms or resources on their own (Turner, 1984, p. 177). Just as hostage taking is a political act for terrorists too weak to cause revolution, in the health-care setting it is a feeling act from people too weak to change what they believe to be grave injustices perpetrated on them by that system (Turner, 1984, p. 172). In other words, these people typically will have very high triage assessment scores when in crisis, and their lethality level will be commensurately high as well.

Dynamics of Hostage Taking

First, hostage takers should be viewed as people who have reached an acute level of frustration. Second, the taking of hostages should be viewed as an attempt at problem solving. Third, hostage takers in most cases see hostages as mere pawns in a larger game and use them as bargaining chips throughout the negotiation process. Finally, the taking of hostages is an attention-seeking behavior to attract an audience, for without an audience the hostage taking is meaningless (Schlossberg, 1980, pp. 113–114).

Dynamically, two general classifications of behavior may be observed in hostage takers: instrumental behavior and expressive behavior. *Instrumental behavior* has some recognizable goal the perpetrator seeks to have fulfilled. Bargaining negotiation is most often used with instrumental types and involves situation-related, substantive objective wants or demands of each party (Hammer & Rogan, 1997). For example, a bank robber caught in the act is willing to exchange a hostage for a getaway car.

Those engaging in *expressive behavior* seek to display their power. Expressive negotiation focuses on the impact of emotion and relationship on the resolution of the crisis (Hammer & Rogan, 1997). Medical personnel held in a hospital by an aggrieved parent who has just lost his child is a demonstration of the hostage taker's ability to gather attention to himself and demonstrate his power. Understanding the dynamics of the hostage taker is extremely important, because it is the expressive (emotion-based) hostage situation that the human services worker is most likely to encounter. Hostage-taking acts that are more likely to result in injuries or fatalities are expressive in nature (Lipsedge & Littlewood, 1997).

Of the two, expressive acts are the more difficult to understand, for such action appears to the casual observer to be senseless. There would seem to be no way that the perpetrators can gain anything except their own or others' destruction (Miron & Goldstein, 1978, p. 10). However, as an expressive gesture, such action is extremely powerful and indicates to the world at large that the perpetrators are able for a short while to take matters and destiny into their own hands. These dynamics combine variously to generate a number of types of hostage takers that the human services worker is likely to encounter.

To further complicate matters, instrumental and expressive acts are sometimes blended and are perpetrated by people with political, economic, and psychological agendas (Hammer, 2007, pp. 36–37). So, although the typologies portrayed in this chapter may be overly simplistic and not so easily type cast, we are mainly concerned with dealing with expressive types.

Types of Hostage Takers

Although Dominick Misino, one of the very best New York Police Department negotiators, proposes that one not get too hung up on diagnostic labels, he still spends time in his book on the different types of hostage takers and how to handle them (Misino, 2004, pp. 110–120). Why does he do this? If a negotiator can ferret out characteristics and identify the particular type of hostage taker being dealt with, then a valid triage assessment can be made and appropriate psychological and behavioral responses constructed. In general, with criminal types who are engaging in instrumental behavior, a rational, problem-solving approach that seeks a compromise in concrete terms is proposed. With psychotic or other emotionally disturbed types who are engaging in expressive behavior, emphasis is on affective techniques that seek to promote affiliation and interdependence between the negotiator and the hostage taker (Donohue & Roberto, 1993). With terrorists who are "emotionally rational," a mix of the two basic techniques is probably best (Miron & Goldstein, 1978, pp. 96–97).

Instrumental and instrumental/expressive hostage takers such as bank robbers, political terrorists, and religious fanatics/cultists have been omitted from this chapter because of the unlikelihood of the worker's encountering these types. However, the instrumental/expressive type, such as the aggrieved or wronged individual, and true expressive types, such as psychotics or those with personality disorders, that the worker is likely to encounter are legion and are frequent recipients of human services.

The Mentally Disturbed

Although earlier research (Fuselier, 1981a; Strentz, 1984) indicated that 50–60 percent of hostage situations involved a person who was mentally ill, newer research indicates that figure is most likely high, with Hammer (2007, pp. 58–59) reporting a rate of 7–19 percent. Indeed, Hammer is critical of the emphasis on psychopathology because he feels that takes away from the core issues of the interactive dynamics of crisis/hostage negotiation. That being said, the people we are most likely to deal with have a high potential for a mental disorder. Mentally disturbed hostage takers suffer from various kinds of psychological maladies. A mentally disturbed person may or may not be in touch with reality. This individual will likely be a loner, acting in obedience to some intensely personal, often obscure impulse (Cooper, 1981, p. 57). This person may believe that taking hostages will carry out some sacred mission or prove that he or she can do something important (Fuselier, 1981a).

The negotiator is likely to encounter a variety of major diagnostic categories of mentally disturbed hostage takers. The problem is that most mentally disturbed individuals do not fall into the nice discrete categories that follow. Many times they are comorbid or have two or more different diagnoses. Some of the most dangerous hostage takers are those who have Axis I psychoses and Axis II personality disorders (American Psychiatric Association, 2000, pp. 28–29), which may also be compounded by substance abuse problems. As Strentz (2006, p. 6) indicates, these are some of the most dangerous individuals a negotiator can come up against. One of the first things that needs to happen is an attempt to determine whether the person has been prescribed antipsychotic or mood-stabilizing medication (Misino, 2004, p. 106) and whether the person has been taking it. The answer to that last question is almost invariably "No." Following are a few of the more common types of hostage taker that human service workers are likely to run into in the course of their work.

The Schizophrenic Personality. In a sense, everybody the negotiator comes in contact with is schizophrenic in that they see the world differently than others do (Misino, 2004, p. 110). However, while people diagnosed with schizophrenia come in a variety of forms, they are all out of touch with reality. They may be recognized by their false system of beliefs and especially by their hallucinations or delusions, disheveled appearance, eccentric dress, ritualistic behavior associated with magical thinking, and their brief, concrete responses to questions. People with paranoid schizophrenia are generally the most dangerous of the various types, and this is further exacerbated if they have a companion diagnosis of antisocial personality disorder (Strentz, 2006, p. 104). They often take hostages in order to carry out what they believe is a "master plan" or to obey "orders from some special person or deity" (Fuselier, 1981a). They are conflicted and have difficulty coping with even minimally stressful situations. They operate out of logic-tight mental compartments that may be extremely bizarre, such as demanding the removal of all white people from the planet within 24 hours (Strentz, 1995, p. 142). One of the frequent symptoms of this type of hostage taker is *ideas of reference*, in which the individual believes that public media broadcasts are addressing him or her personally and transmitting special coded messages that deliver warnings or tell the individual to do things (Strentz, 2006, p. 105).

This combination of frustration, fear, and conflict produces a tremendous amount of anxiety. Excessive anxiety tends to make such people extremely sensitive and volatile, particularly when they are off their medication and their hallucinations and delusions are very active. Real time may be sped up or slowed down for the paranoid schizophrenic. Dissociation from reality is a hallmark of this type, and the negotiator must try to keep the dialogue at an even pace and keep the individual calm enough to stay in touch with the reality of the moment. A very ominous and dangerous turn of events occurs when the paranoid's ideation turns from a collective "they" or "them" against the individual to a specific person or organization (Strentz, 2006, p. 106).

Individuals who have not only paranoid features with schizophrenia but an additional diagnosis of antisocial personality disorder are exponentially more dangerous (Strentz, 2006, p. 103). Their delusions of people or institutions plotting against them means they have to take action first before they are harmed, and they have few moral pangs or guilt feelings about doing so.

Good negotiating strategy calls for reducing anxiety and at the same time attempting to create a problem-solving atmosphere (Maher, 1977, pp. 64–65). Keeping the subject focused on generalities as his target ("they" and "them") is important. Once the subject identifies a specific person or organization as the target, the potential for violence increases a great deal (Strentz, 2006, p. 106). Many times allowing paranoid schizophrenics to ventilate to the point of exhaustion is an effective method of ending the situation (Strentz, 2006, p. 102).

The best approach is to accept the paranoid schizophrenic's statements as true, although the negotiator should not agree with them. The negotiator should not try to convince the person that he or she is wrong (Fuselier, 1981a). Empathic understanding of the beliefs of the paranoid and reflection of the disturbed individual's feelings are appropriate responses. Developing closeness or trust is not likely and indeed may cause the paranoid to become suspicious and distrustful of the negotiator. Because paranoid schizophrenics tend to have sexual identity problems and may become homophobic if a same-sex negotiator is used, it is probably a good idea to have an opposite-sex negotiator. Being sincere and asking questions about the individual's worldviews is helpful in assessing and determining what strategy may be successful (Strentz, 2006, p. 110). In introducing themselves, negotiators need to stay away from references to rank and downplay their officer roles (McMains & Mullins, 2010, p. 318). Like Sgt. Friday of *Dragnet* fame, stick close to the facts and ask for the subject's view of the situation (McMains & Mullins, 2010, p. 327).

Hostage Taker (HT): The radio messages keep coming, even though I've told these people to shut their radios off. They're driving me crazy! You're a cop, you could make them do that.

Negotiator (Neg): Well, I'm a cop okay, but right now I am more a guy trying to see if we can't get you some relief and out of this predicament to the point that you feel safe and can get some peace and quiet. It must be really exasperating that they won't do what you tell them, particularly when all you want is peace and quiet. What are they saying to you that is causing you so much distress?

HT: They are so damn loud. It's the Tea Party, I tell you, and they espouse all this Goody Two Shoes stuff but they want to have sex with me and it's the males for God's sake. They keep sending the messages. Don't you hear them?

Neg: No, I don't hear them, but clearly you do and that's what counts. Can you tell me some more about the messages? Like when you get them. I know they are scaring the hell out of you by the way you are attempting to handle it. Maybe, since they're beaming them into your dorm room, we can find a place that'll seal them off.

While the negotiator never sides with the delusions or hallucinations, they should generally be accepted as real for the subject (Fuselier, 1986). The negotiator uses an empathic response that validates the subject's feeling and proposes a potential way of relieving the painful intrusions by reassuring and attempting to refocus the subject on a proactive solution rather than continue his reactive behavior. The negotiator also shows respect and interest without belittling or making satirical comments about the auditory hallucinations (McMains & Mullins, 2010, p. 328), at the same time attempting to problem-solve (Fuselier, 1986).

The Bipolar Personality. Bipolar hostage takers may be in either a manic or a depressive phase of the illness. When bipolar disorder in the manic stage is overlaid with antisocial personality disorder, the individual is extremely volatile and dangerous (Strentz, 2006, p. 116). He or she will take chances, make threats, and believe that he or she is shrewd enough to escape the police no matter how impossible that might be. Manic individuals need to be kept busy and involved so their attention doesn't focus on the hostages. Their egos also need to be stroked. Active listening skills are critical in allowing the individual with mania to feel that he or she is being heard and is the center of attention. If the person also has antisocial tendencies, then the reality of the situation needs to be made clear as to how far he or she can go before police will take action (Strentz, 2006, pp. 119–121).

Neg: An individual as smart as you certainly understands the difficulty of getting that amount of money together in such a short time. If you start shooting people, that will generate a response that will most likely get you hurt. Surely this is not the day or place you wish to get shot to pieces.

The person with mania needs to be kept on track and grounded. More directiveness can be applied to the situation as it progresses, but the expectation is that the manic will outlast a single negotiator so that a team of negotiators will be needed (Slatkin, 2005, p. 99).

HT: They're gonna drop me down a hole a hundred years deep, so what difference does it make what I do to these people. Say, what happened to Lt. Murphy, and who are you?

Neg: You wore her out. I am Lt. Hansen. Things are certainly not going to be peachy keen after this, and you and I both know that. What you decide to do right now can make a difference in how you fare when you come before a judge, though.

Conversely, hostage takers who are depressed seem incapacitated mentally and may not make clear demands (Strentz, 1995, p. 142). They are very confused and identify themselves by their inability to make a firm decision. They may be characterized by slow, subdued speech, a negative outlook on life, and demands intermingled with references to death. Their hostages are frequently persons known to them. Clinically depressed people are very unpredictable and extremely dangerous. Often they are suicidal and may take a hostage to force the police to shoot them (Strentz, 1984, p. 185) for failing to heed their instructions, or they may fire at the police or fire at a hostage (Strentz, 1984, pp. 193–194).

This phenomenon has become known in law enforcement as "suicide by cop"; it is essentially a tactic depressed individuals employ to commit suicide when they do not have the courage to kill themselves (Strentz, 2006, pp. 137–149). They are extremely dangerous because they will engage in aggressive actions designed to force the police to kill them (Strentz, 2006, p. 137). In cases of depression, a problem-solving approach would most likely be futile. The negotiator must be firm and manipulative but somewhat paradoxically sympathetic and empathic, and listen, listen, listen (Strentz, 2006, p. 121). The negotiator keeps speech slow and subdued to match that of the subject during this initial interaction. The negotiator reflects the subject's loss of a sense of control but also takes a positive, nurturing stance.

HT: I just don't know what to do. It's just a mess.

Neg: I can sense you're feeling like you've lost control of about everything. I understand you've had some problems for a long time and are pretty down about it and feel like there's little if any hope, but you're still here and a long time is not necessarily forever. I also understand you're one of the best mechanics around. There's no reason with some R&R, some medication, and therapy you can't be back to being the best mechanic in Bartlett. Lots of people get down, but "down" isn't necessarily a forever contract. I see lots of people on this job who get down on their luck just like you, and they are walking around right now getting on with their lives. So why not give me a chance to get you some help? Nothing to lose, everything to gain and feel good about yourself again. At least come meet me by the door.

After providing basic understanding and empathic responses, the negotiator challenges the subject's beliefs and provides clear instructions (Slatkin, 1996) targeted at the depressed person's indecision to try to induce mobility. At the same time, the negotiator reframes the depression as a relatively commonplace occurrence that can be handled (McMains & Mullins, 2010, p. 326).

Neg: Look, like I said, most everybody gets down in the dumps. There's no reason at all this can't be taken care of, but holding your kids and everybody else hostage in the day care center is not going to solve that. You can't imagine the effect it will have on the kids if something bad happens to their dad, and I know you are a father who cares very much what happens to his kids. I've done this a long time and have seen its traumatic wake on families. The mess will just get worse if you keep putting yourself deeper in this hole. Send the children out, and then come out and we'll see if we can't get this mess out of the hopeless and into the hopeful arena.

If the individual is suicidal, the negotiator needs to extract a commitment, no matter how tenuous, to keep the person from acting out a threat, and if possible change the subject to get the person's mind off the actions he or she is about to take. In the following dialogue, the negotiator attempts to shift the hostage taker's focus away from suicidal ideation and onto more effective communication. Negotiations in this case involve applying, in a very paced way, the intervention procedures described in the chapter on suicide. A sudden improvement should not be taken as a reflection of the negotiator's fine intervention skills. To the contrary, a positive change in disposition may mean that the depressive has made up his or her mind to commit suicide.

HT: I wonder if you'd see that the picture albums get to the kids?

Neg: I'd be willing to help in any way I can, but I want you to agree to not do anything until we get all these other issues settled.

HT: I really am feeling much better now. I appreciate all you have tried to do.

Neg: Thank you, but if that is true there is no reason you can't put the gun down, let your family and other kids walk out and walk out yourself.

One indication that the hostage taker may be suicidal is the use of hostages to conduct the negotiations. Although getting information from the hostages is a plus, the refusal of the hostage taker to personally negotiate is a bad sign and has a high possibility of ending in violence (Strentz, 1995, p. 142).

Hostage: This is Molly Higgins. I'm a secretary here. He says he doesn't want to talk, that I'm to do his talking.

Neg: Thanks for getting on the line, Molly. If you could tell me who else is there and how they are, I'd appreciate it, if it's OK with Jeb. But I really need to talk to Jeb. So would you tell him to get back on the line, so I can tell him that?

Many times depressed individuals fuel their courage by alcohol. When that happens, one of the better ploys is to wait them out until the alcohol wears off and they are no longer under the influence. Another delaying tactic is to get depressed individuals to start to doubt the decision to kill themselves (Strentz, 2006, p. 141).

Neg: Do you know that most people who attempt suicide by jumping off the Golden Gate Bridge and survive it, later report regretting going through with it as they were flying through the air? You have the rest of your life to kill yourself. I understand you feel the pain is intolerable right now, but forcing us to hurt you isn't the answer to that deep hurt inside of you. I'm not sure what the answer is, but I would sure like for you to put that gas can down, shove your lighter in your pocket, and come out, and let's see if there aren't some other options.

The Inadequate/Dependent Personality. These individuals have come to expect that the authority figures in their life will be critical of them. They don't measure up and generally have to be taken care of by significant others (McMains & Mullins, 2010, p, 301).They have a history of failure and never get things right (Slatkin, 2005, p. 105). They are the born losers in life. They don't graduate from high school, they don't keep jobs, they didn't date the prom queen or anyone else much for that matter, and see themselves as losers. Often they have botched a robbery and have been caught in the process. Because the hostage-taking incident may be the high point of the person's life, the inadequate personality type tends to stretch the situation for all it is worth. Identified by key phrases such as "I'll show them who's boss" and "Now they'll see what I can do," this hostage taker basks in the limelight of the situation. Such pronouncements are indicative of a low self-image. Therefore, the motivation for taking hostages may be to prove that the inadequate type can succeed at something.

Yet in the same instance, he or she may appear contrite and apologetic for the behavior. The inadequate personality type may initially state demands with considerable conviction and then turn around and provide the negotiator with several options (Strentz, 1984, p. 185). Negotiators need to be aware of and seize those options. In the beginning the negotiator's strategy is to be open, empathic, understanding, uncritically accepting, and sympathetic to the many grievances the hostage taker has. Helping the individual find a way to end the situation without failing again is critical. Keeping significant others away from the scene is critical because this type of hostage taker may need to show them he actually can do something—like kill somebody. The primary strategy of the negotiator is to present problem-solving alternatives so that the hostage taker will not feel that he or she has "failed again." The inadequate/dependent person is now involved in something way beyond his or her problem-solving capacity, so after providing ego support, more directiveness is needed . Understand that this individual is impulsive and fatigues easily, so he or she may suddenly give up or take other, more lethal measures to end the situation (Strentz, 2006, p. 89). Playing up to this hostage taker's ego and helping the person find a face-saving alternative are excellent tactics. Those with inadequate personalities have a need to prove themselves to some "significant" others. The "I'll show them" statements indicate this need, and they may murder the hostages if their egos are not handled with extreme care (Slatkin, 2005, p. 106).

HT: I want a personal interview with the news director of Channel 3 right now. I've got some things I want to say. You do that, and I'll let them go.

Neg: I understand how important it is to you to get on television. You let those people go now, and I'll see that you get on the 10 o'clock news.

Reinforcement (Slatkin, 1996) also boosts the inadequate/dependent personality's image and sets the stage for compliance.

Neg: So you made it through Parchman Prison for 7 years. It takes a smart guy to do that. My bet is you'll be just as smart here and make the exchange for the food.

Nurturing the inadequate/dependent's need for approval is a key component in resolving the situation. As such, the negotiator can take a much more directive stance as an attendant, caring, authority figure (McMains & Mullins, 2010, pp. 302–303).

Neg: I think I have enough clout with my boss to make this happen, so it is imperative that you do the following to make this work.

The Antisocial Personality. The person with antisocial personality disorder repeatedly comes into conflict with society and is incapable of having significant loyalty to individuals, groups, or social values. Such people tend to blame others and offer rationalizations for their behavior (American Psychiatric Association, 2000) and are most likely already adjudicated for some crime (Misino, 2004, p. 110). They are deceitful, superficial, grandiose, lacking in empathy, and don't accept responsibility for their actions (Greenstone, Kosson, & Gacono, 2000). The antisocial type is likely to dehumanize the hostages and should be considered extremely dangerous to them because this person will manifest little feeling for their well-being. Although antisocial personalities have not internalized moral values, they do understand their effect on others and are therefore potent adversaries.

While antisocial personality disorders lack emotional depth, they may display a wide range of skillful emotional overlays in place of true emotional responses (Lanceley, 1981, pp. 31–32). The only concern of these hostage takers is for themselves. They do not relate to others, and attempts to empathize with them will do little good. Personal or sensitive information should never be shared with them, particularly about hostages, as they have absolutely no empathy. Therefore, the negotiator should be aware that this type has no compunction about doing anything to anybody.

If at any point this hostage taker decides that hostages are a burden, they will be killed. This individual takes risks and is stimulated, not frightened, by this situation. What frightens others delights the antisocial personality. Because he or she is most likely a criminal and has knowledge of the penal code and system, lying to him or her is not a good idea. Rationalizing the seriousness of the situation and focusing on the mortality of the person is a way of justifying his or her actions and focusing his or her attention on the one thing most desired—not to die! (Strentz, 2006, p. 98).

HT: Don't give me that crap about "more time." You get that car in here, or I start doing some fun things to this little 6-year-old, and her mommy gets to watch.

Neg: I know you're mad about the car, but you know I gotta go through procedures. Surely you know how the bigwigs are and having to be at their beck and call. I understand you could work the kid over, but I wonder if you've thought about the good that'll do you in the long run. It's your hide you're dealing with, too! So let's work on that side of it.

The negotiator does not focus on the hostage but rather focuses directly on the antisocial's profound desire to preserve his or her own best interests, affiliating with the hostage taker from the standpoint that they both suffer injustices at the hands of the powers-that-be (Bradstreet, 1992).

The profound egocentricity of the antisocial type requires constant stimulation. Again, reinforcement (Slatkin, 1996) along with confrontation about negative consequences can induce the antisocial type to become more reasonable. A primary objective in the negotiation process is to keep the holder's attention and avoid having him or her turn attention to the hostages as a source of stimulus.

Neg: You're the man here. You're the one calling the shots. We both know that chance brought the security cop back, and except for that you'd be outta here. I gotta hand it to you, it was a great plan. So use your smarts here too. You and I can work a deal.

This person is not only streetwise but also police-wise, so trickery is not a good idea. Also, the negotiator should avoid references to jail or hospitalization, because antisocial types are likely to become highly agitated if they believe they are going to lose their freedom or it is insinuated that they are crazy. Dealing with this person should never be done in a tentative manner. Such responses will be seen as weakness and will be greeted with contempt. Confidence, assurance, forthrightness, and assertiveness are critical to dealing with the antisocial type. The negotiator may not know the answer, but a waffling "I . . . umh . . . ah . . . well . . . I guess . . . I'll . . . ah . . . have to check that out, okay?" is not the way to handle the antisocial personality.

Neg: You know you have done several things right here to help yourself, but the request for the lawyer to come down here will have to be passed through the site commander. That's just procedure. You know that.

The Borderline Personality. We have already met the hallmark of difficult clients in Chapter 5, people with borderline personality disorder. They are no strangers to contacts with the police in either barricade or hostage situations because of their emotional volatility (Misino, 2004, p. 113). Along with the antisocial personality, they are so numerous and infamous in barricade situations that a number of the negotiators referenced in this chapter have felt obliged to make recommendations on how to handle them (Borum & Strentz, 1992; Lanceley, 2003; McMains & Mullins, 2010; Misino, 2004; Slatkin, 2005; Strentz, 2006).

One of the major problems in dealing with borderline personalities is their ambivalence about people in authority. Given their mercurial "I hate you, don't leave me" feelings, negotiators have their hands full trying to defuse emotionality and maintain contact to keep them from acting on their impulses. Strentz (2006, p. 237) believes this is one of the most dangerous of hostage takers because this person doesn't realize the gravity of the situation and may make inordinate demands and be extremely agitated when they are not immediately met. Further, the subject may start to exhibit psychotic and suicidal/homicidal (Borum & Strentz, 1992; Lanceley, 2003) ideation and indeed act on it. They engage in numerous suicide attempts and have completion rates of about 10 percent. Combine the foregoing characteristics with the additional stressors of a hostage situation, and it is easy to see why Borum and Strentz (1992) think it is important for the negotiators to monitor their own stress levels or, better yet, have another professional monitor them.

Primary components of negotiating strategies with borderline personalities are setting limits, structuring goals, showing empathic understanding, defusing emotions, caringly confronting manipulative behavior, providing support but not eliciting dependence, and staying "with" the subject to control erratic and impulsive behavior. Asking them how the subject feels about a negotiation point is more important than the point itself (Misino, 2004, p. 114).

Calmness, structure, and coolness under extreme emotional conditions are the watchwords. Structuring detail about what normally happens in each stage of the negotiation process and staying in touch with the subject throughout the situation are critical (Lanceley, 2003; Borum & Strentz, 1992). Bonding with and reassuring the subject that help is available and that you will find him or her help are important in massaging that part of the borderline personality that is so needy.

Neg: (*on the telephone*) No, I will not abandon you like your girlfriend or family has. I understand you are extremely distraught over your lover wanting to leave you. But I want you to understand that I can't help you much as long as those day care kids are still in there and you won't put that kitchen knife down and come out and talk to me face to face. If you really do want help, like you say, you can do these things to help yourself. We'll take this one step at a time, and you and I will work this through together. I don't ever quit on folks, and from the way you are talking about how much you care about your girlfriend, I don't think you do either.

In summary, the ideal relationship with the mentally disturbed hostage taker is one in which affiliation and interdependence are high, because those factors lead to mutual trust. It is crucial that the negotiator attempt to establish a trusting relationship early on because research has found that once the tone of the relationship is established (high or low), it tends to stay that way for the duration of the negotiation. When negotiators establish low affiliation, the content of the perpetrator's messages is much more negative and therefore more dangerous (Donohue & Roberto, 1993).

Other Hostage Takers

The Estranged Person. Misino (2004, p. 104) characterizes this hostage taker as highly unpredictable because he or she is driven solely by emotion. A hostage taker who is connected emotionally to the hostage is extremely volatile and dangerous. Invariably, the estranged hostage taker will know the hostage, who will probably be a spouse, a lover, or his or her children. The estranged hostage taker is experiencing a breakdown in his or her interpersonal relationships. These breakdowns lead to domestic quarrels and, in turn, the escalating nature of the quarrels and the feared loss of the significant other lead the estranged person to take the hostage. (Alcohol often provides the liquid courage necessary to carry out the taking.) The estranged hostage taker seeks to coerce the maintenance of the relationship through force. The most distinctive feature of this kind of hostage taking is its intensely personal nature and its unique purpose of continued domination over the significant other (Cooper, 1981, pp. 27–28).

As in any other domestic dispute, the negotiator should be extremely careful of this volatile situation and use empathic listening and responding skills to their fullest. Empathic responding (Slatkin, 1996) that reflects the hurt and despair of the estranged person's feelings demonstrates concern and caring.

Neg: Things really seem to have come unraveled even after you tried your damnedest. It really hurts that she doesn't appreciate what you've done for the family.

Self-disclosure of like problems (Slatkin, 1996) may be a way of creating a bond with the estranged person who is looking for a sympathetic shoulder to cry on.

Neg: I haven't had it as bad as you, but I sure do know about working two jobs to make ends meet and then coming home to a cold shoulder, a cold dinner, and a cold bed. So I do know how it feels.

With this type, the negotiator must contend with the highly personal nature of the hostage taking and the continued denial of reality. Intrinsic to intervention is the negotiator's ability to keep denial from turning into despair. The key to resolution is that the estranged hostage taker needs to be shown a graceful way out (Cooper, 1981, p. 28).

HT: It's not my fault. I've done everything she asked, and then she still jilted me. If I can't have her, nobody will.

Neg: She really hurt you, then. I can start to see why you feel you had to do this. I'm wondering, though, if she can't see now just how strongly you feel. Perhaps you've made your point to her. You certainly have to me!

Because this type of hostage taker often depersonalizes and belittles the hostage in order to make it easier to harm him or her, the negotiator seeks to restore the hostage's dignity and personhood (Misino, 2004, p. 105).

Neg: That "bitch" as you say has seen you through two stints of rehab, as I understand it. So Melanie has stood by you in very tough times, and you know that.

The Institutionalized Individual. Institutionalized hostage takers are inmates who have a grievance, usually about conditions within the system in which they are confined. Hostage takings of this sort are usually deemed instrumental acts planned to produce concrete changes in the institution (Maher, 1977, p. 65). However, an institutional hostage situation invariably also involves expressive elements, and there may be more than one spokesperson among the perpetrators. Therefore, it is extremely important for the negotiator to initiate a dialogue that seeks an empathic understanding of the hostage takers, balanced with focusing on their demands. Because such individuals are wise in the ways of institutional and law enforcement policy, the negotiator needs to be very careful about attempting to manipulate or trick the perpetrators because they are then putting the lives of the hostages in his or her hands, and if caught in a lie, negotiations will crash (Strentz, 2006, p. 157).

HT: Go to hell! We want to see the warden, and we want these 25 demands met, and they ain't negotiable!

Neg: I understand you're pissed that he wouldn't listen to you. I'll certainly convey your message to him, but before I do I want to know that the hostages are all right.

HT: Kiss off! You ain't gettin' nuthin'.

Neg: Look! You know how the game goes. You want something; they want something. So let's get going and see if we can't get what you want.

The Wronged Person. The wronged hostage taker is dissatisfied or aggrieved by the system at large or a particular bureaucracy. Wronged individuals may be identified by the "crosses" they bear and the paranoia associated with their beliefs. These hostage takers feel so grossly discriminated against by the "establishment" that they seek to remake society to their own satisfaction (Cooper, 1981, p. 10).

Aggrieved or wronged individuals are high on the list of potential candidates with whom the human services worker may become involved—if not as a negotiator, then as someone being taken hostage. Aggrieved people feel that no one in a position of responsibility will willingly redress the terrible wrongs that have been done to them. After exhausting a variety of acceptable options within the system and still receiving no redress, such people may do something dramatic (Turner, 1984, p. 178). The wronged individual needs a chance to ventilate his or her feelings to an empathic and sympathetic listener. Summary restatement and reflection (Slatkin, 1996) allow the negotiator to convey to the wronged individual how deeply understood he or she is and that, for once, somebody in authority is listening.

HT: The doctors, nurses, the administrators, the psychologists, the social workers, they're all at fault. She wouldn't have died if they'd done their job. Everybody thinks this is such a hotshot hospital. It's really Murder Incorporated, and people need to know the truth. They killed my wife. She was everything to me. I'm lost without her.

Neg: So what you're saying is that the hospital up and down the line couldn't have screwed things up worse. And in screwing them up they lost your wife. She was the center of your world, and now your world is gone. It really sounds as if the hurt and anger goes bone deep, and the frustration you've felt makes this the only way you can get some respect and command their attention.

Associated with this type of hostage taking is the high priority attached to publicity, because the hostage taker is usually motivated to make the public aware of the wrongs imposed by the particular authorities in question. Proper involvement of the media can enhance the opportunity for releasing the hostages, if the hostage taker perceives that a wrong can be made right by a public airing (Gladis, 1979).

Neg: I realize what a terrible shock her death was, and how you trusted all those people. Yet you believe they let you down and should be exposed for the incompetent blunders they've made. Would you be willing to make a deal? If I can set it up so you can read that statement you've prepared about the hospital, will you let those people out?

Negotiators also need to establish a continuous state of interdependence between themselves and perpetrators who are not classified as "mentally ill." Doing the foregoing is not easy given that perpetrators often undergo mercurial behavioral, cognitive, and affective shifts. Indeed, it may be tempting for negotiators to try quickly to get perpetrators to start thinking more realistically about their problems by getting them to withdraw from the situation or nail down their goals to achieve crisis resolution. However, negotiators need to reject this need for closure and focus on directing and controlling affiliation so that positive affect and mutual liking are developed. In so doing, negotiators can keep the perpetrator talking, gather intelligence, improve leverage, and move to more normative bargaining issues (Donohue & Roberto, 1993).

Alcohol and Substance Abuse. The HOBAS database indicates that about 28 percent of barricade hostage situations involve a person who is intoxicated. Working "wet" certainly makes any negotiation more difficult and potentially more dangerous. Slowing down, being patient, and speaking slowly give the intoxicated subject time to consider what is being asked. Alcohol releases inhibitions, and those inhibitions may range from violence toward hostages to suicide and/or homicide. As a result, the negotiator needs to be alert to indicators that violence potential is increasing whenever alcohol or other mood elevators are used (McMains & Mulllins, 2010, p. 340).

Stages and Dynamics of a Hostage Situation

Throughout the entire hostage episode, emotions of both hostage and hostage taker move on a curve that oscillates between desperation and euphoria. As the episode is protracted, the cycle tends to dampen and retreat from both emotional extremes (Schreiber, 1978, p. 50). It is within this context that the following stages should be examined. There are four stages to a hostage situation: alarm, crisis, accommodation, and resolution (Strentz, 1984, pp. 189–194; 1995, pp. 137–146).

Alarm. The alarm stage is the most traumatic and dangerous and typically lasts about an hour. Whatever the type of hostage takers, in this first stage their emotions are running exceedingly high, their reason may be diminished, and they may be extremely aggressive in their reaction to any perceived threat. To force their will on the hostages, the hostage takers generally believe that hostages must be terrorized into submission. Therefore, hostage takers may be inclined to harass, abuse, or even kill anyone who seems to be interfering with their attempts to consolidate their position (Strentz, 1984, p. 190).

For the unprepared individual who suddenly becomes a hostage, the alarm stage is traumatic in every respect. A previously tranquil situation now becomes a life-and-death one that pivots every minute. For the victim, defenseless and confused, the nightmarish experience takes on an unreal aspect. Many begin to deny the reality of the situation, particularly when people from whom they expect help seem to be doing nothing. The hostage taker becomes the most important person in the life of the victim, and over time his or her actions shape the victim's psychology. The accounts of battered women, abused children, and coerced prostitutes bear an uncanny resemblance to those of hostages, concentration camp survivors, and political prisoners (Herman, 1995, p. 92). From that standpoint, the psychological and behavioral dynamics for these groups during and after their escape or release tend to run parallel. Effective coping at this early stage means immediately putting into place a strong will to survive and not succumbing to panic. It is at this stage that most injuries occur (Strentz, 1995, p. 137). Any sign of panic may cause the perpetrators to overreact and may dramatically diminish the chances of survival (Strentz, 1984, p. 196).

Crisis. The crisis stage marks the beginning of reason for the hostage takers. However, there is still a great deal of unpredictability and danger as they try to consolidate their position. Initial attempts at negotiation at this stage may be marked by outrageous demands and emotional diatribes by the hostage holders. Because they fear assault by the authorities, hostage takers may move hostages to a more secure area or enlist their cooperation in making the area they are in more secure (Strentz, 1984, p. 191). The hostage taker is put at center stage and is tasked with decision making. Although this may seem surprising, there are two reasons why this is done. First, the act of making constant decisions in a stressful situation is extremely fatiguing and wears the hostage taker down. Second, the hostage taker's need for an audience gives him or her a chance to be put in the limelight and focuses attention on the taker and not the hostages (Strentz, 1995, pp. 139–140).

For the hostage, the crisis stage is the most critical because it sets the tone for the remainder of the situation. Hostage–captor interaction at this stage can either enhance or reduce hostages' chances of survival. Although denial by hostages may still be in place as a defense mechanism, the decision to face reality and engage in normal behavior generally provides some emotional relief and mental escape. Hostages who are in positions of responsibility must be very careful not to intimidate their captors. If their captors feel inferior, they may see defiance as the hostage's attempt to humiliate them. In particular, verbal humiliation precipitates violence (Strentz, 1984, p. 203). Fear is also increased by unpredictable outbursts of violence and by inconsistent enforcement of numerous trivial demands and petty rules.

But violence is not the only way the hostage taker gains control over a hostage. The capricious granting of small indulgences may undermine the victim's psychological resistance far more effectively than unremitting deprivation and fear (Herman, 1995, pp. 92–93). There is little difference in these dynamics between the hostage taker and a pimp who controls his prostitutes. In addition to inducing terror, the perpetrator seeks to destroy the victim's sense of autonomy. Deprivations of food, sleep, shelter, exercise, personal hygiene, and privacy are common practices (Herman, 1995, pp. 92–93). These same deprivation tactics are certainly understood and employed by batterers and child abusers.

At this stage, hostages may start to experience three problems: isolation, claustrophobia, and/or the loss of a sense of time. People who are isolated have to come to grips with the fact that the only human contacts they have may be extremely hostile toward them. Claustrophobia can take its toll even if the individual is not isolated and confined to a small cell. And losing a sense of time becomes a very important problem. By this stage, captors have usually removed personal items, including watches, from the hostages.

Sense of time becomes very important to someone held captive who is hoping for rescue. Asking for such small favors as information about time or date puts hostages completely at the mercy of their captors. Hostage takers use such requests to good advantage in earning compliance from their captives (Herman, 1995, p. 93; Strentz, 1984, p. 197). The message is "We can do with you what we want. There is no hope other than what we give you!"

Accommodation. The accommodation stage is the longest and most tranquil. Constantly assessing the mental status of the hostage taker clarifies his or her personality and typology (Strentz, 1995, p. 143). For the hostage, the accommodation stage is marked by time dragging by. Boredom, punctuated only by moments of terror, is the hallmark of this stage. The crests and troughs of emotions that have occurred until this point are likely to induce fatigue in both hostage and hostage taker. With increased control by their captors, hostages suffer from a constriction of initiative and planning. The hostage no longer thinks of how to escape but rather of how to stay alive. With prolonged captivity, constriction becomes habitual. Surviving as a hostage calls for a blend of dignified passivity and nonaggressive, nonhostile actions. To the contrary, being overcompliant also may be risky and taken as a sign of weakness (Strentz, 2006, p. 234).

Thus chronically traumatized people are often characterized as passive or helpless, which certainly lends credence to Walker's (1984) theory of learned helplessness in battered women who are held "captive" by their abusive mates (Herman, 1995, p. 93). If this stage becomes protracted, then there is a likelihood that Stockholm syndrome, named after an aborted bank holdup in Sweden during which one of the hostages fell in love with her captor, will come into operation (Strentz, 1984, p. 198).

Stockholm Syndrome. Unlikely as it may seem, Stockholm syndrome can occur under the most terrifying and horrific of conditions (Speckard et al., 2005; Strentz, 2006, pp. 243–258). Stockholm syndrome is possible if three conditions are met: extended period of time, not being isolated from one's captor, and positive contact between captor and captive (Fuselier, 1981b). The phenomenon comprises the following three elements (Strentz, 1984, p. 198):

1. Hostages generate positive feelings toward the hostage taker.
2. Hostages generate negative feelings toward police and the authorities.
3. Captors generate positive feelings toward their hostages.

Whether the victim is part of a religious cult, a child who has been physically abused by a parent, a political terrorist's hostage, or a customer caught in a bank holdup, the potential for such traumatic bonding is strikingly similar. Evidence seems to support the idea that Stockholm syndrome is not a well-gauged ploy by the hostage to ensure survival. The phenomenon is probably an automatic, unconscious emotional response to the trauma of being taken hostage (Strentz, 1979, p. 2). It seems that as people are thrown together, both captor and captive start to respond to one another on more personal terms. If this occurs, it becomes very hard to regard one another as faceless entities to be despised and used. Familiarity with each other provides a fertile ground for identification with the other's problems, hopes, fears, and outlook on life. If such positive identification by a hostage is reciprocated by the holder, the hostage's chances of survival increase considerably (Ochberg, 1977). During this stage, it is not uncommon for hostages to believe that the authorities are the chief cause of the problem and that if the authorities would only go home, the siege would end (Speckard et al., 2005; Strentz, 1984, p. 200).

Auerbach and associates (1994), using simulated hostage role plays, determined that captives who found their captors most aversive were those who perceived the "terrorists" as most dominant and least friendly. Those "hostages" who had received training in emotion- versus problem-focused coping perceived their "captors" as less threatening and were perceived by the "terrorists" in the same way. The hostage can make use of this phenomenon. In as genuine a way as possible, the hostage should seek to build a positive relationship with his or her captors. The easiest way to do this is to be as real a person as possible by attempting to share the more personal aspects of one's life and to elicit the same from the holders. If hostages make attempts to gain familiarity with the hostage takers, they would probably be wise to avoid political or religious discussions with them, because such discussions accentuate differences between captor and captive (Miron & Goldstein, 1978, p. 92). Eating and exercising are musts. Hostages should take whatever food is offered. Even if it is possible to do only flexibility exercises, hostages should do them regularly (Strentz, 1984, p. 204).

It should be understood that Stockholm syndrome generally does not develop because of the short duration of most hostage situations. Second, most of the hostage situations that human service workers see do not involve strangers. Hostage and hostage taker generally are known to one another and those prior dynamics weigh far more than the dynamics of the hostage taking. However, if this is not the case, the negotiator will many times try to generate a Stockholm syndrome by attempting to personalize the hostages if they are unknown to the taker. That includes using the term "people" rather than "hostages" and always attempting to use personal names. Finally, time is an ally. The more time that passes, the more personal the hostage taking becomes and the more difficult it is to dehumanize the hostages (McMains & Mullins, 2010, pp. 468–469). It is with good reason that Gary Noesner's book (2010) is titled *Stalling for Time*.

Resolution. In the resolution stage, the hostage takers have become fatigued as the long hours or days take their toll. The high expectations that they held early become dashed as they find they have lost most of the bargaining chips. Whether there is a positive or negative resolution now depends on the ability of the negotiator to skillfully bring closure to the situation (Strentz, 1984, p. 193). In particular, it is important to understand the difference between the behavior of a hostage taker who is planning to surrender and one who is planning to commit suicide (see the chapter on suicide for clues indicating whether the hostage taker is also suicidal). If the hostage taker gives any clues at all during this final stage, the negotiator should be prepared to move immediately into a suicide prevention mode. Whatever the type, and however long and arduous the incident, the trained negotiator takes a purposeful and dignified approach to the perpetrator's surrender. Indeed, this is the most critical part of the whole process. Everyone is wary and on edge. If a surrender is to be made, it must occur with every *i* being dotted and *t* crossed so no miscommunication occurs that causes someone to get killed or injured (Misino, 2004, pp. 150–151).

Intervention Strategies

Assessing the motives and emotional status of the hostage taker is an extremely important and delicate task because people's lives are generally at stake. Negotiators must be competent in active listening and relationship skills because the hostage taker cannot be tested or evaluated in any normal way during the period of the emergency (Slatkin, 2005, pp. 19–53). Triage assessment is especially difficult in these circumstances. Often the negotiator has no way of knowing, other than by information that can be obtained verbally, what might be motivating the captor to take such extreme measures. Even then, the negotiator may have to make a determination based only on a verbal assessment taken over the telephone. A compounding problem is that often the negotiator must determine a great deal of personal information beyond the current mental status of the perpetrator, including the expertise and the will to carry out threats. At best, much of this information will be obtained from secondhand sources, such as friends, coworkers, or relatives, who may provide a very biased picture of the captor. Worse, this entire scenario may take place with a great deal of noise, confusion, a crowd, and the media present. Understanding and assessing the degree of mobility/immobility the hostage taker feels are of particular importance because the negotiator needs to decide how directive, collaborative, or nondirective to be.

The following intervention procedures are universally recognized by hostage negotiation teams and can be considered constants in the negotiating process. Yet each hostage situation is unique, and resolution cannot be reduced to any formula that works for all cases. Therefore, the successful negotiator, like other crisis interventionists, is creative but follows a standard procedure, takes risks but proceeds with caution, has empathy but believes in justice, and has patience but moves decisively (Misino, 2004; Slatkin, 2005; Strentz, 2006).

These intervention techniques generally fall within two operational models called REACT (McMains & Mullins, 2010) and S.A.F.E. (Hammer, 2007). REACT is a task model that includes the following steps:

Recognition of the conditions needed to make an incident negotiable involves planning, strategy and tactics, and safety and security.

Engagement is a task that builds rapport and reassurance and facilitates ventilation and validation.

Assessment continuously evaluates the physical risks to all the parties involved.

Contracting/Controlling includes facilitating an agreement on how to resolve the incident; planning out how it will be resolved; helping the perpetrator with his or her ambivalence toward the police, him- or herself, others, and the resolution itself; controlling how the surrender will occur so that nothing goes wrong; and gaining surrender of the hostage taker and release of the hostages.

Terminating/Transferring has to do with what will happen after the surrender, such as arranging for follow-up care with perpetrators who are mentally ill or those known by uniform patrol officers as "frequent fliers" for their constant involvement with the police in such situations. (McMains & Mullins, 2010, pp. 123–202)

The S.A.F.E. model is more a communications model that can be effectively integrated into the REACT tasks. S.A.F.E. has the following components:

Substantive issues are the initial demands and wants made by the subject and consequently the return wants and demands of the negotiator.

Attunement is the degree of relational trust, attraction, liking, respect, and desire to cooperate with another party.

Face is the self-image of the parties that is either threatened or honored (saving face).

Emotion is the degree of emotional distress experienced by both parties. (Hammer, 2007)

As we move through examples and the case study in this chapter, you should see how these interlocking models can work together. The S.A.F.E. model is a reaction to earlier models that focused on instrumental hostage takings from a primarily substantive standpoint and expressive hostage takings from a primarily affective standpoint. This model operates from a more flexible communications basis that recognizes which frame (substantive, attunement, face, emotion) is the main dynamic framework the subject is demonstrating and seeks to match the negotiators' responses to that frame (Hammer, 2007).

Communication Techniques

Throughout the negotiations, basic listening and responding skills critical to any crisis situation are employed (Slatkin, 2005). The first and foremost step is defining the problem. Very clear problem definition is crucial to learning the motives and concerns of the hostage taker, what type of siege operation will occur, what the risks of violence are, and the conditions under which the negotiator will operate (McMains & Mullins, 2010). Use of active listening through clarification and paraphrasing of content, reflection of feelings, summary restatement, and open-ended questions and leads is important in letting the hostage taker ventilate feelings (Slatkin, 1996, 2005). This process also allows assessment of the emotional state and mental condition of the hostage taker (McMains & Mullins, 2010; Strentz, 1995, p. 136). The focus is on the person who most wants and needs to be the center of attention—the hostage taker. The hostage taker is encouraged to tell his or her story in as much detail as he or she needs to do (Strentz, 1995, p. 138). The negotiator uses owning or "I" statements of self-disclosure, immediacy, and reinforcement (Slatkin, 1996) to create a bond between him- or herself and the hostage taker.

Cultural Factors. In an increasingly pluralistic world, particularly in the United States, it is no longer feasible to think of the population in a unitary way. There is a good reason that Chapter 2, Culturally Effective Helping, is in this book. Nowhere does this hold more true than in a hostage/barricade situation. There is a real need to examine cross-cultural comparisons of crisis negotiations because what we have said even in the opening paragraph about basic listening skills may well not apply with people from different cultural backgrounds (Grubb, 2010).

The need to understand what cultural factors are operating in a high-stakes hostage situation is particularly critical for two reasons. First are the social locations (Brown, 2008) we spent a great deal of time describing in Chapter 2. Gary Noesner, a former chief negotiator for the FBI, gives a chilling description of how the Branch Davidian confrontation near Waco, Texas, went horribly wrong because of the social location of a negotiator who tried to go head to head arguing with David Koresh, the Davidian leader, on biblical grounds as to why he should give up, and tactical coordinators whose social locations were clearly based on a confrontational tactical assault location rather than one of negotiation (Noesner, 2010, pp. 94–148).

However, it is not just social location that determines the impact that multiculturalism has on crisis/hostage negotiation. Giebels and Taylor (2009) conducted an in-depth study on how communication occurs in crisis negotiation in low context (LC) and high context (HC) cultures. They focused on a hallmark of crisis negotiation, forcing strategies, which are designed to push resolution through either persuasion or threats. They found that, overall, persuasive arguments replete with factual evidence were more persuasive to LC hostage takers than to HC perpetrators and were more effective in bringing about compromise. Perhaps contrary to stereotypes of HC cultures, which might be supposed to engage in more subtlety as negotiations open, it was found that in the first half of the negotiation they were more immediate in their acceptance of persuasive, fact-based rational arguments. A second finding was that LC perpetrators tended to respond better to persuasive arguments across both first and second parts of crisis intervention, which runs somewhat counter to standard operating procedure of empathic listening and responding, particularly in the case of expressive type barricade/hostage situations.

Further, LC perpetrators were quicker to use direct threats to get needs met, but HC perpetrators, when threatened themselves, responded very vigorously in escalating the crisis and used counterthreats. In this instance, Giebels and Taylor believe that HCs tend to confirm Hammer's (2007) contention that saving face is an important part of negotiation. Because they are concerned with saving face, HCs will respond vigorously to threats to their control, whereas LCs' threat initiators have more to do with coercing the negotiators into accepting their bargaining position. The authors hypothesize that HCs may see this as calling their manhood into question and they have to show the police "who is in charge." They also found that LCs were more immediate in reciprocating information sharing than were HCs, which probably has to do with the LC cultural notion of getting information clear and then using it, as opposed to the more circumspect way information is delivered in an HC culture.

Although Giebels and Taylor's research focused on negotiations that involved more instrumental than expressive crimes, it raises a number of questions about negotiators' strategies when dealing with diverse populations because those "by the book" strategies are used extensively in their training and approach. Nothing is ever simple in the crisis business, particularly when different cultural viewpoints come into play, and that is certainly true in crisis/hostage negotiation.

Recognition and Assessment. In all hostage situations, the initial operating mode between the hostage taker and the negotiator is one of collaboration, wherein the negotiator appears to act as the bargaining agent between the hostage taker and the authorities. Initial tasks are to build rapport and to calm and reassure the perpetrator that things can be worked out (McMains & Mullins, 2010, p. 163). Although the hostages themselves want immediate resolution of the crisis, it is crucial to stretch the time out, wearing down the hostage taker to a point of fatigue (Strentz, 1995, p. 140). As a result, the standard refrain of the negotiator is, "I'm concerned about your problems, and I want you to know I'm going to take all the time that's necessary to understand your concerns." Therefore, letting the hostage taker ventilate for as long as he or she wants may be considered a positive outcome because of the time consumed.

Assessing identity issues is critical. Identity issues come in two forms—personal and social. Personal identity is based on the individual's unique perception of his or her own attributes. Social identity consists of the characteristics and the emotional significance that is attached to one's membership in groups. A suicidal individual barricaded in a house with his sister as a hostage who has just lost his girlfriend and his job is mainly a personal identity issue where the hostage taker is operating in an emotional frame; a political/religious terrorist who takes over a bus and threatens to blow it up has much more of a social identity issue and may be operating from a substantive frame of reference, even though there may be attunement issues (more probably lack thereof) and emotional frames from perceived past injustices. Therefore, depending on what the negotiator is presented with in the way of dynamics and not just content, the Attunement, Face, and Emotion frames are likely starting points. In any of the examples, allowing individuals to save face for either personal or social identity reasons is extremely important. For example, allowing individuals to keep their reputation intact by arranging to not parade them in front of a crowd after their capture may be the most significant point a negotiator can make. In many settings with many types of hostage takers, allowing them to save face by negotiating "honorable" ways out of the barricade situation is a critical piece in resolving the dilemma (Misino, 2004; Strentz, 2006). Therefore, the recognition and assessment stages (McMains & Mullins, 2010, pp. 149–162) are extremely important to understanding what is going on and not rushing in where angels fear to tread.

Controlling and Contracting. As the alarm and crisis stages pass and the accommodation stage develops, the negotiator's strategy changes as well. Action responses (Slatkin, 1996) such as asking closed questions, confronting, interpreting, and giving information and instructions are used to ensure safety, establish a support system, examine alternatives, generate a plan for resolution of the event, and extract a commitment from the hostage taker (Slatkin, 2005, p. 50). The negotiator starts to develop a contract that will lead to surrender. There is a fine line between mandating and gently steering and persuading (McMains & Mullins, 2010, p. 173). The negotiator will use a number of influencing techniques to displace the ambivalence the subject may feel and start moving him or her toward resolution.

Transferring. In the resolution stage, the negotiator will most likely move from a collaborative to a more directive operating mode. Action techniques use directive statements that are designed to elicit commitment and move the hostage taker toward giving up, but also allow him or her to appear in control and save face (Slatkin, 2005, p. 50). Clear plans will be made on how the surrender occurs. Almost without exception, Hammer's Face frame is used here to let the subject believe he or she still has dignity. A good negotiator will not walk off the job as soon as the surrender occurs but will see that guarantees and promises are kept. Keeping credibility is extremely critical in this job, because word will soon be out on the street that the negotiator can't be trusted. That will make everybody's job harder (McMains & Mullins, 2010, pp. 196–197).

Containing the Scene

As in all other law enforcement operations, safety is the foremost consideration. During the Recognition phase of operations, most of the following happens as more information is gained (McMains & Mullins, 2010, pp. 149–162). In a hostage situation, inner and outer perimeters are secured around the hostage scene and a command post is established in the inner perimeter. Although it may appear to the hostages that the authorities are confused and disorganized and are letting their lives run out through the sands of an hourglass, that is not the case at all. Containing and stabilizing the scene prevents the scope of the event from expanding (Schlossberg, 1980). While there may not appear to be much going on in the eyes of the hostages or the eye in the sky beaming the scene to live-feed television, a perfect storm of activity is occurring as a perimeter and command post are set up. While not within the scope of this book, these activities are extensive, complex, and highly coordinated with a number of people playing significant backup roles behind the negotiators.

Gathering Information

The most important and time-sensitive information that the negotiator needs is a profile of the hostage taker. Who is this person? Who are his or her close friends, family, relatives? What kind of criminal record does he or she have? Is there a psychiatric record? Is this person currently obtaining professional help? Is the professional available? What kinds of specialized skills does the hostage taker have? What does the person know about weapons, explosives, electronics? Can the person fly, drive, operate special equipment? Does the hostage taker belong to a religious order? A sect? A gang? What are the individual's deviations? Sexual preferences? Does the person use drugs, alcohol? Is the person on medication? Is it psychotropic? Is he or she taking it? What are his or her immediate problems— money? love life? parole problems? addiction? All these pieces make up the puzzle of who the hostage taker is and will perhaps give the negotiator a clue to a positive solution (Miron & Goldstein, 1978, pp. 92–93).

The next piece of information to be determined is just who the hostages are. Are there really hostages? If so, how many, how old, and what sex are they? What is their current emotional state? Are they intelligent? Do they have potential for aggression? Does anybody need medical assistance or have special requirements? Are they related to their captor or complete strangers (Miron & Goldstein, 1978, p. 93)?

The last piece of initial information needed concerns the hostage site itself. What are safe observation positions? What are the safest approach and escape routes? Are there telephones or other means of communication

present? What amount of space, number of rooms, obstacles, ventilation, and so on, compose the site? What is the access to food, water, toilet facilities? Depending on the situation, collecting this information may be accomplished quickly or take an extended period of time, but gaining this information is critical to prevent injury or loss of life (Miron & Goldstein, 1978, p. 93).

Stabilizing the Situation

The initial tasks of the negotiator are to contain and stabilize the situation (Miron & Goldstein, 1978, p. 95). These first minutes are the most critical for the hostages, and what the negotiating team does now will determine whether the situation is resolved safely (Turner, 1984, pp. 179–180). The negotiator's first goals are to calm the perpetrator and build rapport with him or her (Miron & Goldstein, 1978, p. 95; Misino, 2004, pp. 75–85; Slatkin, 2005, pp. 25–34). An excellent opening strategy is to take a low-key counseling approach that emphasizes reflective listening skills, letting the hostage taker know that the negotiator understands how strongly he or she feels (Donohue & Roberto, 1993).

Neg: From what you're saying, you really feel angry at them. I understand how frustrated you are at the housing authority folks. It's as if they haven't heard a thing you've been saying.

It is important that the negotiator stay calm, especially during these opening gambits (Schreiber, 1978, p. 103). By tone of voice, choice of words, facial expression, and gestures, the negotiator models a calmness that will, one hopes, transfer itself to the hostage taker. Reassurance is part of the attempt to keep the situation tranquil (Miron & Goldstein, 1978, p. 97).

Neg: (*Sits down, takes off coat, pulls out a stick of gum, but not in the same room or within reach of the hostage taker.*) It doesn't seem like we're going any place for a while, so just take your time and tell me what it is you want. I'm sure we can reach a mutually agreeable solution.

The negotiator needs to allow the hostage taker the opportunity to ventilate feelings (Miron & Goldstein, 1978, p. 98; Slatkin, 2005, p. 64). Ventilating provides a number of positive outcomes. The perpetrator's continued talking permits the negotiator to identify the person's mental state and personal problems and to assess the general atmosphere of the situation (Maher, 1977, p. 36). It is also very difficult for the hostage taker to remain emotionally charged and at the same time present lengthy discourses and answer questions about his or her problems to the negotiator (Miron & Goldstein,

1978, p. 98). One of the best ways to keep the perpetrator engaged is to ask open-ended questions.

Neg: I'm not sure I understand what you're really peeved about. How would you like them to set up the tenant grievance procedure with the housing authority? What would you see your role as being in that?

At the same time, the negotiator must be careful not to intrude into the hostage taker's psychological space (Maher, 1977, p. 36). Interpretive statements about the causal dynamics that motivate the hostage taker may generate hostility and increased agitation. To suggest that some personal inadequacy is at the root of the hostage taker's problem is unwise. The following type of statement is *not* suggested.

Neg: So it's really going way back to those inadequate feelings you had as a child. Your mother and father always put you down, so now you're really trying to show them how potent you are, when in fact you really know that it isn't so.

Under no circumstances should the negotiator try to provoke the hostage taker. Arguing, demeaning remarks, outright rejection of demands, and sudden surprises have no place in the dialogue.

Any signs of increased agitation or aggression in the hostage taker should be monitored carefully. Disjointed and speeded-up speech, flared nostrils, flushed cheeks, restlessness, pounding or shaking of fists, are all indicators that the negotiator needs to cool the situation down. One of the best ways to accomplish this is to distract the hostage taker by asking questions totally irrelevant to the situation or suggesting something contrary to what the perpetrator thinks the authorities might want (Miron & Goldstein, 1978, pp. 98–99).

Neg: You said you were interested in pro basketball and the Knicks in particular. Think they've got a chance against the Celtics tonight?

Neg: Well, if you think we're all infidel, godless swine, I guess that's your right. If you feel like you've got to let people know about your feelings, then maybe you ought to go on the radio. (*The negotiator and the media have previously worked out the conditions under which this would happen.*)

By trying to see the problem through the hostage taker's eyes, the negotiator tries to build rapport with the perpetrator. Using owning or "I" statements is one way the negotiator can establish a relationship with the hostage taker. "You" statements tend to be accusatory while "I" statements take ownership and are less threatening (Slatkin, 2005; p. 66). Genuine and noncontrived self-disclosure about the negotiator's own life

as it seems to apply to the conversation is a useful way of establishing the relationship and instigating reciprocal disclosure on the part of the hostage taker (Maher, 1977, p. 41).

Neg: I can sure understand that. I put in long hours, do good work, and still catch hell from the boss even though somebody else screwed up the job. It sure seems like the department isn't very damn grateful for all the effort I put out. Is that about the way you feel about your job?

Pacing the dialogue in a slow and purposeful manner is a key component in the negotiations and works in favor of the authorities. Although hostages may become depressed and question the handling of the situation as time drags by, delay is to their benefit. By not rushing, the negotiator allows the relationship to develop. Also, time wears down the hostage taker's resources faster than it does those of the authorities. Lack of sleep, hunger, thirst, and unrelenting tension focus the hostage taker on the calm reasonableness of the negotiator and aid and abet the problem-solving process (Maher, 1977, p. 13; Miron & Goldstein, 1978, p. 99). Taking a break can work wonders and break an impasse (Misino, 2004, p. 66).

Neg: (*eleven hours into negotiations*) Man! I'm getting tired. Gonna get a cup of coffee and pump some caffeine in my body. How about taking a break off the heavy stuff and just talk some basketball for a while? Maybe if you want some coffee we could talk about that. (*The coffee will have some strings attached.*)

Attunement is critical in building rapport (Hammer, 2007). One of the keys to doing so is not only staying parallel with the hostage taker as he or she frames responses, but creating a closeness and sense of shared responsibility and togetherness in reaching a resolution. Relational closeness markers (Weiner & Mehrabian, 1968) are used to create a "weness" and "nowness" and "thisness" that bonds the subject to the negotiator in real time in relationship to the goal.

Neg: We have worked hard on this and we can agree this is a good deal. It leaves that other stuff out about getting the housing authority heads to roll, but that was sorta tangential anyways. This will get your grievance out in front of the public like you want.

Finally, a good negotiator, like a good therapist, is excellent at restating the hostage taker's ideas back to him. This technique serves to clarify both to the hostage taker and to the negotiator what is really being said. It also builds rapport with the hostage taker because he or she is assured of being listened to very carefully. The hostage taker's words mean something and count for something with the negotiator (Miron & Goldstein, 1978, p. 102).

Neg: OK! Let me see if I understand you correctly. You want to read your manifesto over the radio, but you're worried that they'll ask you some questions you don't want to answer right now. You're also concerned that they'll try to keep your attention diverted so we can pull something on you. Is that about it?

Persuading the Hostage Taker to Give Up

The ultimate mission of the negotiator is to persuade the hostage taker to give up without harming anyone. There are a number of guidelines to which the negotiator should adhere in accomplishing this task. Persuasion should start with agreement with some of the perpetrator's ideas. Agreement in principle tends to soften the hostage taker's resistance to later negotiations (Miron & Goldstein, 1978, p. 103).

Neg: I agree with you. The scandalous conditions in public housing need to be aired, and you've done your research well.

The negotiator should start by negotiating smaller issues first, such as foodstuffs, medicine, cigarettes, and ways of communicating (Miron & Goldstein, 1978, p. 103). However, the negotiator should make it clear from the start that the hostage taker gets nothing without giving something in return (Maher, 1977, p. 13). Once a deal is made, the hostage taker may be squeezed (Slatkin, 2005, p. 58), which is a technique for asking for a bit more after the deal seems to be finalized.

Neg: I'll see about getting the lights turned back on, but I want some indication that the people are all right. By the way, sending the kids out would be a good start on that.

The less attention paid to the hostages in the dialogue, the better. Continuous reference to hostages may exaggerate the hostage taker's sense of importance, turn his or her attention obsessively to them, and steer the dialogue away from resolution (Maher, 1977, p. 12).

Neg: Yes. I understand you'll start shooting one every 30 minutes if we don't comply with your demands, but what I'm not clear about is how you particularly want the transportation provided.

There is one exception to this rule, and that is an attempt by the negotiator to foster the Stockholm syndrome. Any action the negotiator can instigate to emphasize the human qualities of the hostages to the hostage taker should be considered. Most people have difficulty inflicting pain on another unless the victim remains dehumanized (Strentz, 1979, p. 10). Thus, flag words such as "hostage" should never be used (Fuselier, 1981b). The negotiator should attempt to make the captives appear as human as possible.

Neg: I wonder if you could check on Mr. Smith and see how he's feeling. We understand from his wife that he has a heart problem. Also as a good-faith gesture, we'd like you to let Mrs. Jones speak to her children. They don't have a father, and they're pretty scared.

There is always an out to a higher authority (Misino, 2004, pp. 11–24; Slatkin, 2005, p. 58; Strentz, 2006, pp. 37–45). The negotiator does not make the final decision. A field commander does. Tied to this are future conditional and sting strategies. A *future conditional* strategy essentially is "if (the condition) . . . then (doing something in the future)." A *sting* shifts some control back to the negotiator and makes the hostage taker reevaluate his or her position. In a sting, when a demand is made, no matter how large or small, the negotiator reacts with varying degrees of discouragement that range from incredulous to outraged, as if he or she has been "stung" by the request. The negotiator can also use "standard operating procedure" as an out (Slatkin, 2005, pp. 58–59).

Neg: Wow! Both pizzas and smokes. That's a lot to ask. It's really against procedure to dole out smokes. You understand I can't make that decision. It'll have to go up to the chief. But if he agrees, would you consider letting the boy go?

If at all possible, the negotiator should try to convince the hostage takers that their hostages are actually useless (Schreiber, 1978, p. 111). At points like this, closed questions are better than open-ended ones because they force yes-or-no answers and do not allow for a lot of philosophizing or emotional diatribe (Miron & Goldstein, 1978, p. 101).

Neg: How in the world are you going to make your escape with all those people, anyway? Seems to me like the old folks and kids are just going to slow you down. Do you agree?

At some point in the negotiations there comes a time when the most powerful argument can be made to the most telling effect (Schreiber, 1978, p. 112). When that time comes, the negotiator must clearly and with conviction not only state what the facts are, but also give his or her conclusions (Miron & Goldstein, 1978, p. 103). Some things absolutely cannot be negotiated: firearms, exchange of hostages, and generally, drugs (Maher, 1977, p. 67). If drugs are part of the negotiation package, the effects should be carefully evaluated by a physician before they are ever made a bargaining tool (Maher, 1977, p. 39).

Neg: As a total package you've got to realize that it's unacceptable. The guns are not acceptable, for instance. Think about it! The rest of the package is a good one, and we can make a deal on it.

Under most circumstances, friends, relatives, family, clergy, and other associates should not be brought to the scene. This is particularly true if the hostage taker asks for them, because he or she may want to kill them. If people such as these could help, the perpetrator would probably not be in this situation in the first place. If bringing such people to the scene becomes an absolute must, then the negotiator also needs to know clearly what their feelings are and needs to be close enough that he or she can hear what's going on (Maher, 1977, pp. 14–15, 67).

Neg: If we brought your ex-wife down here, how could she help? What would you say to her that's different than when you were married?

The negotiator should argue both sides of any point. By presenting both sides, the negotiator is more likely to be taken seriously by the perpetrator. Furthermore, the negotiator should argue against one or more unimportant aspects of the authorities' position as a way of showing how fair and open-minded the negotiator is (Miron & Goldstein, 1978, p. 104).

Neg: I can understand why you don't like having the area outside the building dark. I know it makes you nervous when you can't see what's going on. However, think about it from our side. The cops are just as nervous as you. What's to keep you from taking a shot at them if they're silhouetted? By the way, that letter you quoted to me that you want to read to the housing authority sounds pretty good. I can't see why the mayor is taking such a hard line in not letting you read it to the media.

A combination of delaying compliance, minimizing counterarguments, and promoting active listening with the perpetrator are excellent techniques when negotiations get down to the finish. In delaying compliance, the negotiator proposes that the perpetrator not make up his or her mind immediately, think it over, and see whether he or she will not see it the negotiator's way at some future point. Immediately, the negotiator should follow up by offering weakened counterarguments to the proposition. Such counterarguments compromise and weaken the captor's own arguments. Finally, passive listening does little for the problem-solving process.

Active listening should be used. The perpetrator should be asked to think about his or her position and what the consequences might be (Miron & Goldstein, 1978, pp. 103–104).

Neg: You've heard what the offer is. I know it's not everything you wanted. I know that reading that letter to the media is nonnegotiable, but what if I could get them to guarantee it right after you give up? The TV crews are all here, and I don't think the city administration could get away with just hustling you off. I believe I could get authorization for you to do that. Think about it for a while. There's no rush.

Although it may seem irrational to do so, the negotiator should agree reluctantly with demands that may in reality benefit the authorities' position because these points may then be used to garner further concessions down the road (Miron & Goldstein, 1978, p. 106).

Neg: OK. If you really want a car instead of a bus, we'll see what we can do, but I don't think my boss is gonna like it. (*The situation is beneficial because fewer hostages can be moved.*)

The negotiator should refrain from making suggestions unless absolutely necessary. This tactic keeps the hostage taker in a decision-making process (Fuselier, 1981b). The perpetrator is then the one who has to make movement. Offering suggestions may also speed up time factors, which may not be advantageous to the negotiator (Miron & Goldstein, 1978, pp. 106–107).

Neg: You're the guy who's in control. You'll have to decide what to come back with. I'm just the go-between.

Two positions the negotiator must take that may seem in opposition to the goal are keeping the hostage taker's hopes alive and realizing that the hostage taker may have to be allowed to escape. The perpetrator must feel, up until the time that all hostages are released, that he or she has not undertaken the seizure in vain and that there is some hope of escape. One way of sustaining this assurance is by continuously reinforcing the hostage taker every time he or she gives in on a point (Miron & Goldstein, 1978, pp. 105–107).

Neg: Personally, I really respect you for letting the old people and children go. I know that wasn't easy, but you did get agreement on your transfer conditions to the airport.

Neg: All right! We're agreed. The Barangan government has agreed to give you asylum and has provided the plane to take you to their country. As soon as you step inside the Baranga National Airliner, the last hostage at the foot of the ladder walks away. You clearly understand that if anything bad happens to that last hostage, that airliner, no matter who's on it, does not leave the airport.

Finally when the surrender is ready to occur, egos should not get in the way from either the police or the hostage taker. Letting the hostage taker feel he has "won" a victory may be important. If providing the hostage taker cigarettes to give up will get the deal done and give the hostage taker a feeling of getting something out of the deal, it should be done, since it helps rather than hinders the process. If the ego of the field commander or any other person in authority gets in the way, it should be clarified that it is not helpful to ending the situation (Misino, 2004, pp. 144–145).

Negotiating in a Hostage Situation: The Case of James

The scene is the diagnostic unit of a large penitentiary. While the basic purpose of negotiations in prisons is similar to other hostage situations (Fuselier, Van Zandt, & Lanceley, 1989), there are differences and some of them apply in this scenario. In a prison hostage situation, initial assessment is whether this is a single contained incident with a single inmate or the start of a riot with a large segment of the population involved. Even if it is only a single inmate, the risk of word spreading and a riot starting are high, so a general lockdown is necessary. There are both advantages and disadvantages to a hostage situation in a correctional facility. A significant advantage is that the hostage taker is well known and most likely so are the hostages, so psychological profiles and criminal backgrounds are readily available. However, on the negative side the inmates know the prison staff they have taken hostage. If they have grudges, as will be seen in this case, that complicates matters enormously and makes for a much more dangerous scenario.

Because prisons are constructed to keep certain people in and certain people out, it may be very difficult to gain tactical control of a hostage situation. When inmates have control of a prison structure, it may be very difficult to physically remove them without incurring significant casualties. Leadership may also become an issue if more than one group of inmates are involved. The inmates may universally hate the guards, but they may also hate each other's gangs. Further, because of the huge publicity that invariably occurs in a prison hostage taking, political pressure mounts and decisions may be made in governors' offices rather than in the command center. Finally, any hostage taking in a prison will be highly charged and more emotional than most domestic situations because prison staff will be trying to protect themselves and retake control and prison officials will be trying to contain the situation and keep more personnel from becoming hostages (McMains & Mullins, 2010, pp. 431–438). Let us now venture into Hardtimes Correctional Facility and watch what is going to turn out to be a very interesting day for a number of people in that facility.

Ricardo Cuervo, a psychologist, has just stepped out of his office. He almost runs into an officer escorting an inmate to some part of the unit. The inmate asks him in a rather abrasive manner, "Who are you?" Ricardo responds civilly, "Do you need to see me?" The response of the inmate is curt: "No! I ain't crazy!" Ricardo reenters his office and thinks, "Something is wrong with that picture!" Stepping back out into the hall, Ricardo sees what was bothering him. First, the officer and inmate are still standing outside his door. There is no reason for the officer and the inmate to be together in the educational unit. Second, the inmate is a half-step in back of the officer and pressing against his back. The officer's face looks like he has seen a ghost, and he shouts, "Do what he says, he's got a shank!" (A shank is a prison-manufactured knife.)

Ricardo does not know it yet, but he is about to become a hostage. The inmate immediately says in a low, menacing voice, "Do what I say, or he gets it right now!" As Ricardo moves down the hall in front of the two another psychologist happens along and becomes part of the procession. Before they are halfway down the hall, another corrections officer and a secretary are commandeered by the inmate. The inmate casts back and forth, looking for a sanctuary, and finally hustles his entourage into a small office of the secretary to the director of social services. The office is approximately 8 feet by 12 feet and has a doorway leading to the director's office. The office secretary, Sandra, is at once seized by the inmate, and the director, alarmed at what he sees taking place out of the corner of his eye, opens the adjoining office door. He is promptly taken captive by the inmate, who now threatens to kill the secretary if anyone does anything. Seven people are now the hostages of James Worthington, convicted of murder of a clerk in a convenience store holdup.

Worthington, with a firm grip on Sandra and the shank pressed below her rib cage, is at the side of the outer door, with a peripheral view of the hallway. Two others, the original corrections officer and Delphinia, another secretary, are in front of Sandra's desk, situated 3 or 4 feet from the door to the hallway. The rest of the hostages, including Cuervo, are behind the desk, sandwiched between it and some file cabinets, away from the door to the director's office. This is the setting as the hostage situation, which is to last 3 hours, begins.

Ricardo: What do you want?

James: (*very aggressive, labile, agitated, with eyes glazed and bulging and rigid posture*) You shut the hell up. I know I'm gonna die today. This is it!

Sandra: (*screaming*) Don't hurt me! I'm afraid! Please put the knife away.

Officer: (*arms waving in a random way*) Yeah, what do you want?

James: (*Becomes violently agitated and yanks the woman tighter to him and screams.*) Shut up, goddamnit! I'm goin' out today, and I'll take every one of you with me. You think I give a shit about you?

At this point a crowd and a lot of confusion invade the hallway. It is apparent that a riot alarm has been set off. A number of custodial officers attempt to get in the doorway.

James: (*shouting at the top of his lungs*) Tell those bastards not to come in here or the woman dies, NOW!

Chorus from hostages: Stay out! He's got a knife! He means business! He'll kill her!

James: (*screaming, with menacing gestures*) I'll stick her. I mean it.

In these early moments of the alarm stage, the hostages make a big mistake by pushing the panic button. The screaming of the secretary and motor movements of the officer are highly agitating to the hostage holder. The attempts by the psychologist and the officer to find out what the problem is are miscalculated. The hostage taker is engaging in expressive behavior, and the instrumental responses of the psychologist and the officer merely agitate James. He is clearly in Hammer's (2007) emotional distress frame and they are not matching it (p. 106). Compounding James's agitation is the confusion in the hallway. The situation out there is far from contained. A custody captain comes to the door and tries to persuade James to throw out the knife.

James: I can't take it anymore—I've had enough of this bullshit!

Captain: (*in a commanding voice*) Don't hurt anyone.

James: If I'm gonna die, I might as well take as many of these mothers with me as I can.

Captain: (*in a more subdued voice*) Tell me what the problem is. Let's see if we can resolve it.

The captain's initial assessment is by the book. He responds in an instrumental way to the hostage taker

by trying to find out what his goal is. However, whatever has happened to James, it is plain that this is the wrong approach at this moment. Dr. Harold Deacon, director of psychology, is now on the scene outside the doorway. Although not trained as a hostage negotiator, Dr. Deacon offers his services to the captain.

Captain: Doc Deacon is out here and would like to talk to you.

James: I told you, I ain't nuts. I don't wanta talk to no shrink.

Deacon makes a quick assessment of the hostage holder's behavior and responds in an expressive mode that targets his emotional distress. James's vehemence about his mental status tells Dr. Deacon that he is going to have to be very careful.

Deacon: Sounds as if you're pretty angry and nobody's listening to you.

James: That ain't the half of it, Doc.

James's response gives Deacon two clues that are critical to assessing the situation in this early stage of engagement, which is a primary task while attempting to keep the subject stabilized (McMains & Muller, 2010, p. 149). First, James responds by acknowledging Deacon's reflective statement. The acknowledgment indicates that the hostage holder has a lot of angry feelings that need ventilating. Second, "the half of it" indicates that the holder does have some kind of agenda, but that there is more of an affective than cognitive basis to it at the moment. The dialogue continues for a few minutes as the holder angrily ventilates, and Deacon responds in a deeply empathic manner. Finally, Deacon takes a risk, one that probably would be seen as tactically unsound in most hostage situations.

Deacon: I'm really having trouble hearing from out here in the hallway. I wonder if I might step into the room?

James: No!

Deacon: I understand how you feel, but I really am having a hard time hearing.

James: Well, OK! But I'm not coming out.

As Deacon enters the room, the original correctional officer taken by James, arms waving wildly, bolts out the door. James is unable to stop the officer because of his hold on Sandra. He immediately flies into a rage. The reaction of the correctional officer is typical. Because of their institutional experience and daily routine, when put in this predicament correctional officers tend to make poor hostages (Strentz, 2006, pp. 150–151).

James: Come back here, you sonofabitch. You tricked me, Doc. Now I'm gonna cut her good.

This foolish, panic-stricken move by the officer is exceedingly dangerous. Although he makes good his escape, he immediately jeopardizes the other hostages. The hostage holder, fearing he may lose control of the rest of the hostages, will invariably feel he has to reassert his power over them in very aggressive ways. Deacon will have to respond quickly with a statement designed to restore some equilibrium to the situation.

Deacon: Hold it! That was stupid. But I'm here now. You've got me, the director of psychology. Frankly, I'm a helluva lot more valuable than he is. So relax. You've come out ahead in the deal.

James: (*still highly agitated*) OK! OK! I got you. It's cool. That jerk was driving me nuts anyways, wavin' his arms around like some freak.

In one respect, the officer's escape helps the situation. His uncontrolled behavior heightened the hostage taker's tension. The officer's inability to get control of himself put the hostages in harm's way, given the high degree of emotional strain that James is experiencing. The officer's departure allows James to divert his attention from controlling the hostages to concentrating on what Deacon is saying.

Generally, going into the room would be unwise because it gives up another person to the situation. However, Deacon's assessment is that as James continues to ventilate, his voice has toned down and he is not swearing as much. Furthermore, Deacon wants to be able to see clearly the hostage holder's nonverbal behavior and measure it against his verbal behavior. Deacon is having a hard time hearing, and although he uses the fact as a ploy to get into the room, it is something the hostage taker can accept as reasonable. More important, at the beginning of any negotiation the negotiator is operating at a trust deficit (Hammer, 2007, p. 85). To build trust and a sense of closeness Deacon wants to engage in a face-to-face discussion, which should give James a better sense of who Deacon is and visually convey the openness and trust the negotiator is trying to build.

Deacon: (*about 30 minutes into the situation*) Something's really hurting. I wonder if you could help me understand why you're so angry. (*Deacon slowly moves to a Substantive frame after he has Worthington stabilized in order to find out what his agenda is.*)

James: (*Slowly, but with increasing speed and vitriol, opens up.*) They wouldn't let me go to my grandfather's funeral. Gave me some jive talk that he wasn't on no relative list in my jacket. The social worker never even come back and give me an explanation after I asked him. No respect, man! None at all! Then last week, Furdy, down in metal shop, says I got me an attitude, says he's gonna lay me up for 6 months without pay. Sent my ass up to the PCC [Prison Classification Committee], which lays a lot of shuck on me—6 months with no pay. Man! How they expect me not to have an attitude, the time hard enough without that? Those be unjust, unrighteous people, man! They don't listen to nothin'. I may be a con, but I deserve some respect, and they really piss me off, man!

Well, look at me and them now. I got seven hostages. Who's got the respect now? They damn sure gonna kill me when this is done, so I might as well take as many with me as I can. Particularly that sucker over there. (*Points to the director of social services.*) He sat there this morning on the PCC and didn't say jack, didn't listen to a word I said. (*Turns menacingly to director of social services.*)

Deacon: (*Seeks to get James's focus of attention off the hostage and back to his feelings about the problem.*) It doesn't have to be that way. (*Rapidly but clearly restates the hostage taker's problems and feelings about the administration's response to them.*)

Deacon's restatement shifts back to an Attunement frame and seeks to affirm and clarify for James that at least someone in the administration is now listening to him. He also seeks to affirm that James is still in good shape, that nothing irreparable has happened. It is extremely important that James understand he still has options at this point and that doing harm to the director will severely limit those options for him. The key feeling seems to be loss of respect (Face frame). Deacon's assessment is that James is not overly angry about what happened as much as with how it happened. The information confirms for Deacon the negotiation approach he has taken with James and gives the psychologist information on areas he will need to pursue.

What Deacon hypothesizes from James's diatribe is that he feels both wronged and inadequate. Deacon needs to reinforce at any opportunity the respect James feels he has lost. He can also use this information to set up a problem-solving situation based on restoration of James's lost self-esteem to resolve the situation. Furthermore, Deacon obtains two pieces of concrete information—the grandfather's death and the confinement to his cell with no work, pay, or privileges—that make James feel he has been unjustly dealt with by the authorities. The combined weight of these two problems, plus James's impulsivity, has pushed him over the edge. James hits three of Slatkin's (2005, p. 117) criteria for prison inmates acting out. He is incarcerated for a long time, he has been put in isolation, and his family is in crisis.

Deacon has another piece of information, which is alarming. The hostage taker has an axe to grind with one of the hostages, the director of social services. For the moment, all Deacon can do is hope to take attention and heat away from the director by refocusing attention to the problem. Deacon also understands from James's rapid mood swings and emotional outbursts that James is on the borderline of having a psychotic breakdown. Those swings need to be contained and stabilized.

A professional negotiator who has just arrived on the scene attempts to communicate with James.

James: I don't want to talk to anybody here. (*to Cuervo*) You, get me the governor on the phone. Or the commissioner of corrections.

Cuervo: I'd be glad to try, but I don't know the number.

James: (*Shouts out the door.*) Hey, I wanta talk to the governor or the commissioner. Somebody get 'em on the line.

Neg: (*outside the room*) They're not available. Tell me what you want and deal with me. Let's see what we can work out.

James: Screw you. I want the governor.

Although the negotiator is technically right in keeping the negotiations contained, his response creates a problem. Deacon has effectively taken over the negotiation role in the eyes of the hostage taker. While psychologists have moved from support to operational roles in hostage negotiation (Hammer, 2007, pp. 26–27; Strentz, 2006, p. 32), they typically do not engage in negotiations for a variety of ethical and legal reasons (Strentz, 2006, pp. 27–35). However, the hostage taker has a lot to say in this endeavor, and given that the psychologist started the dialogue and has bonded with the hostage taker, it is probably wiser to let Dr. Deacon continue instead of arguing over who should be doing the negotiation. Egos and rules should not disallow exceptions. For better or worse, Deacon is the controlling factor, and the professional negotiator is now relegated to a backup role. Deacon immediately picks up on this and regains control.

Deacon: James, it seems like what we have going can be solved between us. Whatever needs to be done, I'll see that it gets done.

James: You'll just say I'm crazy. Think I'm crazy?

Deacon: No, I don't think you're crazy. I believe you're under a lot of stress and feel like no one would listen to you to the point that you had to do something that would get some attention. I can't imagine anyone not being under a lot of stress given all that's happened to you and what's going on right now. I'd be willing to go up before a judge or the institutional administration and go to bat for you, but you have to give up your weapon and walk out if you want that from me.

Cuervo: Dr. Deacon's right. Anybody would feel the stress. I know I do.

James: You shut up! The doc's doin' the talkin'.

Even though Cuervo is also a psychologist, his reinforcement of Deacon does not help the situation. James sees Cuervo and the others as only one thing, bargaining tools. Cuervo and the other hostages would best be advised to be quiet and unobtrusive.

Meanwhile, Deacon has used James's question about being crazy as a wedge. He goes on to give James a plausible, rational reason that speaks directly to James's wounded pride. He is giving James a way out with some honor attached to it (*face framing*) and in the bargain is saying that James has an ally (*attunement framing*). He is also saying that part of the bargain will be no violence (*substantive framing*). What's more, he is shifting attention away from the hostages to James's own well-being. Notice that no time limit is put on dropping the weapon, but Deacon states this as a logical prerequisite to the things that need to happen for James. It is now about an hour into the situation.

Although James is still making some erratic emotional swings, he is much calmer than before. In general, the crisis stage has passed, and the accommodation stage has commenced. Deacon has seated himself on the edge of the desk, rolled up his shirtsleeves, loosened his tie, and put his hands in his pockets. At this point a subtle change occurs in James. He pulls a six-page letter from a back pocket and asks Deacon to look it over.

Deacon: I'm frankly amazed. This is a precise, articulate, well-written letter that clearly spells out the specifics of your complaints. You've obviously thought this out carefully. It surely isn't the typical jailhouse crap I see. This is good information to support your case.

James: (*flicker of a smile, head up*) You really think so, Doc? Would you read it out loud to those guys out there?

Deacon has won a major victory here. The letter from James is well written, and Deacon can legitimately state that. By reinforcing James, he allows the hostage taker to regain some of his lost self-esteem. Deacon reads the letter, and it is decided that a copy of the letter should be made to give to the administration and the commission. James has calmed down quite a bit.

The one major expressive problem still centers on the director of social services, who continuously receives threatening and vicious statements from James. It seems that the director is the focal point for all of James's frustrations. Emotional distress is a major road block in any successful negotiation (Hammer, 2007, pp. 96–108) and Deacon will have to clear this up before going forward with surrender plans.

James: Heeey, Mr. Dye-rec-tore! How you feel now, baby? You ain't so noncommitted now, are you, sucker? How'd you like to get your big fat ego punctured with this? (*Waves knife around.*)

Deacon: Well, my guess is that you're scaring the hell out of him, and if that's your intention you're doing a fine job.

James: Hey, Doc, I just want to make him feel like I did when he was sittin' up there this mornin' playin' God with me.

Deacon: What you're saying is, he made you lose your self-respect, and you hurt because of that. Why don't you ask him how he feels now?

He interprets what James's feelings are and attributes the causality of those feelings directly to the hostage. What the hostage says will determine a lot about how the hostage taker reacts. However, Deacon knows the capabilities of the director of social services and believes the bet is a good one. Involving one of the hostages is risky unless the negotiator knows something about the hostage's personality and response mode under duress (McMains & Muller, 2010, pp. 461–481; Strentz, 1982, 1984).

Director of social services: James, I don't know what else to say but that I'm sorry you feel like I wasn't paying attention to you this morning. I sure wish you'd had the letter and read it, because that would have made a difference. I don't know if you believe I'm sincere or not, but I feel bad about it, particularly since some of these people might get hurt for something I did.

Deacon: James, he said that pretty straight. How do you feel about that?

James: (*visibly calmer*) Yeah, man, well, we all make mistakes, and yours was a big one.

Director of social services: Well, I'd say you're right.

James: How do I know I'll be safe if I let these people go?

It is now more than 2 hours into the situation. This is the first time that James has talked about letting people go and voiced a concern for his own well-being. It is a crucial point in the situation that must not be missed. If Deacon can capitalize on it, the resolution stage is at hand.

Deacon: What's of most concern to you?

James: That I stay alive. I want to be transported to another institution. I don't want any of the guards to get up my backside here. I also want some guarantees that I don't get worked over.

Deacon: I can't guarantee any of that, but let's pass it on to the captain. None of it sounds unreasonable. I can understand your concerns.

Deacon makes no promises, but he owns his feelings about James's position and further increases the bond between himself and the hostage taker. A good deal of negotiation now takes place about the possibility of a transfer, statements to the press, some new demands, how the transfer will take place, recriminations, how the hostages will be released, and a variety of other subjects. This marks a transition from the Contracting and Control stage to the Transfer stage (McMains & Muller, 2010, pp. 196–197). The exchanges proceed with Deacon serving as the conduit between James and the captain and professional negotiator.

Captain: We can do that. I got the OK from the commissioner. We could move you to Starkton.

James: How do I know I can trust you?

Captain: James, you and I have had dealings before, right, man? Did I ever run a game on you? Tell you I could do something and didn't? If I could do it, it got done. Isn't that right?

James: Doc, what do you think about that? Is he runnin' a game on me?

Deacon: I believe him, but how's that square with you? Is he right?

James: I guess that's right. But what about all those other dudes?

Deacon: Look, I'll be willing to walk out of here with you and ride over to Starkton and see you get settled in over there. With me around there's no way that any of the officers would risk working you over.

James: OK. Let's work out the details.

When James checks the situation out with Deacon, it is a good indication that a bond of trust between the two has been established. Deacon serves as James's perceptual check throughout the negotiations but is careful to allow James to continue to feel that he is the person with ultimate responsibility.

Final details are worked out between the captain, Deacon, and James. The women are let go first. The captain and negotiator come into the room and the other men are ushered out. James is given some paper and a pencil to write down some more statements he has to make to the media. To get the paper and pencil, he relinquishes the knife. Once his statement is finished, James is transported to another institution, with Deacon going along to be sure he is safe.

In this hostage situation, although it took place in a penitentiary, James typifies the kind of emotionally overwrought person with whom human services workers are likely to come in contact in the course of their work. Even though Deacon had no formal training in hostage negotiation, he was able to use his considerable therapeutic and crisis intervention skills to resolve the situation. Trained negotiators should be used whenever possible, but a professional negotiator may not always be available. The skills that human services workers such as Deacon bring to the situation may be the best and most expert available. At such times, like it or not, the human services worker becomes a negotiator.

The Crisis Worker as Consultant

Because negotiation strategies are based on psychological principles, it would seem natural to employ social workers, counselors, psychologists, and psychiatrists as negotiators. Still, this is a controversial issue. A number of arguments militate against using mental health professionals as negotiators.

First and foremost, hostage negotiations are law enforcement operations and therefore should be dealt with in terms of immediate resolution of conflict rather than in terms of therapy. There are both ethical and legal considerations in regard to using mental health workers in negotiations (Strentz, 2006, pp. 27–35). Second, the use of mental health professionals supplants the use of a negotiating team approach, particularly if decisive physical action needs to be taken. Third, a mental health professional may not be nearly as capable as a person who has been trained to understand the hostage taker. Fourth, identification of the negotiator as a mental health professional may make hostage takers extremely agitated if they conclude that the authorities believe them to be mentally deranged (Maher, 1977, p. 9). Yet a mental health professional, by virtue of training and personality characteristics, fits many of the criteria Miron and Goldstein (1978, pp. 93–94, 137–166) propose for selection of a negotiator.

The resolution of this dilemma has been to make a psychologist a member of the negotiating team in a consultative capacity (DeBernardo, 2004; Fisher & Ireland, 2010; Hatcher et al., 1998; Slatkin, 2000). As a consultant, the psychologist serves as a resource

person, advisor to the negotiator, intelligence gatherer, debriefer of victims and witnesses, and post hoc evaluator of the total response effort (Hatcher et al., 1998; Powitzky, 1979). According to Butler, Leitenberg, and Fuselier (1993) and Hickman (2010), the psychologist—particularly as a consultant to the negotiator—should:

1. Constantly assess the mental state of the hostage taker, as well as that of the negotiator.
2. Not become directly involved in the negotiations, thereby remaining as objective as possible.
3. Recommend techniques, approaches, or responses that will help resolve the situation.
4. Give postincident critiques.
5. Counsel victims.

The role of mental health consultants has evolved with the continuing development of hostage negotiation techniques. The use of consultants who are knowledgeable in mental health crisis intervention can enhance the management of crisis negotiation (Fisher & Ireland, 2010). Indeed, police departments that do use mental health professionals as consultants have more hostage situations end by negotiated surrender as opposed to a tactical team assault.

If You Are Put in the Role of Negotiator

Often in the mental health business, and particularly in crisis intervention, we are cast into roles that we may not be expert in or necessarily want to assume. However, at the time, we are the proverbial Dutch boy holding his finger in the dike until help arrives. If you happen to be first on the scene of a hostage situation, these 14 points, abridged from Blau (1994, p. 253), are good guidelines to follow.

1. Ensure your own safety; don't be a hero. Stay out of reach or gunshot range of the hostage taker.
2. Avoid soliciting demands the negotiator can't or won't keep.
3. Don't bargain or make concessions the negotiator can't or won't keep.
4. Listen for clues regarding the perpetrator's emotional state and remember them, so you can pass that information on to the negotiator.
5. Don't offer anything to the perpetrator of a material nature. "Anything" ranges from a glass of water to the gold at Fort Knox.
6. You probably can promise that the police won't rush in and storm the building; the last thing they want are dead police officers or dead hostages.

7. Minimize the seriousness of the perpetrator's crime. Things are never as bad as they seem, and any crime can be plea-bargained.

8. Don't refer to anybody as "hostage." Ask about the "people," not the "hostages."

9. Don't try to trick the hostage taker or be dishonest. That subterfuge is sure to be found out and will make the negotiator's job that much harder.

10. Never say absolutely no or yes to a demand. Hedge and be cautious.

11. Don't be creative in making suggestions or putting thoughts in the perpetrator's mind.

12. If the perpetrator seems suicidal, ask about it, and adopt a suicide prevention mode.

13. No relatives, friends, bosses, or anybody else needs to be brought to the scene unless the negotiator decides to do so later. If they are already at the scene, it is probably best to get them away from it.

14. Don't offer to exchange yourself, as Deacon did. You are not a hero for doing so.

If You Are Held Hostage

Frank Bolz (1987 pp. 13–23, 66–71), former chief hostage negotiator for the New York City Police Department, and Dr. Thomas Strentz (1982, 1984; 2006, pp. 229–265), retired FBI agent/hostage researcher, have outlined the following basic ways to protect yourself if you are held hostage.

1. *Don't be a hero.* Accept the situation and be prepared to wait. This may be a challenge for human services workers who are used to being in control. For example, a counselor whom one of your authors knew at a college counseling center tried to take action on behalf of another counselor who was being threatened by a gun-carrying female client, and ended up being shot and killed. The counselor had never seen the woman before and had no idea of her potential for violence. Instead of keeping a low profile, attempting to minimally assess the woman's agitated state, practicing any of the calming techniques in this chapter, or merely waiting for police to arrive, the counselor attempted to physically contain the woman. He attempted to make a heroic rescue and died trying.

2. *Follow instructions.* Particularly in the first minutes after being taken hostage, it is extremely important to follow instructions. Any resistance or hesitation in following directions is likely to indicate to the hostage takers that they must show they are in command of the situation. A clear way of demonstrating that they are now the ones in power is to physically hurt somebody.

3. *Don't speak unless spoken to.* Although the human services worker may make good use of verbal skills when the perpetrator initiates a dialogue, any attempts by the worker to take the lead in a conversation may result in the hostage taker feeling a loss of control.

4. *Don't make suggestions.* Any notion about being "helpful" is likely only to antagonize the captors. Only the authorities have the power to solve the problem. It is their job; they know what they are doing, so let them do it.

5. *Try to rest and eat.* Although it may seem impossible at the time, conserving energy is important. No one can foretell how long the situation may go on. The roller-coaster ride of emotions inherent in the situation is extremely energy draining. Being fully alert and acting in a capable manner requires having the psychic and physical energy to do so, and that requires rest and nourishment.

6. *Carefully weigh escape options.* Any attempt to escape should be weighed very, very carefully against the chances of being caught or provoking harm to other hostages. The odds must be highly in your favor and then weighed against whether you have the wits, physical capability, and energy to escape.

7. *Request aid if needed.* Once the initial takeover is complete and the situation is clearly under the hostage taker's control, it may be appropriate to ask for assistance, such as for medication. Do this directly and quietly to the hostage taker. Do not dwell on this issue, because constant queries may bring unwanted attention to you.

8. *Be observant.* If you are released and others are still held hostage, you may be an invaluable source of information to the authorities. The number of perpetrators, their appearance, what their routine is, what other hostages are in the area, and so on are all important pieces of information that the authorities can use. Furthermore, being observant enables you to keep mentally busy, avoid panic, and adapt to conditions that may change rapidly.

9. *Do not be argumentative.* Argumentiveness is likely to make you stand out and focus attention on you. As such, you may be perceived by your captors as a threat and be treated accordingly. Philosophical, political, religious, or any other emotionally loaded topics should be met with simple agreement and

validation of the captor's beliefs. Hostile language and voicing of hatred or disdain of the captor's beliefs will get you in trouble.

10. *Be patient.* It may appear that nothing is happening to relieve the situation. Remember that time is on the side of the authorities and you.

11. *Avoid standing out.* Besides avoiding verbally standing out, get rid of any identifying information that would make you seem like a threat, an important person, or an object of hatred. Blending in is important because you do not want to be the identifiable example the hostage takers use to show the world that they mean business. You also do not generally show your excellent leadership qualities. You are a member of a cast of thousands unless it is clear you are in imminent danger of being killed.

12. *Treat captors with deference and respect.* One way of establishing the Stockholm syndrome is maintaining eye contact, not assuming a physically aggressive stance, speaking politely when spoken to, and gently establishing a personal relationship with the hostage taker. Remember that no matter how bizarre and ludicrous they may seem, the captors are operating out of an instrumental and/or expressive mode that makes absolute sense to them at the time.

13. *Don't slight the seriousness of the situation by attempting to inject humor into it.* Making humorous remarks about the dilemma may cause the captors to perceive that they are not being taken seriously. Do keep your sense of humor, but keep it to yourself or with others out of earshot and eyesight of the hostage takers.

14. *Be careful of trickery.* Attempting to gain an advantage by resorting to tricks or subterfuge is extremely risky. If the captors find out you are attempting to deceive them, they may use you as a punitive example to other hostages.

15. *Do not embarrass your captors.* Many hostage takers will not have the mental capabilities or the verbal abilities of the human services worker. By engaging in mental or verbal one-upmanship, you run the risk of embarrassing your captors and making them feel foolish.

16. *Keep your confidence and self-esteem.* There is a great deal of evidence that people who survive hostage situations of long duration do not succumb but stay positive in their outlook and take care of themselves physically and mentally.

17. *Keep to routines.* While the situation may be anything but routine, if protracted, settling into a routine of eating, sleeping, washing, personal hygiene, and exercise increases adaption.

18. *Use fantasy, day dreaming, and future planning.* Time will drag by while negotiations are going on. Engaging in daydreaming, fantasizing, and future planning burns time and also gives psychological respite from the hostage situation.

19. *When rescue comes, follow the rescuers' directions precisely.* Rescuers may not know who the captors and hostages are. Staying flat on the ground with hands and arms covering your head lets the rescuers know you are not a threat to them. Many times during a hostage rescue, there will be a lot of noise and confusion, which is purposively designed by the rescuers. Temper the urge to stand up and run with the realization that by so doing you will put yourself in harm's way.

Intervention After Release

For a variety of reasons, a postcrisis may occur after the hostage situation is resolved. There is often a sense that the perpetrator is still present even after liberation. The enforced relationship becomes part of the hostages' inner life and continues to engross their attention after release. Released hostages continue to track their captors and fear them even though they are safely behind bars or otherwise far removed (Herman, 1995, p. 94).

If the Stockholm syndrome was generated, the hostages may hate their rescuers and bitterly protest their captors' treatment. If hostages were killed or injured, there may be unresolved grief resolution. Reestablishing relationships with family and friends that existed prior to captivity may be problematic. Survivors of a hostage situation need to have their sense of power and control returned to them to reduce their sense of isolation and helplessness from being dominated by their captors. Physical rest and proper nourishment, isolation from the media, social support, judicious use of psychotropic medication, and debriefing are all critical to a return to normalcy (Allodi, 1994; McDuff, 1992; McWhirter & Linzer, 1994).

Survivors of a hostage situation indicate that a variety of physical and psychological problems, ranging from paranoia about repeat occurrences and survival guilt to posttrauma anxiety attacks, may appear a long time after the incident (McMains & Mullins, 2010, pp. 470–472). Thus survivors need to be aware that resolving the situation may not necessarily mean the end of their problems associated with being taken hostage (Strentz, 1984, p. 201). The potential for acute stress disorder (American Psychiatric Association, 2000, pp. 429–430) in survivors of a hostage incident is high (Bisson, Searle, & Srinivasan, 1998; Cremniter et al., 1997; Vila, Porche, & Mouren-Simeoni, 1998).

Acute Stress Disorder. Acute stress disorder (ASD) is the younger sibling of its nasty psychological big brother, PTSD (American Psychiatric Association, 2000). Its clinical symptoms look very much like those of PTSD; the major difference is that the disturbance lasts for a minimum of 2 days and occurs within 4 weeks of the traumatic event (American Psychiatric Association, 2000).

ASD certainly is problematic in its own right. However, if individuals are unable to resolve the psychological disturbances that invariably go with traumatic events, they become candidates for PTSD (Classen et al., 1998; Harvey & Bryant, 1998). Although no one can predict who will or will not become a candidate for ASD or PTSD, quick, proactive crisis intervention with individuals who are experiencing acute stress is an excellent vaccination against the virulence of PTSD (Bryant & Harvey, 2000).

Therefore, it is of utmost importance that all individuals who have experienced a traumatic event be given the opportunity to get psychological support as soon after the event as is humanly possible. Two important follow-up activities can do much to help the hostage survivor regain psychological equilibrium quickly: the postincident interview by the police (Strentz, 1995, p. 145) and some type of critical incident stress management (McWhirter & Linzer, 1994).

Postincident Interview. The postincident interview aids both law enforcement and the hostages. It occurs as soon after resolution of the incident as possible before memories fade or are contaminated by the media. Law enforcement officials are eager to know what happened so that they can incorporate their findings into knowledge on how to contain future events and use the information in any legal proceedings against the hostage taker. The length of time interviews take is of no consequence; the interview continues until all participants are satisfied it is over (Strentz, 1995, p. 145). For the hostages, having the undivided attention of law enforcement is an excellent ventilation source. They are also telling their story to someone whom they believe can redress the suffering perpetrated on them and can get even in some small way (Strentz, 1995, pp. 145–146).

Mullins (1988) has provided the following guidelines for postincident interviews with freed hostages, and indeed his guidelines could be used in the debriefing of survivors of any traumatic event (Halpern & Tramontin, 2007; Myers & Wee, 2005; Raphael & Wilson, 2000):

1. Give people a warm reception and assure them they acted properly and that their symptoms are common for going through such an ordeal.
2. Provide a preliminary medical checkup. A hostage situation will most likely exacerbate present medical problems and may cause new ones to develop.
3. Find a warm, comfortable place with food, drink, refreshments, blankets, and clothing if needed. The site of or close proximity to the hostage taking is not the place to do a debriefing.
4. Give them back some control by giving them simple choices such as a soft drink, water, or coffee. Also solicit information about the situation so that hostages believe and feel they have contributed in a meaningful way.
5. Provide psychoeducation about what they may expect and warnings of "blame the victim" phenomena.
6. Give them the opportunity to form a support group if so desired.
7. Provide an opportunity to ventilate feelings if so desired. If not, give assurances that there are mental health professionals willing and able to talk with them when and if they wish to do so.
8. Provide a debriefing of information on what the police did and why they did it, for both the hostages and their families.

Crisis Intervention With Hostage Survivors

It is clear that hostages are not immune from ASD and PTSD. Employee assistance programs (EAPs) are in a unique position to provide services in the aftermath of a traumatic event because of their close working relationship with organizations and their individual employees (Hosie, West, & Mackey, 1993). The following incident is abstracted from McWhirter and Linzer's (1994) report of a crisis intervention after a bank holdup in which bank employees were held hostage, one hostage was subsequently wounded, and the hostage taker was killed by the FBI. This represents a typical comprehensive critical incident stress management process. Depending on the length and severity of the crisis, critical incident stress debriefing may not be enough and additional components of crisis intervention may be warranted, particularly when social and environmental reordering is necessary (Mayer, 1999).

The incident occurred on a Friday, and a crisis team from the bank's EAP was immediately called. After postincident interviews by police, former hostages were given the telephone number for around-the-clock access to the crisis incident stress management (CISM) team. Employees repeatedly used this access until the first debriefing session on Monday morning. Over the weekend, bank officials and crisis team members planned a course of action that included the following:

1. The bank was closed for a week, employees were given paid vacation, and the bank was redecorated.
2. On Monday, a mandatory all-day debriefing for all employees was scheduled at a hotel.
3. On Wednesday, a voluntary 3-hour support group session was held for any employee who wanted to attend.
4. On Friday morning, all employees met at the bank for a reentry orientation with the CISM team.
5. On Friday afternoon, employees met with law enforcement officials to ask questions, raise concerns, and receive feedback from officials regarding their performance while hostages.
6. On the following Monday, CISM team members returned to the bank when it reopened and remained there throughout the day.
7. An 8-week follow-up session was held at the bank.
8. Unlimited individual counseling was provided through the EAP.
9. Ongoing consultation with management was conducted by the CISM team leader.

Initial Debriefing. There is a good deal of debate on whether standard critical incidence stress debriefing (CISD; Mitchell, 1983) is helpful, benign, or may even be harmful (Bryant & Harvey, 2000, p. 163). In this instance the bank employees' initial debriefing was not a standard CISD. Their initial debriefing dealt with psychoeducation about stress responses and processing of the event itself. Employees were given information on the wide range of affective, cognitive, and behavioral reactions to a traumatic event and were assured of the absolute normalcy of the reactions they were experiencing. The employees were taught guided relaxation exercises to reduce stress and were given handouts with information about trauma survivors and support functions for family members (McWhirter & Linzer, 1994).

The informational component of involving an immediate and understanding support system is critically important at this juncture. Observers who have never experienced prolonged terror and who have no understanding of coercive methods of control often assume that they would show greater psychological resistance than the victim in similar circumstances. The survivors' difficulties are all too easily attributed to underlying character problems, even when the trauma is known (Herman, 1995, p. 97), and a "blame the victim" attitude may start to occur within the support system at a time when the survivor needs the most support.

For the bank employees, the fact–thought–feeling critical incident stress debriefing model developed by Mitchell (1983) was used to process the event. First, each group member shared his or her view of the facts of the incident. This fact finding allowed the members to fill in voids in their understanding of the event and why things happened as they did. Next, employees processed their cognitions during the event. Their thoughts had ranged from the mundane ("What'll I fix for dinner if I'm late?") to self-reproach ("I shouldn't be so scared") to bravery ("I ought to do something") to the ridiculous ("This must be some sick joke"). Processing these thoughts allowed employees to understand that they had all experienced a wide range of thoughts during the event and that they were not crazy for having done so.

Employees then processed the event from an affective basis and addressed the wide range of negative emotions they felt at different stages of the event, from terror and anger to apathy and guilt. As is typical in the aftermath of a hostage event, guilt feelings predominated and centered on feeling guilty about not doing something, feeling guilty about somebody else being hurt when they were not, feeling guilty about relief at being freed when others were not, and feeling guilty that the robber had been killed. This progression from facts to thoughts to feelings allowed the group to safely move deeper into self-disclosure and quickly generated group cohesiveness and trust for the process (McWhirter & Linzer, 1994).

After the large group session, employees were separated into two smaller groups: employees released early in the siege and those held until the gunman was killed. Those employees who had been released had specific issues about a coworker being wounded in the shootout, and they had difficulty believing that the gunman was actually dead. Employees held throughout the ordeal had qualitatively and quantitatively different stressors because they had been witness to all the events, including having a gun pointed at them, seeing a fellow employee marched around the bank with a gun at her neck, seeing her wounded, and watching the gunman be killed. These small groups were employee focused and thus allowed everyone to speak to their own evolving issues, rather than following a prescribed model. Finally, individual sessions were also made available for employees who had experienced previous traumatic events and needed assurance that flashing back to remembrances of those past traumas was a normal reaction (McWhirter & Linzer, 1994).

Subsequent Intervention Procedures. On the fifth day after the event, a voluntary group support session was held. Employees were given additional psychoeducational information and the opportunity to process additional thoughts and feelings about the event, including fears about returning to the bank on Friday morning and returning to work on Monday. A week after the event, employees returned to the redecorated bank and were met in the parking lot and given a guided tour through the bank by the CISM team. As employees moved through the bank, the CISM team helped them work through feelings by talking them through their panic while using progressive muscle relaxation techniques. A meeting with law enforcement officials helped answer questions about why the authorities had seemed to be doing nothing.

The employees were also given a great deal of positive feedback by law enforcement officials on their cool demeanor and appropriate responses during the siege (McWhirter & Linzer, 1994). On the following Monday, 10 days after the incident, the bank was reopened with the crisis team on the premises, either to consult individually with employees as the need arose or to merely be present as a comforting resource. As is typical following such a trauma, employees closely monitored every person who walked into the bank, experienced a great deal of silent panic over customers whom they could not clearly hear or see, and were unsettled by repeated intrusive and invasive questioning by curious customers. CISM team members helped employees handle each of these situations when requested (McWhirter & Linzer, 1994).

Finally, an 8-week follow-up found that while there were still some startle responses to loud customers and some anger at customers who made jokes or asked personal questions about the robbery, the employees were tired of thinking about the event and were ready to put it behind them. They reported that although the event had changed their lives forever, they were ready

to move forward (McWhirter & Linzer, 1994). Those who requested it were provided individual counseling on the order of what was described in the chapters on PTSD and sexual assault. As may be seen from this scenario, a comprehensive triage assessment of the group members indicated that a graded crisis intervention approach was needed. That approach ranged from simple postincident interviews and CISD sessions for everybody to specific crisis intervention techniques that included individual therapy (Mayer, 1999).

Crisis Intervention With the Hostage Negotiator

Negotiators are not immune to stress, and hostage negotiation is one of the more stressful occupational pursuits there is (McMains & Mullins, 2010, pp. 523–531). As such, after an incident, tactical and psychological debriefing is a must (Strentz, 2006, p. 53). Engaging in an instant replay and processing of the dynamics not only allows a critical review for a best practices model approach but also allows for ventilation. If this does not happen on a regular basis, long-term problems can occur.

At times other police and the public may blame negotiators for letting the miscreants of heinous crimes survive when slow death would have been too good for them. This outcome may be especially true for police officers if one of their own is killed (Ricketts, 1995). The reason the Memphis Police Department mandates debriefings for all its officers when a traumatic incident occurs is to keep at bay not only PTSD, but also a variety of other personal and social issues that can affect them as well. A debriefing also serves to reinforce for the officers, much like the hostages, that they did their job as well as they could under trying circumstances and as human beings they make mistakes and, as a result, learn from them. They also learn that they are not supermen and superwomen, that the problems they are experiencing are common to all, and that sharing them is one way of alleviating the negative feelings and recriminations. About 95 percent of hostage negotiations end in positive outcomes with no loss of life. Negotiators go into a hostage situation expecting to be successful. When a life is lost, it is the ultimate failure for a negotiator. Yet hostage situations always have that threat hanging over them (McMains & Mullins, 2010, p. 528). No one can be perfect in this business, and feelings of guilt over how one could have handled a situation that had tragic outcomes are commonplace. One can "should have" and "ought to have" oneself to death, and this must not be allowed to happen (Strentz, 2006, p. 53).

SUMMARY

With wide-ranging access to the media as a format to air a variety of grievances, hostage taking has increased tremendously since 1970. A great deal of publicity surrounds terrorist hostage takings, but the human services worker is more likely to become involved with a variety of hostage-taker types who have little to do with worldwide political agendas. Although hostage taking is certainly a crisis-oriented problem, it is unlike other crisis situations in that it is invariably a law enforcement operation and one that deals much more closely with the victimizer than with the victim.

Hostage takers come in a variety of types. Understanding which type the hostage negotiator is dealing with is of critical importance because subsequent negotiating strategies will differ by type. In general, all hostage takers are engaged in either instrumental or expressive behavior or some combination of the two. Instrumental hostage takers are after a very clear, concrete goal. Expressive hostage takers are pursuing power. Hostage taking goes through a fairly linear stage process of alarm, crisis, accommodation, and resolution.

A variety of negotiating techniques are available. These techniques range from the typical active listening and responding skills that most other crisis interventionists would commonly use to some very sophisticated and perhaps somewhat devious methods. In all hostage situations, time is clearly on the side of the negotiators. Therefore, it is imperative that hostage negotiators proceed slowly and with patience.

For hostages, it is clear that keeping a low profile and staying psychologically and physically alert are the best initial moves in the early stages of this crisis situation. If the situation becomes extended, hostages may attempt, in careful and congruent ways, to convey personal aspects of their lives to their captors and attempt to generate the Stockholm syndrome. Becoming a person rather than a bargaining chip in the eyes of one's holders makes it very difficult for them to dehumanize the hostage to the point that he or she can be easily killed. Resolution for the hostage does not necessarily occur when the perpetrators are taken into custody and the hostages are freed; acute and posttrauma stress associated with this crisis may call for extended psychological intervention.

For a fast, readable description of a crisis negotiation team's attempts to get a school shooter to surrender peacefully, we recommend reading *When the Shooting Stopped: Crisis Negotiation at Jefferson High School* (Charles, 2008). This book is a qualitative research study (don't let the words "research" and "study" put you off) of the negotiators at a school shooting that gives you a front row seat on how the incident played out, including what the negotiators did right and did wrong though their eyes and those of the hostages.

 To see some of the concepts discussed in this chapter in action, refer to your *Crisis Intervention in Action* DVD, or see the clips online on the Counseling CourseMate website. To access this site, go to www .cengagebrain.com, where you'll also find an eBook, additional study tools, quizzes, and more. Put yourself in the place of the individuals as you see them going through the abbreviated CISD. Do you think that would be sufficient if you had just been held hostage? CISD is debriefing and not psychotherapy. Do you think it should have been done in a way that was more "therapeutic," rather than the prescriptive way the facilitator conducted it?

REFERENCES

Allodi, F. A. (1994). Posttraumatic stress disorder in hostages and victims of torture. *Psychiatric Clinics of North America, 17*, 279–288.

American Psychiatric Association. (2000). *Diagnostic and statistical manual of mental disorders* (4th ed., Text Rev.). Washington, DC: Author.

Auerbach, S. M., Kiesler, D. J., Strentz, T., & Schmidt, J. A. (1994). Interpersonal impacts and adjustment to the stress of simulated captivity: An empirical test of the Stockholm syndrome. *Journal of Social and Clinical Psychology, 13*, 207–221.

Bisson, J., Searle, M., & Srinivasan, M. (1998). Follow-up study of British military hostages and their families held in Kuwait during the Gulf War. *British Journal of Medical Psychology, 71*(3), 247–252.

Blau, T. H. (1994). *Psychological services for law enforcement.* New York: Wiley.

Bolz, F. A. (1987). *How to be a hostage and live.* Secaucus, NJ: Lyle Stuart.

Borum, R., & Strentz, T. (1992). The borderline personality: Negotiation strategies. *FBI Law Enforcement Bulletin, 61*(8), 6–10.

Bradstreet, R. (1992, September). *Communications: Getting on the right wavelength.* Presented at the San Antonio

Police Department Basic Hostage Negotiations School, San Antonio, TX.

Brown, L. (2008). *Cultural competence in trauma therapy: Beyond the flashback.* Washington, DC: American Psychological Association.

Bryant, R. A., & Harvey, A. G. (2000). *Acute stress disorder: A handbook of theory, assessment, and treatment.* Washington, DC: American Psychological Association.

Butler, W. M., Leitenberg, H., & Fuselier, G. D. (1993). The use of mental health professional consultants to police hostage negotiation teams. *Behavioral Sciences and the Law, 11*, 213–221.

Charles, L. L. (2008). *When the shooting stopped: Crisis negotiation at Jefferson High School.* Lanham, MD: Rowman & Littlefield.

Classen, C., Koopman, C., Hales, R., & Spiegel, D. (1998). Acute stress disorder as a predictor of post-traumatic stress symptoms. *American Journal of Psychiatry, 155*(35), 620–624.

Cooper, H. (1981). *The hostage-takers.* Boulder, CO: Paladin Press.

Cremniter, D., Crocq, L., Louville, P., & Batista, G. (1997). Posttraumatic reactions of hostages after an aircraft hijacking. *Journal of Nervous and Mental Disease, 185*(5), 344–346.

DeBernardo, C. R. (2004). The psychologist's role in hostage negotiations. *International Journal of Emergency Mental Health, 6*(1), 39–42.

Donohue, W. A., Ramesh, C., & Borchgrevink, C. (1991). Crisis bargaining: Tracking relational paradox in hostage negotiation. *International Journal of Conflict Management, 2*, 257–274.

Donohue, W. A., & Roberto, A. J. (1993). Relational development as negotiated order in hostage negotiation. *Human Communications Research, 20*, 175–198.

Federal Bureau of Investigation Crisis Management Unit. (2008). *Hostage Barricade Database System (HOBAS).* Quantico, VA: Author.

Fisher, M., & Ireland, C. A. (2010). Acting as the consultant advisor in a crisis situation: Consultancy and advising in forensic practice: Empirical and practical guidelines. In C. A. Ireland & M. J. Fisher (Eds.), *Consultancy and advising in forensic practice: empirical and practical guidelines, forensic practice* (pp. 91–107). Leicester, UK: Wiley.

Fuselier, G. N. (1981a). A practical overview of hostage negotiations. *FBI Law Enforcement Bulletin, 50* (Pt. 1), 2–6.

Fuselier, G. N. (1981b). A practical overview of hostage negotiations. *FBI Law Enforcement Bulletin, 50* (Pt. 2), 10–15.

Fuselier, G. N. (1986). *A practical overview of hostage negotiations.* Quantico, VA: Federal Bureau of Investigation.

Fuselier, G. N., Van Zandt, C. R., & Lanceley, F. J. (1989). Negotiating the protracted incident: The Oakdale and Atlanta prison sieges. *FBI Law Enforcement Bulletin, 58*(1), 1–7.

Giebels, E., & Taylor, P. J. (2009). Interaction patterns in crisis negotiations: Persuasive arguments and cultural differences. *Journal of Applied Psychology, 94*(1), 5–19.

Gladis, S. D. (1979). The hostage terrorist situation and the media. *FBI Law Enforcement Bulletin, 48*, 10–15.

Greenstone, J. L., Kosson, D. S., & Gacono, C. B. (2000). Psychopathy and hostage negotiations: Some preliminary thoughts and findings. In C. B. Gacono (Ed.), *The clinical and forensic assessment of psychopathy: A practitioner's guide* (pp. 385–403). Mahwah, NJ: Erlbaum.

Grubb, A. (2010). Modern day hostage (crisis) negotiations: The evolution of an art form within the policing arena. *Aggression and Violent Behavior, 15*(5), 342–348.

Halpern, J., & Tramontin, M. (2007). *Disaster mental health: Theory and practice.* Belmont, CA: Brooks/Cole.

Hammer, M. R. (2007). *Saving lives: The S.A.F.E. model for resolving hostage & crisis incidents.* Westport, CT: Praeger.

Hammer, M. R., & Rogan, R. G. (1997). Negotiation models in crisis situations: The value of a communication-based approach. In R. G. Rogan, M. R. Hammer, & C. R. Van Zandt (Eds.), *Dynamic processes of crisis negotiation: Theory, research, and practice* (pp. 9–23). Westport, CT: Praeger.

Harvey, A., & Bryant, R. (1998). The relationship between acute stress disorder and posttraumatic stress disorder: A prospective evaluation of motor vehicle accident survivors. *Journal of Consulting and Clinical Psychology, 66*(3), 507–512.

Hatcher, C., Mohandie, K., Turner, J., & Gelles, M. (1998). The role of the psychologist in crisis/hostage negotiations. *Behavioral Sciences and the Law, 16*(4), 455–472.

Herman, J. L. (1995). Complex PTSD: A syndrome in survivors of prolonged and repeated trauma. In G. S. Everly, Jr., & J. M. Lating (Eds.), *Psychotraumatology: Key papers and core concepts in posttraumatic stress* (pp. 87–100). New York: Plenum Press.

Hickman, D. (2010). An assessment of hostage negotiators' attitudes toward mental health professionals' involvement in hostage negotiation. *Dissertation Abstracts International: Section A. Humanities and Social Sciences, 70*(10), 3392.

Hosie, T. W., West, J. D., & Mackey, J. A. (1993). Employment and roles of counselors in employee assistance programs. *Journal of Counseling and Development, 71*, 355–359.

Kein, J. (1999). Workplace violence and trauma: A 21st century rehabilitation issue. *Journal of Rehabilitation, 65*, 16.

Lanceley, F. J. (1981). The antisocial personality as a hostage taker. *Journal of Police Science and Administration, 9*, 28–34.

Lanceley, F. J. (2003). *On-scene guide for crisis negotiators* (2nd ed.). Boca Raton, FL: CRC Press.

Lipsedge, M., & Littlewood, R. (1997). Psychopathology and its public sources: From a provisional typology to a dramaturgy of domestic sieges. *Anthropology and Medicine, 4*(1), 25–43.

Lord, V., & Sloop, M. W. (2010). Suicide by cop: Police shootings as a method of self-harming. *Journal of Criminal Justice, 38*(5), 889–895.

Maher, G. F. (1977). *Hostage: A police approach to a contemporary crisis.* Springfield, IL: Charles C Thomas.

Mayer, D. (1999, April). *Trauma response planning: An integral part of critical incident stress management.* Paper presented at the Twenty-Third Annual Convening of Crisis Intervention Personnel, Chicago.

McDuff, D. R. (1992). Social issues in the management of released hostages. *Hospital and Community Psychiatry, 43,* 825–828.

McMains, M. J., & Mullins, W. C. (2010). *Crisis negotiations: Managing critical incidents and hostage situations in law enforcement and corrections* (4th ed.). New Providence, NJ: Mathew Bender.

McWhirter, E. H., & Linzer, M. (1994). The provision of critical incidents services by EAPs: A case study. *Journal of Mental Health Counseling, 16,* 403–414.

Miron, M. S., & Goldstein, A. P. (1978). *Hostage.* Kalamazoo, MI: Behaviordelia.

Misino, D. J. (2004). *Negotiate and win.* New York: McGraw-Hill.

Mitchell, J. T. (1983). When disaster strikes: The critical incident stress debriefing process. *Journal of Emergency Medical Services, 8,* 36–39.

Mullins, W. C. (1988). *Terrorist organizations in the United States.* Springfield, IL: Charles C Thomas.

Myers, D., & Wee, D. F. (2005). *Disaster mental health services.* New York: Bruner-Routledge.

Noesner, G. (2010). *Stalling for time: My life as an FBI hostage negotiator.* New York: Random House.

Ochberg, F. M. (1977). The victims of terrorism: Psychiatric considerations. *Terrorism, 1,* 147–168.

Powitzky, R. J. (1979). The use and misuse of psychologists in a hostage situation. *Police Chief, 46,* 30–33.

Raphael, B., & Wilson, J. P. (2000). *Psychological debriefing: Theory, practice and evidence.* Cambridge, UK: Cambridge University Press.

Ricketts, C. (1995). Post incident stress for the negotiator. *Journal of Crisis Negotiations, 1*(2), 9–21.

Roush, M. (2002). Different mindset: Negotiation challenges for today's critical incident responders. *Gazette, 64*(2), 22–24.

Runyan, C. W., Zakocs, R. C., & Zwerling, C. (2000). Administrative and behavioral interventions for workplace violence prevention. *American Journal of Preventive Medicine, 18,* 116–127.

Schlossberg, G. (1980). Values and organization on hostage and crisis negotiation teams. *Annals of the New York Academy of Sciences, 347,* 113–116.

Schreiber, J. (1978). *The ultimate weapon: Terrorists and world order.* New York: Morrow.

Slatkin, A. (1996). Enhanced hostage negotiation: Therapeutic communication. *FBI Law Enforcement Bulletin, 65*(5), 1–6.

Slatkin, A. (2000). Role of the mental health consultant in hostage negotiation: Questions to ask during the incident phase. *Police Chief, 67*(7), 64–66.

Slatkin, A. (2005). *Communication in crisis and hostage negotiations.* Springfield, IL: Charles C Thomas.

Speckard, A., Tarabrina, N., Krasnov, V., & Mufel, N. (2005). Stockholm effects and psychological responses to captivity in hostages held by suicide terrorists. *Traumatology, 11*(2), 121–140.

Strentz, T. (1979, April). The Stockholm syndrome: Law enforcement policy and ego defenses of the hostage. *Law Enforcement Bulletin,* pp. 1–11.

Strentz, T. (1982). The Stockholm syndrome: Law enforcement policy and hostage behavior. In F. M. Ochberg & D. A. Stoskis (Eds.), *Victims of terrorism* (pp. 55–84). Boulder, CO: Westview Press.

Strentz, T. (1984). Hostage survival guidelines. In J. Turner (Ed.), *Violence in the medical care setting: A survival guide* (pp. 183–208). Rockville, MD: Aspen Systems.

Strentz, T. (1995). Strategies for victims of hostage situations. In A. R. Roberts (Ed.), *Crisis intervention and time-limited cognitive treatment* (pp. 127–147). Newbury Park, CA: Sage.

Strentz, T. (2006). *Psychological aspects of crisis negotiation.* Boca Raton, FL: Taylor & Francis.

Turner, J. (1984). Hostage incidents in health care settings. In J. Turner (Ed.), *Violence in the medical care setting: A survival guide* (pp. 171–181). Rockville, MD: Aspen Systems.

Vila, G., Porche, L., & Mouren-Simeoni, M. (1998). Étude longitudinale prospective de la pathologie psychotraumatique après une prise d'otages dans une école. *Annales Medico Psychologiques, 156*(1), 14–20.

Walker, L. (1984). *The battered woman syndrome.* New York: Springer.

Weiner, M., & Mehrabian, A. (1968). *Language within language.* New York: Appleton-Century-Croft.

Human Services Workers in Crisis: Burnout, Vicarious Traumatization, and Compassion Fatigue

Respond to the following questions with a yes or no.

1. Have you left parties early because the occasions offered you no opportunity to counsel?
2. Do you continue to counsel even though it interferes with your earning a living?
3. Do you sometimes have the "shakes" in the morning and find that this unpleasantness is relieved by counseling a little?
4. Do you repeat everything you hear? I mean, do you repeat or paraphrase everything you hear?

These questions are part of Adams's (1989) humorous, satirical test of counseling addiction. Yet the questions may not be too far off target when viewed in terms of another severe problem that strikes many professionals in the human services business—burnout—and its handmaidens, compassion fatigue and vicarious traumatization.

Burnout, though, is far from humorous. Burnout is not just some pop psychology term designed to elicit sympathetic responses from one's coworkers or spouse. It is a complex individual–societal phenomenon that affects the welfare of not only millions of human services workers but also tens of millions of those workers' clients (Farber, 1983, pp. vii, 1). Put in economic terms, billions of dollars are lost each year because of workers in all fields who can no longer function adequately in their jobs. Signs and symptoms of burnout include turnover, absenteeism, lowered productivity, and psychological problems (Golembiewski, Munzenrider, & Stevenson, 1986; Leiter & Maslach, 2005, pp. 3–9). Yet if burnout has been discussed in all occupations, why should it be endemic to the helping professions?

Helping Professionals: Prime Candidates

The bulk of writing and research that has been done on burnout has come from the helping professions. The very nature of the job is to be intensely involved with people, and generally these are people who are not at the highest levels of self-actualized behavior (Maslach, 1982b, pp. 32–33). Burnout tends to afflict people who enter their professions highly motivated and idealistic and who expect their work to give their life a sense of meaning (Pines & Aronson, 1988, p. 11). When many of the clients get worse instead of better despite all of the workers' skill and effort, burnout becomes a high probability for these idealistic people.

Compounding the harsh realities of historically low success rates, the human services business is becoming more difficult. Human services workers are likely to intervene with people with severe psychological and physical traumatic problems connected with sexual and physical assault, murder, Alzheimer's disease, and AIDS. Because of managed care and restricted budgets, human services workers are expected to handle larger caseloads in shorter time periods. These traumatic problems call for tremendous amounts of the worker's energy, resilience, and hardiness. Day in and day out, the severity of these problems and their duration can wear down the optimism and motivation of any worker (McRaith, 1991).

AIDS counselors are an outstanding example of prime candidates for burnout. They must deal with concerns about safe working practices, fear of infection, intensity of counselor/client/significant other relationships over long periods of physical decline to death, the broad range of services needed, transcrisis events involving a variety of issues, increasing numbers of clients, lack of support by other organizations, and shunning by many health-care providers (Miller, 1995; Oktay, 1992).

The foregoing problems are at the core of the helping professions, making them not just some of the most challenging but also some of the most stress-prone occupations. Thus, human services professionals must be able to tolerate a variety of complex problems that are generally couched in ambiguity, deal with conflict from both clients and institutions, and somehow meet a myriad of demands from the ecological framework in which they operate (Paine, 1982, p. 21).

For the crisis worker, this is true many times over. Crisis center work settings are notorious for long and erratic hours, low pay, poorly functioning clients, immediate deadlines, a lack of control over when clients will arrive or phone, few second chances, repeat callers with chronic problems, hostile and emotionally "raw" clients, and interagency red tape. These are only a few of the stressors that assault crisis workers, making them prime candidates for burnout (Distler, 1990). Because the crisis worker is exposed to a high incidence of trauma for extended periods of time, phrases such as "compassion fatigue" (Figley, 1995, 2002), "traumatic" or "event" countertransference (Dahlenberg, 2000, pp. 12–13), "vicarious traumatization" (McCann & Pearlman, 1990; Pearlman & Mac Ian, 1995; Pearlman & Saakvitne, 1995a, 1995b; Saakvitne, 2002), and "traumatoid states" (Thomas & Wilson, 2004) have found their way into the literature to describe what happens when workers are faced over and over with unspeakable trauma.

However, a question arises about whether burnout and its newer derivatives are really dynamically identifiable. Indeed, Hafkenscheid (2005) proposes that the term "vicarious traumatization" is no more than a fancy term made up to excuse therapeutic failure. Paine (1982, p. 11) and Maslach (1982b, p. 29) report that critics propose that burnout is "part of the job," so if a human services professional "can't stand the heat then he or she ought to get out of the kitchen" because there "always has been stress on this job and always will be." Such cursory dismissal of burnout does not consider the major personal, social, and organizational costs that accrue when job stress turns into crisis (Paine, 1982, p. 11). Burnout is connected to loss of job productivity, impairment of inter- and intrapersonal relationships, and a variety of health problems (Golembiewski et al., 1992; Golembiewski & Munzenrider, 1993; Golembiewski, Munzenrider, & Stevenson, 1986). Indeed, there is ominous research accumulating that indicates people who manifest burnout have significant changes in body chemistry that are biomarkers for cardiovascular disease (Grossi et al., 2005; Melamed et al., 2006; Toker et al., 2005). Burnout is not just part of the territory; it has major ramifications for both individuals and institutions (Maslach, 1982b, p. 39). It is a very real problem, with chronic occupational stress as the primary cause (Paine, 1982, p. 16; Tubesing & Tubesing, 1982, p. 156).

Defining Burnout

A historical definition of burnout places it as a child of the 1970s. The term comes from the psychiatric concept of patients who were "burned out" physically, emotionally, spiritually, interpersonally, and behaviorally to the point of exhaustion (Paine, 1982, p. 16). It was first coined as a workplace term by Herbert Freudenberger to describe young, idealistic volunteers who were working with him in alternative health-care settings and who started to look and act worse than many of their clients (Freudenberger, 1974, 1975). Yet defining burnout adequately is not simple.

A very broad definition depicts burnout as an internal psychological experience involving feelings, attitudes, motives, and expectations (Maslach, 1982b, p. 29). Being burned out means that the total psychic energy of the person has been consumed in trying to fuel the fires of existence. This energy crisis occurs because the psychic demand exceeds the supply (Tubesing & Tubesing, 1982, p. 156). It is experienced as a state of physical, mental, and emotional exhaustion caused by long-term involvement in emotionally demanding situations. It is accompanied by an array of symptoms including physical depletion, feelings of helplessness and hopelessness, disillusionment, negative self-concept, and negative attitudes toward work, people, and life itself. It represents a breaking point beyond which the ability to cope with the environment is severely hampered (Pines & Aronson, 1988, pp. 9–10).

Put in plain language, burnout is lost energy. You are exhausted. A good night's sleep is out of the question and sleep aids (including alcohol) don't help much. Aborted attempts to get away don't help and you come back feeling worse than ever. Work is demanding beyond reason and exceeds the best you are able to do.

Burnout is also lost enthusiasm. As Rhett Butler said to Scarlett O'Hara in *Gone with the Wind*, "Frankly my dear, I just don't give a damn!" Passion has been replaced by cynicism. You despise your bosses, the clients, and aren't overly thrilled with your coworkers either. All the zeal, energy, creativity, expertise, and enthusiasm you brought to the job are long gone. Going the extra mile has turned into wondering whether you can go the few yards to the break room. Finally, your confidence has gone out the window. The less effective you become, the more your self-worth shrinks. Why keep going (Leiter & Maslach, 2005, p. 2)? Indeed you are now a candidate for the long shopping list of maladies you'll soon see that come out of this thing called "Burnout!"

Dynamics of Burnout

Burnout is not generally perceived as a crisis event because its onset is slow and insidious. There is no one point or incident that is readily identifiable as the instigating trauma. Rather, it is a slow and steady erosion of the spirit and energy as a result of the daily struggles and chronic stress typical of everyday life and work (Pines & Aronson, 1988, p. 11). Because of the difficulty in identifying burnout, it becomes much easier to chalk it up as a character deficit. A crisis appears only when people are so defeated and exhausted by the environment that they take extraordinary means to find relief, such as quitting a job or occupational field, developing a serious psychosomatic disease, becoming a substance abuser, or attempting suicide. What is even more problematic is that recovery from burnout is not always linear and tends toward chaos and crisis as the individual tries to come to grips with core issues of vocation, personality, and relationships (Kesler, 1990). As a result, the precipitating crisis of job burnout may move toward a more global, existential crisis wherein the person is in a state of crisis over living.

Occupationally, burnout occurs when past and present problems from the job continuously pile up. Leiter and Maslach (2005, pp. 14–19) propose that there are six major sources of burnout: *workload*, when the work is too complex, too much, too urgent, or just too awful; *control* issues from being micromanaged or having ineffective leaders or teams; lack of *reward* in the form of compensation, recognition, or pleasure; an absence of *community* that provides social support; lack of *fairness*, with little justice and lots of arbitrary and secretive decision making and favoritism; and discordant *values*

that indicate you and the organization are severely at odds regarding your belief in the validity and worth of the organization and the organization's belief about your validity and worth. The foregoing problems may vary in degree and kind, but the result is a continuous and grinding interface between the person and the work environment (Pines & Aronson, 1988, pp. 43–44; Riggar, 1985, p. xvi). From the worker's standpoint, no short- or long-term relief is forthcoming.

The body's nonspecific response to any demand is stress. Humans need some stress for optimal performance. However, there comes a point of maximal return for each person. That point is a function of genetic, biological, behavioral, and acquired physiological factors. Beyond that point, stress is harmful (Selye, 1974). Environmental events may either "cause" the activation of the stress response or, more often, set the stage for it through cognitive-affective processing (Everly, 1989, p. 45). The stress response itself involves enervation of neurological, neuroendocrine, and endocrine systems either singularly or in tandem with one another, which in turn activates various physiological mechanisms directed toward numerous target organs (p. 47). In Selye's (1956) general adaptation syndrome, overstimulation and excessive wear of target organs lead to stress-related dysfunction and disease. If the stressor is persistent and there is a chronic drain on adaptive energy, eventual exhaustion of the target organ will occur. The end result physiologically may be as dramatic as a heart attack or as common as a headache.

Stress occurs when there is a substantial imbalance (perceived or real) between environmental demands and the individual's response capability. Burnout occurs when the stress becomes unmediated and the person has no support systems or other buffers to ease the unrelenting pressure (Farber, 1983, p. 14). The outcome is a person affected in every dimension of life by unlimited combinations of symptoms. Such a description very adequately meets the crisis conditions of being in a state of disequilibrium and paralysis.

Cornerstones of Burnout

Let us now look at two human services professionals who are experientially and professionally different, but by almost any definition are in the process of burning out.

Mr. Templeton. Mr. Templeton has worked as a school counselor at Central Junior High School for 2 years. In that time he has instituted some sweeping changes in a guidance program that was, before he came, notorious for running attendance checks and not much more. Mr. Templeton's counseling approach changed all that. Formerly, the last place that students would have gone for help with personal problems would have been the counseling office. By getting out and explaining what his job was all about to students, faculty, parent groups, civic organizations, and anybody else who would listen, and indeed making good on his promises, Mr. Templeton has turned the guidance office into something akin to a land office during the California gold rush. His principal would now fight a circular saw to keep Mr. Templeton around.

What the principal does not know is that Mr. Templeton has fantasies about sending the entire ninth grade to an Outward Bound camp in the Sahara Desert. He has not had a new idea about how to improve the counseling program in 6 months and is wondering if maybe that stockbroker's job that he so capriciously turned down last year was not such a bad idea after all. As he considers all this, he wistfully looks at his wristwatch, then at the ninth-grader sitting across from him, and wonders whether she is in his office because of grade problems or a problem at home. She has been talking for 30 minutes, and he cannot remember two sentences she has said.

Josh. Josh is a social worker at an outpatient clinic for a community mental health center. He has worked there for 5 years. His patient load resembles something on the order of bus traffic to Mecca. He has just received a memorandum from the director further increasing his caseload by 20 percent, along with a rather curt directive to move on some of those old cases and get them off the clinic rolls. Josh is sitting in his friendly local tavern quietly getting drunk and wondering how he is going to put 20 people out on the street with no support. He is also mulling over what response he will make to his wife, who just this morning asked for a separation. Among the complaints she voiced, his job was prominent: the lousy pay for somebody with a master's degree, the long hours with no compensatory time, the emergencies in the middle of the night, and particularly forgetting he is the father of their two children and a husband to her. Josh stares across the bar and orders another drink. While waiting for his order, he swallows an antacid tablet for the dull, burning pain slowly working its way outward from the pit of his stomach.

What do these two human services professionals have in common? They are alike in that they are empathic, sensitive, humane, idealistic, and people oriented

and have been highly committed and dedicated to their profession. However, like most other human services workers prone to burnout, they also tend to be overly anxious, obsessional, enthusiastic, a bit neurotic, extraverted, conscientious, and susceptible to identifying with their clients (Farber, 1983, p. 4; Piedmont, 1993). For both of them, one or more of the following foundation blocks of burnout have been laid (Borritz et al., 2005; Farber, 1983, p. 6; Lee & Ashforth, 1993; Powell, 1994; Sek-yum, 1993; Turnipseed, 1994):

1. *Role ambiguity.* They lack clarity concerning rights, responsibilities, methods, goals, status, and accountability to themselves or their institutions.
2. *Role conflict.* Demands placed on them are incompatible, inappropriate, and inconsistent with values and ethics.
3. *Role overload.* The quantity and quality of demands placed on them have become too great.
4. *Inconsequentiality.* They have a feeling that no matter how hard they work, the outcome means little in terms of recognition, accomplishment, appreciation, or success.
5. *Isolation.* They have little social support either in the institution or outside of it.
6. *Autonomy.* Their ability to make decisions as to what they will do and how they will deal with their clients is co-opted by the bureaucracy of their place of employment.

These foundation stones are not thrown down haphazardly. They are built up slowly but surely over time through a variety of dynamics.

Research on Burnout Dynamics

The following points have been supported to varying degrees by research on burnout (Baird & Jenkins, 2003; Borritz et al., 2005; Carroll & White, 1982; Decker, Bailey, & Westergaard, 2002; Golembiewski & Munzenrider, 1993; Golembiewski, Munzenrider & Stevenson, 1986; Golembiewski et al., 1992; Grossi et al., 2005; Grouse, 1984; Hoeksma et al., 1993; Koeske, Kirk, & Koeske, 1993; Lee & Ashforth, 1993; Linley, Joseph, & Loumidis, 2005; Lyndall & Bicknell, 2001; Maslach, 1982a; Melamed et al., 2006; Piedmont, 1993; Pines & Aronson, 1988; Powell, 1994; Salston & Figley, 2003; Sek-yum, 1993; Toker et al., 2005; Turnipseed, 1994).

1. All stressors are cumulative and can help lead to burnout.
2. Burnout is psychobiological.

3. Environmental factors other than work can be contributors.
4. A lack of effective interpersonal relationships contributes to burnout.
5. Signs of burnout will occur, but recognition of them depends on the observer's astuteness.
6. Symptoms sometimes appear quickly, but most usually occur over time.
7. Burnout is process oriented rather than event oriented.
8. Burnout varies in severity from mild energy loss to death.
9. Burnout also varies in duration.
10. Burnout and resulting crisis can occur more than once.
11. Awareness varies from complete denial to full consciousness of the problem.
12. Burnout is infectious in that it puts additional stress on other workers.
13. Burnout is greatest for beginning and long-term workers and least for mid-duration workers.
14. Men and women are fairly similar in their experiences of burnout.
15. Those who are single experience the most burnout, whereas those with families experience the least.
16. Restorative and preventive measures have to be individually tailored because of the idiosyncratic nature of burnout.
17. Burnout has progressive phases that can be identified by the varying degrees of depersonalization, personal accomplishment (or lack thereof), and emotional exhaustion the individual exhibits.
18. Burnout is not a disease, and the medical model is not an appropriate analytical model.
19. Burnout should not be confused with malingering.
20. Progressive deterioration in physical and mental health occurs as burnout increases.
21. Job autonomy, sense of coherence, and social support buffers are critical to preventing, containing, and reducing burnout.
22. Making time for leisure and using it wisely are as important as any job variable.
23. Burnout can lead to personal and professional growth as well as to despair and trauma.
24. More education, training specific to trauma work, supervision, and institutional support are all related to lower burnout rates.
25. A personal history of trauma is a contributing factor.

Myths That Engender Burnout

Candidates for burnout believe a number of myths about themselves and how they must operate in their environment (Everly, 1989; Friedman & Rosenman, 1974; Kesler, 1990; Maslach, 1982a; Pines & Aronson, 1988; Rodesch, 1994). They tend to distort the reality of the situation in typical type A personality patterns (Friedman & Rosenman, 1974), generating a variety of irrational statements about themselves and their work. These statements are modeled after Albert Ellis's (Patterson, 1980, pp. 68–70) unhealthy thoughts people say to themselves about their predicaments.

1. "My job is my life." This means long hours, no leisure time, and difficulty delegating authority. Anxiety, defensiveness, anger, and frustration are the result when things do not go perfectly.
2. "I must be totally competent, knowledgeable, and able to help everyone." Unrealistic expectations of performance, a need to prove oneself, lack of confidence, and overriding guilt occur when one is not perfect.
3. "To accomplish my job and maintain my own sense of self-worth, I must be liked and approved of by everyone with whom I work." Such workers cannot assert themselves, set limits, say no, disagree with others, or give negative feedback. Therefore, they get manipulated by others in the work setting—including by clients. Self-doubt, passive hostility, insecurity, and subsequent depression are the reward.
4. "Other people are hardheaded and difficult to deal with, do not understand the real value of my work, and should be more supportive." Stereotyping and generalizing about specific problems and people occur, and lack of creativity, wasted energy, and decreased motivation result. The person has a defeatist attitude and a passive acceptance of the status quo.
5. "Any negative feedback indicates there is something wrong with what I do." The person cannot evaluate his or her work realistically and make constructive changes. There is a great deal of anger with critics, which may manifest itself in either passive or aggressive hostility, depending on the person toward whom the anger is directed. Frustration and immobilization are the outcomes.
6. "Because of past blunders and failures by others, things will not work the way they must." Old programs are not carried to fruition, nor are new ones

created. Stagnation and decay in the work setting are the result.

7. "Things have to work out the way I want." The person's behavior is thus characterized by working extra hours and checking up on staff members' work, an inability to compromise or delegate, overattention to detail, repetition of tasks, impatience with others, and an authoritarian style.

8. "I must be omniscient and infallible." The person can never be wrong. The very act of doing therapy with humans in all their infinite ways of behaving means fallibility for the worker, particularly when the client is in crisis.

These dynamics lead to a wide array of symptoms.

Symptoms of Burnout

Burnout is a multidimensional phenomenon, consisting of behavioral, physical, interpersonal, and attitudinal components. Table 16.1 is a ready reference. While the list is lengthy, it is undoubtedly not all-encompassing. Certainly not all human services workers in crisis manifest all the symptoms listed. Yet for the watchful observer, many will become noticeable, particularly if one looks back in time and notes any pronounced changes in the worker.

Levels of Burnout

Burnout can be categorized as occurring at one of three levels: *trait*, *state*, and *activity* (Forney, Wallace-Schutzman, & Wiggers, 1982). At a trait level, it is all-pervasive, encompassing every facet of the worker's life. The worker is completely nonfunctional in regard to person, place, and time. The trait level of burnout is extremely serious and calls for immediate intervention in the worker's life. At a state level, burnout may be periodic or situational. A classic example is what occurs during the period of full moon at a crisis line center. At such times it seems as if every crisis-prone person in town takes a signal from a lunar clock to go berserk. Although problematic, such crisis situations are relieved when the moon wanes, and the crisis line worker returns to some semblance of normalcy. However, over the long term, such state events contribute mightily to anticipatory anxiety, which if not dealt with can precipitate total burnout.

Finally, burnout may be activity based. Any activity that is performed over and over at an intense level, as in encounter group counseling of substance abusers or

serving as a chaplain to the grief-stricken in a trauma center, will invariably wear the armor off the most emotionally bulletproof crisis worker. A simple way of decreasing chances of burnout when the stressor is activity based is to change the routine. However, such change is not always easily accomplished or even recognized as needed.

Stages of Burnout

Another way of characterizing the road to burnout is by stages. Edelwich and Brodsky (1982, pp. 135–136) delineated four stages through which the typical candidate for burnout goes.

Stage 1: Enthusiasm. The worker enters the job with high hopes and unrealistic expectations. If such idealism is not tempered by orientation and training programs that define what the worker can reasonably expect to accomplish, such a rose-colored view of human services work will inevitably lead to the stage of stagnation.

Stage 2: Stagnation. Stagnation occurs when the worker starts to feel that personal, financial, and career needs are not being met. Awareness may come from seeing people perceived as less able moving up the career ladder faster, pressures from home to meet increased financial obligations, and lack of personal intrinsic reinforcement for doing the job well. Astute management policy will head off stagnation by providing a variety of incentives that clearly say to the worker, "You're doing a good job here, and we appreciate it." If intrinsic and extrinsic reinforcement does not occur, the worker will move into the next stage, frustration.

Stage 3: Frustration. Frustration clearly indicates that the worker is in trouble. The worker starts questioning the effectiveness, value, and impact of his or her efforts in the face of ever-mounting obstacles. Because the effects of burnout are highly contagious in the organizational setting, one person's frustration is likely to have a domino effect on others. One appropriate way of meeting frustration is to confront the problem head on by arranging workshops or support groups to increase awareness of the burnout syndrome, and generate problem solving as a group to bring about changes within both the institution and the individual. Catching the problem at this stage may well lead back to a more tempered stage of enthusiasm.

TABLE 16.1 SYMPTOMS OF BURNOUT

BEHAVIORAL	PHYSICAL	INTERPERSONAL	ATTITUDINAL
Reduced quantity or efficiency of work	Chronic fatigue and exhaustion	Withdrawal from family	Depression
Use and abuse of alcohol and illicit drugs	Lower resistance	Compulsion to do all and be all at home	Feeling of emptiness, meaninglessness
Increase in absenteeism	Maladies occurring at organ weak points: ulcers, migraines, gastrointestinal upset, facial tics, etc.	No mature interactions—keeping hidden agendas	Ranging from omnipotence to incompetence
Increase in risk taking	Colds and viral infections	Keeping everyone subservient	Cynicism
Increase in medication	Poor coordination	Feeling drawn to people who are less secure	Paranoia
Clock watching	Insomnia, nightmares, and excessive sleeping	Reduction of significant others to status of clients	Compulsiveness and obsessiveness
Complaining	Muscular tension	Breaking up of long-lasting relationships	Callousness
Changing or quitting the job	Addiction to alcohol and/or drugs	Becoming therapeutically minded and overreacting to comments of friends	Guilt
Inability to cope with minor problems	Increased use of tobacco and caffeine	No separation of professional and social life	Boredom
Lack of creativity	Over- or undereating	Allowing clients to abuse privacy of home by calls or visits at any time	Helplessness and/or hopelessness
Suicidal/homicidal ideation
Loss of enjoyment	Hyperactivity	No opportunity for or enjoyment in just being oneself	Terrifying and paralyzing feelings and thoughts
Loss of control	Sudden weight gain or loss	Loneliness, trust issues	Stereotyping
Tardiness	Flare-ups in preexisting medical conditions: high blood pressure, ulcers, asthma, diabetes, etc.	Loss of authenticity	Depersonalizing
Dread of work	Injury from high-risk behavior	Loss of ability to relate to friends, family, or clients	Pessimism
Vacillation between extremes of overinvolvement and detachment	Missed menstrual cycle	Avoidance of close interpersonal contact	Air of righteousness
Mechanistic responding	Increased premenstrual tension	Switch from open and accepting to closed and denying	Grandiosity
Accident proneness	Injury from accident	Inability to cope with minor interpersonal problems	Sick humor, particularly aimed at clients
Change in or cessation of religious affiliation	Rapid heartbeat	Isolation from or overbonding with staff	Distrust of management, supervisors, and peers
Errors in setting therapeutic boundaries	Breathing difficulties	Increased expression of anger and mistrust	Hypercritical attitude toward institution and coworkers
Errors in judgment and strategy in and outside therapy	Anxiety and panic attacks	Increased vigilance and safety issues for self and loved ones	
PTSD-like symptoms of intrusive thoughts, numbing of affect, sleep disturbance, nightmares, and hypervigilance	Dizziness	Overprotection as a parent	Entrapment in job and relations

TABLE 16.1 (*continued*)

BEHAVIORAL	PHYSICAL	INTERPERSONAL	ATTITUDINAL
Regression	Impaired immune system	Decreased interest in intimacy or sex	Free-floating feelings of inadequacy, inferiority, incompetence, and survivor guilt
Impatient and irritable			Self-criticism and perfectionism
Withdrawn			Rapid mood swings
Losing things			Loss of faith, meaning, purpose
Suicide attempts			Change in religious beliefs
Homicide attempts			Sense of grounding, inner balance lost
			Increased sense of vulnerability to world at large

If the problem is not resolved, then the final stage, apathy, is reached.

Stage 4: Apathy.   Apathy is burnout. It is a chronic indifference to the situation and defies most efforts at intervention. Apathy is truly a crisis stage: The person is in a state of disequilibrium and immobility. Further compounding this stage are denial and little objective understanding of what is occurring. At this point psychotherapy is almost mandatory for reversal to take place.

Worker–Client Relationships

As crisis intervention has spread to more and more areas of psychological trauma, interest in what happens to the workers who deal with these clients has led to the concept of *secondary traumatic stress disorder* (STSD) or what McCann and Pearlman (1990) call *vicarious traumatization* (VT*)* and Figley (1995) calls *compassion fatigue* (CF). These terms are often used interchangeably to describe what is going on when the crisis worker–client relationship becomes pathological. These are the very real, concrete negative effects that occur when human services workers have prolonged exposure to traumatized clients who are in crisis.

Research does indicate that crisis workers experience more negative effects from their work than other types of human services workers (Arvay & Uhlemann, 1996; Blanchard & Jones, 1997; Charney & Pearlman, 1998; Johnson & Hunter, 1997). The potential for STSD is even more pronounced in crisis workers who work with long-term disasters. Wee and Myers (2002) conducted a study of mental health workers who did long-term follow-up

in the Murrah Federal Building bombing in Oklahoma City, and found that about half of the respondents reported being more stressed than doing normal mental health work and being at high risk for both compassion fatigue and burnout. Why is this so?

It is so because trauma work and crisis intervention are so potentially addictive and at the same time so potentially destructive! Much like the "rush" that police officers, paramedics, and other emergency workers experience from being in the middle of traumatic events, crisis workers feel the "adrenaline high" of successful crisis intervention, and this can become highly addictive. As an example, psychologists who worked the aftermath of 9/11 in New York City reported more positive than negative feelings regarding their work (Eidelson, D'Alessio, & Eidelson, 2003). Yet the constant exposure to the "highs" that come with dealing with traumatic events also means that the crisis worker is exposed to a constant barrage of some of the most graphic and horrible physical and psychological ramifications that nature or humankind can visit on people. Two psychological concepts are hallmarks of dealing with crisis clients and, if not understood and dealt with, have the potential to infect the crisis worker and lead to burnout. Those two concepts are countertransference and secondary traumatic stress or vicarious traumatization/compassion fatigue.

Countertransference

Whenever therapy becomes intense, as in crisis work, the potential for countertransference rises dramatically. Countertransference is the attributing to the client, by the crisis worker, of traits and behaviors of past and present significant others or events in the crisis worker's own life. Countertransference responses may be positive or negative, spoken or unspoken, conscious or unconscious. They may include physical, psychological, social, gender, racial, moral, spiritual, cultural, or ecological factors that have impacted the worker through past experiences and are manifested in the "here and now" of therapy by the client. At times, emotional aspects of the client may agitate feelings, thoughts, and behaviors that are deeply buried within the worker's own personality.

When confronted with their own shortcomings, fears, faults, prejudices, and stereotypes as mirrored by the client, human services workers may begin behaving in inappropriate ways. Workers may act in ways designed to meet their own needs and not the clients'. The result is that clients are made to fit neatly into the workers' preconceived patterns for the way things "ought to be," and not necessarily in reference to the client but how they "ought to be" for the crisis worker (Freudenberger, 1977).

The general axiom of psychoanalytic therapy is that countertransference needs to be guarded against, and the therapist's refusal to recognize it and deal with it can, at the least, inhibit the therapist's effectiveness, and at the most, be destructive to the relationship (Dahlenberg, 2000, pp. 1–6). If the phenomenon of countertransference is not recognized and dealt with in positive ways, the human services worker ends up feeling guilty about having negative feelings toward the client and is not even sure why those feelings are occurring. Such feelings are antithetical to what the worker has been taught and believes and can significantly compound the occupational stresses that lead to burnout.

However, Pearlman and Saakvitne (1995a, pp. 22–24) propose that if crisis workers are to deal successfully and understand the pain of their clients in deeply empathic ways, then countertransference is inevitable and necessary. Particularly emotion-laden issues such as physical and sexual abuse of children, terminal illnesses, and chronic suicidal ideation are prime examples of content that may be exceedingly stressful to the worker because of strong feelings and experiences the worker may have about the problem (Dahlenberg, 2000; Fox & Cooper, 1998; Pearlman & Saakvitne, 1995a). The pluses and minuses of countertransference as it applies to trauma appear to balance precariously on a very thin psychological high wire. Main's (2008) study of sexual offender treatment providers found that while they manifested disruptions in cognitions, emotions, and behaviors consistent with those that characterize compassion fatigue and vicarious traumatization, they also possessed many of the components for compassion

satisfaction and reported that their child sexual abuse histories were an advantage in the treatment of sex offenders. As such, one of the critical components to handling countertransference effectively would appear to be close and competent supervision.

Secondary Traumatic Stress/Vicarious Traumatization/Compassion Fatigue

Vicarious traumatization and compassion fatigue are different from the phenomenon of countertransference. As these terms have evolved, they have taken on somewhat different, more discrete meanings. Compassion fatigue is used interchangeably with secondary traumatic stress disorder (STSD). STSD is similar and parallel to PTSD, except that the exposure is to the person relating the event and not the event itself. Compassion fatigue is, as Figley (2002, p. 6) says, "a more user-friendly name" for STSD.

Vicarious traumatization is the transformation that occurs when an individual begins to change in a manner that mimics a client's trauma-related symptoms. It is a constructivist model in which the individual's experience and worldview are changed as a direct result of secondary exposure to trauma though crisis work (Pearlman & Mac Ian, 1995). As an example, in a study conducted by Alexander and associates (1989), researchers who were deeply involved in reading and reviewing rape cases and not actually talking to the victims started to manifest victim pathology. The bottom line is that all of these terms apply to a worker who has been affected by long-term, intense involvement of some type with very traumatized clients.

Vicarious traumatization and compassion fatigue occur as a result of an accumulation of experiences across therapies and clients and are felt far beyond the transference–countertransference issues of a specific client–therapist relationship. Whereas countertransference is temporary, vicarious traumatization and compassion fatigue have the potential to permanently change the psychological constructs of workers who engage in intense and long-term trauma and are an inevitable occupational hazard of trauma work (Saakvitne & Pearlman, 1996, p. 31).

The end result of vicarious traumatization and compassion fatigue is their generalizing effects on countertransference issues. As vicarious traumatization is multiplied and generalized over clients, countertransference reactions become stronger through the human services worker acting them out against the client or submerging them even deeper from awareness

(Saakvitne & Pearlman, 1996, p. 48). For human services workers in general, and crisis workers in particular, vicarious traumatization and compassion fatigue are major mediating factors that lead to burnout.

Maslach (1982b, pp. 36–37) states that the only human services workers who burn out are the ones who are on fire. For such workers, Saakvitne and Pearlman (1996, pp. 26, 49) and Figley (1995) believe that the deep empathy needed to deal with the heart-wrenching situations that often accompany crises makes workers vulnerable to intense and overwhelming feelings and profound disruptions in their beliefs, and assaults the very core of their hope and idealism. Over time, such assaults lead to compassion fatigue (Figley, 1995), wherein the crisis workers' energy is literally wrung out by the incidence and amplitude of dealing with the horrific problems that trauma clients face.

Between a very real dedicatory ethic and at times an insatiable need to assist everyone with any type of problem, the idealistic human services worker sees his or her job as a calling. In an imperfect world, such an idealistic outlook can lead to overinvolvement and identification with the client—often to the worker's detriment (Koeske & Kelly, 1995). As the human services worker becomes more deeply enmeshed in the helping relationship, the worker's strong need to be accepted and liked makes it harder and harder to say no to the client's demands. At this point, the worker has started to take on responsibility for the client.

The worker's overinvolvement with the client may be manifested in a variety of ways. Some of the many indicators that the worker is not paying attention to his or her own needs, or frankly to the client's, include extending the session beyond its usual time limit, taking and responding to phone calls at home at all hours of the night, experiencing hurt feelings over client failures, attempting dramatic cures on impossible cases, becoming panic stricken when well-laid plans go awry, refusing to withdraw from the case when it is clearly beyond the worker's purview, becoming angry, sarcastic, or bored with clients, changing the subject and avoiding the topic, providing pat answers, discounting the client's problems and minimizing distress, not believing clients, fearing what the client will say, silencing client trauma talk, wishing or suggesting the client would "just get over it," feeling numb or avoidant, not being able to pay attention, being constantly reminded of one's own personal trauma events, hoping the client won't show up, becoming frustrated over lack of progress, and losing one's sense of humor over the human

dilemma (Baranowsky, 2002; Dahlenberg, 2000; Van Auken, 1979). The foregoing are all indicators that unresolved countertransference and vicarious trauma/compassion fatigue issues are flourishing.

Under these circumstances, the worker comes to see the helping relationship as a chore, and the client may regress and act out as a way of announcing the client's awareness of the worker's apathetic attitude. As this psychological vortex continues to swirl and the worker becomes even more overwrought and discouraged, the client is likely to terminate the therapeutic relationship (Dahlenberg, 2000; Watkins, 1983). Such negative reinforcement does little to mollify the worker's already bruised ego and may lead to a further downward spiral into burnout. Whether exposure to these occupational hazards has negative or positive outcomes depends a great deal on how both the individual worker and the human services institution deal with them in proactive ways (Dahlenberg, 2000; Deiter & Pearlman, 1998; Figley, 1995; Pearlman & Saakvitne, 1995a; Saakvitne & Pearlman, 1996).

Compassion Satisfaction

Since the previous edition of this book, a great deal of research has focused on the notion of *compassion satisfaction*. Stamm (2005) describes compassion satisfaction as simply the pleasure you derive from being able to do your work well. The reason compassion satisfaction as a construct has gained notoriety is that it appears to be an extremely effective buffer against burnout. Human service workers who are satisfied with the effect they have on clients consistently show low levels of vicarious traumatization and burnout (Conrad & Keller-Guenther, 2006; Eastwood, 2007; Killian, 2008; LaFauci Schutt, 2009; Lawson & Myers, 2011; Ringenbach, 2009; Sullivan, 2004). Therefore, it would seem reasonable that organizations do everything in their power to tell their workers that they are doing a good job and further to get direct feedback from clients that they are satisfied with the care they have been given and the concern they have been shown by the crisis worker.

The Culpability of Organizations

Much of the responsibility for burnout rests with the employing agency and its inability to either recognize or do anything about organizational problems that lead to burnout (Everly, 1989, pp. 295–297; Pines & Aronson,

1988, pp. 97–111; Shinn & Mørch, 1983, p. 238). Savicki and Cooley (1987) compared degree of burnout with work environment and found that those workers who scored highest on burnout indexes felt that they had little impact on procedural and policy issues, lacked autonomy within the guidelines of the job structure, were unclear about agency objectives, had a high intensity of work assignments over extended periods of time, were highly restricted in how they could deal with clients, and felt generally unappreciated by their coworkers or supervisors.

Above all, the organization's inability to clearly define job roles and functions causes role conflict and role ambiguity, and these are two of the best predictors of the workplace's contribution to burnout (Barber & Iwai, 1996). These findings should not be construed as representing "gripes" of the respondents. Numerous other studies (Burke & Greenglass, 1995; Duquette et al., 1994; Jayaratne, Vinokur-Kaplan, & Chess, 1995; Lee & Ashforth, 1993; Sek-yum, 1993; Turnipseed, 1994) have substantiated findings that agencies that do not take pains to communicate clearly with and support their staff have high burnout rates.

One of the most critical support mechanisms for crisis workers is easy access to consultation and supervision. Crisis intervention should never be done in isolation, and the case example presented in this chapter is an excellent example of why that is so. Yet, as Pearlman and Saakvitne (1995a, p. 359) report, unsupervised trauma therapy seems all too common. Pearlman and Mac Ian (1995) found that less than two-thirds of trauma therapists they interviewed reported getting any kind of supervision, although more than 80 percent of those who did receive supervision and consultation found it helpful.

In contrast, those agencies that do allow input into the mission of the organization, are flexible in providing instrumental and emotional support to workers, generate support groups, provide consultation, have job clarity, promote managers with social leadership styles, retain realistic expectations for the progress of their clients, and furnish supervision to help workers solve problems associated with the high stress of their jobs report workers with lower indexes of burnout (Everly, 1989, pp. 299–309; Kahn, 2005; Melchior et al., 1997; Pines & Aronson, 1988, pp. 107–111; Savicki & Cooley, 1987).

Self-Recognition of Burnout

Whatever the degree of burnout, human services workers and their organizations have a notorious blind spot. What they can detect in others and change by therapeutic intervention, they are generally unaware of in themselves. Furthermore, they have extreme difficulty maintaining both the personal and professional objectivity to self-diagnose burnout or muster the discipline and devote the energy to integrate effective intervention strategies into their own lives (Spicuzza & Devoe, 1982).

When they finally are confronted with the fact that something is terribly wrong in their professional lives, their initial maladaptive response is likely to be "What's wrong with me?" rather than "What can I do to change the situation?" Their typical operating mode is not to change the situation but rather to increase the amount of effort and consequently increase the original problem (Pines & Aronson, 1988, pp. 5–9).

Before delving into intervention, your authors want to be very clear that they agree with Watkins (1983) that no one—and we would go a step further and state that *absolutely* no one—who practices in the human services professions is immune to burnout. Furthermore, it has been our experience that human services workers who, like some of you who are reading this passage, think "It'll never happen to me" are invariably the kinds of fellow professionals we end up treating; or, in the absence of treatment, become those who can no longer stand to ply the trade and quit; or, at the extreme, become substance abusers or suicidal or homicidal. In these circumstances, the outcomes range from bad to worse: bad for the profession and worse for you, the professional.

Intervention Strategies

Emphasis in applying the task model in this book will usually focus on the directive end of the continuum because of the depth of the crisis and the client, an "I know more than you do, and I'm not nuts" fellow worker. The crisis interventionist who helps a burned-out human services worker typically must proceed in a very directive manner while confronting the client's irrational beliefs, proposing definite alternatives, and getting the client to commit to specific action steps that will get the person out of the state of immobility. Put in simple terms, fellow human services workers are some of the most stubborn and denial-prone clients there are when they have reached the later stages of burnout.

Intervention for the human services worker suffering from burnout may best be considered in three distinct dimensions: intervention through training, intervention with the organization, and intervention with the individual. Triage assessment of the level of burnout is important in determining the type of intervention to be used. At a trait level, individual therapeutic intervention will clearly be warranted. At a state or activity level, training or organizational intervention may be sufficient. When the organization itself becomes a client, triage assessment would clearly include the administering of both burnout and work-setting instruments to all members of the organization and following up that administration with individual interviews.

Assessment

Three types of instruments are important in determining burnout and compassion fatigue.

Burnout. The first type has to do with determining the degree of burnout in the individual. The most widely used instrument is the Maslach Burnout Inventory–Human Services Survey (MBI-HSS; Maslach & Jackson, 1981a), which is a valid cross-occupational and cross-cultural (Bakker, Demerouti, & Schaufeli, 2002; Gorter et al., 1999) instrument that measures three symptom patterns associated with burnout. The Emotional Exhaustion scale assesses feelings of being emotionally worn out by work. The Personal Accomplishment scale measures feelings of competence and achievement with work. The Depersonalization scale measures unfeeling and impersonal responses toward clients. The scales can also be combined to produce a total frequency and intensity score for burnout. A variation of the scale for professional burnout in general (MBI-GS; Maslach, Jackson, & Leiter, 1996) measures exhaustion, cynicism, and reduced personal efficiency, three components that parallel the original MBI-HSS. There is also a Maslach Burnout Inventory for educators (MBI-ES; Maslach, Jackson, & Leiter, 1996), which uses the foregoing components to measure degree of burnout in educators.

Golembiewski, Munzenrider, and Stevenson (1986) used the Maslach Burnout Inventory's three domains to develop a progressive phase model of burnout. In their model, depersonalization is seen as the least potent and initial burnout phase. It must occur prior to any substantial reduction in feelings of personal accomplishment, which they see as a secondary response and more potent level of burnout. Emotional exhaustion, the third and most potent indicator of burnout (Lee & Ashforth, 1996; Wright & Bonett, 1997), would follow heightening of the prior two stages.

Lee and associates (2007) have developed the Counselor Burnout Inventory. This instrument measures five burnout dimensions: Exhaustion, Incompetence, Negative Work Environment, Devaluing Client, and Deterioration of Personal Life. This instrument attempts to integrate both personal and organizational components of potential burnout factors and determine how much workplace factors contribute to overall burnout. They have attempted to determine what particular patterns of these scales best classify levels of burnout and pattern clusters (Lee et al., 2010). Their research, which sampled counselors who worked in a variety of settings, identified three sets of counselor profiles. A cluster they called "Well-Adjusted Counselors" (WACs) had low scores and flat profiles across all the scales. WACs also reported high job satisfaction, good self-esteem, and decent pay. Their MBI scores correlated with their CBI profiles, with low scores on Emotional Exhaustion and Depersonalization and high scores on Personal Accomplishment.

Lee and his associates (2010) found a second cluster they called "Disconnected Counselors" (DCs), who had medium-level scores on Exhaustion, Negative Work Environment, and Deterioration in Personal Life with high Incompetence and Devaluing Client scores. DCs' scores on the MBI paralleled their CBI scores, with a very high Depersonalization score, low Personal Accomplishment, and midrange Emotional Exhaustion scores. They reported low job satisfaction, poor self-esteem, and low pay.

A third cluster, which the researcher named "Persevering Counselors" (PCs), was characterized by high Exhaustion, Negative Work Environment, and Deterioration in Personal Life, but low scores on the Incompetence and Devaluing Client scales. Of the three groups, the PCs scored far higher on the MBI Emotional Exhaustion scale, in the midrange on Depersonalization, and high on sense of Personal Accomplishment. They reported the most counseling experience, highest positive self-esteem, and highest pay of the three groups, even though they reported the most dissatisfaction with their jobs. The PC cluster is interesting in that they are still performing well, but all the indicators are there for burnout. As such, it would appear that this instrument could identify not only workers who were functioning well as opposed to those who were burning or burned out, but those who were moving in that direction.

Compassion Fatigue and Compassion Satisfaction. Newer tests that specifically target different facets of secondary stress include the Compassion Fatigue Self-Test (Figley, 1995). From Wee and Myers's (2003) preliminary work with this test, it appears that satisfaction with doing crisis intervention work is indeed a counterbalance to compassion fatigue. What they found was that although approximately half the workers sampled had high compassion fatigue scores, almost 90 percent had high satisfaction scores and low burnout scores. The belief is that compassion satisfaction can act as a protective buffer against compassion fatigue and burnout (Collins & Long, 2003).

The Professional Quality of Life Scale (ProQOL; Stamm, 2002, 2005) measures compassion satisfaction, compassion fatigue, and burnout. It is a test for workers in the human services field but is particularly designed for first responders such as police, EMTs, firefighters, and ER personnel. The Compassion Satisfaction and Fatigue Test is of particular interest because it factors in the worker's satisfaction and therapeutic fatigue with clients. Certainly not all crisis workers manifest STSD; many workers are resilient, hardy, and continuously involved in crisis work over long terms with no ill effects. Stamm (2002) hypothesizes that it is because their satisfaction with doing the job counterweights and compensates for the heavy fatigue factors they experience. Therefore, this test gives scores for compassion satisfaction (CS), compassion fatigue (CF), and burnout (BO). Research indicates that indeed compassion satisfaction is an ameliorating factor in both compassion fatigue and burnout.

Work Environment.   The third type of instrument measures the work setting. Typical of this type of assessment device is the Work Environment Scale (Moos, 1981), which measures 10 different dimensions of an organizational component named "social climate." These dimensions are job commitment, support from coworkers, management support, independence in decision making, efficient and planful approaches to tasks, performance pressure, role clarity, degree of control by management, variety and change in job, and physical comfort. Taken together, these various instruments provide a way of examining the degree of burnout in relation to environmental factors within the organization, yield a fairly comprehensive picture of how burned out the worker is, and indicate the degree of intervention necessary (Savicki & Cooley, 1987).

Intervention Through Training

Early in a human services worker's training, and on an ongoing basis when in practice, emphasis needs to be placed on correcting worker attitudes that lead to overinvolvement (Koeske & Kelly, 1995). Although Saakvitne and Pearlman (1996, pp. 25–26) argue that the deep empathy needed for trauma work inevitably begets countertransference and the possibility of vicarious traumatization, at least a part of training should focus on increasing therapeutic detachment and moderating idealism (Warnath & Shelton, 1976). A delicate balance exists between providing empathy and manifesting sympathy for a client.

Beginning human services practitioners need to have their rose-colored glasses gently removed, so they can see that their good intentions are doing neither themselves nor their clients much good (Pines & Aronson, 1988, p. 194). Most particularly, students need to examine their limited insight into their own unresolved issues and conflicts and how those interact with those of their clients, particularly when they are dealing with the often horrific material that is a hallmark of crisis intervention and trauma work (Dahlenberg, 2000; Pearlman & Saakvitne, 1995a, pp. 359–380; Watkins, 1983).

Not all students in the human services field are psychologically equipped to go into crisis work. Although this work is absolutely some of the most gratifying and reinforcing there is in the human services field, it is also some of the most gut-wrenching and heartbreaking. Students who are not exposed to realistic field experiences and good supervision may go blindly into one of the most stressful occupational fields known.

Intervention With the Organization

Much of the literature shows burnout to be situation based (Barber & Iwai, 1996; Kesler, 1990; Melchior et al., 1997; Schaufeli, 2006). Thus, the organization can also be considered as client. When an organization is in danger of burnout, all those who work in the organization should be involved in restructuring working conditions. Indeed, one of the major criticisms of burnout intervention has been the lack of change in the total system (Carroll & White, 1982, p. 56). What makes the major difference in obtaining peak performance from workers as opposed to having them burn out is whether the work environment is supportive or stressful (Pines & Aronson, 1988, p. 48).

Lack of positive reinforcement by the institution is not at all uncommon and fits neatly into an aversive management policy: "There is no such thing as burnout, only staff who don't work and have malicious motives toward the organization." As staff become increasingly burned out, they tend to fulfill management's negative predictions about them (Carroll & White, 1982, pp. 53–54). Although much is mentioned in the burnout literature about eradicating the negative aspects of the work environment, research indicates that a lack of positive features is significantly correlated with burnout independent of the presence of negative work features (Pines & Aronson, 1988, p. 48).

Human services organizations are notorious for having to live continuously on the edge of financial exigency. Lack of physical, human, and financial resources militates against comprehensive service provision and long-term planning. Organizations that face crises such as funding and human resource cutbacks often cope with problems by unwittingly adopting crisis characteristics and operating in a state of disequilibrium and immobility. Just letting the crisis "run its course" is no more appropriate for organizations than for individuals in crisis (Devine, 1984).

Therefore, from an ecological standpoint, the organization needs to move away from piecemeal interventions and apply techniques that have general inputs to the total organization rather than just inputs focused on individuals (Paine, 1982, p. 25). Ideally, interventions should be multifaceted and take into consideration both individual and environmental issues in a balanced and sensitive fashion (Carroll & White, 1982, p. 53). As a start, the administration can take the time to articulate clearly the organization's mission. Cherniss and Krantz (1983) found that organizations that have a clear ideology of purpose have reduced burnout in staff because they minimize ambiguity and doubt about what kind of action is to be taken. Time should be devoted both to establishing positive coworker and supervisory relationships and to reducing the rules, regulations, and paperwork that line staff face as they attempt to provide service to their clients (Savicki & Cooley, 1987). Improved job design, flexible hours, continuous supervision and training, intrinsic and extrinsic reinforcement, and emotional support are a few of many changes that will go a long way toward reducing burnout (Shinn & Mørch, 1983, p. 238).

Most attempts to deal with the organization by people who are burned out are typified by passively hostile actions that include physical, emotional, and mental withdrawal from problems the organization faces (Pines & Aronson, 1988, pp. 91–93). However, effective organizational change rarely is generated solely by the administration or by the individual. Both parties must decide that stopping burnout in its tracks is a good thing to do. To effect change in the organization, each individual must recognize that there is an institutional problem and be responsible for doing something about it. Likewise, administrators and boards of directors must be constantly vigilant and not deny these kinds of problems exist in the organization. Beginning to take responsibility for effecting change in a difficult situation is therapeutic in and of itself simply because it reduces the debilitating effects of the feeling of helplessness.

Yet workers who believe that everything about an organization is wrong and should be changed are the most likely to be burnouts, and administrators and boards of directors who believe the same about their workers are likely to go out of business. Some aspects of the bureaucracy cannot be changed short of destroying it. Thus workers need to develop the ability to distinguish between those aspects of the organization that can be changed and those that cannot (Pines & Aronson, 1988, p. 29).

Burnout-Proofing an Agency.   Probably one of the very best organizations at preventing burnout your authors are aware of is the Exchange Club–Carl Perkins Center for the Prevention of Child Abuse in Jackson, Tennessee, which is used as an example of an exemplary child abuse treatment program in Chapter 9, Sexual Assault. One of the reasons for Carl Perkins Center's excellence is that its directors attempt, to the best of their ability, to burnout-proof the agency and the people in it. As described by East, James, and Keim (2001), they use several strategies to prevent burnout and STSD:

1. Nobody works more than a 40-hour week. Although emergencies may arise, workers will immediately take comp time off after the emergency has passed. Nobody works through lunch. Lunch is downtime and is expected to be taken.

2. The center takes quality time to promote inservice education as a way of continuously updating staff on the most effective and innovative practices available in the field. Quarterly inservices combine staff development, organizational issues, and fun events on skill building.

3. Supervision is continuous and supportive. The supervisor-to-worker ratio is 1:6. Each worker has a weekly session with a supervisor. The role of the supervisor is to listen, provide empathic support, consult, and plan cases.

4. The center expedites logistical problems. Work areas are clean, well lit, with cheerfully decorated

offices and meeting rooms. Therapy rooms have brightly colored carpets and colorful children's murals on the walls. There is a well-stocked resource center with videos, instructional programs, reference books, and a complete, full-sized, Kids on the Block puppet set. There is adequate office and clerical help for all workers, so they do not drown in paperwork. Supplies are adequate and readily available.

5. Case staffings are carefully constructed in a comprehensive manner with team inputs. A clear treatment plan is laid out. There is little confusion about what mission goals are. There is a definite feeling of "we" between the administration and the staff. All supervisors have worked their way up through the organization, so they are acutely aware of the problems and issues staff face.

6. There is a clear delineation between work and home. Home and family are an overriding priority, and the directors of the center are adamant that families come first and work comes second.

7. Faith-based renewal and spiritual growth are encouraged. As one worker stated, "I can't do this alone. I have to give it over to God." This approach is encouraged without regard to denomination. Prayer is a powerful tool for these people, and they use it. There is a saying in war that there are few atheists in foxholes. A parallel can be made to the trauma and crisis business. Finding a sacrosanct spiritual center that one can believe in and retreat to is paramount, given the often heinous nature of crisis work (Collins, 2005; Kennedy, 2006). Because Jackson, Tennessee, is in the "Bible Belt" you may suppose that the staff's deep reliance on faith is a southern cultural artifact. You would be wrong. A good deal of research (Harrison & Westwood, 2009; Lawson & Myers, 2011; Reese, 2009; Simpson, 2006) demonstrates that spirituality is a key component in keeping the nastiness in this chapter out of your life. Short of proselytizing, your authors believe that anybody in this business needs to find some spiritual rock to anchor them. Go to a church, synagogue, mosque. Hug a cypress tree if you are green. Meditate, read theology, worship the Great Spirit, Buddha, God, but get a spiritual foundation in your life. You'll need it if you do this work.

8. Debriefing is used continuously. Whenever a tragedy occurs, such as a child's death or other traumatic event, workers are debriefed, and it is done as expeditiously as possible.

9. The center does not work on an assembly-line basis with repetitive, day-in-day-out work assignments that grind staff down. Workers are expected to schedule variety into their days.

10. The center provides technical support. All of the staff have offices, computers, cell phones, VCRs, and other equipment necessary for optimal performance.

11. The center is well maintained. It is a pleasant place to work with bright colors, nice furniture, individual spacious offices, and conference and therapy rooms that are well lit with good AV and IT facilities and equipment.

12. Workers use a team approach. No one is above getting her or his hands "dirty," and everyone pitches in when something needs to be done. It is not frowned upon to ask for assistance. The center does not deify go-it-alone, heroic martyrs.

13. Safety is the most important product of the center, for both its clients and staff. Clear-cut safety procedures are constantly taught and reinforced to ensure the workers' well-being both at the center and during home visits.

14. The workload is "doable." Over the years, the center has lightened workers' caseloads. As the total number of caseloads rises, more workers are hired. The center has been able to increase staff because its administration is very adept at convincing its constituency that it is doing a great job and should be given the financial support to continue to do so. The administration works very closely with its board and continuously educates it regarding the financial and staffing needs of the center.

15. The center does an excellent job of networking. It serves a large geographic area and therefore has established relationships with other social services agencies (such as schools, police departments, and state welfare agencies) in outlying counties. The center also goes out of its way to provide support for other agencies within its service area. This not only increases the center's credibility with the agencies and institutions, but it also allows for reciprocal perquisites: center employees can utilize office space and the support of staff in other agencies when the employees are far away from their home office.

16. The administration is very thorough in its hiring selection. Candidates are carefully screened to determine how well they will fit into the overall scheme of things.

17. Staff are positively reinforced both intrinsically and extrinsically on a consistent basis. Workers are told they are doing a good job in specific behavioral terms, and they are told often. After a particularly horrific incident in which three sexually abused children all died in a house fire at a foster home, the associate director went to the field office and picked up the workers who had been engaged nonstop in dealing with this tragedy. She piled them into her van and, without a word, took them to a local spa, where they spent the day getting makeovers, massages, aromatherapy, yoga lessons, and a nice lunch. While a day trip to a spa can in no way assuage the grief and stress these workers felt, it does say very clearly, "We care about you!" and that message comes across loud and clear to all of the staff.

The Carl Perkins Center sees its workers as its most important asset and understands the perils of the kind of work it does. The outcomes are proof positive that a proactive program to prevent burnout works. The attrition rate is extremely low. Because this is a fairly young and rapidly expanding agency, many of the workers are young. Research indicates (Meyers & Cornille, 2002) that the demographics and job role of this group would cause them to be at high risk for burnout or STSD. They are not!

The following tests were administered to the Carl Perkins staff: the Los Angeles Symptom Checklist (LASC; King et al., 1995) to measure PTSD symptoms, the Impact of Events Scale (IES; Horowitz, Wilner, & Alvarez, 1979) to measure subjective perceptions of stress experienced by human services workers as a result of working with their clients, and the Maslach Burnout Inventory (MBI; Maslach & Jackson, 1981a) to measure burnout. While the IES indicated that traumatic events have had a high impact on workers, the LASC and MBI scores were very low, indicating that these workers do not have PTSD symptoms and they are not burned out. Particularly noteworthy were their extremely high "personal accomplishment" scores on the MBI (East, James, & Keim, 2001).

In conclusion, the administrative staff at Carl Perkins understand the effects that vicarious traumatization, compassion fatigue, and burnout can have on their organization and set aside time and resources to deal with it. In providing support to staff, the Carl Perkins Center follows very closely the six points proposed by Pines (1983), listed and described in the next section. It would thus appear that even in one of the most stressful of all types of crisis agencies—one that works with traumatized children (Meyers & Cornille, 2002)—the institution can stop burnout dead in its tracks if it has the will to do so.

Social Support Systems. Social support systems act as buffers for the individual and help maintain psychological and physical well-being over time (Pines, 1983, p. 157). They are just as critical to avoiding burnout, whether at home or in the workplace (Distler, 1990; Greenglass, Fiksenbaum, & Burke, 1996; Halbesleben, 2006; Kesler, 1990; Pines & Aronson, 1988; Sullivan, 2004). Family systems are major sources of support (Killian, 2008; Lawson & Myers, 2011; Sullivan, 2004) and can help insulate workers against burnout (Bakker, Demerouti, & Schaufeli, 2005; Halbesleben, 2006; Maslach & Jackson, 1981b). However, it is impossible for one's spouse, partner, family, or friends to fulfill all the support tasks a crisis worker who engages specifically in trauma work will need (Pines, 1983, p. 172). Clearly, the worker needs to have functioning support systems at the job site. How, then, might this occur if it does not happen spontaneously?

In that regard, Golembiewski, Munzenrider, and Stevenson (1986) propose that both instrumental support to achieve an end, such as material assistance, and expressive support to provide a sense of belonging and caring are needed in the workplace (p. 52). They found that employee concern and commitment to the job, peer friendliness and support for one another, and management's support and encouragement of employees all characterized low-burnout groups (p. 189).

Social support systems have six basic functions: listening, technical support, technical challenge, emotional support, emotional challenge, and sharing social reality (Pines, 1983).

1. *Listening.* Periodically, all workers need someone to listen actively to them in an empathic manner without giving advice or making judgments (p. 158).
2. *Technical support.* When confronted with complex client problems, all workers need someone who can affirm confidence in their endeavors. Such a person must have the expertise to understand the complexities of the job and be able to give the worker honest feedback (p. 158).
3. *Technical challenge.* If workers are not intellectually challenged, they will stagnate. Intellectual contact with significant others stretches the worker in a positive way. Such challenges can come only

from people who do not intend to humiliate or gain an advantage and who have professional expertise equivalent to that of the worker (p. 158).

4. *Emotional support.* Workers need someone to be on their side in difficult situations, even if the significant others do not necessarily agree totally with the workers. Professional expertise is not necessary for this function (pp. 158–159).

5. *Emotional challenge.* It is comforting for workers to believe that they have explored all avenues in attempting to resolve their problems. Support persons serve a valuable function when they question such assumptions and confront the worker's excuses. This function should be used sparingly; otherwise it may be construed as nagging (p. 159).

6. *Sharing social reality.* When workers become unsure of the reliability of their own perceptions about the reality of the situation, they need external validation. This function is especially important when workers feel that they are losing the ability to evaluate what is happening with their clients and with the organization (p. 159).

Support Groups. Within the organizational structure, time should be set aside for formal, structured support groups. Structurally, a support group resembles a problem-solving discussion group. The goal of such a group is to build a sense of competence and help workers feel that they can deal with the stresses they encounter in their work situation. A support group is a safe place for workers to disagree and challenge feelings of helplessness.

The group serves as a cathartic agent for releasing pent-up emotions related to the job. Once catharsis occurs, members can realistically examine feelings associated with job stressors. By providing feedback, the support group validates for members that they are not alone in their feelings and reassures them that they are not abnormal in their response to the situation (Sculley, 1983, pp. 188–191).

To do this effectively, a support group not only needs the support of the administration but also must have a consultant/facilitator who is sensitive to the issues involved and can walk a tightwire between allowing the group to vent feelings and keeping the group in a problem-solving model. The buffering effect of a third party consultant/facilitator can help reduce conflict stressors (Giebels & Janssen, 2005). The consultant/facilitator also needs to be in a position to provide the administration with information from the group that will allow

for effective organizational change without becoming a "snitch" in the process (Sculley, 1983, pp. 193–194).

Finally, for those members suffering from vicarious traumatization, compassion fatigue, and the later stages of burnout, referring them for personal counseling should be done with the understanding that these outcomes are indeed occupational hazards no different from carpal tunnel syndrome for keyboard operators or arthritis for concrete finishers. In that regard, organizations must be careful not to secondarily victimize such people as being of weak character or lacking in the "right stuff."

The Individual and the Organization. Vocationally, there are four major maladaptive responses to the onset of burnout. As the level of burnout increases, so does escape avoidance behavior (Thornton, 1992). Workers may attempt horizontal job mobility. They continuously look for the "right" boss or organization when it is the job they are in that is causing their unhappiness.

Others tire of the constant interaction with clients and decide to move vertically up the job ladder into administrative positions. What they fail to realize is that their cynical and jaundiced view of the system will not be left behind but will be carried with them into a whole new set of stresses. It is an understatement to say that these people do not make very good bosses.

There are also people who become what Pines and Aronson (1988, p. 18) call "deadwood." These people have long ago decided that their best bet is to not "rock the boat" so they can make it to retirement. If you have ever read the comic strip *Dilbert*, Wally best represents these individuals. When asked to do something, they politely indicate they are too busy, or agree with every idea put forth but venture none of their own, or contribute only what is minimally necessary to escape notice or censure, or turn the tables and cast incompetence on others to cover up their own failings.

Finally, some people quit their job and the vocation, and in some instances this may be the wisest choice of all.

At this stage of frustration, choices may seem to be limited to job change or job stagnation, but the individual does have other options. First, clearly defining one's role within the organization is a high priority (Kesler, 1990). The worker should conduct a job analysis and determine which tasks are necessary, which are self-imposed, and which contribute to role overload (Pines & Aronson, 1988, p. 109). Through assertive negotiation with the administration, the worker needs to define a reasonable work level and commensurate financial or other rewards for the work performed. Clients should be clearly apprised of the limits of service in regard to time as well as the amount and kind of service to be provided. Although service to clients needs to be a high priority, other tasks should be clearly prioritized. If chores that do not have a high priority cannot be delegated, then serious consideration should be given to dropping them (Leiter & Maslach, 2005).

Finally, if it is apparent that the organization is so entrenched and regressive that little change in policies and programs can be effected, it is probably time to look for greener occupational pastures. It would behoove a worker who is in the frustration stage to consider what a near-future job change entails and start planning for it before reaching the apathy stage. Knowing company severance policies and state unemployment benefits, updating a resume, saving money, and commencing a job search are examples of prudent measures workers may take before they are so mentally, physically, and emotionally exhausted that there is little energy left for a major shift in one's life.

Self-Care

As we have said, burnout is a two-way street with both individual and organizational culpability. There are literally volumes of research that find self-care as *the* critical ingredient for the crisis worker (Alkema, Linton, & Davies, 2008; Eastwood, 2007; Harrison & Westwood, 2009; Killian, 2008; Lawson, 2009; Lawson & Myers, 2011; Morkides, 2009; Ringenbach, 2009; Thomas, 2007). We have already spoken to the significance of support systems and spirituality. What follows sounds a lot like what your mother lectured you on: eating right, sleeping right, getting exercise, taking care of your general hygiene, and after all of those things are done, not forgetting to have fun! One of the toughest parts of this business is doing that.

In William Glasser's reality therapy/control theory (1985), one of the central axes on which his theory revolves is engaging in positive addicting behaviors, and central to those positive addicting behaviors is having fun. The whole notion of Glasser's theory is that when you engage in these positive addicting behaviors your personal world grows much larger, and so does your social world as you interact with it.

Nobody can make you get out of your rut, and it is extremely easy to stay in it, as in the case of one of your authors who right now has been word processing four days in a row on this $!%#@$%#! book and not getting his workouts in and feeling very guilty and even physically edgy about missing his positive addiction. The word "recreate" makes a lot more sense when you break it down into "re-create." So meditate, play rugby, work up your fantasy football team, make a quilt, run a marathon, shoot some pool, play bridge or poker, kill all the video game aliens, go fishing, see a ballgame, weed your flower garden—any of those will do as long as you are having fun, enjoying it, and it has absolutely nothing to do with anything in this book. Hey! You cannot use that as an excuse to your professor that you needed to go recreate and didn't finish this chapter so flunked the exam because you were afraid of burning out!

Private Practitioners and Burnout

The occupational dream of many of our students is to start their own private practice. They fantasize that they could do the kind of therapy they wanted with the clients they selected, be rid of overbearing supervisors and be their own boss, not be bothered with bureaucratic hassles and avalanches of paperwork, set their own hours, and make lots of money! Yet the private practitioner has the potential for even greater problems.

Generally, private practitioners are type A personalities who tend to invest a great deal of time in the job as a means of finding a sense of fulfillment and identity. Competition and achievement serve as guiding values that correlate highly with the need to be seen as worthy and capable (Everly, 1989, p. 105; Pines & Aronson, 1988, pp. 6–9). In a word, they are "driven."

Although the aloneness that pervades a private practice is not the same as the isolation that agency workers sometimes impose on themselves when placed in high-stress situations, it can be more complete. Fenced off from other professionals by ethical and ecological boundaries, the private practitioner has few others with whom to discuss client problems. More important, there are few other individuals with whom they can discuss their own personal problems.

Private practice is clearly a business. As such, it promotes the continuing fear that there will be no clients or that there will never be enough no matter how successfully the business is going (Mitchell, 1977, pp. 145–146). Every client termination raises questions: "Will there be someone to take her place?" "Will he pass the word along that I did him some good?" The private practitioner who is moving toward crisis invariably answers these questions negatively and redoubles his or her efforts to increase client loads and effect cures.

Starting and maintaining a private practice also call for maintaining a public presence. Whether such a presence involves making speeches to the Rotary Club on stress and the businessperson, consulting with the oncology staff on death and dying at the local hospital, or giving a workshop on discipline for Parents Without Partners, the continuous pressure of needing to be seen as active, abreast of current developments, and visible is part of a sales program that must constantly be maintained and upgraded.

Although the private practitioner is his or her own boss, being an independent businessperson also means being completely responsible for maintaining the practice. Long hours and difficult work periods are the rule rather than the exception. Because most clients work regular hours, private practitioners devote many evenings and weekends to their work. Usually there is no one to pick up caseloads, so vacations or even short respites are few and far between. Certainly not all private practitioners suffer from burnout. However, when burnout does occur with human services workers who are in private practice, it is accelerated by the foregoing problems and issues.

Intervention With the Individual: A Case Study

Direct action, in which the worker tries to master the environmental stressors, and palliative action, in which the worker tries to reduce disturbances when unable to manage the environment, are the two positive ways to cope with stress (Pines & Aronson, 1988, p. 144). Direct action is applied externally to the situational stressor in the environment, whereas palliative action is applied internally to one's cognitions and emotions about the stressor. Social support groups, workshops, assertiveness training, flextime, taking time off, salary increase, and role shifts are all examples of direct action. Meditation, relaxation techniques, biofeedback, physical exercise with no ego involvement, adopting positive cognitions, engaging in leisure-time pursuits, adopting better eating habits, reducing addictive substance intake, and adding more humor and joy to one's life are all palliative "decompensation activities" that allow the worker to put stressors aside (Hoeksma et al., 1993; Melamed, Meir, & Samson, 1995; Pines & Aronson,

1988, p. 152; Saakvitne & Pearlman, 1996, pp. 78–87; Stark, 1994).

Whereas workers who are at the frustration stage may well be helped by being involved in self-initiated directive and palliative actions, those at the more serious stage of apathy will not be (Edelwich & Brodsky, 1982, p. 137). In such cases, individual counseling is more appropriate (Baron & Cohen, 1982). Kesler (1990) proposed using Arnold Lazarus's (1976) BASIC ID (behavior, affect, sensation, imagery, cognition, interpersonal relationships, and drugs/biology) paradigm as a treatment approach to burnout. To this formulation Kesler adds an *S* for setting. Given the interactive effects of burnout across multiple facets of the individual, the BASIC IDS approach seems valid for attacking burnout in a comprehensive way.

The following case illustrates the crisis worker using combinations of direct and palliative actions in an abbreviated BASIC IDS approach. It should be clearly understood that neither symptoms nor intervention procedures are all-inclusive. For example, Tubesing and Tubesing (1982, p. 161) listed 36 possible intervention strategies that cover physical, intellectual, social, emotional, spiritual, and environmental components of burnout, and those are not comprehensive by any means. If the client is identified as having more compassion fatigue or vicarious traumatization, a more specific program that focuses on STSD symptoms may be used, such as the Accelerated Recovery Program (ARP; Gentry, Baranowsky, & Dunning, 2002). The case presented is that of a professional with many years of experience and a doctorate, but neophytes should understand that Dr. Jane Lee is genotypical of any human services worker. Her case clearly points out that no worker is immune to burnout, no matter how much experience or expertise that worker may have.

The Client. Dr. Jane Lee is a striking, raven-haired, 43-year-old woman with aquiline features, a low, melodious voice, aquamarine eyes that twinkle, and a smile that could serve as a toothpaste commercial. She is extremely witty and incisive of intellect, is widely read, and can talk as easily with truck drivers as she can with lawyers. At any social function people gravitate toward her. She seems to have been born with the natural empathy and easy familiarity that many people consciously work their whole lives for, yet never quite attain. Divorced for 10 years, Jane has raised her only son while carrying on an exceedingly successful professional life.

Jane has a thriving practice in marriage and family therapy. She has a heavy client load and is clearing approximately $150,000 a year. She is seen by her peers as extremely capable, and her clients speak highly of her. Jane has been in private practice for 8 years. Prior to entering private practice she worked in a community mental health facility. She was so skillful at therapy there that she rose to the directorship of the clinical program.

Jane graduated from a major university with a doctorate in counseling psychology and completed her internship in a VA hospital. She then successfully completed an American Association of Marriage and Family Therapists internship at a private clinic. She has written and published many articles on therapy for anorexics and the families of individuals suffering from catastrophic illnesses. She has also given many inservice programs and presentations at national human services conferences.

By any criteria imaginable, Jane appears to be a highly competent, successful therapist and an exceptionally endowed woman overall. Her ability and demeanor have made her a role model that many in her community aspire to emulate. As Jane sits down with the crisis worker, she is seriously considering drinking a good deal of wine, closing her garage door, climbing into her new Lexus, turning on the ignition, and killing herself.

Jane: I came here today because of what you said to me the other night when we were having a drink. You pretty much have me pegged. I'm burned out even more than what you think, more than what I like to admit. Today I had a decision to make, whether to kill myself or come here. I came here, but I'm not sure it's the right decision. If I killed myself, it seems like it would just be over and done with. I've taken care of everything concerning Bobby, my son. He's practically through with college, and even though we're very close, I really think it'd be better for him if I were gone.

He wouldn't have to put up with my lousy behavior, and believe me, it's lousy right now. There's enough insurance to get him finished up in school, and he could sell the house. He's the only one that really matters besides my clients, and right now I'm not doing worth a damn with them. I'm probably hurting more than I help, and I'm just not up to it anymore. So much pain and so damn little I can do about it. The only thing I can think about now when I go into a cancer ward is how bad the patients smell. Whoever said "You don't have to smell them. All you gotta do is help them!" sure wasn't in this end of the business. I'm also starting to behave like those screwed-up anorexics I work with too. It's starting to seem pretty reasonable to me that they aren't eating. Why the hell should they? Why the hell should *I*? Just sort of fade away and look thin while you're doing it. At least I'd make a great-looking corpse. Anyway, the main reason I came over today was to see if you'd be willing to take my clients. I've thought this over, and you've got what it takes. I think you could help them, and if you agree, I'll start talking to them about coming over to your practice.

CW: What you just said scares the living hell out of me. There's a part of me that wants to run right out of here, because what you're saying is really hitting home with the way I feel at times. There's another part of me that wants to tie you up in log chains until you come to your senses. Finally, there's another part of me that cares for you so much that I'm angry that you've let yourself get into this predicament. Most of all, though, I'm glad I made that reflection the other night and that it finally sank in. I've seen you going downhill for quite a while now. My guess is that you didn't even know it was happening or just laid another piece of armor plate over yourself and said something like "I've got to gut this through" or some of that other irrational garbage I hear you unload on yourself. First of all, I won't even consider what you said about the clients until we agree on one thing, and that is you don't do any harm to yourself until we talk this through. So I want an agreement both as your therapist and as your friend that we shake on that before anything else happens. I won't take no for an answer. If that's not acceptable, we'll negotiate it. No matter what, we're now in this together.

Ethical Issues. The crisis worker is in a difficult position as the client's friend, fellow professional, and now as a therapist dealing with another human being in crisis. When a human service professional who is a colleague becomes impaired, it is the ethical duty of the fellow professional to do something to prevent harm to clients (Harrison & Westwood, 2009; Thomas & Levitt, 2010), and there is research that impaired therapists can hurt clients (Lawson et al., 2007). The overall principle of nonmaleficence (do no harm) comes into play. It is simpler if impairment is due to drugs or alcohol abuse that can be readily observed, or if the professional works in a setting where other professionals can observe the behavior, but it becomes much more difficult when the professional is in private practice or the impairment is burnout, which cannot be smelled or seen in slurred speech or unsteady walking.

Oftentimes close friends and colleagues of burned-out professionals are the first to notice the impairment. Clearly, there are many personal and social dilemmas about "snitching" out one's colleague. The question then becomes, Should colleagues report the impaired professional to the state licensing board or attempt to intervene and help the person by themselves? It is a slippery slope and, as with many ethics questions, there is no clear answer.

Although there are ethical issues in treating a friend and a colleague, when a client is in crisis and lethality is involved, the primary concern is keeping the client safe and returning the individual to a state of equilibrium. Depending on what comes of this crisis intervention, if Jane can regain her psychological equilibrium and manage her own self-care, the crisis worker may do nothing more. If Jane doesn't, the worker is ethically bound to notify a licensing board although that might well spell the end of the friendship (Thomas & Levitt, 2010).

The nuances of this ethical dilemma can be argued after the fact, but right now the crisis worker needs to act. Particularly in small towns where there are essentially no other professionals with the necessary expertise to provide immediate assistance, the appropriate ethical response would be to provide the best level of care as quickly as possible. In that regard, it is most likely that the crisis worker will have some personal or professional relationship with the client.

Because the crisis worker knows the client, she feels free to make some initial owning statements that let the client know exactly how she feels about the situation without becoming sympathetic in the bargain, which she could easily do because she has felt much the same way at prior times in her professional life (countertransference). The crisis worker also makes an initial assessment of the lethality level of the client. Her reflective statement to the client a few evenings earlier was not idle conversation. The crisis worker has seen a slow but steady change coming over Jane in the last 3 months, and as she thinks about it she sees that it was coming a good while before that. Jane has been keeping a stiff upper lip, but there have been indicators that all has not been well lately. She has been rather cynical about clients, as evidenced by her comment about how they smell. She has been suffering a variety of physical maladies that have ranged from unending colds to some severe gastrointestinal problems ominous enough to indicate that surgery might be needed in the near future.

As the crisis worker continues to assess the situation, she further realizes that Jane has truncated relationships with most of her acquaintances and has done this lately with the crisis worker on at least two occasions.

Their relationship had been characterized by an easy rivalry, good comradeship, and just generally a lot of good times together without ever engaging in one-upmanship. Lately, though, the crisis worker has had the feeling that Jane has treated her more as a client than as a friend and has attributed some deeper psychological meaning to even the most innocent conversation.

Assessment. Behaviorally, Jane is in serious trouble. Her performance of daily tasks has become seriously compromised. Her uncharacteristic behavior coupled with her suicidal thoughts places her at a triage level of 7 to 8 on behavior. The only positive behavior she is currently exhibiting is seeking out her colleague. Even though she says she is doing that only to transfer clients, dynamically she is making a clear call for help.

The rather detached, mechanistic way that Jane has reported all this and her blank, hollow look are completely at odds with Jane's usual sparkle, which has been absent the past few months. Performing a quick synthesis of all this background knowledge, what Jane is saying, and the depressed way she is looking and behaving, the crisis worker makes the assessment that Jane is not kidding about killing herself and that the threat must be taken seriously. The crisis worker immediately goes into a suicide prevention mode and institutes a verbal contract with Jane not to kill herself. Even though Jane is a practicing therapist, she is no different from any other client in this regard.

Besides the threat of suicide, a triage assessment of Jane by a worker unfamiliar with burnout might cursorily dismiss her problem as typical whining about one's work. However, the difficult clients she deals with, the amount of time that she has done so, the isolation she has imposed on herself, and the absence of social support systems in her work and at home all lead to a hypothesis of vicarious trauma/compassion fatigue that is rippling out into every component of her life (Figley, 2002, p. 7). Research clearly indicates that the more traumatic clients are and the more often they are seen, the more likely it is that the therapist will experience compassion fatigue, vicarious traumatization, and burnout (Simpson, 2006). In short, Jane is fitting many of the behavioral, attitudinal, emotional, and interpersonal descriptors mentioned earlier in this chapter regarding symptoms of burnout.

Triage assessment for affect is 7 to 8. Although her outward demeanor is calm and collected, her affective responses are uncharacteristically angry and hostile for someone in the helping professions. Jane is using considerable effort to control her feelings. Coupled with the emotional exhaustion that is the most salient factor of burnout, she is close to being acutely depressed. This should come as no surprise, because depression and burnout often go hand in hand (Lawson, 2009; McKnight & Glass, 1995).

Cognitively, Jane is operating at a triage level of 6 to 7. Although Jane is thinking in a linear manner, her logic is twisted, and her belief system is severely compromised by obsessional self-doubt. She is manifesting a great deal of Ellis's (1973) "musturbatory" thinking and demonstrating another hallmark of burnout: a severe decline in her belief in her personal competence, along with depersonalization of her clients. Her complaints go beyond her job and indicate problems with social relationships, physical health, personal integrity, professional identity, belief system, and her total environment. Jane's total triage assessment scale score of 20 to 23 places her in the low to moderate marked impairment range. She is currently functioning between the frustration and apathy stage of burnout and is at a trait level where burnout has become pervasive across her environments. Without intervention, she is likely to move quickly into severe and lethal impairment.

Jane has done one thing right. She has gone to a significant other and is using that trusted other to self-disclose in a very intimate way some of her most troubled feelings (Maslach, 1976; Watkins, 1983). Because Jane's problems have spread out across her environment, the crisis worker will do exploratory counseling across BASIC IDS (Lazarus, 1976) components with the idea that no component of Jane's life is immune to the burnout currently assailing her.

Jane: All right, I can agree to a no-suicide contract. I know that's part of the procedure. Hell, I guess I knew you'd do that when I came in here. Maybe I'm only kidding myself about all this anyway, just a bit of the blues, feeling sorry for myself, and all that crap.

CW: I'm glad you came here, for whatever reason, and I'm also glad you agree to our contract even though you know it's part of the program. I also don't believe that about having the blues, either. I think it's much more than that. I believe right now you're hurting quite a bit. But first I'd like to hear what you think and feel is going on in your life right now.

Intervention. While the crisis worker is acknowledging her regard for Jane, she is also doing quite a bit more. First, she has decided to take a pretty directive stance with Jane for the time being. The worker balances between making emotional challenges to the client and listening closely and accurately to Jane's problems. She also knows Jane is extremely astute at the business they are engaged in, as evidenced by her comment about the contract. She is not going to let Jane play the game ahead of her. Her analysis is that Jane is out of control right now. The crisis worker is therefore going to take control of the situation and will not sit back in a passive mode.

Jane: I don't know. I've dealt with all kinds of problems in my life, and right now there's nothing I can really put my finger on. In comparison to what is going on now, I can tell you that going through the divorce with Jeff, taking off on my own to finish up the doctorate, fighting my way up the ladder in the agency, and then finally making a decision to go out on my own while raising Bobby make what's happening to me now seem like peanuts.

CW: Right! Those were really tough times, and you went through those like Superwoman. But that was then, and we're right here, right now, and from the looks of it you don't much feel like you're Superwoman, and what's happening in your life surely isn't peanuts, or we wouldn't be having this talk right now. So what do you feel like right now?

The crisis worker acknowledges how tough the client has been, but will not let her get stuck in the past. The crisis worker wants to find out what is happening right now. What is more important about this now than it was a year ago? Furthermore, the crisis worker will not let the client discount the problem. It is interesting that if Jane were the counselor here, she would probably ferret out what she has just done—retreating into the past—in a second. The difference is that Jane has really become a client, and she is as blind to the way she talks, thinks, and behaves as any other client. Jane's being a therapist gives her no edge in dealing with her own problems. In fact, her own expertise may militate heavily against her (Kesler, 1990).

Jane: All I can tell you is I'm washed out. Like I get dates and appointments all mixed up. Last week topped that all off. I saw 44 clients last week. I think I got about a dozen appointments mixed up. My appointment book was really screwed up. It was a madhouse, and some of the people got agitated. Nothing like that ever happened before.

CW: Never?

Jane: Well, to a far lesser extent. I've been strung out before, but I could always get it straightened out.

CW: How?

Jane: About every 3 months things would start to get out of hand. I'd just sit back and say, "Janie, old girl, you've got to get out of here for a while." I'd just hop in the car and take off for a weekend in Chicago. Check into a hotel, take in a show, eat some really special meals, and use about half the hotel's hot water washing the clients off of me. Seems like that would clear the cobwebs out of my head.

CW: When was the last time you did that?

Jane: (*wistfully*) About 9 months ago.

CW: Why so long?

Jane: Well, I bought that new office and went in and remodeled the whole thing. I cut the contractor a deal. If I could work on it too, he'd reduce the price.

CW: So being the omnipotent individual you are, you threw out at least one thing that keeps you on an even keel. In fact, rather than getting away from the office, you've been spending almost all your time there. Let's see, we've got a couple of characters running around inside of Jane—Dr. Jane, healer to the world, and Jane the carpenter. Wonder who else is inside there?

The crisis worker is looking for a link between the past and the present. If Jane had some coping mechanisms in the past, what were they? She is specifically looking for coping mechanisms in the past that can be linked to the present and what is happening in the present to keep those coping mechanisms from being put into place. She is also beginning to build a character repertoire with Jane in the hope that Jane can start to see all the various aspects of herself that are now motivating her to do some of the things she does (Butts, 1996). To set the stage for the client's regaining control of her life, the crisis worker proposes a positive character in Jane.

CW: I also heard a character that I'd call Janice, a person who knows when her stress bucket is full and is practical and smart enough to get away from the crap that goes on at that office. Where have you stuck her?

Jane: Back up on the shelf with Janie?

CW: Who's Janie?

Jane: She's the gal who's a little crazy, who can joke with her clients and get up in the middle of the night and go out and start seeding her lawn and sing Chuck Berry songs while she's doing it. (*embarrassed*) There's just no time for them right now. It's not just the new office, but I also needed another car, and since Bobby has changed schools there were a lot of added expenses in that. So I really needed to devote my time to building my caseload up. If I can get through the next 2 years, I can breathe easier.

CW: Well, I'm sure glad to hear you're planning on being around for the next 2 years, anyway. But that's not the question now, is it, because right now it sounds to me as if you're wrung out. You don't have any more energy to give, and you've set up on the wall a couple of people who are pretty important in recharging your batteries. Do you see how important they are and what it's cost you to do that?

The crisis worker is not yet making direct suggestions as to what Jane needs to do; however, she is hoping to raise Jane's consciousness to the fact that she has unconsciously changed her operating method. The crisis worker attempts to get her to recognize this by describing what these very positive characters have done for her. By doing so, the crisis worker is attempting to reintroduce some very healthy defense mechanisms that have previously helped Jane cope well with the stressful life she leads. Three major pathways that keep Jane in equilibrium are currently missing from her life: resiliency, self-management and self-care, and connection with others (Gentry, Baranowsky, & Dunning, 2002). The crisis worker will attempt to reintegrate those into Jane's life.

Jane: I guess so, but I don't know how to get out of it.

CW: What will happen if you don't work on the office this next weekend?

Jane: The new plumbing isn't in. Clients wouldn't be able to use the bathroom. I'd also feel guilty for not working on it.

CW: (*laughing*) Well, the first part of that problem is pretty easily handled. Call the Porta-Potty people. I can imagine a sign that says, "The crap stops here," hanging from the door as clients walk in. (*Jane starts to smile and giggle for the first time since walking in the door.*) The other part of that is, who's the character laying a guilt trip on you? Tell me some more about her.

The crisis worker takes a little bit of a well-gauged risk here by injecting some humor into the situation (Moran, 2002). She does this because humor has been important in Jane's life, is helpful to her in coping, and turns her away from some of the cynicism she feels toward her clients and starts to allow her to laugh at herself a little. The ability to laugh at one's own foibles and some of the bizarre and ridiculously funny things that happen in our clients' lives cannot be overemphasized (Pines & Aronson, 1988, p. 154). Van Auken (1979) extols the judicious use of humor even in the most pathetic of situations. Getting a smile or a laugh from clients is a direct intrusion into the depressive thought processes and behaviors in which they are mired.

The crisis worker also starts to hammer a bit on Jane's guilt. Generally the crisis worker sees guilt as a pretty useless emotion, consumptive of energy that could be used in other, more positive ways. Guilt is invariably an emotion of the past, and whatever was done can never again be retrieved. It is one thing to learn from one's past mistakes and quite another to carry past, unfinished business into the present, particularly when one is feeling guilty about not measuring up.

Jane: That's Mother Superior. I get all kinds of lectures from her. (*bitterly*) She's just like Sister Angeline at St. Mary's, where I went to school. "Say your Hail Mary's and Our Father's. Get your homework done. God doesn't like a shirker. Watch how you dress." Jesus, I hated that!

CW: You hate it, but it sure sounds like you're living it. Small wonder you're feeling so lousy.

The crisis worker starts hooking up feelings with thoughts and actions. The response the crisis worker gets indicates that the burnout has spread out into the client's family life.

Jane: You know, I think that's maybe why Bobby and I are having problems right now. I really sound and act like a Mother Superior to him. My Lord! He's 21 years old, and I've started treating him like he was a 6-year-old. He's about like some of those clients I have to lead around by the nose.

CW: Did you hear what you just said? "He's about like some of those clients I lead around." First of all, I didn't know that was the business you were in. Sounds like Jane the handywoman. Fix 'em up the way you do your office. Second, I wonder how many people outside the office you've decided to fix up and look out for. I have to tell you that's one of the kinds of feelings I've had around you lately.

With this information, the client gives the crisis worker a chance to plunge into some core issues that have definable behavioral outcomes. By stating how she deals with Bobby, Jane is manifesting another of the typical signs of burnout: trying to treat significant others in her life as if they were in the therapeutic situation (Van Auken, 1979). Her relationship with Bobby is extremely important because one way of decreasing burnout is to have a satisfying family life, especially with one's children (Forney, Wallace-Schutzman, & Wiggers, 1982). Worse yet is that she has become autocratic in the therapeutic situation, so it is not surprising that a major component of her life that has been highly reinforcing to her is no longer so and, in fact, has taken on some very negative connotations.

The crisis worker lays that squarely on her. She is mixing up her characters and has replaced Dr. Jane with Jane the handywoman. This state of events is not so surprising since both characters are working in the same office. Jane needs a break in her day-to-day activities and needs to get away from the office to do it (Forney, Wallace-Schutzman, & Wiggers, 1982).

Finally, the crisis worker relates and owns her own experience of having been treated the same way by Jane. She tries to make Jane aware that, like rings on a pond, the ripple effect from her burnout goes far beyond her immediate line of sight (Kesler, 1990).

CW: Indeed, I wonder about your relationships other than those with Bobby, myself, and your clients. Anyone else you're trying to control right now?

Jane: (*frostily*) If you mean men, absolutely no. When I get home at night, I'm so bushed all I want to do is fall asleep, but then all those clients go tumbling around in my head, and I start thinking about car payments, mortgage payments, how to straighten things out with Bobby, and I wind up getting about 2 or 3 hours of sleep a night.

CW: So right now you're so exhausted that you'd just rather be alone.

Jane: That's right, but I feel like I ought to be out mingling with people. I'm so damned isolated anyway.

CW: OK! I can understand that, and I'd agree with you, but let's look at right now. Seems as if you really need some time to just curl up in the fetal position, turn the electric blanket up to nine, and get your batteries recharged. Could you just go home and go to bed, put the answering service on until Monday, and not get up for the whole weekend?

Jane: I suppose.

CW: No supposes. If you don't want to do that, we'll look at something else. But right now you look like *The Grapes of Wrath* and just seem to really need to rest before you think about doing anything else. Are you willing to call the contractor up and tell him you won't be there Saturday and Sunday without feeling guilty about it?

Jane: I could use the rest. All right! I'll give it this weekend.

CW: Fine. But there's one more thing. If you really get to feeling blue, plug the phone in and call me at home. I also want a report next week, so what time do you want to come in?

Jane: Sounds like I'm a client.

CW: Sounds like you're right. (*Laughs.*)

The crisis worker is basically assisting Jane to make a simple commitment to do one thing—get some rest. A critical component in treating burnout is revitalization (Tubesing & Tubesing, 1982, p. 160). Jane is physically fatigued, and the first order of business is to get her physical batteries recharged. A number of other options are available at this juncture, but the crisis worker follows Tubesing and Strosahl's (1976) advice to let the client make the choice of what treatment is appropriate. Keying on the client's own words about needing sleep, the crisis worker follows up and gains commitment to a specific behavior that the client will engage in over the short term. This is not a dramatic first step, but considering the least dramatic steps first is probably the way to go (Van Auken, 1979). The most important objective of this initial encounter is finding some short-term intervention techniques the client is able and willing to use (Freudenberger & Robbins, 1979).

A particular behavior the crisis worker touches on is the use of the telephone. Private practitioners are notorious for taking phone calls from clients at all hours of the night and on weekends. Van Auken (1979) urges human services workers not to let clients run—or, for that matter, ruin—their personal lives. The crisis worker makes sure that Jane follows this dictum, even though the crisis worker herself doesn't practice what she preaches, which leads one to wonder whom the crisis worker may soon need to be talking to about burnout. Finally, the worker provides emotional support, but once Jane is able to ventilate her feelings, the worker moves into a problem-solving mode.

The Next Week

Jane: I'll have to admit I do feel better. Couldn't sleep at all Friday night, but I got 10 hours in Saturday. I can't believe it! I woke up, and I was all curled up in the fetal position. The clients looked somewhat better this week. I can't say it was wonderful, but at least I wasn't an ogre to them. I guess what bothers me most about that is that I've lost all my creativity.

CW: OK! Let's talk about that a bit. You haven't been paying very much attention to the right side of your brain, so what do you expect? What could you do creatively that isn't client involved that'd get the right side of your head going again?

Jane: I've got a couple of articles I've been putting off—how about that?

CW: Got anything to do with clients?

Jane: Yes.

CW: Is that going to help you out?

Jane: I don't guess so, the same old stuff, only I'm writing about it.

CW: What else, then?

Forney, Wallace-Schutzman, and Wiggers (1982) propose that a variety of professional activities may be an excellent coping mechanism; nevertheless, the crisis worker confronts Jane about this suggested alternative. The crisis worker is fairly sure that the client's stress bucket is full to the brim professionally. Jane needs to become less, not more, involved in her professional life.

Jane: Well, there is something else. I bought this sailboat for Bobby and me. The Coast Guard Auxiliary is putting on a sailing class. It would sure surprise Bobby if the next time he came home I could handle that Y-Flyer.

CW: Is that something you want to do? Would like to do it, not need to do it?

Jane: Yes!

CW: And not pile it on top of everything else. Really reserve some time for yourself to enjoy it.

Jane: You sure drive a hard bargain, but I can do it.

This is a wedge in the behavioral repertoire of the client that the crisis worker has been looking to find. Writer after writer in the burnout literature has promoted the use of leisure, particularly physical exercise, as a way of breaking up the dogmatic, work-brittle behavior of just going through the motions that often characterizes the burned-out human services worker (Hoeksma et al., 1993; Melamed, Meir, & Samson, 1995; Savicki & Cooley, 1982).

By proposing for the client a combination of leisure, physical exercise, and quality time with her son, the crisis worker has neatly integrated a number of positive interventions. The crisis worker is moving methodically around Myers, Sweeney, and Witmer's Wellness Wheel (Myers, Sweeney, & Witmer, 2000; Myers & Sweeney, 2005), which has at its center spiritual self-direction, and which Dr. Jane is now mostly without. Specific spokes that radiate out from that wheel that the worker is attempting to put back in place in the client's life are nutrition, exercise, self-care, stress management, a sense of control, realistic beliefs, a sense of humor, renewed creativity, and awareness and coping across her entire ecosystem. With that many spokes missing, it is no surprise that Dr. Jane's psychological vehicle has about lost its spiritual axle as it careens down a crisis cliff that has become a burnout landslide of behavioral, physical, interpersonal, and attitudinal problems.

The crisis worker now takes on the main issue of the client's private practice.

CW: Fine. Let's talk about your practice for a while.

Jane: You know as well as I do about that. Sure, I've got a great caseload now. But who knows, it might dry up next week, and then where would I be?

CW: Has it ever dried up? Even in the last recession?

Jane: No, it hasn't, but I keep expecting the worst.

CW: You've been in private practice 8 years now, right? Has it ever been such that you didn't have enough clients to keep the wolves away from your door?

Jane: No. I guess there's something else. I feel a little foolish saying this, but it's almost like if I don't live up to my reputation and take on those really tough cases, I start feeling like I'm not the queen of the mountain. I mean, in the past I've been real proud of that, but now I don't seem to feel anything but that there's an albatross around my neck.

CW: Sounds like Superwoman again. I frankly admire you for dealing with those terminals' families, and you're right! Not many could do that. But if there's no intrinsic payoff, why are you fooling yourself into thinking you can heal the whole world? See the trap you've put yourself into?

Jane: Well, no! I guess I don't.

CW: OK! I want to try something. Maybe you've used it on some of your clients before. It's a game of "Who Told You?" I want you to move over to my chair and ask that empty chair, which will represent Jane, some questions. I'm going to stand aside and process as we go along, but it'll mostly be up to you. I want you to use all your insight as a therapist and really bore in and go to work on Jane's fictional goals, those crazy things she tells herself that have no counterpart in reality.

Jane as CW: (*Shifts chairs and gets a glitter in her eyes.*) OK, toots! Who told you you had to be Superwoman?

CW: Now shift back.

Jane: Nobody, really, I've just got a lot of responsibilities.

Jane as CW: Responsibilities, my foot! You've been going up that success ladder so fast you've scorched the rungs. Always got to show them. Be number one. My God! You little twerp. You're 43 years old, and you still think you're back on the VA ward. Got to show them you're better than any man. Volunteer for the worst cases. Scared to death you won't succeed. And when you did, you were scared you wouldn't succeed the second time. Who told you that?

Jane: Nobody! It was reality. I had to be better than the men there.

Jane as CW: That was 20 years ago, nerd! The only men you deal with now are your clients. And that's another thing. Is that why you're so afraid of going out with any other man? And don't give me that stuff about getting burned again. You know why that divorce happened, and it sure doesn't have anything to do with having good social relationships now.

Jane: It's just that with the financial obligations for Bobby, I really don't have the time.

Jane as CW: (*really angry and shouting*) I won't have that! How long will you be responsible for him? He's 21 years old. Who supported you when you were 21? I'll tell you who. You did! You just use that as an excuse. Just like you use all those clients as an excuse. You don't fool me, you little martyr. Oh, sure! You get those strokes. (*dripping sarcasm*) Just like Annette here said, "I really admire you,

Jane." You go around fooling everybody, but worst of all you fool yourself. Look at you. Sitting here the pathetic little wretch. You don't fool me. You're not little Miss Goody Two-Shoes. Behind all that depression is a really angry, bitter bitch who's always going around being everybody's servant. So just who told you you had to be that?

Jane: (*Breaks and sobs. The CW goes to Jane, gathers her into her arms, and hugs her for dear life. Five minutes elapse.*) Good Lord! I didn't realize that was all in there. I really got on a roll.

CW: Neither did I, but I figured if anybody could get it out, you could. What have you got out of that?

Jane: Besides spilling my guts, which I haven't done in 25 years, I see now how I got into this. I really set myself up.

CW: What do you want to do?

Jane: Well, I'm not going to kill myself, literally or figuratively. I've got some living to do, and although I'm not going to quit the practice, there sure are going to be some limits put on it.

The "Who Told You?" technique is a combination of Adlerian, rational-emotive behavior, and Gestalt therapy that is extremely powerful. Given a person with the kind of insight Jane has, it often has dramatic results in pointing out the way clients delude themselves. By using Jane as her own therapist, the crisis worker provides no one for the client to rationalize to, attack, manipulate, or otherwise attempt to fool but herself. For a person with Jane's abilities and insight, that seldom happens for very long. Underneath most depression lies anger. If that anger can be mobilized, then the client has taken a major step toward getting back into control of the situation. By putting Jane in a position to view her behavior from outside herself and also giving her a stimulus to attack her irrational ideas by the "Who Told You?" technique, the crisis worker provides an arena in which Jane can combat the apathy she is experiencing.

Such a dramatic shift to being mobile is uncommon among the general populace, and Jane's case is a condensed version of what may generally happen. The crisis worker often must provide the stimulus statements that are the core of clients' irrational ideas because of clients' poor cognition of their own negative self-talk. However, in dealing with highly trained professionals, it is not uncommon for such rapid shifts to occur.

Given the initial stimulus, they may pick up on the technique and provide their own dialogue with little or no help from the crisis worker. When emotional catharsis occurs, the crisis worker then takes a nondirective stance and serves as little more than a sounding board as their fellow professionals put reasonable parameters back into their lives. At that point, human services workers as clients tend to be able to make good decisions quickly about the behavioral, emotional, and cognitive aspects of their lives.

Indeed, if burnout syndrome is successfully overcome, it is not unreasonable to expect that human services workers will come back to their profession with hardier personalities, stronger commitments to self and profession, better self-temperance, a greater sense of meaningfulness, and increased vigor toward their environment (Kobasa, 1979). Furthermore, new coping styles that include greater self-awareness, increased self-insight, and a more direct approach to problem solving are likely to result for those who successfully navigate these treacherous waters (Cooley & Keesey, 1981). Finally, it is our own observation that human services professionals who have successfully conquered burnout respond not only to their work but also to their daily living with calmer and wiser choices, behaviors, and work style.

Summary.   In this vignette the crisis worker uses the BASIC IDS model to deal with multiple, overlapping issues in the client's life (Kesler, 1990). Jane's workload affects her relationship with her family and friends. Her role as mother affects her image of herself. Her image of herself affects her beliefs about her abilities as therapist and mother and finally affects her coping behaviors across the board. The crisis worker links all of these dimensions into a unified whole because each modality interacts with other modalities and should not be treated in isolation (Cormier & Cormier, 1985, p. 153). Jane's sailing expeditions not only will provide her with fun, relaxation, and togetherness with her son, but also are as necessary to her therapeutic functioning as her doctoral training. Achieving balance among the various parts of her life and compartmentalizing them to the extent that they do not start to run into or over one another allow Dr. Jane Lee to be fully functioning in all of them and at the same time limit the stresses inherent in each (Pines & Aronson, 1988, p. 152).

Webb (2007) has listed the following points that can help crisis workers who deal with traumatized children stave off vicarious traumatization, compassion fatigue, and ultimately burnout.

1. Pursue training and professional activities that promote learning. Keeping up in this business is important not only for the knowledge gained and skills learned but for meeting other professionals and continuing to build a professional support system.

2. Work with a variety of clients and limit exposure to trauma in general. It is tempting to specialize in trauma work. Many crisis workers take pride in doing work not everyone can do. It is also an adrenal rush and addictive. However, the old saying "Pride goeth before a fall" is true here. Varied client issues are not only a good way to keep the worker on his or her game but also provide relief from the constant grit and grind of trauma work. One of your authors startled a student he was doing some career counseling with after having worked with five suicidal/homicidal students in a row. His statement, "Thanks for coming in, you're the first normal student I've met today," probably made her wonder just exactly who was enrolling in the university.

3. Create boundaries between work and home, and maintain a personal identity. One of your authors is married to a middle school counselor. Do we talk about our work? Yes! Do we talk about it all the time? Absolutely not! We leave most of it at the door. "It'll be there tomorrow" are words to live by.

4. Find professional friends who understand the stress of this business. You can't have too many professional friends and colleagues. One of your authors makes regular dates to watch baseball games with a psychologist who works at a VA hospital. We talk about psychology, but we also discuss theology and politics, watch baseball, eat peanuts, and sing "Take Me Out to the Ballgame" during the seventh inning stretch.

5. Spend time with people who have not been victimized to maintain a balanced perspective that not all people have pathology. That's why it is important to get into a church, civic organization, fitness center, bridge club, model train club, or benevolent organization where there are just "regular" folks engaged in just "regular" activities.

6. Confront intrusive images and work through them. After reading this chapter you should understand full well that if you start having pop-ups in your mind of the bad stuff you deal with or have nightmares about the stuff, don't punch it back as part of the job. Go get help.

7. Engage in activities that promote a sense of efficacy and empowerment. You may not decide to run for U.S. Senator, but getting involved in a community action program or government committee is an

excellent way of feeling empowered and helping promote causes that give you a sense of self-esteem.

8. Engage in your own psychotherapy. While we do not advocate becoming your own "shrink," what is meant by this point is knowing yourself. If you saw Crazy walking down the other side of the street, would you run over and go lay a body wrap on it? Knowing yourself as to your psychological strengths and weak points is critical in this work.

9. Get supervision from somebody who knows his or her business about trauma work. Your bartender, hairdresser, minister, golfing buddies, or book club members are fine to talk with, but they are "regular" folks up in point 5. You do need somebody who knows this business and how to effectively supervise you as you do it.

Epilogue: Cross-Cultural Comparisons

This chapter is not just for human services workers in the United States. If you are reading this book in Germany, Scotland, Australia, Poland, Austria, Canada, Denmark, China, Korea, Israel, Japan, or some other country, this chapter is also for you. Victor Savicki (2002) conducted a landmark study of child care workers, culture, work environment, and burnout across the United States, Australia, a number of European countries, and Israel and compared them on Maslach Burnout Inventory subscales (Maslach & Jackson, 1981a). What Savicki found when he compared 13 different cultures was that all of you out there don't do well and tend to burn out when there are heavy workloads, unsupportive middle-level managers, an atmosphere in which new ideas and practices are restricted, and inefficiently organized work. Conversely, when the work environment offers encouragement for new ideas, a team of coworkers lends support, and managers set the stage for positive feelings of goal attainment, low burnout scores are the result (Savicki, 2002, pp. 80–87).

However, when culture is factored in, Maslach's three components of burnout change dramatically. For example, Danish and both French Canadian and English Canadian workers have low emotional exhaustion, low depersonalization, and high sense of personal accomplishment scores. Child care workers in what was formerly West Germany have high burnout profiles with a low sense of personal accomplishment and high emotional exhaustion and depersonalization scores.

Interestingly, in what was formerly East Germany respondents had very little sense of personal accomplishment, yet they were not emotionally exhausted nor did they feel much depersonalization. Clearly, even though those are both German populations, the political cultural artifacts left over from what was formerly a communist country seem to play a role in how child care workers operate and what their culture expects from them, in contrast to the democracy of the former West Germany. Now compare the German scores to those of the Israelis, who had very low depersonalization, very high sense of personal accomplishment, but were at the median on emotional exhaustion. Then look at the United States, whose workers scored extremely high in sense of personal accomplishment, but unhappily also had high emotional exhaustion and high depersonalization scores (Savicki, 2002, pp. 78–79).

Both general environmental work measures and individual cultural conformity measures showed significant relationships to the burnout subscales (Savicki, 2002, pp. 88–89). For example, the concept of *power distance* means the amount of control that bosses feel they have over workers and vice versa. High power distances mean that bosses believe they can dictate the behavior of their subordinates. It should come as no surprise that high power distances lead to burn out. Likewise, the *uncertainty avoidance principle* is the degree to which cultures establish rules, procedures, and rituals to compensate for uncertainty and chaos (Savicki, 2002, pp. 38–41). Again it should be no surprise that those cultures with high uncertainty avoidance and many rules to guide the bureaucracy tend to have high burnout scores.

The implications of Savicki's (2002) work would seem to be that not only are the individual worker and the work setting complicit in whether burnout potential is high or low, but also that the overall culture may be a factor as well. If that is true, changing the cultural factor is a tall order indeed! Savicki's (2002) study examines countries whose cultures are generally seen to be more individualist as opposed to collectivist, although arguments could certainly be made for a more collectivist gestalt in what used to be East Germany and other former Soviet bloc countries of Eastern Europe. It would be interesting to see how child care workers from Middle Eastern, African, and Asian cultures that tend to operate more on the collectivist end of the cultural continuum would fare on the Burnout Inventory. Much like avian flu, burnout circles the globe, and you can catch it pretty much anywhere.

SUMMARY

Burnout is not simply a sympathy-eliciting term to use when one has had a hard day at the office. It is a very real malady that strikes people and can have extremely severe consequences. It is prevalent in the human services professions because of the kinds of clients, environments, working conditions, and resultant stresses that are operational there. Because of the intense and stressful nature of crisis intervention, a major contributor to burnout is constant exposure to clients who have had horrific experiences.

Prolonged exposure can induce what is variously called *vicarious traumatization*, *compassion fatigue*, or *secondary traumatization* in the crisis worker. No one particular individual is more prone to experience burnout than another. However, by their very nature, most human services workers tend to be highly committed to their profession, and such commitment is a necessary precursor to burnout. Private practitioners may experience burnout even more severely than their counterparts in organizations because of their professional isolation. All human services workers, public or private, tend to be unable to identify the problem when it is their own. No one is immune to its effects.

Burnout moves through stages of enthusiasm, stagnation, frustration, and apathy. In its end stage, burnout is a crisis situation. The crisis takes many forms. It can be manifested behaviorally, physically, interpersonally, and attitudinally. It pervades the professional's life and can have effects on clients, coworkers, family, friends, and the organization itself.

Recognition of the beginning symptoms of burnout can alleviate its personal and organizational ramifications. Raising consciousness levels in regard to the dynamics of burnout in training programs and conducting on-the-job workshops are important ways of halting and ameliorating its effects. Support groups within the organization that provide instrumental and emotional resources to victims are important. In the past, burnout has been regarded as a malady that resides only within the individual. That view is archaic. Burnout should also be viewed in a systems perspective and as an organizational and cultural problem. At its end stage, burnout is a crisis situation that calls for immediate, direct, and reality-oriented therapeutic intervention. Given corrective remediation, victims of burnout can return to the job and again become productive.

 To see some of the concepts discussed in this chapter in action, refer to your *Crisis Intervention in Action* DVD, or see the clips online on the Counseling CourseMate website. To access this site, go to www.cengagebrain.com, where you'll also find an eBook, additional study tools, quizzes, and more. Now that you've read this chapter, you can sit in the therapist's chair (not the one burned out) or you can sit in the client's chair (the therapist who is burned out). Or, better yet, sit in both of them! Just like Jane, you'll probably try to play the game ahead of the therapist since you are definitely world class in this business yourself. Or, how about the therapist? You've got this other therapist who has this BIG reputation and now you are doing therapy with her. What goes through your head as you sit in one chair and then the other?

REFERENCES

Adams, K. O. (1989). Have you been counseling too hard and too long? *School Counselor, 36*, 165–166.

Alexander, J. G., de Chesnay, M., Marshall, E., & Campbell, A. R. (1989). Parallel reactions in rape victims and rape researchers. *Violence and Victims, 4*(1), 57–62.

Alkema, K., Linton, J. M., & Davies, R. (2008). A study of the relationship between self-care, compassion satisfaction, compassion fatigue, and burnout among hospice professionals. *Journal of Social Work in End-of-Life & Palliative Care, 4*(2), 101–119.

Arvay, M. J., & Uhlemann, M. R. (1996). Counselor stress in the field of trauma: A preliminary study. *Canadian Journal of Counselling, 30*(3), 193–210.

Baird, S., & Jenkins, S. R. (2003). Vicarious traumatization, secondary traumatic stress, and burnout in sexual assault and domestic violence agency staff. *Violence & Victims, 18*(1), 71–86.

Bakker, A. B., Demerouti, E., & Schaufeli, W. B. (2002). Validation of the Maslach Burnout Inventory—General survey: An Internet study. *Anxiety, Stress & Coping: An International Journal, 15*(3), 245–260.

Bakker, A. B., Demerouti, E., & Schaufeli, W. B. (2005). The crossover of burnout and work engagement among working couples. *Human Relations, 58*(5), 661–689.

Baranowsky, A. B. (2002). The silencing response in clinical practice: On the road to dialogue. In C. R. Figley (Ed.), *Treating compassion fatigue* (pp. 155–170). New York: Brunner/Routledge.

Barber, C., & Iwai, M. (1996). Role conflict and role ambiguity as predictors of burnout among staff caring for elderly dementia patients. *Journal of Gerontological Social Work, 26*(1–2), 101–116.

Baron, A., Jr., & Cohen, R. B. (1982). Helping telephone counselors cope with burnout: A consciousness-raising workshop. *Personnel and Guidance Journal, 60*, 508–510.

Blanchard, E. A., & Jones, M. (1997). Care of clinicians doing trauma work. In M. Harris & C. L. Landis (Eds.), *Sexual abuse in the lives of women diagnosed with serious mental illness: New direction in therapeutic interventions* (Vol. 2, pp. 303–319). New Delhi: Harwood Academic.

Borritz, M., Bültmann, U., Rugulies, R., Christensen, K., Viladsen, E., & Kristensen, T. S. (2005). Psychosocial work characteristics as predictors for burnout: Findings from 3-year follow up of the PUMA study. *Journal of Occupational & Environmental Medicine, 47*(10), 1015–1025.

Burke, R. J., & Greenglass, E. R. (1995). A longitudinal examination of the Cherniss model of psychological burnout. *Social Science and Medicine, 40*, 1357–1363.

Butts, S. (Speaker). (1996). *Therapeutic techniques, marriage and family therapy* (Cassette Recording No. 7640-96). Memphis, TN: Department of Counseling, Educational Psychology and Research, University of Memphis.

Carroll, J. F. X., & White, W. L. (1982). Theory building: Integrating individual and environmental factors within an ecological framework. In W. S. Paine (Ed.), *Job stress and burnout* (pp. 41–60). Newbury Park, CA: Sage.

Charney, A. M., & Pearlman, L. A. (1998). The ecstasy and the agony: The impact of disaster and trauma work on the self of the clinician. In P. M. Kleespies (Ed.), *Emergencies in mental health practice: Evaluation and management* (pp. 418–435). New York: Guilford Press.

Cherniss, C., & Krantz, D. L. (1983). The ideological community as an antidote to burnout in the human services. In B. A. Farber (Ed.), *Stress and burnout in the human service professions* (pp. 198–212). New York: Pergamon Press.

Collins, S., & Long, A. (2003). Working with the psychological effects of trauma: Consequences for mental health care workers. *Journal of Psychiatric & Mental Health Nursing, 10*(4), 417–424.

Collins, W. L. (2005). Embracing spirituality as an element of professional self-care. *Social Work & Christianity, 32*(3), 263–274.

Cooley, E. J., & Keesey, J. C. (1981). Relationship between life change and illness in coping versus sensitive persons. *Psychological Reports, 48*, 711–714.

Conrad, D., & Kellar-Guenther, Y. (2006). Compassion fatigue, burnout, and compassion satisfaction among Colorado child protection workers. *Child Abuse & Neglect, 30*(10), 1071–1080.

Cormier, W. H., & Cormier, L. S. (1985). *Interviewing strategies for helpers: Fundamental skills and cognitive behavioral interventions* (2nd ed.). Pacific Grove, CA: Brooks/Cole.

Dahlenberg, C. J. (2000). *Countertransference and the treatment of trauma.* Washington, DC: American Psychological Association.

Decker, J. T., Bailey, T. L., & Westergaard, N. (2002). Burnout among child care workers. *Residential Treatment for Children & Youth, 19*(4), 61–77.

Deiter, P. J., & Pearlman, L. A. (1998). Responding to self-injurious behavior. In P. M. Kleespies (Ed.), *Emergencies in mental health practice: Evaluation and management* (pp. 235–257). New York: Guilford Press.

Devine, I. (1984). Organizational crisis and individual response: New trends for human service professionals (Special issue: Education and training in Canadian human services). *Canadian Journal of Community Mental Health, 3*, 63–72.

Distler, B. J. (1990). *Reducing the potential for burnout.* Paper presented at the Fourteenth Annual Convening of Crisis Intervention Personnel, Chicago.

Duquette, A., Kerouac, S., Sandhu, B. K., & Beaudet, L. (1994). Factors related to nursing burnout: A review of empirical knowledge. *Issues in Mental Health Nursing, 15*, 337–358.

East, T. W., James, R. K., & Keim, J. (2001, April). *The best little vicarious trauma prevention program in Tennessee.* Paper presented at the Twenty-Fifth Annual Convening of Crisis Intervention Personnel, Chicago.

Eastwood, C. D. (2007). Compassion fatigue risk and self-care practices among residential treatment center child-care workers. *Dissertation Abstract International: Section B: The Sciences and Engineering, 67*(10), 2645.

Edelwich, J., & Brodsky, A. (1982). Training guidelines: Linking the workshop experience to needs on and off the job. In W. S. Paine (Ed.), *Job stress and burnout* (pp. 133–154). Newbury Park, CA: Sage.

Eidelson, R. J., D'Alessio, G. R., & Eidelson, J. I. (2003). The impact of September 11 on psychologists. *Professional Psychology: Research and Practice, 34*(2), 144–150.

Ellis, A. (1973). *Humanistic psychology: The rational-emotive approach.* New York: Julian.

Everly, G. S., Jr. (1989). *A clinical guide to the treatment of the human stress response.* New York: Plenum.

Farber, B. A. (Ed.). (1983). *Stress and burnout in the human service professions.* New York: Pergamon Press.

Figley, C. R. (Ed.). (1995). *Compassion fatigue: Coping with secondary traumatic stress disorder in those who treat the traumatized.* New York: Brunner-Mazel.

Figley, C. R. (Ed.). (2002). *Treating compassion fatigue.* New York: Brunner/Routledge.

Forney, D. S., Wallace-Schutzman, F., & Wiggers, T. T. (1982). Burnout among career development professionals: Preliminary findings and implications. *Personnel and Guidance Journal, 60*, 435–439.

Fox, R., & Cooper, M. (1998). The effects of suicide on the private practitioner: A professional and personal perspective. *Clinical Social Work Journal, 26*(2), 143–157.

Freudenberger, H. J. (1974). Staff burn-out. *Journal of Social Issues, 30,* 159–165.

Freudenberger, H. J. (1975). The staff burnout syndrome in alternative institutions. *Psychotherapy: Theory, Research, and Practice, 12,* 73–82.

Freudenberger, H. J. (1977). Burn-out: Occupational hazard of child care workers. *Child Care Quarterly, 6,* 90–99.

Freudenberger, H. J., & Robbins, A. (1979). The hazards of being a psychoanalyst. *Psychoanalytic Review, 66,* 275–296.

Friedman, M., & Rosenman, R. (1974). *Type A behavior and your heart.* Greenwich, CT: Fawcett.

Gentry, J. E., Baranowsky, A. B., & Dunning, K. (2002). ARP: The accelerated recovery program (ARP) for compassion fatigue. In C. R. Figley (Ed.), *Treating compassion fatigue* (pp. 123–137). New York: Brunner/Routledge.

Giebels, E., & Janssen, O. (2005). Conflict stress and reduced well-being at work: The buffering effect of third-party help. *European Journal of Work and Organizational Psychology, 14*(2), 137–155.

Glasser, W. (1985). *Control theory: A new explanation about how we control our lives.* New York: Harper & Row.

Golembiewski, R. T., & Munzenrider, R. F. (1993). Health-related covariants of phases of burnout: A replication. *Organization Development Journal, 11,* 1–12.

Golembiewski, R. T., Munzenrider, R. F., Scherb, K., & Billingsley, W. (1992). Burnout and "psychiatric" cases: Early evidence of an association. *Anxiety, Stress and Coping: An International Journal, 5,* 69–78.

Golembiewski, R. T., Munzenrider, R. F., & Stevenson, J. G. (1986). *Stress in organizations: Toward a phase model of burnout.* New York: Praeger.

Gorter, R., Albrecht, G., Hoostraten, J., & Eijkman, M. (1999). Factor validity of the Maslach Burnout Inventory—Dutch version (MBI-NL) among dentists. *Journal of Organizational Behavior, 20*(2), 209–217.

Greenglass, E., Fiksenbaum, L., & Burke, R. (1996). Components of social support, buffering effects and burnout: Implications for psychological functioning. *Anxiety, Stress, and Coping, 9*(3), 185–197.

Grossi, G., Perski, A., Ekstedt, M., Johansson, T., Lindstrom, M., & Holm, K. (2005). The morning salivary cortisol response in burnout. *Journal of Psychosomatic Research, 59*(2), 103–111.

Grouse, A. S. (1984). The effects of organizational stress on inpatient psychiatric medication patterns. *American Journal of Psychiatry, 141,* 878–881.

Hafkenscheid, A. (2005). Event countertransference and vicarious traumatization: Theoretically valid and clinically useful concepts? *European Journal of Psychotherapy, Counseling and Health, 7*(3), 159–168.

Halbesleben, J. R. (2006). Sources of social support and burnout: Meta-analytic test of the Conservation of Resources model. *Journal of Applied Psychology, 91*(5), 1134–1145.

Harrison, R. L., & Westwood, M. J. (2009). Preventing vicarious traumatization of mental health therapists: Identifying protective practices. *Psychotherapy: Theory, Research, Practice, Training 46*(2), 203–219.

Hoeksma, J. H., Guy, J. D., Brown, C. K., & Brady, J. L. (1993). The relationship between psychotherapist burnout and satisfaction with leisure activities. *Psychotherapy in Private Practice, 12,* 51–57.

Horowitz, M., Wilner, N., & Alvarez, W. (1979). Impact of Events Scale: A measure of subjective stress. *Psychosomatic Medicine, 41*(3), 209–218.

Jayaratne, S., Vinokur-Kaplan, D., & Chess, W. A. (1995). The importance of personal control: A comparison of social workers in private practice and public agency settings. *Journal of Applied Social Sciences, 19,* 47–59.

Johnson, C. N. E., & Hunter, M. (1997). Vicarious traumatization in counsellors working in the New South Wales Sexual Assault Service: An exploratory study. *Work and Stress, 11*(4), 319–328.

Kahn, W. A. (2005). *Holding fast: The struggle to create resilient caregiving organizations.* Philadelphia: Brunner/Routledge.

Kennedy, A. (2006, November). Know when to say "no" and let go. *Counseling Today, 1,* 22–23.

Kesler, K. D. (1990). Burnout: A multimodal approach to assessment and resolution. *Elementary School Guidance & Counseling, 24,* 303–311.

Killian, K. D. (2008). Helping till it hurts? A multimethod study of compassion fatigue, burnout, and self-care in clinicians working with trauma survivors. *Traumatology, 14*(2), 32–44.

King, L. A., King, D. W., Leskin, G., & Foy, D. W. (1995). The Los Angeles Symptom Checklist: A self-report measure of posttraumatic stress disorder. *Assessment, 2*(1), 1–17.

Kobasa, S. (1979). Stressful life events, personality, and health: An inquiry into hardiness. *Journal of Personality and Social Psychology, 37,* 1–11.

Koeske, G. F., & Kelly, T. (1995). The impact of overinvolvement on burnout and job satisfaction. *American Journal of Orthopsychiatry, 65,* 282–292.

Koeske, G. F., Kirk, S. A., & Koeske, R. D. (1993). Coping with job stress: Which strategies work best? *Journal of Occupational and Organizational Psychology, 66,* 319–335.

LaFauci Schutt, J. M. (2009). Personal and environmental predictors of posttraumatic stress in emergency management professionals. *Dissertation Abstracts International: Section A. Humanities and Social Sciences, 69*(1), 483.

Lawson, G., & Myers, J. E. (2011). Wellness, professional quality of life, and career-sustaining behaviors: What keeps us well? *Journal of Counseling & Development, 89*(2), 163–171.

Lawson, G., Venart, E., Hazler, R. J., & Kottler, J. A. (2007). Toward a culture of counselor wellness. *Journal of Humanistic Counseling, Education, and Development, 46,* 5–19.

Lawson, S. K. (2009). Hospice social workers: The incidence of compassion fatigue. *Dissertation Abstracts International: Section A. Humanities and Social Sciences, 69*(8), 4505.

Lazarus, A. A. (1976). *Multimodal behavior therapy.* New York: Springer.

Lee, R. T., & Ashforth, B. E. (1993). A longitudinal study of burnout among supervisors and managers: Comparisons between the Leiter and Maslach and Golembiewski models. *Organizational Behavior and Human Decision Processes, 54*, 369–398.

Lee, R. T., & Ashforth, B. E. (1996). A meta-analytic examination of the correlates of the three dimensions of job burnout. *Journal of Applied Psychology, 81*(2), 123–133.

Lee, S. M., Baker, C. R., Cho, S. H., Heckathorn, D. E., Holland, M. W., Newgent, R. A., et al. (2007). Development and initial psychometrics of the Counselor Burnout Inventory. *Measurement and Evaluation in Counseling and Development,40*(2), 142–154.

Lee, S. M, Cho, S. H., Kissinger, D., & Ogle, N. (2010). A typology of burnout in professional counselors. *Journal of Counseling & Development, 88*(2), 131–138.

Leiter, M. P., & Maslach, C. (2005). *Banishing burnout: Six strategies for improving your relationship with work.* San Francisco: Jossey-Bass.

Linley, A., Joseph, S., & Loumidis, K. (2005). Trauma work, sense of coherence and positive and negative changes in therapists. *Psychotherapy and Psychosomatics, 74*(3), 185–188.

Lyndall, D., & Bicknell, J. (2001). Trauma and the therapist: The experience of therapists working with the perpetrators of sexual abuse. *Australasian Journal of Disaster and Trauma Studies, 5*(1), 1–12.

Main, B. (2008). The effects of treating sex offenders on treatment providers who have a history of child sexual abuse. *Dissertation Abstracts International: Section B. The Sciences and Engineering, 68*(12), 1960.

Maslach, C. (1976). Burned-out. *Human Behavior, 5*, 16–22.

Maslach, C. (1982a). *Burnout: The cost of caring.* Upper Saddle River, NJ: Prentice Hall.

Maslach, C. (1982b). Understanding burnout: Definitional issues in analyzing a complex phenomenon. In W. S. Paine (Ed.), *Job stress and burnout* (pp. 29–40). Newbury Park, CA: Sage.

Maslach, C., & Jackson, S. E. (1981a). *The Maslach Burnout Inventory.* Palo Alto, CA: Consulting Psychologists Press.

Maslach, C., & Jackson, S. E. (1981b). The measurement of experienced burnout. *Journal of Occupational Behavior, 2*, 99–113.

Maslach, C., Jackson, S. E., & Leiter, M. P. (1996). *Maslach Burnout Inventory–GS manual.* Palo Alto, CA: Consulting Psychologist's Press.

McCann, I. L., & Pearlman, L. A. (1990). Vicarious traumatization: A framework for understanding the psychological effects of working with victims. *Journal of Traumatic Stress, 3*(1), 131–149.

McKnight, D. J., & Glass, D. C. (1995). Perceptions of control, burnout, and depressive symptomatology: A replication and extension. *Journal of Consulting and Clinical Psychology, 63*, 490–494.

McRaith, C. F. (1991, April). *Coping with society's secret: Social support, job stress, and burnout among therapists treating victims of sexual abuse.* Paper presented at the Fifteenth Annual Convening of Crisis Intervention Personnel, Chicago.

Melamed, S., Meir, E. I., & Samson, A. (1995). The benefits of personality–leisure congruence: Evidence and implications. *Journal of Leisure Research, 27*, 25–40.

Melamed, S., Shirom, A., Toker, S., Berliner, S., & Shapira, I. (2006). Burnout and risk of cardiovascular disease: Evidence, possible causal paths, and promising research directions. *Psychological Bulletin, 132*(3), 327–353.

Melchior, M., van der Berg, A., Halfens, R., & Abu-Saad, H. (1997). Burnout and the work environment of nurses in psychiatric long-stay care settings. *Social Psychiatry and Psychiatric Epidemiology, 32*(3), 158–164.

Meyers, T. W., & Cornille, T. A. (2002). The trauma of working with traumatized children. In C. R. Figley (Ed.), *Treating compassion fatigue* (pp. 39–55). New York: Brunner/Routledge.

Miller, D. (1995). Stress and burnout among health care staff working with people affected by HIV. *British Journal of Guidance and Counselling, 23*, 19–31.

Mitchell, M. D. (1977). Consultant burnout. In J. W. Pfeiffer & J. E. Jones (Eds.), *1977 annual handbook for group facilitators* (pp. 143–146). La Jolla, CA: University Associates.

Moos, R. H. (1981). *Work Environment Scale manual.* Palo Alto, CA: Consulting Psychologists Press.

Moran, C. C. (2002). Humor as a moderator of compassion fatigue. In C. R. Figley (Ed.), *Treating compassion fatigue* (pp. 139–154). Philadelphia: Brunner/Routledge.

Morkides, C. (2009, May). From burning bright to simply burned out. *Counseling Today.*

Myers, J. E., & Sweeney, T. J. (Eds.). (2005). *Counseling for wellness.* Alexandria, VA: American Counseling Association.

Myers, J. E., Sweeney, T. J., & Witmer, J. E. (2000). The wheel of wellness counseling for wellness: A holistic model for treatment planning. *Journal of Counseling & Development, 78*(3), 251–266.

Oktay, J. S. (1992). Burnout in hospital social workers who work with AIDS patients. *Social Work, 37*, 432–437.

Paine, W. S. (1982). Overview of burnout stress syndromes and the 1980's. In W. S. Paine (Ed.), *Job stress and burnout* (pp. 11–25). Newbury Park, CA: Sage.

Patterson, C. H. (1980). *Theories of counseling and psychotherapy* (3rd ed.). New York: Harper & Row.

Pearlman, L. A., & Mac Ian, P. S. (1995). Vicarious traumatization: An empirical study of the effects of trauma work on trauma therapists. *Professional Psychology, 26*(6), 558–565.

Pearlman, L. A., & Saakvitne, K. W. (1995a). *Trauma and the therapist.* New York: Norton.

Pearlman, L. A., & Saakvitne, K. W. (1995b). Treating therapists with vicarious traumatization and secondary traumatic stress disorders. In C. R. Figley (Ed.), *Compassion fatigue: Coping with secondary traumatic stress disorder in those who treat the traumatized* (pp. 150–177). New York: Brunner-Mazel.

Piedmont, R. L. (1993). A longitudinal analysis of burnout in the health care setting: The role of personal dispositions. *Journal of Personality Assessment, 61,* 457–473.

Pines, A. (1983). On burnout and the buffering effects of social support. In B. A. Farber (Ed.), *Stress and burnout in the human service professions* (pp. 155–173). New York: Pergamon Press.

Pines, A., & Aronson, E. (1988). *Career burnout: Causes and cures.* New York: Free Press.

Powell, W. E. (1994). The relationship between feelings of alienation and burnout in social work. *Families in Society, 75,* 229–235.

Reese, M. T. (2009). Compassion fatigue and spirituality with emergency health care providers. *Dissertation Abstracts International: Section B. The Sciences and Engineering, 69*(12), 7843.

Riggar, T. F. (1985). *Stress burnout: An annotated bibliography.* Carbondale: Southern Illinois University Press.

Ringenbach, R. (2009). A comparison between counselors who practice meditation and those who do not on compassion fatigue, compassion satisfaction, burnout, and self-compassion. *Dissertation Abstracts International: Section B. The Science and Engineering, 69*(6), 3820.

Rodesch, C. K. (1994, April). *Keeping the counselor sane.* Paper presented at the Eighteenth Annual Convening of Crisis Intervention Personnel, Chicago.

Saakvitne, K. W. (2002). Shared trauma: The therapist's increased vulnerability. *Psychoanalytic Dialogues, 12*(3), 443–449.

Saakvitne, K. W., & Pearlman, L. A. (1996). *Transforming the pain: A workbook on vicarious traumatization.* New York: Norton.

Salston, M. D., & Figley, C. R. (2003). Secondary traumatic stress effects of working with survivors of criminal victimization. *Journal of Traumatic Stress, 16*(2), 167–174.

Savicki, V. (2002). *Burnout across thirteen cultures: Stress and coping in child and youth care workers.* Westport, CT: Praeger.

Savicki, V., & Cooley, E. J. (1982). Implications of burnout research and theory for counselor education. *Personnel and Guidance Journal, 60,* 415–419.

Savicki, V., & Cooley, E. J. (1987). The relationship of work environment and client contact to burnout in mental health professionals. *Journal of Counseling and Development, 65,* 249–252.

Schaufeli, W. B. (2006). The balance of give and take: Toward a social exchange model of burnout. *Revue Internationale de Psychologie Sociale, 19*(1), 87–131.

Sculley, R. (1983). The work-setting support group: A means of preventing burnout. In B. A. Farber (Ed.), *Stress and burnout in the human service professions* (pp. 198–212). New York: Pergamon Press.

Sek-yum, S. N. (1993). Occupational stress and burnout among outreaching social workers in Hong Kong. *International Social Work, 36,* 101–117.

Selye, H. (1956). *The stress of life.* New York: McGraw-Hill.

Selye, H. (1974). *Stress without distress.* Philadelphia: Lippincott.

Shinn, M., & Mørch, H. (1983). A tripartite model of coping with burnout. In B. A. Farber (Ed.), *Stress and burnout in the human service professions* (pp. 227–239). New York: Pergamon Press.

Simpson, L. R. (2006). Level of spirituality as a predictor of the occurrence of compassion fatigue among counseling professionals in Mississippi. *Dissertation Abstracts International: Section A. Humanities and Social Sciences, 66*(6), 3223.

Spicuzza, F. J., & Devoe, M. W. (1982). Burnout in the helping professions: Mutual aid as self-help. *Personnel and Guidance Journal, 61,* 95–98.

Stamm, B. H. (2002). Measuring compassion satisfaction as well as fatigue: Developmental history of the Compassion Satisfaction and Fatigue Test. In C. R. Figley (Ed.), *Treating compassion fatigue* (pp. 107–119). New York: Brunner/ Routledge.

Stamm, B. H. (2005). *The ProQOL manual.* Towson, NY: Sidran Press.

Stark, E. (1994). Stress! It's all relative . . . and relatively easy to manage. In R. Yarian (Ed.), *Health 94/95* (15th ed., pp. 62–65). Guilford, CT: Dushkin.

Sullivan, L. (2004). Staff development and secondary traumatic stress among AIDS staff. *Dissertation Abstracts International: Section A. Humanities and Social Sciences, 64*(4), 2365.

Thomas, A. M., & Levitt, D. (2010, August). Self-care: An ethical obligation and preventive tool. *Counseling Today,* 44–46.

Thomas, B. J. (2007). The relationship between affect balance, self-care behavior, and secondary traumatic stress reactions. *Dissertation Abstracts International: Section B. The Sciences and Engineering, 67*(8), 4145.

Thomas, R. B., & Wilson, J. P. (2004). Issues and controversies in the understanding and diagnosis of compassion fatigue, vicarious traumatization and secondary traumatic stress disorder. *International Journal of Emergency Mental Health, 6*(2), 81–92.

Thornton, P. T. (1992). The relation of coping, appraisal, and burnout in mental health workers. *Journal of Psychology, 126,* 261–271.

Toker, S., Shirom, A., Shapira, I., Berliner, S., & Melamed, S. (2005). The association between burnout, depression, anxiety, and inflammation biomarkers: C-reactive protein and fibrinogen in men and women. *Journal of Occupational Health Psychology, 10*(4), 344–362.

Tubesing, D. A., & Strosahl, S. G. (1976). *Wholistic health centers: Survey research report.* Hinsdale, IL: Society for Wholistic Medicine.

Tubesing, N. L., & Tubesing, D. A. (1982). The treatment of choice: Selecting stress skills to suit the individual and the situation. In W. S. Paine (Ed.), *Job stress and burnout* (pp. 155–172). Newbury Park, CA: Sage.

Turnipseed, D. L. (1994). An analysis of the influence of work environment variables and moderators on the burnout syndrome. *Journal of Applied Social Psychology, 24,* 782–800.

Van Auken, S. (1979). Youth counselor burnout. *Personnel and Guidance Journal, 58,* 143–144.

Warnath, C. F., & Shelton, J. L. (1976). The ultimate disappointment: The burned out counselor. *Personnel and Guidance Journal, 55,* 172–175.

Watkins, C. E. (1983). Burnout in counseling practice: Some potential professional and personal hazards of becoming a counselor. *Personnel and Guidance Journal, 61,* 304–308.

Webb, N. B. (2007). *Play therapy with children in crisis: Individual, group, and family treatment* (3rd ed.). New York: Guilford Press.

Wee, D. F., & Myers, D. (2002). Stress response of mental health workers following disaster: The Oklahoma City bombing. In C. R. Figley (Ed.), *Treating compassion fatigue* (pp. 57–83). New York: Brunner/Routledge.

Wee, D. F., & Myers, D. (2003). Compassion satisfaction, compassion fatigue, and critical incidents stress management. *International Journal of Emergency Mental Health, 5*(1), 33–37.

Wright, T., & Bonett, D. (1997). The contribution of burnout to work performance. *Journal of Organizational Behavior, 18*(5), 491–499.

PART IV

No Man's Land

Facing Disaster

The last part of this book is aptly named "No Man's Land" because it deals with the large-scale crisis and megacrisis that result when disaster strikes. The chaos that greets survivors and first responders of large-scale crises or megadisasters is very much like the desolate, wrecked landscape that lies between two battle lines in trench warfare. What has been called the "fog of war" holds true here.

The final chapter of this book is divided into two parts. The first part deals with how the system operates in response to a disaster. Large-scale disaster can never be taken out of the context of its systemic impact. The second part deals with the people who go into that no man's land and the survivors who are there to greet them. It is our belief that a lot of you who aspire to a career in this field will be going into wrecked landscapes like this.

CHAPTER **17**

Disaster Response

A Brief History of Disaster Mental Health Provision

When the first edition of this book was published in 1988, it didn't have a chapter on disaster response. The simple reason was that we would have been hard pressed to fill up three pages of print on theory, research, or practice with regard to the provision of mental health services after a large-scale disaster. Although the federal government has been involved in disaster relief since the 19th century, until recently it has paid very little attention to the psychological aftershocks of a disaster. It wasn't until 1974, as part of a major overhaul of disaster policy, that the Disaster Relief Act was passed. In that bill was section 413, which authorized the National Institute of Mental Health (NIMH) to supply counseling services to victims of disasters and also provided funds to train professionals in the provision of mental health services to disaster victims.

We believe that the notion that people would need mental health assistance after a disaster has roots similar to those of the crisis movement itself. It appears that at least four distinct variables fell into place prior to 2000 to make this happen. First was the birth of community mental health, authorized by the Community Mental Health act of 1963, which put mental health workers in places like Rapid City, South Dakota, Wilkes-Barre, Pennsylvania, and Logan County, West Virginia. These were "hometown" folks, not bureaucrats in some far away capital city, and they would give voice to the mental misery survivors were suffering after a large-scale natural disaster.

Second was the classification of PTSD as a personality disorder in the DSM-III in 1980. That medical classification acknowledged and legitimized the concept of people suffering enduring mental problems after direct exposure to a life-threatening event. That diagnosis can admirably fit survivors of disasters.

Third was the American Red Cross's decision in the early 1990s to establish a mental health certification program after hurricane Hugo and the Loma Prieta earthquake in 1989. Indeed, the American Red Cross separated out disaster mental health from its disaster nursing mainly because of its workers' breaking down from prolonged field placements in the back-to-back disasters of hurricane Hugo and the Loma Prieta earthquake (Morris, 2011).

Fourth was the women's movement during the 1960s and '70s, which brought increased awareness of how often trauma strikes families and what its aftershocks do to a family whose entire belongings have been swept, blown, or burned away. When combined, these variables would play a major role in moving the concept of disaster mental health from an idle backwater into a tsunami of disaster mental health assistance in 2011. Given that movement, you are now going to read a whole lot more in this seventh edition than the few pages we might have scraped together in the first edition.

If you harken back to Chapter 1, where we talked about the coalescing of grassroots movements into a large voice that attracts attention from the media, and soon after that legislatures, you will begin to understand why specific places like Rapid City, South Dakota, Wilkes-Barre, Pennsylvania, and Logan County, West Virginia, became important players in the birthing of disaster mental health. All three of these places suffered terrible flooding in 1972, and Logan County became particularly notorious because of a mining company's failure to maintain the Buffalo Creek dam, which ruptured. The resulting flood waters at Buffalo Creek killed 125 people and wrecked or badly damaged 1,500 homes. To make matters worse, God or Mother Nature didn't cause the disaster but the coal company did, so there was someone to focus attention on that could have prevented the disaster.

Local mental health providers were overwhelmed by survivors needing psychological assistance in all three places, and both state and federal officials were slow to react in providing help. This issue caught the eyes and ears of reporters, and a great deal of publicity was garnered in support of providing mental health assistance to disaster survivors. So, legislators who were already attuned to the notion that victims would need psychological help thought it made good common sense (and particularly good reelection sense) to include mental health funding in the 1974 bill.

There was little research to back up the notion that a lot of people would need psychotherapy after a disaster, but that made little difference given the publicity these three floods received. The few mental health workers that were on scene and their cries for help made good subjects for interviews. One of the best examples of how well disaster mental health assistance could be played in the media was the San Fernando Child Guidance clinic that decided to get into the trauma game after an earthquake struck the San Fernando Valley in California in 1971. The clinic announced that they were offering counseling services for children who had been in the quake area. Over the next few weeks they counseled more than 500 children in the quake area and got the attention of the national media, which generated headlines like "Quake proofing kids." Dr. Stephen Howard, director of clinical services, got nationwide attention when he declared in an interview with the *New York Times* that the American Red Cross's attitude of "keeping a stiff upper lip" wouldn't work and that survivors needed to "talk about their issues" (Morris, 2011).

Return now to Rapid City, South Dakota. The local government's small number of overwhelmed mental health professionals and the federal government's lack of interest in the survivors' plight prompted a call for help from a steering committee the local mayor organized that reached all the way to the Denver, Colorado, office of the National Institute of Mental Health. The NIMH finally responded by sending psychiatric help to the beleaguered city. The problems of adequate mental health provision that were uncovered at Rapid City motivated U.S. senators from the state to become very active in funding these provisions for the Disaster Recovery Act.

In Wilkes-Barre a model program developed by local community mental health providers and the National Institute of Mental Health served as a blueprint for the creation of disaster mental health programs. Called Operation Outreach, one component of this program was the training of outreach workers to go out and meet survivors as they tried to reassemble their lives and provide basic mental health services. Their initial attempts to provide those services were not accepted kindly by the survivors until the workers started giving them assistance in getting the basic necessities of living back in their lives. Then the survivors started to take them into their confidence. Please note that this is a hard lesson to learn for zealous mental health practitioners who volunteer to go to a disaster. Like the workers at Wilkes-Barre, and Dr. Holly Branthoover whom you will get to meet later in the chapter, it is about moving boxes, procuring lice kits, and having your underarm deodorant fail before you ever get to the counseling stage.

Finally, rescue workers in the Buffalo Creek dam failure in Logan County noticed many of the symptoms in survivors that would later be formalized into PTSD criteria. The resulting lawsuit against the mining company whose failed dam had caused the Buffalo Creek disaster brought a number of famous mental health experts into the courtroom. One of them was Robert Lofton, a psychiatrist from Yale, who had done extensive study on Vietnam veterans and would later lay the foundation blocks for what would become PTSD from his work with them. He recognized some of the same pathology in the flood survivors and testified that everybody in Buffalo Creek was affected (Morris, 2011).

A group of people from all three of these disasters were gathered by the medical advisor to the Office of Emergency Preparedness (then the leader in disaster mitigation). There was general agreement that there was not a large outbreak of mental illness, but it was acknowledged that the emotional security of a large number of individuals had been compromised (Morris, 2011). Thus was born the Disaster Relief Act of 1974. This act then evolved into the Stafford Disaster Relief and Emergency Assistance Act of 1986, whose section 416 provided for enhanced mental health services to disaster survivors.

To really understand why mental health generally did not get front row status for a long time, you need to understand that the U.S. government's historical approach to disasters was piecemeal and spread over a variety of agencies. It wasn't until 1978 that the Federal Emergency Management Agency (FEMA) was authorized. It absorbed a variety of agencies that ranged from insurance to weather prediction to civil defense to dam and building safety to counterterrorism. It essentially became a catchall for everything that might create some kind of disaster in the United States. After 9/11, FEMA itself was absorbed into the Department of Homeland Security, becoming the Department of Emergency Preparedness and Response Directorate, which pretty much put FEMA in the back seat politically, financially, and prioritywise. After the debacle of hurricane Katrina, FEMA once again regained standalone status as a department. So, it is not just mental health that has been given short shrift, but the overall coordination of natural and human-made disasters in the United States. So why has all this now changed?

Since 1974 there has been a huge change, so that now psychological services and the people who provide them are seen as an integral part of disaster intervention by the federal government (Dodgen & Meed, 2010). The trauma business meandered along in the 1990s, but school shootings such as Columbine focused attention on disaster in suburbia, the carnage of 9/11 put trauma back up in lights on the national marquee, and the horrific foul-ups by FEMA during hurricane Katrina sealed the notion that mental health would be an important part of any disaster in the 20th century in the United States.

In the aftermath of Katrina, the government poured $52 million for mental health support into Project Recovery in Mississippi, Project Rebound in Alabama, and Louisiana Spirit in Louisiana. That sum of money was second only to the $132 million that went in to mental health services after 9/11 (Morris, 2011).

The emerging concern is how very large intervention systems interact with one another to deal with large-scale crises and megacrises that may arise at the national, state, or community level and directly or indirectly affect neighborhoods, families, and ultimately the individual. Part of the problem is that crisis response systems have not been upgraded along with the times. Remember from Chapter 1 that large disaster relief systems in the United States that are designed to physically aid communities after catastrophes are about 100 years old (Echterling & Wylie, 1999). The field of individual crisis intervention as it is applied in a scientific and systematic manner is about 60 years old (Lindemann, 1944). Systematic and comprehensive intervention by the United States government is about

30 years old (Federal Emergency Management Agency, n.d.). The addition of psychological crisis intervention systems and their incorporation into those large macrosystems are about 35 years old—if we are very generous in our time estimation.

While there has been a great deal of research since 9/11 on what kinds of mental health intervention and techniques work on individuals (Watson, Brymer, & Bonanno, 2011), there has been very little research in large-scale *ergonomics*. Cognitive and organizational ergonomics is the rather exotic scientific discipline concerned with understanding the interactions among humans and other elements of a system. It is the profession that applies theory, principles, data, and methods to product design in order to optimize human well-being and overall system performance—which also applies to coordinating, collaborating, and allocating resources after a disaster. While system interfaces with individuals and ergonomics are pretty cerebral and exotic and not likely to be the topic of discussion over coffee at Starbucks or beer at a sports bar, understanding how those systems work, what effects they have in the fight against terrorism and in large-scale natural disasters, and the mental health issues that go with them is critically important. In a compelling article on this subject, Nickerson (2011) points out that his literature search turned up very little on how ergonomics could help deal with the effects of terrorism when they occur. That research is compelling because, over and over, communication between human beings operating in different systems becomes problematic. Former members of the 9/11 Commission, meeting on the 10th anniversary of that act of terrorism, stated that there were still problems of communication among first responders (Callahan, 2011).

Further, there is little research on how these large systems work—or, in fact, whether they do work—in a palliative psychological manner with various subsystems or individuals (Dziegielewski & Powers, 2005; Litz & Gibson, 2006). Finally, even less is known about what effects vicarious traumatization has on large systems, or indeed what we should do about the effects that instantaneous real-time electronic media can have on various subsystems and the individual (Ursano & Friedman, 2006). How well systems communicate with one another and understanding the effects of rapid changes in technological, geophysical, and societal forces on prevention, intervention, and postvention are key issues in the mitigation of a disaster (Aten et al., 2011; Stokols et al., 2009).

To the contrary, research into evidence-based post-trauma practices for individuals has exploded since 9/11 in the quest to find the best way to help people with mental health issues postdisaster (Watson, Brymer & Bonanno, 2011). The acronym PTSD was known to few people in the first edition of this book in 1988—even our students! Now PTSD has become a household abbreviation for somebody who is traumatized. Professional organizations have ramped up their focus on trauma. Division 56, Trauma Psychology, has been formed by the American Psychological Association and is one of its fastest growing divisions. The Council on Accreditation of Counseling and Related Educational Programs (CACREP), the accrediting body for counselors, has mandated crisis intervention as part of a required curriculum, as has the National Association of School Psychologists. The special September issue of the *American Psychologist*, the main journal of the American Psychological Association, is devoted to the role that psychology has played in disasters since 9/11. Government, government-subsidized agencies, and professional organizations have published psychoeducational materials that range from mental health reactions after a disaster (National Center for PTSD, n.d.b) to talking to children about the Gulf oil spill (SAMHSA, n.d.) and providing schools with memorial guides to 9/11 (American School Counselor Association, 2011). Two centers for dissemination of information and research, the National Center for PTSD (n.d.b) and the National Child Traumatic Stress Network (NCTSN, n.d.), have come into existence in the last 10 years as a direct or indirect consequence of 9/11, Katrina, and Columbine High School.

Where the World Is

The United States is not alone in its changed attitudes toward mental health provision after a natural disaster. Australia has been one of the leaders in the area because of the many natural disasters it has faced. Beverly Raphael, a professor of psychiatry in Australia, has been in the forefront of disaster research and practice with her landmark books *The Anatomy of Bereavement* (1984), *When Disaster Strikes* (1986), and *Disaster Response Handbook* (2000), and dozens of research articles, chapters, and edited books on trauma and disaster.

Europe has established the European Network for Traumatic Stress (TENTS, n.d.) in response to a need for consensus on what evidenced-based outcomes work. TENTS has been funded by the European Union and has built Europewide networks of expertise in the psychosocial management of victims of natural and other disasters. It provides services, expertise, and support to areas of the Union that lack resources and availability of trained personnel (TENTS, n.d.).

Internationally, the United Nations' Inter-Agency Standing Committee (IASC, 2007) has published *IASC Guidelines on Mental Health and Psychosocial Input Support in Emergency Situations*. Those guidelines are being used by countries as small and remote as Nepal to put into operation their disaster responses (Jordans et al., 2010).

International Terrorism and Human-Made Disasters

The ecological, contextual model of crisis intervention, based on ecosystem theory that has emerged on the international scene, is characterized by continuously accelerating events in dynamically changing cultures and environments (Conyne et al., 2003; James, Cogdal; & Gilliland, 2003; James & Gilliland, 2003, pp. 341–342, Myer & Moore, 2006; Norris et al., 2006). Foremost among these events in the United States has been the September 11, 2001, hijackings and terrorist attacks and destruction of the World Trade Center towers in New York City, the attack on the Pentagon, and the crashed airliner in Pennsylvania. These tragedies caused untold grief, loss of property, loss of life, economic damage, and a change in the attitudes of most Americans regarding safety and security (Bass & Yep, 2002; Pyszczynski, Solomon, & Greenberg, 2002). The actions following 9/11 also set in motion other unprecedented events, such as the passage of the Homeland Security Act by the U.S. Congress and the invasions of Afghanistan and Iraq, and placed security in the United States at wartime levels. Practically every American had the feeling of having been individually attacked (Brainerd, 2002) and that we were, indeed, at war.

Add to 9/11 other terrifying events—the bombing of the Murrah Federal Building in Oklahoma City, the attacks on students in high schools from Littleton, Colorado, to Springfield, Oregon, to college students at Virginia Tech University and Northern Illinois University—and there is good reason for most Americans to think the United States is no longer a sanctuary but a battleground. Across the world, events such as the taking of hostages by Chechens and their resulting deaths in a rescue attempt in a Moscow theater and a southern Russian school, Palestinian suicide bombings in the streets of Israel, Muslim radicals' bombing of a nightclub and hotel in Bali and Jakarta and trains in Madrid, drug gang wars in Mexico that approach total war, embassies and nightclubs blown up in Africa and Asia by al Qaida, and the postwar chaos in Iraq and Afghanistan all send clear messages that the world is an unsafe place and that terror may strike unannounced anywhere and at any time. As a result, the hypervigilance of being constantly on guard, the economic loss because of these attacks, and the social and financial expenses of guarding against them cause a variety of previously unknown stressors to appear that impact and crosscut entire nations, cultures, and ecosystems.

Disaster in the form of terrorism has its own special brand of traumatic wake for survivors and has the potential to have metastasizing effects across large systems (Huddy & Feldman, 2011; Morgan, Wisneski, & Skitka, 2011; Ursano & Friedman, 2006). This is true because of the unpredictability of the when, where, and to whom it will happen. Further, the seeming randomness creates fear and anxiety because there is no assurance it will not happen again, and where is anybody's guess. The use of insidious means such as poison gas, germ warfare, or nuclear arms causes horror and incredulity at their seemingly immoral use in the business of mass murder. Information is often inaccurate or highly controlled by the government, which creates uncertainty and anxiety. Increased, constant hypervigilance creates constant and heightened anxiety, which causes both immediate and long-term physical health problems.

Media coverage enhances the horror of gruesome death and injuries. Constant viewing of scenes of death and destruction increases trauma risk. Further compounding the trauma is the aftermath of the terrorist attack with ruinous financial loss and frustration and anxiety at the government's inability to act or bring the perpetrators to justice—particularly when they are outside the country's borders. Finally, there is the added difficulty of finding victim services and mental health professionals who have the know-how to deal with the unique issues that terrorist victims bring with them (Dziegielewski & Sumner, 2005; Myers & Wee, 2005, pp. 247–248). Pastel and Ritchie (2006) aptly call these weapons of mass *disruption* because of the profound psychological ripple effects they cause.

The Israelis are no strangers to terror. Practically all Israeli children carry cell phones so that they can immediately contact their parents and let them know they are safe after bombing or rocket attacks. It is somewhat chilling that one of the favorite children's costumes

during the Israeli Purim holiday (somewhat equivalent to Halloween in the United States) among ultraorthodox Jews was a replica of the "Zaka" uniform. Zaka is an ultraorthodox volunteer organization dedicated to ensuring proper burial according to Jewish rituals. In the immediate aftermath of a terrorist attack, they search for body parts to bring as much of the body as possible to burial (Galai-Gat, 2004). After Galai-Gat delivered the paper just cited at the Annual Convening of Crisis Intervention Personnel, she related how amazed she was that people could come and go so freely from the downtown Chicago hotel where the convention was being held. Thus in a changing world, the question arises, "As go the Israelis, shall the rest of the world go also, and does our mental health system go with it?"

Terrorism brings unique challenges to mental health professionals when weapons of mass destruction are used. The ratio of physical dead and wounded to psychologically afflicted is astounding. Obhu and associates (1997) found that in the Tokyo subway gas attack 11 people died but up to 9,000 people sought medical care because they *thought* they had been gassed. There is also the potential for organic mental disorders along with standard stress reactions given the type of weapon used. Medical isolation and quarantine can create additional stress in individuals who may not be able to receive support from their social systems and in fact may be seen as lepers to be avoided (Flynn, 1998).

The worldview of individuals subjected to terrorist-generated disasters may be very different from others'. There is a good deal of evidence to indicate that these individuals experience PTSD, panic and anxiety disorders, and depression at a far greater and more intense rate than others who are subject to "natural" disasters (U.S. Department of Justice, 2000). While there has been progress, with the counseling field becoming more trauma aware (Shallcross, 2011) and the Red Cross making concerted efforts to provide crisis intervention training to wider segments of first responders, there is as yet little unified training for the sheer number of mental health providers needed in *any* large-scale disaster or megadisaster. This issue is even more pressing with the lack of expertise to deal specifically with terrorist acts (Myers & Wee, 2005, p. 251; Roberts, 2005).

Lastly, the mental health infrastructure itself may be destroyed or disabled by human-made or natural disasters or simply be overwhelmed by the staggering volume of people it will be expected to service. In her pictorial representation of early interventions with survivors of terrorist attacks, Galai-Gat (2004) showed a

Gary Larson cartoon of a crisis center going over a waterfall while on fire—a good analogy for the worldwide state of crisis intervention and what kinds of chaos ecosystemic crises can bring to local agencies, as witnessed by New Orleans mental health facilities attempting to get back into operation after being completely shut down by hurricane Katrina (Shraberg, 2006).

New Directions and New Visions

Crisis intervention is no longer just a one-on-one proposition. We would like to introduce you to what we and some others (Collins & Collins, 2005; Gist & Lubin, 1999; Kilmer et al., 2010; Myer & Moore, 2006; Stokols et al., 2009) believe will characterize more and more of what crisis intervention will become in the 21st century—ecosystemic crisis intervention in the wake of a large-scale crisis or megadisaster (James, Cogdal, & Gilliland, 2003). An ecosystemic crisis is one that reaches out and pervades at a minimum the community and perhaps whole regions or nations. It may be immediate and horrific, like 9/11, with a relatively small loss of life, but have immense ramifications and spread shockwaves around the world. It may slowly and surely spread out across whole continents and have the potential for a tremendous loss of life, such as the African AIDS epidemic or bird flu. It may be human-made, occur dramatically, and then have long-lasting environmental effects that span thousands of years and destroy the social and governing infrastructure of an entire region, such as the Chernobyl nuclear power plant explosion and contamination (Bromet, 1995). It may be malevolent terrorism, creating widespread fear and anger, such as 9/11. It may be a smorgasbord of natural disasters such as the tsunami that struck Japan or hurricane Katrina that drastically alter the landscape and the lives of those in the surrounding area.

In varying degrees, an ecosystemic crisis does all of the foregoing. An ecosystemic crisis not only creates victims who directly experience the traumatic event in widespread numbers, but also creates potential victims because of their vicarious experiencing of the event—even though they may be some geographical or psychological distance from the event itself (Chung et al., 2003; North, 2004; Shallcross, 2011).

This is particularly problematic because often insurance or other mental health-care providers do not recognize these groups of survivors as being in need of assistance (Galai-Gat, 2004). Therefore, the definition of an ecosystemic crisis used in this chapter is somewhat different from the definition of crisis as it applies to individuals that is used in the rest of the book. An *ecosystemic crisis* is any disruptive or destructive event that occurs at a rate and magnitude beyond the ability of the normal social process to control it. Unless dedicated resources are brought to ease the crisis, the integrity of the social fabric is generally degraded in the course of the event such that it becomes very difficult if not impossible to sustain the way of life as it was before the crisis occurred (Ren, 2000).

Although a number of theorists and researchers have examined wide-scale disasters and the collective experiences of the populations who experience them (Freedy & Hobfoll, 1995; Gist & Lubin, 1989; Hobfoll, 1988; Hobfoll & deVries, 1995; Kaplan, 1996), most of the literature focuses on a dissection of the individual's psychological responses (Kaniasty & Norris, 1999). Kaniasty and Norris (1999) propose that the individual's psychological response to disaster cannot be understood without considering the collective response that interacts with the political, cultural, environmental, and social realities of the ecosystem as it operated prior to and after the disaster.

Alternatively, on a very pragmatic and mundane level, the Federal Emergency Management Agency (FEMA) and its various departments spend a great deal of time and energy on providing education, information, and direct service in regard to operational responses to disasters of all kinds (Federal Emergency Management Agency, n.d.). However, what FEMA—or anyone, for that matter—doesn't do is determine how this all goes together, and as you will see in a short while, that had ominous implications when hurricane Katrina came ashore. What one also does not find is a way of making sense out of how crisis intervention strategies interface with the community-wide stressors people experience after a disaster and the various agencies that respond to help them.

Although the impact of community-wide and national traumatic events go back historically at least as far as Pompeii being buried by volcanic explosion nearly 2,000 years ago or the Black Plague killing millions of Europeans in the Middle Ages, the knowledge of those catastrophes and their resulting impact was slow to be felt because news of the disaster traveled only by word of mouth. Likewise, help could come only as fast as responders could spread the word and bring together resources that might arrive in horse-drawn carts or be carried on one's back. Often help was simply unavailable, as there was no known way to mitigate the spread of disease.

Communities were isolated, and when a natural or human-made disaster struck, it was typically felt only at the local level. Further, at the local level, the constituents were essentially of the same race, tribe, or clan, or other social identity and commonly held the same cultural, moral, and religious values. In short, until the 20th century, if Haiti suffered an earthquake, it was known and dealt with by the local community and perhaps the regional ruler. The prevailing philosophy was that people took care of themselves because they were the only ones affected by the traumatic event. In fact, if "strangers" had come to offer help, they probably would have been viewed with distrust and suspicion, given the insular cultural values of the time. The best that could be done proactively was to build cities that wouldn't be washed away by flood or blown away by winds, or to quarantine cities infected with disease. Historically, then, most crisis responses were by passive, preventive means that were meant to minimize the damage before it occurred. Little could be done after the fact to minimize the deaths, economic loss, or societal disintegration.

It should also be understood that there is a rather spirited debate today in world health circles as to whether there is in the Third World any need for a Western world mental health disaster mitigation plan as opposed to the need to obtain basic necessities for survival. PTSD is seen as a Western cultural artifact contrived to justify and propagate the medical mental health model (Summerfield, 2005). To the contrary, others do not see PTSD as a cultural artifact, but indeed a phenomenon that is cross-cultural in nature, and that to deny it would be a terrible professional error and subvert the prevention of suffering (deVries, 1998; Dyregrov et al., 2002).

With the advent of the industrial and information ages, active crisis intervention came to mean that a whole society could be rapidly mobilized and coordinated to reshape the total dynamics of a crisis by using the machines and the command/control/communications/intelligence systems that have evolved in the last two centuries (Ren, 2000). With the condensing of geographic and communication distances, a fundamental but essential trend is that a crisis can no longer be contained within an enclave. The interventionist must necessarily function within and become an integral part of an ecological system that is continually and often richly interwoven with environmental components in the immediate neighborhood, town, district, borough, city, county, parish, canton, state, province, country, continent, hemisphere, and ultimately the world.

This fundamental trend is a melding of systemic crisis intervention strategies that interact in the total environmental and multicultural context of a pluralistic and dynamically changing world. Yet this view is clearly not shared by everyone and may be seen by some as a pretext to impose Western medical practices on the rest of the world. Thus, in the early edition of the Sphere Project world health working paper on disaster response ("Humanitarian Charter," 1998), mental health was not even covered. Indeed the term *psychosocial* has been coined to take away the stigma that a person is mentally ill (Van Ommeren, Saxena, & Saraceno, 2005). Note what the International Interagency Standing Committee Mental Health and *Psychosocial* Support calls itself to make it more palatable to some parts of the international community (IASC, 2007). Indeed, most survivors of a catastrophe may only need social support, and "psychosocial support" is a lot more psychologically palatable than the designator of being "mentally ill." You should thus understand that what is being proposed in this chapter is not universally loved and admired, or even thought to be necessary or right by a number of people.

To that end, this chapter deals with an emerging ecosystemic view of what crisis intervention is becoming as it operates in large systems and deals with metastasizing, large-scale crises and megacrises. *Metastasizing* crises are those that start small but, if not contained both physically and psychologically, can quickly turn into large-scale crises (James, 2006). *Large-scale* crises are those that at a minimum affect whole communities or regions either directly or vicariously. *Megacrises* are defined as those that affect entire countries or the world, either directly or vicariously.

System Overview

The ecological, contextual crisis intervention approach that is described in this chapter reaches far beyond the relational interactions between and among the various members of the crisis client's family, or individuals in the client's workplace and immediate surroundings. Essentially, it is a dynamic, sociocultural, and multicultural view of all ecological influences that impinge upon the individual. It consists of five environmental systems, ranging from the fine-grained inputs of direct communications with social agents (individuals capable of interacting directly with crisis clients) to the broad-based inputs of local community agencies as well as the widespread influences of national imperatives and attitudes and ideologies of the cultures within which these systems operate (Santrock, 1999, pp. 42–44). The approach is continually changing, emerging, evolving, and developing to accommodate the ecological and multicultural contexts within which it exists. It represents a paradigmatic shift: a newly emerging ecosystem that encompasses an interdependency among and within people at all different levels of the total environment. This is not some static amorphous entity. It is very much alive, and as one part is impacted, other parts react.

This ecosystemic view of crisis intervention is adapted from Uri Bronfenbrenner's (1986, 1995; Bronfenbrenner & Morris, 1998; Santrock, 1999, pp. 41–46) ecosystemic theory of human development, and our own (James, Cogdal, & Gilliland, 2003; James & Gilliland, 2003, pp. 336–337, 341–342) and other psychotheorists' (Conyne & Cook, 2003; Conyne et al., 2003; Klotz, 2003) views of ecosystems as they apply to psychotherapy in general and crisis in particular (Collins & Collins, 2005; Norris et al., 2006; Vernberg, 1999). In crisis intervention terms, not only is the individual in crisis affected but also the client's total environment becomes the context that must be considered by crisis workers (Myer & Moore, 2006). Bronfenbrenner (1986, 1995) identified the five environmental components as the microsystem, mesosystem, exosystem, macrosystem, and chronosystem. (See Figure 17.1.)

Microsystem

The microsystem is the setting in which the person in crisis lives. The microsystem setting's contexts may include the individual's family, friends, coworkers, peers, school, neighborhood, and usual haunts. It is within the microsystem that the individual in crisis experiences the most direct social interactions and communications with others. In the microsystem setting, whatever difficulties individuals experience tend to spill over into the family constellation and compound the difficulties caused by the disaster (Green & Solomon, 1995). In the traumatic wake of a disaster, many previous relationships, alliances, partnerships, bonds, and compacts in the microsystem, which were held together in the immediate aftermath as a means of mutual survival, crumble under the weight of compound stresses (Smith & Belgrave, 1995).

The crisis worker adhering to the ecological, contextual, multicultural approach views the person in crisis not as a passive recipient of experiences in those microsystemic settings but as an individual who actively participates in the construction of the settings (Santrock, 1999, p. 42). Reciprocally, the settings have a positive or negative effect on the individual and family and may ameliorate or exacerbate the crisis depending on the person's proximity, relationship to, and perception and meaning of the event (Myer & Moore, 2006).

Mesosystem

In Bronfenbrenner's (1995) developmental system, the mesosystem serves as the communications channel, pathway, or interactive mechanism between components in the microsystem and the exosystem. The mesosystem is essentially the total communications network that allows all individuals and groups within each ecological system to exchange information. It includes every form of communication—from word of mouth to the most sophisticated electronic technology—and is far more than cell phones and television news announcements. In terms of crisis and crisis intervention, the mesosystem and its function as the command-and-control structure of the total system are critical.

The crisis mesosystem is interspersed not only between the microsystem and exosystem (primary mesosystem) but between the exosystem and the macrosystem as well (super mesosystem). Both the primary and super mesosystems play critical roles in resolving ecosytemic crises. These two systems are extremely fluid and may expand very rapidly during a crisis. Think of a lava lamp where, as the oil heats up there are rapid and nonsymmetrical movements of the colored oil. This analogy carries over to a rapidly heating and expanding crisis. (Whether this expansion alleviates or exacerbates the crisis depends a great deal on how and what is communicated by whom and under what circumstances.) One of the major failures in the aftermath of hurricane Katrina was the breakdown of this system at both the primary and super levels. It should be understood that disaster mental health systems are complex mesosystems (networks of other systems) in and of themselves, and what makes them even more complex is that they will be imposed on to host micro- and exo-mental health systems that have their own agendas, vary in preparedness for a disaster, and may well suffer severe disruption themselves due to the disaster (Norris et al., 2006).

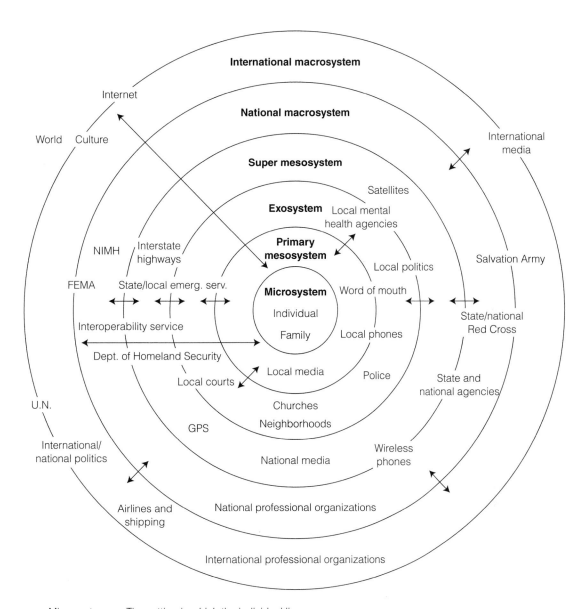

Microsystem: The setting in which the individual lives.
Mesosystem: The relationships, connections, and communication links between individuals and systems.
Exosystem: The experiences in another social setting in which the individual does not have an active
               role; the exosystem does influence the individual's experiences in the immediate context.
Macrosystem: The national and regional systems, attitudes, and ideologies, behavior patterns, beliefs, and
               other products that are passed on from generation to generation and make up the fabric of
               the larger culture.

FIGURE 17.1 Adaptation of Bronfenbrenner's Ecosystemic Model for Crisis.

Local emergency management agencies (LEMAs) expend a great deal of time and effort conducting table-top and on-scene exercises to determine the most effective way of handling a crisis, dealing with logistics, and field-testing communication links (Freeman, 2003; Lane, 2003). These systems directly link crisis interventionists with emergency management agencies. Human service workers trained by NOVA, FEMA, the American Red Cross, and state and local mental health agencies are on call for emergencies, and when a disaster of a magnitude greater than what the local authorities can handle is encountered, these crisis teams are called up and go into action. In the United States, calling up the National Guard is a fair analogy to what happens when a call goes out for crisis workers. Hurricane Katrina is an excellent example of the need for both.

Primary Mesosystem. Communication in the primary crisis mesosystem means having translators to speak to victims whose native tongue is not the national language. It means having ham radio operators and trained weather spotters with two-way radios and crisis response teams and search-and-rescue teams with walkie-talkies to communicate with one another in wrecked buildings or in a blown-down forest. It means establishing clear links from emergency management agencies to media outlets. It means creating integrated communication networks between emergency management agencies and a wide variety of supportive agencies that range from law enforcement and fire departments to heavy equipment operators and mental health professionals.

A primary mesosystem is everything from sign language for a deaf person to the most sophisticated wireless computer satellite uplinks to state and federal emergency management agencies (EMAs) (Freeman, 2003; Lane, 2003). It maintains connections and communications within and among workplaces, schools, churches, families, peer groups, and local social, medical, and governmental services (Bronfenbrenner, 1995; Freeman, 2003; James & Gilliland, 2003, pp. 341–342; Lane, 2003; Santrock, 1999).

For crisis intervention agencies, fast, effective, clear communication is at the center of everything they do. Communication redundancy is critical because if one system fails, another can be substituted. For example, during an electrical storm, the emergency management director of Nassau County, Florida (Jacksonville area), was in her car and attempting to communicate with a member of her staff about storm damage. But she quickly found that communication was impossible because of electrical interference. Despite all of the sophisticated equipment that the county EMA had, the only thing that worked was leaving messages on each other's voice mail (Freeman, 2003). It is not accidental that Jerry Lane, the former emergency manager of the city of Sycamore, Illinois, is a licensed advanced-class amateur radio operator (Lane, 2003). One of the more aggravating problems of hurricane Katrina was that various local agencies used different radio frequencies and could not communicate with one another, nor could they communicate with the super mesosystem. Thus a recurring theme throughout disaster intervention is that communication is vital to the ability to respond in a disaster (Rebman, Carrico, & English, 2008).

Super Mesosystem. Interlinking the macrosystem with all interior systems is the super mesosystem. The super mesosystem that connects the exosystem and the macrosystem serves many of the same coordinating functions, but on a national level. The super mesosystem is composed of information systems that range from the postal service, to national commercial radio and television corporations, to the Internet and its websites, e-mail, instant messaging, and chat rooms, to satellite communication and global positioning systems. Federal agencies such as FEMA, and its parent, the Bureau of Homeland Security, are linked with other governmental agencies such as the Bureau of Justice and private agencies such as the Red Cross and National Organization of Victims Assistance, National Oceanic and Atmospheric Administration weather satellites, the U.S. Weather Service storm prediction centers, supercomputers at national agencies that model and predict disaster scenarios and relief efforts, and the National Emergency Broadcast systems for the public.

National agency and federal department interlinks and downlinks to state EMAs and agencies are all part of the super mesosystem for crisis intervention that operates in the United States. It has major command-and-control centers that can be linked to state communication and control centers, which in turn are linked to local emergency operations centers. These national organizations and agencies have complete mobile command, control, and communications centers that can be rapidly moved on tractor trailers by highway, rail, or ship, or flown into any disaster site. This system was so devastated during hurricane Katrina that the base of operations for repairing the levees and pumping systems in New Orleans was situated in the U.S. Army Corps of Engineers office in Memphis, Tennessee, more than 400 miles up the Mississippi River!

Therefore, the mesosystem is of primary concern to crisis interventionists and the crisis intervention process because it coordinates and drives the dynamic linkages among all components (people, groups, contextual connections, ecological resources). The crisis interventionist—in the role of consultant, collaborator, coordinator, and communicator—is a key resource person operating within the mesosystem.

The advent of smartphones with multiple applications has enhanced the potential of both the primary and super mesosystems in a variety of ways that were unimaginable as little as 5 years ago. Aten and associates (2011) have detailed a number of applications made possible by this new technology:

1. Texting takes far less bandwidth than talking. When other phone systems are plugged up, text messages are likely to get through. Many universities now have text warning systems that can get to any student who has a cell phone on.

2. Smartphone users with weather and news apps can access outside information when they might not otherwise have access to current conditions that affect the crisis.

3. Social networking sites such as MySpace, Facebook, Twitter, Flickr, and LinkedIn allow people to stay in synchronous contact with other net users. Clearly these sites can be used for organizing activities of large groups of people, as witnessed by the recent revolutions in Egypt and Libya which used these devices to organize large demonstrations and avoid police dragnets. These sites would seem to have the same applicability in organizing people during disasters.

4. Global positioning systems (GPS) have proliferated both as hardwired applications in automobiles and trucks and in portable systems such as smartphones. These have tremendous applicability in a disaster for directing traffic, giving directions, providing alternate routes, and locating people who don't know where they are. Onstar is a satellite communication, GPS, and emergency notification communications system hardwired into new General Motors (GM) vehicles. GM has teamed with the American Red Cross to provide information on shelters, medical services, safe routes, food sources, and other services. Aten and associates (2011) reported that Onstar's usage rate went up 30 percent during hurricane Gustave, which is a pretty good indication of how much its subscribers relied on it during what they considered to be an emergency ("GM's Onstar," 2008).

5. When super mesosystems use systems like Onstar, a great many people can access these systems in a hurry, and they don't need an electrical transmission line to do it. The Centers for Disease Control have picked up on this technology and made podcasts that provide "what to do and what to know" information about disease epidemics, safety tips, and other health-related information that can be used by people in disaster areas with no electricity who might otherwise be cut off from critical health information (CDC, n.d.).

The point of all this new technology is that for many people in the primary mesosystem, using it daily is standard practice. Thus super mesosystems like those operated by the federal government or international charitable organizations can use it not only with their own workers when standard communication links are down, but also with a large number of primary system users who are not mystified by the technology and can then spread the information by word of mouth. If these new devices and systems are put to use wisely, they may do much to push the communication problems that have plagued relief efforts into the dustbin of history.

Exosystem

The exosystem exposes the crisis client or clients to experiences in a wider social setting than those encountered in the microsystem context (Bronfenbrenner, 1986, 1995). The exosystem reaches much farther out into the community and may even include state or regional entities. Legal and social welfare services, local mass media, and all governmental agencies and programs that are in a position to impact the individual and to assist persons, families, or groups who are in crisis are part of the exosystem. Crisis workers who live in other parts of the state or province may be called in to help. Typically, in the United States, each local EMA has backup personnel who are in place or on standby support if a crisis arises that temporarily exceeds local capacity to handle the situation.

How effective the exosystem and macrosystem are in providing services depends in large part on how well information passes back and forth through the primary and super mesosystems and how well resources are allocated, delivered, and used based on that information. The FEMA on-site, one-stop-shopping for all related disaster assistance to individuals is an excellent super mesosystem example of direct communication between victims in the microsystem and national providers in the macrosystem.

Macrosystem

The macrosystem includes the national government and all its agencies, and national charitable, religious, service, professional, and benevolent organizations. It encompasses the national rail, air, marine, and highway transportation modalities, and food, fuel, and energy transmission systems. The macrosystem encompasses the total culture in which people live (Bronfenbrenner, 1995). Total culture refers to the behavior patterns, traditions, beliefs, mores, historical artifacts, legal constructs, and all other traits and pursuits that are endemic to a group of people and that are passed on from generation to generation (Santrock, 1999, p. 44). The macrosystem has importance in crisis intervention for two reasons. First and foremost, when a disaster exceeds the normal coping capacity of the disaster impact area, the macrosystem is most likely the place from which help and resources will flow. Second, if the crisis is of a national magnitude such as 9/11, it will be important to do a triage assessment of the national psyche to determine what if any intervention needs to occur with the entire ecosystem.

Disasters do not have to be large in geographic scope or have large numbers of fatalities to be considered macrosystemic. The killing rampage of Seung-hui Cho at Virginia Tech in April 2007 was an isolated incident. Although 32 people were killed, that number pales in comparison to the number of dead on 9/11 in 2001 or the almost daily casualty rate in the Afghan War or the weekly death tolls on U.S. highways. By all objective measures, the Virginia Tech killings were a small disaster. Yet the fact that the tragedy occurred on a quiet college campus, in a place where one's children are supposed to be safe, upset the nation's sense of control much as the Columbine High School shootings did in 1999. The Virginia Tech tragedy quickly turned into a metastasizing crisis that carried far beyond Blacksburg, Virginia. While landline telephone connections jammed up, text messaging, which takes far less bandwidth, did not. Facebook and other social networks were relaying news of the tragedy as it took place and identified danger zones the students needed to stay out of and get away from (Aten et al., 2011).

Most particularly, parents who had sent their children off to college became very concerned about their children's health and well-being, no matter what university or college they attended and no matter what part of the country it was in. Those parents immediately began sending a deluge of phones calls, letters, and e-mails to universities across the country (a national macrosystem), demanding to know what safety measures were in place to protect their children from psychotic gunmen and other potential predators.

Perhaps even more important, the constituency of the universities, students and professors, are highly capable of communicating across the super mesosystem via e-mail, blogs, cell phones, and text messages. That rapidly expanding super mesosystem put the information, conjecture, hypotheses, and rumors about the massacre at Virginia Tech out into the international macrosystem within hours of the shootings. As an example, the dark, violent, and macabre plays that Seung-hui Cho is alleged to have written as a student at Virginia Tech were published in the blogosphere 24 hours after the shootings occurred.

Chronosystem

The Individual. The chronosystem is identified by Bronfenbrenner (1995) as the patterning of environmental events and transactions over the life span as well as the social and historical circumstances that influence the individual, family, peers, coworkers, and others. The essence of the chronosystem is the dynamic influence that time has on events, and time, with its movement, is an absolutely critical variable in regard to disasters. The crisis chronosystem starts with the birth of the traumatic event and not the birth of the person. Although the crisis chronosystem starts with the event, if possible the crisis interventionist needs to backtrack over the personal developmental chronosystem of the individual to determine what, if any, precursors may have contributed to the incident's impact and what antecedent events may cause it to be exacerbated.

In crisis intervention, understanding the part the chronosystem plays in exacerbating or ameliorating the crisis is particularly important. There are two types of disaster trauma—individual and collective (Erikson, 1976). *Individual* trauma hammers the individual psyche and breaks through the person's defense so forcefully and suddenly that reaction is impossible. *Collective trauma* does the same thing, only it does it across the microsystem (the community) to the extent that the social bonds that connect people are torn apart and the community is rent asunder. The chronosystem is important for both individual and collective traumatic responses and can be marked in phases that are generally linear and progressive in nature (see Figure 17.2). Following are brief descriptions of those phases.

Impact. The first few minutes and hours during and immediately after the crisis are critically important. While fear and shock are common, most people behave adaptively and take action to protect themselves and their loved ones. Time may become disoriented and slowed down, with disbelief and denial at what has happened. However, while a good deal of collective chaos may ensue, people react mainly in proactive ways (Myers & Wee, 2005, p. 20). Maslow's hierarchy of needs comes into operation, particularly when the crisis is a disaster

FIGURE 17.2 Pathological Chronosystem of a Crisis Event.

that leaves people without food, shelter, or clothing. As the crisis plays out in the traumatic wake of the next few days, the resolution of problems ranging from having a roof over one's head to communicating or being physically reunited with one's family becomes critical.

Emergency/acute heroic/rescue. Immediately after impact, people spring into action to save others and to save property and regain control of the situation and environment. During this heroic or rescue stage (Myers & Wee, 2005, pp. 20–21; NIMH, 2002; Pennebaker & Harber, 1993) individuals are generally highly energized physically and emotionally, have great morale, cognitively perseverate on the event, and gain relief by talking about their anxieties surrounding the crisis and their responses to it. While individuals are highly energized, problem solving and priority setting are often compromised by the sheer magnitude of the disaster, which many times translates into lots of activity and low efficiency. Seeking or finding out that family members are safe and can be reunited is critical.

Inventory/recovery.   At some point between the impact and the heroic stage an inventory and initial attempts at recovery phase occurs. People conduct an appraisal of the situation and start to plan what they are going to do (NIMH, 2002). They engage in information seeking in regard to finding loved ones, determining whether they are safe or injured, and finding out how well their homes and places of employment have fared (Myers & Wee, 2005, p. 21). Typically there is frustration with the inability to find loved ones or anger at authorities for not letting the survivors back into their neighborhoods to find out about their homes.

Honeymoon.   There is a collective "we are in this together" attitude. This may last anywhere from 1 week to up to 3 months post-impact. The community pulls together. There is optimism about recovery, and the belief that there will be full restitution of financial loss is high. There is a great deal of media coverage and high-level political attention. Public outpouring in the form of physical and financial donations give the community a sense of hope for rebuilding, and there is a strong sense of having shared a horrific experience but having prevailed over the worst of it (Farberow & Frederick, 1978).

At any time from 2 weeks to 2 years, depending on the severity and scope of the event, individuals will experience reintegration and return to a pre-event level of functioning or better, or they may not.

Avoidance.   As individuals work their way through the next few weeks, the kinds of physical and psychological support systems that are provided affect whether acute stress disorder will arise and whether it will eventually turn into posttraumatic stress disorder. As time passes, an avoidance phase generally emerges (Pennebaker & Harber, 1993). People stop talking about the event, but the images and thoughts about it continue to dominate cognitive functioning.

Adaptation.   Whether the pathology of the event continues and the individual enters the adaptation phase (Pennebaker & Harber, 1993) depends a great deal on the resiliency of the individual and the crisis worker's ability to institute a salutogenic model (Antonovsky, 1980, 1991) that emphasizes health and wellness over sickness and pathology. The salutogenic concept affirms what we

historically know about people and crisis. Stress is ever present, and severe stress is going to occur, but people are resilient, recover, and can thrive and grow from it. If people can come to grips with the financial, emotional, and environmental problems they will invariably face, and come to see that no matter what they do things will never quite be the same as they were before but they can move forward, they will have adapted and move on. However, for many adaptation will be difficult because of the disillusionment that sets in.

Disillusionment.   Disillusionment may begin several days or weeks after impact and may last for years, depending on how individuals adjust to their new environment. Disillusionment occurs because the media and politicians go home, bureaucratic red tape slows recovery, insurance money doesn't pay out as much as thought, and multiple other problems arise that say that recovery will be slow if at all. Fatigue finally sets in, and the individual is emotionally and physically exhausted from extended psychological and physical stress. A variety of public health problems may arise from poor living and sanitary conditions, environmental pathogens, and communicable diseases. Stress-related health symptoms, ranging from high blood pressure to exacerbation of preexisting health problems, may occur. Disaster relief workers ironically refer to this period as the *second disaster.* Psychological problems may range from PTSD to panic and anxiety disorders to depression and suicidal ideation (Myers & Wee, 2005, pp. 23).

Anniversary.   As time moves forward into the next year, the anniversary of the occurrence may become significant (Cohen et al., 2006). After a year or more has passed since the incident, a transcrisis state may be reached, depending on whether the individual has resolved the trauma or not. For some victims, the need to talk about and seek help validating their experience will go on and on, much to the dismay of others. This continuing need for catharsis and rumination about the crisis may be met with disapproval and outright anger by others in the victim's support system who seek to distance themselves from it (Smith & Belgrave, 1995). The result is often a perception by the victim of secondary victimization.

Pathogenic to salutogenic shift.   Around the time of the first anniversary of the traumatic event, a benchmark is usually reached. If individuals have put the traumatic event into past context, mourned their losses, and started to rebuild their lives, then they have made a *salutogenic* shift in their lives (a shift that is healthful, wholesome, promoting psychological growth) (Antonovsky, 1980). They have met the challenge the traumatic event posed for them and are able to move on with their lives. In contrast, if individuals have remained mired in the traumatic event long past the acute stage, then they may be said to have made a *pathogenic* (diseased, unwholesome, psychologically debilitating) shift that may become residual and chronic, bringing on a host of physical and psychological maladies. A continuing and contentious issue in the field of trauma therapy is how individuals attain and retain a salutogenic state and if they do or do not need assistance in doing so (Stuhmiller & Dunning, 2000). Antonovsky (1991) has demonstrated that the stronger a person's sense of coherence (the extent to which the stress is deemed manageable, coherent, and meaningful), the more likely he or she is able to cope with life's stressors. If that model is adopted, then much of the role and function of the crisis worker ceases to exist, because in a salutogenic model stress is universal, humans have adapted to it, and they do not necessarily crumble under traumatic stress (Stuhmiller & Dunning, 2000).

Restabilization/reconstruction.   As time passes, decisions have to be made as to whether to rebuild one's life in the same environment or move on to a different place. Rebuilding is not just putting a new house up after an earthquake. It is also about rebuilding and restabilizing one's emotional and social self. Even though there are setbacks, with denied loans, divorce papers, homes that are a total loss, friendships that have been lost, or friends who have died in the disaster, somehow over the months and perhaps years, stabilization and new constructs replace the old.

Therefore, as time moves forward, the survivor needs to engage in a process that is much like Schneider's (1984) transformational model of grief. Monitoring and following up on this transformational process to the client's final acceptance and putting the disaster in perspective may require tracking the client for a year or more. A great deal of discussion is currently occurring on APA's Division 56 (Trauma Psychology) website regarding Richard Tedeschi's and Lawrence Calhoun's notion of posttraumatic growth (Triplett et al., 2011). These two researchers have developed an inventory (Cann et al., 2010, 2011) to assess people's ability to discover new possibilities such as better ways of relating to others, new personal strengths, positive spiritual changes, and stronger appreciation of life in the wake of

a crisis (DeAngelis, 2011). One might say they are putting the empirical test to the Chinese Kanja characters indicating both crisis and opportunity.

The Society.   When we move from the individual to the society at large (the micro-, exo-, or macrosystem), the chronosystem also plays an important part in what is going to happen systemically. In the immediate hours and days of the aftermath of the crisis, all of the resources, agencies, and personnel needed to bring control and equilibrium back to the community are brought to bear, and time becomes acutely important. During this heroic stage (Raphael, 2000), the system responds with unselfishness, self-sacrifice, and heroism in its attempts to rescue people and provide shelter and emergency assistance. Indeed, if there is forewarning, such as the landfall of a hurricane, timelines will extend backward to precede the occurrence.

As an example, the Nassau County Florida Emergency Management Department has a nine-stage sequence that extends from an awareness stage, which starts 72 hours before the hurricane's projected landfall, to a reconstruction stage, which may be continuous and ongoing for weeks or months after the hurricane is over (Nassau County Emergency Management Department, n.d.). During the immediate aftermath, a psychological honeymoon stage (Raphael, 2000) occurs in which there is a great deal of attention by the media, massive intervention by disaster relief agencies, and the notion that things will be set right and services quickly restored. There is an overall "We're all in the same boat, and everybody is equal" attitude.

After all of the emergency crews have finished getting power and phone lines back on, the wonderful outside assistance and resource support have gone home, and the media have moved on to the next disaster, the long-term degrading effects of the disaster are still there and consuming additional resources. When physical facilities—such as churches, schools, parks, and community centers—are gone, activities and interpersonal contacts that were taken for granted may be lost. State and federal bureaucracies and insurance companies seem to have miles and miles of red tape and may deny requests for compensation and support for reconstruction of basic infrastructure. Both for individuals and communities, this phase has often been called the "second disaster" (Myers & Wee, 2005, p. 29).

Losing access to community gathering places has symbolic, social, spiritual, and psychological meaning and may have long-term toxic effects on the community. Rebuilding these structures and reestablishing social links that were severely fractured take a great deal of time and effort (Kaniasty & Norris, 1999). At this point, a disillusionment stage may emerge (Raphael, 2000). There is a sense of frustration, hopelessness, and abandonment that things will never be the same. Widespread posttraumatic stress and depressive symptoms are likely to appear if continuous and long-term mental health assistance is not available. Thus, a very real question arises as to the "when" of provision of services. It is not nearly as glamorous 6 months after a disaster strikes to appear on the scene "ready to help," but it may be as critically important to provide mental health services in the long term as it is in the short term.

The chronosystem, then, represents the development of events in individuals' lives and larger social systems over time, and crisis interventionists need to be aware of how important time and timing are in responding to crises. The phrases "Time changes everything" and "Time is of the essence" appear to capture the flavor of the chronosystem (James & Gilliland, 2003, p. 342).

Defining Principles of a Crisis Intervention Ecosystem

Coming to grips with complex ecosystem service delivery issues is daunting, to say the least. However, Conyne and Cook (2003) and Norris and her associates (2006) have generated the following principles for doing so.

1. *Systems must be interdisciplinary.* No single discipline or "ology" has a corner on this market. Emergency management agencies and crisis intervention systems must rely on a broad spectrum of people, ranging from sanitation workers and electrical linemen to civil and logistical engineers to medical emergency staff and communication workers to law enforcement and fire and rescue personnel to sociologists and psychologists to bankers and economists to ministers and social workers. Further, all of the people in these skills, crafts, trades, and professions must work in an integrated manner. The competent crisis worker integrates seamlessly into this smorgasbord of "ologies"; the pretentiousness sometimes associated with a college degree and the egotism of a particular profession have no place in an ecosystemic crisis. Ecosystemic crisis intervention is the most egalitarian of all mental health

endeavors, and layperson volunteers may be just as effective as psychiatrists. Anyone with an inflated ego will soon be humbled in a large crisis.

2. *The system must be multitheoretical.* If we look at only the psychological component of wide-scale crises, no single psychological theory is presently adequate to deal with the complex swirl of human dynamics that comes out of a crisis. It should be stated absolutely and unequivocally that nobody has a theoretical corner on this market. That includes proselytizers for any of the "alphabet" techniques such as CISD, EMDR, TFT or, alternatively, those who would rail against them. It especially includes the authors of this book! When dealing with large-scale crises or megacrises, psychological theory must at the very least harmonize with logistics, medical, communications, economic, and political theory. To further complicate matters, it is not just which psychological theories and techniques are used, but also when and how those services are delivered.

3. *Individuals are part of the ecosystem.* Like it or not, unless we can somehow find a place in the desert or mountains to become hermits, we are part of the total ecosystem of the world. Our biological makeup, interpersonal relationships, physical environment, and sociological context are all becoming more tightly interwoven into the total ecosystem of the world.

4. *Multiple contexts must be considered.* Micro-, meso-, exo-, and macrosystems are all components of the total ecological system that impact the individual when a megacrisis occurs. To deny that these systems are vectors and forces that impinge on the individual is to have a very parochial view of what this business is about and is to be doomed to fail.

5. *Time is of the essence.* If we believe any of the PTSD research about the deleterious effects the passage of time has on the individual if nothing is done to alleviate the possible effects of the trauma, we need to understand that what occurs in the chronosystem is critical. The availability of adequate physical and psychological resources to deal with a crisis in a timely manner is paramount.

6. *Meaning is important.* What sense we make of the crisis from a broad systemic view is as important as what sense we make of it individually and has much to do with how quickly and effectively it is resolved for both individuals and society.

7. *Parsimonious interventions are needed.* Concordance and coordination within various systems are needed if large amounts of precious time and

energy are not to be wasted. At the federal level, sufficient funding and information resources must be generated and disseminated. At the state level, preparedness plans should address multiple levels of the response across relevant jurisdictions, which includes clear plans on how the state agencies will communicate with the public and providers. Optimal utilization of resources is critical, and collaborative relationships and understanding between agencies need to be formed in advance. Intervention in large-scale crises is extremely expensive in terms of person power and material resources. One of the major balancing acts of local EMAs is to have just enough resources available to bring maximum effort to bear at just the right time to experience maximum effect.

8. *The process is cooperative, collaborative, and consultative.* Just as no single discipline holds sway in a large-scale or megacrisis, cooperation, collaboration, and consultation within, among, and between systems and individuals are paramount. The provision of mental health services is important, but so are getting communication and power systems back on and determining where there is available shelter and whether buildings are safe.

9. *There is a full range of targeted interventions aimed at individuals, institutions, communities, on up to the national level, depending on how widespread the crisis is, and they are ongoing in response to longer-term needs.* Each involved system component, from the individual to the nation, needs to be triaged. Based on that assessment, target-specific interventions need to be made. How things will wind up after a disaster is not just determined in the days after it, but in the months after it. The infrastructure and community as client is as important long range as are individuals.

10. *The service characteristics of credibility, acceptability, accessibility, proactivity, continuance, and confidentiality should be adopted as "cast in stone" goals for service delivery in disaster-stricken areas.* Norris and her associates (2006) found adherence to these characteristics to be one of the most impressive of her findings of the 9/11 response in New York City. Meeting this gold standard of service delivery most likely means that the whole disaster mesosystem is integrated with host systems and running well. To do that effectively requires a variety of organizations and individuals who operate with a high level of cooperation to make that system work.

Overarching all of the foregoing points are planning, more planning, practicing, critiquing, evaluating, and yet more planning. The necessity for vertical and horizontal links in the ecosystem of disaster planning cannot be overemphasized. The result of not having such links became clearly evident after hurricane Katrina. One of the critical components to planning is making sure that disaster mental health planning and activities do not take a backseat to security and safety concerns; people who can make clear decisions must be in place and have the authority to make those decisions (Flynn, 2003). That issue became abundantly clear in the aftermath of Katrina, with local and state leaders bickering about plans that should have been carved in stone long before the hurricane made landfall (Flynn, 2003; Gheytanchi et al., 2007).

National Crisis Response Teams

Perhaps the most important outreach approach has been taken by national agencies in on-site delivery of mental health services at major disasters and the coordination of these services with other relief efforts. Because of past criticism of how both charitable and federal agencies have handled major disasters, those agencies have done a great deal of work to better coordinate their efforts in providing comprehensive disaster relief that cuts across the survivors' total environment (Bass & Yep, 2002; Pyszczynski, Solomon, & Greenberg, 2002; Smith, 2002). Mental health support does little good when people don't have a roof over their heads because it has been blown away in a hurricane. However, it also does little good for survivors to obtain housing but be so traumatized and depressed from the disaster that they cannot begin to regain control over their lives. From plane crashes to university campus shootings, to floods, to post office shootings, to forest fires, to train wrecks, to building bombings, to earthquakes, to school shootings, and to 9/11, some of the most potent and appropriate examples of the ecological nature of crisis intervention have occurred in the United States in the last 10 years, as has a large mobilization, training, and response effort to provide emergency mental health services to victims and survivors of any type of imaginable disaster.

An enormous number of mental health workers from throughout the country, working under the auspices of the American Red Cross, NOVA, FEMA, and state and local EMAs, and supported by the major professional mental health organizations in the United States, have contributed monumental services to the thousands of clients affected by those disasters (Bass & Yep, 2002; Gladding, 2002; Hayes, 2002; Juhnke, 2002; McCarthy, 2002; Modrak, 1992; Morrissey, 1995; Pyszczynski, Solomon, & Greenberg, 2002; Riethmayer, 2002a, 2002b; Smith, 2002; Sullivan, 2002; Underwood & Clark, 2002). Among the comments of hundreds, perhaps thousands, of mental health workers over dozens of major crises, the following is perhaps both descriptive and representative:

> In that capacity, I was an escort who walked with families from the front of the building to the back and talked with them about what they were feeling, what they had felt, or what they anticipated doing in regard to the emotions that would be coming. I also accompanied families to Ground Zero so they could see for themselves the horror and finality of the event. The view from the site helped many individuals begin the process of grieving in depth, as they realized in a stark and striking way that those they had loved and cherished in so many ways were indeed dead and would not be coming back to be with them. (Gladding, 2002, p. 7)

Development of Crisis Response Teams (CRTs). The Oklahoma City federal building bombing, the shootings at Columbine High School, and the 9/11 attacks struck a nerve in the United States. The massive amounts of media coverage of those traumatic experiences and the disaster relief that followed in their wake brought graphic attention to how disasters are handled, including the work of immediate follow-up rapid response teams. These teams did not just spring up full grown at the time of those disasters. Rather, throughout the late 1980s and 1990s, rapid response teams were developed to handle numerous tragedies and disasters, including hurricanes (Shelby & Tredinnick, 1995), serial murders (Wakelee-Lynch, 1990), plane crashes (Modrak, 1992; Shafer, 1989a), bank robberies and hijackings (Brom & Kleber, 1989), campus shootings (Guerra, 1999; Guerra & Schmitt, 1999; Sleek, 1998), and post office shootings (National Organization for Victim Assistance, n.d.).

National Organization for Victim Assistance (NOVA) CRTs. The rapid crisis response team movement received impetus and support on a national level with the establishment of the National Crisis Response Project by the National Organization for Victim Assistance (NOVA) in the late 1980s (Young, 1991).

Originally established to help victims of crime, NOVA, a private, not-for-profit organization, has branched out to offer help to victims of all kinds of disasters through the National Crisis Response Project. It has state and local affiliates throughout the United States. The project set up national crisis response teams (NCRTs) to assist communities following community-wide crises or disasters. One of the first major organized national responses of an NCRT for the specific purpose of providing mental health assistance was on August 20, 1986, when an Edmond, Oklahoma, postal worker shot and killed 14 coworkers and himself.

The main objective of an NCRT in dealing with a local community disaster is to form local crisis response teams that are in a position to deal with the community's grief reactions, stress effects, and posttraumatic stress disorder resulting from the disaster. According to Young (1991), the "project is based on the premise that disasters can cause individual and community-wide crisis reactions and that immediate intervention can provide communities with tools that are useful in mitigating long-term distress" (pp. 83–84).

NCRTs are dispatched at the request of leaders in the affected community. "When a disaster occurs, NOVA is placed in contact with the community in one of two ways: either the community calls NOVA, or NOVA, on hearing of the tragedy, calls the community and offers assistance" (Young, 1991, p. 95). Three types of disaster service are available: (1) providing written material giving details on how to deal with the aftermath of disaster; (2) providing telephone consultation to leading caregivers in the area affected; and (3) sending in a trained team of volunteer crisis workers to assist the community.

The Red Cross. The American Red Cross, like its Red Cross and Red Crescent counterparts around the world, is tasked with dealing with all kinds of disasters. Founded by Clara Barton, the American Red Cross has been in business for about 120 years. It is a private organization that has close ties with local, state, and federal governments. It helped the federal government start the Federal Emergency Management Agency. It is a major contributor to crisis intervention in the wake of large-scale disasters and megadisasters through its training of mental health professionals as members of rapid response teams (Red Cross, n.d.). Professional organizations in counseling, psychology, and social work are closely linked with and provide candidates for its mental health training program.

Federal Emergency Management Agency (FEMA) and the National Institute of Mental Health (NIMH). FEMA was born in 1979 as the result of complaints about federal agencies' slowness, bureaucratic red tape, inefficiency, ineptitude, and duplication of effort in responding to a disaster. Several different agencies were merged into FEMA, and it is now housed in the Department of Homeland Security. FEMA has numerous responsibilities. Among them are education about all kinds of disaster preparedness and coordination between federal, state, and local emergency management agencies in regard to preparedness, training, and disaster mitigation. It provides disaster assistance that ranges from debris removal and rescue efforts to disaster loans for rebuilding and on-site mental health crisis response teams. Its Emergency Management Institute at Emmitsburg, Maryland, is a virtual university of emergency preparedness courses. Courses range from training community emergency response teams (CERTS), made up of ordinary local citizen volunteers who provide support to first responders to aid in rescue efforts, to colloquiums with state mental health service providers on the latest techniques for providing mental health services after a large-scale disaster (Federal Emergency Management Agency, n.d.).

Sometimes more than one agency of the federal government coordinates the work of crisis response teams. Several instances of events during modern times that triggered such a coordinated effort were the earthquakes in both the Los Angeles and San Francisco areas; hurricanes Hugo, Andrew, Floyd, and Katrina that brought devastation and flooding to large parts of the southeastern United States; the nuclear accident at Three Mile Island; and the Love Canal contamination. The response teams were sent in by the National Institute of Mental Health (NIMH) and sponsored and funded by FEMA. In all such national disasters, FEMA and NIMH provide the widely affected areas with instruction, consultation, and expertise in developing local and regional support systems to cope with the enormous aftermath of these disasters (Shafer, 1989b).

Professional Organizations. Professional organizations, such as the American Psychiatric Association, the American Psychological Association, the American Counseling Association, and the National Association of Social Workers, provide volunteers for the Red Cross and NOVA CRTs. These organizations also provide a variety of publications for both professionals and laypersons that can be obtained on their websites or

ordered from them. Their conferences and conventions provide formats for discussion and dissemination of the theory and practice of crisis intervention.

The American School Counseling Association and the National Association of School Psychologists are involved in providing crisis intervention services to schoolchildren and adolescents in the face of a large-scale disaster. As an example, on April 19, 1995, immediately after the Oklahoma City federal building bombing, an American Counseling Association team of Oklahoma school counselors and an art teacher wrote and illustrated *The Terrible, Scary Explosion.* This book, modeled after one written for children after hurricane Hugo in South Carolina, was in the hands of Oklahoma City schoolchildren by April 25, with local school counselors serving as facilitators. The purpose of the book was to help children of all ages process the whole incident and provide a tool to help adults help children (Morrissey, 1995).

The National Association of School Psychologists has national emergency assistance teams (NEATs), which are tied in with NOVA. The mission of NEAT is to develop policies and procedures, disseminate information, provide consultation, and facilitate the training of school-based crisis teams in response to significant emergencies affecting children and adolescents. These NEAT teams go to the scene of school disasters and provide support for local agencies. They are composed of nationally certified school psychologists who have expertise in crisis prevention, intervention, and postvention. The intention of the NEAT team is to help save lives, reduce trauma and injury, facilitate the psychological well-being of students and staff, and allow schools to return to regular activities as soon as possible (Zenere, 1998).

Constructing an Outreach Team. Depending on the nature of the crisis and the ecological setting, outreach teams generally have a diverse occupational range: from psychiatric nurses, paramedics, emergency workers, and psychiatrists to social workers, volunteers, rehabilitation counselors, police officers, and psychologists. These outreach teams are characterized by their multidisciplinary team approach, strong social and community networks, user participation in policy and service delivery, and egalitarianism in the workplace (Gulati & Guest, 1990). Alise Bartley, a private practice licensed professional counselor, describes her experience as a volunteer worker following hurricane Katrina. Based in Gulfport, Mississippi, she slept in a large Navy

Seabee storage facility with 600 other volunteers. She slept two feet from a retired nurse on one side and a Vietnam veteran on the other, both of whom she had just met for the first time in her life (Kennedy, 2007).

Integrative-collaborative teams have a distinctive operational setup and are characteristic of many geographical areas where financial and human resources are not sufficient to form freestanding, specialized crisis units. They are not an ad hoc group collected after a crisis, but rather are trained prior to the crisis. Each member has different skills that, combined, allow the team to respond to a variety of crisis situations. They operate much as a volunteer fire department does. Members typically have primary jobs in other settings, but when a crisis call comes in on a hotline, they immediately leave their regular job, form a crisis team, and go to the crisis site. They are identifiable within the community as the crisis response team and are a cost-efficient and effective way to provide generic crisis intervention (Silver & Goldstein, 1992).

Vertically and Horizontally Integrated Local Emergency Management Systems

Overarching all local agencies involved in crisis after a disaster are the local emergency management agencies. They are the offspring of the old Civil Defense system of the cold war. The examples that follow refer to Florida, where each local agency is directly linked to one of seven regional areas, and Illinois, where there are eight regions linked to the state emergency management agency. In turn, the state agency is linked to FEMA (Freeman, 2003; Lane, 2003).

Role of Local EMA Directors.   Jerry Lane and Nancy Freeman are two public servants whose lives have been anything but simple. They both have run local emergency management agencies.

Jerry was executive director for the Dekalb County, Illinois, Community Mental Health Board and director of the Sycamore, Illinois, Emergency Management Agency. Sycamore is a small town in northern Illinois, located in rolling farmland about 60 miles west of Chicago. It is not famous or notorious for much of anything. However, it does have grain elevator and agricultural chemical warehouse fires, tornadoes, straight-line windstorms, blizzards, and flooding.

But does it really need an emergency management system and a local manager? Listen to Greg Brown, former director of EMT services in White County, Illinois,

and chemical mixing and applications supervisor for Brown Feed and Chemical in Carmi, Illinois. "If you want to talk about the potential for terrorism or accidental disaster, talk about what we have in this warehouse. We easily have enough agricultural chemicals, if used with malice or handled incorrectly, to kill everybody in this town twice over and have some left to spare. You'd better have somebody around who knows what to do with them, and that would apply to about every town in the country that has an agricultural base" (G. Brown, personal communication, December 15, 2004).

For Jerry Lane, living in a small town that may need his skills is the greatest reward of the job. His agency's problems were those of most beginning crisis agencies: inadequate funding, little respect, and a whole lot of politics. Many emergency management jobs were filled by patronage seekers, which may satisfy the needs of a political party but will probably leave a lot to be desired when the crisis starts—as evidenced at the national level with hurricane Katrina. Listen to the comment of a county commissioner in White County, Illinois, about the volunteer EMT program that was asking for an increase in funds from the county board: "Why, they could train a monkey to do that job! Why do they need to be paid any more?" We certainly hope that commissioner doesn't have a heart attack "way out there on Possum Road" because we doubt whether a chimpanzee could make the drive in an ambulance and keep him alive long enough until a life flight arrived, piloted by—we would guess—a baboon.

Although you may consider the commissioner's comment outrageous and patently stupid, this is not an atypical response to any new upstart agency that deals in crisis. Until it becomes politically necessary, little government funding is forthcoming to support crisis intervention programs. Certainly 9/11 and hurricane Katrina put a new perspective on the need for local emergency management agencies and competent people to run them.

Nancy Freeman is a retired deputy director of the Nassau County, Florida, Emergency Management Agency. Nassau County is next to Jacksonville, Florida. Nancy got into the emergency management business doing research analysis for hazard mitigation while she was a graduate assistant at the University of North Florida. While doing research for various counties in north Florida, she learned enough about the business of emergency management that she applied for a job with one of the counties and got it! Besides being adjacent to a large urban population—with all of its potential hazards for disaster—Nassau County is situated on the shore of the Atlantic Ocean, with all of the hurricane risks attendant to that locale. To add a little more to the hazardous, potential-for-disaster mix, the county also has military facilities with nuclear capabilities. Suffice it to say that the Nassau County EMA is very, very interested in hurricanes and their potential effects under a variety of conditions.

Nancy's world is defined by the term "networking" and, as is true for most emergency managers, it is a double-edged sword. On the one hand, Nancy sees networking with a variety of very committed professionals as one of the most rewarding parts of her job. On the other hand, when egos, turf guarding, and politics get involved, it can be one of her major headaches.

These managers are a new breed of technocrat that is being placed in charge of coordinating a welter of activities, agencies, and logistical problems in regard to managing every conceivable emergency you might imagine and then some. If you'd like a job like this, you had better be good with acronyms and know what they stand for. Want to be able to do a HHVA (hospital hazard vulnerability analysis) or get a RACES (radio amateur civil emergency system) up and running? Curious to know what the difference between cold, warm, and hot zones are, or whether you need a Level A protection suit when you venture into one of them? Does that sound like an interesting job? Think you'd like to do that?

Background and Training.   What are the qualifications? you may ask. What university do I need to attend to major in that "stuff"? In the previous edition of this book, which in real time would be about four and a half years ago, there were 6 doctoral programs, 29 master's programs, 14 bachelor's degree programs, and 16 associate degree programs in the United States, Australia, England, and Turkey that offered a degree in emergency management. Specifically in regard to mental health crisis intervention, the University of South Dakota had established the first doctoral program with a specialty track in clinical/disaster psychology. Now, if you go to www.chds.us/?partners/institutions, which is the website for the Center for Homeland Defense and Security, you will find 321 programs that range across associate, bachelor's, master's, doctorate, and certification programs in just about any type of emergency management program with any type of focus you can imagine. You should understand that the content of these degrees varies quite a bit because as of yet there is no clear consensus on what all that "stuff" should be. If you sought to earn an interdisciplinary bachelor's degree with a major in emergency management from Western Carolina

University, for example, your courses could range from International Terrorism to Crisis Communications to the Politics of Budgeting (Western Carolina University Emergency Management Institute, n.d.).

However, as Nancy Freeman (2003) says, "My bachelor's degree and graduate work is in the humanities, with an emphasis in interior design, history, and historical preservation, and you wouldn't think that would be anything like what you'd need for this job, but I learned about architecture in that program, and I can read a building plan and know what 'load bearings under initial impact' means, and that is critically important when we are designing evacuation and safety plans. I also know how to do research and that is critically important in this job."

Jerry Lane holds a master's degree in community mental health. Jerry sort of wandered into this business by being an amateur radio operator and weather spotter. As Jerry says, "I'm kind of a rare breed. Most emergency managers don't have a mental health background. They tend to be retired military and have a pretty good handle on how to handle logistics problems, which is indeed important in this job" (Lane, 2003).

Both of these directors have taken many courses through the Federal Emergency Management Association's Emergency Management Institute, which has a campus in Emmitsburg, Maryland, and various correspondence and Internet courses. Besides critical incident stress debriefing and PTSD training, you might also be required to take Preparedness Planning in a Nuclear Crisis, Mortuary Services in Emergency Management, Hazardous Materials Basic Awareness, and Executive Analysis of Fire Service Organization and Emergency Management. If you are getting the idea that you had better be a Jack or Jill of all trades and a master of many, you are right!

There is a national certification process and an international association of emergency managers. In Florida, emergency managers must be certified through a combination of course work, training, and work experience. They must also take 150 hours of education courses every 4 years to retain their certification. There is continuous ongoing training in management tools resources, new technology, and communications. There are two annual conferences managers are expected to attend, one of which covers general emergency preparedness. Lots of training exercises are developed at the national and state levels and then are brought down to the local level to be used in training exercises (Freeman, 2003). Still interested in this job?

What Do Emergency Managers Do? Certainly, disasters don't happen every day. Does that mean that emergency managers sit around playing pinochle, drinking coffee, eating doughnuts, pitching horseshoes, and polishing the fire engine, waiting for something to happen? Local EMAs are in the business of preparing for, preventing, intervening in, and mitigating the effects of any and all kinds of disasters. To do that takes a great deal of planning and coordinating. Direct your attention to the matrix of city and county agencies and the support functions they engage in as primary or secondary supports in a disaster (see Figure 17.3). While you might think of roads, bridges, potable water, and sewage disposal as being critical, the last thing you might think of would be animal issues. But if you had severe flooding after a hurricane, animals—both alive and dead—would be a very real problem.

Planning for Disasters. There are two types of disasters, those that have prior warning time and those that do not. As a result, local EMAs have various disaster plans that are implemented in stages. Although there might be very little warning in the case of a tornado or a chemical spill from a derailed train, hurricanes and forest fires generally do have lead time for preparation. Nassau County has a very complex and lengthy hurricane plan that is divided into 10 stages. A brief description of those stages follows to give you an idea of just how involved this business is (Nassau County Emergency Management Department, 2003). For each stage, a particular action is noted and the responsible section is designated to implement it. Those sections are emergency operation center (EOC) command, planning, logistics, operations, administration, recovery task force, and elected policy makers.

Awareness stage. 72–60 hours Estimated Land Fall (ELF) of hurricane. Activate emergency command center. Establish liaison with the National Weather Service, state department of emergency management, surrounding counties, media, utility services, law enforcement, fire agencies. Conduct vulnerability analysis. Activate alert phone system. Prepare primary evacuation routes. Notify all gas and diesel wholesalers to restock retail outlets within 12–24 hours. Test EOC communications equipment.

Standby stage. 60–48 hours ELF. Activate emergency broadcast system. Notify amateur radio group to go on standby. Use local media and National Weather Service bulletins to advise boat owners, home owners, drawbridge operators, and motel and hotel managers, and detail causeway and bridge closings and evacuation routes. Coordinate establishment of emergency worker shelters. Secure EMS ambulances, transport vehicles, oil spill trailers, heavy equipment.

Decision stage. 48–45 ELF. Activate traffic control plan and emergency transport plan. Declare state of emergency and activate county emergency plan. Recommend/order evacuation. Designate nonessential businesses to close. Coordinate decision-making actions and link all municipalities, law enforcement agencies, fire districts, utility companies, hospitals, and medical care facilities with State Division of Emergency Management and the National Hurricane Center.

Preparation stage. 45–36 ELF. Begin implementing evacuation plan for "at risk" populations such as mobile homes, people with special needs, tourists, campers, people without transportation, and low-lying areas. Activate all EOC communication systems. Announce public closings. Implement 24-hour operation of fleet management garage and fueling resources. Activate emergency transportation plan. Prepare shelters for opening.

Evacuation stage. 36–4 ELF. Issue evacuation orders. Identify areas at risk. Announce shelter openings and transportation pickup points. Request National Weather Service to broadcast information on road closures. Activate/coordinate shutdown of electric power services. Maintain communications with public shelters, emergency worker family shelters, special care centers, emergency transportation, area hospitals, animal emergency care facilities, power, water, sewage, utilities, fire districts, law enforcement, and public works. Begin preplanning post-storm activities.

Storm/emergency stage. Monitor storm/emergency characteristics. Continue preplanning post-storm activities. Continue communications with other agencies.

Immediate emergency stage. Commence local emergency response activities. Determine long-term human service needs, including mental health-care counseling. Determine information and referral services. Assess temporary housing needs. Distribute resources: food, water, clothing, cleanup kits. Activate recovery task force and review damage reports. Recommend implementation of appropriate moratoriums and adoption

P = Primary / S = Support Agencies	ESF 1 Transportation	ESF 2 Communication	ESF 3 Public Works	ESF 4 Fire Fighting/Emerg. Medic	ESF 5 Information & Planning	ESF 6 Mass Care	ESF 7 Resource Support	ESF 8 Health and Medical	ESF 9 Search & Rescue	ESF 10 Hazardous Materials	ESF 11 Food & Water	ESF 12 Energy	ESF 13 Military Support	ESF 14 Public Information	ESF 15 Volunteers & Donations	ESF 16 Law Enforcement	ESF 17 Animal Issues
All local media														S			
Amateur Radio Emerg. Serv.		S			S									S			
Acme County Medical Center				S	S			S						S			
Goodwill Industries Center														S	S		
Midville City Public Works Dept.	S		S		S		S					S		S			
Midville City Fire Department		S		S	S				S	S				S			
Midville City Police Department		S			S									S		S	
Midville City Planning Department					S									S			
Civil Air Patrol		S			S									S			
Contracted Medical Examiner								S						S			
State Dept. of Law Enforcement													P	S			
State Highway Patrol													S			P	
State National Guard Forces													S	S			
State Power and Light Dept.												S		S			
State Public Utilities Dept.												P		S			
Animal emergency care centers														S			S
Home Health Care Agencies								P						S			
Regional Electrical Authority		S					S					S		S			
Medical Supply Companies								S						S			
Acme County Building Dept.		S			S		S							S			
Acme County Cattleman's Assoc.														S			S
Acme County Clerk of Court							S							S			
Acme County Coordinator														S			
Acme County Council on Aging	S				S		S	S						S			
Acme County Emergency Mgmt.			S	P	S	S	S		S	S	S		S	P	S		S
Acme County Engineering Services			S		S		S							S			
Acme County Extension Agency				S	S						S			S	P		S
Acme County Facilities Maintenance			S		S		S							S			
Acme County Fire/Rescue		S		P	S		S		P	P				S			
Acme County Geog. Info. Systems					S		S							S			
Acme County Health Dept.						S	S	P						S			
Acme County Humane Society														S			P
Acme County Jail							S							S			
Acme County Library System														S			
Acme County Planning Dept.					S		S							S			
Acme County Risk Management							P			P				S			
Acme County Road & Bridge Dept.	S		P		S		S					S		S			
Acme County School Board	P				S	P	S	S						S			
Acme County Sheriff's Office	S	P		S	S		S	S	S	S	S			S		P	S
Acme County Solid Waste Dept.		S			S		S							S			
Acme County Veterinary Society														S			S
Acme County Volunteer Center							S							S	S		
Regional American Red Cross						P		S			S			S	S		
State Parks & Recreational Services													S	S			
Private businesses											S			S			
Salvation Army				S							S			S	S		
Mental health centers								S						S			
Volunteer organizations											S			S			

FIGURE 17.3 Midville City/Acme County Emergency Support Function Matrix. SOURCE: Adapted from Nassau County, Florida, Emergency Management Department (Freeman, 2003).

of emergency resolutions and ordinances. Determine if curfew needed. Activate Damage Assessment Teams. Monitor public health conditions.

Evaluation stage. Determine if primary threat still exists. Conduct/coordinate initial impact assessment effort. Reaffirm and/or reestablish communications with all shelters, hospitals, towns, state emergency operations, law enforcement, public works, fire districts, and surrounding counties. Enact emergency resolutions. Determine initial mutual aid requirements and request assistance from state EOC. Discuss emergency ordinances to be enacted. Issue news media releases. Establish times for briefings/planning meetings. Report accidents to date, update status. Assess damage to areas with existing or potential hazardous materials. Summarize current operational activities underway. Discuss current strategy. Review human resource needs. Determine additional resources needed. Implement rest and rotation policies for emergency workers. Assess logistics of transportation routes opened, distribution sites, feeding procedures, available sleeping facilities.

Reconstruction stage. Perform long-term activities or projects focused on improving or strengthening community's economy. Complete restoration of services. Dispose of debris and allocate resources to cleanup chores. Focus on community recovery planning, building and construction issues, environmental/ecological issues. Continue/complete human service delivery assistance of information and referral, resource distribution, health-care delivery, mental health-care counseling, and transportation assistance. Complete activities for presidential disaster declaration. Perform hazard mitigation projects to reduce community's susceptibility and vulnerability to hurricanes. Repair, replace, modify, or relocate public facilities in hazard-prone areas.

Restoration stage. Perform assessment of community needs and economic damage. Address the following restoration issues: economic and job base assessment, community recovery planning, building and construction issues, public information and citizen outreach, environmental issues and ecological concerns. Provide health-care delivery for both pre- and postdisaster needs, including home health-care management and case referral. Put mental health-care counseling into operation. Determine victims' counseling needs by triage assessment. Determine training needs for mental health professions on disaster-related issues. Place mental

health professions/CISD team members on community assessment teams. Determine where counseling services will operate. Determine transportation needs to public feeding sites, shelters, and disaster service sites. Reestablish and implement public transportation service. Chore service needs assessment for cleanup. Determine needs and coordinate with volunteer groups for debris cleanup, interior home cleanup, window repair, etc. Coordinate with FEMA to set up Disaster Field Office and Disaster Application Centers. Assist in establishing temporary housing sites. Establish a federal public assistance office to coordinate all disaster relief efforts to clients. Participate in interagency hazard mitigation team and hazard mitigation survey activities. Complete after-evacuation report and county incident report. Critique the management of the storm emergency.

Throughout the unfolding stages of the disaster, constant needs assessment should occur. A community mental health needs assessment formula (Flynn, 2003, p. 23) that constantly updates the dead, hospitalized, nonhospitalized injured, homes destroyed, homes with major and minor damage, unemployed due to job loss, and other losses will give a good indication of the potential numbers of people in need of crisis counseling services. The same community-wide assessment should continuously occur in regard to mental health (Katz, 2011). Nancy Freeman was asked when she would know that the crisis is over. She stated, tongue in cheek, that she'd know because no one had called and everyone had found his or her dog and Aunt Nellie. In reality, the immediate crisis is considered passed when everyone's safety is assured from any effects of the disaster, public works are back in operation, and services are returning to normal. That's when the EOC can get a doughnut and some sleep!

The foregoing plan for hurricanes can be adapted to any kind of disaster, whether natural or human-made. While timelines may be very compressed or in some instances operations may start at the emergency stage, the format is replicable with just about any kind of community-wide crisis. Although local EMAs have very little preparation time for other types of disasters, they do not stand idly by waiting for something to happen. Continuous interagency tabletop exercises give them practice in responding to a variety of potential disasters. Assessment of particularly vital and vulnerable public sites, ranging from water treatment plants to nursing homes, is made to determine what needs and weak points there may be. Jerry Lane spends a fair amount of time working with individual agencies to develop their own internal disaster plans to fit with the overall one that the local EMA has.

Mental Health Components of Local EMAs

Any local mental health clinic should have a prototype disaster response plan (Lane, 2003). While each community will have variations due to its own particular regional and state systems of mental health delivery, geographic locale, and population differences, they should generally follow along with what Hartsough (1982) has outlined for mental health agencies' typical response to a disaster.

The following points are abstracted from Hartsough (1982), Lane (2003), and the Norfolk, Virginia, Community Services Board Model SCB Disaster Plan (2003). First of all, the centers must have a plan that assumes that they may be victims themselves and have breakdowns in communications; loss of or inability to find staff; loss of equipment, supplies, and records; inability of staff to cope with loss; and problems recognizing their functional limits. The mental health center must be prepared to provide services in two situations—a localized but traumatic event and a large-scale disaster. A localized event can be responded to without affecting operations to any great degree. A disaster will most likely disrupt operations to some degree, while drastically increasing the demand for services. A clear chain of command with redundancy features is mandatory. There should be an assessment of population groups in the area with regard to high-risk groups such as children, non-English-speaking, elderly, and low socioeconomic groups. Interagency cooperative agreements should be made. A specific mental health liaison person should be named to the local EOC.

Predisaster training encompasses development of outreach programs that target "normal people acting normally in an abnormal situation." Training specifically targets practitioners who have not had formal training in outreach or who historically perform poorly when they have to rely on their formal training. Consideration should be given to sending local clinicians to Red Cross training. Drills and tabletop exercises should be developed and conducted in coordination with the local EOC.

Personnel. Volunteers who would function as reserve crisis counselors should be recruited and trained in crisis intervention skills. Specified workers should be selected for multidisciplinary crisis response teams. A chief of operations should be nominated and will be the individual actually running the disaster response. There should also be an emergency preparedness coordinator who will be responsible for planning and preparation prior to a disaster and will function as a consultant to the chief of operations during an actual emergency. This person will be the liaison to the local EOC.

An outside clinical consultant should be retained to assess the physical and mental condition of the staff. A command-and-control and communications center should be established and staffed by a team leader and other staff necessary for it to function effectively. A historian should keep an ongoing journal of activities that occur as a result of the disaster. The decisions, events, problems, and information should include details, names and addresses, times, and issues that can later be used for debriefings, psychological autopsies, system improvements, grant requests, or reimbursement.

A personnel liaison will assist the chief of operations in assessing, making, and tracking staff and volunteer assignments. A media/information liaison will provide information to the media and local government, develop press releases, and distribute general information regarding service delivery. Staff may be made available to the local EOC to provide psychological support.

Transdisaster (0–14 Days). The mental health unit needs to initiate immediate mental health services when the disaster occurs; restore services to clients served during normal times; act as the disaster mental health advisor to the local government; provide outreach programs and coordinate resources for the delivery of disaster mental health services from the Red Cross, NOVA, FEMA, and other religious and philanthropic organizations; coordinate the responses of any contractors for services with particular emphasis on evacuation of residential facilities; target specific areas, such as evacuation centers, emergency relief centers, and FEMA "one-stop" service centers; provide support services for disaster workers; and assist with mental health emergencies in hospitals with victims requiring medical or psychiatric care.

Postdisaster (15–365 Days). Evaluate and assess the need for postdisaster services; implement prepared immediate services grant and prepare regular services grant if a presidential disaster is declared; establish linkages with American Red Cross mental health workers to hand off clients requiring longer-term care; monitor for long-term psychological effects; educate the public regarding disaster-related psychological phenomena; evaluate program response, both short and long term; perform psychological autopsy on total crisis response and debrief workers.

In the foregoing sections of this chapter you have read about the overall composition of disaster planning and infrastructure. In an ideal world, even in a world of disasters, all of this runs smoothly. While 9/11 certainly had its share of chaos and confusion (Halpern & Tramontin, 2007, pp. 171–197; Kaul & Welzant, 2005; Norris et al., 2006), order came out of that maelstrom fairly quickly, and everybody thought they had learned a lot of lessons. Then along came hurricane Katrina and everything got turned upside down.

What Happened With Katrina?

In any disaster there is invariably an attempt to fix blame. If blame can be fixed, then people may start to believe that the impossible, out-of-control, insane, unbelievable, chaotic, and unfathomable event can be contained, made sense of as to the reasons it occurred, and a sense of control regained as to what went wrong and how it can be made right the next time. In that sense hurricane Katrina is no different from multitudes of other natural disasters that have hit other countries. Indeed, in comparison to typhoons and earthquakes that have plagued Asia and the Middle East, it is a relatively small event, and certainly so in regard to loss of life. Yet the recriminations from hurricane Katrina are unending and rub raw nerves from the standpoints of socioeconomic, racial, political, and even interstate rivalries. While it is expected, rightly or wrongly, that there will be disasters in countries like Bangladesh, it "cannot happen" in the United States. We pride ourselves on controlling our destiny through science and industry, up to and including controlling nature. After Katrina, apparently not!

This is not an exposition about who's to blame or what's to blame. The emerging facts suggest that there is plenty of blame to pass around and share. However, what Anahita Gheytanchi and her associates (2007) have compiled is worth reporting as a way of looking at how the various systems within a disaster ecosystem operate, or in the case of hurricane Katrina . . . don't! Gheytanchi and her associates report 12 key failures of response.

1. *Lack of efficient communication.* The sine qua non of disaster mitigation is communication. Both within and between the primary and super mesosystems, communication failed. At least four separate command structures were operating in

Katrina's aftermath: two command structures in FEMA and two military command structures. That's at least two too many and resulted in crossed communications, duplicated or incomplete efforts, and generally clouded decision making.

2. *Poor coordination plans.* Coordination is about moving assets to where they are most needed. The inability to coordinate relief efforts ranged from not utilizing one of the finest hospital ships in the world, the U.S.S. *Bataan,* which sat idly offshore, to an inability of FEMA to find buses and drivers and move people out of the Superdome, to hundreds of trucks filled with ice sitting idly in Memphis freight yards with no place to go, to thousands of house trailers sitting in Arkansas when they were desperately needed in Mississippi and Louisiana.

3. *Ambiguous authority relationships.* The Department of Homeland Security remained on a "pull" basis, which means that the state had to request federal assets, rather than a "push" basis, which means that assets would be immediately made available to the state. The National Response Plan Catastrophic Incident Annex (NPR-CIA) should have been invoked prior to landfall, but in fact was never invoked. The prevarication and waffling by Louisiana state and local governments on instituting mandatory evacuation because of the cost, even though they were getting intense pressure from federal authorities to do so, caused severe problems that culminated in the Superdome fiasco.

4. *Who's in charge?* Factious political fights plagued relief efforts. The shifting of blame from the mayor of New Orleans to the governor of Louisiana to the president of the United States settled nothing. Lessons from previous hurricanes about coordination among federal, state, and local governments have not been learned or at least not been put into practice. Laws that govern the use of the armed forces in the continental United States also severely hamstring efforts to quickly deploy military personnel and need to be changed.

5. *Counterterrorism versus all-hazards response.* Money, staff, and other assets have been drained out of FEMA and moved to Homeland Security efforts to combat terrorism. A natural disaster the size of hurricane Katrina dwarfs any terrorist attack up to a nuclear detonation or release of the plague. Yet Homeland Security funded disaster preparedness for terrorism as opposed to natural disaster at a 7-to-1 ratio pre-Katrina.

6. *Ambiguous training standards and lack of preparation.* Across the board, training and experience with disasters were lacking. While the aforementioned FEMA training to become a certified LEMA manager sounds good, the reality is that the training requirements to become an emergency manager and become certified were cumbersome and difficult to complete. Standards for accreditation of response agencies were also vague and not tied to any performance-based evidence.

7. *Where is the "learning" in lessons learned?* A multiagency hurricane exercise that very closely resembled Katrina was completed prior to the storm. Outcomes closely paralleled what actually happened. Yet failure of local and state governments to follow up and take advantage of the exercise doomed it to collect dust on the shelf. This is not the first instance of failure to heed learning from the past. Putting into practice all of the procedures necessary to stave off a disaster like Katrina is difficult, costly, and time consuming; it demands expertise and interagency cooperation at the local level and vertical integration with state and federal agencies. Tackling the logistical and tactical problems involved in implementing those procedures takes a backseat when the danger is not imminent.

8. *Performance assessment was not integrated into the process.* In an evidence-based world, continuous performance assessment should be built into disaster relief efforts, but that is not the case. Performance evaluation is especially lacking in mental health provision. An assessment device that provides benchmarks and rubrics to gauge how relief is proceeding and how well it is going is sorely needed so that best practices models may be generated. There was discussion about that after 9/11, but it still hadn't happened seven years later. To this day there still is no clear way of systematically evaluating the services rendered (Watson, Brymer, & Bonanno, 2011).

9. *The geography of poverty.* Are race and socioeconomic status response factors? While race became a factor because the majority of the poor in New Orleans were black, the fact is that disaster plans as they are currently formulated put the poor, the elderly, the sick, and other disenfranchised individuals who are not financially or physically able to evacuate, relocate, or rebuild at extreme risk without regard to race, creed, color, national origin, religion, sexual preference, or any other distinctive human quality.

10. *Rumor and chaos.* Urban legend and rumor, the bane of any disaster, ran rampant in New Orleans. No clearly designated official spokesperson appeared, giving clear, unconflicted, factual messages that could be believed. Exaggeration by elected officials of armed violence was given airtime by the media, and these rumors then turned into "facts" and took on a life of their own. At its best rumor served to warn people and put them on their guard. At its worst it turned into a self-fulfilling prophecy that slowed rescue efforts. Concrete, factual, up-to-the-minute information by an official spokesperson with both face and content validity was essentially absent. Above all else, an ironclad rule in any disaster is that one highly valid, knowledgeable spokesperson gives facts out in a timely manner and dispels rumors as they arise.

11. *Personal and community preparedness.* There was clearly a sharp divide between what happened in Louisiana and Mississippi in regard to recovery efforts. Both states suffered an equal amount of catastrophic devastation along their coast. However, for whatever reasons, and there are many variables to be examined, Mississippi was more resilient. Whether the majority of its people had better resources and support systems is a different question from whether they were prepared. However, that question needs to be examined carefully, for both physical and psychological differences and perhaps even cultural differences that were demonstrated and heavily influenced long-term outcomes in the two states.

12. *Disaster mental health and the role of mental health professionals.* What actually works for reducing mental health problems in people afflicted with a disaster like Katrina is still not clear, and a great deal of research needs to be done to find out what evidence-based practices do work. Critical incident stress debriefing (CISD), which has been used and most certainly abused as a panacea, appears not to be the ultimate answer. Further, attributions that label survivors as suffering from a mental illness don't work very well either. The preferred operating mode now is the use of psychological first aid and social support (Watson, Brymer, & Bonanno, 2011). Self-efficacy models that foster self-reliance, coping, and problem-solving skills, focus on individual needs, seek to extinguish PTSD at early onset,

and concentrate on functional recovery rather than looking for pathology seem to hold promise (Ruzek, 2006).

Psychological First Aid and Psychosocial Support as Applied to Disaster Survivors

As detailed in Chapter 1, the National Institute of Mental Health (2002) defines psychological first aid (PFA) as establishing safety of the client, reducing stress-related symptoms, providing rest and physical recuperation, and linking clients to critical resources and social support systems. Psychological first aid has now been adapted and modified from its initial use by Raphael (1977) into a first-order, evidence-based approach to working with survivors of mass disasters (Brymer et al., 2006; Hobfoll et al., 2007). It may be taught to paraprofessionals and nonprofessionals. For example, it is one of the training modules (CERT, 2011) that volunteer CERT workers get as part of their search and rescue work training.

Psychological first aid as it is applied in a disaster is designed to reduce distress, generate short- and long-term adaptive functioning, and link survivors with additional services (Watson, Brymer, & Bonanno, 2011). *The Field Operations Guide for Psychological First Aid* developed by the National Child Traumatic Stress Network and the National Center for PTSD (NCTSN/NCPTSD, 2006) is considered state-of-the art in that regard (Webber, Mascari, & Runte, 2010). Delivery of PFA includes a number of core actions (NCTSN/NCPTSD, 2006): make initial respectful contact by a warm engaging presence; gather and provide information in regard to supports needed to deal with immediate physical and safety concerns; provide and direct people in regard to practical assistance needed; provide for their safety and comfort both from a physical and psychological standpoint by linking them with social services; teach them basic coping skills if requested; get information and help that will connect them to social supports, such as reuniting them with family and other social groups with which they are involved.

The job of CFA workers is not to attempt to engage in therapy or elicit details of the tragedy; rather, it is to reduce acute psychological distress by their supportive and compassionate presence through basic active listening and responding skills (Everly & Flynn, 2005). Initiating contact involves the notion of "just being there" or "compassionate loitering" (Webber, Mascari, & Runte, 2010), which emphasizes careful observation, a nonintrusive presence, and caring, respectful contact.

One example is the crisis workers who were available in the dining halls of Virginia Tech residence facilities and classrooms immediately after the shootings there. Volunteers had handouts on normal reactions to tragedies, self-care tips about trauma, and resource lists. Workers were instructed to engage and support students who seemed to be struggling by a respectful, nonintrusive introduction as a way to offer their support. They wore purple armbands to identify their presence. They reported that students initially would not speak to them, but as time went by and students started coming to terms with their grief, they would stop by and thank them for being there (Lawson, Bodenhorn, & Welfare, 2010).

Even doing the foregoing may not be necessary as most people are pretty resilient after a disaster (Hobfoll et al., 2007). As indicated in Chapter 2, Culturally Effective Helping, insistence on participating in "psychotherapy" may be met with anger and extreme resistance. In support of the concept of voluntary participation, Bonanno, Westphal, and Mancini (2011) found that a "one size fits all" intervention might hold no advantage over, and could even undermine, the self-efficacy and resiliency of survivors. For many others, PFA may be both necessary and sufficient. Finally, for some few others, PFA may be necessary but not sufficient.

When More Than PFA Is Needed

It was first thought that severity of exposure to the event and severity of postevent stress and adversity would be the greatest factors indicating the need for more in-depth intervention for serious and chronic psychological problems (Norris, 2006). However, since 9/11 it is clear that degree of exposure or proximity to the attacks does not explain all of the persons presenting with severe psychological problems after a disaster. An individual waving an American flag for hours and hours over an interstate highway 1,000 miles from the impact sites, and refusing to come down for safety, is one example among literally thousands of individuals across the country who "lost it" after 9/11 and needed something more than PFA. In other words, vicarious traumatization through exposure to merely seeing or hearing about disaster events could instigate maladaptive psychological responding. As a consequence, Watson, Brymer, and Bonanno (2011) have compiled a laundry list from their own and a number of other researchers that total 22 risk factors for adults and 13 for children. We believe it doesn't make a lot of sense to try to go through that list and winnow out significant variables. What we do believe in is knowing how to use the Triage Assessment Form in this book. People scoring 20 or more are going to need something more than PFA for sure; they are going to need someone to monitor them closely until they regain some precrisis equilibrium and most likely should not be turned loose on their own. People in the high 20s, who are potentially lethal to themselves or others either by intended commission of unsafe acts or unintended omissions of activities needed to keep them safe, should not be turned loose. People in the high teens will most likely profit from PFA *and* a good deal of on-site psychosocial support so that they don't escalate into the 20s. People in the low teens are probably ideal candidates for PFA. Anybody in the single digits on the TAF probably needs to counsel us!

The Current State of Affairs

The problem with this latter approach, however, is twofold. First, it assumes that a large enough number of practitioners have the necessary crisis intervention skills to do this. If mental health practitioners are not available, then paraprofessionals or laypersons like those who operate in Community Emergency Response Teams (CERTs) and are taught psychological first aid as part of their training may be initial providers of psychological support. That may be stretching it a bit. With all due respect to CERT volunteers, we spend a lot of time teaching these "first aid" techniques to graduate students. They are not easy to implement, particularly when faced with a person in crisis, and we wonder if the estimated learning time of 1 hour and 15 minutes (including video) will be sufficient (CERT, 2011).

You will soon hear from a licensed professional counselor who was deployed in Louisiana post-Katrina. This counselor has extensive training and practice in crisis intervention. She is still the exception rather than the rule. Given her background and training, she struggled and reevaluated her therapeutic worldview as she went through her tour of duty. Her story is not much different from that of many others who were there with her. While the American Red Cross crisis counseling training program has trained thousands of practitioners, that resource was clearly not enough for hurricane Katrina. The Red Cross and government agencies were forced to suspend their standards and bring in any licensed counselor, psychologist, social worker, psychiatric nurse, or psychiatrist they could get their hands on.

FEMA's crisis counseling assistance and training program (CCA-TP) is available to state mental health authorities once an area has been declared a disaster area by the president. That is a lot like closing the barn door after the horse has escaped. Way too many things are happening to stop and say, "OK, we now have a large, metastasizing disaster on our hands; let's do some training!" This training occurred in Memphis approximately a month after Katrina. To say it was mostly useless is being kind. We believe that training should come prior to any catastrophic event and follow-up refresher courses should go with it. After a congressional inquiry into this program's problems in south Florida, a critical review of it was instigated and a number of worthwhile recommendations were made to tighten it and beef it up—particularly in regard to coordination activities (Department of Homeland Security, 2008). None of those recommendations made clear whether a municipality can actually get training prior to a disaster, though.

Young and his associates (Young, 2006; Young et al., 2006) have developed a comprehensive predisaster training program that holds much promise. It has a conceptual framework that differentiates natural and human-caused disaster and examines effects on both individuals and communities. It has both practitioner and administrative training components and specific modules on high-risk client populations and interfaces with other organizations. This fine program is time consuming, most likely expensive, and requires trainers who have expertise in both disaster mental health practice and administration. Those are difficult commodities to find.

Consistent and comprehensive training for mental health providers in crisis intervention as they matriculate through professional training programs has been piecemeal at best (Coke-Weatherly, 2005), as clearly described by Roberts (2005). That appears to be changing to some extent. The Council for Accreditation of Counseling and Related Educational Programs and the National Association of School Psychologists both require the teaching of crisis intervention in their accrediting criteria. While that may now be seen as necessary, it remains to be seen whether what is taught will be sufficient. Other professional accreditation agencies appear to make the provision of crisis intervention training voluntary.

Most certainly, Katrina was a megacrisis that had metastasizing effects far beyond its geographic landfall and a physical scope that had never before been experienced, with disenfranchised people shipped all over the United States. The terrorist attack on 9/11 probably had the widest range of vicarious psychological effects ever experienced in the United States, with the possible exception of the Japanese attack on Pearl Harbor.

A number of national committees issuing from both 9/11 and Katrina have made numerous recommendations in regard to the provision of crisis services to individuals following these human-made and natural disasters. These recommendations have been summarized by Watson, Brymer, and Bonanno (2011) in their article on postdisaster psychological intervention since 9/11.

1. Be proactive ahead of time with pragmatic, flexible plans that match appropriate services to each phase of the recovery period.
2. Promote a sense of safety, connectedness, calm, hope, and efficacy.
3. Participate in groups with stakeholders to coordinate and learn from others, minimize duplication, and mend gaps in service.
4. Be culturally sensitive and consider human rights.
5. Be willing to undergo evaluation and open to scrutiny of practices.
6. Stay up to date on evidence-based practices.
7. Maximize participation by local populations and find and use local resources and capabilities.
8. Integrate activities and programs into larger systems to reduce stand-alone services, reach more people, and be more sustainable over time and space.
9. Use a stepped approach that focuses early efforts on practical help and pragmatic support, with psychological first aid for a generally resilient population.
10. Use triage assessment and focused care for those with specialized needs who require increased levels of intervention.
11. Provide technological assistance, consultation, and training to local providers.
12. Conduct needs assessment of the community with ongoing monitoring of services and program evaluation.
13. Support community-based cultural rituals, memorial services, and spiritual healing practices.

Priscilla Dass-Brailsford's book *Crisis and Disaster Counseling: Lessons Learned From Hurricane Katrina and Other Disasters* (2010) examines many of these recommendations, and the lack of their in-depth implementation. The book places particular emphasis on cultural variables (Boyd, Quevillon, & Engdahl, 2010; Boyd-Franklin, 2010; Dass-Brailsford, 2010) that affected mitigation efforts post-Katrina. How the worker interacts in the first few minutes and hours of contact will most likely determine how effective intervention is and can profoundly affect the recovery course of survivors (Miller,

2010). You should understand that this is why we included a chapter on multiculturalism in this book—not just to be politically correct, but because this is one of the most important variables in disaster crisis intervention.

You should also understand that, as yet, we believe the foregoing 13 principles are neither well known nor practiced regularly by a sufficient number of folks in this business to handle a megadisaster or a pandemic. That is particularly true of pandemics, in which the needs will be exponentially greater than in local megadisasters like Katrina (Webber & Mascari, 2010).

Crisis intervention is not the major occupational definition of most of the people who are called to a mass disaster, nor are you going to find it named in the Dictionary of Occupational Titles. Until that happens, there are likely to be, both on an individual and systemic basis, problems from people attempting to ply this trade who don't know what they are doing or, worse yet, think they do but don't. Frankly, the mere fact that you are reading this book most likely makes you more knowledgeable about crisis intervention than a lot of other professionals who hold Ph.D.s in the helping services fields. The recent birth of Division 56 (Trauma Psychology) of the American Psychological Association and the requirements of counseling and school psychology accrediting agencies for the provision of crisis intervention are a start, along with the American Red Cross's view to expand its psychological intervention curriculum and conduct outreach to more constituencies. Evidence-based treatment practices are starting to be published, but the real-time chaos of disasters makes it hard to do much other than do ex post facto studies. We agree with Silverman, Allen, and Ortiz (2010) that with all due respect to PFA, which appears to have replaced CISD as the treatment de jour, we would like to see a whole lot more outcome studies on its effectiveness, particularly in regard to whom it is applied to, by what kinds of people, under what kinds of conditions. Please forgive us for being flinty-eyed about panaceas, but 40 years in this business have seen a lot of cure-alls come and go.

The People of Disasters: Responders and Survivors
Crisis Workers at the Disaster

Crisis workers have a wide range of duties after a disaster. Foremost is simply being available for survivors to talk with, listening to their experiences, empathizing, and processing with them as they attempt to make sense of it. These activities fall mostly within provision of psychosocial support services and psychological first aid. Workers may help survivors locate significant others, help relatives with identification of victims, or help make arrangements for the deceased. They may provide information on the affective, behavioral, cognitive, interpersonal, and physiological responses to traumatic events (Friedman, Ritchie, & Watson, 2006).

Crisis workers may help relatives through the grieving process, promote social support systems for survivors, and devise a plan of action to mobilize the survivors' resources. They may make appropriate referrals and provide follow-up services. They may also provide debriefing to other emergency service workers (Walker, 1990), prepare food, find clothing, wash dishes, move rubble, help people find lost puppies, talk about how a family who has just lost everything is going to get their 17-year-old into the private college they had planned sending her to but now have no money to do so, administer first aid, help people figure out insurance and FEMA claim procedures, help determine what to do with a grandmother whose nursing home is now full of black mold, conflict-resolve angry feelings between tired, hot, smelly inhabitants of a disaster shelter, and do a thousand other things that lend physical and psychological support—all while dining on military MREs, contracting head lice, going without a bath for a *very* long time, getting bitten by fire ants, and seeing a dermatologist for an unknown skin condition after their tour of duty. Following are some reflections by Dr. Holly Branthoover (personal communication, October 18, 2006) on her experience post-Katrina.

Thoughts of a Mental Health Worker on Katrina One Year Later

Dr. Holly Branthoover, Licensed Professional Counselor and Associate Professor of Counseling, Indiana University of Pennsylvania

I was recruited by the National Board for Certified Counselors via e-mail on Sunday, September 4, 2005, to respond to hurricane Katrina for the Red Cross. I filled out the application packet immediately, faxed it back, and expected to hear from them in a few weeks. The Red Cross contacted me 2 days later, on Tuesday, September 6, asking, "When can you leave?" I garnered permission from the university, prepared coverage for my classes, and flew out on Saturday, September 10. Preparation for the trip included a Red Cross phone orientation and faxed material providing me instructions.

I flew into Baton Rouge, Louisiana, and completed my "in processing" with the Red Cross. I slept in a staff shelter in Baton Rouge that evening and received my assignment the next morning. I was assigned as a part of a team of three mental health workers—a team leader who was a licensed clinical social worker and another team member who was also a licensed professional counselor. We drove to Covington, Louisiana, to the regional Red Cross headquarters for the eastern region of Louisiana. At Covington, we were given our field assignment—to live and work with evacuees at Pearl River High School in Pearl River, Louisiana (275 residents), and to also service three other shelters: Riverside Elementary (25 residents), 6th Ward Elementary (36 residents), and Abita Springs Middle School (35 residents). We also added 5th Ward Elementary (50 residents) when we got to the field.

I stayed in Louisiana for 2 weeks, leaving on Saturday, September 24. However, my departure was very stressful as hurricane Rita arrived on Friday, September 23, closing the Baton Rouge airport and necessitating a drive to Jackson, Mississippi, to catch a flight. Here are some of the points I feel are important if you decide to do disaster mental health work:

In addition to my initial mental health team of three, we received another mental health team member and heavily utilized some local mental health people who had volunteered. The local people were very important in that they were a potential constant in people's lives, whereas we could only be available for a short time. So we had them handle people or families that were potentially staying in the area. It worked very well. I believe this use of local resources is paramount to a successful operation on this scale.

Another thing that I feel very strongly about after my experience is that roving teams may work for medical personnel, but they do not work for mental health. You must join the system. My team lived in the shelter. We ate from the ERV [emergency response vehicle]. We showered (or didn't, in some cases) in the same showers as the residents. Although we certainly did not share their experience of loss, we did share their experience of the frustration of living in a shelter, and I believe it helped them to develop a rapport with us that facilitated assistance.

When we first got to Pearl River High School, we were assigned a counseling room in which to see people. How many people came to that room? Not one! People in crisis do not present for counseling; they are not looking for self-actualization. We had to be out there, in the shelter, sitting with them, talking to them, listening to their stories. As previously mentioned, our team was covering several other shelters, not just Pearl River High School. Our team leader made a wise decision that we needed to provide a constant presence there, as well, so the same people traveled to the same shelters on a daily basis.

One of the things that crisis textbooks talk about is that crisis responders should have the quality of flexibility—I never realized the importance of this until my experience in Louisiana. I had no idea where I was going when I boarded the plane to Louisiana. I had to call a phone number when I landed to get more information. Talk about an adventure! After I reached my assignment in Pearl River, communication was terrible. Even 2 weeks after the storm, cell phone service, landline phone service, TV, Internet, electricity, and so on were all unreliable or nonexistent. Information was carried by courier in some instances, and by the time a directive reached us, it could be wrong or changed.

Misinformation was rampant. We spent some time on rumor control. We actually traveled by car to sites that we "heard" were providing services—like water, cleaning kits, food, blue roofs (tarpaulins to cover damaged roofs), and so on. We tried to confirm what information was factual and pass that to our residents. Who would want to use the last of their gas to drive to a site for assistance and find there is no assistance available? We also acted as a liaison with FEMA representatives in the area, getting accurate information and facilitating services. Much of our time was spent in linking clients to assistance—more social work than counseling.

Medical services are also a part of what the Red Cross provides during a disaster. The mental health staff worked closely to assist the medical staff. Some people were in crisis because of their injuries (e.g., a woman with a severe vaginal infection from being in the floodwater who thought she was dying). Some were in crisis because they could not get their medication (everything from life-sustaining medication to methadone). We detoxed half a dozen people from their methadone in the shelter. Lack of medication was a big issue. Since we, as a team, had a car, we tried to barter and borrow supplies and medication when we came into contact with staff at other locations or on trips to regional headquarters. Things like hand sanitizer and lice kits were quite a commodity.

Working with the children in the shelters was another important activity that we engaged in. One of the members of my team was the head of a day care center

in New York, so she was very invested in setting up children's programs. Again, we did very little counseling here. Our team member set up children's activities three times per day at Pearl River. Activities included arts and crafts, games, movies, and the like. This served two positive purposes, providing structure to the children's day (the shelter is a boring place) and giving parents a break. We had to put boundaries on the parent break because some took advantage. For example, we had to make a rule that parents could not leave the shelter while children's activities were going on (so they could be available if there was a problem). Although it varied by developmental level, children began to express their feelings about the hurricane and their current life situation via the artwork and games.

When we first arrived, and periodically throughout, we worked with disaster relief services staff a great deal. Staff were stressed and burned out. At some of the smaller shelters, we were the only professional mental health service providers that the disaster relief staff had seen since the hurricane. At one shelter, several medically needy residents had died, and staff needed to talk about and process this experience. They were angry at the lack of supplies and communication—so much food was available that it was sometimes thrown away, but there was a great lack of medical supplies. At times, staff members got into arguments, and we would mediate. Sometimes, staff was just stressed and needed to talk. Our team leader consulted often with the shelter manager, assisting in administrative decisions about shelter services. I believe this was a strength of our shelter manager—getting mental health input on shelter operation. In one instance, I was asked to talk with a staff member who had violated Red Cross policy and was going to be relieved of her duties and sent home early.

In the shelter, we had National Guard protection for only the first 2 days. From then on, we had 24-hour protection from local law enforcement—parish sheriffs, with at least two on duty at all times. We worked closely with the sheriffs—assisting with resident arguments, and so on. There were two cocaine arrests at the shelter, with those residents being taken to jail. We had two domestic violence incidents—we worked with security to come up with a safety plan for all residents (this meant moving the two offending husbands to a different shelter). I spoke personally with a least two people who were suicidal, and we worked with security to observe them since there were no inpatient mental health facilities available.

Another incident that was particularly scary happened 2 nights before I left. When hurricane Rita was coming, a mandatory evacuation of New Orleans resulted in our shelter numbers swelling to close to 500 people. Many were Hispanic workers from construction crews who spoke little or no English. A local person and a worker got into a fight in the cafeteria, and a gun was pulled. Although security directly dealt with the gun issue, we assisted with crowd control and calming everyone down afterward—including staff!

Some of my philosophies of crisis intervention were challenged as a result of this experience. The goal of crisis intervention is to return clients to their precrisis state of functioning. In this case, the majority of the clients in the shelter had a precrisis state of functioning that was dysfunctional! By 2 weeks poststorm, most of the residents left in shelters were people who had little before the storm in the way of resources—both personal and financial. People with family support systems or money were already gone. The majority of our residents had supported themselves via public assistance or SSI disability. Many were involved with community mental health, child protective services, and the legal system. Several were inmates from the county jail who had been released as the storm approached. Drug abuse, child abuse, and domestic violence were prevalent. Given the demographics, it was hard to tell when crisis intervention should end! I also found it important to help people problem-solve within the context of their culture. One man felt trapped about making a decision to go back to work. He did not want to leave his wife alone at the shelter, as he felt it was his duty to protect her. His wife had been called back to work, too. However, he did not want her working while he was not (who would watch their stuff?), and his duty as a man was to provide. I had to work within these values—not my own.

My last two thoughts are related to actually being a part of a team response. Just because you are "mental health" doesn't mean that you are not part of the entire shelter team. Pitch in! I did kitchen work, carried and moved things, and cleaned. Each night, after residents went to bed (curfew at 10 P.M.), the whole shelter was disinfected. I helped with this every night. Working alongside someone can give a great opportunity for them to share their feelings or vent. It also allowed us to be part of the staff—not separate. This said, I do not minimize the benefit of doing mental health things for staff. The second week I was there, a local pizza place opened. The mental health team organized a pizza

party for staff for after residents went to bed. It turned out to be a great stress reliever.

Last, all of the things I have talked about are occurring while you are living the experience of a disaster and trying to help people at the same time. I slept on a cot, showered only once the first week, and tried to avoid getting lice (which I did, luckily, because the thought alone freaked me out!). In our travels, we saw the horrific devastation in Slidell, Louisiana, which borders Pearl River and was where the eye of the hurricane passed through. We also traveled, on our day off, into New Orleans, again witnessing the loss and devastation of the storm. During our trip to the city, we got free pizzas from Dominos (they were passing them out) and water. We drove around the city to different National Guard troops, firemen, and EMS companies, passing out pizza and water, and spent time just talking to them—something they were grateful for when they found out we were "mental health." It was scary to be in a city that looked like a ghost town, patrolled by military personnel with M16s. We got to see the Superdome and the Convention Center. I believe it was important to have this R&R even though we were still, in a way, doing our mental health job. There were several times in the 2 weeks when I got really stressed out (like when I asked for lice kits at headquarters and was told we couldn't have lice at our shelter—because they hadn't gotten a report of it!). So it is important to find a way to take care of yourself—phone calls home, camaraderie with other staff, watching a DVD (after the power is back on!), and so on. You can't help others if you are a stressed-out, burned-out mess!

Now switch to Memphis, Tennessee, 450 miles away.

Lessons I Learned From Katrina

Dr. Richard James, Licensed Professional Counselor, Psychologist, National Board Certified School Counselor, Department of Counseling, Educational Psychology and Research, University of Memphis

When Katrina hit the Gulf Coast, little did mental health providers in Memphis, Tennessee, realize that they also would be in the eye of the hurricane. As the magnitude of the disaster started to become clearer and the flow of evacuees moved away from the coast, one thing became very clear in a hurry. We were not prepared for the onslaught of people with wide-ranging mental and medical problems that were about to descend on us. Compounding the problems those medically and mentally fragile people brought into our community were 13,000 homeless individuals who were essentially living out of their cars or motels for the first 2 weeks post-Katrina. As it became clearer that these people were not going back home immediately, a variety of crisis situations arose.

Three anecdotes will give you a pretty good idea of how ill prepared the city of Memphis and Shelby County, Tennessee, were to deal with a major disaster as far as provision of mental health service was concerned. This is probably more ominous when considering that the scene of the actual disaster was more than 400 miles away from us.

On September 3, 2006, I was helping my daughter and her fiancé load my truck with gasoline, lantern and cooking fuel, lanterns, cooking equipment, firearms, meals ready to eat, sleeping bags, and other supplies as they prepared to go back to see what was left of their home in Long Beach, Mississippi, after hurricane Katrina sent a 5-foot wall of water through it. At 10:00 A.M. I received a phone call from a harried Shelby County Red Cross director of medical services who had located me by word of mouth and was told I might be able to help since "I knew everything about crisis intervention." He asked if I could provide assistance to the crew of the *American Queen* sternwheeler passenger liner that was docked in Memphis with a crew of 250 very agitated individuals. The boat and crew all shipped out of New Orleans, and they had no word of their families or homes because they had been on the Mississippi River since Katrina hit. The problem was that no one could find this 400-foot-long boat—in Memphis, not even the police. Finally, the riverboat was located at 5 P.M. I got another counselor and headed for the boat. Now the problem was that the boat was set to sail at 6 P.M., passengers were filing on board, and dinner was being served, so no one could come to talk to us. That was the start of what came to be a deluge that we were ill prepared to handle and caused us to reevaluate every facet of our disaster preparedness and mental health provision system in Memphis.

The bishop of the Memphis Catholic diocese had witnessed Katrina firsthand from a hotel room as he saw his car go floating away in Bay St. Louis, Mississippi. He immediately flung open the doors of all the Catholic schools in Memphis and welcomed any and all families from the coast to enroll their children tuition free in the Memphis Catholic school system. Many of these children came from very poor families with extreme deficits in their educational backgrounds. A lot of these kids were the toughest of the tough to teach and found their way into new Catholic inner-city Jubilee schools, which operate on very tight budgets with little support staff. Since I was "the guy who knew all about crisis" and was also a school counselor educator, I was asked to put a workshop together for the private schools in Memphis on dealing with traumatized children. On September 10, together with Dr. Jo Epstein, a National Certified School Counselor and an elementary school counselor with the city of Memphis, I delivered a workshop at the University of Memphis that was attended by 31 counselors and teachers from 19 private schools. After we finished delivering a 3-hour workshop on trauma and what they might expect to see in their school buildings, I looked out over the room and saw that many of those faces looked like deer caught in the headlights of an oncoming truck! I immediately knew that I would need help in dealing not only with evacuees but also with teachers and counselors, who would be suffering from secondary traumatization from attempting to deal with those children. For the next 6 months these teachers and counselors met with me for supervision as they valiantly attempted to deal with these high-risk children and stave off compassion fatigue and burnout.

It quickly became apparent that we didn't have enough mental health professionals to deal with the people coming into our city with a host of medical and mental issues. We also did not have anyone in charge of handling these people. The coordinator of the local crime victims' assistance center, a licensed clinical social worker, and another LCSW at one of the local mental health clinics stepped into the breach and started to make order out of what was rapidly turning into a classic example of chaos theory at work (see Chapter 1, Approaching Crisis Intervention). Picture your author sitting in a reception center talking with a methadone maintenance heroin addict from New Orleans.

Addict: "Hey, man, they won't give me any methadone, say I got to have a prescription. If I don't get some methadone pretty damn quick, I'll go rob a liquor store and get the real deal!"

By the middle of September we had approximately 13,000 expatriates from New Orleans and the Gulf Coast in our city. All thoughts about licensing and certifying mental health workers for disaster work went right out the window with Katrina. The faculty at our university mobilized 200 students in the counseling, school psychology, and social work departments, and with faculty supervisors they started working in the shelters. These students and faculty served up to

2 months in this capacity until some semblance of order could be restored.

The bottom line was that we too were not prepared for this megadisaster. The outcome of this disaster was the establishment of a planning committee for the Greater Memphis Area Emergency Preparedness for Mental Health. That committee's composition ranges from mental health personnel from hospitals, community agencies, and human service provision organizations to religious leaders, school system personnel, city and county officials, the police, fire, and EMT departments, charitable organizations, homeland security, medical facilities, and universities. This is certainly a work in progress. Will we be better prepared than we were for Katrina? That's a good question! Wherever you are in this country, or any other country for that matter, you might ask yourself the same question. The ripple effects of a disaster this large flow far out from the epicenter. Disasters that affect such a great number of people need all of the professions mentioned above if successful crisis intervention is going to occur, as you will soon see.

Case Study of the Benefield Family

Now meet the Benefield family, who are about to experience the crisis of their lives. The Benefields typify, in an encapsulated way, how the ecosystemic crisis intervention model *should* (note the emphasis on "should") operate when a large-scale disaster afflicts a family.

Tuesday, April 21, 14:00 Hours Military Time (2:00 P.M. CDT)

An F-4 tornado has hit Midville, Tennessee, a town with a population of approximately 40,000 in the south-central United States. The storm cut across the town and left a path of destruction about one-quarter to one-half mile wide for a distance of more than 5 miles. It effectively cut a path through the industrial park, damaging numerous buildings but particularly wreaking havoc on the automotive plant, which employed more than 1,000 people. The plant is close to a total loss. The storm continued through several residential areas and a housing development, hopscotched, and then hit the main elementary school of Midville and reduced it to rubble. All 600 students were inside the building at the time, under cover in the hallways.

The water plant received a direct hit from the storm and can no longer keep water pressure up or produce potable drinking water. The power grid has been disrupted by downed power lines and wrecked substations, and the city is currently without power. Both cellular and landline telephone systems are inoperable because of downed towers and lines. The local hospital has received minor damage but is still in operation. Local fire, police, and emergency services have emerged largely unscathed and are close to fully operational. There has been a significant loss of life in addition to injuries that appear to be in the hundreds.

Now meet the Benefield family: Travis Benefield, age 33, a machinist at the local automobile plant; Sara Lee Benefield, age 32, a dental assistant; Jason Benefield, age 13, an eighth-grader at Midville Middle School; Lou Ann Benefield, age 11, a sixth-grader at Midville Middle School; Shawn Benefield, age 6, a first-grader at Midville Elementary School; and Loretta Benefield, age 54, the mother of Travis.

April 21, 14:15 Hours Military Time (2:15 P.M., 15 minutes after the tornado)

Travis Benefield is emerging from the rubble of the automobile plant. He has no major injuries, just minor cuts and bruises from falling and flying debris. While frantically helping dig others out, he is also attempting to reach his wife on his cell phone, but that is not working. Sara Lee Benefield is currently upside down in her van in a water-filled ditch. She is there because she heard the tornado siren and, instead of taking cover in the dentist's office where she worked, became hysterical and was on her way to school to pick up her children. She is semiconscious, bleeding, and clearly in need of rescue and medical assistance.

Jason Benefield is currently looking for his sister, Lou Ann, in the melee that is now Midville Middle School. No one was hurt in either the middle school or the high school, and neither school was significantly damaged. Everyone in both the middle and high schools had been protected in the hallways; however, chaos now reigns as teachers attempt to control panic-stricken students who heard the tornado go over and can now see the destructive path it has made. Lou Ann is likewise attempting to find her brother Jason. She is also hysterical because she has seen that the tornado essentially destroyed the elementary school that her brother Shawn attends. Shawn is currently missing, probably buried somewhere under the rubble of the elementary school. Loretta, the grandmother who resides with the family, is currently lying in a field, dead from a broken neck and back, about one-quarter mile from where the family lived in a manufactured home that has been blown away and no longer exists.

April 21, 14:25 Hours, Emergency Command Center

LEM director, Thaddeus Washington: (*on short-wave radio to all ham operators and state police emergency and state emergency broadcast systems*) It appears we have had a major tornado disaster here involving most of Midville. We currently have no power or cellular or landline telephone communication. It appears that there is a large path of destruction throughout the city, and there is also a very high casualty rate as we had less than 15 minutes' warning time. We have ruptured gas lines and water lines and have no ability to pump water. We have at least two fires. We are requesting immediate assistance from the region IV and state emergency management network. We are making a damage assessment now. Instructions will follow in about 30 minutes.

As the reports from police cars and ham radio operators start to come into the center, the director has to make several quick decisions about the magnitude of the disaster. From the initial reports he decides to alert the regional and state emergency management coordinators. He also needs a better assessment of what is going on in the community. He therefore asks for a state police helicopter and instructs his emergency preparedness manager to get airborne and conduct an assessment.

April 21, 14:35 Hours, Midville Middle School, School Crisis Response Team Meeting in Cafeteria

Linda Gidcome, Assistant Superintendent, Crisis Response Coordinator: It appears that we have a major crisis involving not only the elementary school but the whole town. The police are over at the elementary school, but we have many children trapped in there. Undoubtedly there are casualties in that building. Jackson Little, the elementary school counselor and our crisis intervention coordinator, is not yet accounted for. Until he is found, Jim Constansis, the high school vocational coordinator, is his backup and in charge of intervention. We also have some other missing people, so, Jim, I want you to get backups for them. I am going to turn the meeting over to Jim.

Jim Constansis, Crisis Intervention Coordinator: We also have to deal with our children here and in the high school to be sure they are safe. We need to get everybody back in their rooms and run the roll. Right now we don't have any good information about where "safe" is. As such, we are going to hold all middle and secondary school students in their respective buildings. It appears that right now there is no way into the school from outside due to debris on the roads. I want to get backups for all the missing members of the team. Our first priority is to run the rolls and see

who is missing. So we need to take the TO GO boxes' primary hard copy and send three teams (Red, Blue, Green) over to the elementary school, while the Orange Team stays here and the Purple Team stays at the high school to start receiving kids. We will bring K through third grades here and fourth and fifth grades to the high school. Red has K and 1, Blue has 2 and 3, and Green has 4 and 5. They are going to need medical assistance over there, so I want the Orange Team to pull all of our available medical supplies out of the sports facility storage and set up a dispensary in the cafeteria.

Luda Sarapokin, our school nurse, will be running that. We're going to get on the radio and let OEC know what our condition is just as soon as the building engineer can get the generator hooked up to it and running. All of you pick up your two-way radios. Things are going to get pretty hectic, so remember your radio manners and protocol. We have done this in an exercise; the only difference was that the middle school was the target. We can do this. Let's go to work!

The Incident Command System has been in place for 2 years in the Midville School District. It has a clear incident command system (Thomae, 2002) that has been activated on the tornado's departure. Its first and primary job is to account for all the children. Any parents who could somehow manage to get to the school would be taken to a waiting area before any children would be released. The parents have been informed of this plan and know what to expect and what to do.

April 21, 15:05 Hours, above Midville in a helicopter

Saria Wickeramasaka, Emergency Preparedness Coordinator: (*in a state police helicopter above Midville, on the radio speaking to the LEM director*) The Packard engine plant is completely ruined; the total building is involved. I can see human movement, but there are undoubtedly people trapped in the plant. I do not see any evidence of fire. We will need heavy equipment including cranes and hoists. We will need EMTs and rescue equipment and units. The Hi Power petroleum bulk plant got hit and there is leakage from their storage tanks. It appears both gasoline and fuel oil are being discharged, although the berms seem to be containing the fuel at present. We will need a containment and cleanup crew there along with fire equipment and spillage trucks. I see no evidence of fire. The elementary school has received a direct hit. The middle of the building has sustained a great deal of damage and the east wing has collapsed. I can see movement, and it appears the school CRTs are working at the elementary school. There are undoubtedly many casualties.

The roads to the school are currently impassable. We will need heavy equipment including teams with chain saws to get in there. I would recommend this as our first priority. We do have two house fires, one on Appleton at Branch and one on Sycamore past Hoover. The one on Sycamore is in danger of involving an apartment complex. It should be fought immediately. The street is blocked from the north, but trucks can come in from the east side and through the apartment complex.

The waterworks is a total loss with the pumping station and filter house completely wrecked. You can probably assume that the available water supply is what is currently in the two north and south standpipes, which appear to have sustained no damage. The sanitary works is operational. The path of the tornado is pretty steady from southwest to northeast approximately one-quarter to one-half mile wide running from state highway 37 to just south of I-69 for a stretch of about 5 miles. There are some skips, but it has pretty much gone through Midville from the industrial park on the southwest side of town through the west side of town. Before it went back up in the air, it got the mobile home park on Breezemore Road. There are mobile homes blown apart and on top of one another. I can see human movement here also, but there are going to be lots of casualties.

I estimate about 200 homes destroyed or heavily damaged and 600 more with some damage. We need to notify Midville Central and St. Andrew's hospitals that they need to go to Code Red [highest emergency status]. We are going to need Tennessee Valley Power to do the same, as it appears we have a complete power outage across the city. Midville Power and Light will not be able to handle this outage alone.

As this assessment comes into the emergency operations center (EOC), information is relayed through the regional EOC coordinator and transmitted to the state EOC. As the magnitude of the disaster unfolds, the governor is notified and mobilizes National Guard units. Word goes out to FEMA, the Red Cross, and the Salvation Army, and these groups begin mobilizing human resources to go to Midville. Within 1 hour and 10 minutes, a massive mobilization effort is underway. Food, drinking water, medicine, medical supplies, emergency medical personnel in the form of EMTs and fire departments, rescue teams, and heavy equipment all move toward Midville.

As Lane (2003) indicates, if roads are impassable and it is possible, someone with the EOC needs to get airborne and conduct a visual assessment of the extent of the damage and relay information to the center about what and who are going to be needed where and under how high a priority.

April 21, 15:21 Hours, Command Center

As the LEMA director sends out mobilization orders, a number of workers you will soon meet swing into action. In these first few hours and days they will be administering what is generally construed to be psychological first aid as they attempt to gain control over the chaotic scenes and traumatized individuals who are survivors of the disaster. As they enter the setting, they will be sensitive to the culture and diversity of the populations they are servicing. They will also be aware of and looking for at-risk populations. They are, first and foremost, interested in the immediate physical safety of survivors. To that end, they will attempt to provide a sense of predictability, control, comfort, and safety to survivors by providing straightforward and easily understood information about disaster response activities and services. They will attempt to protect survivors from additional traumatic experiences and trauma reminders while they go about their work. Major tasks will be reuniting children with their caregivers, stabilizing emotionally overwhelmed survivors, and providing support for acutely bereaved persons (National Center for PTSD, n.d.a).

To accomplish the foregoing tasks, the workers will engage in a great deal of information gathering in regard to current needs and concerns about the following:

1. Nature and severity of experiences during the disaster
2. Death of a family member or close friend
3. Concerns about immediate postdisaster circumstances and ongoing threat
4. Separations from or concern about the safety of loved ones
5. Physical illness and need for medications
6. Losses incurred as a result of the disaster (home, school, pets, personal property, etc.)
7. Extreme feelings of guilt or shame
8. Thoughts about causing harm to self or others
9. Lack of adequate supportive social network
10. Prior alcohol or drug use
11. Prior exposure to trauma or loss
12. Prior psychological problems (National Center for PTSD, n.d.a)

When the workers have the foregoing information, they will identify and clarify the most immediate needs of the survivor, discuss an action plan with the person, and then act to address the identified needs. Integral to this process is providing information on traumatic stress and coping mechanisms to help alleviate the stress and linking the individual with the disaster relief services they will need (National Center for PTSD, n.d.c). Follow these crisis workers now as they put the foregoing points into action.

April 21, 15:51 Hours, Midville Elementary School

Jack Tankersly, School CRT Blue Team member at Midville Elementary: (*helping a dazed boy with some cuts and blood on him out of the rubble of the east hallway of Midville Elementary School*) I'm Mr. Tankersly from the middle school. How are you doing?

Shawn: Iah guess Ah'm okay, Iah dunno. . . . Whaaat happened?

Jack: There was a tornado, but you are going to be all right. If you can walk okay, we are going to take you to the middle school and get you checked out. Can you do that?

Shawn: Yeah, I guess. I jest got some little cuts on my arms. There's some other kids hurt bad back in the hallway, though. Jamie's eyes were shut and he wasn't talkin' even when I shook him. He was hurt real bad, maybe even dead or somethin'.

Jack: Yes, I know, and we will get them out. So don't worry about that. Right now let's focus on you. Can you give me your name and tell me who your teacher is?

Shawn: Shawn Benefield. Ah'm in Mrs. Cruz's first-grade class.

Jack: (*Checks over the two-way radio with the documentation leader on the student in the central elementary To Go box.*) Good. You have a brother and a sister in the middle school, Jason and Lou Ann, right?

Shawn: Yes.

Jack: I am going to have someone take you up to the middle school and get those cuts cleaned up and check you out. I'll let them know you are coming, so your sister and brother will know you are okay.

One of the critical components in any disaster in a school is keeping track of and accounting for children. Nowhere is the concept of the school as *in loco parentis* (in place of the parent) more important. Portable, centralized, and redundant To Go boxes (Thomae, 2002) are critical to such an endeavor; they hold classroom lists, student names, addresses, telephone numbers, medical issues, release forms, and parent and guardian names. Moving a school full of injured, confused, and terrified students is an undertaking that must be done carefully and precisely so that no student is lost or unaccounted for. While there is a school Critical Incident Stress Management Team to deal with students' psychological concerns, it is separate and distinct from the incident command system and will not come into

operation until the physical safety of the students is assured. Particularly important staff members on this team are bus drivers, secretaries, and custodians who have knowledge of children and building facilities that educators do not (Allen & Sheen, 2005). Reuniting missing children with parents is a critical component and one of the highest priorities in any disaster (National Center for PTSD, n.d.a). As an example, one of the Herculean efforts accomplished by the National Center for Missing and Exploited Children after hurricane Katrina was reuniting all 5,192 children reported missing with their families (Missing Children, 2006).

April 21, 15:30 Hours, EOC Command Center

Thaddeus Washington: (*addressing command center staff*) We have a Class One disaster. We are going to be overwhelmed with dead, wounded, and people needing shelter, food, water, clothing, and mental health assistance. We are setting a shelter up at the National Guard Armory. We are going to set up a morgue at the Seabrook Packing Plant. The high school and the middle school are going to be reception and clearing centers, so we can get people sorted out and families reunited.

We may have to turn them into shelters too. As soon as we get that done, we will probably set up for the Red Cross and FEMA teams here at the Civic Center. Our first priority is to get the kids out of the elementary school. Preliminary reports indicate that there are a number trapped in the building.

We need to get the roads opened so we can get heavy equipment in there. The EMAs from Sawyer, Plainfield, and Cumberland are sending fire and rescue units. The state EOC has been notified and informed the governor, who is going to call for a presidential disaster order. We need to get the road opened, so get all of Howell Paving and Construction and the State Highway department equipment on the road and heading in that direction, and get three of our CERT teams to help them clear trees, so let them know we have to have chainsaws. Saria landed and says we will need at least one and possibly two tracked cranes.

Our second priority will be the Packard plant. I want Cassius Mendoza, the construction superintendent for Norton Metal Frame Buildings, to go out there and tell us what we need. We also need to get people out there to help organize them—although Joel Pickard, the plant superintendent, and I have gone over their emergency plan and they seem to be functioning pretty well given the way the whole thing came down. Get the rest of the CERT teams spread out along the line from state route 37 up to I-69. Be sure we get one team up to the mobile home park on Breezemore. We need to get the water system back on line. It appears most of our staff at the waterworks, including Joe Mulvidge, the chief engineer, and Hack Townsend, the superintendent, have been injured. I have asked staff from the Sawyer water system to come and give us an assessment. Until further notice we will ration water and put a boil order out because we are bound to lose pressure on the system. I have a feeling that this is going to be really bad. I hope our practices have paid off. Dr. Benjamin, we are going to need to get your mental health team assembled. I am afraid there is going to be work for them. OK, everybody, you know your jobs, let's go to work!

April 21, 15:35 Hours

Dr. Yolanda Benjamin, Executive Director of Hatchie County Mental Health Center and mental health liaison to the Midville EOC: (*speaking to Ester Carey, her secretary, at the mental health center on an emergency band radio*) How many staff have we got that are at the center? OK, good! They know what to do. We are going to need counselors at the National Guard Armory and out at Seabrook Packing. We are also going to need to send counselors out to both hospitals to work with the chaplains out there. As soon as they open the road to the schools, I'll go out there and see what kind of assistance they need there. There are going to be Red Cross counselors coming in, but right now we are it.

Both Washington and Benjamin are going to have to balance between being responders and coordinators. For the present, they are in the responding business, but as more outside assistance arrives, their job will change to consulting and coordination with the external support systems that are going to flood into the area (Lane, 2003). It is critically important that integration of mental health services with other disaster responders occurs and that it is recognized as a critical component to overall relief efforts, as exemplified by Mr. Washington and his immediate referral to Dr. Benjamin and her mental health teams (Ørner et al., 2006).

April 21, 17:12 Hours

Juanita Sanchez, leader of Community Emergency Response Team (CERT) 10: (*Looking for survivors, she clambers down a steep ravine into a muddy creek bottom where Sara Lee Benefield's SUV is upside down. Sara is barely conscious and keeps rambling incoherently about needing to get her kids.*) (*speaking into her two-way radio*) Jake, notify the medical OEC that CERT 10 has a woman pinned in her car at the bottom of Rutledge Creek at the Brunner Street Bridge. We are going to need medical assistance, a wrecker, and an extraction team. (*speaking to*

Sara Lee) Can you hear me? I want you to talk to me. OK? We are getting help here for you. Can you tell me your name? Mine is Juanita. I am on a CERT team. I found you down here where the tornado blew you and your car. We are going to get you out of here.

Sara Lee: I . . . need mah children . . . Shawn and . . . I cain't remember . . . (*Eyes roll back.*)

Juanita: OK, I understand that is what you need to do. Now you stay with me. Stay awake! We will help you with that. Do you hurt anywhere?

Sara Lee: (*slow, measured, and staggered speech in a low voice*) Mah . . . legs . . . are . . . numb and mah chest hurts. Iah cain't move. Iah need to git mah kids. Where . . . are . . . mah . . . kids? Iah need . . . some . . . hep!

Juanita: There are people at the school right now taking care of all of the kids. Good! Great! You are talking to me! Stay awake! (*Radios information back to the team.*) I am not going to leave you. My name is Juanita Sanchez. Can you say my name?

Sara Lee: Juanita . . . Juanita Ramras.

Juanita: Close enough! (*Starts to conduct a head-to-toe basic medical assessment. Covers Sara and keeps her talking to postpone shock and unconsciousness.*)

CERT volunteer teams are common everyday citizens who have undergone FEMA training as a rapid and immediate reaction force to help save lives. The FEMA training teaches volunteers skills needed to assist before, during, and after a disaster, such as fire suppression, diagnosing and dealing with the three major killers of injured—airway obstruction, bleeding, and shock—first aid, light search-and-rescue operations, disaster psychology and team organization, and disaster simulation exercises (Emergency Management Institute, n.d.). Juanita is a volunteer who has gone through CERT training. Her occupation is a bookkeeper at a local auto dealership.

April 21, 18:23 Hours

Allie Tran Nyguen, CERT Team 4 member: (*in a field 300 yards northeast of the Breezemore Mobile Home Park, speaking into his two-way radio*) I have a female, approximately age 50, who is unresponsive and who has no pulse, lying about 150 yards north of Breezemore Road. We need to get her ID'ed. She has no identification on her. Can we get her transported? We will need a four-wheel drive.

Carl Hanratty, Team 4 leader: I'll send Sheila, Jon, and Jerry over there with the 4 × 6 ATV. EOC is setting up a morgue at the Seabrook Packing Plant. We'll get her out of the field and then they can pick her up. Write down her description and the details of where she was found and we'll attach that to her bag.

April 21, 19:02 Hours, Midville Civic Center

Travis Benefield: (*at the Civic Center, stunned, irate, and half-hysterical, speaking rapidly and loudly to Kate Mc-Clain, mental health counselor*) I NEED SUM BY-GOD HEP HERE AND RITE NOW! I cain't git to mah house. Iah heared that everything in the Breezemore Park has done blowed away. Mah momma was at our home there sleepin'. I don't know where mah wife is, there weren't no one at the dentist's office 'cause it was all beat up from the twister. Iah heared that everybody at the elementary school done got kilt, and Iah got kids there, but they won't let me near there neither. Iah walked and hitched a ride into here 'cause Iah ain't got no vehicle 'cause part of the Packard plant is on top of it. And Iah cain't find mah dad-burned tools nowheres.

Kate: (*deescalating Travis*) I see how upset you are. I am Kate McClain. I do not know your name.

Travis: Ah'm Travis Benefield. Iah work out to the Packard plant and mah wife's Sara Lee and she works at Doc Collard's office. She's his dental assistant, and Iah got three kids out to the schools—Shawn, Lee Ann, and Jason, and then there's mah momma, Loretta, and Iah been out at the Packard plant pullin' folks outta there, and there's a lotta people bad hurt, and Iah lost all mah durn tools, and Jim Houston, the other millsetter, is dead under a stamping machine, and . . . I'm ahm ABOUT TO GO NUTS AND AH NEED SOME DAD GUM HEP! (*Rapid, panting breathing, eyes rapidly moving back and forth, fists clinched pounding hand in fist, rapid, random pacing verging on hysteria.*)

Kate: (*Gently interrupting his continuous, escalating, out-of-control verbiage, she starts with enough command in her voice to get Travis's attention, then rapidly diminishes her voice level.*) TRAVIS! T-R-A-V-I-S. IF I AM TO HELP YOU, I NEED YOUR FULL ATTENTION. (*Travis gives a startled look, but slows down and attends to the worker.*) Thank you, Travis. I want you to take a deep breath and just listen to me for a moment. Good. Just take a deep breath. Again, I understand all the confusion. It is a mess, but we will get it straightened out. I hear how concerned you are about all your family and how terrifying that is not knowing anything. I need you to get grounded here so I can be of the most help. To do that I need for you to have your wits about you. OK! So humor me here a moment. Tell me where you are right now, tell me what time it is on that clock behind me, and tell me what they're doing over there in the corner?

Travis: Ah, well, we'uns are here into the com-mun-it-ee center and it's ah well . . . I think that thar clock has done stopped. Them ladies is settin' up what looks like some sammiches 'n' sodas 'n' water and what-not.

Kate: Excellent. I just wanted to get your feet planted back on the ground here so we can make some headway. OK?

Travis: (*rather sheepishly*) Yes'um, I do indeed have my wits about me now. I do apologize for my unseemly behavior thar.

Kate: Thank you. You have every right to be upset. That is normal. But we will get this squared away. I am a counselor here, and I am going to help you. Right now I need you to help me, though. How about let's go over here and sit down and let me get Jodell Brown over here. She is one of the coordinators, and we will see what we can start to find out, and get you reunited with your family. I bet you haven't had anything to eat or drink since the tornado hit. I need you to be calm and collected, so we can get the information we need, so do you suppose you could sit here and maybe eat a sandwich and have a soda and tell me and Jodell what we need to know to help you?

Travis: Well, OK. Ah'm jest so scared, though. It were purely awful out there to the plant, and Iah cain't find out nuthin'. Iah done pulled people out of there as much as Iah could until they done got there with the heavy equipment, then Iah didn't want to leave but Iah had to find out about mah family.

Kate: So you did what you could out there. It is certainly understandable that you want to find out about your family and get them together. Not knowing is really the worst part, but here is Jodell, and she is going to get the information she needs from you, and then we will be able to tell you something. And that's really what you want to know, isn't it? Let me go get you a sandwich and a soda and just tell Jodell.

In the preliminary stage of a crisis, mental health counselors need to understand that they can best help by providing very practical support (Ørner et al., 2006). A central information area will be a trip into Bedlam with people attempting to reunite with families. Getting order and direction is a first priority. This is not a time to attempt to do "counseling." Help is what is needed, and the mental health crisis worker can best do that by calming and defusing people who are very distraught, angry, grief stricken, and in shock.

Kate is helpful in deescalating and defusing a very distraught individual who has been severely traumatized and is now terrified that his family has fared even worse. She uses two standard techniques with excitable and distraught clients. First is *entrainment* and then *grounding* (Webber, Mascari, & Runte, 2010). She raises her voice in a command level manner, but not quite as loud as the client's; she then tails off her decibel level and speaks more slowly This tactic catches the client's attention but then hopefully models for him to tone down and slow down. She uses simple calming techniques of introducing herself and asking for his name. She then asks him to take a deep breath to slow him down. She does a quick reality orientation that refocuses him into his present environment. She then offers him food and drink and a place to sit. All of these are basic calming and grounding techniques that are simple but effective. Her negative interrogative question is generally a very bad counseling technique because it implies agreement, but in this case Kate specifically uses it to get agreement and further stabilize and get Travis under control.

April 21, 19:22 Hours, Civic Center Reception and Clearing Area

Jodell Brown, clearing coordinator: (*Kate McClain, mental health crisis worker, is also present.*) Mr. Benefield, here is what I have. All of your children are safe. Shawn had some minor cuts and bruises, but he has received medical attention for those and is fine. They are all at the middle school. They are getting supper served to them. We will relay to them that you are safe also. Your wife is in the hospital. She was pinned in her car, but they got her out. She had to have one leg operated on because it was fractured. She has two fractured ribs, but she is okay and in stable condition. She already knows the children are safe, and we are now relaying to her that you are safe. From what we now know, I am sorry to tell you that there are no homes left standing in Breezemore Park. There were many people who were killed and there were many injured out there, and presently it is off limits as they sort through the debris looking for survivors. We have no one identified as Loretta Benefield at any hospital. As of now we are listing her as missing. We will have transportation here to take you to the children. If you do not have any friends' or relatives' home you can go to, then we can take you to the National Guard Armory for tonight. There will be a FEMA field office set up tomorrow, and there will be all of the major insurance carriers here in mobile disaster units by tomorrow morning. As soon as we have any word about your mother, we will let you know. Now Kate will go with you and get you out to the children. Do you have any questions for me?

Travis: (*Dazed, taking in all of that information, hesitates and thinks. The crisis worker waits patiently.*) Well, no, I don't rightly guess. I guess mah sister over to Crowley could take we'uns in, but I don't know how to git word to her. I guess fer tonight we'uns just best go to the Armory. Ah'm sick to death about not knowing about momma. But I do thank you for findin' out all the rest. I 'preciate it most kindly, ma'am.

Jodell: You are welcome, Mr. Benefield. If you will give me her phone number and address, we will try to get in touch with her. Just so I can be sure that you have gotten all that, could you sort of summarize it so I'm sure that I haven't left anything out or have been unclear?

The crisis worker very carefully and specifically goes through the items she needs to cover. She then asks Travis to recapitulate what she has said so that they all have a clear understanding of what has been covered and what is going to happen. Kate will see that Travis and his children are reunited and will hand him off to another crisis worker at the shelter. This is basic psychological first aid that is designed to slow things down, get some control back in the situation, provide support and reassurance, and improve short-term functioning (Halpern & Tramontin, 2007, pp. 203–218).

April 22, 08:35 Hours, National Guard Armory Disaster Shelter

Ollie Naifeh, MSW, Red Cross disaster counselor from Memphis: Mr. Benefield, hello, I am Oliver Naifeh, a Red Cross counselor from Memphis. You can call me Ollie. I just got your name as one of my people. How did your night go?

Travis: Well, not real well, sir. Iah didn't sleep much, but the kids did. Iah'd like to git over to see Sara Lee. And Iah'd shore like to find out about momma.

Ollie: We have contacted your sister, and she is on her way over here now. The whole city has been declared a disaster area, so it is going to take her some time to get here. I do not have any good news to tell you about your mother, Travis. She was not among the survivors. I am sorry to tell you that a woman answering the description you gave us was found in a field about 300 yards from your home, and she was deceased when she was found. She is at a temporary morgue. This is a terrible task, but we need you to go down there and see if the person is your mother. There will be another counselor there. His name is Jeffrey Chung. He knows you are coming, and he will be there to help you if indeed it is your mother. I will stay with you until your sister comes, and we will talk about what you will need to do about housing and insurance and any other assistance you may need. There will be counselors at the FEMA One Stop to help you with any questions you may have or assistance you may need.

April 22, 09:42 Hours, Seabrook Packing Plant Temporary Morgue

Travis Benefield and Jeffrey Chung, Licensed Professional Counselor from Hatchie County Community Mental Health Center and grief specialist, look on as a medical assistant gently unzips a body bag.

Travis: (*Recoils in shock, then gently touches his mother's cheek.*) Oh Lordy, momma! You have done gotten yourself kilt dead. I told you and done told you to go to the shelter if'n a twister was comin', but you didn't never pay no mind to me. Oh, dear God! Mah momma is dead! (*Starts sobbing.*)

Jeffrey: (*Nods to the attendant and gently turns Travis away.*) I am terribly sorry for your loss. Come on, let's go outside and sit down and talk.

Travis: (*crying*) Did she . . . do you . . . know . . . ah . . . suffer much?

Jeffrey: The field report said she was dead when they found her, and the autopsy shows she died of a broken neck, so I would say no. (*The counselor waits patiently while Travis weeps.*)

Travis: (*head in his hands*) Iah jest . . . it is jest too much. Iah don't know . . . cain't think. Too much.

Jeffrey: (*Uses STOP technique. Slowly and easily puts his hand on Travis's shoulder and gently guides him out of morgue and over to a chair, where he sits down with him. After a while of letting Travis sob quietly, he begins speaking very gently and slowly while making eye contact.*) It is overwhelming, and that's why I am here. I would be happy to get the paperwork together and move your mother to a funeral home if you would like. Or we can keep her here for a while and give you some time to decide what kind of arrangements you would like to make. Oliver Naifeh is your counselor, so he will work with me. Given all you have gone through, it is understandable that you feel overwhelmed. Anyone would. It is a common response to an awful, abnormal situation. You may feel guilty about not doing enough to get your mom to go to a shelter, but that was her choice. (*Sits patiently and gently touches Travis's forearm while he silently sobs.*) Do you have a minister or anybody else I could call?

Travis: Oh . . . OK. If'n you could do that. Our family has always done gone to Kittinger's Funeral Home. Iah guess you could call them up. Iah hadn't even thought about church. We'uns go to the First Baptist Church. Pretty near every Sunday. Reverend Dehl is the minister, but I 'spect he is right busy about now. I guess he'd like to know 'bout Loretta 'cause she sang in the choir and was a pretty staunch member. If'n you could take care of it, Ah'd 'preciate it most greatly. Seems like Iah cain't take care of mah family what's alive right now hardly a'tall, let 'lone what's done and gone.

The morgue counselor does three things. First he implements the STOP technique, which for a morgue counselor is standard operating procedure given the further trauma people will experience when they identify loved ones. STOP is an acronym for Sit, Think, Observe, Plan (Webber, Mascari, & Runte, 2010). The counselor slowly moves the client away from his mother and guides him over to a chair where they sit down. He gauges that it will be okay to put his hand on Travis's shoulder given what he has observed about the cultural norms of the area in times of grief. He observes that indeed Travis will need basic assistance and starts to plan out what he will need to help him with. Being in charge of a morgue at a disaster site takes a great deal of compassion and sensitivity, and the STOP system is a sort of default way of slowing things down and gently moving the bereaved in helping them to get mobilized.

Second, he offers to provide very specific help with details concerning Travis's mother's death. Jeffrey's triage rating of Travis is in the low 20s. He sees a person who is cognitively overwhelmed and behaviorally and emotionally exhausted, has narrowly escaped death as has the rest of his family, and now has to identify his mother's body. As a result, Jeffrey needs to gently but firmly provide support and direction. How access to the dead is provided to loved ones and the interaction that occurs while this is happening are often critical to the survivors' ability to integrate the traumatic event and avoid further psychological injury (Shalev et al., 1998).

Finally, the worker suggests help from his church. Faith-based organizations play huge roles in disaster relief (Phillips & Jenkins, 2010). The worker is fairly sure that, given the culture of the area, Travis's church and minister can and will provide a great deal of support to him. Thus, he asks if he can contact his church.

The morgue counselor is further aware of the stages of survivor grief (see Chapter 12, Personal Loss: Bereavement and Grief) and empathically responds to Travis's shock, sadness, anxiety, and guilt without judging Travis's ability to "handle" all of it. Further, Jeffrey does not judge what Travis has or has not done, nor does he offer meaningless platitudes about Travis's losses. The scenario is played out over and over with other families in the immediate aftermath of a disaster. Local crisis workers work closely with Red Cross, NOVA, and FEMA crisis workers to provide an integrated, efficient, and seamless operation. While these crisis workers will provide immediate mental health assistance, it will be most often in terms of support. This support provides for both the family's survival needs and emotional needs.

April 24, 11:00 Hours, Hatchie County Mental Health Center

Sara Lee Benefield: Well, we'uns are in a fine fix right now. We are both out of work and livin' with Travis's sister, and we still have funeral arrangements to make fer Loretta. It's like we don't know where to start. We did have some home insurance, but Iah don't think it will be near enough. There isn't a thing left of our home, so we'uns have to start all over again. About what we've got is the clothes on our backs and $437.12 in the bank. Travis hasn't even got his tools, which he cain't seem to quit worryin' about all along with the other stuff.

Ollie Naifeh, social worker: OK, I am going to drive you over to the Civic Center, and we will go to the Disaster Recovery Center. I am going to introduce you to some people I know in the Red Cross and the Salvation Army. They can help with immediate assistance for food and shelter and maybe even tools. We can go to the FEMA One Stop and see about getting you a home loan to get you back on your feet and a roof over your heads. They will send an inspector out there really quickly and get the ball rolling, and they will work with your insurance company. They will also work with you on what is called disaster unemployment compensation. It is not quite your paycheck, but it will help out a good bit. Jeffrey has gotten your mother taken care of, and we can talk about funeral arrangements for your mother, Travis. I am guessing that money may be a problem?

Travis: Well no, momma had one of them universal burial policies, although I don't have no idea where it is, and she had about $5,000 put back. Reverend Dehl said he would be proud to preach momma's funeral as soon as we let him know, and there was Wednesday night services, and everybody done gave us their condolences and said what a fine person Loretta was and not to worry over much, that they would hep take care of things.

The crisis counselor does very little mental health counseling at this juncture. He is far more concerned with just getting the basic survival needs of this family met (Ruzek, 2006). There will be time enough for the other later on. As soon as external crisis workers help the community regain control after the immediate aftershock of the crisis, they will leave and turn their clients back over to the local mental health unit.

April 25, 18:00 Hours, High School Gymnasium

Eva Jane Walters, Superintendent, Midville Public School District: (*speaking to about 500 parents*) Thank you for being here under the tough circumstances you are facing. I know many of you have lost your homes or have your home heavily damaged. I know this because I have been sleeping with many of you at the National Guard Armory as my own home is heavily damaged. We are now four days post-tornado. It is Friday. It is time to get your children back to learning. I also know we are going to have school Monday morning, and that includes all the elementary school students. We have been working this week to make those arrangements happen. At the end of my talk there will be a number of teachers in the cafeteria with homerooms, children's names, and new attendance centers for them. St. Benedict's Catholic Church and Midville First Baptist have graciously opened their doors to us, and we are going to hold classes there. That will be in walking or carpooling distance, and we will have buses at the shelters for those children still housed there. Some of your children will have different teachers because their teachers are dead or injured. We are going to have school counselors trained in crisis intervention from Saline,

Wahatchie, and Forked Deer counties' schools here working with our counselors, school psychologists, and school social workers from the Tennessee River Special Education District will be here as well, and teachers to deal with any emotional issues children have. We are composing a series of classroom guidance meetings, which should go a long way towards helping us identify and work through problems that children are having. We are going to work very closely with you in this regard, and we want you to work very closely with us. We know this community does not lack for courage and mental toughness, and we know you and your children are tough minded and resilient, but there is toughness and there is smartness and we want to be smart about taking care of your children's academic, social, and emotional needs because we know if those other needs are taken care of we get better academic results, and in the end that is what we are about, the best academic success we can get. Midville schools have long been outstanding and part of the glue that holds this city together and gives it pride. We are not stepping back from that one inch, but to do that we are going to need all of the cooperation this community can bring to bear on getting these schools up and running. If you have any questions, I will be happy to take them now or talk with you or individually later on.

I also want to say something about our loss, not only of a building but of teachers and students who made it into the viable academic community it was and will be again. We are now planning with the PTA a commemorative memorial service in the Civic Center that will take place before school is out at the end of May. We understand that many of you are dealing with your own personal grief and loss right now and we want to give you time to work through that. We want to be supportive of you in any way we can because we know it is important to you and your children. The Hatchie Mental Health Center and grief counselors will be available if you or your children have need of them. You can call the Hatchie clinic or call us at the high school counselor's number. All the calls will be kept confidential. Thank you for coming. If you have questions now, there are teachers who will bring you a microphone so everybody can hear. I have the rest of the schools' administrative staff here, so if I don't have the answer one of them probably will. When we are done here, we'll exit towards the cafeteria where you can pick up your child's school, room, and teacher assignment. We will have e-mail as power becomes available again but are not sure when that will happen. So we've resurrected some old mimeograph machines and you grandparents will recognize the purple bulletins. Welcome back to the 1950s, but we'll get information to you, rest assured. This is not going to be easy, but with your help we will get the Golden Eagles back up and running.

The superintendent does five things that are critical when a school suffers a calamitous event. First, the "whole child" is the focus. Academic, social, and emotional components are all targeted. Second, she is intent on moving the school and the community as quickly as possible back to day-to-day living and a sense of "normalcy." Third, she seeks to develop a strong sense of community with the families whose children attend the school. Fourth, she has the school function as a valid and reliable source of information by telling parents specifically what is happening and keeping a communication line open to them so that they know there is a centralized and trusted source of information that they can go to when the rumor mill gets going (Kilmer, Gil-Rivas, & MacDonald, 2010).

The superintendent also does something else that is critical in the face of a disaster in which children's lives are lost. Students' ability to work though the grieving process is in part a social phenomenon that is anchored in their peer group when friends are lost (Worden, 2002). Therefore, school needs to get started again to serve as the place where they come together to grieve friends' loss. Providing not only counselors to deal with adjustment problems but grief counselors who can work with the whole family to help them come to terms with their loss is not an easy sale at times. However, providing the common ground of the school as a brokerage for such deeply personal issues can go a good way toward easing the stigma of having to seek help with one's loss. Even if parents have not lost a relative, many people will have lost houses, places of employment, or social gathering places such as churches, clubs, and organizations that play integral parts in their lives, fracturing both their micro- and to a large extent their exosystem supports. We are fully aware that a school system should not get into the funeral business (see Chapter 13, Crises in Schools). However, when faced with a large-magnitude disaster that affects the whole community, the school system certainly needs to provide a process for students to grieve and move on. It also needs to take part in memorial exercises that are inclusive of all students and parents as a way of acknowledging the loss, allowing expression of feelings, and effecting reengagement with school (Kerr, 2009, pp. 130–132). You may wonder why we included this piece about schools here and not in the school chapter. It is important to understand how critical a school is in the fabric of a community and its recovery in disaster (Kilmer, Gil-Rivas, & MacDonald, 2010). To not have

one example of the part the school plays in disaster mitigation is to leave out a critical part indeed of the exosystem of a community.

April 30, 16:00 Hours, Hatchie County Mental Health Center

Kate McClain, licensed professional mental health counselor: How are things going? I spoke with Ollie before he left, and he said things were moving along. How do you feel about that?

Sara Lee: Well, we have done got the loan approved, and the insurance company has been real good about things. We have got us temporary housing assistance and have a place over in Crowley. The kids want to stay here with their friends, so we'uns are gonna bring them over here every day. Mah dentist office is gonna open up next week. But we don't know when or if the Packard plant will reopen, so Travis is gonna be on unemployment.

Travis: Maybe y'all could talk to Shawn some. He is wakin' up at night screamin'. Iah don't think he is near over the school fallin' in and his best friend gittin' kilt. It was tough buryin' momma, but we got that done, and the church really hept.

Sara Lee: And maybe you could talk to Travis here too about him feelin' so durn guilty about leaving the plant to come look fer us. And Iah don't suppose it would hurt for me to talk some too, seein' as how I feel so stupid about runnin' off like a chicken with mah head cut off and makin' things even worse, durn fool that Iah am.

Kate: OK, I will be glad to do that. I think you are making progress and showing me that you have some strong fiber, that you are moving forward rapidly to getting things back to some kind of normalcy. Maybe your minister has told you, but there is going to be a community-wide meeting put on by NOVA. It's called "Y'all come" for all those who were in the tornado or affected by it, kind of a community memorial, talking, and bonding service. That might be something you would want to go to. That really sort of helps when people come together to talk about their experiences. I would also like our psychologist to give you some tests that will tell us how much this is affecting you. Those will help me better plan what we might want to do. Some of what you are experiencing is quite common. We just don't want it to turn into PTSD. (*Explains the difference between ASD and PTSD and what they are all about. She puts a positive view on the disorders by explaining that while most people start out with these symptoms, they tend to go away, particularly when people are proactive about doings things like what she is proposing to the Benefields.*) We are having some small support groups meet, and you are welcome to join them immediately.

I will also contact Shawn's school counselor, Janet Beverly from the middle school, who is filling in there since Mr. Little is still in the hospital, and see if we can set up something for Shawn. We have worked pretty closely together. We might want to have you all in as a family. I know she is starting some family groups there for people whose kids are having some problems. I also want to tell you that I really respect your observations and request for help about your children. That tells me you are truly caring parents. That is going to be really important in the days and months ahead.

The counselor does some psychoeducation with the Benefields in regard to ASD and PTSD. While there is limited evidence about the benefits of psychoeducation, particularly self-help materials in regard to trauma, Wessely and associates (2008) recommend that any psychoeducation should promote resilience and adaptability rather than pathology. Therefore, the counselor commonizes and attempts to allay fears that this means they are losing their minds rather than having a naturally occurring response to what they have been through. For many people, the psychological symptoms of hypervigilance, startle responses, nightmares, and the like, are as scary or more so than what they have just been through. While the education does not make the symptoms disappear immediately, it is calming to know they are common occurrences and that these survivors are not losing their minds.

The counselor also seeks to get them involved in a group. It is one of the best ways to share experience, bond with other survivors, and start back on the road to recovery. Finally, the counselor reinforces the mother for thinking about her children and husband. It is extremely important that caregivers provide a supportive, understanding environment in which children may manifest symptoms, can process thoughts and feelings without fear of recrimination, and otherwise attempt to integrate the trauma into their lives and come to terms with it (Gil-Rivas et al., 2010). Many times caregivers' ability to support their children will be compromised by their own trauma-related issues (Gil-Rivas et al., 2007).

May 8, 09:00 Hours, Midville Baptist Church (Temporary Site for Midville Elementary School)

Janet Beverly, elementary school counselor: Shawn, I wonder how you are getting along?

Shawn: Yes, ma'am. All right, I guess.

Janet: I looked at some of your drawings you made when we had the classroom meeting about the tornado. (*Shows him one of his drawings.*) I wonder if you could tell me about this?

Shawn: Yes, ma'am. That's me and that there's Jamie and that's Leotis. They were mah best friends. Jamie was right next to me in the hall when the tornado hit, but he's dead now.

Ah'm red 'cause I thought I was all bloody, but it was really his blood. Leotis was with Mrs. Cruz. And he and her both got kilt, and Iah don't know why. Ma says it was God's will, but Iah jest don't rightly know. Iah don't think much of God if he done let this happen, to tell the truth. Ma wouldn't like me sayin' that, but Iah reckon that's how Iah feel. Iah don't sleep too good at night neither, and Iah shore don't like storms. Sometimes Iah think Iah hear Jamie and Leotis. We used to play a lot together, soldiers and stuff down by Brunner's Creek. Iah miss them somethin' terrible.

Janet: I wonder if you might like to come to a group I am starting, Shawn. It is for a bunch of kids who have friends who died or got hurt or lost other things, who just plain feel sad and maybe a little lonely right now.

Shawn: Yes, ma'am. Iah guess that'd be OK. Iah sure wish Jamie and Leotis could come. Iah miss mah grandma too. She used to have cookies made when Iah'd git home.

As indicated throughout this book, when children are involved with traumatic events, as Stacy Overstreet, a Tulane University school psychology student who worked with post-Katrina students in the New Orleans school, stated, "There are two vital keys to recovery: social support and putting experiences in context" (Dingfelder, 2006). This is exactly what the school counselor is doing with Shawn when she uses expressive arts and group counseling to help him start to come to terms with his traumatic experiences, put them in his past, and grow from them (Malchiodi, Steele, & Kuban, 2008, p. 299). Groups are powerful ways to bring children together to share commonality of experience, own feelings that range from scared to angry to guilty, decrease isolation, enhance coping and adaptation, seek commonalities, build cohesion and trust, and help members cope with those bad feelings (Nisivoccia & Lynn, 20007). There is not a lot of outcome evidence on postdisaster groups for children, but at least two studies indicate that they do help to reduce posttrauma stress symptoms (Chemtob, Nakashima, & Hamada 2002; Salloum & Overstreet, 2008).

A child with traumatic grief can get "stuck" on the traumatic aspects of the death, which then interferes with the normal grieving process (DeAngelis, 2011). The fact that Shawn was covered with the blood of his close friend and lay there with his friends' bodies admirably fits such criteria. Chapter 7, Posttraumatic Stress Disorder, describes how, by using trauma-focused cognitive-behavioral therapy in creating a trauma narrative using a combination of stress management, play therapy, and cognitive behavior techniques to monitor and control emotional dysregulation, children can move through both their grief and the posttrauma stress symptoms that often accompany it (Cohen, Mannarino, & Deblinger, 2006).

Indeed, if intervention is used as indicated in Chapter 13, Crises in Schools, the school can become a post-disaster anchor for children (Clark et al., 2006; Munsey, 2006). The CD-ROM *Transcending Trauma After a Disaster: A Guide for Schools* (Clark et al., 2006) provides an excellent example of how a school district can mobilize its resources after a disaster to help normalize and bring a modicum of control into an anything-but-normal situation.

May 15, 16:00 Hours, Hatchie County Mental Health Center

Kate McClain, licensed professional mental health counselor: (*meeting with Sara Lee and Travis*) I have talked with Janet Beverly, the school counselor. She is recommending that Shawn go into one of her counseling groups. Her report and what the psychologists report is that he has had a pretty rough time and is suffering from what we call acute stress disorder. (*Reiterates what ASD is and why it is important for it to be dealt with before it becomes PTSD.*) I am also going to recommend that you all come to the clinic as a family. I think it will be helpful for all the kids to talk about some of this stuff and see that, even though you have suffered some severe losses, your family is still together.

Sara Lee: I 'spect you're right. I don't suppose Travis will own up to it, but he's not the same, and neither am I. Shawn isn't the only one havin' nightmares. I jump near outta mah skin every time there's a thunderstorm. Travis and I have never had a hard word with one another, but the other night we done had a huge fight over nuthin'. It was jest nuthin'. (*Tears start to well up in her eyes.*) It was awful. It was in front of his sister's family and the kids. (*Starts to cry.*) He went and apologized, and so did I, but that is not like us a t'all. I don't know what we're becomin', and it scares me half to death.

Travis: (*Puts his arm comfortingly around his wife.*) Iah 'spect you're right, honey. Iah still cain't git them durn tools off mah mind, and that is plumb ridiculous. Iah got a whole new set, though. The church has really hept out and all, but it jest seems like things keep tumblin' through mah mind, and Iah cain't git no peace with them. That's why Iah got mad 'cause Sara Lee kept tellin' me to git over it, that we had other things to think about. And Iah got mad. Iah don't like it much neither.

Kate: I want to assure you that those are perfectly normal responses to an abnormal situation. But that doesn't make them any easier to bear. I would really like you to go to the NOVA "Y'all come" meeting. The ministerial association is going to put on some stuff along with it. I think you will

find it helpful to hear and share some of the things you have gone through. You are strong folks, but everyone could use a little help and support, and I think this would be good.

The counselor is very interested in how her client family is dealing with the traumatic wake of the disaster. She coordinates her efforts with the school counselor and the clinic psychologist. The NOVA meeting and the church provide community support, but there are specific individual mental health issues that assail this family that need to be worked on so that the family does not fracture (Myers & Wee, 2005, p. 33). While most people are resilient in a disaster and will recover, it is critically important to intervene when there are indicators things are not going well (Ruzek, 2006). This emergency mental health is set up on a Family Assistance Center model (Halpern & Tramontin, 2007, pp. 190–191; Leskin et al., 2006), in which one person acts as a broker and communicator to deal with the many social, psychological, and financial issues that will assail them. Getting all the family into therapy is a positive move because no one then feels the stigma of being the identified "sick" person when everybody else is doing well.

May 22, 16:00 Hours, Hatchie County Mental Health Center

Travis: Well, we went to that "Y'all come" meeting, and I would say it was hepful. Sort o' gives you a sense of pride 'n' hope, I guess. Kinda like we'uns are all in this together. They had a pretty good community church memorial service and all afterwards. Eighty-three dead and over 600 hurt. Lord A'mighty!

Sara Lee: Iah'd agree. But what Iah really liked was our first family meeting. Iah talked to the kids afterwards. Lee Ann and Jason both didn't want to come, but they both said afterwards they wouldn't mind coming again, which means they really did like it. Iah jest feel a little more peaceful somehow. Like we'uns are on the right track.

Travis: Iah guess it is like gittin' back in control. Ain't felt like that much.

Kate: I am glad to hear that. We will take this slow and easy. We have plenty of time. We will work on this as long as you feel the need to.

The counselor seeks to reinforce the Benefields for their courage and willingness to commit to some pretty arduous mental health work in addition to all the other challenges they face. She reemphasizes that there is no rush to working through their problems. Kate is now working on what is called *second phase* crisis intervention in the crisis chronosystem. The immediate crisis is over. Basic physiological needs have been met. At this point, the crisis worker is more concerned about possible long-term effects on the whole family; therefore, she is treating the family system as a client. She seeks to coordinate her efforts with other human services workers both from an individual perspective, as in the case of Shawn, and a wider community perspective, such as helping support the NOVA and the community church program. The more social support that can be generated, the more likely the victims are to use it to help with the distress (Yates, Axsom, & Tiedeman, 1999).

April 25 (1 year and 4 days after the tornado), 16:00 Hours, Hatchie County Mental Health Center

Sara Lee: Iah guess we'uns are ready to say good-bye, Kate. We'uns really 'preciate what you have done fer us. We'uns couldn't have done this a t'all without you. We all went to the big memorial service last week at the Civic Center. It'll always be part of our lives, but it is behind us now, and we kin go on. Shawn is really doing well. He is off antidepressants and has a couple of new friends. We'uns couldn't go back to Breezemore. Jest too many bad memories, but we done got a lot out south o' town and put our new manufactured home on it, and there are some new kids out there Shawn met at Southside Elementary. None of us are having any nightmares either, although Iah still don't like thunderstorms, and we have a tornado shelter by our home now.

Travis: Iah guess Ah'd agree. Iah shore do appreciate what y'all have done fer us. It was tough, but Iah think we'uns are better fer it as a family. We're a whole lot tighter than before. Iah don't even think about mah tools no more, and even though Iah got mah head shrunk it feels better. (*Laughs.*) Durndest thing about them tools. We got momma buried beside paw out to Big Prairie Cemetery. Got her a nice stone, too. Pink marble. She always liked pink. She's at peace . . . and I guess fer that matter, so am Iah—as fer as one could be, given the circumstances. We are about ready to reopen the engine works, and Iah been workin' gittin' the machines all set up.

Kate: I am glad to have worked with you. I agree. I think we are ready to get divorced. (*Everybody laughs.*) I expect I will see you around town, so I look forward to seeing you out and about. I also want to tell you I really respect you for what you have done. I have learned from you, probably as much as you have learned from me, and I appreciate you coming into and touching my life. It makes me feel even more sure that this is the business I was meant to do.

Sara Lee: Well Iah think the good Lord put you in the right job. Thanks and good-bye.

Travis: Amen to that. (*Both hug Kate and go out the door and on with their lives.*)

Over the long haul, most people, even when they suffer comprehensive and horrific loss like the Benefields,

are resilient and equal to the task of moving on with their lives (Gist, Lubin, & Redburn, 1999). What the crisis counselor provides is not so much therapy as information and programs that help families like the Benefields normalize an abnormal situation and address their material resource losses (Farberow & Frederick, 1978). The crisis worker also takes precautionary steps to monitor this family very closely for a while. While people sometimes do develop PTSD, the vast majority are amazingly resilient and do not (Drabek, 1986).

The major role that the crisis worker initially plays is one of victim advocate by facilitating the return of basic services to survivors (Salzer & Bickman, 1999). The crisis worker then shifts from problem-focused to more emotion-focused coping (Lazarus & Folkman, 1984) and seeks to help the family move forward and reframe the crisis and distance themselves from it through preventive and support therapy (Chemtob, 2000).

Often the lack of use of mental health services by families like the Benefields is not happenstance (Norris & Alegria, 2006). There are many reasons, some good and some bad, why mental health services are underused after a disaster (Yates, Axsom, & Tiedeman, 1999). Some individuals see the use of such services and facilities as a sign of mental illness and therefore a major character flaw that would label them as "nut" cases. To avoid being perceived as outcasts by peers, these individuals may be very loath to use mental health services (Bethel & Oates, 2007). If such services are poor, uncoordinated, culturally insensitive, and intrusive, they indeed may do more harm than good. In this instance, good mesosystem coordination and communication among a number of local and national agencies in the micro-, exo-, and macrosystems worked to provide nonintrusive help and support. The sensitivity, caring, support, and unconditional positive regard of a variety of different helping professionals working in close coordination—including social workers, psychologists, licensed professional counselors, school counselors, and "just plain folks"—helped make the Benefields' experience with mental health services a positive one.

The anniversary of the disaster is a benchmark for positive resolution, and like most people, the Benefields are resilient and capable of moving forward with a little help. The tornado has left an indelible imprint on their lives that will never go away, but like the Chinese symbols that start every chapter in this book, they have found opportunity in the crisis and have come out of it stronger than they were before.

While the Benefields represent the stereotype of a white, Anglo-Saxon, fundamentalist Christian, blue-collar family in the south-central United States, you might gather from the surnames of some of the people who came to their assistance or who worked on the overall disaster that they represented a rainbow coalition of Americans of all races, ethnicity, and cultural backgrounds. That was not done to be politically correct. The fact of the matter is that even in rural west Tennessee, we are becoming a melting pot of races, ethnicity, and divergent cultural backgrounds. As such, a multicultural perspective is critical to any crisis intervention—and, indeed, people with just such divergent surnames work on crisis teams with which we are involved. A final word on multiculturalism: The worker should also understand that his or her own cultural biases have an even higher potential for surfacing when faced with oppositionally defiant clients who may not think, talk, act, look, or even smell like the worker. For example, more than one of the editors of this book has queried the author when reading the dialogues of the Benefield family.

Editors have questioned words such as *we'uns* (which literally means "we ones") and *fer* (meaning "far" or "for") because they were unsure themselves of the meaning and were equally unsure that you, the reader, would understand what was being said. Those words were intentionally used in the dialogues to test readers' responses to the deep southern rural dialect of Travis Benefield and his family. If you were put off by that dialect, found it hard to understand, and knew it was not proper English, then you might be put off by Travis as an "ignorant redneck" as well. Despite all your good works and good intentions, you might then unintentionally treat him with less respect than you would a person who talked like a 6 o'clock network news broadcaster. As a result, do you suppose Travis's reaction to you would be different than it was to the social workers, licensed professional counselors, and other crisis workers who were culturally sensitive to him and treated him respectfully despite his language? Cultural sensitivity is displayed when the worker translates into primary language that the client can understand (Myers & Wee, 2005, p. 62), whether that be Spanish, Urdu, or English with a deep southern accent.

Although you might think that Travis's obsessive concern about his tools is somewhat bizarre, in fact it has a deep cultural basis. Bethel and Oates (2007) have found that an Appalachian male like Travis, the patriarchal head of his family, is expected to be a good "hunter" who provides for and takes care of his family by supplying them with food, shelter, and clothing. The loss of his tools strikes at the very heart of who Travis

is and how his culture defines him as an independent, hardworking, self-reliant provider for his family. In Travis's world, a blue-collar job in which a man can be skillful with tools may be more valued than a white-collar job. It is no accident that Travis persists in brooding on the loss of his tools, for those tools are in fact symbolic of his very identity as a man. The wise and culturally sensitive crisis worker will understand that the loss of his tools is as critical to Travis as the loss of his house, and that worker will be empathic and supportive, placing a high priority on helping Travis get his "durn" tools replaced.

The deep roots that the Benefield family has in their religion and spiritual values should also be understood as a significant part of their life and culture. To not use and honor their religion and spiritual values to help salve the wounds of their losses would be a grave mistake indeed (Bethel & Oates, 2007; Stambor, 2005). Thus, ecological dynamics are a two-way street. Being aware of the impact that the ecology exerts on both participants (client and crisis worker) and the interactive effect it has on each is crucial if the relationship is going to progress and the crisis is to be resolved.

Focus on the Worker
Debriefing

"Debriefing is an intervention designed to assist workers and survivors in dealing with intense thoughts, feelings, and reactions that occur after a traumatic event, and to decrease their impact and facilitate the recovery of normal people having normal reactions to abnormal events" (Myers & Wee, 2005, p. 173). Probably no emergent technique in crisis intervention has created more controversy than debriefing procedures. The attacks on debriefing psychotherapy (Gist & Lubin, 1999) have been some of the most vituperative we have seen in 40 years in the field of counseling, and while there are several different models of debriefing (Armstrong, O'Callahan, & Marmar, 1991; McWhirter & Linzer, 1994; Myers & Zunin, 1994), these attacks have been especially virulent in regard to Mitchell and Everly's (1995a) critical incident stress debriefing (CISD) model and their lack of hard research evidence to demonstrate its effectiveness (Gist, Lubin, & Redburn, 1999). Further, like most wishful searches for a panacea in dealing with an intractable problem, debriefing has been hailed as a potent vaccination against PTSD. However, research indicates it is not (Bisson & Deahl, 1994; Bisson, Jenkins, & Bannister, 1997; Deahl, 1999; Hobbs et al., 1996; Kenardy et al., 1996; Lee, Slade, & Lygo, 1996; Raphael, Meldrum, & McFarland, 1995). It has come to the point that psychological debriefing cannot be endorsed for use with survivors (Brymer et al., 2009; Gray & Litz, 2005).

In fact, Mitchell and Everly have not been able to provide scientific evidence that CISD does much of anything beneficial for workers or victims (Gist, Woodall, & Magenheimer, 1999), and at least one study found it to be harmful (Avery & Orner, 1998a, 1998b). Further, caustic rebukes have rained down on CISD as a get-rich-quick scheme for "quack" therapists and a "get out of jail free" (or almost free) card for businesses and insurance companies who can claim it is an effective vaccination against PTSD and therefore do not have to pay for much more expensive rehabilitation procedures to employees who come down with PTSD symptoms (Gist, Woodall, & Magenheimer, 1999; Raphael, 1999). CISD has also been roundly criticized for mandating that all workers who were victims of the crisis obtain CISD, even though it may be personally or culturally inappropriate (Silove, 1999; Weisaeth, 1999). Finally, there is a serious ethical question as to the blanket use of CISD for all kinds of populations for all kinds of trauma under all kinds of conditions (Raphael, 1999). At the National Institute of Mental Health consensus conference, the following recommendation was approved:

> Early intervention in the form of a single one-on-one recital of events and expression of emotions evoked by a traumatic event (as advocated in some forms of psychological debriefing) does not consistently reduce risks of later developing PTSD or related adjustment difficulties. Some survivors (e.g., those with high arousal) may be put at heightened risk of adverse outcomes as a result of such early interventions. (National Institute of Mental Health, 2002, p. 8)

On the other side of the debate, adherents absolutely believe in its effectiveness, and there are studies to support that (Chemtob, 2000; Jacobs, Horne-Moyer, Jones, 2004; MacDonald, 2003; Pender & Prichard, 2008, 2009; Robinson, Sigman, & Wilson, 1997; Wagner, 2005). Many of its adherents tend to be frontline workers. Their responses to those who would vilify CISD are that it does work—if the procedure is used correctly and if the people who do it are trained to use it the way Mitchell and Everly (1999) propose (Freeman, 2003; Lane, 2003; Montano & Dowdall-Thomae, 2003). One of the major issues has been its profligate use for *anybody for any kind of traumatic event*. Mitchell and Everly (1999) never intended it to be that. It was intended to be applied directly to emergency service workers,

firefighters, and police officers to help them quickly integrate feelings and thoughts so that the experiences would lose their potential to become disturbing. Part of why it has been so successful (and so abused and misapplied) is that at face value it *should* work, survivors appreciate that someone cares enough about them to listen, and talking bad stuff out is a good way to get rid of it (Halpern & Tramontin, 2007, pp. 265–266).

Sharing experiences is one way of bonding through an adverse experience. If you don't believe that, get invited to an American Legion bar and talk to some ex-marines, or spend some time with police officers at "choir practice" after a tough drug bust where shots were fired. Debriefing objectives of ventilation of feelings, reordering and reorganization of cognitions, normalization of experience, increased group support, verbal reconstruction and integration, and screening for traumatic stress referral would seem to be laudable goals for postintervention with any disaster worker (Halpern & Tramontin, 2007, pp. 267–268; Myers & Wee, 2005, pp. 172–174).

Your authors tend to be in guarded agreement with the use of CISD for specific populations of first responders. We have seen this technique work in powerful ways with some very cynical and tough police field commanders who were very much in need of debriefing a multitude of traumatic events and the stress and pent-up emotions that went with them (Addy & James, 2002). It is also worth noting that when we do role-play CISD shooting scenarios with our students (Dr. James is certified as a CISD-trained debriefer), they almost universally agree that they thought the debriefing was helpful. Having presented the foregoing arguments for and against, the fact stands that different types of debriefing strategies still predominate in the field of trauma work. For that reason alone, the following description of debriefing emergency workers is presented.

Debriefing Emergency Workers

Critical Incident Stress Debriefing (CISD). CISD was developed by Jeffrey Mitchell, a firefighter and paramedic in Baltimore County, Maryland, as a result of his own responses to the traumatic incidents he continuously witnessed. Originally designed to deal only with firefighters and EMTs who were first responders to fires, accidents, and other events where they saw and dealt with horrific sights, sounds, and smells, CISD is now used with a variety of people who have suffered trauma (Morrissey, 1994). CISD teams are typically composed of two members who must hold a minimum of a master's degree in the mental health professions and who have undergone training and received certification in CISD. Debriefing is designed to mitigate the psychological impact of a traumatic event, restore homeostasis and equilibrium, prevent PTSD from developing, and identify people who will need professional mental health follow-up (Mitchell & Everly, 1995a, p. 270).

Informal Defusing. Informal defusing is a first-order intervention following traumatic incidents and is typically performed by CISD-trained on-site personnel. The goal of defusing is to lessen the impact of a traumatic event and accelerate the normal recovery process by providing a brief, time-limited format to air feelings and thoughts of the event (Myers & Wee, 2005, p. 167). This three-stage intervention is a shortened version of a full-scale debriefing and usually takes about 1 hour. First, team members introduce themselves and then explain the process and delineate expectations. Second, the traumatic experience is explored via participants' disclosure of facts, cognitive and emotional reactions, and finally symptoms of distress related to the traumatic event. Third, participants receive information to normalize the dissonant cognitions of the event and educate them with regard to stress, stress management, and trauma (Mitchell & Everly, 1995a, p. 275).

Formal Debriefing. The formal debriefing process has seven stages and typically takes place within 24 hours to 7 days after a traumatic event. It is generally 2 to 3 hours long. It is a combination of psychological and educational elements formatted in a structured group setting, and it involves personnel who have been directly affected by a traumatic event such as police officers, firefighters, EMTs, and ER staff. It is not intended for use with the general public (Pender & Prichard, 2008). Debriefing helps make the transition from processing facts about the event to emotional responses to the event and, finally, back to cognitive information about reactions and coping with traumatic experiences. It is not psychotherapy, but rather a controlled meeting that allows participants to discuss their emotions and thoughts about the event in a non-threatening environment (Mitchell & Everly, 1995b).

The seven stages are described as follows:

1. *Introduction.* The introduction is crucial to setting the tone of the debriefing. Besides introducing team members and explaining the process and guidelines for the CISD, the introduction also seeks to lower resistance and motivate the participants by discussing sensitive issues such as confidentiality (Mitchell & Everly, 1995a, p. 271).

2. *Fact finding.* Facts are discussed first because they are easiest to deal with and are typical of what may be discussed with emergency workers after a traumatic event. The leaders typically start by making statements such as "We only have a sketch of what happened. We'd like you to fill us in on what happened. So we can get an overall picture, we'd like everyone—no matter what part you played—to give us your perspective on it. If you don't feel ready to do that, that's OK too. Just shake your head, and we'll move past you. We need to know who you are, what your involvement was, and what happened from your point of view." Order doesn't matter; the episode will sort itself through the facilitative ability of the CISD leaders (Mitchell & Everly, 1995a, p. 272).

3. *Thoughts.* The CISD leaders ask the participants for their initial or most poignant thoughts about what happened. Moving from facts to thoughts starts to personalize the event and allows emotions to surface. As participants voice their thoughts, the leaders should elicit those emotions that come naturally with their thinking about the situation and that allow for movement into the next phase, reaction (Mitchell & Everly, 1995a, p. 272).

4. *Reaction.* This phase is the most emotionally powerful for participants. Questions that elicit responses are variations on a theme of "What about the situation was most bothersome to you? If you could change one part of it, what would it be?" Leaders will act more as passive facilitators at this point, as participants spontaneously speak to their affective responses to the event (Mitchell & Everly, 1995a, pp. 272–273).

5. *Symptoms.* The symptom phase is used to shift the group back to more cognitive material. The discussion deals with what went on both during and after the event. The leaders ask the group to describe their experience in terms of affective, behavioral, cognitive, or physical experiences they had. To get the group going, the leaders may give examples such as "My whole body was shaking for 5 minutes after the firing quit; I was under control, but I kept thinking I can't stand another minute of this; I wanted to say something, but my tongue was tied; I'm scared to death, but I know I have to go back into that building so my feet move me there somehow" (Mitchell & Everly, 1995a, p. 273).

6. *Teaching.* Leaders may point out that what the participants have talked about fits precisely into the symptoms of acute stress. The leaders let the

participants know that these are normal, typical reactions, that they are not losing their minds or otherwise somehow not equal to the task. The participants are instructed in how to recognize and understand symptoms that might not have surfaced yet. Participants are also given information in stress management techniques. This phase moves the participants even farther away from the emotional content they have worked through in the reaction phase (Mitchell & Everly, 1995a, p. 274).

7. *Reentry.* The reentry phase is a final opportunity to summarize and bring closure to all the issues that have been discussed. The CISD team's job at this time is to answer questions, provide reassurance, reflect on any agendas they believe have not been brought out, dispense handouts, and provide referral sources for extended psychological work (Mitchell & Everly, 1995a, p. 274).

In summary, the CISD derives its effectiveness from early intervention, the opportunity to experience catharsis in safety, the opportunity to verbalize the trauma, a definite behavioral structure, group and peer support, and a provision for follow-up if needed (Mitchell & Everly, 1995b, p. 41).

Debriefing Crisis Workers

Whether one buys the CISD model or not, it seems abundantly clear that *some* kind of debriefing process is indispensable in assisting crisis workers themselves to regain a state of emotional, cognitive, and behavioral equilibrium following their intensive intervention work in the aftermath of a chaotic crisis. The detailed procedures that follow are provided because it is essential for crisis workers to know how to debrief disaster workers as well as to understand the value of being debriefed themselves. The techniques and perspectives offered here may even enable the crisis worker to debrief the debriefers.

The Need for Debriefing.   Throughout this book crisis intervention is often depicted as complex and chaotic. Natural disaster, mechanical or human-caused large-scale accidents, mass murders resulting from terrorism, or death and destruction from floods and tornadoes all create the confused and chaotic disorder that, much like a battle, are so disorienting that, for crisis workers, there are no scripts and little time for reflection, planning, or rehearsal. It is not surprising that crisis workers themselves tend to suffer psychological problems from the same trauma they are trying to alleviate in others. What the crisis worker sees, hears, smells, and touches may also rattle long-buried skeletons in the worker's own emotional closet. This phenomenon is known as vicarious traumatization (Saakvitne & Pearlman, 1996) or compassion fatigue (Figley, 2002), wherein the worker unwittingly absorbs and internalizes the very trauma that the client manifests (see Chapter 16, Human Services Workers in Crisis, for more on this phenomenon).

CERT team members are all citizens with different occupations. They are not therapists and they do not receive supervision. Corey-Souza (2007) conducted a study of 96 members of the Florida Crisis Responses team on measures of compassion fatigue and compassion satisfaction. She found a strong negative correlation between compassion fatigue and compassion satisfaction, and that burnout is one of the strongest predictors of compassion fatigue. So put yourself in the place of Jeffrey Chung, the Midville morgue counselor, or any of the CERT team members who found Loretta Benefield. Do you think you would be up for some kind of psychological debriefing? Finally, compounding it all, mental health crisis workers may be called on to debrief other emergency personnel who have been up to their arms in blood, gore, wreckage, and a panoply of human tragedy. It is important, then, that crisis workers themselves go through debriefing and that certain precautions are taken to arm them against the multiple stressors they will face when doing disaster work (Armstrong, O'Callahan, & Marmar, 1991). As an example, Leffler and Dembert (1998) conducted a study of U.S. Navy divers involved in the recovery of wreckage and passenger remains from TWA Flight 800, which crashed en route to Paris in 120 feet of water off the coast of Long Island, New York. They reported that divers who were exposed to human remains, especially those of children, found that experience to be far more stressful than the safety hazards they encountered.

First responders to the twin towers of the World Trade Center manifest all of the themes of what Robert Lifton (1983) calls the psychology of survival—psychic numbing, guilt over having not done enough or living when others did not, paranoia over attempts to provide psychological help, vivid death imprints, and futile and abortive attempts to make sense out of what they saw, heard, smelled, and touched (Henry, 2004). If this sounds to you suspiciously like PTSD or the vicarious traumatization you read about in the Chapter 16 on burnout, you are correct. Compound this with Henry (2004) and Addy and James's (2002) research, which found that responders such as police officers tend to be very wary of "head shrinkers." If you are an EMT, firefighter, or police officer, just to admit you may have some kind of mental problem puts you at risk because your partners may fear that your inability to function under pressure may harm them (Henry, 2005). So what is to be done? Above all else is self-care (Merlino, 2011), which means knowing you are not a super crisis worker, nor is anyone else, and having enough sense to look out for yourself and your team both physically and psychologically.

Precautions. First of all, crisis work of this kind is done in teams. Whether at the scene with a number of specialists or in an after-action debriefing, workers do not act in isolation. Using the buddy system allows workers to rotate with difficult clients, ventilate to one another, check out perceptions, watch each other for signs of fatigue, and give each other a break (Hayes, Goodwin, & Miars, 1990; Mitchell & Everly, 1995b; SAMHSA, 2003; Talbot, Manton, & Dunn, 1995, p. 286; Walker, 1990).

Second, crisis workers in a disaster need to take time off to sleep and decompress. An 8-hour shift under disaster conditions is a long time (Hayes, Goodwin, & Miars, 1990). Crisis workers need to be rotated out of high-stress jobs, such as body identification and survivor notification, on a regular basis and be given less stressful duties (Walker, 1990). They also need time off between crises to rest and recuperate physically and psychologically (Talbot, Manton, & Dunn, 1995, p. 293). The U.S. Department of Mental Health proposes a maximum of 12-hour shifts followed by 12 hours off. They also propose that work rotations should change from high-stress to lower-stress functions (SAMHSA, 2003).

Third, as trite as it sounds, it is important to have plenty of water and nutritious food at the scene (SAMHSA, 2003). One of your authors has been in a crisis negotiation situation in which he and two police officers were unable to get food or water. The salvaged contents of the lunchbox of one of the officer's children that had been left in the backseat of her squad car was a lifesaver after we had been there from 5 P.M. until 3 A.M. without food and with very little water!

Fourth, have a clear chain of command with clear role and function statements. Nothing is worse or potentially more lethal than going into a disaster without a clear understanding of what one is going to do and to whom one is going to report. Correlative to the foregoing is having adequate and timely supervision to process what one is doing (SAMHSA, 2003).

Fifth, on-site crisis workers should not debrief one another (Spitzer & Neely, 1992; Talbot, Manton, & Dunn, 1995, p. 286). Another team of crisis workers who have not been at the scene should be brought in to lead debriefing. In this manner, the leaders cannot be construed as engaging in recriminations, second-guessing, or accusations about who did or didn't do what.

Sixth, the debriefing should be held away from the crisis scene if possible (Talbot, Manton, & Dunn, 1995, p. 286). Moving away from the scene physically allows the crisis workers to move away psychologically.

Seventh, the organizational context within which the group operates should be taken into consideration because it too plays a part in how the group is affected (Talbot, Manton, & Dunn, 1995, p. 286). The way the organization—and this includes even charitable organizations such as the Red Cross—runs its disaster relief program is critically important to how the individual handles stress at the disaster site.

Eighth, the crisis workers need to be in excellent physical and mental health themselves. From both a physical and mental standpoint, they will be stretched to the limit. Diving into the wake of a traumatic event is no place for someone who is out of shape either physically or mentally (Walker, 1990). But even if a crisis worker is in excellent physical and psychological condition, no one is immune from the cumulative and acute onset of stress (see Chapter 16, Human Services Workers in Crisis).

Although overuse of the procedure and policies requiring mandatory CISD attendance can create passive participation and even negative resentment, it would seem that a standing operational order for all emergency workers and crisis workers should be some kind of regular debriefing (not necessarily the CISD model). There are a variety of models that focus on different aspects of the event, such as positive reframing (Charlton & Thompson, 1996), group processing (Dyregrov, 1997), intensive follow-up after the debriefing (Solomon, 1995), multiple stressor debriefing (Armstrong, O'Callahan, & Marmar, 1991), dynamic understanding of the event (Talbot, Manton, & Dunn, 1995), and disaster debriefing (Myers & Zunin, 1994).

While there are concerns that traditional CISD may sabotage personal integrity in favor of victim status by emphasizing pathology over resiliency and trauma over strength, Echterling, McKee, and Presbury (2000) believe that linking people in crisis, hearing one another's crisis stories, normalizing reactions, and facilitating the group's coping are positive outcomes that are critical to resolution. Your authors absolutely agree. Debriefing should be the natural and final act of the emergency and crisis workers' job and should be no less expected than that of a fighter pilot after a combat mission.

Dynamics of Debriefing. The debriefers of crisis workers are dealing with a matrix of issues: the crisis event and its victims, the response to that event by the crisis workers, the individual crisis worker's personal and professional response to the survivors, the dynamics of the group as it goes through the debriefing process, and developing a collective plan for handling the next crisis (Echterling, McKee, & Presbury, 2000; Silove, 1999; Talbot, Manton, & Dunn, 1995, p. 286).

From a professional standpoint, each crisis worker needs to understand and evaluate the usefulness of his or her interventions, explore alternatives, and plan future courses of action. Focusing on survivor aspects rather than victimization is important in refocusing the individual on perseverance, creativity, and sensitivity, which often fade into the background in the face of the pain, anguish, and helplessness that the worker feels (Echterling, McKee, & Presbury, 2000). Individual crisis workers also need to look at how they operate as members of the group. Group dynamics and cohesiveness impart a powerful influence on each worker, so the group as client may need to be examined. Such dynamics may, in fact, parallel the dynamics of the victim group and are referred to as *parallel processing* (Talbot, Manton, & Dunn, 1995, p. 291).

On a personal basis, the debriefers need to explore with workers their own personal issues that may intrude into their crisis intervention work. Particularly, parallel processing and countertransference issues need to be examined. As opposed to the CISD approach of Mitchell and Everly (1995b), which does not delve into the personal dynamics of emergency workers, Talbot, Manton, and Dunn (1995) believe that psychological understanding and integration are exceedingly important to crisis workers, because this is the stuff they are made of and how they operate. The personal history of the individuals in the group and of the group itself may also be of importance. Past baggage of the group, or the individual workers' issues with the group, may carry over into the present, and everyone needs to acknowledge that baggage and be helped to set it down and leave it.

Confidentiality. A continuing issue in debriefings centers on ethical concerns about acts of commission or omission, issues of responsibility or integrity, and even larger questions concerning life-and-death decisions (Walker, 1990). In that regard, all debriefings of emergency workers or mental health workers should be absolutely confidential, and that fact should be stated and enforced from the beginning (Mitchell & Everly, 1995a).

Understanding. One of the main tasks of the debriefer is to make psychological sense of what is going on and to help the crisis workers absorb that knowledge. Thus debriefers should be well grounded in group dynamics, group functioning, and group counseling skills. They need to be able to compliment workers on their respective strengths—accentuating the positive rather than the multitude of negatives that can easily pervade a crisis (Echterling, McKee, & Presbury, 2000).

The debriefer needs to summarize, and allow people to verbalize, what they have learned from the crisis and the debriefing, in order to minimize workers' vulnerability to the phenomenon of vicarious traumatization (Saakvitne & Pearlman, 1996). Crisis workers need to have a sense of mastery over what they have done as well as to feel positive about themselves as they take leave of the traumatic event and the debriefing (Echterling, McKee, & Presbury, 2000; Silove, 1999; Talbot, Manton, & Dunn, 1995, p. 296).

Qualifications to be an excellent debriefer do not come from one weekend workshop such as one of your authors went through. An excellent debriefer, according to Jordan (2002), will have experience not only in crisis intervention but in trauma counseling as well. Jordan proposes that anyone who does trauma supervision needs to have not only an excellent understanding of what trauma is about, but also an understanding of oneself as he or she operates in a traumatic situation both with people who are suffering from trauma and with those who are intervening with the traumatized. Knowing how secondary traumatization affects first responders and mental health workers is critical. Also knowing what to do about secondary traumatization and how to convince hardheaded veteran first responders and mental health workers is the zenith of this business, and not many achieve those heights.

In summary, the combined processes that Mitchell and Everly (1995a), Echterling, McKee, and Presbury (2000), and Talbot, Manton, and Dunn (1995) describe derive their effectiveness from:

1. An early intervention before the trauma is concretized and becomes a disease reservoir
2. An opportunity for catharsis by ventilating emotions in safe surroundings with a structured environment and a knowledgeable and trusted facilitator

3. An opportunity to verbalize the traumatic event and the parts played by reconstructing it, making sense of it, and integrating it into awareness

4. The provision of structure through the debriefing procedure of a definite beginning and a definite end that provides a clear, linear sequence of events that leads to closure, as opposed to the chaos so recently encountered

5. The dispelling of myths that one must be able to "handle" all things and that emotions are liabilities

6. Peer support from others who belong to the same "club"

7. Provision of follow-up if the traumatic stress and the symptoms are not expunged

8. Education about the effects of stress and the concept that it is a naturally occurring process and not a "weakness"

9. Dynamic understanding of both past and present motivators and causative factors that actuate specific responses in each individual

10. Reframing and emphasizing the positive outcomes and strengths demonstrated by the worker

11. The knowledge that such debriefings allow individuals not only to survive job stress but to do their jobs better

Final Thoughts

It has now been 24 years since we wrote the first edition of this book. Burl Gilliland, coauthor of the book, has been dead for 10 years, so these final thoughts will be those of your other coauthor, Richard "Dick" James. Claire Verduin, our editor at Brooks/Cole at the time of the first edition in 1988, remarked with some humor and some cynicism that it would probably be a nice onetime edition that would wind up gathering dust on library bookshelves, and that would be it. At that time there were three or four books on crisis and very little research or theory that made it into professional journals. Burl Gilliland started a crisis class at the University of Memphis back in 1975 with little more than pamphlets, mimeographed handouts, and guest speakers from various grassroots organization that were doing crisis work of different kinds. Crisis intervention was a psychological backwater that had few adherents and even fewer practitioners. Almost none of the material that appears in this closing chapter was in existence at that time. In fact, most of the material in the entire book was not! That should give you an idea about how much this field has grown in that short time.

I was on a panel of Brooks/Cole authors at the 2007 American Counseling Association convention in Detroit. That panel met with students to discuss careers in the field of human services. I started out in my professional life as a junior high school counselor 40 years ago, and I am still the coordinator of the school counseling program at the University of Memphis. Those have both been great experiences, but they pale in comparison to the field of crisis intervention. I got into the crisis business through sheer dumb luck and the inability to say no to a request to start the Crisis Intervention Team program with the Memphis Police Department that has since become world renowned. That has been the best career decision I ever made. There is now little question in my mind that crisis intervention is in the mainstream of psychotherapy. That's what I told the students in Detroit. If you want a career that will give you the ride of your life, get into this business!

SUMMARY

This chapter is predicated on emergent trends that encompass the total ecological and cultural environments in which we live and work. It is a multisystemic approach to crisis intervention. The five-dimensional circle and cylinder of systems that impact crisis workers and the individuals and groups who are their clients include the microsystem, mesosystem, exosystem, macrosystem, and chronosystem. These five systems, based on the Bronfenbrenner model, make up the arena in which crisis workers intervene in situations that may include individuals, families, groups, and organizations in a variety of crises at the local level as well as in widely dispersed geographical areas and cultural settings.

The rise of the Federal Emergency Management Agency (FEMA) and the various state and local emergency management agencies has given a great deal of impetus to the integration of emergency services and the crisis intervention that goes along with them. The case study of the Benefield family as a model of integrated crisis intervention services is the ideal and demonstrates how these various systems interface and act on individuals in the microsystem. Given hurricane Katrina's traumatic wake, it appears that ideal state of service has not yet been reached.

To see some of the concepts discussed in this chapter in action, refer to your *Crisis Intervention in Action* DVD, or see the clips online on the Counseling CourseMate website. To access this site, go to www.cengagebrain.com, where you'll also find an eBook, additional study tools, quizzes, and more. Watching Christopher and Monica on video, imagine that you are not sitting in a nice easy chair, but are sitting in a student desk in a middle school that is being used as a shelter for homeless tornado survivors. Further imagine that there is no power, no hot water, and you are sleeping in that shelter and eating military MREs. Also notice that you haven't had a bath in three days of 90-degree-plus days and 80-degree-plus nights with no AC. How do you feel about getting into the disaster relief business now? Do you think your attitude might be a little different toward Christopher and Monica?

Crisis workers and first responders to disasters and other traumatic events themselves need a format to air their thoughts and feelings, to ventilate and decompress from the horrific work they engage in. In response to this need, defusing and debriefing strategies have been developed. Chief among them has been critical incident stress debriefing (CISD). CISD in particular has come under sharp criticism as being not helpful and in some cases harmful to go through. However, adherents just as vehemently state that it is absolutely necessary to keep them sane. From that standpoint, it appears that some model of debriefing for crisis workers is imperative. However, at the start of the 21st century one thing is abundantly clear: Crisis intervention is a growth industry, and it is here to stay.

REFERENCES

Addy, C., & James, R. K. (2002, April). *Lieutenants in the crosshairs: Alternative approaches in the treatment of crisis and trauma in field command level staff.* Paper presented at the 25th Annual Convening of Crisis Intervention Personnel, Chicago.

Allen, M., & Sheen, D. (2005). *School-based crisis intervention: Preparing all personnel to assist.* New York: Guilford Press.

American School Counselor Association. (2011). *9/11 memorial teaching guide.* Available at www.schoolcounselor.org/content.asp?contentid=645

Antonovsky, A. (1980). *Health, stress, and coping.* San Francisco: Jossey-Bass.

Antonovsky, A. (1991). The structural sources of salutogenic strengths. In C. Cooper & R. Payne (Eds.), *Personality and stress: Individual differences in the stress process* (pp. 67–104). London: Wiley.

Armstrong, K., O'Callahan, W., & Marmar, C. (1991). Debriefing Red Cross disaster personnel: The multiple stressor debriefing model. *Journal of Traumatic Stress, 4,* 581–593.

Aten, J. D., Leavell, K., Gonzalez, R, Luke, T., Defee, J., & Harrison, K. (2011). Everyday technologies for extraordinary circumstances: Possibilities for enhancing disaster communication. *Psychological Trauma, Theory, Research, and Practice, 3*(1), 16–20.

Avery, A., & Orner, R. (1998a, Summer). First report of psychological debriefing abandoned—The end of an era? *Traumatic Stress Points, 12*(3), 1112.

Avery, A., & Orner, R. (1998b, July). More on debriefing: Report of psychological debriefing abandoned—The end of an era? *Australian Traumatic Stress Points,* pp. 4–6.

Bass, D. D., & Yep, R. (2002). *Terrorism, trauma, and tragedies: A counselor's guide to preparing and responding.* Alexandria, VA: American Counseling Association.

Bethel, B., & Oates, J. A. (2007, March). *The untold story of the Beverly Hillbillies.* Paper presented at the Thirty-first Convening of Crisis Intervention Personnel and the Contact USA Conference, Chicago.

Bisson, J. I., & Deahl, M. P. (1994). Psychological debriefing and prevention post-traumatic stress—More research is needed. *British Journal of Psychiatry, 165,* 717–720.

Bisson, J. I., Jenkins, J. A., & Bannister, C. (1997). Randomized controlled trial of psychological debriefing for victims of acute burn trauma. *British Journal of Psychiatry, 171,* 78–81.

Bonanno, G. A., Westphal, M., & Mancini, A. D. (2011). Resilience to loss and potential trauma. *Annual Review of Clinical Psychology, 7,* 511–535.

Boyd, B., Quevillon, R. P., & Engdahl, R. M. (2010). Working with rural and diverse communities after disasters. In P. Dass-Braillsford (Ed.), *Crisis and disaster counseling: Lessons learned from hurricane Katrina and other disasters* (pp. 149–163). Thousand Oaks, CA: Sage.

Boyd-Franklin, N. (2010). Families affected by hurricane Katrina and other disasters: Learning from the experiences of African-American survivors. In P. Dass-Braillsford (Ed.), *Crisis and disaster counseling: Lessons learned from hurricane Katrina and other disasters* (pp. 67–82). Thousand Oaks, CA: Sage.

Brainerd, A. M. (2002). Tragic events and the effects on all of us. In D. D. Bass & R. Yep (Eds.), *Terrorism, trauma, and tragedies: A counselor's guide to preparing and responding* (pp. 111–112). Alexandria, VA: American Counseling Association.

Brom, D., & Kleber, R. J. (1989). Prevention of posttraumatic stress disorders. *Journal of Traumatic Stress, 2*, 335–351.

Bromet, E. J. (1995). Methodological issues in designing research on community-wide disasters with special reference to Chernobyl. In S. E. Hobfoll & M. W. de Vries (Eds.), *Extreme stress and communities: Impact and intervention* (pp. 307–324). Dordrecht, Netherlands: Kluwer.

Bronfenbrenner, U. (1986). Ecology of the family as a context for human development: Research perspectives. *Developmental Psychology, 22*, 723–742.

Bronfenbrenner, U. (1995). Developmental ecology through space and time: A future perspective. In P. Moen, G. H. Elder, Jr., & K. Luscher (Eds.), *Examining lives in context: Perspectives on the ecology of human development* (pp. 619–647). Washington, DC: American Psychological Association.

Bronfenbrenner, U., & Morris, P. A. (1998). The ecology of developmental processes. In W. Damon & R. M. Lerner (Eds.), *Handbook of child psychology* (5th ed., Vol. 1, pp. 993–1028). New York: Wiley.

Brymer, M. J., Steinberg, A. M., Vernberg, E. M., Laynes, C. M., Watson, P. J., Jacobs, S. A., et al. (2009). Acute interventions for children and adolescents. In E. Foa, T. Keane, M. Friedman, & J. Cohen (Eds.), *Effective treatments for PTSD* (2nd ed., pp. 106–116). New York: Oxford University Press.

Callahan, R. (2011, September 16). Sept. 11 panelists still see threats. *Memphis Commercial Appeal*, A3.

Cann, A., Calhoun, L., Tedeschi, R. Taku, K., Vishnevsky, T., Triplett, K., et al. (2010). A short form of the Posttraumatic Growth Inventory. *Anxiety, Stress, & Coping: An International Journal, 23*(2), 127–137.

Cann, A., Calhoun, L., Tedeschi, R., Triplett, K., Vishnevsky, T., & Lindstrom, C. (2011). Assessing posttraumatic cognitive processes: The Event-Related Rumination Inventory. *Anxiety, Stress, & Coping: An International Journal, 24*(2), 137–156.

Centers for Disease Control (CDC). (n.d.). *Podcasts at CDC*. Retrieved September 16, 2011, from www.2c.cdc.gov/podcasts

CERT. (2011). *Community Emergency Response Team training manual module 7: Psychological First Aid*. Available at www.citizencorps.gov/cert/training_mat.shtm.#CERTIG_IG_unit7_Jan2011.doc

Charlton, P. F. C., & Thompson, J. A. (1996). Ways of coping with psychological distress after trauma. *British Journal of Psychology, 35*, 517–530.

Chemtob, C. M. (2000). Delayed debriefing after a disaster. In B. Raphael & J. P. Wilson (Eds.), *Psychological debriefing: Theory, practice, and evidence* (pp. 227–240). New York: Cambridge University Press.

Chemtob, C. M., Nakashima, J. P., & Hamada, R. S. (2002). Psychosocial intervention for postdisaster trauma symptoms in elementary school children: A controlled community field study. *Archives of Pediatric and Adolescent Medicine, 156*, 211–216.

Chung, M. C., Easthope, Y., Farmer, S., Werrett, J., & Chung, C. (2003). Psychological sequelae: Post-traumatic stress reactions and personality factors among community residents as secondary victims. *Scandinavian Journal of Caring Science, 17*(3), 265–270.

Clark, J., Hayes, R. L., Hayes, L., Millner, V. S., Sharpe, T., & Waltman, R. (2006). *Transcending trauma after a disaster: A guide for schools* [CD]. Mobile: University of South Alabama and Mobile County Public School System.

Cohen, J., Mannarino, J. A., & Deblinger, E. (2006). *Treating trauma and traumatic grief in children and adolescents*. New York: Guilford Press.

Cohen, P., Kasen, S., Chen, H., Gordon, K., Berenson, K., Brook, J., et al. (2006). Current affairs and the public psyche: American anxiety in the post 9/11 world. *Social Psychiatry and Psychiatric Epidemiology, 41*(4), 251–260.

Coke-Weatherly, A. (2005). *An analysis of where and how crisis intervention is taught and learned*. Unpublished doctoral dissertation, University of Memphis, Memphis, Tennessee.

Collins, B. G., & Collins, B. G. (2005). *Crisis and trauma: Developmental-ecological intervention*. Lahaska, PA: Lahaska Press.

Conyne, R. K., & Cook, E. P. (2003, March). *Understanding persons within environment: An introduction to ecological counseling*. Program and paper presented at the annual meeting of the American Counseling Association, Anaheim, CA.

Conyne, R. K., Cook, E. P., Wilson, R. F., Tang, M., O'Connell, W. P., McWhirter, B. T., et al. (2003, March). *Ecological counseling: An approach for the 21st century*. Program and paper presented at the annual meeting of the American Counseling Association, Anaheim, CA.

Corey-Souza, P. (2007). Compassion fatigue in members of the Florida Crisis Response Team: A consequence of caring. *Dissertation Abstracts International: Section B. The Sciences and Engineering*, 2695.

Dass-Brailsford, P. (Ed.). (2010). *Crisis and disaster counseling: Lessons learned from hurricane Katrina and other disasters*. Thousand Oaks, CA: Sage.

Deahl, M. (1999). Debriefing and body recovery: War grave soldiers. In B. Raphael & J. P. Wilson (Eds.), *Psychological debriefing: Theory, practice, and evidence* (pp. 108–117). New York: Cambridge University Press.

DeAngelis, T. (2011). Helping kids cope in an uncertain world. *Monitor on Psychology 42*(8), 67–70.

Department of Homeland Security. (2008). FEMA's crisis counseling assistance and training program: State of Florida Project Hope. Available at www.dhs.gov/xoig/assets/mgmtrptsl/OIG_08-96_Sep08.pdf

deVries, F. (1998). To make a drama out of trauma is fully justified. *Lancet, 351*, 1579–1580.

Dingfelder, S. F. (2006). New needs in New Orleans schools. *Monitor on Psychology, 37*(6), 28–29.

Dodgen, D., & Meed, J. (2010). The federal government in disaster mental health response: An ever-evolving role. In P. Dass-Brailsford (Ed.), *Crisis and disaster counseling: Lessons learned from hurricane Katrina and other disasters* (pp. 181–195). Thousand Oaks, CA: Sage.

Drabek, T. E. (1986). *Human systems response to disaster: An inventory of sociological findings.* New York: Springer.

Dyregrov, A. (1997). The process in psychological debriefings. *Journal of Traumatic Stress, 10,* 589–605.

Dyregrov, A., Gupta, L., Gjestad, R., & Raundalen, M. (2002). Is the culture always right? *Traumatology, 8,* 1–10.

Dziegielewski, S. F., & Powers, G. T. (2005). Designs and procedures for evaluating crisis intervention. In A. R. Roberts (Ed.), *Crisis intervention handbook* (3rd ed., pp. 742–773). New York: Oxford University Press.

Dziegielewski, S. F., & Sumner, K. (2005). An examination of the U.S. response to bioterrorism: Handling the threat and aftermath through crisis intervention. In A. R. Roberts (Ed.), Crisis intervention handbook (3rd ed., pp. 262–290). New York: Oxford University Press.

Echterling, L. G., McKee, E. J., & Presbury, J. (2000, March). *Resolution-focused crisis debriefing for traumatized groups.* Paper presented at the American Counseling Association Conference, Washington, DC.

Echterling, L. G., & Wylie, M. L. (1999). In the public arena: Disaster as a socially constructed problem. In R. Gist & B. Lubin (Eds.), *Response to disaster: Psychosocial, community, and ecological approaches* (pp. 327–352). Philadelphia: Brunner/Mazel.

Emergency Management Institute. (n.d.). *Community emergency response team overview.* Retrieved August 8, 2003, from www.training.fema.gov/EMIWeb/CERToverview.asp

Erikson, K. T. (1976). *Everything in its path: Destruction of community in the Buffalo Creek flood.* New York: Simon & Schuster.

Everly, G. S., & Flynn, B. W. (2005). Principles and procedures of acute psychological first aid training for personnel without mental health experience. *International Journal of Emergency Mental Health, 8*(2), 93–100.

Farberow, N. L., & Frederick, C. J. (1978). *Training for human service workers in major disasters.* Rockville, MD: National Institute of Mental Health.

Federal Emergency Management Agency. (n.d.). *History of FEMA.* Retrieved August 6, 2003, from www.fema.gov

Figley, C. R. (Ed.). (2002). *Treating compassion fatigue.* New York: Brunner-Routledge.

Flynn, B. W. (1998, April). *Terrorist events using weapons of mass destruction: Confronting the mental health consequences.* Paper presented at the Third Harvard Symposium on Complex Humanitarian Disasters, Disaster Medical Response: Current Challenges and Strategies, Boston.

Flynn, B. W. (2003). *Mental health all-hazards planning guide.* Rockville, MD: National Technical Assistance Center of the National Association of State Mental Health Directors.

Freedy, J. R., & Hobfoll, S. E. (Eds.). (1995). *Traumatic stress: From theory to practice.* New York: Plenum Press.

Freeman, N. (Speaker). (2003, May 28). *Ecological disaster crisis management* (Cassette Recording No. 052803). Fernandina Beach, FL: Nassau County Emergency Management Department.

Friedman, M. J., Ritchie, E. C., & Watson, P. J. (2006). Overview. In E. C. Ritchie, P. J. Watson, & M. J. Friedman (Eds.), *Interventions following mass violence and disasters: Strategies for mental health practice* (pp. 3–15). New York: Guilford Press.

Galai-Gat, T. (2004, April). *Early interventions with survivors of terrorist attacks in Jerusalem.* Paper presented at the 28th Annual Convening of Crisis Intervention Personnel and 2nd Collaborative Crisis Centers Conference, Chicago.

Gheytanchi, A., Joseph, L., Gierlach, E., Kimpara, S., Housley, J., Franco, Z., et al. (2007). The dirty dozen: Twelve failures of the hurricane Katrina response and how psychology can help. *American Psychologist, 62*(2), 118–130.

Gil-Rivas, V., Kilmer, R. P., Hypes, A. W., & Roof, K. A. (2010). The caregiver–child relationship and children's adjustment following hurricane Katrina. In R. P Kilmer, V. Gil-Rivas, R. G. Tedeschi, & L. G. Calhoun (Eds.), *Helping families and communities recover from disaster: Lessons learned from hurricane Katrina and its aftermath.* (pp. 55–76). Washington, DC: American Psychological Association.

Gil-Rivas, V., Silver, R. C., Holman, E. A., McIntosh, D., & Poulin, M. (2007). Parental response and adolescent adjustment to the September 11th terrorist attacks. *Journal of Traumatic Stress, 20,* 1063–1068.

Gist, R., & Lubin, B. (Eds.). (1989). *Psychological aspects of disaster.* New York: Wiley.

Gist, R., & Lubin, B. (Eds.). (1999). *Response to disaster: Psychosocial, community and ecological responses.* Philadelphia: Brunner/Mazel.

Gist, R., Lubin, B., & Redburn, B. G. (1999). Psychosocial, ecological, and community perspectives on disaster response. In R. Gist & B. Lubin (Eds.), *Response to disaster: Psychosocial, community and ecological responses* (pp. 1–16). Philadelphia: Brunner/Mazel.

Gist, R., Woodall, S. J., & Magenheimer, L. K. (1999). And then you do the Hokey Pokey and you turn yourself around . . . In R. Gist & B. Lubin (Eds.), *Response to disaster: Psychosocial, community and ecological responses* (pp. 269–290). Philadelphia: Brunner/Mazel.

Gladding, S. T. (2002). From Pier 94, near Ground Zero, New York City. In D. D. Bass & R. Yep (Eds.), *Terrorism, trauma, and tragedies: A counselor's guide to preparing and responding* (pp. 7–9). Alexandria, VA: American Counseling Association.

GM's Onstar, American Red Cross partner to provide emergency services in crisis situations. (2008, September). *Domain B.* Available at http://domain-b.com

Gray, M. J., & Litz, B. T. (2005). Behavioral interventions for recent trauma: Empirically informed practice guidelines. *Behavior Modification, 29,* 189–215.

Green, B. L., & Solomon, S. D. (1995). The mental health impact of natural and technological disasters. In J. R. Freedy & S. E. Hobfoll (Eds.), *Traumatic stress: From theory to practice* (pp. 163–180). New York: Plenum Press.

Guerra, P. (1999, May). Counselors help victims of school shooting. *Counseling Today, 41,* 12–14.

Guerra, P., & Schmitt, S. M. (1999, June). Reactions to Littleton shooting. *Counseling Today, 41,* 26–27.

Gulati, P., & Guest, G. (1990). The community centered model: A garden-variety approach or a radical transformation of community practice? *Social Work, 35,* 63–68.

Halpern, J. & Tramontin, M. (2007). *Disaster mental health theory and practice.* Belmont, CA: Brooks/Cole.

Hartsough, D. (1982). Planning for disaster: A new community outreach program for mental health centers. *Journal of Community Psychology, 10,* 255–264.

Hayes, G. (2002). Intervening with school students after terrorist acts. In D. D. Bass & R. Yep (Eds.), *Terrorism, trauma, and tragedies: A counselor's guide to preparing and responding* (pp. 63–65). Alexandria, VA: American Counseling Association.

Hayes, G., Goodwin, T., & Miars, B. (1990). After disaster: A crisis support team at work. *American Journal of Nursing, 2,* 61–64.

Henry, V. E. (2004). *Death work: Police, trauma, and the psychology of survival.* New York: Oxford University Press.

Henry, V. E. (2005). In A. E. Roberts (Ed.), *Crisis intervention handbook* (3rd ed., pp. 171–199). New York: Oxford University Press.

Hobbs, M., Mayou, R., Harrison, B., & Worlock, P. (1996). A randomised control of psychological debriefing for victims of road traffic accidents. *British Medical Journal, 313,* 1438–1439.

Hobfoll, S. E. (1988). *The ecology of stress.* New York: Wiley.

Hobfoll, S. E., & deVries, M. W. (Eds.). (1995). *Extreme stress and communities: Impact and intervention.* Dordrecht, Netherlands: Kluwer.

Hobfoll, S. E., Watson, P. J., Bell, C. C., Bryant, R. A., Brymer, M. J., Friedman, M. J., et al. (2007). Five essential elements for immediate and mid-term crisis in mass trauma intervention: Empirical evidence. *Psychiatry, 70,* 283–315.

Huddy, L., & Feldman, S. (2011). Americans respond politically to 9/11: Understanding the impact of terrorist attacks and their aftermath. *American Psychologist, 66*(5), 455–467.

Humanitarian charter and minimum standards in disaster response. (1998). *Sphere Project.* Geneva: World Health Organization.

Inter-Agency Standing Committee (IASC). (2007). *IASC guidelines on mental health and psychosocial input support in emergency situations.* Geneva: Author.

Jacobs, J., Horne-Moyer, H. L., & Jones, R. (2004). The effectiveness of critical incident stress debriefing with primary and secondary trauma victims. *International Journal of Emergency Mental Health, 6,* 5–14.

James, R. K. (2006, May). *Four hundred miles from landfall: Lesson learned from Katrina.* Paper presented at the Thirtieth Annual Convening of Crisis Intervention Personnel and the Contact USA Conference, Chicago.

James, R. K., Cogdal, P., & Gilliland, B. E. (2003, April). *An ecological theory of crisis intervention.* Paper presented at the American Counseling Association convention, Kansas City, MO.

James, R. K., & Gilliland, B. E. (2003). *Theories and strategies in counseling and psychotherapy* (5th ed.). Boston: Allyn & Bacon.

Jordan, K. (2002). Providing crisis counseling to New Yorkers after the terrorist attack on the World Trade Center. *The Family Journal, 10*(2), 139–144.

Jordans, M., Upadhaya, N., Tol, W., Shrestha, P., Doucet, J., Gurung, R., et al. (2010). Introducing the IASC mental health and psychosocial support guidelines in emergencies in Nepal: A process description. *Intervention, 8*(1), 52–63.

Juhnke, G. A. (2002). Intervening with school students after terrorist attacks. In D. D. Bass & R. Yep (Eds.), *Terrorism, trauma, and tragedies: A counselor's guide to preparing and responding* (pp. 55–58). Alexandria, VA: American Counseling Association.

Kaniasty, K., & Norris, F. (1999). The experience of disaster: Individuals and communities sharing trauma. In R. Gist & B. Lubin (Eds.), *Response to disaster: Psychosocial, community and ecological approaches* (pp. 25–62). Philadelphia: Brunner/Mazel.

Kaplan, H. B. (1996). *Psychosocial stress: Perspectives on structure, theory, life course and methods.* San Diego, CA: Academic Press.

Katz, C. L. (2011). Needs assessment. In F. J. Stoddard, A. Pandya, & C. Katz (Eds.), *Disaster psychiatry: Readiness, evaluation, and treatment* (pp. 49–68). Arlington, VA: American Psychiatric Publishing.

Kaul, R. E., & Welzant, V. (2005). Disaster mental health: A discussion of best practices applied after the Pentagon attack. In A. R. Roberts (Ed.), *Crisis intervention handbook* (3rd ed., pp. 200–220). New York: Oxford University Press.

Kenardy, J., Webster, R., Lewin, T., Carr, V., & Carter, G. (1996). Stress debriefing and patterns of recovery following natural disaster. *Journal of Traumatic Stress, 9,* 37–49.

Kennedy, A. (2007, July). Responding to the call. *Counseling Today.*

Kerr, M. M. (2009). *School crisis prevention and intervention.* Upper Saddle River, NJ: Pearson.

Kilmer, R. P., Gil-Rivas, V., & MacDonald, J. (2010). Implications of major disaster for educators, administrators, and school-based mental health professionals: Needs, actions, and the example of Mayfair Elementary. In R. P. Kilmer, V. Gil-Rivas, R. G. Tedeschi, & L. G. Calhoun (Eds.), *Helping families and communities recover from disaster: Lessons learned from hurricane Katrina and its aftermath* (pp. 167–191). Washington, DC: American Psychological Association.

Kilmer, R. P., Gil-Rivas, V., Tedeschi, R. G., & Calhoun, L. G. (Eds.). (2010). *Helping families and communities recover from disaster: Lessons learned from hurricane Katrina and its aftermath.* Washington, DC: American Psychological Association.

Klotz, J. M. (2003). *Welcome to ecological counseling.org.* Retrieved April 21, 2003, from www.ecologicalcounseling.org

Lane, J. (2003). *Ecological crisis management* (Cassette Recording No. 082803). Memphis, TN: University of Memphis.

Lawson, G., Bodenhorn, N., Welfare, L. (2010). Virginia Tech: A campus and a community respond. In J. Webber & J. B. Mascari (Eds.), *Terrorism, trauma, and tragedies: A counselor's guide to preparing and responding* (3rd ed., pp. 73–76). Alexandria, VA: American Counseling Association Foundation.

Lazarus, R. S., & Folkman, S. (1984). *Stress, appraisal, and coping.* New York: Springer-Verlag.

Lee, C., Slade, P. & Lygo, V. (1996). The influence of psychological debriefing on emotional adaption in women following early miscarriage: A preliminary study. *British Journal of Medical Psychology, 69*, 37–49.

Leffler, C. T., & Dembert, M. L. (1998). Posttraumatic stress symptoms among U.S. Navy divers recovering TWA Flight 800. *Journal of Nervous & Mental Disease, 186*, 574–577.

Leskin, G. A., Huleatt, W., Jerrmann, J., Ladue, L., & Gusman, F. (2006). Rapid development of family assistance centers: Lessons learned following the September 11 terrorist attacks. In E. C. Ritchie, P. J. Watson, & M. J. Friedman (Eds.), *Interventions following mass violence and disasters: Strategies for mental health practice* (pp. 257–277). New York: Guilford Press.

Lifton, R. J. (1983). *The broken connection: On death and the continuity of life.* New York: Basic Books.

Lindemann, E. (1944). Symptomatology and management of acute grief. *American Journal of Psychiatry, 101*, 141–148.

Litz, B. T., & Gibson, L. E. (2006). Conducting research on mental health interventions. In E. C. Ritchie, P. J. Watson, & M. J. Friedman (Eds.), *Interventions following mass violence and disasters: Strategies for mental health practice* (pp. 387–404). New York: Guilford Press.

MacDonald, C. M. (2003). Evaluation of stress debriefing interventions with military populations. *Military Medicine, 168*, 961–967.

Malchiodi, C., Steele, W., & Kuban, C. (2008). Resilience and posttraumatic growth in traumatized children. In C. Malchiodi (Ed.), *Creative interventions with traumatized children* (pp. 285–301). New York: Guilford Press.

McCarthy, J. J. (2002). How a school district crisis response team can help. In D. D. Bass & R. Yep (Eds.), *Terrorism, trauma, and tragedies: A counselor's guide to preparing and responding* (pp. 53–54). Alexandria, VA: American Counseling Association.

McWhirter, E. H., & Linzer, M. (1994). The provision of critical incident services by EAPs: A case study. *Journal of Mental Health Counseling, 16*, 403–414.

Merlino, J. P. (2011). Rescuing ourselves: Self-care in the disaster response community. In F. J. Stoddard, A. Pandya, & C. Katz (Eds.), *Disaster psychiatry: Readiness, evaluation, and treatment* (pp. 35–48). Arlington, VA: American Psychiatric Publishing.

Miller, L. (2010). On-scene crisis intervention: Psychological guidelines and communication strategies for first responders. *International Journal of Emergency Mental Health, 12*(1), 11–19.

Missing Children. (2006). Missing Children: Getting home after disaster strikes. *Challenge, 14*(1), 1–2.

Mitchell, J. T., & Everly, G. S., Jr. (1995a). *Advanced critical incidents stress debriefing.* Ellicott City, MD: International Critical Incidents Stress Foundation.

Mitchell, J. T., & Everly, G. S., Jr. (1995b). Critical incidents stress debriefing (CISD) and the prevention of work-related traumatic stress among high risk occupational groups. In G. S. Everly, Jr., & J. T. Lating (Eds.), *Psychotraumatology* (pp. 267–280). New York: Plenum Press.

Mitchell, J. T., & Everly, G. S., Jr. (1999). Critical incident stress management and critical incident stress debriefings: Evolutions, effects, and outcomes. In B. Raphael & J. P. Wilson (Eds.), *Psychological debriefing: Theory, practice, and evidence* (pp. 71–90). New York: Cambridge University Press.

Modrak, R. (1992, January). Mass shootings and airplane crashes: Counselors respond to the changing face of community crisis. *Guidepost, 34*, 4.

Montano, R., & Dowdall-Thomae, C. (2003, June). *Are you ready for the crisis?* Paper presented at the American School Counselor Association Convention, St. Louis, MO.

Morgan, G. S., Wisneski, D. C., & Skitka, L. J. (2011). The expulsion from Disneyland: The social psychological impact of 9/11. *American Psychologist, 66*(5), 447–454.

Morris, A. J. (2011). Psychic aftershocks: Crisis counseling and disaster relief policy. *History of Psychology, 14*(3), 264–286.

Morrissey, M. (1994, June). ACA, Red Cross to work together to help disaster victims. *Guidepost, 36*, 1, 6.

Morrissey, M. (1995, June). Members write children's book to help youngsters cope with Oklahoma City tragedy. *Counseling Today, 37*(12), 20.

Munsey, C. (2006). Schools: A post-Katrina anchor for children. *Monitor on Psychology, 37*(9), 46–47.

Myer, R. A., & Moore, H. (2006). Crisis in context theory: An ecological model. *Journal of Counseling & Development, 84*(2), 139–147.

Myers, D., & Wee, D. F. (2005). *Disaster mental health services*. New York: Brunner–Routledge.

Myers, D., & Zunin, L. (1994). Debriefing and grief: Easing the pain. *Today's Supervisor, 6*(12), 14–15.

Nassau County Emergency Management Department. (2003). *Storm time and event schedule*. Fernandina Beach, FL: Author.

National Center for PTSD. (n.d.a). *Mental health effects following disaster: Risk and resilience factors*. Available at www.ptsd.va.gov/professional/pages/effects-disasters-mental-health.asp

National Center for PTSD. (n.d.b). National Center for PTSD home. Retrieved September 17, 2011, from www.ptsd.va.gov

National Center for PTSD. (n.d.c). Psychological first aid manual for mental health care providers. Available at www.ptsd.va.gov/professional/manuals/psych-first-aid.asp

National Child Traumatic Stress Network (NCTSN). (n.d.). National Child Traumatic Stress Network. Retrieved September 16, 2011, from www/nctsn.org

National Child Traumatic Stress Network and National Center for PTSD (NCTSN/NCPTSD). (2006). *Psychological first aid: Field operations guide* (2nd ed.) Available at www.ptsd.va.gov/professional/manuals/manual-pdf/pfa/PFA_V2.pdf

National Institute of Mental Health (NIMH). (2002). *Mental health and mass violence: Evidence-based early psychological intervention for victims/survivors of mass violence: A workshop to reach consensus on best practices*. Washington, DC: Author.

National Organization for Victim Assistance. (n.d.). *NOVA's mission, purposes, accomplishments, and organizational structure*. Retrieved August 8, 2003, from www.trynova.org/Victims/mission.html

Nickerson, R. S. (2011). Roles of human factors and ergonomics in meeting the challenge of terrorism. *American Psychologist, 66*(6), 555–566.

Nisivoccia, D., & Lynn, M. (2007). Helping forgotten victims: Using activity groups with children who witness violence. In N. B. Webb (Ed.), *Play therapy with children in crisis: Individual, group, and family treatment* (pp. 294–321). New York: Guilford Press.

Norfolk, Virginia, Community Services Board. (2003). *A model CSB disaster plan*. Retrieved May 16, 2003, from www.jmu.edu/psychologydept/csbplan.htm

Norris, F. H. (2006). Disaster research methods: Past progress and future directions. *Journal of Traumatic Stesss, 19*(2), 173–184.

Norris, F. H., & Alegria, M. (2006). Promoting disaster recovery in ethnic-minority individuals and communities. In E. C. Ritchie, P. J. Watson, & M. J. Friedman (Eds.), *Interventions following mass violence and disasters: Strategies for mental health practice* (pp. 319–342). New York: Guilford Press.

Norris, F. H., Hamblen, J., Watson, P., Ruxek, J., Gibson, L., Pfefferbaum, B., et al. (2006). Toward understanding and creating systems of postdisaster care. In E. C. Ritchie, P. J. Watson, & M. J. Friedman (Eds.), *Interventions following mass violence and disasters: Strategies for mental health practice* (pp. 343–364). New York: Guilford Press.

North, C. S. (2004). Approaching disaster mental health research after the 9/11 World Trade Center terrorist attacks. *Psychiatric Clinics of North America, 27*(3), 589–602.

Obhu, S., Yamashina, A., Takasu, N., Yamaguchi, T., Murai, T., Naknbao, K., et al. (1997). Sarin poisoning on the Tokyo subway. *Southern Medical Journal, 90*, 587–593.

Ørner, J. R. J., Kent, A., Pfefferbaun, B., Raphael, B., & Watson, P. (2006). The context of providing immediate postevent intervention. In E. C. Ritchie, P. J. Watson, & M. J. Friedman (Eds.), *Interventions following mass violence and disasters: Strategies for mental health practice* (pp. 121–133). New York: Guilford Press.

Pastel, B. H., & Ritchie, E. C. (2006). Mitigation of psychological weapons of mass destruction. In E. C. Ritchie, P. J. Watson, & M. J. Friedman (Eds.), *Interventions following mass violence and disasters: Strategies for mental health practice* (pp. 300–318). New York: Guilford Press.

Pender, D. A., & Prichard, K. K. (2008). Group process research and emergence of therapeutic factors in Critical Incident Stress Debriefing. *International Journal of Emergency Mental Health, 10*, 39–48.

Pender, D. A., & Prichard, K. K. (2009). AGSW best practices guidelines as a research tool: A comprehensive examination of critical incident stress debriefing. *Journal of Specialists in Group Work, 34*(2), 175–192.

Pennebaker, J. W., & Harber, K. D. (1993). A social stage model of collective coping: The Loma Prieta earthquake and the Persian Gulf War. *Journal of Social Issues, 49*, 125–146.

Phillips, B., & Jenkins, P. (2010). The roles of faith based organizations after hurricane Katrina. In R. P Kilmer, V. Gil-Rivas, R. G. Tedeschi, & L. G. Calhoun (Eds.), *Helping families and communities recover from disaster: Lessons learned from hurricane Katrina and its aftermath* (pp. 215–238). Washington, DC: American Psychological Association.

Pyszczynski, T., Solomon, S., & Greenberg, J. (2002). *In the wake of 911: The psychology of terror*. Washington, DC: American Psychological Association.

Raphael, B. (1977). Preventive intervention with the recently bereaved. *Archives of General Psychiatry, 132*, 3–10.

Raphael, B. (1984). *The anatomy of bereavement.* New York: Basic Books.

Raphael, B. (1986). *When disaster strikes: How individuals and communities cope with disaster.* New York: Basic Books.

Raphael, B. (1999). Conclusion: Debriefing—Science, belief, and wisdom. In B. Raphael & J. P. Wilson (Eds.), *Psychological debriefing: Theory, practice, and evidence* (pp. 351–359). New York: Cambridge University Press.

Raphael, B. (2000). *Disaster mental health response handbook: An educational resource for mental health professionals involved in disaster management.* New South Wales, Australia: New South Wales Institute of Psychiatry.

Raphael, B., Meldrum, L., & McFarland, A. C. (1995). Does debriefing after psychological trauma work? *British Medical Journal, 310*, 1479–1480.

Rebmann, T., Carrico, R., & English, J. F. (2008). Lessons public health professionals learned from past disasters. *Public Health Nursing, 25*, 344–352.

Red Cross. (n.d.). Emergency disaster response. Retrieved August 21, 2003, from www.redcross.org/services/intl/edr.html

Ren, C. H. (2000). Understanding and managing the dynamics of linked crisis events. *Disaster Prevention and Management, 9*(1), 12–17.

Riethmayer, J. (2002a). Dealing with the impact of trauma. In D. D. Bass & R. Yep (Eds.), *Terrorism, trauma, and tragedies: A counselor's guide to preparing and responding* (pp. 107–109). Alexandria, VA: American Counseling Association.

Riethmayer, J. (2002b). Explaining terrorism to children. In D. D. Bass & R. Yep (Eds.), *Terrorism, trauma, and tragedies: A counselor's guide to preparing and responding* (pp. 27–31). Alexandria, VA: American Counseling Association.

Roberts, A. R. (2005). The ACT model: Assessment, crisis intervention, and trauma treatment in the aftermath of community disaster and terrorism attacks. In A. R. Roberts (Ed.), *Crisis intervention handbook* (3rd ed., pp. 143–170). New York: Oxford University Press.

Robinson, H. M., Sigman, M. R., & Wilson, J. P. (1997). Duty-related stressors and PTSD symptoms in suburban police officers. *Psychological Reports, 81*, 835–845.

Ruzek, J. I. (2006). Models of early intervention following mass violence and other trauma. In E. C. Ritchie, P. J. Watson, & M. J. Friedman (Eds.), *Interventions following mass violence and disasters: Strategies for mental health practice* (pp. 16–36). New York: Guilford Press.

Saakvitne, K. W., & Pearlman, L. A. (1996). *Transforming the pain: A workbook on vicarious traumatization.* New York: Norton.

Salloum, A., & Overstreet, S. (2008). Evaluation of individual and group grief and trauma interventions of children post disaster. *Journal of Clinical Child and Adolescent Psychology, 37*, 495–507.

Salzer, M. S., & Bickman, L. (1999). The short- and long-term psychological impact of disasters: Implications for mental health interventions and policy. In R. Gist & B. Lubin (Eds.), *Response to disaster: Psychological, community and ecological approaches* (pp. 63–82). New York: Brunner/Mazel.

Santrock, J. W. (1999). *Life-span development* (7th ed.). Boston: McGraw-Hill.

Schneider, J. (1984). *Stress, loss, and grief: Understanding their origins and growth potential.* Baltimore, MD: University Park Press.

Shafer, C. (1989a, September). Counselors offer crisis intervention at Iowa crash site. *Guidepost*, pp. 1, 3, 6.

Shafer, C. (1989b, December). Recent disasters trigger NIMH response. *Guidepost*, pp. 1, 5.

Shalev, A., Sahar, T., Freedman, S., Peri, T., Lick, N., Brandes, D., et al. (1998). A prospective study of heart rate response following trauma and the subsequent development of posttraumatic stress disorder. *Archives of General Psychiatry, 55*, 553–559.

Shallcross, L. (2011). A day that changed the nation and a profession. *Counseling Today, 54*(3), 36–40.

Shelby, J. S., & Tredinnick, M. G. (1995). Crisis intervention with survivors of natural disaster: Lessons from hurricane Andrew. *Journal of Counseling and Development, 73*, 491–497.

Shraberg, M. (2006, May). *Disaster planning for a crisis center.* Paper presented at the Thirtieth Convening of Crisis Intervention Personnel/Contact USA Conference, Chicago.

Silove, D. (1999). A conceptual framework for mass trauma: Implications for adaptation, intervention, and debriefing. In B. Raphael & J. P. Wilson (Eds.), *Psychological debriefing: Theory, practice, and evidence* (pp. 337–350). New York: Cambridge University Press.

Silver, T., & Goldstein, H. (1992). A collaborative model of a county intervention team: The Lake County experience. *Community Mental Health Journal, 28*, 249–253.

Silverman, W. K., Allen, A., & Ortiz, C. D. (2010). Lessons learned from hurricane Katrina and other devastating hurricanes: Steps necessary for preparedness, response, and intervention. In R. P. Ryan, V. Gil-Rivas, R. G. Tedeschi, & L. G. Calhoun (Eds.), *Helping families and communities recover from disaster: Lessons learned from hurricane Katrina and its aftermath* (pp. 289–311). Washington, DC: American Psychological Association.

Sleek, S. (1998, August). Experts scrambling on school shootings: School violence in rural areas could worsen. *APA Monitor, 29*, 1, 35–36.

Smith, H. B. (2002). The American Red Cross: How to be a part of the solution, rather than a part of the problem.

In D. D. Bass & R. Yep (Eds.), *Terrorism, trauma, and tragedies: A counselor's guide to preparing and responding* (pp. 37–38). Alexandria, VA: American Counseling Association.

Smith, K. J., & Belgrave, L. L. (1995). The reconstruction of everyday life: Experiencing hurricane Andrew. *Journal of Contemporary Ethnography, 24*, 244–269.

Solomon, R. M. (1995). Critical incidents stress management in law enforcement. In G. S. Everly (Ed.), *Innovations in disaster and trauma psychology: Applications in emergency services and disaster response* (pp. 123–157). Baltimore, MD: Chevron.

Spitzer, W. H., & Neely, M. K. (1992). Critical incident stress: The role of hospital-based social work in developing a statewide intervention system for first-responders delivering emergency services. *Social Work in Health Care, 18*, 39–58.

Stambor, Z. (2005). Responders must consider victim's culture, experts say. *Monitor on Psychology, 36*(11), 28.

Stokols, D., Misra, S., Runnerstrom, J. M., & Hipp, J. A. (2009). Psychology in an age of ecological crisis: From personal angst to collective action. *American Psychologist, 64*(3), 181–193.

Stuhmiller, C., & Dunning, C. (2000). Concerns about debriefing: Challenging the mainstream. In B. Raphael & J. P. Wilson (Eds.), *Psychological debriefing: Theory, practice, and evidence* (pp. 305–320). New York: Cambridge University Press.

Substance Abuse and Mental Health Services Administration (SAMHSA). (2003). *Tips for emergency and disaster response workers stress prevention and management approaches for rescue workers in the aftermath of terrorist acts.* Retrieved August 30, 2003, from http://mentalhealth .org/cmhs/EmergencyServices/stress.asp

Substance Abuse and Mental Health Services Administration (SAMHSA). (n.d.). *Tips for talking to children & youth about the oil spill disaster: Interventions at home for preschoolers to adolescents.* Available at www.oilspilldistress .samhsa.gov/node/3845

Sullivan, J. (2002). How should HR and managers react in the aftermath of terrorism events? In D. D. Bass & R. Yep (Eds.), *Terrorism, trauma, and tragedies: A counselor's guide to preparing and responding* (pp. 67–68). Alexandria, VA: American Counseling Association.

Summerfield, D. (2005). What exactly is emergency or disaster "mental health"? *Bulletin of the World Health Organization, 83*(1), 76.

Talbot, A., Manton, M., & Dunn, P. J. (1995). Debriefing the debriefers: An intervention strategy to assist psychologists after a crisis. In G. S. Everly, Jr., & J. M. Lating (Eds.), *Psychotraumatology* (pp. 281–298). New York: Plenum Press.

TENTS (n.d.) *TENTS–TP: The European Network for Traumatic Stress—Training and Practice.* Available at www .tentsproject.eu

Thomae, C. (2002). *The incident command system and standard operating procedures for a school crisis team.* Tucson: Arizona School Counselor Association.

Triplett, K., Tedeschi, R., Cann, A., Calhoun, L., & Reeve, C. (2011). Posttraumatic growth, meaning in life, and life satisfaction in response to trauma. *Psychological Trauma: Theory, Research, Practice, and Policy, 14*, 35–68.

Underwood, M. M., & Clark, C. (2002). Using metaphor to help children cope with trauma: An example from September 11th. In D. D. Bass & R. Yep (Eds.), *Terrorism, trauma, and tragedies: A counselor's guide to preparing and responding* (pp. 33–36). Alexandria, VA: American Counseling Association.

Ursano, R. J., & Friedman, M. J. (2006). Mental health and behavioral interventions for victims of disasters and mass violence: Systems, caring, planning and needs. In E. C. Ritchie, P. J. Watson, & M. J. Friedman (Eds.), *Interventions following mass violence and disasters: Strategies for mental health practice* (pp. 405–414). New York: Guilford Press.

U.S. Department of Justice. (2000). *Response to terrorism victims: Oklahoma City and beyond.* Washington, DC: Author.

Van Ommeren, M., Saxena, S., & Saraceno, S. (2005). Mental and social health during and after acute emergencies: Emerging consensus? *Bulletin of the World Health Organization, 83*(1), 71–75.

Vernberg, E. M. (1999). Children's responses to disaster: Family and systems approaches. In R. Gist & B. Lubin (Eds.), *Response to disaster: Psychosocial, community and ecological approaches* (pp. 193–210). Philadelphia: Brunner/Mazel.

Wagner, S.L. (2005). Emergency response service personnel & the critical incident stress debriefing debate. *International Journal of Emergency Mental Health, 7*, 33–41.

Wakelee-Lynch, J. (1990, October). Florida crisis elicits aid from college officials and counselors. *Guidepost*, pp. 1, 3.

Walker, G. (1990). Crisis-care in critical incident debriefing. *Death Studies, 14*, 121–133.

Watson, P. J., Brymer, M. J., & Bonanno, G. (2011). Postdisaster psychological intervention since 9/11. *American Psychologist, 66*(6), 482–494.

Webber, J., & Mascari, J. B. (Eds.). (2010). *Terrorism, trauma, and tragedies: A counselor's guide to preparing and responding* (3rd ed.). Alexandria, VA: American Counseling Association Foundation.

Webber, J., Mascari, J. B., & Runte, J. (2010). Psychological first aid: A new paradigm for disaster mental health. In J. Webber & J. B. Mascari (Eds.), *Terror, trauma, and tragedies: A counselor's guide to preparing and responding* (3rd ed., pp. 201–205). Alexandria, VA: American Counseling Association Foundation.

Weisaeth, L. (1999). Briefing and debriefing: Group psychological interventions in acute stressor situations. In B. Raphael

& J. P. Wilson (Eds.), *Psychological debriefing: Theory, practice, and evidence* (pp. 43–57). New York: Cambridge University Press.

Wessely, S. C., Bryant, R. A., Greenberg, N., Earnshaw, N., Shapley, J., & Hacker-Huges, J. (2008). Does psychoeducation help prevent post traumatic psychological distress? *Psychiatry, 71*(2), 287–302.

Western Carolina University Emergency Management Institute. (n.d.). *College degree offering for emergency management.* Retrieved April 15, 2007, from www.wcu.edu/2686.asp

Worden, J. W. (2002). *Grief counseling and grief therapy: A handbook for the mental health practitioner* (3rd ed.). New York: Springer.

Yates, S., Axsom, S., & Tiedeman, K. (1999). The help-seeking process for distress after disasters. In R. Gist & B. Lubin (Eds.), *Response to disaster: Psychosocial, community, and ecological approaches* (pp. 133–166). Philadelphia: Brunner/Mazel.

Young, B. H. (2006). The immediate response to disaster: Guidelines for adult psychological first aid. In E. C. Ritchie, P. J. Watson, & M. J. Friedman (Eds.), *Interventions following mass violence and disasters: Strategies for mental health practice* (pp. 134–154). New York: Guilford Press.

Young, B. H., Ruzek, J. I., Wong, M., Salzer, M. S., & Naturale, A. J. (2006). Disaster mental health training: Guidelines, considerations, and recommendations. In E. C. Ritchie, P. J. Watson, & M. J. Friedman (Eds.), *Interventions following mass violence and disasters: Strategies for mental health practice* (pp. 54–79). New York: Guilford Press.

Young, M. A. (1991). Crisis intervention and the aftermath of disaster. In A. R. Roberts (Ed.), *Contemporary perspectives on crisis intervention* (pp. 83–103). Upper Saddle River, NJ: Prentice Hall.

Zenere, F. (1998, Fall). NASP/NEAT community crisis response. *Newsletter of the Florida Association of School Psychologists.*

Index

A

Abstinence, 352, 365
Abuse, 297, 354–355. *See also specific kinds of abuse*
Academic problems, 490
Accelerated Recovery Program (ARP), 630
Acceptance, 83
  communication of, 87
  PTSD recovery and, 170–171
  of responsibility, 389–390
Accessibility, 120
Accidents, 213, 351–352
Accommodation stage, hostage crisis, 589–590
ACOAs. *See* Adult Children of Alcoholics
Acoustic startle response, 160
Acquaintance rape, 253–255
Acquired Capability for Suicide Scale, 219
Acting in crisis intervention, 87–93
  action strategies, 89–93
  collaborative counseling, 89
  directive counseling, 88–89
  networking, 93
  nondirective counseling, 89
  referral resources, 92
Acting-out children, 286, 364
Action continuum, 59
Active listening, 592, 597
ACT model, 20
Acute crisis, 70
Acute stress disorder (ASD), 149, 150, 606, 693
Adaptational theory, 15
Adaptive model of grief, 422, 437–438
Addiction
  aftercare programs for, 399–402
  assessment of, 375–381
  crisis points in treating, 381–385
  defense mechanisms displayed in, 356–358

definition of, 355
denial of, 390–391
detoxification process and, 385
dynamics of, 356–360
dysfunctional family rules about, 361–363
enabling and codependency in, 358–360, 397
family therapy for, 396–399
models of, 352–354
positive behaviors as, 629
principles of treatment for, 385–402
relapse prevention and, 399–402
summary review of, 402–403
treatment approaches to, 365–371, 385
  See also Chemical dependency; Substance abuse
Addiction Severity Index (ASI), 376
Addictive behavior, 355
ADDRESSING model, 33, 34
Adlerian psychotherapy, 560
Administration
  of burned-out organizations, 625
  of telephone crisis lines, 134
Adolescents
  bereavement and, 428–429, 523–525
  juvenile offenders as, 488–499
  sexual abuse of, 261–287
  suicide committed by, 210, 499–509
  trauma experienced by, 190
  See also Children
Adult Children of Alcoholics (ACOAs), 363–365
  effects of childhood roles on, 364
  facts about, 363
  feelings experienced by, 363–364
  potential problems faced by, 364–365
Adults
  children of alcoholics as, 363–365
  PTSD treatment process for, 164–178

sexual abuse survivors as, 261–271
suicide intervention strategies for, 222–240
Advocacy, 318
Affect dysregulation, 153
Affective development, 491
Affective severity scale, 65–66
Affective-state-dependent retention, 155
Affective states
  assessment of, 60, 65–66
  memory recall and, 155
  See also Emotions; Feelings
Affective strategies, 437
Affect regulation, 261
Affirmation, 277
Afghanistan war veterans, 163–164
Aftercare programs, 399–402
After-school programs, 484
After the Death of a Child: Living with Loss Through the Years (Finkbeiner), 445
Age
  bereavement and, 430
  caregiver population and, 425
  domestic violence and, 305
  suicide counseling and, 231–232
  violent clients and, 547
AIDS
  bereavement process and, 430–431, 456–457
  confidentiality issues and, 114
  crisis issues related to, 456–457
  See also HIV clients
Alarm stage, hostage crisis, 588–589
Alcadd Test, 376
Alcohol abuse, 351–352
  addiction models and, 352–354
  adult children of alcoholics and, 363–365
  aftercare programs for, 399–402
  assessment of, 375–381

children in families of, 360–365, 399
controlled drinking and, 374–375
crisis points in treatment for, 381–385
date rape and, 254
denial of, 356, 390–391
detoxification process and, 385
diagnosis of, 371–372
domestic violence and, 305, 331, 336
dysfunctional family rules about, 361–363
environmental cues and, 395–396
family therapy for, 396–399
hostage takers and, 588
institutional violence and, 547
intervention strategies for, 372–385
medications for, 401
mental illness and, 371–372
motivation to change, 372–374, 377
principles of treatment for, 385–402
relapse prevention and, 399–402
statistics on, 349–350
summary review of, 402–403
treatment approaches to, 365–371, 385
See also Chemical dependency;
    Substance abuse
Alcoholics Anonymous (AA), 4, 5, 365–366, 367, 402
Alcoholism, 5, 355
Alexithymia, 269
Altered states of consciousness, 490, 493
Alternatives
    considering with clients, 56, 71, 91
    exploring in telephone counseling, 124
Altruistic suicide, 212
Ambiguous loss, 417
American Association of Suicidology (AAS), 218, 219, 509
American Counseling Association (ACA), 511, 667, 702
American Medical Association (AMA), 351
American Psychiatric Association (APA), 150, 151, 229, 488, 581, 667
American Psychological Association (APA), 478, 511, 542, 652, 667, 678
American Psychologist journal, 652
American Red Cross, 45, 649, 666, 673, 677
American School Counselor Association (ASCA), 509, 511, 667
Americans With Disabilities Act (1990), 115, 512, 513, 544
Anatomy of Bereavement, The (Raphael), 652
Anchoring
    of geriatric violent clients, 566–567
    of mental health clinic clients, 100
Anger
    adult children of alcoholics and, 364
    childhood trauma and, 192
    choice making and, 333, 334

deflection of, 559–561
depression and, 637
juvenile offenders and, 490
physical cues of, 333–334
programs for managing, 330–338
rape based on, 250
sexually abused children and, 277–278
Anger: How to Live With It and Without It (Ellis), 334
Anger management, 330–338
    assessment process for, 331
    children/adolescents and, 483–484
    goals of, 330–331
    intake interview for, 331–332
    motivation of clients in, 332
    overview of sessions in, 332–337
    success of, 337–338
Angry Man: "Why Does He Act That Way?" (Stoop & Arterburn), 335
Animated guilt, 177
Anniversary of crises, 662
Anomic suicide, 212
Anonymity, 120, 121
Antidepressants, 172
Antisocial batterer, 307
Antisocial personality disorder, 585–586
Anxiety, 10
    reactions based on, 106
    reducing, 172, 525, 527
    See also Fear
Apathy, 619
Appeasement, 559
Applied crisis theory, 16–17
Artwork
    EMDR and, 194–195
    violent, 494
Aryan nation gangs, 479–480
ASI-MV test, 376
Assaulted Staff Action Program (ASAP), 571
Assaultive behavior
    crisis workers as victims of, 541, 569–571
    domestic violence and, 297–298
    See also Violence
Assertion statements, 79, 335–336
Assertiveness
    importance of, 22–23
    training children in, 278
Assessment, 59–72
    of affective states, 60, 65–66
    of alternatives, 71
    of behavioral functioning, 60, 66
    of burnout, 623–624, 632–633
    of chemical dependency, 375–381
    of childhood sexual abuse, 264–265, 275–276
    of cognitive states, 60, 66–67
    of coping mechanisms, 71
    of crisis severity, 60, 61–67

of disaster response, 675
of domestic violence, 309–312, 331
of EMDR clients, 186, 187
of emotional functioning, 70–71
of geriatric violent clients, 564–565
of grief, 423
of homicide potential, 71–72
of hostage crises, 591, 593
of institutional violence, 546
of lethality, 130–131, 220–222, 495, 496
of psychobiology, 69–70
of PTSD, 164–169, 192–193
of school crises, 520–521
of self, 90
of spirituality, 377
of suicide potential, 71–72, 130, 217–222
of support systems, 71
See also Medical assessments; Triage assessment
Assisted suicide, 211
Assumptions, culturally biased, 29–30
At-risk students, 480–481
Attachment theory, 301, 420, 439
Attentiveness, 84
Attitude Towards Women Scale, 309
Attunement, 595
Authority issues, 674
Automatic thoughts, 451
Autonomic hyperarousal, 160
Autonomy, 57, 615
Autopsy, psychological, 237, 241, 570
Aversive imagery technique, 503–505
Avoidant personality disorder, 128
Awareness, 81, 670

B
Balance of power, 328
Bartley, Alise, 667
Barton, Clara, 666
Basic crisis theory, 13–14
BASIC IDS approach, 630, 638
Battered Woman Scale, 309
Battered woman syndrome, 300, 302–303
Battering, 297, 338
    children and, 322–324
    courtship/dating partners and, 325
    crisis worker guidelines on, 314–315, 317–318
    cycle of violence and, 307–308, 334
    gay/lesbian partners and, 326–329
    intervention for rape and, 255–261
    myths about, 306–307
    personality types prone to, 307
    programs for perpetrators of, 300, 329–338
    psychological factors related to, 304–305
    PTSD symptoms and, 310
    safety for victims of, 315–318
    theories on causes of, 300–304
    transcrisis states and, 318

Battering (*continued*)
  women's shelters and, 318–322
  See also Domestic violence; Physical
    abuse
Beck Depression Inventory (BDI), 219
Befrienders International, 136
Behavioral clues, 218
Behavioral couples therapy, 397
Behavioral emergencies, 8
Behavioral functioning
  assessment of, 60, 66
  burnout and, 618–619
  comparing precrisis ratings of, 67
  displaced behaviors and, 191
  skill building and, 270
Behavioral learning model, 352
Behavioral rehearsal, 276
Behavioral severity scale, 66
Behavioral strategies, 437–438
Behavioral telehealth, 135–141
Beliefs, cultural, 38, 44
Benefield family case study, 683–696
Bereavement, 414–464
  adaptive model of, 422, 437–438
  adolescents and, 428–429, 523–525
  assessing grief and, 423
  attachment theory and, 420, 439
  children and, 425–428, 447–449,
    523–525
  cognitive-behavioral approaches to, 438
  complicated/prolonged grief and,
    433–435
  conceptual approaches to, 420–423
  crisis workers and, 461–462
  cultural dynamics of, 417–418
  definition of, 416
  dual process model of, 421–422, 437
  Dutro's model of, 421
  DVD/web resources on, 464
  elderly people and, 429–430, 454–456
  HIV/AIDS clients and, 430–431,
    456–459
  intervention strategies for, 435–461
  job loss and, 431–432
  narrative therapy and, 438–439
  parents and, 425, 442–447
  pet owners and, 433, 453–454
  school crises and, 523–525
  separation/divorce and, 432–433,
    449–453
  sociocultural mores and, 418–419
  spirituality/religion and, 419–420,
    446–447
  spousal death and, 423–424, 439–442
  stage/phase models of, 420–421
  suicide and, 238–240, 508–509
  summary review of, 463–464
  survivor's guilt and, 162
  traumatic grief and, 434–435
  types of, 423–435

  uncomplicated, 416
  See also Grief; Loss; Mourning
Bias, cultural, 29–30
Bibliotherapy, 445, 454
Biochemical malfunction, 213
Biologically derived crises, 17
Biopsychosocial models, 352
Bipolar disorder, 127, 583–584
Blank, Arthur, 150
Blood alcohol content (BAC), 350
Body scan, 187
Bolz, Frank, 604
Bonding, 158
Borderline personality disorder, 108–111,
  128, 331, 586
Boundary issues, 284
Bowlby's attachment theory, 420
Boys
  female sexual abusers of, 273–274
  myths about sexual assault of, 252–253
  See also Children
Brady, Matthew, 6
Branthoover, Holly, 650, 679–681
Bridging exercises, 287
Briefing, 522
Brief therapy, 10, 13
Broaching, 34–35
Bronfenbrenner, Uri, 656, 657, 660
Broset Violence Checklist (BVC), 546
Brown, Greg, 668
Brown, Laura, 28, 33, 42, 297
Bullying, 485–488
  cyberbullying as, 486–487
  interventions for, 487–488
  juvenile offenders and, 490
Burnham, Joy, 487
Burnout, 612–640
  assessment of, 623–624, 632–633
  BASIC IDS approach to, 630, 638
  case study on working with, 630–638
  compassion fatigue and, 461, 619,
    620–621, 623–624
  compassion satisfaction and, 621, 623–624
  cornerstones of, 614–615
  countertransference and, 619–620
  culpability of organizations for, 621–622
  cultural factors related to, 639
  definition of, 613–614
  DVD/web resources on, 640
  dynamics of, 614–619
  ethical issues related to, 631–632
  grief work and, 461–462
  helping professions and, 612–613
  intervention strategies for, 622–629
  levels of, 617
  major sources of, 614
  maladaptive responses to, 628–629
  myths that lead to, 616–617
  organizational interventions for,
    624–629

  prevention strategies for, 625–627, 629,
    638–639
  private practitioners and, 629–630,
    636–637
  research on, 615–616
  school crises and, 528
  secondary traumatic stress disorder and,
    619, 620
  self-recognition of, 622
  social support systems for, 627–628
  stages of, 617, 619
  stress and, 614
  suicide ideation and, 632–633
  summary review of, 640
  support groups for, 628
  symptoms of, 617, 618–619
  training as intervention for, 624
  treatment approach to, 630–638
  vicarious traumatization and, 461, 619,
    620–621
  worker–client relationships and,
    619–621
Burst stress, 43

C
CAGE test, 376
Calhoun, Lawrence, 462, 663
Calming techniques, 688–689
Caplan, Gerald, 3, 13
Caregivers
  importance of self-care for, 461–462
  loss experienced by, 424–425
Care teams, 440
Caring, 83
Carl Perkins Center, 278–287, 625–627
Case examples
  of adult survivors of sexual abuse,
    263–271
  of anger management groups, 332–337
  of burnout interventions, 630–638
  of childhood sexual abuse, 278–281
  of disaster-based crises, 683–696
  of domestic violence, 312–318, 319–322
  of ecosystemic crisis intervention,
    683–696
  of geriatric violent clients, 564–569
  of hostage crises, 598–603
  of institutional violence, 555–569
  of juvenile offenders, 493, 495–498
  of rape and battery intervention,
    255–261
  of substance abuse assessment,
    378–381
  of suicide crisis counseling, 222–231,
    232–234, 239–240, 501–505
  of transcrisis intervention, 525–527
Case handling, 95–116
  confidentiality in, 112–115
  crises in long-term therapy, 105–108
  difficult clients and, 111–112

long-term vs. crisis, 95–98
people with borderline personality
   disorder, 108–111
walk-in crisis facilities and, 96, 98–101
See also Crisis case handling
Catharsis, 81, 628, 637
Cavanaugh, James, 570
Centers for Disease Control (CDC), 499,
   545, 659
Ceremonial events, 454
Change
   crises and seeds of, 10
   motivation to, 372–374, 377
Chaos theory, 15–16, 213, 216
Charlatans, Internet, 137
Chavez, Larry, 555
Chemical dependency, 349–403
   addiction models and, 352–354
   adult children of alcoholics and,
      363–365
   aftercare programs for, 399–402
   alcohol and, 351–352
   assessment of, 375–381
   children in families of, 360–365, 399
   confrontation and, 383, 384, 391–393
   controlled drinking and, 374–375
   crisis points in treatment for, 381–385
   defense mechanisms displayed in,
      356–358
   denial of, 356, 390–391
   detoxification process and, 385
   diagnosis of, 371–372, 378
   DVD/web resources on, 403
   dynamics of, 356–360
   dysfunctional family rules about,
      361–363
   enabling and codependency in,
      358–360, 397
   environmental cues and, 395–396
   family interventions for, 384–385
   family therapy for, 396–399
   goals for treatment of, 385–386
   group therapy for, 388–389
   individual therapy for, 387–388
   intake analysis example, 378–381
   intervention strategies for, 372–385
   irrational mental sets and, 394–395
   juvenile offenders and, 490
   limit testing and, 393
   medications for, 401
   mental illness and, 70, 371–372
   motivation to change, 372–374, 377
   principles of treatment for, 385–402
   protocol for treatment of, 386–387
   relapse prevention and, 399–402
   relationship skills and, 389
   responsibility acceptance and, 389–390
   sociocultural determinants of, 350
   statistics on, 349–350
   summary review of, 402–403

telling "secrets" about treatment for,
   393–394
terminology associated with, 354–356
treatment approaches to, 365–371, 385
triage assessment and, 378
See also Addiction; Alcohol abuse;
   Substance abuse
Chemical dependent, 355
Child Abuse Prevention and Treatment
   Act (1974), 272
Child Behavior Checklist, 193
Child Protective Services, 283
Child PTSD Symptom Scale, 193
Child rapists, 275
Children
   alcoholic families and, 360–365, 399
   assessing PTSD in, 192–193
   bereavement and, 425–428, 447–449,
      523–525
   cognitive-behavioral therapy for, 193
   counseling of, 283–287
   death of, 425, 442–447
   disaster trauma and, 693–694
   domestic violence and, 322–324,
      334–335
   EMDR used with, 194–195
   family therapy and, 399
   grief counseling for, 427–428,
      447–449
   interviewing, 281–282
   juvenile offenders as, 488–499
   natural disasters and, 693–694
   neuropathology in, 155
   parental suicide and, 238
   play therapy for, 193–194, 323–324, 428
   preparing for legal testimony, 282
   sexual abuse of, 261–287
   suicide committed by, 210, 499–509
   support systems for, 188–189
   symptoms of PTSD in, 152–153, 155,
      188–192
   treatments for PTSD in, 193–195
   See also Adolescents
Child sexual abuse, 261–287
   adult survivors of, 261–271
   assessment of, 264–265, 275–276
   boundary issues and, 284
   case examples of, 278–281
   cognitive restructuring and, 268–269
   confronting perpetrators of, 269–270
   counseling process and, 283–287
   criminal justice system and, 282
   date rape and, 254
   disclosure of, 275, 279
   discovery and admission of, 265–266
   dynamics of, 272–274
   educating children about, 278
   extinguishing trauma caused by,
      267–268
   false memories and, 262–263

family issues and, 273–274, 282–283,
   284, 285
female abusers and, 273–274
grief related to, 269, 277
grounding victims of, 266–267
group therapy and, 270–271, 283–284
home interventions and, 286–287
immediate aftermath of, 279–281
intergenerational transmission of, 273
intervention strategies for, 275–287
interview process and, 281–282
juvenile offenders and, 489–490
long-term consequences of, 261–262
myths about, 252–253
phases of, 274–275
prevention of, 278, 284
psychoeducation about, 266
psychological trauma caused by, 249,
   261–262
PTSD and, 262, 264, 266, 272
reporting of, 271–272
revictimization issues and, 262
signs and symptoms of, 272
skill building for survivors of, 270
summary review of, 288
therapy for, 265–271, 276–277
validation of, 267, 277
See also Rape; Sexual assault
Cho, Seung-hui, 115, 216, 479, 493, 512,
   513, 543, 550, 660
Choice, 10, 333, 334
Christian Stephen ministry, 438
Chronic crisis, 70–71, 96, 98–99
Chronological Assessment of Suicide
   Events (CASE), 220
Chronosystem, 660–664
   individuals and, 660–663
   society and, 663–664
Churchill, Winston, 135
CISD. *See* Critical incident stress
   debriefing
CIT program. *See* Crisis Intervention
   Team (CIT) program
Civilian adjustment, 158
Classical conditioning, 478
Claustrophobia, 589
Clery, Jeanne, 544
Clery Act (1990), 476, 544
Clients
   assessment of, 59–72
   commitments from, 58, 93
   connecting with, 52–53
   dealing with the loss of, 241
   difficult, 111–112
   disoriented, 564–569
   gay and lesbian, 326–329, 485
   geriatric violent, 564–569
   HIV/AIDS, 114, 327, 430–431, 456–457
   manipulative, 108, 132
   motivation of, 332, 372–374, 377

Clients (*continued*)
  predispositioning, 52, 138–140
  safety of, 55–56, 90, 123
  seclusion of, 562–563
  sedation of, 563–564
Clinical interview
  domestic violence assessment and,
      310–311, 331–332
  substance abuse assessment and, 377
  suicide risk assessment and, 219–220
Clinician-Administered PTSD Scale
      (CAPS-1), 165
  children's version (CAPS-C), 193
Clinician's Guide to Treating Stress After War
      (Whealin, DeCarvalho, & Vega), 196
Closed-ended questions, 76
Cluster suicides, 505–506, 507
Cobain, Curt, 215
Cochran, Johnnie, 297
Cochran, Sam, 102
Codependency, 355, 358–360, 397
Coercive control, 301
Cognitive-behavioral therapy
  alcohol abuse and, 366, 401
  child sexual abuse and, 276
  domestic violence and, 330
  grief counseling and, 438
  PTSD and, 193, 261
Cognitive development, 491
Cognitive dissonance, 439
Cognitive model, 17–18, 352
Cognitive restructuring, 268–269
Cognitive severity scale, 66–67
Cognitive state assessment, 60, 66–67
Cognitive strategies, 438
Coherent narrative, 439
Collaboration, 226, 665
Collaborative Assessment and Management
      of Suicidality (CAMS), 220
Collaborative counseling, 89
Collaborative owning statements, 77
Collective trauma, 660
Collectivism, 31
College counseling centers, 543–544
Columbine High School shootings, 479,
      493, 660
Combat fatigue, 150
Commitment
  of clients to inpatient facilities, 99
  obtaining from clients, 58, 93, 124–125
Communication
  of acceptance, 87
  of empathy, 83–86
  failures of, 674
  of genuineness, 86–87
  hostage crises and, 592–593
  nonverbal, 85–86
  school crises and, 519–520
  silent, 86
  verbal, 84–85

Community Emergency Response Teams
      (CERTs), 667, 676, 677, 687
Community liaison, 518
Community Mental Health Act (1963), 3,
      96, 101, 115, 649
Community mental health clinics,
      99–101
  anchoring process in, 100
  intake interview in, 100
  mobile crisis teams from, 101
Community outreach programs, 484
Community Reinforcement Approach
      (CRA), 368–369
Community Reinforcement Approach
      and Family Training (CRAFT), 369
Compassionate Friends, 443, 445
Compassion fatigue, 461, 619, 620–621,
      623–624
Compassion Fatigue Self-Test, 623–624
Compassion satisfaction, 621, 623–624
Compassion Satisfaction and Fatigue
      Test, 624
Compensation neurosis, 150
Complex PTSD, 153
Complicated grief, 416, 433–435, 457–461
Comprehensive Soldier Fitness (CSF)
      program, 163–164
Conferences, 6
Confidentiality issues, 112–115
  debriefing process and, 701
  duty to warn principle and, 113–114,
      509–510
  HIV clients and, 114
  Internet counseling and, 137
  principles bearing on confidentiality,
      112–113
  telephone counseling and, 141
Conflict avoidance, 558–559
Conflict Tactics Scale, 331
Confrontation
  in anger management groups, 333
  in chemical dependency counseling,
      383, 384, 391–393
  of difficult clients, 112
  of sexual abuse perpetrators, 269–270
  of violent clients, 558–559
Congruency, 83
Conjugal terrorism, 301
Connecting with clients, 52–53
Constructive thinking patterns, 56
Consultation, 510–511, 603, 665
Contagion suicides, 505–506, 507
Contextual-ecological model, 18–19
Contingency management (CM), 368
Continuous Data Questionnaire
      (CDQ), 378
Contracts
  daily sobriety trust, 397
  hostage negotiation, 593
  no-harm/stay-alive, 229–230

Control issues
  anger management and, 335
  caregivers and, 462
  hostage negotiation and, 593
  planning process and, 56–57
  psychoeducation and, 57–58
  sexually abused children and, 277–278
  telephone counseling and, 120
Controlled drinking, 374–375
Coordination plans, 674
Coping mechanisms, 56, 70, 71, 92
Coping with Crisis: Lessons Learned
      (Poland), 528
Copycat gangs, 479
Copycat suicides, 500, 507
Core listening skills, 53
Council on Accreditation of Counseling
      and Educationally Related Programs
      (CACREP), 527, 652
Counseling
  chemical dependency, 381–385
  childhood sexual abuse, 283–287
  collaborative, 89
  confidentiality issues in, 112–115
  difficult clients, 111–112
  directive, 88–89
  gang members, 481
  grief, 435–461
  Internet, 119, 135–141
  multicultural, 38–46
  nondirective, 89
  peer, 483
  suicide, 222–240, 501–505
  telephone, 119–135
  university, 543–544
  women at shelters, 319–322
  worker burnout, 630–638
  See also Therapy
Counselor Burnout Inventory (CBI), 623
Counselors. *See* Crisis workers
Countertransference, 461, 619–620
Courtois, Christine, 6
Courtship violence, 325
Covert callers, 131
Covert modeling, 133–134
Crawford, Robert, 511
Creativity, 22
Crime Awareness and Campus Security
      Act (1990), 544
Criminal behavior, 490–491
Criminal justice system
  child sexual abuse and, 282
  domestic violence and, 329
  See also Legal issues
Crisis
  characteristics of, 10–11
  chemical dependency, 383–385
  choice and, 10
  chronic, 70–71, 96, 98–99
  chronosystem of, 660–664

creating in clients, 383–385
danger/opportunity inherent in, 10
definitions of, 7–9, 23
developmental, 16
disaster-based, 649–703
ecosystemic, 17, 654–655
existential, 17
hostage, 579–609
idiosyncrasy of, 10
quick fixes and, 10
school, 474–529
seeds of growth/change in, 10
severity of, 60, 61–67, 69
situational, 16–17
social/environmental, 99
symptomology of, 11
theories of, 13–17
transcrisis states and, 11–13
universality of, 10
Crisis and Disaster Counseling (Dass-
    Brailsford), 678
Crisis case handling, 95–116
    assessment in, 98
    client functioning in, 97
    compared to long-term case handling,
        95–98
    confidentiality issues in, 112–115
    difficult clients and, 111–112
    Internet and, 119
    long-term therapy and, 105–111
    objectives of, 97
    principles of, 96
    summary review of, 115–116
    telephone crisis lines and, 119–135
    walk-in crisis facilities and, 96, 98–101
Crisis counseling assistance and training
    program (CCA-TP), 677
Crisis incident stress management (CISM)
    team, 607, 608
Crisis interveners, 518–519
Crisis intervention
    acting mode in, 87–93
    ACT model of, 20
    assessment process in, 59–72
    basic strategies of, 81–83
    burnout and, 622–629, 630–638
    child sexual abuse and, 275–287
    climate of human growth in, 83–87
    cognitive model of, 17–18
    consistency of, 511
    contextual-ecological model of, 18–19
    dealing with failure of, 241
    debriefing process and, 696–702
    developmental-ecological model of, 18
    disaster response and, 649–703
    domestic violence and, 309–318
    eclectic theory and, 20–21
    ecosystemic, 654–678
    emerging trends in, 654–655
    equilibrium model of, 17

gangs and, 480–485
gay and lesbian violence, 327–329
grassroots movements in, 4–5
grief and, 435–461
historical overview of, 3–7
hostage crises and, 591–604, 605–608
hybrid model of, 51–59
institutionalism of, 5–6
Internet-based, 119, 135–141
listening skills in, 75–81
models of, 17–20
multiculturalism in, 28–46
networking in, 93
police and, 101–105
psychological first aid in, 19–20
psychosocial transition model of, 18
PTSD victims and, 169–170
referral resources in, 92
rewards inherent in, 23
school crises and, 522
sexual assault and, 255–261
societal impetus for, 6–7
substance abuse and, 372–385
suicide and, 222–240, 499–509
telephone counseling as, 119–135
volunteerism and, 5, 673
Crisis intervention coordinator, 517
Crisis Intervention in Action DVD, 46
Crisis Intervention Team (CIT) program,
    6, 102–105
    concept of, 102–103
    success of, 105
    training component of, 103–105
Crisis management, 225–228
Crisis plans, 515–523
    implementing, 519–523
    logistics and, 519–520
    physical requirements and, 519
    planning committee and, 516–517
    response steps and, 520–523
    school crisis response team and, 517–519
Crisis response coordinator, 517
Crisis response planning committee,
    516–517
Crisis response teams (CRTs), 506–507,
    517–519, 666
Crisis stage, hostage crisis, 589
Crisis theories, 13–17
    adaptational, 15
    applied, 16–17
    basic, 13–14
    chaos, 15–16
    developmental, 16
    eclectic, 20–21
    ecosystems, 14–15
    expanded, 14–16
    interpersonal, 15
    psychoanalytic, 14
    summary of, 24
    systems, 14

Crisis therapy, 19
Crisis workers
    action strategies for, 89–93
    alliance building by, 255
    assault statistics for, 541
    assertiveness of, 22–23
    battered women guidelines for, 314–315,
        317–318
    burnout in, 461, 612–640
    compassion fatigue in, 461
    creativity of, 22
    debriefing of, 241, 570, 699–702
    effective, 21–23
    empathic listening by, 436
    energy and resiliency of, 22
    failure of crisis intervention by, 241
    flexibility of, 22
    grief in, 461–462
    HIV/AIDS clients and, 430–431
    hostage crises and, 603
    life experiences of, 21–22
    long-term therapists compared to,
        95–96
    mental reflexes of, 22
    multicultural competency of, 29, 39–40
    personal experiences of, 679–683
    poise of, 22
    post-disaster duties of, 678–679
    security/safety strategies for, 549–552
    self-defense procedures for, 561–562
    substance abuse assessment by, 375–378
    suicide intervention guidelines for,
        235–236
    training of, 552–555
    vicarious traumatization of, 461
    victims of violence as, 541, 569–571
    volunteers as, 5, 673
Critical incident stress debriefing
    (CISD), 19
    criticisms of, 696–697
    cultural factors and, 36
    emergency workers and, 697–699
    hostage crises and, 607
    institutional violence and, 570
    mental health issues and, 675
    school crises and, 521
    See also Debriefing process
Cross-cultural counseling, 39–40. *See also*
    Multiculturalism
Cubic model, 212
Cues
    environmental, 395–396
    motoric, 548
Cultural adaptation, 45
*Cultural Competence in Trauma Therapy:
    Beyond the Flashback* (Brown), 28
Cultural factors
    bereavement and, 417–418
    biased assumptions and, 29–30
    burnout dynamics and, 639

Cultural factors (*continued*)
domestic violence and, 300–301
ecological dynamics and, 35–36
effective helping and, 38–46
emic vs. etic models and, 32–35
geographic locale and, 43–44
high- vs. low-context cultures and, 31–32
hostage negotiations and, 592–593
individualism vs. collectivism and, 30–31
language barriers and, 40
occupations and, 42–43
outreach services and, 40
PTSD and, 35–36, 655
rape dynamics and, 250
religion/spirituality and, 40–42
self-awareness of values and, 29
substance abuse and, 350
support systems and, 42
training related to, 45
See also Multiculturalism
Culture, definition of, 28
Cyberbullying, 486–487
Cybercounseling. *See* Online counseling
Cyberstalking, 326, 486
Cyberthreats, 486

D
Daily sobriety trust contract, 397
Dass-Brailsford, Priscilla, 678
Date rape, 253–255
alcohol use and, 254
prevention of, 254–255
risk of, 254
Date violence, 325
Davis, Scott, 482–483, 497–498
Death
of children, 425, 442–447
cultural responses to, 417–418
disasters and, 689–690
elderly people and, 454–456
euthanasia and, 211
imprint of, 161
of parents, 457–461
of pets, 433, 453–454
philosophical views of, 210
religion/spirituality and, 419–420
sociocultural mores and, 418–419
of spouses, 423–424, 439–442
sudden, 439
suicidal, 210–211
traumatic, 415, 434–435, 442–447
See also Bereavement; Grief
Debriefing groups, 178
Debriefing process, 696–702
confidentiality and, 701
controversy about, 696–697
crisis workers and, 699–702
dynamics of, 701
effectiveness of, 701–702

emergency workers and, 697–699
formal vs. informal, 698–699
hostage crises and, 607–608
institutional violence and, 570
loss of clients and, 241
need for, 699–700
precautions about, 700–701
school crises and, 522
war veterans and, 158
De-escalation techniques, 104
Defense mechanisms
of chemical dependents, 356–358
of enablers/codependents, 359–360
Deficiency model, 211
Deflection, 559–561
Defusing techniques, 104
Deinstitutionalization, 542
Delayed PTSD, 150
Delusions, 129
Demobilizing, 522–523
Denial
of addiction, 356, 390–391
of alcohol abuse, 356, 390–391
of institutional violence, 544–545
in PTSD, 159–160, 169, 173–175
Denigration, 486
Dependence, 355. *See also* Chemical dependency
Dependency issues, 121
Dependent personality disorder, 127
Depression
alcoholism and, 357–358
anger related to, 637
assessment of, 65
battered women and, 314, 321
hostage takers and, 583–584
juvenile offenders and, 491
suicide and, 211
Desensitization, 162, 186–187, 193, 525
DESNOS classification, 153
Detoxification, 385
Developmental crises, 16
Developmental-ecological model, 18
Developmental issues
bereaved children and, 426–428
childhood trauma and, 190
sexual abuse and, 278
suicide and, 211
Developmental theory, 16
Developmental Trauma Disorder (DTD), 272–273
Deviance, 492
Diagnosis
of chemical dependency, 371–372, 378
of PTSD, 152–153
Diagnostic and Statistical Manual of Mental Disorders (DSM), 11, 29, 150, 152, 434, 522
Diagnostic Interview for Children and Adolescents (DICA-R), 193

Dialectical behavior therapy (DBT), 224
Differential vulnerability, 41
Difficult clients, 111–112
Digital natives, 135
Directive counseling, 88–89
Disaster-based crises, 649–703
case study on, 683–696
crisis worker duties in, 678–679
debriefing process after, 696–702
DVD/web resources on, 703
ecosystemic model and, 655–665
failures of response to, 674–676
human-made or terrorist, 652–654
local emergency management systems for, 668–674
mental health provision for, 649–652
national response teams for, 665–668
natural disasters and, 17, 160, 674–676
new trends in responding to, 654–655
personal accounts of workers in, 679–683
psychological first aid in, 676–677
recommended interventions for, 678
summary review of, 702–703
training counselors for, 677
Disaster mental health, 649–652
brief history of, 649–652
global attitude changes about, 652
Hurricane Katrina lessons about, 674–676
local EMA components for, 673–674
Disaster planning, 670–673
mental health services and, 673–674
role of LEMA directors in, 668–669, 670
Disaster Relief Act (1974), 649, 650
Disaster Response Handbook (Raphael), 652
Disclosure of child sexual abuse, 275, 279
Disconnected Counselors (DCs), 623
Disease model of addition, 353
Disenfranchised grief, 416, 459
Disequilibrium, 10, 50, 149
Disillusionment, 662, 664
Disinhibition effect, 136
Disoriented clients
mild disorientation in, 564–567
severe disorientation in, 568–569
validation therapy for, 568–569
Disowned statements, 77–78
Displacement, 191, 356–357, 359
Disposition, 100
Dissociation, 153, 160, 359
Distance, professional, 129–130
Distancing, 83–84
Disturbed crisis-line callers, 128–131
Divorce
bereavement and, 432–433
grief counseling and, 449–453
referral resources and, 450

Domestic violence, 297–339
  advocacy and, 318
  anger management and, 330–338
  assessment of, 309–312, 331
  case example of, 312–318, 319–322
  children and, 322–324, 334–335
  cognitive-behavioral treatment for, 330
  components of intervention for, 312–318
  courtship behavior and, 325
  criminal justice system and, 329
  crisis worker guidelines for, 314–315,
    317–318
  cultural factors in, 300–301
  cycle of, 307–308, 334
  depression and, 314, 321
  dynamics of, 300–309
  emerging approaches to, 299–300
  ensuring safety in cases of, 315–318
  facilitating movement in victims of,
    313–315
  families of origin and, 334–335
  feminist-based treatment for, 329–330
  financial consequences of, 334
  gay/lesbian partners and, 326–329
  grief process and, 320–321
  incidence of, 298–299
  institutional violence and, 547–548
  intake interview for treating, 331–332
  intervention strategies for, 309–318
  lethality assessment, 318, 323
  myths about, 306–307
  overview of, 297–298
  personality types prone to, 307
  psychological factors in, 304–305
  realities for women of, 308–309
  shelters and, 318–322
  social factors in, 300–301
  stress and, 305–306, 333–334
  substance abuse and, 305, 331, 336
  summary review of, 338–339
  telephone hotlines for, 135, 311–318,
    338–339
  terror in victims of, 321
  theories on causes of, 300–304
  transcrisis perspective on, 318
  treatment programs for, 300, 329–338
  See also Battering; Physical abuse
Drugs
  business of, 349
  date rape and, 254
  definition of, 355
  domestic violence and, 305, 336
  institutional violence and, 547
  mental health and, 69–70
  statistics on use of, 349–350
  See also Medications; Substance abuse
Dual diagnosis, 371–372
Dual process model, 421–422, 437
Duluth model, 299, 329, 337
Durkheim, Emile, 212

Dutro's model of grief, 421
Duty to warn principle, 113–114, 509–510,
  513–514
DVD/web resources, 46
DWI schools, 367
Dying with dignity, 213
Dynamic Appraisal of Situational
  Aggression (DYAS), 546
Dysfunctional families, 305, 361–363
Dysphoric/borderline batterer, 307

E
*Early Warning, Timely Response: A Guide
  to Safe Schools* (Dwyer, Osher, &
  Warger), 489
Eclectic crisis intervention theory, 20–21
Ecological factors, 35–36
Ecological/integrative theory, 213
Economic crises, 17
Economic stress, 305
Ecosystemic crises, 17, 654–655
Ecosystemic crisis intervention, 654–678
  case example of, 683–696
  chronosystem and, 660–664
  defining principles of, 664–665
  diagram illustrating, 657
  exosystem and, 659
  failures of response in, 674–676
  historical examples of, 654–655
  large system view of, 655
  macrosystem and, 659–660
  mesosystem and, 656–659
  microsystem and, 656
  system overview, 655–664
Ecosystems theory, 14–15
Education
  childhood sexual abuse and, 266, 278
  crisis counseling and, 677–678
  domestic violence and, 305
  emergency management training and, 669
  institutional violence and, 556–558
  suicide prevention through, 236–237
  See also School crises; Training
    programs
Egoistic suicide, 212, 216
Elderly people
  bereavement and, 429–430, 454–456
  grief counseling for, 454–456
  homicidal clients as, 231, 234–235
  pattern of neglect toward, 44
  reminiscence therapy for, 565–566
  suicide intervention for, 231–235
  violent clients as, 543, 564–569
  See also Geriatric violent clients
Ellis, Albert, 334, 616
Embedded therapy, 43
EMDR. *See* Eye movement desensitization
  and reprocessing
Emergency management agencies
  (EMAs), 658

Emergency management education/
  training, 669
Emergency operations center (EOC),
  670, 685
Emergency/outcry phase of PTSD, 169,
  172–173
Emergency telephone crisis hotlines, 134–135
Emergency worker debriefing, 697–699
Emic model, 32–35
Emoticons, 138
Emotional enmeshment, 162–163
Emotional replenishment, 461–462
Emotional status assessment, 70–71
Emotional strength, 71
Emotional support/challenges, 628
Emotions
  assessment of, 60, 65–66
  coping stamina and, 70
  deflection of, 559–561
  juvenile offenders and, 491
  online expression of, 138
  relearning of, 269
  slowing down of, 128–129
  suicide and, 237–238
  See also Feelings
Empathic presence, 436
Empathy, 83–86
  attentiveness and, 84
  distancing error, 83
  grief work and, 436
  nonverbal communication of, 85–86
  reflection of feelings and, 85
  silence and, 86
  sympathy vs., 83
  verbal communication of, 84–85
Empirically derived scales, 168
Employee assistance programs (EAPs),
  228, 606–607
Empty chair technique, 177–178, 459
Enabling, 356, 358–360, 397
Encyclopedia of Psychological Trauma
  (Reyes, Elhai, & Ford), 5–6
Enthusiasm, 617
Enticement, 274
Entrainment, 688
Entrapment, 274, 303
Environmental cues, 395–396
Epitaph exercise, 524–525
Epstein, Jo, 682
Equilibrium, 50
Equilibrium model, 17
Ergonomics, 651
Escape to therapy, 359
Escapist suicide, 211
Estranged hostage taker, 586–587
Estranged violent juvenile offenders
  (EVJOs), 488–499
  acting in response to, 498–499
  case examples of, 493, 495–498
  interviewing potential EVJOs, 495–498

Estranged violent juvenile
   offenders (*continued*)
  screening methods for identifying,
     493–494
  traits, characteristics, behaviors of,
     489–493
Estrangement, 162
Etched memories, 189–190
E-therapy. *See* Online counseling
Ethical issues
  burnout and, 631–632
  confidentiality and, 112–113, 509–510
  duty to warn and, 113–114, 509–510
  Internet counseling and, 137, 141
  school violence and, 509–515
  telephone counseling and, 141
Etic model, 30
Euphoria, 401–402
European Network for Traumatic Stress
   (TENTS), 652
Euthanasia, 211
Evacuation orders, 670
EVJOs. *See* Estranged violent juvenile
   offenders
Exchange theory, 301–302
Existential-constructivist model, 212–213
Existential crises, 17
Exosystem, 659
Expanded crisis theory, 14–16
Expansion, 82
Expectations, realistic, 129
Experimentation, 15–16
Exposure treatment, 175, 261, 268–269
Expressive behavior, 101, 209, 580–581
Externalizing problems, 444
External locus of control, 491
Extinguishing trauma, 267–268
Extreme right-winger gangs, 479–480
Eye movement desensitization and
   reprocessing (EMDR), 184–188
  controversy over, 184–185
  development of, 185
  PTSD and, 184–188, 261
  traumatized children and, 194–195
  treatment components in, 185–188

F
Face validity, 551
Facilitative assessment, 71
Facilitative listening, 79–81, 312
Facilitative responding, 79–80, 312
Facilitator role, 441
Faith, 446–447
False memories, 262–263
Families
  alcoholic, 360–365
  chemical dependency treatment and,
     384–385, 396–399
  child sexual abuse and, 273–274,
     282–283, 284, 285
  cycle of violence in, 307–308, 547–548

dysfunctional, 305, 361–363
effect of child's death on, 442
PTSD treatment for, 184
responses to PTSD in, 160–161
shelters for, 318–322
suicide guidelines for, 236–237
support systems in, 188–189
Family Educational Rights and Privacy Act
   (1974), 115, 511, 512
Family mascot role, 361, 364
Family-only batterer, 307
Family therapy
  children and, 399, 448
  grief counseling and, 448
  PTSD and, 184
  session example, 398–399
  substance abuse treatment and, 396–399
Family Trouble Center (FTC) program,
   332, 334
Family violence. *See* Domestic violence
Fantasy, 357
Fatalistic suicide, 212
Fear
  in adult children of alcoholics, 363–364
  in battered women, 321
  in hostage crisis captors, 589
  in students at school, 477
  See also Anxiety
Federal Emergency Management Agency
   (FEMA), 3, 651, 654, 658, 667, 673,
   677, 702
Feedback
  motivational interviewing and, 373
  online counseling and, 136
Feelings
  anger management and, 335
  deflection of, 559–561
  owning of, 77–79
  reflection of, 85
  relearning, 269
  See also Emotions
Feil, Naomi, 568, 569
Female sexual abusers, 273–274
Feminist theory, 302
Figley, Charles, 165, 415
Final common pathway, 353
Finkbeiner, Ann, 425, 445
Finkelhor, David, 272
Fishbowl discussions, 104–105
Flaming, 486
Flexibility, 22
Flooding, 175, 193
Fluoxetene or Prozac, 172
Focused view of multicultural
   counseling, 30
Focusing strategy, 82
Follow-up process, 58
Foreshortened future, 190–191
Forgiveness, 460
Formal debriefing, 698–699

Freeman, Nancy, 668–669, 672
Freud, Sigmund, 150, 211
Freudenberger, Herbert, 613
Freyd, Pamela and Peter, 262
Frustration, 490, 617
Functioning. *See* Behavioral functioning
Future conditional strategy, 596

G
Gang rape, 251
Gangs, 479–485
  community and, 484–485
  institutional violence and, 543
  intervention approaches to, 480–485
  SARA model for dealing with, 485
  school system problems and, 484
  suburban and rural emergence of, 480
  types of, 479–480
Gateway model of addiction, 353
Gay and lesbian clients
  crisis intervention with, 327–329
  partner violence among, 326–329
  school bullying of, 485
  treatment issues for, 328–329
Gender inequality, 250
General adaptation syndrome, 614
Genetic predisposition model, 353
Gentle conversation, 436
Genuineness, 83, 86–87
Geographic factors
  cultural issues and, 43–44
  domestic violence and, 305
  poverty issues and, 675
Geriatric violent clients, 564–569
  anchoring of, 566–567
  assessment of, 564–565
  case examples of, 564–569
  eliciting trust from, 565
  illusions/hallucinations of, 567–568
  mild disorientation in, 564–567
  pacing behavior of, 565
  reality orientation of, 565
  reminiscence therapy and, 565–566
  remotivation of, 568
  security blankets for, 567–568
  severe disorientation in, 568–569
  sundown syndrome and, 567
  validation therapy with, 568–569
  See also Elderly people
Gestalt techniques, 177–178, 459
Gheytanchi, Anahita, 674
Gilliland, Burl, 702
Glasser, William, 629
Global positioning system (GPS), 659
Goals
  of chemical dependency treatment,
     385–386
  of domestic violence treatment,
     330–331
Grassroots movements, 4–5

Grief
adaptive model of, 422, 437–438
adolescents and, 428–429, 523–525
assessment tools for, 423
attachment theory and, 420, 439
battered women and, 320–321
being there for, 436–437
children and, 425–428, 447–449, 523–525
cognitive-behavioral approaches to, 438
complicated, 416, 433–435, 457–461
crisis workers and, 461–462
definition of, 416
disaster survivors and, 690
disenfranchised, 416, 459
dual process model of, 421–422, 437
Dutro's model of, 421
elderly people and, 429–430, 454–456
employees and, 432
institutionalization of, 419
intervention strategies for, 435–461
job loss and, 431–432
narrative therapy for, 438–439
parents and, 425, 442–447
pet owners and, 433, 453–454
prolonged, 416, 433–435
resolution of, 269
Schneider's model of, 421
school crises and, 523–525
separation/divorce and, 432–433, 449–453
sexual abuse and, 269, 277
spousal death and, 423–424, 439–442
stage/phase models of, 420–421
suicide and, 238–240, 508–509
traumatic, 416, 434–435, 693–694
See also Bereavement; Mourning
Grief Experience Inventory (GEI), 423
Grossman, David, 478
Grounding process, 266–267, 688–689
Group therapy
adolescent bereavement and, 524–525
chemical dependency and, 388–389
childhood sexual abuse and, 270–271, 283–284
children of domestic violence and, 324
elderly people and, 454
family treatment and, 184
HIV/AIDS clients and, 457
life adjustment group and, 183–184
nonoffending parents and, 284
parental grief and, 442–443
pet owner's grief and, 453–454
PTSD and, 178–184
same-sex couples and, 328
school crises and, 524–525
separation/divorce and, 450
spousal grief and, 440–441
suicide survivors and, 238–239
See also Support groups

Growth
climate of, 83–87
model of loss and, 421
posttraumatic, 195
Guidance
provided by crisis workers, 82
school-based programs of, 483
Guided imagery, 525, 527
Guilt
ACOAs and, 364
animated, 177
burnout and, 634–635
survivor's, 158, 161–162
Gulf War veterans, 152

H
Habituation, 356
Hallucinations, 129, 567
Hara-kiri, 212
Harassment, 486
Harris, Eric, 479, 493
Hazard prevention/control, 550–552
HCR-20 assessment instrument, 546
Health Insurance Portability and Accountability Act (HIPAA), 115, 137, 512
Helplessness, 302–303
Heroic/rescue stage, 661–662
Hero role, 360–361, 364
High-context cultures, 31–32
Histrionic personality disorder, 127
HIV clients
bereavement process and, 430–431, 456–457
confidentiality issues and, 114
crisis issues for, 456–457
partner abuse and, 327
See also AIDS
Hogan Grief Reaction Checklist (HGRC), 423
Homegrown gangs, 479
Home interventions, 286–287
Homeland Security Act, 652
Homicide
assessing potential for, 71–72, 130
confidentiality issues related to, 113
elderly people and, 231, 234–235
expressive acts of, 209
failure of crisis intervention for, 241
notes left about, 215–216
school violence and, 476, 479
suicide and, 215–216
See also Violence
Homosexual clients. *See* Gay and lesbian clients
Honeymoon stage, 662, 663
Hope Kit, 234
Hopelessness, 211–212
Hopelessness Scale, 219
Hostage Barricade Data System (HOBAS), 580

Hostage crises, 579–609
accommodation stage in, 589–590
alarm stage in, 588–589
assessment of, 591, 593
case example of, 598–603
communication techniques for, 592–593
containing the scene of, 593–594
crisis stage in, 589
debriefing process after, 607–608
DVD/web resources on, 609
dynamics of, 580–591
employee assistance programs and, 606–607
gathering information during, 594
intervention strategies for, 591–604
interviewing hostages after, 606
mental health professionals and, 603
negotiating in, 591–604
overview of, 579–580
perpetrator characteristics in, 581–588
persuasion strategies in, 596–598
post-release interventions after, 605–608
resolution stage in, 590–591, 593
self-protection rules in, 604–605
stabilizing the situation, 594–596
stages of, 588–591
Stockholm syndrome and, 590, 605
stress disorders from, 606
summary review of, 609
survivor interventions and, 606–608
Hostage takers
estranged, 586–587
institutionalized, 587
mentally disturbed, 581–586
negotiating with, 591–604
persuading to give up, 596–598
substance abuse by, 588
suicide committed by, 580, 583, 591
types of, 581–588
wronged or aggrieved, 587–588
Hotlines. *See* Telephone counseling
Howard, Stephen, 650
Hughes, Francine, 300
Human–Animal Bond and Grief, The (Lagoni, Butler, & Hetts), 454
Human-made disasters, 17, 652–654
Human services
violence dynamics in, 546–549
worker burnout in, 461, 612–640
Humor, 634
Hurricane Katrina, 674–678
failure of response to, 674–676
mental health support following, 651
personal accounts of, 679–683
Hybrid model of crisis intervention, 51–59
assessment and, 59
clarifying intentions in, 53
connecting with clients in, 52–53
examining alternatives in, 56
follow-up process in, 58

Hybrid model of crisis
    intervention (*continued*)
  illustration of, 59
  obtaining commitment in, 58
  planning to reestablish control in, 56–57
  predispositioning clients in, 52
  problem exploration in, 53–54
  providing support in, 54–56
  psychoeducation used in, 57–58
  safety as default task in, 55–56
  summary of, 59, 72
Hypersensitivity, 491
Hypervigilance, 157, 160
Hypochondriasis, 360
Hysterical neurosis, 150

I
Identity issues, 593
I Hate You—Don't Leave Me (Kreisman &
    Straus), 108
Illness, terminal. *See* Terminal illness
Illusions, 567
Imagery
  aversive, 503–505
  guided, 525, 527
  intrusive, 159, 169, 173
Immigration issues, 40
Immobility, 50
Impact assessment, 520
Impact of Events Scale (IES), 168, 627
Impact stage
  of disasters, 660–661
  of rape, 255–257
Implementing crisis plans, 519–523
Impulsivity
  juvenile offenders and, 491
  suicide ideation and, 503
Inadequate/dependent personality, 584–585
Incest. *See* Child sexual abuse
Inconsequentiality, 615
Indirect behavioral emergencies, 8
Indirect suicide, 214
Individual crisis, 7–8, 23
Individual differences, 89–90
Individualism, 30–31
Individualist/collectivist continuum,
    30–31
Individual therapy
  for chemical dependency, 387–388
  for grief, 440, 448, 450, 453, 454, 524
  for PTSD, 172–178
  for worker burnout, 630–638
Individual trauma, 660
Informal defusing, 698
Informational support, 55
Inpatient treatment, 367
Installation phase of EMDR, 187
Institutionalism, 5–6
Institutional violence, 541–571
  admission time and, 548

appeasement and, 559
assessment of, 546
bases for, 546–549
case examples related to, 555–569
college counseling centers and, 543–544
conflict avoidance and, 558–559
deflection and, 559–561
denial of, 544–545
DVD/web resources on, 571
dynamics of, 546–549
education of clients and, 556–558
family history and, 547–548
follow-up with staff victims of, 569–571
geriatric clients and, 564–569
hazard prevention/control, 550–552
hostage takers and, 587
institutional culpability in, 543–545
interactive participants and, 548
intervention strategies for, 549–564
legal liability and, 545
motoric cues to, 548
multiple indicators of, 548–549
physical environment and, 550–552
precautionary guidelines on, 553–555
precipitating factors in, 542–543
predisposing history and, 547
program evaluation and, 555
psychological disturbance and, 547
reporting incidents of, 555
restraints and, 563
seclusion and, 562–563
security planning and, 549
sedation and, 563–564
show of force and, 561–562
social stressors and, 547
staff culpability in, 545
stages of intervention for, 555–564
substance abuse and, 542
summary review of, 571
time-outs and, 561
training workers about, 552–555
work history related to, 548
worksite analysis for, 549–550
Instrumental behavior, 101, 209, 580, 581
Instrumental grieving, 422
Insurance issues, 137
Intake interview, 100, 331–332, 377
Integration, 169, 177–178
Integrity, 79
Intellectualization, 357, 359
Intensive long-term outpatient treatment
    (ILTOT), 367
Intent to harm and duty to warn principle,
    113–114, 509–510
Interactional theory of suicide, 213, 216
Inter-Agency Standing Committee
    (IASC), 652
Interdisciplinary systems, 664
International Society for Mental Health
    Online (ISMHO), 119

International Society for Traumatic Stress
    Studies, 172, 193
International terrorism, 652–654
Internet
  access code to resources on, 46
  crisis services on, 119, 135–141
  gang-related sites on, 480
  legal/ethical issues, 141
  netiquette rules, 137–138
  stalking behavior on, 326
  See also Online counseling
Interpersonal Needs Questionnaire, 219,
    223, 228
Interpersonal theory, 15, 212
Interpretation, 174–175
Intervention. *See* Crisis intervention
Interviews
  battered woman, 310–311
  children with PTSD, 192
  clinical, 219–220, 310–311
  domestic violence, 331–332
  intake, 100, 331–332, 377
  juvenile offender, 495–498
  motivational, 373–374
  post-hostage crisis, 606
  sexually abused children, 281–282
  structured, 165
Intimate partner violence (IPV), 297.
    See also Domestic violence
Intimate terrorism, 301
Intimidating behaviors, 485
Intraindividual theory, 302
Intrusive thoughts/images, 159, 169, 173
Intuitive grieving, 422
Inventory of Complicated Grief
    (ICG), 423
Inventory/recovery phase, 662
Inward aggression, 211
Iraq war veterans, 163–164
Irrational mental sets, 394–395
Isolation
  burnout and, 615
  domestic violence and, 305
  suicide and, 233
Israel, terrorism in, 653

J
James, Richard, 32, 681–683
Jealousy, 327, 336
Job loss, 431–432
Johnson, Vernon, 384
Joiners, 360
Journaling, 176–177
Journal of College Counseling, 544
Juvenile offenders, 488–499
  acting in response to, 498–499
  case examples of, 493, 495–498
  interviewing, 495–498
  screening, 493–494
  trait comparison of, 489–493

K

Karpman Drama Triangle, 397
Kids on the Block system, 278
Kinkel, Kip, 511
Klebold, Dylan, 479, 493
Koch, Andy, 493
Korean War veterans, 150
Koresh, David, 592
Kübler-Ross, Elisabeth, 420
Kushner, Harold, 445

L

Lane, Jerry, 658, 668, 669, 672
Langman, Peter, 488
Language
  barriers related to, 40
  Internet rules of, 137–138
Large-scale crises, 655
Larson, Gary, 654
Laws. *See* Legal issues
Lazarus, Arnold, 630
Leakage, 493–494
Learned helplessness, 302–303
Learning theory, 302
"Least restrictive environment"
    movement, 542
Legal issues
  bereavement process and, 419
  childhood sexual abuse and, 282
  confidentiality and, 112
  domestic violence and, 298, 329
  duty to warn and, 113–114, 509–510,
    513–514
  institutional violence and, 545
  Internet counseling and, 137, 141
  mental illness and, 513–514
  privacy rights and, 512
  school violence and, 509–515
  telephone counseling and, 141
Legitimization of violence, 250
Leisure, 636
Lesbian clients. *See* Gay and lesbian
    clients
Lethality
  assessing, 130–131, 220–222, 495, 496
  burnout and, 632–633
  domestic violence and, 318, 323, 331
  gay/lesbian partner violence and, 328
  HIV-infected clients and, 456
  intervention failure and, 241
  overview of, 209
  school, 474–529
  See also Homicide; Suicide; Violence
LGBT students, 485
Licensing issues, 137
Life adjustment group, 183–184
Life experiences, 21–22
Lifestyle model of addiction, 353
Lifton, Robert, 178, 650, 699
Likert scales, 193

Limits
  setting, 79
  testing, 393
LINC network, 121
Lindemann, Eric, 3, 13
Lisek, David, 249
Listening
  crisis intervention process and, 75–81
  domestic violence interventions and, 312
  hostage crises and, 592, 597
  social support systems and, 627
Listening skills, 53, 75–81
  closed-ended questions, 76
  empathic listening, 436
  facilitative listening, 79–81
  open-ended questions, 75
  owning feelings, 77–79
  restatement, 76
  summary clarification, 76–77
Local consultation dilemma, 44–45
Local crisis hotlines, 135
Local emergency management agencies
    (LEMAs), 657, 668–674
  disaster planning by, 670–673
  mental health components of, 673–674
  role of directors in, 668–669, 670
Locus of control, 491
Logistical support, 54
Loneliness, 430
Long-term case handling
  assessment in, 98
  borderline personality disorder and,
    108–111
  client functioning in, 97
  crisis case handling vs., 95–98
  dealing with crisis states in, 105–108
  objectives of, 97
  principles of, 96
  See also Crisis case handling
Long-term disposition, 100
Lorenz, Edward, 15
Los Angeles Symptom Checklist (LASC), 627
Loss
  ambiguous, 417
  dealing with, 439–461
  definition of, 66, 417
  due to caregiving, 424–425
  human experience of, 415
  personal stories about, 414–415, 462–463
  primary vs. secondary, 417
  Schneider's model of, 421
  stigmatized, 456
  terms related to, 416–417
  types of, 423–435
  See also Bereavement
Loss and grief map, 453
Loss orientation, 421–422
Lost child role, 361, 364
Low-context cultures, 31–32
Ludic suicides, 214

M

MacAndrew Alcoholism Scale, 375
Macrosystem, 659–660
Male dominance/supremacy, 250, 300
Manic depressives, 127
Manipulative clients, 108, 132
Marriage
  domestic violence and, 297–339
  effect of child's death on, 442
  separation/divorce and, 432–433,
    449–453
  spousal death and, 423–424, 439–442
Maslach Burnout Inventory (MBI), 623, 627
Masochism, 303
Masquerading, 486
Massachusetts Coalition of Battered
    Women, 299, 314
*Mass Trauma and Emotional Healing
    Around the World* (Kalayjian &
    Dominique), 46
Meaning
  importance of, 664
  making of, 438
Media
  contagion suicides and, 506
  crisis awareness and, 6
  domestic violence and, 300
  hostage crises and, 609
  information liaison to, 673
  school crisis liaison to, 517–518
  suburban/rural gangs and, 480
  terrorism covered in, 653
  violence in, 478
Medical assessments
  of child sexual abuse, 281–282
  of domestic abuse, 298–299, 311
Medical liaison, 518
Medications
  alcohol abuse, 401
  determining usage of, 129
  mental disorders and, 69–70
  psychotropic, 69, 172
  PTSD, 69, 172
  See also Drugs
Meditation training, 172–173
Megacrises, 655
Megagangs, 480
Memories
  etched, 189–190
  false, 262–263
  traumatic, 155
Memory Moments exercise, 524
Memphis Police Department, 102–105
Mental disorders
  antisocial personality, 585–586
  bipolar disorder, 127, 583–584
  borderline personality, 108–111, 128,
    331, 586
  inadequate/dependent personality,
    584–585

Mental disorders (*continued*)
posttraumatic stress disorder, 149–196
schizophrenia, 581–583
Mental health services, 649–652, 673–674, 675–676
Mental illness
chronic, 96, 98–99
crisis line callers and, 127–128
hostage takers and, 581–586
institutional violence and, 542, 547
juvenile offenders and, 491
legal rights and, 513–514
police role in dealing with, 101–102
substance abuse and, 70, 371–372
suicide and, 500
Mental reflexes, 22
Mental sets, 394–395
Mesosystem, 656–659
Messiahs, 360
Metaphors, 444
Metastasizing crises, 9, 655
Michigan Alcohol Screening Test (MAST), 375
Microsystem, 656
Middle Eastern war veterans, 163–164
Mild disorientation, 564–567
Military trauma, 150–152, 156, 157–159
Millon Clinical Multiaxial Inventory, 331
Minimizing, 357
Minnesota model, 367
Minnesota Multiphasic Personality Inventory (MMPI), 168, 219, 309, 375
Miracle question, 455
Misino, Dominick, 581
Missing persons hotline, 134–135
Misuse, 356
Mitchell, Jeffrey, 697
Mobile crisis teams, 101
Mobility, 50
Mobilization, 82
Modeling
behavior, 479
covert, 133–134
Molesters, 274
Moral model of addiction, 353
Moral principles, 113
Mortality
facing one's own, 462
spousal death and rates of, 424
Mothers Against Drunk Driving (MADD), 4, 351
Motivational interviewing, 373–374
Motivational stance behaviors, 373
Motivation of clients, 332, 372–374, 377, 568
Motivation to change model, 372–373
Motoric cues, 548
Mourning
complicated grief and, 433–434
definition of, 417
suicide and, 508–509
See also Bereavement; Grief

Multiculturalism, 28–46
cultural biases and, 29–30
current state of, 45–46
ecological factors and, 35–36
effective helping and, 38–46
emic vs. etic models of, 32–35
geographic locale and, 43–44
high- vs. low-context cultures and, 31–32
hostage negotiation and, 592–593
individualist/collectivist continuum and, 30–31
language barriers and, 40
local consultation and, 44–45
necessity of acting and, 45
occupational factors and, 42–43
online counseling and, 140
outreach services and, 40
religion/spirituality and, 40–42
self-awareness of values and, 29
shortcomings of, 36–38
summary of, 46
support systems and, 42
training related to, 45
universal vs. focused views on, 30
See also Cultural factors
Multidisciplinary team approach, 667–668
Multiphasic/multimodal treatment, 171–172
Multitheoretical systems, 664
Multivariate diagnosis, 371–372
Murder. *See* Homicide
Myths
battering, 306–307
burnout-creating, 616–617
faith-related, 446
rape, 251–253
suicide, 216–217

N
Narcissists, 127
Narrative coherence, 190
Narrative therapy, 438–439
National Association of School Psychologists (NASP), 652, 667
National Association of Social Workers (NASW), 667
National Center for Education Statistics, 475
National Center for Health Statistics, 499
National Center for PTSD, 652
National Child Traumatic Stress Network (NCTSN), 652
National Coalition Against Domestic Violence (NCADV), 299
National Comorbidity Study, 350
National Crisis Response Teams (NCRTs), 665–668
National Domestic Violence Hotline, 338–339

National emergency assistance teams (NEATs), 667
National hotlines, 135
National Incident Management System, 516
National Institute of Mental Health (NIMH), 19, 649, 650, 667, 697
National Institute on Alcohol Abuse and Alcoholism (NIAAA), 351, 376
National Organization for Victim Assistance (NOVA), 521–522, 666
National Organization for Women (NOW), 4, 299
National Response Plan Catastrophic Incident Annex (NRP-CIA), 674
National Save-a-Life League, 3, 119
National Violence Against Women Survey, 248
Natural disasters, 17, 160, 674
case study on, 683–696
failures of response to, 674–676
personal accounts of, 679–683
See also Disaster-based crises
Needs
assessment of, 516
hierarchy of, 19, 65
Negative role models, 492
Negotiation, hostage, 591–604
case example of, 598–603
guidelines for conducting, 603–604
intervention strategies for, 591–598
negotiator debriefing after, 608
use of crisis workers in, 603
See also Hostage crises
Neo-Nazi gangs, 479–480
Nested ecological theory, 303
Netizens, 137
Networking, 93
Neurochemical malfunction, 213
Neuropathology, 155
Neurotransmitters, 69
Noble savages, 7
Noesner, Gary, 590, 592
No-harm contracts, 229–230
Noncompliance, 110–111
Nondirective counseling, 89
Nonverbal communication, 85–86
Noonan, Peggy, 479
Nostalgia, 150
NOVA model, 521–522, 666
Nuisance callers, 131
Numbing, 159–160, 169, 173–175

O
Oblative suicides, 214
Obsessive-compulsive disorder, 127
Occupational factors, 42–43
Occupational Safety and Health Administration (OSHA), 543, 544, 545, 549, 550
Odd/bizarre beliefs, 492

Older adults. *See* Elderly people
Onetime situational crisis, 70
On Killing (Grossman), 478
Online counseling, 119, 135–141
    appeal of, 136
    effectiveness of, 141
    netiquette rules, 137–138
    predispositioning in, 138
    problems of, 136–137
    session example, 138–140
    summary review of, 142
    training needs for, 140
    virtual reality and, 140–141
    See also Telephone counseling
Onstar system, 659
Open-ended questions, 75, 133
Operant conditioning, 478
Operation Outreach program, 650
Operations/communications center, 519
Order, implementing, 82
Outing or trickery, 486
Outpatient treatment, 367
Outreach programs
    constructing teams for, 667–668
    crisis response teams and, 665–668
    cultural issues related to, 40
    safety precautions for, 553–555
Overlap model of suicide, 214
Overstreet, Stacy, 693
Owning statements, 77–79

P
Pacing behavior, 565, 595
Painful and Provocative Events Scale, 219
Parallel processing, 701
Paranoia, 127
Paranoid schizophrenics, 582
Parasuicide, 8, 214
Parental influence model, 353
Parent liaison, 518
Parents
    child sexual abuse and, 273–274, 284, 285
    child suicide and, 238
    complicated grief and death of, 457–461
    effects of a child's death on, 425, 442
    grief counseling for, 442–447
    groups for nonoffending, 284
Parsimony, 376
    in assessment, 376
    in intervention, 664–665
Partner violence. *See* Domestic violence
Passive aggression, 128, 359–360
Passive suicide, 233
Pathogenic shift, 663
Pathological chronosystem, 661
Pathology, 492
Pedophiles, 252
Peer-cluster model, 353
Peer counseling, 483

Peer deaths, 428
Peer mediation, 483
Peer referral, 494
Perception, 10–11
Performance assessment, 675
Peritraumatic stress symptoms, 257
Persevering Counselors (PCs), 623
Personal identity, 593
Personality model of addiction, 354
Personality tests, 309–310, 375
Personality traits, 400
Personnel liaison, 673
Persuasion strategies, 596–598
Perturbation, 214–215, 222
Pet Loss and Human Bereavement
    (Kay et al.), 454
Pet owners
    bereavement process for, 433
    grief counseling for, 453–454
Phantom students, 481
Phone counseling. *See* Telephone
    counseling
Phone tree, 520
Physical abuse
    assessment of, 309–312
    children and, 322–324
    courtship behavior and, 325
    intervention strategies for, 255–261
    juvenile offenders and, 489–490
    PTSD symptoms and, 310
    See also Battering; Domestic violence
Physical problems, 492, 493
Physician's Desk Reference (PDR), 100, 129
Physiological responses in PTSD,
    154–155, 191
Pizzey, Erin, 299
Placaters, 361, 364
Planning
    action steps, 91–92
    disaster, 670–673
    to reestablish control, 56–57
    school crises and, 515–523
    security and safety, 549–552
    telephone counseling and, 124
Play therapy, 193–194, 276, 323–324, 428
Poise of crisis workers, 22
Police, 101–105
    changing role of, 101
    CIT program and, 102–105
    mentally ill persons and, 101–102
    occupational barriers and, 43
    school resource officers as, 482–483
    triage assessment checklist for, 68
    using for suicide, 105, 214, 580, 583
Politically based crises, 17
Pornography, 250
Positive reinforcement, 78–79
Positive thinking patterns, 56
Postdisaster services, 673–674
Postmodernist constructivist therapies, 438

Posttraumatic growth, 195, 663
Posttraumatic stress disorder (PTSD),
    149–196
    acute stress disorder and, 149, 150,
        606, 693
    adult treatment process for, 164–178
    affective-state-dependent retention
        and, 155
    assessment of, 164–169
    battering and, 310
    chemical dependency and, 371
    children and, 152–153, 155, 188–195
    complex, 153
    conflicting diagnoses of, 153
    cultural factors and, 35–36, 655
    death of children and, 442
    denial/numbing and, 159–160, 169,
        173–175
    diagnostic categorization of, 152–153
    dissociation and, 160
    DVD/web resources on, 196
    dynamics of, 152–155
    EMDR for treating, 184–188, 194–195
    emergency/outcry phase of, 169, 172–173
    family responses to, 160–161, 184
    group treatment for, 178–184
    helping other victims of, 195
    hostage crises and, 606
    importance of acceptance in, 170–171
    incidence of, 156
    individual treatment for, 172–178
    initiating interventions for, 169–170
    institutional violence and, 569, 570
    integration phase of, 169, 177–178
    intrusive thoughts/images in, 159, 169,
        173
    maladaptive patterns of, 161–163
    medical classification of, 649
    medications for treating, 69, 172
    multiphasic/multimodal treatment of,
        171–172
    nervous system arousal in, 160
    numbing/denial and, 159–160, 169,
        173–175
    overview of, 149–152
    physiological responses in, 154–155, 191
    preexisting psychopathologies and,
        153–154
    psychobiological effects of, 69
    psychoeducation about, 266
    rape trauma and, 249, 261
    recovery phases for, 169, 172–178
    reflective-transition phase of, 169,
        175–177
    residual impact of, 156
    risks of treatment for, 171
    sexual abuse of children and, 262, 264,
        266, 272
    summary review of, 196
    symptoms of, 152–153

Posttraumatic stress disorder (*continued*)
    terrorist acts and, 653
    transcrisis states compared to, 11–12
    trauma type and, 156–157
    war veterans and, 10, 150–152, 154, 156,
        157–159, 163–164
Postvention strategies, 239–240, 505–509
Poverty issues, 675
Power distance, 639
Power issues, 335, 462
Power rapist, 250
Pranksters, 131
Prayer, 460
Preadolescent suicide, 500–501
Precautions
    on debriefing process, 700–701
    on institutional violence, 553–555
Predispositioning, 52, 138–140
Pregnancy, 305
Preschoolers, bereaved, 426
Prescriptive model, 354
Presenting problems, 109
Prevention strategies
    for burnout, 625–627, 629, 638–639
    for child sexual abuse, 278, 284
    for date rape, 254–255
    for substance abuse relapse, 399–402
    for suicide, 3, 119, 210, 235–236, 499–509
Primary intervention, 9
Primary loss, 417
Primary mesosystem, 658
Primary prevention, 9
Privacy rights, 512
Private practitioners
    burnout in, 629–630, 636–637
    telephone calls taken by, 636
Prizing, 83
Problem behavior model, 354
Problem definition, 53–54, 90–91
    in hostage crises, 592
    in juvenile offender interviews, 495
    in telephone counseling, 122–123
Problem exploration, 53–54
Problem-saturated story, 443–444
Professional distance, 129–130
Professional journals, 5
Professional organizations, 667
Professional Quality of Life Scale
    (ProQOL), 624
Prohibition, 349
Projection, 357
Projective techniques, 193
Prolonged exposure, 268–269
Prolonged grief, 416, 433–435
Protection, 82
Prozac, 172
Psychache, 212, 216
Psychic trauma. *See* Posttraumatic stress
    disorder
Psychoanalytic model of addiction, 354

Psychoanalytic theory, 14
Psychobiological assessment, 69–70
Psychodynamic approach, 174–175, 211
Psychoeducation, 57–58, 266, 276, 570, 693
Psychological autopsy, 237, 241, 570
Psychological connection, 52–53
Psychological contact, 122
Psychological dependence, 355
Psychological entrapment, 303
Psychological factors
    alcohol abuse and, 351
    domestic violence and, 304–305
    institutional violence and, 547
    rape dynamics and, 250–251
    suicidal behavior and, 211–212
Psychological first aid (PFA), 19–20, 56,
    119, 257, 521, 676–677
Psychological support, 54
Psychosocial model of addiction, 354
Psychosocial transition model, 18
Psychosocial vs. mental health support,
    655
Psychotic breaks, 108
Psychotropic drugs, 69, 172
PTSD. *See* Posttraumatic stress disorder

Q
Questions
    closed-ended, 76
    open-ended, 75, 133

R
Rage, 192
Railway spine, 150
Rape, 249–261
    case example of, 255–261
    date and acquaintance, 253–255
    definitions of, 249
    dynamics of, 249–253
    impact stage of, 255–257
    intervention strategies for, 255–261
    male victims of, 252–253
    myths about, 251–253
    psychological factors and, 250–251
    recovery process following, 259–261
    responses of victims to, 259
    secondary victimization following,
        257–259
    social/cultural factors and, 250
    support for victims of, 257–259, 260–261
    trauma caused by, 249, 261
    See also Child sexual abuse; Sexual
        assault
Raphael, Beverly, 652
Rappers, 131
Rapport building, 595
Rational-emotive behavior therapy
    (REBT), 452–453
Rationalization, 357
Rational Recovery method, 401

Rational suicide, 213
Reaction formation, 357, 359, 401–402
REACT model, 591
Realistic expectations, 129
Reality orientation, 565
Reality therapy, 481
Realness, 83
Reasons for Living (RFL) scale, 220, 233
Reconstruction stage, 663, 672
Record keeping, 510, 555
Red Cross, 3, 45, 666, 673, 677
Reenactment of trauma, 191
Referral resources, 92
    elderly people and, 454
    separation/divorce and, 450
Reflection, 85, 169, 175–177
Reflective-transition phase of PTSD, 169,
    175–177
Refocusing, 80
Reframing, 268
Regression, 106–107, 357
Regular crisis-line callers, 126–128
Rehabilitation Act (1973), 512, 513, 544
Reinforcement
    cultural, 301
    positive, 78–79
Reinforcement-Based Treatment (RBT),
    369–370, 397
Relapse, 356, 399–402
Relational markers, 77, 595
Relationship skills, 389
Relaxation training, 172–173, 276, 525, 527
Religion/spirituality, 40–41, 419–420,
    446–447
Reminiscence therapy, 565–566
Remotivation therapy, 568
Repression, 357, 359
Rescue fantasy, 462
Resiliency, 10, 22
Resolution stage, hostage crisis, 590–591
Resource/facilities person, 519
RESPECTFUL model, 33
Responsibility, accepting, 389–390
Restatement, 76
Restoration orientation, 422
Restoration stage, 672–673
Restorying process, 449
Restraints, physical, 563
Revitalization, 635
Risk-needs-responsivity (RNR) model, 552
Risks
    date rape, 254
    PTSD treatment, 171
    suicide, 218, 219–220, 500
Rogers, Carl, 36
Role models, 492
Roles
    of adult children of alcoholics, 364
    of children in alcoholic families, 360–361
    of human service workers, 615

Roosevelt, Teddy, 304
Ruane, Michael, 493
Rumors, 675
Runaway hotlines, 135
Rural areas
    gangs in, 480
    outreach services in, 43
    telephone crisis lines in, 121
Rush, Benjamin, 349

S
Saccades, 186
Sadistic rapist, 250
Sadness/melancholy
    assessment of, 65
    grief and, 435
    See also Depression
SAD PERSONS scale, 219
S.A.F.E. model, 591–592
Safe sex, 457
Safety
    of battered women, 315–318
    of clients in counseling, 55–56, 90, 123
    of individuals threatened by clients,
        113–114
    of public service workers, 549–555
    of schools, 484, 496
    of sexually abused children, 277
Salutogenic shift, 663
Salvation Army, 3
Sanctioned-use model of addiction, 354
SARA model, 485
Savicki, Victor, 639
Scapegoat role, 360
Schizophrenia, 127, 581–583
Schizotypal behavior, 127
Schneider's growth model, 421
*School-Based Crisis Intervention: Preparing
    All Personnel to Assist* (Heath &
    Sheen), 528
School counselors, 527–528
School crises, 474–529
    assessment of, 68, 520–521
    bereavement and, 523–525
    bullying and, 485–488
    demobilizing after, 522–523
    DVD/web resources on, 529
    gangs and, 479–485
    group grief work and, 524–525
    juvenile offenders and, 488–499
    legal and ethical issues related to,
        509–515
    lethality assessments and, 495, 496
    logistics of dealing with, 519–520
    natural disasters and, 683, 684, 686,
        691–692, 694
    planning for, 515–523
    problems leading to, 484
    school facilities and, 474–476, 519
    statistics on, 476–478

steps in responding to, 520–523
    suicide interventions and, 499–509
    summary review of, 528–529
    training related to, 528
    transcrisis interventions and, 525–527
    university counseling centers and,
        543–544
    violent behavior and, 476, 478–479,
        509–515
School Crisis Prevention and Intervention
    (Kerr), 528
School crisis response teams (SCRTs),
    506–507, 517–519, 522
School resource officers (SROs), 482–483
*School Shooter: A Threat Assessment
    Perspective, The* (O'Toole), 489, 495
Scream Quietly or the Neighbors Will Hear
    (Pizzey), 299
Screening juvenile offenders, 493–494
Seclusion of violent offenders, 562–563
Secondary intervention, 9
Secondary loss, 417
Secondary stressors, 192
Secondary traumatic stress disorder
    (STSD), 619, 620
Secondary victimization, 257–259, 309,
    544–545
Second disaster, 662, 663
Secrecy of child sexual abuse, 275
Security analysis/planning, 549–552
Security blankets, 567–568
Security liaison, 518
Sedation, 563–564
Self-assessment, 90
Self-care, 461–462, 629
Self-defeating behavior patterns, 127–128
Self-defense procedures, 561–562
Self-disclosure, 22, 37, 42, 587, 595
Self-efficacy models, 675–676
Self-knowledge, 29
Self-managed behavioral technique, 453
Self-murder, 211
Self-organizing systems, 15
Self-reports, 165–168
Separation
    bereavement and, 432–433
    grief counseling and, 449–453
    referral resources and, 450
Serious violent juvenile offenders (SVJOs),
    488, 489–493
Severe disorientation, 568–569
Severely disturbed crisis-line callers,
    128–131
Severity of crisis, 60, 61–67, 69
Sexual acting out, 286
Sexual assault, 248–289
    boundary issues and, 284
    case example of, 255–261
    childhood victims of, 261–287
    date and acquaintance, 253–255

DVD/web resources on, 289
    intervention strategies for, 255–261
    male victims of, 252–253
    myths about, 251–253
    psychological factors in, 250–251
    recovery process from, 259–261
    social/cultural factors in, 250
    statistics on, 248–249
    summary review of, 288
    support following, 257–259, 260–261
    survivors of, 249, 261–271
    trauma caused by, 249, 261–262
    underreporting of, 249
    See also Child sexual abuse; Rape
Sexual Assault Nurse Examiner (SANE)
    program, 258
Sexual behavior
    domestic violence and, 336
    HIV-positive clients and, 457
    telephone crisis lines and, 132
Sexually Victimized Children (Finklehor), 272
Sexual problems, 132
Shapiro, Francine, 185, 194
Shatan, Chaim, 178
Shell shock, 150
Shelters, 318–322
    counseling women at, 319–322
    dynamics of, 319–320
    emotional feelings common at, 320–321
    follow-up care after leaving, 322
Shneidman, Edwin, 3, 209, 210, 212, 214,
    216, 237
Short-term disposition, 100
Short-term outpatient programs (STOP), 367
Show of force, 561–562
Silence, 86
Silent callers, 132
Silent sufferers, 360
SIMPLE STEPS method, 221, 223
Simpson, O. J., 297
Situational clues, 218
Situational crises, 16–17
Situational supports, 56
Skill building, 270
Slips, 356
Smartphones, 659
Smorgasbord home boy gangs, 480
Social constructivists, 29
Social disorganization, 250
Social/environmental crisis, 99
Social exclusion, 486
Social factors
    bereavement and, 418–419
    crisis intervention movement and, 6–7
    domestic violence and, 300–301, 305
    institutional violence and, 547
    rape dynamics and, 250
    substance abuse and, 350
    See also Cultural factors
Social identity, 593

Social integration theory, 212
Social learning, 478
Social locations, 33
Social networking sites, 659
Social reality, 628
Social status, 492
Social support, 42, 54–55, 627–628, 675
Sociobiology, 303
Sociocultural models, 354
SOCRATES assessment measure, 377
Solution-focused brief therapy (SFBT), 384, 385, 401
Somatization, 153
Sommers-Flanagan, John and Rita, 481
Space, providing available, 436
Spirituality, 40–41, 67, 377, 419–420, 446–447
Spiritual strategies, 437, 438
Spousal abuse. *See* Domestic violence
Spousal death
    grief and, 423–424
    intervention strategies for, 439–442
    support groups for, 440–441
Stafford Disaster Relief and Emergency Assistance Act (1986), 650
Stagnation, 617
Stalin, Joseph, 350
Stalking behavior, 325–326
Stalling for Time (Noesner), 590
Stay-alive contracts, 229–230
Stern, Adolph, 108
Stigmatized loss, 456
Sting strategy, 596
Stockholm syndrome, 303, 590, 605
STOP technique, 690
Stowe, Harriet Beecher, 3
Strentz, Thomas, 604
Stress
    burnout and, 614
    chemical dependency and, 354, 387–388
    domestic violence and, 305–306
    hostage crises and, 606
    institutional violence and, 547
    management of, 333–334
    occupational factors and, 43
    physiological responses to, 154–155
    traumatic death and, 442
    See also Posttraumatic stress disorder
Stress-coping model of addiction, 354
Stress inoculation, 387–388
Stressors
    persistent, 614
    secondary, 192
Stress response syndrome, 442
Structured interviews, 165
Subjective Units of Discomfort (SUDs) scale, 186
Substance abuse
    addiction models and, 352–354

adult children of alcoholics and, 363–365
aftercare programs for, 399–402
alcohol and, 351–352
assessment of, 375–381
children in families of, 360–365, 399
controlled drinking and, 374–375
crisis points in treatment for, 381–385
date rape and, 254
denial of, 356, 390–391
detoxification process and, 385
diagnosis of, 371–372, 378
domestic violence and, 305, 331, 336
DVD/web resources on, 403
dysfunctional family rules about, 361–363
environmental cues and, 395–396
family therapy for, 396–399
hostage takers and, 588
institutional violence and, 542, 547
intervention strategies for, 372–385
juvenile offenders and, 490
medications for, 401
mental illness and, 70, 371–372
motivation to change, 372–374, 377
principles of treatment for, 385–402
relapse prevention and, 399–402
sociocultural determinants of, 350
statistics on, 349–350
summary review of, 402–403
terminology associated with, 354–356
treatment approaches to, 365–371, 385
Vietnam War veterans and, 158
See also Addiction; Chemical dependency
Substance Abuse Subtle Screening Inventory (SASSI), 331, 336
Suburban gangs, 480
Sudden deaths, 439
Sudden infant death syndrome (SIDS), 425
Suicide, 209–242
    adolescents and, 210, 499–509
    age factors in, 231–232
    alcohol abuse and, 352
    assessing potential for, 71–72, 130, 217–222
    assisted, 211
    burnout and, 632–633
    case examples about, 222–231, 232–234, 239–240, 501–505
    characteristics indicative of, 214–215, 216
    children and, 210, 238, 499–509
    clues indicative of, 217–219
    cluster or contagion, 505–506, 507
    complicated grief and, 458
    coping with the loss of clients by, 241
    counseling clients with ideas of, 222–240, 501–505
    crisis response teams and, 506–507

DVD/web resources on, 242
dynamics of, 211–216
elderly clients and, 231–235
existential-constructivist model of, 212–213
expressive acts of, 209
failure of crisis intervention for, 241
family/friend/associate guidelines on, 236–237
grief related to, 238–240
homicide and, 215–216
hostage takers and, 580, 583, 591
impulsivity and, 503
interpersonal theory of, 212
intervention strategies for, 222–240, 499–509
juvenile offenders and, 492
management "don'ts" relative to, 235–236
moral dilemma of, 210–211
myths about, 216–217
national hotline for, 242
notes left about, 215–216
parent survivors of, 238
police-assisted, 105, 214, 580, 583
postvention strategies, 237–240, 505–509
prevention of, 3, 119, 210, 235–236, 499–509
psychological theories of, 211–212
risk factors for, 218, 219–220, 500
school-based, 499–509
sociological theory of, 212
statistics on, 209–210
summary review of, 241–242
survivor support groups, 238–239
telephone hotlines, 119, 135
theories of, 211–213
warning signs of, 218–219
Suicide by cop, 105, 214, 580, 583
Suicide Risk Assessment Decision Tree (SRADT), 220
Suicide Status Form III, 223, 228
Summary clarification, 76–77
Sundown syndrome, 548, 567
Super mesosystem, 658–659
Support
    assessing systems of, 71
    counselor burnout and, 627–628
    domestic violence interventions and, 312–313
    family systems of, 188–189
    juvenile offenders and, 497–498
    providing to clients, 54–55, 81–82, 90
    rape victims and, 257–259, 260–261
    same-sex relationships and, 328
    social, 42, 54–55, 627–628, 675
    telephone, 121, 123–124, 312–313
Support groups
    for bereaved teens, 524–525

for burnout, 628
for disaster survivors, 693
for divorce, 450
for HIV/AIDS clients, 457
for parental grief, 442–443
for PTSD, 178–184
for sexual abuse survivors, 270–271
for spousal grief, 440–441
for suicide survivors, 238–239
See also Group therapy
Support systems, 42
Suppression
of addiction problems, 359
of childhood sexual abuse, 275
Survivalist gangs, 479–480
Survivor's guilt, 158, 161–162
SVJOs. *See* Serious violent juvenile
offenders
Sympathizing/placating, 130
Sympathy vs. empathy, 83
Symptomology of crises, 11
Symptom substitution, 400
Syndromatic clues, 218
Systemic crisis, 8–9, 23
Systems theory, 14, 303–304

T

Tarasoff case (1976), 113–114, 221, 230, 509
Target-specific interventions, 665
Task model. *See* Hybrid model of crisis
intervention
Teachers
student threats to, 477
suicide of, 508–509
Technical support/challenges, 627–628
Technological innovations, 659
Tedeschi, Richard, 462, 663
Teenagers. *See* Adolescents
Telephone counseling, 119–135
advantages of, 119–121
confidentiality issues in, 141
covert modeling in, 133–134
dealing with difficult clients in, 133–134
defining problems in, 122–123
domestic abuse and, 135, 311–318,
338–339
DVD/web resources on, 142
effectiveness of, 141
emergency hotlines and, 134–135
ensuring safety in, 123
errors and fallacies about, 125–126
ethical and moral issues in, 141
exploring alternatives in, 124
formulating administrative rules for, 134
legal issues in, 141
listening skills in, 312
national vs. local, 135
obtaining commitment in, 124–125
planning process in, 124
private practitioners and, 636

problem callers and, 131–134
providing support in, 122, 123–124,
312–313
psychological contact in, 122
regular callers and, 126–128
severely disturbed callers and, 128–131
strategies for, 121–126
summary review of, 142
switching crisis workers in, 133
terminating abusive behavior in, 133
time-limited hotlines and, 134–135
See also Online counseling
Temperance movement, 349
Terminal illness
bereavement process and, 430–431,
456–457
crisis issues related to, 456–457
Termination problems, 107
Terrifying Love (Walker), 300
Terror
in battered women, 321
See also Fear; Trauma
Terrorism, 652–654
Terroristic batterer, 307
Texas Revised Inventory of Grief (TRIG),
423
Text messages, 659
Therapeutic relationship
borderline patients in, 109–111
confidentiality issues in, 112–115
counselor burnout and, 619–621
difficult clients in, 111–112
manipulative clients in, 108, 132
Therapy
brief, 10
chemical dependency, 387–388
childhood sexual abuse and, 265–271
cognitive-behavioral, 193, 261, 276, 330,
366, 401, 438
crisis in, 107–108
domestic violence, 329–338
EMDR, 184–188, 194–195
escape to, 359
family, 184, 396–399, 448
narrative, 438–439
play, 193–194, 276, 323–324, 428
PTSD sequence of, 169, 172–178
reminiscence, 565–566
remotivation, 568
validation, 568–569
See also Counseling; Group therapy;
Individual therapy
Thinking patterns, 56
Thoughts
automatic, 451
intrusive, 159, 169, 173
technique for stopping, 175–176
Threat Assessment Teams, 494, 514, 550
Threats, 66, 113–114, 275, 477, 486,
495, 541

Time
chronosystem and, 660–664
PTSD and passage of, 664
Time-limited hotlines, 134–135
Time-outs, 561
Toddlers, bereaved, 426
Tolerance, chemical, 356
Tornado disaster case study, 683–696
Training programs
burnout prevention, 624
CIT program, 103–105
cross-cultural, 45
disaster counseling, 677–678
emergency management, 669
institutional violence, 552–555
volunteer worker, 673
See also Education
Trajectory model of suicide, 212
Transactional Analysis theory, 397
Transcendent phase of intervention, 287
*Transcending Trauma After a Disaster: A
Guide for Schools* CD-ROM, 694
Transcrisis states, 11–13
chemical dependency and, 372
domestic violence and, 318
long-term therapy and, 105–108
posttraumatic stress disorder vs., 11–12
school crises and, 525–527
suicide survivors and, 239
transcrisis points and, 12–13
Transference, 171
Transgression, 66
Transients from megagangs, 480
Transparency, 83
Transposition, 191
Trauma
childhood, 155, 188–192
disaster, 693–694
extinguishing, 267–268
grief and, 416, 434–435
helping other victims of, 195
hostage crises and, 606
individual vs. collective, 660
military, 150–152, 156, 157–159
posttraumatic growth from, 195
psychic disequilibrium from, 149–150
rape or sexual, 249, 261
response to, 152
self-reports about, 165–168
staff victims of violence and, 569–571
types of, 156–157
vicarious, 241, 461, 619, 620–621
See also Posttraumatic stress disorder
Traumagram protocol, 165–168
Trauma psychology, 6
Trauma Symptom Checklist for Young
Children, 192–193
Trauma Symptom Inventory, 193
Traumatic bonding theory, 301
Traumatic death, 415, 434–435, 442–447

Traumatic grief, 416, 434–435, 693–694
Trauma tourism, 7
Treatment noncompliance, 110–111
Triage assessment, 61–69
    of bereaved individuals, 439–440
    of chemical dependency, 378
    of crisis worker burnout, 632–633
    of disaster survivors, 677
    of lethality, 220–222
    of PTSD, 180
    of school crises, 514–515, 520–521
Triage Assessment Checklist for Law
    Enforcement (TACKLE), 68
Triage Assessment Form (TAF), 61–69
    affective severity scale, 65–66
    alternate forms of, 67–69
    behavioral severity scale, 66
    cognitive severity scale, 66–67
    illustrated sample of, 62–65
    precrisis functioning comparison, 67
    rating clients on, 67
Triage Assessment Severity Checklist–
    Civilian (TASC-C), 68
Triage Assessment System for Students in
    Learning Environments (TASSLE),
    68, 514, 515
Trust, eliciting, 436, 565
Tunnel vision, 400
Twelve-step programs, 365–366
Type I/II childhood traumas, 189, 190–192

U
Uncertainty avoidance, 28, 32, 639
Uncle Tom's Cabin (Stowe), 3
Uncomplicated bereavement, 416
Understanding, conveying, 78
Unemployment, 431–432
Unfinished business, 459, 460, 566
Universal view of multicultural
    counseling, 30
University counseling centers, 543–544
URICA assessment measure, 377

V
Validation
    of childhood sexual abuse, 267, 277
    of geriatric violent clients, 568–569
Validation therapy, 568–569
Validity of Cognition (VOC) scale, 186
Value judgments, 78
Van Praagh, James, 423
Verbal abuse, 133
Verbal clues, 218
Verbal communication, 84–85
Verduin, Claire, 702
Veterans. *See* War veterans
Veterans Administration (VA) hospitals, 153

*Veterans and Active Duty Military
    Psychotherapy Treatment Planner, The*
    (Moore & Jongsma), 196
Vicarious traumatization, 241, 461, 613,
    619, 620–621
Victim/victimizer dynamic, 157–158
Video games, 478, 479
Vietnam War veterans
    assessment of, 168–169
    civilian adjustment for, 158
    impact of antiwar sentiment on, 159
    intrusive-repetitive thoughts in, 159
    PTSD in, 4–5, 150–152, 156, 157–159
    substance abuse among, 158
Violence
    alcohol abuse and, 351
    bases for profiling, 546–549
    crisis workers as victims of, 541,
        569–571
    cycle of, 307–308, 334
    ethical issues related to, 113–114,
        509–515
    geriatric clients and, 564–569
    graphic/written indicators of, 494
    intervention strategies for, 255–261
    juvenile offenders and, 491
    legal issues pertaining to, 113–114,
        509–515
    legitimization of, 250
    predictors of, 491, 546
    predisposing history of, 547
    preoccupation with, 492
    school crises and, 476, 478–479, 509–515
    security/safety issues and, 549–552
    shelters as protection against, 318–322
    stages of intervention for, 555–564
    terrorism and, 652–654
    See also specific forms of violence
Violence Against Women Act (1994), 299,
    326
Violence Screening Checklist–Revised
    (VSC-R), 546
Violent/antisocial batterer, 307
Virginia Tech shootings, 115, 216, 479, 493,
    511–512, 513, 543, 660
Virtual reality, 140–141
Volunteer workers, 5, 673

W
Walker, Lenore, 300, 302
Walk-in crisis facilities, 96, 98–101
    anchoring process in, 100
    community mental health clinics as,
        99–101
    intake interview in, 100
    mobile crisis teams from, 101
    types of presenting crises in, 96, 98–99

Wannabe gangs, 479
War neurosis, 150, 154
Warning signals, 400
War veterans, 10, 150–152, 154, 156,
    157–159, 163–164
Weapons, 492–493
Web resources
    book's access code to, 46
    See also World Wide Web
Wednesday's Children (Young), 272
Well-Adjusted Counselors (WACs), 623
When Bad Things Happen to Good People
    (Kushner), 445
When Disaster Strikes (Raphael), 652
"Who Told You?" technique, 637
Wife abuse. *See* Domestic violence
Wilson, Bill, 365
Winter, Betty, 43, 332
"Wishing and hoping" syndrome, 313
Withdrawal, 356
Witness role, 441
Women
    assessing abuse in, 309–312
    child sexual abuse by, 273–274
    domestic violence and, 299–300
    institutional violence and, 542–543
    realities of physical abuse for, 308–309
    sexual assault of, 249
    shelters for, 318–322
Women's movement, 649
Work Environment Scale, 624
Work history, 548
Working alliance, 255
Workplace
    burnout assessment in, 624
    security/safety planning in, 549–552
    violence in, 541, 545
Worksite analysis, 549–550
World Wide Web
    access code to resources on, 46
    crisis services on, 119, 135–141
    gang-related sites on, 480
    legal/ethical issues, 141
    netiquette rules, 137–138
    stalking behavior on, 326
    See also Online counseling
Wronged/aggrieved hostage takers,
    587–588

Y
YAVIS clients, 44–45
Young, Leontine, 272

Z
Zero tolerance policies, 511, 549